A
TURKISH–ENGLISH
DICTIONARY

A
TURKISH–ENGLISH
DICTIONARY

BY
H. C. HONY

WITH THE ADVICE OF
FAHİR İZ

SECOND EDITION

OXFORD
AT THE CLARENDON PRESS

Oxford University Press, Ely House, London W. 1

GLASGOW   NEW YORK   TORONTO   MELBOURNE   WELLINGTON
CAPE TOWN   SALISBURY   IBADAN   NAIROBI   LUSAKA   ADDIS ABABA
BOMBAY   CALCUTTA   MADRAS   KARACHI   LAHORE   DACCA
KUALA LUMPUR   HONG KONG   TOKYO

FIRST EDITION 1947
REPRINTED LITHOGRAPHICALLY 1949, 1953, 1954

SECOND EDITION 1957
REPRINTED LITHOGRAPHICALLY 1958, 1960, 1967

PREFACE TO THE SECOND EDITION

THE first edition of this dictionary was completed in 1946. During the next five years my collaborator and I were occupied in compiling our English–Turkish dictionary. In the course of this we naturally came across a large number of words and phrases which we had overlooked or which had come into more general use, and which obviously should be included in any new edition of the Turkish–English dictionary.

Moreover, the original edition, as explained in the preface, was compiled under exceptional difficulties owing to the war and there were many errors of omission and commission. It is hoped that most of these have been eliminated in the present work.

In order to include the extra material without greatly enlarging the size of the work, it has been rearranged by putting all compound words as far as alphabetically possible under the main word, or at least in groups where they naturally come together. A good number of now obsolete words have been omitted.

I have adhered to the principle, adopted in the original edition and in the English–Turkish dictionary, that the inclusion of common phrases and idioms is far more important than the inclusion of large numbers of comparatively rare words.

H. C. H.

September, 1956

PREFACE TO THE FIRST EDITION

A MODERN Turkish–English dictionary is badly needed. When this dictionary was started there was only one inadequate and rather inaccurate little dictionary, published in Turkey. Just as the work was finished, there appeared a large dictionary published by the Turkish Ministry of Education. This is a very useful work, but it includes great numbers of invented words, few of which are likely to survive, and many unnecessary phrases. Moreover it was written primarily for Turks and therefore omits many phrases and idioms which are incomprehensible to an Englishman, though readily understood by a Turk. In the present dictionary a large number of these difficult idioms have been included, because they are commonly used and their meaning is often impossible to guess even if one knows the separate words of which they are composed.

The work has been done under circumstances of exceptional difficulty, because, on account of the war, it was impossible to get necessary reference books from Turkey. The lack of these has greatly increased my labour, and war-time duties have preoccupied me.

The writer of a Turkish dictionary is faced with the further difficulty that there exists no court of appeal such as the *Oxford English Dictionary* provides for English. No good Turkish dictionary has been written since those of Shemseddin Samy Bey in 1885 and Sir James Redhouse in 1890, and all subsequent dictionaries mainly derive from them. But changes in the Turkish language during the past sixty years have put much of their content out of date. Besides, the reform of the language brought about by Mustafa Kemal in 1928 not only involved change in the alphabet but greatly encouraged the movement, already under way, to rid Turkish of Arabic and Persian words. Such a purification was badly needed and has brought the written language into line with the spoken. Unfortunately, reformers, carried away by their zeal, have tried to reintroduce great numbers of obsolete Turkish words, and, what is worse, have invented hundreds of new words. The effect is to produce a new written language as far removed from spoken Turkish as the old literary language was. To expunge the word *mekteb*, which is as much part and parcel of the Turkish language as 'school' is of English, and to put in its place the invented word *okul* (to sound like the French *école*) can hardly be regarded as an improvement of the language.

In view of all these difficulties I feel justified in craving the indulgence of the reader for inevitable errors of omission and commission.

My thanks are due to the Delegates and staff of the Clarendon Press for encouragement and advice. Above all I am grateful to my Turkish collaborator, Fahir İz, of Istanbul University and now a lecturer at the School of Oriental Studies; Fahir İz is not only a master of his own tongue, but also a versatile linguist, and if this dictionary bears the mark of real scholarship, the credit is mainly due to him.

H. C. H.

December 1946

INTRODUCTION

I. SPELLING

TURKISH spelling is still in a rather unsettled state. In this new edition I have adopted the more logical way of spelling words of Arabic origin, that is to say I have retained the original voiced consonants at the end of words instead of changing them into voiceless consonants, although it is admitted that the Turks do in fact sound them as voiceless, that is to say they change a final **b, d, c** into **p, t, ç**; I have also retained the voiced consonants in front of voiceless ones, that is to say: I write **ibtida, idhal, ictima,** and not **iptida, ithal, içtima** and so forth. Of course in conversation these voiced consonants tend to become voiceless even in English; the 'b' in 'obtain' is not the same as the 'b' in 'obdurate'. The reason for the retention of the original consonants is that the final ones will in any case occur when the word is declined and followed by a vowel, and the others will occur in other forms of the same Arabic root. The present-day Turk may not always realize that **ithal** has anything to do with **dahil,** or **içtimai** with **cemaat,** though naturally he will, if he knows his own language properly. For the foreigner it is a great advantage to be able to detect the relationship of words springing from the same root.

There is an uncertainty about the spelling of many other words, especially in the vowels. The following table includes the most common variations.

u and **ü**

ü ,, **ö**

a ,, **e**

i ,, **ı**

ğ ,, **v**

p ,, **b**

t ,, **p**

ç ,, **c**

The use of the circumflex over the long **a** and of the ' to represent the Arabic *hamza* or *'ain* is very variable and the addition or omission of these should not worry the reader.

2. VOCABULARY

(i) *French and English words*

The first edition took it for granted that any student of Turkish would know enough French to identify and understand the innumerable French words used in Turkish. (This fondness for French words is in marked contrast with the official attempts to eradicate all Arabic and Persian words, which have been for centuries an integral part of the language.) It is now clear, however, that this is not the case. I have therefore included the most commonly used French words though the student must expect to meet many others, used mainly for ostentation, in inferior journalism. English words, mostly to do with games or ships, have been generally included as they are often not easy to recognize in their Turkish garb; it took me a long time to find out that **nakavt** was the Turkish for 'knock-out'.

(ii) *Invented words and meanings*

It is now easier to see which of these words are likely to survive. As was foreseen in the first edition, very few of the thousands invented have caught on; even these few are mostly of no benefit to the language and many of the invented new meanings for old words are positively harmful and have done nothing but impoverish the language, e.g. the use of **sağlık** for **sıhhat,** of **savaş** for **harb,** of **basmak** for **tab'etmek,** of **çevirmek** for **tercüme etmek** and a score of other senseless innovations.

(iii) *Plants, trees, birds, and fishes.*

Since the first edition it has been possible, largely through the help of the late Dr. Malcolm Burr, to get more information on these subjects. On fishes and trees the information is fairly complete, but it has been impossible to get much reliable information about plants and birds. There seems to be no one in Turkey who can be regarded as an expert on these subjects. It has been necessary to put a query (?) to many translations.

3. ARRANGEMENT

(i) *Compound words*

In the early days of the language reform it was customary to write compound words as one word. Later they were generally written as two. Now both methods are in use. It would certainly be better to follow the earlier method and write all compounds as one word, or at any rate adopt the English method of using a hyphen. As in this edition all compound words are placed under the heading of the main word as far as possible, there should be no difficulty in finding the compound word required, whether written as one or as two words.

(ii) *Verbal forms*

The passive, causative, reciprocal, and other forms, which can be made of every verb, have not as a rule been inserted, unless they bear some special meaning or unless their form makes it difficult to identify them with the original verb. The student of Turkish simply must learn these forms, which are very much used; he will not make much progress until he can translate at once **sevişdirilemediklerinden.**

(iii) *Phrases, sayings, and proverbs*

Idioms form one of the greatest difficulties in all languages; Turkish has perhaps more than most and, in addition, the Turks are particularly fond of proverbs and folk-sayings; many of the latter are unintelligible to someone who does not know their background of reference, and a whole story, probably from Nasreddin Hodja, would have to be told to make them understood; in this edition I have added an Appendix giving the original story of some of the commonest and most difficult to understand. For others I have simply put the nearest English equivalent. The ideal in the treatment of idioms and phrases would be to put them under each of the principal words which form them; but this would greatly add to the size of the dictionary. They have therefore, for the most part, been put under one of the main words. I have gone rather against the current practice, which is to put them under the commonest word, and have put them under the most uncommon word; this has two advantages: (*a*) the uncommon word is the one most likely to be looked out in any case, and (*b*) it helps to prevent the overcrowding of such common words as **baş, yüz, el,** *etc.,* which often makes it difficult to find a phrase under such words.

(iv) *The suffix* **-ane.**

Adjectives and adverbial derivatives ending in the Persian suffix **-ane** have mostly been omitted; see **-ane** in the text.

4. GRAMMAR

There was a good deal of adverse criticism of the grammatical terms employed in the first edition. I feel that this was largely justified. Our grammatical terms were meant originally to apply to Latin and Greek; they are often quite inapplicable to languages of a different family and of a construction so different as Turkish. Various new grammatical terms have been invented to describe the various parts of speech of such languages, but the use of these is by no means standardized and they are mostly known only to professional philologists. I have therefore decided to omit most grammatical terms, except to show which verbs are active and which neuter and, in certain cases, to distinguish between substantives and adjectives where the English words may be either.

5. PRONUNCIATION AND STRESS

Turkish is not a difficult language to pronounce. The new phonetic alphabet is fairly satisfactory, with the exception of the ill-devised dotless i (ı). A truly phonetic alphabet is impossible without using some fifty or sixty signs. There is little difficulty about the consonants, but even in Turkish the great Redhouse estimated that there are some twenty-two different vowel sounds, and after all it is usually in the vowels that foreigners fail to pronounce the language as a native would. As we know in English it is the vowels, not the consonants (with the exception of 'r'), that enable us to decide, not merely what part of the country a man comes from, but the class to which he belongs.

It is not the function of a medium-sized dictionary such as this to go into the niceties of pronunciation, which can in any case only be properly learnt from a native, but some help is given the student by showing which vowels are long and which short and where the stress falls. In the first edition this was done by means of signs and accents over the actual words; but this gave the words an unnatural appearance and may even have been confusing to those, perhaps the majority, who possess a sight memory. So in this edition the information is given in brackets after the word. In purely Turkish words all vowels are short and the stress is practically always on the last syllable. In such cases there is no indication of the pronunciation; where, however, there is an exception to this rule, short vowels are indicated by a dot (·), long vowels by a dash (–), and the stress by an accent over the stressed syllable. The final long syllable of many Arabic words becomes short in Turkish, but when such words are declined and followed by a vowel that syllable becomes long; such syllables are represented by an asterisk; thus **hayat** (·٭) is pronounced (·١) but the accusative **hayatı** is pronounced (·–١). This rule applies to all Arabic plurals in **-at**; these are not all marked, but enough of them are marked to remind the reader of the rule. As stated above, the stress in purely Turkish words usually falls on the final syllable; exceptions to this rule are:

(i) In compound words the stress falls on the last syllable of the first component, e.g. **arıkovanı** (·١···), **başkâtib** (١···). The stress mark has not been shown for all compound words, but again enough examples are given to remind the reader.

(ii) In all persons of the imperative the stress falls on the verb root if this is monosyllabic, or on its last syllable if it is polysyllabic, e.g. **yazma** (do not write !) is (١·) and **okumasın** (let him not read!) is (·١···); **yazma** (·١), **okuma** (···١) are verbal nouns (writing) and (reading).

In foreign words the stress is usually the same as in the original language, e.g. **manevra** (·١·) (manœuvre), **fayrap** (١·) (fire up, full steam ahead!). In all cases the stress in Turkish is light as in French and not at all like that in English, where it is often so strong as to obliterate the unstressed syllables.

The vowels are *approximately* as follows:

(i) *Soft or Front Vowels.*

   e as in *bed*.
   i (·) as in *hit*.
   i (–) as *ee* in *see*.
   ö as French *eu* in *peu*.
   ü as French *u* in *tu*.
   â (after **k, g, l**) as in *bad*, but see **k, g, l**.
   û (after **k, g, l**) as *u* in *cute*.

(ii) *Hard or Back Vowels.*

   a (·) as *u* in *sun*.
   a (–) and **â** (when denoting the long Arabic **a**) as in *far*.
   ı something between the *i* in *big* and the *u* in *bug*.

o as *o* in *doll* or *au* in *author*.

u (·) as in *bull*.

u (–) as in *rule*.

The consonants are as in English, except:

c as *j* in *jam*.

ç as *ch* in *choke*.

ġ as in English, but when it is followed by **â** or **û** it is palatalized: thus **gâ** is very nearly *gya*.

ğ with hard vowels is sometimes a very guttural but hardly perceptible *g*, as in **dağ** = *dagh*, and sometimes very little more than a prorogation of the preceding vowel, as in **ağa** = *aa*; with soft vowels it is a consonantal *y*, as **eğer** = *eyer*.

j as the French *j* in *je*.

k with soft vowels is frontal like the *k* in *kill*; with hard vowels it is backward like the *c* and *ck* in *cuckoo*, but it is more pronouncedly frontal or backward than in the English examples; when followed by **â** or **û** it is highly palatalized and at times very nearly *ch*.

l followed by a hard vowel is much like the English *l*, but before a soft vowel it is more frontal and rather like the German *l*.

v is something between the English *v* and *w*, though in some words it is practically the same as **ğ** and indeed is interchangeable; thus **dövmek** (to beat) may also be written **döğmek**.

6. PUNCTUATION

The Turks are not yet quite used to European punctuation or perhaps it would be fairer to say that, owing to the great difference in the structure of their sentences, their punctuation is often very puzzling to us. If you are completely bewildered by some sentence, try cutting out all the punctuation marks and often you will find it quite easy to translate.

ABBREVIATIONS

a. adjective.
abb. abbreviation.
abl. ablative.
acc. accusative.
adv. adverb.
App. Appendix.
approx. approximately.
Ar. Arabic.
arith. arithmetic.
bot. botanical.
caus. causative mood.
cf. compare.
coll. colloquial.
comm. commercial.
comp. comparative.
cont. contemptuously.
corr. corruption.
dat. dative.
dial. dialect.
elect. electricity.
Eng. English.
err. error; erroneously.
esp. especially.
etm. etmek.
fig. figuratively.
fin. financial.
Fr. French.
gen. genitive; generally.
gram. grammar.
impers. impersonal.
inf. infinitive; infantile.
interj. interjection.
iron. ironically.
iz. izafet.
jur. juridical.
lit. literally.
math. mathematics.
mech. mechanical; mechanics.

med. medical.
mil. military.
mus. music.
n. noun.
neg. negative.
naut. nautical.
num. numeral; numeral adjective.
olm. olmak.
opp. opposed.
orig. origin; originally.
part. participle.
pass. passive.
Pers. Persian.
pl. plural.
pop. popular.
prep. preposition (in Turkish, post-position.).
prop. n. proper noun.
q.v. quod vide, see.
sing. singular.
sl. slang.
s.o. someone.
stg. something.
superl. superlative.
v. verb; vide, see.
va. verb active.
verb. verbal.
vn. verb neuter.
vulg. vulgarly.
⌐ ¬ proverb or proverbial expression.
* the word so marked must have the appropriate personal pronominal suffix, *e.g.* **beli* kırılmak**, to be exhausted; I was exhausted = **belim kırıldı.**
⸾‖ invented word or invented new meaning for an old word.

A

ab (–) Water; rain; river, ~ u hava, climate.

aba Coarse woollen stuff; Arab cloak. ~ altından değnek göstermek, to threaten with soft words: ···e ~yı yakmak, to be 'gone on' s.o.

âba (–͟) pl. of eb. Fathers.

âbad¹ (–͟) Prosperous; flourishing. ~an (––͟), prosperous; a flourishing place. ~ani (–––͟), prosperity; flourishing place.

âbad² (–͟) pl. of ebed. Eternities (in the future).

abadi (––͟) A kind of soft yellow writing-paper.

abajur (Fr. abat-jour) Lampshade.

abalı Wearing an aba; poor, wretched. ⌐vur ~ya!⌐, attack the weak!; put the blame on s.o. who can't defend himself!

abamak va. Refuse; resist.

abandırmak va. caus. of abanmak: make an animal kneel.

abanî (––͟) A mixed tissue of cotton and silk, generally with a yellow design.

abanmak vn. (with dat.) Lean over or against stg.; push against.

abanoz Ebony. ~ kesilmek, to become as hard or as black as ebony.

abartmak va. Exaggerate.

abazan Hungry (esp. for love). Hunger; craving for love.

Abbas A name of men. ⌐~yolcu⌐, said in allusion to one who is going away or being dismissed his post.

abdal¹ Silly fool; saint. (also ~sı, ~ımsı) imbecile; feckless.

abdal² Exchange.

abdest, –ti Ritual ablution. ~ almak, to perform such ablution: ~ bozmak, to relieve nature: ~i* gelmek, to want to relieve nature. ~hane (···͟), latrine, water-closet. ~siz, not having performed ritual ablution; impure: ~ yere basmamak, to be exceedingly religious.

abdülleziz Earth-nut.

Abdürrahman ⌐Koyun bulunmadığı yerde keçiye ~ Çelebi denir⌐, 'where a sheep is not to be had great respect is paid to a goat', i.e. (i) make the best of what you have got; (ii) ⌐a Triton among minnows⌐.

abdüsselâm (····͟) Mandrake.

abe (–͟) Used to call attention; v. also ağabey.

âbede (–·͟) pl. of âbid. Worshippers; devotees.

abes Useless and low-down. Useless thing; nonsense. ~le uğraşmak, to pass one's time with trifles: ~ yere, in vain, to no purpose.

abıhayat (–··͟), –tı The water of life; water of a legendary spring; any excellent water. ~ içmiş, said of one who never grows old.

abırevan (–··͟) Flowing water.

abıru (–·͟) Honour; self-respect. ~ dökmek, to abase oneself by toadying, to truckle.

abi Elder brother.

abid, –bdi Slave; mortal.

âbid (–͟), –bdi Worshipper; devotee.

âbide (–·͟) Monument.

abla (͟·) Elder sister; elderly domestic.

ablak Only in ~ yüzlü, round-faced.

abli Sheet of a small sail. ~yi kaçırmak, to lose control of oneself.

abluka (·͟·) Blockade. ~ kaçağı, blockade-runner: ~yı yarmak, to run the blockade.

abone (·͟·) (Fr. abonné) Subscriber; subscription.

aborda (·͟·) In ...e ~ etm-, (of a ship) to go alongside another ship etc.

abramak va. Control; manage.

abraş Speckled; piebald; (leaf) spotted by chlorosis.

abuhava (–··͟) Climate.

abuksabuk (·͟·͟) Incoherent nonsense.

abullabut Stupid; loutish.

abur cubur (·͟·͟) Incongruous mixtures (foods etc.); trash. ~ kimseler, riffraff.

abus (·͟) Sour-faced; grim; frowning.

abüdane (–·–͟) Water and grain; one's daily bread; Providence; destiny.

acaba (͟··) I wonder!; is it so?

acaib v. acayib.

acar Bright (child); self-reliant; plucky; enterprising.

acayib (·–͟) pl. of acibe. Marvels. Wonderful; strange. How strange!; you don't say so! (often iron.).

aceb v. acaba.

acele Haste, hurry. Hasty; urgent. ~ etm., to hasten, to be in a hurry: ~ye gelmek, to be done in a hurry and carelessly: ···ye getirmek, to profit by another's haste (to cheat him): ⌐~ işe şeytan karışır⌐, haste is of the Devil; ⌐more haste less speed⌐. ~ci, in a hurry; impatient, restless (person).

acem Persian. ~ kılıcı, a double-edged sword. Acemistan (...͟), Persia.

acemi Tyro, novice; raw recruit. In-experienced, raw. ~ **oğlan,** a recruit in the Janissaries. ~**lik,** inexperience; a being a tyro.

acenta (·¹·) Agent (commercial).

aceze *pl. of* **âciz.** The destitute; waifs and strays.

acı¹ Bitter; sharp, pungent; rancid (butter, oil); glaring (colour); dismal, pitiable. ~ **bakla,** lupin: ~ **kabuk (kök),** quassia: ~ **su,** hard water; brackish water. ~**ağac,** quassia tree. ~**hiyar,** colocynth.

acı² Pain, ache; grief, sorrow. ~**sını çekmek,** to pay the penalty *of an action*: ~**sını çıkarmak,** to indemnify oneself for a loss, to take revenge for stg; **ben bunun** ~**sını tependen çıkarırım,** I'll make you pay for this: ~ **görmüş,** who has suffered much: ~**sı tepesinden* çıkmak,** to suffer great pain: **can** ~**sı,** physical pain: **evlâd** ~**sı,** grief for the loss of a child: **içler** ~**sı,** heart-rending.

acık Grief, sorrow; tragedy. ~**lı,** tragic; touching.

acık·mak *vn.* Feel hungry. **karnım acıktı,** I am hungry. ~**tırmak,** to make hungry, give a keen appetite.

acı·lanmak *vn.* Become bitter, pungent *or* rancid. ~**lık,** bitterness. ~**msı, ~mtrak,** rather bitter.

acı·mak *vn.* Feel pain; ache; hurt; feel pity, be sorry. *va.* Grudge *stg.*; regret its loss or waste; pity. ~**nmak,** to be pitied: be regretted; grieve. ~**nacak,** pitiable; deplorable, regrettable.

acırga Horse-radish.

acırganmak *vn.* Feel compassion.

acıtmak *va.* Cause pain *or* suffering; hurt.

acib (·¹) Wonderful; strange. ~**e** (·—¹) strange or wonderful thing: ~**i hilkat,** monster, monstrosity.

âcil (—¹) Hurried; hasty; urgent; prompt; pressing. ~**en** (⸜··), promptly; hastily, urgently.

aciz, –czi Incapacity; impotence; poverty.

âciz (—¹) Incapable; weak; impotent; poor, humble. ~**leri,** your humble servant: ···**den** ~ **kalmak,** to be incapable of. ~**ane** (—··—¹), ~**zî** (—·⸜), humble; modest; *used as polite or modest way of expressing* 'my', *e.g.* **tarafı âcizanemden,** from my part, from me.

acul (·⸜) Impatient; precipitate.

acur Kind of cucumber.

acuze (·⸜·) Old woman; hag.

acyo (¹·) Agio; premium. ~**cu** speculator.

aç¹ *imperative of* **açmak.**

aç² Hungry, destitute; covetous, insatiable. ~ **açına,** without food, without having a meal: ⌐~ **ayı oynamaz⌐,** a hungry bear

won't dance; a discontented man won't work well: ~ **bırakmak,** to starve (*va.*): ~ **biilâc,** starving, utterly destitute· ~ **durmak,** to be able to stand hunger; to fast: ~ **karnına,** on an empty stomach: ~**ından ölmek,** to die of starvation; to be fearfully hungry: ⌐~ **tavuk kendini arpa ambarında sanır⌐,** the hungry hen dreams she is in the barley barn (pleasant illusions, wishful thinking).

açalya (·¹·) Azalea.

açar Implement for opening; key; condiment, appetizer.

açevele (··¹·) (*naut.*) Span; stretcher of a hammock.

açgözlü (¹··) Covetous, avaricious; insatiable.

açık Open; uncovered; clear; cloudless; vacant, unoccupied; light (colour); free in manner; impudent; obscene (book); audible; distinct, plain, clear; blank (bill, endorsement). Open air; open country; open sea, the high seas; vacant space; deficit; outside (football). ~**tan açığa,** openly, frankly: **açığı çıkmak,** to show a deficit; **memurun yüz lira açığı çıktı,** the official was £100 short in his accounts: **açığa çıkmak,** to lose one's post, to be without a job: ~ **durmak,** to stand aside, not to interfere: ~ **itibar,** overdraft: ~**ta kalmak,** to be out in the cold; to be uncared for; to be without a job: ~**lar livası,** the unemployed (*iron.*): ~**tan para kazanmak,** to get an unexpected and unearned addition to one's income: **açığa satış,** short sale: **açığa varmak,** to go out into the open sea: **açığa vurmak,** to proclaim to the world; to declare openly: ~ **yer,** open space; vacant post: **başı** ~, bareheaded: **eli** ~, open-handed, generous: **gözü** ~, wide awake, vigilant: **gözü** ~ **gitti,** he died without seeing the fulfilment of his hopes: **yolun** ~ **olsun!,** I wish you a pleasant journey; good luck to you!

açık·ağız (·¹··), babbler; imbecile; astonishment; rocket (flower). ~**ça** (·¹·), openly; clearly: ~**sı,** in plain words. ~**göz, ~gözlü,** wide awake, sharp, cunning; 'bright fellow', 'cunning chap'. ~**gözlülük,** a being wide awake: ~ **etm.,** to be wide awake and practical; to 'have an eye on the main chance'. ~**kapı** (·¹··), way of escape; open door (*commercially*). ~**lamak,** to make public, divulge; become public, become common knowledge; throw off disguise *or* concealment. ~**lı,** *in* ~ **koyulu,** with light and dark colours; variegated; dappled. ~**lık,** open space; interval; freedom of manner; indecency; clearness (of weather *or* expression); lightness (of colour); open; spacious.

~**meşreb,** libertine; immoral. ~**saçık** (·¹··), immodestly dressed; indecent (words *etc.*); disorderly, untidy.

açılış Opening; inauguration; clearance.

açılmak *vn.* Be opened; be discovered; be widened; become more spacious; be amused; be refreshed; escape from boredom; recover *from faintness etc.*; (of weather) to clear; (of a post) to become vacant; be cleaned; open out; develop; throw off restraint, become more easy in manner; be morally corrupted; draw away from, shun; put to sea; (of a swimmer) to go far out. **açılıp saçılmak,** to be immodestly dressed: **araları açıldı,** they have quarrelled: **başi* ~,** to begin to get thin on top: **birine ~,** to open one's heart to s.o.: **içi* ~,** to be cheered up.

açkarnına (¹···) *adv.* Fasting; on an empty stomach.

açlık Hunger; greed. ~**tan nefesi* kokmak,** to be destitute.

açma Act of opening; field cleared of bushes *etc. ready for cultivation.*

açmak *va.* Open; begin (a discussion, a war *etc.*); reveal (secret); solve (difficulty); undo, unravel; whet (the appetite); unfold; set (sails); clear away (obstruction); sink (well); rub up, polish; uncover; bring into cultivation; explain *a subject* more fully; suit, become. *vn.* (Of a flower) to bloom; (of the sky *or* weather) to clear. ꜛaç gözünü açarlar gözünüꜞ, keep your eyes open or you will have them opened for you: **başına* iş** (*or* **oyun**) ~, to create a difficulty for s.o.: **bayrak ~,** to unfurl the flag of revolt: **el ~,** to beg: **elektriği** (**radyoyu**) ~, to turn on the light (wireless): **telefon ~,** to make a telephone call; **yanlış açmışınız,** you've got the wrong number: **yer ~,** to make room for (*dat.*).

açmalık Soap; detergent.

açmaz Difficult situation (in chess *etc.*). ~**a düşmek,** to fall into a trap: ~**a getirmek,** to play a trick on, to lay a trap for: ~ **oynamak,** to lay a trap.

açtırmak *va. caus. of* **açmak.** Cause to open *etc.*; clear (land). **göz açtırmamak,** to give no peace; not to give *anyone* a chance to recover himself.

ad¹ Name; reputation. ~**ına,** in the name of, on behalf of, for: ~**ı nedir?,** what is his name?: ~**ını ağza almamak,** to refuse to mention s.o.'s name, to have nothing more to do with him: ~**ı* batmak,** to pass into oblivion: ~**ı bile okunmamak,** to be of no importance: ~**ı* çıkmak,** to get a good (bad) name: ~**ı* ···e çıkmak,** to be known as ...; to get the reputation of ...: ~**ı sanı,** one's name and reputation; ~**ı sanı yok,**

of no account, of no repute: ~**ıyle sanıyle,** by his (its) well-known name: ~ **takmak,** to give an unpleasant name: ~**ı var,** it exists only in name, *not in reality*: **çocuğun** ~**ını koymak,** to give a child a name; to come to a decision; to define precisely, to make clear.

ad², –ddi A counting *or* esteeming; number; computation.

ada Island; ward *of a town.* **Adalar,** the Aegean Archipelago: **Büyük Ada,** the island of Prinkipo.

âda (·¹) *n. pl. of* **adu.** Enemies.

âdab (–¹) *n. pl. of* **edeb.** Customs; proprieties. ~**ı milliye,** national traditions *or* customs: ~**ı muaşeret,** rules of behaviour, 'savoir vivre': ~**ı münazara,** the rules of debate.

adaçayı (·¹··), **–ni** Garden sage.

âdad (–¹) *n. pl. of* **aded.** Numbers.

adak Vow; votive offering; threat.

Adalardenizi, –ni Aegean Sea.

adalât (···¹), **–tı** *n. pl. of* **adale.**

adale Muscle. ~**li,** muscular.

adalet (·–¹), **–ti** Justice. ~**li,** just. ~**siz,** unjust. ~**sizlik,** injustice.

adalı Islander, *esp.* Aegean islander.

adalî (··¹) Muscular.

adam Man; human being; person; good, fine man; serving-man; agent; partisan. ~**a dönmek,** to become presentable *in dress etc.*: ~ **etm.,** to make a man of, to bring up well: ~ **evlâdı** (**oğlu**), a well-bred man: ~ **içine çıkmak,** to go out in public: ~**ına göre,** according to the individual (*as regards status, worth etc.*): ~ **olmaz,** hopeless, incorrigible: ~ **sen de!,** come along!, you can do it!; don't worry!: ~ **sırasına geçmek,** to become an important person (*iron.*): ~ **yerine koymak** *or* ~**dan saymak,** to hold in esteem; to count as a person of consequence.

adamak *va.* Vow; offer *stg.* in fulfilment of a vow. ꜛ~**la mal tükenmez**ꜞ, promises cost nothing.

adamakıllı (·¹···) Proper; reasonable. Thoroughly, fully. ~ **ıslattım,** I gave him a sound thrashing: ~ **yorulmuş,** thoroughly tired.

adam·ca (·¹·), **adamcasına** (·¹···) In a human manner; in the proper way; as a man should. ~**cağız,** the good fellow; the poor chap. ~**cıl,** *lit.* 'not afraid of man', *and thus* 'liable to attack man', man-hater; misanthrope; vicious (horse); *but also* 'not afraid of man' *and thus* 'tame'. ~**cılayın,** ~**cılayn** (·¹···), as a man should, properly, decently. ~**lık,** decent and honest behaviour; Sunday-best clothes. ~**otu** (·¹··), **–nu,** mandrake. ~**sız,** without servants; without help.

adasoğanı (·¹···), **–nı** Squill.

adaş Of the same name; namesake.

âdat (–¹), **–tı** pl. of âdet. Customs.

adatavşanı, –nı Rabbit.

adavet (··–¹), **–ti** Hostility, enmity; hate.

‖**aday** Candidate.

add·etmek (¹··), **–eder** va. Count; enumerate; esteem. **~olunmak** (¹···), to be counted.

aded Number; numeral. bir **~**, one piece, one: yüz **~**, a hundred head of: **~i** tam or **~i** salih, whole number: kesirli **~**, fractional number. **~î** (··–¹), numerical.

adem Non-existence; lack of; absence; (followed by izafet and noun it can generally be translated by in-). **~i** kabiliyet, incapacity; **~i** emniyet, insecurity (such phrases are often written as one word): **~i** kabul, non-acceptance (of a bill).

âdem (–¹) Adam. beni **~**, mankind. **~î** (–·–¹) a., human. **~iyet, –ti**, humanity. **~zade** (–·–¹), mankind.

adese Lens.

âdet (–¹), **–ti** Custom, habit; menstruation. **~** etm., or edinmek, to contract a habit: **~** görmek, to menstruate: **~** üzere, according to custom; as usual: **~** yerini bulsun diye, as a mere formality. **~a** (–·–), as usual; simply; merely; sort of; nearly; as good as: walk! (riding command).

adım Step; pace; pitch of a screw. **~ ~**, step by step, gradually: **~** açmak, to lengthen the step, to go faster: **~ını*** alamamak, to be unable to refrain from doing sig.: **~** atmak, to step, to walk; to take the first step, to begin: **~** başında, at every step, frequently: **~ını** tek almak, to proceed with caution: cimnastik **~**, at the double. **~lamak**, to measure by pacing. **~lık**, a distance of so many steps: bir **~** yer, only a step away, quite near.

âdi (–¹) Customary, usual; commonplace, common; vulgar, mean. **~** gün, an ordinary day (as opp. to festivals, holidays etc.).

adid (·–¹) Numerous.

adil (¹·), **–dli** Justice; equity. kâtibi **~**, Notary Public.

âdil (–¹) Just; legally competent witness.

adîl (·–¹) Equal; equivalent; like; match. bi **~**, matchless.

adi·leşmek vn. Become common or inferior. **~lik**, commonness, vulgarity; baseness.

adîm (·–¹) Lacking; without; (followed by Arabic article and noun) in-, e.g. **~ülihtimal**, improbable; **~ülimkân**, impossible.

adin Eden. cenneti **~**, the Garden of Eden, Paradise.

ad·lamak va. Give a name to. **~lanmak**,

to be named. **~lı**, named; famous: **~ adıyle**, by its (his) well-known name: **~** sanlı, celebrated.

adlî (·–¹) Pertaining to justice; judicial. **~ye** (··–¹), Ministry of Justice.

adres Address. **~** rehberi, address book; directory.

adsız Nameless; unknown; without reputation. **~** parmak, the ring-finger.

aduv, adu Enemy.

af, –ffı Pardon; exemption; excusal; dismissal. **~** olunmaz, unpardonable: **~fı** umumî, general amnesty.

afacan Unruly, undisciplined; 'gamin', whipper-snapper, urchin.

âfak (–¹), **–kı** pl. of ufuk. Horizons. adı **~ı** tutmak, to get a great reputation.

âfaki (–––¹) Foreign; vagabond; here and there; on this side and that; superficial; futile (language); objective (opp. to enfüsî, subjective).

afallamak, afallaşmak vn. Be astonished, taken aback, stupified.

afât (–¹), **–tı** pl. of âfet.

aferide (···–¹) Created.

aferim, aferin (–·–¹) Bravo!, well done! (often used ironically to express disappointment). **~** almak, to obtain an honourable mention (in a school etc.).

âfet (–¹), **–ti** Disaster, calamity; bane, blight; person of bewitching beauty. **~zede**. stricken by disaster.

affetmek (¹··), **–eder** va. Pardon, forgive; excuse; give leave to go; dismiss. **affedersiniz!**, I beg your pardon!

affı v. af.

afi Showing off, swagger. **~** kesmek or yapmak, to cut a dash, to swagger. **~li**, swaggering.

afif (·–¹) Chaste; virtuous; innocent.

afiş (·–¹) (Fr. affiche) Advertisement, poster.

afitab (–·–¹) Sun; beautiful face. **~** perest, sun-worshipper; sunflower.

afiyet (–·–¹), **–ti** Health. **~** ola!, 'bon appetit!': **~** olsun!, may it do you good! (said to one about to eat or drink, have a bath or a shave etc.): **~le** yemek, to eat with a good appetite.

aforoz Excommunication.

afsun (·–¹), **efsun** Spell, charm, incantation; crafty tale. **~cu**, sorcerer. **~ger**, sorcerer, witch. **~lamak.** to bewitch.

aftos (sl.) Sweetheart. **~piyos** (¹·¹), useless, worthless.

afur tafur (·¹··) With a superior air.

afyon Opium. **~keş**, opium addict. **~ruhu, –nu**, laudanum.

ağ Net; web (of spider); fly (of trousers). **~** gözü, mesh: **~** gemisi, mine-sweeper.

ağa Obsolete title given to an illiterate man; lord, master, gentleman; obs. title of many officials. **ak** ~, white eunuch: **harem** ~sı, black eunuch who used to supervise the harem: **köy** ~sı, village headman: ⌐**gidene** ~**m gelene paşam**⌐, 'you say "Sir" to your outgoing superior, but "My Lord" to his successor' (said of a toady): ⌐**sen** ~ **ben** ~ **koyunları kim sağa?**⌐, 'you are a gentleman, I am a gentleman, who is to milk the sheep?'

ağababa (·¹··) Important person; senior; old-fashioned man.

ağabey (·¹·), **abe, abey** Elder brother; senior (colleague etc.).

ağac Tree; wood, timber. Wooden. ~**çileği, –ni,** raspberry. ~**kakan,** woodpecker. ~**kavunu, –nu,** citron. ~**kurdu, –nu,** wood-boring maggot. ~**lamak,** ~**landırmak,** to plant with trees, afforest. ~**lık,** wooded place; copse: well-wooded.

agâh (–⹁) Aware; informed; vigilant. ~ **etm.,** to inform; to put s.o. on his guard.

ağa·lanmak vn. Become proud like an Agha; give oneself airs. ~**lık,** state of being an Agha; title of Agha, pride; generosity, magnanimity.

ağar·mak vn. Become white or pale; become light (dawn). **ortalık ağardı,** the dawn broke. ~**tı,** a growing grey; whiteness; curd; milk residues. ~**tmak,** to whiten; clean; clear s.o.'s honour: ⌐**sakalımı değirmende ağartmadım**⌐, 'it was not in a flour-mill that my beard became white', i.e. I am grey with experience: ···**in yüzünü** ~, to do honour to ....

ağaz (–⹁) Beginning.

ağbanı Cotton stuff embroidered with yellow silk.

ağda A semi-solid sweet made of sugar, honey etc. ~ **koymak,** to apply this sticky substance to the skin to remove hairs. ~**lanmak,** ~**laşmak,** to become of the consistency of thick syrup. ~**lı,** of the consistency of thick syrup; heavy, involved speech or writing.

ağdırmak va. Cause to become semi-solid by boiling; cause to rise.

ağı, ağu Wealth; jewels; poison. ~ **otu,** hemlock. ~**lamak,** to poison.

ağıl Pen, fold; halo. ~**lanmak,** to be folded or penned; to be surrounded by a halo.

ağım Ascent; instep. ~**lı,** high in the instep.

ağır Heavy; weighty; serious, dignified; slow; lazy; unwholesome; offensive (words); severe (illness, punishment); valuable; painful; fatiguing; pregnant. ~ **almak,** to be slow or lazy in doing stg.: ~**dan almak,** to avoid excess; not to be too keen: ~ **ayak,** heavy with child: ~ **basmak,** to have influence, to be able to 'pull strings': ~ **ceza mahkemesi,** Criminal Court: ~ **davranmak,** to act in a slow or reluctant manner: ~ **esvab (mal),** expensive clothes (goods): ~ **gelmek,** to be hard to bear, to be trying or humiliating: **ağrına* gitmek,** to give offence, to hurt the feelings of: ~ **gövde,** fat: ~ **hapis cezası,** imprisonment with hard labour: ~ **hava,** unhealthy weather or climate: ~ **işitmek,** to be hard of hearing: ~ **satmak,** to put on an air of importance: **eli (eline)** ~, slow at work; lazy; slow in paying debts; heavyhanded; severe: **kulağı** ~, hard of hearing. **ağır·başlı,** (of a man) grave, serious, dignified. ~**canlı,** lazy, indifferent. **–ezgi,** slowly. ~**kanlı,** lazy, torpid. ~**lamak,** va. to treat with respect, honour; entertain, show hospitality to: vn. to become slow. ~**laşmak,** to become heavier, more difficult, slower, more serious; (of food) to begin to go bad; (of weather) to become overcast: **dili** ~, (of a drunkard etc.) to be incoherent in speech: **kulakları*** ~, to become hard of hearing. ~**lık,** weight, heaviness; slowness; stupidity; seriousness; hardness of hearing; nightmare; oppression caused by heat or boredom; trousseau; baggage; heavy transport of an army: ~ **basmak,** for sleepiness to come upon one; for a nightmare to oppress one; to feel uneasy.

ağırşak Disk; anything round and swollen; bobbin. **diz ağırşağı,** knee-cap.

ağıt Lament; mourning. ~**çı** professional mourner.

ağız, –ğzı Mouth; speech, manner of speaking, dialect; opening; edge (of a knife); biestings (colostrum); each successive baking in an oven, hence **ilk** ~, the first attempt at anything, e.g. the first child. ~ **ağza,** brimful; ~ **ağza vermek,** (of two people) to speak close to each other so that no one else may hear: **ağzından,** verbally, by hearing, unauthentic: **ağzı* açık kalmak,** to gape with astonishment: ⌐**ağzını açacağına gözünü aç!**⌐, instead of gaping with astonishment open your eyes (and understand what is happening): **ağzını* açmak,** also to give vent to one's feelings: **ağza almak,** to mention stg.: **ağza alınmaz,** uneatable; unmentionable, obscene: **ağzını* aramak** or **yoklamak,** to sound s.o.; to try to discover s.o.'s intentions: **ağzına* bakmak,** to hang on s.o.'s lips; to act in accordance with s.o.'s words: **ağzına beraber,** brimful: ~ **birliği etm.,** to tell the same tale: ~ **bozmak,** to vituperate, to swear:

⌐ağzından çıkanı kulağı Işitmiyor¹, he does not realize what he says; he is very stupid : ağzından* dökülmek, to be clear from a man's speech *that he is lying etc.*: ağza düşmek, to become a matter of common talk, to be the subject of scandal : ~ etm., to speak one's mind; to try to talk *s.o.* over; to talk in a theatrical manner: ağzına* geleni söylemek, to say disagreeable things; to speak without due reflection : ağzını* havaya açmak, to be disappointed; to get nothing : ···in ağzının içine bakmak, to hang on the lips of ...: ~dan işitme, hearsay, as a rumour only : ağzı kara, who delights in giving bad news; inclined to make the worst of anything he hears : ~ kokusu, foul breath; moodiness, caprice; ben herkesin ağzının kokusunu çekemem, I can't put up with everyone's whims *or* criticism : ağzı kulaklarına varmak, to grin from ear to ear, to be exceedingly pleased : ~ kullanmak, to explain away a matter: ⌐ağzile kuş tutsa faydası yok¹, even if he does the impossible it will be of no use : ağzından lâf (söz) almak, *by dint of talking of this and that* to get a person to say what one wants : ağzına lâyık, fit for your mouth, *i.e.* something really good to eat : ağzını poyraza açmak, *v.* ağzını havaya: ağzının* suyu akmak, for one's mouth to water, to long for something : ~ tadı, *v.* ağıztadı: agzını topla!, behave yourself!, don't be impudent! ···den ağzı* yanmak, to suffer loss or trouble from ...: ~ yapmak, to try to make out that *stg.* is other than what it really is: dört yol ağzı, cross-roads: düşman ağzı, calumny : halk ağzı, rumour, canard : ilk ~da, at the first shot, at the first attempt: kaymak ağzı, the crust of clotted cream. ağız·ağza, full to the brim; completely, utterly. ~bağı, mousing (of a hook). ~dolusu, without restraint, unreservedly; at the top of one's voice. ~kalabalığı, –nı, a spate of words· ~na getirmek, to disconcert by a flow of words. ~lık, mouthpiece (of a pipe *etc.*); cigaretteholder; muzzle; stone surround *of a well*; cover of leaves *over a basket of fruit.* ~otu, –nu, priming *of a gun.* ~persengi, –ni, constant refrain; anything constantly harped upon. ~sız, submissive, docile, meek. ~suyu, –nu, spittle. ~tadı, –nı, enjoyment of a meal; general feeling of satisfaction; *often written in two words and* ağız *with possessive suffix, e.g.* ağzımın tadı.

ağla·mak *vn.* Weep: grieve. ⌐ağlarsa anan ağlar, gerisi yalan ağlar¹, 'if anyone weeps it will only be your mother, the others will only

pretend to weep', *i.e.* don't expect others to worry about you : anası ~, to suffer great pain or misfortune : ⌐hem ağlarım hem giderim¹, *used of s.o. who pretends to be unwilling when he is really keen*: kan ~, to weep bitterly. ~malı, on the verge of tears. ~şma, a weeping together : bir ~ faslı başladı, they all started to weep. ~şmak, to weep together; to complain continually. ~tmak, to cause to weep : anasını* ~, to give a good hiding to; to ill-treat. ~yış, weeping, complaint.

ağleb Very prevalent; most. ~i ihtimal, in all probability : alal~, generally, for the most part.

ağma Star; shooting star.

ağmak Rise; evaporate.

ağnam (··⸜) *pl. of* ganem. Sheep; goats; flocks. ~ vergisi, sheep tax.

ağniya (···⸜) *pl. of* gani. Wealthy people.

Agop (*Armenian*) Jacob. ⌐Agobun kazı gibi ne bakıyorsun?¹, why do you stand and stare in that stupid way and do nothing?

ağraz (··⸜) *pl. of* garaz. Aims; objects.

ağrı Pain; ache. ~sı tutmak, for the pains of childbirth to come on : baş ~sı, headache; nuisance, pest : ilk göz ~sı, one's first love; one's first child. ~lı, ~klı, aching, painful. ~mak, to ache, hurt : başım ağrıyor, my head aches. ~sız, without pain : ~ baş, a man without cares : ~ başına derd açmak, to bring unnecessary trouble on s.o. ~tmak, to cause pain to, hurt.

Ağrıdağı Mount Ararat.

ağu *v.* ağı.

ağucuk (*iron.*) Baby; dolly; overgrown boy. ~ bebecik, naughty boy!, shame!

Ağustos August. ⌐~ta suya girsem balta kesmez buz olur¹, 'if I try to bathe in August, an axe wouldn't break the ice', *i.e.* I am always unlucky. ~böceği, –ni, cicada; chatterbox.

ağuş (–⸜) Embrace.

ağyar (·⸜) *pl. of* gayr. Others; strangers; rivals. ~a karşı, before others, publicly : yar ve ~, (lover and rivals) friend and foe, all the world.

ağzı *v.* ağız. ~açık, gaping idiot. ~bir, talking the same language; in agreement. ~bozuk, foul-mouthed, blasphemous. ~gevşek, talkative, indiscreet. ~kara, hypocritical; calumnious; bearing bad tidings. ~pek, who can keep a secret, discreet.

ah¹ Sigh; curse. ~ çekmek *or* etm., to sigh : ~a gelmek *or* ~ına uğramak, to suffer one's due retribution : ~ı* kalmamak, for s.o.'s curse to take effect sooner or later : ~ı* tutmak, for one's curse to take effect.

ah² Ah!; oh! ~ **deyip** ~ **işitmek**, to be alone and helpless: ~ **minel'aşk!**, alas! what a tyrant is love!: ~ **minelmevt!**, ah! cruel Death!

âhad (–·–) Units;individuals. **~ınas** (––·–·), the common people.

ahadiyet, –ti Oneness; the unity of God; monotheism.

ahali (·–·) *pl.* *of* ehil. Inhabitants; people; the public.

ahar White face-paint; size *for giving a finish to paper etc.*

âhar (–·) Other; different. **emri ~a kadar,** pending further instructions.

ahbab (·⁴) *pl.* *of* hıb. Friends; (*usually as sing.*) acquaintance. **~lık,** acquaintance-ship, friendship: **göz ahbablığı,** a knowing s.o. by sight.

ahcar (··–) *pl.* *of* hacer. Stones.

ahçı, aşçı Cook. ~ **başı,** head-cook: ~ **dükkânı,** eating-house. **~lık,** cooking; the profession of cook.

ahdar Green. **Hilâli Ahdar,** *now* **Yeşil Ay,** the Green Crescent (Turkish Temperance Society).

ahd·en (¹·) By treaty; as a pact. **~etmek** (¹··), **–eder,** *vn.* to take an oath; solemnly promise; make an agreement: *va.* contract to do *stg.*; undertake to do; enjoin. **~i,** *v.* **ahid.** **~î** (·–·), pertaining to a pact *or* contract. **~üpeyman** (····–) **etm.,** to take a solemn oath.

ahen (–·) Iron (*n.*). **~ger,** smith. **~in** (–··), iron (*a.*); robust, strong.

ahenk (–·) Purpose, intention; accord, harmony; music. ~ **kaidesi,** the law of vowel harmony in Turkish. **~li, ~tar,** harmonious, in accord; in time; in order.

aheste (–··) Slow; gentle; calm; 'piano' (*mus.*). ~ **beste,** slowly (*iron.*).

ahetmek (¹··), **–eder** *vn.* Utter a curse; sigh.

ahfad (·¹) *pl.* *of* hafid. Grandsons; descendants.

ahfeş One who sees better by night; *only in* ⌐**~in keçisi gibi başını sallamak**⌐, to agree with everything that s.o. says.

ahım şahım (–¹–·) *In* ~ **değil,** (*iron.*), anything but beautiful *or* excellent.

ahır Stable.

âhır *v.* âhir.

ahi (*Formerly*) member of a trade guild.

ahibba (···–) *pl.* *of* habib. Friends.

ahid, –hdi Oath; promise; pact; undertaking; solemn injunction; period, epoch. **~leşmek,** to take an oath together; to enter into a solemn agreement with one another. **~li,** bound by promise or contract. **~name** (···–), pact, agreement. **~şiken,** violating an agreement.

ahir (·–·), **âhir** (–·) (*There is considerable confusion between these two forms of the Arabic root.*) The end. Last; latter. ~ **zaman,** the latest time, the present age. **~en** (·–·), lastly, recently. **~et** *v.* ahret. **~in** (–·–·), last ones, contemporaries. **~ülemir,** at the end of the matter, at last, finally.

ahize (–·–·) Receiver (telephone *etc.*).

ahkâm (·⁴) *pl.* *of* hüküm. Judgements; dispositions; laws, rules; opinions; inferences *from omens or astrological observations*; absurd opinions *or* suppositions. ~ **çıkarmak,** to draw arbitrary conclusions; to put forward ridiculous suppositions: **~ından geçilmiyor,** he is unbearably puffed-up· ~ **kurmak,** to lay down the law in a conceited manner.

ahlâf (·–·) *pl.* *of* halef. Successors; descendants; posterity.

ahlâk (·⁴), **–kı** *pl.* *of* hulk. Moral qualities; morals; character. **hüsnü ~,** goodness of character; good morals: **ilmi ~,** moral philosophy, ethics. **~çı** (·–·), moralist. **~î** (·–·), pertaining to morals, moral. **~ıyat** (·–·⁴), **–tı,** ethics. **~ıyun** (·–·–·), moralists. **~sız,** immoral; amoral.

ahlamak *vn.* *In* ahlayıp vahlamak, to sigh and moan.

ahlat, –tı Wild pear; boor. ⌐**~ın iyisini dağda ayılar yer**⌐, 'the bears in the mountains eat the best of the pears'; the best things go to those who do not deserve them.

ahlât (·–·), **–tı** *pl.* *of* hilt. Humours (of the body).

ahmak Silly fool, idiot. **~lık,** stupidity, foolishness. **~ıslatan,** a fine drizzle.

ahmer *a.* Red. **Bahri ~,** the Red Sea.

ahrar *n.* *pl.* *of* hür. Free men; liberals.

ahret, –ti The next world, the future life. **~te on parmağım yakanda (olacak),** you'll pay for this in the next world; it's most unfair: ~ **suali,** endless questions, a 'regular' cross-examination: **~e varmak,** to go to the next world, to pass away. **~lik,** anything pertaining to the next world; devout man; an orphan brought up by well-to-do people as a servant.

ahsan, ahsen Better; best; more *or* most beautiful.

ahşa (·–·) *n.* *pl.* *of* haşa. Guts, intestines.

ahşab Wood. Wooden.

ahtapot, –tu Octopus; polypus; cancerous ulcer.

ahter Star; fortune, luck.

ahu (–·–) Gazelle. ~ **gözlü,** with beautiful eyes. **~baba** (–·–··), a nice old fellow; spook. **~dudu** (–·–··), **–nu,** raspberry.

âhü·enin (–···–), **~vah, ~zar** (–·–·) Moaning, lament; complaint.

ahval (·⸍), **-li** *pl. of* **hal.** Conditions; circumstances; the state of a person's health. ∼**i âlem**, the state of the world : ∼**i hazıra**, the present state of affairs : ∼ **ne merkezde?**, how are things going?

ahvel Squinting, squint-eyed.

ahyan (·⸍) *n. pl. of* **hin.** Times; moments. ∼**en**, at times, occasionally.

ahzetmek (⸍··), **-eder** *va.* Take; receive.

ahzisar (··⸍) **etm.** *vn.* Take revenge.

ahzüita (···—⸍) *Lit.* 'giving and taking'; buying and selling; commerce.

aid (−⸍) Relative to; concerning; belonging; competent (authority *etc.*). ···**e** ∼ **olm.**, to belong to, to concern.

aidat (−·⸍), **-tı** *n. pl.* Revenues; income; contribution; allowance; remuneration.

aidiyet (−··⸍), **-ti** A belonging to; a concerning; competence (of a court *etc.*). **bize bir** ∼**i yoktur**, it has nothing to do with us.

aile (−·⸍) Family; wife. ∼**vî** (−··⸍) *a.*, family, domestic.

ajan Agent. ∼**s**, news agency.

ajur (*Fr. à jour*) Open-work embroidery; hemstitch.

ak, **-kı** *a.* White; clean. *n.* White; white *of an egg or an eye.* ∼ **akçe**, silver money : ⸢∼ **akçe kara gün içindir**⸣, 'save up for a rainy day!' : ∼**ı** ∼ **karası kara**, with a white complexion but black eyes and hair; ∼**la karaya seçmek**, to have the greatest difficulty to do stg. : ∼ **pak**, bright and clean : **saçına*** ∼ **düşüyor**, his hair is beginning to turn white : **yüz** ∼**ı**, honour; **yüzü*** ∼, his conscience is clear : **yüzünü** ∼ **çıkarmak**, to be a source of pride : **bu işten yüzümün** ∼**ile çıktım**, I have come out of this affair without a stain on my honour.

akabe Steep road; pass; dangerous moment.

akabinde (⸍···) *adv.* Immediately afterwards; subsequently.

akağa (⸍··) White eunuch.

akağac (⸍··) A kind of birch; (?) = **akçaağac.**

akaid (·−⸍) *n. pl. of* **akide.** Articles of faith, religious precept; catechism.

akamber (⸍··) Ambergris.

akamet (·−⸍), **-ti,** Sterility.

akar[1] Flowing; running (water); leaky. ∼ **yakıt**, liquid fuel.

akar[2] (·⸍) Landed property; real estate. ∼**at** (·−⸍), **-tı** *or* ∼**et** (·−⸍), **-ti**, houses or flats built by a public institution to let. ∼**etçi**, landed proprietor.

akarsu Running water; a single necklace of diamonds or pearls.

ak·asma (⸍··) White climbing rose; clematis. ∼**baba** (⸍··), vulture. ∼**balık** (⸍··), dace (?). ∼**benek** (⸍··), leucoma. ∼**ciğer** (⸍··), lungs.

akasya (·⸍·) Acacia.

akça[1] Whitish; *v.* **akçe.** ∼ **kavak**, white poplar : ∼ **ağac**, maple : ∼ **pakça**, rather pretty.

akçe, akça[2] Coin; third of a para; money; sum of money. ∼ **etmez**, of no value, of no account : ∼ **kesmek**, to have a mint of money : **geçer** ∼, good currency, genuine : **ufak** ∼, small change.

akçıl Whitish; faded.

akdah (·⸍) *pl. of* **kadeh.** Cups; goblets; bowls.

akdem *comp. of* **kadim.** More ancient; prior; senior; more important. *adv.* Before. **bundan** ∼, some time back; formerly. ∼**ce** (·⸍·), formerly; not long ago; already.

Akdeniz (⸍··) Mediterranean.

akdes Most holy.

akdetmek (⸍··), **-eder** *va.* Bind, tie; conclude (bargain, treaty); contract (marriage); set up, establish (council); organize (meeting).

ak·diken (⸍··) Hawthorn. ∼**doğan** (⸍··), gerfalcon (?). ∼**günlük** (⸍··), oil of savin (juniper). ∼**haşhaş** (⸍··), white poppy *from which a syrup (diacodium) is made.*

âkıbet (−·⸍), **-ti** End; consequence, result; the near future; destiny. *adv.* (⸍··) Finally. ∼**bin** (···⸍), ∼**endiş** (···—⸍), far-sighted, prudent. ∼**ülemir**, in the end.

akıcı *a. & n.* Fluid; flowing; fleeting. ∼**lık**, fluidity; fluency.

âkıd (−⸍) Contracting. ∼**eyn**, the two contracting parties.

âkıl (−⸍) Wise; intelligent.

akıl, **-klı** Reason, intelligence, sense, wisdom; comprehension; prudence; memory; opinion. ∼ **almaz**, incomprehensible; incredible : **aklı* başına* gelmek**, to come to one's senses; **aklı başında**, he knows what he's about, he's 'all there'; **aklı başında olmamak**, to be incapable of clear thought; **akli* başından* gitmek**, to lose one's head : **aklını* bozmak**, to lose one's reason : **aklı* durmak**, to be dumbfounded, to be incapable of thought : ∼ **etm.**, to think *of a plan etc.* : **aklı evvel**, very clever : **aklına* gelmek**, to come to one's mind, to occur to one : **aklına* getirmek**, to remind *s.o.*; to recollect : **aklı* kesmek**, to decide, judge; **bu işi aklım kesmiyor**, I am not clear about this matter : **aklına* koymak**, to have quite made up one's mind : ∼ **öğretmek**, to give advice : **bu aklı kim sana öğretti?**, who put this idea into your head? : **aklı sıra**, according to him (*iron.*); if he is to be believed. ∼**da tutmak**, to bear in mind : ⸢∼ ∼**dan üstündür**⸣, there is always a better brain to be found: ⌐~ **var izan var**⌐ *or* ⌐~ **var yakın var**⌐, it's quite obvious, it's only common sense: **akla yakın,** reasonable, clear: **bir işe aklı* yatmak,** to be satisfied about a matter. **akıl·balığ** (··–ᐟ), having reached years of discretion. ~**dişi, –ni,** wisdom tooth. ~**hocalığı, –nı,** a being *s.o.'s* adviser; the giving of pretentious advice: ~ **istemem,** I don't want any outside advice; I want nobody's interference in this matter. ~**hocası, –nı,** mentor, pretentious adviser. ~**kutusu, –nu,** trusty adviser; one fertile in expedients. ~**lı,** clever, intelligent; reasonable; prudent. ~**lılık,** wisdom, intelligence. ~**sız,** stupid: ⌐~ **başın zahmetini ayak çeker**⌐, 'little wit in the head makes much work for the feet'.

akın Raid; foray; rush; stream *of people etc.* ~ ~, in crowds, in streams: **hava** ~**ı,** air-raid. ~**cı,** raider; (*formerly*) a corps of light cavalry in the Turkish army.

akıntı Current, stream, flow. ~**ya kürek çekmek,** to row against the current; to waste one's efforts: ~ **zaviyesi,** leeway (due to current).

akış Course; inclination; trip, *e.g.* **iki** ~**ta bin uskumru tuttuk,** in two runs we caught a thousand mackerel.

akıtma Blaze (on a horse); a kind of pancake.

akıtmak *va.* Make *or* let flow; shed (tears). **kanını içine** ~, to hide one's resentment.

akib (·ᐟ) Following; consequent. ···**in** ~**inde,** immediately after *or* behind . . .

akid, –kdi A tying; tie, knot; compact, treaty; bargain; marriage.

âkid (–ᐟ) Contracting party, signatory. ~**in,** the contracting parties.

akide (·–ᐟ) Religious faith, creed; sugar candy. ~**yi bozmak,** to go counter to one's faith or convictions.

akif (–ᐟ) Assiduous, persevering.

akik (·ᐟ) Agate.

âkil (–ᐟ) Eating. ~**ülbeşer,** cannibal: ~**ülhaşerat,** insectivorous. ~**e** (–·ᐟ), corroding ulcer.

akim (·ᐟ) Sterile, barren; without result.

akis, –ksi Opposite; contrary; reflection (in water *etc.*); reverse side; reverberation. **aksine anlamak,** to understand exactly the opposite of what was said: **aksi gibi,** 'just to spite one', *e.g.* **o gün aksi gibi yağmur yağdı,** of course it *would* rain that day.

ak·kefal (ᐟ··) Grey mullet. ~**kuyruk** (ᐟ··), a kind of tea, (?) orange pekoe.

akla·mak *va.* Whiten; put a white mark on; clear *s.o.'s* honour; acquit. ~**tmak,** to cause to be whitened: ···**in yüzüna** ~, to bring honour upon ....

aklen (ᐟ·) Reasonably, intelligently.

akletmek (ᐟ··), –**eder** *va.* Think of.

aklı¹ *v.* akıl.

aklı² Spotted *or* mixed with white. ~ **karalı,** with white and black spots; piebald.

aklık Whiteness; white face-paint; innocence.

aklısıra (·ᐟ··) *Used ironically to imply what was in the mind of the person concerned;* according to him; if he is to be believed: ~ **şıklaştı,** she dressed in what she thought was a chic way.

akl·î (·ᐟ) Pertaining to the mind or reason; reasonable; mental. ~**iselim,** common sense. ~**iyat** (··ᐟ), –**tı,** matters solved by reasoning and not based on tradition. ~**iye,** mental diseases; mental clinic. ~**iyeci,** mental specialist.

akma Flow; current. Flowing. ~ **yıldız,** shooting star.

akmak *vn.* Flow; ooze; drip; (of textiles) to become frayed or unravelled; (of a stocking) to ladder. ··· **e** ~, to go as far as ... : ⌐**akmazsa da damlar**⌐, 'even if it does not flow, it drips', *i.e.* don't despise even a small profit; it brings in something, if not a lot: ⌐**akan sular durur**⌐, 'flowing waters stop', there is nothing more to be said; that clinches the argument: **gönlü*,** to feel an attraction towards *stg.*: **gözü*,** to be blinded (by accident); ⌐**iki gözüm önüme aksın!**⌐, may my eyes fall out (if what I say is not true); **gözümden uyku su gibi akıyor,** I am terribly sleepy: ... **yüzünden akıyor,** it is obvious that he ... ; you can see by his looks that . . .

akord (*Fr. accord*) A being in tune. ~ **etm.,** to tune *a musical instrument.* ~**cu,** tuner.

akraba (··ᐟ) *pl. of* karib. Relatives; *also as sing.* relative. ~**lık,** relationship.

akran (·ᐟ) *pl. of* kırn *and* (*wrongly*) *as pl. of* karîn. Equals, peers; people of the same age, contemporaries; companions. ⌐~ ~**dan azar**⌐, bad habits are infectious: ~**ından kalmak,** to be behind one's fellows *in success etc.*: **ben** ~, people of my own age.

akreb Scorpion; hour-hand *of a clock.* ⌐**akrabanın akrabaya** ~ **etmez ettiğin**⌐, no scorpion treats a man as relations do each other.

aksa (·ᐟ) More *or* most distant; utmost. ~**yı Şark,** the Far East.

aksak Lame; limping; lop-sided. ~**lık,** lameness; limping behind others; hitch, defect. ~**sız,** without limping; without a hitch.

aksakal (ᐟ··) Village elder.

aksam (·ᐟ) *pl. of* kısım. Parts.

aksamak *vn.* Limp; falter; have a hitch.

aksan Accent.

aksata v. ahzüita.

aksatmak va. Cause to limp; hinder, delay.

akse (Fr. accès) Fit; attack; paroxysm.

akset·mek (ˌ··), **-eder** va. & vn. Reflect; be reflected; reverberate; come to the hearing of s.o. ~**tirmek**, va. reflect; echo.

aksır·ık Sneeze. ~lı tıksırıklı, sneezing and coughing; old and in bad health. ~**mak**, to sneeze. ~**tıcı**, sternutatory, sneeze-provoking.

aksi¹ v. akis.

aksi², **aksî** (·ˌ) Contrary; perverse, contrary; unlucky. ~ **çıkmak**, to happen contrary to expectation : ~ **takdirde**, in the opposite case; on the other hand. ~**lenmek**, to show resentment, to bridle. ~**lik**, perversity, contrariness; obstinacy; difficulty, hitch; misfortune, mishap. ~**ne**, on the contrary; in a contrary manner. ~**seda** (···ˌ), echo. ~**tesir** (···ˌ), reaction, counterstroke.

aksoy (ˌ·), ~**lu** Noble, well-born.

aksöğüt (ˌ··) White willow.

aksu (ˌ·) Amaurosis.

aksülâmel (···ˌ) Reaction.

aksülümen Corrosive sublimate.

akşam. Evening. In the evening. ~ı etm., to stay till the evening : ~ **sabah**, constantly, all the time : ~ **sabah demez gelir**, he comes at all sorts of times (without any consideration for one) : ~a **sabaha**, very shortly, at any moment : ~**üstü** or ~ **üzeri**, towards evening : ~ **yediği sabah unutmak**, to be very absent-minded. ~**cı**, one who spends his evenings drinking; worker on a night-shift. ~**lamak**, to spend the whole day doing stg. or going somewhere; to pass the night at a place. ~**latmak**, va. to put s.o. or stg. off till the evening; to keep s.o. busy, or a job going, all day; to entertain for the night. ~**layın** (·ˌ··), in the evening. ~**lık**, evening clothes etc.

aktar¹, **attar** Druggist, herbalist; dealer in small wares, haberdasher, mercer.

aktar² n. pl. of kutur. Sides; regions.

aktarma Change (of train); transhipment; plagiarism. ~**k** va., to move from one receptacle to another; to tranship; to move from one train to another; to turn topsy-turvy : **damı** ~, to re-tile a roof.

aktavşan (ˌ··) Jerboa.

akur (·ˌ) Exasperated, furious; mad (dog).

akval (·ˌ) n.pl. of kavil. Assertions, opinions; promises.

akvam (·ˌ) n. pl. of kavım. Peoples. **Cemiyeti** ~, the League of Nations (there are four other Turkish phrases for this).

akvaryum Aquarium.

akya A fish of the mackerel family (Lichia amia).

al¹ (·) Red, vermilion, crimson; chestnut (horse). Red colour; rouge; erisipelas, puerperal fever. ~ **basmak**, to blush; to be stricken with puerperal fever : ~ı **al moru mor**, red in the face from exertion or confusion : ~ **sancak**, the Turkish flag.

al² (·) Fraud, trick.

al³ (·) In ~ **aşağı etm.**, to knock down.

âl¹ (–) Dynasty, line; family of an important man. ~**i resul**, the posterity of the Prophet.

âl² (–) High.

ala- prefix (Fr. à la). ~**turka**, in the Turkish style : ~**franga**, in the European style.

ala Of various colours; speckled; pied. ~**bacak**, with white socks (horse). ~**balık**, trout.

âlâ (–ˌ) a. comp. of ali. Higher; highest; good, excellent. **ne** ~!, what a good thing! ; also iron. what a shame! : **pek** ~, very good!, alright!, excellent!

alabanda (···ˌ) The inside of a ship's side; broadside; order to 'about ship!'; violent abuse; severe scolding. ~ **etm.**, to put the helm hard over : ~ **iskele** (sancak), hard to port (starboard) : ~ **yemek**, to get a good 'dressing down'.

alabildiğine (ˌ·····) adv. To the utmost. ~ **koşmak**, to run at full speed : ~ **şişman bir adam**, 'the fattest man you ever saw' : **göz** ~, as far as the eye can see.

alabros (Fr. à la brosse) a. (Hair) cut very short.

alabura (···ˌ), **albura**. ~ **etm.**, to hoist a flag (naut.); to give a nautical salute by raising oars on end; to furl sails· ~ **olm.**, to capsize.

alaca¹ Of various colours; motley; piebald. A kind of striped stuff. ~ **basma**, chintz : ~ **dostluk**, a fickle friendship : ~ **karanlık**, twilight; dawn : ~**sı içinde**, sly, shifty; ⌐**hayvanın ~sı dışında, insanın ~sı içinde**⌐, you can judge a horse by its exterior, you can only know a man by his internal qualities : **deli** ~**sı**, crude and clashing colours. ~**bulaca** (··ˌ··ˌ), daubed with incongruous colours.

alaca² In ~ **verece**, the completion of a purchase.

alacak 3rd pers. sing. fut. of almak. n. Money owing; credit. **ondan alacağım var**, he owes me money : **alacağı olsun!**, 'I'll make him pay for it!' : ⌐**~la verecek ödenmez**⌐, a debt you owe cannot be paid by a debt owed to you. ~**lı**, creditor.

alacı, **alaçı** Executioner.

alaçık Tent of felt or wattle used by nomads.

aladoğan (·¹··) Buzzard (?).
alafranga (··¹·) In the European fashion.
alageyik (·¹··) Fallow deer.
alâim, alâyim (·–¹) pl. of alâmet. Signs. ~i sema, rainbow: ~i cevviye, meteor.
alâka (·–¹) Connexion; relationship; attachment; love; interest. ···le ~sı* olm., to be interested in: kat'i ~ etm., to break off relations, to sever connexion. ~bahş (·–·¹), interesting. ~dar (·–·⊥), connected, concerned, interested; pl. ~an, those concerned, those interested: ~ etm., to interest. ~landırmak, to interest, to affect. ~lı, in love; connected, interested; also (in journalese) interesting.
alâkaderilimkân (¹·····⊥) As far as possible.
alakarga (·¹··) Jay.
alâküllihal (··¹··) Only in ~ geçinmek or yaşamak, to have just enough to live on: ~ geçiniyoruz, (politely) 'we're not too badly off'.
âlâm (–⊥) pl. of elem. Pains; sorrows.
alamana (··¹·) Small lugger, fishing-smack; large trawl-net.
alâmeleinnas (·–¹··⊥) In public.
alâmeratibihim (·–·⊥···) According to their rank.
alâmet (·–¹), –ti Sign; mark; symbol; symptom; trace. Enormous; monstrous. ~i farika, distinguishing mark; trademark.
alan¹ Who takes or receives; purchaser.
alan² Clearing in a forest; open space; square in a town; sphere of work etc. spor ~ı, sports ground, playing-field.
alantalan, alantaran (·¹·¹) In utter confusion.
alarga (·¹·) Open sea. Distant, apart. ~!, push off!; keep clear!: ~da, in the offing; clear of: ~ durmak, to remain aloof: ~ etm., to put out to sea.
alaşağı (¹···) etm. va. Beat down, knock down; depose, dethrone.
alât (–⊥) pl. of alet. Instruments, tools. ~ı cinsiye, genital organs.
alaturka (··¹·) In the Turkish fashion.
alavere (··¹·) Utter confusion; jumble; passing or throwing a thing from hand to hand; a kind of gangway for loading coal on to a ship. ~ tulumbası, force-pump.
alavire (··¹·) Speculation (financial). ~ci, speculator.
alay Troop; crowd; procession; regiment; great quantity; joke, derision. ~ ~, in great numbers: ~a almak, to make fun of: ···le ~ etm., to make fun of ...: ~ etme!, 'joking apart', 'tell me seriously': ~ malay, the whole outfit: bir işin ~ında olm., not to take a matter seriously: ~ sancağı, regimental flag; ~ sancakları, flags for dressing

ship, celebrations etc. ~cı, joker; mocker: mocking, derisive. ~lı, ceremonious; pompous; mocking: officer risen from the ranks, as opp. to mekteblî, hence as a., amateur (iron.).
alâyım v. alâim.
alâyiş¹ (––¹) Pomp, display; showiness.
alâyiş² (·–¹) Defilement, pollution.
alaz Flame. ~lama, erythema. ~lamak, to scorch, singe; brand; speak a few friendly words to s.o. ~lanmak, to be singed or branded; (of the skin) to be inflamed or to come out in spots.
albastı Puerperal fever.
albatr Alabaster.
albay Colonel; captain (naval); group captain (air).
albeni (¹··) Attractiveness, charm.
albura v. alabura.
alçacık (¹··) Rather low.
alçak Low; short; vile, base, abject; cowardly. ~tan almak, to adopt a friendly, modest attitude; to change one's tone: ~tan görüşmek, to speak in a quiet, modest manner: ~ gönüllü, humble, modest; but ~ tabiatli, of a base nature: ~ ses, low voice; (mus.) low-pitched voice. ~lamak v.a., to despise, to treat with contempt: vn. to become low; to stoop. ~latmak, to lower, lessen, humiliate. ~lık, lowness, shortness; baseness, meanness, cowardice.
alçalmak vn. Bend down, stoop; abase oneself; condescend.
alçarak Lowish.
alçı Plaster of Paris. ~lamak, to cover with plaster of Paris. ~taşı, –nı, gypsum: sert ~, anhydrite.
aldanmak vn. Be deceived; be enticed; be taken in; be mistaken.
aldat·ıcı Deceptive; deceiving; cheating. ~maca, trick, 'sell', catch. ~mak, to deceive, dupe, cheat.
aldır·ış ~ etm., to pay attention, to take notice (usually in the negative). ~mak, va. caus. of almak q.v.; to make stg. fit into stg. else; vn. to take notice; to pay attention (to = dat.): göze ~, göze almak, v. göz. ~mamak (·¹··), va. & vn. neg. of above: to take no notice; to pretend not to see or hear: aldırma!, pay no attention!, take no notice!; don't worry!: burnundan kıl ~, to be very stand-offish and superior; not to yield an inch. ~mamazlık (·¹··), indifference: ~tan gelmek, to be indifferent, not to care.
aleddevam (¹··–) Continuously.
alel·âcayib (¹····) Strange; surprising. ~âcele (¹····), in haste. ~âde (¹·–·), ordinary, normal, usual. ~ekser (¹···),

for the most part. ~**fevr** (ˡ··), on the instant; impulsively. ~**hesab** (ˡ···–), on account (payment). ~**husus** (ˡ···–), especially. ~**ıtlak** (ˡ···–), absolutely; unreservedly; universally. ~**ûmum** (ˡ···–), generally, in general. ~**ûsul** (ˡ···–), in the customary manner; as a mere formality.

alem Sign; mark; flag; proper name; high mountain; peak of a minaret; the crescent and star on top of a mosque. ~ **olm.**, to become a distinctive name or epithet for ...; to be known as .... ~**dar** (··ˡ), standard-bearer.

âlem (–ˡ) World; universe; all the world, everyone; class *of beings*; state of health; amusement, entertainment, party; a surprising state of affairs. ~**de**, *expresses a fervent wish, e.g.* ~**de o kitablar benim elime geçmeliydi!**, really I *ought* to have got hold of those books; ~**i ervah**, the world of spirits, the next world: ~**i gaib**, the occult world: ~**i mâna**, ~**i ruya**, the world of dreams: **böyle yapmanın** ~**i yok**, one shouldn't do this sort of thing: **fahri** ~, the Glory of the World, Mohammed: **kendi** ~**de olm.**, to be occupied with one's own affairs; to live quietly and contentedly: **ne** ~**desiniz?**, how are you getting on?: **o bir** ~**!**, he's quite a character!

âlem·gîr (–·ˡ) World-conquering; universal. ~**şümul** (–··ˡ), world-embracing; mondial; universal.

alen·en (ˡ··) Publicly, openly. ~**î** (··ˡ), public; openly said *or* done. ~**iyet**, –**ti**, publicity.

alerresivelâyin (··ˡ··–·) *Lit.* 'on my head and eyes!', *i.e.* 'with the greatest pleasure!'

ales·sabah (ˡ···) In the morning. ~**seher** (ˡ···), at dawn. ~**seviye** (ˡ····), on an equality; uniformly; to all alike.

alesta (·ˡ·) Ready; prepared. ~**!**, stand by! ready!

alet (–ˡ), –**ti** Tool; instrument; member *of the body.*

alet·tafsil (ˡ···–) In detail; circumstantially. ~**tevali** (ˡ···––), continuously, without a break.

alev Flame; pennant. ~ **almak** *or* **kesilmek**, to catch fire; to flare up *in a passion*: ~ **makinesi**, flame-thrower. ~**li**, flaming; in a passion.

alevî (··ˡ) Partisan of Ali; Shiite.

aleyh Against. ~**inde**, against him *or* you: ~**imizde**, against us. ~**dar** (··ˡ), opponent: ~**lık**, opposition. ~**te**, unfavourable.

aleykümselâm (··ˡ·ˡ) Peace be to you! (*in reply to the Moslem salutation* **selâmaleyküm**).

alfabe Alphabet.

algarina (··ˡ·) Floating crane; sheer-hulk.

algınlık *In* **soğuk algınlığı**, a chill.

algoncar Sloe; bullace.

alıc Neapolitan medlar.

alıcı Buyer, customer; receiver (telephone, wireless). Dazzling; attractive. ~ **gözü ile bakmak**, to look at *stg.* as a genuine purchaser; to regard earnestly, with serious intention, carefully: ~ **kuş**, bird of prey.

alık Crazy; imbecile.

alıkomak, alıkoymak (·ˡ··) *va.* Keep; detain; stop.

alım *n.* Taking; buying, purchase; attraction: range. ~ **satım**, business, trade: **göz** ~**ı**, distance the eye can see. ~**cı**, creditor; tax-collector. ~**lı**, attractive. ~**sız**, unattractive, ugly.

alın, –**lnı** Forehead, brow; face; front; boldness, shamelessness. **alnı açık**, honest, honourable: **alnı ak**, innocent, blameless: **alnının akıyle**, without a stain on his character: **alnını* çatmak**, to frown: ~ **damarı çatlamak**, to lose all sense of shame: **alnını* karışlamak**, to challenge, defy; '**alnını karışlarım!**', 'I defy you to do it!': ~ **teri**, the sweat of the brow, hard work: **ben hayatımı alnımın teriyle kazanırım**, I earn my living by the sweat of my brow: ~ **yazısı**, destiny: **güneşin alnı**, the heat of the day.

alıngaç, alıngan Touchy.

alınlık Ornament worn on the forehead; inscription *or* sign on the front of a house.

alınmak *vn. pass. of* **almak**. Be taken *etc.*; take offence. **kimse üstüne alınmasın**, let no one think that this refers to him.

alınteri *v.* **alın**.

alış Action of taking *etc., v.* **almak**; ~ **veriş**, buying and selling, trade; connexion; relation.

alış·ık Accustomed to; used to; tame; familiar; regular (customer *etc.*); working smoothly (machine). ~**kan**, accustomed; familiar: ~**lık**, a being accustomed; familiarity. ~**mak**, to be accustomed; become familiar; become tame; work smoothly. ~**tırmak**, to accustom, familiarize; tame; instruct; train; get into running order. ···**i alıştırarak haber vermek**, to break the news gently *to s.o.*

alışveriş *v.* **alış**.

Ali *prop. n.* Ali. ~ **kıran baş kesen**, bully, despot: ~ **Paşa vergisi**, a present the return of which is demanded: ~ **Veli**, Tom, Dick, and Harry.

âli (–ˡ) High; exalted. ~**cah** (––ˡ), high in rank. ~**cenab** (––·ˡ), majestic; eminent; magnanimous, generous. ~**lık**, magnanimity, generosity. ~**güher**, of a noble nature *or* essence. ~**himmet**, high-minded, high-principled. ~**kadir**, high

in value, esteemed. ~makam, ~mekân
(——·⸱), of high position or rank. ~şan
(——⸱), eminent, illustrious. ~tebar (——·⸱),
of high lineage.
alicengiz In ~ oyunu oynamak, to play a
dirty trick.
âlihe (—·⸱) n. pl. of ilâh. Gods.
alikıran v. Ali.
alil (·⸱) Ill; invalid; blind.
âlim (—⸱) Learned; scholar. ┌bin ~in
bilmediğini bir ârif bilir┐, a wise man knows
what a thousand learned men do not.
alimallah (·⸱·—) By God!; God knows!; I
warn you!
alivre (Fr. à livrer) For future delivery.
aliyülâlâ (··⸱——) a. The very best.
alize (Fr. alizé) Trade-wind.
alkım Rainbow.
alkış Applause. ~lamak, to applaud.
alkol, –lü Alcohol. ~ik, alcoholic.
Allah (·⸱) God. ~~!, by God!, Good Lord!:
~ın ···i, often used as a euphemism for
'God-forsaken' cf. English 'blessed': ~tan
or ~tanki, (i) natural(ly), inborn; (ii) thank
Goodness that, it's a good thing that . . .,
e.g. '~tan şemsiyeyi yanıma almıştım!',
'thank Heaven I had taken my umbrella
with me!': ~ü âlem, probably, God knows
(deprecatingly): ~ aşkına, for the love of
God, for God's sake!: ~ bir, I swear:
~ından bulsun!, may God punish him!
(for I cannot): ~ derim, words fail me!, it's
hopeless!: ┌~ dokuzda verdiğini sekizde
almaz┐, what Fate has decreed cannot be
altered: ~ın evi, mosque; heart: ~ göstermesin!, God forbid!: ~ için, used to strengthen an assertion: ~a ısmarladık, good-bye!:
~tan kork!, shame! don't do it!: ~tan
korkmaz, impious; unjust, cruel: ~
lâyığını (müstahakkını) versin!, may God
give him his deserts!, curse him!: ~ ne
verdiyse, (of food etc.) whatever is at hand,
'pot-luck': ~ vere, God grant that, let's
hope that …: ~ vergisi, talent: ~ vermesin!, God forbid!: ~ versin, (i) as ~
vere; (ii) reply to a beggar when refusing
alms; (iii) an ironical congratulation:
~a yalvar!, said to one who complains about
stg. for which he is himself to blame, or who
insists on doing stg. wrong: 'well then, God
help you!: bilenler (görenler) ~ için
söylesin!, phrase calling others to witness
that what one says is true.
allahlık (·—⸱) Useless but harmless (man);
beyond the comprehension of man; beyond human power to remedy; imbecile.
allâk Tricky, deceitful; fickle.
allak bullak (·⸱·⸱) Pell-mell; all over the
place; in utter confusion, topsy-turvy.
allâme (·—⸱) Very learned.

allem kallem (·⸱·⸱) Vague words (such as
'so-and-so'); tricks, dodges. ~ etm., to
put s.o. off with words; to trifle with s.o.:
allem etmek kallem etmek, to try all sorts
of tricks to attain one's purpose.
allı In ~ pullu or ~ güllü, brightly coloured
and decorated.
allık Redness; red colour; rouge.
alma (·⸱) Word of command to stop rowing,
'easy all!'
almak, –lır va. Take; get, obtain; receive;
accept; buy; take in, contain; comprehend;
conquer, capture. vn. Take fire; (of a
(contagion) to take hold, to affect. al benden de o kadar, it's the same with me;
'same here!': alip yürümek, to make swift
progress; to become the vogue, to 'catch
on': ateş ~, to catch fire: boynuna* ~,
to undertake, to assume responsibility for:
···in etrafını ~, to surround: gözün ala-
bildiği kadar, as far as the eye can reach;
~den kendimi alamadım, I could not help…,
I could not refrain from …: kız ~, to
marry: ödünc ~, to borrow: söz ~, to
receive a promise: üstüne* ~, to take
upon oneself: yol ~, to take the road, to
travel; to advance.
alman German. ~ca (·⸱·), German (language). **Almanya** (·⸱·), Germany.
alnı v. alın.
alp, –pı Hero; brave.
alt, –tı Lower or underpart of a thing;
underside; bottom. Lower, under. ~ ~a
üst üste, one on top of the other; ~ ~a üst
üste boğuşma, tough struggle: ~ında*,
under him, it etc.: ~tan, from below: ~tan
~a, by implication, between the lines; in
an underhand way; ~tan ~a anlatmak,
to hint at, to imply: ~ına almak or ~ına
alıp dövmek, to give a good thrashing to:
~ başında, near, next: ~ başından, from
the very bottom: ~ etm., to conquer, to
overthrow: ~ına etm., to foul one's clothing or bed: ~ından girip üstünden çıkmak,
to put things in disorder; to squander all
one's money: ~ta kalmak, to get the worst
of it; ┌~ta kalanın canı çıksın!┐, vae victis!,
woe to the conquered!: ~ında kalmamak,
not to be outdone; not to be under an
obligation: ~ olm., to be overcome: ~
tarafı, the underside; the sequel; 'bunda
düşünecek ne var? Alt tarafı beş lira',
'Why hesitate? After all, it's only a matter
of five pounds': ~ını üstüne getirmek, to
turn topsy-turvy: ayak ~, the sole of the
foot; the ground under the feet: el ~ından,
in an underhand or secret manner.
altabaşo (··⸱·) ~ yakası, the foot of a sail.
altı Six. ~lık, consisting of six (piastres,
pounds, etc.), ~ncı┐, sixth.

altın Gold; gold coin; wealth. Golden. ~ adını bakır etm., to bring dishonour upon an honoured name. ~**babası, –nı,** immensely wealthy; a Croesus. ~**baş,** the name of a choice kind of melon : ~ kefal, the Golden Mullet (*Mugil auratus*). ~**cı²,** goldsmith. ~**kökü, –nü,** ipecacuanha root. ~**lamak,** to gild. ~**otu, –nu,** hart's-tongue fern. ~**sarısı,** golden blonde. ~**top, ~pu,** trollius. ~**topu, –nu,** (golden ball), *expression used to describe a pretty chubby baby.*

altıparmak Very large palamut *q.v.*

altıpatlar (··¹·) Six-shooter, revolver.

altışar Six each; six at a time.

altlı *In* ~ üstlü, topsy-turvy; upside-down.

altlık Something put under as a support; pad *put under writing paper.*

altmış Sixty. ~**altı** (··¹·), *a kind of card game;* ~**ya bağlamak,** to put *s.o.* off with vague promises; to come to an agreement which satisfies both parties. ~**ar,** sixty each; sixty at a time. ~**ıncı,** sixtieth. ~**lık,** sixty years old; containing sixty parts; worth sixty ... .

alttaraf (¹··) Continuation; sequel.

altüst (¹·) Upside-down; topsy-turvy.

alûd (–⁻) *Pers. suffix.* Contaminated with, affected by, *e.g.* hâb~, sleepy; hun~, bloody. ~**e** (––¹), soiled, contaminated.

alüfte (–·¹) Tart, cocotte.

alyans (*Fr. alliance*) Wedding-ring.

am (·) Vulva.

âm (–) General; universal; public; common, ordinary.

ama, amma (¹·) But; *sometimes expresses surprise or exaggeration.* ~**sı yok** *or* ~**sı maması yok,** there's no 'but' about it; 'but me no buts!'

âmâ (–⁻) Blind. **amâ** (·⁻), blindness.

amac Target; aim, object.

âmade (––¹) Ready; prepared. **emre** ~, at (your) disposal; available.

âmak (–¹), **–kı** *pl. of* umk. Depths; profundities.

âmal (–⁻), **–li** *pl. of* amel. Actions, deeds.

âmâl (–⁻), **–li** *pl. of* emel. Desires, hopes; ambitions.

aman (·⁻) Pardon, mercy. ~**!,** help!; mercy!; alas!; for goodness sake : ~ dilemek, to ask for quarter : ···ı ~**a düşürmek,** to make *s.o.* cry for mercy : ···in önünde ~**a gelmek,** to be helpless in the face of ... : ~ vermek, to grant quarter : ~ zaman dinlemez, merciless; ~**ı zamanı yok!,** there's no getting out of it; you must! ~**ın, ~!,** help! ~**sız,** pitiless, without mercy.

Amasya (·¹·) *prop. n.* Amasia. ⌐~**nın bardağı biri olmazsa biri daha¹,** 'there are

as good fish in the sea as ever came out of it', *or* 'it doesn't matter, I can easily get another'.

ambalaj (*Fr. emballage*) Packing; wrapping.

ambar, anbar Granary; storehouse; magazine; hold *of a ship;* barn; bin *for measuring sand, stones, etc.* ~ ağzı, hatchway : ~ kapağı, hatch (on a ship). ~**cı,** storekeeper; warehouseman.

ambargo (·¹·) Embargo.

amber Ambergris. ~ balığı, spermaceti whale : ~ çiceği, musk-mallow; muskseed. ~**baris** (··⁻·), barberry, berberis.

ambreyaj (*Fr. embrayage*) Clutch. ~ yapmak, to let in the clutch.

amca, amuca (¹·) Paternal uncle. ~**zade** (···¹), cousin.

amden (¹·) Intentionally; deliberately.

amedci (–·¹), **amedî** (–·⁻) *Formerly the head of the office at the Sublime Porte dealing with correspondence with the Palace; he was also Chief Secretary to the Council of Ministers.*

amel Action, deed; work; execution; action of the bowels, diarrhœa; practice; performance. ~ etm., to act, to proceed : ~ olm., to have diarrhœa : ilm ve ~, theory and practice.

amele *pl. of* âmil. Workers; *also used as sing.* workman, labourer.

amelî (··⁻) Practical (*as opp. to* nazarî, theoretical). **ameliyat, –tı,** *pl. of* ameliye, practical deeds (*as opp. to theories*); operations (*mil., etc.*); *as sing.,* surgical operation. **ameliye,** surgical operation; operation; work; chemical process.

amelmanda, amelimanda Incapable of work; past work, retired; invalid.

amenna (–¹–) *interj.* Admitted!, agreed!

amerikalı (·¹···) *n.* American. **amerikan** (···⁻) *a.* American : ~ bezi, unbleached calico.

amik (·⁻) Deep; profound.

âmil (–¹) Doing; working; active. Workman; factor; manufacturer.

amîm (·⁻) Universal, general.

amin (–¹) Amen!, so be it! ~ alayı, *ceremony observed by a school for a new pupil.*

aminen (–·¹) Safely and soundly.

âmir¹ (–¹) Commanding. Commander; superior; chief. ~**lik,** authority; command; a being a chief *or* superior.

âmir² (–¹) Flourishing, prosperous; belonging to the Government, official.

amiral, –li Admiral. ~ gemisi, flagship.

amirane (–··¹) In an imperious *or* commanding manner.

âmiyane (–·–¹) Vulgar, common.

-amiz (–-) *Pers. suffix.* Mingled with ...; provoking .... hikmet~, mingled with wisdom: fitne~, seditious. **amiziş**, association; intercourse.

amma (¹·) But. *v.* ama.

amme (–¹) The public; everyone. **âmme** (–¹) *fem. of* âm, *a.* general; public: menfaatı ~, the public interest: ~nin malûmu, known to all.

âmmi (–¹) Paternal uncle.

amortisör (*Fr. amortisseur*) Shock-absorber.

ampirik (*Fr. empirique*) Empirical.

ampul (·–-) (*Fr. ampoule*) Electric light bulb.

amuca (¹··) *v.* amca.

amud (·–-) Pole; column, pillar; perpendicular. ~**en** (·–-·), vertically. ~**dî** (·—–-), perpendicular, vertical. ~**ufıkarî** (·—··—-), spine, backbone.

amyant (*Fr. amiante*) Asbestos.

ân (–) Beauty, attractiveness; nuance.

an¹ (·) Moment, instant. bir ~ evvel, as soon as possible: el ~, at the moment, at present; even now: her ~, at any moment.

an² (·) Mind, intelligence; perception; memory.

an³ (·) *In* ~ san, renown, reputation.

-an (–) *Pers. plural termination.*

ana Mother; the principal part *or* main body *of a thing.* Main, principal; basic. ~ akçe *or* para, the principal (financial): ~ baba, parents; ~m babam, my father and mother; *sometimes* 'my dear fellow!'; ~ baba gün, great confusion: ~ baba evlâdı, a darling child: ~dan doğma, stark naked; ~dan doğma kör, born blind: ~sını satarım, (*sl.*) I don't care two hoots!: ~ yarısı, one who takes the place of a mother.

anac¹ Capable of looking after itself (animal or child); grown up, big; brought up to a business; experienced; shrewd.

anac² Stock *for grafting.*

Ana·dolu (·¹··) Anatolia. ~**dolulu** (·¹···), ~**dollu** (¹···), Anatolian.

anafor Eddy; something got for nothing; illicit gain; bribe. ~**cu**, one who lives at another's expense, parasite; profiteer; one who makes illicit gains. ~**lamak** (*sl.*), to make illicit gains, to profiteer.

anahtar Key; spanner; electric switch. ~**cı**, keeper of keys, warden.

analık Motherhood, maternity; a motherly woman; adoptive mother.

ananas Pineapple.

an'ane *pl.* **an'anat** (··¹) Tradition. ~**sile**, with full details. ~**vî** (···-), traditional.

ananet (·–¹), **-ti** Impotence.

anarşi Anarchy.

anasıl (¹··) By origin, originally.

anasır (·–¹) *pl. of* unsur. Elements.

anason Aniseed.

anat (–-), **-tı** *pl.* Shades of meaning.

anavata (··¹·) A kind of embroidery.

anayasa (·¹··) Constitution.

anayol (·¹·) Main road.

anayurd (·¹·) Mother country; original home.

anbean (¹··) From moment to moment; from time to time; gradually.

anca (¹·) Hardly, barely; only; just: ⌐~ beraber kanca beraber⌐, inseparable *friends etc.*; 'we must stick together'.

ancak (¹·) Hardly, barely, only, just. But; on the other hand, however.

and Oath; vow. ~ bozmak, to violate an oath: ~ etm. *or* içmek, to take an oath: ~ vermek, to conjure, to adjure. ~**laşma**, treaty, covenant. ~**laşmak**, to take an oath with another. ~**lı**, who has taken an oath.

‖**andaç, andıç** Gift; souvenir.

andavallı (*sl.*) Simpleton.

andelib (··-) Nightingale.

andetmek (¹··), **-eder** *vn.* Take an oath; pledge.

andır·an Reminiscent of. ~**mak**, to bring to mind; to bear a striking resemblance to.

andız Elecampane; thicket outside a town; brothel quarter.

andıçmek *vn.* Take an oath, swear.

ane Pubes; private parts.

-ane (–¹) *Pers. suffix* (i) *turning adjectives into adverbs, e.g.* mest, drunk; mestane, in a drunken manner; (ii) *turning an adjective describing a person into one describing an act or an inanimate object, e.g.* âlim, learned (man); âlimane, learned (book); (iii) *turning a noun into an adjective or adverb, e.g.* peder, father; pederane, paternal *or* in a paternal manner.

anele Ring of an anchor.

anenfeanen *v.* anbean.

anfi (*abb. Fr. amphithéâtre*) Lecture-room.

angarya (·¹·) Forced labour; unpaid job; hard task; fatigue (*mil.*); burden, infliction. Carelessly, perfunctorily; unwillingly.

angıt, angut The Ruddy Sheld-duck; (*sl.*) fool.

angudi (·—-) Orange-brown.

anha minha (¹·¹·) Approximately.

anılmak *vn. pass. of* anmak. Be mentioned; be called; be remembered.

anırmak *vn.* Bray; boast.

‖**anıt** Monument; memorial.

anıvahidde (–·—··) At once, immediately.

anız Stubble. ~ bozması, the breaking up of stubble.

anî (−⌣) Instantaneous; momentary; sudden, unexpected. ∼**de** (⌣−·), on the instant, instantly.

anif (·⌣) Violent, rough; severe; brutal.

ânifen (⌣··) Above (mentioned); before; not long ago.

anilmerkez (¹···) Centrifugal.

anjin Angina.

anka (·⌣) A legendary bird; phoenix; imaginary thing; will-o'-the-wisp.

ankarib (¹·−) Shortly, soon.

ankasdin (¹··) Intentionally; with malice prepense.

ankebut, −**tu** Spider.

ankesman (*Fr. encaissement*) Paying-in.

anket, −**ti** (*Fr. enquête*) A series of interviews by a journalist on some particular subject.

anlamak *va.* Understand. ···**den** ∼, to understand, to know about; to appreciate; to find pleasure in: **bu ilâcdan hiç bir şey anlamıyorum,** I don't think much of this medicine: **senin anlıyacağın,** (i) you know what I mean; (ii) in short; to cut a long story short: **söz (lâf)** ∼, to be reasonable, sensible: **söz anlamaz,** unreasonable; wilful.

anlaşamamazlık (··¹···) Misunderstanding.

anlaşıl·an So it seems; probably; apparently. ∼**ır** *a.*, intelligible, clear. ∼**mak,** to be understood, be evident. **anlaşılır,** it is clear that; it can be inferred that; **anlaşılır anlaşılmaz,** imperceptible: **şimdi anlaşıldı,** now the matter is clear.

anlaşma Agreement, understanding. ∼**k,** to understand one another; to come to an agreement.

anlat·ılmak *vn.* Be recounted; be explained. ⌐**anlatılışa göre fetva verilir**¬, judgement is given in accordance with the way the case is presented. ∼**ış,** mode of explaining; explanation; description: ⌐∼**tan** ∼**a fark var**¬, it makes a difference according to how a case is presented. ∼**mak,** to explain, expound; narrate; make known. **söz** ∼, to persuade.

anlayış Understanding; intelligence; sagacity. ∼**lı,** intelligible; intelligent.

anmak *va.* Call to mind; mention. **adını hayır ile** ∼, to speak well of s.o. after his death.

anne (¹·) Mother. ∼ ∼, maternal grandmother. ∼**ciğim** (¹···), dearest mother; mummy!

anonim Anonymous. ∼ **şirket,** joint-stock company.

anormal Abnormal.

ansamimikalb (¹·−··) From the bottom of the heart; sincerely.

ansız (¹·), ∼**ın** (¹··) Sudden; suddenly; without warning.

antepfıstığı (·¹···), −**nı** Pistachio nut.

antika (·¹·) Antique, rare; comic; eccentric. Figure of fun; hemistitch. ∼**cı,** dealer in antiques. ∼**lık,** eccentricity.

antrasit Anthracite.

antre (*Fr. entrée*) Entry; entrance-fee.

antrepo (*Fr. entrepôt*) Bonded warehouse.

antrenör (*Fr. entraîneur*) Trainer.

anud Obstinate.

apaçık (¹··) Wide open; very evident *or* clear.

apansız (¹··), ∼**ın** All of a sudden.

apar topar (·¹·¹) With surprising suddenness; headlong; helter-skelter.

aparmak *va.* Carry off; make off with.

apartıman, apartman Block of flats; flat.

apartma Something taken; plagiarism.

apaşikâr (¹−·−) Very evident.

apayrı (¹··) Quite different; quite distinct.

apaz Closed hand *or* fist; handful. ∼**lama,** beam wind. ∼**lamak,** to grasp with the hand; to sail with a beam wind.

apış Fork of the body. ∼ **açmak,** to stand with the legs apart. ∼ **arası,** *polite for* the 'private parts'. ∼**ık,** with legs a-straddle; (of a horse) too tired to move; weary; dejected; dazed: **apışıp kalmak,** to be completely nonplussed. ∼**tırmak,** to tire *a horse* out completely; to bring *s.o.* into a state of weariness and helplessness; to moor a *ship* fore and aft.

apiko (·⌣·) A ship's having the anchor taut ready to haul up. Ready; on the qui vive, alert, smart.

apolet, −**ti** Epaulet.

apre (*Fr. apprêt*) Finishing (of textiles).

apse Abscess.

apşak *v.* **apışık.**

aptal, aptes *v.* **abdal, abdest.**

apukurya (··¹··) (Gr. ἀποκρέα) Carnival; shrove-tide.

apul apul (·¹·¹) In a swaying manner; waddling.

âr (−) Shameful deed; shame, bashfulness; modesty. ∼ **etm.,** to be ashamed: ⌐∼ **yılı değil, kâr yılı**¬, (i) of course one wants to make a profit; (ii) (*sarcastically*) he won't miss a chance of making money!

ar¹ (·) (*Fr. art*) Art.

ar² (·) (*Fr. are*) Are (100 sq. metres = 119·6 sq. yds.).

ara Interval *or* space *of place or time*; relation *or* understanding *between two persons*; (*with possessive pronoun and* -**da**) among, amongst; (*with poss. pron. and after two nouns connected by* **ile**) between. ∼**dan,** in between (of time), meanwhile: ∼**ları***

açık, their relations are strained, they are not on good terms: ~ya almak, to surround, to hem in: ~da bir, here and there: ~larını* bozmak, to create a rift between ... : ~ bulmak, to find a way or opportunity: ~sını bulmak, to find a way of arranging a matter; to reconcile: ~da çıkarmak, whilst otherwise occupied to find an opportunity of doing some necessary thing: ~dan çıkarmak, to remove stg.; to get one job out of the way in order to be able to do others: ~dan çıkmak, to go away from the midst of others, to have nothing more to do with them; not to interfere; to take no further part in stg.: ~ya girmek, to act as mediator; to interfere; to prevent by interference: ~da gitmek, to pass unnoticed amongst many others: ~ya gitmek, to be lost; to be sacrificed: ~sı* iyi olmamak, not to like s.o. or stg.: ~da kalmak, to be mixed up in an affair: ~ kapı, connecting door between two buildings or rooms: birini ~ya koymak, to put in s.o. as intermediary: ~da sırada, now and again: ~ vermek, to pause; to make a break; ~ vermeksizin, without interruption: bir ~da, at the same time, simultaneously; in the same place together: bir ~ya gelmek, to come together, to meet in one place: bu ~da, at this moment; at this place; including, amongst these: bunlar ~sında, amongst these: ⌐işin ~sı soğudu⌐, the matter has been neglected too long to do much about it now: söz ~sında, in the course of conversation or of a speech.
âra (−⸴) pl. of rey. Opinions; votes.
-âra (−⸴) Pers. suffix. Adorning ... .
arab Arab; Ethiopian; nigger. ~ aklı, stupidity: ak ~, the true Arab (not black): ⌐anladımsa ~ olayım⌐, 'hanged if I understand!': ⌐kırk ~ın aklı bir incir çekirdeğini doldurmaz!⌐, 'the wits of forty negroes would not fill a fig-seed!': ⌐ne Şamın şekeri ne Arabın yüzü⌐, 'better forgo something pleasant if it involves something unpleasant'. ~sabunu, soft soap. ~saçı, −nı, woolly hair; any tangled affair; mess: ~ gibi, tangled, confused, intricate.
araba Carriage; cart; wagon; slide-rest (lathe). ~sını düze çıkarmak, to put matters straight, to get over difficulties: ⌐~ kırılınca yol gösteren çok olur⌐, there is plenty of help to be had when it is too late: bir ~ lâf, a lot of talk: çek ~yı!, be off with you!, clear out! küçük ~, top-slide (lathe). ~cı, driver, coachman; maker of carts, etc. ~lık, coach-house, cart-shed; cartload.
arabağı (·⸴··), −nı Septum.
arabî (···⸴) (Arab; Arabian; Arabic. ~yat (···⸴), −tı, Arab literature and science.
Arabistan (····⸴) Arabia.

arabozan (·⸴··) Mischief-maker.
arabulan (·⸴··) Peacemaker; mediator.
Araf (−⸴) Purgatory.
arak Sweat; raki. ~iye (·−·⸴), soft felt cap worn under a turban; a kind of fife.
arak·çı Pilferer, thief. ~lamak, to remove or steal adroitly; filch.
aral Archipelago. **Aral**, Sea of Aral.
aralamak va. Make a space between two things; half-open; leave ajar.
aralık Space; interval in place or time; chink, crevice; opening; passage; interruption, break. Scattered; at intervals; half-open, ajar. ~ (ayı), (formerly) the month of Zilkade, (now) December: ~ etm., to leave half open, to leave ajar: aralığa gitmek, to fall between the cracks, i.e. to be lost or put away: ~ vermeden konuşmak, to talk continuously: bir ~, for a while; at a suitable moment; at some time or other: bu ~, at this time; then; meanwhile.
âram (−⸴) Rest; quiet. ~gâh (−−⸴), place of respose; retreat.
aramak va. Seek, look for; look s.o. up; search; examine; hope for, long for; miss (feel the absence of). ağız ~, to endeavour to get s.o. to tell stg.: ⌐sen arıyorsun, şimdi dayağı yersin⌐, 'you're just asking for a hiding, now you shall have one': ⌐bizde para pul arama!⌐, 'don't think we've got any money!': birini arayıp sormak, to make inquiries about s.o.'s health, circumstances etc.
âran (−⸴) Moderation.
aranmak vn. Be sought; be searched; search oneself, one's pockets etc.; search one's mind; be sought after; be desired or appreciated too late; be missed.
ararot, −tu Arrowroot.
arasıra (·⸴··) At intervals; now and then.
arasız Without a break, uninterruptedly.
arasta (·⸴·) Street in a bazaar devoted to one trade; fair; sutlers' camp.
araste (·−⸴) Decorated.
araşid Peanut, earth-nut, ground-nut.
araştırma Research; investigation. ~k, to search; investigate; make researches into.
aratmak va. Make anyone regret or long for stg.
arattırmak Cause s.o. to search etc.; try to get s.o. to take stg. which is not so good as that first offered. ⌐gelen gideni arattırır⌐, 'the newcomer makes one long for his predecessor'.
arayıcı Seeker; Customs inspector; man who makes a living by searching for things washed up by the sea or on rubbish heaps, beachcomber. Wandering about as if

searching for stg. ~ **fişeği**, jumping cracker.

arayış *n.* Searching.

ârayiş ($\stackrel{\perp}{-}\cdot$) Adornment; embellishment.

âraz ($-\stackrel{\perp}{}$) *pl. of* **arz** *or* **araz.** Non-essential attributes; symptoms; accidents. Breadths; latitudes. ~î ($--\stackrel{\perp}{}$), accidental, fortuitous; incidental.

araz Accidental or non-essential attribute; symptom; accident; fortuitous gain; worldly goods, property.

arazi ($\cdot-\stackrel{\perp}{}$) *pl. of* **arz.** Lands, countries; estates, real property. ~**i memlûke,** freehold land: ~**i miriye,** Crown lands.

arbede Quarrel; noise; row.

ard Back; behind; hinder part; sequel, end. ~**ımca,** ~**ıma,** ~**ımda,** behind me, after me: ~**ı arası kesilmeden,** continuously, uninterruptedly: ~**ı arkası gelmiyen,** endless: ~**ına bak!,** look behind you!: ~**a düşmek,** to lag behind: ~**ında gezmek,** to run after *s.o.,* to try to obtain *stg.*: ~**ına kadar açık,** wide open: ~**da kalmak,** to remain behind; to survive, to outlive: ~**ı kesilmek,** to cease, to come to an end: ···**in ~ından koşmak,** to run after ...: ~**ı sıra,** one behind the other, in a series; ···**in ~ı sıra,** immediately following ...: ~**ı sıra yürütmek,** to send as escort or companion: ⌐**elinden geleni ~ına koyma!**⌐, 'do your worst!'

arda A turner's chisel; a peg *for marking.*

ardala Bell *attached to the last camel of a caravan*: cushion *for the back of an animal*; pillion.

‖**ardcı** Rearguard.

ardıc Juniper. ~ **kuşu,** thrush: ~ **katranı,** oil of savin.

ardın ardın ($\cdot\stackrel{\backprime}{}\cdot\stackrel{\backprime}{}$) Backwards.

ardısıra *v.* **ard.**

ardiye Rent for storage in a warehouse; demurrage; warehouse.

ardsız In ~ **arasız,** uninterruptedly.

arduvaz (*Fr. ardoise*) Slate.

arefe *v.* **arife.**

argaç Woof *of a tissue.*

argımak *vn.* Grow thin.

argın Thin; exhausted. ~**lık,** emaciation; exhaustion.

argıt Mountain pass.

arı[1] Bee. ~**beyi, -ni,** queen-bee. ~**cı,** beekeeper. ~**kovanı** ($\cdot\stackrel{\backprime}{}\cdots$), -**nı,** beehive. ~**kuşu, -nu,** bee-eater.

arı[2] Clean; innocent. ~**kan** ($\cdot\stackrel{\backprime}{}\cdot$), pureblooded; blood (horse). ~**lamak,** to cleanse. ~**lık,** cleanliness.

arık Lean, emaciated; clean, pure, honourable.

arış Warp *of a tissue*; forearm, cubit; pole *of a ox-wagon.*

arıtmak *va,* Cleanse; purify.

ârız ($-\stackrel{\backprime}{}$) That which occurs or befalls; accidental; intercepting, impeding, obstructing. Cheek. ~ **olm.,** to happen, to befall. ~**a,** accident; incident; defect; obstruction. ~**alı,** uneven, broken (country); full of difficulties and obstacles; defective. ~**asız,** unobstructed; level; free from difficulties; without hitch; without defects, undamaged. ~**î** ($-\cdot\stackrel{\perp}{}$), accidental; adventitious; casual; temporary.

arî ($-\stackrel{\perp}{}$) Aryan.

âri ($-\stackrel{\perp}{}$) Naked; destitute; lacking, free from.

ârif ($-\stackrel{\backprime}{}$) Wise; intelligent; skilled, expert. ⌐**e tarif ne hacet?**⌐, there is no need to explain to a sensible man. ~**ane** ($-\cdot-\stackrel{\backprime}{}$), skilful, clever (*of an inanimate object or an act*).

arifane ($-\cdot-\stackrel{\backprime}{}$) A picnic or feast to which each one supplies his share.

arife, arefe Eve *of a fesitval etc.*; threshold *of an event.*

arina Sand for scouring.

ariyet ($-\cdot\stackrel{\backprime}{}$), -**ti,** anything borrowed *or* lent. ~ *or* **ariyeten kullanmak,** to make temporary use of *stg.*

ariz ($\cdot\stackrel{\perp}{}$) Broad, wide. ~**u amik,** fully and in great detail.

ariza ($\cdot-\stackrel{\backprime}{}$) Petition; letter from an inferior to a superior.

Arjantin ($\cdot\stackrel{\backprime}{}\cdot$) Argentina.

ark, -kı Irrigation canal.

arka Back; back part; reverse side; sequel, end; protection, support; supporter, backer. ~ ~**ya,** one after the other; ~ ~**ya vermek,** to stand back to back *for mutual protection*: ~**dan** ~**ya,** behind the back, secretly: **bir işin ~sını almak,** to put an end to a matter: ~**sından dolaşmak,** to follow up *a matter etc.*: **bir işin ~sına düşmek,** to follow a matter up to its conclusion: **birinin ~sına düşmek,** to go in pursuit of, to run after *s.o.*: ~**sını getirememek,** to be unable to carry out an enterprise *which has been started*: ~**sından gezmek,** *v.* ~**sından dolaşmak:** ~**da kalanlar** (~**dakiler**), those left behind: ~**sı kesilmek,** to be cut off, terminated; to come to an end; to become extinct: ~**sı*** **olm.,** to have s.o. behind one, to have a 'backer', to have 'influence' in one's career: **birine** ~ **olm.,** *or* ~**sını vermek,** to support *or* protect s.o.: ~**dan söylemek,** to speak of *s.o.* behind his back, to backbite: ~ **tarafı,** continuation, sequel: ~ **üstü yatmak,** to lie on one's back: ~**sı var,** to be continued; *also* to have 'backing': ~**sı yere gelmez,** he can't be 'downed'; he has powerful backers: **ardı** ~**sı kesil-**

meden, incessantly: ⌐elinden geleni ∼na koyma!⌐, 'do your worst!': gözü* ∼da kalmak, not to be at rest about a matter; to feel unhappy about stg. not done.

arka·çantası, –nı, haversack, knapsack. ∼**daş,** companion, friend; colleague. ∼**daş-lık,** comradeship, friendship. ∼**lamak** va., to support, to back, to protect. ∼**lı,** who has supporters or 'friends at court'. ∼**lıç,** porter's saddle. ∼**lık,** as ∼**lıç;** a kind of jacket; carrier *of a bicycle;* back *of a chair etc.*: ∼**sıpek,** strong; warmly clad; having protectors.

arkış Caravan; messenger.

arlanmak vn. Be ashamed. **arlanmaz,** shameless, brazen-faced.

arma (¹·) Armorial bearings; rigging of a ship. ∼ **soymak,** to dismantle the rigging: ∼ **uçurmak** *or* **budatmak,** (of a storm) to carry away the rigging.

armador Rigger.

armağan Present, gift.

armatör (*Fr. armateur*) Ship-owner; belaying-pin; cleat.

armoz, armuz Seam between the planks of a boat. ∼**lu,** carvel-built.

armud Pear; (*sl.*) stupid. ⌐∼ **piş ağzıma düş!**⌐, 'pear, ripen and fall into my mouth!' (*purporting to be the prayer of one who hopes to obtain stg. without effort*): ⌐∼**un sapı var üzümün çöpü var demek**⌐, to be very hard to please; always to find fault with everything: ⌐**benim elim de** ∼ **devşirmiyor da**⌐, 'my hand is not engaged either in picking pears', *i.e.* I can hit back, I can look after myself.

arnavud Albanian. ∼ **kaldırımı,** cobbled street. **Arnavudluk,** Albania.

arpa Barley. ⌐∼ **ektim darı çıktı**⌐, it was a bitter disappointment; I was disillusioned: **bir** ∼ **boyu,** a very short distance: ⌐**atın ölümü** ∼**dan olsun**⌐, you can't have too much of a good thing: **frenk** ∼**sı,** pearl-barley. ∼**cı,** seller of barley: ∼ **kumrusu,** a kind of domestic dove; ∼ **kumrusu gibi,** pensive and sad.

arpacık Stye; foresight of a gun. ∼ **soğanı,** (?) Spanish leek.

arpağ Incantation, charm. ∼**cı,** wizard, sorcerer.

arpalama (i) Founder (disease of horses' feet); (ii) the curing of a stye by a charm. ∼**k,** to be overfed with barley; to be sick.

arpalık Field with good barley; barley bin; a kind of fief; mark on a horse's teeth *by which his age can be told.*

arpasuyu (·¹··), **–nu** Beer.

arsa (¹·) Building plot.

arsız Shameless; impudent; importunate.

arslan v. **aslan.**²

arş¹ Forearm; cubit; warp *of a tissue.*

arş² *mil. command.* March!

arş³ The Throne of God; pavilion, booth; roof, ceiling.

arşın Turkish yard (= *about 27 in.*). ⌐(**bezi) herkesin** ∼**a göre vermezler**⌐, 'you won't always be taken at your own evaluation'. ∼**lamak** va., pace out; measure by yards: vn. step out, walk quickly; **sokakları** ∼, to loaf, to stroll about. ∼**lık,** *anything* sold by the yard; *anything* a yard in length.

arşiv (·¹) Archives.

art v. **ard.**

artakalmak (·¹··) vn. Remain over. **bin belâdan** ∼, to have suffered much.

artamak vn. Remain over; survive.

artık Left, remaining; superfluous. What is left, residue, remnant. More. (¹·) Well now!, come now!, enough! ∼ **eksik,** deficiencies; more or less; under or over: **kılıç** ∼**ları,** those who escaped the sword. ∼**lık,** superfluity, redundancy.

artırma, arttırma Act of increasing; economizing; overbidding; auction.

artırmak, arttırmak va. Increase, augment; economize, save, put by; raise a bid *at an auction;* collect; go too far, exceed the bounds. **boğazdan** ∼, to economize by cutting down one's food.

artma verb. n. of **artmak.** Left over, remaining. Residue.

artmak vn. Increase, multiply; remain over; rise (of prices, the tide *etc.*). **yeter de artar,** enough and more than enough.

arus (·¹) Newly married bride.

arusek (·–¹) Doll; a very iridescent kind of mother-of-pearl.

aruz Prosody.

arya (¹·) *In* ∼ **etm.,** to dip flag.

arz¹ The earth; land; country.

arz² Width, breadth; latitude. ∼ **dairesi,** a parallel of latitude: ∼**ı şimalî (cenubî),** northern (southern) latitude. ∼**an** (¹·), in width; in latitude. ‾∼**anî** (·–¹), transverse, cross.

arz³ Representation; petition; expression of opinion; submission *of stg. for consideration.* ∼**ı hürmet ederim,** I present my respects: ∼ **ve taleb,** supply and demand. ∼**etmek** (¹··), **–eder,** va., to present *a petition;* submit *a proposal;* offer *an opinion;* express *a sentiment;* present *one's respects.*

arzî¹ (·¹) Terrestrial. ∼**yat, –tı,** geology.

arzî² (·¹) Latitudinal.

arziye v. **ardiye.**

arzu (·¹) Wish, desire. ∼ **etm.,** to wish, to desire: **bir şey yapmak** ∼**sunda olm. (bulunmak),** to have a wish to do stg.

~**keş,** ~**lu,** wishful, desirous. ~**lamak,** desire, long for.

arzuhal, –li Written petition *or* representation. ~**ci,** writer of a petition; street letter-writer.

arzullah *In* ~**i vâsia,** a spacious place; vast.

as¹ Myrtle.

as² Ermine (animal).

as³ Ace.

||**as-** Second-; vice-. ~**teğmen,** second-lieutenant : ~**başkan,** vice-president.

asâ (·-¹) Stick; baton; sceptre. ~**yı Musa,** the rod of Moses.

–âsâ (−¹) Like .... **devâsâ,** like a giant, gigantic.

asab Nerve; *pl.* **âsab** (–¹). ~**î** (··¹), nervous; neurotic; irritated; on edge. ~**iyeci,** neurologist. ~**iyet, –ti,** nervousness; nervous irritation; (*formerly*) fanaticism; sensitiveness. ~**ileşmek,** to have one's nerves on edge, become irritable.

asabe Paternal relations; heirs.

asakir (·–¹) *pl. of* **asker.** Soldiers.

asalet (·–¹), **–ti** Nobility of birth; performing a duty in person; personal appearance in court. ~**en** (·¹··), in person; acting as principal (not as representative).

asam Deaf; surd.

âsan (–¹) Easy.

asansör Lift, elevator.

asar ((−¹) *pl. of* **eser.** Works; monuments; signs, traces, remains; legends. ~**ı atika,** ancient monuments, antiquities.

âsar (−¹) *pl. of* **asır.** Centuries; ages.

asas *v.* **ases.**

asayiş Quiet; repose; security.

||**asbaşkan** (¹··) Vice-president.

aselbend Benzoin. ~ **mahlûlü,** friar's balsam.

ases Night-watchman; night patrol; (*formerly*) Chief of Police.

asgar *comp. of* **sagir.** Smaller; smallest. ~**î** (··¹), smallest; minimum.

ası¹ Profit, benefit. ~**lı,¹** profitable, advantageous.

ası² Suspension.

asığ, asık¹ Profit; advantage. ~**lı,** useful.

asık² Cross; gruff. ~ **yüzlü,** sulky.

asıl, –slı Foundation; base; origin; source; root; race, stock; essential part *or* substance. Real; true; essential; main; fundamental; original. **aslına bakarsan,** the truth of the matter is : **aslı faslı yok,** entirely unfounded, devoid of all truth; **aslîle mukabele etm.,** to compare with the original : **aslı nesli,** his origin and family : **aslı yok,** it is without foundation; untrue.

asılacak About to be hanged; gallows-bird, criminal.

asılı² Hanging; suspended; (arm) in a sling; hanged (executed).

asılmak *vn.* Hang; be hung; be suspended; stretch out; lean over; insist; be obstinate; (*with dat.*) cling to; pull.

asılsız Without foundation; untrue.

asılzade (···–¹) Nobleman; aristocrat.

asım Place difficult of access *or* to which access is forbidden.

asım takım (·¹·¹) Ornaments.

asıntı A putting-off, a delaying; unpaid debt.

asır, –srı Age; time; epoch; century. ~**dide** (···–¹), age-old, immemorial. ~**lık,** (so many) centuries old.

asi (–¹) Rebel, insurgent; brigand; sinner. Rebellious; refractory. ~**lik,** rebellion.

âsib (–¹) Disaster, calamity.

asid Acid.

aside (··–¹) A dish made of rice or barley meal, meat and okra (**bamya**).

asîl (·¹) Of noble birth; noble. Principal (*as opp. to agent*). ~ **memur,** real *as opp. to acting* official. ~**lik,** nobility.

âsim (–¹) Offender; criminal.

asîr (·¹) Difficult, arduous.

asitan (−·¹) Threshold; court *of a prince.* **Asitane,** Istanbul.

asiyab (−·¹) Water-mill.

asker Soldier. ~**î,** military. ~**lik,** military service.

askı Anything hanging *esp.* a bowl for flowers; pendant; bunch of fruit *hung up to ripen*; braces, suspenders; sling (*med.*); king-post; delay, postponement; suspense, doubt. ~**ya almak,** to prop up, support : ~**da bırakmak,** to leave in doubt *or* suspense : ~**da kalmak,** to remain in suspense, to await conclusion : **kâğıdları** ~**ya çıkmış,** their banns have been put up (before marriage).

aslâ (¹–) Never; in no way. Never!, decidedly not!

aslan¹, aslen (¹·) Originally; fundamentally; essentially.

aslan², arslan Lion; brave man. ~ **payı,** the lion's share : ~ **sütü, raki :** ⌜**ağzile** ~ **tuttuğunu söylemek⌝,** to boast of incredible performances: **gemi** ~**ı,** a ship's figure-head: ⌜**her yiğidin kalbinde bir** ~ **yatar⌝,** everyone has an ambition. ~**ağzı, –nı,** snapdragon; stone tap *in the form of a lion's mouth.* ~**lık,** great bravery. ~**pençesi, –ni,** lady's mantle, alchemilla.

aslı *v.* **asıl.**

aslî (·¹) Fundamental; radical; essential; substantive (rank). ~**ye,** *fem. of* **aslî.** Court of First Instance.

asma Suspended; pendent. Vine *esp. on a trellis.* ~ **kat,** entresol: ~ **kilid,** padlock:

~ köprü, suspension bridge: **~ merdiven**, gangway. **~kabağı, –nı**, a kind of gourd grown on a trellis. **~lık**, place planted with vines. **~yaprağı, –nı**, vine leaves *used in cooking* dolma.

asmak *va*. Hang; suspend; put off paying *a debt*; cease *work*; play truant *from school*, '*cut*' *a lecture etc*. **asıp kesmek**, to behave in an arbitrary and despotic manner: **astığı astık kestiği kestik olm.**, to wreak one's will, to be answerable to no one for one's actions: **kulak ~**, to pay attention; **kulak asmamak**, to take no notice: **surat ~**, to scowl.

aso Ace; star performer.

asrı *v*. asır. **~hazır**, the present epoch of history, *i.e. subsequent to the French Revolution*.

asrî (·¹) Modern; up-to-date. **~leşmek**, to modernize. **~lik**, modernization; a being up-to-date.

‖assubay Junior officer.

astar Lining; priming, undercoat (paint). ⌜**~ı yüzünden pahalı**⌝, 'its lining costs more than the outside material', an accessory that costs more than the main thing; an enterprise the cost of which is greater than the gain; the game is not worth the candle; **bir işin aslı ~ı**, the real truth of a matter: **aslı ~ı yok**, there is no foundation whatever for it: **yüzü ~ı bellisiz bir adam**, a doubtful character: ⌜**yüz verirsen ~ını da ister**⌝, if you give him an inch he will take an ell. **~lık**, material for lining; suitable for lining.

‖asteğmen (¹··) Second-lieutenant. **deniz ~i**, midshipman.

astragan Astrakhan.

asude (−−¹) Tranquil; at rest. **~gi**, tranquillity.

asurî (−−⌐) , **asurlu** Assyrian.

asüman (−·⌐) The heavens; sky. **~î** (−·−⌐), celestial.

asyaî (···−⌐) Asiatic.

aş Cooked food. ⌜**~ deliye kalıyor**⌝, when the wise fall out, the fool profits; 'duobus certantibus tertius gaudens': **~ (y)ermek**, (of a pregnant woman) to long for unusual food: **~ta tuzu bulunmak**, to make a contribution, however small, to stg.: **ağzının ~ı mı?**, it is something he could not do: ⌜**azıcık ~ım, kavgasız başım**⌝, not rich but free from care: ⌜**pişmiş ~a soğuk su katmak**⌝, to add cold water to cooked food, *i.e*. to spoil everything at the last moment.

aşağı Down; below. Lower; low, common, inferior. The lower part. **~da**, below· **~ya**, downwards, down: **~dan almak**, to begin to sing small; to return a soft answer: **~ görmek (tutmak)**, to under-

estimate; to despise: **~ yukarı**, up and down; to and fro; roughly speaking, more or less; **Ahmed ~ Ahmed yukarı**, it's nothing but Ahmed Ahmed all the time; **kedi ~ kedi yukarı**, *she talks about* nothing but her cat: **baş ~**, headlong; upside-down, topsy-turvy: **beş ~ beş yukarı**, close bargaining: **bir ~ bir yukarı**, up and down, to and fro.

aşağı·lamak *va*., lower, degrade; treat as inferior: *vn*. come down; come lower; fall in esteem, be discredited; become cheap *or* common. **~lı, in ~ yukarılı**, both upstairs and downstairs. **~lık**, lowness: inferior, base, common.

âşar (−⌐) *pl. of* üşür, Tenths; tithes. **~at** (··⌐), **–tı**, decimals; tens. **~î** (−−⌐), decimal.

aşayir (·−⌐) *pl. of* aşiret, Tribes.

aşçı *v*. ahçı.

aşere Ten.

aşermek *v*. aş.

aşevi (¹··), **–ni, aşhane** (·−⌐) Cook-house; kitchen; restaurant; soup-kitchen.

aşı Graft; vaccination, inoculation. **~ kalemi**, slip for grafting, scion.

aşıboyası (·¹···) **–nı** Red ochre paint.

aşık Knuckle-bone; helmet. **~ atmak**, *lit*. to play knuckle-bones; to compete *with an idea of daring and of not being likely to succeed*: **aşığıcuk oturmak**, to be lucky, to be successful. **~kemiği, –ni**, ankle-bone (astragalus).

âşık (−¹) In love. Lover; wandering minstrel. **Hak aşığı**, platonic lover; disinterested person.

aşı·kalemi (·¹···), **–ni** Cutting used for grafting. **~lamak**, graft, bud; inoculate, vaccinate; cool with ice. **~lı**, grafted; inoculated.

aşındırmak *va*. Wear out *by friction*. **birinin kapısını ~**, to be always visiting s.o.; to pester s.o. by frequent visits.

aşınma Depreciation, wear and tear (*accountancy*); erosion. **~k**, to be worn away *by friction*; to be effaced; to depreciate.

aşırı The space beyond a thing; overseas. Excessive, beyond bounds. **~ gitmek**, to go beyond the bounds, to exceed the limit: **gün ~**, every other day.

aşırma Conveyed over; smuggled; stolen. Plagiarism; theft.

aşırmak *va*. Convey over a height; pass over; escape (danger); go beyond (limit); smuggle; steal, pilfer; get rid of *s.o*. **gün ~**, to get through a bad day.

aşırtma *verb. n. of* aşırtmak. Passed over; stolen; saddlegirth. **~ topçu ateşi**, indirect fire (*mil*.).

aşifte, aşüfte (−·ͻ) 'Fast' woman.
aşikâr (−·ͺ) Clear, evident. ~e (−·−ͻ), clearly; openly, publicly.
aşina (−·ͺ) Acquaintance. As Pers. suffix, expert in ..., understanding ...; e.g. lisanaşina, linguist. ~lık, ~yi, acquaintance; intimacy; expert knowledge: ···le aşinalığı olm., to know s.o. to speak to.
âşir (−ͻ) Tenth. Tenth part; intimate friend; wife.
aşir, −şri, Ten.
aşiret (·−ͻ), −ti Tribe, esp. a nomadic tribe.
aşiyan (−·ͺ) Nest; abode, home.
aşk, −kı Love; passion. ~a gelmek, to get excited : ~ olsun!, bravo!, well done!; also expresses disappointment, that's too bad of you!: Allah ~ına!, for God's sake!
aşketmek (ͻ···), −eder va. In such phrases as: bir tokat ~, to give s.o. a box on the ears.
aşkın Passing over or beyond; excessive; furious, impetuous. iş başımdan ~, I am up to the ears in work.
aşlamak v. aşılamak.
aşmak va. Pass over or beyond; (of a stallion) to cover. vn. Pass the limit; be extravagant; overflow. iş başından* ~, to be overwhelmed with work.
aşna fişne (··ͻ) Coquetry, flirting.
aşnalık v. aşinalık. ~ etm.; to greet, to salute.
aşoz Rabbet.
aşub (−ͺ) Confusion, tumult. In compounds, exciting; disturbing.
aşure (·−ͻ) The tenth of Muharrem; sweet dish prepared for that day.
aşüfte v. aşifte.
aşvades (·ͻ·) Cockle (shell-fish).
aşyermek v. aş.
at, −tı Horse. ~lar anası, large masculine woman : ͼ~la arpayı dövüştürmekͻ, 'to make the horse quarrel with his barley', to try to set friends at loggerheads : ~ başı beraber gitmek, to be on a level with, to be neck and neck : ~a binmek, to ride a horse : ͼ~ bulunur meydan bulunmaz, meydan bulunur ~ bulunmazͻ, stg. one needs is sure to be lacking : ͼ~a deveye değil ya!ͻ, it won't be a great expense: ͼ~a et, ite ot vermekͻ, to give the wrong thing to the wrong man : ~ hırsızı gibi, his appearance is against him : ͼ~tan inip eşeğe binmekͻ, to lose position; to come down in the world : ~ kafalı, stupid : ~ oynatmak, (i) to have complete mastery of a subject; (ii) to have authority in a place.
ata Father; ancestor. ~lar sözü, proverb.
atâ (·ͺ·) Gift.
atabey, atabek Name formerly given to a

prince's tutor; title given to various small rulers.
atak Testy; irritable, quick to take offence.
atalet (·−ͻ), −ti Idleness; inertia.
ataya (·−ͺ) pl. of atiye. presents.
atbalığı (ͻ···), −nı Silure (?).
atcambazı (ͻ···), −nı Circus-rider; rough-rider; horse-dealer.
atebe Threshold; step, stair; royal Court.
ateh Senility, dotage. ~ getirmek, to reach one's second childhood.
aterina (··ͻ·) Sand smelt.
ateş Fire; heat; ardour, vehemence; fever, temperature. ~ almamak, to misfire : ͼ~ almağa mı geldiniz?ͻ, said to one who comes to a house etc. and only stays a minute : ~ bacayı (saçağı) sarmak, lit. for a fire to catch the chimney (eaves), i.e. to have got beyond control : ~ basmak, to feel hot from shame or anger : ~ ten gömlek, ordeal : ~ kesmek, to cease fire : ~ pahasına, at an exorbitant price : ~e vermek, to set on fire; to cause a panic : kendini ~e atmak, to sacrifice oneself.
ateş·balığı, −nı, sardine. ~böceği, −ni, fire-fly; glow-worm. ~çi, stoker; fireman. ~feşan, erupting fire. ~gede, fire-temple. ~î (−·ͺ), fiery; fiery red; infernal. ~in (−·ͺ), hot; fiery. ~kayığı, −nı, a kind of large rowing-boat. ~kes, cease-fire. ~leme, firing; spark of a petrol engine. ~lenmek, to catch fire; to fly into a passion. ~li, burning, fiery; passionate; having a temperature. ~pare (···ͻ), spark; man full of fire. ~perest, −ti, fire-worshipper.
atfen (ͻ·) With reference to; considering.
atfetmek (ͻ···), −eder va. Direct, incline; attribute; impute.
atıcı Marksman, good shot; braggart, swaggerer. ~lık, marksmanship.
atıf, −tfı Inclination; a turning towards; favour; an attributing or ascribing; the joining of two words or two sentences to each other.
atıfet (−·ͻ) −ti Benevolence; affection; sympathy, pity, mercy. ~en (−ͻ··), out of kindness.
atık Small churn.
âtıl (−ͻ) Idle, lazy; inactive. ~ kalmak, to be inactive; to be out of use or abandoned.
atılgan Dashing, reckless, bold. ~lık, dash, pluck.
atılmak vn. pass. of atmak. Be thrown, discharged, thrown away; be discredited; be dismissed from an office; burst in upon a conversation; rush; hurt oneself on stg.
atım Discharge (gun); range of a gun : charge of powder and shot; round. bir

~lık barutu* kalmak (olm.), to be down to one's last round, to have nothing in reserve.

atış Act of firing *a gun.* ~ **meydanı** (sahası), rifle *or* artillery range.

atışmak *vn.* Quarrel; have a tiff.

atıştırmak *va.* Bolt (food). *vn.* Begin to snow *or* rain.

ati (−⸗) Future; subsequent. The future. ~**de**, in the future; below (what follows): **ber vechi** ~, in the following manner.

atik Quick, alert, agile.

atîk (·⸗) Ancient. **asarı** ~**a**, ancient monuments.

Atina (·¹·) Athens.

atiyen (⸗··) In the future; subsequently; as mentioned below.

atiyye (·−¹) Gift; largesse.

atkafalı (¹···) Stupid.

atkestanesi (¹····), −**ni** Horse-chestnut.

atkı Woof, weft; hay-prong; shawl; shoe-buckle.

atlama Jump, spring; the omission *or* skipping *of a passage.* ~ **ipi** skipping-rope: ~ **taşı** stepping-stone.

atlamak *va.* Jump over; skip, omit; narrowly escape *a danger etc.* *vn.* Leap, spring.

atlanmak[1] *vn. pass. of* atlamak.

atlanmak[2] Get a horse; mount a horse.

atlas Atlas; satin. **A**~ **okyanusu**, the Atlantic Ocean. ~**çiçeği**, −**ni**, Cactus.

atlatmak *va.* Cause to jump; pass over; overcome *a danger or an illness*; put off; deceive; put off *or* get rid of *a person* by empty promises.

atlayış Jump.

atlet Athlete.

atlı Rider, horseman. Mounted on horseback; having *so many* horses. ~**karınca** (*more correctly* atlıkaraca), roundabout, merry-go-round.

atma Strap of a shoe.

atmaca Sparrow-hawk.

atmak *va.* Throw; throw away; drop; put into; postpone; fire (gun); shoot (an arrow *etc.*); blow up (a bridge *etc.*); aim at; give *a kick*; step *a pace*; cast *an imputation*; tell *lies*; drink off *a glass of beer etc.* *vn.* Splinter, crack, split; (of a gun) to go off; (of a magazine) to blow up; (of the heart) to beat; boast; invent stories; tell lies; (of the dawn) to break; (of a colour) to fade. ⌐atma Recebl¬, 'don't tell such tales to me!': **atıp tutmak**, to rant, declaim, inveigh: ⌐attığını vuruyor¬, he never fails to hit the mark, he always attains his object: **başından*** ~, to reject, to refuse; to get out of *a task*: **can** ~, to desire ardently; to save one's life *by taking refuge*: **çenesi attı**, his

jaw fell (*at the moment of death*): **lâf** ~, to talk, chat, chatter; to make remarks *to a girl* in passing: **söz** ~, to make remarks and innuendos to a girl: ···**e taş** ~, to make insinuations against ... .

atmasyon (*sl.*) Bragging, boast; bluff.

atmeydanı (¹·−·), −**nı** Hippodrome; *name of a famous square in Istanbul.*

atölye (·¹··) (*Fr. atelier*) Workshop; studio.

atsineği (¹···), −**ni** Horsefly, gadfly.

atsız Horseless; on foot.

atş Thirst; desire. ~**an** (·⸗), thirsty; dried up; ardently desirous.

attar *v*, aktar.

atuf Affectionate; kindly. ~**etlû** (···⸗), *former official form of address to certain ranks.*

av The chase; hunting, shooting, fishing; game; prey; booty. ~ **aramak**, to hunt for game; to search for *stg.* to lay hands upon: ~**a çıkmak**, to go out hunting; to form a line of skirmishers: ~ **havası**, good hunting weather; thieves' opportunity: ~ **uçağı**, fighter plane.

avadanlık (Artificer's) set of tools.

avakıb (·−¹) *pl. of* akıbet. Ends, results.

aval[1] Half-witted.

aval[2] *In* ~ **etm.**, to back *a bill.*

avalim (·−¹) *pl. of* âlem. Worlds *etc.*

avam (·⸗) *pl. of* amme. The public, the common people. **Avam Kamarası**, the House of Commons: **halkın** ~ **tabakası**, the lower classes: **lisanı** ~, the popular speech. ~**ferib**, ~**firib** (·−·⸗), one who deceives the public, demagogue.

avamil (·−¹) *pl. of* âmil. Agents; causes.

avanak Gullible. Simpleton.

avans Advance (money).

avanta (·¹·) Advantage; profit, *esp.* illicit profit. ~**cı**, one who makes illicit gains.

avara (·¹·) Cast off!; shove off! (*naut.*); clear out! Free, not in gear. ~**ya almak**, to throw out of gear, to disengage: ~ **kasnak**, loose pulley: ~**lı kavrama**, loose coupling: ~ **kolu**, lever for striking gear *used with fast-and-loose pulleys.*

avare (−−¹) Vagabond; good-for-nothing; out-of-work; gadabout; wild (child). ~ **etm.**, to interfere with s.o.'s work by *talking etc.* ~**lik**, idleness, vagrancy.

avarız (·−¹) *pl. of* ârıza. Obstacles *etc.*

avarya (·−¹) Damage to goods in transit; average.

avatıf *pl. of* atıfet. Kindnesses.

avaz Loud voice. ~ **çıktığı kadar**, at the top of one's voice.

avcı Hunter; skirmisher (*mil.*); fighter *plane or pilot.* ~ **kuş**, bird of prey. ~**lık**, hunting; shooting.

avdet, −**ti** Return. ~ **etm.**, to return.

avene, avane Helpers; accomplices.

avenk (−¹) *v.* **hevenk.**

-âver (−¹) *Pers. suffix.* Bringing ...; causing ...; possessing ...; **cengâver**, warlike, brave.

avgın, avgun Small watercourse.

avize (−−¹) Chandelier; hanging-lamp. ~ **ağacı**, yucca.

avizo (·¹·) Dispatch-boat.

avköpeği (¹···), **-ni** Sporting dog.

avlak Good hunting-ground.

av·lamak *va.* Hunt; shoot; fish for; entice, allure. *vn.* Go out hunting *etc.* **gafil** ~, to catch unawares: **gönül** ~, to attract: **sinek** ~, to idle about. ~**lanmak**, to be hunted; to be caught; to go out hunting.

avlu Courtyard.

avniye *A kind of* coat *worn in the nineteenth century.*

avrat, -tı, -dı Wife; woman.

avret, -ti The private parts.

avruk Crooked; warped.

Avrupa (·¹·) Europe. ~**lı**, European. ~**laşmak**, to become europeanized.

avuc Palm of the hand; handful. ~ **açmak**, to beg: ~ **içi**, the hollow of the hand: ~ **içi kadar yer**, a tiny place: ~**unun* içine almak**, to have *s.o.* completely in one's power: ~**unu* yalamak**, to go away empty-handed: ~**unu yala!**, you'll get nothing!: **ele** ~**a sığmaz**, uncontrollable, intractable: **elinde* ~unda* nesi varsa**, everything he (you) possesses. ~**dolusu**, handfuls (of), heaps (of). ~**lamak**, to grasp in the hand; to take a handful of.

avukat, -tı Advocate; lawyer. Loquacious.

avundurmak *v.* **avutmak.**

avunmak *vn.* Be put off *or* deceived; have the attention distracted; have the mind taken off stg.; (of a cow) to be in calf.

avurd Hollow inside the cheeks. ~**u** ~**una çökmüş**, with sunken cheeks: ~ **etm.** *or* **satmak**, to give oneself airs: ~ **şişirmek**, to puff out the cheeks with conceit: ~ **zavurd**, bluster, self-assertion: ~ **zavurd etm.**, to assume a blustering and superior air. ~**lu**, puffed up; conceited; swaggering.

Avustralya (··¹··) Australia.

Avusturya (··¹··) Austria.

avutmak *va.* Keep *a child* quiet by amusing it; delay *or* distract *s.o. by some pretence*; delude; console.

ay Moon; month; crescent; beautiful face. ~ **başı**, the first of the month: ~ **dede**, *personification of the moon*: ~ **dedeye misafir olm.**, to sleep in the open: ~ **doğdu**, the new moon; ~**ın ondördü**, the full moon: ~**ın ondördü gibi**, very beautiful (girl): ~ **parçası**, a beauty: ~ **tutulmak**, for the

moon to be eclipsed: ~**da yılda bir**, very rarely.

aya¹ Palm of the hand; sole of the foot.

aya² (¹·) (Gr. ἁγία) Holy. **Aya Sofya**, St. Sophia.

âya (−·) I wonder whether; maybe, perhaps.

ayağınaçabuk (·¹···¹) Agile.

ayak Foot; leg; step; foot (measure); stair; round *of a ladder*; outlet *of a lake*; tributary *of a river*. ~**la**, afoot, by walking: ~**ta**, on foot, standing: ~**tan**, 'on the hoof': ···**den ayağını* alamamak**, to be unable to give up ...: ···**e ayağı* alışmak**, to frequent *a place*: ~ **altı**, just under one's feet; in one's way: ~ **altında kalmak**, to be trodden underfoot: ~ **basmak**, to set foot *in a place*: to put the foot down, to insist: **ayağını* çabuk tutmak**, to hurry: ···**den ayağını çekmek**, to give up going *somewhere*: ~ **diremek**, to put the foot down, to insist: **ayağına* gelmek**, (of luck, success *etc.*) to come to one without any efforts on one's own part: **ayağına* kadar gelmek**, to condescend to visit *s.o.*: 'ayağıma kadar geldi', 'he was good enough to come and see me': 'ben senin ayağına gelemem!', 'you don't expect me to come and see you, do you?' (*sarcastically*): **kendi ayağıyle gelmek**, to come of one's own accord: **ayağını* giymek**, to put one's shoes on: **ayağına* ip takmak**, to try to discredit *s.o.*: ~ **işi**, light work; errand: (**ortalığı**) **ayağa kaldırmak**, to instigate *or* arouse *or* alarm people: **ayağa kalkmak**, to rise to one's feet, to stand up: ···**in ayağına kapanmak** (**düşmek, sarılmak**), to implore *s.o.* for mercy: ···**den ayağını* kesmek**, to cease going *somewhere or other*: **birinin ayağını kesmek**, to prevent *s.o.* from going: **ayağı* kesilmek**, to be prevented from going: **ayağı* suya ermek** (**girmek**), to understand the position, to realize the truth: ~ **takımı**, the common herd, the rabble: ~ ~ **üstüne almak**, to cross the legs: **ayağı* yere basmamak**, to jump for joy: ~ **yerden kesilmek**, to find some means of transport other than walking: ⌐**bin bir** ~ **bir** ~ **üzerinde**¬, all treading on each other's toes, very crowded: **bir** ~ **evvel**, as soon as possible: **bir** ~ **üzerinde**, quickly: **söz ayağa düşmek**, for affairs of importance to get into the hands of the rabble.

ayak·altı (·¹··), **-nı**, the sole of the foot; ground under the feet; much frequented place: ~**nda**, on this very spot. ~**bastı**, ~ **parası**, toll or tribute levied on travellers or passers-by. ~**çı**, servant employed on light outdoor jobs; errand-boy; man employed for a particular job. ~kabı, foot-wear, boots, shoes *etc.*: ayakkablarını çevir-mek, to give s.o. a hint that it is time he went: ˹sağlam ~ değil˺, he is not to be trusted; a bad lot; (woman) 'no better than she should be'. ~lamak, to trample on; to measure by pacing. ~lanmak, to rise to the feet; to rise in rebellion *or* remon-strance. ~lı, having feet; on foot; long-legged (animal); movable, ambulatory: ~ kütübhane, (a walking library) a very learned man: ~ canavar, (walking man-eater) a perfect brute. ~lık, anything serving as a foot; anything a foot in length; stilts. ~takımı, –nı, the lower classes, the rabble. ~taş, ~daş, companion, comrade; accomplice. ~teri, –ni, doctor's fee; fee *paid to anyone called away from his home to attend to a job.* ~üstü, standing; in haste; frequented: ~ anlatılmaz, it can't be explained all in a moment. ~yolu, –nu, latrine, water-closet.

ayal, –li *pl. of* aile. Families; dependants; *as sing.,* wife; family. evlâdü~ sahibi, a family man.

ayan Manifest, evident. ~ beyan, very evident; clearly; in every detail.

âyan (–ᴵ) Notables; chiefs; senators; *as sing.,* village headman. ~ meclisi, Senate.

ayar Standard of fineness *of gold or silver;* carat; gauge; accuracy *of a weighing-machine or watch;* degree; grade; disposi-tion, temper; *in conjunction with another noun can usually be translated by* regulating ..., *e.g.* ~ musluğu, regulating cock: ~ valfı, regulating valve: ~ bobini, tuning-coil (wireless): ~ etm., to regulate *a watch etc.* ~lamak, to assay; to test; to adjust; to regulate; to verify correctness *of weights* and stamp them. ~lı, of stan-dard fineness; regulated (watch); adjust-able: ~ bomba, time-bomb.

ayar·mak *vn.* Go astray. ~tmak, to lead astray, pervert; entice; seduce.

Ayasofya (·ᴵ·) *The great mosque of that name, formerly St. Sophia, in Istanbul.*

ayaz Frost *on a clear winter night or* dry cold *on a winter day.* ~a kalmak, to miss stg. by being too late: ~da kalmak, to be exposed to frost; to wait in vain: ˹~ Paşa kol geziyor˺, it's frightfully cold: işler ~ gitti (*sl.*), things have gone 'to pot'. ~lamak, to pass a frosty night in the open; to be cold; to wait in vain. ~lan-mak, (of the night) to become clear and frosty; to catch a chill.

ayazma (·ᴵ·) Sacred spring.

aybar Imposing *or* majestic air.

aybaşı (ᴵ··), –nı The first day of a month; menstruation.

ayçiçeği (ᴵ···), –ni Sunflower.

aydın Light; moonlight. Bright; luminous; clear; brilliant; enlightened. gözünüz ~!, I wish you joy!, *said on hearing good news concerning the person addressed:* göz ~a gitmek, to pay a visit of congratulation. ~latmak, to illuminate, enlighten. ~lık, light; daylight; skylight.

ayet, –ti Sign; miracle; verse of the Koran. ~ülkürsü, *the name of a verse of the Koran usually recited in times of danger.*

aygın *In* ~ baygın, languid; half asleep.

aygır Stallion; violent man. deniz ~ı, sea-horse, hippocampus: su ~ı, hippopotamus.

ayı Bear; boor; clumsy lout. ~ gibi, huge: ˹~ya kaval çalmak˺, 'to play a flute to a bear', to try to make a stupid person under-stand: ˹~yı vurmadan postunu satmak˺, 'to sell the bearskin before killing the bear': ˹köprüyü geçinceye kadar ~ya dayı demek˺, 'to call the bear "uncle" until you have crossed the bridge', to treat anyone with respect as long as he can be useful or harmful to you. ~balığı, –nı, seal. ~cı, bear-leader; coarse rough man (*esp. in games*).

ayıb Shame; disgrace; something 'not done'; fault, defect. Shameful, disgrace-ful; unmannerly. ~dır!, for shame!; you ought to be ashamed of yourself: ~ ara-mak, to seek an excuse for blaming: ~ değil, there's no harm in it; it's quite per-missible: sormak ~ olmasın, I hope you don't mind my asking. ~lamak, to find fault with, censure. ~sız, without defect; irreproachable; innocent.

ayık In full possession of the senses; wide awake; sober *after being drunk.* ~lık, soberness; recovery *from fainting etc.;* consciousness.

ayıklamak *va.* Clear of refuse; clean; clean off; pick and choose, select. ˹gel, ayıkla pirincin taşını˺, 'come and pick the stones out of the rice!', *i.e.* 'here's a pretty mess!'

ayılmak *vn.* Recover *from drunkenness etc.;* come round *after fainting.*

ayırd Difference. ~etm., to distinguish; make a difference between. ~lamak, to separate; distinguish; select.

ayır·mak *va.* Separate; sever; disconnect; set apart, reserve; choose; distinguish; discriminate. ···den göz ayırmamak, not to take the eyes off *stg.*: yerinden ~, to move from its place. ~tmak, to put aside; reserve.

ayışığı (ᴵ···), –nı Moonlight.

âyin (–ᴵ) Rite; ceremony. ~icem, '*cere-mony in honour of Jem (considered the in-ventor of wine)',* hence: a Bacchic feast, drinking-bout.

ayine (––᷄) Mirror; *v. also* **ayna**. ⌐~si iştir kişinin, lâfa bakılmaz⌐, a man's worth is known by his deeds, not his words: ⌐bakalım, ~yi devran ne gösterir⌐, let's see what the future will show.

aykırı Crosswise, transverse, athwart; incongruous; perverse; eccentric. ···e ~, not in accordance with ...: ~ gitmek, to swerve from the straight path; to go on in an extravagant manner.

aylak Unemployed; involuntarily idle. Loafer, tramp. ~çı, casual labourer.

aylık Monthly; a month old; lasting a month; Monthly salary. ~çı, one who receives a monthly salary.

ayn Eye; spring; well; exact copy, counterpart. ~ını çıkarmak, to make a copy of *stg.*

ayna Mirror; lathe chuck; *v. also* **ayine**. üç ayaklı ~, 3-jaw chuck. ~lı, having a mirror; (*sl.*) fine, excellent. ~lık, transom *of a boat*: ~ tahtası, the back of a stern thwart. ~sız (*sl.*), unpleasant; policeman.

Aynaroz Mount Athos.

aynen (᷄··) In exactly the same way; without any change; textually; integrally; in kind (payment).

aynı (᷄··) *v.* **ayn**. Identical; the same; veritable. ~ zamanda, at the same time.

aynî (·᷄) Ocular; (*legal*) real *as opp. to personal.*

aynile (᷄···) *v.* **aynen**.

ayniyat (···᷄), –tı Goods in hand; inventory; payment in kind.

ayniye[1] *fem. of* **aynî**. Eye clinic.

ayniye[2] *In* eşyayı ~ gümrüğü, *department of the Custom House, where goods were sold which had been received by the Customs in kind in lieu of cash payment.*

ayniyet, –ti A being identical.

ayol (᷄··) *Friendly but slightly reproachful acclamation.*

ayran *Drink made with* yoğurt *and water mixed with snow or ice;* buttermilk. ~ı kabarmak, to lose control of oneself from *temper or drink;* to be infuriated: ⌐~ yok içmeğe, tahtla gider sıçmağa⌐, *said of one who, although penniless, wishes to show off:* ⌐hiç kimse ~ım ekşi demez⌐, no one runs down his own wares; no one cries 'stinking fish!': ⌐sütten (çorbadan) ağzı yanan ~ı üfler de içer⌐, ⌐a scalded cat fears cold water⌐. ~lı, quick-tempered, fiery.

ayrı Apart; separated; alone; isolated; other. Separately; one by one; by oneself. ~ basım, reprint (of an article *etc.*): ~ gayrı yok, no need for ceremony; indiscriminately, without any exception, all alike: ~mız gayrımız yok, we have everything in common; we don't stand upon

ceremony: ~ seçi, difference, disparity: ~ seçi yapmak, to differentiate the treatment of people, to discriminate.

ayrı·ca (᷄··), separately; apart; otherwise; in addition. ~k, separated; wide apart (eyes); parted (hair): ~ otu, couch grass. ~lık, separation; isolation; difference; absence: ~ çeşmesi, well outside a village, *where it is customary to bid farewell to those departing.* ~sız, indiscriminately.

ayrılmak *vn.* Be separated, parted; differ, be distinguished; disagree; depart; crack, split open.

aysberg Iceberg.

Ayşe *A name of women, esp. of Mohammed's second wife Ayesha.* ~ kadın fasulyesi, French beans.

ayva Quince. ekmek ~sı, a juicy kind of quince. ~lık, quince orchard.

ayvaz Steward, major-domo. ⌐~ kasab hep bir hesab⌐, it all comes to the same thing.

ayyar (·᷄) Crafty, deceitful.

ayyaş Given to drink; toper.

Ayyuk (·᷄), –ku The star Capella; the highest point of the heavens. sesi ~a çıkıyordu, he was shouting at the top of his voice.

az Little; few; insignificant. Seldom. ~ buçuk, somewhat: ~ buz şey değil, it is no small matter: ~ çok, in some degree, more or less; a certain number; ~a çoğa bakmamak, to make the best of it: ~ daha (kaldı), all but: ~ görmek, to deem too little: ~ günün adamı değil, he is a man of experience: bir ~, a little, rather: bir ~dan, in a moment, soon.

âza (–᷄) *pl. of* **uzuv**. Limbs; members; *as sing.* member. ···e ~ kaydolunmak, to be enrolled as a member of ... .

azab[1] Bachelor; marine *in the old Ottoman navy.*

azab[2] (·᷄) Pain; torture. ~ vermek, to cause pain *or* annoyance: ⌐şeytan ~da gerek⌐, it serves him (me) right!; (*hum.*) 'no peace for the wicked!'

azacık (᷄··), *v.* **azıcık.**

azad Free; freeborn. Liberation; dismissal *of children from school;* the giving of a holiday. ⌐~ buzad cennette bizi gözet!⌐, 'we set you free, you look after us in Paradise!', *phrase used by children when setting free a captured bird.* ~e (––᷄), free; released; absolved: ~ ser, independent. ~egi (–––᷄), liberty, freedom. ~etmek (·᷄··), –eder, ~lamak, to set free, emancipate; to let *children* out of school. ~lı, set at liberty. ~sız, who cannot be freed.

azalık (––᷄) Membership.

azal·mak *vn.* Diminish; be reduced; be

âzam lowered. ~**tmak,** va. to diminish; lessen; lower.

âzam (−¹) *Comp. of* azim. Greater, greatest. ~**î** (−·¹), greatest; maximum: in the greatest degree. **haddi** ~, the extreme limit.

azamet, −ti Greatness; grandeur; pride, conceit; ostentation. ~**füruş,** ostentatious; who gives himself airs. ~**li,** great, magnificent, imposing; proud, ostentatious.

azar¹ Reprimand; reproach. ~**lamak,** to scold, reprimand, reproach.

azar² azar (·¹·¹) Little by little, gradually.

azdırmak Lead astray; spoil (a child); rouse, excite; allow a small evil to become serious.

Azerî (−·¹) Native of *or* belonging to Azerbaijan.

azgın Furious; mad; unbridled; extreme, excessive; rebellious; astray; (river) in flood.

azı, azıdişi (·¹··) Molar tooth; tusk. **gemi** ~**ya almak,** to take the bit between the teeth, to get out of hand.

azıcık (¹··) *Dim. of* **az.** A very little.

azık Food; provisions; fodder.

azılı Furnished with tusks; ferocious, savage; dangerous; violent; unbridled.

azım, −zmı Bone.

azımsamak, azınsamak Think *stg.* insufficient.

‖**azınlık** Minority.

azışmak vn. Become aggravated.

azıtmak vn. Grow excessively; overflow; rebel; go astray; go too far; become unreasonable; become insolvent. *Sometimes* va. *as in* **işi azıttı,** he went too far. **kedi (köpek)** ~, to take an unwanted cat (dog) right away and leave it in a distant place.

azil, −zli Dismissal; removal *from office.*

azim, −zmi Resolution, determination; firm intention. ~**kâr** (··¹), resolute, determined.

âzim (−¹) Resolved *to do stg.* ~ **olm.,** to set out on a journey; to engage to do stg.

azîm (·¹) Great, vast, immense; important; powerful.

azimet (·−¹), −**ti** Departure; setting out on a journey.

aziz (·¹) Dear; precious; rare; highly priced; mighty; glorious; saintly. Saint. −**e,** *fem. of* **aziz.** ~**lik,** practical joke; annoyance caused for amusement.

azletmek (¹··), −**eder** va. Dismiss *from an office.*

azlık Scarcity; paucity; minority.

azlolunmak (¹···) vn. Be dismissed; be placed in retirement.

azma Hybrid; monstrosity.

azmak vn. Go astray; become furious, mad, unmanageable; become depraved; be on heat, rut; (river) be in flood. *n.* River in spate; overflow of a river dam. **düş** ~, to have nocturnal emissions.

azman Monstrous, enormous; hybrid. Baulk of timber.

azmetmek (¹··), −**eder** va. Resolve upon; intend.

azmış Enraged; excited; furious; on heat.

azot, −tu Nitrogen.

Azrail (·−¹) The Angel of Death.

azvay ·¹·) Aloes.

B

bab (−) Door; gate; chapter; subdivision; class, category; connexion; subject. **bir** ~ **ev,** one house: **bu** ~**da,** on this head, in this connexion.

baba Father; forefather; venerable man; head of a religious order; a kind of fit *peculiar to negroes;* knob; post of a staircase; bollard. ~**larımı ayağa kaldırma!,** do not infuriate me!: ~ **dostu,** an old friend of the family: ⌐~**sının hayrına değil ya¬,** not 'just for love', not in a disinterested manner: ~**dan kalma,** inheritance; inherited: ~ **ocağı,** family house: ~**m da olur** *or* **bunu** ~**m da bilir (yapar** *etc.***),** that's easy; anyone knows (can do *etc.*) that: ~**na rahmet!,** *a form of thanks:* ~**sı tutmak** *or* ~**ları üstünde olm.,** (of negroes only) to have a kind of fit; to run amok: ~ **yurdu,** paternal home: **ha** ~**m ha!,** *an expression of encouragement or emphasis:* **iskele (şam, trabzan)** ~**sı,** *terms used of a father whose authority is not respected:* **konuşur** ~**m konuşur,** he talks and talks.

baba·anne, paternal grandmother. ~**can,** kindly, good-natured, easy-going (man). ~**ç,** big cock; turkey-cock; swaggering. ~**fingo** (··¹·), top-gallant sail *or* yard. ~**hindi** (·¹··), turkey-cock. ~**lı,** having as father ...; running amok; irascible: **dokuz** ~, bastard. ~**lık,** paternity; fatherly affection; adoptive father; guardian; simple old man: good and sincere; simple, ingenuous. ~**yani** (··−¹), fatherly, unpretentious, free-and-easy; shabby. ~**yiğit,** full-grown strong young man, 'stout fellow': brave; virile: ···**lerin en** ~**i,** the best of....

Babıali (−·−¹) The Sublime Porte.

Babil ($\stackrel{\_}{\cdot}$) Babylon; Babel.

baca Chimney; skylight; funnel *of a steam-ship*. ~ **başı,** stone mantelpiece: ~ **kulağı,** small stone shelf by the side of a fireplace: ~ **tomruğu,** the part of the chimney above the roof: ~**sı tütmez,** (of a family) in an evil plight, destitute: **fikri** ~**dan aşmış,** peculiar, eccentric: **kapı** ~ **açık,** open to all, unguarded: ⌐**kapıdan atsalar** ~**dan düşer**⌐, a bore from whom one cannot escape: **kapısı** ~**sı yok,** a tumble-down or jerry-built building.

bacak Leg; thigh; knave (cards). ~ **kadar,** knee high (of a child): ~ **kalemi,** fibula: ⌐**her koyun kendi bacağından asılır**⌐, every-one must answer for his own misdeeds: 'iki bacağından tutup ayırıverim!', 'I'll make mincemeat of you!' ~**lı,** long-legged; having *such-and-such* legs. ~**sız,** short-legged; squat; naughty (child).

bacanak Brother-in-law (*only of one of two men who have married sisters*).

bacı Elder sister; wife; *title of respect for elderly women*; negro nurse; wife of the chief of a religious order.

baç, –çı Toll; tax; customs duty.

bâd (–) Wind; breath.

badana ($\cdot\stackrel{\_}{\cdot}\cdot$) Whitewash; distemper. ~**lamak,** to whitewash *or* distemper. ~**lı,** whitewashed, distempered; much made-up (woman).

badaş Grain mixed with earth and stones *left on the ground after threshing*.

badaşmak *vn.* Come to an agreement; make up a quarrel, be reconciled; get on well with one another.

badat Jerusalem artichoke; (?) white truffle.

bade¹ (–¹) Wine-glass; wine; raki.

bade–² ($\stackrel{\_}{\cdot}\cdot$) *prefix.* After .... ~ **harabül Basra,** *v.* Basra: ~**hu** ($\stackrel{\_}{\cdot}\cdot$–), after that, then: ~**ma** ($\stackrel{\_}{\cdot}\cdot\cdot$), henceforth: ~**lmilâd** ($\stackrel{\_}{\cdot}\cdot\cdot$–), after Christ, A.D.: ~**ssalat,** after prayers: ~**ttasdik,** after confirmation.

badem (–¹) Almond. Almond-shaped. ~**cik,** tonsil. ~**ezmesi, –ni,** almond paste, marzipan. ~**î** (–·$\stackrel{\_}{\cdot}$), almond-shaped. ~**içi, ~ni,** kernel of the almond. ~**lik,** almond orchard. ~**şekeri, –ni,** sugar almonds. ~**yağı, –nı,** almond oil.

baderna ($\cdot\stackrel{\_}{\cdot}\cdot$) Parcelling *of a rope*.

bâdısaba ($\stackrel{\_}{\cdot}\cdot\cdot$¹) Zephyr; gentle cool wind.

badi A kind of duck. ~ ~, waddling.

bâdi (–$\stackrel{\_}{\cdot}$) Causing; originating. *n.* Beginning.

badik Tiny. ~**lemek,** to waddle.

badire (–·¹) Unexpected calamity; difficult situation.

badiye (–·¹) Desert; wilderness.

bâdnüma (–·$\stackrel{\_}{\cdot}$) Vane; weathercock.

badya (–¹) Large wooden *or* earthen bowl; tub.

bafon *Corruption of* **vakfon** *q.v.*

bağ¹ Bond, tie; bandage; impediment; restraint; bundle. **ayak** ~**ı,** tether; moral restraint, restraining influence: **ayağının** ~**ını çözmek,** to divorce one's wife.

bağ² Vineyard; orchard; garden. ~ **bahçe sahibi,** a man of property: ~ **bozumu,** the vintage: ~ **budamak,** to prune a vine-yard: ⌐**bakarsan** ~ **olur bakmazsan dağ olur**⌐, if you look after your property it will be a garden, if not, a wilderness; suc-cess depends upon effort. ~**cılık,** vini-culture.

bağa *Generic name for batrachians and chelonians*; tortoise; tortoiseshell.

Bağdad ($\stackrel{\_}{\cdot}\cdot$) Baghdad. ⌐~ **harab oldu**⌐, I am very hungry: ⌐**sora sora** ~ **bulunur**⌐, you can get anywhere by asking: ⌐**yanlış hesab** ~**dan döner**⌐, an error will be found out sooner or later. ~**i,** a native of Bagh-dad; made of lath and plaster.

bağdalamak *va.* Trip (in wrestling).

bağdaş Sitting cross-legged in oriental fashion. ~ **kurmak,** to sit thus.

bağdaşmak *v.* ba̤daşmak.

bağı Spell, incantation. ~**cı,** sorcerer.

bağır, –ğrı The middle part of the body; bosom; internal organs; middle *or* front *of anything*. **bağrına taş basmak,** to re-strain or hide one's grief: **bağrı yanık,** afflicted, distressed: **göğüs** ~ **açık,** with the shirt open, carelessly dressed; disorderly.

bağırış *n.* Shouting, yelling. ~**mak,** to shout together; to clamour, bawl, raise an outcry.

bağır·mak *vn.* Shout, yell; cry out. ~**tı,** a shouting.

bağırsak Intestine; (*comm.*) casing.

bağırtlak The Desert Grouse (*Pterocles*), *also used for the* Sand Grouse (*Syraptes paradoxus*).

bağış Gift; donation. ~**lamak,** to give gratis; to give in charity, donate; pardon; spare the life of: **adını*** ~, to tell one's name: **gençliğine** ~, to put *stg.* down to one's youth and forgive on that account.

bağî (–$\stackrel{\_}{\cdot}$) Rebellious, unruly.

bağlama *verb. n. of* **bağlamak;** a kind of lute. Tied, bound; *in conjunction with another noun,* connecting ..., coupling ... .

bağlamak *va.* Tie, bind, fasten, attach; bandage; form (skin, ice, seed *etc.*); assign (an income *etc.*); do up (parcel); dam (a stream). ···**e** ~, to end up by ...: **başını** ~, to give in betrothal or marriage: **başını*** **bir yere** ~, to find a job for s.o.; to save him from destitution: **cerahat** ~, to sup-purate: ···**e gönül** ~, to set one's heart on;

to fall in love with: **göz** ~, *err. for* **göz**
bağmak, *q.v.*: **kabuk** *or* **yüz** ~, (of meat or
milk) to form rind or skin; (of a wound)
to heal up: **bir işi mukaveleye** ~, to make
a contract about stg.: **şarta** ~, to make
stg. depend üpon a condition, *i.e.* to attach
a condition to *stg.*: **tane** ~, (of a plant)
to form seed: **yağ** ~, to put on fat.
bağlan A kind of wild goose.
bağlanmak *vn. pass. of* **bağlamak**. Be tied
etc.; be obliged; be engaged *to do stg.*:
basireti* ~, to be blind *or* to lack perception as to one's own interests: **kızının**
kısmeti bağlandı, somehow the girl has
never found a husband.
bağlı[1] Bound; tied; impotent; settled,
concluded (agreement *etc.*); assigned (income *etc.*): ···**e** ~, dependent on, connected
with: **adama** ~, depending on the man
concerned: **başı** ~, married; settled; connected *with some office etc.*: **eli kolu** ~, tied
hand and foot; who has cut the ground
from under his own feet by some injudicious admission: **gözü** ~, blindfolded;
bewitched; stupid; inexperienced.
bağlı[2] Having vineyards. ~ **bahçeli**, rich,
well-to-do.
bağlılık A being bound; attachment,
affection.
bağmak *va.* Bewitch. **göz** ~, to hoodwink.
bağrı *v.* **bağır**.
bağrışmak *vn.* Shout together.
bağteten (¹··) Suddenly; unexpectedly.
bâh (–) Sexual intercourse. **münebbihi** ~,
aphrodisiac.
baha *v.* **paha**.
bahadır (·–¹) Brave. Hero.
bahane (·–¹) Pretext; excuse. ~**sile**, on
the pretext that: ~ **etm.**, to make an idle
excuse.
bahar[1] (·–⁴) Spring (season), *more usually*
ilk~, *as opp. to* **son**~, autumn.
bahar[2] (·–⁴) Spice. *pl.* ~**at**, –**tı**, spices:
~ **katılma**, seasoning. ~**lı**, spiced, aromatic.
bahçe Garden. **nebatat** ~**si**, botanical garden: **hayvanat** ~**si**, zoological garden.
~**lik**, full of gardens; pertaining to a
garden; garden-plot.
bahçivan (··¹) Gardener.
bahî (–⁴) Erotic.
bahir, –**hri** Sea; a poetical metre.
bahis, –**hsi** Discussion; inquiry; subject of
discussion or inquiry; bet, wager. **bahsi**
geçen, above-mentioned: **ne bahsine ister**
sen girerim, I'll bet anything you like:
~ **tutmak**, to bet.
bâhis (–¹) Investigating, *or* treating of, *a*
subject.

bâhname (——¹) Pornographic or obscene
writing.
bahren (¹·) By sea.
bahr·i *v.* **bahir**; (?) grebe. ~**î**, maritime,
naval, nautical. **Bahri·ahmer**, the Red
Sea. ~**lut**, the Dead Sea. ~**muhit**, the
ocean. ~**kebir**, the Pacific. ~**müncemid**,
the Arctic Ocean. ~**sefid**, the Mediterranean. ~**siyah**, the Black Sea.
bahriye *fem. of* **bahrî**. Navy. **düveli** ~,
the naval powers: **ticareti** ~, maritime commerce: ~ **Nezareti** (**Vekâleti**), the Ministry
of Marine: ~ **zabiti**, naval officer. ~**li**,
sailor belonging to the navy.
bahs·etmek (¹··), –**eder** *va.* (*with abl.*)
Discuss; mention; treat of; bet. ~**i**, *v.*
bahis: ~ **müşterek**, totalizator, pari
mutuel.
bahş Gift. *As suffix*, giving ...; forgiving
.... ~**ayiş** (·–¹), a giving; a pardoning.
~**etmek** (¹··), –**eder**, to give, grant; forgive, remit. ~**iş**, tip, gratuity; gift.
baht, –**tı** Luck, fortune; good luck; destiny. ···**den** ~**ı* açık olm.**, to be lucky
in ...: ~**ı kara**, unlucky: **ne çıkarsa** ~**ına**,
v. **peşrev**. ~**iyar** (··⁴), lucky; happy.
~**iyarlık**, good fortune; happiness.
bahusus (⁴··) Especially; particularly;
above all.
baid (·⁴) Far distant; improbable.
bâis (–¹) Cause; motive. ···**e** ~, causing .... .
bakakalmak *v.* **bakmak**.
bakalorya (··¹·) (*Fr. baccalauréat*) . (*For*
merly) school leaving certificate.
||**bakan** Minister. ~**lık**, Ministry.
bakanak Cloven hoof.
bakar[1] *aor. of* **bakmak**.
bakar[2] Ox. ~**î** (··⁴), bovine.
bakaya (·–⁴) *pl. of* **bakıye**. Residues
arrears.
bakıcı Soothsayer. ||Attendant; nurse.
bakılmak *vn. pass. of* **bakmak**. Be attended to; be looked after; be considered;
be followed as a rule; (of a lawsuit) to be
heard.
bakım Look, glance; attention; upkeep.
bir ~**dan** *or* ~**a**, in one respect; from one
point of view. ~**evi**, –**ni**, crèche; hospital
for children; home for old people. ~**lı**,
well-cared for; plump. ~**sız**, neglected.
bakındı (¹··) *For* **bak imdi!**, just look!
bakınmak *vn.* Look around; be bewildered.
bakır Copper; copper utensil. ~ **çalmak**,
to taste of copper *from being cooked in an*
untinned copper vessel: ~ **pası**, verdigris:
dişi ~, soft copper; **erkek** ~, hard copper:
⌐**yer demir gök** ~¬, a hopeless outlook.
~**cı**, coppersmith.
bakış Look; care. ⌐**adam olacak çocuk**

~ından bellidir⌐, you can tell by his looks the child who will make a fine man : kuş ~ı, bird's-eye view. ~lı, having *such and such* a way of looking, *e.g.* cin ~, having a look of malicious cunning : şahin ~, hawk-eyed.

bakıye Remainder, residue; arrears; balance; sequel. ~tüsseyif, (left by the sword), the survivors of a battle.

baki (−⸳−) Permanent, enduring, lasting; remaining. Remainder. Finally; as to the rest. ~ **kalmak**, to remain over, survive; ⌐~ **kalan bu kubbede bir hoş sada imiş⌐**, 'all that is left in this dome is a pleasant sound' (*a pun on the name of Baki, the poet who wrote this line*); (i) only a happy memory remains; (ii) try to leave something to be remembered by.

bakir (−⸳) *a.* Virgin; untouched. ~e, *n.* virgin.

bakkal Grocer. ~iye, groceries.

bakkam Logwood; a kind of non-fast dye.

bakla Bean, *esp.* broad-bean; link (of a chain). ~yı ağzından* çıkarmak, to let out something that one has hitherto kept back : ~ dökmek, to tell fortunes by beans : ağzında ~ ıslanmaz, indiscreet talker, chatterbox : senin ağzında bir ~ var, you are keeping something back. ~çiçeği, a dirty yellowish-white colour. ~giller, leguminous plants. ~kırı, dapple-grey(horse).

baklava A kind of pastry *made of flake pastry with walnuts and almonds, generally cut into lozenge-shaped pieces.* Lozenge-shaped.

bakliye Leguminous. *pl.* bakliyat, legumes, peas and beans.

bakmak *vn.* & (*with dat.*) *va.* Look; look at; examine; look after, tend; attend to, see to; look to for guidance; face towards, look out on. bakalım, we'll see! (*according to context implies doubt, hesitation, threat, or encouragement*) : bakarsın, in case; it may be, *e.g.* şemsiyeni unutma, bakarsın yağmur yağar, don't forget your umbrella, it may rain : bakar mısın?, *a polite way of calling attention* : baka kalmak, to stand in astonishment or bewilderment : bakar kör, a blind man whose eyes appear normal; one who fails to perceive what is going on around him : bana bak!, look here!; hi!: baná bakma!, never mind what I do!; don't count on me!: işe ~, to attend to one's job : kusura bakma!, excuse me!: yüzüne* bakmamak, to have no further consideration for s.o., to have nothing more to do with s.o.: bu iş yüz liraya bakar, this is a matter of say, £100.

bakrac Copper bucket.

baksana (·⸳·) Look here!; listen to me!

bakteri Bacterium, microbe.

baktırmak *va. caus. of* bakmak. Make *or* let look; show; cause to look after.

bal, -lı Honey; syrup. ~ alacak çiçek, one from whom something is likely to be had; an act likely to be profitable : ~ başı, the purest honey : ⌐~ dök yala⌐, very clean (*cf.* a floor 'off which one could eat one's meal') : ~ gibi, pure as honey, unadulterated; easily, properly, certainly : ~ gibi yalan, a lie pure and simple : ⌐~ tutan parmak yalar⌐, 'who touches honey licks his fingers', he is getting something out of it : ağzından ~ akıyor, he is quick-witted and intelligent : ⌐ağzına bir parmak ~ çalmak⌐, to try to silence a man with a grievance by offering him something quite inadequate in return or by some empty compliment : ⌐bir eli yağda, bir eli ~da⌐, very comfortably off, well-to-do : bir parmak ~ olm., to be the subject of gossip : sözünü ~la kestim, excuse my interrupting!

bâl¹ (−), **-li** Wing; fin; arm.

bâl² (−), **-li** Heart; mind. fariğül~, easy in mind.

bala Child, baby.

balâ (−⸳−) High, eminent; above. ~daki, above-mentioned.

balaban Tame bear; enormous man *or* animal; large drum. ~ kuşu, bittern. ~laşmak, to become very large or fat.

baladör Sliding-gear.

balak *v.* malak.

balan Porch.

balansine (··⸳·) Main boom topping-lift.

balâpervaz (−−·−) High-flying; ambitious; arrogant.

balar Thin board.

balarısı (⸳···), **-nı** Honey-bee.

balâter (−−⸳) Higher.

balayı (⸳··), **-nı** Honeymoon.

balcı Dealer in honey.

balçak Guard of a sword-hilt.

balçık Wet clay; potter's clay; sticky mud. ~ hurması, crushed dates : ⌐güneş ~la sıvanmaz⌐, 'the sun cannot be coated with clay'; ⌐truth will out!⌐

baldır Calf of the leg. ~ı çıplak, a rough, rowdy : ~ kemiği, tibia, shinbone. ~ak, the lower part of the trouser leg. ~ıkara, maidenhair fern.

baldıran Hemlock.

baldız Wife's sister, sister-in-law.

balgam Mucus; phlegm. ~ taşı, jasper : bir ~ atmak, to drop a malicious hint.

balık Fish. ⌐~ baştan kokar⌐, 'the fish begins to stink at the head', *i.e.* corruption starts at the top : balığa çıkmak, to go out fishing. ~ağı, **-nı**, fishing-net. ~ane, ~hane, custom-house for dues on fish brought into Istanbul market. ~çı, fisherman; fishmonger. ~çıl, piscivorous; heron. ~eti, well fleshed, neither fat nor thin. ~lama, dive (head foremost); headlong. ~lava, fishing-ground. ~nefsi, –ni, spermaceti. ~pulu, –nu, fish-scale. ~sırtı, –nı, ridge; road with a steep camber; hog-backed (road). ~yağı, –nı, fish-oil; cod-liver oil. ~yumurtası, –nı, fish-roe.

baliğ (–ᵎ) Reaching, attaining; amounting (to); adult, mature; perfect. Amount, sum. ~ olm., to reach the age of puberty: ···e ~ olm., to amount to ... .

balina (·ᵎ·) Whale; whalebone. ~ çubuğu, whalebone.

balkabağı (ᵎ···), –nı Sweet gourd; idiot.

balkan Chain of wooded mountains. Balkan yarımadası, the Balkan Peninsula.

balkımak vn. Shimmer, glitter; throb slightly.

ballan·dırmak Smear with honey; extol extravagantly. ballandıra ballandıra anlatmak, to relate in terms of extravagant praise. ~mak, to become thick like honey; become sweet and attractive.

ballı Honeyed. ~baba, dead-nettle.

balmumu (ᵎ···), –nu Wax. ~ yapıştırmak, to stick wax on stg., to note down a thing to be remembered; to mark s.o. down for revenge or punishment: kırmızı dipli ~ile davet, (an invitation with red sealing-wax), a formal invitation (only used ironically); ⌐kırmızı dipli ~ile çağırmadım ya¬, 'nobody asked you to come!'

balo (ᵎ·) Ball, dance.

balon Balloon; ship's fender: balloon flask.

baloz Low-class café chantant.

balpeteği (ᵎ···), –ni Honeycomb.

balsıra Manna; a disease of tree leaves.

balta Axe. ~yı asmak, to worry, to have a down on, to keep on at s.o.: ~ burun, a curving nose: bir işe ~ ile girişmek, to set about stg. in a clumsy and tactless manner: ~ görmemiş (girmemiş) orman, virgin forest: ~ olm. or ~yı kapıya asmak, to be tiresome, to bore, to pester: bir ~ya sap olm., to find a career: ~yı taşa vurmak, to do or say something unseemly; to make a faux pas: ~sı varmış, (of a girl) she has a young man.

balta·baş, the bow of a straight-stemmed ship. ~cı, maker or seller of axes; woodcutter; sapper or pioneer (mil.); halberdier in the old Palace Guard of the Sultans; fireman equipped with axe. ~lamak, to cut down with an axe; extirpate, demolish; cut away (hopes etc.); sabotage. ~layıcı, saboteur. ~lık, district within which the inhabitants of a village have the right to cut wood.

baltrap Clay pigeon trap.

balya (ᵎ·) Bale. ~lı, baled.

balyemez An ancient kind of gun.

balyos Old title of Venetian Ambassador, applied vulgarly also to foreign consuls.

balyoz Sledge-hammer.

bambaşka (ᵎ··) Utterly different.

bambu Bamboo.

bambul Chafer (Anisoplia).

bamteli (ᵎ··), –ni Bass note; whiskers, imperial; vital point; sore spot. ~ne basmak, to tread on s.o.'s corns, to touch him on a sore spot.

bamya (ᵎ·) Okra, gumbo.

–ban (–) Pers. suffix. Keeper of ..., e.g. der~, door-keeper.

bana dat. of ben. To me. ~ bakma, v. bakmak: ~ mısın dememek, to be very thick-skinned; to have no effect.

bandıra (ᵎ··) Flag (not used of Turkish flag).

bandırma Sweetmeat made of grape-juice and walnuts.

bandırmak va. Dip into a fluid, soak.

bandırol, bandrol Stamped paper attached to certain monopolies.

bando (ᵎ·) Musical band.

bangır bangır Yelling, screaming.

bâni (–ᵎ) Builder, constructor; founder.

banka (ᵎ·) Bank (comm.). ~cı, banker.

bankiz (Fr. banquise) Ice-floe, ice-pack.

banliyö (Fr. banlieue) Suburb.

banmak v. bandırmak.

banotu (ᵎ··), –nu Henbane.

banyo (ᵎ·) Bath, developing dish; development of a negative.

bâr (–) Load, burden; time, turn; fruit. ···e ~ olm., to be a burden to ... .

bar¹ (·) Drinking bar; low cabaret.

bar² (·) Name of a popular dance in E. Anatolia.

–bar (–) Pers. suffix. Spreading ...; pouring ..., e.g. eşk~, shedding tears.

bar bar (ᵎ·) In ~ ~ bağırmak, to shout loudly, to keep on shouting.

baraj Barrage (dam); barrage (mil.).

barak Long-haired (animal); thick-piled (stuff). Plush; a kind of climbing vine.

baraka (·ᵎ·) Hut, shed.

baran (–ᵎ) Rain.

barata (·ᵎ·) Cloth cap formerly worn by the Bostanjis (Sultan's guards); Turk's-Cap Lily. haseki ~sı, columbine.

barbar Barbarian.

barbata Parapet.

barbunya (·ᵎ·) Red Mullet; a kind of bean.

barbut, –tu A gambling game with dice.

barça Galley; ancient war-ship.

barçak Guard of a sword hilt.

barda Cooper's adze.

bardak Drinking mug; glass for water. **~ eriği,** egg-plum: **bir bardak suda fırtına,** a storm in a tea-cup: ⌐**bunun üstüne bir ~ soğuk su iç!**¬, you can write that off!, you'll never see it again!

barem (*Fr. barême*) Ready reckoner; scale of official salaries. **~ kanunu,** law regulating official salaries: **hayat ~i,** cost of living.

barğam A fish of the bass family.

barı·mak *va.* Shelter; shield; assist. **~nak,** shelter; hiding-place. **~ndırmak,** to give shelter to, to lodge (*va.*). **~nmak,** to take refuge *or* shelter; to lodge (*vn.*).

barış Reconciliation; peace. **~ (görüş) olm.,** to be reconciled. **~ık,** at peace; reconciled; in agreement. ···**le yıldızı ~ olm.,** to be on good terms with ...: ⌐**yedi kıralla ~**¬, on good terms with everyone, *but more frequently used of* a woman with many lovers. **~mak,** to be reconciled; to make peace.

barî (−ᴸ) God.

bari (ᴸ·) For once; at least. **~ haberini alsam,** if only I could get news of him!

barid (−ᴸ) Cold.

bârika (−·ᴸ) Flashing *of a sword etc.*; lightning.

barikad Barricade.

bâriz (−ᴸ) Manifest; prominent.

bark *Only in* **ev ~ sahibi** *or* **evli ~lı bir adam,** a family man. **~lanmak,** to set up house, start family life.

barka (ᴸ·) Large rowing-boat.

barko (ᴸ·) Barque.

barlam Hake.

baro (ᴸ·) The (legal) Bar.

barsak Intestine. **~ askısı,** mesentery: **ince ~,** small intestine: **kalın ~,** large intestine: **kör ~,** appendix.

barsam Sting-fish, weever.

baru (−ᴸ), **barı** Rampart; refuge.

barudî (·−ᴸ) Of the colour of gunpowder; slate-coloured.

barut, −tu Gunpowder; very pungent drink; hot-tempered man. **~ hakkı,** charge of powder: **~ kesilmek,** to fly into a rage: ⌐**~ yoktu kaptanım**¬, 'no further explanation is needed'; *v. App.* **~hane** (···−ᴸ), powder factory; powder magazine. **~luk,** powder-flask.

baryum (ᴸ·) Barium.

bâs (−) Mission; resurrection. **~übâdelmevt,** the resurrection of the dead.

basamak Step, stair; tread, round *of a ladder*; column (of figures).

basan Pressing; treading. Nightmare; printer.

basar Sight; mental perception. **zaafı ~,** weak sight. **~î,** optical.

basarık Treadle.

basbayağı (ᴸ···) Very common *or* ordinary. Altogether, entirely.

basık Compressed; low, dwarf; mumbling.

basılı Stamped; printed.

basılmak *vn. pass. of* **basmak.** Be pressed *etc.*; be overcome; be extinguished.

||**basım** *n.* Printing. **~evi, −ni,** printing-house, press.

||**basın** The Press.

bâsır (−ᴸ) Who sees; sharp-sighted; quick-witted. **~a,** the visual faculty.

basil (*Fr. bacille*) Bacillus.

basir (·ᴸ) Intelligent, discerning. **~et,** (·−ᴸ), **−ti,** perception, insight; circumspection; foresight. **~i* bağlanmak,** to lose one's common sense; to be blind to the consequences of one's actions.

basit Simple; plain; elementary; vast, extensive. **~a** (·−ᴸ), sundial. **~e,** ordinary (*i.e. non-leap*) year. **~leştirmek,** to simplify.

baskı Press; stamp; printed copy; oppression; restraint. **~ altında,** under discipline; under pressure.

baskın Heavy; overpowering; superior, surpassing. Sudden attack; night attack; raid *by the police etc.* **~ çıkmak,** to come out best; ···**dan ~ çıkmak,** to get the better of: **~ etm.,** to make a surprise attack *or* raid: **su ~ı,** flood.

baskül (*Fr. bascule*) Weighing-machine, weighbridge.

basma *verb. n. of* **basmak.** Print; printed goods, *esp.* printed cotton hangings. Pressed; printed. **bakır ~sı,** copperplate printing: **taş ~sı,** lithograph.

basmak *va.* (*with acc.*) Stamp, print; attack suddenly, surprise; raid; overpower; give (a blow); utter (a cry): (*with dat.*) press; tread on; oppress. *vn.* Tread; be oppressive; settle, sag; (cold *or* darkness) set in; (water) flood, overflow; (of a number of people) to arrive suddenly, to crowd in. **bas!,** 'go to hell!': **basıp gitti,** he went off *without caring a straw*: **ağır ~,** to press heavily; to impose one's will; to reprimand: **ayak ~,** to put down the foot; to set foot *in a place*: to insist: **çürük tahtaya ~,** to run into danger; to compromise oneself: **el** *or* **kitaba el ~,** to take an oath: **kahkahayı ~,** to burst out laughing: **sikke ~,** to coin money: **tam üzerine ~,** to 'hit the nail on the head': **on sekiz yaşına bastı,** he has reached the age of 18: **yaygarayı ~,** to cry out loudly.

basmakalıb (·ᴸ··) Stereotyped (remark *etc.*); cliché.

baso (ᴸ·) Bass (*mus.*).

Basra (ᴸ·) Basra. **~ Körfezi,** the Persian

Gulf: bade harabül~, (after the destruction of Basra), too late!

bast, ~tı Detailed explanation.

bastarda (·¹·) Ancient war-galley. Flagship.

bastı Vegetable stew.

bastıbacak Short-legged; squat; *used ironically of a child behaving like an adult.*

bastırmak *va. caus. of* basmak. Push down, press; overwhelm; extinguish; repress; suppress; hide, hush up (scandal *etc.*); catch unawares; tack (sew); relieve (stomach); cry out; give a decisive *reply etc.* (Of cold *etc.*) set in. ateş ~, for a fever to set in.

bastika (·¹·) Snatch-block.

baston Stick; jib-boom. ~ francalası, long French bread: ~ yutmuş gibi, 'as stiff as a poker'.

basur Piles, haemorrhoids. ~ otu, lesser celandine: kanlı ~, dysentery.

bâsübâdelmevt (—·—·¹) The resurrection of the dead.

baş Head; top; knob; bow *of a ship*; beginning, source; head *of cattle, etc.*; leader; intelligence, understanding; moneychanger's charge. *a.* Head, chief (*generally written with noun as one word, e.g.* başvekil, Prime Minister; *often used as a preposition meaning* near, by, *e.g.* ocak başı, by the fire; *often used where English would use a personal pronoun, e.g.* ~ıma gelenler, the things that happened to me; ~ına belâ getirmek, to bring trouble upon him. ~ ~a, together, tête-à-tête, face to face; confidentially; ~ ~a kalmak, to be in consultation with; ~ ~a vermek, to have a tête-à-tête, to collaborate, to put their heads together: ~a ~, entirely, completely; just enough; *v. also* başabaş: ~ta, at the top; at the head; first; before everything: ~tan, again, from the beginning: ~tan ~a, from end to end; entirely: ~ı açık, bareheaded: ~ açmak, to uncover the head: ···den ~ alamamak, to be too busy with stg. *to be able to do anything else*: ~ını* alıp gitmek, to go off without notice: ~ının* altından çıkmak, (of a plan *etc.*) to be hatched out in s.o.'s head: ~ aşağı, head first, headlong; upside-down; ~ aşağı gitmek, (of a business, *etc.*) to go steadily down; ~tan aşağı, from head to foot; entirely: ~ından* atmak, to put off *or* get rid of *s.o.*: ~ı boş, vagabond; not tied up (animal); free, unfettered: ~ımla beraber, 'with the greatest pleasure!': ~ına* bitmek, to pester: ~ çekmek, to take the lead, to guide: ~tan çıkarmak, to seduce *or* pervert: ···i ~a çıkartmak, to make a lot of s.o.: ···le ~a çıkmak, to cope with, to

master, to succeed with; ~ına* çıkmak, to presume on s.o.'s kindness: ~tan çıkmak, to throw off restraint, to get out of control; to be led astray: ~döndürücü, vertiginous: ~ dönmesi, giddiness: ~ı dönük, giddy; bewildered: ···le ~ edebilmek, to cope with ...; ···le ~ edememek, to be unable to cope with ...: ~ etm., to succeed, to overcome: ~tan geçen, event, adventure: ~ından* geçmek, (of an event *etc.*) to happen to one: ~a gelmek, to happen; ┌~a gelen çekilir┐, ┌what can't be cured must be endured┐: ~ göstermek, to appear, to arise; (of a revolt *etc.*) to break out: ~ına* hal gelmek, to be hard put to it: ~ı* için, for the sake of: ~ kaldırmak, to rise in revolt: ~ kaldırmamak, to work unceasingly: ~tan kara etm., (of a ship) to run ashore; to make a last desperate effort: ~tan kara gitmek, to head for disaster: ~ kesmek, to bow: ~ından* korkmak, to be afraid of being involved in stg. *for fear of the consequences*: ~ında* olm., (of a job) to be on one's hands; ~ımda bu iş var, I've got this job to do: ~ı önünde, harmless and submissive: ~ınız sağ olsun!, 'may your head be safe', *the recognized formula of sympathy to one who has lost a relative by death*: ~ı taşa geldi, he has had a bitter experience. ···e ~ tutmak, to head *a ship* towards ...: ~ tutmamak, (of a ship) not to hold her course: ~ ucunda at his side, *or, more usually*, at his bedside: ~ üstünde tutmak, to honour highly; ~ üstünde yeri olm., to be highly venerated *or* loved: ~ üstüne!, 'at your service!', 'with pleasure!', 'very good!': ~ vermek, (i) to give one's life; (ii) to show its head, to begin to appear: ~ vurmak, (i) to have recourse to; (ii) (of a fish) to bite: ~ına* vurmak, (of drink, wealth *etc.*) to go to one's head: ~ yastığı, pillow: ~ı* yerine gelmek, to collect oneself, to recover one's wits: ~ yukarıda (havada), proud, ambitious: adam ~ına, per man, per head: alt ~, the lower end of a thing; alt ~tan başlamak, to begin at the end: bir ~tan, all at once, all together: büyük ~, cattle: küçük ~, sheep and goats: iş ~ı, place of business: iş ~ında bulunmak, to be at work, to be at one's place of business: kendi ~ına, of his own accord; on his own, independently: saat ~ında, at the end of every hour, for every hour: yeni ~tan, afresh, all over again.

baş·abaş (¹··), at par: ~tan yukarı (aşağı), above (below) par: *v. also* başa baş. ~ağrısı, -nı, headache; nuisance, worry. ‖~bakan, Prime Minister. ~buğ, Commander-in-Chief; head of irregular troops; leader. ~çavuş, sergeant-major. ~çı, seller of cooked sheep's-heads. ~gedikli, sergeant-major. ~göz, ~ etm., to marry: ~ yarmak, to bungle, to make a mess of things; to do something unseemly. ~ıbozuk, irregular soldier; not in uniform; civilian. ||~kan, president; chairman. ~kâtib, first secretary; chief clerk. ||~kent, -tı, capital (of a country). ~kumandan, Commander-in-Chief. ~lı, having a head; principal, important; rounded; with a knob; (ship) down by the head: ~ başına, independent, on his own; independently: belli ~, eminent, well-known; principal: koyun ~, stupid. ~lık, headship; presidency; headgear; helmet; cowl; bridle; title of a book; heading of an article; top of a mast; (in parts of Anatolia) sum paid to a bride's father by the bridegroom: harb başlığı, war-head of a torpedo. ~muharrir, editor-in-chief. ~murakıb, Controller-in-Chief (financial). ~örtü, ~örtüsü, -nü, headgear; veil. ~sağlığı, -nı, a saying 'başınız sağ olsun!', (form of condolence on a bereavement): ~ dilemek, to offer one's condolences. ~sız, without a head; without a leader. ~vekil, Prime Minister. ~yazar, principle leader-writer.

başak Ear of corn. ~ bağlamak or tutmak, to come into ear: ~ samanı, chaff. ~çı, gleaner. ~lı, in ear, bearing spikes.

||başarı Success. ~cı, ~lı, successful, enterprising.

başarmak va. Bring to a successful conclusion; succeed in; accomplish.

başgöstermek v. baş.

başka Other; another; different; apart. ···dan ~, other than; besides: ~ ~, separately, one by one: gelmedi, o ~, the fact that he did not come is beside the point: ~sı, another; s.o. else. ~ca (·¹·), separately, independently; rather different; otherwise; further. ~laşmak, to alter, to grow different. ~lık, diversity; alteration; change of appearance.

başla·mak vn. va. (with dat.). Begin. ~ngıc, beginning; preface. ~nmak¹, to be begun. ~tmak, to cause or let begin; to put a child to school. ~yış, beginning.

başlanmak² vn. Form a head or a root (as of an onion etc.).

başlı etc. v. after baş.

başmak Shoe; slipper. ~çı, shoemaker; man who looks after the removed shoes of those entering a mosque. ~lık, material for making slippers; allowance paid to Sultan's mother or daughter.

başparmak (¹··) Thumb; great toe.

baştarda v. bastarda.

başvurmak (¹··) vn. Have recourse (to); (of a ship) to pitch.

bataet, -ti Slowness, tardiness.

batak Quagmire; bog, marsh. Boggy; fraudulent; about to sink or perish; desperate (condition, affair). ~çı, fraudulent borrower; swindler; cheat: ⌐~ya mal kaptırmış gibi¹, 'as if a swindler had got hold of your property' (said to a person anxious to get back what he had just lent to a friend). ~hane (··−¹), gambling den; den of thieves; dangerous spot. ~lı, marshy. ~lık, marshy place, bog; quicksand.

bâtapu (⌐··) Holding an authentic title-deed. ~ sahib, owner by virtue of a legal title-deed.

batarya (·¹·) Battery of artillery.

batası A form of the 3rd pers. sing. of the subjunctive of batmak, only used in curses; yere ~ âdet, an accursed custom; adı ~, 'that damned fellow'; adı ~ hastalık, that confounded illness.

batı The West; west wind.

batık Submerged.

batıl (−¹) False; erroneous; vain; useless. ~ itikad, superstition.

batın, -tnı Abdomen, stomach; family; clan; generation. bir ~da üç çocuk, three children at a birth.

bâtın (−¹) Inward, internal; hidden; mystical. Interior, inside; secret; mystery. ~en (⌐··), internally; inwardly; secretly. ~î (−·⌐), hidden; mysterious; pertaining to the inside; spiritual; esoteric.

batır Brave.

batırmak va. Submerge; sink; thrust into; ruin; reduce to bankruptcy; decry, speak ill of.

batış A sinking; decline; ruin; setting of the sun.

bati (·⌐) Slow, tardy; slothful.

Batlamyos Ptolemy. Ptolemaic.

batmak vn. Sink; go to the bottom; (of the sun or a star) set; (of money) be lost; be destroyed; pass out of existence; go bankrupt. va. (with dat.) Penetrate; enter deeply; prick, sting; get on the nerves of, irk. bata çıka, 'sinking and rising', i.e. with the greatest difficulty: boğazına* kadar borca ~, to be up to one's ears in debt: göze ~, to attract unfavourable attention, to offend the eye: kan tere ~, to sweat profusely: para ~, (of money) (i) to be lost; (ii) to burn a hole in one's pocket.

batman Measure of weight varying from 2 to 8 okkas = 5½ to 22 lb.

batnî (·⌐) Abdominal.

battal Abrogated, cancelled, void; use

less, worthless; unemployed, idle; large and clumsy. Large-sized paper; documents no longer valid. ~ **etm.**, to render null and void; to cancel.

battaniye (·—·ˈ) Blanket.

batur Brave.

bav A training for the chase. ~**cı**, trainer of dogs *or* hawks.

bavul Traveller's trunk.

bay (*Originally*) a rich man; (*now*) ‖ a gentleman. ~ **A.**, Mr. A.

bayağı (··ˈ) Common, ordinary; rough, coarse. (ˈ··) Simply, merely, just. ~ **günler**, ordinary days (*as opp. to Sundays and holidays*).

‖**bayan** Lady. ~ **A.**, Mrs. *or* Miss A.

bayat Stale; not fresh; insipid; out-of-date. **hayatı* gidip ~ı* kalmak**, to be overcome with enthusiasm about stg. ~**î**, *in such expressions as*: **bizimki yine ~ faslından başladı**, our friend started to harp on the same old string.

baygın Fainting; unconscious; languid; faint; heavy (smell). ~**lık**, swoon, fainting condition; languor; drooping (of a flower). **mide baygınlığı**, sinking sensation at the stomach.

bayıl·mak *vn.* Faint, swoon; droop. *va.* Pay; spend. ···**e ~**, to be passionately fond of *or* addicted to stg.: **gülmeden ~**, to be sick with laughing: **içi ~**, to feel faint from hunger: **imam bayıldı**, a dish of stuffed aubergines: **parayı ~**, to pay up, to 'hand over the cash'. ~**tıcı**, sickly (taste, smell). ~**tmak**, *caus. of* bayılmak: **içini ~**, (of food) to be sickly, to cause slight nausea.

bayındır Prosperous; developed. ~**lık**, prosperity; development. ‖ ~ **Bakanı**, Minister of Public Works.

bayır Slope; ascent, slight rise.

bayi (–ˈ), -**yii** Vendor.

baykuş Owl. Ill-omened.

bayrak Flag, standard. ~ **açmak**, to unfurl a flag; to collect volunteers; to defy; to revolt; ~**ları açmak**, to become insolent and abusive: ~ **koşusu**, relay race. ~**lı**, **eli ~**, insolent and abusive. ~**tar**, standard-bearer.

bayram Religious feast day (*esp.* the festival following the fast of Ramadan). ~**dan ~a**, seldom: ‘~ **değil**, **seyran değil** ...’, *v. App.*: ~ **etm.**, to be very delighted: ˈ~**dan sonra şekeri nidem?**ˈ, ‘what can I do with sweets after the feast (**Şeker Bayramı**)?’, *i.e.* it's no use to me now. ˈ**deliye her gün ~**ˈ, to a fool every day is a holiday: **kara ~**, a day of mourning: **millî ~**, national fête day. ~**laşmak**, to exchange appropriate greetings on a feast day. ~**lık**, pertaining to a festival; new

clothes for a feast day; present given on a feast day.

baysungur A bird of prey (? Lammergeier).

baytar Veterinary surgeon.

bazan, bazen (⊥·) Sometimes; now and then.

bazı (⊥·) Some; a few; certain. Sometimes. ~**lar**, some of them; ~**nız**, some of you: ~ ~, at times now and then: ~ **adam** *or* **adamlar**, some people, certain people: ~ **kere**, sometimes.

baziçe (—·ˈ) Toy, plaything; laughing-stock. **birsinin elinde ~ olm.**, to be a mere tool of s.o.

bazirgân *v.* bezirgân.

bazlamaç A kind of Anatolian pastry.

bazu (–⊥) The upper arm; strength. ~**bend**, armlet, brassard.

be Hi!, I say!

beanşartki (··ˈ·) On condition that.

bebek Baby; doll. **göz bebeği**, pupil (eye); apple of the eye: **sakallı ~**, one who behaves in a manner unsuitable to his years: **taş ~**, (of a woman) a mere doll; pretty but cold.

beberuhi (··⊥·) Pygmy; dwarf.

bebr Tiger.

beca (·⊥) In place; proper.

becayiş (·—ˈ) Exchange of posts between two officials. ~ **etm.**, to exchange posts.

becelleşmek. Struggle *or* fight with one another.

becerik Resourcefulness; tact; ability. ~**li**, resourceful; capable, efficient; clever. ~**siz**, maladroit, incapable.

becermek *va.* Carry out stg. skilfully; do stg. with success; (*iron.*) spoil, ruin.

becit Necessary.

beç *In* ~ **tavuğu**, guinea-fowl.

bed, bet Bad; ugly; unseemly. ~**ine* gitmek**, to vex, annoy.

bedahet (·–ˈ), -**ti** A being obvious; improvisation, extempore speech.

bedava (·–ˈ) Gratis, for nothing; very cheap, for next to nothing. ~**cı**, one who expects to get stg. for nothing.

bedavet (·–ˈ), -**ti** Nomadic existence.

bedayi (·–ˈ) *pl. of* bedia. Beautiful *or* precious things.

bedbaht Unfortunate; unhappy. ~**lık**, misfortune.

bedbin Pessimistic; cynical. ~**lik**, pessimism, cynicism.

beddua (··⊥) Curse, malediction. ···**e ~ etm.**, to curse s.o.

bedel Substitute; equivalent; price; sum paid for exemption from military service (*also* ~**i nakdî**); military substitute who serves for somebody else. ···**e ~**, in place of ...; in exchange for ...; as a substitute for ...: dünyalara ~, worth almost anything: icar ~i, rental: bir ömre ~, worth a life. ~ci, ~li, one who has paid military exemption tax.

beden Trunk; body; wall of a castle; bight of a rope. ~ bağı, rolling hitch. ~en (·¹·), in person; personally; physically. ~î (··¹), bodily; corporeal.

bedendiş (··¹) Having evil intentions, malevolent.

bedesten Covered market *for the sale of valuable goods*; drapery market.

bed'etmek (¹··), **-eder** *vn.* Begin.

bedevî (··¹) Bedouin; nomad.

bed·hah (·¹) Malevolent. ~hu (·¹), ill-natured; vicious.

bedi, -dii The science of figures of speech in writing.

bedia (·−¹) A great work of art.

bedih·e (·−¹) Axiom; impromptu; repartee. ~i (·−¹), obvious, self-evident: ~dir, it goes without saying.

bediî (·−¹) Aesthetic. ~yat, ~tı, aesthetics.

bedir, -dri Full moon.

bed·maye (·−¹) Wicked. ~mesti, ~mestlik, intoxication. ~nam (·¹), of ill repute. ~zeban (··¹), foul-mouthed, scurrilous.

begayet (·−¹) Extremely.

beğendi A dish of aubergines.

beğenmek *va.* Like; approve; admire; select. beğenmemek, not to like; to be particular about *stg.*: beğen beğendiğini!, choose whichever you like, take your choice!: beğenmiyen beğenmesin!, if you don't like it you may lump it!: kendini ~, to think a lot of oneself; to be presumptuous: 'kime rastgelsem beğenirsiniz', 'guess whom I met': yer ~, to select a place for oneself.

beha *v.* paha.

behane *v.* bahane.

behemehal (·¹··) In any case; whatever happens.

beher To each; for each. ~ine, for each one, per head: ~ gün, daily.

behey *Interj. expressing irritation.* Hi, you there!

behim·e (·−¹) Animal; brute. ~î, pertaining to brutes; animal *i.e. sexual feelings etc.* ~iyet, -ti, bestiality *esp. sexual.*

behişt, -ti Heaven, paradise.

behre Share, lot, portion; advantage; knowledge; capacity. ~dar (··¹), ~li, possessing a share *of goods or knowledge*; fortunate. ~siz, without a share; unfortunate; poor; incapable.

beht, -ti Amazement, bewilderment, perplexity.

beis Harm. ~ yok!, no matter!: 'tab'ında ~ yoktur', 'no objection to its being

printed' (*formula stamped on a manuscript after passing the censor in Abdul Hamid's time*).

beka (·¹) Permanence; stability; what remains; sequel. darı~, darül~, the next world.

bekâr Celibate. Bachelor; provincial living alone in a large town. ~et (·−¹), -ti, virginity. ~lık, celibacy; a being unmarried.

bekaya (·−¹) *pl. of* bakiye. Arrears of state revenue; recruits due for military service, but not called up.

bekçi Watchman, *esp.* night-watchman; sentry; forest guard.

bekir *A man's name.* ⌐yırtılan Deli ~in yakası⌐, it is I who will suffer.

bekle·mek *va.* Await; watch; guard; lie in wait for; expect, hope for. *vn.* Wait; remain in expectation. beklemiş et, meat that has been kept or hung: ···in yolunu ~, to lie in wait for *s.o.* ~nmek, ~nilmek, *pass. of* beklemek. ~şmek, to wait or keep watch together. ~tmek, to cause to wait; to have *s.o. or stg.* watched or guarded.

bekri Habitual drunkard; toper.

Bektaşi (·−¹) Belonging to the Bektashi sect of dervishes; freethinker; dissolute. ~ sırrı, a great mystery: ~ üzümü, gooseberry.

bel¹ Waist; loins; middle of the back; midship; mountain pass. ~i* açılmak, to feel the need to urinate: ~i anahtarlı kadın, a careful and efficient housewife: ···e ~ bağlamak, to rely upon, to trust to: ~ini* bükmek, to break the back of, to defeat; (of an illness) to cripple; (*sl.*) to make short work *of a piece of meat etc.*: ~ vermek, (of a building) to sag, to show signs of collapse: eli ~de, alert, ready for action: yarı ~e kadar, to the waist.

bel² Spade; gardener's fork.

belâ (·¹) Trouble; misfortune; calamity; grief; difficulty; punishment; curse. ... ~sı, for the sake of .... *e.g.* namus ~sı, for honour's sake: ~sını* bulmak, to get the punishment one deserves: ~ çıkarmak, to start a quarrel: ⌐~ geliyorum demez⌐, misfortunes give no warning: ~lar mübareği, a blessing in disguise: ~yı satın almak, to ask for trouble; to get into difficulty with one's eyes open: ~ya uğramak, to get into trouble, to meet with misfortune: Allahın ~sı, a 'perfect pest': Allah ~sını versin!, may God punish him!; curse him!: baş ~sı or başa ~, a source of trouble and annoyance: bin ~ ile, only with the greatest difficulty: dilinin* ~sını çekmek, to get into trouble from inability to hold one's tongue.

belâgat (·–¹), **-ti** Eloquence.

belağrısı (¹···), **-nı** Lumbago.

belâhet (·–¹), **-ti** Stupidity; idiotcy.

belâlı (·–¹) Troublesome; difficult; calamitous; quarrelsome. Man kept by a prostitute; (*jokingly*) man who believes himself to be the favourite of a girl.

belâya (·–⸱) *pl. of* **beliyye**. Plagues *etc.*

belbel (¹·) *In* ~ **bakmak**, to look about one stupidly.

Belçika (·¹·) Belgium. ~**lı**, Belgian.

belde Town; country.

beledî (··⸱) Belonging to a town; local; municipal; civic. ~**ye**, municipality; ~ **reisi**, mayor.

beleş (*sl.*) Gratis. ~**çi**, one who gets stg. for nothing, sponger.

‖**belge** Document; certificate.

beli (¹·) Yes.

beliğ (·⸱) Eloquent.

belik Plait of hair.

belir·mek *vn.* Become conspicuous; appear; gaze with eyes wide open *from fear or anger*. ~**siz**, indistinct, not clear; uncertain: **adı** ~, an unimportant person: **belli** ~, hardly perceptible: **ne idügü** ~, a doubtful character of unknown antecedents. ~**ti**, mark; sign; proof. ~**tmek**, to make conspicuous or clear; to make known; to expound; to point out; to open *the* eyes in astonishment *etc.*

beliyye Trial; trouble; calamity.

belkemiği (¹···), **-ni** Backbone.

belkemikli (¹···) Vertebrate.

belki (¹·) Perhaps; may be. Even, but. ~ **de**, as likely as not.

belleme Numnah; horse-blanket.

bellemek¹ *va.* Commit to memory, learn by heart.

bellemek² *va.* Dig with a spade.

bellenmiş¹ Dug with a spade.

bellenmiş² Committed to memory; well-known.

belli Known; evident, clear. ~ **başlı**, eminent, notable; chief: ~ **beyan**, very evident. ~**siz**, unknown; imperceptible: **belli** ~, almost invisible.

bellütiye The oak-tree family; Cupuliferae.

belsoğukluğu (¹····), **-nu** Blennorrhoea; gonorrhoea.

bembeyaz (¹··) Extremely white.

bemol Flat (*mus.*).

ben¹ I. ~**im diyen** *in such phrases as*: ~**im diyen adam bu işi yapamaz**, this is not just anybody's job. '~ **ettim sen eyleme (etme)!**' *a humble entreaty or apology.*

ben² Mole; beauty-spot.

benam (·⸱) Named; famous.

benat (·⸱), **-tı** *pl. of* **bint**. Daughters; girls. ~**ı Havva**, daughters of Eve.

bence (¹·) In my opinion; as for me.

bencileyin (¹···) Like me (*deprecatingly*).

bend Bond, tie, fastening; dyke, dam, reservoir; paragraph; article *in a paper*. *Suffix*, binding ...; bound by .... ~**etmek**, **-eder**, to bind, fasten; attach to oneself.

bende Slave; servant. ~**niz**, 'your humble servant' (*a polite form of the first pers. sing.*). ~**gân** (··⸱) *pl. of* **bende**, slaves, servants; household servants of a princely house. ~**hane** (··–¹), *deferential way of saying* 'my house'.

bender Commercial port; fortress protecting a seaport or a strait. ~**ek**, small seaport.

benek Spot on the skin *or* coat. ~**li**, spotted.

‖**bengi** Eternal.

beni·âdem (···–¹) Sons of Adam, mankind. ~**beşer**, human beings.

benim *gen. of* **ben**. Mine, my. ~**ki**, the one belonging to me, mine: **o sokak senin, bu sokak** ~ **dolaştı**, he walked about from street to street. ~**semek**, to appropriate *or* lay claim to *stg. that does not belong to one*; to adopt as one's own; to assume as a personal obligation or interest.

beniz, **-nzi** Colour of the face. **benzi* atmak**, to turn pale: **benzinde* kan kalmamak**, to look very pale.

benk, **-ki** Narcotic drug made from hemp, bhang.

benli¹ Having moles on the face or body.

benli² *v.* **senli**.

benlik Egoism; personality; self-respect. ~ **davası**, self-conceit; a feeling of personal superiority: **milli** ~, national pride; national character.

bensiz Without me; without my assistance. Without a mole.

benzemek *vn.* (*with dat.*) Be like; resemble; *with a participle in the dat.*, to look as if ..., *e.g.* **ümid kesmişe benziyor**, it looks as if he had given up hope. **bir şeye benzemiyor**, it's useless (*cf. our* 'it's like nothing on earth'); **işte şimdi bir şeye benzedi**, now it's beginning to look like something, *i.e.* it's all right, *but* **işte şimdi tam benzedi**, look at the mess it's in now!

benzer Resembling. *n.* Like; copy. ~**i yok** *or* ~**siz**, unique: **tam** ~**i**, an exact similar. ~**lik**, resemblance, similarity.

benzetmek *va.* Liken; compare; make an imitation *or* copy of; mistake *a person for another*; see a resemblance. '~ **gibi olmasın!**', I don't wish to make a comparison, *said when making a comparison with a dead person or one who is ill or when the comparison might seem to be uncomplimentary to one of the parties*: ···**i bir şeye** ~, to make *stg.* look 'something like', to put in order: **mektebden kaçan çocuğu babası iyice benzetmiş**, his father gave the truant a good hiding.

benzeyis Resemblance.

benzi *v.* beniz.

benzin Petrol; benzine.

ber *Pers. prep.* On; in; according to. **bermutad**, according to custom: **bervechi ati**, in the following manner.

–ber *Pers. suffix.* Carrying away ..., *e.g.* **dilber** (ravisher of hearts), beautiful: ... breasted, *e.g.* **semenber**, silver-breasted.

beraber (·–¹) Together; in company with. Abreast, equal; in the same direction *or* on the same level. ∼**e bitmek**, to finish in a dead heat: ∼**e kalmak**, to be equal in a game: **bununla** ∼, at the same time, nevertheless: **yerle** ∼ **olm.**, to be razed to the ground, to be utterly destroyed. ∼**lik**, a being equal *or* abreast; solidarity, cooperation.

beraet, –ti Innocence; acquittal. ∼ **etm.**, to be acquitted: ⌜∼**i zimmet asıldır**⌝, a man is to be presumed innocent until his guilt is proved: ∼**i zimmet mazbatası**, certificate of discharge of an official leaving a post.

berakis On the contrary.

berat (·⁴), –**tı** Patent; warrant; order conferring a dignity *or* decoration. ∼ **gecesi**, *the Moslem Feast (15th of Shaban), celebrating the revelation of his mission to Muhammad.* ∼**lı**, patented.

berayi (·–·) *Pers. prep.* For; for the purpose of; for the sake of.

berbad Destroyed; scattered; ruined; spoilt; filthy; soiled. ∼ **etm.**, to spoil, to ruin.

berber Barber. ∼ **aynası**, hand-mirror.

Berber, berberî Berber.

berceste Select; choice.

berdel'acuz (···–·) (Old woman's cold), spell of cold weather at the end of March.

berdevam (··–·) Lasting; continuous. Continuously, uninterruptedly. ···**de** ∼**dır**, he continues to ...: ∼ **olm.**, to continue to exist.

bere¹ Bruise; dent. ∼**lemek**, to bruise.

bere² Beret.

bereket, –ti Abundance, increase; blessing. ∼ **versin**, may God bless you (*a form of thanks*); fortunately, as good luck would have it. ∼**li**, fruitful, fertile; abundant.

bergüzar Memento; gift for remembrance.

berhane (·–·) Large rambling house.

berhava (··–·) Carried into the air; destroyed; annihilated. ∼ **etm.**, to blow *stg.* up: ∼ **olm.**, to be blown up; to be annihilated.

berhayat (··–·) Alive.

berhurdar, berhudar (··–·) Enjoying the fruits of one's labour; successful, prosperous. ∼ **ol !**, I wish you prosperity, *meaning* 'I thank you'.

berî (·–·) Free from; exempt; absolved; acquitted.

beri The near side (*as opp. to* öte, the far side); this side; here, hither; the time since; until now. Since. ∼**deki**, that which is on this side: ∼ **taraf**, this side: **geldiğimden** ∼, since I came: **o günden** ∼, since that day. 'yarın olsun da hayrı ∼ gelsin', let's wait till tomorrow and hope for the best. ∼**ki**, nearest; last mentioned.

berk¹ Hard; firm; solid; rugged.

berk², **–ki** Lightning.

berk³, **–ki** Leaf.

berkarar (··–·) Stable; constant; durable. ∼ **olm.**, to remain unchanged.

berkemal (··–·) In perfection; complete.

berkitmek *va.* Render solid *or* firm; strengthen; back, support; confirm, affirm.

berlam Hake.

bermucibi (¹–··) In conformity with; as required by.

bermurad (··–·) Satisfied; happy. ∼ **olm.**, to have one's wish.

bermutad (¹––) As usual.

berrak Clear; limpid; sparkling.

berr·en (¹·) By land. ∼**î** (·–·), terrestrial; land. **asakiri** ∼**ye**, land forces (*as opp. to* maritime). ∼**iye**, land forces; desert.

bertaraf Aside; out of the way; putting aside; apart from. ∼ **etm.**, to put aside; to get rid of: ∼ **olm.**, to be put aside; to disappear: **şaka (lâtife)** ∼, joking apart.

bervechi (·¹·) In the manner of. ∼ **ati**, in the following manner, as follows: ∼ **peşin**, in anticipation; ready money being paid.

berzah Connecting interval between two things or states; period between death and resurrection; any place *or* state of anxiety and suffering; isthmus; precipice. **belâyı** ∼, a great difficulty; a cursed nuisance.

besa (¹·) Truce (*esp. in a blood-feud*); compact.

besalet (·–¹), **–ti** Courage, bravery.

besatet (·–¹), **–ti** Simplicity.

besbase (·–¹) Mace (of nutmeg).

besbedava (¹···) Absolutely gratis.

besbelli (¹··) Very clear *or* evident.

besbeter (¹··) Very much worse.

besi¹ Support, prop.

besi² Place in which animals are fattened; the fattening of animals. ∼**ye komak**, to put an animal out to fatten. ∼**li**, fattened; well-nourished.

besle·me Act of feeding *or* fattening; domestic servant *brought up in a house from* *childhood.* ~ **kılıklı,** slatternly. **~mek,** to nourish; to fatten; to rear *an animal;* to support, prop; to take into one's service: **can ~,** to be a gourmet. **~yici,** feeder, fattener; nutritious, wholesome.

besmele *The formula* 'bismillah!' (in the name of God). ~ **okumak** *or* **çekmek,** to pronounce this formula *before doing stg.* **~siz,** of evil omen; rogue.

beste Bound; fastened; obliged; congealed. Tune; musical composition. **~kâr** (··⸗), musical composer. **~lemek,** to compose music, to set to music. **~li,** with music.

beş Five. ~ **aşağı ~ yukarı,** close bargaining. ~ **aşağı ~ yukarı uyuşmak,** to come to some sort of an understanding: ~ **kardeş,** a slap, a box on the ear; ⌐~ **kardeşin tadını tatmamış**⌐, he wants a good smacking: ~ **para etmez,** worthless: ⌐ ~ **parmak bir değil**⌐, all men are not alike.

beşaret (·−⸗), **−ti** Good news; beauty; innovation.

beşaşet (·−⸗), **−tı** Having a smiling face, joy.

beşbıyık Medlar.

beşer¹ Five each.

beşer² Mankind. **~î** (··⸗), human. **~iyet, −ti,** humanity; human nature.

beşere Epidermis.

beşibirlik, beşibiryerde (···⸗·) Turkish gold 5-lira piece, *used as ornament.*

beşik Cradle. ~ **kertme nişanlı,** engaged to one another while yet in the cradle.

beşinci Fifth.

beşir One who brings good tidings.

beş·kardeş *v.* **beş.** **~li,** having five parts; the five (in cards). **~lik,** five-piastre piece; worth five piastres; five *yards long etc.* **~me,** a kind of cloth with stripes of five colours. **~pençe,** starfish. **~yüzlük,** Ltq. 500 note.

beşuş Smiling; happy.

bet¹, −ti *Only with* **beniz.** **~i benzi kalmamış,** he has no colour left.

bet² *Only in* ~ **bereket,** abundance, prosperity.

bet³ *v.* **bed.**

betelemek *va.* Quarrel with *s.o.*

beter *comp. of* **bed.** Worse. **~in ~i var,** there is always something worse.

beton Concrete. **~arme,** reinforced concrete.

bev·il, −vli Urine. **~letmek, −eder,** to urinate. **~lî,** uric.

bevvab Door-keeper; porter.

bevval *In* **~ı zemzem,** the man who urinated into the sacred well of Zemzem to acquire notoriety.

bey *Formerly a title inferior to Pasha and* *superior to Aga;* gentleman; prince; chief; ace (cards). **küçük ~,** the son of the house, the 'young master'.

beyaban (·−⸗) Desert; the wilds.

beyan (·⸗) Declaration; explanation; expression; style. ~ **etm.,** to announce, declare, explain. **~at** (·−⸗), **−tı,** *pl. of* **beyan;** declarations; *as sing.,* discourse, speech: **~ta bulunmak,** to hold forth, make a speech, give an explanation, make an announcement. **~name** (·−−⸗), manifesto; affidavit.

beyarı (⸗··) Queen bee.

beyaz White. White colour; white *of the eye, of an egg etc.;* fair copy. **~a çekmek,** to make a fair copy: **~a çıkarmak,** to stand up for *s.o.,* to clear his character. **~ımsı, ~ımtrak,** whitish. **~lı,** with white in it.

beyefendi (⸗···) *Term of respect in addressing a person;* sir!

beygir Horse; horse-power. **~ci, ~ sürücüsü,** a man who lets horses out on hire *or* attends to hired horses: **bostan ~i gibi dönmek (dolaşmak),** to walk aimlessly round and round; to stick to routine, to make no progress.

beyhude (·−⸗) Vain, useless. In vain.

bey·i (⸗··) *n.* Selling, sale. ~ **ve şira,** buying and selling, trade. **~î** (·⸗), connected with selling. **~iye,** certificate of sale; seller's commission.

beyin, −yni Brain; intelligence. **beyni* atmak,** to fly into a passion: **beyni* sulanmak,** to become senile *or* muddle-headed: ~ **tavası,** brain fritters. **~siz,** brainless, stupid.

beyit, −yti Couplet, verse.

beylerbeyi (⸗···) *(Formerly)* Governor of a province.

beylik Title or status of Bey; gentle birth; district governed by a Bey; 'the Government'. Belonging to the State; conventional, stereotyped. Small blanket *issued to soldiers.* ~ **gemi,** a government ship: ~ **satmak,** to behave like a little lord, to give oneself airs. **~çi,** *the head of an office, which, in Imperial Turkey, issued diplomas and commissions and ratified foreign treaties.*

beyn *As Turkish* **ara.** **~imizde,** amongst us, between us; **~lerinde,** amongst them *etc.* **ıslahı ~ etm.,** to promote a good understanding. **beyn−,** *Ar. prefix.* inter-; between ...: **~ehüma,** between them: **~elmilel,** international: **~ennas,** in common.

beynamaz (−·⸗) *(err. for* **binamaz).** One precluded from prayer *on account of canonical uncleanness;* unbeliever. ~ **özürü,** a lame excuse: *v.* **cami.**

Beyoğlu (¹··), **-nu** Pera.

beyt, -ti House; dwelling. ~**ullah,** the Cubical House at Mecca. ~**utet** (·–¹), ~ etm., to pass the night. ~**ülharam** (···–¹), as beytullah. ~**ülmal,** (*formerly*) the Public Treasury (*esp.* the branch connected with inheritance under the Canon Law).

beyyine Proof; evidence.

beyza Egg. **beyzâ,** white: narı ~, white heat.

beyzade (·–¹) Son of a Bey; noble.

beyzî (·–¹) Oval.

bez¹ Linen *or* cotton material; cloth; duster; canvas. **Amerikan** ~**i,** calico: yelken ~**i,** sail-cloth: ⌐**kenarına bak** ~**ini al, anasına bak kızını al**⌐, 'before buying stuff look at a sample, before marrying a girl look at her mother'.

bez² Gland.

bezdirmek Annoy, plague.

bezek Ornament; decoration. ~**çi,** woman who dresses brides; decorator.

bezelye (·¹··) Pea(s).

beze·mek *va.* Deck out; adorn. ~**n,** ornament; embellishment. ~**nmek,** to be adorned.

bezesten *v.* bedesten.

bezgin Tired of life; disgusted; discouraged.

bezim, -zmi Convivial gathering; feast; orgy. **bezmi muhabbet,** a reunion of friends: **bezmi Cem,** a drinking party.

bezir Linseed; linseed oil. ~**yağı, -nı** Linseed oil.

bezirgân (···–¹) Merchant *or* pedlar (*esp.* Jewish. **din (politika)** ~**ı,** one who exploits religion (politics) for his own ends. ~**lık,** cunning dealing.

bezl A giving or spending without stint; use, employment: ~**i himmet,** a making every endeavour: ~**i nefis,** expenditure of one's energy. ~**etmek** (¹··), **-eder,** to lavish *favours, compliments etc.*

bezmek Become weary and discouraged. ···**den** ~, to become sick of ..., disgusted with ... .

bezminus (···–¹) Drinking orgy.

bezzaz Linen-draper.

bıcıl Knucklebone.

bıcılgan (··¹) Cracked heels (in a horse); *perhaps also* malanders.

bıçak Knife. ⌐~ **kemiğe dayandı**⌐, (the knife has come up against the bone), it can no longer be borne; it has reached the limit: ~ **sırtı kadar,** a very small difference; ölmesine ~ **sırtı kalmış,** he all but died: ~ **silmek,** to finish off a job: **ağzını** ~ **açmıyor,** he is very depressed. ~**çı,** cutler; a bit too ready with his knife; quarrelsome. ~**lamak,** to stab, to knife. ~**lı,**

armed with a knife: **kanlı** ~ **olm.,** to be at daggers drawn. ~**yeri, -ni,** scar of a knife wound.

bıçılgan¹ *v.* bıcılgan.

bıçılgan², bıçırgan Burnisher.

bıçkı Cross-cut saw. ~ **talaşı,** sawdust: ~ **tezgâhı,** saw-mill.

bıçkın A quarrelsome rough; vagabond, ne'er-do-weel.

bıdık Short and tubby.

bıkkın Disgusted; satiated; bored.

bıkmak *vn.* Be disgusted *or* satiated. ···**den** ~, to be sick of *stg.*: **bıktım!,** I'm sick of it!; I've had enough of it!

bıldır (¹·) Last year; a year ago.

bıldırcın Quail; plump and attractive little woman.

bıllık bıllık Plump.

bıngıl *In* ~ ~, quivering like a jelly, well-nourished, fat. ~**dak,** soft spot on the skull of a new-born baby, fontanelle. ~**damak,** to quiver like a jelly.

bırakmak *va.* Leave; leave go; release; quit, abandon; put off; put down; deposit; leave off, cease from; entrust *sig. to s.o.*: allow; grow (moustache *etc.*); divorce; bequeath; keep *a boy* in a class, not to promote him. *vn.* (Of stg. stuck on) to come away, to come unstuck. **akıl bırakmamak,** to upset *s.o.'s* thoughts: ···**e etmediğini*** **bırakmamak,** to leave nothing undone to harm *or* annoy *s.o.*: **kendini** ~, to cease to take an interest in oneself (one's dress, one's business *etc.*): **kâr** ~, to show a profit: **mektubu postaya** ~, to post a letter.

bıyık Moustache; whisker *of a cat*; tendril. ~ **altından gülmek,** to laugh in one's sleeve: **bıyığını balta kesmez olm.,** to be a 'tough' fellow, to fear no one: ~ **burmak,** to curl the moustache; (of a young man) to swagger slightly, to show himself off to the girls: ~**larını ele almak,** to become a man. ~**lı,** having a moustache: ~ **balık,** barbel.

bızır Clitoris.

bi- (–) *Pers. suffix.* Without ..., -less.

biaman (––¹) Pitiless.

biat (–¹) Oath of allegiance; homage; (*only correctly used with reference to the Caliph*).

bibaht (–¹) Unfortunate.

bibehre (–·¹) Portionless; without a share of knowledge *or* capacity; unfortunate; incapable.

biber Pepper; pimento. ~**iye,** rosemary. ~**lik,** pepper-pot.

biblo (*Fr.* bibelot) Trinket; curio; knick-knack.

bicili *In* cicili ~, gaudy; all decked out.

biçare (––¹) Without help; poor, wretched.

biçilmek *vn. pass. of* **biçmek.** Be cut *etc.* **biçilmiş kaftan,** appropriate, well-adapted, 'cut out' for the job; 'just made' for *s.o.*

biçim Cut *of a coat*; form, shape; manner, sort. **~e sokmak,** to put in order : **ne ~ ...?,** what sort of ...; **bu ne ~ şey?,** what's this?; this is odd! **~li,** well-cut, well-shaped. **~siz,** ill-shaped, unsymmetrical, ugly.

biçki Cutting-out *of clothes etc.*

biçmek *va.* Cut out; cut up; divide; reap, mow. **ekin ~,** to harvest crops : **kesip ~,** to consider and decide : **ölçüp ~,** to measure and cut out; to take in *stg. (a room etc.)* at a glance : **paha ~,** to estimate a price : **pay ~,** to apportion a share; to deduce a conclusion.

bid' Vulva; coition.

bidar (—$\cdot$) Awake, alert.

bid'at, -tı Innovation *which is evil from a religious point of view*; heresy. **ehli ~,** heretics.

bidayet ($\cdot$—$\cdot$), **-ti** Beginning. **~ mahkemesi,** Court of First Instance.

bidon (*Fr.*) Can, drum.

bi·edeb (—$\cdot$$\cdot$) Unmannerly, ill-bred. **~esas** (—$\cdot$$\cdot$), without foundation.

biftek Beefsteak.

bi·gâh (—$\cdot$) Unseasonable, untimely. **~gam** (—$\cdot$), free from sorrow or care.

bigâne (—$\cdot$) Foreign; strange; aloof; uninterested, indifferent.

bigayrihakkin ($\cdot$$\cdot$$\cdot$$\cdot$) Unjustly, without right.

bi·günah (—$\cdot$$\cdot$) Innocent, blameless. **~haber,** unaware, ignorant. **~had,** without limit; infinite : **~ü bihesab,** endless, innumerable.

bihakkin ($\cdot$$\cdot$$\cdot$) Rightly, deservedly; as it should be; perfectly.

bi·haya (—$\cdot$$\cdot$) Shameless. **~hengâm** (—$\cdot$$\cdot$), ill-timed, untimely. **~hesab,** countless. **~hod,** beside oneself *from fear or ecstasy.* **~hude,** *v.* beyhude. **~huş,** (—$\cdot$), unconscious, bewildered. **~huzur** (—$\cdot$$\cdot$), uneasy, uncomfortable : **~ etm.,** to worry. **~hüner,** without skill or ability. **~ilâc** (—$\cdot$$\cdot$), **in aç ~,** utterly destitute, starving.

biiznihüda ($\cdot$$\cdot$—), **biiznillah** ($\cdot$$\cdot$$\cdot$) God willing.

bikes (—$\cdot$) Friendless; destitute; orphan.

bikir,-kri Virginity; virgin. **izalei ~ etm.,** to deflower.

bilâ– ($\cdot$$\cdot$) *Ar. prefix.* Without ....

bilâd ($\cdot$$\cdot$) *pl. of* **beled** and **belde.** Countries, regions; cities; townships.

bilâfasıla ($\cdot$—$\cdot$) Uninterruptedly.

bilâhara ($\cdot$—$\cdot$) Later on.

bilâistisna ($\cdot$—$\cdot$—) Without exception.

bilâkaydüşart ($\cdot$—$\cdot$$\cdot$) Unconditionally.

bilâkis ($\cdot$$\cdot$) On the contrary.

bilâmucib ($\cdot$—$\cdot$) Without reason *or* motive.

bilânço Balance sheet.

bilâperva ($\cdot$—$\cdot$$\cdot$) Without fear; boldly; freely.

bilârdo Billiards.

bilâ·sebeb ($\cdot$—$\cdot$) Without cause *or* reason. **~ücret,** without payment *or* reward. **~vasıta** ($\cdot$—$\cdot$$\cdot$), directly, without intermediary. **~veled,** without issue.

bilbedahe ($\cdot$—$\cdot$) Impromptu; all at once.

bilcümle ($\cdot$$\cdot$) All. In all; totally.

bildik *Past part. of* **bilmek.** Known; not a stranger. Acquaintance. **~ çıkmak,** to turn out to be an old acquaintance : **bildiğini okumak,** to go one's own way, to follow one's own judgement without asking the opinion of others : **bildiğinden şaşmamak,** not to be deterred by others from going one's own way.

bildirmek *va.* Make known; communicate; notify.

bile[1] Even. Together with. **~mce,** in company with me; **~since,** in company with him.

bile[2] *In* **~ ~,** knowingly; with one's eyes open.

bile[3] *v.* **bilye.**

bileği Instrument for sharpening. **~ çarkı,** grindstone : **~ kayışı,** strop : **~ taşı,** whetstone.

bilek Wrist; pastern. **~ damarı,** pulse : **~ gibi akmak,** to flow abundantly : **ayak bileği,** ankle; tarsus : **bu işte kimse onun bileğini bükemez,** nobody can equal him in this. **~li,** strong-wristed.

bilemek Sharpen, whet, grind. **···e diş ~,** to cherish a grudge against *s.o.*, to await a chance of revenge against *s.o.*

bilet, -ti Ticket. **~ kesmek,** (of tram-conductor *etc.*) to give a ticket. **~çi,** ticket collector, tram-conductor.

bileyici Knife-grinder.

bilezik Bracelet, bangle; collet; stone forming the mouth of a well; ring of metal round a column *or* a gun. **altın ~,** gold bracelet; skill *or* trade *enabling a man to earn his livelihood.*

bilfarz ($\cdot$$\cdot$) Supposing that.

bilfiil ($\cdot$$\cdot$) In fact, actually.

bil·ge Learned and wise. **~gi,** knowledge. **~giç,** pedant; pretending to be learned. **~giçlik,** pedantry : **~ satmak,** to make a parade of one's knowledge. **~gili,** learned. **~gin,** learned man, scientist.

bilhassa ($\cdot$$\cdot$) Especially, in particular. **~ ve ~,** above all.

bililtizam ($\cdot$$\cdot$$\cdot$) On purpose.

bilin·mek *vn. pass. of* **bilmek.** Be known, recognized *etc.*; be acceptable, gratefully received. **~mez,** unknown; incomprehensible.

‖**bilirkişi** Expert.

bilistifade (¹·--·) Profiting by, taking advantage of.

biliş A knowing; knowledge; acquaintance. **~ tanış,** friends and acquaintances. **~mek,** to know one another, be acquainted; strike up an acquaintance.

bilittifak (¹·--) By common agreement; unanimously.

bilkuvve (¹··) Inherent; virtual; virtually; potentially.

bilküllıye (¹···) Entirely, wholly.

billahi (¹-·) *In* **vallahi ~!,** I swear by God.

billur Crystal; cut-glass. Crystal-clear.

bilmece Riddle, enigma.

bilmedik (¹··) Who does not know; unknown. **~ kimse kalmadı,** everyone knows it.

bilmek, –ir *va.* Know; learn; recognize; guess; consider; believe; *(with the gerund in -a, -e,* to be able to ..., *e.g.* **yapabilmek,** to be able to do; **gidebilmek,** to be able to go. *v. also* **bildik** *and* **bile. bilmemezlikten gelmek,** to pretend not to know: **çektiklerimi ben bilirim!,** you can't think what I suffered!: ⌐**kendi bilir!**¬, (i) just as he wishes!; it's up to him!; (ii) on his head be it!: **kendini bilmez,** insensible; confused; who does not know his place, arrogant, insolent: **kendimi bildim bileli,** from the time I was capable of thinking: ⌐**siz bilirsiniz!**¬, 'as you will!': ⌐**ya Rabbi, sen bilirsin!**¬, 'O my Lord, you know!', *said under one's breath and generally to oneself to express annoyance*: **(bunu yapmayın!) yaparsanız orası artık sizin bileceğiniz iştir,** if you do it, you will do it at your own risk.

bilmez Who does not know; ignorant; ungrateful. **~lik,** ignorance; feigned ignorance: **~den** *or* **bilmemezlikten gelmek,** to feign ignorance.

bil·misil (¹··) In a like manner. **mukabele ~,** tit-for-tat, retaliation. **~mukabele** (¹·--·), in return, in retaliation. **~muvacehe** (¹·--·), confronting *two people* with one another. **~münasebet** (¹·--··), by the way, in this connexion. **~münavebe** (¹·--·), alternately; by turns. **~ûmum** (¹·-), in general; on the whole; all. **~vasıta** (¹·--), indirectly. **~vesile** (¹·--·), on the pretext of; profiting by the occasion.

bilye (¹·) Marble (child's plaything); billiard ball; ball *(mech.).* **~ yatağı,** ball-bearing.

bimâna (--⌐) Meaningless; without significance.

bimar (-¹) Ill. **~hane** (--·¹), lunatic asylum.

bimisil (-·¹) Peerless.

bimuhaba (⌐·--) Without respect *or* consideration; impartial. Dauntlessly, unsparingly.

bin¹ Thousand; a great many. **~lerce,** in thousands: **~i bir para,** abundant; very cheap: **~de bir,** very rarely: **~ can ile,** with the utmost eagerness: ⌐**~ dereden su getirmek**¬, to make all sorts of excuses: ⌐**~in yarısı beş yüz (o da sende yok)**¬, *said to one deep in thought, stg. like* 'a penny for your thoughts!', *but meaning rather more* 'what have you got to worry about that you are so pensive?': **~ yaşasın,** long live ...!

bin² Son; *chiefly in Arab names, e.g.* Ali bin Hassan, Ali the son of Hassan.

–bin (-) *Pers. suffix.* -seeing. **durbin,** far-sighted; telescope.

bina Building, edifice; act of building, construction; a basing *a claim etc. on some fact*: chapter on indeclinable words in Arabic grammar; ⌐**benim oğlum ~ okur, döner döner yine okur**¬, *used about one who keeps harping on the same subject or about stg. which makes no progress*: **~ etm.,** to build.

bîna (-¹) Seeing; able to see; clear-sighted.

binaberin (·⌐··) Consequently; therefore.

binaen (·⌐·) On account of; in consequence of; based on. **~aleyh,** consequently, therefore.

binam (-⌐) Nameless. **~ ve nişan,** without a trace.

binamaz (--⌐) *v.* **beynamaz.**

binbaşı (¹··) Major; commander (navy); squadron-leader.

bindallı Purple velvet embroidered with leaves and flowers.

bindirme *verb. n. of* **bindirmek.** Joint; overlap. Mounted on, resting on; clinker-built.

bindirmek *va. caus. of* **binmek.** Cause to mount *etc.*; cause to rest on *or* overlap; (of a ship) to collide with, to ram. **üzerine ~,** to fall on; to increase violence; to blame (wrongly).

binefsihi (·¹··) Of himself; in himself.

binek Connected with riding. A mount (horse *etc.*). **~ arabası,** carriage: **~ otomobili,** passenger car. **~atı, –nı,** saddle-horse.

biner A thousand each.

bingözotu (·¹··), **–nu** Scammony.

binici A good horseman; jockey. **~lik,** horsemanship.

binihaye (--·-) Infinite, endless.

bininci Thousandth.

biniş Act *or* method of riding; ancient ceremonial riding dress; long full cloak *worn formerly by ulema.*

binlerce In thousands; thousands of.

binlik Large bottle holding 1,000 dirhems; a 1,000-lira note.

binmek *va. (with dat.)* Mount; ride; go on (a train or ship); overlap; assume an attitude *or* condition. **iş fenaya bindi,** the affair has taken a bad turn.

binnefs (ˈ·) In person, personally: itself.

binnetice (ˈ·—·) Consequently; as a result.

binnisbe (ˈ··) Relatively.

bint, –ti Daughter; girl.

bipayan (——ˈ) Endless; infinite; everlasting.

biperva (—·ˈ) Fearless; unscrupulous.

bir One; a; the same; equal; in such a way; once; alone, only; *sometimes* = just, *e.g.* ~ **gidip bakalım,** let's just have a look; *sometimes adds emphasis, e.g.* ~ **yağmur** ~ **yağmur!,** you never saw such rain!; ~ **döğdü ki,** he gave him such a beating. ~**den,** suddenly; together: ~ **de,** in addition, furthermore: ~ **başına,** alone; on his own: ~**e bin kazanmak,** to make an enormous profit: ~**e** ~ **gelmek,** to be the one and only cure, to be 'just the thing': ~ **dediği iki olmaz,** highly esteemed and beloved; **karısının** ~ **dediğini iki etmiyordu,** he could refuse nothing to his wife: ~ **iki demeden,** (i) without hesitation; (ii) suddenly: ~ **olm.,** to be at one, to agree: ⌜~ **olur, iki olur**⌝, once or twice *but not always*: ~ **şey,** something: ~ **şey değil,** don't mention it!; it's nothing, it does not matter: ~ **şeyler,** something or other; lots of things: ⌜~ **varmış** ~ **yokmuş**⌝, 'once upon a time' *(beginning of a fairy story)*; 'that's all a happy memory now': **bu evlerin ikisi de** ~, these houses are identical; it makes no difference which house: **gelmesi ile gitmesi** ~ **oldu,** he no sooner came than he went: **neler çektiğimi** ~ **ben bilirim** (~ **de Cenabı Hak),** what I went through is only known to me and to God: **seninle** ~ **daha konuşursam iki olsun,** I'll never speak to you again: **yerle** ~ **olm.,** to be razed to the ground.

bira (ˈ·) Beer. ~**hane** (···ˈ), beerhouse; public house; brewery.

birader (·—ˈ) Brother.

biraz (ˈ·) A little, rather. ~**dan,** in a short while, soon; shortly afterwards.

birbiri, –ni One another.

birçok (ˈ·) A good few; a lot.

birden Together; at the same time. **hepsi** ~, all together; the whole of. ~**bire** (·ˈ··), all of a sudden; all at once.

birdirbir Leap-frog.

birdüziye (ˈ···) Continuously.

bire *v.* bre.

birebir (ˈ··) Most efficacious (remedy); equal to the occasion; 'just the thing'.

birer One apiece, one each. ~ ~, one by one: ~ **ikişer,** one or two each: ~ **kuruşa,** at one piastre each.

biri One of them; an individual. ~ ~, one another: ~**miz,** one of us: ~ **gelir** ~ **gider,** one goes, another comes: **herifin** ~, some fellow or other.

biribiri, –ni One another.

biricik (ˈ··) Unique; one only; a small one; a pet one.

birikinti Accumulation; heap; garbage. **su** ~**si,** puddle.

birik·mek *vn.* Come together, assemble; accumulate. ~**tirmek,** *va.* collect; assemble; amass; save up (money); let *work etc.* accumulate. **içine** ~, to bury *insults or sorrows* in one's heart.

‖**birim** Unit.

birinci First; chief. ~**lik,** first prize; first place.

birisi *v.* biri.

birkaç A few; some. ~ **defa,** several times.

birleş·ik United. ~**mek** *vn.,* unite; reunite; assemble; agree; be reconciled. ~**miş,** united: ~ **milletler,** United Nations.

birli Ace *of cards*; the one *in dominoes etc.*

birlik Unity; union; agreement; association; equality; similarity; identity. ~**te,** together, in company: **ağız birliği,** unanimity of expression: **el birliği,** unity in action, co-operation.

birörnek (ˈ··) Of the same pattern.

birsam Hallucination.

birşey *v.* bir.

birtakım (ˈ··) A quantity; some.

birteviye (ˈ···) Continuously; regularly.

birtürlü (ˈ··) *(with neg. verb)* By no means; in no way.

bisiklet, –ti Bicycle.

bisküvit, –ti Biscuit.

bismillâh (···ˈ) In the name of God! *(said by Moslems before starting on any undertaking).*

bit, –ti Louse. ~**i kanlanmak (canlanmak),** to recover one's spirits, one's money *etc.*; to become uppish. **yaprak** ~**i,** aphis.

bitab (—ˈ) Exhausted; without strength. ~**u takat,** utterly exhausted. ~**i** (——ˈ), exhaustion; weakness.

bitaraf (—·ˈ) Impartial; neutral. ~**lık,** impartiality; neutrality.

biteviye (ˈ···) All of a piece; complete. Uninterruptedly.

bitik Worn out; exhausted.

bitirim End; conclusion. *(sl.)* 'topping'. ~ **yeri,** gambling den.

bitirmek *va. caus. of* **bitmek.** Finish; complete; terminate, bring to an end; destroy; cause to grow *or* sprout. **işini** ~, to finish s.o.'s business; to kill him.

bitiş·ik Touching; contiguous; neighbouring. Next-door house; neighbour. ~mek, to be contiguous; to join; adhere.

||bitki Plant.

bitkin Exhausted, worn out.

bit·lemek va. Delouse. ~lenmek, to be infested with lice; to be deloused. ~li, lousy.

bitme verb. n. of bitmek. yerden ~, short, squat.

bitmek vn. Come to an end, finish; be exhausted; be ruined or destroyed; sprout, grow: ~e ~, to be very fond of ... : olup ~, to happen; olup bitenler, events; ⌐oldu da bitti, maşallâh!⌐, 'well that's done and finished with!' (said when s.o. has been rushed into giving their unwilling consent); ben oldum bittim, ever since I can remember.

bitmez Interminable, endless.

bit·otu (¹··), –nu Lousewort. ~pazarı, –nı, old clothes market. ~sirkesi, ~ni, nit.

bittabi (¹··) Naturally, of course.

bitüm Bitumen.

bityeniği (¹···), –ni Lit. louse-bite; tender spot; secret anxiety due to some wrong done. bu işin içinde bir ~ var, there is stg. fishy about this.

bivaye (––¹) Without shelter, homeless; disappointed.

bivefa (–·¹) Faithless; inconstant.

biyel (Fr. bielle) ~ kolu, connecting-rod.

biz¹ We. ···le ~bize kalmak, to have a tête-à-tête with ... .

biz² Awl.

bizaa, bizaat (·–¹) Ability.

bizar (–⸴) Tired, wearied; sick of a thing. ~ etm., to distress, annoy.

bizatihi (·⸴··) In itself; intrinsically.

bizim Our. ~ için, for us. ~ki, ours; my wife or my husband.

bizzarur (¹·–), bızzarure Forcibly, necessarily.

bizzat (¹–) In person, personally.

blöf Bluff.

blûz Blouse.

bobin Bobbin; spool; coil (elect.).

boca (¹·) Act of pouring or decanting. ~ etm., to turn over; transport; pour out, empty; tilt; veer (ship). ~ alabanda tiramola etm., to wear ship. ~lamak vn., veer, bear away; turn from side to side; lurch, stumble, falter, vacillate; fail; get confused when speaking.

bocurgat Capstan; winch. bu adam ~sız iş görmez, this man will only work under pressure.

bocurum Mizzen sail of a yawl.

bodoslama Stem or stern post of a ship.

bodrum Subterranean vault; dungeon; cellar. ~ katı, basement.

bodur Short, dwarf, squat.

bofa ~ balığı, lamprey.

boğa Bull. ~ güreşi (dövüşü), bull-fight.

boğaça (·¹·) Flaky pastry.

boğası Thin twill used for linings.

boğaz Throat; mountain pass or defile; strait; mouth of a river; mouth requiring food; food in general; board of a servant or animal. ~dan bahsetmek, to talk about food: ~ını çıkarmak, to earn just enough for one's food: ~ derdine düşmek, to be mainly concerned with the question of food: ~ından* geçmemek, to be unable to enjoy a meal because s.o. was absent: ~ ~a gelmek, to fly at one another's throats, to quarrel violently: ~da kalmak, to stick in the throat: ~ kavgası, a quarrel about food: ~ olm., to have swollen glands: ~ına* sarılmak or ~ını* sıkmak, to take s.o. by the throat, to throttle; to put pressure on, insist: ~ tokluğuna hizmet etm., to give service in return for food: ~dan yatmak, to be laid up with a sore throat: ~ını* yırtmak, to shout oneself hoarse: ⌐can ~dan gelir⌐, one must eat to live: canı* ~ına* gelmek, to come to the end of one's tether, to lose one's patience: sık ~ etm., to 'keep on at' s.o. to get stg. done.

Boğaziçi (·¹··) –ni The Bosphorus.

boğaz·kesen (·¹··) Fortress commanding a strait; fortress surrounded by water; narrow street; mountain gorge. ~lamak, to cut the throat of; strangle. ~lanmak, pass. of boğazlamak: to acquire a good appetite; (sl.) to be cheated. ~lı, gluttonous. ~sız, who eats little.

boğmaca (¹··) or ~ öksürüğü Whooping-cough.

boğmak¹ Node; joint, articulation; a kind of lark.

boğmak² va. Constrict; choke; strangle; suffocate; drown. şakaya ~, to ridicule, to make a jest of stg.

boğucu Suffocating; stuffy; (sl.) cheating.

boğuk Suffocated; hoarse (voice). beli ~ bardak, a narrow-waisted glass.

boğulmak vn. pass. of boğmak. Be choked, drowned etc.; gasp for breath; choke with laughter or anger; be fleeced.

boğum Node; articulation; choke (gun). ~lu, articulated; knotty; wrinkled.

boğun As boğum; hole in the roof for smoke or ventilation.

boğuntu Suffocation; oppression; swindling, cheating at a game. ~ya getirmek, to squeeze money out of s.o. by putting him in an embarrassing position: lâfı ~ya getirmek, to twist words, to quibble.

boğuşmak *vn.* Fly at one another's throats; quarrel; fight.

bohça Square piece of stuff for wrapping; bundle; parcel; square shawl; selected and finely cut tobacco. ~ **etm.**, to wrap up in a bundle: ~**sını koltuğuna vermek**, to 'sack' *s.o.*: **parça** ~**sı**, rag-bag: **parça** ~**sı gibi**, made of ill-assorted pieces. ~**cı**, woman pedlar of small draperies, *who used to visit harems*. ~**lamak**, to wrap up, make a parcel of.

bok, –ku Excrement; ordure. Worthless. ~**tan**, made of rubbish, useless: ~**u** ~**una**, in vain, senselessly: ~**unu çekmek**, to suffer the evil consequences of s.o. else's action: ~**u çıkmak**, for the ugly side of a man or a thing to be revealed: ~**unda inci aramak**, to over-estimate *s.o.*: ~ **püsür**, rubbish: ~ **yemek**, to commit an indiscretion, to make a mistake: ~ **yoluna gitmek**, to lose one's life unnecessarily for a worthless reason: **aklı** ~**una karışmak**, to be frightened out of one's wits.

bok·böceği, –ni, dung-beetle. ~**lamak**, to soil, befoul; besmirch, bring into disrepute; mismanage. ~**laşmak**, become bad *or* difficult; be annoyed *or* bored; meddle. ~**lu**, fouled with dung, filthy. ~**luca**, thicket: ~ **bülbülü**, wren; pert and talkative person. ~**luk**, dungheap; filthy place; state of disorder *or* misery: ⌐**nerede çokluk orada** ~¬, too many people spoil a party *etc.*; *sometimes* ⌐**too many cooks spoil the broth**¬.

boksit, –ti Bauxite.

bol¹ Wide; loose; ample, copious, abundant. ~ **ahenk**, fond of gaiety: ~ ~ *or* ~ **bolama**, abundantly; generously: ~ **bulamak**, to lay on thickly; to give abundantly: ~ **keseden**, generously; ~ **keseden atmak**, to make extravagant promises; to talk wildly about spending money: ~ **paça**, wide trouser legs. ~**lanmak**, to become wide *or* loose; become copious or abundant. ~**luk**, wideness; looseness; easiness of fit; abundance, plenty: ~ **bir memleket**, a land of plenty: '**nerede bu** ~?', *a reply to an excessive demand or statement*, 'that's a bit stiff, isn't it?'

bol², –lü A drink of mixed liqueurs and fruit-juice.

bol³, –lü The game of bowls.

boliçe (·¹·) Jewess.

bomba (¹·) Bomb. ~**lamak**, to bomb.

bombarda (·¹·) A kind of sailing boat *used in the Aegean*.

bombardıman Bombardment; bombing.

bombok (¹·) Utterly spoilt; quite useless.

bombort, bonbort Bombardon.

bomboş (¹·) Completely empty; utterly nonsensical.

boncuk Bead (*esp. a blue bead in a child's hair or a horse's mane to avert the evil eye*). ~ **illeti**, infantile convulsions: ⌐**mavi** ~ **kimde ise benim gönlüm ondadır**¬, *phrase from a Nasreddin Hodja story meaning* 'to please both parties', *v. App.*

bonfile Best undercut of beef.

bonjur Morning-coat.

bono (¹·) Bond; bill. **açık** ~, blank cheque; 'carte blanche'.

bonservis (*Fr. bon service*). Certificate of good character.

Bor¹ A town in Anatolia. ⌐**geçti** ~'**un pazarı, sür eşeği Niğde'ye**¬, (i) it's too late now to do anything; (ii) things have changed now.

bor² Waste *or* uncultivated land. Wine.

bor³ Boron.

bora (¹·) Squall, tempest; violent reproach *or* abuse. ~ **yemek**, to be exposed to a storm of wind *or* words. ~**ğan** (··¹), whirlwind; tempest.

borani *A dish of vegetables and rice.*

borazan Originally 'trumpeter', now only trumpet. ⌐**sesine (nefesine) güvenen** ~**cı başı olur**¬, 'by all means do it, if you think you can!'

borc Debt; loan; duty, obligation. ~**a alışveriş etm.**, to buy on credit: ~ **almak**, to borrow: ~ **bini aşmak**, to have a pile of debts: ~ **etm.**, to incur a debt: ~ **gırtlağa çıkmak**, to be up to the ears in debt: ~ **harc**, getting money by hook or by crook: ~ **vermek**, to lend: **boynunun*** ~**u**, one's first duty. ~**lanmak**, to become indebted. ~**lu**, indebted; debtor. Under obligation: **uçan kuşa** ~ **olm.**, to be in debt all round.

borda (¹·) Ship's side; broadside. ~ ~**ya**, alongside (*naut.*).

bordro (¹·) (*Fr. bordereau*). Memorandum; account; docket.

borsa (¹·) Bourse; stock-exchange.

boru Tube; pipe; trumpet; idle tale, nonsense. ~ **değil**, it's no small matter: ~**su ötmek**, to be the 'big noise', to be the most important person in a place: **kalk** ~**su**, reveille: ⌐**yem** ~**su çalmak**¬, to put off with empty promises. ~**çiçeği, –ni**, datura.

bos *Only in conj. with* **boy**. Figure; stature.

Bosna (¹·) Bosnia.

bostan Vegetable garden (*esp.* melon garden); cucumber; melon. ~ **dolabı**, irrigation water-wheel: ~ **korkuluğu**, scarecrow; lazy *or* incapable person. ~**cı**, gardener; (*formerly*) one of the Sultan's body-guards: ~ **başı**, officer commanding the Sultan's body-guards.

boş Empty; empty-handed; vain, useless; unoccupied; unemployed; divorced; loose, untethered. **~ta,** unemployed: **~una,** in vain: **~unu almak,** to take up the slack; to trim an unlikely story so as to make it plausible: ⌐**~ atıp dolu tutmak**⌐, to 'draw a bow at a venture' and unexpectedly to hit the mark; to make a lucky shot; to learn something one wants to know by subtle questions: **~ bulunmak,** to be taken unawares; to be surprised: **~a çıkmak,** to come to nothing, to fail: **~ düşmek,** (of a woman) to be divorced: **~ eli,** empty-handed; at leisure: **~ gezmek,** to idle about, to be without work: ⌐**~ gezenin ~ kalfası**⌐, ne'er-do-weel, vagabond. **~ kâğıdı,** a written declaration of divorce: **~ olm.,** to be empty; to be useless; to be unoccupied: **~ vermek,** to pay no attention: **~ yere,** in vain: **başı ~,** without bridle or halter; vagabond; not in any occupation, independent: **eli ~ durmak,** to remain idle: **vakti ~una geçirmek,** to waste time.

boş·almak vn. Be emptied; run out; (animal) get loose. **~altmak** va. empty; pour out; discharge (firearm). **~ama,** divorce. **~amak,** to divorce. **~anmak,** to be loosed, break lose, escape; be poured; pour with rain; (firearm) be discharged; be emptied; be divorced; empty one's heart; burst into tears: **bardaktan boşanırcasına yağmur yağıyor,** it's raining in torrents: **sinirler ~,** to be unable to refrain from laughing. **~atmak,** to make or let a wife be divorced. **~boğaz,** garrulous, indiscreet. **~boğazlık,** idle talk, indiscreet babbling. **~lamak,** to loose, let go; abandon, neglect. **~luk,** emptiness; vacant space; vacuum; vanity; uselessness; leisure.

Boşnak Bosnian.

bot, ~tu Dinghy.

boy[1] Length; height; depth; stature; size. **~ ~,** of different sizes or qualities: **~dan ~a,** from end to end; completely: **~una,** lengthwise; continually; along: **~unca,** lengthwise; according to its length; along; **sahil ~,** along the shore: **tarih ~,** in the course of history; v. also **boylu: ~ almak** (atmak, çekmek, sürmek), to increase in stature: **~u bosu,** v. **boybos: ~a çekmek,** (of a child) to keep growing taller without growing proportionately broader: **~u*** **devrilsin!,** (a curse) 'may he die!': **~ göstermek,** to put in an appearance and do nothing; but 'gelsin **~unu göstersin!**', let him come and we will see what he is made of: **~unun* ölçüsünü almak,** to get one's deserts; to learn by painful experience: **~ ölçüşmek,** to compete with s.o.: **~undan utan!,** you should be ashamed to do this at

your age: **dere burada ~ vermez,** the river is out of one's depth here.

boy[2] Branch of a race. **Türklerin Oğüz ~u,** the Oguz branch of the Turkish race.

boya Dye; paint; colour. **~ tutmak,** to take a dye; (of a dye) to become fast: **~ vurmak,** to paint or dye: **atmaz ~,** fast dye: **göz ~sı,** eyewash: **her ~dan boyamak,** to be a jack-of-all-trades: **kundura ~sı,** boot polish: **~cı,** dyer; colourman; shoe-black: **~ küpü,** dyer's vat; ⌐**~ küpü değil**⌐, 'it's not so easy as all that!' **~hane** (···—⌐), dye-house; colourman's shop. **~lı,** painted; dyed; coloured. **~ma,** action of painting etc.; coloured, painted, dyed; false, imitation. **~mak,** to paint, dye; swear at s.o.: **göz ~,** to hoodwink: **birbirinin gözünü ~,** (of two parties) to pretend to believe stg. when each knows the other does not believe it.

boyan Liquorice plant. **~balı, ~nı,** liquorice. **~kökü, ~nü,** the root of the liquorice plant.

boy·bos (⌐·), acc. **boyu bosu.** Stature. **boyu bosu yerinde,** tall and well-built. **~ca** (⌐·), as regards height or length: **~ evlâd,** a practically grown-up child: **~ günaha girmek,** to commit a great sin. **~lamak,** to measure the length or height of; to traverse the length of; (sl.) to betake oneself to: **ahreti ~,** to die: **elliyi boyluyorum,** I am getting on for fifty: **mahkemeyi ~,** to have to appear in court. **~lanmak,** to grow, to become long or tall. **~latmak,** to make growth in height or length; to make s.o. go to a distant place. **~lu,** possessing length or height: **~ boslu,** well-built, well-developed: **~ boyuna,** at full length: **~boyunca,** in its entire length: **uzun ~,** tall. **~suz,** short in stature.

boyna Single oar used over the stern to steer or scull a boat. **~ ile yürütmek,** to scull a boat.

boynu v. **boyun.**

boynuz Horn; cupping-glass. **~ çekmek,** to cup: ···**e ~ taktırmak,** to make a cuckold of s.o.: **~ vurmak,** to gore. **~lu,** horned; cuckold; pimp; procuress. **~otu, ~nu,** hellebore.

boyotu (⌐··), **~nu** Fenugreek.

boyun[1] gen. of **boy.**

boyun[2], **~ynu** Neck. **boynuna* almak,** to take upon oneself: **boynu altında kalsın!,** (a curse) 'may he perish!': **boynuna* atmak,** to impute to: **boynuna* binmek,** to dun, to persecute: **~ borcu,** a binding duty: **~ eğmek,** to bow the neck, to submit; to humiliate oneself: **boynu* eğri,** hanging the head in shame, humiliated: **~ kesmek,** to bow the head in respect or *humility*: 'boynum kıldan ince', I am at your mercy; upon my head be it!: ~ noktası, the point where two hills join: boynu* tutulmak, to have a stiff neck: ~ vermek, to obey: boynunu* vurmak, to decapitate: günahı boynuna*, on his head be it!

boyuna 1. *Dat. of* **boyun.** 2. *Dat. with possessive suffix of* **boy,** *q.v.*

boyun·atkısı, –nı, neckerchief, scarf. **~bağı, –nu,** necktie; scarf; dog-collar. **~buran,** wryneck. **~ca,** *v.* boy. **~duruk,** yoke: **boyunduruğa vurmak** *or* ~ **altına almak,** to put under the yoke, to reduce to servitude *or* submission. **~luk,** scarf; collar.

boz Grey. Uncultivated land.

boza (¹·) Boza, *a fermented drink made of millet.* **ensesinde ~ pişirmek,** to torment; to inflict punishment on.

bozarmak *vn.* Become grey; become brown or sunburnt. **kızarıp ~,** to turn red and pale alternately *from fear, rage, or shame.*

bozca Greyish. Uncultivated land. **Bozca Ada,** Tenedos.

bozdoğan Grey falcon; (?) merlin; a kind of pear.

bozgun Routed, defeated. Rout, defeat. ~ **vermek** *or* **~a uğramak,** to be routed. **~cu,** defeatist. **~culuk,** defeatism.

bozkır Pale grey. Steppe.

bozkurt Grey wolf; *legendary wolf said to have led the Turks across a mountain barrier into the open world.*

bozlak A tune of folk music.

bozma Act of spoiling *etc.* Spoilt; demolished; made out of old materials, reconstructed. **~cı,** one who buys old things to use the materials again.

bozmak *va. & vn.* Derange; spoil; ruin, destroy; deprave, corrupt; deflower; disconcert; cancel; break (oath, treaty); change (money); defeat, rout; gather final crop of *grapes etc.*; break up and reconstruct into stg. else; go mad; (of weather) to deteriorate. **abdest ~,** to relieve nature: **ağız ~,** to abuse, vituperate: **aklını* ~,** to go off one's head: **and ~,** to violate an oath: **bağ ~,** to gather in the vintage: **birisile ~,** to 'have a down on' s.o.: **bir şeyle ~,** to have a bee in one's bonnet about stg., to be obsessed by stg.: **efkârini* ~,** to pervert s.o.: **ordugâh ~,** to break camp: **oruc ~,** to break a fast: **şakaya ~,** to turn into a jest, to make a mockery of: ⌜**Allah yazdıysa bozsun!**⌝, God forbid!: **yapıp ~,** to make and remake, to constantly reconstruct.

bozrak Of a light greyish colour.

bozuk¹ A kind of musical instrument *with nine strings.*

bozuk² Destroyed; spoilt; out of order; ruined; broken; depraved, corrupt. ~ **para,** small change: **ahlâkı ~,** depraved: **başı ~** (başıbozuk), irregular soldier; civilian: **keyfim ~,** my health is bad. **~düzen,** disordered, irregular. **~luk,** ruin; a being out of order or broken down; defeat; small change.

bozulmak *vn. pass. of* **bozmak.** Be spoilt *etc.*; get out of order; break down; deteriorate; (meat *etc.*) go bad; be disconcerted; look vexed; grow thin; become pale and ill.

bozum *verb. n. of* **bozmak.** ~ **olm.,** to be disconcerted: ~ **havası,** the embarrassment caused in company by anyone's discomfiture: **bağ ~u,** the vintage.

bozumca A kind of lizard.

bozuntu Discomfiture, embarrassment; old materials, scrap; *also as* **bozma** *q.v.* **~ya uğramak,** to be embarrassed or discomfited: **~ya vermemek,** not to let oneself be disconcerted: **şair ~su,** a mere parody of a poet, a so-called poet.

bozuş·mak *vn.* Quarrel with one another; become estranged. **~uk,** who has quarrelled; on bad terms.

böbrek Kidney. ~ **yağı,** suet.

böbür Tiger; *sometimes* leopard. **~lenmek,** to assume an arrogant air, to boast.

böcek Insect; bug; crayfish (spiny lobster). **~kabuğu, –nu,** bright greenish-blue colour: shot, iridescent. **~lenmek,** to be infested with insects.

böğ A kind of poisonous spider.

böğrülce (·¹·) Kidney-bean.

böğür, –ğru Side; flank· **boş ~,** the small of the back: **eli böğründe,** discouraged, disheartened; unable to do anything.

böğürmek *vn.* Bellow; low.

böğürtlen Blackberry.

‖**bölge** District; zone.

bölme Bulkhead; partition; dividing wall. **su ~leri,** watertight compartments.

bölmek *va.* Separate; divide; cut up. **ikiye ~,** to divide into two.

bölük Part; subdivision; fragment; compartment; company, squadron (*mil.*).

bölüm Act of dividing; portion; slice; chapter; article.

bölünmez Indivisible.

bölüşmek *va.* Divide up; share out.

bön Silly; naïve; vacant; imbecile.

börek *Name given to various kinds of* pastry *or* pie. **Nemse böreği,** fritter.

börtmek *vn.* Be slightly cooked, be half cooked. **sıcaktan ~,** to be half broiled in the heat.

börülce Kidney-bean.

böyle (ˌ·) Such; similar to this. So, thus, in this way. ~ **iken,** while it is or was thus; notwithstanding: ~ **ise,** if so, in that case: **bundan** ~, henceforth: **şöyle** ~, so so, not too well. ~**ce** (ˌ··), somewhat in this fashion. ~**likle** (··ˌ·), in this manner.

branda Sailor's hammock; awning or hood of a lorry etc. ~ **bezi,** canvas.

bre Now then!, hi, you!; sometimes in admiration, wonderful! **bekle** ~ **bekle,** he (we etc.) waited and waited.

Brehmen Brahmin.

briçka (ˌ·) A kind of open carriage; britska.

brik Brig.

brom Bromium. ~**ür,** bromide.

bronş (Fr. bronche) Bronchus, windpipe. ~**it, -ti,** bronchitis.

broş Brooch.

bu This; pl. **bunlar,** these.

bû Smell, odour.

bucak Corner; angle. ~ ~ **aramak,** to hunt in every hole and corner: **birine dünyanın kaç** ~ **olduğunu göştermek,** to teach s.o. a lesson, to give him 'what for': **ucu bucağı yok,** vast.

buçuk Half (only after numerals). **az** ~, just a little: **bir** ~, one and a half: **saat iki** ~, the time is half-past two: **üç** ~ **atmak** (sl.), to be frightened.

bud v. but.

bûd Being; existence.

Buda (ˌ·) Buddha.

budacık Twig; shoot; small knot (wood).

budak Twig; shoot; knot in timber. **gözünü** ~**tan sakınmamak,** to be fearless. ~**lanmak,** to send forth shoots; become knotty or snaggy; become complicated or difficult. ~**lamak,** to bud-graft.

budala Silly fool; imbecile; greedy. **futbol** ~**sı,** mad on football.

buda·mak va. Prune; lop, trim. ~**nmak,** to be pruned or trimmed; to apply oneself assiduously to stg.

Buğdan (ˌ·) Old Turkish name for Moldavia.

buğday Wheat. ~ **benizli,** light-complexioned: **mısır** ~**ı,** maize.

buğu Steam; vapour; mist. ~**hane** (··ˌ·), vapour bath; sterilizer; oven for killing silkworms. ~**lanmak,** to be enveloped in vapour or steam; (glass) to be misted over.

bugün (ˌ·) Today. ~**e** ~, adds emphasis to the succeeding statement, 'don't forget that…': ~**ü* yarınına* uymamak,** for one's circumstances (one's mood etc.) to be liable to change. ~**edek** (ˌ···), up till today. ~**kü** (ˌ··), of today, today's. ~**lük** a., just for today: ~ **yarınlık,** that may happen any moment.

buğz Hatred, malevolence, rancour. ~ **bağlamak,** to bear ill will, to cherish a hatred.

buhar (·ˌ) Steam; vapour; exhalation.

buhran (·ˌ) Crisis. ~**î** (·—ˌ), critical.

buhur (·ˌ) Incense; fumigation. ~**dan** (·—ˌ), ~**luk,** censer. ~**umeryem,** cyclamen.

bukadar v. **kadar.**

bukalemun (···ˌ) Chameleon; fickle or changeable person; shot silk.

buket, ~**ti** Bouquet.

bukle (Fr. boucle) Lock of hair; curl.

bulak Spring; source.

bulama Grape-juice boiled down to the consistency of honey.

bulamac Thick soup made with flour, butter, and sugar.

bulamak va. Smear; bedaub; dirty, soil; mix; coat or cover (with = dat.).

bulan·dırmak va. Render turbid or muddy; cloud (the eye or mind); turn (the stomach). ~**ık,** turbid; cloudy; overcast. ~**mak,** to become cloudy or turbid; become nauseated; (of the eye) to become bloodshot or opaque; (of the eye or mind) to be clouded or dimmed. ~**tı,** nausea.

bulaş·ıcı Contagious, infectious. ~**ık,** smeared over; soiled, dirty; infected; contagious; suspect after being in contact with infection; compromised; (ship) not having a clean bill of health. Dirt; contagion; dirty kitchen utensils: ~ **bezi,** dish-cloth: ~ **suyu,** dirty water; dishwater. ~**ıkçı,** dishwasher.

bulaş·mak vn. Be smeared or stuck; become dirty. ···**e** ~, to come into contact with contagion; be involved in an affair; take in hand; have to do with. ~**tırmak,** to smear; stick on; dirty; infect; involve in stg. unpleasant: **yüzüne gözüne** ~, to make a mess of stg., to fail.

buldok Bulldog.

bulgari A kind of guitar.

bulgur Boiled and pounded wheat. **ebe** ~**u,** fine hail.

Bulgurlu In ⌐~**ya gelin mi gidecek?**⌐, 'why all this unnecessary fuss?'

bullak v. **allak.**

bulmaca Cross-word puzzle.

bulmak, -ur va. Find; invent; obtain; reach. **buldukça bunamak,** to be never content but always to ask for more: **Allahtan bulsun!,** may God punish him!: **aradığını buldu,** he got what he was asking for, i.e. his deserts: **belâsını*** ~, to meet with well-merited punishment: **bilmem neden buldu buldu da beni buldu,** I don't know why he picked on me (of all people): **ettiğini*** ~ to pay for one's misdeeds:

fena ~, to die; to come to an end : **seksenini** ~, to reach the age of eighty : **vuku** ~, to happen : **yerini** ~, to reach its proper place : **yüz** ~, to have the presumption, to dare.

bulundurmak *va.* Make *or* let be present; have ready; have in stock.

bulun·mak *vn. pass. of* bulmak. Be found *etc.*; be present; be (*cf. Fr. 'se trouver'*); ···**e** ~, to assist. ~**maz**, not to be found; rare, choice : ~ **Hind Kumaşı,** *used ironically of stg. erroneously thought to be rare or precious.*

buluş Act of finding; invention, discovery.

buluş·mak *vn.* Be together with others; meet. ~**turmak,** to bring together; arrange a meeting of : **bulup** ~, to find at any cost.

bulut, –tu Cloud. ~ **gibi sarhoş,** dead drunk. ~**lanmak, t**o become cloudy *or* opaque : **gözleri** ~, to be on the verge of tears. ~**lu,** cloudy, overcast.

bulûz Blouse.

bûm (–) Owl.

bumba (¹·) Boom (*naut.*).

bumbar Intestine; sausage; draught excluder.

bun Anxiety, distress; crisis. ~**lu,** anxious, distressed.

buna *dat. of* bu.

bunak Imbecile; in one's second childhood, senile.

bunalmak *vn.* Be stupified; be suffocated *with smoke etc.*: be utterly bored *or* wearied.

bunamak *vn.* Reach one's dotage. **buldukça** ~, to be always grumbling, never to be satisfied.

bunca (¹·) In this fashion; this much. ~ **kere,** so many times : ~ **zaman,** so long a time. ~**layın** (¹···), so much, so many; in this way.

bundan *abl. of* bu. ~ **böyle,** from now on, henceforth : ~ **dolayı,** on account of this.

bunluk Uneasiness; crisis.

bunu *acc. of* bu.

bunun *gen. of* bu. ~**la beraber,** however, in spite of this : ~ **üzerine,** then, thereupon.

bura (¹·) This place; this condition; this point. ~**m,** this part of me : ~**ya,** to this spot, here : ~**dan,** from here : ~ **ahalisi,** the people of this place.

burağan *v.* borağan.

Burak Celestial steed *used by Mohammed.*

buralı (¹··) Belonging to this place.

buram ~ ~, whirling, eddying; like a whirlpool; excessively : ~ ~ **terlemek,** to sweat profusely.

buran Whirlwind; whirling tempest *of rain or snow.*

buranda (·¹·) Canvas hammock.

burası (¹··) This place, here. ~ **neresi ?,** what place is this?

burc[1] Tower; sign of the Zodiac.

burc[2] Mistletoe.

burçak[1] Vetch.

burçak[2] Screwed; wound round itself.

burçun Female roedeer.

burgacık (¹··) *In* **kargacık** ~, bad scrawling (writing); crooked, twisted.

burgu Auger; gimlet; corkscrew.

burjuvazi Bourgeoisie.

burkulmak *vn.* Be sprained. **içi*** ~, to feel a pang *of remorse, pity, or envy.*

burkutmak *va.* Sprain.

burma Act of twisting; castration; screw; convolution; griping of the stomach; sweet *made of dough, oil, and sugar.* Screwed; twisted; spiral; castrated.

burmak *va. & vn.* Twist; wring; castrate; dislocate; (of the bowels) to gripe; bore a hole. **dudak** ~, to screw up the lips.

burnu *v.* burun.

burnuz Burnous, woollen Arab cloak; bath robe.

burs (*Fr. bourse*) Scholarship.

burtlak Suckling pig.

buruk Twisted; sprained; acrid, sour.

burulmak *vn. pass. of* burmak. Be twisted; writhe with pain; be offended.

burum Torsion; contortion. ~ ~, contorted; griped.

burun, –rnu Nose; beak; promontory; pride, arrogance. **burnu* büyümek,** to become conceited : **burnunu* çekmek,** to sniff; to go away empty-handed : **burnuna* çıkmak,** to become intolerable : **burnunun* doğrusundan ayrılmamak,** to be above taking anyone's advice, to be too conceited to listen to others : **burnundan düşen bin parça,** very conceited; unapproachable; in the worst of tempers : ʳ(**hık demiş) burnundan düşmüş**ʼ, the very spit of ... (*usually in a derogatory sense*) : **burnumdan* geldi,** it completely spoilt my pleasure : **burnundan* getiririm,** I'll make you sorry for it : **burnuna* girmek,** to come too close to s.o. : ~ **kanı,** bloodred : **burnunun* kemiği sızlamak,** to feel very sad : ~ **kırmak,** to screw up the nose *in dislike or contempt* : **burnunu* kırmak,** to take the conceit out of s.o. : **burnunun* ucunda,** right under one's nose : **burnunun ucunu görmemek,** to be blind with pride; to be very drunk : ʳ**ağzından* girip burnundan* çıkmak**ʼ, to try all sorts of tricks on s.o. to gain one's end : **canım* burnumdan* geldi,** I was dead tired.

burun·deliği, –ni, nostril. ~**duruk,** twitch *for holding an unruly horse.* ~**kanadı,**

–nı, outside of the nostril, ala. **~luk.** nose-ring *of a bull*; iron toe-cap of a boot. **~salık,** muzzle.

buruntu Colic.

buruş·mak *vn.* Be wrinkled, creased *or* puckered; have the teeth set on edge. **~turmak,** to crease, wrinkle; corrugate; frown; set the teeth on edge. **~uk,** puckered; wrinkled; ruffled.

buse, puse (–¹) Kiss.

but, bud Thigh; leg of meat. ⌐eti ne, budu ne ?¬, what can you expect from that poor, weak creature?

butlan Error; a being null and void. Cancelled, not in force.

buud, –u'du Distance; dimension.

buymak *vn.* Freeze; freeze to death.

buyruk, buyuruk Order, command. **başına ~,** who goes his own way without asking others' permission or advice; who is his own master.

buyrultu Order; decree; nomination paper *for lower officials*.

buyurmak *va.* Order; deign or condescend to do; *used as an auxiliary instead of* etmek *when addressing a person of rank or when wishing to be polite*; **buyurunuz!,** please *sit down, lead the way etc.*; **ne buyurdunuz?,** I beg your pardon, what did you say?; **ne buyururlar** (*politely*) what is your opinion? (*sarcastically*) what have you got to say about that?: ⌐**buyurun cenaze namazına**¬, (come to the funeral!), we are done for!: ⌐**tembele iş buyur, sana akıl öğretsin**¬, 'offer work to a lazy one, let him give you good advice', *said of or to a man who tries to get out of doing stg. by suggesting a different course of action*: **teşrif ~,** to do the honour of visiting.

buz¹ *v.* az.

buz² Ice. Very cold; frozen. **~ gibi,** very cold; new and clean; fresh and tender (meat); *also* 'of course', 'as a matter of course': **~ bağlamak,** to form ice, to freeze over: **~ kesmek,** to feel very cold: **~ kesilmek,** to be frozen; to be petrified *with fear, etc.*: **~ üstüne yazmak,** to do stg. which will not last, to build on sand: **~ yalağı,** a depression where snow lies. **~hane,** ice-factory; ice-house. **~kıran,** ice-breaker. **~lanmak,** to become ice; be covered with ice; lose polish, become dull. **~lu,** iced; dulled; ground (glass). **~lucam** (·¹·), ground glass. **~luk,** ice-factory; ice-house; ice-box.

buzağı Sucking-calf.

‖**buzul** (·¹) Glacier.

bücür Short, squat, dwarf; 'cute' (*of a child, or of an insignificant person from whom one would not expect 'cuteness'*).

büğrü *v.* eğri.

büğü Sorcery.

bühtan (·–¹) False accusation; calumny. **~cı,** calumniator.

bükâ (·–¹) Weeping.

büklüm Twist; curl. **iki ~,** bent double with age.

bükmek Twist; spin; curl; contort; bend. **belini ~,** *v.* bel: **boyun ~,** to bow; **boyunu* ~,** to resign oneself to the inevitable; to be bowed down by grief: **dudak ~,** to curl the lip *in disdain or contempt*: **kol ~,** to twist the arm; to overcome: ···**in kulağını ~,** to drop a hint to *s.o.*

bükük Curved; twisted. **boynu ~,** wretched: **kulakları ~,** warned beforehand.

bükül·mek *vn. pass. of* bükmek. Be twisted *etc.* **beli ~,** to be bent double with age; to be handicapped by *stg.* **~ü,** bent; twisted; spun.

büküm Act of twisting *or* spinning; torsion; twist; once spun wool *etc.*; skein; yarn.

büküntü Fold; twist; knot; hemstitch.

bülbül Nightingale ⌐**~ün çektiği dili belâsıdır**¬, one's tongue is apt to get one into trouble. **~ gibi,** fluently.

bülend High. **~ avaz,** loud-voiced: **~pervaz,** ambitious; presumptuous.

bülheves Capricious; fickle; libidinous.

bülten Bulletin.

bülûğ (·–¹) Puberty; maturity; age of discretion. **~a ermek,** to reach the age of puberty.

bünyan (·–¹) Act of building; construction; building.

bünyat (·–¹) Foundation.

bünye Edifice; structure (of the body *etc.*); constitution.

bürgü Covering; cloak; veil.

bürhan (·⸳) Proof; evidence.

büro Bureau; office.

bürudet (·–¹), **–ti** Cold; coldness.

bürülü Wrapped up; enfolded.

bürüm A wrapping up, folding; fold. **~cek,** anything wrapped up like a cocoon. **~cük,** raw silk; crêpe; gauze.

bürümek *va.* Wrap; enfold; cover up; invade, infest. **gözünü* kan ~,** to be near murder with anger; to see red.

bürüncük *v.* bürümcük.

bürünmek *vn.* Wrap oneself up.

büsbütün (¹··) Altogether; quite.

bütçe Budget.

bütün Whole, entire, complete. Wholly, completely. The whole. **~ gün,** the whole day. **~leme,** a second examination for those who failed the first time. **~lemek,** to complete; to repair. **~leyin** (·¹··) completely.

büvelek, büye, büyelik Gad-fly.
büyü Spell, incantation; sorcery. ~**yü bozmak,** to break a spell: ~ **otu,** thorn-apple (datura): ~ **yapmak,** to practise sorcery, to cast a spell. ~**cü,** sorcerer, magician. ~**lemek,** to cast a spell on, to bewitch. ~**lü,** bewitched; having magic powers.
büyük Great, large; high; important; elderly. ~ **ana (anne),** grandmother: ~ **baba,** grandfather: ~ **kafalı,** highly intelligent: ~ **söylemek,** to dogmatize; to be too cocksure; to talk in a manner for which one will be sorry later: **gözü*** ~**te olm.,** to aim high, to have great ambitions.
Büyükada (·¹··) The island of Prinkipo.
büyültmek va. Make great; exaggerate.
büyümek vn. Grow large; grow up; increase in importance. **büyülmüş de küçülmüş,** (of children) appearing to be much older than they are, precocious:

gittikçe burnu büyüyor, he gets more conceited every day: **gözleri büyümüş bir halde,** with eyes starting out of his head *with terror etc.*
büyütmek va. Make great; enlarge; exaggerate; nourish and cherish; bring up. **gözde** ~, to exaggerate the importance of *stg.*
büzgü Pucker; pleat.
büzmek Constrict; pucker. ⌐**her kesin ağzı torba değil ki büzesin¬,** you can't stop people talking: **lâkırdıyı ezip** ~, to hum and haw without being able to express one's meaning.
büzük Constricted; puckered. Anus.
büzülmek (··¹) vn. Contract; shrink; shrivel up; cower, crouch. **bozulup** ~, to be disconcerted and 'retire into one's shell': **ezile büzüle,** humbly, apologetically.

C

caba (¹·) Thrown into the bargain. ~ **etm.,** to give gratis: ... **da** ~**sı,** and into the bargain ...: **bu da** ~, and what's more, and into the bargain. ~**cı,** sponger, parasite.
cabeca (²·—) In places; here and there.
cacık A drink *made of* **ayran** *q.v., with pieces of cucumber in it.*
cadaloz A spiteful old hag.
cadde Main road; thoroughfare; highway. ~**yi tutmak,** to 'clear out'.
cadı Witch; hag; vampire.
cafcaf Pompous or pretentious speech; ostentation. ~**lı,** pompous; showy; elegant.
cağ Spoke of a wheel. ~ **torbası,** spare nosebag *for a horse.*
−cağız, −ceğiz *Suffix implying smallness or affection.* **evceğiz,** our little house: **adamcağız,** the good fellow; the poor man.
cah (−) High position; dignity, rank.
cahil (−¹) Ignorant; inexperienced; uneducated; young. **kara** ~, utterly ignorant. ~**iyet, −ti,** the Age of Ignorance, *i.e.* prior to Mohammed. ~**lik,** ignorance; inexperience; youth.
caiz (−¹) Lawful; permitted, admissible; possible. ~**e,** mark, dash, tick; present, reward.
caka (¹·) Ostentation; swagger. ~ **satmak (yapmak),** to swagger, to show off. ~**cı,** ~**lı,** swaggering.
câli (−¹) False; imitation; insincere.
câlib (−¹) Attracting; attractive; causing.
câlis (−¹) Sitting on the throne; reigning.

Calût (−¹) Goliath.
cam Glass; photographic plate. ~ **evi (yuvası),** rebate or groove for glass. ~**cı,** glazier. ~**lı,** glass-covered, glazed.
câm (−) Wine-glass.
camadan Double-breasted waistcoat; chest for clothes or linen; valise; reef-point. ~ **bağı,** reef-knot: ~**ı fora etm.,** to shake out a reef: ~ **vurmak,** to take in a reef.
cambaz Acrobat; circus-rider; horse-dealer; swindler. ~**hane** (··—¹), circus.
cam·dolab (·¹·) Glass-fronted case *for books etc.* ~**ekân,** shop-window; showcase; garden frame; dressing-room of a bath. ~**göbeği,** glass-green. ~**göz** (·¹), tope; avaricious.
cami (−¹), **−ii** *or* **−yi** Mosque. ⌐**eceli gelen köpek ~ duvarına siyer (işer)¬,** 'the dog who is doomed to die makes water against the wall of a mosque', ⌐**quem deus vult perdere, prius dementat¬,** ⌐**iki ~ arasında beynamaz¬,** 'who hesitates between two mosques, thereby missing service at either', ⌐**falling between two stools¬.**
câmi (−¹) Collecting; bringing together; containing. ~**a,** assembly of people; the community.
camid (−¹) Frozen; solid; inorganic, mineral. A solid; an inorganic substance.
cam·lamak va. Cover with glass; glaze. ~**lık,** anything covered with glass; shop-window.
camus (·¹) Water buffalo.
can Soul; life; a soul, a living person;

darling, beloved friend; a member (of certain Moslem sects); force, vigour, zeal. Agreeable, pleasant. ~**dan**, very sincerely: ~ım!, (i) 'my dear fellow!', 'my good man!' (*expresses a mild reproof*); (ii) *as an adj.*, beloved: ~ **acısı**, fearful pain: ~ **acıtmak**, to cause suffering, to oppress: ~ı* **ağzına*** **gelmek**, to be half-dead *from anxiety or fatigue*: ~ **alacak yer**, the most sensitive spot; ~ **alacak** *or* **alıcı nokta**, a vital point: ~ını **almak**, to take *s.o.*'s life: ~ **atarcasına**, ardently: ···e ~ **atmak**, to desire passionately: ~ı **aziz**, one's own dear self: ~**la başla**, with heart and soul: ~ ~**a baş başa**, each for himself, 'sauve qui peut': ~ı* **çekilmek**, to feel extreme pain: ~ **çekişmek**, to be in the throes of death: ~ı* **çekmek**, to long for: ~ını **çıkarmak**, to exhaust, to ruin, to ill-treat: ~ı* **çıkmak**, to die; to be very tired: (of clothes) to be very worn; ⌐~ **çıkmayınca huy çıkmaz**⌐, ⌐what's bred in the bone won't out of the flesh⌐: ~ **damarı**, the vital spot, the the most important point: ~ **dostu**, a very sincere friend: ~ **düşmanı**, a mortal enemy: ~ **evi**, the heart; the pit of the stomach; any vital spot: ~**dan gelmek**, to die: ~**ü gönülden**, most willingly: ~ı* **istemek**, to feel (physically) like doing *stg.*, *but* ~ın **isterse !**, 'all right!', 'as you will!': ~**ına*** **işlemek** (**kâr etm.**), to become intolerable: ~ **kalmamak**, to have no life left in one, to be utterly exhausted: ~**a** ~ **katmak**, to make one feel more alive, to refresh, to delight: ~ **kurtaran yok mu?**, 'help!': ~ **üstünde olm.**, for one's life to be in danger: ~ını* **yakmak**, to hurt (*esp.* the feelings): ~**ına yandığım**, the cursed ... (*sometimes used in admiration*): ~ı* **yanmak**, to suffer pain *or* loss: **ne** ~ı **var?**, he's not got much strength left: **vay** ~**ına !**, by Heaven!, by Jove!: ⌐**çok veren maldan, az veren** ~**dan**⌐, it is not the gift that matters, but the spirit in which it is given; 'the widow's mite'.

canalıcı (¹···) The Angel of Death; Azrail; *v. also under* **can**.

canan (−¹) Sweetheart. ⌐**evvela can sonra** ~⌐, everyone thinks first of his own interests; ⌐**number one comes first**⌐.

canatış (¹··) Passionate desire.

canavar Monster; brute; wild beast; wild boar. ~ **düdüğü**, a warning syren. ~**lık**, savagery, ferocity, barbarity. ~**otu**, **-nu**, broom-rape.

canciğer *In* ~ (**kuzu sarması**), people very dear to each other.

candar Living creature; defender. Alive; animated.

caneriği (¹···), ~**ni** A sweet and juicy kind of green plum.

canevi (¹··), **-ni** Any vital part of the body; pit of the stomach; seat of the affections.

canfes Taffeta. Made of taffeta.

cangil cungul (·¹·¹) Ding-dong; noisily.

canhıraş (−·¹) Harrowing; disagreeable.

cani (−¹) Criminal.

canib (−¹) Side; direction; party *to a transaction*. ... ~**inden**, on the part of ...: ... ~**ine**, towards ...: **her** ~**den**, from all quarters. ~**dar** (−·¹), troops protecting the flank.

can·kulağı (¹···), **-nı** Rapt attention. ~**kurtaran**, lifebuoy, lifebelt. Life-saving: ~ **otomobili**, motor ambulance. ~**lanmak**, to come to life; to become active *or* lively. ~**lı**, alive; lively; active; vigorous: **iki** ~, pregnant: **yedi** ~, having seven lives; invincible: **para** ~**sı**, a lover of money. ~**pazarı** (¹···), ~**nı**, a situation where life is at stake. ~**sağlığı**, **-nı**, health; *v. also* **sağlık**. ~**sıkıntısı**, **-nı**, boredom. ~**siz**, lifeless; weak, slack, dull. ~**siperane** (····−¹), self-sacrificing (act).

cant, **-tı** (*Fr. jante*) Felloe; rim *of a bicycle*.

car¹ Woman's shawl or cloak.

car² Neighbour.

car³ ~ ~, *used to express loud and continuous noise or talk.* ~**car**, chatterbox.

cari (−¹) Running, flowing; current (money *etc.*); valid; occurring, present; usual.

carih (−¹) Wounding. **alâtı** *or* **eslihai** ~**a**, cutting weapons, cold steel. ~**a**, *fem. of* **carih**; limb *or* organ of the body; beast of prey.

caris Shrewish.

cariye (−·¹) Female slave; concubine; *politely for* 'my daughter'.

carlamak *vn.* Talk loudly and incessantly.

cart *Imitates the sound of something being torn.* ~ **curt etm.**, to use threatening words. ~**adak**, suddenly and noisily.

carta Fart. ~**yı çekmek** (*sl.*), to die.

cascavlak (¹··) Completely naked *or* bald. ~ **kalmak**, to be left desitute *or* helpless.

-casına, **cesine** *Suffix denoting* 'in the manner of', *e.g.* **hayvancasına**, in a bestial way; **delicesine**, like a madman; *also with verbs, e.g.* **pek eskiden tanışırmışçasına el sıkıştık**, we shook hands in the manner of people who had known one another a long long time.

casus (−¹) Spy. ~**luk**, espionage.

cavalacos Worthless.

cavid (−¹), **cavidan** (−−¹) Eternal; celestial. ~**i**, eternity.

cavlak Naked; bald; featherless, hairless. **cavlağı çekmek**, (*sl.*) to die. ~**lık**, nudity; baldness; utter desitution.

cay- Place *or* point (*only in compounds with izafet*), *e.g.* ~ı **sual**, questionable point.

caydırmak *va. caus. of* **caymak.** Cause *s.o.* to renounce *or* change his purpose.

cayır *In ~ ~, denotes continuous and rather violent action*; willy-nilly; 'jolly well': ~ ~ **yanmak,** to burn furiously. **~damak,** to crackle *or* creak. **~tı,** noise of tearing *or* creaking *or* the crackling of flames.

cayiğir (−·⌐) Established; existing.

caymak *vn.* Swerve; deviate *from a purpose,* change one's mind.

cayro (¹·) Gyro-.

caz Jazz. **~bant,** jazz band.

cazgır Referee *in a wrestling match.*

cazib (−¹) Attracting; attractive. **~e,** *fem. of* cazib; attractiveness; attraction; charm; the force of gravity. **~eli,** attractive.

−ce, −çe, −ca, −ça *Suffix denoting* on the part of; in the manner of; according to. *With an adjective it forms the diminutive*: hükûmetçe, on the part of the government: adamca, in the manner of a man: bence, according to me; for my part: soğukça, rather cold.

ceb Pocket; purse. **~i delik,** penniless: birini **~inden çıkarmak,** to out-do s.o.: ⌐istemem yan **~ime koy!**⌐, *said to or of a person who pretends not to want stg. which he really does want.*

cebanet (·−¹), **−ti** Timidity; cowardice.

cebbar (·⌐) Omnipotent (of God); tyrannical. Tyrant.

cebe Cuirass; armour; munitions of war. **~ci,** armoured infantryman; armourer (of the Janissaries). **~li,** man-at-arms; provincial soldier; local mounted police *serving as escort to travellers.*

cebel Mountain. **−î** (··¹), pertaining to mountains; mountaineer. **Cebelitarık** (···−¹), Gibraltar.

cebelleşmek *v.* cedelleşmek.

cebellezi (·¹··) *In ~* **etm.,** to appropriate what does not belong to one.

ceberut (···⌐) The majesty of God; despotism, tyranny. Tyrant; bully.

cebhane (·−¹) Powder magazine; ammunition; munitions of war. **~lik,** ammunition store.

cebharçlığı (¹···), **−nı** Pocket-money.

ceb·he Front; forehead. **~den taarruz,** frontal attack: ···e karşı **~ almak,** to take the field against ... . **~hî** (·⌐), frontal.

cebiboş, cebidelik Without a sou, penniless.

cebin (·⌐) Cowardly. Forehead.

cebir, −bri Force; violence; compulsion; algebra. cebrile, by force, compulsorily. **~e** (·−¹), surgeon's splint.

Cebrail (·−−⌐) The Archangel Gabriel.

cebr·en (¹·) By force. **~etmek** (¹··),

−eder, to force, compel. **~î** (·⌐), done by force; compulsory; algebraical. **~inefis, ~fsi,** self-control, self-restraint: ···den ~ etm., to restrain one's desire to ..., to refrain from ... .

ced, −ddi Grandfather; ancestor. **~di âlâ,** a remote ancestor, the founder of one's family: ~ **beced,** from one generation to another: **~dine rahmet !,** well done!: yedi **~dine,** *adds emphasis to the succeeding word, e.g.* yedi **~dine lânet !,** curse and damn him!; yedi **~ine tövbe etm.,** to forswear for good and all. **~danî** (·−⌐), atavistic. **~de,** grandmother; ancestress.

cedel Dispute; argument. **~leşmek,** to dispute, debate, argue; struggle.

Cedi (·⌐) Capricorn.

cedid (·⌐) New; modern.

cedre Goitre.

cedvel Canal; ruled paper *or* book; tabulated form, table, list, schedule; ruler. **~e geçirmek,** to tabulate.

cefa (·⌐) Ill-treatment, unkindness, cruelty. ~ **etm.,** to ill-treat, torment. **~kâr** (·−⌐), *(orig.)* cruel; *(now)* who has suffered much. **~keş** (·−¹), suffering, tormented; long-suffering.

ceffelkalem (¹···) Offhand, without reflection.

−ceğiz *v.* **−cağız.**

cehalet (·−¹), **−ti** Ignorance.

cehd A striving; endeavour. **~etmek** (·¹··), **−eder,** to strive.

cehennem Hell; inferno. ~ **dibi,** a remote and inaccessible place: ⌐~e kadar yolu var!⌐, he can go to hell for all I care!: ~ **kütüğü,** a hardened sinner: ~ **ol !,** clear out!, go to hell!: canı **~e !,** damn him! **~î** (···⌐), hellish; damned. **~lik,** worthy of hell; hardened sinner; stoke-hole *of a Turkish bath.* **~taşı, −nı,** nitrate of silver.

cehil, ⌐hli Ignorance. **cehli basit,** acknowledged ignorance *as opposed to* **cehli mürekkeb,** ignorance posing as wisdom.

cehiz *v.* **cihaz.**

cehre Spindle; reel.

cehr·en (¹·) Loudly; clearly; publicly. **~î,** loudly, clearly *or* publicly read *or* spoken.

cehri Madder root *and* the dye derived therefrom.

ceket, −ti Jacket, coat.

celâdet (·−¹), **−ti** Sturdiness; intrepidity; moral courage.

celâl (·⌐) Majesty (*esp.* of God); glory; wrath. **~lenmek,** to get into a rage. **~li,** quick-tempered, irascible.

celâli (·−¹) *Originally* a provincial rebel; *hence* a rebellious person.

celb A procuring; attraction; summons.

~etmek (¹··), –eder, to attract, bring, procure; supply; import; summon; drive; transport. ~name (·–¹), summons, citation.

celeb Drover; cattle-dealer.

celi (·⸜) Clear, evident. hattı ~, large cursive style of Arabic writing.

celil (·⸜) Illustrious.

cellâd (·⸜) Executioner. Merciless.

celse A sitting; session.

Cem Jemshid (a legendary Persian king); a name of Solomon.

cem, -mmi Crowd. ~mi gafir, a great multitude.

cemaat (·–¹), –ti Community; party; group; congregation.

cemadat (·–⸜), –tı pl. of cemad. Inorganic substances.

cemahir (·–⸜) pl. of cümhur. Only in ~i Müttehidei Amerika, the U.S.A.

cemal (·⸜), –li Beauty.

cem'an (¹·) In all; as a total. ~ yekûn, the sum total.

cemaziyel·âhir (·⸜···¹) The sixth month of the Moslem year. ~evvel (·⸜··¹), the fifth month of the Moslem year. ~ini bilmek, to know all about s.o.'s antecedents (not to his credit).

cem·etmek (¹··), –eder va. Bring together; collect; add up. ~i, –m'i, a collecting, bringing together, adding; plural; total. ~î (¹–), all; everyone; the whole. ~'î (·⸜), collective.

cemil (·⸜) Beautiful; charming, gracious. ~e (·–¹), a kind or gracious act; compliment. ~ekâr (·–⸜), kind, attentive.

cemiyet, –ti Assembly; meeting; society; association; wedding. ~i Akvam, League of Nations: ~i belediye, municipal council. ~li, full of people, crowded; comprehensive.

cemre (lit. a burning ember); the gradual increase of warmth in February. ~ düşmek, (of the weather) to get warmer.

cenab (·⸜) Majesty; excellency. ~ları, his Excellency (of foreigners only). C~ı Hak, God.

cenabet (·–¹), –ti A state of impurity; a person in that state; (as a term of abuse) foul brute.

cenah (·⸜) Wing; fin; flank (mil.).

cenaze (·–¹) Corpse. ~ alayı, funeral procession. canlı ~, a living skeleton.

cenb Pleura. ~î (·⸜), pleural.

cenbiye An Arabian dagger.

cendere (¹··) Press; roller press; narrow gorge; crowded place, squash. ~ baklası, a very thin kind of bean: ~ye koymak, to oppress, torture.

ceneralya (··⸜·) Cineraria.

ceneviz (·¹·) Genoese; artful, cunning.

cengâver (·–¹) Warlike; brave.

cenge Spark; firefly.

cengel, cangal Jungle.

cenin (·⸜) Foetus, embryo. ıskatı ~, miscarriage.

cenk War; battle; quarrel. ~cu (·⸜), warlike; quarrelsome. ~leşmek, to make war, fight, struggle.

cennet, -ti Paradise. ~li, belonging to paradise; the late ...; 'of happy memory'. ~lik, deserving of Heaven. ~mekân ···⸜), 'of happy memory'; in paradise.

centilmen Gentleman. ~ce, in a gentlemanly way.

cenub (·⸜) The South. ~u garbî, South-West; ~u şarkî, South-East. ~en (·⸜·), to or from the South. ~î (·–⸜), southern.

cepane v. cebhane.

ceph– v. cebh–.

cer, -rri A pulling or drawing; jack; crane; derrick. ~ atölyesi, railway repair shop; ~re çıkmak, (of religious students) to go to the provinces and preach to gain money for their studies.

cerahat (·–¹), –ti Pus. ~li, suppurating.

ceraid (·–¹) pl. of ceride. Newspapers.

ceraim (·–¹) pl. of cerime. Crimes; sins; penalties.

cerbeze Quick-wittedness; readiness of speech; push, go; wiliness. ~li, go-ahead; loquacious, having 'the gift of the gab'; able to get what he wants by talking.

cereb Mange; itch, scabies.

cereme Fine, penalty; amends. ···in ~sini çekmek, to pay the penalty of ... .

ceres Bell attached to the neck of an animal ; cow-bell.

cereyan (··⸜) A flowing; a movement; current; draught; an occurring; course. ~ etm., to happen, occur; flow; conform.

cerh A wounding; a refusing to accept evidence; confutation. ~etmek (¹··), –eder, to wound; to declare evidence to be invalid; to refute, contradict.

ceride (·–¹) Newspaper; journal; register.

ceriha (·–¹) Wound.

cerime (··¹ or ·–¹) v. cereme.

cerrah (·⸜) Surgeon. ~î (·–⸜), surgical. ~lık, surgery.

cerrar (·⸜) Mendicant preacher; importunate beggar.

cerr·etmek (¹··), –eder va. Pull; drag. ~i, v. cer. ~ieskal, the science of dynamics or mechanics.

cesamet (··¹), –ti Largeness; hugeness; size; importance; grandeur. ~li, huge, grandiose.

cesaret (··¹), –ti Boldness, daring; courage. ···e ~ etm., to dare stg.

cesed Corpse.

cesim (·⸣) Enormous; grandiose; of great importance.

–cesine v. **casına.**

ceste In ~ ~, little by little; gradually; by instalments.

cesur (·⸣) Bold, daring; courageous.

cet v. **ced.**

cev, –vvi Space; the vault of heaven.

cevab (·⸣) Reply, answer. ~ı dikmek, to give a sharp and decisive reply: reddi ~ etm., to give a reply; red ~ı, a negative reply, refusal: sudan ~, an unsatisfactory reply. ~en (·⸣·), in reply. ~î (·—⸣), replying: ~ mektub, letter in reply. ~lı, having or needing a reply. ~name (·—⸣), letter in reply.

cevahir (·—⸣) pl. of **cevher.** Jewels; as sing. jewel. ~ yumurtlamak, to say some pricelessly silly things. ~ci, jeweller.

cevami (·—⸣) pl. of **cami.** Mosques.

cevari (·—⸣) pl. of **cariye** q.v.

cevaz (·⸣) A being permissible or lawful; permission. ~ vermek, to regard as permissible.

cevelân (···⸣) Revolution; circuit; circulation; a going for a stroll. ~gâh (···—⸣), place where a circuit is made; round-up of game.

cevf Cavity; hollow space; interior.

cevher, güher Essence; substance; nature; disposition; mineral ore; jewel; damascening of steel. ~ini* tüketmek, to be at the end of one's tether. ~î (···⸣), pertaining to jewels or ores; essential, natural, innate. ~li, talented; naturally capable; set with jewels; damascened; containing ore.

cevir, –vri Injustice; oppression; tyranny.

ceviz Walnut; (naut.) crown or wall knot. (büyük) Hindistan ~i, coco-nut: (küçük) Hindistan ~i, nutmeg: ⸢kırdığı ~ bini aştı (geçti)⸥, his errors or stupidities are past counting.

cevval (·⸣) Active, lively, energetic.

cevv·i v. **cev.** ~ihava (···⸣), the atmosphere. ~î (·⸣), atmospheric.

Cevza (·⸣) The constellation Gemini.

ceyb Sine.

ceylân (·⸣) Gazelle.

ceyş Army.

ceyyid Good; fresh; excellent.

ceza (·⸣) Punishment; fine; retribution; apodosis. ~sını bulmak (çekmek), to get one's deserts: ~ evi, prison: ~ kanunu, criminal code: ~ kesmek, to fine: ~ zaptı tutmak, to report a dereliction of duty on the part of an official: Allah ~sını versin !, damn him! ~en (·⸣·), by way of punishment. ~lanmak, to be punished. ~yinakdî (·—···⸣), fine.

cezair (·—⸣) pl. of **cezire.** Islands.

Cezayir (·—⸣) Algiers; Algeria. ~ dayısı gibi kurulmak, to put on an air of importance: ~ menekşesi, periwinkle (flower).

cezb Attraction; allurement; drawing-in of breath. ~u def, attraction and repulsion. ~e, ecstasy, rapture; mystical contemplation. ~etmek (⸣··), –eder, to draw, attract; imbibe; draw in.

cezim, –zmi Definite decision; resolution.

cezir¹, –zri Root; source; square root. cezri mikâb, cube root: cezri murabba, square root.

cezir², –zri Ebb.

cezire (·—⸣) Island; Mesopotamia. şibih ~, peninsula.

cezmetmek (⸣··), –eder va. Resolve on; decide to.

cezrî (·⸣) Radical; thorough.

cezve Pot with long handle for making coffee.

Cezvit, –ti Jesuit.

cezzar (Lit.) butcher; bloodthirsty man; tyrant.

cıcık Stuffing, only in cıcığını çıkarmak, to damage by use, to wear to pieces; cıcığı çıkmış, worn out, in pieces.

cıdağu, cıdav Withers of a horse.

cıgara (·⸣·) Cigarette.

cıkcık Squeak.

–cılayın v. **cileyin.**

cılgar Extra yoke of oxen used for ascending a hill.

cılız Puny; thin; delicate; badly formed writing.

cılk Addled; rotten; inflamed, festered. ~ çıkmak, to be addled; to come to nought.

cılkava Fur made from the neck of wolves or foxes; a kind of wolf.

cıllık v. **cıcık.**

cımbız, cımbıstra Tweezers.

cınak Talon or claw of a bird or beast of prey.

cıngır Expresses a ringing sound.

cır Song.

cırboğa Jerboa; puny child.

cırcır Chirping or creaking sound; cricket; babbler. ~lık, chattering, loquacity.

cırlak Cricket; shrike; shrew; person with a screeching voice.

cırlamak, cırtlamak vn. Screech; sing; chatter.

cırtlak Braggart; v. also **cırlak.**

cıva (⸣·) Mercury, quicksilver. ~lı (⸣··), containing mercury; loaded (dice).

cıvadra (·⸣·) Bowsprit.

cıvata (·⸣·) Bolt (screw). ~ anahtarı, spanner.

cıvık Wet; sticky; viscid; clammy; tiresome, importunate, silly and facetious. Any viscid or sticky substance.

cıvıl *In ~ ~, imitates the peeping and twittering or the gathering of small birds.* **~damak,** to twitter, chirp. **~tı,** twittering, chirping.

cıvı·mak *vn.* Become soft *or* sticky; become insipid *or* tiresome; become too familiar or impertinent; be 'done for', be hopelessly spoilt. **'yüz verme, cıvır',** 'don't encourage him, he'll take advantage of it'. **~tmak,** to make soft *or* sticky; spoil; become soft *or* sticky; become tiresome or over-familiar *like a drunkard etc.*

cıyak *In ~ ~, imitates the cry of a kite or the high-pitched shouting of a child.*

cıyırdamak, cıyırtı *v.* cayırdamak, cayırtı.

cız *Imitates a sizzling noise.* ~ sineği, gadfly: **yüreği* ~ etm.,** to be deeply affected *by sudden bad news etc.* **–bız,** grilled meat; a sort of toffee. **~ıktırmak,** to scrawl. **~ıldamak,** to sizzle. **~ıltı,** a sizzling noise. **~ır, ~ ~,** imitates the sound of sizzling meat, of breaking glass, of the scratching of a pen. **~ırdamak,** *v.* cızıldamak. **~ırtı,** *v.* cızıltı. **~lamak,** to burn with a sizzling noise: **yüreği* ~,** to be deeply affected *by sudden bad news etc.*

cızlam *In* ~ı çekmek (*sl.*), to go away.

–ci, –cü, –cı, –cu *Suffix which, added to a noun, forms the agent, maker or seller connected with that noun, e.g.* **gemi,** ship, **gemici,** sailor; **yol,** road, **yolcu,** traveller; **saat,** watch, **saatçi,** watchmaker, seller or repairer of watches.

cibayet (·–ᵃ), **–ti** Collection of rents *or* taxes.

cibillî (···ᵃ) Natural; innate, inborn. **~yet, –ti,** nature; innate character. **~yetsiz,** of base character.

cibinlik Mosquito-net.

cibre Residue of fruit after pressing.

Cibril *v.* Cebrail.

cici (*Childish language*) Good; pretty. Toy; trinket; trifle. **~m,** my darling. **~li,** gaudily decked out with trifles: ~ bicili, glaring, gaudy.

cicim Light carpet *for hanging as a curtain or on walls; v. also* cici.

cicoz *Only in* para ~, not a penny left!

cidal (·–ᵃ), **–li** Dispute; combat.

cidar (·–ᵃ) Wall.

Cidde Jeddah.

cidd·en (¹·) Seriously; in earnest; greatly, exceedingly. **~î** (·–ᵃ), earnest; serious, not joking; strenuous. **~iyet,** seriousness.

cife (–ᵃ) Carcass, carrion; anything disgusting.

cifir, –fri Art of divination.

ciğer Liver; lungs; heart; vitals; affections. **ak~,** lungs: **kara~,** liver: ~ acışı, a

bitter grief: **~i* ağzına* gelmek,** to be terribly frightened: **~i beş para etmez,** a worthless fellow: ~ **hastalığı,** consumption: ~ **köşesi,** darling, well-beloved: **~i* yanmak,** to be greatly grieved or upset. **~ci,** seller of livers. **~otu, –nu,** rock lichen; sea-moss. **~pare** (···ᵃ), darling.

ciğlör (*Fr. gicleur*) (Carburettor) jet.

cihad Holy War *against non-Moslems*; a fight in any good cause (*cf.* English 'crusade').

cihan (·ᵃ) World; universe. ~ **harbi,** World War: iki ~, this world and the next. **~dide** (·–ᵃ), who has seen the world; experienced. **~gir** (·–ᵃ), world conqueror. **~nüma** (·–·ᵃ), map of the world; terrace with extensive view. **~şumul,** world-embracing, mondial: ~ **şöhret,** world-wide reputation.

cihar (·ᵃ) Four (at dice).

cihat (·ᵃ), **–tı** *pl. of* cihet. Sides, directions *etc.*

cihaz Apparatus; outfit; equipment; trousseau; funeral equipment.

cihet, –ti Side; quarter; direction, bearing; motive, consideration. o **~ten,** from that direction, from that consideration *or* that point of view: ~ ~, from that side and this: ~ **tayini etm.,** to take one's bearings: **bir ~lı bir bitaraflık,** a one-sided neutrality: **ez her ~,** from every direction, in every respect.

–cik, cuk *etc.* *Suffix forming a diminutive either of a noun or an adjective.*

cilâ (·ᵃ) Brightness, lustre; polish, varnish. ~ **etm.,** to polish, burnish: ~ **vurmak,** to varnish. **~cı,** polisher, varnisher. **~lı,** polished, shining, varnished.

cilâsin (·–ᵃ) Hero. Brave; dexterous; well-built.

cilbend Large pocket-book; portfolio.

cild Skin; hide; binding *of a book*; volume. **~î** (·ᵃ), pertaining to the skin, cutaneous. **emrazı ~iye,** skin diseases. **~lemek,** to bind (book). **~li,** bound (book); in volumes: **iki ~ kitab,** a book in two volumes. **~siz,** unbound (book).

~cileyin (·ᵃ·), **–cılayın** *Suffix.* Like ..., in the manner of ...; **adamcılayın,** in the manner of a man; **buncalayın,** to this degree; **bencileyin,** like me.

cilve Grace, charm, coquetry; phenomenon, spectacle. **kaderin ~si,** the irony of Fate; **tabiatın ~si,** the manifestations of Nature. **~kâr** (···ᵃ), graceful; charming; coquettish. **~li,** graceful; coquettish; capricious.

cim *The Arabic letter* jim, *now* c *and called* '*jeh*' (*jay*). ~ **karnında bır nokta,** a nonentity; a matter of no importance.

cima (·$\dot{-}$), **-aı** The sexual act.

cimbekuka (·$\dot{)}$··) Ill-shaped, deformed (man).

cimcime A kind of small water-melon. Small and dainty.

cimri Mean, miserly.

cin Genie, djinn, demon, sprite; spirit; intelligent man. ~**i başına* toplanmak**, to become furious: ~ **çarpmak**, to have a stroke, be paralysed: ~ **gibi**, clever and agile: ~ **mısırı**, a dwarf kind of maize: ~ **taifesi**, the family of demons and sprites: ⌐~**ler top (cirid) oynuyor**⌐, 'the demons play ball', *i.e.* deserted, haunted: ~**i** *or* ~**leri tutmak**, to go mad.

cinaî (·$-\dot{-}$) Criminal.

cinas Pun.

cinayet (·$-\dot{)}$), **-ti** Crime. ~**kâr** (·$-$·$\dot{-}$), criminal.

cinfikirli ($\dot{)}$···) Shrewd; ingenious.

cingil Each individual stalk of a bunch of grapes.

cingöz Shrewd; crafty, sly.

cinnet, -ti Madness; insanity. ~ **getirmek**, to become insane.

cinnî (·$\dot{-}$) Pertaining to djinns and demons. Djinn, demon.

cins Genus; species; class; race; kind, variety; sex; gender. Pure bred, thoroughbred. ~ ~, of various kinds. ~**i latif**, the gentler sex. ~**î** (·$\dot{-}$), generic; sexual. ~**ibir**, of the same genus or kind. ~**iyet, -ti**, the belonging to a race *or* genus; nationality; characteristic of sex, sexuality.

ciranta (·$\dot{)}$·) Endorser *of a bill.*

cirid Stick *used as a dart in the game of jerid*; the game itself; javelin (in modern athletics). ~ **oynamak**, to move about freely.

cirm Body (*not living*); volume, size. ⌐**ateş olsa** ~**i kadar yer yakar**⌐, 'there's nothing to be feared from him!'

ciro ($\dot{)}$·) Endorsement. ~**lu**, negotiable. ~**suz**, not negotiable.

cisim, -smi Body; substance; material thing. **cismi basit**, simple substance: ⌐**ismi var cismi yok**⌐, 'it has a name but no substance', stg. known by name but in fact non-existent.

cism·anî (·$-\dot{-}$) Corporeal; material. ~**en** ($\dot{)}$·), as regards the body; in size.

civan (·$\dot{-}$) A youth; young man. Youthful. ~ **kaşı**, a kind of embroidery. ~**lık**, youth, adolescence. ~**merd**, generous, munificent. ~**perçemi, -ni**, yarrow, milfoil.

civar (·$\dot{-}$) Neighbourhood; environs. Neighbouring. ···**in** ~**ında**, in the neighbourhood of, near to ... .

civciv Chick; chirrupping of birds; chatter,

noise. ~**li**, noisy; lively; crowded; numerous.

civelek Strong lively lad; youth in the service of the Janissaries. Brisk, lively, playful.

ciyadet (·$-\dot{)}$), **-ti** Excellence; freshness; cleanness.

Cizvit *v.* **Cezvit.**

cizye Tribute; poll-tax.

coğraf·î (·$-\dot{-}$) Geographical. ~**ya** (·$\dot{-}$·), geography.

cokey ($\dot{)}$·) Jockey.

Con Ahmed Bey (*Name of a man who claimed to have invented perpetual motion*); scientific quack.

conta ($\dot{)}$·) Gasket.

cop, -pu Truncheon.

corum Shoal of fish.

coşkun Ebullient, boiling over; overflowing; exuberant; furious; anxious. ~**luk**, ebullition; overflowing; exuberance; enthusiasm; exaltation.

coşmak *vn.* Boil up; overflow; become exuberant; be enthusiastic.

cömerd Generous. ~**lik**, generosity.

cönk Anthology; miscellany (*lit.*).

cudam Useless sort of person. ⌐**adam değil,** ~⌐, 'don't call him a man!'

cuma (·$\dot{-}$) Friday. ~ **alayı,** (*formerly*) *the ceremonious procession of the Sultan to a mosque on Fridays, the* **selâmlık.** ~**lık,** pertaining to Friday: ~ **elbise,** one's Sunday best clothes. ~**rtesi** (·$\dot{-}$··), Saturday.

cumba ($\dot{)}$·) Any projecting part of a building; bow-window; balcony.

cumbadak ($\dot{)}$··) Falling suddenly into water *or* an abyss; *imitates the noise of such a fall.*

cumbul, cumbur ~ ~, *imitates the noise of stg. falling into water.*

cumbur·tu Plop; loud noise. ~**lop,** plop!, splash!

cumhur (·$\dot{)}$) The mass of the people; populace; republic. ~ **Reisi,** ~ **Başkanı,** the President of the Republic. ~**a uymak,** to follow the majority. ~**î** (·$-\dot{-}$), republican. ~**iyet** (·$-$·$\dot{-}$), **-ti,** republic. ~**iyetçi,** ~**iyetperver,** upholder of the Republic, republican.

cunda ($\dot{)}$·) End of a gaff, peak.

cuppadak ($\dot{)}$··) *v.* **cumbadak.**

cura Two- or three-stringed lute; a small kind of hawk; (*sl.*) cigarette stump. ~ **zurna,** a small shrill horn.

curcuna (·$\dot{)}$·) Drunken revel; disorderly dance; orgy; brawl; confused medley.

curnal *v.* **jurnal.**

curnata (·$\dot{-}$·) Mass arrival of quails.

cuş (–), **cuşiş** (–$\dot{)}$) Effervescence; commotion; enthusiasm. ~**a** ~, full of

excitement: ~u huruş, commotion, excitement, enthusiasm: ebkem ~, idiot.
cübbe v. cüppe.
cüce Dwarf.
cücük Sweet, pleasant; tender. The heart of an onion; tuft of beard (imperial); chick.
cücümek vn. Become sweet.
cüda (·⸌) Separated; separate; alone. ~ düşmek, to get separated from s.o.
cühelâ (··⸌) pl. of cahil. Ignoramuses.
cülûs (·⸌) Accession to the throne.
cümbür In ~ cemaat, all in a body; the 'whole caboodle'.
cümbüş Amusement, entertainment, jollity; a kind of metal mandolin. ~ etm., to make merry, to enjoy oneself. ~lü, with jollity and amusement.
cümcüme Skull.
cümle A total, a whole; category; phrase, sentence. ~si, all of them: ~yi asabiye, the nervous system: ~ kapısı the main or front door of a biggish house: ⌐~nin maksudu bir, amma rivayet muhtelif⌐ they all mean the same thing but they call it by different names: bu ~ ile nevertheless: ez in ~ or bu ~den, as an instance of this: kara ~, simple arithmetic; kara ~si bozuk half illiterate, very ignorant. ~ten (¹··), wholly, entirely.

cümudiye (·—·¹) Glacier; iceberg.
cündî (·⸌) Expert horseman.
cünha Serious offence, crime.
cünun (·⸌) Insanity.
cünüb Canonically unclean.
cüppe Robe with full sleeves and long skirts.
cür'a A draught or gulp of drink; dregs.
cür'et, –ti Boldness, daring. ···e ~ etm., to dare to ... . ~li, ~kâr, bold, daring.
cürmümeşhud (···⸌) Flagrant offence. ~ halinde 'in flagrante delicto': ~ yapmak, to lay a trap to catch s.o. red-handed.
cüruf (·⸌) Slag; scoriae.
cürüm, –rmü Crime; fault; sin; v. cürmümeşhud.
cüsse Body, trunk. ~li, big-bodied; huge.
cüz, –z'ü Part; section; piece, fragment; one of the thirty sections of the Koran; section of a book; pamphlet. ~ kesesi, a case containing extracts from the Koran, carried by pupils in old Turkish schools: ~'ü lâyetecezza, atom.
cüzam Leprosy. ~lı, leprous.
cüzdan Pocket-book; wallet; portfolio. hesab ~ı, pass-book.
cüz'î (·⸌) Trifling, insignificant; partial; fragmentary. ~ce (·⸌·), somewhat small, petty.
cüzü·ferd Atom. ~tam, unit.

Ç

çaba·lamak Strive; struggle; endeavour. nafile çabalama!, don't waste your efforts!; it's no use! ~lanmak, to move one's limbs about in an agitated manner; struggle.
çabucak (¹··), **çabucacık** (·¹··) Quickly.
çabuk Quick; agile. Quickly; in a hurry; soon. ~ olm., to hurry: eline ~, quick at his work. ~luk, speed; agility; haste. el çabukluğu, sleight-of-hand.
çaça Sprat; very small mackerel.
çaçaron Talkative person; charlatan.
çadır Tent. ~ kurmak, to pitch a tent: kıl ~, horsehair or felt tent used by nomads.
çağ¹ Time; age, period; stature. orta ~, middle-age; the Middle Ages.
çağ² Sink; drain.
çağan Camel fetter.
çağanak, çağnak (¹·) Only in çalgı ~, a noisy musical party.
çağanoz Crab.
Çağatay The Chagatay branch of the Turkish race. ~ca, the Chagatay language.
çağdaş Contemporary.
çağıl In ~ ~, imitates the noise of running

water; burbling. ~damak, to burble, to murmur as running or boiling water. ~tı, the murmur of running water.
çağırmak va. & vn. Call out; call; invite; sing.
çağırtkan Decoy bird.
çağla (¹·) Green almond or other unripe fruit; dull greyish-green colour.
çağla·ma Murmuring of water. ~mak, v. çağıldamak. ~r, natural cascade. ~yan, artificial cascade. ~yık, bubbling spring; hot spring.
çağlı Reaching a certain stage of maturity or height. pehlivan ~, built like a wrestler; strong, robust.
cağnak Castanet; v. çağanak.
cağrılmak vn. Be called out; be shouted; be called; be invited; be sung. geriye ~, to be recalled, to be removed from office.
çağrışmak vn. Cry out together; call one another; make a row.
çak¹ Imitates the sound of clashing metal or a hammer blow.
çak² Torn; cracked. ~ ~, full of rents or cracks; all in pieces.

çak³ Exactly, precisely. ~ ortasında, exactly in the middle of it.

çakal Jackal. ~ eriği, wild plum.

çakaloz Small cannon *formerly nsed for shooting pebbles.*

çakar *v.* çakmak. Phosphorescence caused by moving objects in water.

çakı Pocket-knife. ~ gibi, keen and active.

çakıçak *v.* çak çak.

çakıl Pebble. ~ döşemek, to pave with pebbles. ~dak, ball of dried dung *hanging on the tail or belly of a sheep*; clapper *of a mill*; rattle. ~damak, to make a clattering sound. ~lık, pebbly place; court paved with pebbles. ~tı, clattering rattling noise.

çakılmak *vn. pass. of* çakmak. Be stuck *in a place.* çakılmadan (*sl.*), without anyone noticing.

çakın, çakın Lightning; flash; spark.

çakır¹ Any intoxicating drink. ~cı¹, wine-merchant; innkeeper. ~keyf (·¹·), half-tipsy.

çakır² Grey with blue streaks; greyish-blue. Merlin. ~cı², falconer. ~dikeni, -ni, burdock; burr. ~kanad, teal. ~pençe, grasping, avaricious.

çakır³ *In* ~ çukur, rattling noise; broken ground. Full of pot-holes, uneven.

çakış·mak *vn.* Fit into one another; be united; collide with one another; (of poets) to compete with one another. ~tırmak, *caus. of* çakışmak; *vn.*, to drink, to booze; to make merry with drink.

çakma Flash; stamp *on silver etc.*

çakmak¹ *va.* (*with acc.*) Drive in by blows; nail; tether by a peg; strike *a flint or a match*; snap *the teeth*; palm off *false coin*; fit *one thing into* another; guess, perceive: (*with abl.*) understand, know about *stg.*; be 'ploughed' in *an exam. vn.* Be ostentatiously deferential; (of lightning) to flash; carouse. çakar almaz, that which misfires, *hence* that which does not work: 'birer tane çakalım' (*sl.*), 'let's have a drink'.

çakmak² Steel for striking on a flint; pocket-lighter; trigger. gözleri ~ ~, heavy-eyed *from sleeplessness or fever.* ~lı, flintlock (gun). ~taşı, -nı, flint.

çakşır Trousers *with broad band round the waist and light leather boots attached to the ankles*; feathers *round the legs of some birds.*

çaktırmak *va. caus. of* çakmak (*sl.*), çaktırmadan, without attracting anyone's attention; without being noticed.

çal Escarpment.

çal-, çala *Prefix indicating repeated action of the verb* çalmak, *e.g.* çalçene, 'chin-wagger', talkative; çalakürek, (rapidly striking with the oar) rowing hard.

çalak (−¹) Quick, agile. ~i, agility.

çala·kalem (¹···) With flowing pen; scribbling hastily. ~kaşık (¹···), ~ yemek, to eat greedily. ~kürek (¹···), rowing hard.

Çalap God.

çalapa Jalap.

çalarsaat (·¹··), -ti Striking clock; repeater (watch); alarm clock.

çalçene Chatterbox, babbler.

çaldırmak *va. caus. of* çalmak. Cause to strike, steal, play *etc.*; let *a thief* steal; lose by theft. altını ~, to give oneself away.

çalgı Musical instrument. ~ çalmak, to play a musical instrument: ~ takımı, an orchestra *or* band; their instruments. ~cı, musician. ~cılık, music (*as a profession or art*).

çalı Bush, shrub; thicket. kara ~, *v.* karaçalı; one who causes bad blood between others: süpürge ~sı, heather. ~çırpı, brushwood; sticks and thorns *used for fencing.* ~fasulyesi, -ni, climbing kidney-beans; runner beans. ~kavak, pollarded poplar *used in basket-making.* ~kuşu, -nu, (?) golden-crested wren. ~lık, thicket.

çalık Slanting, awry; walking sideways; tainted, spoilt; dismissed, expelled; dazed, deranged. Sheep scab. aklı ~, crazy: rengi ~, discoloured, faded.

çalım Stroke, blow; swagger. ~ına getirmek, to find a suitable opportunity: ~ satmak, to swagger, to give oneself airs. ~lı, swaggering, arrogant.

çalınmak *vn. pass. of* çalmak. Be struck *etc.*; ···e ~, smell *or* taste of *stg.*; reach *the ear.*

çalışkan Industrious, hard-working.

çalış·mak *vn.* Work; try, strive; study; (of wood) to warp. çalışıp çabalamak, to strive hard, to do one's best. ~tırmak, to make or let *s.o.* work *or* try; set to work, employ.

çalkalamak *v.* çalkamak.

çalkama *verb. n. of* çalkamak; omelet.

çalkamak *va.* Agitate; shake *or* toss about; rinse; wash out (mouth); gargle; beat (eggs); churn (milk); (of a hen) to turn *its eggs*; (of tainted milk) to turn the stomach of. göbek ~, to shake the belly *in Oriental dance.*

çalkan·mak *vn. pass. of* çalkamak. Be agitated *or* shaken about; (of a ship) to roll; (of the sea) to become rough; sway about while walking; become addled; fluctuate; (of news) to spread like wildfire. ~tı, agitation; a shaking; a tossing about *of the sea*; rapids *of a river*; rolling *of a ship*; disturbance *of the stomach.*

çalkar Anything that upsets the stomach;

purgative; gin *for separating seeds from
cotton.*

çalmak *va.* Give a blow to; knock (on a
door); strike (the hour); ring (bell); play
(musical instrument); (of a referee) to blow
his whistle for a foul *etc.*; smear (butter
etc.); mix; steal; have a flavour *or* smell *of
stg. else*; verge on (a colour); have a *certain*
accent; (of the sun or wind) to scorch.
çalmadığım kapı kalmadı, (there is no door
that I have not knocked on), I have left
no stone unturned, I have made every
effort: **çalmadan oynar,** over-cheerful;
gushing; officious: ˹**bunu al da başına
çal!**˺, (*phrase used in returning in anger to
s.o. stg. you have received from him*) 'here,
take it back, I don't want it!': **süt** ~, of
milk, to upset *a baby*: **yere** ~, to throw to
the ground.

çalpara Castanet; swimming crab. ~**lı**
tulumba, chain-pump.

çalyaka (ˑ‥) Seizure *of s.o.* by the collar.
~ **etm.,** to seize by the collar.

çam Fir; pine. ~ **devirmek,** to 'drop a
brick', to put one's foot in it: ˹**eski** ~**lar
bardak oldu**˺, (old fir-trees have been made
into mugs), things are not what they were:
~ **yarması gibi,** *said of a strongly built man.*

çamak Freshwater bream.

çamaşır Underclothing; linen; soiled
linen; the washing. ~ **değiştirmek,** to
change one's linen: **bir kat** ~, a change of
linen: **birinin kirli (iç)** ~**larını ortaya
çıkarmak,** to reveal *s.o.*'s misdeeds. ~**cı,**
laundryman. ~**cılık,** profession of laun-
dering; white goods. ⋯**hane** (⋯–ˑ),
laundry. ~**lık,** linen-cupboard; laundry;
washing-tub; stuff for making underclothing.

çamçak Wooden vessel for water; (?) roach.

çam·fıstığı (ˑ⋯), –**nı** Pine kernel. ~**lık,**
pine wood. ~**sakızı** (ˑ⋯), –**nı,** pine
resin; an unescapable bore: sticky. ˹**çoban
armağanı** ~˺, 'a shepherd's present is a
bit of resin', *said when giving a small
present.*

çamuka (ˑⁱ·) Sand-smelt.

çamur Mud; unmannerly person; 'a bad
lot'. ~ **atmak,** to vituperate: ~**a bulamak,**
to cover with disgrace: ~**dan çıkarmak,**
to help *s.o.* out of the mud, to help out of a
difficulty: ~**a düşmek,** to fall into adversity: ~ **sıvamak,** to cast aspersions: ~**a
taş atmak,** to invite abuse from an impudent or aggressive person: ˹(**yan bastı**)~**a
yattı**˺, *v.* **yan basmak:** **çömlekçi** ~**u,** potter's clay. ~**cuk,** tench. ~**cun,** teal.
~**lamak,** to cover with mud; to slander.
~**lu,** muddy. ~**luk,** muddy place;
gaiters; mudguard; boot-scraper.

çan Bell. ~ **çalmak,** to ring a bell; to trumpet abroad: ~ ~ **etm.,** to chatter unceasingly: ~**ına* ot tıkamak,** to confound an
opponent; to muzzle; to render impotent:
kulağına ~ **çalmak,** to din *stg.* into s.o.'s
ears.

çanak Earthenware pot *or* pan; beggar's
alms-bowl. ~ **çömlek,** pots and pans,
crockery: ~ **tutmak,** by one's own words or
deeds to bring down insult on oneself; to
'ask for it': ~ **yalamak,** to agree with s.o.
in order to please him; ~ **yalayıcı,** lickspittle, toady: **kan çanağı,** barber's bleeding basin; an eye red with rage. ~**çı,**
potter.

Çanakkale (·ˑ‥) Dardanelles (town). ~
Boğazı, the Dardanelles Straits.

çanaklık Top of a mast; crow's-nest.

çançan Loud and continuous chatter.

çançiçeği (ˑ⋯), –**ni** Campanula.

çandır A cross between the **dağlıç** and
karaman breeds of sheep and the mutton
thereof.

çangıl çungul *Imitates a harsh broken
speech or a foreign or provincial accent.*

çangır ~ **çungur,** clink-clank; jingle-
jangle. ~**damak,** to make a clanking or
jangling sound. ~**tı,** clanking, jangling
sound.

çankulesi (ˑ⋯), –**ni** Belfry.

çanta (ˑ·) Bag; case; valise; knapsack.
~**da keklik,** a partridge in the bag, *i.e.*
something safely secured: **arka** ~**sı,** haversack: **para** ~**sı,** purse. ~**cı,** maker *or*
seller of bags *etc.*; porter employed to carry
official correspondence to ministers *etc.*

çap, –pı Diameter; bore; calibre (*also used
fig. as in English*); plan showing size and
boundaries of a building or piece of land.

çapa (ˑ·) Hoe; mattock; mortar larry;
anchor (with flukes). **fırtına** ~**sı,** sea-
anchor, drogue. ~**cı,** hoer.

çapaçul Slovenly; untidy; tatterdemalion.

çapak Crust round the eyes *in 'blear-eye'*;
rough skin *on metal castings*; burr.
~**balığı, –nı,** freshwater bream.

çapalamak *va.* Hoe.

çapan, çapar One who gallops; courier.

çapanak Booty; pillage; smuggled goods.

çapanoğlu (·ˑ‥) *In* ˹(**işi kurcalama**), **alt
tarafı** ~ **çıkar**˺, (better not meddle with the
matter) there's a 'fly in the ointment',
'there's a snag somewhere', 'it might raise
awkward questions'.

çapar Albino. *v.* **çapan.**

çaparı Multi-pointed fish-hook; lure.

çaparız Obstacle; entanglement. Perverse.
~ **etm.,** to create a difficulty, to block the
way.

çapıcı Raider, marauder.

çapkın Vagabond, rascal; scamp; rake; dissolute; ne'er-do-well; swift horse. **~lık,** profligacy, debauchery, rascality.

çaplı Of a *certain* calibre. **büyük ~,** of a large bore *or* big calibre.

çapmak *vn.* Ride fast, gallop; gad about. Raid, pillage.

çaprak Saddle-cloth.

çapraş·ık Crosswise; complicated, entangled. **~mak,** to be interlaced; be involved *or* difficult.

çapraz Waistcoat *etc.* fastened by frogs; anything fastened crosswise. Saw-set. Crossing, crosswise; double-breasted (coat). **~lama, ~vari,** crossed obliquely.

çapul Raid; booty, plunder. **~ etm.,** to sack, pillage; to go on a raid. **~cu,** raider. **~lamak,** to go raiding; to pillage, sack.

çaput, -tu Rag; patch.

çar Czar. **~lık,** reign *or* government of a Czar : **~ idaresi,** the Czarist régime.

çarçabuk (ᵔᵔ) Very quickly; in haste.

çarçur In a wasteful or squandering manner. **~ etm.,** to squander : **~ olm.,** to be wasted.

çardak Hut *built of brushwood on supports*; trellis; pergola; gallows.

çare (−ᵔ) Remedy; means; measure; help. **~ bulmak,** to find a remedy *or* a means : **bundan başka ~ yok,** there is no other way out; this is the only thing one can do : **başının ~sine baksın,** let him look out for himself *or* look after himself : **ne ~?,** what can one do? : **ne ~ ki ...,** inevitably ..., it can't be helped but .... **~saz** (−ᵔ−), who finds a remedy *or* a means. **~siz,** irremediable; inevitable; necessary; helpless, without means. **~sizlik,** lack of means; urgency; poverty; helplessness.

çarhetmek (ᵔᵔ) *v.* çark.

çarık Sandal of raw-hide or rope *worn by peasants*; drag for a cart-wheel. **~lı,** wearing sandals; ignorant and illiterate : **~ diplomat,** *said of a peasant who, though illiterate, is pretty shrewd*; shrewder than one would suspect.

çariçe (ᵔᵔ) Czarina.

çark, -kı Wheel; paddle-wheel; fly-wheel; anything that revolves; machinery; the celestial sphere; fate, destiny. **~ı bozulmak,** to have one's affairs upset, to meet with misfortune : **~ çevirmek,** to wander around : **~ etm.,** to wheel, to turn : **~a etm.** *or* **çekmek,** to put *a tool* to the grindstone : **~ işi,** machinery; machine-made : **~ işletmek,** to work a machine; to work a scheme for one's own advantage. **~çı,** engineer, mechanic, engine-driver; knifegrinder; **~başı,** chief engineer. **~ıfelek,**

the sphere of heaven; destiny; Catherine-wheel; passion-flower. **~lı,** with paddle-wheels.

çarmıh Cross *on which malefactors were crucified*; *v.* çarmık. **~a germek,** to crucify.

çarmık Shroud *of a mast.*

çarnaçar (ᵔ−·) Willy-nilly; of necessity.

çarpan A fish of the Weever family (*Trachinus radiatus*).

çarpı Whitewash.

çarpık Crooked; awry; bent; warped; slanting; deviating; struck with madness *or* paralysis; ill-omened. **~ bacaklı,** bandy-legged : **~ çurpuk,** crooked; deformed; deviating in all directions.

çarpılmak *vn. pass. of* çarpmak, become crooked *etc.*; be struck with madness *or* paralysis; meet with divine punishment *for blasphemy etc.*; have a fit; behave oddly. **iki yıl sürgün cezasına çarpıldılar,** they were punished with two years' banishment.

çarpın·mak *vn.* Struggle; get flustered. **~tı,** shock; palpitation.

çarpışma Collision; conflict; clash. **~k,** to strike one another; come into collision; fight.

çarpıtmak *va.* Make crooked *or* awry. **yüzünü gözünü ~,** to make a wry face.

çarpma Blow; stroke; multiplication; rough-cast. **cin ~sı,** paralytic stroke *or* sudden attack of insanity.

çarpmak *va.* Strike; knock; strike mad *or* paralytic; carry off, burgle; hold up *for robbery*; pick *s.o.'s* pocket; multiply. *vn.* Bump; come into collision; (of the heart) to palpitate; (of wine) to go to the head; (of the sun) to give a sunstroke. **cin ~,** for an evil spirit to possess one and cause madness *or* paralysis : **göze ~,** to strike the eye, to be conspicuous : **kömür ~,** for charcoal fumes to affect one : **kuran (evliya) ~,** for the Koran (or a saint) to punish a profane act : **yere ~,** to knock down : **yerden yere ~,** to discredit, to run down : **yüzüne* ~,** to cast in *s.o.'s* teeth.

çarptırmak *va. caus. of* çarpmak. Cause to collide *etc.*; allow to pillage; have one's pocket picked. **cezaya ~,** to have punished.

çarşaf Sheet (of a bed); dress with veil *formerly worn by Turkish women in public.*

çarşamba Wednesday. **~dır ~ demek,** to insist that one is right : **~ karısı,** witch, hag; a very untidy woman, a 'regular fright' : ⌐**ayın dört ~sı bir araya gelmiş⌐,** 'the four Wednesdays of the month have all come together', *i.e.* difficulties or work have come with a rush : **ağzını ~ pazarına çeviririm** (*sl.*), I'll smash your face in : **çıkmaz ayın son ~sı,** the Greek Kalends.

çarşı Market; bazaar; street with shops. ~ya çıkarmak, to expose for sale: ~ya çıkmak, to go shopping.

çasar Caesar; Kaiser.

çaşıd Spy.

çat *Imitates a sudden noise.* ~ diye, all of a sudden: ~ kapı, unexpectedly, suddenly: ~ orada ~ burada, now here now there (*of a person or thing always in a different place*): ~ pat, *v.* çatpat.

çatak Point of intersection; an impenetrable thicket at the bottom of a valley; defile. Involved; twin-kernelled (nut).

çatal Fork, prong; dilemma. Forked; bifurcated; with a double meaning (word); difficult, delicate (matter); hoarse (noise). ~ çekiç, claw-hammer: ~ iş, a vexed question, dilemma: ~ tırnak, cloven hoof: ~ görmek, to see double: geyik ~ı, antler. ~laşmak, ~lanmak, to bifurcate; to become ambiguous *or* complicated. ~lı, forked; ambiguous, doubtful.

çatana (·\·) Small steamboat.

çatı Framework; skeleton; roof. ~ katı, attic; top story: aynı ~ içinde *or* bir ~ altında, under the same roof; intimate with one another; 'in the same box'.

çatık Touching; contiguous; fitted together; intimate; sour-faced, scowling. ~kaş, with eyebrows that join: sulky face.

çatır ~ ~, *imitates a crackling or clashing noise*; willy-nilly. ~damak, to make a chattering or clattering noise; dişleri* ~, (of the teeth) to chatter. ~tı, clattering *or* chattering noise.

çatışmak *vn.* Bump into one another, collide; (of joints) to fit into one another; (of animals and insects) to mate; to come up against one another *in dispute or competition.*

çatkı Bandage round the head; pile *of rifles.* ~lık, pole connecting the yokes of two oxen.

çatkın Protégé, favourite; bound by ties of interest or friendship; puckered, creased; frowning. ~lık, grumpiness, sour looks.

çatlak Crevice; crack; fissure. Split; cracked; 'cracked' (crazy); chapped (hand); hoarse (voice). damarı ~, brazen-faced, shameless.

çatla·mak *vn.* Crack; split; (of a wave) to break; (of an animal) to die from exhaustion; burst *with rage or heat etc.*; weep *or* groan bitterly. ~tmak, to split; crack; make one's head ache; make *s.o.* nearly burst *with rage etc.*: ride *a horse* to death; pronounce in an exaggerated and pedantic manner.

çatma *verb. n. of* çatmak. Action of putting together *etc.*; anything put together like framework; parts temporarily and roughly put together; a thick silk cloth *used for furnishing.* Assembled, put together; loosely sewn together. ~kaş, *v.* çatıkkaş: derme ~, loosely put together; jerry-built; odds and ends, scraps *of news, knowledge, etc.*

çatmak *va. & vn.* Fit together; build; set up; pile (arms); load (an animal); bump up against, collide with; come up against (a difficulty); meet; have a lucky encounter with *an influential man or one who can be of use to one*; tack, sew coarsely; (of a season) to come round; become aggressive. çattık !, 'we're up against it!': ···e ~, to seek a quarrel with ...: adamına ~, (of a quarrelsome man) to meet his match: 'tam adamına çattık', 'we've struck just the one man *who can help us* (*or ruin us*)': başına ~, to bind on the head: gelip ~, (of a time or a regular event) to be due, to come round; (of an unpleasant event) to befall, to happen to one: sağa sola ~, to seek a pretext for a quarrel.

çatpat (\·) Now and then, rarely; somewhat. ~ fransızca konuşmak, to have a smattering of French: ~ konuşmak (of a child) to be able to talk a little.

çatra (\·) *In* ~ patra, with a clatter. ~ patra söylemek, to speak *a language* incorrectly or with difficulty.

çav The genital organs of a horse.

çavdar Rye. ~ mahmuzu, ergot.

çavşir Opopanax.

çavuş Sergeant; doorkeeper; messenger; uniformed attendant *of an ambassador or consul.* ~kuşu, –nu, hoopoe. ~üzümü, –nü, a kind of large and sweet grape.

çay[1] Stream; tributary of a river.

çay[2] Tea. ~ üzümü, bilberry. ~danlık, teapot. ~hane (·–\), tea-shop; tea-garden.

çayır Meadow; pasture; pasture grass. ~a çıkarmak (salmak), to put out to grass. ~kuşu, –nu, lark. ~latmak, to pasture, to put out to grass. ~lık, pasture, meadowland. ~otu, –nu, meadow grass; grass cut and fed green. ~peyniri, –ni, cream cheese.

çayır çayır *v.* cayır cayır.

çaylak Kite; avaricious, grasping person. acemi ~, a clumsy beginner, *v. App.*

çeç Heap of winnowed grain.

çeçe Tsetse.

Çeçen The Tchetchen tribe *of NE. Caucasus*; talkative.

çedik *In* ~ pabuc, yellow morocco slipper.

çegane (·–\) Rattle *of metal disk on a wire used by dancers*; tambourine.

çehiz *c.* cihaz.

çehre Face, countenance; sour face. ~si* **atmak** or ~ **etm.**, to make a wry face, to sulk: ~ **eğmek**, to show disapproval: ~ **züğürdü**, ugly: **ne bu** ~?, why do you make such a face? ~**li**, having *such and such* a face; scowling.

Çek, –ki, Çekli Czech.

çek, –ki Cheque.

çekçek Small four-wheeled handcart.

çekecek Shoehorn. **çizme çekeceği**, bootjack.

çekeme·mek (·¹··) *va.* Be unable to tolerate; envy. ~**mezlik** (·¹···), intolerance, envy.

çeki A measure of weight (about 500 lb.) *for wood etc.*; horse-load (*of firewood etc.*). ~**ye gelmez**, very heavy; unbearable, intolerable; unseemly: ~ **taşı gibi**, very heavy, ponderous: **her** ~**ye gelir**, who can adapt himself to any situation, opportunist, turncoat.

çekic Hammer. **şeytan** ~**i**, a very bright child. ~**hane** (··—¹), steam-hammer shop *of a factory*.

çekidüzen Orderliness, tidiness; toilet. **kendine** ~ **vermek**, to tidy oneself up; to put one's house in order.

çekik Elongated; slanting (eyes). ~ **çene**, receding chin.

çekilir Endurable, tolerable.

çekil·mek *vn. pass. of* **çekmek**. Be pulled *etc.*; withdraw, retire; draw back; shrink; contract; (of water) to recede; to dry up. **çekil oradan !**, clear out of there! ~**mez**, unendurable, intolerable.

çekinecek Which is to be avoided *or* guarded against.

çekingen Timid; shy; reserved; retiring.

çekinmek *vn.* Beware; take precautions; draw back; recoil *through fear or dislike*; refrain *from*; hesitate.

çekirdek Stone *or* pip *of a fruit*; grain (in weight), nucleus. ~ **içi**, kernel: ~ **kahve**, coffee beans: ~**siz**, stoneless, pipless; ~**siz kuru üzüm**, sultana: ~**ten yetişmek**, to be accustomed to *or* trained to *stg.* from an early age: **iki dirhem bir** ~, over-elegantly dressed; dressed up to the nines.

çekirge Grasshopper; locust; cricket.

çekiş·mek *vn.* Pull one another about; struggle; scramble for stg.; quarrel, dispute, litigate. **çekişe çekişe pazarlık etm.**, to make a bargain after long haggling: **can** ~, to be in the throes of death: **halat** ~, to have a tug-of-war. ~**tirmek**, to slander; criticize; reproach; curse.

çekitaşı (·¹··), –**nı** The counterweight for weighing a **çeki** *q.v.* ~ **gibi**, very heavy, ponderous.

çekme Act of drawing *etc.*; drawer; till; overalls; shrinkage. Rolled (iron *etc.*); well-formed; *clothing or boots* that draw on. ~**ce**, drawbridge; drawer, till, small coffer; desk; small port of refuge.

çekmek *va.* Pull, draw, attract; drag; pull on (boots, trousers *etc.*); withdraw; trace (a line); undergo, suffer, bear, endure, support; cause to support; decline, conjugate; inhale; absorb; (*sl.*) drink; weigh; make a copy of; mate (an animal). *vn.* Contract, shrink; weigh; last, take *so long*. ···**e** ~, to resemble; **babasına çekiyor**, he takes after his father: **çek !**, (*to a chauffeur etc.*) 'go on!': **çek arabayı !**, 'clear out!': **çekip çekiştirmek**, to gossip maliciously about *s.o.* (as a servant about her mistress): **çekip çevirmek**, to run (a house *etc.*); to know how to treat (a person): **çekip çıkarmak**, to pluck out, eradicate: **çekip uzatma**, prolixity: **canı*** ~, to long for: **duvar** ~, to set up a wall *between two places*: ···**den el** ~, to relinquish, renounce, give up *stg.*: **enfiye** ~, to take snuff: **bir fiili** ~, to conjugate a verb: **güçlük** ~, to have difficulty, to suffer difficulties: **ispirto** ~, to distil alcohol: **kafayı** ~, to drink heavily: **kâğıda (deftere)** ~, to copy on to paper (into a notebook): **kahve** ~, to grind coffee: **odun** ~, to weigh wood; **yaş odun ağır çeker**, wet wood weighs heavy: **perde** ~, to separate by a curtain; **perdeyi** ~, to draw the curtain: **resim** ~, to take a photograph: **sözümü fenaya çekti**, he put a bad interpretation on my words: **telgraf** ~, to send a telegram: **bu yol iki saat çeker**, this journey takes two hours: **zahmet** ~, to suffer trouble; to take trouble: **ziyafet** ~, to give a feast.

çekmen *v.* **çepken**.

çekmez Unable to bear; unshrinkable.

çektiri Ancient war-galley, *propelled by sails or oars*.

çektirme Large boat with sails and oars *used in coastal trade*; = **çektiri**.

çektirmek *va. caus. of* **çekmek**. ···**i işten el** ~, to remove *s.o.* temporarily from an office.

çelebi *Formerly a title of* a royal prince; educated man; gentleman; *title given to men of certain religious orders*. Well-mannered, courteous.

çelenk Wreath; plume; bejewelled aigrette.

çelik[1] Short piece of tapered wood; tipcat; belaying-pin; marlinspike; cutting *of plant*. Clipped; bevelled; diverted; ousted. ~ **çomak**, the game of tipcat.

çelik[2] Steel. ~**hane** (···—¹), steel foundry.

çelim Form, shape. ~**li**, well-made; strong. ~**siz**, misshapen; uncouth; scraggy; infirm, frail.

çelme *verb. n. of* **çelmek**. Trip (with the foot). ~ **takmak (atmak)**, to trip up.

çelmek Strike lightly; clip, lop; divert the mind; persuade; dissuade; confute, rebut *a statement*. **aklını*** ~, to captivate the mind, to bias, to persuade, dissuade; **ayağı** ~, to trip up: **gönlünü*** ~, to try to gain s.o.'s affection.

çeltik Unhusked rice; rice-field; Glossy Ibis.

çember Hoop; ring *of wood or metal*; fillet; neckerchief; the vault of heaven; fortune's wheel. Rounded. ~ **içine almak**, to encircle (*mil.*): **feleğin** ~**inden geçmek**, to experience vicissitudes of fortune, to have much experience of the world. ~**lemek**, to fit with hoops; to encircle.

çemçe Wooden ladle; skate, ray.

çemen Cummin. *v. also* **çimen**.

çemre·mek *va.* Tuck up (clothes); roll up (sleeves *etc.*). ~**nmek.** to tuck up one's sleeves; to prepare for action.

çendele Cheese-cloth.

çene Jaw; chin; loquacity; end of a ship's keel. **birinin** ~**sini açmak**, to give an opening to speak to one *who you would rather did not speak*: ~**si atmak**, to drop the jaw at death, to die: ~ **çalmak**, to chatter: ~**si düşük**, very talkative: ~ **kavafı**, chatterbox: ~**ye kuvvet**, by force of words, by dint of speaking: ~**si* oynamak**, to eat: ~**sini* tutmak**, to hold one's tongue; ⌐~**n tutulsun!**¬, 'may your jaw be stuck!' (*a curse on one who speaks in an ill-omened way*): ~ **yarışı**, a prolonged argument: ~ **yarıştırmak**, to enter on a prolonged argument: ~ **yormak**, to talk in vain, to waste one's breath: ⌐**alt** ~**den girip üst** ~**den çıkmak**¬, to talk s.o. over.

çene·altı, **–nı**, the under side of the chin; dewlap. ~**baz**, ~**li**, ~**sidüşük**, garrulous, talkative. ~**kemiği**, **–ni**, jaw-bone.

çengel Hook. Hooked; crooked. ~**lemek**, to hang on a hook: **kafamda bir sual çengellendi**, a question-mark arose in my mind. ~**li**, hooked: ~ **iğne**, safety-pin. ~**sakızı**, **–ni**, chewing-gum *made from a species of cardoon*.

çengi Public dancing-girl. ~ **kolu**, a troop of dancing-girls: **bir kol** ~, one who talks too loudly and heartily.

çenk Hand, paw, talon; harp. ~ **çalmak**, to lay hands on; to play the harp: **çengü çegane**, a musical entertainment.

çent A few, some. Cent.

çentik. Notch; defect. Notched.

çentmek *va.* Notch, nick; mince.

çepçevre (ˑ··), **çepeçevre** (·ˑ··) All around.

çepel Foul (weather); gloomy, dull;

muddy; mixed, adulterated. Storm of wind, rain and sleet; muddy season; mud, dirt; extraneous material.

çepiç Year-old goat.

çepin Trowel.

çepken A kind of short overcoat with wide sleeves.

çer *In* ~**den çopten**, flimsy.

çerağ¹ Lamp; candle; torch.

çerağ² *v.* **çırak**.

çerçeve Frame; window-frame. **kanunun** ~**sine sığmaz**, it is not in accordance with the law. ~**li**, framed.

çerçi Pedlar.

çerez Appetizer; hors-d'œuvre. ~**lenmek**, to partake of an appetizer.

çerge, **çergi** Gipsy tent. ~**ci**, stallholder in a market.

çeri Soldier; military force. **yeni** ~, Janissary. ~**başı** *in error for* **çergibaşı**, gipsy leader.

Çerkes, **Çerkez** Circassian. ~**tavuğu**, **–nu**, a dish of chicken with walnuts.

çermik Thermal waters.

çerviş Cooking fat; suet; tallow.

çeşid Sort; variety; sample; set *of cups etc*. ~ ~, of various sorts: ~ **düzmek**, to buy various sorts of a thing. ~**li**, various, assorted.

çeşm Eye; sight. ~**ibülbül**, *glassware or stuff* decorated with small coloured spots.

çeşme Fountain. ⌐**iki gözü iki** ~¬, in floods of tears.

çeşni Taste; flavour; small portion eaten to judge the flavour; sample; assay. ~**sine bakmak**, to test the flavour of *stg*.: ~ **olur**, it would be a pleasant change. ~**ci**, person who tests the flavour of foods; assayer; a municipal inspector of standards and samples. ~**lenmek**, to be properly flavoured. ~**li**, tasty; properly flavoured; fired by a percussion-cap.

çete Band (of brigands, rebels *etc.*). ~**ye çıkmak**, to go forth on a marauding raid: ~ **muharebesi**, guerilla warfare. ~**ci**, member of a **çete**; comitadji.

çetele Tally-stick.

çetik *v.* **çedik**.

çetin Hard; difficult; harsh; perverse; obstinate. ~ **ceviz**, an obstinate and difficult person.

çetrefil The speaking of a language (*esp.* Turkish) in an ungrammatical way and with a bad pronunciation; mispronunciation. Badly spoken (language); complicated; difficult to understand.

çevaliye Basket *for loading coal*.

çevgen Polo; polo-stick.

çevik Quick, agile, adroit; sound.

çevirme Piece of meat roasted on a spit

or skewer; kebab; a kind of thick jam; turning movement (*mil.*); translation. Translated.

çevirmek *va.* Turn; turn round; change *one thing* into *another*; translate; recant; surround, enclose. **çekip** ~, to manage *a business etc.*; to know how to deal with *a person*: **dolab** (hile, iş *etc.*) ~, to be up to some mischief: **şaşkına** ~, to dumbfound: ···**den yüz** (baş) ~, to withdraw one's favour from; to abandon (a project, an opinion).

çevkân (·-̱) *v.* **çevgen.** Stick with bells on the end, *used in the old Turkish bands.*

çevre Circumference; circuit; surroundings; contour; embroidered handkerchief. ~**sini dolaşmak**, to go all round about *a place*: ···**in** ~**sini sarmak,** to surround. ~**lemek,** to surround.

çevrik Turned round; surrounded; overturned.

çevrilmek *vn. pass. of* **çevirmek.**

çeyiz Bride's trousseau. ~**çemen,** *as* **çeyiz.**

çeyrek Quarter; quarter of an hour; five-piastre piece.

çıban (·̱) Boil; abscess. **Bağdad** ~**ı,** the Baghdad boil *or* Aleppo button. ~**başı, –nı,** head or apex of a boil: **çıbanın başını koparmak,** to bring matters to a head.

çıfıt Jew (*contemptuously*); mean, stingy. ~ **çarşısı,** like a jumble-sale: **içi** ~ **çarşısı,** evil-minded, malevolent.

çığ Avalanche.

çığa Sterlet.

çığıltı Confused noise of animal cries.

çığır, –ğrı Track left by an avalanche; path, way. ~ **açmak,** to start a new method, to open the way to stg. new; ···**e** ~ **açmak,** to open the way to ..., to give an opportunity to ...: **çığrından çıkmak,** to get off the rails, to fall into disorder.

çığır·mak *v.* **çağırmak.** ~**gan,** ~**tkan,** decoy bird; tout; noisy fellow. ~**tma,** a kind of fife.

çığlık Cry, clamour; scream.

çığrış Clamour, outcry. ~**mak,** to cry out together *or* against one another.

çığsak Damp.

çıkagelmek (·̱··), ~**ir** *vn.* Appear suddenly.

çıkar Profit, advantage; way out. Leading to success; (of a street) leading to another street. ~ **yol bulmak,** to find a way out: ~ **yolu yok,** there is no way out of it: **bir işte** ~**ı olm.,** to have an axe to grind: **kendi** ~**ına bakmak,** to seek one's personal advantage, to 'look after number one'.

çıkarmak *va.* Take out, extract; remove;

expel; export; take off (clothes *etc.*); bring out; publish; raise; produce; bring out and offer (food *etc.*); certify *as unfit etc.*; make out, get the sense of; derive, deduce; last *or* serve for *a season etc.* **baştan** ~, to seduce, lead astray: **bulup** ~, to invent, find out, discover: **dil** ~, to put out the tongue in derision: **diş** ~, to extract a tooth; (of a child) to cut a tooth: **ekmeğini** ~, to gain one's livelihood; **ekmeğini taştan** ~, to be capable of earning his livelihood from anything: **elden** ~, to part with, dispose of, lose: **gözden** ~, to reckon on the loss of *stg.*, to be prepared to sacrifice *stg.*: **birini haklı** ~, to prove s.o. right; to maintain that s.o. is right, to take his part: **hizmetten** ~, to dismiss from service: **iş** ~, to raise difficulties; **işten** ~, to dismiss from a post *etc.*; **işten iş** ~, to raise unnecessary objections: 'köyü bugün çıkarırız', 'we'll make the village today': **bir sözden mâna** ~, to misinterpret a word *or* stg. said: **masrafını** ~, to recover one's expenses: **mesele** ~, to make a fuss, raise a difficulty; to seek a cause for a quarrel: **meydana** ~, to show, to bring to light, discover: **ortaya** ~, to divulge; to produce: ···**e taş** ~, to give points to, to be far superior to: **taşın suyunu** ~, to be extremely strong *or* energetic: **yalancı** ~, to prove *s.o.* to be a liar; to make *s.o.* look like a liar *by telling him a thing which he repeats and which then turns out to be untrue*: **bu palto kışı çıkarır,** this overcoat will last me the winter, *but* **bu palto kışa çıkarır,** this overcoat will last till the winter. **kışı Mısırda çıkardı,** 'he passed the winter in Egypt'.

çıkartma Transfer (of a coloured print to another surface).

çıkartmak *va. caus. of* **çıkarmak.** Cause *or* let remove *etc.*

çıkaryol (·̱·) Road leading to another road; the right way out *or* of doing stg.

çıkı *v.* **çıkın.**

çıkık Projecting; dislocated (limb). ~**çı,** bone-setter.

çıkın Something (*esp.* money) wrapped up in a cloth or handkerchief; small bundle; hoard of money. **kirli çıkı,** one who has accumulated money by stinginess. ~**lamak,** to tie up in a bundle.

çıkıntı Projection; salient; projecting balcony; marginal note. ~**lı işaret,** caret (ʌ): **girintili** ~**lı,** serrated, zigzag.

çıkış Method of going out; exit; start (of a race); sortie (*mil.*); scolding.

çıkış·mak *vn.* Enter into competition *or* rivalry with another; undertake something beyond one's power; reach; suffice; burst out into anger or reproach; scold. ~**tır-**

mak, to make (money) suffice *for stg.*; procure; cause to reach.

çıkma *verb. n. of* **çıkmak.** Act of going out *etc.*; exit; promontory; balcony; bow-window; invention; marginal note *or* word; loin-cloth *used in coming out of a Turkish bath.* Newly appeared *or* invented. ~ **takımı,** bath linen: **yeni** ~ **âdet,** newfangled custom.

çıkmak *vn.* Come *or* go out; issue; appear; come into existence; come to pass; result; turn out to be; jut out, be prominent; (*month, season etc.*) pass, be over; set forth, start; come *or* go up, ascend, rise; make, suffice for (a coat *etc.*); (of a rumour) to get about; (of a joint) to be dislocated. ···**den** ~, to leave *one's job,* resign from ...; pass out of *a school, university etc.*: ···**e** ~, amount to ...; fall to the lot of; start on *a journey*; compete with *s.o.*; be received in audience by ...; play the part of, *e.g.* Otelloya çıktı, he played the part of Othello: **çık bakalım!** (*sl.*), 'fork out!', 'pay up!': '**çıkmadık candan ümid kesilmez¹,** 'while there's life there's hope': **adı* fena(ya) çıkmak,** to get a bad name: ···**le başa** ~, to cope with ...: **başına** ~, to presume on *s.o.'s* kindness, to take liberties with *s.o.*: **dediğin çıktı,** it has turned out as you said: **dışarı** ~, to go out, to go out to the lavatory: **dörtten iki çıkarsa,** if two be substracted from four: **evden çıkmak,** to leave a house, *esp.* to leave for good, to give up a house: **kış çıktı,** winter is over: **bu kumaştan bir palto çıkar mı ?,** will this cloth suffice for an overcoat?: **ne çıkar !,** what does it matter!: **bir şey çıkmaz,** it doesn't matter: **pahaya** ~, to rise in price: **paradan** ~, to incur expense: **vekile (elçiye)** ~, to go and see a Minister (Ambassador): **yalan** ~, to turn out to be untrue: **yola** ~, to set forth on a journey; **yoldan** ~, to get off the road, to lose one's way: **bu yol nereye çıkar?,** where does this road lead to? **bu işte kimse ona çıkamaz,** nobody can compete with him in this.

çıkmaz Blind alley; dead-end; impasse.

çıkolata (··⌐·) Chocolate.

çıkra Thick undergrowth.

çıkrık Winding-wheel (of a well *etc.*); windlass; pulley; reel; lathe; spinning-wheel.

çılan A large kind of jujube.

çılbır Dish of poached eggs and yoghourt; chain or rope attached to a halter; lunge.

çıldır cıldır (·¹··) With bright staring eyes. ~ ~ **bakmak,** to gaze about one in a distracted manner: ~ ~ **etm.,** (of eyes) to flash.

çıldırmak Go mad; go off one's head.

çılgın Mad; insane; raging.

çıma (¹·) Hawser; cable; fall of a tackle; end (*as opp. to* '*bight*') of a rope. ~ **dikişi,** short splice. ~**çı** (¹··), quayside hand.

çımarıva (··¹·) Ceremonial manning of the yards or decks by a ship's crew.

çımkırık A bird's evacuation of faeces; gardener's watering-can.

çın çın *Imitates the noise of tinkling glass or thin metal.* ~ ~ **ötmek,** to make an empty, ringing sound; to be empty *or* deserted.

çınakop, çinekop Young lufer fish.

çınar Plane-tree.

çıngar Quarrel; dispute; lawsuit.

çıngıl Small bunch of grapes on a side shoot.

çıngır ~ ~, tinkle tinkle. ~**damak,** to give out a ringing sound, to tinkle. ~**tı,** ringing or clinking sound.

çıngırak Small bell.

çınlamak *vn.* Give out a ringing *or* clinking sound; have a singing in the ear. **kulağı çınlasın!,** 'may his ears be singing!', *said when making a kind reference to one who is absent.*

çıplak Naked; bare; destitute. ~**lık,** nudity, bareness: **vakayı bütün çıplaklığile anlattı,** he related the event omitting no details.

çıplatmak *va.* Strip bare; denude.

çıra (¹·) Resinous wood; torch; kindling wood. ~**lı,** resinous.

çırak, çırağ Apprentice; pupil; pensioner; *formerly a person brought up as a servant in a great house and subsequently set up in life, usually by being married off;* favourite. ~ **çıkmak (olunmak, edilmek, çıkarılmak),** to quit the service of s.o. with provision for the future; ~ **etm.,** to pension off or set up in life a çırak. ~**lık,** apprenticeship; fee paid by an apprentice; allowance from a patron.

çırakma Candlestick. ~**n,** beacon *lighted to attract fish by night*; a kind of lighthouse.

çıramoz Torch-holder *for attracting fish by night.*

çırçıplak (¹··), **çırılçıplak** Stark naked; utterly destitute.

çırçır Cotton-gin; rivulet: a kind of wrasse.

çırpı Twig; chip; clipping; skim coulter *of a plough*; chalk-line *for marking straight lines on timber.* ~**dan çıkmak,** to get out of line: ~**ya getirmek,** to put into line, to make straight: ~ **ipi,** carpenter's chalk-line: ~ **vurmak,** to mark a straight line with the chalk-line: **bir** ~**da,** easily and quickly; **işi bir** ~**da çıkarmak,** to make nothing of a job, to do a thing easily: **çalı** ~, brushwood.

çırpıcı Fuller; man who washes printed stuffs in the sea *to make their colours fast.*

çırpın·mak *vn.* Flutter; struggle; fuss about; be all in a fluster. ~**tı,** flurry; fretting *of small waves.*

çırpış·mak *vn.* Flutter. ~**tırmak,** to strike lightly with a small stick; to scribble hastily.

çırpmak *va.* Strike lightly with a series of small blows; tap; pat; beat (carpet); clap (the hands); flutter (the wings); rinse; bleach; trim *the ends of stg.* **çalıp ~,** to pilfer.

çırt, –tı Irrigating device, *by which a leather bucket is alternately lowered and raised by an animal.*

çıt *Imitates the sound of a small thing breaking.* ~ **etmek,** to keep perfectly quiet: ~ **yok,** there is not a sound to be heard.

çıta Border, moulding; long narrow strip of wood; bar *for high-jump.* ~**lı geçme,** tongue-and-groove joint.

çıtak Speaking Turkish with a foreign accent; *name given to the Turkish-speaking people of the Balkans;* swashbuckler.

çıtarı A kind of sea-bream (*Box salpa*).

çıtçıt, –tı Press-button.

çıtıpıtı Graceful; pretty; dainty.

çıtır ~ ~, *imitates a crackling sound.* ~**damak,** to crackle. ~**pıtır** *imitates the agreeable speech of a child or young girl.* ~**tı,** slight sound.

çıtkırıldım Effeminate; weak, fragile.

çıt·lamak *vn.* Make a slight cracking sound. ~**latmak,** *caus. of* çıtlamak: to hint at: **parmak ~,** to crack a finger. ~**pıt,** percussion cap *which goes off when trodden on.*

çıvgar Additional animal *for ploughing, or for hauling a gun.*

çıyan Centipede. ~ **gözlü,** with cold reptilian eyes: **sarı ~,** *used of a fair-complexioned but unpleasant looking person.* ~**cık,** little centipede; bistort.

çızıktırmak *va.* Scribble; scrawl.

çiçek Flower; small-pox; fickle *or* tricky man. **çiçeği burnunda,** quite fresh, brand new; in the full bloom of youth: **aman ne ~ !,** *said of a girl who unexpectedly becomes rather forward and flighty:* **ne ~ olduğunu bilirim,** I know the sort of fellow he is: **su çiçeği,** chicken-pox. ~ **aşısı, –nı,** vaccine. ~**bozuğu, –nu,** pock-mark; pock-marked. ~**çi,** florist. ~**li,** in bloom; decorated with flowers; with a flowery pattern (stuff); suffering from small-pox. ~**lik,** flower garden; flower vase; conservatory. ~**suyu, –nu,** orange-flower essence, neroli.

çifaide (¹···) What's the use?

çift, –ti Pair; couple; mate; yoke of oxen; pair of pincers. Even (number); double. ~**bir altı,** double one six (*in giving a telephone number*): ~ **çubuk,** *v.* **çiftçubuk:** ~**e gitmek,** to go ploughing: ~ **koşmak,** to harness to the plough: ~**e koşmak,** *to use for ploughing an animal normally used for other purposes:* ~ **sürmek,** to plough: **bir ~, a pair: sana bir ~ sözüm, var,** I want a word or two with you.

çift·çi, ploughman; farmer. ~**çilik,** agriculture. ~**çubuk,** general work of the farm *or* vineyard; agriculture: **çiftine çubuğuna bakmak,** to look after one's farm *or* estate.

çifte Paired; doubled. Double-barrelled gun; pair-oar boat; horse's kick with both hind feet; a double whorl on a horse's forehead (*accounted unlucky*). ~ **atmak,** (of a horse) to lash out with both hind feet: ~ **kumrular,** a pair of inseparable friends: ~ **telli,** belly-dance: **iki ~ kayık,** boat with two pairs of oars. ~**kaatlı,** cigarette rolled in double paper. ~**lemek,** (of a horse) to lash out. ~**li,** kicking (horse); unlucky, ill-omened; treacherous, deceitful. ~**nağra,** double-drum.

çifter Having a pair each.

çiftleşmek, *vn.* Mate (of animals).

çiftlik Farm.

çiğ¹ Dew.

çiğ² Raw, uncooked; unripe; crude, inexperienced. ~ ~ **bakmak,** to look around in an uncouth and boorish manner: ~ **toprak,** neglected, uncultivated land: ···**i** ~ ~ **yemek,** to tear *s.o.* to pieces (*fig.*); to nourish a bitter enmity against *s.o.*: ⌐~ **yemedim ki karnım ağrısın¬,** 'I've done nothing that I should be blamed': ⌐**hatır için** ~ **tavuk yenir¬,** one would do almost anything for friendship's sake: ⌐**insan** ~ **süt emmiştir¬,** 'to err is human'.

çigan Gipsy.

çiğdem Crocus; saffron.

çiğdene A kind of pinewood.

çiğid Cotton-seed; freckle.

çiğlik Rawness; tactlessness.

çiğnemek *va.* Trample on, crush; masticate, chew; ignore. '**bizi çiğneyip geçtiniz**', 'you passed us without even condescending to notice us (*jokingly*)'; **müdürü çiğneyip umum müdüre çıkmış,** he ignored (*or* passed by) the director and went straight to the Director-General: **bir kanunu (kaideyi) ~,** to ignore a law (rule): **lâkırdıyı ~,** to mumble.

çiğnemik Food masticated *and then fed to a baby.*

çihar Four (*these Persian numerals are chiefly used in calling the throws of dice*).

çiklet, –ti Chewing-gum.

çil Bright; shiny; speckled, freckled. Spot; freckle; grey partridge. ~ **yavrusu gibi dağılmak,** to scatter like a covey of partridges, to be utterly routed. ~**li,** speckled; freckled.

çile[1] Period of forty days religious retirement and fasting; period of penitence; trial; suffering. ~ **çekmek (çıkarmak, doldurmak),** to pass through a severe trial: ~**den çıkarmak,** to infuriate: ~**den çıkmak,** to be exasperated.

çile[2] Hank or skein of silk etc.; bowstring.

çilek Strawberry. **ağac çileği,** raspberry.

çile·keş Suffering; (of a dervish) undergoing period of solitude and fasting. ~**siz,** carefree.

çilingir Locksmith. ~ **sofrası,** small table with drinks and hors-d'œuvres on it.

çillenmek vn. Become freckled or speckled.

çim Turf; short grass; grass plot; moss.

çimdik Pinch. ~**lemek,** to pinch.

çimen Meadow; lawn; turf. ~**lik,** ~**zar,** grassy spot; expanse of lawn; meadow.

çimensiz In **çehizsiz** ~, (girl) without dowry; without means.

çimento Cement.

çimlenmek vn. Sprout; become grassy; have a nibble; get perquisites or pickings.

çimmek vn. Plunge into water; bathe.

çimrenmek vn. Tuck up one's trousers before entering water; gird oneself up for some enterprise.

çin v. **çın.**

Çin China. ~**ce,** Chinese language. ~**li,** Chinese.

–çin Pers. suffix. Picking up ...; collecting ... .

çingene, çingâne Gipsy; low, mean, cunning fellow, very small **palamut.** ~ **borcu,** a debt, the repayment of which is hard to get; ~ **borcları,** petty debts: ⌐~ **çalar Kürd oynar⌐,** 'the gipsy plays, the Kurd dances', one is as bad as the other; a disorderly party: ~ **düğünü,** a disorderly, riotous assembly: ~ **sarısı,** very bright yellow. ~**lik,** mode of life and habits of a gipsy; vagabondage; meanness, shabbiness: ~ **etm.,** to behave in a mean, miserly way.

çini Porcelain; encaustic tile; enamel ware; indian ink. Tiled (stove etc.). ~ **mavi,** bright blue. ~**li,** decorated with painted tiles.

çinko Zinc.

çintan, çintiyan Wide trousers worn by peasant women in Turkey.

çipil Blear-eyed; dirty (weather).

çipo Anchor-stock.

çiriş Shoemakers' or bookbinders' paste;

size. ~ **gibi** or ~ **çanağı gibi,** sticky and bitter: **işim** ~ (sl.), I am in a mess. ~**lemek,** to smear with paste or size. ~**otu, –nu,** asphodel.

çirkef Sink; sewer; dirty water; ill-bred, badly-behaved man. ~**e taş atmak,** to do stg. to invite the abuse of an insolent person.

çirkin Ugly; unseemly; unpleasant. ~**lik,** ugliness; nasty habit or behaviour. ~**semek,** to find stg. ugly or unpleasant.

çiroz Dried mackerel; person who is mere skin and bone.

çis Honeydew; manna.

çis·elemek, ~**imek** vn. Drizzle. ~**inti,** fine drizzle.

çiş Urine. ~ **bezi,** baby's diaper: ~**im* geldi,** I want to make water.

çişik (·¹) Leveret.

çit[1], **–ti** Chintz.

çit[2], **–ti** Fence of hurdles or brushwood. ~ **çekmek,** to make a fence round a place: **yerli** ~, permanent fence; hedge: ~ **kuşu,** wren.

çitari A Mediterranean sea-bream (Box salpa).

çiti Act of putting together; darning.

çitilemek va. Squeeze or rub stg. while washing it.

çitişmek vn. Become tangled or matted.

çitlembik Terebinth berry. ~ **gibi,** (of a girl) small and dark.

çitlik Material suitable for making a hedge; place enclosed by a hedge.

çitmek va. Put together; darn; as **çitilemek.**

çitmik One sprig of a bunch of grapes; a pinch of stg.

çitsarmaşığı (¹····), **–nı** Convolvulus.

çivi Nail. ~ **gibi,** brisk, alert: ~ **kesmek,** to shiver with cold: ⌐~ ~**yi söker⌐- ⌐set a** thief to catch a thief⌐; (sl.) 'another little drink won't do us any harm'. ~**dişi, –ni,** canine tooth. ~**leme,** dive (feet foremost). ~**lemek,** to nail; to stab. ~**lenmek,** to be nailed; to be glued to the spot.

çividî Indigo blue.

çivit, çivid Indigo; washing-blue. ~**lemek,** to dye with indigo; to treat laundry with blue.

çivmek vn. Miss the mark.

çiy v. **çiğ.**

çizecek Scriber.

çizgi, çizik Line; mark; scratch; trace; stripe; wrinkle; dash in Morse code (dot = **nokta**); hopscotch. ~**li,** striped; ruled (paper).

çizi As **çizgi;** furrow. ~**nti,** small scratch or mark.

çizme Top-boot; Wellington. ⌐~den yukarı çıkmak⌐, to meddle with things you don't understand (cf. 'shoemaker, stick to your last!'). ~li,wearing top-boots: ⌐(orduda) sarı ~ Mehmed Ağa⌐, any unknown ordinary person, 'Tom, Dick, or Harry'.

çizmek va. Draw a line or mark; sketch; rule with lines; scratch; erase, cancel. yan ~, to slip away; to 'cut' s.o.: işten yan ~, to shirk one's work: yan çizilecek iş değil, it is not a job to be scamped.

çoban Shepherd; rustic; boor. ~ armağanı, an unpretentious present: ~ etm., to shepherd, (iron.) to look after children etc.: ~ köpeği, sheepdog. ~aldatan, goatsucker. ~çantası, -nı, shepherd's-purse. ~kebabı, -nı, bits of meat threaded on a stick and cooked over a wood fire. ~lık, the calling of a shepherd; a shepherd's pay. ~püskülü, -nü, holly. ~süzgeci, -ni, goose-grass, cleavers. ~tarağı, -nı, teazle. ~yıldızı, -nı, the planet Venus.

çocuk Infant; child; boy. ~ almak, (of a doctor) to deliver a child: ~ aldırmak, to have a child delivered or aborted: ⌐~tan al haberi⌐, if you want to know the truth listen to what children say; 'little pitchers have long ears': ~ düşürme, abortion: ~ oyuncağı, a toy, a matter of no account; child's-play (very easy thing): çoluk ~, wife and children, the whole family.

çocuk·cağız, the poor little child. ~ça (·⌐·), childish(ly). ~laşmak, to be or become childish. ~lu, having children. ~luk, childhood; childishness, folly, silly deed. ~su, childish.

çoğalmak vn. Increase, multiply.

çoğan v. çöven.

çoğu The greater part; most; v. çok. ~ kimse, most people.

‖çoğunluk Majority.

çoğumsamak va. Deem too many or too much.

çok Much; many; too much, too many; very. çoğu, the greater part, most; çoğumuz, most of us: ~tan or ~tan beri or ~tandır, for a long time, since long ago: ~ bilmiş, (of a child) precocious, who knows more than he should; (of a man) who 'knows a thing or two': ~ gelmek, to seem excessive: ⌐çoğu gitti azı kaldı⌐, it won't be long before ...; the end is near: ~ görmek, to deem excessive; to grudge: çoğa kalmaz, it won't be long before ...: bu iş ~ ~ bir saat sürer, this business won't take more than an hour at the most: ~ sey!, how odd!; 'you don't say so!': ~ yaşa!, long live!

çokal Coat of mail.

çokbilmiş v. çok.

çokça A good many; a good deal; somewhat.

çokluk Abundance; multiplicity; crowd. Often. ⌐nerede ~ orada bokluk⌐, 'where there is a crowd there is also filth'; too many are a nuisance.

çolak With one arm missing or paralysed.

çolpa With one leg damaged; clumsy; untidy.

çolukçocuk Wife and children; all the family; junior and unimportant people. çoluğa çocuğa karışmak, to become a family man.

çomak Club; cudgel.

çomar Large watch-dog; mastiff; (sl.) old publican.

çopra Backbone of a fish; impenetrable thorn-patch; hyssop. ~ balığı, (?) loach.

çopur Pock-mark. Pock-marked.

çorab Stocking. ~ söküğü gibi, 'like the unravelling of a stocking', i.e. proceeding easily and quickly or in rapid succession; birinin başına ~ örmek, to play a dirty trick on s.o. ~cı, hosier. ~cılık, hosiery.

çorak Arid; barren; brackish (water). An impervious kind of clay; saltpetre bed. ~lık, land impregnated with salt.

çorba Soup; medley, mess. ~ etm., or ~ya döndürmek, to make a mess of, to turn upside-down: ~ gibi, muddy; sloppy; in disorder: ~da tuzu* (maydanozu*) bulunmak, to participate in a small way. ~cı, Christian notable (now used jokingly about non-Moslems); official entertainer of guests in a village. ~lık, anything suitable for making soup.

çotra Flat wooden bottle or mug. ~ balığı, file-fish.

çöğür A species of eryngium. A kind of lute.

çökelek Skim-milk cheese.

çöker·mek, ~tmek va. Make a camel kneel; cause to collapse. diz ~, to make kneel. ~tme, a kind of fishing-net; breakthrough (mil.).

çök·mek vn. Collapse; fall down; give way; (of sediment) to settle, be deposited; be prostrated by age or fatigue; (of darkness, fog, sorrow etc.) to descend upon one. acısı yüreğine* ~, for a loss etc. to be deeply felt: diz ~, to kneel. ~türmek, v. çökermek.

çök·ük Collapsed; fallen down; caved in; sunk, depressed; precipitated. ~üntü, sediment, deposit; debris, dilapidation; depression; subsidence. ~üşmek, to fall down together; to run in from all sides and fall upon stg.

çöl Desert; wilderness. ~lük, desert tract of country.

çömelmek *vn*. Squat down on one's heels.

çömez Boy who works in return for board and lodging; hodja's assistant; follower, disciple; (*school sl.*) swat, sap. papas ~i, novice *in the priesthood*.

çömlek Earthenware pot. ~ hesabı, clumsy work; accounts made by an illiterate person, *v, App.*: ~ kebabı, meat roasted in a pipkin: çanak ~, pots and pans. ~çi, potter. ~çilik, earthenware.

çöp, -pü A fragment of vegetable matter; chip; straw; sweepings, litter, rubbish. ~ arabası, dustcart: ~ atlamamak, to let nothing escape one, to pay the utmost attention: ~ gibi, very thin: ~ kebabı, small bits of meat grilled on a skewer: ~ ~ üstüne koymamak, not to do a stroke of work: ağzıma ~ koymadım, I haven't eaten a morsel: gözünü ~ten sakınmaz, dare-devil, intrepid: ⌐sakınan göze ~ batar⌐, overcaution is often dangerous.

çöp·atlamaz, punctilious, meticulous. ~çatan, predestination, fore-ordination (*only in connexion with marriage*); woman who acts as go-between in arranging a marriage. ~çatmak, to arrange a marriage. ~çü, dustman, scavenger. ~leme, hellebore. ~lenmek, to pick up scraps for a meal; to get pickings *from another's business or in virtue of an official position*. ~lük, rubbish-heap; dustbin. ~süz, without a stalk: ~ üzüm, a person without relatives (*usually of a marriageable girl or boy who has no relatives and is therefore desirable*).

çör Used only in conjunction with çöp. ~çöp, sticks and straws; brushwood: ~den çöpten, 'made of matchwood', flimsily built.

çördek Halyard. ~ yakası, head *of a sail*.

çördük Hyssop.

çörek A kind of shortbread *in the shape of a ring*; anything ring-shaped. ~lenmek, to be coiled up; to coil oneself up. ~otu, çöreotu, seeds of *Nigella sativa*, *used to flavour* börek.

çöven[1], çoğan Soapwort (*the roots of which are used by sweetmakers*).

çöven[2] *v.* çevgen.

çözgü Warp; cotton sheeting.

çözme A kind of silk tissue.

çöz·mek *va.* Untie; unravel; undo; solve (problem, cipher). ~ük, untied; disentangled; loose; thawed. ~ülmek, to be untied *etc.*; (*mil.*) to withdraw from contact with the enemy, to disengage; melt; thaw: dili* ~, to recover one's speech. ~üntü, a going to pieces; downfall; *débâcle.*

çubuk Shoot, twig; staff; metal rod; pipe;

stripe (in a textile). çubuğunu tellendirmek, to take it easy: çubuğunu tüttürmek, to smoke one's pipe; to be lazy and indifferent: tüfek çubuğu, ramrod. ~lamak, to beat (a carpet *etc.*). ~lu, striped (cloth *etc.*). ~luk, cupboard *or* rack for pipes.

çuha Cloth. ~çiçeği, -ni, polyanthus.

çuhadar Lackey *or* footman *formerly employed in the houses of the great.*

çuka Sterlet.

çukur Hole; hollow; ditch; cavity; tomb; dimple. Hollowed out; sunk; concave. ~a düşmek, to meet with misfortune: ···in ~unu kazmak, to prepare the ruin of s.o.: bir ayağı ~da olm., to have one foot in the grave: bostan ~u, manure-pit: göz ~u, eye-socket: gözleri* ~a kaçmak, to have sunken eyes, to wear a haggard look. ~luk, place full of hollows *or* ditches.

çul Hair-cloth; horse-cloth; badly made clothes. ~u tutmak, to become rich, to come into property: ~ tutmaz, spendthrift, shiftless. ~ha, weaver: ~ kuşu, long-tailed tit. ~lama, food covered with dough and then baked. ~lamak, to cover *a horse* with a rug; (of waves) to break right over a ship. ~lanmak, to be covered with a horse-cloth; to put on new clothes; to become rich; (*with dat.*) to hurl oneself upon *s.o.*, to fall upon; to pester.

çulluk Woodcock. kervan çulluğu, curlew: su çulluğu or efendi çulluğu, snipe: ~ tersi, woodcock 'trail'.

çulpa *v.* çolpa.

çulsuz Destitute.

çultarı Quilted saddle-cloth.

çultutmaz Shiftless, improvident.

çurçur A kind of wrasse.

çutal *In* çatal ~, confused, all mixed up.

çuval Sack. ⌐açtırma ~ın ağzını⌐, don't insist *or* don't pursue this subject (*you may provoke unpleasant revelations*). ~dız, packing-needle: ⌐iğneyi kendine ~ı karşındakine (başkasına)⌐, try it on yourself first, *or sometimes,* be sure you are not to blame before blaming others.

çük Little boy's penis.

çünki, çünkü Because.

çürük Rotten; unsound; spoilt; worthless; unsound (argument); unfit for military service. Bruise. ~ buhar, waste steam: ~ çarık, utterly rotten: ~ çıkmak, to turn out rotten, to prove to be unsound *or* false; çürüğe çıkmak, (of a soldier) to be invalided out of the army: ~ tahta, a risky business: ~ tahtaya basmak, to suffer loss, to be cheated: ipi ~, undependable: yaprak çürüğü, leaf-mould. ~lük, rottenness; putrefaction; rot-heap; common grave in a cemetery.

çürü·mek *vn.* Rot; decay; spoil; become worthless *or* unsound; be unsound in credit; (of a soldier) to be rejected for unsoundness; show the mark of a bruise. **~tmek,** to cause a rot *etc.*; to show *an argument etc.* to be unsound, to refute, rebut.

çüş *Sound made to stop an ass or to deride a man behaving like one.*

D

–da, –de, –ta, –te *Particle forming the locative case or the equivalent of a preposition.* In; on.

da¹, de, ta, te And; also; but. **sen de, ben de,** both you and I : **her kes gitti, o da kaldı,** everyone went, but he remained; **üşüdüm de giyindim,** I was cold, so I put on my clothes : **mektub gelse de meraktan kurtulsak,** if only a letter would come and relieve our anxiety : **görsem de tanıyamam,** even if I were to see him I should not recognize him : **ne iyi ettin de geldin,** you've done well to come : **gelse de gelmese de faydası yok,** it's useless whether he comes or not : **anlamadım da sordum,** I didn't understand, so I asked : 'Niçin sordun?' 'Anlamadım da', 'Why did you ask?' 'I didn't understand, that's why'.

da² (–) *In compounds*: disease, illness. **~ülkelb,** rabies : **~üssıla,** nostalgia.

dâd (–) Gift; sale; munificence; justice; lament. **~ı Hak,** a gift of God, talent : **~ü feryad,** a cry of lament : ⸢**onun elinden ~ bir feryad iki**⸣, I'm sick of him!

dadanmak *va. with dat.* Acquire a taste for; get fond of; visit *a place* frequently; frequent; make too free use of, abuse.

dadaş Village 'blood' (*in E. Anatolia*).

dader (–ꞌ) Brother.

dadı, dada Nurse.

dafi (–ꞌ) Repelling, warding off. **tayyare ~ topu,** anti-aircraft gun.

dafire (·–ꞌ) Plexus (*med.*).

dağ¹ Mountain; *as an attributive noun it often merely means* 'wild', *e.g.* **~ elması,** crab-apple. **~ adamı,** mountaineer; rough fellow : **~lar anası,** a huge woman : **~ ayısı,** mountain bear; uncouth, boorish fellow : **~ babaları,** brambling : **~ başı,** top of the mountain; wild, remote spot : **~da büyümüş,** bucolic; country bumpkin : **~ deviren,** coarse and clumsy, a 'bull in a china shop' : **~lara düşmek,** to be in a destitute condition : **~ eteği,** foothill, lower slopes of a mountain : ⸢**~dan gelip bağdakini kovmak**⸣, of a new arrival to treat the old inhabitants with contempt, *or*, of an upstart official to treat the old stagers cavalierly : **~ gibi,** huge; a great amount of *anything* : **~a kaldırmak,** to kidnap : ⸢**~ ~a kavuşmaz (ulaşmaz)** insan

insana kavuşur (ulaşır)**⸣, mountains don't meet but men do, *i.e.* you'll run up against him some day : **~ taş,** all around; in great quantities; greatly; ⸢**~lara taşlara**⸣, *an expression used when talking of a calamity, meaning* 'may such a thing be far from us!': ⸢**~ ~ üstüne olur, ev ev üstüne olmaz**⸣, two families can't live under the same roof : **aralarında ~lar kadar fark var,** there is a world of difference between them.

dağ² Brand; mark; cautery; scar. **~ basmak,** to brand : **~ı dil** *or* **~ı derun,** great sorrow.

dağar Wide-mouthed earthenware jar.

dağarcık Leather bag *or* wallet, *used by shepherds etc.* **dağarcığındakini çıkarmak,** to bring out a remark one has prepared beforehand.

dağdağa Trouble and turmoil; confusion; noise. **~lı,** noisy, confused; troublesome.

dağdar Afflicted, grieved; branded, stigmatized.

dağ·ılmak *vn.* Scatter, disperse; fall to pieces; be spread, be disseminated; be distributed; (of a room *etc.*) to be untidy. **~ınık,** scattered; dispersed; wide apart; disorganized; unorganized; untidy. **~ nizam,** open order (*mil.*). **~ınmak,** *v.* **dağılmak.** **~ıtmak** *va.,* scatter, disperse; distribute; break to pieces; create a mess *in a room etc.*

dağlamak *va.* Brand; cauterize; (of heat or cold) to scorch; wound the feelings, grieve.

dağlı¹ Mountaineer; uncouth, bucolic.

dağlı² Branded; scarred; sore at heart.

dağlıç A kind of sheep; the mutton therefrom.

dağlık Mountainous country. Mountainous.

dağsıçanı (ꞌ···), **–nı** Marmot.

daha More; a greater number. More, again, besides; further; yet; *preceding an adjective it forms the comparative thereof.* **~ bu sabah geldi,** he only arrived this morning : **~ dün,** only yesterday : **~ erken,** earlier; it is still early : **~ neler!,** what next!, how absurd! : **~sı var,** that's not all; to be continued : **bir ~ gitmem,** I'll go no more : **bir ~ sene,** next year : **bir ~ yaz!,** write once again! **iki üç ~ beş eder,** two plus three makes five.

dahame (·–¹) Enlargement; hypertrophy.

dahdah Gee-gee.

dahi And; also; furthermore; too; even. **ve ~ duralar**, and that was the end of it!

dâhi (–¹) A genius. **bir ~nin dehası mektebde keşfedilmez**, the genius of a genius is not discovered at school. **~lik**, the state or quality of a genius.

dahil (·¹) Only in '~ek ya resulallah!', I take refuge in thee, O Prophet!

dahil (–¹) Who or which enters; who or which is inside; inner; interior; inside; included. **~ etm.**, to include: **~ olm.**, to be included: **bir şeyin ~inde**, inside a thing. **~en** (¹··), internally; in the interior (of a country). **~î** (–·¹), internal; inner. **~iye** (–··¹), *fem. of dahilî*; Ministry of the Interior; clinic for internal diseases: **~ zabıtı**, officer employed in the administration of a military school. **~iyeci**, official of the Ministry of the Interior; specialist in internal diseases.

dahiyane (–·–¹) Of genius (book, action etc., *but not used of a person*).

dahiye (–·¹) Calamity; man of great genius or intelligence.

dahl, –li Entry; interference; participation. **···de ~i olm.**, to have a part in, to be implicated in.

dahme Tomb, mausoleum.

dai, da'i (–·¹) That which invites or causes; one who calls men to religion; missionary; emissary. **~i şübhe**, a cause for suspicion.

daim (–¹) Enduring, permanent; continuous. **~a** (¹·–), always; perpetually. **~î** (–·¹), constant; permanent; perpetual.

dair (–¹) Revolving. (*with dat.*) Concerning; about; relating to. **~e** (–·¹), circle; suite of rooms; department; offices (of an administration); limit (of jurisdiction *etc.*); tambourine. **edeb ~sinde**, in a decent, mannerly way: **makine ~si**, engine-room. **~en** (¹··), in a circle. **~enmadar** (¹··––), all round. **~evî** (–··¹), circular.

daiye (–·¹) Motive; claim, pretension.

dakik (·¹) *a.* Minute; delicate; subtle, accurate, precise. Flour.

dakika (·–¹), **dakka¹** (·¹) *n.* Minute. **~sı ~sına**, to the very minute, very punctually.

dakka² (¹·) *In* ⌐men ~ dukka¬, (who strikes is struck) 'the biter bit'.

daktilo (·¹·) Typist; typewriting. **~ etm.**, to type.

dal¹ Branch, bough; twig; spray *of diamonds etc.* **~dan ~a atlamak**, to jump from one subject to another: **~ budak salmak**, to send out ramifications, to grow

in size or importance: **~ gibi**, graceful, slender: **bindiği* ~ı kesmek**, to cut the ground from under one's own feet: **bir ~da durmaz**, fickle, capricious: **güvendiği ~lar elinde kalmak**, to be 'let down', to be deceived.

dal² Shoulder; back. **~ına* basmak**, to irritate s.o.: **~ına* binmek**, to put pressure on s.o., to pester.

dal³, dâl (–) Indicating, denoting; symptomatic. **~ olm.**, to signify, indicate.

dal⁴ Bare; naked.

dalak Spleen; honeycomb. **~ olm.**, to have inflammation of the spleen.

dalâlet (·–¹), **–ti** A going astray; deviation, error.

dalamak *va.* Bite; sting; prick.

dalaş Quarrel. **ağız ~ı**, a bickering, wrangle. **~mak**, to bite one another; to wrangle.

dalavere, dalavera (··¹·) Trick; deceit; intrigue.

dalbastı *In* ~ kiraz, lit. 'cherries that weigh down the branch', *seller's cry* 'Fine cherries!'

daldırmak *va. caus. of* **dalmak.** Plunge *into a liquid*; put *into the ground*; layer (a shoot).

dalga Wave; undulation; watering (of silk *etc.*); (*sl.*) trick, deceit. **~yı başa almak**, (of a boat) to turn to meet a wave; to breast the waves (*also fig.*): **~ geçmek**, to be lost in reverie, to be wool-gathering; (*sl.*) to pretend to be doing some work: **···le ~sı olm.**, (*sl.*) to have a love affair with … .

dalga·cı, a wool-gatherer; one who pretends to be working; tricky fellow: **~ Mahmud**, a lazy chap. **~kıran**, breakwater. **~lanmak**, (of the sea) to become rough; (of a flag) to wave; undulate; become corrugated. **~lı**, covered with waves; rough (sea); undulating; corrugated; watered (silk).

dalgıç Diver.

dalgın Plunged in thought; absent-minded; somnolent. **~lık**, reverie; brown study; absence of mind; distraction.

dalkavuk Toady; sycophant; parasite. **~luk**, sycophancy; flattery; fawning.

dalkılıc Who has bared the sword; with bared sword; warrior; swashbuckler.

dallan·dırmak *va.* Cause to ramify; complicate; render difficult; exaggerate. **~mak**, to become branched, ramify; become complicated. **dallanıp budaklanmak**, to spread out in all directions, to have far-reaching effects.

dallı Branched. **~ budaklı**, complicated; intricate.

dalmak *vn.* Plunge, dive; be lost in thought; be absorbed in an *occupation*. **dala çıka**, sinking and rising, *i.e.* with the greatest difficulty: **hasta gene daldı**, the patient has become unconscious again: **içeri ~**, to insinuate oneself into a place unexpectedly: **uykuya ~**, to drop off to sleep.

daltaban Bare-footed; destitute; vagabond.

dalya¹ (ˡ·) Dahlia.

dalya² (ˡ·) Tally. ~ **on**, that makes ten.

dalyan Fishing nets, *fastened to poles, on one of which stands a look-out to observe the entry of fish*; fishpond; reserved fishery. **~ gibi**, well set-up: **~ tarlası**, the area enclosed by the **dalyan**.

dam¹ Roof (*in Anatolia only a flat roof*); roofed shed; small house; outhouse; stable; prison. **~ altı**, any place covered by a roof, *esp.* a loft *or* garret: **~dan düşer gibi**, suddenly; untimely; out-of-place (remark *etc.*): ⌐**~dan düşen halden bilir**⌐, the only ones who can sympathize with a man's misfortunes are those who have suffered similarly, *v. App.*

dam² Trap; snare; net. **~ı iğfaline düşürmek**, to entrap s.o.

dam³ (*Fr. dame*) Lady partner *in a dance*.

dama (ˡ·) The game of draughts. **~ demek**, to give up, to accept defeat: **~ taşı**, draughtsman; **~ taşı gibi**, who is constantly moving from place to place. **~cı**, draughts-player.

damacana (··ˡ·) Large wicker-covered bottle; demijohn.

damad (−ˡ) Son-in-law; bridegroom; title given to the son-in-law of a Sultan; a kind of duck.

damak Palate. **~ eteği**, the roof of the mouth: **damağını* kaldırmak**, to reassure *a frightened person*: **tadı damağında* kalmak**, to be remembered with longing. **~lı**, having a palate: **~ diş**, dental plate with artificial palate.

damalı Having a check pattern.

damar Vein; seam (of coal *etc.*); disposition, character; bad humour. **~ı atmak**, of a vein to pulsate: ···**in ~ına basmak**, to tread on *s.o.'s* corns, to exasperate *s.o.*: ···**in ~ını bulmak**, to find out *s.o.'s* weak spot: ···**in ~ına girmek**, to ingratiate oneself with *s.o.*: **~ı* tutmak**, to have a fit of bad temper; to be capricious *or* obstinate: **hasislik ~ı tuttu**, he had a fit of avarice, he was overcome by avarice; (*if used of a normally good quality this idiom is ironical, e.g.* **vazife ~ı tuttu**, his sense of duty called him (*iron.*); **~ iltihabı**, phlebitis: ⌐**akacak kan ~da durmaz**⌐, what is fated will happen.

damar·lı, veined; with swollen veins; obstinate; perverse. **~sız**, without veins; shameless.

damdazlak (ˡ··) Completely bald.

damen (−ˡ) Skirt of a garment.

damga Instrument for stamping; stamp; mark; stigma. **ayar ~sı**, hallmark: **soğuk ~**, embossed stamp. **~lamak**, to mark with a stamp; to stigmatize. **~lanmak**, to be marked *or* stamped; to be disgraced. **~lı**, stamped, marked: **~ eşek**, *said in contempt of a person known to everyone*. **~pulu, −nu**, stamp (paper); revenue stamp.

damıtmak *va.* Distil.

damız Breeding-shed; breeding establishment. **~lık**, animal kept for breeding; stallion: used for propagating: **~ fidan**, nursery plant.

damkoruğu (ˡ···), **−nu** Houseleek.

damla Drop; paralytic stroke: gout. (Medicine) taken with a dropper. **~ inmek**, to have a stroke; *also sometimes* to have an attack of gout: **~ yakut**, ruby of the finest water. **~lık**, medicine dropper; space between two houses on which the eaves drip. **~lamak**, to drip; to appear suddenly, to turn up (when not wanted); to frequent habitually. **~latmak**, to pour out drop by drop; to distil.

damping (ˡ·) Dumping *of goods*.

−dan, −den *Particle forming the ablative case or the equivalent of the prepositions* from, by.

−dan *Pers. suffix.* Receptacle, case, *e.g.* **şam~**, candlestick.

−dan *Pers. suffix.* Knowing ..., *e.g.* **nükte ~**, witty.

dana Calf. **~ eti**, veal: ⌐**~nın kuyruğu kopmak**⌐, for the crucial moment to come, for the worst to happen: **anasıyle ~**, mother and child. **~burnu, ~nu**, cockchafer grub; whitlow.

dâna (−ˑ) Learned, wise.

dandini (ˡ··) *Word used when dangling a baby.* **~ bebek**, effeminate dandy, childish person: **ortalık ~**, everything is in a mess.

dan dun Bang! bang!

dane (−ˡ) *v.* **tane.**

dang Dengue fever.

dangalak Loutish, boorish, stupid.

dangıl *In* **~ dungul**, boorish: **~ dungul konuşmak**, to speak with an ugly provincial accent.

danışık Consultation. **~lı**, *in* **~ dövüş**, a 'put up job', a plan previously concocted to deceive s.o.

danışmak *va. & vn.* Consult, ask advice; confer. **bu işi kime danışmalı ?**, whom should one consult about this ? : **gönlüne ~**, to take counsel with one's heart, to ponder.

||**danıştay** New name of the old Şurayı Devlet; Court which tries cases between private persons and the government.

Danimarka (··¹·) Denmark.

daniska (·¹·) The best of anything. **bunun** ~sını bilir, he knows this from A to Z.

dank¹ v. dang.

dank² In kafasına* ~ demek (etmek), suddenly to understand from some incident something that had previously puzzled one; kafama ~ dedi, the truth dawned upon me; kafasına ~ dedi also means 'he has learnt his lesson'.

dans Dance. ~ etm., to dance.

dantelâ (·¹·) Lace.

dapdaracık (¹···) Very narrow, tight or scanty.

dar Narrow; tight; difficult; scanty; short (of time). Narrow place; straits; difficulty. ~a ~ or ~ ~ına, with difficulty, hardly: ~a boğmak, to take advantage of s.o.'s difficulties: ~da bulunmak, to be in financial straits: ~a düşmek, to be in a difficulty: ~a gelmek, to be pressed for time; to be forced by circumstances: ~a gelemem, I won't be rushed!: ~a getirmek, to hurry or 'rush' s.o. into doing stg.: ~da kalmak, to be in difficulties: ~ kurtulmak, to narrowly escape: ~ yetişmek, barely to reach: ···e canını* ~ atmak, to manage to take refuge in ...: eli ~, close-fisted; not having enough to live on (also eli ~da): içi ~, impatient, hasty: kendisini* bir yere ~ atmak, to make hastily for a place: sabahı ~ etti, he waited impatiently for the morning.

–dar (–) Pers. suffix. Holding ...; possessing ...; e.g. hisse~, shareholder; bayrak~, standard-bearer.

dâr (–) House; habitation; country. ~ı beka, the next world: ~ül fena or şu ~ı dünya, this world: ~ü diyar, house and home, one's own country: ~ ül İslâm, the Moslem world.

dara Tare (weight). ~ya atmak or çıkarmak, to regard as unimportant, to take no notice of. ~sız, net (weight), excluding the tare.

daraban (··⌐) Pulsation; palpitation.

darabat (··⌐) pl. of darbe. Blows; reverses.

daracık (¹··) Rather narrow or tight; somewhat scanty.

daradar (¹··) With difficulty; only just.

darağacı (¹···), ~nı Gallows; sheer-legs.

daralmak vn. Become narrow or tight; shrink; become scanty; become difficult; be restricted. nefesi* ~, to be short of breath: vakit daraldı, there is not much time.

dârat (–⌐), –tı Pomp; magnificence; display.

darb Blow; minting of coins; multiplication (arith.). ~e, blow, stroke; turn of fortune; chance: ~i hükûmet, coup d'état. ~elemek, to give blows. ~etmek, ~eder, to strike; to mint money; to multiply (arith.).

darbimesel Proverb.

darbuka (·¹·) Earthenware kettle-drum.

dardağan Scattered; in utter confusion. ~ darısı, the seeds of the tamarisk: ~ darısını saçmak, to sow discord; to sow the seeds of evil.

dardarına (¹···) With difficulty; only just.

dargın Angry; irritated, offended. ~ olm., sometimes means to pretend not to care about stg. (because one cannot afford it or for some such other reason). ~lık, irritability, anger.

darı Millet. ~sı başına, 'may he (you) follow suit!'; may his turn come next for a piece of good luck: dibine ~ ekmek, to squander, consume, utterly exterminate.

darılmaca In ~ yok, 'you must not get angry'; 'I am warning you beforehand that you may be disappointed'.

darılmak va. Scold. vn. Get cross.

darifülfül (–··¹) Long pepper.

darkafalı (¹···) Narrow-minded.

dar·lanmak, ~laşmak vn. Become narrow or confined; be in straits. ~latmak, ~laştırmak, to make narrow; restrict; oppress.

darlık Narrowness; narrow place; trouble; poverty. el darlığı, parsimony: gönül darlığı, worry, depression: nefes darlığı, shortness of breath; asthma.

darmadağın (¹···) In utter confusion; all over the place.

dar·ülâceze (–···¹) Poorhouse, infirmary. ~ülfünun (–··⌐), university. ~ülharb (–·¹), theatre of war. ~üşşafaka (–···¹), school for orphans. ~üşşıfa (–··⌐), mental hospital.

darvincilik Darwinism.

dasitan (–·⌐) Story; legend; ballad; epic; adventure; spell. dillerde ~ olm., to be the general topic of conversation. ~î (–·⌐), epic, legendary.

–daş Suffix implying fellowship or participation, e.g. yol~, fellow-traveller; din~, co-religionist.

da·ülkelb (–·¹) Hydrophobia. ~ülmerak (–··¹), ~kı, hypochrondria. ~üsseher (–·¹), insomnia. ~üssıla (–··¹), nostalgia.

dâva (–⌐) Lawsuit; trial (law); claim; petition; problem; thesis; matter, question. ···e ~ açmak or ···i ~ etm., to bring a suit at law against s.o.: ~ başı, the main argument: ~sında bulunmak, to claim that ...:

~ **etm.**, to claim, to pretend to; to be arrogant: ···**in ~sını tutmak**, to take the side of, to adhere to the cause of: ~ **vekili**, advocate, barrister: **şairlik ~sına düştü**, he sets up to be a poet.

dâva·cı, claimant; plaintiff: **~yım!**, I'll have the law of you, I'll sue you! **~lı**, which is claimed; who *or* which is the subject of a lawsuit; defendant; pretentious; (book *etc.*) written to uphold a theory.

davar Flocks of sheep or goats; beasts of burden. **kara ~**, cattle.

davet (**−**ᴵ), **−ti** Summons; invitation; feast. ~ **etm.**, to invite; to incite, cause. **~iye**, card of invitation. **~li**, one who is invited, guest.

davlumbaz Paddle-box *of a steamer*; hood *of a forge*.

davranış Behaviour; attitude.

davranmak Bestir oneself; prepare for action; resist; behave; take pains. **davranma!**, don't stir!: **silâha ~**, to prepare to use a weapon.

davudî (**−−**ᴵ) Bass *or* baritone voice; fine manly voice.

davul Drum. **~a dönmek**, to swell: **alnı ~ derisi**, shameless: ⌜**hem kaçar hem ~ çalar**⌝, 'he runs away but at the same time plays the drum', *said of one who, while pretending not to like it, continues to do stg.*: ⌜**kulağına ~ mu çalınıyor?**⌝, 'are you deaf?': ⌜**uzaktan ~un sesi hoş gelir**⌝, 'oh! the brave music of a *distant* drum!'

dayak Prop; support; beating (*esp.* bastinado). ~ **atmak**, to give a thrashing: ~ **vurmak**, to put up a prop *to a wall etc.*: ~ **yemek**, to get a thrashing: **kapı dayağı**, piece of timber put behind a door to keep it shut. **~lamak**, to shore *or* prop up. **~lık**, suitable as a prop; deserving a beating.

dayalı Propped up; leaning against; **döşeli ~**, completely furnished.

dayamak *va.* Prop up; support: lean *a thing against stg. as support to it*: (*sl.*) to give (*with an idea of cheating or with some other derogatory sense*). **eline ~**, to thrust into s.o.'s hand.

dayanık·lı Lasting, enduring; strong. **~sız**, not lasting; temporary; weak.

dayanmak *vn.* Endure, last, hold out; (*with dat.*) lean on; rely on; confide in; resist; support; push; (of a road) to end in *a place*; succeed in reaching a place. **can olsun dayansın!**, it's more than flesh and blood can stand!: **mahkemeye dayanmışlar**, they ended up in court: **polis kapıya dayandı**, the police came on the scene: **ucuza dayanmamak**, to be unable to resist stg. offered cheap or gratis.

dayatmak *va. caus. of* **dayamak**. Cause to lean against *or* prop up; fling (an accusation *or* a refusal) in s.o.'s face. *vn.* Be obstinate in refusing to do stg. '**ben bunu yapmam dedi dayattı**', he insisted that he would not do it.

dayı Maternal uncle; captain of a ship; 'a good fellow'. ⌜**dümende ~sı var**⌝, (his uncle is at the helm), he has powerful supporters, 'he's got influence'. **~zade** (···−ᴵ), cousin.

dâyin (−ᴵ) Creditor.

daz Baldness. Bald. **~lak**, bald.

dazara dazar (··ᴵ ·ᴵ) Hurrying and scurrying.

de[1] And; also; *v.* **da**[1].

de[2] Hi!; now then! ~ **bakalım!**, now then!; well, how about it!

deavi (·−ᴵ) *pl. of* **dâva**. Suits; matters; claims.

debağat (·−ᴵ), **−tı** The trade of a tanner.

debbağ (·ᴵ) Tanner.

debbe Copper vessel *with handles and lid*.

debboy *v.* **deppoy**.

debdebe Noise, clamour; pomp, display. **~li**, magnificent, resplendent, showy.

debe Ruptured, suffering from hernia. **~lik**, rupture, hernia.

debelenmek *vn.* Struggle and kick.

Debreli *In* ⌜**at martini, ~ Hassan, dağlar inlesin!** ⌝,'fire your gun, D.H., and let the mountains echo!', *used about one who is drawing the longbow.*

debreyaj (··ᴵ) (*Fr. débrayage*) ~ **yapmak**, to declutch.

decace (·−ᴵ) The constellation Cygnus.

dede Grandfather; old man; dervish. ⌜**kendisi muhtacı himmet bir ~, nerde kaldı gayriye himmet ede**⌝, 'himself an old man in need of help, how can he help another?'

dedik *v.* **düdük** *and* **demek**.

dedikodu Tittle-tattle, gossip.

dedirgin *v.* **tedirgin**.

dedirmek, dedirtmek *va. caus. of* **demek**. Make *or* let say; give occasion for stg. to be said.

dedveyt *In* ~ **tonluk**, deadweight tonnage, *i.e. carrying capacity of a ship as opp. to displacement tonnage (weight of the ship itself).*

def *v.* **tef**.

defa Time; turn. **bir kaç ~**, on several occasions: **çok ~**, often: **iki ~**, twice. **~at, −tı**, *pl. of* **defa**, times: **~le**, repeatedly. **~ten** (ᴵ··), all at once.

defetmek (ᴵ··), **−eder** *va.* Drive away; expel; eject; abolish.

defi, −f'i A repelling; expulsion; removal; refutation. **def'i belâ kabilinden**, to do stg.

merely as a precaution against some possible evil: **def'i hacet (tabii) etm.**, to relieve nature: **tayyare ~ topu**, anti-aircraft gun.

defin, -fni Burial.

define (·–¹) Buried treasure; unexpected wealth; 'a real treasure' *of a servant etc.* **~ci**, impostor, who gets money out of 'suckers' by pretending to have found a treasure or to have inherited great wealth, confidence trickster.

defne (¹·) Bay-tree. **~ yaprağı**, bay leaf; very small lüfer fish.

defnetmek, -eder *va.* Bury.

defolmak (¹··), **-olur** *vn.* Be removed; go away. **defol!**, clear out!

defter Register; account-book; notebook; list; catalogue. **~ açmak**, to open a list *of subscriptions etc.*: **~i kapamak**, to close the account, to finish with a matter: **eski ~leri karıştırmak**, *v.* **Yahudi. ~dar**, *(formerly)* Finance Minister; *(now)* head of the financial department of a vilayet; accountant. **~emini, -ni**, Director of the Registry of Landed Property. **~hane** (··–¹), office of the Land Registry.

değdirmek *va. caus. of* **değmek**. Cause to reach *etc.*: cause to be worth: have *stg.* valued.

değer Value, worth, price; talent. Worth; worthy of. **~li**, valuable; estimable (man). **~siz**, worthless.

değil *Negative particle.* Not; not only; not so. **~(-dir)**, he is not: **ben yazdım, sen ~**, it is I who wrote, not you: **evi ~, bahçeyi görmedim**, it is the garden, not the house, that I did not see: **böyle yapanlar yok ~dir**, people who do thus are not wanting, there are many who do thus: **~ ... hattâ ...**, not merely ..., but even ... .

değin, dek Until; up to. **Ankaraya ~**, as far as Ankara: **bugüne ~**, up till today: **o gelinceye ~**, until he comes.

değirmek *v,* **değdirmek.**

değirmen Mill. **···in başında* ~ çevirmek**, to worry *or* disturb *s.o.*: ⌈**bu sakalı ~de ağartmadım**⌉, 'it was not in a mill that I got this white beard', *i.e.* I am old and experienced: **~de sakal ağartmak**, to be inexperienced and immature; not to have learnt from experience.

değirmi Round; circle; square piece *of stuff.* Roundish *or* squarish.

değiş Exchange. **~ etm.** *or* **~ tokuş etm.**, to exchange, to barter. **~ici**, changeable; changing. **~ik**, changed; changeable; varied; fickle; new, unusual: **bu çocuk ~ olmuş**, this child must be a changeling. **~iklik**, alteration; variation: **ağız değişikliği**, a change of food; a change *in general.*

değişmek *va. & vn.* Change, alter, vary. Exchange.

değme Ordinary; chance; any; every; *(sometimes)* the very best, 'super': *(with neg.)* hardly any; not just any; *v. also* **değmek. ~de** (¹··), probably not, I suppose not.

değmek *va. (with dat.) & vn.* Touch; reach; attain; be worth. **değmez !**, it isn't worth while: **değme gitsin**, *in such phrases as:* **öyle bir telâş ki değme gitsin !**, a fearful confusion: **öyle bir ziyafet ki değme gitsin !**, you never saw such a feast!: ⌈**değme keyfine !**⌉, now he should be happy!: **canına* ~**, to be enjoyable; ⌈**babanın canına değsin !**⌉, *phrase used when giving thanks for a kind action*: **eli* ~**, to have an opportunity *or* to find time *to do stg.*; **elim değmişken**, while I have the chance; while I am about it: **el değmemiş**, untouched; virgin: **nazar (göz) ~**, for the evil eye to strike one; **nazar değmesin!**, absit omen!; 'touch wood!': '**bu kahve değdi doğrusu !**, 'I did enjoy that coffee!' *v. also* **değme.**

değnek Stick; rod; beating. **~ yemek**, to get a beating: ⌈**dokuz körün bir değneği**⌉, a most precious thing: **koltuk değneği**, crutch: ⌈**kör değneğini bellemiş gibi**⌉, 'as a blind man knows his stick', he does it as a matter of course, *i.e. without troubling to think whether it is the best course.* **~çi**, official of a guild: '**işsizlerin ~si miyim ?**', 'am I responsible for looking after the unemployed ?'

deha (·–¹) Great ability; genius. **~kâr** (·–¹), possessed of genius.

dehalet (·–¹), **-ti** Submission. **~ etm.**, to take refuge; (of rebels *etc.*) to give oneself up.

dehan Mouth.

dehir, -hri Period, age; eternity; providence, fortune.

dehlemek Urge on *an animal with cries of* '**deh!**'; chase away.

dehliz Entrance-hall; vestibule; corridor; ear-passage.

dehne Jasper; malachite.

dehrî (·–¹) Secular, mundane. Materialist; atheist.

dehşet, -ti Terror. **~ salmak**, to spread terror. **~li**, terrible: **~ sıcak**, 'frightfully' hot.

dek¹ *v.* **değin.**

dek² Trick, fraud. **~ etm.**, to play a trick on, deceive.

dekaik (·–¹), **-ki** *pl. of* **dakika**. Minutes; niceties, fine points, subtleties.

dekan Dean *of a faculty.*

dekor Stage scenery.

delâil (·–¹) *pl. of* **delil.** Proofs *etc.*

delâlet (·–¹), **–ti** Acting as a guide *or* pilot; guidance; indication. ~**le**, through, by the agency of; care of (c/o): ~ **etm.**, to guide; to indicate, show, signify.

deli Mad; insane; crazy; foolish, rash; wild (*also* of plants *etc.*); violently addicted to, 'mad on'. Madman. ~ **bal**, honey made from poisonous plants: ⌜~ **balkabağından olmaz ya!**⌝, he must be off his head!: ~ **baş**, pig-headed: ~ **bayrağı açmak**, to be in love: ~ **canlı**, restless; capricious: ~ **divane**, utterly mad: ~**nin eline değnek vermek**, to give an opportunity to one who is capable of doing harm: ⌜~ ~**den hoşlanır, imam ölüden**⌝, 'the madman likes another madman, the Imam likes a dead man (because he gets a burial fee)', everyone is wrapped up in his own concerns: ~ **ırmak**, a furious, violent river: ... ~**si olm.**, to be 'mad on' *stg.*: ~ **orman**, a dense forest: ~ **saçması**, absolute nonsense 'utter rot': ⌜~**nin zoruna bak!**⌝, what an extraordinary idea!: **ne oldum** ~**si**, one whose head is turned by unexpected good luck.

deli·alacası, –nı, a wild mixture of colours. ~**bozuk**, erratic, unstable, eccentric. ~**ce**, rather mad; poisonous (mushroom *etc.*); ergot; darnel; (·¹·) furiously, madly, like a madman. ~**dolu**, who talks at random and without reflection. ~**duman**, foolhardy, reckless; crazy, good-for-nothing. ~**fişek**, unbalanced, flippant.

delik Hole; opening; (*sl.*) prison. Bored; pierced. ~ **deşik**, full of holes: ~ **kapamak**, to make good a deficiency: **deliğe tıkmak**, to 'put into clink': **kulağı** ~, who keeps his ears open; wide awake.

delikanlı (·¹··) Youth; young man. Young; sprightly. ~**lık**, youth; youthfulness.

delik·deşik (·¹··) Full of holes; honeycombed. ~**li**, having a hole *or* holes; perforated: ~ **taş**, well-curb formed of one stone. ~**siz**, without holes; sound: ~ **bir uyku**, a sound sleep.

delil Guide, pilot; proof, evidence; indication, sign.

delilik Madness.

delinmek *vn. pass. of* **delmek**. Be holed *or* perforated; be worn through.

delir·mek *vn.* Go mad; become insane; be furiously angry; be mad *with love or desire*. ~**tmek**, to drive mad.

delişmen A bit crazy; wild (youth *etc.*).

delk, –ki Friction.

dellal *v.* **tellal**.

delme A piercing *or* perforating. Perforated, holed.

delmek *va.* Pierce; hole; bore. **delip geç-**

mek, to make a hole and go right through: **kulak** ~, to make an ear-splitting noise.

delv Bucket; the constellation Aquarius.

dem¹ Blood.

dem² Breath; vapour; alcoholic drink; moment, time. ~ **çekmek**, to drink wine *etc.*; (of birds) to sing sweetly: ~ **tutmak**, to accompany music: ···**den** ~ **vurmak**, to talk at random and vaguely about *stg.*; to claim; '**bu evi almak istiyorum, fakat sahibi on bin liradan** ~ **vuruyor**', 'I want to buy this house, but the owner talks about £10,000 (*which is absurd*)'; '**Amerikaya gitmekten** ~ **vuruyor**', 'he talks airily about going to America': **her** ~, every moment, continually.

dembedem (¹··) From time to time.

dembeste Speechless.

‖**demeç** Statement; words; speech.

demek (**der, diyor, diyecek, diyen**) *va.* Say; tell; mean; call *or* give a name to. **dediği dediktir**, he abides by what he says; he is an obstinate fellow; ⌜**dediği dedik düdüğü (çaldığı) düdük**⌝—*said of a spoilt child whose every whim is satisfied, or of one who expects such treatment*, 'a little despot': **deme gitsin**, indescribable, unbounded; *v. also* **değmek**: **der demez**, just at that moment, he had no sooner spoken than ...: **derken**, *lit.* 'even as he spoke', *i.e.* just then, all at once: ... **deyip, geçme**, 'don't think you can dismiss it by saying ...', don't think ... of no account: ~ **ki** *or* ~ **oluyor ki**, that means to say that: ⌜**bana mı(sın) demedi**⌝, it had no effect: **bu ne** ~?, what does that mean?: **türkçede buna ne dersiniz?**, what do you call that in Turkish?: **ne** ~!, 'how so?' (*to express disapproval*); 'not at all!', 'certainly you may!' (*as terms of politeness*): **ne dedim de oraya gittim?**, why on earth did I go there?: ⌜**kimin ne demeğe hakkı var?**⌝, 'who can object to that?': ⌜**ne oldum dememeli ne olacağım demeli**⌝, 'don't boast about your present unless you are sure of your future': ⌜**yaşı ben diyeyim 17, siz deyiniz 18**⌝, his age is 17, maybe 18: **yaz demez kış demez**, whether it be winter or summer: ... **diyor da (başka) bir şey demiyor**, he thinks of nothing but ...: **diye** *v.* **diye**.

demet, –ti Sheaf; bunch; faggot; bundle. ~**lemek**, to tie up in a bunch *or* a faggot.

demevî (··¹) Pertaining to the blood; full-blooded, sanguine.

dem·i Tears. ~ **'î**, lachrymal.

demin (¹·) Just now; not long ago. ~**cek** (¹··), just a moment ago.

demir Iron; anchor; iron *part of anything*, barrel *of a gun*, blade *of a knife etc.* ~ **almak**, to raise anchor: ~ **atmak**, to cast anchor, to anchor: ~ **boku**, iron slag: ~ **kazık**, the Pole Star: ~ **resmi**, anchor dues: ~ **üzerinde**, with the anchor up, ready to sail: ···**i** ~**e vurmak**, to put in chains.

demir·baş, iron head *of an implement*; persistent *or* obstinate man; movable stock *of a farm or* furnishings *of a shop, let to the tenant to be accounted for to the owner*: ~ **erzak**, iron rations: ~ **yemek**, a standing dish. ~**ci**, blacksmith. ~**hindi**, tamarind. ~**kapı**, gorge of a river; fortified defile. ~**lemek**, to anchor; to bar (a door). ~**li**, at anchor. ~**yeri**, **–ni**, anchorage. ~**yolcu**, railwayman. ~**yolu**, **–nu**, railway.

demle·mek, ~**tmek**, ~**ndirmek** *va.* Steep (tea). ~**nmek**, to drink (spirits *etc.*); (of tea) to be steeped.

demlik Tea-pot.

demokrasi Democracy.

–den, **–ten**, **–dan**, **–tan** *Particle forming the ablative case or equivalent to a preposition.* From; than; on account of *etc.*

denaet (·–ᵃ), **–ti** Mean or low-down action; meanness. ~**kâr** (·–·ᵃ), mean, vile.

deneme Trial; test. ~**k**, to try, test.

denî (·ᵃ) Vile, base. ~**lik**, vileness, baseness.

denilmek *vn. pass. of* **demek**. Be said; be called.

deniz Sea; wave; storm. ~ **olm.**, to be rough (sea): ~ **onu tutuyor**, he is sea-sick: **açık** ~. the open sea. ~**altı**, **–nı**, *n.* submarine; *a.* submarine; open to the sea, exposed. ~**anası**, **–nı**, jelly-fish. ~**aşırı**, overseas. ~**aygırı**, **–nı**, sea-horse, hippocampus. ~**ayısı**, **–nı**, walrus. ~**ci**, seaman, sailor: seaworthy. ~**cilik**, profession of sailor; aquatic sports; sailing; seaworthiness. ~**kadayıfı**, **–nı**, a kind of seaweed. ~**kızı**, **–nı**, mermaid. ~**köpüğü**, **–nü**, meerschaum. ~**lik**, sloping board on the rail of a boat *to keep the water out*; window-sill. ~**mili**, **–ni**, nautical mile. ~**otu**, **–nu**, seaweed. ~**piresi**, ~**ni**, crayfish. ~**yolları**, **–nı**, sea-ways; shipping lines.

denk Bale; half a horseload; balance, equilibrium; trim; counterpoise. In proper balance; equal. **dengi dengine**, to everyone his due: ~ **etm.**, to make into bales; to pack up; to trim (boat *etc.*); **dengine getirmek**, to choose the psychological moment: **ayağını** ~ **almak**, to be careful where one is going, to 'watch one's step': **bu adam senin dengin değil**, this man is not your equal (in position *or* capacity): **bu kız o gencin dengi değil**, this girl is not a good match for that young man: **kafa dengi bir insan**, a man of one's own sort, a kindred spirit.

denk·leşmek, to be in equilibrium, be balanced *or* trimmed. ~**leştirmek**, *caus. of* **denkleşmek**; *also* to manage to find (money). ~**siz**, unbalanced; awry.

denli[1] Good-tempered, tractable; careful.

denli[2] Of *a certain* kind *or* manner; of *a certain* degree. **ne** ~, what sort; whatever sort.

denmek, **–nir** *vn. pass. of* **demek**. Be said; be named. **buna ne denir?**, what is this called?: **hemen hemen yok denecek kadar az**, so few that one might almost say there were none.

densiz Peevish; refusing to listen to reason.

depo (ᴵ·) Depot; warehouse. **benzin** ~**su**, petrol tank.

depozito (··ᴵ·) Deposit; security.

deppoy Military store; depot.

||**deprem** Earthquake.

depre·mek, ~**tmek** *va.* Move; stir. ~**nmek**, ~**şmek** *vn.*, move; be stirred; rise.

der Gate; door. **Der Saadet** *or* **Der Aliye**, *old names of* Istanbul.

deraguş (·–ᵃ) Embrace.

derakab (ᵃ··) Immediately afterwards.

derbeder Vagabond; bohemian; living an irregular life; careless *in dress, etc.*

derbend Defile; pass.

derc Insertion. ~**etmek**, to insert; to inscribe.

derceb etm. *va.* Pocket; put in the pocket.

derd Pain; suffering; grief; trouble; grievance; obsession; chronic disease; boil. ~**e girmek**, to fall into trouble: ~**i günü**, one's pet grievance, obsession: ~**i* ne imiş?**, what's his trouble?; what does he want?: ~ **ortağı**, fellow sufferer; one to whom one confides one's woes: **(bir şeyin)** ~**ine düşmek**, to be quite taken up with *stg.*: **başına*** ~ **açmak**, to bring trouble on s.o.'s head: **başı*** ~**e düşmek**, to get into trouble: **başı* (kendi)** ~**ine* düşmek**, to be completely preoccupied with one's own troubles: **canının*** ~**ine düşmek**, for one's vital interests to be at stake: ⌐**elin** ~ **görmesin!**⌐, 'may you be free from trouble!', *a form of thanks for help given*: **içine*** ~ ~ **olm.**, to be a thorn in one's side; to cause regret or remorse.

derd·daş, one to whom one confides one's troubles. ~**etmek**, to let *stg.* prey on one's mind. ~**lenmek**, to ache; to be pained, be sorrowful. ~**leşmek**, to pour out one's grief to another *or* to one another; to sympathize with one another. ~**li**, pained; sorrowful; aggrieved. ~**siz**, free from pain *or* sorrow; free from cares: ⌐~ **başa derd almak**⌐, to bring unnecessary trouble upon oneself.

derdest, –ti In hand; in possession; in course of being made *or* done. Arrest. ~ **etm.**, to arrest; to sequestrate : **mallar ~i irsaldır,** the goods are in the course of being dispatched.

dere Valley; stream. ~ **tepe,** hills and valleys; ~ **tepe dolaşmak,** to wander over hill and dale; ⌐~ **tepe demedik yürüdük gittik¬,** we stopped at no obstacle; ~**den tepeden konuşmak,** to have a long chat about all sorts of things : ⌐**bin ~den su getirmek¬,** to make all kinds of excuses, to raise innumerable difficulties.

derebey·i (·\··), **–ni** Feudal chieftain; despot; bully. ~**lik,** feudalism : ~ **devrinde,** in the feudal age.

derece Step, stair; degree; rank; grade; thermometer. ~ ~, by degrees : ~ **koymak,** to take *s.o.'s* temperature : **çekilmez ~ye kadar,** to an intolerable degree : **son ~,** in the highest degree, utterly.

dereke The lowest stratum; descending degree; degree below zero. **bu ~ye sukut etmiş,** so low had he sunk.

dereotu, ~nu Fennel; dil.

dergâh (·⌐) Court of a king; dervish convent.

dergi Collection (of poems *etc.*); review, magazine.

derhal (\·) At once, immediately.

derhatır ((·–⌐) **etm.** *va.* Call to mind; recollect.

deri Skin; hide; leather. ~**sine sığmamak,** to be 'too big for one's boots' : **bir ~ bir kemik,** nothing but skin and bones. ~**lenmek,** (of a wound *etc.*) to heal up.

deriğ *v.* **diriğ.**

derilmek *vn. pass. of* **dermek.** Be collected; collect oneself.

derin Deep; profound. Deep place. ~**den ~e,** from far away; minutely, profoundly : ~**den sesler geliyor,** there are far-off sounds. ~**lik,** depth; profundity; hollow.

derk, ~ki Comprehension. ~**etmek** (\··), to understand.

derkâr (·⌐) At work, busy; manifest, evident.

derken *Lit.* 'while speaking'; even as he spoke; and then; at that moment.

derkenar Marginal note; postscript.

derle·mek *va.* Gather together, collect. ~ **toplamak,** to tidy up, to clear away (dishes *etc.*). ~**nmek,** *pass. of* **derlemek :** ~ **toplanmak,** to pull oneself together.

derli toplu Gathered together and arranged; in order; compact; tidy.

derman (·⌐) Strength; energy; remedy. ~ **bulmak,** to find a remedy : ~**ım yok,** I am exhausted; I have not the means. ~**sız,** feeble, debilitated; exhausted.

derme Gathered together; collected. ~ **çatma,** hastily collected and put together; jerry-built; (soldiers) collected at random; scraps of, odds and ends of. **fransızcası pek ~ çatma,** he has only a smattering of French.

dermek *as* **derlemek.**

dermeyan In the midst; under discussion; on the *tapis.* ~ **etm.,** to bring forward, to put forward (a proposal *etc.*).

dernek Gathering, assembly, party; society.

derpiş etm., *va.* Take into consideration; suggest.

ders Lecture; lesson. ~**i asmak,** to play truant : **bu ~i sana kim verdi?,** who put that idea into your head? ~**hane** (·–⌐), class-room. ~**iam** (··⌐), a public lecture *or* lecturer *in a mosque.*

dert *v.* **derd.**

dertop *In* ~ **olm.,** *or* **büzülmek,** to curl oneself up : ~ **etm.** *(sl.),* to round up, to catch.

deruhde Undertaken; assumed. ~ **etm.,** to undertake, to take upon oneself.

derun (·⌐) Inside; heart, soul; conscience. ~**î** (·–⌐), internal; intrinsic; cordial, sincere.

dervent *v.* **derbend.**

derviş Poor man, pauper; beggar; dervish. Simple; contented; humble. ⌐~**in fikri neyse zikri odur¬,** 'the dervish keeps reciting that formula of prayer which best coincides with his own thoughts', *i.e.* he has a bee in his bonnet about that, he can't keep off that subject : ~ **meşreb,** unconventional : ⌐**bekliyen ~ muradına ermiş¬,** 'everything comes to those who wait'.

derya (·⌐) Sea; ocean; very learned man. **deniz ~ ayak altında,** *phrase used to describe a fine view near the sea.* ~**dil,** large-hearted, magnanimous; always looking at the best side of things.

derz Seam; suture; pointing *of a wall.*

desene (·\·), **desenize** (·\··) *Optative of* **demek** *with a vocative ending;* 'isn't it so?'; it seems that . . . : you mean . . . .

desise (·–⌐) Trick, ruse; intrigue. ~**kâr** (·–·⌐), intriguing, plotting, tricky. ~**ci,** tricky, cunning, intriguer.

despot Greek bishop, Metropolitan; despot. ~**hane** (··–⌐), office and residence of Greek Metropolitan.

dessam (·⌐), **dessame** (·–⌐) Valve *of the heart.*

dessas Intriguing, deceitful.

dest, –ti Hand.

destan *v.* **dasitan.**

destar Turban.

deste Handle; hilt; bunch; packet; quire;

pestle. ~ ~, in packets, by dozens, in heaps; ~ başı, choice specimen put on the top of a heap of goods.

destek Beam; prop; stand; support. ~ **vurmak** or ~**lemek,** to prop or shore up; to support.

destere *v.* testere.

desti *v.* testi.

destgâh *v.* tezgâh.

destres olm. *va. (with dat.)* Acquire; reach.

destur Formula; code; permission. ~**!,** by your leave!, make way!; *also said superstitiously when entering an unpleasant or dangerous place.* ~ **var mı?,** have I your permission? ~**un!,** 'excuse the expression!'

deşelemek *va.* Scratch up *the ground.*

deş·ik Hole. Pierced. **delik** ~, full of holes. ~**ilmek,** to be pierced; (of an abscess) to be opened up; to burst *of its own accord.* ~**mek,** to open by incision, lay open; unearth; open up (a sore point, a vexed question).

dev Giant. ~ **anası,** giantess, huge woman: ~ **gibi,** huge.

deva (·⌐) Medicine; remedy. **her derde** ~, a panacea: ~**yı kül,** panacea. ~**î** (·—⌐), medicinal, remedial.

devair (·—ⸯ) *pl.* of **daire.** Offices *etc.*

devali (·—⌐) Varicose veins.

devam (·ⸯ) A continuing; continuation; permanence; assiduity; regular attendance at work. ~ **etm.,** to continue, last; persevere; *(with dat.)* to continue *stg.*; frequent (a place); attend *or* follow (a course of lectures *etc.*). ~**lı,** continuous, assiduous. ~**sız,** without continuity; inconstant; unenduring; not persevering; irregular at work. ~**sızlık,** lack of continuity *or* perseverance; irregular attendance at work, absenteeism.

devâsa (·—⌐) Gigantic.

devaynası, ~**nı** Magnifying mirror. ⸢**kendini** ~**nda görmek**⸣, to exaggerate one's own importance.

deve Camel. ⸢~ **bir akçe** ~ **bin akçe**⸣, 'there are cheap camels and dear camels', *i.e.* it all depends by what standard you are reckoning: **(yok)** ~**nin başı!,** incredible!, impossible!, out of the question!: ~ **döşlü,** thin in the loins, tucked-up (horse): ⸢~**yi hamudu ile yutmak**⸣, 'to swallow the camel, bridle and all'; *has the same meaning as* ~ **yapmak** *q.v., but is used about a large-scale affair:* ~ **hamuru,** 'camel dough', *said of some indigestible food:* ~ **kini,** rancour; the nourishing of a grudge: ~**de kulak,** stg. very small in relation to the whole, a mere trifle: ~ **yapmak,** to acquire

by deceit, *used generally about public property:* ⸢~**ye yokuşu mu seversin ...**⸣, *v. App.*: ⸢**ata** ~**ye değil ya!**⸣, not so very expensive after all: **bu adama lâf anlatmak** ~**ye hendek atlatmaktan zor,** it's impossible to convince this man: ⸢**ya bu** ~**yi gütmeli, ya bu diyardan gitmeli**⸣, 'you must pasture this camel or leave this country'; one must adapt onself to circumstances.

deve·bağırtan, (that makes the camel cry out), a steep and stony road. ~**boynu, –nu,** S- *or* U- shaped tube; saddle between hills. ~**ci,** camel-driver; camel owner. ~**dikeni, –ni,** thistle. ~**dişi,** having large seeds or grains. ~**kinli,** who nourishes an old and bitter grudge. ~**kuşu, –nu,** ostrich. ~**tabanı, –nı,** coltsfoot. ~**tımarı, –nı,** hastily and negligently performed job. ~**tüyü, –nü,** camel hair; light brown colour.

deveran (··ⸯ) Revolution, rotation; circulation. ~ **etm.,** to go round, rotate, circulate. ~**î** (··—ⸯ), revolving: **hareketi** ~**ye,** circular motion. ~**ıdem** (··—·ⸯ), circulation of the blood.

devir, –vri Rotation; revolution; cycle; circuit; tour; period, epoch; transfer *of a thing from one receptacle to another.* ~ **etm.,** *or* **devretmek,** to revolve, circulate; turn upside down; turn over to another: **devri saadet,** the age of Muhammad, the Golden Age: **devri sabık,** the old régime: **devrin valisi,** the Vali of the day, the then Vali.

devirmek *va.* Overturn; reverse; knock down; pull down; drink *a glass etc.* to the dregs. ···**e gözlerini** ~, to look daggers at ... .

devlet, –ti State; government; kingdom; prosperity, success, good luck. ~**le,** prosperously; *(as interj.)* 'good luck to you!': ~**ü ikballe,** *(as a parting wish)* 'good luck and prosperity!': ~ **memuru,** government official: **dinü** ~, Church and State: **ne** ~**i,** what good luck! ~**çi,** one who favours state control. ~**çilik,** the policy of state control. ~**hane** (··—ⸯ), 'the house of prosperity' *(very polite for* 'your house'). ~**kuşu, –nu,** unexpected good luck; ~**leşmek,** to become nationalized. ~**li,** prosperous, wealthy; *distinguished title formerly given to certain high officials.* ~**lû,** *title given only to the highest officials.*

devralmak (ⸯ··) *va.* Take over.

devran (·ⸯ) Time; epoch; the wheel of fortune; fate.

devre Cycle; generation; period; session *of Parliament*; period *of an election*; electrical circuit. **kısa** ~, short circuit.

devren (ⸯ·) By cession; while making a round *of inspection.* ~ **kiralık,** subletting.

devretmek (¹··) *v.* devir.

devri *v.* devir.

devrî Rotatory. **senei** ~ye, anniversary.

devrik Turned back on itself. ~ **yaka**, turned-down collar.

devrilmek *vn. pass. of* devirmek. Be overturned. ⌐**boyu devrilesi!**¬, 'curse him!'

devriye A certain class of circuit judges (ulema); police round; patrol. ~ **gezmek**, to patrol.

devrü·ferağ etm. *va.* Cede, transfer. ~**teslim**, transfer (of a trust); handing over (of a post *etc.*).

devşirme Act of gathering *or* collecting; (*formerly*) the selection of boys to be brought up as Janissaries. Collected together. **derme** ~, collected anyhow, rubbish.

devşirmek *va.* Gather, pick; roll up (carpet *etc.*); collect oneself.

devvar Revolving continuously; fickle. ~ **tulumba**, rotary pump.

deyiş A kind of folk-song.

deyn Debt; obligation.

deyyus Cuckold; pander.

dığdığı Who pronounces 'r' like 'g'.

dılı, –l'ı Rib; side of a triangle.

dımdızlak (¹··) Stark naked; destitute; quite bald; (*sl.*) stony-broke.

Dımışk *Old name of* Damascus.

dıngıldatmak *va.* Clang.

dırahoma (·¹··) *v.* drahoma.

dıral *Only in* ⌐~ **dedenin düdüğü gibi kalmak**¬, to be at a loss; not to know what to do.

dır·dır Continuous tiresome chatter *or* grumbling. Who thus chatters. ~**ıltı**, continuous and annoying chatter; slight squabble: ~ **çıkarmak**, to have a slight quarrel. ~**lamak**, ~**lanmak**, to babble tiresomely; make annoying noises; nag. ~**laşmak**, to squabble in undertones.

dış Outer; exterior. Outside, exterior; outward appearance. **içi** ~**ı bir**, uniform; sincere; consistent: **içi* dışına* çıkmak**, for one's clothes to become dishevelled.

dışarda, dışardan *v.* dışarı.

dışarı *n.* Outside, exterior; the provinces; the country (*as opp. to town*); abroad. *adv.* Out; outside; abroad. **dışarda**, outside; abroad: **dışardan**, from without; from abroad: ~ **çıkmak**, to go out; to go to the closet: ~**ya gitmek**, to go into the provinces; to go abroad: **gözü** ~**da olm.**, to be discontented with one's job and on the lookout for another: **şehrin** ~**sında**, outside the town: ~ **vurmak**, to show; to reflect. ~**lık**, the provinces. ~**lıklı**, provincial.

dışı *Used as a suffix*; outside of ...; extra-.

evlilik ~ **birleşmeler**, extramarital unions: **kanun** ~, outside the law, illegitimate: **memleket** ~ **haklar**, extraterritorial rights.

‖**dışişleri** (¹···) *In* ~ **Bakanı**, Minister of Foreign Affairs.

dışkı Excrement.

dışlı Pertaining to the outside; possessing an outside. **içli** ~, familiar, intimate.

dışyüz (¹·) Outer surface; outside; appearance.

dızdık *Only in* **dızdığının dızdığı** (dış-kapının mandalı), a distant relative.

dız·dız Buzzing, whizzing; pickpocketing. ~**dızcı**, a pickpocket *who takes advantage of a hubbub to rob s.o.* ~**ıltı**, a humming *or* buzzing. ~**lamak**, to hum, buzz.

dızlak Naked; bald.

diba (–⁻) Silk tissue with a flowery pattern.

dibace (––¹) Preface to a book; first pages of a book *adorned with paintings and gilding*.

dibek Large stone or wooden mortar. ~ **kahvesi**, coffee ground in a mortar.

didar (–⁻) Eye; sight. **arzı** ~ **etm.**, to appear.

Dicle The Tigris.

dide (–¹) Eye. ~**ler ruşen olsun!**, May your eyes be bright! (*a form of congratulation*).

–dide (–¹) *Pers. suffix.* Having seen ...; *e.g.* **cihandide**, who has seen the world, experienced.

didik Teased out, pulled to shreds. ~**lemek**, to tease out into fibres or shreds; pick to pieces; cut to shreds. **birbirini** ~, to tear one another to pieces (*fig.*).

didilmek *vn.* Be picked *or* worn to shreds.

didinmek *vn.* Wear oneself out; toil; be excessively eager *or* anxious, fret.

didirgin *v.* tedirgin.

didişmek *vn.* Push each other about; quarrel; struggle.

didon (*From 'Monsieur Dis donc', popular name for a Frenchman*); ~ **sakallı**, wearing an imperial.

difteri Diphtheria.

diğer (⁻·) Other; another; altered, different; next (day). ~**endiş**, ~**kâm** (··⁻), altruistic.

diğeren Pitchfork.

dik Perpendicular; upright; straight; steep; uncompromising, opinionated. ~~ **bakmak**, to glare, to look daggers: ~ **durmak**, to stand upright: (**suyun**) ~**ine gitmek**, to do just the opposite *of what one is asked etc.*, to be pig-headed: ~ **ses**, harsh, loud voice: ~ **sözlü**, who does not mince his words: ~**ine tıraş**, shaving against the grain; utterly boring or exaggerated talk. ~**başlı**, pig-headed, obstinate.

dikel Long-handled digging-fork. ~eç, dibber.

diken Thorn; sting *of an insect*; obstacle. **tüyleri*** ~ ~ olm., for one's hair to stand on end: ⌜gülü seven ~ine katlanır⌝, 'no rose without its thorns'. ~dudu, -nu, blackberry. ~li, thorny; prickly: ~ tel, barbed wire.

dikence Stickleback.

dikici Cobbler.

dikili Sewn, stitched; planted; set up. ~ ağacı yok, he has no children *or* no home: ~ taş, obelisk: ⌜ağzında torba ~ değil ya!⌝, why don't you speak openly?

dikilmek *vn. pass. of* dikmek. Be sewn; be planted; stand stiff and immobile; (of the eye) to be intently fixed on; (of a horse) to jib. **baş ucuna ~**, to pester s.o.

dikim Act of sewing *or* planting. ~hane (···⌐), sewing workshop (*esp. a government shop*).

dikiş Sewing; planting; stitch; seam; splice. **(bir yerde)** ~ tutmak, to take root or settle down in a place: ~ tutturamamak, to be incapable of settling down to a job *or* keeping a post: **bir ~te içmek**, to drink off at a draught: **düşmesine ~ kaldı**, he only just saved himself from falling. ~çi, seamstress.

dikiz Roguish look; observation. ~ etm. *or* geçmek, to watch intently: ~ aynası, observation mirror; mirror of a motor-car. ~lemek, to keep under observation; spy upon.

dikkafalı (¹···) Obstinate, pig-headed.

dikkat,-ti Attention; care; fineness; subtlety. ~le, with care; attentively: ~ etm., to pay attention; to be careful: ~ kesilmek, to pay great attention: ···i nazarı ~e almak, to take into consideration: ···e nazarı ~i celbetmek, to call attention to .... ~li, attentive; careful; carefully made. ~siz, inattentive; careless. ~sizlik, inattention; carelessness.

diklemesine Perpendicularly.

diklik A being upright *etc. v.* dik. **aklın dikliğine gitmek**, to be obstinately perverse.

dikme *verb. n. of* dikmek. Act of sewing *etc.*; young plant; prop; derrick. Sewn; stitched; spliced.

dikmek *va.* Sew; stitch; splice; set up; plant; drain (a cup); fix (the eyes *upon stg.*); stick *a thing into stg.*; prick up (the ears); (of hair) to stand on end. **göz ~**, to glare; to cast envious glances on *stg.,* to long to possess *stg.*: **şişeyi ~**, to drink straight from the bottle.

dikmen Peak; summit.

dikte (*Fr. dicté*). Dictation. ~ etm., to dictate.

dil¹ Tongue; language; spit of land; index *of a balance*; sheave *of a block*; bolt *of a lock*; reed *of an oboe etc.*; a prisoner of war captured in order to obtain information. ~i* açılmak, for the tongue to be loosed; (of a person hitherto silent) to start talking: ⌜~inin* altında bir şey var⌝, there is something he is keeping back *or* hesitates to say: ~i bağlı, silent, raising no objections: ~ bilmez, he does not know Turkish: ~ çıkarmak, to put out the tongue at s.o.: ~i* dolaşmak, to talk in a confused manner *from drunkenness or fear*: ~ dökmek, to talk *s.o.* round: ~i* döndüğü kadar, *to explain* as well as one can: ~i* dönmemek, to be unable to pronounce a word: ~e *or* ~lere düşmek, to become the subject of scandal: ~inden* düşürmemek, to never cease talking about *stg.*: ~i ensesinden çekilsin!, (a curse), 'may his tongue be pulled out!: ~e gelmek, to become the subject of scandal; to begin to speak: ~e getirmek, to cause to be talked about; to give utterance to *stg.*: ~ini* kesmek, to become silent: ~ine sağlamdır, (i) he does not use bad language; (ii) he is discreet: ~ini* tutmak, to hold one's tongue: ~i* tutulmak, to be speechless *from fear etc.*: ~e vermek, to talk openly about *stg. which should be kept secret*: ~ ini yutmak, *as* küçük ~ini yutmak *but also* 'to appear to have lost the use of one's tongue': ⌜ağzı var ~i yok⌝, 'he has a mouth but no tongue', *said (approvingly) of a very silent person*: ⌜Allah kimseyi ~ine düşürmesin!⌝, 'may God preserve anyone from his tongue!': küçük ~, uvula; küçük ~ini* yutmak, to be overcome by great surprise or fear.

dil² Heart. ~ü can, heart and soul.

dilak Clitoris.

dilaltı (¹··), -nı Pip (in fowls); pustule under the tongue.

dil·âra (·—⌐) Pleasing; seductive. ~âver (·—¹), courageous. ~aviz (···¹), ravishing. ~azar (·—¹), vexatious.

dilbalığı (¹···), -nı Sole (fish).

dil·baz (·¹) Talkative and coquettish; (a woman) who can always talk a man over. ~ber, captivating, charming; sweetheart, darling: ~dudağı, a kind of sweet cake. ~beste, attached to; in love.

dilcik Little tongue; clitoris; pointer *or* needle *of a gauge etc.*

dil·cu (·¹) Desirable, sought after. ~dade (·—¹), beloved; lover; coloured handkerchief *bound round the head.*

dilebesi (¹···), -ni Talkative, glib.

dilek Wish, desire; request. ~ kuyusu, wishing-well. ‖~çe, petition, formal request.

dilemek *va.* Wish for, desire; ask for. özür ~, to ask pardon.

dilen·ci Beggar. ~ çanağı gibi, full of odds-and-ends : ~ vapuru, steamer that stops at every port of call. ~cilik, mendicancy, begging. ~mek, to be a beggar, to beg.

dil·firib (··⌐) Ravishing. ~füruz (··⌐), delightful; joy-giving. ~gir (·⌐), displeased; sad. ~hah (·⌐), desire, wish; heart's desire. ~hiraş, heart-rending. ~hun (·⌐), deeply vexed; sore at heart.

dilim Slice; strip. ~ ~, in slices.

dil·keş, fascinating. ~küşa (··⌐), pleasant, exhilarating.

dillenmek, dilleşmek *vn.* Find one's tongue; become chatty; grumble; talk indiscreetly *or* rudely; be the object of talk, be criticized.

dilli Having a tongue *etc.*, *v.* dil¹; who chatters pleasantly. ~ dişli, sharp-tongued : ağu ~, stuttering : tatlı ~, pleasant-spoken : uzun ~, indiscreet in speech. ~düdük, talkative, chatterbox.

dilmek *va.* Cut in slices *or* strips.

dil·nişin Agreeable, pleasant. ~nüvaz, tender, kind; soothing. ~pesend, admirable; pleasing.

dilpeyniri (¹···), **-ni** *Kind of* cream cheese *made in long strips.*

dil·pezir Agreeable. ~riş, sore at heart. ~rüba (··⌐), ravishing. ~saz (·⌐), agreeable, affable. ~sitan, fascinating.

dilsiz Dumb; mute. ~lik, dumbness.

dil·suhte (·—¹) Sore at heart; afflicted. ~suz (·⌐), touching, moving; compassionate. ~şad (·⌐), happy, contented. ~şikâr (··⌐), seductive. ~şikeste, broken-hearted.

dimağ (·⅄) Brain; intelligence. ~çe, cerebellum. ~î (·—⌐), cerebral.

dimdik (¹·) Bolt upright; quite perpendicular; very steep (downwards).

dimi A kind of textile, (?) dimity.

Dimyat *prop. n.* Damietta. ⌐~a pirince giderken evdeki bulgurdan oldu¹, 'while going to Damietta to get rice, he lost the crushed wheat at home', *i.e.* to lose what one has in the effort to get more or better.

din Religion, faith (*esp.* the Moslem). ~i bir uğrunda, for the sake of Islam : ~i bütün, sincerely religious, good and honest : ~den imandan çıkmak, to lose all patience, to become exasperated : ~ine yandığım (*sl.*), the cursèd.

dinar An ancient gold coin; Serbian franc; Persian and Iraki coins.

dinc Vigorous; robust. başı* ~, at peace. ~elmek, to become vigorous, recover one's strength. ~leşmek, to feel refreshed. ~lik, robustness; good health.

din·dar Religious, pious. ~darlık, piety. ~daş, co-religionist.

dindirmek *va. caus. of* dinmek. Cause to cease; stop (bleeding *etc.*); calm, quieten.

dingil Axle. ~demek, to rattle, to wobble.

dingin Exhausted (animal).

dinî (−⌐) Pertaining to religion; religious.

dini·bütün Good; pious. ~ müslüman, a true Moslem. ~mübin, Islam.

diniyri (·¹··) Diamonds (at cards).

dink Fulling-mill.

dinlemek *va.* Listen to; hear; pay attention to; obey. başını* (kafasını*) ~, to rest (mentally) : kendini o kadar dinleme !, don't fuss so much about yourself : söz ~, to listen to advice, to be docile; söz dinlemez, disobedient.

dinlen·dirmek *va.* Make *or* let rest; calm. kafasını* ~, to rest oneself : kalıbı ~, to die. ~mek, to rest; to become quiet; be heard, be listened to.

dinletmek *va.* Cause to hear; make listen; bore; recount (a tale); sing *a song etc.* well. ⌐külahıma dinlet!¹, 'tell that to the Marines!' : sözünü* ~, to make oneself listened to; to be obeyed.

dinleyici Listener. ~ler, the audience.

dinmek *vn.* Cease; leave off (rain, bleeding *etc.*); calm down.

dinsiz Without religion; impious; cruel. ⌐~in hakkından imansız gelir¹, 'a villain will be worsted by a greater villain'; 'diamond cut diamond'.

dip, −bi *n.* Bottom; lowest part; foot (of a tree *etc.*); anus. *a.* Bottom; lowest. **dibe çökmek,** (of a deposit *etc.*) to sink to the bottom : ~ göstermek *or* sömürmek, to drink to the dregs : dibinden traş, a clean shave : burnunun dibinde, under one's nose, very close : tencere dibi, food adhering to the bottom of a saucepan : ⌐tencere tencereye dibin kara demiş¹, 'the pot called the kettle black'.

dipçik Butt of a rifle. ~ kuvvetile, by force.

dipdiri (¹··) Full of life; very robust; safe and sound.

dipkoçanı (¹···), **−nı** Counterfoil.

dipsiz Bottomless; unfounded, false; inconstant. ~ testi, spendthrift.

dirahmi The Greek coin 'drachma'.

dirahşan (··⌐) Bright; sparkling.

dirayet (·—¹), **−ti** Comprehension; intelligence; ability. erbabı ~, people of intelligence; shrewd, clever man. ~li, capable, intelligent. ~siz, stupid; incapable; unintellectual.

direk Pole; pillar; column; mast; septum; very tall man. ~ ~ bağırmak, to shout at the top of one's voice : ana ~, lower mast :

burnunun* direği kırılmak, to be quite overcome by a smell: burnunun* direği sızlamak, to be very sad: can direği, the sound-post of a violin: ⌐gökün ∼leri alındı⌐, utter ruin ensued: yarış direği, 'greasy pole'. ∼li, masted: üç ∼, three-masted.

direksiyon Steering-wheel and mechanism of a motor-car.

diremek va. In ayak ∼, to 'put one's foot down'.

diren Large-pronged fork, esp. winnowing-fork.

direnmek vn. Disagree; dissent emphatically; insist.

dirhem 400th part of an okka; ancient Arab coin; shot (in a sporting gun). ∼ kadar, a very small quantity: ⌐ağzından söz ∼le çıkıyor⌐, it's hard to get anything out of him: kendini ∼ ∼ satmak, to give oneself airs: elli (yüz) ∼lik, bottle of raki containing 50 (100) dirhems.

diri Alive; fresh, not faded (salad, leaf); energetic, lively; sharp (words); not properly cooked. ∼lik, a being alive; vitality; brusqueness.

diriğ (·⸚) Refusal, reluctance; regret, sorrow. ∼ etm., to refuse, withhold, grudge. ∼!, alas!, a pity!

diril·mek vn. Come to life; be resuscitated. ∼tmek, to bring to life, resuscitate; re-invigorate; enliven.

dirim Life. ölüm ∼ meselesi, a matter of life and death.

dirisa, dirise The training of a gun.

dirlik A living in amity. ∼ düzenlik, harmonious life, good fellowship. ∼siz, cantankerous (man); inharmonious (family life).

dirsek Elbow; bend; knee of timber; crank; bracket; outrigger of a rowing-boat. ···e ∼, çevirmek, to take a dislike to; to 'drop' s.o. when he can be of no further use to one: ∼ çürütmek, to wear out the elbows with study.

diş Tooth; cog; thread of a screw; clove; any tooth-shaped thing; (sl.) a pinch of stg. ···e ∼ bilemek, to nourish a hatred for ..., to watch for a chance to harm ...: ∼ çıkarmak, to pull out a tooth; to cut a tooth: ∼e değmedi, (of food) there was very little of it: ∼e dokunur, profitable, worth while; enjoyable: ···e ∼ geçire-memek, to be unable to influence or harm ...: ∼e gelir, an easy prey: ∼ine göre, to one's taste: ∼ ∼ kar, snow, which, instead of lying smoothly, assumes a granular appearance, each flake seeming to stand out by itself: ∼ kırmak, to put hashish in a cigarette: ∼ kirası, v. dişkirası: canını* ∼ine*

takmak, to take one's life in one's hands; to make desperate efforts: ⌐işten artmaz ∼ten artar⌐, better to save money by economical living than to try to make more out of one's job.

diş·bademi, -ni, soft-shelled almond. ∼budak, ash tree. ∼çi, dentist; ∼lik, dentistry. ∼eti, -ni, gums. ∼fırçası, ∼nı, toothbrush. ∼hekimi, -ni, dental surgeon.

dişi Female; soft, yielding. ∼ demir, soft iron.

diş·karıştıracağı, -nı Toothpick. ∼kirası, -nı, (lit. 'hire of teeth'); formerly a fee demanded by Janissaries for eating, free, at an eating-house; then, by tax-gatherers who were guests at a tax-payer's house; then, a present given to guests at a banquet at a great house, but nowadays only as slang, meaning salary for a sinecure. ∼lek, having prominent teeth; having gaps in one's teeth. ∼lemek, to take a bite out of stg. ∼li, toothed; cogged; jagged; having sharp teeth, formidable; influential; hustling; who gets things done. ∼ or ∼ çark, cog-wheel: ∼ olm., to 'show one's teeth': ∼ tren, cog-wheel railway. ∼macunu, -nu, toothpaste. ∼otu, -nu, sage. ∼tabibi, -ni, dental surgeon. ∼tacı, -nı, crown of a tooth. ∼tozu, -nu, toothpowder.

ditmek va. Pick into fibres; tease; card; (of birds of prey) to tear to pieces.

dival Embroidery in gold thread or cotton, mounted on cardboard.

divan (-⸚) Council of State; public sitting of a governor or council; collection of poems by one author; (·⸝) divan, sofa. ∼a çekmek, to summon into one's presence: ∼ durmak, to stand in a respectful position with hands joined in front: ∼ taburu, parade for inspection: ayak ∼ı, an urgently assembled Council of State.

divane (−−⸝) Crazy, insane. ∼lik, madness.

divan·hane (−·−⸝) Council-chamber; hall. ∼âli (−−−·−⸚), High Court before which only Ministers and other high officials are tried. ∼ıharb, courtmartial. ∼ımuhase-bat (−−−··−⸝), -tı, Council charged with the examination of the expenditure of Ministries.

divanî (−−−⸚) Large style of Arabic writing formerly used for firmans. Pertaining to the Council of State.

divik White ant, termite.

divit Case for reed pens and ink for Arabic writing.

diyabet, -ti Diabetes.

diyakos Deacon.

diyanet (·–ı), **–ti** Piety; religious affairs.

diyar (·ı̊) *pl. of* **dar.** Houses; countries; *used as sing.,* country; district.

diyare Diarrhoea.

diye *Gerund of* **demek**; *lit.* 'saying'; *used following direct speech, where it can best be rendered by inverted commas; otherwise it is used to express purpose, reason, hope, supposition etc., eg.* ⌐**yanlışlık olmasın ~ acele etmem**⌐, 'I do not hurry for fear of making a mistake'; ⌐**her müdüre otomobil tahsisatı ~ para verilir**⌐, 'every director is given money as car allowance'; *the exact shade of meaning is easier to obtain, if it be remembered that* **diye** *represents what a person is supposed to say to himself when doing stg.; e.g.* ⌐**ne ~ bunu yapmış?**⌐, 'what was his reason for doing this?'; *whereas* 'why did he do this?' *would not necessarily mean quite the same thing.*

diyet¹, **–ti** Blood-money; ransom. **~ istemek**, to demand retaliation by the law of talion.

diyet², **–ti** Diet.

diyez (*Fr. dièse*) Sharp (*mus.*).

diz Knee. **~inin* bağı çözülmek**, to give way at the knees *from fear etc.* : **~ boyu**, knee-deep; all-pervading: **~ çökmek**, to kneel: **~ çukuru**, shallow rifle-pit: **~ini* dövmek**, to repent bitterly: **~e gelmek (varmak)**, to kneel in entreaty: **~lerine* kapanmak**, to embrace s.o.'s knees in supplication: **~leri* kesilmek**, to give way at the knees from fatigue: **~lerini* kırarak selâm vermek**, to curtsy: **~ üstü**, on the knees, kneeling.

dizanteri Dysentery.

dizbağı, **–nı** The tendons of the knee; garter.

dizdize Knee to knee.

dizel Diesel.

dizgin Bridle; rein. **~leri ele vermek** *or* **~leri başkasına kaptırmak**, to hand over the reins to another, to let another take control: **~ini kısmak**, to hold in, to curb: **~leri toplamak**, to rein in, to curb: **dolu ~**, at a gallop, with the utmost speed.

dizi Line; row; string (of beads *etc.*); file (of soldiers); progression (*math.*). **~ci**, one who arranges; compositor. **~li**, arranged in a line *or* row; on a string *or* a skewer; set up (type).

dizkapağı, **–nı** Knee-cap.

dizlik Trousers *or* drawers reaching to the knee; knee-cap (protective covering).

dizmek *va.* Arrange in a row; string (beads *etc.*); set up (type).

dobra dobra (ı̊.ı̊.) Bluntly, frankly, without beating about the bush.

doçent Lecturer or assistant professor in a university.

doğan Falcon. **~cı**, falconer.

doğma Birth. Born, by birth. **~ büyüme buralıyım**, I was born and bred here: **anadan ~**, stark naked; **anadan ~ kör**, born blind. **~ca**, by birth; native.

doğmak *vn.* Be born; (of sun or stars) to rise; come to pass. **doğduğuna pişman**, 'who wishes he had never been born'; tired of life; 'born tired': ⌐**gün doğmadan neler doğar**⌐, 'ere the day break many things may happen': **içime* doğdu**, I had a presentiment.

doğram Slice. **~ ~ kesilmek**, to be cut up in slices. **~a**, act of slicing; parts of a house made by a carpenter (doors, windows *etc.*): **dişi ~**, dovetail. **~acı**, carpenter.

doğramak *va.* Cut up into pieces *or* slices. **bol ~**, to make great promises, to brag.

doğru¹ *For* **doğu**. East; east wind.

doğru² *a* Straight; upright; level; direct; right; true; honest, faithful, straightforward. *n.* The right; the truth. ···**e ~**, towards, near: **~dan ~ya**, directly, without intermediary: **~su**, the truth of the matter: **~dan ayrılmak**, to swerve from the path of right: **~ çıkmak**, to come true; to prove to be right: **~ durmak**, to behave oneself: **~ya ~ eğriye eğri**, good for good and evil for evil: **~ oturmak**, to sit still, to keep quiet: ⌐**~söyliyeni dokuz köyden kovarlar**⌐, 'he who tells the truth is chased out of nine villages'; home truths are not welcomed: **daha ~su**, or, to be more exact: **ellisine ~**, not far off fifty: **İstanbulun kışı yaza ~dur**, Istanbul's winter is towards summer, *i.e.* very late.

doğru·ca (ı̊··), directly; straight. **~lamak**, to correct; to confirm. **~lmak**, to become straight, level *or* true; sit up; come true, be realized: ···**e ~**, to set out for, go towards. **~ltmak**, to put straight *or* right; correct; (*sl.*) to manage to earn. **~luk**, straightness; rectitude; honesty; truth. **~su**, in truth: **daha ~**, or, to be more exact.

doğu The east; the East.

doğum Birth; confinement. **~ kâğıdı**, birth certificate. **~evi**, **–ni**, maternity home. **~lu**, born in *such and such* a year: **1920 ~**, the 1920 class (*mil.*).

doğur·mak *va. & vn.* Give birth (to); bring forth; breed. **~tmak**, to cause to give birth; to assist delivery.

doğuş Birth; sunrise. **~lu**, by birth; well-born: **iyi ~**, of good family; of noble character.

dok¹, **–ku** Dock.

dok², **–ku** Duck (material).

doka, duka (ı̊·) Duke.

doksan Ninety. ~ **dokuzluk tesbih,** rosary of 99 beads. ~**ıncı,** ninetieth. ~**ar,** ninety each; ninety at a time.

doktor Doctor. ~**luk,** profession of medicine; title of doctor. ~**a,** degree of doctor.

||**doku** Tissue.

dokuma Weaving; woven tissue; cotton fabric. Woven. ~**cı,** weaver. ~**cılık,** textile industry.

dokumak va. Weave. ⌈**ince eleyip sık** ~⌉, to examine too minutely; to be too exact and meticulous.

dokunaklı Touching, moving; biting, piquant; harmful; strong (tobacco etc.).

dokundurmak va. caus. of **dokunmak²**. Make or let touch; hint at.

dokunmak¹ vn. pass. of **dokumak**. Be woven.

dokunmak² va. (with dat.) Touch; come in contact with; (of a fish) to bite; affect; have an evil effect on; injure; meddle with; vex; concern. ···**in** ···**e faydası** ~, to be of use to: ···**in** ···**e yardımı** ~, to help, to contribute to: **namusa** ~, to slur the honour of, to insult: **namusuna** or **ırzına** ~, to violate a woman: ···**in** ···**e zararı** ~, to do harm to: ⌈**bir dokun bin ah dinle kasei fağfurdan**⌉, 'touch the china bowl once and you will hear a thousand sighs', used of stg. about which there are numerous complaints, or of s.o. who is full of complaints.

||**dokunulmazlık** Immunity from arrest.

dokunur Touching; affecting; harming. ~ **dokunmaz,** scarcely touching.

dokurcun Stack of hay or corn; a game played with beads or pebbles, merels.

dokuş In **değiş** ~, exchange, barter.

dokuşmak v. **tokuşmak**.

dokuz Nine. ⌈~ **ayın çarşambası bir araya gelmek**⌉, 'for the Wednesdays of nine months all to come at the same time', for a great accumulation of work to arise: ~ **babalı,** whose father is unknown: ~ **doğurmak,** to fret with impatience; to suffer hardship: ~ **doğurtmak,** to hustle: ⌈~**unda ne ise doksanında da odur**⌉, 'what he was at nine he is at ninety', he'll never improve: ~ **yorgan eskitmek,** 'to wear out nine blankets', to live to a great age.

dokuz·ar Nine each; nine at a time. ~**taş,** the game of nine men's morris or merels. ~**lu,** containing nine parts etc.; the nine (at cards). ~**uncu,** ninth.

dolab Anything that revolves; water-wheel; treadmill; turnstile; cupboard; trick, plot. ~ **çivisi,** medium-sized nail: ~ **kurmak** or **çevirmek,** to set a snare, to lay a trap: ~**a girmek,** to fall into a trap, to be cheated. ~**cı,** plotter, intriguer. ~**lı,** furnished

with cupboards; tricky, deceitful: ~**saat...,** grandfather clock.

dolak Puttee.

dolam One turn of any coiled thing; fold of a turban. ~**a,** act of winding; a kind of wrap; whitlow.

dolamak va. Twist; wind round; encircle; bandage; lay a burden or duty on s.o. **başına*** ~, to saddle s.o. with stg. ···**i diline** ~, to repeat constantly, to make stg. the main topic of one's conversation: to be always running s.o. down: ···**i parmağına** ~, to have an 'idée fixe' about stg., to have 'a bee in one's bonnet' about stg.

dolambaç Winding; sinuous; flexible; twisting (road). Tortuosity. ~**lı,** not straightforward, tortuous: ~ **yer,** labyrinth.

dolamık Net; snare.

dolan Deceit. **yalan** ~, a pack of lies. ~**dırıcı,** swindler; swindling.

dolan·dırmak va. Make to go round; surround; cheat, swindle; acquire by fraud. ~**mak,** to revolve; circulate; saunter about. ···**e** ~, to surround.

dolâr Dollar.

dolaş Tangle; obstacle. Tangled; involved. ~**ık,** tortuous; intricate; confused. ~**ıklık,** tortuosity; intricacy; obscurity of style etc.

dolaşmak va. & vn. Go around; walk about; go a round of visits etc.; make a tour; become tangled or confused; (of a street or river) to wind about. ···**in ayaklarına** ~, to be a hindrance or handicap to s.o.; **ayakları*** **birbirini** ~, to be thrown into confusion; **ettiği fenalık ayağına dolaştı,** he paid for his mistake; his misdeeds were visited upon him: **dili*** ~, to be tongue-tied or to stammer from surprise or confusion; to speak thickly when drunk; **dillerde** ~, to be talked about everywhere: **dört** ~, to be in a quandary: **zihni*** ~, to be confused or bewildered.

dolay Surroundings; outskirts. ···**den** ~**ı,** on account of, due to: ~**sile,** on account of; in connexion with; as regards; indirectly; consequently.

doldurmak va. Fill; complete; stuff; load (a gun etc.); prime (a person); fill up (a hole); charge (an accumulator); (of a child) to foul its clothes. **çile** ~, to undergo suffering: **denizi** ~, to reclaim land from the sea: **diş** ~, to stop a tooth: **gününü*** ~, to complete one's sentence in prison: **kulağını*** ~, to prime s.o.: **kuzu** ~, to stuff a lamb for roasting: **yerini*** ~, to fill a post, to perform the duties of it properly.

dolgu The filling or stopping of a tooth.

dolgun Full, filled; stuffed; abundant; high (wages); spiteful, full of wrath. **etine** ~

plump: **kulağı ~**, well-informed. **~luk**, fullness, plenitude; a being overfull; anger, spite: **kulak dolgunluğu**, knowledge acquired by listening to others: **mide dolgunluğu**, oppression of the stomach, indigestion.

dolma A dish of meat or vegetables stuffed with rice and forcemeat; anything stuffed; reclaimed land; embankment; lie, invention. Stuffed; filled up with earth or stones. **~ kalem**, fountain-pen: **~ yutmak**, to swallow a lie, to be taken in: **ağızdan ~ top**, muzzle-loading gun: **kabak ~sı**, stuffed vegetable marrow: **yaprak ~sı**, vine leaves wrapped round forcemeat.

dolmak vn. Fill, become full; swell; be completed; be full of anger or spite. **dolup dolup boşalmak**, (of a place) to be thronged with people: **gözleri* ~**, to have the eyes full of tears.

dolmuş Filled; stuffed. Vehicle or boat that only starts when all the seats are taken.

dolu¹ Full; solid (not hollow); loaded (gun). Contents (of a bottle etc.); charge, load (of a gun). **~ dizgin gitmek**, to ride at full speed: **ağız ağıza ~**, brimful: **avuc ~su**, handful: ⌜**boşa koydum dolmadı, ~ya koydum almadı**⌝, I couldn't find any solution of the problem.

dolu² Hail. **~ yağmak**, to hail: ⌜**yağmurdan kaçıp ~ya tutulmak**⌝, 'out of the frying-pan into the fire'.

doluk Hide used as a waterbottle or a float.

dolun·ay (·¹·) Full moon. **~mak**, (of the sun) to set; (moon) to be full.

domalan Tumour, abscess; truffle.

domalmak vn. Project as a hump; bend down with the back protruding; (animal) to lie humped up.

domates (·¹·) Tomato.

dombay Female buffalo.

dombaz v. **tombaz**.

domuz Pig, swine; obstinate and disagreeable man. **~una**, out of spite; (sl.) thoroughly: **~ gibi**, obstinate; swinish: strong, healthy; **~ gibi** or **~una çalışmak**, to work like a nigger: **~ herif**, 'stout fellow': ⌜**~dan kıl çekmek (koparmak)**⌝, to get something out of a stingy or unfriendly man: **~ tırnağı**, crowbar, jemmy: **~ topu**, a kind of torture: **hind ~u**, guinea-pig.

domuz·ayağı, –nı, corkscrew; caltrop (mil.). **~budu, –nu**, leg of pork, ham. **~lan**, dung bettle (?). **~luk**, swinish behaviour; pig-headedness; pigsty. **~yağı, –nı**, lard.

don¹ Clothing; pair of drawers; coat or colour of a horse. ⌜**ata ~a bakma binmiş cana bak !**⌝, never mind his horse or his

clothes, look at the rider!: ⌜**ayağında ~u yok başına fesleğen takar**⌝, 'he has no pants on but wears a sprig of sweet basil on his head', i.e. he spends money on luxuries when he cannot afford the necessaries of life.

don² Frost. **~lar çözülmek**, for a thaw to set in.

donakalmak (·¹··) vn. Be petrified with horror or fear.

donanım Rigging.

donanma A being decked out with flags etc.; illumination; fleet; navy.

donanmak vn. Be decked out, illuminated, equipped, rigged.

donatmak va. Deck out, ornament; equip; rig; illuminate; dress (ship); (sl.) abuse. **tepeden tırnağa ~**, to curse s.o. up and down.

dondurma Frozen; set (concrete). Ice-cream; concrete. **~cı**, ice-cream vendor, **~k**, va., to freeze.

donmak vn. Freeze; become frozen; (of cement) to set.

donsuz Without pants; destitute person, vagabond.

donuk Frozen; frosted (glass); matt; dull; dim; torpid.

donyağı, –nı Tallow. **~yle pekmez**, incompatible.

dopdolu (¹··) Chock-full.

doru Bay (horse). **açık ~**, light bay: **kestane ~su**, chestnut bay: **yağız ~**, brown bay.

doruk Summit; peak. Piled up into a cone. **~lama**, heap; in a heap, piled up.

dosa Gangway plant (naut.).

dosdoğru (¹··) Absolutely straight; straight ahead; perfectly correct.

dost, –tu Friend; lover; mistress. Friendly. ⌜**~ ağlatır düşman güldürür**⌝, the friend brings tears, the enemy smiles; friends criticize, enemies flatter: ⌜**~lar alışverişte görsün**⌝, for the sake of appearances, v. App.: ⌜**~lar başına!**⌝, may the same befall all my friends!, said when speaking about another's success: **iyigün ~u**, a fair-weather friend.

dost·ane (·–¹), **~ça**, friendly, amical. **~luk**, friendship; friendly act; favour. **bir ~ kaldı**, 'that's the last lot' (said by a shopman).

dosya (¹·) Dossier, file.

doy Feast. **~gun**, satiated; who has all his needs satisfied; of independent means. **~ma**, satiety; saturation.

doy·mak vn. Be satiated; be sick of stg. **~ bilmez**, insatiable. **~maz**, insatiable, greedy. **~ulmak**, to have enough of (of = dat.); be satiated.

doyum Satiety. **sonbaharın güzelliğine ~ olmaz,** one never gets tired of the beauty of autumn: ⌈**size ~ olmaz!**⌉, 'one can't have enough of you', *said jokingly when taking leave of s.o.; the reply is:* ⌈**size de inan olmaz**⌉ (*I don't believe you*). **~luk,** quantity sufficient to satiate; plunder, booty.

doyurmak *va.* Satiate; satisfy; nourish; be beneficial; corrupt by generosity.

doz Dose. **~unu kaçırmak,** inadvertently to mix a medicine too strong; (*fig.*) to overdo it.

döğ– *v.* **döv–.**

dökme Act of pouring or casting; a metal casting. Cast (metal); poured out in a heap (wheat *etc.*); (liquid) in bulk. **~ci,** founder, moulder.

dökmek *va.* Pour; scatter; throw away; cast (metal); shed (tears, leaves); come out in skin eruptions (small-pox, measles); reject, 'plough' *in an exam.*; change, turn into. **büyük su ~,** to empty the bowels: **dil ~,** to talk s.o. round: ⌈**···in eline su dökemez**⌉, he can't hold a candle to …: ⌈**işi alaya dökme!**⌉, 'don't turn the matter into a joke!': **kâğıda ~,** to put on paper, to write down: **para ~,** to pour out money: **su ~,** to make water: **tüyünü ~,** (of a bird) to moult: **yüzsuyu (âbiru) ~,** to demean oneself, to humiliate onself *by asking for stg.*

döktürmek *va. caus. of* **dökmek;** (*sl.*) write *or* speak well and easily.

dökük saçık Dishevelled, unkempt.

dökülmek *vn. pass. of* **dökmek.** Be poured *etc.*; fall into decay; disintegrate, go to pieces; (of leaves) to drop off, fall; (of teeth, hair) to fall out; be 'ploughed' *in an exam.* **dökülüp saçılmak,** to unburden oneself, to tell everything; to throw off one's clothes *in undressing*; to spend lavishly: **ağzından dökülüyor,** from the way he speaks it is obvious *that he is lying etc.*: **denize ~,** (of a river) to run into the sea: **kırılıp ~,** to coquet: **iş yeni bir kalıba döküldü,** the affair has taken a new turn: ⌈**tepemden (başımdan) aşağı kaynar sular döküldü**⌉, I felt hot all over (from shame *etc.*): **üstünden* ~,** (of clothes) to be unbecoming: **yola ~,** to take *a certain* course: **yollara ~,** for everyone to come out into the streets.

döküm A pouring out; a casting; a shedding (of leaves *etc.*). **~hane** (···ᵊ), foundry.

dökünmek *vn.* Throw water over oneself. **soyunup ~,** to undress.

döküntü Debris; remnants; reef; stones thrown into the sea *to make a breakwater*; dregs (of the population *etc.*); skin eruption.

döl Foetus; semen; germ; race, stock. **~ döş,** progeny, descendants: **~ tutmak,** (of animals *only*) to become pregnant. **~yatağı, –nı,** womb.

döndürmek *va. caus. of* **dönmek.** Turn round *or* back; turn inside out; reverse; 'plough' *s.o. in an exam.*

dönek Untrustworthy; who never keeps his word; (boy) who always fails in his exams.

dönemec Corner; bend. **~li yol,** a winding road.

döngel Medlar.

dönme Act of turning; retreat; conversion; Jewish convert to Islam. Convert; renegade. **~ dolab,** revolving cupboard *in a wall for conveying food from one room to another*; revolving wheel *at a fun fair.*

dönmek *vn.* Turn; turn back; return; change, be transformed; change one's religion; swerve *from a course*; fail to keep *an agreement*; fail *in an exam.*; fail to be promoted to a higher class. **döne döne çıkmak,** to ascend in a spiral: **dönüp dolaşıp,** in the long run, after all: **başı* ~,** to turn giddy: **beyninden* vurulmuşa ~,** to be terribly shocked *by bad news etc.*: **dili* dönmemek,** to be unable to pronounce a word: **gözü* ~,** to be blind with anger or passion; **gözleri* ~,** (i) *as* **gözü ~;** (ii) for the eyeballs to be turned up *when at the point of death*: **sözünden ~,** to go back on one's word.

dönük With the back turned; turned away. **rengi ~,** faded.

dönüm¹ *Superficial measure* 40 *arshins long by* 4 *arshins wide* = *about* 97 *sq. yards.* **yeni ~,** one hectare (*about* 2½ *acres*).

dönüm² Turn; revolution; a time. **~ noktası,** the turning-point: **gün ~ü,** the solstice: **yıl ~ü,** anniversary.

dönüş Act of turning *or* returning; return journey.

dördayak (¹··) On all fours. ⌈**kedi gibi her zaman ~ üzerine düşmek**⌉, 'like a cat always to fall on one's feet', *i.e.* always to emerge successfully from a difficulty. **~lı,** quadruped.

dörd·er Four apiece; four at a time. **~üncü,** fourth.

dört Four; (*largely used to express totality, e.g.*: **~ el ile,** with the greatest energy; **~ gözle beklemek,** to await with the greatest impatience; **~ nala gıtmek,** to go at full speed; **~ taraftan,** from every quarter; **~ bir yana,** in every direction; **~ yanına bakmak,** to look all round *etc., etc.*): **~ayak,** *v.* **dördayak:** **~ başı mamur,** prosperous, flourishing; well-appointed: **~ dönmek,** to turn a place upside down; to search everywhere; to think of every possible means *of doing stg.*: ~ ucunu koyuvermek (bırakmak), to lose heart about *stg.*, to give *stg.* up.

dört·kaşlı, with bushy eyebrows; with a budding moustache. ~**köşe**, square. ~**lü**, possessing four ...; the four *of a suit at cards.* ~**lük**, that which is worth *four piastres etc.*, or weighs four *pounds etc.*; quatrain. ~**nal**, gallop; ~**a**, at a gallop, at full speed. ~**yolağzı, –nı**, four crossroads.

döş Flank; breast; withers. ~ **tarafından et**, scrag end of meat. **döl** ~, a man's progeny and descendants.

döşek Mattress; bed. ~ **döşemek**, to spread a bed; to make up a bed. ~**li**, furnished with a bed; having a broad base; broad and flat-bottomed (boat).

döşeli Spread; laid down (carpet *etc.*); furnished; ornamented. ~ **dayalı**, fully furnished.

döşeme Floor covering; pavement; furniture; upholstery. ~**ci**, furniture dealer; upholsterer.

döşe·mek *va.* Lay down, spread (carpet *etc.*); carpet; pave; furnish with carpets. **döşeyip dayamak**, to furnish fully. ~**nmek**, to be spread out; be laid down; take to one's bed; 'let oneself go', give vent to one's feelings. ~**tmek**, *va. caus. of* **döşemek**.

dövdü Hammer; mallet; back of an axe.

döven Flail; threshing-machine.

döviz (*Fr. devise*) Foreign bills; foreign exchange.

dövme, döğme Wrought (iron *etc.*); tattooing.

döv·mek *va.* Beat; hammer, forge; thresh; thrash; bombard; pound. ~**ünmek**, to beat oneself; beat the breast *from pain or sorrow*, lament.

dövüş, döğüş Fight. ~**ken**, warlike, bellicose, combative. ~**mek**, to fight against one another; struggle.

dragon Dragoon.

drahoma (·¹·) Dowry.

dram Drama; tragedy.

drednot, –tu Dreadnought.

drezin (*Fr. draisienne*) Platelayer's trolley.

dua (·¹) Prayer; blessing; desire. ~ **etm.**, to pray; to bless; to ask for a blessing on: **hayır** ~, benediction: ⌐**olmıyacak ~ya amin demem**⌐, I can't agree to an impracticable suggestion. ~**cı**, one who prays for another: ~**nız**, your humble servant. ~**han** (·–¹), ~ **olm.**, to pray.

duba (¹·) Barge; pontoon; floating bridge. ~ **gibi**, very fat.

dubara (·¹·) Deuce at dice; trick, fraud. ~**cı**, trickster, cheat.

duçar (–¹) Face to face; subject to; afflicted with; exposed to. ···e ~ **olm.**, to be subject *or* exposed to ...; to contract *a disease.*

dudak Lip. ~ **dudağa**, lip to lip: ~ **çukuru**, the groove in the upper lip: ~ **kıpırdatmak**, to open the lips, to utter a word.

dudu Old Armenian woman. ~ **kuşu**, parrot.

duhul (·¹), –**lü** Entrance; inclusion; importation. ~**etm.**, to enter; to be included; to begin: to be imported; to consummate the sexual act. ~**iye**, entrance fee; ticket of admission; import duty.

duka Duke; ducat.

dul Widowed. Widow; widower. ~**luk**, widowhood.

dulavratotu (··¹··), –**nu** Burdock.

dum *v.* **tım.**

duman Smoke; mist; condensation *on a glass of cold water etc.* ~**ı üstünde**, with the bloom still upon it, quite fresh: **birine** ~ **attırmak**, to defeat s.o. utterly, to have him at one's mercy: ⌐**(bacası eğri olmuş) ~ı doğru çıksın**⌐, (no matter if the chimney be crooked) as long as the smoke gets out, *i.e.* no matter as long as the result is good: **işi ~dır**, he is in a bad way; he is ruined: **kafa** ~ **olm.**, to be befuddled: **sonu*** ~**dır**, he'll come to a bad end: **tozu ~a katmak**, to raise a dust, to proceed at great speed.

duman·lamak *va. & vn.*, give out smoke; cover with mist; render turbid: **kafayı** ~, to become fuddled. ~**lanmak**, to be filled with smoke *or* mist; be smoked *or* cured; become confused in mind; become fuddled: **gözü*** ~, to be blind with rage. ~**lı**, smoky, misty; tipsy: **başı*** ~, fuddled with drink; deranged by passion: ⌐**kurd ~ havayı sever**⌐, the wolf likes foggy weather, evil-doers shun the light.

dumlu Cold.

dumur Only in ~**a uğramak**, to be atrophied; to disappear.

dun Low; base; lower, inferior.

dur Halt!; stop! **selâm** ~!, present arms!; *v.* **durmak**.

dûr Far; distant. ~**u dıraz**, long and prolix, at great length.

durac Francolin.

dûradur (––¹) Far away, distant. Over a long distance; at long intervals.

durak Stopping-place; halt; pause; residence. Stationary. ~ **su**, stagnant water. ~**lama**, standstill. ~**lamak, ~samak**, to hesitate; to break off, to come to a stop.

duralar *v.* **dahî.**

dûrbin (–¹) Far-sighted; provident.

durdurmak *va. caus. of* **durmak**. Stop; make to stand; cause to wait. **akıllar ~**, to dumbfound.

dûrendiş (–·¹) Far-sighted; prudent.

durgun Stationary; stagnant; calm; fatigued; perplexed; at a standstill. **~luk**, a being stationary; stagnation; quiet; heaviness; prostration; anxiety; amazement. **akıllara ~ verecek derecede**, to an astounding degree.

durmak, –ur *vn.* Stop; cease; stand; wait; remain; endure; continue; dwell *on a subject*; (*as an auxiliary verb it expresses continuous action, e.g.* **bakadurmak** *or* **bakıp ~**, to keep on looking). **durup dinlenmeksizin**, unceasingly: **durup durma!**, 'don't keep standing there!': ⌈**durup dururken**⌉, without any reason; without provocation: **durmuş et**, meat that has been kept a few days: **dura kalmak**, to be bewildered *or* aghast: **durmuş oturmuş bir hal**, a settled mature state; a being too old for one's years and having the manners of an experienced man: ⌈**dur yok otur yok**⌉, no respite, not a moment's peace: **ayakta ~**, to stand: **boş ~** to remain idle: **gözüne dizine ~**, to be punished for one's ingratitude: **hiç durmadan**, uninterruptedly; without a moment's hestiation: **içi* durmamak**, not to feel comfortable until stg. is done; to feel bound to do stg.: **işler duruyor**, business is stagnant: **karşı ~**, to oppose: **mideye ~**, to lie heavily on the stomach: **sözünde* ~**, to abide by one's word: **... şöyle dursun ..., ...** let alone ..., *e.g.* ⌈**yabancı dil şöyle dursun kendi dilini bile bilmiyor**⌉, 'he doesn't even know his own language, let alone a foreign one': **···in üzerinde ~**, to dwell upon *a subject etc.*: **yüzüne* duramamak**, to be unable to refuse.

durmaksızın (·¹··) Unceasingly.

duru Clear; limpid. **~lamak**, to rinse in clean cold water.

durubuemsal (·–··¹), **-li** *pl. of* **darbımesel**. Proverbs.

durulmak¹ *vn. impers. of* **durmak**. **burada durulmaz**, one can't stop here; 'no stopping here!'

durulmak² *vn.* Become quiet, settle down; become well-behaved; (of liquids) to become clear. **dibe ~**, (of particles in a liquid) to settle to the bottom: **ortalık duruldu**, it became quiet.

durum Position; attitude.

duruş Posture; attitude; aspect; behaviour. **yan ~u**, side view, profile.

duruşma Sitting *or* hearing of a court.

duruşmak *vn.* Confront one another (in combat *or* argument).

dûş Shoulder.

duş Douche; shower-bath.

dut Mulberry. ⌈**~ yemiş bülbül gibi**⌉, 'like a nightingale that has eaten mulberries', *i.e.* taciturn: ⌈**sabırla koruk helva, ~ yaprağı atlas olur**⌉, 'by patience sour grapes are turned into a sweetmeat, the mulberry leaf into satin'; anything can be done by patience. **~luk**, mulberry garden: full of mulberry trees.

dût Smoke; fog.

duvak Veil *worn by brides or new-born babies*; stone or earthenware lid. **duvağına doymamak**, of a newly married bride to die or be separated from her husband: **~ düşkünü**, a newly married bride who becomes a widow.

duvar Wall. **~ arpası**, wild barley: **~ ayağı**, the foot *or* foundation of a wall: **~ çekmek**, to build a wall round: **~ gibi**, very solid; as deaf as a post: ⌈**~a yazıyorum**⌉, don't forget that I have told you this; some day you will learn that I am right: **kapı ~**, no one opened the door; there was no answer *to a knock or ring*.

duygu Perception; feeling; sense; sensation; a thing heard *or* perceived; information, knowledge. **~lu**, sensitive, impressionable; perceptive, intelligent; well-informed. **~suz**, insensitive; apathetic; ignorant.

duy·mak *va.* Feel; perceive; hear; get information of. **~maz**, who does not perceive; imperceptive; insensitive: **vurdum ~**, thick-skinned; 'slow in the uptake'. **~ulmadık** (·¹··), unheard-of, strange. **~ulmak**, *pass. of* **duymak**, to be heard *or* felt; be heard of; be known; be promulgated, made public. **~urmak**, to make heard, felt *or* perceived; to make known, divulge. **~uş**, impression, feeling.

duziko Greek raki flavoured with mastic.

dü Two (at dice). **~ beş**, double fives.

Dübbü·asgar, the Little Bear, Ursa Minor. **~ekber**, the Great Bear, Ursa Major.

dübür, –brü Arse; anus; back.

düdüçkin Sandpiper.

düdük Whistle, pipe, flute; long hollow tube; silly fellow. Very long and slender. **~ gibi kalmak**, to be left alone and helpless (through one's own fault): **~ gibi kiyafet**, clothes too small and tight: **canavar düdüğü**, siren, warning whistle: ⌈**dediği dedik düdüğü ~**⌉, (*said of a child whose every whim is satisfied or of a person who expects to be so treated*): ⌈**parayı veren düdüğü çalar**⌉, 'who pays the piper calls the tune'.

düğme Button; knob; pimple. **~li**, with buttons, buttoned. **~lemek**, to button up.

düğüm Knot; bow; knotty problem. ~ noktası, crucial or vital point.

düğün Feast *on the occasion of a wedding or circumcision.* ~ bayram, feast, merrymaking: ~ evi gibi, *place* full of merrymakers: ⌐~pilaviyle dost ağırlamak⌐, to entertain s.o. at another's expense; to take credit for what has been done by others. ~çiçeği, –ni, buttercup, ranunculus.

dühan (·⸗) Smoke; tobacco.

dükkân Shop. ikindiden sonra ~ açmak, to open a shop late in the day, *i.e.* to undertake stg. when it is too late. ~cı, shopkeeper.

düldül *Humorous name for a* horse; nag.

dülger Carpenter; builder. ~balığı, –nı, John Dory.

dümbelek Small drum; idiot.

dümdar Rearguard.

dümdüz Absolutely flat, level *or* straight.

dümen Rudder. ~i eğri, walking about in a zigzag manner; acting aimlessly and without plan: ···in ~i elinde olm., to be in charge of ...: ~ kırmak, to change course; kır ~i, 'get out!', 'clear off!': ~ neferi, the last man in a file; anyone who is left behind others, *e.g.* the laziest boy in a class: ~ suyu, the wake of a ship: ⌐dayısı ~de⌐, 'his uncle is at the helm', *said of one who gets on by favour.* ~ci, helmsman; *also as* dümen neferi.

dümtek *In* ~ vurmak, to beat time by slapping the knees with the hands.

dün Yesterday. ⌐~ bir bugün iki⌐, only just arrived; of recent occurrence; *also used of a new arrival getting above himself,* 'what cheek!': ~den bugüne, in a short time: ~ değil evvelsi gün, the day before yesterday: ~den hazır (razı, teşne), only too glad; just waiting for it. ~kü, of yesterday: ~ gün, yesterday: ~ çoçuk, still only a beginner; young and inexperienced.

dünür *The* relationship *between the parents of a husband and those of his wife and vice-versa; such a* relation-at-law. bir kıza ~ düşmek, to ask for the hand of a girl on behalf of s.o. else: ~ gezmek, to try to find a girl as wife for s.o.: ~ gitmek, to go and see a girl and ask for her hand on behalf of another. ~cü *v.* görücü.

dünya World; the Earth; this life; worldy goods. ~da (*with neg.*), never in the world, on no account: ~nin ···i, a vast quantity of ..., *e.g.* ~nin parası, a mint of money: ~ âlem, all the world, everybody: ~lar benim oldu, I felt on top of the world: ~ durdukça, as long as the world lasts: ~ evi, marriage: ~yı gözü* görmemek, to be completely obsessed by one idea: ~ gözüyle görmek, to see *stg.* before one dies: ~

güzeli, extremely beautiful *woman*: ~ kadar, a world of; very large; ~ kelâmı etm., to talk about things, to talk *in general*: ~lar kendisinin olmuş gibi sevindi, he was overcome with joy: ~ varmış!, *expression of relief or pleasure*, good!, that's better!: ~sından* vazgeçmek, to give up all interest in everything, to neglect one's affairs, one's person *etc.*: şöhreti ~yı tutmak, to become world-famous.

dünya·lık Worldly goods, wealth; money. ~perest, worldy-minded.

dünyevî Worldly, mundane.

düpedüz (⸗··) Absolutely flat; quite level; utterly. ~ delilik, sheer madness: 'herif ~ beni tahkir etti', 'the fellow flatly insulted me'.

dür, dürdane Pearl.

dürbin, dürbün Far-sighted. Telescope; field-glasses.

dürmek *va.* Roll up. dürüp bükmek, to fold.

dürt·mek *va.* Prod; goad; incite. ~ücü, one who prods or goads; inciter, instigator. ~üklemek, to prod. ~üş, push, prod; incitement. ~üşmek, to prod one another; to incite. ~üştürmek, to keep pushing one another; keep on inciting or goading *s.o. to do stg.*

düruğ (·⸗) Untruth, lie. ~u maslahatâmiz, a white lie.

dürü Roll; anything rolled up.

dürüm Fold; pleat. ~ ~, in folds or pleats: ~ü bozulmamış, never unfolded, brand new.

dürüst Straightforward, honest; correct, accurate. doğru ~ konuşmak, to speak correctly; to speak decently; to speak frankly.

dürüşt Coarse; severe; brutal.

Dürzi Druze.

dürzü *A term of abuse implying treachery or cruelty.*

düstür Principle; formula; code of laws; register; precedent; permission; authority; book of medical prescriptions. ~ülâmel (·–·–⸗), in force (of a law *etc.*): register of precedents; guiding principle. ~uledviye (·–··⸗), book of prescriptions.

düş Dream. ~ü azmak, to have a seminal emission during sleep.

düşeş Double six (at dice); an unexpected bit of luck.

düşgelmek *va.* (*with dat.*) (*sl.*) Meet by chance.

düşkün Fallen; broken down, decayed; fallen on bad times, 'come down in the world'; addicted; a slave (to). boğazına ~, gluttonous; fırsat ~ü, opportunist, 'with an eye to the main chance', profiteer:

kıyafetine ~, particular about his dress,
but kıyafet ~ü, poorly dressed : kumara ~,
addicted to gambling : vücudden ~,
emaciated : yıldızı ~, whose star has set,
unfortunate. ~lük, decay, poverty; misfortune; excessive addiction.

düşman Enemy, foe. ~ ağzı, calumny :
⌐eski dost ~ olmaz¬, only old friends are
reliable : kaşık ~ı, wife (*sl. and jokingly*) :
⌐su uyur ~ uyumaz¬, always be on your
guard against an enemy. ~lık, enmity,
hostility.

düşme Act of falling *etc.* elden ~, secondhand.

düşmek *vn.* Fall; fall down; fall *in price,
esteem or position*; fall on evil days; fall
away in health; (*naut.*) drift; fall to one's
lot, befall, happen; befit, become, be suitable; fall for, take to *a thing* (*dat.*); appear
suddenly; give the impression of being
odd, silly etc.; (of a baby) to be aborted.
va. Subtract, deduct. düşe kalka, with
great difficulty, after great efforts : ⌐düş-
mez kalkmaz bir Allah¬, 'only God is free
from the vicissitudes of Fate' : ···le düşüp
kalkmak, to live with ..., to be intimate
with ... : 'düş önüme!', 'come along with
me!' (*usually used by policemen etc.*) :
birinin arkasına ~, to follow s.o. about : bu
bana düşmez, it is not for me to say *or*
do this : çiğ ~, to seem crude : dile ~, to
become the object of gossip : garba düşer, it
is more to the west : hesabdan ~, to be
deducted from *or* not included in an
account : birisine işi* ~, to have recourse
to s.o. : küçük ~, to look small, to feel
foolish : sırası düştü, the moment has come
to do stg. : ev yolun soluna düşüyor, the
house is on the left side of the road : suya ~,
to come to nought : bir işin üstüne ~, to
persist in a matter; to be very keen on
stg. birinin üzerine ~, to 'keep on at' a
person; to be unduly concerned about s.o. :
yere ~, to fall to the ground, to come to
nought : yollara ~, to set forth *in quest of
s.o. or stg.* : halk yollara düştü, the people
poured out on to the roads.

düşnam (·⸗) Vituperation.

düşük Fallen; drooping; low; 'come down
in the world'; loose, disconnected (writing); aborted. ~ etek, untidy, slovenly.
~lük, looseness *of style*; faultiness *of
rhythm etc.*; fall *in prices*.

düşüm Stamped piece of wood *formerly
used by tax-collectors.*

düşünce Thought, reflection; anxiety.
~li, thoughtful; pensive; worried. ~siz,
thoughtless, unreflecting.

düşünmek *va.* Think of; remember;
ponder over. *vn.* Be pensive; reflect; be

worried. bir şeyi yapmağı ~, to think of
doing stg.; bir şeyi yapmağa ~, to hesitate
about doing stg. (to be reluctant) : düşünüp
taşınmak, to ponder stg. well : 'düşünün
bir kere!', 'just think for a moment! :
'çok düşünüyor', 'it's very pensive' (*said
of an animal that is looking ill*).

düşünüş Mode of thinking; reflection.

düşürme Act of dropping *or* causing to
fall; miscarriage. elden ~, a chance of
buying cheaply; a bargain.

düşürmek *va. caus. of* düşmek. Cause to
fall; drop; beat down; bring down (an
airplane); cause to meet; pass *from the
body* (a worm *etc.*) : ağzından* düşürmemek,
never to cease talking about *stg.* : birbirine
~, to set two people at loggerheads : cahil
~, to show up s.o.'s ignorance : çocuk ~, to
have a miscarriage : elden ~, to get cheap,
to get a bargain : elden düşürmemek, to
use *stg.* continually : fırsatını (sırasını) ~,
to seize an opportunity : itibardan ~, to
discredit s.o. : küçük ~, to make s.o. look
small : ⌐bu yüzüğü ellili raya düşürdüm¬,
'I had the luck to get this ring for fifty
lira'.

düşürtmek *as* düşürmek.

düşüş Fall; manner of falling.

düşvar (·⸗) Difficult; disagreeable.

düt *Only in* 'herkesin ~ dediği keçi olmaz',
one doesn't get all one wants.

düttürü (⸗··) Oddly dressed. Odd dress.
D~ Leylâ, *the personification of* an eccen-
trically dressed person; one whose clothes
. are too tight and too short.

düve Heifer.

düvel *pl. of* devlet. Powers; states. ~i
muazzama, the Great Powers. ~î (··⸗),
pertaining to states; diplomatic.

düyun (·⸗) *pl. of* deyn. Debts. ~u
umumiye, the Public Debt : ~u gayri
muntazama, floating debt.

düz Flat; level; smooth; straight; uniform.
Flat level place. ayak ~e basmak, to reach
safety, to get out of difficulties. ~ayak,
on a level with the street or ground; without stairs, on one floor. ~cesi, frankly;
to tell the truth.

düz·elmek *vn.* Be arranged; be put in
order; be improved. ~eltmek, ~etmek,
to make smooth *or* level; put in order;
arrange; correct; embellish; set on the
right road.

düzen Order; regularity; harmony; tidiness; toilet; invention, lie, trick. ~i
bozuk, out-of-tune : ~ kurmak, to use
cunning : ~ vermek, to put in order, to
tune. ~baz, tricky, deceitful : cheat,
impostor. ~li, in order; orderly, neat,
tidy; harmonious; tricky; fictitious. ~lik,

harmony: **dirlik** ~, harmonious and quiet life: ⌐**Allah dirlik** ~ **versin!**¬, *said in wishing happiness to a newly married couple.* ~**siz**, in disorder; untidy; out-of-tune; without guile, straightforward. ~**sizlik**, disorder, untidiness; discord.

düzetmek *v.* **düzeltmek.**

düzgün¹ Smooth; level; in order; arranged; correct; in tune; in unison. **eli** ~, skilful: **eli yüzü** ~, rather pretty (woman). ~**lük**¹, order, regularity.

düzgün² Face-paint. ~ **sürmek**, to make up *the face*. ~**lü**, made-up, painted (face). ~**lük**², receptacle for cosmetics.

düzine Dozen.

düzlemek *va.* Smooth; flatten; level.

düzlük Smoothness; levelness; flatness; plainness, simplicity; flat level plain.

düzme, düzmece Made up; false; counterfeit; sham.

düzmek *va.* Arrange; prepare; put in order; invent (tale *etc.*); counterfeit, forge; know carnally. **düzüp koşmak**, to arrange and put together.

düztaban Flat-footed; ill-omened man, a 'Jonah'.

düzü *Only in* **bir** ~**ye**, uninterruptedly, continuously.

düzülmek *vn. pass. of* **düzmek**; **yola** ~, to set out on a journey.

E

eali (·—ᴗ́) *pl. of* **âlâ**; Highest; *as n.* The upper classes; high society.

eazim *pl. of* **âzam**; Greatest; *as n.* Great people.

eb, ebu Father. ~**aanced**, ancestrally; from one generation to another.

ebabil (·—ᴗ́) *Birds mentioned in the Koran*; (?) 'the souls of the damned' (Bosphorus Shearwater).

eb'ad (·ᴗ́) *pl. of* **buud**. Dimensions.

ebcem *In* ~ **çüş**, stupid and uncouth.

ebced *The first mnemonic formula of Arabic letters according to their numerical value, e.g.* **elif** = 1, **be** = 2, **jim** = 3, **dal** = 4. *There are eight of these formulas in all.* ~ **hesabı**, numeration by letters of the alphabet.

ebe Midwife; 'he' *in such games as* 'catch', 'touch-last' *etc.* **dil** ~**si**, garrulous person; quick at repartee. ~**gümecı, –nı**, marshmallow. ~**kuşağı, –nı**, rainbow. ~**lik**, midwifery.

ebed Eternity in the future (*as opp. to eternity in the past* = **ezel**). ~**en** (ᴗ··), eternally; (*with neg. or as interj.*) never (*very emphatic*). ~**î** (··ᴗ́), eternal; without end. ~**iyen** (···ᴗ́·), eternally. ~**iyet**, –**ti**, eternity in the future.

ebenced (ᴗ··) *v.* **ebaanced**.

ebeveyn *dual of* **eb**. Parents.

ebher Aorta.

ebleh Imbecile, stupid.

ebkem Speechless.

ebna (·ᴗ́) *pl. of* **bin**. Sons; descendants.

ebniye *pl. of* **bina**. Buildings.

ebr Cloud.

ebru¹ (·ᴗ́) Eyebrow.

ebru² (·ᴗ́) Marbled (paper). Marbling; marbled paper. ~**lu**, ~**lî**, marbled; changing colour.

ebucehil karpuzu, –nu Colocynth.

Ebusuud *In* ~ **torunu**, a very devout person.

ebühevl Sphinx.

ecanib (·—ᴗ́) *pl. of* **ecnebi**. Foreigners.

ecdad (·ᴗ́) *pl. of* **ced**. Grandfathers; ancestors.

ecel The appointed hour of death; death. ~ **beşiği**, a regular death-trap (vehicle): ~**i* gelmek**, for one's hour of death to have come: ~**i kaza**, accidental death: ~**i mev'ud**, natural death: ~**iyle ölmek**, to die a natural death; 'cinayet mi ~ mi?', 'was it a crime or a natural death?': ~**ine susamak**, to run into the jaws of death, knowingly to face death: ~ **teri dökmek**, to be in mortal fear.

echel *superl. of* **cahil**. Very ignorant.

echize *pl. of* **cihaz**. Outfits.

ecil, –cli Cause, reason.

ecinni Genie; evil spirit.

ecir, –cri Reward; recompense. ⌐**Allah** ~ **sabır versin!**¬, 'may God recompense you and give you patience!' (*said when expressing sympathy for a death*): ~ **sabır dilemek**, to offer one's condolences.

ecîr (·ᴗ́) Hireling; day labourer; salaried person; employee.

eciş bücüş Shapeless; crooked; bent double with age. ~ ~ **yazı**, scrawl, bad handwriting.

eclâf (·ᴗ̇) *pl.* Rowdies; hooligans; rabble.

ecnas (·ᴗ̇) *pl. of* **cins**. Kinds.

ecnebi Foreign. Foreigner; stranger.

ecram (·ᴗ̇) *pl. of* **cirm**. Bodies; planets.

ecsam (·ᴗ̇) *pl. of* **cisim**. Bodies; substances. ~**ı lâtife**, pleasant bodies (*sometimes used for* 'fairies').

ecsad (·ᴗ̇) *pl. of* **cesed**. Corpses; bodies.

ecvef Hollow; cavernous; ignorant, foolish.

ecza ($\cdot\stackrel{1}{-}$) *pl. of* cüz. Parts; components; drugs, chemicals; unbound sections of a book. **~cı**, chemist, druggist. **~hane** ($\cdot--$^{1}), **~ne**, pharmacy, chemist's shop.

eda ($\cdot^1$) Payment; execution (of a deed, a duty); air, tone, manner; affectation. ~ etm., to pay (debts); perform (duty). **~lı**, gracious, seductive, charming; having *such and such* an air; affected: **ciddî** ~, with a serious air.

edani ($\cdot-\stackrel{1}{-}$) Lowest. Low vile people or things.

edat, –tı Particle (*grammar*).

edeb Breeding; manners; education; the science of letters; modesty, shame. ~ **erkân**, good manners: **~i kelâm**, euphemism: ~ **öğretmek** (**göstermek, vermek**), to teach *s.o.* manners, to chastise: ⌜**~dir söylemesi**⌝, 'excuse the expression!': **~ini takın** *or* **~inle otur!**, behave yourself!: **~ü terbiye**, good upbringing: ~ **yeri**, the private parts. **~lenmek**, to be *or* become well-behaved. **~li**, well-behaved, with good manners. **~siz**, ill-mannered; rude; shameless. **~sizlik**, bad manners; rudeness; impertinence; shameful act or behaviour.

ededurmak *va.* Continue to do. ⌜**sen itiraz ededur o yine istediğini yapar**⌝, 'you can object as much as you like, he will still do as he wishes'.

edevat ($\cdot\cdot$$\flat$), **–tı** *pl. of* edat. Tools; particles.

edib ($\cdot$$\flat$) Literary man. Polite, gentlemanly. **~ane** ($\cdot--$^{1}), in a polite, well-brought-up manner; in a literary manner.

edici Making; doing; *usually used with other adjectives to form a compound adjective, e.g.* **mest**, drunk; **mestedici**, intoxicating.

edik Soft unsoled house boot.

edille *pl. of* delil. Proofs *etc.*

edilmek *vn. pass. of* etmek. Be done; be made; *forms the passive of compound verbs made with* etmek, *e.g.* **zannetmek**, to think; **zannedilmek**, to be thought.

edinmek *va.* Get, procure. **âdet** ~, to acquire a habit: **dost** ~, to get friends, to make a friend of ...: **oğlu** ~, to get a son; to adopt as a son.

Edirne ($\cdot^1\cdot$) Adrianople.

ediş Manner of doing *or* making.

edna *comp. of* deni. Lower; lowest; least; minimum; most trifling; ordinary; the poorest quality of. The rabble.

edvar ($\cdot$$\flat$) *pl. of* devir. Revolutions, periods *etc.*

edviye *pl. of* deva. Drugs.

edyan ($\cdot$$\flat$) *pl. of* din. Religions.

ef'al ($\cdot$$\flat$), **–li** *pl. of* fiil. Actions; verbs.

efe *Title borne by Zeybek notables*; Zeybek; swashbuckler. **~lik**, braggadoccio, 'side'.

efendi ($\cdot^1\cdot$) Master; *formerly used after a name as* 'Mister'; gentleman. **~m**, Sir!; I beg your pardon!; what did you say?; *or just put in for politeness like the French* '*monsieur*': ⌜**~m nerede, ben nerede**⌝, *expression used ironically when the person, to whom you are speaking, quite fails to get your meaning*: ⌜**~ime söyliyeyim**⌝, *expression used to link two sentences in speech,* ... and then ...; *sometimes denotes hesitation,* 'what was I going to say?' **~lik**, gentlemanly behaviour.

efgan ($\cdot\stackrel{1}{-}$) Moan; lamentation.

Efgan ($^1\cdot$), **efganlı** Afghan.

efkâr ($\cdot$$\flat$) *pl. of* fikir. Opinions; ideas; *as sing.* thinking; anxiety; intention. ~ **etm.**, to be worried about stg.: **~ı umumiye**, public opinion. **~lanmak**, to become thoughtful *or* anxious. **~li**, anxious, worried.

eflâk ($\cdot$$\flat$), **–ki** *pl. of* felek. Spheres *etc.* **~e ser çekmek**, to be sky high.

Eflak Wallachia; Wallachian.

Eflâtun[1] Plato; learned man.

eflâtun[2] Lilac-coloured.

efrad ($\cdot$$\flat$) *pl. of* ferd. Individuals; private soldiers. ⌜**~ını câmi, ağyarını mâni**⌝, 'assembling all the essential points and eliminating everything extraneous', *i.e.* very exact and precise.

efrenc *n.* European. **~î**, *a.* Frank, European; syphilitic.

efsane ($\cdot-$^{1}) Fable; idle tale. ~ **ve efsun**, idle talk; wild stories.

efser Crown.

efsun *v.* afsun.

efsus Wrong, injury; pity. **~!**, alas!

efzun Increasing; more, many. **hadden ~**, beyond measure; exceeding all bounds.

Ege ($^1\cdot$) Aegean.

eğe[1] File. ~ **kemiği**, rib. **~lemek**, to file.

eğe[2] Master; guardian; relation.

eğer[1], **eyer** Saddle.

eğer[2] ($^1\cdot$) If; whether. **~çi**, although; granted that; it is true that.

eğic Wooden hook (*for gathering fruit etc.*).

eğik Inclined; slanting.

eğilmek *vn.* Bend; incline; bow; lean out of a window *etc.* **eğilip bükülmek**, to bow and scrape: ⌜**ağac yaşken eğilir**⌝, the green twig is easily bent; 'as the twig is bent the tree is inclined'.

eğin, –ğni Upper part of the back. **eğne binmek**, to bully.

eğinc Wen; tumour.

eğindirik Large turned-down collar; tippet.

eğinti Filings.

eğirmek *va.* Spin.

‖eğit·im Education. **~mek**, to educate. **~men**, village teacher.

eğlemek *va.* Stop; retard; delay.

eğlen·ce Diversion; amusement; plaything; joke; useless *or* unimportant thing; very easy matter. **~celi**, diverting, amusing. **~celik**, *such things as sweets, salted almonds etc. eaten merely as tit-bits for amusement rather than nourishment.* **~mek**, to be diverted *or* amused; amuse oneself; joke; stop; wait; be put off.

eğleşmek *vn.* Amuse oneself; rest oneself; reside.

eğmek, iğmek *va.* Bend; incline; persuade. **boyun ~**, to bow the neck, submit.

eğre Felt saddle-pad.

eğrek Ditch; small watercourse.

eğreltiotu, -nu Fern.

eğreti *v.* iğreti.

eğri *v.* iğri.

eğrim Felt saddle-cloth; small whirlpool.

egsos, egzos Exhaust (of an engine).

ehem, -mmi Most *or* more important. **~miyet, -ti**, importance. **~le**, efficiently; with interest. **~miyetli**, important. **~miyetsiz**, unimportant.

ehil, -li Family, household; friends; people; husband, wife. Possessor of, endowed with. **ehli idrak**, a man of intelligence : **işinin ehli adam**, a man who knows his job : **söz ehli**, eloquent.

ehli·beyt, the Prophet's family. **~dil**, wise; wise men, sages; as rint *q.v.* **~hibre**, expert. **~keyf**, one who knows how to enjoy life properly, *bon viveur.* **E~salib**, the Crusaders. **~vukuf**, connoisseur, expert.

ehlî Tame; domesticated. **hayvanatı ~ye**, domestic animals.

ehliyet, -ti Capacity; competence. **~li**, capable; competent; qualified; skilled. **~name** (····ı), certificate of competence.

ehram¹ (·ı) The Pyramids; a pyramid.

ehram² *v.* ihram.

Ehrimen Ahriman; devil.

ehven Easiest; cheapest; lesser (evil). **~i şer**, the lesser of two evils. **~leştirmek**, to cheapen. **~lik**, cheapness.

ejder, ejderha Dragon; monster.

ek, -ki Joint; patch; scar; suffix. **~ini belli etmemek**, to dissimulate; not to give oneself away; to hide the true state of affairs : **~ten pükten**, made of odd pieces put together.

ekâbir (·—ı) *pl. of* ekber. Great persons; important people.

ekal *comp. of* kalil. Lesser; least. **en ~**, the very least. **~liyet, -ti**, minority.

ekalim (·—ı) *pl. of* iklim. Regions; countries.

ekanim (·—ı) *pl. of* uknum. Substances : persons of the Holy Trinity (**~iselâse**).

ekber *comp. of* kebir. Greater; greatest; elder, eldest. **Allahü ~**, Allah is the greatest.

ekici Sower; cultivator.

ekid (·—ı) Strong; firm; peremptory. **~en** (·—·), vigorously; urgently.

ekil, -li Food.

ekili Planted; sown.

ekim Sowing; ‖ October.

ekin Sowing; cultivation; crops. **~ biçmek**, to reap the harvest : **~ vakti**, seed-time. **~ci**, sower, cultivator.

ekip, -pi (*Fr. équipe*) Team; crew; gang.

ekle·mek *va.* Join *a piece* on to *stg.* : increase by adding a piece; join together; deal (a blow). **~nti**, something added on; suffix. **~tmek¹**, caus. of eklemek.

ekler (*Fr. éclair*) Zip-fastener.

ekletmek², -eder *va.* Eat.

ekmek¹ *va.* Sow; scatter; drop (and lose); deal (blows); give *s.o.* the slip.

ekmek² Bread; food; livelihood, profession. **~ çarpmak**, for ingratitude to be punished : **ekmeğe el basmak**, to swear upon bread (*as stg. sacred*) : ⌐**~ elden su gölden**⌐, 'bread from a stranger, water from the lake', to live without working, to get one's living free : ···**i ekmeğinden etmek**, to take the bread out of *a person's* mouth; to cause *s.o.* to lose his job : **~ kapısı**, the place where one works for one's living : **ekmeğinden* olm.**, to lose one's job : ⌐**ekmeğini taştan çıkarmak**⌐, to be able to get one's living out of anything : ⌐**ekmeğine yağ sürmek**⌐, *lit.* to butter his bread, *i.e.* to help s.o. inadvertently when one would rather not have helped, to 'play into s.o.'s hand' : **eli* ~ tutmak**, to earn one's own living : ⌐**yediğin ~ gözüne dizine dursun!**⌐, *an imprecation on an ungrateful person.*

ekmek·çi Baker. **~çilik**, baking, the trade of a baker. **~içi, -ni**, the inside of a loaf; the crumb of bread. **~kabuğu, -nu**, the crust of bread. **~kadayıfı, -nı**, sweetmeat *of thin layers of bread soaked in syrup with clotted cream on top.* **~lik**, suitable for making bread; (*sl.*) a job by which one can live. **~ufağı, -nı**, crumb.

ekmel *comp. of* kâmil. More *or* most perfect *or* excellent. **~iyet, -ti**, perfection.

ekran (*Fr. écran*) Screen (of a cinema *etc.*).

ekser¹ Large nail.

ekser² (·ı) *comp. of* kesir. More *or* most numerous or frequent; most usual. The majority; the most part. **~î** (ı·—), for the most part. **~iya** (ı···), generally; more frequently; for the most part. **~iyet, -ti**, majority; greatest part; quorum.

eksibe *pl. of* kesib. Sand-dunes.

eksik Deficient; lacking, absent; defective; incomplete. Deficiency; deficit. ~ **etek,** woman, 'petticoats': ~ **etmemek,** not to deprive *s.o.*; always to have in stock: ~ **gedik,** small deficiencies; **bir şeyin eksiğini gediğini yoklamak,** to inquire into the defects of stg.: 'eksiği ne?', 'what is there to complain of?': ┌~ **olma!**┐ *or* ┌**Allah ~ etmesin!**┐, 'may you never be wanting!' (*expresses gratitude*): ~ **olmamak,** (of a person) always to turn up *at a party, a meeting etc.*: ┌~ **olsun!**┐, 'better without!', 'I would rather not have it!': **artık ~,** over or under, more or less: **on para ~,** ten paras short.

eksik·lemek, to render deficient *or* defective. ~**lik,** deficiency; defectiveness. ~**siz,** without defect; complete; perfect; permanent; continuous.

eksilmek *vn.* Grow less, decrease; be absent. **bunu yapmasa nesi eksilir?,** if he doesn't do it what would he miss?

eksiltme A putting up to tender; an asking for the most reduced terms for carrying out a contract. ···**in inşaatı kapalı ~ye konmuştur,** the construction of ... has been put up to secret tender.

eksiltmek *va.* Diminish; reduce.

eksiz Without an addition; in one piece; seamless.

eksper Expert.

ekşi Sour; acid; fermented; sour-faced. Any sour substance; pickle; leaven. ~**mek,** to become sour; ferment; become cross or disagreeable; (of the stomach) to be upset; to feel foolish *when proved to have been in the wrong*: to become stale or hackneyed. **başına* ~,** to be a burden to *s.o.*: **bu iş elinde ekşidi,** he has let this matter drag on, has neglected it. ~**mik,** cheese made from skim milk. ~**msi,** ~**mtrak,** sourish. ~**suratlı,** sour-faced. ~**tmek,** ~**lemek,** to render sour; cause to ferment; make *s.o.* look foolish *by exposing his error*; **çehreyi (yüzü)* ~,** to frown, to look cross.

ekti Tart; morose; miserly. ~ **püktü,** hanger-on.

ekûl, –lü Gluttonous, voracious. Glutton.

ekyeri (¹··), **–ni** Line where one thing is joined to another.

ekzos Exhaust (of an engine).

el¹ Hand; forefoot; handle; handful; one discharge *of a firearm*; deal *at cards*. ~**de,** in possession; in hand, in the course of being done: ~**den,** by hand (*as of a letter*); cash payment; directly, without an intermediary, *e.g.* **bir muameleyi ~den takibetmek,** to follow up a matter personally instead of in an official manner: ~**i açık,**

open-handed, generous. ~ **açmak,** to beg *for alms*: ~**e alınmak,** (of a reason or excuse) to be accepted; ~**e alınmaz,** bad in quality; unacceptable: ~ **almak,** (of a novice in an order of mystics) to receive permission to initiate others: ~**e almak,** to show (mercy, severity *etc.*); ┌**bir az insafı ~ al!**┐, 'be a bit reasonable, show a little fairness!': ~**inin* altında,** in one's power: ~ **altından,** in an underhand way, secretly: ~ **atmak,** to lay hands upon; **bir işe ~ atmak,** to start, to take a matter up: ~ **ayak çekildi,** everyone had retired; the streets were deserted: ~**den ayaktan düşmüş,** crippled by illness *or* old age: ~**i ayağı tutar,** sound of limb, sturdy: ~ **bağlamak,** to join hands together *in a respectful attitude*: ~ **bakmak,** to read the hand *in palmistry*: ···**in ~ine bakmak,** to read *s.o.'s* hand; to depend on *s.o.* for one's living: ~**de bir,** a sure thing, a 'dead cert.'; **o ~de bir,** that's all right; there is no doubt we'll get it: ~**den bırakmak** (**çıkarmak**), to put down; to relinquish; to surrender *stg.*; 'insafı ~**den bırakma!**', 'don't be unreasonable!': ~**i boş,** empty-handed; without work; without means of subsistence: ~ **bulmak,** to find a helping hand: ~**i çabuk,** dexterous: ···**den ~ini (ayağını) çekmek,** to give up doing *stg.*; to withdraw from ...: **işten ~ çektirmek,** to suspend *s.o.* from a post: ~**den çıkarmak,** to get rid of *stg.*: ~**den çıkmak,** to be lost, to pass out of one's possession: ~**imde* değil,** it is not within my power; I can't help *doing stg.*: ~**den düşme,** secondhand, a bargain: ~**de baş başta,** in great confusion; very embarrassed: ~ ~**e,** hand in hand; ~ ~**e vermek,** to cooperate: ~**de etm.,** to obtain, to get hold of: **birine ~ etm.,** to beckon to *s.o.*: ~**den geçirmek,** to examine and clean or repair *stg.*: ~**den geçmek,** to be examined; to be overhauled: ~**e geçmek,** to come into one's possession: **ele geçmez,** not easily come by, not often met with: ~**den gelmek,** (i) to be possible for one; (ii) to tip; to pay: ~**inden* gelmek,** to be possible for one, to be within one's power: ┌~**den ne gelir?**┐, 'what can one do?': ~**lerde gezmek,** to be the fashion, to be the rage: ~**inden* gitmek,** to pass out of one's possession, to be lost: ~ **kaldırmak,** to show fight: ~**de kalmak,** to be left over; to remain unsold: ~**inde kalmak,** to remain undone; to be spoilt by delay: ~ **koymak,** to commandeer, to requisition: ~**inde* olm.,** to be within one's power: ~**inde* olmamak,** to be beyond one's power; ~**inde olmıyarak güldü,** he could not help laughing: **bir işte ~i***

olm., to have a finger in a matter : bir elden satılmak, to be sold *en bloc or* at one go : ~inden tutmak, to help : ~le tutulur, tangible : ~ üstünde gezmek, to be popular or beloved by the people : ~ üstünde tutmak, to treat with honour : ~de var bir (beş), ... and carry one (five) (*arith.*) : ~e vermek, to deliver up; betray, 'give away' : ~ vurmak, to clap the hands; to interfere, meddle with : işe ~ vurmamak, not to lift a finger to do stg. : ~de yapmak, to do *stg.* easily or offhand.

el² One other than oneself; people outside one's own family; people *in general* : a people, tribe : the country of a people or tribe; stranger. ~ evi, another's house : ~e (güne) karşı, in the presence of others, before all : babam ~ kapısında çobanlık etti, my father was a shepherd in another's service : ⌐~in geçtiği köprüden sen de geç¹, do as others do.

elâ Light-brown (eyes). açık ~, greenish-grey : gök ~, bluish-grey.

elâlem All the world, everybody; strangers.

elaltından (¹···) Secretly; in an underhand way.

el'aman Enough! ···den ~ demek, to have enough of, to be absolutely sick of.

el'an, elân Now, at present; still.

elarabası (¹····), –nı Hand-cart.

elâstikî Elastic. ~yet, –ti, elasticity.

elayak (¹··) *In* ~ çabalamak, to make every effort : ~ çekilmek, to be deserted (of streets at night) : ~ yürümek, to walk on all fours.

elbet (¹· *or* ·¹), **elbette** (··¹ *or* ¹··) Most certainly; decidedly.

elbezi (¹··), –ni Napkin; towel.

elbirliği (¹···), –ni Agreement; co-operation.

elbise *pl. of* libas. Clothes, garments.

Elcezire Mesopotamia.

elçabukluğu (¹····), –nu Sleight-of-hand; dexterity.

elçi Envoy; ambassador. büyük ~, Ambassador : orta ~, Minister.

eldeğirmeni (¹····), –ni Coffee-grinder.

eldiven Glove.

elebaşı (·¹··) Chief (of a bandit gang); ringleader.

eleğimsağma *For* alâimi sema, Rainbow. ~ altından geçmek, *v. App.*

elek Sieve. ~ten geçirmek, to sieve; to examine minutely.

elektrik Electricity. ~li, electric; live (wire).

elele (¹··) *In* ~ vermek, to shake hands; to agree; to work together.

elem Pain; suffering; illness; sorrow. ~ çekmek, to suffer pain or grief.

eleman Element; personnel.

eleme Sieved; sifted; selected. Act of sieving. ~ imtihanları, preliminary examination.

elemek *va.* Sift; sieve; inspect *or* search carefully; select : wind *yarn* into hanks.

elfatiha (·¹··) The opening chapter of the Koran; *the word engraved on every Moslem tombstone, hence* ~ *means* 'good-bye for ever' *to s.o. or stg.*

elfaz (·ᵛ) *pl. of* lâfız. Words *etc.*

elhak Truly, really, indeed.

elhamdülillah (·¹···) Thank God!

elhan (·¹) *pl. of* lâhin. Musical sounds; melodies.

elhasıl (¹–·) In short; in brief.

elhazer For God's sake, no!; beware!

elif The letter 'A' *in the Arabic alphabet; (elif is a vertical straight line, hence it gives the idea of thin and straight vertically).* ⌐~i görse mertek (direk) sanır¹, 'if he sees an elif he thinks it a post', *i.e.* quite illiterate : işin ~ini dahi bilmiyor, he doesn't know the rudiments of the business : saat ~i ~ine dokuz, it is exactly nine o'clock.

elifbe, elifba (··¹) Alphabet.

elîm (·¹) Painful; grievous.

elinsaf (···¹) 'Be reasonable!'

elişi (¹··), –ni Manual labour; handicraft. Hand-made.

elkab (·ᵛ) *pl. of* lâkab. Titles; nicknames.

elkâsibü *In* ⌐~ habibullah¹, 'an (honest) tradesman is beloved by God'.

ellem *In* ~ kömürü, hand-picked, selected charcoal.

elle·mek *va.* Handle; feel with the hand; pick out by hand; take by the hand and turn out. ~şmek *vn.* Take each other by the hand; shake hands; come to blows; try one another's strength by hand-grips.

elli¹ Having hands; having a handle.

elli² Fifty. ~nci, fiftieth. ~şer, fifty at a time; fifty each.

elma Apple; round thing. ~ şarabı, cider : ⌐bir ~nın bir yarısı biri, bir yarısı biri¹, as like as two peas : kızıl ~, *name given to a legendary and ideal land, sometimes referring to Rome* : ⌐yarım ~ gönül alma¹, 'a trifling present wins the heart' *(said when offering a present or stg. to eat).*

elma·baş, pochard. ~cık, small apple; hip-bone; high part of the cheek : ~ kemiği, cheek-bone. ~kürk, fur made of the cheek pieces of fox-skins. ~lık, apple orchard.

elmas Diamond; precious; beloved. ~çı, diamond-merchant. ~traş, cut glass; diamond glass-cutter; diamond-cutter (man).

elmasiye (·—¹) Fruit jelly.

eloğlu (¹··), –nu Stranger; outsider; other people.

elpençe *In* ~ **divan durmak,** to stand in an attitude of respect, *with the hands clasped in front.*

elsine *pl. of* **lisan.** Languages.

elti *The relationship between the wives of two brothers*; sister-in-law. ⌐**ortak gemisi yürür,** ~ **gemisi yürümez**⌐, fellow wives can get on with each other, but the wives of two brothers can't.

elulağı (¹···), **-nı** Anything the hand can reach; a thing at hand; tool; servant; assistant.

elvah (·⁴) *pl. of* **levha.** Tablets; plates.

elvan (·⁴) *pl. of* **levin.** Colours. Of various colours.

elveda (···¹) Farewell!, good-bye!

elveriş Sufficiency; suitability. ~**li,** sufficient; suitable, well-adapted; useful; convenient; profitable. ~**siz,** unsuitable; inconvenient.

elvermek *vn.* Suffice; be suitable; be useful; be convenient; happen; be current. **elverir!,** that's enough! : **fırsat elvermemek,** not to have the opportunity : **keseye elvermemek,** to be beyond one's means.

elviye *pl. of* **liva.** Banners; provinces.

elyaf (·⁴) *pl. of* **lif.** Fibres.

elyazısı (¹···), **-nı** Handwriting; manuscript.

elyevm Today; now.

elzem *comp. of* **lâzım.** More *or* most necessary. ~**iyet, -ti,** extreme urgency or necessity.

em'a (·¹) *pl. of* **mea.** Bowels, intestines.

emakin (·–¹) *pl. of* **mekân.** Places; houses.

emanat (·–⁴), **-tı** *pl. of* **emanet.** Deposits; sacred relics.

emanet (·–¹). **-ti** Anything entrusted to another; deposit; a government office receiving or paying out government money. ~ **hesabı,** deposit account : ~**e hiyanet,** breach of trust : **Allaha** ~**!,** farewell!; good-bye to ... . ~**çi,** person with whom a thing has been deposited for safe keeping or deliverance. ~**en** (·¹··), for safe keeping; on deposit; through the government direct, not by a third party.

emare (·–¹) Sign; mark; token; circumstantial evidence.

emaret (·–¹), **-ti** Chieftainship; territory of an emir.

emaye (*Fr. émaillé*) Enamel ware.

embiya *v.* **enbiye.**

embube (·–¹), **enbube** Pipe; tube.

emcik Nipple; teat.

emece By common effort; collectively.

emek Work; labour; trouble; fatigue. **emeği* geçmek,** to have contributed great efforts towards achieving *stg.* : ~**le ekmeği* kazanmak,** to work for one's living : ~

vermek (**çekmek**), to labour, to take great pains : **el emeği,** manual labour; workmanship. ~**çi,** worker; one who takes pains. ~**dar,** old servant; veteran. ~**daş,** fellow workman. ~**lemek,** to walk with difficulty; (of a baby trying to get about) to shuffle along. ‖~**li,** retired *officer etc.*; who has been long in service : pensioner : ~**ye ayırmak,** to pension off. ~**siz,** free from labour *or* fatigue; easy (life).

emel Longing; desire; ambition; thing wished for, ideal. ~ **etm.,** to long for; to aspire to. ~**siz,** unambitious.

emi *In such phrases as*: **kimseye söyleme** ~**!,** don't tell anyone, will you! ; **unutma** ~**!,** now don't forget!

emin Safe, secure; sure, certain; trustworthy. Steward; custodian; superintendent; controller. **bölük** ~**i,** quartermaster : **sandık** ~**i,** chief cashier.

emir, -mri Order, command; matter, business; event, case. ~ **atlısı,** mounted orderly : ~ **eri,** orderly; batman : **emri gaib,** the 3rd pers. sing. of the imperative : **emri hazır,** the 2nd pers. of the imperative : **emre hazır,** at hand for use; at disposal : ~ **kulu,** one who is under orders : ~ **subayı,** adjutant : **evvel** ~**de,** in the first place; first of all.

emîr (·¹) Emir; chief; commander. ~**ülmu'minin,** Commander of the Faithful (*title of the Caliphs*).

emirber Bearer of an order; orderly (*mil.*).

emircik kuşu, -nu Kingfisher.

emirname (···–¹) Written command; decree; *polite form for* 'your letter'.

emlâh (·⁴) *pl. of* **milh.** Salts.

emlâk, -ki *pl. of* **mülk.** Lands; possessions. ~**i miriye,** Crown lands.

emles Smooth.

emmare (··–¹) Imperious. **nefsi** ~, lust of the flesh.

emme Act of sucking. ~ **tulumba** suction pump.

emmek *va.* Suck. ⌐**anasından emdiği (süt) burnundan geldi**⌐, 'he paid for it'; 'he suffered for it' : **kanını** ~, to suck the blood of, to exhaust *or* despoil *s.o.*

emnüselâmet Peace and security.

emniyet, -ti Security; safety; confidence. ···**e** ~ **etm.,** to trust; ···**i** ···**e** ~ **etm.,** to entrust *stg.* to *s.o.* ~ **müdürü,** Chief of Police : ~ **somunu,** lock-nut. ~**li,** safe; trustworthy, reliable. ~**siz,** untrustworthy; insecure; unsafe; distrustful. ~**sizlik,** untrustworthiness; lack of confidence.

emoraji Haemorrhage.

emraz (·⁴) *pl. of* **maraz.** Illnesses; diseases.

emred Beardless; young.

emretmek (ᵛ··), **–eder** va. Command, order.

emri v. emir. **~hak, –kkı,** God's will, euphemism for 'death'. **~vaki** (···–ᵛ), 'fait accompli'; accomplished fact. **~yevmi,** order of the day.

emsal (·⁴), **–li** pl. of misil and mesel. Similars; likes; equals; proverbs, tales; coefficients; used as sing. a like; precedent. **~i misillû,** as in similar cases : ~ olmamak şartile, provided it is not regarded as a precedent : **~i var,** there are precedents for it : **~i yok,** there is no precedent; he has no equal : ⌈Allah **~i** kesiresile müşerref etsin!⌉, -may God honour us by many similar occasions! (said when visiting people on feast-days) : mevkice **~ler,** people of equal station in life. **~siz,** peerless; unequalled; unprecedented.

emtaa, emtia pl. of meta. Goods.

emvac (·⁴) pl. of mevc. Waves.

emval (·⁴), **–li** pl. of mal. Possessions; goods; riches.

emvat (·ᵛ) pl. of meyyit. The dead.

emzik Nipple; teat; baby's bottle; spout. **~lemek,** to fit a spout to a vessel. **~li,** having a teat or spout; with a child at breast (woman).

emzirmek va. Suckle.

en¹ Width; breadth. **~ince,** according to its width; across its width : **~ine boyuna,** widthwise and lengthwise; fully; tall, well-built (person) : ⌈**~ine çekmiş, boyuna çekmiş, buna karar verdi**⌉, 'he looked at it from all angles and then decided on this' : **~i konu** (gen. as one word), at length, fully, thoroughly : **~i sonu,** the long and the short of it : **~inde sonunda,** in the end, at last : ⌈**kimi ~ine çeker kimi boyuna**⌉, everyone has his own opinion.

en² Most; forms the superlative. **~ evvel,** before everything; first of all.

enam A book of prayers.

en'amlı Soft and tender.

enaniyet, –ti Egoism; pride; selfishness.

enayi Credulous. Fool. ~ **dümbeleği,** a prize idiot.

encam (·–ᵛ) End; result. ~ **bulmak,** to end, result : ~ **vermek,** to bring to an end, conclude. **~kâr** (·–ᵛ), at the end, finally.

encek, encik Puppy, kitten, cub; shin.

encümen Meeting; council; committee; assembly; heap.

endaht, –tı A throwing; a firing; discharge of a firearm.

endam (·–ᵛ) Body; shape; figure; symmetry; stature. arzı ~ **etm.,** to make an appearance, to present oneself. **~aynası, –nı,** full-length mirror. **~lı,** well-proportioned, graceful.

endaze (·–ᵛ) Measure; proportion; measure of about 26 in.

ender comp. of nadir. More or most rare; used between two adjectives to give emphasis, e.g. harab ~ harab, utterly ruined.

enderun Women's apartments of a palace; interior.

–endis Pers. suffix. Thinking of ...; **dur~,** far-sighted; **diğer~,** (who thinks of others) altruistic.

endişe (·–ᵛ) Thought; anxiety; doubt. **~li,** thoughtful, anxious, troubled.

endüstri Industry.

enek Castrated.

enemek va. Castrate.

enfes comp. of nefis. Most pleasing; choice, delightful, delicious.

enfiye Snuff. ~ **kutusu,** snuff-box.

enfüsî (···–ᵛ) Subjective (as opp. to âfakî, objective).

engebe Unevenness of ground; broken ground. **~li,** steep and broken (ground).

engel Obstacle; difficulty; handicap; rival.

enger, engersakızı Mastic; chewing-gum made from wild artichoke.

engerek Adder, viper. **~otu, –nu,** Viper's bugloss.

engin, Vast, boundless; the open sea; the high seas.

enginar Artichoke.

enhar (·⁴) pl. of nehir. Rivers.

enik The young of a carnivorous animal, whelp, cub, puppy etc.

enikonu Fully; at length. ~ **yoruldum,** I am thoroughly tired.

enin (·–ᵛ) Moan, groan.

enine v. en¹.

enis (·–ᵛ) Sociable. Companion.

enişte (·ᵛ·) Husband of an aunt or a sister.

enkaz Ruins; debris; wreck, wreckage. **~cı,** ship-breaker; house-breaker.

enli Wide, broad.

enmuzec (·–ᵛ) Specimen; pattern; model; type.

ensab¹ (·⁴) pl. of neseb. Relationships; races; origins.

ensab² (·⁴) pl. of nisbet. Ratios; proportions.

ensal (·⁴), **–li** pl. of nesil. Generations; children etc. **~i atiye,** future generations.

ense Back of the neck, nape; back. **~sine*** binmek, to persecute, to tyrannize : **~sinden*** gitmek, to follow s.o. closely : **~si kalın,** well-off; care-free; influential : ~ **kökü,** the lower part of the neck : ~ **kökünden gelmek,** to be very close behind one, on top of one : ⌈**~sine vur ekmeğini al elinden**⌉, 'hit him on the neck and take the bread out of his hand', used to describe a very mild person : ~ **yapmak,** to lead a lazy and comfortable life : **top** ~, hair kept full at the back.

enselemek *va.* Seize by the neck; collar.

enser Large nail.

ensice *pl. of* **nesic.** Tissues.

ensiz Without width; narrow.

entari Loose robe. **gecelik** ~, night-gown.

entipüften Insignificant; ridiculous; futile; flimsy.

entrika (·¹·) Intrigue; trick. ~ **çevirmek,** to resort to tricks, to intrigue.

enva (·−¹), **–aı** *pl. of* **nevi.** Sorts, kinds.

envanter Inventory.

enzar (·−¹) *pl. of* **nazar.** Looks; favours.

epcet *v.* **ebced.**

epey (¹·) Pretty good, pretty well; a good many; a good deal of. ~**ce** (¹··), fairly; to some extent; pretty well.

epher, epkem *v.* **ebher, ebkem.**

eprimek *vn.* (Of clothes) to wear thin.

epsem *v.* **ebkem.**

er¹ Man; male; husband; private *soldier* : a manly man; a capable man. ⌐~ **oyunu birdir¹,** once is enough; no need to try again : ~**e varmak,** (of a woman) to marry : ~**e vermek,** to give *a girl* in marriage : ~**oğlu** ~, hero : **iş** ~**i,** a good man for work : **oturduğu mevkiin** ~**i oldu,** he was fit to hold the position he did : **sözünün** ~**i,** a man of his word.

er² Early; soon. ~ **geç,** sooner or later.

eracif (·−¹) *pl. of* **ercaf.** False rumours; calumnies.

eramil (·−¹) *pl. of* **ermel.** Widows; poor women.

‖**erat, –tı** *pl. of* **er.** Private soldiers.

erazil *pl. of* **rezil.** Low, vile people.

erbaa Four.

erbab (·⅄) *pl. of* **rab.** Masters; *as Turkish sing.,* expert; *with izafet,* possessing ..., gifted with ..., *e.g.* ~**ı hüner,** talented, skilful. ~**ı bilir,** (the connoisseur knows it), first-class : **her işi** ~**ından sormalı,** in every matter one should take the advice of an expert : **işlerinin** ~**ı,** masters of their craft.

erbain Forty; *only used in Turkish to mean* the forty days of severe winter, *i.e.* 21 Dec. to 30 Jan. : ~**e girmek,** to hibernate.

‖**erbaş** Non-commissioned officer, N.C.O.

erce¹ (¹·) In a manly way.

erce² (·¹) Somewhat early.

erdeb *An Arab corn measure of* about 5 bushels.

erdemlik Virtue; ability.

erdirmek *va. caus. of* **ermek.** Cause to reach *or* attain. ···**e akıl** ~, to come to understand *stg.*

Erdun Jordan. **Maverayı** ~, Trans-Jordania.

Erem *v.* **İrem.**

eren One who has arrived at the truth; wise and virtuous man; *the pl. is used in the same sense and as a mode of address among dervishes.*

Erendiz The planet Jupiter.

erfane *v.* **arifane.**

erganun Organ (*mus.*).

ergeç¹, erkeç (·¹) Billy-goat.

ergeç² (¹·) Sooner or later.

ergen Youth of marriageable age; batchelor, celibate. ~**lik,** the pimples of puberty.

ergin Mature; ripe; adult.

erguvan Judas-tree; purple colour. ~**î** (···−¹), purple.

erik Plum.

erike Throne; bed; sofa.

erimek *vn.* Melt; fuse; pine away; (of a boil *etc.*) to subside, pass away; (of textiles) to wear out.

erincik Lazy; bashful, timid.

erinmek *vn.* Melt away; flag.

erişmek *vn.* Arrive; attain; mature; reach the age of marriage.

erişte (·¹·) Freshly made vermicelli.

eritmek *va.* Melt; dissolve; cause to waste away; squander.

erkân (·⅄) *pl. of* **rükün.** Rules; recognized rules of procedure or behaviour; high officials. ~ **heyeti,** staff (*mil.*) : ~ **kürkü,** fur cloak formerly presented by the Sultan to those promoted to the rank of Vezir : **usul** ~, the rules of good behaviour, 'savoir vivre'. ~**iharbiye,** General Staff (*mil.*).

erkeç, –çi He-goat.

erkek Man; male. Manly; virile; courageous; honest and true. ~ **canlısı,** a woman who is always running after men : ~ **demir,** hard iron. ~**lik,** masculinity, virility; manliness; courage. ~**si,** masculine (woman). ~**siz,** (of a woman) husbandless, without support.

erken Early. ~**ce,** rather early. ~**ci,** early-rising; who comes early.

erlik Masculinity; virility; bravery.

ermek *vn.* Reach; attain; arrive at maturity; reach religious perfection, become a saint. ···**e aklı*** ~, to comprehend or grasp *stg.* : ⌐**ayağı* suya** ~¹, for the feet to reach water, *i.e.* to know where one stands, to realize the position : ⌐**el ermez güc yetmez¹,** an impossibility : **kemale** ~, to reach perfection or completion.

Ermeni Armenian. ⌐~ **gelini gibi kırıtmak¹,** 'to be as coy as an Armenian bride', *i.e.* to hang back *or* be slow in doing stg. ~**ce,** the Armenian language. ~**stan,** Armenia.

ersiz Husbandless; destitute (woman).

erte, ertesi The following day *or* year, *etc.* **harb** ~**si**, post-war: **yarın** ~**si**, the day after tomorrow. ~**lemek**, to remain over till the next day; for the morrow to come.

ervah (·⸰) *pl. of* **ruh**. Spirits; souls. **ham** ~, coarse-minded.

erzak (·⸰), –**kı** *pl. of* **rızık**. Provisions; food.

erzan Cheap; worthy, proper, due. ~ **buyurmak**, to permit, to see fit.

erze, erz Cedar.

erzel *comp. of* **rezil**. More *or* most despicable.

esafil (·—⸰) The rabble, the lower classes.

esame Register of names, muster roll. ~**li**, enrolled.

esami *pl. of* **isim**. Names. ~**si okunmaz**, he is of no consequence.

esans (*Fr. essence*) Perfume.

es'ar (·⸰) *pl. of* **siir**. Current prices.

esaret (·—⸰), –**ti** Captivity; slavery.

esas (·⸰) Foundation; base; principle; essence. Principal, basic. ~**ında**, fundamentally: ~**ı yok**, there is no foundation for it (of a rumour *etc.*). ~**en** (·⸌·), fundamentally; essentially; in principle; from the beginning; besides; anyhow. ~**î**, fundamental; essential; principal: **kanunu** ~, constitution. ~**lanmak**, to be established; to be founded. ~**lı**, based; founded; secure; true; sure; principal; fundamentally right. ~**sız**, baseless; unfounded.

esatir (·—⸌) *pl.* Legends; stories; myths; mythology. ~**î** (·—–⸌), legendary; mythological.

esbab (·⸰) *pl. of* **sebeb**. Causes; reasons; means; requisites; materials. ~**ı mucibe**, motives; justification: ~**ı muhaffife**, extenuating circumstances: ~**ı mücbire**, 'force majeure'.

esbak Former; late; ex-.

esed The constellation Leo. ~**iye**, the felines.

esef Regret. ~ **etm.**, to regret, to be sorry. ~**â**, a pity!

esen Blowing; hale, hearty, robust. ~**lik**, health, soundness.

eser Sign; mark; trace; remains; monument; work (of art, literature *etc.*); effect; action. ... ~ **olarak**, as the result of ...: **bir talih** ~**i**, a piece of good fortune: **buralarda sudan** ~ **yok**, there is no trace of water hereabouts. ~**icedid** (····⸌), ~ **kâğıdı**, foolscap paper.

esfel *comp. of* **safil**. Lower, lowest. ~ **essafilin**, the lowest of the low.

eshab (·⸰) *pl. of* **sahib**. Possessors; companions; companions and disciples of the Prophet. ~**ı devlet**, men of wealth: ~**ı mesalih**, men of affairs, business men;

petitioners to a public office: ~**ı seyif**, men of the sword, warriors.

esham (·⸰) *pl. of* **sehim**. Arrows; shares, *esp.* shares of companies.

esinti Breeze.

esir Captive; prisoner of war; slave; a slave *to drink etc.* ~ **almaca**, the game of 'prisoners' base': **yatak** ~**i**, bed-ridden. ~**ci**, slave-dealer. ~**firaş** (····⸌), bed-ridden.

esîr The ether.

esirge·mek *va.* Protect; spare; grudge. ⸢**Allah esirgesin!**⸣, 'may God protect us!', 'God forbid!': **bunu benden esirgeme!**, do not grudge me this!: **dille ve parayla yapılacak hiçbir şeyi esirgemezdi**, he left nothing undone that words or money could do: **sözlerini esirgemedi**, he did not mince his words. ~**yici**, who protects or spares; grudging; stingy.

esirî Ethereal.

eskal[1] (·⸰), –**li** Heavy weights; burdens; baggage.

eskal[2] *comp. of* **sakil**. Very heavy; indigestible; very disagreeable (man); very ugly.

eski Old; ancient; chronic; out of date; worn; secondhand. ~**ler**, the ancients: ~**den**, of old: ⸢~ **ağza yeni taam (kaşık)**⸣, *said when eating the first dish of fruit etc. of the year*: ~**den beri**, from of old, for a long time past: ~**si gibi**, as of old: ~ **kafalı**, old-fashioned (person): ~ **maden**, genuine material; old china.

eski·ci, dealer in secondhand goods; old-clothes man; cobbler. ~**mek**, to be worn out; to grow old in service. ~**püskü**, old clothes; old and tattered things. ~**tmek**, to wear out; to cause to grow old.

eskrim (*Fr. escrime*) Fencing.

eslâf (·⸰) *pl. of* **selef**. Predecessors.

eslem *comp. of* **salim** and **selim**. More *or* most safe; most sure *or* certain.

eslemek *va.* Listen to; hear. **söz** ~, to take advice; to be obedient.

esliha *pl. of* **silâh**. Arms, weapons; armament *of a warship*. ~**i nariye**, fire-arms.

esma *pl. of* **isim**. Names; nouns; attributes of God. ⸢~**yı üstüne sıçratmak**⸣, to bring trouble upon oneself.

esman (·⸰) *pl. of* **semen**. Prices.

esmek *vn.* Blow (of the wind *etc.*); come by chance; (of unexpected good fortune) to befall; come into the mind. **esip savurmak**, to shout and bluster: **aklına*** ~, to occur to one: **akıllarına esti İstanbula gittiler**, they took it into their heads to go to İstanbul: **aklına eseni söylüyor**, he says whatever comes into his head.

esmer Dark complexioned; brunette.

esna Course; interval; time. ... ~**sında**, in

the course of ..., during ...: ~yı ikammette, in the course of the stay: o ~da, at that time, meanwhile.

esnaf *pl. of* sınıf. Classes; kinds; trades; guilds; *as sing.* tradesman; artisan; prostitute. ~ zihniyeti, the mentality of a shopkeeper; being commercially minded: ayak ~ı, pedlar. ~ça, mercenary; utilitarian.

esnan *pl. of* sin. Teeth; years of life; class of recruits.

esnek Elastic. ~lik, elasticity.

esne·mek *vn.* Yawn; stretch and recover shape; bend; yield. ~tmek, to cause to yawn; bore; to stretch; bend. ~yiş, yawn; elasticity.

esrar[1] *pl. of* sır. Secrets; mysteries. ~ kutusu (küpü) a man of mystery; mysterious person. ~engiz, ~lı, mysterious.

esrar[2] Hashish. ~keş, hashish addict.

esre Arabic vowel point for i.

esrik, esrük Drunk; over-excited. **esrimek** *vn.* Become drunk *or* very excited.

estağfurullah (·¹···) 'I ask pardon of God', *phrase used in reply to a compliment or an expression of politeness such as* 'bendeniz'; 'don't mention it!'

estaizübillâh (··¹···) 'I take refuge with God', *used to express indignation.*

estek *Only in conjunction with* köstek. ~ köstek etm., *or* ~ etmek köstek etm., to make all sorts of excuses to get out of doing stg.

ester Mule.

esvab *vulg.* espap. Clothes, clothing. ~cı, ready-made clothes merchant; secondhand clothes dealer. ~ başı, Keeper of the Wardrobe. ~lık, suitable for clothes.

esved Black.

eş One of a pair; a similar thing, a thing that matches another; mate; fellow; husband; wife. ~ dost, one's friends and acquaintances: ~i emsali görmemiş, unprecedented: ~ etm., to match: ~ olm., to be a match: ~ tutmak, to choose a partner: ~i yok, peerless.

eş'ar (·⁴) *pl. of* şiir. Poems.

eşarp (*Fr. écharpe*) Scarf; sash.

eşas (*Fr. échasse*) Stilt.

eşbeh *comp. of* şebih. More *or* most similar *or* suitable.

eşcar (·⁴) *pl. of* secer. Trees.

eşek Donkey, ass. ~ arısı, wasp, hornet, bumble-bee: ⌐~ başı mıyım?⌐, 'am I not worth listening to?' (*said as a reproach to those paying no attention to the speaker*): ⌐~ başı mısın?⌐, 'why don't you use your authority?': ⌐eşeğin kuyruğu gibi ne uzar ne kısalır⌐, 'like a donkey's tail he neither grows longer nor shorter', *said of people who make no progress* (*from incapacity or*

bad luck): ⌐~ sudan gelinceye kadar dövmek⌐, to thrash soundly: ~ şakası, a coarse practical joke: eşeğe ters bindirmek, to pillory, to show *s.o.* up: ⌐dilini ~ arısı soksun!⌐, 'may a wasp sting his tongue!' (*used when talking of a foul-mouthed person*).

eşek·çi, donkey driver. ~hıyarı, ~nı, squirting cucumber. ~lenmek, to make an ass of oneself. ~lik, silliness, asininity.

eşelemek *va.* Stir up; scratch about; hunt for; rummage. bir meseleyi ~, to rake up some matter; to seek out and inquire into it.

eşgal (·⁴), **~li** *pl. of* şügul. Occupations; affairs. tatili ~, strike *of workmen.*

eşhas (·⁴) *pl. of* şahıs. Persons; characters *in a play.*

eşik Threshold; entrance to a palace; bridge (of a violin *etc.*). eşiğini aşındırmak, to frequent a place constantly: birinin eşiğine gelmek, to petition *or* importune s.o.

eşinmek (Of animals) to scratch up the ground.

eşirra (···¹) *pl. of* şerir. Evil. Scoundrels.

‖**eşit** Equal, equivalent; the same.

eşk, ~ki Tears, weeping.

eşkâl, ~li *pl. of* şekil. Forms; figures. 'adamın ~ini tarif et!', 'describe the man's appearance!'

eşkıya *pl. of* şaki. Rebels; brigands; *also as sing.* Brigand. ~lık, rebellion; brigandage.

eşkin Canter. Cantering. ~ gitmek (yürümek), to canter.

eşkina, eşkine A Mediterranean fish (*Corvina nigra*).

eşme Shallowly dug. Water-hole.

eşmek *va.* Dig lightly; scratch up the ground. *vn.* Hurry off *to war or other duty.*

eşraf (·⁴) *pl. of* şerif. Descendants of the Prophet; notables *of a town etc.*

eşref *comp. of* şerif. More *or* most noble or eminent. ~ saat, the propitious moment.

eşsiz Matchless, peerless; without a mate.

eşya *pl. of* şey. Things; objects; furniture; luggage; belongings; goods. ~lı, furnished. ~sız, unfurnished.

et, ~ti Meat; flesh; pulp of a fruit *etc.* ~ bağlamak, (of a wound) to begin to heal up: ~i budu yerinde *or* ~ine dolgun, well-covered but not fat: ⌐~i ne, budu ne?⌐, what's the use of him; he's a poor creature: ⌐~i senin, kemiği benim⌐, 'his flesh is yours, his bones mine' (*said by a parent handing his son over to the care of a schoolmaster and meaning stg.* like 'don't spare the rod!'): ~le tırnak gibi, a very near relation; ~ tırnaktan ayırmak, to separate s.o. from his closest relations: başının* ~ini yemek, to worry the life out of s.o., to nag at him.

etabli (*Fr. établi*) *Only in* ~ Rumlar, Greeks settled in Istanbul.

etba, -aı *pl. of* tâbi. Followers; attendants; servants.

etek Skirt *of a garment*; foot *of a mountain*. eteği belinde, industrious, active (woman): ~ dolusu, in abundance: eteğine* düşmek, to fall at *s.o.'s* feet in entreaty; to turn to *s.o.* for help: eteği düşük, slovenly, slatternly: eteğine* sarılmak, to entreat *s.o.*: eteği temiz, honest: ~leri* tutuşmak, to be exceedingly alarmed: ~leri* zil çalmak, to be frightfully pleased: dünyadan elini* eteğini* çekmek, to retire from active life; to go into seclusion: eksik ~, woman, 'petticoats', eline eteğine doğru, chaste.

etek·lemek To kiss the skirt of *s.o. in respect or congratulation*; flatter; fan with the skirt. ~lik, skirt; material for a skirt.

etem *comp. of* tam. More *or* most perfect *or* complete.

etepetâ (·¹·–) Precocious (child); affectedly serious (adult).

eter Ether.

etfal, -li *pl. of* tıfıl. Children.

Eti Hittite.

etibba *pl. of* tabib. Physicians.

etiket, -ti (*Fr. étiquette*) Label, ticket; etiquette.

etinedolgun (·¹·) Plump, well-covered.

etkafalı (¹···) Thickheaded.

etkesimi (¹···) Carnival before Lent.

||etki Effect.

etli With meat in it (pilaf *etc.*); fleshy, plump. ~ budlu, well-furnished with flesh, strong: ~ye sütlüye karışmamak, not to worry about other people's affairs, to mind one's own business.

etmek (eder, ediyor, edecek *etc.*) *va.* Do; make; be worth; fetch *a certain price.* Etmek *is the verb most commonly used to make a composite verb, chiefly with Arabic nouns, e.g.* zannetmek, to think; sarfetmek, to spend; *when the noun is of two syllables, the noun and the verb are usually written separately, e.g.* hizmet etmek, to serve; telefon etmek, to telephone. ⌐eden bulur⌐, one pays for what one does: çocuk oynamadan edemez, a child must play, cannot do without games: insan susuz nasıl edebilir?, how can a man live without water?: birini bir şeyden ~, to cause s.o. to lose stg., to deprive s.o. of stg.

etraf (·⁴) *pl. of* taraf. Sides; ends; directions; regions; surroundings; the world around; relatives; details; circumstances. ···in ~ında, around ...: ~ta, in the neighbourhood, around: ~tan, from all around, from all directions: ···in ~ını almak, to surround: ~u eknaf, all the surrounding

country: ~a haber vermek, to give general notice: bu ~ ahalisi, the people of these parts. ~lı, detailed; long-winded. ~lıca (·¹··), fully, with all details; (···¹), fairly detailed; in rather a detailed manner.

etsiz Without meat; thin.

etsuyu (¹··), -nu Gravy; meat broth.

ettirmek *va. caus. of* etmek. Cause to do *etc.*

etvar (·⁴) *pl. of* tavır. Modes; manners. ~ satmak, to give oneself airs.

etyaran Deep-seated whitlow.

ev House, dwelling; home; household; family; compartment, pigeon-hole. ~ açmak, to set up house: ~ bark, house and family: ~ bark sahibi, a family man: ~ ekmeği, home-made bread: ~ eşyası, household effects: ~ kadını, housewife, a woman who looks after her home properly: ~ halkı (takımı), household (family and servants): ~ sahibi, master *or* mistress of a house; proprietor of a house, landlord: ⌐~lere şenlik!⌐, 'joy to houses!', *a phrase used when mentioning a death or disaster and meaning stg. like* 'may Heaven save you from such disaster!': ~ yapıcı, bringing domestic happiness: ~ yıkmak, to cause domestic infelicity, to break up a home: ahret ~i, the next world: kara ~, tent of black felt *used by the nomad tribes of Central Asia.*

evail (·–¹) *pl. of* evvel. Beginnings; early times; first ten days of a month; the ancients; chief men. ~da, in ancient times.

evamir (·–¹) *pl. of* emir. Commands; edicts.

evani (·–⁴) *pl. of* aniye. Vessels, pots, dishes.

evbaş *pl. of* vebeş. Roughs, hooligans.

evc Apogee; summit.

evca (·⁴), -aı *pl. of* veca. Pains.

evce, evcek (¹·) All the family. With *or* by all the family.

evci Boarder at a school who spends the week-end at home.

evcimen¹, evciment (*for* encümen). Thronged; full.

evcimen² Fond of one's home, domesticated; thrifty.

evdirmek *v.* ivdirmek.

evel *and derivatives v.* evvel *etc.*

evermek *va.* Cause to marry; give in marriage.

evet (¹·) Yes. ~efendimci, yes-man. ~lemek, to say 'yes'; to keep saying 'yes, yes!'

evgin, ivgin Hurried; in a hurry.

evham (·⁴) *pl. of* vehim. Apprehensions; illusions; hypochondria. ~ getirmek, to become a hypochondriac, to have a nervous breakdown. ~lı, full of false apprehensions; hypochondriac.

evirmek va. Only in ~ çevirmek, to turn stg. over and over; look about one in hesitation; explain in the wrong way; invert, turn inside out. evire çevire dövmek, to thrash soundly: bir şeyi dilinin altında ~ çevirmek, to have stg. one wishes to say but can't get out.

ev'iye pl. of **via**. Blood-vessels; veins.

evkaf (·⁴) pl. of **vakıf**. Pious foundations; estates in mortmain; the government department in control of these estates.

evlâ (·⁻) Better; preferable; most suitable.

evlâd (·⁴) pl. of **veled**. Children; descendants; as sing. child, son. ~ acısı, grief for the loss of a child: ~ edinmek, to become a parent; to adopt a child. ~iyelik, heirloom; a thing that will last for many years. ~lık, quality of a child; adopted child: evlâdlığa kabul etm., to adopt.

evlek Furrow; the quarter of a dönüm; draining ditch in a field.

evlenme Marriage. ~k, to marry: ... üstüne ~, to marry in addition to ... .

evleviyet, -ti Preference. ~le, all the more; so much the sooner.

evli Married; having houses. ~ barklı, married and having a family: elli ~ köy, a village of fifty houses.

evliya (···⁻) pl. of **veli**. Guardians; relatives; saints; as sing. saint. ~ otu, sainfoin: ~yı umur, the heads of the administration. ~lık, saintliness; fitted to be a saint; innocent, ingenuous.

evrad (·⁴) pl. Flowers; roses.

evrak (·⁴), -kı pl. of **varak**. Leaves; documents, papers, archives. ~ ~, in sheets: ~ı nakdiye, paper-money: ~ı resmiye, official documents.

evram (·⁴) pl. of **verem**. Tumours; consumptives.

evrenk, evrent. Throne.

evsaf (·⁴) pl. of **vasıf**. Qualities; qualifications.

evvel, evel (evel and its derivatives can be spelt with one **v** or two) First; former; foremost; initial. The first part; beginning. Before. First; ago; formerly. ~den, from former times; beforehand, previously: ~ Allah sonra .... 'firstly God, then ...', in such sentences as: '~ Allah sonra sizin sayenizde bu işi buldum', 'it is solely due to you (after God) that I got this job': ~ ve ahır, formerly; on several occasions: ~ ve ahırını bilirim, I know him very well; I know all about him (it): ~ zaman, in olden times, long ago: aklı ~, very clever: beş sene ~, five years ago: bir an ~, as soon as possible: bundan ~, before this,

previously: en ~, first of all, before anything else: gitmezden (gitmeden) ~, before going.

evvel·â (¹··) firstly. ~allah (··¹–), (with the help of God), certainly, surely; v. also under **evvel**: ⌈~bu işi iki günde yaparım⌉, 'I don't think there is any doubt I can do this job in two days'. ~beevvel (·¹···), first of all. ~ce (·¹·), a little time before; previously; a little way in front. ~emirde (·¹···), in the first place, first of all. ~i, previously, of old. ~iyat, -tı, origins; rudiments, first principles, preamble. ~ki, ~si (·¹·), first, former: ~ gün, the previous day; the day before yesterday: ~ sene, the previous year; the year before last.

evza, -aı pl. of **vaz'ı**. Postures; gestures. ~ satmak, to give oneself airs.

ey O!; well!; hi!: eh!

eyalet (·–¹), -ti Province.

eyer Saddle.

eyi, eyici v. **iyi, iyici**.

eylemek va. Do; used in compound verbs as etmek; neyleyim?, what shall I do?; what am I to do!

eylûl, -lü September.

eytam (·⁴) pl. of **yetim**.

eytmek va. Say; recite.

Eyub The prophet Job; a suburb of Istanbul, wherein is situated the Mosque of Eyub.

eyvah Alas!

eyvallah (¹··) Yes; so be it!; thanks! ~ı olmamak, to be obliged to no one: buna da ~, God's will be done!: kimseye ~ etmezdi, he sought nobody's favour: her şeye ~ demek, to agree with everything that is said.

eyyam pl. of **yevm**. Days. ~ı bahur, the dog days: ~ reisi, fair-weather sailor; time-server: bir ~, at one time, formerly.

ez Pers. prep. From.

eza¹ Vexation; torment.

eza², ezacı for **ecza, eczacı**.

ez'af¹ (·⁴), pl. of **zııf**. Multiples; doubles.

ez'af² comp. of **zayıf**. Most weak; poorest.

ezan The call to prayer by a muezzin.

ezber By heart. ~den, (i) by heart; (ii) without knowing: ~ etm., to learn by heart: ~e gitmek, to proceed blindly without knowing where one is going: ~e konuşmak, to talk about stg. without understanding it: ~ okumak, to recite from memory. ~ci, one who learns by heart easily or in a parrot-like way. ~lemek, to learn by heart, to con.

ezcanüdil (··⁻··) With heart and soul; from the bottom of the heart.

ezcümle (¹··) For instance; among other things.

ezdad (·ᵛ) *pl. of* zıd. Opposites; contraries.

ezel Eternity in the past. ∼den, without hesitation. ∼î (···⸜), eternal (without beginning). ∼iyet, −ti, having the quality of eternity in the past: ∼aten ebediyete, from all past time till all future time; without beginning or end.

ezgi Tune, song. ⌐ince ∼ fıstıkı makam⌐, lazily and slowly.

ezgil A kind of medlar.

ezgin Crushed; trampled on; oppressed.

ezhan (·*) *pl. of* zihin. Minds; opinions.

ezhar (·ᵛ) *pl. of* zehir. Flowers.

ezher From every ... : ∼ cihet, from every direction; in every respect.

ezici Crushing. ∼ faikiyet, crushing superiority.

ezik Crushed: squashed. ∼büzük, (fruit) spoilt by crushing in transit.

ezilmek *vn. pass. of* ezmek. Be crushed, oppressed *etc.* içi (yüreği) ∼, to feel a sinking sensation in the stomach *from hunger etc.*

ezinti Sensation of sinking in the stomach; faintness; breakdown.

eziyet, −ti Injury; ill-treatment; pain; vexation; torture. ∼li, fatiguing; vexatious; painful.

ezkaza (ᵗ··) By chance; by hazard; accidentally.

ezkiya *pl. of* zeki. Clever people.

ezme Action of crushing *etc.*; something crushed; paste. **badem** ∼si, almond paste: **patates** ∼si, mashed potatoes.

ezmek *va.* Crush; pound; triturate; bruise; reduce to poverty *or* impotence. ⌐ez de suyunu iç!⌐, (i) 'take it back, I don't want it!' (*in returning a gift in anger or rejecting an offer*); (ii) 'you can write that off!', 'it's worthless!'

ezmine *pl. of* zaman. Times.

Ezrail (·−ᵗ) The angel of death.

ezrak Blue.

ezvak (·ᵛ), −kı *pl. of* zevk. Tastes; pleasures.

F

faal (·⸜) Active; industrious. ∼iyet (·−ᵗ), −ti, activity; energy; industry.

fabrika (·ᵗ·) Factory. ∼ işi, machinemade goods. ∼cı, manufacturer.

facia (−·ᵗ) Tragedy; drama; disaster. ∼lı, tragic; terrible.

fâcir (−ᵗ) Dissolute.

faça (ᵗ·) A turning about; volte-face.

façeta (·ᵗ·) *v.* faseta.

façuna (·ᵗ·) The serving or whipping *of a rope.*

fağfur *Ancient title of the Emperor of China:* porcelain. *v.* dokunmak.

fahim, −hmi Charcoal; coal; carbon.

fahîm (·⸜) Great, grand; illustrious. ∼ane (·−−ᵗ), in a grand or majestic manner; illustrious: zatı ∼iniz, Your Highness.

fahir, −hri Glory; pride; excellence. fahri âlem, 'the glory of the world', *i.e.* Mohammed.

fâhir (−ᵗ) Who glories in his deeds; glorious; sumptuous.

fahiş (−ᵗ) Immoral; obscene; excessive. ∼e (−·ᵗ), harlot.

fahiz, −hzi Thigh.

fahrî (·⸜) Honorary.

fahur (·⸜) Boasting; self-glorifying.

faide (−·ᵗ) *v.* fayda.

faik (−ᵗ) Superior; preferable; excellent. ∼iyet (−··ᵗ), −ti, superiority; excellence.

fail (−ᵗ) Who does or acts; author; agent;

maker; subject *of a verb.* ismi ∼, present participle active; noun of the agent. ∼iyet (−··ᵗ), −ti, action; activity; efficiency; influence.

faiz (−ᵗ) Interest *on capital.* ···i ∼i işlemek, for stg. to bear interest : ∼e yatırmak, to put out at interest : yüzde on ∼, interest at ten per cent.

fak *Only in* ∼a basmak, to make a false step, to be deceived.

fakat (ᵗ·) But; only; exclusively.

fakfo German silver.

fakırn, krı Poverty.

fakîh, fakıh Moslem jurist; learned.

fakir Poor. Pauper; 'your humble servant'. ∼ane (···ᵗ), pertaining to a poor man; poor; humble. ∼hane (···ᵗ) 'the poor man's house', *i.e.* my house. ∼lik, poverty.

fakr·üddem Anaemia. ∼ühal, ∼ kağıdı, certificate showing the holder is without means of subsistence. ∼u, ∼ sefalet, utter poverty.

fal Omen, augury; fortune. ∼ açıcı, soothsayer, fortune-teller: ∼ açmak *or* ∼a bakmak, to tell a fortune: ∼ tutmak, to take an omen, to draw a lot: el ∼ı, fortune told from the hand: falı hayır, good omen; of good omen. ∼cı, fortune-teller: el ∼lığı, palmistry.

falaka (·ᵗ·) Piece of wood to which the

feet of the victim of bastinado are tied; whippletree. ~ya çekmek, to subject *s.o.* to bastinado.

falan *v.* filân.

falçeta (·¹·) Curved shoemaker's knife.

falname (·–¹) Book of omens or oracles.

falso (¹·) False note; error. ~ vermek, to make a slip; to fall into error.

faltaşı (¹··), –nı A pebble or bean from which an omen is taken. gözünü ~ gibi açmak, to stare in amazement: gözü ~ gibi açılmak, to learn by bitter experience.

falya (¹·) Touch-hole of a muzzle-loading gun. ~ çivilemek (tıkamak), to spike a gun.

fâm (–) Colour; shade.

familya (·¹·) Family; wife.

fanfan *Popular expression for* talking French.

fâni Transitory; fleeting; decaying; mortal. ~lik, a being transitory *or* perishable.

fanilâ (·¹·) Flannel; flannel vest; blanket.

fantaziye Ostentation, display; fancy goods.

fantezi Fancy goods; (*rarely*) fancy, imagination.

fanus (–¹) Lantern; lamp-glass.

far (*Fr. phare*) Head-light *of a motor-car.*

faraş Dust-pan; dust-bin; sweeper; unchaste woman.

faraz·a (¹··) Supposing that .... ~î (··¹) hypothetical. ~iye, *pl.* ~iyat, supposition, hypothesis.

farbala (¹··) Furbelow; flounce; fringe.

fare (–¹) Mouse; rat. ⌈~ deliğe sığmamış, bir de kuyruğuna kabak bağlamış⌉, 'the mouse couldn't squeeze into the hole and anyhow he had a pumpkin tied to his tail' (*to describe a complication to an already difficult situation*): ⌈ki (içine) ~ düşse başı yarılır⌉, 'so (empty) that if a mouse fell in he would crack his head'.

farfara Empty-headed braggart; windbag. ~lık, frivolity; idle brag.

fariğ (–¹) Who transfers (property *etc.*); free from work, at leisure; exempt from; empty; at peace. ~ olm., to cease from work; to be free from; to cede possession; to renounce.

farik (–¹) Distinguishing; separate; distinctive. ~a (–·¹), *fem.* of farik: peculiarity; character: alameti~, distinctive mark; trade mark. ~avî (–··¹), characteristic.

faris (–¹) Mounted. Horseman.

Faris (–¹) The province of Fars; Persia. ~î (–·¹), Persian. ~iyat (–··¹), –tı, Persian literature and culture.

fariza (·–¹) Religious duty; binding obligation; legal share of inheritance.

fark, –kı Difference, distinction; dis-

crimination. ~ gözetmek, to discriminate, treat differently: ~ında mısın?, do you notice?; do you realize?: ~ında olm., to be aware: ~ına varmak, to become aware, to perceive, realize, understand: ~ vermek, to give change (money): akçe ~ı, rate of exchange. ~etmek (¹··), –eder, to distinguish, perceive; differ; alter. ~lı, different; changed; better: ~ farksız, hardly distinguishable: ~ tutmak, to discriminate, to treat differently. ~sız, indistinguishable; without difference; equal. ~sızlık, resemblance; equality.

farmason Freemason. ~luk, freemasonry.

Fars Persia; ~ça, Persian language.

fart, –tı Excess; abundance; exaggeration. ~ı mesai, overwork: ~ı nezaket, overpoliteness.

farta furta (¹···) Brag; empty threats. ~ ~sız, simply; without bragging.

farz Religious precept; binding duty; hypothesis, supposition. Binding, obligatory. ~ı ayın, a duty which must be observed by all: ~ı kifaye, a religious duty, the observance of which by some will absolve the rest, *hence* stg., the performance of which is not very important, *or* a duty which is sure to be fulfilled by some and therefore neglected by others: ~ı muhal, supposing the impossible; in the improbable event of.

farzetmek (¹··), –eder *va.* Suppose. farzedelim, let us suppose.

Fas Morocco; Fez. ~lı, Moroccan, Moorish.

fasafiso (··¹·) Nonsense.

fasahat (·–¹), –tı Purity of speech; correctness *in speaking a language*; eloquence.

faseta (·¹·) Facet.

fasıl, –slı Subdivision; chapter; section; decision; season; musical performance; slander. ·· in hallü faslı, the settlement *of a dispute etc.*: ~ heyeti, the orchestra (in Oriental music).

fâsıl (–¹) Separating, dividing. hattı ~, dividing line, boundary. ~a, separation; partition; interval; interruption: ~ vermek, to have an interval or a temporary stop; to interrupt: bilâ ~, uninterruptedly. ~alı, with breaks or interruptions: with partitions. ~asız, continuous, uninterrupted.

fasır *In such expressions as*: çocuğun bütün vücudü ~ ~ kabardı, swellings came out all over the child's body.

fâsid (–¹) Corrupt; vicious; perverse; false; mischievous. ~ daire, vicious circle.

fasih (·¹) Correct and distinct (speech); eloquent.

fâsik (–¹) Impious; lewd; depraved.

fasile (·–ᴵ) Botanical order; classification.
fasletmek (ᴵ··), **–eder** va. Separate; divide; decide (a case); solve (a problem); malign, traduce.
fassal Backbiter; one who always 'runs down' others.
fasulya, fasulye (·ᴵ·) Bean. **ayşe kadın ~sı** or **taze ~**, French beans: **çalı ~sı**, runner-beans: ⌐**kendini ~ gibi nimetten saymak**⌐, (to think that one is a heaven-sent gift like beans), i.e. to think oneself very important.
faş (–) Divulged; commonly talked about. **aman ~ olmasın!**, I hope to goodness it doesn't get about. **~etmek, –eder,** to divulge; to betray (a secret).
faşır faşır Imitates the noise of splashing water. **~tı**, a splashing noise.
fatanet (·–ᴵ), **–ti** Intelligence.
fâtır (–ᴵ) Creator.
fâtih Conqueror; the title of Mahomet II, the conqueror of Constantinople; the quarter of Istanbul round the Fatih Camii, the Conqueror's Mosque. **~a** (–·ᴵ), the opening chapter of the Koran; opening or beginning of an undertaking; decision: ···**e ~ demek**, to 'say good-bye' to s.o. or stg., to give up as lost: **~ okumak**, to recite the fatiha, to pray for the soul of s.o.; to give up as lost. **~ân** (–·⁻ᴵ), conquerors, i.e. those who were present at the conquest of Constantinople: **~ evlâdındandı,** he belonged to a family that came in with the conquest (as we say 'his family came over with the Conqueror').
fatin Intelligence. (·⁻ᴵ) Intelligent; sagacious. **Fatin Hoca**, weather prophet (allusion to a Director of the Istanbul Observatory, who bore that name).
Fatma Fatima (Mohammed's daughter). ⌐**kabaramazsın kel ~** (annen güzel sen çirkin⌐, rhyme chanted by children to annoy a turkey and make it puff itself out, used of petty attempts to annoy.
fatura (·ᴵ·) Invoice; book of samples.
fava Broad beans mashed and eaten cold with oil and lemon juice.
favl Foul (in a game).
favori Whiskers.
fay (Fr. faille) Geological fault.
fayda, faide Use; profit; advantage. **~?**, what's the use?: **~ yok**, it's no use; there's nothing to be done: ···**in ~sı dokunur**, it is useful or profitable. **~cılık**, utilitarianism. **~lanmak**, ···**den ~**, to derive a profit from; to make use of; to profit by. **~lı**, useful; profitable; advantageous. **hem ~ hem istifadeli**, both useful and profitable. **~sız**, useless; in vain; unprofitable.

fayrap, faryap (ᴵ·) (Fire up!), order to a ship's engineer to stoke up for maximum speed. **~ etm.**, to stoke up; to get to work quickly on a thing.
faz Phase (elect.).
fazahat (·–ᴵ), **–tı** Shame; disgrace.
fazail (·–ᴵ) pl. of fazilet. Virtues; good qualities.
fazayih (·–ᴵ) pl. of faziha.
fazıl, –zlı Superiority; merit; ability; learning; munificence. **erbabı ~**, men of culture. **fâzıl** (–ᴵ), virtuous; munificent; erudite.
faziha (·–ᴵ) Shameful act; crime.
fazilet (·–ᴵ), **–ti** Merit; excellence; superiority. **~kâr, ~li**, virtuous, excellent.
fazla Remainder; balance; excess. Excessive; superfluous. Beside; more (than). Too much; very much. **~sile**, abundantly: ⌐**~ mal göz çıkarmaz**⌐, you can't have too much of a good thing: **~ olarak**, moreover, furthermore: ⌐**her şeyin ~sı ~**⌐, 'enough is as good as a feast'. **~laşmak**, vn. to increase.
febiha (ᴵ·–) Well and good!; so much the better!
fecaat (·–ᴵ), **–ti** Calamity.
fecayi (·–ᴵ), **–ii** pl. of facia. Disasters; tragedies.
feci (·⁻ᴵ) Painful; tragic. **~a** (·–ᴵ), grievous calamity, tragedy.
fecir, –cri Dawn. **Fecri âti,** name given to a school of writers about the beginning of the 20th century: **fecri kâzib**, false dawn: **şimal ~i**, Aurora Borealis.
feda (·–) Ransom; sacrifice. **~ etm.**, to sacrifice: **~ olm.**, to be sacrificed: **~ olsun**, I will gladly make this sacrifice. **~i** (·–⁻ᴵ), one who sacrifices his life for a cause; patriot; revolutionary. **~ilik** (·–·ᴵ), self-sacrifice; devotion. **~kâr**, (·–ᴵ), self-sacrificing; self-denying; devoted. **~kârlık**, self-sacrifice; abnegation; devotion.
feddan Superficial measure used in Egypt, being as much as a pair of oxen can plough in a day, about 1 acre.
fehamet (·–ᴵ), **–ti** Greatness; eminence. **~lû**, title given to the Grand Vizier; His Excellency, His Highness.
fehim, –hmi Understanding; intelligence. **fehîm** (·⁻ᴵ), intelligent.
fehmetmek (ᴵ··) va. Understand.
fehva (·⁻ᴵ) Tenor, import. **~sınca**, as the saying goes; with the meaning of.
fek¹, –kki Jaw.
fek², –kki Dislocation; a breaking; a setting free; redemption (of a pledge). **~ki rabıta**, rupture of relations; also physical separation. **~ketmek** (ᴵ··), **–eder,** to dislocate, break open; undo.

felâh (·⁴) Prosperity; deliverance; security. ~ **bulmaz,** hopeless (drunkard *etc.*).

felâhat (·–¹), **–ti** Agriculture.

felâket (·–¹), **–ti** Disaster, catastrophe. ~**li,** disastrous. ~**zede,** victim of a disaster; involved in a calamity.

felâsife (·–·¹) *pl. of* **feylesof.** Philosophers.

felc Paralysis. ~**e uğramak,** to be paralysed (of a public service *etc.*).

felek The firmament; the heavens; fortune, destiny. ~**ten bir gün aşırmak (çalmak),** to pass a very enjoyable day: ⌈~ **bunu da çok gördü**⌉, fate has denied me this: **feleğin çemberinden geçmiş,** who has suffered the ups and downs of fortune; who has seen life: ~**ten kâm almak,** to have a very good time: ⌈~ **kimine kavun yedirir, kimine kelek**⌉, Fate deals kindly with some, unkindly with others: **feleğin sillesini yemiş,** who has suffered the buffetings of fate. ~**iyat, –tı,** astronomy. ~**zede,** unlucky, unfortunate.

Felemenk (·¹·) Holland; Dutchman. ~**li,** Dutch; Dutchman. ~**taşı** (··¹··), **–nı,** diamond.

felenk *v.* **filenk.**

felfelek Betel-nut.

fellâh Agriculturalist; Egyptian peasant; Egyptian; negro.

fellek, fellik ~ ~, running confusedly in all directions. ~ ~ **aramak,** to search high and low.

felsef·e Philosophy. ~**î** (··¹), philosophical. ~**iyat, –tı,** philosophical science *or* works.

fem, –mmi Mouth; opening. ~**mî,** oral.

fen, –nni Science; art; sort, variety; branch of science; ruse. ~**ni harb,** the art of war: ~ **kıt'ası,** technical troops.

fenâ (·⁻) Extinction; dissolution; death. ~ **bulmak,** to come to an end, to die, to decay. **darı ~,** this transient world.

fena (·⁻) Bad; ill; unpleasant. Bad thing. **işin ~sı bu ki,** the worst of it is that: ~**ya çekmek,** to take stg. in a bad sense: ~ **etm.,** to do evil; to do *stg.* badly: ~ **olm.,** to feel bad; to feel like fainting: ~**ya sarmak,** to take a turn for the worst: ~**ya varmak,** to go from bad to worse: **bu iş ~ma gitti,** this business has exasperated me. ~**laşmak,** to become worse, deteriorate, be aggravated; go bad. ~**lık,** evil; bad action; injury: **birine ~ gelmek,** for s.o. to feel ill.

fend (*corr. of* **fen**) Trick, ruse. ⌈**kadının ~i erkeği yendi**⌉, 'woman's wiles are too much for a man'.

fener Lantern; street-lamp; lighthouse; pinion *of a shaft.* ~ **alayı,** torchlight procession: ~ **çekmek,** to light the way with a lantern: ~ **dubası,** lightship: ~

gövdesi, headstock *of a lathe*: ~ **kasnak,** cone-pulley: ~ **mili,** spindle *of a lathe,* mandrel: ⌈~**i nerde söndürdün?**⌉, 'where did you put your lantern out?', *said jokingly to one who arrives late.* **gündüz ~i** (*sl.*), negro. ~**balığı, –nı,** angler fish. ~**böceği, –ni,** (?) glow-worm; (?) a kind of moth. ~**li,** having a lantern; member of the **Fenerbahçe** Sports club; Phanariot (member of the old Greek aristocracy).

Fenike (·¹·) Phoenicia. ~**li,** Phoenician.

fenimelmatlûb (·¹·–) So much the better!

fenn·en (¹·) Scientifically; technically. ~**enmek,** to be experienced (in evil). ~**î** (·⁻), scientific; technical.

fer Pomp; display; splendour, radiance; lustre; ornament.

ferace (·–¹) *A kind of* overall *formerly worn by Turkish women when they went out*; cloak *worn by ulema.* ~**lik,** material suitable for such garments.

ferağ (·⁴) Renunciation; cession (of property *etc.*); leisure; tranquillity. ~ **etm.,** to cede, transfer, give up. ~**at** (·–¹), **–tı,** abandonment (of a project, of work *etc.*); renunciation; self-sacrifice; abnegation; a being free from care or work: ~ **etm.,** to abdicate, renounce, give up; be at ease: ~**i nefis,** self-sacrifice; abnegation. ~**atkâr,** self-sacrificing: ~ **mesai,** devoted efforts.

ferah Spacious; open; roomy; cheerful. Easily, with room to spare. Cheerfulness, joy, pleasure. ~ ~, amply: **içi* ~,** cheerful, in a good humour. ~**feza** (·¹·–), pleasant. ~**lanmak,** to become spacious or airy; become cheerful; enjoy oneself. ~**lık,** spaciousness, airiness; cheerfulness, enjoyment; distraction; relief. ~**nak,** cheerful, gay; an air in Oriental music.

ferahi (·–¹) Small metal disk *formerly worn by soldiers on the fez*; metal plate *worn by military police on the collar.*

feraiz (·–¹) *pl. of* **fariza.** Sacred duties; shares of inheritance *allowed by Moslem law.* **ilmi ~,** the branch of Moslem jurisprudence dealing with inheritance.

fer'an, fer'en (¹·) As a side issue; as a secondary matter.

feraset, –ti Sagacity, intuition. ~**li,** sagacious, perspicacious.

ferc Vulva.

ferce Gap; breach; opening. ~**yab** (··⁻), finding a respite; finding a means or opportunity of escaping.

ferd Person, individual; odd number. Single; unique, peerless; odd (number). ~**en** (¹·), individually, one by one (*also* **ferdaferd**). ~**î,** *a.,* individual. ~**iyet, –ti,** individuality. ~**iyetçi,** individualist. ~**iyetçilik,** individualism.

ferda (·-́) The morrow, the next day; the future. ∼**sı,** the next day.

fere Chick of any game bird.

feres Horse; knight *at chess.* ∼**i a'zam,** the constellation Pegasus. ∼**î** (··-́), equine.

ferhenk Wisdom; knowledge; lexicon.

feri, -r'i Branch, ramification; secondary matter. **fer'î** (·-́), derived; secondary. **mahsulü** ∼, by-product.

feribot (¹··), **-tu** Ferry-boat; train ferry.

ferid (·-́) Solitary; unique.

ferifte Deceived, duped.

ferih (·-́) Cheerful, happy. ∼ **fahur yaşamak (geçinmek),** to live in great comfort, to be very well off.

ferik¹ (·-́) Divisional General.

ferik² Chick of any game bird; toasted grains of wheat; any small thing. ∼ **elması,** a kind of small apple.

-ferma (·-́) *Pers. suffix.* Commanding ...; compelling ...; *e.g.* **hande**∼, mirth-compelling, ridiculous.

ferma (¹·) *In* ∼ **etm.,** *or* **durmak,** (of a sporting dog) to point or set.

ferman Command; firman; decree; imperial edict. ∼ **sizin,** with pleasure; as you will: **hasbül**∼, in accordance with the Imperial command: ⌐**tozdan dumandan** ∼ **okunmuyor¹,** the situation is so confused that one can do nothing.

ferman·ber, one who faithfully carries out an order. ∼**dih,** ∼**ferma,** who issues commands; rulers. ∼**lı,** provided with an imperial order; one against whom an edict has been issued; outlaw.

fermejüp Snap-fastener.

fermene (¹··) Short waistcoat ornamented with braid.

ferraş (·-́) Servant who makes beds, beats carpets *etc.*; sacristan.

fers Horse; knight *at chess.* ∼**ülbahir,** hippopotamus.

-fersa (·-́) *Pers. suffix.* Rubbing ...; corroding ...; wearing out ...; **tahammül**∼, (exhausting the endurance), unbearable; **can**∼, (fretting life), annoying.

fersah League; an hour's journey. ∼ ∼, greatly (*cf. Eng.* 'miles' better): ···**i** ∼ ∼ **geçmek,** to be miles ahead of ...: ∼**larca uzaktan,** miles away.

fersiz Without radiance; dull. ∼ **gözler,** lack-lustre eyes.

fersude (·-¹) Worn out, old.

ferş Act of spreading or laying (carpets *etc.*); carpet; bed; the face of the earth. ∼ **sahası,** floor space: **minel** ∼ **ilelarş,** from the earth to the heavens. ∼**etmek** (¹··), **-eder,** to spread; to lay (rails *etc.*); to carpet (a room). ∼**iyat, -tı,** the laying *of rails, pipes etc.*

fertik *In* **fertiği çekmek,** to sneak away ∼**lemek,** to make off.

fertut (·-́) Decrepit. ∼**luk,** decrepitude.

feryad (·-́) A cry; wail; cry for help. ∼ **etm.,** to cry out; to call for help: ∼**ı vermek,** to let oneself be mastered *by love, drink etc.*: ∼**a yetişmek,** to go to the rescue of one calling for help. ∼**cı,** who calls for help; wailing.

ferz The queen *at chess.* ∼ **çıkarmak,** to give the queen (as handicap): ∼ **çıkmak,** (of a pawn) to queen.

fes Fez. ∼ **tarağı,** fuller's teazle.

fesad (·ᵛ) Depravity; corruption; duplicity; malice; intrigue; sedition; disorder. ∼**ı ahlâk,** bad morals, demoralization of character: ∼ **kazanları kaynamak,** for mischief to be brewing: ∼ **kurmak,** to plot mischief: ∼ **kutusu,** mischief-maker, conspirator: **ehli** ∼, conspirator(s), intriguer(s): **mide** ∼**ı,** stomachic disorder. ∼**cı,** mischief-maker; engaged in subversive activity; conspirator. ∼**cılık,** subversive activity, intrigue, conspiracy.

fesane (·-¹) Legend, fable; idle talk.

fesh, -shi Abolition; cancellation; dissolution. ∼**etmek** (¹··), **-eder,** to abolish, annul; abrogate; dissolve (parliament *etc.*).

fesîh Wide; spacious.

fesleğen Sweet-basil; *v.* **don.**

festekiz *Only in* **filàn** ∼, this, that and the other (was said).

fesübhanallah (¹·-·-·) 'Then praise to God!'; good God alive!

feşafeş (·-¹) *Imitates the noise of waves lapping against stones.*

feşmekân *As* **festekiz.**

fetanet (·-¹), **-ti** Intelligence.

fetebarek (¹···) 'May (God) be blessed!', *an expression of pleasure or congratulation.*

fetha Opening; *the vowel sign for a and e in Arabic.*

fethetmek (¹··), **-eder** *va.* Conquer.

fethî (·-́) Victorious.

fethimeyyit, -ti Autopsy.

fetih, ∼**thi** Conquest. ∼**name** (··-¹) Bulletin announcing a victory; poem celebrating a victory.

fettan Seducer. Alluring; cunning. ∼ **civelek,** scapegrace, rascal.

fetva Opinion or decision on a matter of Canon Law *given out by a* mufti. ∼**hane** (···-¹), *formerly the official residence of the Sheikhulislam.*

fevaid (·-¹) *pl.* of **fayda.** Uses; advantages.

fevc Group *or* troop of men. ∼ ∼, in groups; in troops.

feveran A boiling; effervescence; eruption. ∼ **etm.,** (of a volcano) to erupt; to boil over with anger.

fevk, -kı Top; upper part. bunun ~ında, above this. ~alâde (¹···), extraordinary: ~den terfi etmiş, he got special promotion. ~alâdelik, singularity; a being extraordinary. ~albeşer (¹···), superhuman. ~algaye (¹···), extremely. ~alhad (¹··), beyond the limit. ~almemul (¹···), beyond what was hoped for, unexpected. ~anî (·—¹), upper, superior. ~attabia (¹·····), supernatural.

fevr Haste, hurry. alel~, in a hasty manner, on the instant. ~en (¹··), quickly, promptly; suddenly. ~î (·—⁴), sudden; speedy; impulsive.

fevt, -ti Irreparable loss; death. ~i fırsat etm., to lose an opportunity. ~etmek (¹··), **-eder**, to lose *an opportunity etc.* ~olmak (¹··), to die.

fevvare (·—¹) Gushing spring; fountain.

fevz Attainment of an object; success; escape.

feyezan Overflowing; flood; abundance.

feylesof Philosopher.

feyyaz (·—⁴) Overflowing; abounding; flourishing; munificent.

feyz Abundance; munificence; progress. ~ almak (bulmak), to make progress, to be successful: ···den ~ almak, to profit by...: ~ü bereket, abundance *of harvest etc.*: Allah ~ini artırsın!, I wish you all success. ~li, abundant; prosperous; successful; bountiful.

feza (·—⁴) Vast empty space; space (firmament).

-feza (·—⁴) *Pers. suffix.* Increasing... .

fezahat v. fazahat.

fezail (·—¹) *pl. of* fazilet. Qualities *etc.*

fezleke Résumé; précis; substance of a police report.

fıçı Cask, barrel; tub. ~ balığı, salted fish in barrels: ~ dibi (*sl.*), low pub: ~ gibi, very fat: ~ üzümü, grapes brought to the market in barrels. ~cı, cooper.

fıkara, fukara *pl. of* fakir. Poor; the poor; pauper. ~lık, poverty.

fıkarî Vertebral; vertebrate. ~ye, the vertebrates.

fıkdan (·¹) Absence (of *stg.*); need; privation.

fıkıh, -khı Moslem jurisprudence.

fıkır ~ ~, *imitates the sound of boiling water*; coquettishly. ~dak, coquetry: flirtatious. ~damak, to make a bubbling noise; skip about; sparkle; flirt. ~tı, a bubbling noise.

fıkra Vertebra; sentence; paragraph; article *in a paper*; anecdote.

fıldır fıldır Skipping about; rolling the eyes. ~ ~ aramak, to hunt around feverishly for stg.

fındık Hazel-nut. ~ kurdu, nut maggot; tiny (woman). ~çı, seller of nuts; girl who uses her charms to get stg. out of a man. ~î, nut-brown. ~kıran, nutcrackers. ~sıçanı, -nı, common house-mouse.

fır A whirr; a circuit. ~ ~ dolaşmak, to go whirring round: birinin etrafında ~ dönmek, to hover round s.o.

Fırat, -tı (¹·) The Euphrates.

fırça (¹·) Brush.

fırdolayı (¹···) All around.

fırdöndü (¹··) Swivel; lathe carrier.

fırfır v. firfir.

fırıl *In* ~ ~ aramak, to search high and low. ~dak, weather-cock, vane; spinning-top; ventilator; whirligig; deception, ruse: ~ çevirmek, to be up to some mischief; to intrigue. ~dakçı, trickster, cunning fellow. ~danmak, to spin round; to move around hurriedly and anxiously.

fırın Large oven. ⌐bunu yapman için kırk ~ ekmek yemen lâzım¬, it will be a long long time before you are capable of doing that: yüksek ~, blast-furnace. ~cı, one who looks after a furnace; baker. ~kapağı, -nı, thick-skinned; unruffled.

fırışka (·¹·) Light breeze; cat's-paw.

fırka Group; party; military division; squadron of a fleet. ~ ~, in separate parties.

fırkat v. firkat.

fırkata (·¹·) Frigate.

fırlak Protruding.

fırla·ma Act of flying off; bastard. ~mak, to fly off into space; fly out; leap up; rush; (of prices) to soar. ~tmak, to hurl. ~yış, a leaping up; rush; upward rush *of prices.*

fırsat, -tı Opportunity; chance. ~ düşkünü, opportunist; one whose eye is firmly fixed on the main chance: ~ı kaçırmak, to miss an opportunity: ~ yoksulu, one who would do evil if he had a chance; waiting for an opportunity. ~çı, ~çu, who seeks an opportunity; on the look out for a profitable chance.

fırt *Imitates the sound of a bird's flight.* ~ ~ girip çıkmak, to be continuously going in and out.

fırtına (·¹·) Gale; storm. ~lı, stormy.

fıs, fısfıs Whisper. In a whisper. ~ıldamak, ~lamak, to whisper. ~ıltı, whisper.

fısır fısır *Imitates the noise of a pipe being smoked.*

fısk, -kı Sin; immorality. ~u fücur, debauchery.

fıskıye Jet of water; fountain.

fıslamak *va. & vn.* Whisper.

fıstık Pistachio nut; ground-nut; peanut; pine-kernel; (*more specifically* şamfıstığı or **antepfıstığı** = pistachio nut; yerfıstığı =

groundnut; peanut; çamfıstığı = pine-kernel). ~ çamı, stone pine : ~ gibi, plump and healthy. ~i, pistachio green, light green : ˹her boyadan boyadı, ~si kaldı˺, 'he's tried every paint, there only remains pistachio green', *sarcastic remark when there is a suggestion of doing stg. absurd and out-of-place* : ˹ince ezgi ~ makam˺, *(musical terms)*, in slow time; 'taking his time about it' *(rather sarcastically)*.

fış fış *Imitates a hissing or rustling sound.*

fışfış *In* hacı ~, *a nickname for Arabs.*

fışıl ~ ~, *imitates a splashing sound.* ~**damak**, to make a splashing sound; rustle. ~**tı**, a splashing *or* rustling sound.

fışır ~ ~, *imitates a gurgling or rustling sound.* ~**damak**, to gurgle; to rustle. ~**tı**, a gurgling *or* rustling noise.

fışkı Horse dung; manure.

fışkın Sucker; shoot.

fışkır·ık Squirt; syringe. ~**mak**, to gush out; to spurt out; (of a plant) to spring up.

fıta¹ (¹·) Racing skiff.

fıta² (¹·), **futa** Apron; loin-cloth.

fıtık, –tkı Hernia, rupture.

fıtır, –trı The breaking of a religious fast. idi ~, Moslem festival at the end of the Ramazan fast.

fıtnat, –tı Intelligence.

fıtr·at, –tı Creation; nature; natural character. ~**aten** (¹··), by nature, naturally. ~**î** (·¹), natural; innate.

fi¹ Price.

fi² *Ar. prep.* In; on. filcümle, on the whole : filhakikat, in truth : ~ tarihinde, in the days of yore, long ago.

fiat (–¹), **–ti** Price; value. **maktu** ~, fixed price.

fidan Plant; sapling; shoot. ~ gibi, straight, well set-up (boy *etc.*). ~**lık**, nursery-garden; newly planted vineyard.

fide (¹·) Seedling plant *for planting out.* ~**lemek**, to plant out *seedlings.* ~**lik**, nursery-bed.

fidye, ~inecat, –tı Ransom.

fiğ *v.* fik.

figan (·⁴) Cry of distress, wail.

fihris, fihrist, –ti Index; catalogue; list.

fiil Act, action, deed; verb. ~**e gelmek**, to become a fact; to be done : ~**e getirmek**, to execute, to carry into effect : **kuvveden** ~**e getirmek**, to turn a potentiality into a fact, to carry out a project; realize *an ambition etc.* ~**en** (¹·), actually, really. ~**î** (·¹), actual, real; de facto *(as opp. to* hukukî, *de iure*). ~**iyat, –tı**, deeds.

fik, –ki Wild vetch.

fikir, –kri Thought, idea; mind; memory. fikrimce, in my opinion : fikri dağınık, distracted; preoccupied : fikrine* gelmek, to

come into one's mind : fikre getirmek, to recall to mind : fikrine* koymak, to decide *to do stg.* : birinin fikrine koymak, to put into the mind of another, to suggest to him : fikri sabit, fixed idea : fikrinde* saklamak, to bear in one's mind : fikre varmak, to ponder, to give oneself up to reflection : aklı* fikri* birbirine karışmak, to be bewildered.

fikir·li, having ideas; intelligent; thoughtful : cin ~, very shrewd. ~**siz**, thoughtless; unintelligent.

fikr·en (¹·) Thoughtfully, after taking thought. ~**et, –ti**, thought, reflection. ~**etmek, –eder**, to think of; ponder. ~**i,** *v.* fikir. ~**î,** intellectual; mental.

fil Elephant; bishop *at chess.* ˹deveden büyük ~ var˺, there is a still greater one to be found.

filâdur Lanyard *of a shroud.*

filâma *v.* flâma.

filân So and so; such and such. ~ festekiz (feşmekân), *he said* this, that and the other : ~ fıstık, this and that; and so forth : 15 lira ~, somewhere about 15 lira. ~**ca,** so and so; s.o. or other. ~**ıncı,** numbered so-and-so; the 'so manyeth'.

filândıra *v.* flândıra.

filâriz Mallet for beating out flax.

filbahar, filbahri Mock orange, philadelphus.

filcan *v.* fincan.

fildekos (*Fr. fils d'écosse*) Lisle thread; garments made of the same; vest.

fildişi (¹··), **–ni** Ivory.

file Net; netting.

filen *v.* fiilen.

filenk Cross-piece of timber on the ways of a launching slip; boat-chock.

fileto (·¹·) Fillet *of beef etc.*

filhakika (¹···) In truth, truly.

filî *v.* fiilî.

Filibe (·¹·) Philippopolis; Plovdiv.

filibit, –ti Phlebitis.

filigran Watermark in *paper.*

filik Finest quality mohair.

filika (·¹·) Ship's boat. ~ demiri, grapnel.

filim, –lmi Film (cinema). filmini almak, (i) to film; (ii) to X-ray : filme çekmek, to film.

filinta (·¹·) Carbine.

filispit ('Full-speed'); (*sl.*) dead drunk.

Filistin (·¹·) Palestine.

filiyat *v.* fiiliyat.

filiz Tendril; bud; young shoot; cutting. ~**i,** bright green. ~**kıran,** cold East wind, *which blows in May.* ~**lemek,** to prune. ~**lenmek,** to send forth shoots, to sprout.

filo (¹·) Fleet; squadron *of ships.* ~**tillâ** (··¹·), flotilla.

filoş¹ Floss silk. ~otu, a kind of reed *used for wickerwork.*

filoş² Flush (at cards).

filoz Small buoy *made of a gourd or of cork.*

filozof Philosopher.

filvaki (¹··) In fact, actually.

fimabaid (¹···) Hereafter.

fincan Cup; porcelain insulator. ~cı, seller of cups: ⌜~cı katırlarını ürkütmek⌝, to bring unnecessary trouble upon oneself, *v. App.*

finfon *v.* fanfan.

fing, fink *Only in* ~ atmak, to saunter about and enjoy oneself; to flirt around.

fingir *In* ~ ~, with a swaying motion; coquettishly. ~ ~ etm., to walk thus. ~dek, frivolous; coquettish. ~demek, to behave frivolously and coquettishly. ~ti, flirtation; noisy party.

fino (¹·) Pet dog; lap-dog.

firak (·⁴), –kı Separation; sorrow at separation. ~lı, sad, melancholy.

firar (·⁴) Flight; desertion. ~ etm., to fly, escape, desert. ~i (·–¹), deserter.

firaşkin Luff-tackle.

Firavun Pharaoh; a proud and obstinate man. ~ faresi, ichneumon: ~ inciri, Sycamore fig.

firdevs Paradise; garden.

fire (¹·) Loss of weight by evaporation; inevitable loss or wastage. ~ vermek, to suffer such wastage.

firfir Purple; blossom of the Judas tree. ~î, purple.

firik Wheat grains plucked green and dried.

firkat, -ti Separation; absence; nostalgia.

firkateyn Frigate.

firkete (·¹·) Hairpin.

firma (¹·) Commercial firm.

firuz (·–¹) Lucky. ~e (·–¹), turquoise.

Fisagor Pythagoras.

fisebilillah (¹····) (In God's way); gratis; for nothing.

fisk *v.* fısk.

fiske Flick; flip with the fingers; bruise made by a flip; small blister. ~ dokundurmamak, to protect *s.o.* from the slightest aggression: ~ ~ kabarmak (olmak), to be covered with small bruises: ~ vurmak, to give a flip.

fisket, –ti Boatswain's pipe. ~ çalmak, to pipe (on board ship).

fiskos A whispering with evil intent; insinuation. ~ etm., to whisper insinuations; to plot under one's breath.

fislemek *v.* fıslamak.

fistan Kilt; skirt, petticoat.

fis (*Fr. fiche*) Counter (for games); slips of paper or cards *for an index etc.*; peg; plug (electric). ~lemek, to make a card index.

fişek Cartridge; rocket; roll of coins; (*sl.*) sexual intercourse. **deli** ~, madcap: **kestane fişeği**, squib. ~hane (··–¹), cartridge factory. ~lik, cartridge-belt; bandolier; ammunition pouch.

fit¹, –ti Instigation, incitement; an equivalent gain or loss at a game of chance. ~ olm., to be quits; to come to an agreement about price; to consent: ~ vermek, to put a mischievous idea into another's head, to spread discontent: ⌜bir ~ bin büyü yerine geçer⌝, a malicious hint can do a power of evil: **dünden** ~, only too glad; only too ready. ~çi, mischief-maker.

fit² *In* ~ tulumbası, feed-pump.

fitil Wick; fuse; seton; piping (of dress); (*coll.*) incitement. Drunk. ~i* almak, to get into a rage, to flare up; to become alarmed: ~ gibi, as drunk as a lord: ~ vermek, to work *s.o.* up to great excitement; to incite *s.o.* against another: **burnundan*** ~ ~ gelmek, utterly to spoil one's pleasure. ~lemek, to light the fuse of a mine, a bomb *etc.*; to enrage; to incite one against another.

fitle·mek *va.* Denounce; incite, instigate; set one person against another. ~yici, inciting, instigating.

fitne Instigation; disorder; sedition; mischief-making. Mischief-maker, instigator. ~ fücur, a dangerous mischief-maker: ~ kopmak (basmak), for disorders or sedition to break out: ~ olm., to be a temptation; to be an intriguer; for troubles to break out: ~ vermek, to make a mischievous suggestion. ~ci, trouble-maker; seditious person. ~lemek, to instigate trouble; to make a mischievous remark.

fitre Alms given at the close of the Ramazan fast.

fitret, –ti Interval between two successive events; interregnum; languor.

fittulumbası (¹····), –nı Feed-pump.

fiyaka (*sl.*) Showing-off; ostentation. ~sı bozulmak, to look sheepish when one's showing-off is ridiculed: ~ yapmak (satmak), to show off.

fiyat *v.* fiat.

fiyonga, fiyongo Bow-tie; bow knot.

fizik Physics; temperament; constitution; physique. Physical (*also* fisikî).

flâma (¹·) Pennant; surveyor's pole.

flândıra (¹·) Ship's pennant; red band-fish.

flâsa (¹·) Rope-yarn.

flâvta (¹·) Flute.

flok, –ku Jibsail. **balon** ~, spinnaker.

floka (¹·) Felucca.

florcin, flûrcun (?) Hawfinch.

floş Floss silk; flush (at cards).

flört, –tü Flirt.

flûrya (ᵛ·) Greenfinch; a yellow scented flower.

flusahmer v. fülusiahmer.

fob F.o.b., free on board.

fodla (ᵛ·) A kind of flat round loaf *formerly distributed by theological colleges to the poor.* ~cı, one who takes a job merely to get food *etc.*

fodra (ᵛ·) Lining or padding *of a coat.*

fodul Vain; presumptuous; egotistical. ⌐hem kel hem ~¬, bald but vain, *i.e.* proud though with nothing to be proud of; in the wrong but proud of it.

fokur ~ ~, *imitates the sound of boiling water.* ~damak, to bubble noisily, to boil up.

fol Nest-egg. ⌐ortada ~ yok yumurta ~¬, nothing on which to base a claim or to prove anything. ~luk, sitting-box (for hen).

folya v. fulya.

fondo (ᵛ·) Bonds of a country; the funds.

fondo, fonda (ᵛ·) Let go the anchor!

font Cast-iron.

fora (ᵛ·) Out!; open!; unfurl (sails)! Open; opened up. ~ etm., to take down, open up (engine *etc.*); draw (a weapon); unfurl (flag); set (sails): ~ kürek !, ship oars !

forma (ᵛ·) Compositor's forme; folio; 16 pages of a book; number, part (publication); school uniform; colours *of a sporting club.* ~ ~ çıkmak (of a publication) to come out in parts.

foroz The catch of fish in one cast of the net. ~kayığı, –nı, small boat *used for getting out the fish from a fixed fishery* (dalyan).

fors[1] Personal flag *flown on a ship;* national *or* personal emblem.

fors[2] (*Fr. force*) Power; prestige.

forsa (*Fr. forçat*) Galley-slave; convict.

fos False; bad.

fosfor Phosphorus. ~lu, phosphorous, phosphoric.

foslamak vn. (*sl.*) Fail; be disconcerted.

fosur fosur ~ ~, *imitates the noise of smoking a narghile etc.* ~datmak, to smoke noisily and with enjoyment.

fota v. futa.

fotin Boot. ~bağı, –nı Bootlace.

fotograf Photograph; camera. alaminüt ~, 'while-you-wait' photo.

foya (ᵛ·) Foil (for setting off a gem); eyewash; fraud. ~sı meydana çıkmak to be shown up: ~ vermek, to give oneself away.

frak, –kı Tail-coat.

francala (ᵛ··) Fine white bread; roll.

frank, –gı Franc. ~lık, a franc's worth of *stg.*

Fransa (ᵛ·) France. ~lı, French, Frenchman.

fransız French. ~ca, the French language; in French.

fren (*Fr. frein*) Brake. ~lemek, to brake.

frengi Syphilis; a kind of lock. ~ deliği, scupper-hole. ~li, syphilitic.

frengî Europeanized. **frengistan,** Europe.

frenk, –gi European. ~gömleği, –ni, stiff shirt. ~inciri, –ni, prickly pear. ~üzümü, –nü, red currant.

freze (ᵛ·) Milling cutter. ~ makinesi, milling-machine.

fribort (ᵛ·) Freeboard.

frilya (ᵛ·) Greenfinch.

frumaye (– – ᵛ) v. fürümaye.

fuar (*Fr. foire*) Fair.

fufel Areca-nut; betel-nut.

fuh·şiyat, –tı Obscenities; immoralities. ~uş, –hşu, immorality; indecency; prostitution.

fukara v. fıkara.

ful, –lü A small kind of bean; mock-orange, syringa.

fulya (ᵛ·) Jonquil. ~balığı, –nı, eagle ray.

fund Pound (weight).

funya (ᵛ·) Primer (artillery).

furgon Luggage-van.

furş (*Fr. fourche*) Fork *of a bicycle.*

furu v. füru[1].

furuş v. fürüş.

furya (ᵛ·) Rush; glut.

fus Lobe.

futa (ᵛ·) Apron; long cask for grapes; skiff.

futbol, –lü Football.

fuzul Silly meddlesome man. ~en (· ᵛ·), superfluously; without right; unjustly. ~lî (· –ᵛ), meddling; officious; exceeding his rights; excessive; superfluous. ~iyat (· –·ᵛ), –tı, superfluous words *or* deeds.

füc'eten (ᵛ··) Suddenly (*esp. of dying*).

fücur (·ᵛ) Immorality, debauchery; incest.

fülusiahmer (·ᵛ···) *In* ~e muhtac olm., not to have 'a red cent'.

fünun (ᵛᵛ) *pl. of* fen. Sciences; arts. darül~, university : mecmuai~, encyclopedia; very learned man.

fürce Breach, gap; leisure. ~yab olm., to find an opportunity.

füru, –uu *pl. of* feri. Branches; subdivisions; distant relations. usul ve ~, fundamental and subordinate questions; close relations and distant relations : usul hem de ~, root and branch.

füruht, –tu Sale.

–füruş (·ᵛ) *Pers. suffix.* Selling ...; hod~, (who sells himself) braggart.

–füruz (·ᵛ) *Pers. suffix.* Enlightening ...; dil~ that cheers the heart.

füruzan (·–ᵛ) Bright; shining.

fürümaye (··–ı) Low-down; ill-bred.

füshat, –ti Spaciousness; wide space; ample time; delay, respite. ~ **vermek,** to grant a delay, give a respite.

füsun (·ı) Charm; enchantment, sorcery.

fütuhat (·–ı), **–tı** *pl. of* **fetih.** Victories, conquests. ~**çı,** conqueror; imperialist.

fütur (·ı) Languor; abatement. ~ **gelmek,** to be languid or lukewarm; to be discouraged. ~**suz,** indifferent; regardless of public opinion; undeterred.

fütüvvet, –ti Youth; youthful folly; generosity, magnanimity; *name of a semireligious guild in the Middle Ages.*

füyuzat (·–ı), **–tı** *pl. of* **feyz.** Bounteous gifts; divine blessings.

G

gaasıb Who seizes by violence; usurper.

gabari (*Fr. gabarit*) Template.

gabavet (·–ı), **–ti** Stupidity; obtuseness.

gabi (·ı) Stupid; obtuse.

gabin, –bni Fraud; overcharge.

gabya (ı·) Topsail. ~ **çubuğu,** topmast.

gaco (*sl.*) Sweetheart; very small **palamut,** *q.v.*

gacur *In* ~ gucur, a creaking noise.

gaddar Cruel; perfidious; exorbitant. ~**ane** (·––ı), in a cruel way; cruel (*not of persons*); deceitful; exorbitant. ~**lık,** cruelty; perfidy; sale at exorbitant prices.

gadir, –dri Cruelty; tyranny; injustice; perfidy; breach of trust.

gadretmek (ı··), **–eder** *vn.* Do a wrong; act unjustly; commit a breach of trust.

gadubet, –ti *v.* gudubet.

gaf (*Fr. gaffe*) Gaffe, blunder.

gaffar Forgiving; indulgent (God).

gafil (–ı) Careless; inattentive; unwary. ~ **avlamak,** to catch unawares, take by surprise; cheat the unwary: ~ olm. (bulunmak), to take no heed, pay no attention; be unaware.

gafir (·ı) *In* cem'i ~, a great multitude.

gaflet, –ti Heedlessness; inattention; somnolence. ~ **basmak,** ~**e düşmek,** to be heedless *or* unaware: ~ etm., to be negligent; to commit a mistake through absentmindedness; to be unaware of what is going on: ···den ~ üzere bulunmak, to be unaware of... (that...). ~**ten** (ı··), inadvertently; without reflection; absent-mindedly; unawares.

gaga Beak. Aquiline; hook-nosed. ~ **burun** aquiline nose: ~**sından yakalarım,** I'll settle his hash. ~**lamak,** to peck. ~**laşmak,** to peck one another; (of birds) to caress one another with their bills.

gâh, kâh (–) A time; moment. ~ ~ at times, now and then: ~ ..., ~ ..., at one time ..., at another ...: ~**bigâh,** in season and out of season: ~**u nagâh,** at every moment. ~**i** (ı·), sometimes, at times.

–gâh (–) *Pers. suffix indicating* place of ...,

e.g. ordu~, (place of an army) encampment; ikamet~, place of residence.

gaî (–ı) Having regard to the end or purpose; teleological.

gaib (–ı) Absent; invisble; hidden; lost. The invisible world; the 3rd person (*gram.*). ~**dedir,** he has disappeared: ~**den haber almak,** to practise divination, to foretell the future: ~**e ihtar,** warning published in the papers that if a certain person does not present himself before the court he will be tried by default: ~**lere karışmak,** to disappear, abscond: ulûmu ~**e,** the occult sciences.

gaile (–·ı) Anxiety; trouble; difficulty; war. hizmetçi ~**si var,** there is the servant problem. ~**li,** troubled, worried. ~**siz,** without worries, carefree.

gait (–ı) Human excrement.

gaklamak *vn.* Croak.

galâ (·ı) Dearness; dearth.

galat, –tı Error; erroneous expression, barbarism. ···den ~, a corruption of *a word*; an erroneous version of ...: ~**ı elvan,** colour-blindness: ~**ı hilkat,** a freak of nature, monster: ~**ı his,** illusion: ~**ı meşhur,** a solecism consecrated by use: ~ **söylemck,** to use an erroneous expression: ~**ı rüyet,** optical illusion.

galebe Victory; superiority, predominance; uncontrollable ferocity. ~ etm. (çalmak), to conquer, overcome.

galeta (·ı·) Hard biscuit.

galeyan Ebullition; effervescence; rage; excitement. ~ etm., to boil, effervesce; boil with rage.

gali (–ı) High-priced; precious; exorbitant.

galib (–ı) Victorious; superior; dominant; prevailing; most usual; probable. ~ olm. (gelmek), to be victorious, win, surpass. ~**a** (ı·–), probably; presumably. ~**iyet** (–··ı), **–ti,** victory; superiority.

galibarda (··ı·) Bright scarlet colour.

galiye A perfumed black hair ointment; black.

galiz (·ı) Coarse; thick; rude.

galle Income; rental.

galsame Gills *of a fish.*

gam¹, -mmı Care, anxiety; grief. ~ yemek, to be oppressed with anxiety or sorrow: def'i ~ etm., to console oneself, distract oneself: ne ~ !, what matter !: ⌐ölsem de ~ yemem⌐, (if only I can do this) I don't mind what happens.

gam² (*Fr. gamme*) Gamut; scale.

gamalı (¹··) *In* ~ haç, swastika.

gamalûd (.-¹) Sad.

gamba (¹·) Kink *in a rope*; upper part of a boot or stocking.

gambot, -tu Gunboat.

gamız¹, gaamız (-¹) Obscure; abstruse.

gamız², -mzı Wink; tale-telling, denunciation. ~lamak, to spy upon and tell tales about; denounce.

gam·lanmak *vn.* Be grieved; fret. ~lı, sorrowful, grieved; anxious.

gammaz Telltale, sneak, informer. ~lamak, to tell tales about; to spy upon; inform against.

gamnak (·-¹), **gamkin** Anxious, sad.

gamsele (¹··) Mackintosh, oilskin.

gamsız Free from grief; carefree.

gamze Wink; significant look; twinkle; dimple.

ganaim (·-¹) *pl. of* ganimet. Spoils *etc.*

ganem Sheep *or* goats; a flock of sheep.

ganga (¹·) A kind of tambourine.

gangaloz Old hag.

gangıran, gangren Gangrene.

gani Wealthy; independent; free from want; abundant; generous. ~ ganimet, abundance of spoil *or* anything to be had for the taking: ~ gönüllü, generous: ⌐Allah ~ ~ rahmet etsin⌐, 'may God rest his soul' (*only used when mentioning a good deed of a deceased person*).

ganimet, -ti Spoils, booty; windfall, godsend. fırsatı ~ bilmek, to seize an opportunity.

gar¹ (*Fr. gare*) Station.

gar² Cavern.

garabet (·-¹), **-ti** A being a stranger; absence from home; exile; strangeness; curiousness, singularity.

garaib (·-¹) *pl. of* garibe. Strange things *etc.*

garam (·-¹) Passionate love.

garaz, garez Selfish aim or motive; spite, rancour, grudge. ···e ~ bağlamak, to nourish a spite against ... : ~ ..., the thing is that... : bir ~a mebni, for some private end; because of a spite: ~ tutmak, to bear a grudge: erbabı ~, people with ends to serve; selfish. ~kâr (···¹), ~lı, selfish, interested; spiteful, malicious. ~kârlık, malice, spitefulness; evil intent. ~sız, disinterested; without ulterior motive.

garb The West; Europe. ~cı, one who desires the westernization of Turkey. ~en (¹·), westwards. ~î (·¹), western. ~iyun (··¹), westerners; Europeans. ~lı, western; European. ~lılaşmak, to become westernized.

gardfren (*Fr. garde-frein*) Brakesman.

gardırop (*Fr. garde-robe*) Wardrobe; cloakroom.

garet (-¹), **-ti** Raid; plundering incursion; sack of a city; booty. ~ etm., to raid, pillage; carry off as booty.

garez *v.* garaz.

gargar Porous bottle *or* jar.

gargara Gargling; gargle.

garib (·¹) Stranger; away from his own country; poor, needy; strange; curious. ~i ... the strange part of it is that ...: ~ine* gitmek, to appear strange, to strike one as odd: ~ yiğiti young man fresh from the country. ~lik, being a stranger; a being without friends; poverty. ~semek, to find a thing strange; to feel lonely *or* a stranger.

garik (·¹) Drowned; submerged; immersed.

garim (·¹) Creditor.

gariye ~ fasilesi, the Laurel family.

garizi (·-¹) Natural; innate. ~ hararet, the normal temperature of the body.

gark, -kı A being submerged; drowning; a being overwhelmed. ~ etm., to submerge; to overwhelm (with presents or favours): ~ olm., to be submerged; be drowned; be covered *or* overwhelmed.

garnizon Garrison.

garsetmek (¹··), **-eder** *va.* Plant.

garson (*Fr. garçon*) Waiter.

gasb Wrongful seizure; usurpation. ~etmek (¹··), **-eder**, to seize by force; snatch away.

gaseyan Vomiting.

gâsıb *v.* gaasıb.

gas·il, -sli Washing, *esp.* canonical washing and washing of the dead. ~letmek (¹··), **-eder**, to wash. ~sal, a washer of the dead.

gaşy, gaşiy Fainting, swoon; ecstasy. ~etmek (¹··), **-eder**, to cause to faint; enrapture. ~olmak (¹··), to swoon; be in an ecstasy.

gavail (·-¹) *pl. of* gaile. Troubles *etc.*

gavamız (·-¹) *pl. of* gamıza. Obscure matters; abstruse points; niceties; minutiae, fine points. bir şeyin ~ına aşına olm., to know a thing minutely.

gâvur Non-Moslem; ghiaour; infidel; atheist. ~ etm., to waste utterly; to ruin: ~ gibi inad etm., to refuse obstinately: ~ olm., to be a renegade. ~luk, quality of being a non-Moslem; irreligion; Christian fanaticism; cruelty. ~ca (·ı·), in the manner of an infidel; cruelly; in a European language.

gavvas Diver.

gaybî (·⸰) Pertaining to the unknown or occult.

gaybubet (·–ı), **–ti** Absence; disappearance; alibi. ~ etm., to absent oneself; disappear.

gayda A kind of bagpipes, *used by Bulgars.*

gaye (–ı) Aim, object; end.

gayet (–ı), **–ti** Extremity, end; limit; object, purpose. Extremely. ~le, extremely: ~ülgaye, to the very utmost degree: ~i irtifa, meridian height. ~siz, endless, infinite.

gayr, –rı *or* **–ri** Another thing *or* person; *used with the izafet it forms à negative prefix,* *e.g.* ~icaiz, illicit; ~ikâmil, imperfect; *(these adjectives are written as one word and the commonest will be found under* gayri*).* ~ım, another than I, s.o. else: ~e muhtac, in need of another: ayrımız ~ımız yok, we have everything in common; there is no difference between us: ondan ~i, other than that; moreover, besides: onun ~i, a different one: bi ~i hakkın, unjustly.

gayrendiş (··⸰) Altruistic.

gayret, –ti Zeal; energy; perseverance; jealousy of one's rights or honour. ⌜~ dayıya düştü⌝, 'it is for uncle to make the effort', 'well, if no one else can do it you (I) must!': ~ine dokunmak to goad s.o. on by reminding him of his duty, his honour *etc.*: ~i elden bırakmamak, to persist: ~ etm., to display zeal or energy, to bestir oneself: ~ vermek, to inspirit, encourage. ~keş, jealous of one's rights or honour; partisan; zealous. ~li, zealous, persevering. ~siz, without enthusiasm; slack.

gayrı¹ (ı·) Henceforth; at length, finally.

gayrı², **gayri** *v.* gayr. *As neg. prefix = un-, in- etc. (for pronunciation see the simple adjective; the main stress falls on the first syllable of* gayri*).* ~caiz, illicit; improper. ~ihtiyari, involuntary, willy-nilly. ~ilmî, unscientific. ~kabil, impossible. ~kâfi, insufficient. ~mahdud, indefinite. ~mahsûs, imperceptible. ~memnun, displeased. ~menus, unfamiliar. ~meşru, illegitimate. ~meş'ur, unconscious. ~muktedir, incapable; impotent. ~muntazam, irregular; disorderly. ~ mübadil, not subject to change; not subject to exchange (of populations); established. ~mümkün, impossible. ~samimî, insincere. ~tabiî, unnatural, abnormal. ~uzvî, inorganic. ~vâkı, that did not happen. ~vakıf, unaware.

gayur Very zealous; indefatigable.

gayya A well in Hell; 'the bottomless pit'.

gayz Anger. ~ü gasb, fury and wrath.

gaz¹ Gauze.

gaz² Gas; paraffin.

gaza (·⸰), **gazve** War on behalf of Islam, Holy War; victory over infidels.

gazab Wrath. ~ etm. *or* ~a gelmek, to get angry: ~a getirmek to make angry, infuriate. ~lanmak, to become infuriated. ~lı, ~nak, angry.

gazal, –li Gazelle.

gazanfer Lion; brave man.

gazeb *v.* gazab.

gazel¹ Lyric poem. ~iyat, –tı, lyrics.

gazel² Withered leaves. ~ vakti, autumn, fall. ~lenmek, (of leaves) to wither and fall.

gazete (·ı·) Newspaper. ~ci, journalist; newsvendor.

gazi (–ı) One who fights for Islam; veteran of a war; *title taken by a victorious Moslem general or ruler.* ⌜Ey ~ler, yol göründü⌝, it's about time we were going!

gazî Gaseous.

gaziye A sweet-smelling yellow-flowered tree (? *Acacia dealbata*).

gaz·lemek *va.* Gas (*mil.*). ~li, gaseous; worked by *or* mixed with gas *or* paraffin.

gazoz Fizzy lemonade or gingerbeer.

gazub Angry.

gazubet *v.* gudubet.

gazve *v.* gaza.

gebe Pregnant. ⌜geceler ~dir⌝, 'wait, things may be better tomorrow!'

gebermek *vn.* Die (*of animals or, contemptuously, of men*). ~tmek, to kill.

gebeş Thick-headed; awkward, uncouth.

gebre¹ Hair-cloth glove *for grooming horses.*

gebre² Caper; caper tree.

gece Night. Last night; tonight; by night. ~ baskını, night raid (by a burglar or footpad); night attack (*mil.*): ~ gündüz (demeden), day and night, continuously: ~kuşu, owl; nightbird (of a man): ~ yarısı, midnight: ~ yatısı, who passes the night at a place; hospitality for the night; ~ yatısına buyurun!, pray come and stay the night!. ~ci, night worker; nightwatchman. ~lemek, to pass the night; to become night. ~leyin (·ı··), by night. ~lik, pertaining to the night; night-dress, night-gown; food for the night. ~sefası (·ı···), –nı, Marvel of Peru.

gecik·mek *vn.* Be late. ~tirmek, to cause to be late; be slow in doing *stg.*

geç Late. ~ kalmak, to be late: ⌜~ olsun da güç olmasın⌝, 'better late than never'; better there should be a delay than a difficulty: **Allah gecinden versin!**, (*used when speaking to a person of his own death*), I hope it won't be for many years.

geçe¹ Past (*only in telling the time*); onu çeyrek ~, a quarter past ten.

geçe² Side, flank.

geçelim 1*st pers. pl. optative of* **geçmek**. Let's pass that by; let's not talk about that.

geçen Passing; past; last. **~lerde**, recently: ~ **gün**, the other day: ~ **sene**, last year.

geçer Current (coin *etc.*); saleable. Current value.

geçici Passing; temporary; infectious.

geçid Place of passage, pass, ford; fairway (*naut.*); act of passing. ~ **resmi**, military review; march past: ~ **vermek**, (of a river) to be fordable; (of a pass) to be open.

geçil·mek *vn. pass. of* **geçmek**. Be passed; be passable; be given up *or* renounced. **buradan geçilmez**, no passage! **~mez**, impassable; not to be given up: impasse.

geçim A living together in agreement; a 'getting on' with one another; compatibility; current value, currency; livelihood. ~ **derdi**, the struggle to earn one's daily bread: ⌜~ **dünyası bu!**⌝, 'one's got to live!': ~ **seviyesi**, the standard of living. **~li**, easy to get on with; affable. **~siz**, unable to get on with others. **~sizlik**, inability to get on with others or with each other; incompatibility.

geçinecek Means of subsistence; income.

geçinmek *vn.* Live; exist; subsist; get on well with others; pass for, have the reputation of. **alınterile** ~, to live by the sweat of one's brow: **birisinden** ~, to live on s.o. else, to sponge on s.o.

geçirmek *va. caus. of* **geçmek**. Make *or* let pass; transport over *stg.*; get rid of (pain *etc.*); go through, experience; appoint (to a post); see off (a friend *etc.*); insert, fit into; pass off as good *or* current; cause to renounce. ... **başına*** ~, to hit *s.o.* over the head with ...: **dar** ~, narrowly to escape: **diş** ~, to get one's teeth into, injure, annoy: **ele** ~, to get into one's power: **evini başına geçiririm**, I'll bring the house down about his ears (*a threat*): **gözden** ~, to scrutinize: **o hastalığı geçirdim**, I have got over that illness; **bu hastalığı bana geçirdiniz**, you have passed this disease on to me, have given me this disease: **hesaba** ~, to enter to an account: **vaz** ~, to persuade *or* make *s.o.* give up *stg.*: **zihinden*** ~, to ponder.

geçirtmek *va. caus. of* **geçirmek**.

geçiştirmek *va.* Get over (an illness); escape *or* survive (an accident). **lâkaydane (sükûtla)** ~, to pass over *stg.* with indifference (in silence).

geçkin Over-ripe; past the prime; not so young; over-matured (wood); former, previous (holder of an office); past (a certain age).

geçme *verb. noun of* **geçmek**. *a.* Fitting into *stg.* else; made in sections. **sandık ~si**, dovetail.

geçmek *vn.* Pass; pass along, over, into *etc.*; pass away, come to an end, expire; deteriorate; fade; (fruit) be over-ripe; be transferred; move; pass as current; be in vogue. *va.* (*with acc.*) Pass (overtake); go beyond; skip, leave out; (*sl.*) denounce, tell tales about; talk about; (*sl.*) *used as an auxiliary to replace* **etmek**, *e.g.* **alay** ~, to mock; **işaret** ~, to make signs. ···**den** ~, to pass, pass by, through *etc.*; give up, abandon, renounce: ···**e** ~, undertake; take over, succeed to *a post etc.*; penetrate: **geç !**, don't take any notice!; ignore that!: **geçelim**, let's pass by that; let's not talk about that: **geçmez**, *v.* **geçmez**: **geçmiş**, *v.* **geçmiş**: **geçtim olsun !**, I'll drop the idea: **adı** ~, to be mentioned: **adi (bahsi) geçen**, the aforementioned: **artık bizden geçti** *or* **biz artık geçtik**, I'm past that sort of thing, I'm too old for that: **başa** ~, to come to the fore, to become chief: **başından*** ~, to happen to one: **birbirine** ~, to fit into one another; to intertwine; to fall into confusion; to quarrel with one another: ⌜**bu da geçer**⌝, 'this too will pass !'; never mind !: **candan** ~, to sacrifice one's life *or* be ready to give one's life: **çok geçmeden**, before long: **ele** ~, to be arrested; to be obtained: **eline*** ~, to come into one's possession: **gün geçmez ki**, not a day passes but...: **gün geçtikçe**, as the days pass, in course of time: **hatırından*** ~, to pass through the mind: **ismi geçen**, the aforementioned: **iş işten geçti**, it's all over; there's nothing one can do now: **kendinden*** ~, to lose consciousness; to be beside oneself *with joy etc.*: **kendinden geçmiş** (of a man) no longer of any use: **sözü* geçiyor**, his word carries weight: **yere** *or* **yerin dibine** ~, to sink into the ground from shame.

geçmez That does not pass; non-current; incurable; non-infectious. **su** ~, impermeable; waterproof.

geçmiş Past; past the prime; passed away; deceased; over-ripe. **~i kınalı (kandilli)**, damn the fellow !; that scoundrel: ⌜**~e mazi (yenmişe kuzu)**⌝, that was a long time ago; things aren't the same now: ~ **ola**, it's too late now: ⌜~ **olsun!**⌝, *said to congratulate s.o. on recovery from an illness or escape from an accident*: **birisile ~i olm.**, to have common experiences or memories with s.o.

geda (·⸗) Beggar.

gedik Breach; notch; gap; warrant; tenure; *a kind of* leasehold; a licence *for certain trades*. With teeth missing. ~ **kapamak**, to fill a gap : eksik ~, any kind of deficiency : eksik ~ tamamlamak, to make everything good : ⌐taşı gediğine koymak¹, to give as good as one gets; to make a clever retort. ~li, breached; notched; having a gap; *property* held under a gedik; possessing the warrant or licence known as gedik; regular (customer, visitor), habitué. Regular n.c.o. (*mil.*).

gedilmek *vn.* Become notched *or* jagged; have a gap.

geğe, geğeç Stinging, biting. ~lemek, to sting, bite, peck.

geğir·mek *vn.* Belch. ~ti, belch.

geğrek Lower rib; false rib. ~ ağrısı (batması), stitch in the side.

gelberi Iron rake *for a fire.*

gelecek About to come; future. ~ ay, next month, *but* ~ salı, Tuesday after next (*next Tuesday* = bu salı *or* önümüzdeki salı).

gelen Coming; comer. ~ geçen, coming and going. Passers-by.

‖**gelenek** Tradition.

gelgeç Fickle, inconstant. ~ hanı, a place where people come and go.

gelgelelim (¹···) All the same; and yet; however.

Gelibolu Gallipoli.

gelici geçici Transient, passing.

gelin Bride; daughter-in-law. ~ gibi sallana sallana yürümek, to walk slowly and lazily : ~ odası gibi, very tidy: ⌐kendi kendine ~ güvey olm¹, (i) to set out to decide a matter without the authority or the competence to do so; (ii) to be ridiculously self-important; (iii) to reckon without one's host : ⌐kızım sana söyliyorum, ~im sen anla!¹, to talk 'at' s.o.; to make remarks intended for s.o., but not directly addressed to him.

gelince (·¹·) Regarding; as for. bana ~, as for me, as far as I am concerned.

gelin·cik *Dim. of* gelin; weasel; poppy; three-bearded rockling (fish). ~ illeti, *popularly used to describe* any illness causing swelling of the legs, *e.g.* dropsy. ~havası, –nı, fine calm weather. ~kuşu, –nu, a species of lark. ~lik, quality of a bride; marriageable girl; anything suitable for a bride.

gelinmek *vn. impers. of* gelmek. bir saatte gidilir gelinir, you can go there and back in an hour : hakkından gelindi, he (it) was got the better of, was overcome.

gelir *aor. of* gelmek. Income, revenue. ~li, having such and such an income; having a fixed income.

geliş Act *or* manner of coming; gait; the way a thing comes *or* happens. söz ~i,

supposing that; for example; apropos : sözün (lâfın) ~i, in the course of conversation. ~igüzel (··¹··), by chance, at random; haphazard.

gelişme Development.

gelişmek *vn.* Grow up; develop; grow healthy *or* fat; make progress.

gelme Act of coming. Come, arrived. Avrupadan ~ oyuncaklar, toys imported from Europe : uşaklıktan ~, an ex-servant.

gelmek, –ir *vn.* Come; suit, fit, answer *a purpose*; seem, appear; sham, pretend; endure, bear; (*with the gerund in* –a *or* –e) happen habitually, *e.g.* edegelmek, to do habitually; olagelmek, to happen constantly. geldi geleli, ever since he came : gel gelelim, *v.* gelgelelim: gelip gitmek, to come and go, to go to and fro : gelsin yemek, gitsin yemek, there was heaps of food; gelsin Ali gitsin Ali, it was always Ali, Ali (who had to do everything) : gel de kızma !, 'how could anyone not be angry ? '; ⌐gel de bu adama bir daha yardım et !¹, 'how could one help this man again (after the way he behaved last time)!' : güleceğim geldi, I wanted to laugh: Istanbulu göreceğim geldi, I long to see Istanbul: görmemezlikten geldi, he pretended not to see : işitmemezlikten geldim, I pretended not to hear : yağmur altında durmağa gelmez, it doesn't do to stop out in the rain: bu kumaş yıkamağa gelmez, boyası çıkar, this stuff won't wash, its colour runs: bu adamla munakaşa etmeğe gelmez, it doesn't do to argue with this man : ⌐geleceği varsa göreceği de var !¹, 'let him come and see what's waiting for him!'; 'let him try it on!' : bana öyle geliyor ki, it seems to me that... : başına* ~, to happen to one : çıka ~, to appear suddenly : işe ~, to be suitable for the job : işine* ~, to suit one's purpose or desires : yola ~, to think better of *stg.*; to come round to the right way of thinking; to submit.

gem Bit (of a horse). ~ almak, to submit to the bit: ~ almaz, uncontrollable: ~i azıya almak, to take the bit between the teeth, to get out of control: ···e ~ vurmak, to curb ... .

gemi Ship. ~de teslim, free on board (f.o.b.) : ~ yatağı, ship's berth; port of shelter. ~ci, sailor: ~ nuru, St. Elmo's fire. ~cilik, the profession of a sailor; art of managing a ship; navigation.

gemrenmek *vn.* Be gnawed *or* nibbled; (of a horse) to champ the bit: gnash the teeth.

gen Broad; vast; abundant. ~lik, comfort; easy circumstances.

genc¹ Young. Young man. ~elmek,

~**leşmek,** to become youthful or vigorous.
~**lik,** youth; youthful folly: **gencliğine* doyamamak,** to die young.
genc², gencine (·−ı) Treasure; treasury; storehouse.
gene¹, yine (ı·) Again; moreover; still.
gene² Tick; castor bean. **buğday ~si,** weevil.
||**genel** a. General. ~**kurmay,** General Staff.
geniş Wide; vast; extensive; abundant; generous, magnanimous; at ease, free from care. **eli ~,** generous: **içi ~,** easy-going; phlegmatic: **bir işi ~ tutmak,** to do stg. on a broad scale: **gönlünü ~ tut !,** don't worry !, don't take it too seriously ! ~**gönüllü,** not easily upset, possessing equanimity. ~**lemek,** to widen, extend, ease; become spacious or wide; be at ease, in easy circumstances: **nefis ~,** to feel more at ease. ~**lik,** width, spaciousness; abundance; ease of mind; easy circumstances.
geniz, -nzi Nasal passages. ~**e kaçmak,** (of food) to go down the wrong way: ~**den söylemek,** to speak through the nose.
ger Hen bird.
–**ger** Pers. suffix. Maker, worker, doer. **ahenger** (worker of iron) blacksmith.
gerçek True; actual; genuine; truthful; in the right. In truth; in earnest; really. Truly!, really! The truth. ~**ten,** truly, really; true, genuine: **gerçeğini söylemek,** to tell the truth of it. ~**lenmek, ~leşmek,** to turn out to be true.
gerçi (ı·) Although; granted that; it is true that.
gerdan Neck, throat, front of the neck. ~ **kırmak,** to put on coquettish airs; to bow. ~**kıran,** (neck-breaking) stumbling (horse); wryneck. ~**lık,** necklace; neckband.
gerdek Nuptial chamber.
gerdel Wooden or leather bucket.
gerdun (·−ı) The Heavens; sky; the wheel of fortune. ~**e,** wheeled vehicle.
gerek¹ A necessary, a requisite. Necessary, needed; fitting, proper, due; with the conditional tense gerek conveys probability, e.g. **pek de yanlış olmasa ~,** and it is probably not far off the truth. ~**se,** if it be necessary; if it be proper: ~**tir,** it is necessary; it is right: **gereğince,** as far as necessary; as required; if need be; in accordance with: **gereği gibi,** as is due, properly: **nene ~ ?,** why worry ?, it doesn't concern you!: **neme ~ ?,** what's that to me ?, what do I care ? : ⌈**yolcu yolunda ~**⌉, a traveller's place is on his road.
gerek² ~ ... ~..., whether ... or ...: ~ **büyük ~ küçük,** whether large or small.

gereklik Necessity; fitness.
gerekmek vn. Be needful, necessary; be lacking; be fitting or suitable; be worthy of.
geren Stiff clay soil that cracks with drought.
gergedan Rhinoceros; rhinoceros horn.
gergef Embroiderer's frame.
gergi Instrument for stretching; weaver's bar; stretcher of a rowing-boat.
gergin Stretched; taut; strained (relations). ~**lik,** tension.
geri Behind; back; again. Hinder part; rear; remainder. Hinder; posterior; back; backward. ~ **almak,** to take back: ~**sini almak,** to complete stg.: ~ **basmak,** to reverse (a car): ~**ye bırakmak,** to put off, postpone: ~ **dönmek,** to turn back: ~ **durmak,** to abstain, refrain; not to interfere: ~ **gelmek,** to come back, return: ~ **gitmek,** to go back, recede, decline: ~ **kalmak,** to remain behind, be late: ~ **kalan,** the rest, the remainder: ~ **komak,** to put back; leave undone; postpone: ~ **olm.,** (of a watch) to be slow: ~ **vermek,** to give back: ~**sin ~ye yürümek,** to walk backwards: **ayakları* ~ ~ gitmek,** to draw back in fear etc.; to go unwillingly: **ilerisini ~sini düşünmek,** to weigh all considerations.
geridon (Fr. guéridon) Round pedestal table.
gerilemek vn. Recede; be slow; be late; remain behind; make no progress.
geri·li Stretched; taut. ~**lme,** tension; ~ **kuvveti,** tensile strength. ~**lmek,** pass. of germek. ~**nmek,** to stretch oneself.
geriz Sewer, drain.
germ Warm, hot. ~**ü serd,** hot and cold; the pleasant and unpleasant sides of anything.
germe Tension; strain. ~ **somun,** turnbuckle.
germek va. Stretch; tighten. **göğüs ~,** to put on a good face, to feel confident: ···**e göğüs ~,** to stand up to, resist: **göğsünü gere gere,** proudly, confidently: **haça ~,** to crucify.
germi (·−ı) Warmth; ardour, eagerness.
geştügüzar (···−ı) Walking or riding about; journey.
getire In **hak ~,** nil; nothing more; finished; that's all !
getirmek va. Bring; produce; import. **dile ~,** to mention; to make the subject of talk or censure: **hatıra ~,** to remember, think of: **imana ~,** to convert to the faith: **meydana (vücude) ~,** to bring into existence, create: **yerine ~,** to carry out, fulfil; put in its place; replace: **yola ~,** to bring to reason; put to rights.

getirtmek *va.* Cause to be brought, imported *or* transported; order (book *etc.*).

getr Gaiter.

gevelemek Chew; hum and haw.

geven Tragacanth shrub.

geveze Talkative; chattering; gossiping; indiscreet, unable to keep a secret. ~**lik**, babbling, gossip; indiscreet talk.

gevezit Wood-louse; (?) bombardier beetle.

gevher Jewel; essence of a thing; jewel of speech; clever, witty saying.

geviş Chewing the cud, rumination. ~ getirmek, to chew the cud.

gevrek Friable; brittle; crackly. Biscuit. ~ ~ gülmek, to laugh in an easy, self-satisfied way.

gevremek *vn.* Become crisp and dry.

gevş·ek Loose; slack; lax; soft; feeble; weak in health; lukewarm, lacking in zeal. ~ ~ gülmek, to laugh in a vulgar and rather too free-and-easy a manner : ağzı ~, one who cannot hold his tongue : bir işi ~ tutmak, not to take a matter seriously. ~**emek**, ~**eklemek**, ~**elmek**, to become loose, slack, feeble, lukewarm; become too familiar. ~**etmek**, to loosen; slacken; weaken; be slack about *stg.*, neglect.

geyik Deer; stag. ala *or* yağmurca ~, fallow-deer : ulu ~, red deer. ~**dili**, –**ni**, hart's-tongue fern.

gez Notch in an arrow; backsight of a gun (*foresight* = arpacık); rope with knots at intervals for measuring ground; plumb-line. ~e vurmak, to level.

gezdirmek *va. caus. of* gezmek, *q.v.*; göz ~, to cast the eye over *stg.*

gezgin Travelled; who has seen much of the world. ~**ci**, *as* gezgin; itinerant pedlar.

gezi[1] Tissue of mixed silk and cotton.

‖**gezi**[2] Promenade; excursion.

gez·ici Travelling, touring; itinerant. ~**il-mek**, to be gone round; to be visited *or* inspected. ~**inmek**, to go about aimlessly; stroll. ~**inti**, excursion; walk, stroll; place where one strolls; passage, corridor.

gezlemek *va.* Notch (an arrow); measure (ground); adjust, set straight.

gezlik Pocket-knife; a kind of curved sword.

gezme *verb. n. of* gezmek; patrol; watch-man.

gezmek *vn.* Go about; travel; walk about (*esp. with a view to seeing things or for enjoyment*); go about and inspect : dillerde ~, to be on everyone's tongue : ellerde ~, to pass from hand to hand, to be a common object : el üstünde ~, to be highly valued : pek ileride ~, to put forward great pretensions : ⌜ne gezer⌝, by no means, not at all; 'not likely!'; out of the question : ⌜nere-

lerde geziyor !⌝, 'what on earth is he about!'

gıbta Longing; envy (without ill will). ~ etm., to envy : şayanı ~, enviable.

gıcık A tickling sensation (*esp. in the throat*). gıcığı* tutmak, to have a tickling of the throat, to wish to cough. ~**lamak**, to cause an irritation in the throat.

gıcır A kind of chewing-gum. ~ ~, very white and clean, brand new; *imitates the sound of chewing gum or gnashing the teeth or creaking.* ~**damak**, to creak; to rustle; to give out the sound of gıcır. ~**datmak**, to make creak; gnash the teeth. ~**tı**, a creaking *or* rustling noise.

gıda (·–) Food; nourishment; amount of food or drink usually taken. ~**aî**, nutritious; alimentary. ~**lanmak**, to be fed or nourished. ~**lı**, nutritious. ~**sız**, not nutritious; without food; undernourished.

gıdak *In* gıt gıt ~, *imitating the noise of a hen that has laid an egg.* ~**lamak**, to cackle.

gıdık Tickling; the under side of the chin. ~**lamak**, to tickle.

gık *In* ~ bile demedi, without a murmur : bir şeyden ~ demek, to be sick of stg. : ~ dedirtmek, to cause *s.o.* to be sick of stg. : ~ dedirtmemek, not to give *s.o.* a chance to speak; not to give *s.o.* a breathing-space; to listen to no objections.

gıla (·–) High price. kahtu ~, scarcity and dearth, famine.

gılâf Covering; case; *v.* kılıf.

gıllügış Malice; rancour; treachery. ~**tan** âri, utterly sincere. ~**lı**, malicious; untrustworthy. ~**sız**, free from malice; open, sincere.

gılman *pl. of* gulâm. Boys; slaves; the beautiful youths of Paradise. ~ ve cevarı, male and female slaves.

gılzet, –**ti** Coarseness; rudeness; thickness.

gına[1] (·–) Wealth; contentment; sufficiency; satiety; disgust. ~ gelmek, to have had enough; to be surfeited.

gına[2] (·–) Nasal twang; song through the nose.

gıpta *v.* gıbta.

gır *The sound of a* snarl, a snore *etc.* ~**gır**, snarling; snoring; tiresome noise; small motor-boat; zip-fastener; bag-shaped fishing-net : ~ söylemek, to harp querulously on stg.

gırıl·damak (Of the stomach) to rumble. ~**tı**, a rumbling noise (*esp. of the stomach*).

gıriv (·–) Cry, wail, shriek.

gıriz·e (·–) Natural disposition; instinct. ~**î** (·–), natural; instinctive.

gırla (¹·) Abundantly; incessantly; too much.

gırlamak v. gırıldamak.

gırlı Humming, buzzing; noisy.

gırt *Imitates the noise of cutting stg. thick with scissors.*

gırtlak Windpipe; throat. gırtlağına* basmak, to force s.o. to do stg.: gırtlağına düşkün, greedy: ~ gırtlağa gelmek, to be at one another's throats: ~ kemiği, Adam's apple. ~lamak, to strangle.

gışa (·ⸯ) Membrane; covering; veil.

gıt v. gıdak.

gıyab (·⸌) Absence; default. ~en (·ⸯ·), by default; in the absence of: ~ tanımak, to know s.o. by name. ~i (·—ⸯ), defaulting; not present in court: ~ hüküm, judgement given in default.

gıybet, –ti Speaking ill of s.o. in his absence; backbiting; absence; alibi. ~ etm., to slander, backbite. ~çi, slanderer, backbiter.

gıygıy *Imitates the sounds of a violin.*

gibi The similar; the like. Similar, like. As; as soon as; just as; as though. geldiği ~, as soon as he came *or* comes: onun ~, like him; benim ~ler, people like me: bu ~ler, the likes of these; people like this: gereği ~, as it should be: ne ~ ?, what sort of ?, how ?: bir ses duyar ~ oldum, I thought I heard a voice: bilmez ~ soruyor, he asks as though he does not know, pretending not to know: yağmur yağacak ~ görünüyor, it looks as though it were going to rain: bu işin sonu iyi olmıyacak ~me geliyor, I have a feeling that this won't turn out well: kızmış ~ye gelen bir mâna ile baktı, he gave an angry look.

gider *aor. of* gitmek; expenditure, outlay. ~ayak (·⸌··), at the last moment; at the moment of going. ~ek, gradually.

gidermek va. Remove; cause to go; satisfy (a desire).

gidi Pander; *interj. expressing abuse, often mild, sometimes almost affectionate.* seni ~ !, scoundrel !; you little rascal !: hey ~ günler!, oh ! the good old days !

gidilmek *Impers. of* gitmek. oraya gidilmez, one can't go there.

gidiş A going; movement, gait; conduct. ~ o ~, that was the last that was seen of him: ~ini beğenmiyorum, I don't like his conduct. ~at, –tı, *pseudo-Arabic pl. of* gidiş; goings-on.

gidişmek vn. Itch.

gidon (*Fr. guidon*) Burgee; handlebar of a bicycle.

–gil *Suffix meaning* belonging to the family of ... .

giran Heavy; disagreeable; costly. ~baha (···ⸯ), costly; precious.

girdab Whirlpool; dangerous place.

girdi *In such phrases as*: bir işin ~sini çıktısını bilmek, to know the ins and outs of a matter: bu işin daha bir çok ~si çıktısı var, there are a lot more complications in this matter.

girdibad (··ⸯ) Whirlwind.

girgin Who knows how to ingratiate himself; pushing. ~lik, pushfulness; ability to worm one's way into favour.

giriban (·—⸌) Collar. elinden ~ını kurtardı, he escaped.

girift Interlaced (writing); involved, intricate. Small flute.

giriftar (··ⸯ) Captive; afflicted with; subject to; exposed to. ~ olm., to be struck down *by an illness etc.*; to be exposed to.

girilmek *impers. of* girmek. girilmez, no entry !

girinti Recess; indentation. ~li, having recesses: ~ çıkıntılı, wavy, zigzag, indented.

giriş Entry; entrance. ~ supapı, inlet valve. ~ken, enterprising, pushful.

girişmek vn. (*with dat.*) Penetrate; mix oneself up with *a matter*, meddle, interfere; set about, undertake.

Girit (⸌·) Crete. ~li, Cretan.

girive (·—⸌) Blind alley; winding road; impasse, difficulty; whirl of amusement; press of business.

girizgâh Introduction *to a subject*: introductory part of a poem.

girme Act of entering; a breaking into the enemy's position.

girmek vn. (*with dat.*) Enter; go into, be contained by; enter upon, begin; come into, join, participate. girdi çıktı, v. girdi: ⸢girmiş çıkmış⸣, (who has entered a lunatic asylum and come out again), a bit queer, with a screw loose: araya ~, to mediate: birbirine ~, to be intermixed, confused; to become embroiled, to come to blows: eline* ~, to fall into s.o.'s hands, to be caught: yola girmek, to come right somehow.

girme·li Having an entrance; having a recess. ~ çıkmalı, having places for entrance and exit; indented; zigzag. ~lik, ticket of admission; entrance fee.

giry·an a. Weeping. ~e, n. Weeping, tears: ~ etm., to weep.

gişe Guichet; ticket-window; grille; pay-desk.

gitgide (⸌··) Gradually; in the course of time.

gitmek, gider vn. Go; go away; go on *doing*; fade; perish, die; (*with dat.*) suit, fit; be sufficient for; gitmek *is sometimes used with another verb to express finality or certainty, e.g.*: anlıyamadım gitti, I just *couldn't* understand; **doktor gelinceye kadar yaralı ölüp gidecek,** the wounded man will certainly die before the doctor comes. **gide gide,** gradually: **gide gele,** by continually going and returning; with great insistence: **gider ayak,** at the last moment; at the moment of going: ⌐**gitti gider dahi gider**¬, they are gone for ever: **bu elbise iki sene gider,** this suit will last two years: **elden ~,** to be lost: **öyle ... ki deme (sorma) gitsin !,** you never saw such a ...: ⌐**sen giderken ben geliyordum**¬, while you were going I was coming back; I've forgotten more than you ever knew; you can't take me in: **yola ~,** to set out on a journey.

gittikçe (·¹·) By degrees, gradually; more and more.

giy·dirmek *va.* Put on (clothes); clothe, dress; abuse, reproach. **~ecek,** clothing, dress. **~ilmek** (of clothes) to be put on, to be worn. **~im,** garment; clothing, dress: **~ kuşam,** clothes, *esp.* one's best clothes; finery: **bir ~ nal,** a set of horseshoes. **~inmek,** to dress oneself, put on one's clothes: **giyinip kuşanmak,** to dress oneself up, to put on one's best clothes.

giyme (*Fr. guillemet*) Inverted commas.

giymek *va.* Wear, put on (clothes). **mahkemenin hükmünü ~,** to be condemned by a court.

giz¹ A time. **bu ~,** this time; for this once: **her ~,** always; (*with neg.*) never.

giz² Flagstaff *at the stern of a ship.*

gizleme Concealment; camouflage.

gizlemek *va.* Hide; conceal; secrete.

gizli Hidden, concealed; secret. **~ din taşımak,** to have a hidden religion (*also fig.*): **~ kapaklı,** very secret, clandestine: **~siz kapaklısız,** frankly, openly: **~ sıtma,** pruritis, itching; a slight tickling of the throat; one who acts in a sly and underhand manner. **~ce,** in a secret manner, secretly.

gocuk Sheepskin cloak.

gocunmak *v.* kocunmak.

gogoriko (··¹·) Very odd.

gol, –lü Goal (football).

gomalaka (¹···) Shellac.

gomalâstık India-rubber (for erasure).

gomba (¹·) Mat made of rushes *or* fibres; coir rope.

gomene Cable (measure).

gonca *v.* konca.

goril Gorilla.

goygoycu Blind beggar, *who was led round to collect provisions for the 10th of Muharrem.*

göbek Navel; belly; paunch; centre; heart (of a plant); central ornament; generation. **~ adı,** *the name given to a Turkish child at birth, later inscribed on his identity papers,*

but not necessarily used: **~ atmak,** to dance the belly-dance: **~ bağlamak (salıvermek),** to develop a paunch; **~leri beraber kesilmiş,** inseparable friends: **göbeği* çatlamak,** to exert oneself to the utmost: **göbeği* düşmek,** to develop an umbilical hernia; to carry heavy weights: **göbeğini kesmek,** to cut the navel-string: **kendi göbeğini kendi kesmek,** to rely only on oneself for everything: **göbeği sokaktan kesilmiş,** a vagabond: ⌐**onunla göbeğiniz bitişik değil ya!**¬, 'must you always do everything together ?', 'can't you do this by yourself ?': **Parisin göbeğinde,** in the heart of Paris: **yetmiş yedi göbeğinden beri asîl olan Türk,** a Turk whose family has been noble for generations.

göbek·lenmek, to become paunchy; (of a cabbage *etc.*) to develop a heart. **~li,** with a central boss; having a paunch. **~taşı, –nı,** the raised central platform in a Turkish bath.

göç Migration; change of abode. **~ etm.,** to migrate; to strike tents; to pass over to the next world. **~ebe,** nomad. **~er,** nomadic; movable. **~kün,** emigrant.

göçen, göçken Leveret; stoat.

göç·mek *vn.* Strike tents and move off; change one's abode; die; (of a building) to fall down, cave in. **karnı* ~,** to have the belly sink in from starvation. **~men,** emigrant; refugee. **~ük,** the caving-in *of a mine.* **~ünmek,** to pass on, to die. **~ürmek,** *caus. of* göçmek.

göğde, göğermek *v.* gövde, gövermek.

göğsü *v.* göğüs.

göğüs, –gsü Breast, chest, bosom; flare of of a ship's bow. **~ çukuru,** the pit of the stomach: **~ geçirmek,** to sigh, groan: **~ germek,** to face, stand up to: **~ göğse gelmek,** to come to hand-to-hand fighting: **~ göğse muharebe,** hand-to-hand fight: **~ göğse vermek,** to embrace: **~ illeti,** consumption; asthma: **göğsü* kabarmak,** to swell with pride: **~ tahtası,** breastbone, sternum: **elini* göğsüne* koymak,** to lay one's hand on one's heart, to search one's conscience. **~lemek,** to breast (waves *etc.*). **~lü,** broad-chested; having a flared bow (ship): **~ bindirme,** scarf. **~lük,** bib, apron; breastplate; breast harness.

gök, –kü, –ğü Sky; heavens. Blue, sky-blue; beautiful. ⌐**~te ararken yerde bulmak**¬, to meet in an unexpected way *s.o.* one has been searching for: to obtain *stg.* in an unexpected manner: **göğe çıkarmak,** to laud to the skies: **göğe çıkmak,** to fall into a towering rage: **~ gözlü,** blue-eyed (*supposed in Anatolia to be ill-omened*): **~ gürlemek,** to thunder: ⌐**~ten ne yağar**

de yer kabul etmez[1], 'what is there that rains from heaven and the earth does not accept?', one must submit to the decrees of Providence: **başı* göğe ermek**, to be in the seventh heaven of delight: **başı göğe erdi sanıyor**, he thinks he has done stg. wonderful: ⌐**tecrübeyi göğe çekmemişler**¬, 'no harm in trying': **yerden göğe kadar**, utterly, completely: **yeri göğü birbirine katmak**, to move heaven and earth (to do (stg.): **yerle ~ bir olsa**, even if the heavens should fall; no matter what happens.

gök·çe, somewhat blue; pleasant: rock-dove. **~çeağac**, a kind of willow. **~çek**, **~çen**, pretty; pleasant. **~çül**, inclining to blue. **~dere**, the Milky Way. **~elâ**, bluish-grey (eyes). **~gürültüsü, –nü**, thunder. **~kır**, blue-grey, ashen. **~kubbe**, the vault of heaven; the universe. **~lük**, blueness, blue colour. **~remek**, to become blue; become green; sprout; (of a bruise) to become black and blue. **~taşı, –nı**, turquoise. **~yüzü, –nü**, firmament, heavens.

göl Lake; pond; puddle. **~ ayağı**, the outlet of a lake. **~başı, –nı**, head of a lake, stream feeding a lake. **~cük**, pond, puddle. **~ek**, pond, puddle; gnat.

gölge Shadow; shade; shading (drawing); protection. **~de bırakmak**, to overshadow, surpass: **~ etm.**, to cast a shadow; to trouble, become an obstacle: **el ~si**, a letter of recommendation. **~altı, –nı**, shady place, shade. **~lenmek**, to sit in the shade; become shady. **~li**, shaded, shady. **~lik**, shady spot; arbour.

gölotu (¹··), **–nu** Water-lily.

gömgök Intensely blue; dark blue.

gömlek Shirt; layer; cover; sleeve (*mech.*); gas mantle; skin of a snake; generation. **~ değiştirmek**, (of a snake) to change its skin; (*fig.*) to change one's opinions *etc.*: **~ değiştirir gibi**, inconstant, unstable: **~ taşı**, facing-stone: **ateşten ~**, a pitiable situation, *esp.* poverty: **bir ~ farklı olm.**, to be little, if any, superior: **şimdiki hali eskisinden bir ~ iyidir**, his present condition is hardly any better than his old one: **dosya gömleği**, file cover. **~lik**, shirting. **~sarması, –nı**, lamb's liver stuffed with rice.

gömme Act of burying. Buried; let-in, recessed, inlaid; flush.

gömmek *va*. Bury; hide by burying; let in; inlay.

gömüldürük Bow of an ox-yoke; breast-band.

gömül·mek *vn*. Be buried; sink deeply *into stg*. **~ü**, buried; hidden; underground; flush.

gön Leather.

gönder Pole; boom; gaff; goad; flag-staff.

göndermek *va*. Send.

gönlü *v*. gönül. **~nce**, after one's heart; as desired.

gönül, gönlü Heart; feelings; affection, *esp.* amorous affection; mind; inclination; courage. **~ açıklığı**, peace of mind, happiness: **gönlü* açılmak**, to feel at ease, to feel serene, to be cheered up: **~ açmak**, to cheer *s.o.* up: **gönlü* akmak**, to feel attracted by, to fall in love with: **~ almak**, to please, to content, to make up to *a child etc. after being severe*: **gönlünü avlamak**, to try to get the attentions *of a girl etc.*; to run after *a girl*: **~ bolluğu**, generosity: **~ budalası**, hopelessly in love: **gönlü* bulanmak**, to feel sick, nauseated; to feel suspicious *about stg. or s.o.*: **~ bulandırmak**, to nauseate; to arouse suspicion: **gönlü* çekmek**, to desire: **~ darlığı**, foreboding, anxiety: **~ delisi**, one who keeps falling in love; blindly in love: **gönlüne* doğmak**, to have a presentiment: **~ eğlencesi**, pleasure; a toy of love; solace: **gönlünü* etm.**, to please, conciliate; to induce *s.o.* to do *stg.*: **gönlünden* geçirmek**, to meditate *doing stg.*, to entertain *an idea*: **~ gözü**, perception, the power of seeing the truth: **gönlünü* hoş tutmak**, to try to make oneself forget trouble; not to worry: **~ hoşluğu ile**, willingly: **gönlü* kalmak**, (i) to feel resentment, to feel hurt; (ii) to hanker after *stg.*: **~ kırmak**, to hurt the feelings: **gönlünden* kopmak**, (of a present or tip) to be given gladly; '**gönlünüzden ne koparsa veriniz !**', 'give what you feel like giving !': '**gönlümden koptu fakire bir lira verdim**', 'I gladly gave the poor fellow a lira': **gönlü* olm.**, to agree (*to* = ···**e**); to be in love (*with* = ···**de**): **gönlü var**, he is willing; he is in love: **~ vermek**, to give one's heart, to fall in love: **gönlünü* yapmak**, to console; to satisfy: **gönlü yok**, he is unwilling; he is not in love: **canü ~den** *or* **candan ve ~den**, with all one's heart and soul: **iki ~ bir olm.**, for two hearts to beat as one; to be in full agreement.

gönül·lü Willing; self-assertive. Volunteer; lover; beloved. **alçak ~**, meek, modest; affable. **~süz**, without pride. modest; affable; disinclined, unwilling, **~süzlük**, disinclination, unwillingness; modesty, lack of self-assertiveness.

gönye Square (drawing instrument). **~sinde olm.**, to be at right angles.

göre (*with dat.*) According to; respecting; about; considering; suitable for.

göre göre *v*. göz.

görenek A doing stg. because others do it; fashion.

göresi *In* ~ gelmek, to long to see, to miss. ~mek, to long for.

görgü Experience; breeding, good manners. ~lü, well-bred, having good manners. ~süz, ill-bred, common; without manners; uncouth.

görme Act of seeing, sight. Seeing; seen. sonradan ~, upstart, parvenu. ~ce, subject to the condition of being seen (of a sale); estimated by sight only.

görmek, -ür *va.* See; deem; visit; experience; *used as an auxiliary verb with the gerund in* ···e, ···a *it signifies continuous action, e.g.* söyliyegörmek, to go on speaking. görerek ateş, direct fire (*mil.*); görmiyerek ateş, indirect fire: ⌐gören Allah için söylesin !¬, *stg. like* 'I swear it's true!': görmüş geçirmiş, a man of great experience: vaktile görmüş geçirmiş, one who has seen better days: görmemiş *v.* görmemiş: ⌐göreyim seni!¬, 'let's see what you are made of': görsün *v.* görsün: çok ~, to deem too much; to regard as being beyond s.o.'s deserts: harcını ~, to defray the expenses of *stg.*: hizmet ~, to serve; to render a service: hoş ~, to tolerate, condone: iş ~, to work: münasib ~, to deem fit; to think it a fitting moment *to do stg.*: rüya ~, to dream: tahsil ~, to study: terbiye ~, to be educated: zarar ~, to suffer loss: 'onun azametini görme!', 'you never saw anything like his conceit !'

görmemezlik (¹···), a feigning not to see; indifference; connivance. ~ten *or* görmemezliğe gelmek, to pretend not to see.

görmemiş Inexperienced; parvenu. ⌐~in oğlu olmuş (çekmiş çükünü koparmış)¬, *said of s.o., esp. a parvenu, who spoils stg. which he cannot properly appreciate.*

görsün *3rd sing. imperative of* görmek. Let him see ! gelmiye ~ !, wait till he comes (and then you'll see)!: bir kere kızmaya ~, if he *does* get angry (then you'll regret it)!: yazmıya ~, he's only got to write about it (and that would settle the matter).

görücü Woman sent to find or inspect a prospective bride.

görüm Sight; look. yüz ~ü, the bridegroom's first sight of his bride's face (*in former times*). ~ce, husband's sister, sister-in-law. ~lük, stg. to be seen: yüz görümlüğü, present given by the bridegroom to the bride.

görün·mek *vn.* Show oneself; appear; seem; be visible. ⌐görünen köye kılavuz istemez¬, 'no guide is needed to a village that is in sight', *i.e.* it is too obvious to require explanation: görünmez olm., to disappear. ~ür, apparent; visible: ~lerde yok, it is not in sight. ~üş, appearance;

show, parade: ~ü böyle, such are the appearances: ~ etm., to make a show: ~te, apparently.

görüş Mode *or* act of seeing; point of view. ilk ~te, at first sight: onun son ~üm oldu, that was the last I saw of him. ~me, interview; talk, conversation.

görüş·mek *vn.* See one another; meet and converse; become acquainted. *va.* Discuss. görüşeni karışanı olmamak, to be free from interference by others, to be independent: gene görüşürüz inşallah, I hope we shall meet again ! ~türmek, to introduce to one another.

gösteriş Appearance; aspect; imposing appearance; show, ostentation, display; demonstration; eyewash. kuru ~, mere show. ~li, of striking appearance; stately, imposing. ~siz, poor looking, unimposing.

göstermek *va.* Show; indicate; expose *to the sun etc. vn.* Appear. baş ~, to show its head, to appear: Allah göstermesin !, God forbid ! : kendini* ~, to prove one's worth: sana gösteririm !, I'll show you ! (I'll teach you not to do that again !) : ufak ~, to look younger than one is.

göstermelik Worth exhibiting; for show only (of goods in a shop window).

göt, -tü Behind, arse; courage, audacity. ~ün ~ün, backwards.

götürmek *va.* Take away; carry off; lead *or* conduct to; hold, contain; bear, endure, support. bu mesele su götürür, that is an open question: bu iş şaka götürmez, this is not a joking matter: içi* götürmemek, to be unable to bear the misfortunes of others.

götürü In a lump sum. ~ almak, to buy in the lump, to contract at a lump price: ~ bina, a building put up by contract; wretchedly built: ~ pazarlık, a bargain for the whole lot.

gövde Body; trunk; whole carcass. ~ye atmak, to eat, swallow: kan ~yi götürüyor, there's a regular massacre going on; 'there's a hell of a mess'. ~li, bulky; corpulent.

gövelâ *v.* gökelâ.

göver·mek *vn.* Turn blue *or* green. ~ti, a blue spot on the skin.

göya *v.* gûya.

göymek *va.* Burn.

göz Eye; the evil eye; hole; mesh; opening; drawer; compartment; pigeon-hole; tray *of a balance*; spring; arch *of a bridge*; bud. ~ ~, all holes; porous; reticulated: ~ü açık, wide awake, shrewd: ~ü açık gitmek, to die disappointed: ~ünü açıp kapamadan *or* kapayıncaya kadar, in the twinkling of an eye: ~ açtırmamak, to give *a person* no respite, to give no chance to recover himself *or* take action: ~ alıcı, striking, dazzling: ~e almak, to envisage, to bring oneself to *or* resign oneself to *stg.*: ···e ~ atmak, to glance at: ~ünü* bağlamak, to blindfold; to hoodwink: ~ bağmak, to cast a spell, to bewitch: ~ boyamak, *v.* boyamak: ~den çıkarmak, to be prepared to pay *or* sacrifice *stg., e.g.* ⌐bu seyahat için yüz lirayı ~den çıkarmak lâzım⌐, 'you will have to be prepared to spend 100 lira on this journey': bir şeyin ~ünü çıkarmak, to reject stg. good (for stg. inferior): ~den çıkmak, to fall from favour, to fall in consideration: ~ü çıkmak, to lose an eye: ~ü daldan budaktan esirgememek (sakınmamak), to disregard dangers: ~den düşmek, to fall into disesteem: ~ etm., to wink: ~üne* girmek, to ingratiate oneself with *s.o.*, to curry *s.o.'s* favour: ~ göre göre, what is obvious to all, *e.g.* ~ göre göre çalmak, to steal openly; ~ göre göre yalan söylemek, to tell a barefaced lie, to tell a lie although one knows that everyone knows it is a lie; ~ göre göre inkâr etm., to deny what one's auditors have already heard one admit; yüzlerce genci ~ göre göre ölüme sevk etmek, to send hundreds of young men to an obvious death: ~ ~ü görmez (karanlık), pitch dark: ~ hapsi, a being under surveillance *or* detention; ~ hapsine almak, to keep under observation *or* under open arrest: ~ünün* içine bakmak, (i) to cherish dearly; (ii) to be at the beck and call of *s.o.*; (iii) to look entreatingly at *s.o.*: ~ü* kalmak, to hanker after *stg.*, to envy *stg. possessed by another*: ~ü* yollarda kalmak, to have been waiting a long time *for s.o. or stg.*: ~ kapağı, eyelid: ~ü kara, desperate, beside himself: ~ karası, the iris of the eye: ~ kararı, judgement by the eye; guess; roughly speaking: ~ü* kesmek, to think oneself capable *of doing stg.*; to like; to think suitable: ~üne* kestirmek, to think oneself capable of ...; to have an eye on *stg.* as suitable, to mark down as a desirable possession; to pick out a suitable *one*: ~ koymak, to cast covetous eyes upon *stg.*: ~ kulak olm., to be all eyes and ears, to be on the qui-vive; ⌐bu çocuğa ~ kulak oluver!⌐, 'just keep a sharp eye on this child': ~ nuru, work that strains the eyes; ~ nuru dökmek, to engage on work that strains the eyes: ~ünün* nuru, the light of one's eyes, darling: ~de olm., to be in favour, to be much thought of: ···de ~ü* olm., to desire *stg.* strongly: ~ü* olmamak, to have no particular desire for: ~ önünde bulundurmak, to keep in view, to bear in mind: ⌐~ünü seveyim!⌐, please!; *sometimes* 'well done!': ~üne* sokmak, to thrust *stg.* under *s.o.'s* eyes by way of re-

proof or accusation: ~de tutmak, to hold in favour: ~ü* tutmak, to take a fancy to: ~ ucu, the corner of the eye: iki ~üm, my dear: iki ~ arasında, in the twinkling of an eye: yüz ~ olm., to be unduly intimate. göz·ağrısı, –nı, eye-ache; ilk ~, one's first love. ~akı, –nı, the white of the eye. ~bağı, –nı, magic, spell. ~bağıcı, magician; conjuror. ~bebeği, –ni, pupil of the eye; 'the apple of one's eye'. ~cü, watchman, sentinel; spy. ~cülük, watch; keeping guard; spying. ~çukuru, –nu, eye-socket. ~dağı, –nı, intimidation; fright: ~ vermek, to intimidate; to act as a deterrent. ~de, favourite, pet. ~demiri, –ni, bower anchor.
gözen Fallow-deer.
gözer Sieve, riddle, screen.
gözetleme Observation (*mil.*). ~k, to observe, spy upon.
gözetmek *va.* Mind, look after, take care of; watch; pay regard to; observe (duty); keep under observation; envisage. hatır ~, to respect the feelings of.
göz·evi, –ni, eye-socket. ~gü, mirror. ~leme, an eyeing, a watching for; fritter, pancake. ~lemek, to watch for, wait for; keep an eye on. ~lü, having eyes; having drawers *or* pigeon-holes: beş ~, (bridge) having five arches: para ~, fond of money. ~lük, spectacles: ~ otu, honesty (plant). ~lükçü, optician. ~lüklü, bespectacled. ~taşı, –nı, copper sulphate. ~ükmek, to appear, show oneself. ~yaşı, –nı, tears: ~ dökmek, to shed tears. ~yılgınlığı, –nı, dread, terror.
grandi (¹·) Mainmast.
grev Strike. ~ci, striker.
griva Cat-head. demiri ~ya almak, to cat the anchor.
gron A kind of heavy silk cloth.
grup, –pu Group.
gubar (·⌐) Dust; pollen. ~alûd, covered with dust.
gube A kind of sardine.
gudd·e Gland. ~î (·⌐), glandular.
gudruf (·⌐) Cartilage.
gudubet (·–⌐), –ti Ugly face. ~ bozuntusu, hideously ugly.
gufran Mercy (*of God only*).
guguk Cuckoo; cry of derision.
gugurik Odd; ridiculous.
gul Ghoul, ogre.
gulâm (·⌐) Boy; youth; male slave. ~para, pederast.
gulfe Foreskin.
gulgule Clamour; gurgling noise.
guluklamak *vn.* (Of a hen) to cluck.
gulyabani (···⌐) Ogre.
gumena (¹··) Cable (length).

gûna (·-̣·) Sort; way, manner. ~**gûn**, of various sorts.

gunne Nasal twang.

gupilya (·¹·) Split pin.

gûr *n.* Grave.

gurab (·-̣) Crow.

gurama (··-̣) *pl.* Creditors. taksimi ~, the distribution of a debtor's goods among his creditors.

gurbet, -ti Absence from home; exile; foreign travel. ~ **çekmek**, to feel homesick. ihtiyarı ~ **etm.**, voluntarily to exile oneself, to emigrate. ~**zede**, exiled; living abroad.

gureba (··-̣) *pl. of* **garib**. Strangers; people living out of their own country; paupers; *the name of certain cavalry units in former times.* ~ **hastanesi**, infirmary.

gurk Broody (hen); turkey-cock.

gurlamak, guruldamak *vn.* Rumble.

gurre First night of a lunar month; brightness; first glow of dawn; star on a horse's forehead.

gurub Sunset; setting of a star ~ **etm.**, to set.

gurultu Rumbling noise.

gurur Pride, vanity; conceit. ~**lu**, arrogant; vain.

gussa Sorrow; anxiety.

gusül, -slü Ritual ablution. ~**hane** (··-¹), bath for ritual washing.

gûş Ear.

gûya As if, as though; it seemed that; one would think that; supposedly.

gübre Dung; manure. ~ **şerbeti**, liquid manure. ~**lemek**, to dung, manure. ~**lik**, dung-hill.

güc Strength; force, violence; difficulty. ~**üne* gitmek**, to offend, annoy, hurt *s.o.'s* feelings: ~**ü* yetmek**, to be strong enough, to be able: **iş** ~, business, occupation (*generally written in the nominative as one word but declined as two words, e.g.* **işine* ~üne bakmak**, to attend to one's work; **işi ~ü yok**, he has no occupation).

güc·enmek, to be offended, hurt *or* angry. ~**lü**, strong; violent: ~ **kuvvetli**, very strong and healthy: ⌐**hem suçlu hem ~**¹, not merely at fault but offensive about it. ~**süz**, *in* **işsiz** ~, out-of-work, without a job: ~ **kuvvetsiz**, without strength. ~**süzlük**, weakness; slackness; unemployment.

güç Difficult, hard. With difficulty. ~ **belâ** *or* ~ **hal ile**, with great difficulty: **sabahı** ~ **etm.**, to wait impatiently for the morning.

güderi Chamois leather; deerskin.

güdük Tailless; docked; stumpy; incomplete. ~ **kalmak**, to be incomplete *or* unfinished; to be childless.

güdümlü Controlled, *esp.* government controlled. ~ **mermi**, guided missile.

güft·e The words of a song. ~**ügû**, conversation; gossip.

güğül Cocoon (from which the moth has emerged).

güğüm Copper vessel with a long handle.

güher *v.* **gevher**.

güherçile Saltpetre.

gül Rose; dial *of a compass.* ~ **gibi**, neat; charming; finely, 'swimmingly': ⌐**ü tarife ne hacet !**¹, you needn't tell me, I know all about the fellow: ⌐**al ~üm ver ~üm**¹, 'take it, my pet, give it, my pet!', *said about one who is over-polite:* ···**in üstüne ~ koklamaz**, he wouldn't dream of making love to anyone but ... .

gül·ab (·-̣), rose-water. ~**bayramı, -nı**, the Feast of Tabernacles; Feast of Pentecost. ~**beşeker** (·¹··), conserve of roses. ~**çehreli**, rosy-cheeked. ~**dan**, vase for flowers.

gülbank, -kı Prayer *or* song uttered by many in unison; chant; slogan; war-cry.

güldür güldür *Imitates fluent reading or steady burning.*

güldür·mek *va.* Make laugh; amuse. **kendini âleme** (**her kese**) ~, to be a laughingstock: **yüzüne*** ~, to rejoice the heart of. ~**ücü**, causing to laugh, amusing.

gülecek Laughable; ridiculous.

güleç Smiling.

güler Smiling; given to laughter. ~ **yüz**, a smiling cheerful face: ⌐~ **yüz, tatlı söz yılanı deliğinden çıkarır**¹, a smiling face and pleasant words will lure a snake from his hole. ~**yüzlü**, merry, cheerful; affable.

güleş *v.* **güreş**.

gül·gün Rosy, rose-coloured ~**hatmi**, hollyhock. ~**istan**, rose-garden. ~**istanlık**, *in* ⌐**dünyayı güllük ~ görmek**¹, to see everything through rose-coloured glasses. ~**kurusu, -nu**, dried rose leaves *for jam*; the colour of dried rose leaves.

güllâbi, güllâbici Warden in a lunatic asylum. ⌐**ben deli ~si değilim**¹, 'I can't deal with idiots'.

güllaç Sweet *made with starch wafers, filled with cream and flavoured with rose-water.*

gülle Cannon-ball; shell; bar-shot; any very heavy thing. ~ **atmak**, to put the weight.

gül·lü Surrounded by *or* decorated with roses. ~**lük**, rose-garden.

gülmek *vn.* Laugh; smile; be pleased. ⌐**güle güle!**¹, 'good-bye and good luck!': **güle güle** (*with a verb*) to do anything happily or with success; **güle güle kullanınız (giyiniz)!**, *said to one who has just acquired stg. new;* **güle güle kirleniniz !**, *a* *greeting to one just out of a bath*: **bir gözü* ~**, to have mixed feelings: **yüze ~**, to feign friendship, to dissimulate: **yüzü* ~**, to be merry and cheerful.

gülmez Sullen; sour-faced; severe.

gül·rengi (¹··), **–ni** Rose colour. **~suyu** (¹··), **–nu**, rose-water.

gülümsemek *vn.* Smile.

gülün·ç Ridiculous. **~ecek**, ridiculous; odd **~mek**, to laugh to oneself; to be a subject of laughter: **buna gülünmez**, this is not a thing to laugh about.

gülüstan Rose-garden.

gülüşmek *vn.* Laugh together; laugh at one another.

gül·yağı (¹··), **–nı** Attar of roses. **~yanaklı** (¹···), rosy-cheeked **~zar** (·¹), rose-garden; flower garden.

güm[1] A thing buried; ruin. **~e gitmek** (*sl.*), to go to ruin; perish.

güm[2] Hollow booming noise.

güman Doubt; suspicion.

gümbür ~ ~, *imitates* a booming noise. **~demek**, to boom, thunder, reverberate; (*sl.*) to 'pop off', die. **~tü**, a booming noise: '**seyreyle sen ~yü !**', now for the crash!, now there will be a to-do!

gümec Honeycomb.

gümlemek *As* gümbürdemek.

gümrah[1] Astray; having lost the way; depraved.

gümrah[2] Dense; copious; luxuriant. **~lık**, abundance, luxuriance.

gümrük Customs; custom-house. ⌜**~ten mal kaçırır gibi**⌝, unnecessarily hurried and flustered: **~ resmi**, customs dues: **kara gümrüğü**, octroi. **~çü**, customs officer.

gümüş Silver. **~ kaplama**, silver-plated: **~ takımı**, silver plate, set of silver. **~balığı**, **–nı**, sand smelt. **~lemek**, to silver-plate. **~selvi**, reflection of the moon on water. **~suyu**, crystal-clear water. **~ü**, silver grey; silvery: **~ fanilâdan pantalon**, grey flannel trousers.

gün Day; time; sun; light; feast-day. **~den ~e**, from day to day: **~lerden bir ~**, once upon a time: **~ü ~üne**, to the very day: **~ünü ~ etm.**, to enjoy oneself properly; to make the best use of one's time (*iron.*): **~ün ~ü var**, the day may come (when we shall need it): **~ aşırı**, every other day: **~ün birinde**, then, one day (unexpectedly): ···**e ~ doğmak**, for *s.o.'s* day to come, *e.g.* ⌜**muallim gelmedi, çocuklara ~ doğdu**⌝, 'the teacher did not come, it was a great day for the children'; ⌜**harb çıktı muhtekirlere ~ doğdu**⌝, 'war broke out, it was the profiteers' chance': **~ geçmek**, for a day to pass; for the sun to scorch *or* tan: **~ görmez**, sunless (place): **~ görmüş**, who has seen better

days; who has held important posts or been a man of consequence: **~ görmemiş**, of no standing, with no career behind him: **~ünü görürsün !**, (*a threat*) 'you'll pay for this !': **bir ~ evvel**, as soon as possible: **ele ~e karşı**, before all, publicly: **geçen ~**, the other day, not long ago: **iki ~de bir**, every third day: ⌜**ne ~e duruyor?**⌝, 'why not use it?'; 'why not do this?': **o ~ bugündür**, ever since that day: **öbür ~**, the day after tomorrow: **öteki ~**, the day before yesterday; the other day.

günah Sin; fault. ⌜**~ı boynuna!**⌝, 'well, *you* must take the consequences!': **~ çıkarmak**, (of a priest) to hear a confession: **bu ~ına (bile) değmez**, the game is not worth the candle: **~ından* geçmek**, to pass over *s.o.'s* sin, to forgive him: **~a girmek**, to sin: **~ına* girmek**, to accuse wrongfully, to wrong: **~ vebali**, the whole responsibility for an evil deed: ⌜**beni ~a sokma!**⌝, 'don't drive me to blasphemy (or other sin)!'; 'don't insist upon this!'

günah·kâr, sinner; culpable; prostitute. **~kârlık**, sinfulness; guiltiness; prostitution. **~lı**, culpable; sinful. **~sız**, blameless; without sin.

gün·aşırı, every other day. **~aydın**, good morning ! **~balığı**, **–nı**, rainbow wrasse. **~batısı**, **–nı**, sunset; West; west wind. **~begün**, day by day. **~delik**, daily wage; daily (paper *etc.*); everyday (wear); ephemeral. **~delikçi**, day-labourer. ||**~dem**, agenda. **~doğrusu**, **~doğuşu**, **–nu**, East; south-east wind. **~dönümü**, **–nü**, solstice. **~düz**, daytime; by day: **~ feneri**, a nigger. **~düzlü**, *in* geceli **~**, going on night and day, continuous. **~düzse**. **fası**, **–nı**, convolvulus. **~düzün**, by day; in the daytime.

güneş Sun; sunshine. ⌜**~i balçıkla sıvamak**⌝, (to plaster over the sun with clay), to try to hide the truth: **~ gibi**, plain, manifest: **~ tutulmak**, for the sun to be eclipsed: **~ vurmak**, for the sun to cause sunstroke: **başına ~ geçmiş**, he is feeling the effect of the sun. **~lenmek**, to bask in the sun; sunbathe; be spread in the sun to dry. **~lik**, sunny place; sunshade; sun-hat; peak *of a cap*.

||**güney** South.

gün·kü Of the day. **geçen ~ gazete**, the paper of a few days ago: **her ~**, everyday. **~lemek**, to pass the day *in a place*. **~lük**[1], sufficient for *so many* days; *so many* days old; **on ~ zahire**, provisions for ten days; **iki ~ çocuk**, a two-day-old baby: **~ emir**, order of the day (*mil.*): **~ güneşlik**, bright sunny weather: **~ yumurta**, new-laid egg. **~lük**[2], liquidambar tree; incense, frankincense.

~**übirlik,** day visit (without spending the night). ~**ügününe,** to the very day; right on time.

günye *v.* gönye.

güpegündüz (ᐟ···) In broad daylight.

güpeşte *v.* küpeşte.

gür[1] Abundant; dense; rank. ~ sesli, with a fine strong voice.

gür[2] *In* ~ ~, imitates a gurgling or a humming noise.

gürbüz Sturdy; robust. ~**lük,** sturdiness; healthiness.

Gürcü Georgian. ~**stan,** Georgia.

güreş Wrestling. ~**ci,** wrestler. ~**mek,** to wrestle. başa ~, to wrestle for the championship; (*fig.*) to concern onself only with important matters.

gürgen Hornbeam; made of hornbeam; beautiful; showy; (*commercially* gürgen *is often used for* beechwood).

gürleme Loud noise. gök ~, thunder. ~**k,** to make a loud noise: gök ~, to thunder.

gürlük Abundance; exuberance; luxuriance. ⌐**Allah son gürlüğü versin !**⌐, 'may God give him happiness and prosperity in the end !'

güruh Class, group (*always derogatory*). ⌐~**u lâyeflehun**⌐, 'an incorrigible lot'.

gürül *In* ~ ~, bubbling, gurgling; in a loud and rich voice. ~**demek,** to make a loud noise; to thunder; (of cattle) to low.

gürültü Loud noise; uproar; confusion. ~**ye gitmek,** to be lost in the confusion; to suffer punishment or loss through no fault of one's own; for the innocent to suffer with the guilty. ~**ye pabuc bırakmamak,** not to be intimidated by mere threats. ~**cü,** noisy; boisterous (person). ~**lü,** noisy, tumultuous, crowded. ~**süz,** noiseless, quiet.

gürz Iron club; mace.

güsüm *Name of* a violent wind *on the Black Sea coast*.

güteperka (··ᐟ·) Guttapercha.

gütmek, –der *va* Drive before one; drive *an animal* to pasture; cherish; nurse (a project or a grievance) hedef ~, to pursue an aim: kan ~, to nurse revenge for a murder, to have a blood feud.

güve Clothes-moth.

güvec Earthenware cooking-pot; casserole. türlü ~, meat and vegetables *cooked in such a pot.*

güven Confidence; reliance ||~**lik,** security. ~**mek,** (*with dat.*) trust in; rely on; be confident; dare: ⌐**güvendiğim dağlara kar yağdı**⌐, I have been let down, sadly disappointed.

güvercin Pigeon. ~ gerdanı, shot colour. ~**lik,** dove-cot, pigeon-loft; small cupboard *in the stern of a boat*; small fort *in the form of a tower.* ~**otu, –nu,** vervain; verbena.

güverte (·ᐟ·) Deck. ~ yolcusu, deck passenger (without a cabin). ~**li,** decked.

güvey Bridegroom; son-in-law. ~ feneri, winter-cherry: ~ girmek, to marry.

güveyeniği (·ᐟ···), –**nı** Moth-eaten place.

güz Autumn.

güzaf (·ᐟ̱) Idle talk; bombast. lâfü ~, empty words; brag.

–güzar (·ᐟ̱) *Pers. suffix.* Performing ...; passing ..., *e.g.* maslahat~, (who carries on the business) Chargé d'Affaires.

güzel Beautiful, pretty; good; nice. A beauty. ~ hava, fine weather: çok ~ !, very good ! ~**avratotu** (···ᐟ··), –**nu,** deadly nightshade; belladonna ~**ce** (··ᐟ), pretty fair; fairly well; (·ᐟ·), thoroughly. ~**im,** that beautiful (thing) of mine, or his *etc.* ~**lik,** beauty; goodness, agreeableness; fragrancy; happiness: ~ ile, gently, without using force: ⌐**zorla ~ olmaz**⌐, *lit.* 'good cannot be imposed by force', *but the meaning is rather* 'this is something which cannot be achieved by force'.

güzeran (··ᐟ̱) Passing. Passage. ~ etm., to pass.

güzergâh Place of passage; ford; ferry; route (of a bus *etc.*).

güzeşte Past; outstanding, in arrears.

güzey Shade; shady side.

güzi·de (·—ᐟ) Choice; elect; select. ~**delik,** choice part, the best part. ~**n** (·ᐟ̱), chosen; choice.

güz·lük Autumn-sown (crops). ~**ün** (ᐟ·), in the autumn.

H

ha *interj. Calling attention, expressing surprise, asking a rhetorical question; as English* 'ah!', 'hi!', 'ha!' ~ babam konuşuyor !, he talks and talks!: ~ bügün ~ yarın, either today or tomorrow, it doesn't matter which: ⌐~ bügün ~ yarın yaparım

diye beni oyaladı⌐, 'he put me off by saying he would do it within the next day or two': ⌐~ deyince bulunmaz⌐, you can't find it on the spur of the moment: ⌐böyle söyledi ~ ?⌐, 'so he said that, did he ?': ⌐gitti ~ ?⌐, 'he's gone, has he ?': herkes harb ~ çıktı ~

çıkacak diye telaş içinde idi, everyone was perturbed about the probability of war: **manzara da manzara ~ !**, what a wonderful view!

hâb (–) Sleep. **~ı gaflet**, lack of vigilance.

habaset (·–¹), **–ti** Wickedness; vice; act of villainy.

habazan Greedy, gluttonous; hungry for. **~lık**, hunger.

habbe Grain; seed. **~ değmez**, worthless: **~si kalmadı**, there was nothing left: ⌐**~yi kubbe yapmak**⌐, 'to make a mountain out of a molehill': **su ~si**, bubble.

haber Knowledge, information; news; anecdote; predicate (*gram.*). **~ almak**, to receive information, to learn; to make inquiry: **~ etm.**, to inform, give notice: **~im olmadan**, unknown to me, without my knowing: **~im var**, I know, I am aware: **~im yok**, I know nothing about it; I have not heard: **kara ~**, bad news. **~ci**, messenger; telltale. **~dar**, possessed of information: **~ etm.**, to inform, to bring to the knowledge of. **~leşmek**, to keep one another informed; to correspond.

Habeş, habeşî Abyssinian; dark-olive coloured. **~istan**, Abyssinia.

habib (·–¹) Lover, beloved; friend.

hâbide (––¹) Sleeping.

Habil (–¹) Abel. **~ ile Kabil**, Cain and Abel.

habir (·–¹) Informed; aware; erudite.

habire (·–¹) Continuously.

habîs (·–¹) Wicked; abominable; vicious; malignant (tumour). Wretch, scoundrel.

habt·etmek (¹··), **–eder** *va.* Get the better of in an argument; reduce to silence. **~olmak** (¹··), to be reduced to silence.

hac, –ccı The pilgrimage to Mecca. **~ca gitmek (varmak)**, to make the pilgrimage.

hacalet (·–¹), **–ti** Shame; mortification.

hacamat, –tı A bleeding or cupping.

haccetmek (¹··), **–eder** *vn.* Make the pilgrimage to Mecca.

hâcegân *pl. of* hoca. Hodjas. **~lık**, *an office in the Moslem priesthood.*

hacer Stone. **~i semavî**, meteorite: **~ şecer**, useless things; useless people, the masses. **~iesved**, the Black Stone *in the Kaaba at Mecca*: **~ gibi muallakta**, *said of some matter kept in suspense.*

hacet (–¹), **–ti** Need; necessity; requirement, want; prayer *to God or some supernatural power, asking for stg.* **~ dilemek**, to make such a prayer: **~ kapısı (penceresi)**, door *or* window of a saint's tomb, *where people pray for the fulfilment of a wish*: **~ yok**, there is no need for it: **defi ~ etm.**, to relieve nature: **ne ~ ?**, what need is there?; for what purpose?

hacı One who has made the pilgrimage to Mecca, Hadji; pilgrim. **~m**, my dear fellow: ⌐**~sı hocası**⌐, 'all the ecclesiastics': ⌐**seni gören ~ olur**⌐, 'you're quite a stranger'. **~ağa**, a provincial nouveau riche. **~baba**, a venerable old man who has made the pilgrimage. **~laryolu**, the Milky Way. **~otu, –nu**, mandrake plant. **~yağı, –nı**, a kind of cheap perfume. **~yatmaz**, *a toy loaded at the bottom, so that when knocked over it gets up again*, tumbler; restless, mischievous child.

hacım *v.* hacim.

hacil Ashamed; mortified.

hacim, –cmi Volume, bulk; tonnage. **hacmi istiabî**, cubic capacity *of a container.*

hacir, –cri Prohibition, interdiction, *esp. the legal interdiction of a person's control over property etc.*

Hacivad *A character in Karagöz representing the official type.*

haciz, –czi Sequestration; distraint.

hacle Bridal chamber.

hacmen (¹·) In volume; in size.

haç, –çı Cross; crucifix. **~ çıkarmak**, to cross oneself. **~lamak**, to crucify. **~lı**, having a cross: **~lar**, the Crusaders.

had, –ddi Boundary; limit; degree, rank; term (of a syllogism or mathematical equation). **~dini* bilmek**, to know one's place: **~dini* bilmemek**, to be above oneself, to presume: ···**e ~dini bildirmek**, to put s.o. in his place, to teach him how to behave: **~ çizmek**, to set a limit to: **~dim değil**, it is not for me (to say *or* do *stg.*): **~dine mi düşmüş !**, he wouldn't dare!: **~di geçmek**, to overstep the bounds, to go beyond the limit: **~dim olmıyarak**, if I may be so presumptuous; although it is not for me to say: **~dim yok**, I dare not, I have no right: **~di zatında**, in itself, essentially: **~den ziyade**, beyond the limit, excessively: **kimin ~dine?**, who would dare?: **ne ~dimize !**, how could I presume to do such a thing?; I wouldn't dare.

hâd (–) Sharp; pungent; acute (illness). **zaviyei ~de**, acute angle.

hâdde Wire-drawer's plate; rolling-mill; acute angle. **~den geçirmek**, to examine minutely.

haddi *v.* had.

hadebe Hump; protuberance; solar prominence.

hadeka Pupil *of the eye.*

hademe *pl. used as sing.* Servant (*in offices, schools, etc*).

hadım Eunuch. **~ etm.**, to castrate. **~ağası, –nı**, chief eunuch in a palace or great house; black eunuch.

hadi (¹·) *v.* **haydi.**

hadid¹, haziz Perigee; perihelion.

hadid² Irascible; violent. Iron. **~ülmizac,** choleric, hot-tempered.

hadika (·−¹) Garden; pleasure-ground.

hadim (−¹) Servant.. Serving.

hâdim (−¹) Destroying.

hadis (·⁻¹) Religious tradition of the Prophet.

hâdis (−¹) New; recently appeared; of recent occurrence. **~ olm.,** to occur; to come into existence. **~ e** (pl. **hâdisat),** event; incident; accident, mishap : **~ çıkarmak,** to provoke an incident.

hadnaşinas (·−·¹) Who is above himself, who does not know his place.

hads Intuition. **~î,** intuitive.

hadsiz Unbounded, unlimited. **~ hesabsız,** innumerable.

haf Half-back (football).

hafakan Palpitation. **~lar basmak (bozmak),** to be exasperated.

hafaya (·−⁻¹) *pl. of* **hafi.** Secrets.

hafazanallah (··¹··) 'May God preserve us !', *used when talking about a disaster.*

hafız (−¹) Keeper; protector; one who has committed the Koran to memory; (*sl.*) simpleton : **kuvvei ~a,** memory : **~ı kutub,** librarian. **~a** (−·¹), memory.

hafi (·⁻¹) Hidden; secret.

hafid (·⁻¹) Grandson. **~e** (·−¹), granddaughter.

hafif Light; easy; flighty. **~ten almak,** tó make light of, not to take seriously : **~ tertib,** slightly, just a little. **~lenmek,** to become lighter *or* easier; to lose weight; diminish. **~lik,** lightness; flightiness; relief, ease of mind. **~meşreb,** flighty, frivolous; dissolute. **~meşreblik,** levity, frivolity; looseness of morals.

hafir, –fri Excavation.

hafi·ye Detective; spy; secret agent. **~yyen** (·⁻¹), secretly; stealthily.

hafr·etmek (¹··), **–eder** *va.* Excavate. **~iyat, –tı,** excavations.

hafta Week. **~larca,** for weeks on end : **~sına,** the same day the following week : **~sına kalmaz,** within a week : **~ya,** a week today. **~başı, –nı,** the first day of the week; pay-day. **~lık,** weekly; per week: weekly wages. **~lıkçı, ~lıklı,** worker paid by the week.

haftaym (¹··) Half-time (football).

haham Rabbi. **~başı, –nı,** Chief Rabbi.

hahiş (−¹) Wish, desire. **~ger,** desirous.

hahnahah (⁻−−) Willy-nilly.

haib (−¹) Disappointed; frustrated. **~ü hasir,** disillusioned and nonplussed.

haif (−¹) Fearful, timorous.

hail¹ (−¹) Interposing. Obstacle; partition.

hail² (−¹) Terrible, frightful. **~e** (−·¹), tragedy (play). **~nüvis,** tragic author. **~evî** (−··⁻¹), tragic.

hain (−¹) Traitor. Treacherous; deceitful; ungrateful; mischievous. **tuz ekmek ~i,** who repays his host with ingratitude. **~ane** (−·−¹), treacherous, ungrateful (*of deeds, not men*); in a treacherous manner. **~leşmek,** to become a traitor, behave treacherously. **~lik,** treachery, perfidy; an act of treachery.

haiz (−¹) Possessing; obtaining; furnished with. **bu şeraiti ~ olanlar,** those who fulfil these conditions.

hâk (−), **–ki** Earth, soil. **~i helâke sermek,** to make *s.o.* bite the dust (in death) : **~ ile yeksan etm.,** to raze to the ground.

hak¹ (·), **–kki** Engraving; erasing. **fenni ~,** the art of engraving.

hak² (·), **–kkı** Truth; right; justice; due; respect, relation. Right; true; proper; equitable. **~kında,** concerning; **bunun ~kında,** concerning this : **~kını* almak,** to get one's due, to get one's fair share : **···in ~kından gelmek,** to get the better of *s.o.* or *stg.*; to pay *s.o.* out: **~kı* için,** for the sake of : **~ kazanmak,** to be proved right; to deserve : **~kı sükût,** hush-money : **~kı tarik,** right of way, toll : **~ üzere,** according to equity, by rights : **~kı* var,** he is right; **onda bir lira ~kım var,** he owes me a lira : **···e ~ vermek,** to acknowledge *s.o.* to be right : **···in ~kını* yemek,** to cheat *s.o.* of his rights, to wrong *s.o.* : **~ yerini buldu,** justice prevailed : **~kı yerine getirmek,** to make right prevail, to do justice : **ana (baba, hoca) ~kı,** the debt one owes to one's mother (father, teacher) : **namusum ~kı için,** upon my honour : **telif ~kı,** copyright : 'vazifeyi ihmal etmeniz ~kınızda iyi olmaz', 'it will be bad for you if you neglect your duty'.

Hak³, –kkı *or* **Cenabı ~,** God.

hakan (−⁴) Oriental potentate; Sultan. **~î** (−−⁴), royal, imperial.

hakaret (·−¹), **–ti** Insult; contempt. **~ etm.,** to insult : **~ görmek,** to be insulted. **~amiz** (·−·−¹), insulting.

hakayik (·−¹) *pl. of* **hakikat.** Truths.

hakem Arbitrator; referee, umpire.

haketmek (¹··), **–eder** *va.* Deserve; be entitled to.

hakeza (−·⁻) Thus, in this manner; ditto.

hakgû Veracious; just.

hakî (−⁻) Earth-coloured; khaki.

hakikat (·−¹), **–ti** Truth; reality; sincerity. Truly, really. **~ülemir** *or* **~i hal,** the truth of the matter. **~en** (·⁻··), in truth; really. **~li,** true; sincere; faithful. **~perest,** who worships the truth. **~siz,** false; insincere.

hakikî (·—ᴗ) True; real; genuine; sincere. ~ **mermi**, live cartridge.

hâkim (—ᴗ) Ruling; dominating; overlooking. Ruler; governor; judge. ~**i mutlak**, absolute ruler: ···e ~ **olm.**, to overlook a place etc. ~**ane** (—·—ᴗ), lordly; as befits a ruler. ~**iyet** (—··ᴗ), –**ti**, sovereignty; domination; rule: ~**i milliye**, the sovereignty of the people. ~**lik**, the office of a judge or ruler; domination.

hakîm (·—ᴗ) Very wise or learned. Sage; philosopher; *the same word written and pronounced* **hekim** *means* doctor. ~**ane** (·—–ᴗ), wise; prudent; philosophic: in a wise, prudent or philosophic manner.

hakîr (·—ᴗ) Despicable; of no account; 'your humble servant'. ~ **görmek**, to despise. ~**ane** (·—–ᴗ), humble, modest: in a humble or modest way.

hakkâk (·—ᴗ), –**ki** Engraver.

hakk·alinsaf (ᴗ···) In a fair and just manner. ~**aniyet** (·—·ᴗ), –**ti**, justice; equity. ~**aniyetli**, just, equitable.

hakketmek (ᴗ···), –**eder** va. Engrave; erase.

hakk·ı v. hak. ~**ında**, concerning; with regard to. ~**ısükut**, –**tu**, hush-money. ~**ile**, ~**iyle**, rightfully, properly.

hakkuran In ~ **kafesi**, a tumble-down house.

hak·lamak va. Destroy; finish (a meal or a man). ~**laşmak**, to settle mutual accounts; to be quits.

hak·lı Right; who is right; having a right. ~**perest**, loving truth and justice. ~**sız**, unjust; wrong; having no rightful claim. ~**sızlık**, injustice, wrong. ~**şinas**, who knows the truth; just.

Haktaalâ (···—ᴗ) God most High.

hal,[1] –**li** Condition; situation, state, circumstance; strength; quality; attribute; ecstasy; trouble; the present time; present tense (*gram.*); case (*gram.*). ~**de** (*following a participle*), although, *e.g.* **geleceğimi bildiği** ~**de beklememiş**, although he knew I was coming he did not wait: ~ **ile**, consequently; as a matter of course: ~**den anlamak**, to be capable of understanding and sympathizing with others: ⌐~**e bak!**¬, (*referring to an impudent claim*) 'what cheek !'; (*referring to a well-deserved failure*) 'ah! look at the result !', *or* 'what a lesson !': ~**ine bakmadan**, to do or say stg. without regard to one's abilities or circumstances: ~ **böyle iken**, and yet, and even under these circumstances: ~**i hazır**, the present time; the present tense; the 'status quo': ~**i* kalmamak**, to have no strength left: ~ **olm.**, (of dervishes etc.) to be in a trance, to be in convulsions; ⌐**sana bir** ~ **olmuş !**¬, 'what's come over you?', 'what on earth

has happened to you *that you should behave thus* ? '; ⌐**şayed bana bir** ~ **olursa**¬, 'if anything should happen to me'; ᴗ**çocuğu susturuncaya kadar bir** ~ **oldum**¬, 'I had a job to quieten the child': ···**in** ~**ini sormak**, to inquire after *s.o.*, to ask after his health etc.: ~ **hatır sormak**, to ask formal questions showing a general interest in a person or his family: ⌐**senin** ~**in neye varacak !**¬, 'what will become of you I don't know (if you go on like this)': ᴗ**ne** ~**in varsa, gör !**¬, 'well, go your own way !': ⌐**aşağı inmeğe** ~**im yok**¬, 'I don't feel like coming downstairs': ~**e yola** (*or* ~**ine yoluna**) **koymak**, to put to rights, to put in order: ᴗ**bu adamın** ~**lerini beğenmiyorum**¬, 'I don't like the way this man carries on': ⌐**onun her** ~**i sinirime dokunuyor**¬, 'everything about him gets on my nerves': **başına*** ~**ler gelmek**, for misfortunes to befall one: **her** ~**de**, in any case; at any rate: **kendi halinde**, quiet and inoffensive; insignificant: ⌐**onu kendi** ~**ine bırak !**¬, 'let him be!', 'leave him alone!': ⌐**kimse** ~**in nedir demedi**¬, 'no one took any interest in me': **o** ~**de**, in that case: **şimdiki** ~**de**, under present circumstances.

hal,[2] –**lli** Solution *of a question or problem*; the untying *of a knot etc.*; a melting, liquefaction.

hal,[3] –**li** (*Fr.* halles) Covered market-place.

hâl, –li Mole (on the body).

hala (ᴗ·) Paternal aunt.

halâ (·—ᴗ) Void, vacuum; latrine, closet.

hâlâ (—ᴗ—) At the present time; now; just; up till now; still; yet.

halâs (·ᴗ) Deliverance; salvation; safety. ~ **bulmak**, to be saved: ~ **etm.**, to save, deliver. ~**kâr** (·—ᴗ), saving; saviour, deliverer.

halat, –tı Rope; hawser.

halât, –ti *pl. of* **halet**. Circumstances; conditions.

halâvet (·—ᴗ), –**ti** Sweetness; agreeableness. ~**li**, sweet; agreeable. ~**siz**, disagreeable, ugly.

halayık Female servant or slave.

halazade (···—ᴗ) Cousin (child of a paternal aunt).

halbuki (·ᴗ·), **halbuyse** However; nevertheless; whereas.

hale (—ᴗ) Halo *round the moon*.

Haleb (ᴗ·) Aleppo. ~ **çıbanı**, the Aleppo button or boil: ⌐~ **orada ise arşın burada**¬, 'well, prove it !'; 'let's put it to the test !': ⌐**işte geldik, gidiyoruz, şen olsun** ~ **şehri**¬, *a line from a folklore story, said when leaving a place after a short stay, sometimes implying a vague disappointment.*

halecan Palpitation *of the heart*; excitement, agitation, anxiety. ~**lanmak,** to be agitated or excited.

halef Successor; posterity; substitute. ~ **selef olm.,** to succeed *another in office etc.* ~**iyet, -ti,** succession; subrogation.

halel Defect; injury; prejudice. ~ **gelmek,** for injury *or* prejudice to occur: ···e ~ **getirmek (vermek),** to cause harm to, to prejudice. ~**dar,** harmful, prejudicial.

halen ($\stackrel{\perp}{\cdot}$) Now; at present. ~ **ve kalen,** in manner and speech.

halet (−¹), −**ti** Situation; state; condition. ~**i ruhiye** *or* **ruh** ~**i,** state of mind.

hal'etmek (¹··), −**eder** *va.* Dethrone, depose.

halezon *v.* helezon.

halhal, -li Anklet *or* bangle *worn by women.*

halı Carpet. ~**cı,** maker *or* seller of carpets.

hali¹, -l'i Dethronement, deposition.

hali², hâli (−¹) Vacant, empty; unoccupied. ~**den** ~, free from, exempt from: ~ **etm.,** to quit, cease from; empty; leave vacant: **bir şey yapmaktan** ~ **kalmamak,** not to fail to do; not to give up doing stg.: ~ **vakitte,** in leisure moments: **iki ihtimaldan** ~ **değildir,** it is not exempt from two probabilities, *i.e.* it must be one or the other: **kurunu** ~**ye,** bygone ages.

halib (−¹) Ureter.

halic Strait; estuary; canal. **H**~, the Golden Horn.

halife (·−¹) The Caliph. ~**lik,** the Caliphate.

hali·harb State of war. ~**hazırda** ($\stackrel{\perp}{\cdot}·−··$), at the present moment.

halik (−¹), −**kı** Creator.

halil¹ Intimate friend. ~**e,** intimate female friend; wife.

Halil² *A proper name of men.* ⌐**kesesinde** ~ **İbrahim bereketi var**⌐, 'he knows how to make his money go a long way'.

halîm (·$\stackrel{\perp}{\cdot}$) Mild; gentle; patient. ~ **selim,** quiet and good-tempered.

halis (−¹) Pure, unadulterated; genuine; sincere. ~ **muhlis,** true, authentic. ~**ane** (−·−¹), sincere (words *etc.*); sincerely; without ulterior motive. ~**üddem** ($\stackrel{\perp}{\cdot}···$), pure-blooded, thoroughbred.

halita (·−¹) Mixed substance; alloy.

hali(y)le Consequently; as a matter of course.

halk, -kı People; crowd; the common people. **ev** ~**ı,** the household.

halka Ring; hoop; circle; door-knocker; link *of a chain.* ~**yı burnuna takmak,** to bring into submission: ~ **olm.,** to form a ring: **ayın** ~**sı,** halo round the moon: **ders** ~**sı,** a class of students. ~**lamak,** to furnish with a ring; encircle; fasten with a ring on to a hook (door *etc.*). ~**lı,**

ringed; linked; in coils. ~**vî,** ring-shaped, annular.

halkâri Robe embroidered with gold.

halkçı An upholder of the rights of the people; democrat. ~**lık,** democracy.

halketmek (¹··), −**eder** *va.* Create.

halkevi (¹··), −**ni** 'The People's House', *name of social institutes now being set up all over Turkey.*

halkıyat, -tı Folklore.

hallac Wool-carder. ~ **pamuğu gibi dağıtmak,** to scatter about in all directions.

Hallak (·$\stackrel{\perp}{\cdot}$), −**kı** The Creator.

hall·enmek *vn.* Manifest interest *in a thing or a person.* ~**eşmek,** to confide troubles to one another, to have a good talk.

halletmek (¹··), −**eder** *va.* Undo; solve (a question); explain; dissolve; analyse.

halli¹ *acc. of* hal², *q.v.*

halli² Of *or* in a *certain* condition. **orta** ~, not too well-off; lower-middle-class *but with reference to financial rather than social circumstances.* ~**ce,** slightly better; pretty well-off.

hallihamur (···¹) Of the same substance; one with; 'part and parcel' (of = ile).

halsiz Weak; exhausted, tired out. ~**lik,** exhaustion.

halt, -tı Impertinence; stupid and improper speech or deed. ~ **etm.,** *v.* **haltetmek:** ~ **karıştırmak (yemek),** to make a great blunder, to 'put one's foot in it' badly. ~**etmek** (¹··), −**eder,** to do or say stg. stupid *or* out-of-place: ⌐**ne halteder ağanın beygiri !**⌐, 'what an absurd mess !' *or* 'how are we to get out of this mess ?': ⌐**ne haltetmeğe oraya gittin?**⌐, 'what the dickens did you go there for?': **ona** ~ **düşer!,** he has no right at all to interfere; it's nothing to do with him!: **yanında haltetmiş,** he is nothing in comparison.

halter (*Fr.* haltère) Dumb-bell.

halûk (·$\stackrel{\perp}{\cdot}$) Of good character; well-disposed, decent.

halükâr (−·$\stackrel{\perp}{\cdot}$) *In* **her** ~**da,** in all circumstances.

halva *In* ⌐**helva demesini de bilirim** ~ **demesini de**⌐, 'I can adjust myself to all circumstances'.

halvet, -ti Solitude; retirement; privacy; lonely place, wilderness; private room; cell for religious exercises; hermitage; private room in a bath. ~**e dönmek,** (of a room) to become hot and stuffy: ~ **etm.,** to make a room private by turning out other persons; to retire into a private room (*also* ~**e girmek**). ~**güzin** (···$\stackrel{\perp}{\cdot}$), ~**nişin** (···$\stackrel{\perp}{\cdot}$), recluse, hermit.

ham Unripe; immature; raw, crude; inexperienced, tyro; out of training; vain, useless; unreasonable. ~ **halat,** coarse, clumsy (man): ~ **toprak,** uncultivated land: hayali ~, vain illusion; hopeless task.

hamail (·–ˡ) Band or cord worn over one shoulder *for carrying a weapon etc.*; amulet *thus worn*; any amulet or charm. **~î,** suspended by a cord or belt worn over one shoulder and under the other.

hamak Hammock.

hamakat, –ti Stupidity; folly.

hamal Porter; carrier; common coarse fellow. ~ **camal,** the lowest class of people. **~başı** (·ˡ··), **–nı,** foreman of a group of porters. **~iye,** porterage. **~lık,** profession of a porter; coarse behaviour; toiling and slaving; unnecessary burden.

hamam Bath, *esp.* a Turkish bath. ~ **anası,** a huge woman: ⌐~da deli var!¬, *phrase used to describe a sudden commotion:* **~kubbesi,** the domed chamber of a Turkish bath; a noisy talker: ~ **otu,** depilatory: ~ **takımı,** bath towels: ⌐eski ~ eski tas¬, 'the same old bath, the same old cup (used for throwing water over oneself)', the same old thing; just the same as ever. **~böceği -ni,** the so-called 'German' cockroach. **~cı,** proprietor of a public bath: canonically unclean and in need of a ritual bath.

hamarat Hardworking, industrious.

hamas·et (··–ˡ), **–ti** Heroism. **~î,** epic. **~iyat,** epic poem.

hamd A giving thanks and praise to God. **~etmek** (ˡ··), **–eder,** to give thanks and praise to God. **~olsun** (ˡ··), thank God!; thanks be! **~üsena** (···–ˡ), thanks and glory to God!

hamel The Zodiac sign Aries.

hamhalat (ˡ··) Loutish, boorish.

hamhum Humming and hawing. ~ **şarolop,** a lot of nonsense; swindle.

hâmız (–ˡ) Acid; sour. **~î,** acid. **~iyet, –ti,** acidity; sourness.

hami (–ˡ) Protecting, guarding. Protector; patron.

hamî (–ˡ) Hamite. Hamitic.

hamil, –mli Pregnancy; burden; crop (of a tree); act of loading; imputation. **vaz'ı ~,** parturition: ~ **vakti,** the moment of parturition.

hâmil (–ˡ) Bearing; bringing. Bearer (of a document *etc.*). **~e,** pregnant woman: ···den ~ **kalmak,** to be with child by .... **~en,** (–ˡ··) (*with acc.*) having with one; furnished with.

haminne (·ˡ·) 'Grannie'.

hamir, –mri Wine.

hâmis (–ˡ) Fifth. **~en,** fifthly.

hâmiş (–ˡ) Marginal note; postscript.

hamiyet, –ti Zeal; public spirit; patriotism. **~li,** public-spirited; philanthropic.

hamlac Blowpipe.

hamlacı Chief rower; stroke oarsman; *title of the Palace boatmen in former times.*

hamlamak, hamlaşmak *vn.* Get out of condition *or* out of practice; become soft from lack of work.

hamle Attack, onslaught; effort; dash, 'élan'; turn (at chess, draughts *etc.*). ~ **etm.,** to attack; make a great effort: **ilk ~de,** at the first onslaught; 'at the first go'.

hamletmek (ˡ··), **–eder** *va.* Load; ascribe, impute (to = *dat.*).

hamlık Unripeness; crudeness; inexperience; lack of condition.

hampa *v.* **hempa.**

hamse Five. Work consisting of five parts.

hamsi Anchovy (fresh).

hamsin Fifty; the last fifty days of winter; the hot summer wind of Egypt.

hamud Collar *of a horse's harness.*

hamul Patient, forbearing, long-suffering. **~e** (·–ˡ), cargo; load; charge.

hamur Dough; leaven; essence, nature; quality (of paper); anything of the consistency of dough. Half-baked (bread). **~açmak,** to roll out dough: ~ **gibi,** limp, flabby: ~ **işi,** pastry: ~ **tutmak,** to knead dough *for bread or pastry:* ⌐elinin ~iyle erkek isine karışmak¬, to set out to do stg. beyond one's power; (of a woman) to try to do a man's job: hal ve ~, *v.* **hallihamur.**

hamur·kâr, baker's assistant. **~lamak,** to cover with dough; lute. **~lu,** covered or made with dough; leavened; fermented. **~suz,** unleavened: unleavened bread: ~ **bayramı,** the Jewish Feast of Passover.

hamuş (·–ˡ), **hamuş** (–ˡ–) Silent; extinguished; docile. **~i** (·–ˡ), silence; extinction.

han¹ Sovereign; *oriental title of princes etc.,* Khan.

han² Inn; caravanserai; large commercial building. ~ **gibi,** vast: ~ **hamam sahibi,** a man of property: ⌐burası yol geçen ~ı değil¬, 'where do you think you are!'; 'you must behave yourself here!' **~cı,** innkeeper: ⌐ben ~ sen yolcu iken¬, you may be glad of my help some day.

hançer Dagger.

hançere Larynx.

hand·an Laughing, gay, cheerful. **~e,** laugh; joke.

handiyse (·–ˡ·) Shortly; any moment now.

hane (–ˡ) House; dwelling; family *or* household; compartment; subdivision; column (for figures); square *of a chessboard;* sign of the Zodiac. ~ ~, in separate compartments. *Used as a suffix and often abbreviated to* –ane *or after an* a *to* –ne, house of ..., place of ..., *e.g.* **hastahane** *or* **hastane,** hos-

pital; **postane**, post office. **~berduş** (with his house on his back), homeless, vagabond.
hanedan (—·$\underline{\cdot}$) Great family; dynasty. Of illustrious descent, noble; courteous; hospitable. **~lık**, the courteous hospitality of a gentleman.
hanefi (··$\underline{\cdot}$) Of the Hanefi sect; orthodox.
haneharab (—··$\underline{\cdot}$) Whose home is ruined; miserable; good-for-nothing.
haneli (—·$\underline{\cdot}$) Having *so many* houses; in squares, check (pattern). **dört ~ rakam**, a four-figure sum: **kırk ~ köy**, a village of forty houses.
hanende (—·$\underline{\cdot}$) Singer.
hangi ($\underline{\cdot}$·) Which?; whichever. **~niz**, which of you?; whichever of you: **~si**, which of them?; which ever of them: ⌐**~ taş pekse başını ona vur!**⌐, 'whichever stone is hardest, knock your head on it!', *said to a person who demands to be helped out of a difficulty for which he himself is responsible*; 'you got yourself into the mess, get out of it yourself!': **~ vakitte**, at what time?; at whatever time.
hanıkah (—·$\underline{\cdot}$) Dervish convent.
hanım Lady. **~ evlâdı**, mollycoddle; a rather too well-behaved child. **~böceği**, **–ni**, ladybird. **~efendi**, madam. **~eli**, **–ni**, honeysuckle. **~hanımcık**, a model housewife; a 'perfect little lady' (according to old Turkish standards). **~ördeği**, **–ni**, shelduck.
hani[1] Sea-perch; comber.
hani[2] ($\underline{\cdot}$·) Where?; well?; you know!; and then. **~ bana?**, what about me?, where do· I come in?: **~dir**, it's a long time now since ... : ⌐**~ dün bize gelecektin**⌐, 'I thought you were coming to see us yesterday (but you didn't)': **~ o günleri!**, (*expressing regret*) 'ah! those days are over!'; 'I only wish we could!'; (*iron.*) 'what an idea!'; 'out of the question!': ⌐**~ yok mu?**⌐, 'you know what I mean': **güzelliğine de güzel ~!**, there's no question about her beauty!
hânis (—$\underline{\cdot}$) Perjured. **yemininden ~ olm.**, to violate one's oath.
haniya *v.* hani.[2]
hanlık Title or territory of a Khan; khanate.
hantal Big; clumsy; badly made; coarse; clownish, boorish.
hanüman (··$\underline{\cdot}$) Home; family and belongings. **~ı harab**, whose home is ruined. **~suz**, home-destroying.
Hanya ($\underline{\cdot}$·) Canea (in Crete). ⌐**~yı Konya'yı anlamak**⌐, to learn by bitter experience: ⌐**sana ~yı Konya'yı göstererim!**⌐, I'll teach you a lesson! (*threateningly*)'.
hap, **–pı** Pill. **~ı yutmak**, to be 'done for': ⌐**tam mânasile ~ı yuttuk**⌐, we're properly

'in the soup'; it's all up with us! **~ıcık**, *in ~* **yapmak**, to catch *a sweet, a cherry etc.* in the mouth.
hapis, **–psi** Confinement, imprisonment; prison. Imprisoned; detained. **~ giymek**, to be sentenced to prison: ···**i göz hapsinde tutmak**, not to let *s.o.* out of one's sight; to keep under observation. **~hane**, **~ane** (··—$\underline{\cdot}$), prison.
hapsetmek ($\underline{\cdot}$··), **–eder** *va.* Imprison; confine.
hapş·u *Imitates a sneeze*, 'atishoo!' **~ırmak**, to sneeze.
haptetmek *v.* habtetmek.
har[1] (—) Hot. **mıntakayı ~re**, the tropical zone.
har[2] (—), **–rı** Thorn.
har[3] (·) Ass.
har[4] (·) *In* ⌐**~ vurup harman savurmak**⌐, to spend money prodigally, to 'blue' one's money.
–har (—) *Pers. prefix.* Eating-; drinking-; *e.g.* **şarab~**, a wine-bibber; **hun~**, bloodthirsty.
hara[1] (·$\underline{\cdot}$) Stud farm; stock farm.
hara[2] (—$\underline{\cdot}$) Marble; moiré; watering (of silk *etc.*).
harab (·$\underline{\cdot}$) A ruining *or* destroying. Ruined, devastated; decayed; desolate. **~ etm.**, to destroy, devastate: **~ olm.**, to be devastated; to fall into ruin; to be impoverished; to be desperately in love: ⌐**bade ~ül Basra**⌐ *or* ⌐**Basra ~ olduktan sonra**⌐, too late!: **hali* ~**, he is ruined; he is in a bad way.
harab·at (·—$\underline{\cdot}$), **–tı** *pl. of* **harabe**. ruins; *as sing.* tavern. **~atı** (·—$\underline{\cdot}$), (*originally*) dissolute drunkard; (*now*) careless about his dress and unconventional in his habits; bohemian. **~e** (·—$\underline{\cdot}$), a ruin; tumble-down house or town. **~ezar** (·—·$\underline{\cdot}$), place of ruins. **~i** (·—$\underline{\cdot}$), ruin; poverty, misery. **~iyet** (·—·$\underline{\cdot}$), **–ti**, **~lık**, a state of ruin; destruction.
harac Tax; tribute; public auction; (*formerly*) tax paid by non-Moslems in lieu of military service. **~ ~!**, going! going! (*at an auction*): **~a çıkarmak**, to put up to auction: **~a kesmek**, to levy a tribute on *a place*; to extort heavy taxes; to oppress: **~ mezad**, selling by auction. **~güzar**, tributary. **~cı**, collector of tribute.
haram (·$\underline{\cdot}$) Forbidden by religion; unlawful; sacred, inviolable Forbidden deed. **~ etm.**, to forbid the use or enjoyment *of stg.*: **~ mal**, property unlawfully acquired; ill-gotten gains: ⌐**~ olsun!**⌐, 'may Heaven punish you!' (*said to one who wrongfully seizes another's property*): **~ yemek**, to enrich oneself unlawfully **~i** (·—$\underline{\cdot}$), brigand,

thief. ~lik (·——¹), brigandage. ~zade (·——¹), bastard; scoundrel.

harar Large sack made of haircloth.

hararet (·—¹), **-ti** Heat; fever, temperature; thirst; fervour, exaltation. ~ **basmak**, to feel thirsty: ~ **söndürmek**, to quench one's thirst: ~ **vermek**, to make thirsty. ~li, irascible; heated (argument); feverish; enthusiastic.

haraza Quarrel.

harb, –bi War. ~ **hali**, state of war: ~ **ilânı**, declaration of war: ~**in sevk ve idaresi**, the conduct of war, the waging of war: ~ **zengini**, war profiteer. ~cû, ~ci, warlike; warmonger. ~e, javelin, pike. ~en (¹··), by war, by force of arms. ~etmek (¹··), **-eder**, to go to war, fight. ~i, ramrod. ~î (·—¹), pertaining to war, military. ~iye, War Academy; Ministry of War: **erkânı** ~, General Staff: **sefinei** ~, warship. ~sonrası, –nı, ~sonu, –nu, post-war period; aftermath of war.

harbak, –kı Hellebore.

harc Expenditure, expenses, outlay; raw material; ingredients; trimmings (braid *etc.* for a dress); anything within one's power or means; mortar, plaster; soil mixture, compost. ~ı **âlem**, within everybody's means; in common use, ordinary, everyday: **akıllı adamın** ~ı, the way a wise man would act: **benim** ~ım **değil**, that's not for me; it's beyond my means: **mahkeme** ~ı, legal costs: **Yunanistanı zaptetmek İtalyan ordusu** ~ı **değil**, to conquer Greece is beyond the power of the Italian army: **zengin adamın** ~ı, only within·the means of a rich man.

harc·amak, to expend, spend; use; designedly to put a person in danger, get rid of, kill. ~etmek (¹··), **-eder**, to spend, disburse. ~ıâlem, *v.* harcı âlem. ~ırah, journey-money, travelling expenses. ~lı, made with mortar *or* compost; trimmed *with* braid *etc.*; expensive. ~lık, pocket-money.

hardal Mustard. ~ **lâpası**, mustard poultice: ~ **yakası**, mustard plaster. ~iye (·——¹), grape-juice flavoured with mustard. ~lık, mustard-pot.

hare (–¹) Moiré; watering (of silk *etc.*).

harekât (··ᴗ), **-tı** (i) *pl. of* hareket. Movements. (ii) *pl. of* hareke. Vowel points.

hareke Vowel point (in Arabic writing). ~lemek, to insert the vowel points. ~li, with the vowel points inserted

hareket, –ti Movement; act; behaviour; departure; excitement. ~i **arz**, earthquake: ~ **etm.**, to move, act; set out: ~e **gelmek**, to begin to move; to come into play: ~e **getirmek**, to set in motion: ~ **kolu**, starting-handle: ⌐**nerede** ~ **orada**

bereket⌐, activity brings prosperity. ~siz, motionless. ~sizlik, immobility.

hareli (–·¹) Watered (silk *etc.*), moiré.

harem The women's apartments *in a Moslem house*; a sacred territory *esp. that of Medina and Mecca.* ~ **selâmlık olm.**, for men and women to form separate groups. ~ağası, –nı, black eunuch. ~eyn, the two sacred places of Islam, Mecca and Medina. ~işerif (····—¹), the Prophet's tomb at Medina.

harf, –fi Letter *of the alphabet*; particle *(gram.)*; word; speech, language; allusion; witticism. ~i ~ine, to the very letter; word for word: ~ inkılâbı, the reform of the alphabet, *i.e. the change from Arabic to Latin script* (1928). ~endaz, who makes insulting remarks to women in the street. ~endazlık, the offence of doing so: ~ta **bulunmak**, to make such remarks. ~î (·—¹), pertaining to letters, literal. ~itarif (····—¹), the definite article *(gram.).* ~iyen (·¹·), literally.

harhara Death-rattle.

harharyas Porbeagle

harıl *In* ~ ~, assiduously; ~ ~ **yanmak**, to burn furiously and continuously. ~tı, loud and continuous noise *esp. that of burning.*

haric (–¹) The outside, exterior; abroad. External, outside; not included. ~ **etm.**, to exclude: ~ **olm.**, to be excluded: ~ **ez kanun**, extra-legal: ~ **ez memleket**, extraterritorial: **harb** ~i **kalmak**, to remain out of the war: **hasmı muharebe** ~i **bırakmak**, to put the enemy out of action: **ihtimalden** ~, improbable.

~en (ᴗ··), externally. ~î (–·¹), external; foreign; heretic. ~kısmet, **-ti**, quotient. ~iye (··ᴗ¹), foreign affairs; external diseases: ~ *or* **Vekaleti** ~, Ministry of Foreign Affairs. ~ciyeci, member of the Foreign Service; specialist in external diseases.

harif (·—¹) Autumn.

harik (·—¹), **-ki** A fire; conflagration.

harika (–·¹) Wonder; miracle. Marvellous; extraordinary.

harikulâde (ᴗ··–·) Extraordinary; unusual.

harikzede Injured by fire; rendered homeless by a fire. ~gân, victims of a fire.

harim (·—¹) Most intimate and private place; any place that a man is bound to protect and defend. Private; intimate.

harin Restive, refractory (horse); obstinate. ~lamak, (of a horse) to become restive after staying too long in the stable.

harir Silk.

haris (·—¹) Greedy; avaricious; ambitious. ~icah, inordinately ambitious.

harita (·⌣·) Map; plan. ~da.olmamak, to be unexpected, unforeseen (of difficulties *etc.*)

harl·amak *vn.* Be in flames; burn furiously. ~ı, burning furiously.

harman Operation of threshing grain; heap of grain for threshing; threshing-floor; harvest time; blend (of tea, tobacco *etc*); heap of printed leaves *ready to be put into a book.* ~ dökmek, to thresh: ~ döveni, a kind of sledge driven over the grain to thresh it out: ~ etm., to blend; to sort and arrange: ~ savurmak, to winnow: ~ sonu, residue of grain *mixed with stones and dust, left after threshing*; remnants of a fortune or business: ~ yeri, threshing floor.

harmancı Thresher; blender *of tobacco etc.*

harmani (·—⌣) Long cloak.

harman·lamak *va.* Blend (tea, tobacco *etc.*). ~lanmak, ay ~, for a halo to form round the moon.

harnıb *v.* harub.

harp¹, –pı, harpa (⌣·) Harp.

harp² *v.* harb.

harrangürre (⌣·⌣·) In a disorderly and noisy manner. ·

harre (—⌣) *Fem. of* har. Hot. memaliki ~, the tropics.

harrü (⌣·) *In* ⌜ya ~ ya marrü⌝, 'well, we'll have a shot at it; perhaps it will come off, perhaps it won't'.

hars Culture; education. ~î (·⌣), cultural. ~iyat, –tı, cultural matters.

harşef Fish-scales; artichoke, cardoon. ~iye, ·the artichoke family, cynara. ~iyülcenah, lepidoptera.

harta (⌣·) Map; plan.

hartadak *Imitates the sound of stg. being bitten or suddenly seized.*

hartuç Cartridge (for cannon).

harub Carob, locust-bean. ~iye, a drink made of locust-beans.

has (—), –ssı Special; peculiar *to*; private; pure, unmixed; fast (dye). The upper class; *formerly* a fief of a yearly value of over 100,000 akçe.

hasad Reaping; harvest. ~ etm., to reap.

hasail (·—⌣) *pl. of* haslet. Moral qualities.

hasais (·—⌣) *pl. of* hasisa. Innate virtues *or* qualities.

hasar (·⌄) Damage; loss. ~a uğramak, to suffer loss or damage. ~at (·—⌄), –tı, losses.

hasb·elicab (⌣···) According to need; necessarily. ~eliktıza (⌣····—), according to the requirements of the case. ~ellüzum, according to need. ~elvazife (⌣··—·), as required by duty. ~ennezake (⌣··—·), out of politeness.

hasbetenlillah (⌣····) (For the sake of God); disinterestedly; without expecting anything in return; just for the love of it.

hasbıhal, –li Private and friendly chat. ~ etm., to have a friendly chat; to exchange confidences.

hasbi (·⌣) Disinterested; gratuitous; without reason. ~ geçmek (*sl.*), not to care.

haseb Personal qualities; merit. ~ ve neseb, distinction by personal qualities as well as by birth.

hasebi(y)le By reason of ....

hased Envy; jealousy. ~ etm., to envy. ~ci, envious; jealous.

haseki (*Formerly*) one of the Sultan's personal bodyguards; favourite wife of the Sultan. ~ küpesi, columbine, aquilegia.

hasen Beautiful; good. ~at, –tı, good works, pious deeds; charitable institutions.

hasıl Barley cut green for fodder.

hâsıl (—⌣) Resulting; happening; produced; growing. Produce; product; crop; result; profit. ~ı *or* ~ı kelâm, to sum up, in short. ~ etm., to produce; to acquire: ~ olm., to result, ensue; be produced, be obtained: ~ı tahsil etm., (to produce what has already been produced), to waste one's time or energy: ~ulemir, the sum and substance of a matter.

hasıl·a (—·⌣), produce. ~at (—·⌄), –tı, produce; products; revenue; profit: safi ~, net profit. ~atlı, productive; profitable. ~lanmak, (of children and crops) to grow up. ~sız, producing or yielding nothing; unprofitable; useless.

hasım, –smı Enemy, adversary. ~lık, enmity, hostility.

hasır¹ (—⌣), –srı A restraining; restriction; a devoting or consecrating to one purpose.

hasır² Rush mat *or* matting. ~ eskileri, remains of old mats, *jokingly used instead of* hazretleri: ~ kaplamak, to cover with wickerwork: ~ koltuk, wicker chair: ~ şapka, straw-hat. ~altı (·⌣··), (*lit.* 'under the mat'): ~ etm., to hide; to leave *a request* unanswered; to shelve *a matter*; to hush *stg.* up. ~lamak, to cover with matting. ~lı, covered with matting; made of wickerwork: large bottle covered with wickerwork. ~otu, –nu, rush.

hâsir (—⌣) Longing *or* grieving for an absent person *or* thing; deprived; destitute.

hasis (·⌣) Stingy; vile; mean, petty. ~lik, stinginess, vileness.

hasiyet (—·⌣), –ti A special quality *or* virtue; good effect on the body. ~li, having a special quality; beneficial to the health; savoury.

haslet, –ti, haslat Moral quality; character.

hasm·ane (·—⌣) Hostile (attitude *etc.*). ~ıcan, a deadly foe, a mortal enemy.

hasna (·⌣) A beauty (woman); an agreeable kind woman. ~ müstesna, an exceptional beauty.

haspa Minx; rascal (*used affectionately and generally of a girl*).

hasren (¹·) Limited to (*dat.*).

hasret, –ti Regret *for stg. lost*; longing *for stg. not yet gained*; longing *for a person or place*. Feeling a loss. ···in ~ini çekmek, to long to see *a person or thing* again: ···e ~ kalmak, to feel the loss *or* absence of .... ~li, ~keş, suffering from separation; longing for s.o. *or* stg.

hasretmek (¹··), –eder *va.* Restrict; restrain; appropriate; devote *or* consecrate to one thing.

hassa¹ Quality; property; peculiarity.

hassa² (–¹) *fem. of* has. A ruler's bodyguard; anything especially belonging to the sovereign. hazinei ~, the Privy Purse, the Civil List.

hassas (·¹) Very sensitive; delicate in feeling; scrupulous, conscientious. ~iyet (·—·), –ti, ~lık, sensibility; perceptivity; sensitivity; touchiness; quickness of response; delicacy of feeling; care and interest in what one does.

hassaten (¹··) Specially, particularly.

hâsse (–¹) Sense; each of the five senses.

hasta Sick, ill. ~bakıcı, hospital attendant; trained nurse. ~lık, illness, disease. ~lıklı, ailing; in ill health. ~ne (·–¹), ~hane (···–¹), hospital.

hasud (·¹) Jealous, envious.

haşa Saddle-cloth.

hâşa (–¹) God forbid !. ~ minhuzur (minelhuzur *or* huzurdan), 'with all due respect'; 'excuse the expression!'

haşarat (···♭), –tı *pl. of* haşere. Insects; reptiles; small creeping things; vermin; mob; blackguards.

haşarı Wild; dissolute; out-of-hand; naughty. ~lık, unruly behaviour, wild prank.

haşeb Wood. ~î (···¹), wooden.

haşefe Glans penis.

haşem *n. pl. Only in* hadem ve ~ (*or, erroneously but more common* hademe ~e), servants and retinue.

haşere Creeping thing; insect.

haşhaş Poppy. ~iye (·—·¹), the poppy family, Papaveraceae.

haşır *v.* hışır *and* haşir.

haşin Harsh; rough; bad-tempered.

haşir, –şri The assembly of all men for the Day of Judgement; the Day of Judgement. haşre kadar, till the Day of Judgement: ···le ~ neşir olm., to be in close contact with ..., to be cheek by jowl with ... .

haşiş Hashish.

haşiv, –şvi Redundant words; padding.

haşvi kabih, a redundancy which ought to be cut out: haşvi melih, a parenthetical clause adding beauty to a sentence.

haşiye (–·¹) Marginal note; comment; postscript.

haşlama Boiled. Boiled meat.

haşlamak *va.* Boil; scald; (of an insect) to sting; (of frost) to nip; scold severely.

haşmet, –ti Majesty; pomp. ~li, majestic, grand. ~lû, *title given to European sovereigns*, His Majesty. ~meab (···¹), Your Majesty.

haşr·etmek, –eder *va.* Collect people together; to assemble mankind for the Last Judgement. ~üneşr *v.* haşir.

haşviyat (··♭), –tı Redundant words; verbiage.

haşyet, –ti Fear; awe.

hat¹, –ttı Scratch; line; railway line; mark; writing; decree. ~tı batıl, line of cancellation: ~tı divanî, large engrossing style of writing *formerly used for official documents*: ~tı fâsıl, dividing line: ~tı hareket, line of conduct, method of proceeding: ~tı rik'a, ordinary cursive handwriting *formerly used by Turks*: ~tı şerif *or* humayun, royal mandate *sent by the Sultan to the Grand Vizier*: ~tı talik, the Persian style of writing: dar ~, narrow-gauge railway: geniş ~, normal gauge railway: hüsnü ~, calligraphy.

hat² *v.* had.

hata (·¹) Mistake; fault; offence. ~ etm., to err; to miss (in shooting). ~en (·¹·), by mistake, in error. ~lı, erroneous.

hatab Wood; timber.

hatar Danger. ~nak (···¹), perilous.

hatem (–¹) Seal. ~ülenbiya, the last of the prophets, *i.e.* Mohammed.

hatıl Beam *or* course of bricks in a stone wall.

hatır¹ Thought; idea; memory; mind; feelings; influence; the consideration that one person expects from another. ~ını* almak, to content s.o.; to have a kindly though for s.o.: ~dan çıkarmak, to forget: ~ından* çıkmak, to pass out of one's mind, to be forgotten: ~ına* gelmek, to occur to one's mind: ~ına* getirmek, to remind s.o.: ~a gönüle bakmamak, to act independently, to be impartial: ~ gönül bilmemek, to take no account of others' feelings: ~ gözetmek, to have regard for. the feelings: ~ını* hoş tutmak, to keep one's mind at ease about stg.; to keep *another* satisfied: ~ için, as a favour; ···in ~ı için, for the sake of ..., out of regard for ...: ~ı* kalmak, to feel hurt, to be offended: ~nız kalmasın !, don't be offended!: ~ı* olm., to be of account, to be considered, *e.g.* ⌐~ım yok mu?⌐, 'have I no weight, don't I count for anything?': ~larda olm., to be in everyone's mind, to be generally remembered: ~ı* sayılmak, to have one's feelings respected; to have influence; ~ı sayılır, respected; considerable: ~ saymak, to take another's feelings into account; to esteem: ~ sormak, to inquire about *s.o.'s* health: ~da tutmak, to bear in mind: ~ını* yapmak, to placate, to make amends to *s.o.*: sefai ~la, with tranquillity; with pleasure.

hatır² *In* ~ ~, *imitates the noise of eating a raw vegetable etc.*; raw, crude. ~ hutur, coarse, unpolished (man).

hâtıra (−·¹) Memory; remembrance; souvenir. ~ defteri, diary: ···in ~sı olarak, in memory of.... ~at, −tı, memories; memoirs.

hatır·lamak *va.* Remember. ~latmak, to remind. ~lı, influential; who must be considered; esteemed. ~nişan, impressed on the memory. ~nüvaz, ~şinas, considerate, obliging, courteous.

hatiat (··⸱), −tı *pl.* of hatie.

hatib Preacher; orator. ~lik, oratory.

hatie Fault, mistake; sin, offence.

hatif (−¹) An invisible speaker, a mysterious voice; echo.

hatim, −tmi A reading or reciting the Kuran from end to end. ~ duası, prayer after reading the whole Kuran: ~ indirmek, to finish the reading of the Kuran: hatmi kelâm etm., to finish speaking.

Hâtim Taı (−¹−¹) *The name of an Arab chief, renowned for his generosity.*

hâtime (−·¹) End, conclusion; epilogue; peroration. ~ çekmek, to conclude.

hatire (·−¹) *err. for* hazire. Graveyard in the precincts of a mosque.

hatiye *err. for* hatie.

hatmetmek (¹··), −eder *va.* Conclude; complete; read through *the Kuran or any other book* from end to end; to read *a book* again and again.

hatmi Marsh-mallow; hollyhock.

hats, hatsî *v.* hads, hadsî.

hattâ (¹·) Even; so much so that; to the extent that.

hattat, −tı Calligrapher; ~lık, calligraphy.

hattı *v.* hat. ~dest, −ti, handwriting. ~humayun (···−¹), royal mandate. ~istiva, ~üstüva (····¹), the Equator. ~şerif (····¹), royal mandate.

hattî (·¹) Lineal, linear. resmi ~, geometrical *or* mechanical drawing.

hatun (−¹) Lady; woman. ~ kişi, woman.

hatve Step; pace; pitch (of a screw). ~ atmak, to go forward

hav Down (feathers); nap; skin (of a peach).

hava Air; weather; wind; atmosphere; climate; tune; liking, desire, whim, fancy; hobby. ~dan, for nothing, gratis; as a windfall: ~ almak, (i) to take the air, to have an airing; (ii) to let in air; (iii) to get nothing: ~ çalmak, to play a tune: ⌐herkes bir ~ çalıyor⌐, everyone expresses a different opinion: ~ya gitmek, to be in vain, to be wasted: ~ ve heves, fancies; pleasures: ~ oyunu, speculation on the Stock Exchange: ~ parası, a tax on the enhanced value of land due to building; premium charged by landlords in addition to rent: ~ payı, room (space); ~ payı bırakmak, to leave a loophole (*fig.*): ~dan sudan mevzular, subjects of no importance: ⌐bana göre ~ hoş⌐, it's all the same to me; it suits me: başı* ~da, proudly: kendi ~sında* olm., to follow one's own fancies; to think only of oneself.

hava·cı, aviator, airman. ~cılık, aviation. ~cıva, alkanet; trifles; nought. ~dar, airy; desirous; in love. ~fişeği, −ni, rocket (*mil. signal*): ~gazi, −ni, coal-gas. ~î (·−⸱), aerial; fanciful, flighty; sky-blue: ~ fişek, rocket: ~ hat, aerial railway: ~ meşreb, not serious, frivolous. ~ilik (·−−¹), flightiness, frivolity. ~iyat (·−·⸱), −tı, futilities; trifles. ~lanmak, to take the air; be aired; be ventilated; take to the air, fly, be airborne; (of a girl) to become flighty and frivolous.

havadis (·−¹) *pl. of* hadise. Events; news.

havale (·−¹) Assignment; the referring *or* transfer *of a matter*; bill of exchange; infantile convulsions; eclampsia; lattice fence; overhang. ~ etm., to transfer (a debt, a business *etc.*); to refer *a matter to another person or department*; to point *a weapon* towards *s.o.*: ~ olm., to be referred *to s.o.* else; (of an infant) to have convulsions.

havale·li (·−·¹), docketed; unwieldy, bulky, top-heavy, overhanging; (ship) with a high superstructure; surrounded by a palisade; given to convulsions. ~name (·−·−¹), order for payment; bill of exchange; money order. ~ten (·¹··), by bill of exchange; being referred *to s.o.*

havalı Airy; having *such and such* a climate.

havali (·−¹) Environs, neighbourhood.

havan Mortar *for pounding*; mortar (gun); tobacco-cutting machine. ~ eli, pestle: ⌐~da su dövmek⌐, to engage in useless discussions *or* fruitless work: ~ topu, mortar, howitzer.

havari (·−¹) Apostle (*pl.* ~yun, the Apostles).

havas¹ (·¹) *pl. of* has and hassa. The upper classes; people of distinction; intimate friends; special qualities; private domains of the Sultan. ~ ve avam, the upper and the lower classes.

havas², –ssı pl. of hasse. Senses. ~sı hamse, the five senses.

havasız Airless, badly ventilated, close.

havayic (·–¹) pl. of hacet. Necessities; wants. ~i zaruriye, the bare necessities of life.

havayolları, –nı Air Lines; Airways.

haves v. heves.

havf Fear. ~nak (·–¹), afraid; fearful, frightful.

havhav n. Barking; baying.

havi (––¹) Containing … (with acc.). ~ olm., to contain.

havil, –vli Horror; terror. can havliyle, in terror of one's life, desperately.

havlamak vn. Bark.

havlı Downy; having a nap or pile. Towel.

havli v. havil.

havlican Galingale (aromatic root).

havlu Towel. v. also avlu.

havra Synagogue; 'bedlam'. ~ya dönmek, (of a place) to become very noisy and crowded.

havruz Chamber pot, po.

havsal·a Pelvis; crop of a bird; gizzard; comprehension, intelligence. ~sı* kavrı-yamamak, to be unable to comprehend: ~ya sığmaz, incomprehensible. ~î (··–¹), pelvic.

havsız Without down or nap; shiny (clothes).

havşa Countersink. ~ açmak, to counter-sink, counterbore. ~lı, countersunk.

havuc Carrot. yaban' ~, parsnip.

havut Camel pack-saddle.

havuz Artificial basin or pond; dock. sabih ~, floating-dock. ~lamak va., to dock (a ship).

Havva (·–¹) Eve.

havya (¹·) Soldering-iron.

havyar Caviare. ~ kesmek, to idle around, moon about.

havza River-basin, catchment area; sphere; domain; territory of a state or town.

hay¹ Alive.

hay² Hey!; alas! ~ ~, certainly! by all means!; right ho!

hay³ In ⌈~dan gelen huya gider⌉, 'easy come, easy go' (money).

haya Testicle.

hayâ (·–¹) Shame; modesty, bashfulness. ~lı, bashful; modest. ~sız, shameless, impudent.

hayal (·¹) –li Spectre, phantom; reflection; image; fancy, imagination; shadow panto-mime. ~ etm., to imagine stg.: ~ kuvveti, the power of imagination, a lively imagina-

tion: sukutu ~ (inkisarı ~, ~ kırgınlığı), disappointment.

hayal·at (·–¹), –tı vain imaginings: ~a kapılmak, to be fed on illusions. ~ci, giver of a puppet-show; visionary, day-dreamer. ~en (·–¹·), in imagination. ~et (·–¹), –ti, phantom, ghost, apparition. ~hane (·––¹), imagination, fancy. ~î (·–¹), fantastic, imaginary : puppet-player. ~ifener, (orig.) a magic lantern; a 'mere skeleton'. ~meyal, like a spectre, hardly perceptible: ~ görmek, to be hardly able to make stg. out from darkness or distance: ~ hatırlamak, to remember faintly. ~perest, visionary; castle-builder.

hayat¹, –tı Covered court; vestibule.

hayat² (·⁴), –tı (·–¹) Life; living. kaydı ~ şartile, for life (appointment etc.). ~bahş, life-giving. ~î (·–¹), vital. ~iyat (·–·⁴), –tı, biology. ~iyet (·–·¹), –ti, vitality.

hayda·lamak, ~mak¹ va. Drive on animals with loud shouts. ~mak², cattle-lifter, marauder; vagabond.

haydar Lion; courageous man. ~ane (···–¹), like a lion, courageous.

hayderî (···–¹), ~ye Kind of waistcoat formerly worn in the house.

haydi, hadi, haydin (¹·) Come!; be off! ~ ~, all the more; at the most; easily: ~ gidelim, come along!, let's be going!: ~ git!, clear out! ~sene (···¹), come along!

haydud Brigand. ~ yatağı, brigands' den. ~luk, brigandage.

hayfaki (·–¹·) Alas!, unfortunately.

hayhay Certainly!, by all means!

hayhuy v. hayühuy; also hay³.

hayıf Alas!; what a pity! ~lanmak vn., to bemoan, lament.

hayır¹ (¹·) No!

hayır², –yrı Good; prosperity; health; ex-cellence; profit, advantage. Good; advantageous; auspicious. ~lar!, all well! (as an answer to 'ne var ne yok?'): hayra alamet değil, it bodes no good: hayrı dokunmak, to be of use, to serve a useful purpose: ~ dua, a blessing, benediction: hayrını gör-mek, to enjoy the advantages or profit of stg.: çocuklarının hayrını görmedi, his children turned out badly; hayrını gör!, may it bring you good luck! (said by the vendor to the purchaser); (sarcastically) well, I wish you the luck of it!; hayrını görme!, bad luck to you!: ~ hasenat, pious or charitable institutions: ~dır inşallah!, I hope all is well!, I hope there is nothing the matter!: hayrı kalmamak, to be no longer of any use; (of a man) to have become useless by having been spoilt or through intemperance etc.: ~ ola!, 'good news, I hope!': ~ sahibi, a philanthropist: hayrı yok, there is no

good to be expected of him (it); **gemiden
~ yoktu**, there was no hope of saving the
ship: ⌐**ağzını hayra aç¹**⌐, 'say something
cheerful for a change!' (*as a rebuke to one
who utters gloomy forebodings*).
hayır·hah, benevolent. **~hahlık**, benevolence. **~laşmak**, to conclude a sale
with the formula 'harını gör!'. **~lı**, good;
advantageous; auspicious: **~ olsun!** *or*
haydi ~sı!, let's hope for the best; good
luck to it! **~sız**, useless, good-for-nothing;
unproductive; ill-omened.
hayıt Agnus-castus tree.
hayız, –yzı Menstruation.
hayide (--ꞌ) Chewed; stale (joke);
hackneyed (expression).
haykırış, haykırma A shouting, bawling.
haykırmak *va. & vn.* Shout, bawl, cry out.
haylaz Idle, lazy. Lazy man; vagabond.
hayli (ꞌ·) Much; many; very; pretty
(fairly). **~den ~ye**, a lot of; very much.
~ca (ꞌ··), a good many; considerably.
haylûlet (·–ꞌ), **–ti** Arrival; appearance;
intervention.
haymana (ꞌ··) A large open plain where
animals are turned out to graze. **~ beygiri
gibi dolaşmak**, to wander about aimlessly.
hayme Tent. **~nişin**, dwelling in tents;
nomad.
hayran (·ꞌ) Astonished; perplexed; filled
with admiration. ⌐**ben sana ~, sen cama
tırman**⌐, *a meaningless expression used to
describe an impracticable and purely romantic
idea.* **~lık**, amazement; admiration.
hayrat (·Ꞌ), **–tı** Pious deeds; pious foundations. **eski ~ı berbad etm.**, in trying to
improve a thing to make it worse.
hayret, –ti Amazement, stupor; admiration. **~e bırakmak**, to astound: **~ etm.**, to
be perplexed; to be lost in admiration *or*
astonishment (at = *dat.*): **~te kalmak**, to
be lost in amazement.
hayrı *v.* **hayır.**
hayrola Good news, I hope!; well, how did
it go off?
hayrülhalef Worthy successor.
haysiyet, –ti Personal dignity; amour
propre. **~ divanı**, a court of honour *to
decide on questions relating to the conduct of
members of a profession or an association.*
~li, jealous of his personal honour; self-
respecting. **~şiken**, that hurts one's self-
respect.
hayt, –tı Fibre; filament.
hayta (*Formerly*) a mounted guard, *who
escorted a caravan*; armed and mounted
brigand; out-of-hand, mischievous child;
young hooligan.
hayühuy (–·ꞌ·), **hayıhuy** Worries and
troubles; the humdrum of everyday life.

hayvan Living creature; animal; beast of
burden; stupid fool. **~at** (·–ꞌ), **–tı**,
animals: **~ bahçesi**, zoological garden.
~ca (·ꞌ·), **~casına**, like an animal;
bestially; stupidly. **~cı**, cattle-dealer *or*
breeder. **~î** (·–ꞌ), animal, bestial. **~iyet,
–ti**, **~lık**, quality of an animal; bestiality;
stupidity; stupid *or* brutal action.
hayyalesselâ 'Hasten to prayer!' (*the end
of the call to prayer*). **~ demek** *or* **~yı
çekmek**, to say one's last word.
hayyiz Place; space; *err. in* **hayzü mekân**,
space (infinity).
haz, –zzı Pleasure; contentment; enjoyment. **~ duymak**, to feel pleasure: **~zı
nefs**, sensual pleasure; luxury.
hâzâ (Ꞌ–) *Lit.* 'this (is)', *used in such expressions as*: **~ kibar**, a real gentleman; **~ ev**,
a perfect house; **~ sersem**, a complete idiot.
hazain (·–ꞌ) *pl. of* **hazine.** Treasures.
hazaket (·–ꞌ), **–ti** Skill, ability (*esp. in
medicine*). **~li**, skilful in one's profession.
hazan Autumn. **~ yaprağı gibi titremek**,
to tremble like an aspen leaf.
hazar¹ Big saw. **su ~ı**, sawmill worked by
water.
hazar² Peace. **~ mevcudu**, peace establishment *of an army*. **~î** (·.Ꞌ), peaceful: **~
kuvvet**, peacetime strength of the army.
hazele Rogues. **~ bezele**, hooligans.
hazer Precaution. **···den ~ etm.**, to be on
one's guard against ... .
hazerat (·–Ꞌ), **–tı** *pl. of* **hazret.** Excellencies.
Hazerdenizi (·Ꞌ···), **–ni** The Caspian Sea.
hazf, –fi Elision; suppression. **~etmek**
(Ꞌ··), **–eder**, to elide; suppress.
hazık (–ꞌ) Skilful (doctor *etc.*).
hâzım (–ꞌ) Who digests; digestive; long-
suffering. **hazım, –zmı**, digestion;
patience under insult. **~lı**, patient, long-
suffering; tolerant. **~sız**, indigestible;
irritable, touchy. **~sızlık**, indigestion.
hazır Present (not absent); present (time);
ready, prepared; ready-made. **~ ekmek
yemek**, to live without working: **~ etm.**,
to prepare: **~a konmak**, to settle down to
enjoy what is already prepared; to enjoy
the fruits of others' labours: **~ olm.**, to be
ready; to be present; ⌐**~ ol!**⌐, 'attention!'
(*mil.*); 'get ready!': **~ para**, money in hand,
the sum of money that a man has at his
disposal; ⌐**~ paraya dağlar dayanmaz**⌐, no
one can long go on living on his capital: **~
yemek**, food already prepared (*such as
tinned soups etc.*); **~dan yemek**, to live on
one's capital: **~ yiyici**, one who lives on his
capital; as **hazırcı** (ii): ⌐**~ sokağa giderken
şu mektubu da postaya atıver!**⌐, 'since you
are going out anyhow, just post this letter
for me!'

hazır·cevab, quick at reply and repartee. **∼cı,** (i) seller of ready-made clothes; (ii) one who likes the good things of this world if he can get them without trouble to himself. **∼lamak,** to prepare. **∼lık,** readiness; preparedness; preparation: **∼ görmek,** to make preparations: **∼ tahkikatı,** preliminary investigations (legal). **∼lop,** hard-boiled egg; a lucky find. **∼ol,** attention! (*mil.*): **∼ vaziyetinde durmak,** to stand at attention. **∼un** (−·−), *pl. of* **hazır;** those present.

hazin Sad; melancholy.

hazine (·−) Treasure; treasury; buried treasure; storehouse; reservoir, cistern; chamber of a gun. **∼i humayun,** the Imperial Treasury: **∼li tüfek,** magazine rifle. **∼dar,** treasurer. **∼ievrak, -kı,** state archives (*now* **devletin evrak ∼si**).

haziran (·−) June.

hazire (·−) Graveyard in the precincts of a mosque.

haziz *v.* **hadid.**

hazm·etmek (··), **-eder** *va.* Digest; swallow (an affront). **∼î** (·−), digestive.

hazne *v.* **hazine.** Tank, reservoir.

hazret, -ti Excellency (title); *title of the earlier Caliphs.* **∼i Peygamber,** the Prophet: **∼leri,** His Excellency (*after a title*); *used as a jocular address to a friend* 'old fellow!', 'old man!'

hazzetmek (··), **-eder** *vn.* Rejoice; be pleased; ···**den ∼,** to be fond of ... .

heba (·−) Waste; loss. **∼ etm.,** to waste; spoil: **∼ olm.,** to be wasted; to be sacrificed in vain.

hebenneka *The name of an historic fool; a fool who thinks himself clever.*

heccav Satirist.

hece Syllable. **∼ vezni,** metre based on the number of syllables. **∼lemek,** to spell out by syllables. **∼li,** having *so many* syllables.

hecin Dromedary. **∼ süvar,** member of a Camel Corps.

hedaya (·−−) *pl. of* **hediye.** Presents.

hedef Mark; target; object, aim. **∼e isabet etm.,** to hit the target; to attain one's object.

heder A considering of no account; the shedding of blood with impunity; vain expenditure of life or effort. **∼ etm.,** to treat as of no account; to leave blood unavenged: **∼ olm.,** to go for nothing; to be sacrificed uselessly; to be a pity.

hedik Snowshoe.

hedim, -dmi Demolition.

hediye Present, gift; price. **∼lik,** fit for a present; a choice thing. **∼ten** (·−··), as a present.

hedmetmek (··), **-eder** *va.* Demolish.

hekim Doctor. **∼lik,** profession of doctor; medical science.

hektar Hectare (= 2·471 *acres*).

helâ (·−) Closet, privy.

helâk (·-), **-ki** Destruction; death; exhaustion. **∼ etm.,** to destroy; to wear out with fatigue: **∼ olm.,** to perish; to be utterly done up.

helâl (·-), **-li, -lı** A permitted *or* legitimate act *or* person; lawful spouse. Lawful; legitimate. **∼im,** my lawful property; my lawful spouse: **∼inden,** legitimately; honestly earned; as a free gift: **∼ etm.,** to declare *stg.* lawful; to give up a legitimate claim to another: ⸢**∼i hoş olsun**⸣, *affectionate expression used when mentioning an absent person*: **∼ olsun!,** may it be your lawful right and property! (*said when concluding a bargain or when giving stg.*): **∼ süt emmiş,** entirely trustworthy: ⸢**anamın sütü gibi ∼ olsun!**⸣, you are quite entitled to it; you need have no qualms about accepting it: '**bunu yaparsan sana her hakkım ∼ olsun!**', if you do this, I will forgive you everything: **kanı ∼,** outlaw, proscribed person.

helâl·î (·-·), a tissue of silk with cotton or wool; old-fashioned pinchbeck watch. **∼laşmak,** mutually to forgive one another (*when dying or setting out on a long journey*). **∼lık,** forgiving an unlawful act; person whom one may legitimately marry; lawful spouse: **helâllığa almak,** to take as one's lawful wife: **∼ dilemek,** to ask forgiveness for an unlawful act. **∼zade** (···−), legitimate offspring; an honest man.

helâvet *v.* **halâvet.**

hele (··) Above all, especially; at least; at last. Hi! listen to me!; now just look here! **∼ ∼,** now tell me truly!: **∼ bir göreyim,** just let me see!: **∼ bunu yapma, sana göstererim!,** don't you dare do it, or I'll give you what for!

helecan *v.* **halecan.**

helezon Snail; snailshell; spiral; propeller. **∼î** (···−), spiral, helical.

helile (·−) Myrobalan (*used as a purgative*).

helke Pail; bucket.

helme Thick liquid or paste *made by boiling starchy substances.* **∼ ∼ olm.,** to become like paste: **∼ dökmek** *or* **∼lenmek,** to become a jelly, become like paste.

helva Sweetmeat *made of sesame flour, butter, and honey; there are many kinds such as* **koz ∼sı** (with walnuts), **badem ∼sı** (with almonds), *etc.* **∼ sohbeti,** a social gathering *where* **helva** *is offered to the guests*: **kudret ∼sı,** manna **∼cı,** maker or vendor of **helva**: **∼ kabağı,** a kind of white-fleshed pumpkin. ~hane (···–ᴵ), large shallow pan in which helva is made.

hem And also; too. ~ ben ~ sen, both you and I: ve ~de, and moreover.

hem– *Pers. prefix indicating similarity or company.* ~ahenk, harmonious. ~asır, contemporary. ~ayar, of the same standard *or* class; alike. ~cins, of the same kind *or* race. ~civar, neighbour; neighbouring. ~dem, constant companion; crony; confedetate. ~derd, fellow sufferer.

hemece *v.* emece.

hemen (ᴵ·) At once; exactly; just; just now; continually; about, nearly; only just; only. ~ ~, almost, very nearly. ~cecik (·ᴵ··), ~cek (ᴵ··), at once.

hem·fikir Like-minded. ~hal, –li, in the same condition; fellow sufferer. ~hudud, having the same boundary or frontier; contiguous. ~meşreb, alike in character. ~pa (·ᴸ), accomplice, confederate. ~paye (·–ᴵ), of equal rank; of the same standing. ~raz (·ᴸ) *n.*, intimate; confidant. ~sin, –sinni, one of the same age. ~şeri, fellow townsman; compatriot.

hemşire Sister, trained hospital nurse. ~zade (···–ᴵ), sister's child, nephew, niece.

hem·ta (·ᴸ) Equal. Match. bi~, matchless. ~zaman, contemporaneous. ~zeban, speaking the same tongue; unanimous in expression.

hendek Ditch; moat; trench.

hendes·e Geometry; mathematics. ~eli, ~î (···ᴸ), geometrical.

hengâm Time; season; period.

hengâme Uproar; tumult.

henüz (·ᴵ) Yet; still; (*with neg.*) not yet: (ᴵ·) just now; a little while ago.

hep All; the whole. Wholly; always. ~imiz, all of us; ~iniz, all of you: ~ten, entirely: ~ altındır, it is all gold: ~ bitti, it is entirely finished ~si, the whole of it; all of it; all of them: ~nden ziyade, above all. ~yek, double-one (in dice).

her Every; each. *Many of the compound expressions of* her *are variously written as one word or as two or three. Those which are almost always written as one are given separate headings, q.v.* ~ an, always, any moment: ~ bir, every; each; each one; whoever; anyone of: ~ gün, every day; continually: ~ günkü, everyday: ~ günlük, everyday clothes: ~ halde, in any case, under any circumstances; for sure; apparently: ~ kim, whosoever, whoever: ~ nasıl, in whatever way: ~ nasılsa, in whatever way may be; somehow or other: ~ ne, whatever; ~ ne hal ise, well anyhow …: ~ ne pahasına olursa olsun, at whatever cost: ~ nedense, for some reason or

other; I don't know why: ~ nekadar, however much: ~ nerede, wherever: ~ ne türlü, of whatever kind; in whatever way: ~ ne vakit, whenever; every time that …: ~ neyse, whatever it be; however it be; anyhow: ~ yerde, everywhere: ~ zaman, every time; always.

heragıl (·–ᴵ) *pseudo-Arabic pl. of* hergele. Roughs, hooligans.

herbar (·ᴸ) Every time; always.

hercai (·–ᴵ) Ubiquitous; roving; inconstant. ~ menekşe, pansy.

herc Confusion; turmoil. ~ümerc, a confused, disordered mass.

herçibadabad (ᴵ·––––) Come what may!; at all costs.

herdem (ᴵ·) At every moment. ~taze (·ᴵ–·), evergreen; ageless.

herek Prop *for vines etc.*; temporary platform *for drying raisins, tobacco etc.*

herem Feeble, decrepit. Decrepitude.

herfane (·–ᴵ) *v.* arifane².

hergele Herd of animals; a lot of roughs; rough coarse fellow; street urchin. ~ci glossy ibis.

herhangi (·ᴵ·) Whoever; whatever.

herif Fellow (*always derogatory*). ~in biri, some fellow or other. ~ci, in ~ oğlu, (*an insulting expression*) 'the fellow'.

herkes (ᴵ·) Everyone.

hernedense (··ᴵ·) *v.* her.

herrü *v.* harrü.

Hersek Herzogovina.

herze Nonsense. ~ yemek, to talk nonsense. ~gû (··ᴸ), who talks nonsense. ~vekil, busybody; twaddler.

hesab (·⁴) A counting; reckoning; calculation; account; bill; accounts; arithmetic. ~ını bilmek, to be careful and economical: ~a çekmek, to call to account, to hold responsible: ~ etm., to calculate: ~a *or* ~ına* gelmek, to suit; ~a gelmez, countless; unbounded: ~ görmek, to have a reckoning, to settle up: ~ işi, (sewing) not judging by eye where to insert needle, but counting the threads in the stuff sewn: ~ı kesmek, to settle an account definitely; to sever relations with s.o.: ~ kitab, after full consideration; ~a kitaba uygun, suitable to one's means; ~ı kitabı yok (bilmez), uncontrolled; unlimited: ~ meydanda, it's quite obvious: ⌜evdeki ~ çarşıya uymaz⌝, things don't turn out as one reckons; 'don't count your chickens before they are hatched'.

hesab·ca (·ᴵ·), according to the reckoning; normally, properly speaking. ~cı, calculating; careful; miserly. ~î (·–ᴸ), pertaining to accounts; who calculates; economical; stingy. ~lamak, to reckon; estimate.

~lı, calculated; well considered. ~sız, countless; uncertain, problematical; without reflection; ~ kitabsız, uncontrolled (expenditure *etc.*); casual, at random, thoughtlessly.

hetepete In a stumbling *or* stammering manner.

hethüt *Imitates a loud and menacing way of speaking.* ~ etm., to behave in a bullying manner, to browbeat.

hetk, –tki A rending; violation. ~i ırz, violation, rape: ~i perdei namus, the violation of one's honour.

hevam (·—·) *pl. of* hamme. Creeping things; insects.

hevenk, –ği Bunches *of grapes etc.* hung up.

heves Desire; inclination; mania; zeal. ~ini almak, to satisfy a desire. ~at (··—·), –tı, *pl. of* heves. ~kâr, ~li, desirous; eager; having aspirations; dilettante. ~kârlık, a passing desire; longing; hobby. ~lendirmek, to awake the desire *in s.o. to do stg.* ~lenmek, to long for, desire. ~siz, disinclined.

hevil, –vli Horror; terror. ~nak (··—·), terrible; horrifying.

hey Hi!; *also expresses regret, reproach or admiration.*

heyamola (··ᴗ·) *Cry in unison of sailors at work*; with much difficulty and fuss. ~ ile iş görmek, to work only when hustled.

heybe Saddle-bag; wallet.

heybet, –ti Awe; majesty; imposing air. ~li, imposing, majestic; awe-inspiring.

heyecan Excitement; enthusiasm; emotion. ~a gelmek (~ bulmak), to get excited, be enthusiastic. ~lı, excited; exciting; enthusiastic.

heyelân Landslide.

heyet, –ti Shape, form; state, aspect; assembly, commission, committee; astronomy. ~i mecmuası itibarile, taken as a whole; ~i teşriiye, legislative assembly: ~i umumiyesile, taken as a whole; ~i vükela *or* vekile, Council of Ministers, Cabinet; ehli ~, astronomers. ~şinas, astronomer.

heyhat Alas!

heyhey¹ Amusement; orgy; song.

heyhey² *In* ~ler geçirmek, to be very agitated, to have a fit of nerves: içime ~ler geliyor, I can't stand it any longer; I shall have a nervous breakdown.

hey'î (·—·) Astronomical.

heykel Statue. ~traş, sculptor. ~traşlık, sculpture.

heyulâ (—·—·) Matter (the substance of which all is formed); spectre, bogy. ~yî, like a terrifying apparition.

hezar¹ (·—·) Thousand. ~fen, –fenni, Jack-of-all-trades; omniscient; versatile.

hezar² (·—·) Nightingale.

hezaren Cane, rattan; delphinium.

hezel Joke, jest; comedy; comic tale; indecent verse. ~iyat, –tı, comic stories or verses.

hezen arısı Bumble-bee.

hezeyan Talking nonsense; delirium. ~ı mürteiş, delirium tremens.

hezimet (·—·), –ti Utter defeat, rout.

hıçkırık Hiccough; sob. ~ tutmak, to have the hiccoughs. ~mak, to sob.

hıdırellez, hıdrellez The beginning of summer (6th of May).

hıdiv (·—·) Khedive. ~î (·—·—·), Khedivial. ~iyet, –ti, Khediviate.

hıfız, –fzı A guarding *or* protecting; protection; a committing to memory; committing the Koran to memory. hıfza çalışmak, to be trained in learning the Koran by heart.

hıfz·etmek (ᴗ··), –eder *va.* Protect; preserve; commit to memory. ~ısıhha, hygiene.

hık *In* 「~ demiş burnundan düşmüş」, he is the very spit of him; *v. also* hınk.

hık mık etm. *vn.* Hum and haw. hık da dese, mık da dese faydası yok, whatever he said it was no use: hık mık yok, there is no question about it !

hil'at, –ti Robe of honour.

hımbıl Silly; slow.

hımhım Talking through the nose. 「~la burunsuz birbirinden uğursuz」, 'birds of a feather'.

hınc Rancour; hatred. ~ beslemek, to nourish a grudge: ···den ~ını çıkarmak (almak), to take revenge on, to vent one's spleen on ... : ···in ~ını çıkarmak, to take revenge for ... .

hıncahınç Chock-a-block.

hınk *In* 「kahve döğücünün ~ deyicisi」, one who only helps by making a lot of noise; one who, to curry favour, agrees with all another says.

hınzır Swine; foul fellow; *sometimes used in joking admiration.* Swinish. ~lık, a dirty trick.

hır Row, quarrel. ~ çıkarmak, to start a quarrel.

hırçın Ill-tempered; (of the sea) angry. ~lık, bad temper; obstinacy.

hırdavat, –tı *pl.* Small wares; ironmongery. ~çı, seller of small wares, pedlar; ironmonger.

hırgür Snarling; noisy quarrel.

hırhıra *In* ~ kemiği, the Adam's apple.

hırhıryas Porbeagle.

hırıl·damak *vn.* Growl; purr; have a rattle (râle) in the throat. ~daşmak, to snarl at one another; quarrel without reason.

~**tı**, growling, snarling; squabble; râle, death-rattle.

hırızma (·¹·) Nose-ring worn by Arab women; nose-ring (of animals). ~**sı çıkmış**, all skin and bones.

hıristiyan Christian. ~**lık**, Christianity.

hırka Short cloak, *usually quilted*; dervish's coat. **Hırkai Şerif**, the Prophet's Mantle, *preserved as a relic at Istanbul*: ⌐**bir lokma bir** ~¬, a morsel of food, a rag of clothing, *i.e.* enough to keep body and soul together.

hırla·mak *vn.* Growl, snarl. ~**nmak**, to growl or snarl (*of a man only*). ~**şmak**, to snarl at one another; to squabble noisily.

hırlı *Only in* ~ **hırsız**, honest men and thieves.

hırpa·lamak *va.* Ill-treat; misuse. ~**lanmak**, to be ill-treated; be upset.

hırpani (·–¹) Ruffled; untidy, unkempt.

hırpo (*sl.*) Big clumsy fellow.

hırs Inordinate desire; greed; ambition (bad); anger. ~**ındanʿ çatlamak**, to be ready to burst with anger: ~**ınıʿ ···den çıkarmak**, to vent one's spleen on ... . ~**ıcah**, inordinate ambition.

hırsız Thief. Thieving. ~ **feneri**, dark-lantern: ~ **malı**, stolen goods: ~**a yol göstermek**, imprudently *or* inadvertently to help a wrongdoer. ~**lama**, stealing; like a thief, furtively, stealthily, surreptitiously. ~**lamak**, to steal. ~**lık**, theft, thieving. ~**yatağı**, **–nı**, thieves' den; receiver of stolen goods.

hırs·lanmak *vn.* Get angry. ~**lı**, angry; desirous; avaricious.

hırt Coarse and vulgar yet conceited.

hırtıpırtı Trifles, rubbish; old clothes.

hırtlamba (·¹·) Poorly and untidily clothed; weakly and coughing and spitting. ~**sı çıkmış**, in rags and tatters; thin and bony: ~ **gibi giyinmek**, to be untidily dressed with an excess of clothing.

hırva Castor-oil plant, ricinus.

Hırvat Croat; Croatian; great big man. ~**istan**, Croatia.

hısım, **–smı** A relative. ~**lık**, relationship.

hışıl·damak *vn.* Make a wheezing *or* rustling noise. ~**tı**, a wheezing *or* rustling noise.

hışım, **–şmı** Anger; indignation. **hışmına**ʿ **uğramak**, to be the object of *s.o.'s* anger.

hışır Unripe melon; rind of a melon. Stupid and gullible. ~ ~ **etm.**, to make a harsh grating sound. ~**damak**, to make the noise produced by dry leaves, by paper or silk, or a snake moving in dry grass. ~**tı**, such a noise.

hıtta Region; country.

hıyaban (·–¹) Alley; avenue.

hıyanet *v.* hiyanet.

hıyar Cucumber; dolt. Uncouth and stupid. *v. also* hiyar. **yabanı** ~, squirting cucumber. ~**cık**, bubo; tumour.

hız Speed; impetus. ~ **almak**, to get up speed; *but* ~**ını almak**, to slow down; to take it easy: ~**ını alamamak**, to be unable to slow down, not to be able to stop oneself.

hızar *v.* hazar¹.

Hızır *A legendary person who was reputed to arrive and help in critical moments.* ~ **gibi yetişmek**, to be a 'deus ex machina', a timely help; to come as a godsend: ⌐**kul daralmayınca (sıkışmayınca)** ~ **yetişmez**¬, *said when unexpected help arrives to one in difficulties.*

Hızırilyas *v.* hıdirellez.

hız·lanmak *vn.* Gain speed or impetus. ~**lı**, swift; violent; loud.

hibe Gift.

hibre Knowledge; experience; experiment. **ehli** ~, expert.

hicab (·⅄) Modesty, shame. ~**ı haciz**, diaphragm. ~**lı**, veiled; modest; bashful.

Hicaz¹ Hedjaz.

hicaz² *or* ~**kâr** A mode in Oriental music.

hicir, **–cri** *v.* hicran.

hiciv, **–cvi** Satire; lampoon.

hicran (·⅄) Separation; absence from one's family; mental pain; bitterness of heart.

hicr·et, **–ti** Abandoning one's country; emigration; *the emigration of Mohammed from Mekka to Medina, i.e.* the Hegira (A.D. 622). ~**î** (·⅃), pertaining to the Hegira: **senei** ~**ye**, any year of the Hegira era.

hicv·etmek (¹··), **–eder** *va.* Satirize. ~**î** (·⅃), satirical. ~**iye**, satire, satirical poem (*pl.* hicviyat).

hiç No. Nothing. Not at all; never; (*without neg.*) ever. ~ (*or* ~ **bir**) **kimse**, nobody: ~ **bir şey**, nothing at all: ~ **değilse** (**olmazsa**), at least: ~ **mi** ~, absolutely nothing :ʿ~ **olur mu**ʾ?, does it ever happen?, is it possible?: ~**e saymak**, to hold of no account: ~ **yoktan** (**yüzünden**), for no reason.

hiç·lik, nullity. ~**ten**, *abl. of* hiç; sprung from nothing, parvenu; useless; got for nothing; trifling, insignificant: ~ **sebeblerle**, under absurd pretexts.

hidayet (·–¹), **–ti** The right way, *esp.* the way to Islam; a searching for the right way.

hiddet, **–ti** Violence; impetuosity; anger, fury. ~**e gelmek**, to fly into a passion. ~**lenmek**, to become angry. ~**li**, angry; violent.

hidemat (··⅄), **–tı** *pl. of* hizmet. Services, *etc.* ~**ı mesbukasına mebni**, for his past services: ~**ı şakka**, hard labour (penal).

hidiv *v.* **hıdiv.**

hiffet, –ti Levity, frivolity; idiocy. ~ göstermek, to behave frivolously: aklına ~ getirmek, to go off one's head.

hikâye A relating, narration; story; novel. ~ etm., to tell, narrate. ~ci, story-teller; short-story writer. ~cilik, the art of story-telling.

hikemî (···⌐) Rational; philosophical; physical. ~yat (···–ı), –tı, philosophical writings; wise sayings.

hikmet, –ti The ultimate hidden cause *for existence or occurrence*; the Divine Wisdom; inner meaning or object; wisdom; philosophy; wise saying; reason; physics. Allahın ~i or ~i Huda, the divine dispensation; 'Heaven knows why!'; 'strangely enough!'; 'for some mysterious reason': işin ~ini bilmiyorum, I don't know the real truth of the matter: ~inden sual olmaz (olunmaz), 'Heaven only knows why!': bu çocuk bir ~ !, this child is hopeless; there's something wrong about this child: her gün gelirdi ne ~se bugün gelmedi, he has been coming every day, it's odd he hasn't come today: ⌐pahalıdır ~i var, ucuzdur illeti var⌐, 'if it is dear, there is a good reason for it; if it is cheap, there is something wrong with it', *i.e.* it always pays to buy the best.

hikmet·ivücud, (····⌐), –dü, the real reason; the *raison d'être*. ~şinas, sage; natural philosopher.

hilâf (·⌐) The contrary, opposite; contravention; opposition; lie. ~ına, contrary to ..., against ...: ~ı hakikat, contrary to the truth: ~ım varsa, if I lie.

hilâfet (·–ı), –ti The Caliphate.

hılâf·gir (·–ı) Opposing; adversary. ~ınca (·–ı·), in opposition to, in contravention of.

hilâl[1] (·⌐), –li Toothpick; earpick.

hilâl[2] (·ı), –li Crescent. Hilâli Ahmer, the Red Crescent (Turkish equivalent of the Red Cross, now Kızılay). ~î (·–⌐), crescent-shaped; *v. also* helâlî. ~iye, celandine.

hile (–ı) Trick; wile; stratagem; fraud. ~ etm., to make use of a trick: ···den ~ sezmek, to suspect ... of laying a trap: ~i şeriye, a way of getting round the law. ~baz, ~li, ~kâr (–·⌐), wily, deceitful; fraudulent. ~kârlık (–·–ı), deceit, trickery, fraud. ~siz, genuine; aboveboard.

hilim, –lmi Mildness; gentleness; forbearance.

hilk·at, –ti Creation; natural form *or* disposition. ~aten (ı··), by nature. ~î (·⌐), natural, inborn, congenital.

himaye (·–ı) Protection; defence. ~ etm.,

to protect: ~ usulü, protectionist system (*as opposed to free trade*). ~kâr, protective; patronizing. ~li, escorted (convoy *etc.*)

himmet, –ti Effort, zeal, endeavour; influence; moral support; benevolence. ~inizle, thanks to your assistance: ~ etm., to exert oneself, to take trouble: ~ etmemek, to be unwilling to help, to make no effort. ⌐~i hazır nazır olsun!⌐, 'may his support be always at hand!' (*used superstitiously when speaking of a holy man*).

hin[1] Moment; special *or* appointed time. ~i hacette, when the need occurs.

hin[2] A kind of djinn. ~oğlu hin, son of the devil, scoundrel; very crafty fellow.

Hind India. ~istan, India. ~î (·⌐), Indian.

hindi Turkey (bird).

hindiba (···⌐) Chicory.

hindistancevizi, –ni (Büyük) ~, coconut; (küçük) nutmeg.

hinihacette (ı····) When the need arises.

hinoğlu (ı··), –nu *v.* hin.[2]

hint·kumaşı (ı···), –nı Very rare and precious thing (*usually used jocularly*). ~tavuğu, –nu, turkey. ~yağı, –nı, castor-oil.

hirfet, –ti Trade; craft. ehli ~, artisan; tradesman.

his, –ssi Sense; perception; faculty; feeling, sensation; sentiment. ~lerine* kapılmak, to be swayed by one's feelings.

hisa (ı·), etm. *va.* Hoist (flag *etc.*); toss (oars).

hisar Castle; fortress.

hisli Sensitive.

hisse Share; allotted portion; share *in a company*. ···den ~ kapmak, to learn a lesson from ...: ~ senedi share certificate: ~i şayia, co-ownership: kıssadan ~, the moral of the story is .... ~dar, participator; shareholder: (*pl.* ~daran; ~ meclisi, shareholders' meeting). ~li, having shares; divided into portions; belonging to various people. ~leşmek, to divide into portions; to share together. ~mend, having a share; having an interest; who profits.

hisset, –ti Avarice; stinginess; a stingy person.

hiss·etmek (ı··), –eder *va.* Feel; perceive. ~î (·⌐), perceptible; that can be felt; psychological; sentimental. ~ikablelvuku, –uu (*err. for* hisskablelvuku) premonition; presentiment. ~iyat (··ı), sensations; feelings; perceptions.

hissiz Insensitive, unfeeling, callous.

hiş, hişt *Interj. used to call attention*; hist! ~ piş etm., to call out 'hist!'; to call out to a girl.

hitab (·⸜) An addressing a person; address; allocution. ~ etm., to address; to make a remark to: ⸢bu adam kabili ~ değil *or* gayrikabili ~dır⸣, 'one can't talk to this man' (he's too stupid or he can't be trusted). ~e (·—⸜), address, speech. ~en (·⸜·), addressing: bana ~, addressing me. ~et (·—⸜), –ti, office of a preacher; oratory.

hitam (·⸜) Conclusion; completion. ~ bulmak, to come to an end: ···e ~ vermek, to bring to an end.

hitan (·⸜) Circumcision.

hiyanet (·—⸜), –ti Treachery, perfidy. Perfidious; basely ungrateful. ~i vataniye, high treason. ~lik, malicious act.

hiyar (·⸜) Option. hakkı ~, the right of option: *v. also* hıyar.

hiyel *pl. of* hile. Wiles.

hiyerarşi Hierarchy.

hiza (·⸜) The point opposite *or* on the same level; line; level. ···in ~sına, on a level with ..., in a line with ...: ~sını almak, to take the bearing *or* the level of ...: ···in ~sına kadar, up to the level of ...: ~ya gelmek, to get into line: bir ~da, in one line, on one level. ~lamak, to be *or* become level with; be in a line with; arrange in a line.

hizib, –zbi Clique; party; portion of the Koran.

hizmet, –ti Service; duty; employment; function. ···in ~inde bulunmak, to be in the service of ...: ···e ~ etm., to render service to ...: ~ini görmek, to serve for, take the place of. ~çi, servant. ~cilik, the position and duties of a servant: ~ etm., to be a servant *with s.o.* ~kâr (··⸜), servant.

hoca (⸜·) Moslem priest; hodja; schoolmaster. akıl ~sı, one who sets up to give good advice to others: ⸢ha ~ Ali ha Ali ~⸣, it's much of a muchness. ~lik, the quality *or* profession of a hodja *or* schoolmaster: ahlâk hocalığı etm., to set oneself up as a guardian of morals: akıl hocalığı yapmak, to give good advice (pretentiously). ~nım, *for* hoca hanım, woman teacher.

hodan Borage.

hod·bin Egotistical, selfish; conceited. ~binlik, self-conceit; selfishness. ~endiş, selfish. ~gâm, ~kâm, wilful; egotistical. ~perest, egotistical. ~pesend, self-satisfied, conceited.

Hodiri (⸜··), **Hodri, Hodori** *In* ⸢~meydan⸣, 'come and try!' (*a challenge*).

hohlamak *va.* Breathe upon.

hokka Inkpot. ~ ağızlı, with a small pretty mouth: şeker ~sı, sugar-bowl: tükürük ~sı, spitoon.

hokkabaz Conjuror; cheat, knave. ~lik, conjuring; trickery.

hol, –lü Hall.

Holanda (·⸜·) Holland. lı, Dutchman.

homur·danmak, *vn.* Mutter; grumble. ~tu, a muttering, grumbling.

hona Stag.

hop *In* ~ oturup ~ kalkmak, to keep on jumping up and down *from excitement*. ~lamak, to jump about.

hoparlör (*Fr. haut parleur*) Loudspeaker.

hoppa Volatile, flighty, flippant. ~lik, levity, flightiness.

hoppala (⸜··) *Used when dangling a child*; 'up she goes!'; *exclamation of surprise*. ~ bebek, a childish person.

hopurdatmak *v.* höpürdetmek.

hor Contemptible. ~a geçmek, to be appreciated: ~a gelmez, that will not stand rough usage: ~ görmek (bakmak), to look down upon, to treat as of no account: ~ kullanmak, to misuse; to use for the commonest purposes.

hora (⸜·) A kind of round dance; noisy party. ~ tepmek, to dance the hora; to dance about noisily and clumsily (*as of a lot of tipsy people*).

horan A kind of folk dance *on the Black Sea coast*. ~ etm., *as* hora tepmek.

Horasan (·⸜·) Khorasan. horasan, mortar made of brickdust and lime. ~î (·—⸜), native of Khorasan; kind of turban formerly worn by government clerks; santonin; dull red colour.

horata Noisy party; loud noise.

horlamak[1] *vn.* Snore.

hor·lamak[2] *va.* Treat with contempt; ill-treat. ~luk, contemptibility.

horon *v.* horan.

horosbinâ Butterfly blenny.

horoz Cock; hammer *of a gun*. ~ akıllı (kafalı), hare-brained. ⸢~u bile yumurtlar⸣, 'even his cock lays eggs', *i.e.* everything succeeds with him. ~ işi, badly made, trash: ~dan kaçmak, (of a girl) to be coy and bashful: ~ kuyruğu, cock's tail; French bean: ~ mantarı, chanterelle: ~ şekeri, a sweet in the form of a cock *stuck on the end of a stick*: ⸢~ ölmüş, gözü çöplükte kalmış⸣, 'the cock is dead, but his eye remains on the dung-heap' (*a pun, since* 'gözü arkada kalmak' *means* 'to look back regretfully'), *used of one who looks back regretfully to things that are now lost to him*: ~ yumurtası, a very small egg, pullet's egg: çöplük ~u, one with low-down tastes: yabani ~, blackcock.

horoz·ayağı, –nı, cartridge-extractor. ~cuk, a little cock; youth; tansy (?). ~gözü, –nü, a kind of camomile. ~ibiği, –ni, cock's-comb (*Celosia*); hoopoe; bright red; *when meaning a cock's comb it is written*

as two words. **~lanmak,** to strut about.
~oğlu, abnormal, crazy.

hort·lak *A corpse which is vulgarly supposed to arise from its grave and frighten people in the dark;* spook; vampire. **~lamak,** to rise from the grave and haunt people.

hortum Elephant's trunk; hose-pipe; waterspout.

hortzort *v.* zartzurt.

horul *Imitates the noise of snoring.* ~ ~ **horlamak,** to snore noisily: ~ ~ uyumak, to sleep soundly; to be supine. **~damak,** to snore. **~tu,** snore, snoring.

hoş Pleasant, agreeable; quaint. *conj.* Well; even. ~ **geçinmek,** to get on well *with s.o.*: ⌐~ **geldiniz!**⌐, 'you are welcome!', *greeting to one just arrived, the correct reply being* ⌐~ **bulduk!**⌐: ~ **gelmek,** to be agreeable, to be liked, *e.g.* bu bana ~ geliyor, I like this: ~ **görmek,** to condone, overlook, tolerate; ~ **görürlük,** tolerance: **~una* gitmek,** to please, to be agreeable to: ⋯**le bası*** ~ **olmamak,** to dislike: bir ~ olm., to feel uncomfortable; to be disconcerted *or* offended: ⌐iyi misiniz ~ musunuz?⌐, 'I hope you are well!': ⌐~ **ben gitmiyecektim ya!**⌐, 'well, I shouldn't have gone anyhow!': ⌐~ **gelse ne faydası var?**⌐, 'even if he does come what use will it be?'

hoş·amedi (·—·⌐) *n.* Welcome. **~beş,** friendly greeting; friendly chat. **~bu** (·—⌐), pleasantly scented. **~ça** (⌐·), pleasantly, nicely: ~ **kalın!,** good-bye! **~etmek** (⌐··), **–eder,** *in* ⋯in hatırını (gönlünü) ~, to satisfy *or* please *s.o.* **~lanmak,** ⋯dan ~, to like. **~laşmak,** to get to like (*with abl.*); to like one another; to be disconcerted *or,* offended; (of food) to turn sour. **~luk,** pleasantness; happiness; comfort; quaintness: bir hoşluğum var, I am feeling rather queer: gönül hoşluğu ile, gladly, willingly. **~nud,** contented, pleased. **~nudluk,** contentment; pleasure. **~nudsuz,** discontented, displeased. **~nudsuzluk,** discontent, dissatisfaction. **~sohbet, –ti,** good company; conversationalist.

hoşaf Fruit in syrup. ⌐eşek ~tan ne anlar?⌐, 'it's throwing pearls before swine': ⋯de ~ın yağı kesilmek, to be dumbfounded.

hoşmerim *A dish made with unsalted fresh cheese.*

hoşt *Noise made to frighten away a dog.*

hoşundu (⌐··) How odd!

hotkâm *etc. v.* hodkâm *etc.*

hotoz (*Corr. of* kotaz = yak); yak's tail *as a banner;* crest *of a bird;* a kind of ancient headgear for women; bun, topknot (hair).

hov Hawking, falconry. **~ağası,** falconer. **~lamak,** to throw a hawk.

hovarda Scapegrace; rake; spendthrift; rich lover of a prostitute. **~lık,** dissoluteness; rakishness; being free with money.

hoyrat Vulgar; rough; coarse and clumsy man.

höcre *v.* hücre.

hödük Boorish; clumsy. Lout; bumpkin.

hökelek Peevish; contrary; boastful.

höpürdetmek *va.* Drink noisily.

hörgüç Hump *of a camel;* any protuberance. **~lük,** camel saddle.

höykürmek *vn.* Intone religious formulae.

höyük *v.* öyük.

hu Hi!; I say!

hub, –bbu Love. **~bu vatan,** love of one's country.

hûb (–) Good.

hububat (·–⌐), **–tı** Cereals.

hubut, –tu Descent; fall.

Huda (·⸜) God. ~ **nekerde,** God forbid!: biavni ~, with the help of God. **~dad** (·—⸜), given by God.

hud'a Fraud; deceit.

hudavend (·—⌐) Lord; master. **~igâr** (·—··⸜), ruler, *esp.* the Sultan Murad Ist; God; (*formerly*) the province of Brusa.

hudayinabit (·—·—⌐) That which grows by itself; of spontaneous growth; in its natural and wild state; (of children) running wild; untaught; amateur.

huddam *pl. of* hâdım = servants, *but used to mean* spirits. sahibi ~ *or* ~lı hoca, a man who claims to be able to communicate with spirits.

hudud *pl. of* had. Boundaries; limits; *as sing.* frontier.

hudus Occurrence; creation.

huffaş Bat. ⌐rencide olur didei ~ ziyadan⌐, 'the eyes of the bat are hurt by the light', *i.e.* the ignorant dislike the truth.

hufre Ditch; excavation; pit.

huğ Mud hut.

hukuk (·⸜), **–ku** *pl. of* hak. Rights; dues; laws. **~u düvel,** international law: ~ Fakültesi, the Law Faculty: kat'ı ~ etm., to break off relations: ⌐onunla aramızda ~umuz var⌐, 'we are old friends'. **~çu,** jurist. **~î** (·—⸜), legal; juridical; 'de jure'. **~şinas,** jurist.

hulâsa (·—⌐) The extract *of a substance;* quintessence; abstract, summary. In short, in fine. **~sını almak,** to sum up: ~ etm., to summarize, to make a précis of: **~i kelâm,** the sum and substance of what has been said, in short. **~aten** (·⸜··), in short; to sum up.

hulefa (··⸜) *pl. of* halife. Successors; Caliphs; *formerly* superior clerks in a government office. **~yi Raşidin,** the first four Caliphs.

hulf, –fü Failure to keep one's word; breach of promise. ~**etmek** (¹··), **–eder,** not to abide by one's word.

hulk, –ku Moral quality; character.

hulkum (·⁴) Pharynx; gullet. ~**î** (·–¹), guttural.

hulûl (·⁴), **–lü** An entering *or* penetrating; appearance; beginning *of a season*; reincarnation; osmosis. ~ **etm.,** to penetrate into; to enter (another body); to occur; to gain ascendancy over another: ~**i muslihane,** pacific penetration: ~ **siyaseti,** the policy of penetration.

hulûs (·⁴) Sincerity; devotion; esteem *for a superior*; flattery. **birine** ~ **çakmak,** to toady to, to make up to s.o. *by subtle flattery.* ~**kâr,** sincere; sincere friend; hypocritical; sycophant.

hulya (·–¹) Day-dream. ⌐~ **bu ya¹,** 'if by any possible chance ...'; 'let's suppose that ...'. ~**lı,** dreamy, romantic.

humar Drunken headache; 'hang-over'.

humayun *v.* hümayun.

humbara *v.* kumbara.

humk, –ku Stupidity.

humma (·–¹) Fever; typhus; typhoid. **kazıklı** ~, tetanus: **lekeli** ~, purpura; typhus; cerebrospinal meningitis. ~**lı,** feverish.

hummaz Sorrel; *also* = **loğusa şekeri,** *q.v.*

humus¹, –msu A fifth.

humus² Mashed chickpeas.

humuz (·–¹), **–mzu** Oxide (*pl.* humuzat). ~**iyet, –ti,** oxidization.

hun Blood. ~**har,** ~**riz,** bloodthirsty.

huni Funnel (*for pouring liquids*).

hunnab *v.* hünnab.

hunnak, –kı, –ğı Quinsy; angina.

hunsa (·–¹) Hermaphrodite.

hurac *pl.* Boils.

hurada *v.* kurada.

huraf·e (·–¹) Silly tale; superstition; myth. ~**at, –tı,** superstitions. ~**eperest,** superstitious.

hurc Large leather saddle-bag; hold-all.

hurd *In* ~ **hurdavat,** old rubbish. ~**a,** old iron, scrap metal; small, fine: ~ **fiatine,** at scrap price; for the value of the materials. ~**acı,** secondhand metal-dealer. ~**lanmak,** to be broken into small pieces. ~**avat,** *v.* hırdavat.

hurde Trifle; small bit; fine point, nicety. Small; trifling; minute. ~**bin,** microscope; acutely perceptive; hypercritical. ~**binî** (···–¹), microscopic. ~**haş** (···¹), in fragments.

huri (–¹) Houri; beautiful girl.

hurma Date (fruit). ~**dorusu,** of a brown bay colour (horse). ~**lık,** date-grove.

hurrem Happy, gay.

huruc (·⁴) An issuing forth; exit; sortie; rebellion; start of a new movement. ~ **etm.,** to come out; to make a sortie; to rise in rebellion.

huruf (·⁴) *pl. of* harf. Letters. ~**at** (·–⁴), **–tı,** types.

huruşan (·–¹) Roaring; clamorous.

hurya *v.* hürya.

husran *v.* hüsran.

husuf (·⁴) Eclipse of the moon.

husul (·⁴), **–lü** An occurring, appearing *or* being produced; attainment. ~ **bulmak** *or* ~**e gelmek,** to be accomplished *or* attained; ~**e getirmek,** to accomplish.

husumet (·–¹), **–ti** Enmity, hostility. **izharı** ~ **etm.,** to assume a hostile attitude.

husus (·⁴) Particularity; peculiarity; matter; connexion; particular. ~**iyle,** especially: ~**unda,** with reference to: **bu** ~**ta,** in this matter, in this connexion. ~**at** (·–⁴), **–tı,** *pl. of* husus: ~**ı sairede,** in other matters, in other particulars. ~**î** (·–¹), special, particular, private, personal. ~**îlik** (·–·¹), a being peculiar. ~**iyet** (·–·¹), **–ti,** peculiarity; speciality; intimacy.

husye Testicle.

huş¹ Reason; sense.

huş² Birch-tree.

huşu (·–¹), **–uu** Deep and humble reverence.

huşunet (·–¹), **–ti** Harshness; roughness; coarseness.

huşyar (·–¹) Reasonable; sober-minded.

hut, –tu Fish; the constellation Pisces.

hutbe The sermon and prayer delivered by the official preacher in a mosque on Fridays. **sikke ve** ~, the right of minting coins and being prayed for in the hutbe (*the special prerogatives of the Sultan as Caliph*).

hutut (·⁴), **–tu** *pl. of* hat. Lines *etc.*

huval Shoemaker's last; wedge for stretching a boot.

huveynat, –tı *pl.* (*err. for* hüveynat). Micro-organisms.

huy¹ Outcry; hue and cry; tumult.

huy² Disposition; temper; habit; bad habit. ~**unu husunu bilmiyorum,** I don't understand his temperament: ~ **edinmek,** to acquire a habit: ~ **kapmak,** to contract a bad habit: ⌐~ **canın altındadır¹,** you can't eradicate what is innate, 'what's bred in the bone will out in the flesh': ~**u** ~**uma suyu suyuma uygun,** his disposition is the same as mine, we get on very well together: ···**in** ~**una suyuna gitmek,** to treat *s.o.* tactfully. ~**etmek** (¹··), **–eder,** to contract the bad habit of ... . ~**lanmak,** to get into bad habits; (of an animal) to become restive or obstinate; (of a person) to become touchy or nervous. ~**lu,** of such-and-such a temper; suspicious, touchy;

bad-tempered, fractious : **iyi** ∼, good-tempered, well-behaved : ∼ **huyundan vazgeçmez,** it is difficult to get out of a bad habit. ∼**suz,** bad-tempered, fractious. ∼**suzluk,** bad temper; obstinacy.

huzme Bundle; parcel; bunch; pencil *of rays.*

huzu (·⸗) Humility; deep respect.

huzur (·⸗) Presence; repose, quiet, freedom from anxiety. ···**in** ∼**una çıkmak,** to enter the presence (of a great man), to have an audience with ... : **hakkı** ∼, honorarium *paid to the member of a Commission.* ∼**lu,** at ease; comfortable; tranquil. ∼**suz,** uneasy, troubled.

huzuzat (··⸗), **-tı** *pl.* of **haz.** Pleasures *etc.*

huzzar (·⸗) *pl.* of **hazır.** Those present; spectators.

hübub (·⸗) The blowing of the wind.

hüccet, -ti Argument; proof; title-deed. ∼**im elinde,** I am your slave.

hüceyre Small cell.

hücra (·⸗) Remote, solitary (place).

hücre Small room; cell; cell (biology); niche, alcove. ∼**vî** (··⸗), cellular.

hücum (·⸗) Attack, assault; rush *of blood.* ···**e** ∼ **etm.,** to attack.

Hüd *v.* **Hüt.**

hüda[1] *v.* **hidayet.**

Hüda[2] *v.* **Huda.**

hüddam *v.* **huddam.**

hükema (··⸗) *pl.* of **hakim.** Sages.

hükkâm *pl.* of **hâkim.** Rulers; judges.

hükm·en (¹·) By the decision of a judge; legally; in accordance with rules or regulations. ∼**etmek** (¹··), **-eder,** *vn.* (*with dat.*) *va.,* decide on; judge; exert influence; master; rule; command. ∼**î** (·⸗), judicial; done in accordance with a rule; nominal (*as opp. to actual*) : ∼ **şahıs,** juridical person. ∼**ünce** (·¹·), in conformity with; according to the requirements of.

hükûmet, -ti (*pl.* **hükûmat**) Government; administration; state; authority. ∼ **darbesi,** coup d'état : ∼ **etm.,** (**sürmek**), to rule, govern : ∼ **kapısına düşmet,** to have dealings with the Government.

hüküm, -kmü Rule; authority; government; command, edict; judicial sentence or decision; judgement; tenor, import; effect, influence; importance. ∼**den düşmek,** to be no longer valid : **hükmünü geçirmek,** to assert one's authority : **hükmü* geçmek,** (of a person) to have authority, for his word to carry weight; (of an order) to be enforceable, *but also* to have lost its validity (*the tense of* **geçmek** *would probably decide which of these contradictory meanings is the right one*) : ∼ **giydirmek,** to pass sentence : ∼ **giymek,** to lose one's case at law; to be condemned : **hükmü* olm.,**

for one's word to go, to be of importance; to be valid *or* effective : **hükmünde olm.,** to be equivalent to, to have the same effect as : ∼ **sürmek,** to reign; to prevail : **fırtınanın hükmü geçti,** the worst of the storm is over : ⌐**ne hükmü var?**⌐, 'what does it matter ? ', 'it's of no importance !'

hüküm·dar, monarch, ruler. ∼**darlık,** sovereignty. ∼**ferma** (···⸗), ruling, prevailing, predominating. ∼**name** (···¹), written decision *or* sentence of a court. ∼**ran,** ruler, sovereign. ∼**ranlık,** ∼**rani,** sovereignty, dominion. ∼**süz,** no longer in force; null.

hülle A suit of clothes; a mock marriage *which enables a divorced woman to return to her previous husband.* ∼**ci,** *the man whom she marries on this occasion and who then divorces her.*

hüma (·⸗) A fabulous bird of good omen; phoenix; good luck.

hümayun (·–⸗) Felicitous; imperial.

hüner Skill; dexterity; ability; art; talent. ∼**li,** skilful; talented; cleverly made. ∼**siz,** without talent; inartistic; clumsily made.

hüngür *In* ∼ ∼ **ağlamak,** to weep bitterly. ∼**demek,** to sob. ∼**tü,** sobbing.

hünkâr Sultan. ∼ **imamı gibi,** with an air of great importance. ∼**beğendi,** *a dish made with aubergines and cheese.*

hünnab Jujube.

hünsa (·⸗) Hermaphrodite.

hür, -rrü Free; well-born.

hürmet, -ti Respect; veneration. ···**e** ∼ **etm.,** to respect, honour. ∼**en** (¹··), out of respect (*for = dat.*). ∼**kâr,** respectful. ∼**li,** worthy of respect, venerable; respectable; rather big (*iron.*); ∼**ce,** *only in the ironical sense.* ∼**siz,** irreverent; disrespectful.

hürriyet, -ti Freedom, liberty. ∼**perver,** loving liberty; liberal.

hürya In a rush; in a sudden burst (of a crowd *etc.*).

hüsnü *v.* **hüsün.** *As prefix,* good-. ∼**ahlâk, -kı,** good morals; morality; good character. ∼**hal, -li,** good conduct : ∼ **varakası** (**kâğıdı**), certificate of good conduct. ∼**hat, -ttı,** calligraphy. ∼**kabul, -lü,** friendly reception. ∼**kuruntu,** fond imagination; wishful thinking. ∼**muamele,** good treatment. ∼**netice,** good result. ∼**niyet, -ti,** good intention; goodwill. ∼**tabiat, -tı,** good taste. ∼**tabir** (···–), a happy expression (*only used ironically*). ∼**tefsir,** favourable interpretation. ∼**tesadüf** (····–), a happy coincidence. ∼**tesir** (···–), good impression. ∼**yusuf,** Sweet-William. ∼**zan, -nnı,** good opinion : ⌐**bu sizin** ∼**nınız !**⌐, 'that's what *you* think (*but you're wrong*) '.

hüsran (·ᵈ) Moral loss; disappointment; frustration.

hüsün, –snü Goodness; beauty; agreeableness. hüsnü halde, in good condition, in good repair.

Hüt Only in ~ dağı gibi, very swollen.

hüthüt kuşu, –nu Hoopoe.

hüve (¹·) He. ~ ~sine, exactly like; the self-same.

hüveyda (··ᴸ) Evident, manifest.

hüveynat (··ᵈ), –tı pl. Micro-organisms.

hüviyet, –ti Identity. ~i mechul, identity unknown: ~ cüzdanı (varakası), identity papers.

hüyük, höyük Mound; barrow (ancient grave).

hüzün, –znü Sadness, melancholy, grief. ~lenmek, to be grieved or sad. ~lü, sad.

hüzzam A mode in Oriental music.

I

ıblık Capon.

ıcık v. icik.

ıçkırık, ıçkırmak v. hıçkırık.

ıdlâl v. izlâl.

ığıl ığıl Gurgling.

ığrıb A medium-sized fishing-smack.

ıh Cry used to make a camel kneel. ~lamak, to call out 'ıh !' to make a camel kneel; to breathe loudly. ~latmak, ~tırmak, to make a camel kneel by saying 'ıh !'

ıhlamur Lime-tree; made of lime wood; infusion of lime flowers.

ık v. hık.

ıkın·mak vn. To hold the breath when making a great physical effort. ıkına sıkına, grunting and groaning; with great effort. ~tı, great effort.

ıklamak vn. Breathe with difficulty; sigh, groan.

ıklım v. iklim.

ıldırgıç Deceit, swindle.

ılgar Gallop; cavalry charge; foray, raid. ~cı, raider. ~lamak, to make a raid.

ılgım, ılgımsalgım Mirage.

ılgın Tamarisk.

ılgıncar Wild cherry.

ılı Tepid, lukewarm. ~ca, hot spring. ~cak, ~k, tepid. ~mak, to become lukewarm; to cool down. ~ndırmak, ~tmak, ~ştırmak, to make tepid, to cool.

ımızganmak vn. Doze; (of a fire) to be almost out.

ıncalız A kind of wild bulb used for pickling.

ır Song; tone or pitch of voice.

Irak¹, –kı Irak; Mesopotamia. ~lı, inhabitant of Irak.

ırak² Distant. ⌈dostlar başından ~ !⌉, 'may it be far from our friends !' (formula used on hearing of a catastrophe) : üstümüzden ~ !, said on hearing news of a misfortune.

ırga·lamak, ~mak va. Move, shake. ~lanmak, ~nmak vn., to move, be moved; vibrate; be shaken.

ırgat Labourer; workman; bricklayer; capstan, windlass. ~ pazarı, place where labourers collect to be hired. ~başı, –nı, foreman. ~lık, profession or pay of a labourer.

ırıp Large fishing net.

ırk, –kı Race; lineage. ~an (¹·), by race, racially. ~çılık, racialism. ~î, (·ᴸ), racial.

ırlamak va. & vn. Sing.

ırmak¹ Large river.

ırmak² va. Scatter; rout.

ırz Honour; chastity; modesty. ~ düşmanı, a vicious rake: ~ına* dokunmak, to dishonour: ~ına* geçmek (tecavüz etm.), to violate.

ırza (·ᴸ) etm., va. Satisfy, content; get to consent.

ıs Master; owner; any mark of human habitation.

ısdar (·ᴸ) etm. va. Issue; put forth.

ısgara (·¹·) Gridiron; grill; grate; grating; any framework in the form of a grating. Grilled (meat etc.).

ısı Heat. Warm. ~lık, heat; heat-spots; rash.

ısın·dırmak va. Warm, heat; cause to like. gönül ~, to warm the affections, to cause to have friendly feelings. ~mak, to grow warm: ···e ~, to have a warm affection for; to get accustomed to; ⌈yeni mahallemize ısındık⌉, 'we found our new quarter very congenial'.

ısırgan Nettle.

ısırgın Heat-spots; rash.

ısırık Mark or wound made by a bite.

ısır·mak va. Bite. dilimi ısırdım, I all but said ...: ···i gözüm ısırıyor, I feel I know that man etc.: parmak ~, to be surprised, to marvel. ~tmak, caus. of ısırmak: parmak ~, to astonish.

ısıtmak va. Heat. yerini ~, to be unwilling to give up one's post.

ıska Miss. ~ geçmek, to miss the ball at football etc.; to fail; to fail to see or hear.

ıskaça (·¹·) Step of a mast.

ıskala (·¹·) Musical scale.

ıskalara (··¹·) Ratlines *of a ship*; port gangway (of a man-of-war).

ıskara *v.* ısgara.

ıskarça (·¹·) Stowed tight, packed.

ıskarmoz Rowlock; thole pin; rib *or* frame of a ship; barracuda (*sphyræna*).

ıskarta (·¹·) Discard (in card games) Discarded, scrapped ~ya çıkarmak, to discard; to scrap.

ıskat¹ (·⁴), –tı A throwing down. ~ı cenin, miscarriage : ~ etm., to throw down, to bring to nought; dispossess; annul; reject.

ıskat², –tı Alms given on behalf of the dead *as compensation for neglected religious duties*. ~çı, priest or beggar receiving such alms.

ıskorpit, –ti, ıskorbüt Scurvy.

ıskota (·¹·) Sheet *of a sail.* ~ bağı, sheetbend : ~ yakası, clew *of a sail.*

ıslah (·⁴) Improvement, reform. ~ etm., to improve, put to rights, reform : ~ı beyn etm., to reconcile. ~at (·—⁴), –tı, improvements, reforms. ~atçı, reformer. ~atperver, reformist. ~hane (··—¹), reformatory.

ıslak Wet. ~ karga, a chicken-hearted fellow.

ısla·mak, ~tmak *va.* Wet; punish; flog. ~nmak, to become wet; be wetted.

ıslık Whistle. ~ çalmak, to whistle. ~lamak, to boo (*Fr. siffler*).

ısmarlama Ordered; bespoken. A thing ordered *or* made to order; a stereotyped expression *etc.*

ısmarlamak *va.* Order; bespeak; commend; recommend. Allaha ısmarladık (*pronounced* Allahsmalladık), good-bye!

ıspanak Spinach.

ısparçana (··¹·) Serving of a cable; strand of a rope. ~ etm., to serve *a rope.*

ısparı (·¹·) Kind of sea-bream (*Sparus annularis*).

ısparmaca (··¹·) Fouled cables.

ıspatı Clubs (in cards).

ıspavlı (·¹·) Twine.

ıspazmoz Spasm.

ıspor Sport.

ısrar (·⁴) Insistence. ~ etm., to insist.

ıssız Lonely, desolate (place); without an owner; without signs of man, deserted. ~lık, desolation.

ıstağfurullah *v.* estağfurullah.

ıstampa (·¹·) Inking-pad.

ıstavroz Cross; sign of the cross. ~ çıkarmak, to cross oneself.

ıstıfa (··—) A choosing; selection; natural selection (survival of the fittest). ~ etm., to choose, to prefer.

ıstılah (··⁴) Technical term; conventional name. ~ paralamak, to use unusual or scientific language. ~at (···¹), –tı, technical terms.

ıstırab, ıstırar *v.* ıztırab, ıztırar.

ışık Light; lamp. Bright, light.

ışıl ~ ~, shining brightly; sparkling. ~amak, ~damak, to shine, sparkle, flash. ~atmak, ~datmak, to cause to shine, flash. ~dak, searchlight; torch. ~tı, brightness; shining; flash.

ışımak *v.* ışılamak.

ışın Gleam; flash.

ışkırlak The pointed cap worn by Karagöz, *q.v.*

ıştın Eathenware lamp.

ıtır, –trı Perfume, aroma; fragrant plant (*esp.* the Rose-scented Geranium). ~nak (···⁴), perfumed, aromatic. ~şahı, sweetpea. ~yağı, –nı, attar of roses.

ıtlak (·⁴) Liberation; divorce; repudiation; a taking *stg.* in its widest sense; an applying a name to. ~ etm., to set free; to divorce; remit (debt); repudiate; qualify or give a name to.

ıtma (·⁴), –aı Incitement; temptation. ~ etm., to tempt; to make *s.o.* covet.

ıtnab (·⁴) Verbosity; prolixity. ~ etm., to be verbose.

ıtrah (·⁴) etm. *va.* Discard; eliminate.

ıtrî (·⁴) Perfumed; aromatic. ~yat, –tı, perfumes; perfumery. ~yatçı, perfumer.

ıttıla (···⁴), –aı Information; cognizance. ~ hasıl olm., for information to be acquired : kespi ~ etm., to get information.

ıttırad (···⁴) Regularity; uniformity. ~ üzere, regularly.

ıvır zıvır Rubbish, nonsense; unimportant things. Nonsensical.

ızam (·⁴) *pl.* of azm. Bones.

ızbandut Bandit; brigand; huge terrifying man.

ızgara *v.* ısgara.

ızhar *v.* izhar.

ızlâl *v.* izlâl.

ızmar (·⁴) Dissimulation. ~ etm., to hide one's feelings.

ızrar (·⁴) A causing harm. ~ etm., to harm, prejudice.

ıztırab (··⁴) Distress; anxiety; pain.

ıztırar (··⁴) Need; compulsion. ~ında kalmak, to find oneself compelled *to do stg.* ~an (··⁴·), from sheer necessity. ~î (··—⁴), forced; involuntary.

İ

iade (·−ı) Restoration; giving back; repetition. ~ **etm.,** to give back, return: to restore (peace *etc.*): ~**i muhakeme,** retrial. ~**li,** *in* ~ **taahüdlü mektub,** registered letter receipt of which is returned to the sender.

iane (·−ı) Help; subsidy; donation, subscription *to a charitable fund etc.* ~ **toplamak,** to collect subscriptions. ~**ten** (·−··), as a help *or* donation.

iare (·−ı) Loan. ~ **etm.,** to lend.

iaşe (·−ı) Subsistence; victualling. ~ **etm.,** to sustain, feed.

iba (·−ı) Refusal; non-compliance.

ibad *pl. of* **abid.** Servants; servants of God, men. ~**ullah** (·−··), 'servants of God!', *used to express satisfaction*; a lot of *stg., e.g.* ⌐**bu sene uskumru** ~⌐, this year there is an abundance of mackerel.

ib'ad (·−ı) A removing to a distance. ~ **etm.,** to remove to a distance, to send away.

ibadet (·−ı), −**ti** Worship, prayer. ~**gâh,** ~**hane,** place of worship.

ibaha (·−ı) A making lawful; the removal of a prohibition.

ibare (·−ı) Sentence; clause.

ibaret (·−ı) Consisting (of); composed (of). ···**den** ~ **olm.,** to consist of ...; to be equivalent to ...; to be nothing but ... .

ibate (·−ı) Lodging. **iaşe ve** ~, board and lodging.

ibcal, −**li** An honouring *or* respecting.

ibda (·−ı), −**aı** A creating; an inventing.

ibham[1] Thumb.

ibham[2] Obscurity, ambiguity.

ibik Comb (of a cock *etc.*).

ibin, −**bni** Son.

ibiş Idiot.

ibka (·−ı) A making permanent; a keeping an official in his post. ~ **etm.,** to maintain; to confirm *a person* in his office; to keep *a pupil* in the same class without promoting him. ~**en** (·−··), by way of permanency; ~ **intihab etm.,** to re-elect.

iblağ (·−ı) **etm.** *va.* Cause to reach; cause to amount to; communicate (to).

iblis (·−ı) Satan; devil; devilish man.

ibne Catamite.

ibni Son of ... . ~**vakit,** −**kti,** opportunist.

ibra (·−ı) Discharge. ~ **etm.,** to discharge *a debt*; to free from claim; to pass *accounts.* ~ **kâğıdı** *or* ~**name** (·−−ı), certificate of receipt *or* discharge.

ibram (·−ı) Request; insistence. ~ **etm.,** to insist; to be over-persistent in making a request.

ibranî (·−−ı) Hebrew. ~**ce** (·−−·), Hebrew (language).

ibraz (·−ı) Manifestation; display (of feelings *etc.*); presentation (of documents).

ibre Needle, *esp.* magnetic needle; pointer; stamen.

ibret, −**ti** Example; warning; admonition. ~ **almak,** to take warning: ~ **gözüyle (çeşmile) bakmak,** to look at *stg.* in order to get a warning or a lesson from it: ~ **kudreti,** odd and ugly: ···**e** ~ **olm.,** to be a lesson to ...: **bu adam bir** ~!, what an impossible man! ~**amiz** (···ı), offering a warning; exemplary. ~**bahş,** giving a warning. ~**en** (ı··), as an example; as a warning: ~ **lissairin,** as a warning to others.

ibrik Vessel with a handle and spout; kettle; ewer. ~**tar,** *a former official whose duty was to superintend the Sultan's ablutions.*

ibrişim Silk thread. Made of silk thread.

ibtal (·ᵛ), −**li** A rendering null and void. ~ **elm.,** to annul; to bring to nought: **hissi** ~ **etm.,** to anaesthetize.

ibtida (···ı) Beginning. As a beginning. ~ **etm.,** to begin. ~**î** (···−ı), primary; primitive; elementary: **mevaddı** ~**ye,** raw materials.

ibtidar (···ı) **etm.** *va.* Set oneself to work *on stg.*

ibtihac Rejoicing.

ibtihal, −**li** Supplication.

ibtilâ (···ı) Addiction. ~ **etm.,** to be addicted to *stg.*

ibtina (···ı) **etm.** *va.* Base oneself on, rely on.

ibtisam etm. *vn.* Smile.

ibtizal, −**li** A becoming of little account *from being in abundant supply*; depreciation. ~**e düşmek (uğramak),** to become commonplace *or* vulgarized.

ibzal (·−ı) **etm.** *va.* Give without stint.

icab (−ı) A rendering necessary, a requiring; exigency. ···**in** ~**ı,** through, on account of, as required by, *e.g.* **arkadaşlık** ~**ı,** as friendship requires: ~**ında,** in case of need: ~**ına bakmak,** to do what is necessary; ⌐~**ına bakarım**!⌐, 'I'll settle his hash!'; 'I'll soon settle that!': ~ **etm.,** to render necessary, require; to be necessary: ~ **eden tedbirler almak,** to take the necessary measures: ~**ı hale göre,** as required by circumstances: ~**ı var,** it is needed, necessary.

icabet (·−ı), −**ti** Acceptance; favourable

answer. ~ etm., to accept (an invitation); to accede (to a request).

icad (–⌣) Invention; fabrication. ~ etm., to invent; fabricate, trump up.

icar (–⌣) A letting *or* leasing. ~ etm., *or* ~a vermek, to let out, to let out on lease. ~e (·–⌣), rent, rental : ~ muaccele, rent paid in advance : ~ müeccele, rent paid in instalments. ~eteyn (·–·⌣), (*lit.* 'two rents); property let on payment of an initial rent or 'fine' and a yearly rent.

icaz¹ (–⌣) Abridgement; conciseness, terseness. ~ etm., to render concise; to compress (writing, speech) : ~ tarikile, concisely, laconically.

icaz² (–⌣) Overwhelming superiority; wonder, miracle; transcendence. ~kâr (––⌣), masterly, unsurpassed.

icazet (·–⌣), –ti Authorization; formal permission; certificate, diploma. ~name (·–·–⌣), diploma; authorization to teach.

icbar (·⌣) A compelling, constraining. ~ etm., to force, compel.

icik cicik *In* iciğini ciciğini bilmek, to know a thing inside out.

iclâl (·⌣) An honouring *or* exalting.

iclâs (·⌣) Enthronement.

icma (·⌣), –aı Agreement. ~ı ümmet, a consensus of opinion *on religious matters*.

icmal (·⌣), –li Summary; *résumé*; adding up. ~ etm., to summarize. ~en (·⌣·), in a summarized form; briefly.

icra (·⌣) Execution; performance; accomplishment. ~ etm., to carry out, perform, execute : ~ heyeti, committee charged with the execution of judicial decisions : ~ kuvveti, the executive power : ~ memuru, executive officer (judicial official) : ~ vekilleri heyeti, Council of Ministers, Cabinet. ~at, –tı, operations, performances; judicial acts; affairs. ~î (·–⌣), executive.

ictihad (·⌣) Interpretation *of a legal or religious point*; doctrine; legal ruling; opinion, conviction. ... ~ında bulunmak, to be of the opinion that ... : ⌐~ kapısı kapandı¬, the last word has been said upon that point.

ictima (·⌣), –aı Assembly, gathering, meeting. ~î (·⌣), social. ~ileşmek, to be social, to adapt oneself to the life of the community. ~iyat, –tı, social sciences, sociology. ~iyun, sociologists.

ictinab (·⌣) Avoidance; abstention. ~ etm., to avoid, abstain from : ~ı gayrikabil, inevitable, unavoidable.

ictisar (·⌣) Daring. ~ etm., to dare, to take the liberty of.

iç Inside, interior; stomach; heart. Inner, interior. [iç *is often used where English would use a personal pronoun, e.g.* içi sıkıldı,

he was bored; içim bulanıyor, I feel sick]. ~ ~e, one within the other; *one room* opening into another : ~ten ~e, secretly; to the innermost recesses : ~imde, within me : ~imizde, amongst us : ···in ~inde, inside ..., within ...; üc gün ~inde, within three days : ~ler acısı, tragic, heartrending : ~ açıcı, cheering (news *etc.*) : ~ açmak, to cheer up, to set at ease; ~ini* açmak, (i) to cheer s.o. up; (ii) to unburden oneself : ~ine almak, to contain; to include : ~i* almamak, to feel an aversion for *some kind of food* : ~ine* atmak, to endure in silence : ~i* bayılmak, to feel faint *from hunger etc.* : ~ bezelye, shelled peas : ~i* bulanmak, to feel nauseated; to wish to vomit : ~ çamaşırı, underclothing : ~ *or* ~ini* çekmek, to sigh : ~i* çekmek, to long for : ~inden çıkamamak, to be unable to get at the root of *a matter*; to be unable to settle *stg.*; ~inden çıkılmaz bir mesele, an insoluble problem, an incomprehensible matter : ~inden* doğmak, to have a sudden impulse to do *some good act*; ~ine* doğmak, to have a feeling or presentiment *that stg. will happen* : ~ini* dökmek, to unburden oneself : ~i* dönmek, to be nauseated : ~ etm., to 'bag', to appropriate to one's own use : ~i* geçirmek, to sigh; ~inden* geçirmek, to review in one's mind : ~i* geçmek, to doze; (of a fruit) to become over-ripe; ~inden* geçmek, to pass through the mind, to occur to one : ~i geçmiş, lethargic : ~inden* gelmek, to feel (mentally, not physically) like doing *stg.* : bir şey için ~i* gitmek, to desire a thing strongly : ~i* götürememek, not to have the heart to : ~i* kalmak, for the gorge to rise, to have a feeling of nausea : ~i* kan ağlamak *or* ~inden* kan gitmek, to grieve bitterly, to pine away from grief : ~inden okumak, to read to oneself : ~i* rahat olm., to feel at ease about *stg.* : ~i* sıkılmak, to be bored : badem ~i, the kernel of an almond : ekmek ~i, the crumb of bread : işin ~inden iş çıkarmak, to keep raising difficulties : işin ~inden çıkmak, to get out of a difficulty; ⌐... deyip işin ~inden çıktı¬, 'he avoided further discussion by saying ...' : işin ~inde iş var, there's something behind it all.

içecek Drinkable. Drink, beverage.

içerde, içeride Within; inside.

içeri The inside; interior; stomach. In; to the inside. ~den, from the inside : ~si, his (its) interior : ~ye, to the inside : ~(ye) buyurun !, please come in ! : ~ girmek, to enter; bin lira ~ girdim (*sl.*), I have lost £1,000.

içerlek Standing back (of a house); secluded.

içerlemek *vn.* Be grieved; be annoyed, be angry *without showing it.*

içgüvey, içgüveyisi, –ni Husband who lives with his wife's parents. ⌐~sinden hallice⌐, so so, not too well.

içiçe *v.* iç.

içim[1] *v.* iç.

içim[2] A draught *of water etc.* bir ~ su, delicious *(generally of a woman)*; bir ~ suya gitmek, to go for next to nothing: bu suyun ~i iyidir, this water has a good taste. ~li, pleasant to the taste (of a drink).

için[1] For; on account of; in order to. Allah ~, for God's sake: bunun ~, for this reason; for this purpose: onun ~, for him; for his sake; on account of him *or* that: yaşamak ~, in order to live: meşgul olduğum ~, because I was busy: ne için, for what reason, why.

için[2] *In* ~ ~, internally; secretly; in a hidden and imperceptible manner.

içinde, içinden, içine *v.* iç.

içindekiler The contents.

içirmek *va. caus. of* içmek. Cause to drink *etc.*; add a liquid so that it is absorbed.

içkale (¹··) Citadel.

içkapı (¹··) Inner door.

içki Drink, *esp.* alcoholic drink. ~ye düşkün, addicted to drink. ~li, licensed to sell alcoholic drinks.

içlenmek *vn.* Be affected (emotionally). büsbütün içleniyorum, I am quite overcome by my feelings.

içli Having an inside, a kernel, a pulp *etc.*; reticent; sensitive; touching; emotional; sad, hurt. ~ dışlı, intimate, familiar.

içlik Pertaining to the inside.

içme *verb. n. of* içmek; spring of mineral water *(gen. used in the pl.).*

içmek *va. & vn.* Drink. ⌐içtikleri su ayrı gitmez⌐, they are very intimate friends: and ~, to take an oath: ⌐bunun üstüne soğuk su iç!⌐, 'you can write that off!', 'you'll never see that again!': çok içer, he drinks a lot, he is a toper: tutun ~, to smoke (tobacco).

içoğlanı (¹···), **–nı** A young page *in training for domestic service.*

içre (¹·) Interior. In, within, among.

içsıkıntısı (¹····), **–nı** Boredom.

içten *v.* iç; sincere, from the heart.

içtihad *etc. v.* ictihad *etc.*

içyağı (¹··), **–nı** Suet.

içyüz (¹·) The inside of a matter; the inner meaning; the real truth.

id (–) Festival. ~i adha, the festival of Kurban Bayram: ~i fıtır, the festival of breaking the fast of Ramazan: ⌐~iniz said olsun!⌐, *formula of greeting on a festival.*

ida (–¹), **–aı** A depositing for safe keeping.

idadi (––¹) Preparatory; secondary. ~ *or* idadiye, secondary school.

idam (–¹) Capital punishment; execution. ~ etm., to condemn to death.

idame (··–¹) Continuance. ~ etm., to preserve; to prolong.

idare (·–¹) Management, direction, superintendence; administration; economizing; night-light. ~ etm., to administer, manage, take charge of; to economize, make ends meet; suffice; bir adamı ~ etm., to handle a man carefully *(because he is easily upset, etc)*; to keep an eye on a man *(because he is not to be trusted to do a thing properly)*; otomobil ~ etm., to drive a motor-car: ~i beytiye, domestic economy: ~ ile geçinmek, to live economically: ~ kandil, night-light: ~i maslahat etm., to be a skilful negotiator, to be clever at dealing with difficult situations; to get along somehow or other: ~ meclisi, board of management of a business: kendini ~ etm., to manage for onself; kendini ~den âciz, utterly incapable.

idare·ci, a good manager; a tactful person; administrator, organizer; specialist in administrative law. ~hane (·–·–¹), office; administration. ~li, economical; good at managing; efficient. ~siz, wasteful; who manages badly. ~ten (·–··), administratively; departmentally.

idarî (·–¹) Pertaining to the administration; administrative.

idbar (·⁴) Adversity; a falling into disgrace.

iddet, –ti *The three months interval during which a Moslem woman may not remarry.*

iddia (··¹) Claim; pretension; assertion; bet. ~ etm., to claim, to set up a pretension: İddia Makamı, the Public Prosecutor (as a party in a trial): ~ya tutuşmak (girişmek), to assert *stg. in contradiction of another's assertion*: kabili ~, maintainable (theory, opinion). ~cı, obstinate; assertive; dogmatic. ~lı, on which a bet has been made; about which claims or disputes have arisen. ~name (··––¹), the formal charge *against a person in a Court of Law.* ~sız, unpretentious.

iddihar (··⁴), **idhar** A laying up in store. ~ etm., to store up *(esp.* to buy up and store for future profit)*; to hoard.

idgam (·⁴) The pronouncing of a double consonant. ~lı konuşmak, to speak too accurately, to be pedantic in one's speech.

idhal (·⁴), **–li** An introducing, importing, inserting. ~ etm., to import, introduce, insert. ~at (··–¹), **–tı**, imports.

idhar *v.* iddihar.

idil Idyll.

idiş, idiç Gelding. Castrated; emasculated. ~ etm., to geld.

idman (·ᵢ) Physical exercise; training; sport. ~lı, in good training; well-trained; accustomed.

idrak (·ᵢ), **-ki** Perception, intelligence; collection, getting-in (of harvest). ~ etm., to catch up, overtake, reach; be contemporaneous with; perceive, comprehend. ~li, intelligent, perceptive. ~siz, dense, unintelligent.

idrar (·ᵢ) Urine. ~ yolu, urethra: ~ zorluğu, retention of urine.

idrojen Hydrogen.

idüğü *Used officially for the past. part. of* imek, *and in the phrase* ⌐ne ~ belirsiz bir adam⌐, a man of doubtful antecedents; a man of no consequence.

ifa (—᳟) Performance; fulfilment; payment. ~ etm., to execute, fulfil, pay.

ifade (·—᳝) Explanation; expression; deposition *of evidence.* ~ etm., to express, explain, depose, instruct: ~i meram, the exposition of thought *or* intention: ~i meram etm., to express oneself.

ifakat (·—᳝), **-tı** Convalescence. ~ bulmak, to convalesce, to get well. ~yâb (·—·᳟), recovered from an illness.

ifate (·—᳝) Loss; waste of time.

iffet, **-ti** Chastity; honesty, uprightness. ~li, chaste; virtuous; loyal. ~siz, unchaste, dissolute; dishonest.

ifham (·ᵢ), **etm.** *va.* Cause to be understood, explain.

iflâh (·ᵢ) Salvation. ~ı kesilmek, to be exhausted : Allah ~ etsin!, may God reform him!: bu adam ~ olmaz, this man is incorrigible.

iflâs (·ᵢ) Bankruptcy, insolvency. ~ etm., to go bankrupt.

ifna (·᳟) Destruction. ~ etm., to destroy, annihilate.

ifrağ (·᳟) A casting, moulding, shaping; excretion. ~ etm., to transform, convert; to excrete.

ifrat (·ᵢ), **-tı** Excess; doing too much (*as opp. to* tefrit = *doing too little*). ~la, excessively: ~ etm., to overdo, to go to excess.

ifraz (·᳟) A separating; secretion. ~ etm., to secrete (a liquid *etc.*); to allot, set aside. ~at (·—᳝), **-tı**, secretions *of the body.*

ifrit, **-ti** Demon. Malicious, devilish. ~ olm. (kesilmek), to be mad with fury.

ifsad (·ᵢ) A spoiling, corrupting, inciting. ~ etm., to corrupt, seduce, incite to revolt. ~at (·—᳝), **-tı**, *pl. of* ifsad. ~cı, agitator, political inciter.

ifşa (·᳟) Divulgation; disclosure. ~ etm., to divulge, reveal. ~at (·—᳝), **-tı**, revelations: ~ta bulunmak, to reveal, divulge.

iftar (·ᵢ) The breaking of a fast; the meal taken at sundown *during the fast of Ramazan.* ~ etm., to break one's fast: ~ topu, the gun fired at sunset during Ramazan. ~ iye (·—·᳝), light food suitable for breaking the fast; present made to guests at the iftar. ~lık, suitable to the breaking of the fast; hors-d'œuvres *etc.* eaten at the iftar.

iftihar (··ᵢ) Laudable pride. ···le ~ etm., to glory in, to be proud of: Nişanı ~, *name of a former decoration.*

iftikar (··ᵢ) Poverty; destitution; need. ···e ~ etm., to have need of.

iftira (··᳟) Slander; fabrication, forgery. ~ etm., to slander.

iftirak (··ᵢ), **-kı** Dispersion; absence; separation.

iftitah (··᳟) Act of opening; beginning. ~î, opening (speech *etc.*), inaugural.

iğ Spindle. ~ ağacı, spindle-tree: ~ taşı, millstone.

iğbirar (··ᵢ) Annoyance; disappointment.

iğde Wild olive, oleaster.

iğdiç, **iğdiş** *v.* idiş.

iğfal (·ᵢ), **-li** Deception; seduction. ~ etm., to delude; to take advantage of another's negligence; seduce. ~kâr, who deludes *or* seduces.

iği *v.* iğ.

iğlâk (·ᵢ), **-kı** A rendering obscure.

iğmaz (·ᵢ) A winking *or* closing of the eye. ~ı ayn etm., to wink, to connive at, pretend not to see: ~dan gelmek, to be indifferent.

iğmek *v.* eğmek.

iğne Needle; pin; thorn; sting; pintle *of a rudder;* fish-hook; hypodermic injection; (*fig.*) pinprick. ⌐~ atsan yere düşmez⌐, a very crowded place: ~ deliği, the eye of a needle: ⌐~ deliğine kaçmak⌐, to hide oneself in confusion: ~ iplik, mere skin and bone; ~den ipliğe kadar, everything required: ~den ipliğe (sürmeye) kadar, with full details, in a circumstantial way: ⌐~ ile kuyu kazmak⌐, to use a needle to dig a well, *i.e.* to do stg. in an unpractical way *or* to undertake stg. requiring great care and much time: ~ yemek, to have an injection: ~ yutmuş köpek gibi, exhausted, upset.

iğne·ardı, **-nı**, back-stitch. ~cik, pintle *or* brace of a rudder. ~dan, ~lik, needle-case. ~lemek, to fasten with a pin; to prick; to give a hypodermic injection; to wound with words. ~leyici, stinging, pricking. ~li, having pins; having a needle *or* a sting; biting (words).

iğrek (*Fr. y-grec*) The *y* in algebra.

iğrelti Fern.

iğrenc Disgust, loathing. Disgusting, loathsome, repulsive.

iğren·mek *vn.* Be disgusted; feel aversion. ~**ecek,** disgusting.

iğreti Borrowed; makeshift; temporary; false, artificial. ~ **almak,** to borrow for temporary use; ~**ye almak,** to prop up temporarily: ⌐~ **ata binen tez iner**⌐, 'one doesn't enjoy the use of a borrowed thing for long', *i.e.* a temporary job is not as good as a permanent one.

iğri, eğri Crooked; bent; awry; perverse. Curved timber *esp. of a ship.* ~ **büğrü,** twisted; gnarled: ~ **gitmek,** to deviate; to go wrong: ~ **kalem,** carving chisel. ~**bacak,** bow-legged. ~**lik,** crookedness; curvature; perversity; dishonesty. ~**lmek,** to become bent, to incline. ~**ltmek,** ~**tmek,** to make crooked; bend; twist: **çehre** ~, to put on a sour face.

iğtinam (··ᵛ) Seizure; booty. ~**etm.,** to seize as booty: ~ı **fırsat etm.,** to seize an opportunity.

iğtişaş (···ᐟ) Riot, disturbance.

iğva (·ᐟ) A leading astray. ~ **etm.,** to tempt, to lead astray. ~**at, -tı,** temptations: ~**a kapılmak,** to yield to temptation, to be led astray.

iğzab (·ᐟ) **etm.,** *va.* Provoke, anger.

ihafe (·–¹) Intimidation. ~ **etm.,** to frighten.

ihale (·–¹) A referring *or* delegating; adjudication. ~ **etm.,** to hand over, transfer, refer, delegate; award (contract). ~**ten** (·ᐟ··), by award, by adjudication.

iham (–¹) Ambiguity.

ihanet (·–¹), -**ti** Treason; infidelity.

ihata (·–¹) A surrounding *or* embracing; comprehension; erudition, comprehensive knowledge. ~ **etm.,** to embrace; surround; comprehend. ~**lı,** widely read, erudite.

ihbar (·ᵛ) A communicating; notification; denunciation. ~ **etm.,** to communicate, convey (information, news); inform; warn; denounce. ~**iye** (··–·¹), reward for giving information *or* for denouncing a person; official notice. ~**name** (···–¹), notification; declaration.

ihda (·ᐟ) **etm.** *va.* Give as a present.

ihdas (·ᵛ) **etm.** *va.* Produce; invent; raise (difficulty); introduce (a new thing); create (a new post).

ihfa (·ᐟ) **etm.** *va.* Hide, secrete.

ihkak (·ᵛ) *In* ~ı **hak etm.,** to see that the right prevails, to ensure justice: **bizzat** ~ı **hak etm.,** to take the law into one's own hands.

ihlâl (·ᵛ), -**li** A spoiling; infraction (of the law, of a treaty); non-observance. ~ **etm.,** to spoil; to violate (treaty), break (the law).

ihlâs (·ᵛ) Sincerity.

ihlil Urethra.

ihmal (·ᵛ), -**li** Negligence. ~ **etm.,** to neglect; to act negligently, be careless. ~**ci,** ~**kâr,** negligent, careless.

ihnak (·ᵛ) **etm.** *va.* Strangle.

ihrac (·ᵛ) Extraction; exportation; expulsion; emission; disembarkation. ~ **etm.,** to emit, expel, export, disembark: ···**in suretini** ~ **etm.,** to make a copy of. ~**at** (·–¹), -**tı,** exports. ~**atçı,** exporter.

ihrak (·ᵛ) A burning. -**iye** (·–·¹), fuel; fuel allowance.

ihram Woollen cloak *worn by Arabs and pilgrims at Mecca*; sofa covering.

ihraz (·ᐟ) **etm.** *va.* Obtain; attain.

ihsai (·–ᐟ) Statistical. ~**yat** (·–·ᐟ), -**tı,** statistics.

ihsan (·ᵛ) Kindness; favour; benevolence. ~ **etm.,** to do a kindness; bestow *a favour*; give *a present.*

ihsas (·ᵛ) Sensation. ~ **etm.,** to cause to feel; inspire; hint, insinuate; feel, perceive.

ihtar (·ᵛ) A reminding; warning ~ **etm.,** to remind; to call attention; to warn. ~**name** (···–¹), written warning; official warning *to cease a practice.*

ihtısas (···ᵛ) Specialization. ~ **kesbetmek,** to specialize: ~ **mahkemesi,** (*formerly*) court for the suppression of contraband: ···**de** ~ **peyda etm.,** to specialize in ...: ~ **sahibi olm.,** to be a specialist in .... ~**sız,** non-specialist: ~ **işçi,** unskilled labourer.

ihtibas Imprisonment; retention of urine; repression (psychological).

ihticab Concealment; a being hidden by a veil or curtain; *the sun's* being clouded over.

ihticac (···ᵛ) A proving; a giving a reason. ~ **etm.,** to adduce as proof: ~**a salih,** valid as evidence.

ihtida (···ᐟ) Conversion to Islam.

ihtifa (···ᐟ) **etm.** *vn.* Hide oneself.

ihtifal (···ᵛ), -**li** Ceremony *in memory of s.o. or on some anniversary.* ~**ci,** the organizer of such a ceremony.

ihtikan (···ᵛ) Administration of a clyster; enema; congestion (*med.*).

ihtikâr (···ᵛ) Cornering for profit; profiteering. ~**ci,** profiteer.

ihtilâc Agitation; convulsion.

ihtilâf (···ᵛ) Difference; disagreement. ~ı **manzara,** parallax. ~**lı,** controversial.

ihtilâl (···ᵛ), -**li** Riot; rebellion; revolution. ~ **çıkarmak,** to raise a rebellion: ~**i şuur,** mental disturbance. ~**ci,** revolutionary.

ihtilâm (···ᵛ) Nocturnal emission.

ihtilâs (···ᵛ) Embezzlement; malversation.

ihtilât (···ᵛ), -**tı** Confusion; complication (of diseases *etc.*); social intercourse. ~ **etm.,** to mix, to mingle with others.

ihtimâl, –li Probability; possibility; hypothesis. Probable; possible. Probably, most likely. **~at** (···–ᵥ), **–tı**, probabilities: **~ kaidesi**, the law of probabilities. **~î** (···–ᵥ), probable.

ihtimam (··ᵥ) Care; carefulness; taking pains; solicitude. **~ etm.**, to take pains, work carefully. **~kâr, ~lı**, taking pains; solicitous.

ihtimar (··ᵥ) Fermentation.

ihtinak (··ᵥ), **–kı** A being throttled *or* suffocated.

ihtira (···–ᵥ) Invention. **~ beratı**, patent: **~ etm.**, to invent. **~î** (···–ᵥ), inventive.

ihtirak (··ᵥ), **–kı** Combustion; approach of a planet to the sun. **~ etm.**, to become burnt.

ihtiram (··ᵥ) Respect, veneration. **~ etm.**, to respect, venerate, honour.

ihtiras (··ᵥ) Violent longing; passion; greed; ambition.

ihtiraz (··ᵥ) Precaution; avoidance, abstention. **~ etm.**, to guard against, take precautions; avoid: **~ kaydı**, reservation.

ihtisab (··ᵥ) *Formerly* an inland customs office; a kind of *octroi* tax.

ihtisar (··ᵥ) Abbreviation; reduction of a fraction. **~ etm.**, to shorten, abridge. **~en** (··–ᵥ·), in brief; in an abridged form.

ihtisas (··ᵥ) Sensation; impression.

ihtişam (··ᵥ) Pomp; magnificence.

ihtiva (···–ᵥ) **etm.** *va.* Hold, contain; include.

ihtiyac (··ᵥ) Want; necessity; poverty; need. ···e **~ı*** olm., to be in need of ....

ihtiyar¹ (··ᵥ) Old. Old man. **~ heyeti** council of elders (village council). **~lamak**, to grow old. **~lık**, old age.

ihtiyar² (··ᵥ) Choice, selection; option. **~ etm.**, to choose, prefer; incur (expense, trouble): **~ı elden gitmek.**, to be overcome by emotion; to lose one's self-control: **~ı sükût etm.**, to prefer to say nothing: **~ı zahmet etm.**, to take the trouble to: **bilâ ~**, without option; **bilâ ~ bunu söylemiş**, he could not help saying this: **masraf ~ etm.**, to go to the expense *of doing stg.*

ihtiyarî (···–ᵥ) Optional; voluntary; not obligatory.

ihtiyat (··ᵥ), **–tı** Precaution; providing oneself with a reserve; reserve (*also mil.*). **~ akçesi**, reserve fund: **~ ordusu**, reserve of troops: **kaydi ~la**, with reserve. **~en** (··ᵥ·), by way of precaution; as a reserve. **~î**, precautionary. **~lı, ~kâr**, cautious, prudent. **~sız**, imprudent; improvident; incautious. **~sızlık**, imprudence; improvidence.

ihtizar (···–ᵥ) **etm.** *vn.* Be at the point of death.

ihtizaz (··ᵥ) Vibration.

ihvan (·ᵥ) *pl.* Brethren; friends. **~ı vatan**, fellow countrymen: **cümle ~**, everyone. **~üssefa**, brother devotees.

ihya (·–ᵥ) A bringing to life, resuscitation. **~ etm.**, to bring to life, reinvigorate, enliven; load with benefits.

ihzar (·ᵥ) Preparation; a causing to be present. **~ etm.**, to cause to be present, summon, cite: **~ emri** *or* **müzekkeresi**, summons to appear before a court. **~î** (·–ᵥ), preparatory. **~iye**, fee for a summons.

ika (–ᵥ) **etm.** *va.* Cause; bring about; commit (crime).

ikad (–ᵥ) A setting fire to. **~ etm.**, to light (fire *etc.*).

ik'ad (·ᵥ) **etm.** *va.* Enthrone; instal.

ikame (·–ᵥ) A setting up *or* establishing; substitution. **~ etm.**, to set up; to post sentinel *etc.*); to substitute: **dâva ~ etm.**, to bring an action *against s.o.*

ikamet (·–ᵥ), **–ti** Residence; dwelling; a staying at a place. **~ etm.**, to dwell, to stay: **~e memur**, ordered to reside *at a certain place*: **~ tezkeresi**, permit to reside. **~gâh** (·–·ᵥ), place of residence.

ikan (–ᵥ) Certainty; comprehension.

ik'ansese (*A complicated Arabic word of which no one knows the meaning*); useless; worthless.

ikaz (–ᵥ) A rousing; warning. **~ etm.**, to awake, arouse; caution, warn.

ikbal (·ᵥ), **–li** Good fortune; success; prosperity; (*formerly*) a slave girl about to become the Sultan's concubine. **~perest**, ambitious.

ikdam (·ᵥ) Perseverance; effort. **~ etm.**, to persevere.

iken While being; while; though; (*when joined to a participle it is generally abbreviated to* -ken, *e.g.* giderken, while going). **yazacak ~**, while on the point of writing *or* instead of writing: **hal böyle ~**, even though this was the situation; in spite of this situation.

iki Two. **~miz**, both of us: **~si**, both of them: **~ baştan olm.**, to be possible only if both parties show goodwill: **~de bir (birde)**, at frequent intervals, constantly: **~ ···de bir**, one in two ..., every other ..., *but* (*illogically*) **~ günde bir**, every third day; *also* frequently; every now and again: **~ canlı**, pregnant: ⌐**~ el bir baş içindir**⌐, 'two hands are for one head', *i.e.* one must work oneself and not depend on others: **~si ortası olmaz**, there is no middle course: **bir ~ derken**, then all of a sudden; ⌐**bir ~ derken işler fenaya varır**⌐, if you allow small faults to pass unnoticed they will become bad habits.

iki·ağızlı, two-edged (sword). ~**çenek-
liler,** dicotyledons. ~**çifte,** boat with
two pairs of oars. ~**lemek,** to make two;
to get another *thing in addition to the one
which one already has.* ~**li,** having two
(parts *etc.*); the two *of a suit of cards.*
~**lik,** consisting of two; costing two
(piastres *etc.*); disunion.

ikin Eh!; I wonder!

ikinci Second.

ikindi The time of the afternoon prayer;
afternoon. ⌐~**den sonra dükkân açmak¬,**
to leave doing a thing until too late. ~**yin**
(·¹··), in the afternoon.

ikişer Two each; two at a time. ~ ~ **koşmak,** to harness a pair of horses *or* oxen *to
a cart etc.*

ikiyüzlü (·¹··) Having two faces; double-
faced; hypocrite.

ikiz Twins. Twin. ~**leme,** ~**li,** having
twins; double.

iklil Crown; diadem.

iklim Region; country; climate. **yedi** ~
dört bucak, all over the world.

ikmal (·⌐), –**li** Completion. ~ **etm.,** to
complete: ~ **efradı,** (*mil.*) draft, replace-
ments: ~ **hatları,** (*mil.*) lines of communication: ~ **kolları,** (*mil.*) supply columns:
gününü ~ **etm.,** (of a convicted man) to
complete his sentence: **noksanı** ~ **etm.,** to
make good a deficiency. ~**ci,** pupil who
has to undergo a second examination after
failure at the first.

ikna (·⌐) **etm.** *va.* Satisfy; convince; persuade.

ikrah (·⌐) Disgust, loathing. ~ **etm.,** to
loathe. ~**en** (·⌐·), with loathing; much
against one's will.

ikram (·⌐) A showing honour and respect
(*esp. to a guest*); kindness; gift; discount,
abatement on price. ~ **etm.,** to show
honour to; to give *a present;* to offer (a
cigarette *etc.*); to make a reduction in price.
~**iye** (·–·¹), bonus; gratuity; prize *in a
lottery.* ~**lı,** hospitable.

ikrar (·⌐) Declaration; confession; acknowledgement. ~ **etm.,** to confess, acknowledge.

ikraz (·⌐) Loan. ~ **etm.,** to lend money.
~**en** (·⌐·), as a loan.

iks The *x* (in algebra).

iksa (·⌐) **etm.** *va.* Clothe.

iksir Elixir; philosopher's stone; any magic
substance; cordial.

ikta' (·⌐) Fief.

iktibas (·⌐) Quotation; adaptation *of a
novel or play.* ~ **etm.,** to borrow; to use as
a quotation. ~**en** (··⌐·), quoting; as a
quotation.

iktida (··⌐) **etm.** *va.* Follow; be guided
by; imitate.

iktidar (··⌐) Ability, capacity; power. ~**ı***
olm., to be capable of, able to do: ~**da
olm.,** (of a political party) to be in power:
~ **partisi,** the party in power, the government: **ademi** ~, impotence. ~**lı,** capable.
~**sız,** incapable.

iktifa (··⌐) **etm.** *vn.* Content oneself (with
= **ile**); be satisfied; suffice.

iktiham (··⌐) **etm.** *va.* Surmount; overcome; endure.

iktiran (··⌐) Conjunction *of planets;* approach. ··**e** ~ **etm.,** to meet with (approval
etc.): **karara** ~ **etm.,** to be decided: **iyi bir
neticeye** ~ **etm.,** to be brought to a successful conclusion: **tasdiki âliye** ~ **etm.,** to
receive the approval or signature of the
head of the state.

iktisa (··⌐) **etm.** *va. & vn.* Wear. Be
clothed.

iktisab (··⌐) Acquisition, gain. ~ **etm.,** to
acquire.

iktisad (··⌐) Economy; political economy.
~ **etm.,** to economize. ~**cı,** economist.
~**î** (··–⌐), economic; pertaining to economics. ~**iyat** (··–·⌐), –**tı,** economics. ~**iyun**
(··–·⌐), economists.

iktitaf (··⌐) Compilation. ~ **etm.,** to cull;
to compile; to reap the benefit of.

iktiza (··⌐) Necessity; requirement. ... ~**sı,**
on account of ..., as rendered necessary by
... : ~**sınca,** according to its requirements:
~**sına göre,** as may be necessary, as occasion
requires: ~ **etm.,** to be requisite: ~ **ettirmek,** to render necessary, require: ~**sı olm.,**
to be necessary.

il Province; country; || vilayet; (*for* **el**)
people.

ilâ¹ *Arabic prep.* Up to; to; towards; until;
(*in purely Arabic phrases it is generally
joined to the article and/or noun, e.g*
ilelebed, to all eternity; **ilânihaye,** to the
end).

ilâ² A raising or exalting. ~ **etm.,** to raise,
exalt.

ilâahiri *v.* **ilâhiri.**

ilâc (·⌐) Remedy; medicine; device. ~
için yok, *said of stg. not to be found:* **la** ~,
through sheer necessity, there being no
way out. ~**lı,** medicated. ~**sız,** incurable.

ilâh¹ *Abb. for* **ilâahiri.** Etcetera.

ilâh² God. ~**e** (·–¹) goddess. ~**i** (·–¹),
hymns, chants; *interj. expressing admiration or astonishment.* ~**î** (·–⌐), divine.
~**ici,** singer of chants, dervish. ~**ileştir-
mek,** to deify. ~**iyat** (··–·⌐), –**tı,** theology.
~**iyun** (·–·⌐), theologians.

ilâhiri Etcetera.

ilâm (–⌐) Sentence; judicial decree; official
decision. ~ **etm.,** to notify officially.

ilân (–⌐) Declaration, notice, announce-

ment, proclamation; advertisement. ~ı
harb, declaration of war : ~ etm., to declare,
proclaim, announce : ~ pulu, revenue
stamp on advertisements. ~at, -tı, advertisements : ~ idarehanesi, advertising
agents. ~cılık, publicity, advertising.
ilânihaye (¹·—·) To the end.
ilâve (·—¹) Addition; supplement; postscript; exaggeration. ~ etm., to add. ~li,
having an addition or supplement. ~ten
(·⸱·..), in addition; as an addition.
ilbas (·⸱) etm. va. Clothe.
ilca (·⸱) Constraint, compulsion. ~ etm.,
to compel.
‖ilçe Administrative district formerly
known as a kaza.
ile, ilen (–le, –yle) With; by means of;
and. benimle refikam, my wife and I :
kalemle, with a pen; kalemile or kalemiyle,
with his pen : söylemekle, by saying : bunu
söylemekle beraber, while saying this, in
spite of saying this : bunu söylemesile
beraber, just as he had said this, he had
hardly said this when ... .
ilel pl. of illet. Illnesses etc.
ilelebed (¹···) For ever.
ilelmerkez (¹···) Centripetal.
ilen·c Curse. ~mek, to curse.
iler Only in ~ tutar yer bırakmamak, to
tear to tatters, to maltreat, to ' take it out
of' one; and ~ tutar yeri kalmamak, to be
torn to tatters, to be in a pitiable condition.
ilerde, ilerden v. ileri.
ileri The forward part; the front; the
future. Advanced; in advance; forward;
in front; future; fast (of a clock). ~ almak,
to promote (a person); to put forward (a
clock) : ~ gelmek, to come forward, to
make progress, to surpass; v. also ilerigel-
mek : ~ gelenler, notables, important
people : ~ gitmek, to go too far : ···in ~sine
gitmek, to follow a matter up; to go deeply
into stg.: ~ geri sözler, unseemly, in-
appropriate, fault-finding words : ~ sürmek, to drive forward; to advance (a
reason, an argument); to advance a person
in rank. ~ varmak, to go ahead; to go too
far.
iler·ide In front; in future. ~iğelen
(··¹··), notable; important person. ~iğel-
mek (··¹··), ···den ~, to result from, be
caused by; v. also ileri. ~leme, advance,
progress; feed (of a tool). ~lemek, to
advance, progress; (of a clock) to be fast.
~letmek, to cause to advance; make progress in (an art etc.); put forward (clock).
iletmek va. Send or give to another; send to
a place; carry off, make off with.
ilga (·⸱) Abolition; annulment. ~etm., to
abolish, annul, abrogate.

‖ilği Interest. ~lenmek, to be interested
(in = ile). ~li, interested; connected with.
ilh Abb. for ilâahiri. Etcetera.
ilhad (·⸱) Atheism; heresy.
ilhak (·⸱), -kı Annexation. ~ etm., to
annex; join on.
ilham (·⸱) Inspiration. ~ etm., to inspire.
ilhan Prince; emperor.
ilik¹ Loop for button or hook; buttonhole.
~lemek, to button up; to fasten by hook
and eye. ~li¹, buttoned; fastened by hook.
ilik² Marrow. Delicious. ~ gibi, tasty,
appetizing : iliğe işlemek, (of cold etc.) to
penetrate to the marrow; to make a great
impression : iliğini* kurutmak, to wear s.o.
out. ~li², containing marrow.
ilim, –lmi Knowledge; science. ilmi hukuk,
jurisprudence.
ilinti Roughly sewing together, tacking;
knot.
ilişik Connexion; relation; bond; impediment, hitch; suspense account; liability,
obligation. Connected; relative; attached;
enclosed herewith. ilişiği* kalmamak, (of
a matter) to be settled up; (of a person) to
sever his connexion, to have no further
interest : ilişiğini* kesmek, to sever one's
connexion with; to sever s.o. else's connexion, i.e. dismiss, discharge. ~siz, un-
attached, free.
iliş·mek va. Touch; interfere with. vn. Be
fastened to; hold on slightly to; sit un-
comfortably on the edge of stg.; remain a
short time; have a disagreement, quarrel.
çaketim çiviye ilişti, my coat caught on a
nail : göze ~, to catch the eye. ~tirmek,
to fasten, attach.
ilk First; initial; primary (school); beginning. ~ ağızda, at the first attempt, at the
first shot : ~ önce, first of all.
ilka (·⸱) A throwing or dropping into; suggestion. ~ etm., to suggest, put an idea
into s.o.'s head; sow (discord); throw into
danger; lower a boat into the sea.
ilkah (·⸱) Fertilization; insemination.
ilk·bahar (¹··) The spring. ~çağ (¹·),
ancient times. ~in (¹·), first; in the first
place. ~mekteb, ‖~okul (¹··), primary
school. ‖~söz (¹·), preface.
illâ (¹·) v. also ille. Except; or else; whatever happens; without fail. ~ ki oraya
gitmiyesin !, whatever you do, don't go
there! : ~ velâkin, but on the other hand :
bunu böyle yapmak lâzımdır ve ~ felâ, you
must do it this way or not at all.
illallah (¹···) Expresses annoyance or disgust.
~i ve resulihi !, I am sick to death of it
(you etc.) : senden ~ !, I'm sick of you!
ille (¹·) v. also illâ. Absolutely; just; especially. ~ bu gün mü olmalı ?, must it be

today? : ~ **gideceğim diyor,** he says he simply must go : **ne zaman sokağa çıksam ~ yağmur yağar,** whenever I go out it's sure to rain.

illet, -ti Disease; defect; cause, reason. ~ **edinmek,** to acquire a tiresome habit : **frengi ~i,** syphilis. ~**li,** ill, diseased; defective; having some annoying habit.

illiyet, -ti Reason; causality.

illiyin (···⌐) The Highest Heaven; Paradise.

ilmek, ilmik Loop; bow; noose; slip-knot. ~**lemek,** to tie loosely. ~**li,** lightly tied; in a bow.

ilmi v. ilim. ~**hal,** book for teaching to children the elements of religion. ~**ye,** a member of the hierarchy of Moslem jurisprudents and religious teachers.

ilmî (·⌐) Scientific; pertaining to knowledge. **tariki ~,** the career of the professors of Islamic canon law; the hierarchy of such.

ilmik v. ilmek.

ilmühaber Identity papers; certificate; receipt.

ilmülemraz Pathology.

ilsak (·⌐) **etm.** va. Join on; attach.

iltibas (··⌐) Confusion of one word or phrase with another. ~**a mahal kalmamak için,** to avoid any ambiguity. ~**lı,** ambiguous.

iltica (···⌐) **etm.** vn. Take refuge; ask for quarter, surrender. ~**gâh,** place of refuge, asylum.

iltifat (··⌐) **-tı** Courteous or kind treatment; favour. ~ **etm.,** to take notice of, greet; treat with kindness. ~**çı,** kind, affable. ~**kârane,** courteous; in a kind and affable manner.

iltihab (··⌐) Inflammation, ~**î** (···—⌐), inflammatory. ~**lanmak,** to become inflamed.

iltihak (··⌐), **-kı** Action of joining or attaching oneself. ···**e ~ etm.,** to join; to connect oneself with; to adhere to.

iltima (···⌐) A flashing or shining.

iltimas (··⌐) Request, prayer; recommendation; favouritism. ~ **etm.,** to request, solicit; ask a favour for a protégé, recommend him for a post. ~**çı,** one who asks such favours, patron, protector. ~**lı,** one who gets a job through favouritism.

iltisak (··⌐), **-kı** Contiguity; junction; adherence. ~ **borusu,** union (mech.) : ~ **etm.,** to adhere, be joined; be contiguous. ~**î** (···—⌐), agglutinative (language).

iltiva (···⌐) A being coiled or wound about sig.; meandering (of a river); torsion; plication (geology).

iltiyam (··⌐) Healing of a wound; cicatrization. ~ **bulmak,** (of a wound) to heal up.

iltizam (··⌐) A looking after the interests

of s.o.; a farming of a branch of the public revenue. ~ **etm.,** to take the part of, uphold, prefer, favour; to farm a branch of the revenue: ~**a vermek,** to lease out the collection of certain revenues: **sükûtu ~ etm.,** to prefer to keep silent. ~**cı,** one who farms a branch of the revenue. ~**en** (···⌐·), on lease, by farming out; in support; on purpose; by preference. ~**î** (···—⌐), done on purpose; showing favour, partial, sympathetic : optative tense (yazayım, gideyim) : ~ **olarak,** on purpose, designedly.

ilzam (·⌐) **etm.** va. Silence by argument.

ima[1] (—⌐) Allusion, hint. ~ **etm.,** to allude to, hint at.

ima[2] A kind of wild goat.

imal (—⸰), **-li** Manufacture; making. ~ **etm.,** to make, manufacture, produce, prepare : ~**i fikir etm.,** to go into a matter deeply, to think it out. ~**at** (——⸰), **-tı,** manufactured goods; production of same. ~**athane,** factory, workshop.

imale (·—⸰) A bending or inclining; the pronunciation of a short vowel as a long one for the purposes of prosody. ~ **etm.,** to incline, persuade, convince : ···**e ~i nazar etm.,** to examine stg.

imali (——⸰) Alluding to; containing a hint or implication. **bu ~ sözler,** words alluding to this, these sort of words.

imam (·⸰) Leader in public worship; religious leader; Imam. ⌐~ **evinden aş ölü gözünden yaş**⌐, 'you might as well expect tears from a corpse as food from an Imam' (allusion to their alleged stinginess) : ⌐**cami** (or **cemaat) ne kadar büyük olsa ~ bildiğini okur**⌐, 'however large the mosque (congregation) the Imam will read the appointed prayers', i.e. rules are rules; also sometimes 'he goes his own way without paying attention to others'.

imam·bayıldı, a dish of aubergines with oil. ~**e** (·—⸰), stem of a rosary; mouthpiece of a pipe; turban. ~**et** (·—⸰), **-ti,** quality and office of an Imam. ~**suyu** (·⸰··), **-nu,** raki. ~**zade** (···—⸰), son of an Imam.

iman (—⸰) Belief; faith; religion. ~**ım,** a term of address among the lower classes : ~**ı*** **ağlamak** (sl.), to suffer, to undergo hardship : ~ **etm.,** to have faith in God (esp. in accord with Moslem tenets) : ~**a gelmek,** to be converted to the true faith; to see reason : ~**a getirmek,** to convert to Islam; to bring s.o. to see reason : ···**e ~ getirmek,** to believe in a dogma etc.: ~**ı gevremek** (sl.), to undergo hardship; to be exhausted : ~**ına kadar,** to the utmost degree : ~ **tahtası,** the breast : ~**ı yok,** a term of abuse.

im'an (·╵) Scrutiny; investigation. **nazarı** ~ **ile**, with careful scrutiny.

imansız (—·╵) Unbelieving; atheist; cruel, inhuman.

imar (—╵) Improvement by cultivating or building. ~ **etm.**, to improve; to render prosperous. ~**et** (·—╵), **-ti**, prosperous condition; kitchen for the distribution of food to the poor; ~ **çorbası**, soup supplied by such kitchens; stg. got for nothing.

imbat¹, -tı A cool sea-breeze *which prevails in the Aegean in the summer.*

imbat² *v.* **inbat.**

imbik Retort, still. ~ **etm.** *or* ~**ten çekmek**, to distil.

imbisat *v.* **inbisat.**

imdad (·╵) Help, assistance; reinforcement. ~ **etm.**, to come to *s.o.*'s help: ~**a yetişmek**, to come to the help of, to reinforce. ~**cı**, one who comes to another's help; reinforcement.

imdi (╵·) Now; in a short time; thus; and so.

imece Work done for the community by a whole village; corvée. By the united efforts of the community.

imha (·╵) Destruction; effacement. ~ **etm.**, to obliterate, destroy, cancel.

imhal, -li Postponement. ~ **etm.**, to grant a delay, postpone.

imik Soft place on a baby's skull, fontanel.

imizgenmek *vn.* Doze; (fire) to be nearly out.

imkân (·╵) Possibility; practicability. ~ **dahilinde**, within the bounds of possibility, as far as possible: ~**ı yok**, it is impossible. ~**lı**, possible. ~**sız**, impossible. ~**sızlık**, impossibility.

imlâ (·╵) Action of filling; spelling, orthography. ~ **etm.**, to spell; to dictate: ~ **makinesi**, dictaphone: **bu çocuk** ~**ya gelmez**, this child is incorrigible. ~**sız**, misspelt.

imparator Emperor. ~**içe** (···╵·), empress. ~**luk**, title and position of emperor; empire.

imrar (·╵) **etm.** *va.* Pass (time *etc.*). ~**ı eyyam etm.**, to pass one's days, live.

imrenmek *va.* (*with dat.*) Long for; envy, covet.

imsak (·╵), **-ki** Fasting; abstention; abstinence, continence; the hour at which the Ramazan fast begins each day. ~ **etm.**, to fast, abstain, refrain. ~**li davranmak**, to be moderate, to avoid excess. ~**iye**, timetable giving the hour when the fast begins, *v.* **imsak.**

imtidad (···╵) Extension, prolongation. ~**ınca**, all along, throughout its length: ~ **bulmak**, to be prolonged.

imtihan (···╵) Trial, test; examination. ~**a**

çekmek, to examine *a pupil* thoroughly: ~ **etm.**, to examine (a pupil *etc*): ~**a girmek** *or* ~ **olm.**, to sit for an exam.: ~**da kalmak**, to fail in an exam.: ~ **vermek**, to pass an exam.

imtilâ A being full; repletion; congestion. ~ **etm.**, to be replete.

imtina (··╵), **-aı** Avoidance; refusal. ~ **etm.**, to refuse; to avoid.

imtinan A being under an obligation.

imtisal (··╵), **-li** A conforming to rule. ···**e** ~ **etm.**, to conform to; comply with; follow *an example*. **nümunei** ~, an example to follow, exemplary. ~**en** (··╵·), conformably, in compliance with.

imtisas (··╵) Sucking; absorption. ~ **etm.**, to be absorbed.

imtiyaz (··╵) Distinction; privilege; concession; autonomy; diploma. ~ **bulmak**, to acquire distinction: ~ **sahibi**, concessionaire; privileged person. ~**at** (···╵), **-tı**, ~**ı ecnebiye**, the Capitulations (*abolished 1914*). ~**lı**, distinguished; privileged; autonomous.

imtizac (··╵) A blending; a fitting together; a getting on well together. ···**le** ~ **etm.**, to blend with, fit, get on well together with; get accustomed to. ~**lı**, harmonious; well-fitting (door *etc.*). ~**sızlık**, incompatibility of temperament.

imza (·╵) Signature. ···**i** ~ **etm.**, ···**e** ~ **atmak** *or* **koymak**, to sign: ~ **sahibi**, signatory. ~**lamak**, to sign.

in¹ Human being, *only used in conjunction with cin*. ⌐~ **misin cin misin nesin**⌐, whatever you are, a man or a spirit: ⌐~ **cin yok**⌐, there's not a soul there.

in² Den *or* lair *of a wild beast.*

inabe (·—╵) Appointment of a deputy; entrance into a religious fraternity.

inad (·╵) Obstinacy. ~**ına** (·—·╵), out of obstinacy; out of contrariness; just to spite one; it would just happen that; as luck would have it: ···**e** ~, despite ...: ~ **etm.**, to be obstinate, to persist: ···**in** ~**ına yapmak**, to do *stg.* just to spite *s.o.*: ⌐**iş** ~**a bindi**⌐, it is a matter of sheer obstinacy; we'll see who can hold out longest, *v. App.* ~**cı**, obstinate, pig-headed.

in'am (·╵) **etm.** *va.* Bestow *a favour*; do *a kindness.*

inan Belief; trust. ~ **olsun!**, believe me!, rest assured that .... ‖~**c**, belief; confidence. ~**dırmak**, to cause to believe; persuade; deceive: **Allah inandırsın!**, believe me! ~**ılacak**, ~**ılır**, credible. ~**ılmaz**, incredible. ~**ış**, belief; credulity.

inanmak *va.* (*with dat.*) Believe; trust.

inas (·╵) *pl.* Females. ~ **mektebi**, (*formerly*) school for girls.

inayet (·–¹), **–ti** Kindness; favour; grace; care, effort. ~ **ola!**, *said to a beggar when refusing to give alms.* ~**en** (·⸴··), as a favour. ~**kâr, –li**, kind; gracious; obliging.

inba, imba (·⸴) Communication. ~ **etm.**, to give news of, to communicate *stg.*

inbat¹ *v.* imbat.

inbat², imbat (·⸴) A causing to grow. ~**î** (·–⸴), vegetative.

inbias (··⸴) etm. *vn.* (*with abl.*) Be caused by; proceed from.

inbisat (··⸴), **–ti** Act of spreading *or* expanding; cheerfulness. ~ **etm.**, to be dilated, extended; open out; be at one's ease.

incaz (·⸴) Performance *of a request*; fulfilment *of a promise.*

ince Slender; thin; fine; slight; subtle; delicate. ~**den** ~**ye**, minutely; in a subtle manner: ~ **elemek**, to pass through a fine sieve; ⌐~ **eleyip sık dokumak⌐**, to be too particular, to be very meticulous: ~ **hastalık**, tuberculosis: ⌐~**sini ipe kalınını çöpe dizmek⌐**, to go into details, to be too particular.

ince·cik (¹··), very slender *or* fine; minutely, finely. ~**lemek**, to examine minutely; go into *a matter* carefully. ~**lik**, fineness; delicacy; refinement; subtlety; ingenuity. ~**lmek**, to become fine *or* thin; be refined *or* delicate; be too subtle, quibble. ~**ltmek**, to make fine *or* slender; refine; subtilize; make nice distinctions. ~**rek**, slender, elegant; rather thin. ~**saz**, Turkish orchestra of stringed instruments.

inci Pearl. ~ **dizisi**, a string of pearls: ~ **balığı**, bleak. ~**çiçeği, –ni**, lily of the valley.

incik¹ Shin.

incik² Slightly bruised or broken. Sprain; bruise.

incil Gospel, New Testament.

incilâ (··–¹) Brightness; manifestation. ~ **etm.**, to be manifest, appear.

incimad (··⸴) A being frozen *or* solidified. ~ **etm.**, to be frozen *or* congealed.

incinmek *vn.* Be hurt; be offended.

incir Fig. ~ **çekirdeğini doldurmaz**, trifling, insignificant: ⌐**bir çuval ~i berbad etm.⌐**, to undo everything, to 'upset the applecart': **frenk** ~**i**, prickly pear: **kavak** ~**i**, purple fig: **lop** ~**i**, green fig: **ocağına** ~ **dikmek**, to break up a home; to ruin, exterminate. ~**ağacı, –nı**, fig-tree. ~**kuşu, –nu**, beccafico.

incitici Harmful; hurting; offending.

incitmek *va.* Hurt; touch; offend, vex.

incizab (··⸴) A being attracted; gravitation.

ind Side. benim ~**imde**, in my opinion; onun ~**inde**, in his opinion.

indel·hace (¹···), ~**iktiza**, ~**ıztırar**, ~**lüzum** In case of need.

indî (·–¹) Personal; subjective; arbitrary.

indifa (··–¹), **–aı** Eruption (volcanic). ~ **etm.**, to erupt. ~**at, –tı**, skin eruptions. ~**î**, eruptive.

indinde *v.* ind.

indiras (··⸴) Ruin; obliteration.

indirme Act of lowering; unloading (from a ship *etc.*); landing of troops from the air.

indirmek *va.* Cause to descend; lower; calm; give (a blow). **denize** ~, to launch *a ship.*

indiyat (··–¹), **–tı** *pl.* Assertions founded only on personal opinion.

inek Cow. ~**çi**, cowman, cowherd. ~**lik**, cowshed; idiotic behaviour.

ineze Sickly, debilitated.

infak (·⸴) etm. *va.* Keep others at one's own expense; maintain.

infaz (·⸴) Execution of an order. ~ **etm.**, to carry out *an order.*

infial (··⸴), **–li** Annoyance; anger, indignation. ~ **etm.**, to be annoyed or indignant.

inficar (··⸴) A bursting forth; breaking of the dawn; (*silk industry*) the hatching of the caterpillars.

infikâk (··⸴), **–ki** Separation. ~ **etm.**, (of an official *etc.*) to leave his post.

infilâk (··⸴), **–kı** Explosion. ~ **etm.**, to burst, to explode: **mevaddı** ~**iye**, explosives.

infirad (··⸴) Isolation. ~ **etm.**, to be isolated. ~**cı**, isolationist.

infisad (··⸴) A becoming corrupt *or* spoilt.

infisah (··⸴) Disintegration; dissolution; cancellation. ~ **etm.**, (of an assembly) to be dissolved.

infisal (··⸴), **–li** Separation; resignation *from a post.* ~ **etm.**, to be severed *or* separated; to be removed *or* to retire *from a post*; to go away.

ingiliz English. Englishman; pound sterling. ~ **anahtarı**, spanner. ~**ce**, English language; in English; in the English fashion.

İngiltere (··¹·) England.

inha (·–¹) Official memorandum to a superior department recommending the appointment *or* promotion of an official.

inhidam (··⸴) A falling down; a being demolished. ~ **etm.**, (of a building) to collapse.

inhilâl (··⸴), **–li** A being undone, solved, dissolved. ~ **etm.**, to be dissolved, decomposed; to become void.

inhimak (··⸴), **–ki** Addiction. ···**e** ~ **etm.**, to give oneself up to *stg.*; to have a weakness for *stg.*

inhina ($\cdots\stackrel{1}{\cdot}$) A being curved *or* bent; abasement.

inhiraf ($\cdots\stackrel{1}{\cdot}$) Deviation. ~ etm., to deviate; to be altered. ~ı hatır, displeasure: ~ı mizac, indisposition.

inhisaf ($\cdots\stackrel{1}{\cdot}$) Eclipse of the moon.

inhisar ($\cdots\stackrel{1}{\cdot}$) Monopoly; limitation, restriction. ~a almak *or* kendine ~ ettirmek, to monopolize: ···e ~ etm., to be restricted to ... .

inhitat ($\cdots\stackrel{1}{\cdot}$), –tı Decline; degradation; degeneration.

inhizam ($\cdots\stackrel{1}{\cdot}$) Defeat, rout.

ini Younger brother.

inik¹ Cub; pup.

inik² Lowered (of a tent *etc*).

in'ikad ($\cdots\stackrel{1}{\cdot}$) Conclusion of an agreement; setting up (of an assembly *etc*.). ~ etm., to be concluded; to be assembled *or* established.

inikâs ($\cdots\stackrel{1}{\cdot}$) Reflection.

inildemek *vn.* Echo; resound; moan.

inilmek *vn. impers. of* inmek. buradan inilir, one goes down here.

inilti Moan, groan; echo.

inim inim With groans and laments.

iniş Descent; slope; decline; landing *of an aeroplane*. ~ çıkışlar, ups and downs.

in'itaf ($\cdots\stackrel{1}{\cdot}$) Deflection. ~ etm., to be deflected, to turn away; to direct one's glance *to*, to look.

inkâr ($\cdot\stackrel{1}{\cdot}$) Denial; refusal. ~ etm., to deny, ı refuse.

inkıbaz ($\cdots\stackrel{1}{\cdot}$) Constipation. ~a uğramak, to be constipated.

inkılâb ($\cdots\stackrel{1}{\cdot}$) Radical change; revolution; transformation. ~atı devran, the vicissitudes of life: ···e ~ etm., to be transformed or turned into ...: ~ geçirmek, to undergo a transformation: harf ~ı, the reform of the alphabet.

inkıraz ($\cdots\stackrel{1}{\cdot}$) The decline and extinction (of a family or dynasty). ~ bulmak, to become extinct.

inkısam ($\cdots\stackrel{1}{\cdot}$) A being divided. ~ etm., to be divided up: kabili ~, divisible.

inkıta ($\cdots\stackrel{1}{\cdot}$), –aı Cessation; interruption. ~a uğramak, to cease; to be interrupted.

inkıyad ($\cdots\stackrel{1}{\cdot}$) Submission; obedience. ~ etm., to submit, obey (*with dat.*).

inkıza ($\cdots\stackrel{1}{\cdot}$) Termination; expiration. ~ etm., to expire, mature, terminate.

inkisar ($\cdots\stackrel{1}{\cdot}$) A breaking; refraction; vexation; curse. ~etm., to refract; to be vexed; to curse. ~ı hayal, disappointment: ~ı* tutmak, for one's curse to take effect.

inkişaf ($\cdots\stackrel{1}{\cdot}$) A being discovered; development. ~ etm., to be discovered, to appear; to develop.

inle·mek *vn.* Moan, groan. ~tmek, to cause to moan; oppress; make resound.

inme Act of descending; landing of an aeroplane; launching of a ship; fall; apoplexy, stroke. Fallen, dropped. gökten ~, heavensent. ···e ~ inmek, to have a stroke.

inmek *vn.* Descend; fall down; alight; (aeroplane) land; subside; (price) fall; (apoplexy) attack, strike. *va.* Plant (a blow); strike: yüreğine* ~, to die of a heart attack; to suffer a terrible blow; az daha yüreğime iniyordu, I nearly died of shame.

inmeli Struck by apoplexy; paralysed.

insaf ($\cdot\stackrel{1}{\cdot}$) Justice; moderation; reasonableness, fairness. ~ !, 'be reasonable !', 'be fair !': ~ etm., to act with justice: ~a gelmek, to come to reason; to be fair; to show moderation *or* pity: artık ~ına kalmış, it now all depends on his sense of fairness; it is at his discretion. ~kâr, ~lı, just, equitable; humane; reasonable, fair. ~sız, unjust; unfair; without a conscience; cruel. ~sızlık, injustice; inhumanity; unfairness.

insan Human being, man; fine type of man. Humane; upright. ~ içine çıkmak, to go out in public, to mix with one's fellow-beings. ~ca ($\cdot\stackrel{1}{\cdot}\cdot$), humane: as a man should. ~iyet ($\cdot-\stackrel{1}{\cdot}$), –ti, ~lık, humanity; humankind; kindness. ~iyetli, humane. ~iyetsiz, inhuman, cruel. ~oğlu, –nu, man, mankind.

insıraf ($\cdots\stackrel{1}{\cdot}$) A being declinable (*gram.*).

insicam ($\cdots\stackrel{1}{\cdot}$) Coherence *in speech or writing*; harmony; regularity. ~lı, coherent. ~sız, incoherent.

insidad ($\cdots\stackrel{1}{\cdot}$) A being closed *or* blocked up.

insiyak ($\cdots\stackrel{1}{\cdot}$), –kı A being driven *or* guided; instinct. ~î ($\cdots-\stackrel{1}{\cdot}$), instinctive.

inşa ($\cdot\stackrel{1}{\cdot}$) Construction; creation; literary composition; book giving models for letter writing. ~ etm., to construct, build: hali ~dâ, in course of construction. ~at ($\cdot-\stackrel{1}{\cdot}$), –tı, buildings; works: bahrî ~, naval constructions, shipbuilding. ~î ($\cdot-\stackrel{1}{\cdot}$), pertaining to building *cr* shipbuilding.

inşad Recitation; repetition (in a school). ~ etm., to recite.

inşallah ($\stackrel{1}{\cdot}\cdots$) *Lit.* 'if God pleases'; I hope; it is to be hoped that.

inşia' ($\cdots\stackrel{1}{\cdot}$) Radiation.

inşiab ($\cdots\stackrel{1}{\cdot}$) Subdivision; ramification.

inşikak ($\cdots\stackrel{1}{\cdot}$), –kı A being split *or* cracked.

inşirah ($\cdots\stackrel{1}{\cdot}$) Cheerfulness; exhilaration; relief.

intac ($\cdot\stackrel{1}{\cdot}$) etm. *va.* Result in; cause; bring to a conclusion; bring forth *young*.

intak ($\cdot\stackrel{1}{\cdot}$), –kı A making speak; God's endowing man with speech. ~ı Hak, 'as though God had put the words into his mouth'; condemned out of his own mouth.

intan (·ᵼ) Internal microbic infection (pneumonia *etc.*). ~î (·—ᵼ), infectious.

intaş (·ᵼ) Germination.

intıba (··ᵼ), –aı Impression; feeling.

intıbak (··ᵼ), –kı Adaptation; adjustment. ~ etm., to be adapted, to adapt or adjust oneself; to conform. ~ melekesi, adaptability. ~sızlık, lack of adaptability.

intıfa (··ᵼ) Extinction (of a fire). ~ etm., to be extinguished.

intibah (··ᵼ) An awakening; vigilance; circumspection. ~ devri, the Renaissance: şayanı ~, worth paying attention to; worth taking note of *as a warning.*

intifa (··ᵼ), –aı Gain, advantage; usufruct. ~ etm., to profit: kaydi hayat ile ~ hakkı, life-interest.

intiha (··ᵼ) End; limit. ~ bulmak, to come to an end. ~î (··—ᵼ), final; extreme.

intihab (··ᵼ) Selection, choice; election; preference. ~ dairesi, electoral district, constituency: ~ etm., to choose; elect; prefer. ~at, ~tı, elections.

intihal (··ᵼ), –li Plagiarism. ~ etm., to plagiarize.

intihar (··ᵼ) Suicide. ~ etm., to commit suicide.

intikad Literary criticism.

intikal (··ᵼ), –li Transition; passing from one place to another; transfer of property (by sale or inheritance); passing away to another world; perception, understanding. ~ etm., to pass to another place; pass away (die); (of a conversation) to change to another subject; perceive: sürati ~, quickness of perception.

intikam (··ᵼ) Revenge. ···den ~ almak, to revenge oneself on, take revenge on ...: ~ını almak, to avenge .... ~cı, vindictive.

intisab (··ᵼ) Relation; attachment. ~ etm., to be connected with; to join *a political party etc.*: to enter (a career).

intişar (··ᵼ) Publication; dissemination; ~ etm. *or* bulmak, to be spread *or* disseminated.

intizam (··ᵼ) Regularity; order; arrangement. ~ bulmak, to become well arranged, be set in order: ~ üzere olm., to be in good order *or* well disciplined. ~sız, irregular; disordered.

intizar (··ᵼ) Expectation; (*sl.*) abuse, curse. ~ üzere olm., to be on the lookout for something. ~en (··ᵼ), pending, while waiting (for = *dat.*).

inzal (·ᵼ), –li Emission *of semen.* ~etm., to cause to descend.

inzar (·ᵼ) Prognosis (*med.*).

inzibat (··ᵼ), –tı Discipline. ~ memuru, military policeman. ~î (··—ᵼ), disciplinary.

inzimam (··ᵼ) Act of being added *or* joined to. ~ etm., to be added: ~ı rey, consent; concurrence.

inziva (··ᵼ) A retirement into seclusion; a leading the life of a hermit. ~ya çekilmek, to retire into seclusion.

ip, **–pi** Rope; cord; string. ~ atlamak, to skip: ~ cambazı, tight-rope walker: ~ ~le çekmek, 'to string up', hang: ···i ~le çekmek, to await *stg.* anxiously: ~ini çözmek, to sever *s.o.'s* connexion with *stg.*: ~e gelmek, to come to the gallows: ~ kaçkını, jailbird: ~e kazığa vurmak, to execute by hanging or impaling: ~ten kazıktan kurtulmus, gallows-bird: ~i kırık, vagabond: ~ini* kırmak, to slip away; to get out of hand: ~ koparmak, to break the link *with stg.*: ~ini* koparmak, to make off: ⌐onun ~iyle kuyuya inilmez⌐, he is not to be relied on: ~i sapı yok *or* ~e sapa gelmez, without connexions, vagabond; incoherent, irrelevant (*also* ipsiz sapsız); ~ ucu, *v.* ipucu; ~in ucunu kaçırmak, to lose the thread of *stg.*; to lose control of *stg.*: ~e un sermek, to make vain excuses; to be lazy; *v. App.*: ~ini üstüne atmak (*sl.*), to give s.o. his head, to leave him to his own devices: ayağına* ~ takmak, to run *s.o.* down, to gossip maliciously about *s.o.*

ipek Silk; silken. ~ kozası, silk cocoon: ham ~, raw silk. ~böceği, –ni, silkworm. ~çi, silk merchant or manufacturer; ~çilik, silk industry. ~çiçeği, –ni, the portulaca and mesembryanthemum classes of flowering plants. ~hane (··—ᵼ), silk factory. ~li, of silk.

ipeka (·ᵼ·) Ipecacuanha.

ipham *v.* ibham.

ipipullah (·ᵼ··) *In* ⌐~ sivri külâh⌐, stony-broke, destitute.

ipiri Huge.

ipka *v.* ibka.

iplemek *va.* Bind with a rope; (*sl.*) respect, pay attention to.

iplik Thread; sewing-cotton. Made of linen. ~ ~, thread by thread; ~ ~ olm., to become frayed or threadbare: ipliği* pazara çıkmak, to get a bad name; to be shown up: anasının ipliğini pazara çıkarmış, an unprincipled scoundrel: pamuk ipliğile bağlamak, to settle *a matter* in an unsound manner.

iplik·cik, threadlike worm *attacking the flesh of human beings in hot countries* (? *filaria*). ~hane (··—ᵼ), spinning-mill. ~lenmek, to become unravelled. ~peyniri, –ni, *a kind of cheese showing the marks of the cheese-cloth.*

ipotek Mortgage.

ipsit Felloe.

ipsiz Having no connexions, vagabond. ~ **sapsız,** without house or home; irrelevant.

iptal, iptida *etc. v.* ibtal, ibtida *etc.*

ipucu (ˡ··), **–nu** Clue; motive. *v. also* ip.

irab (–ˡ) The declension of an Arab word; the case-endings. ~**da mahalli yok,** of no account, insignificant.

irad (–ˡ) Income, revenue; a citing *or* quoting. ~ **etm.,** to quote; deliver (a speech); adduce (proof): **Hazineye** ~ **kayd-edilmek (yazılmak),** (of a deposit *etc.*) to be forfeited to the Treasury: **sabıt** ~, fixed income.

irade (·–ˡ) Will; will-power; command, decree. ~**i cüz'iye,** the limited freewill of man: ~**si* elden gitmek** *or* ~**sine* hâkim olmamak,** to lose one's self-control: ~**si haricinde,** over which he had no control: ~**i milliye,** the national will: ~**i seniye,** imperial rescript. ~**li,** strong-willed.

iradî (·–ˡ) Voluntary.

irae (·–ˡ) *etm. va.* Show, manifest; indicate.

irak *v.* ırak.

İran Persia (ˡ·), ~**î** (——ˡ), ~**lı,** Persian.

iras (·ˡ) *etm., va.* Cause.

irca (·ˡ), **–aı** A sending back. ~ **etm.,** to cause to return; to refer; to ascribe: ~ **kısmı,** recuperator (artillery).

irem, irembağı A fabulous paradise in Arabia; the garden of Eden.

irfan Knowledge; culture; refinement; spiritual knowledge.

iri Huge; voluminous; coarse. ~ **yarı,** big, powerfully built *man.* ~**baş,** tadpole. ~**ce,** somewhat large or coarse. ~**leşmek,** to become large. ~**li,** *in* ~ **ufaklı,** mixed large and small, fine and coarse. ~**lik,** largeness; size.

irin Pus; filth. ~**lenmek,** to suppurate.

iriş Warp *of a tissue;* pole *of a wagon.*

irkâb (·ˡ) *etm. va.* Cause to ride; mount; embark.

irk·ilmek *vn.* Be startled, draw back *in fear;* (water) collect, become stagnant; become inflamed. ~**inti,** stagnant pool. ~**mek,** (of water) to collect and stagnate.

İrlânda Ireland. ~**lı,** Irish.

irmik Semolina.

irs Inheritance; hereditary quality. ~**en** (ˡ·), by inheritance. ~**î** (·ˡ), hereditary.

irsal (·ˡ), **–li** Act of sending. ~ **etm.,** to send, dispatch.

irşad (·ˡ) Act of guiding, showing the right way; enlightenment. ~ **etm.,** to direct; guide with advice; initiate (a novice). ~**at** (·–ˡ), **–tı,** *in* ~**ta bulunmak,** to give advice.

irtibat (··ˡ), **–tı** Connexion; tie; communication (*mil.*); liaison. ~ **hatları,** lines of communication.

irtica (··ˡ), **–aı** A going back; political reaction. ~**î** (··–ˡ), reactionary.

irtical (··ˡ), **–li** A speaking extempore; improvisation. ~**en** (··–ˡ·), extempore.

irtidad (··ˡ) Apostasy.

irtifa (··ˡ), **–aı** Elevation; height, altitude. ~**en** (··–ˡ·), in altitude.

irtifak (··ˡ), **–kı** *In* ~ **hakkı,** easement (legal).

irtihal (··ˡ), **–li** A passing away. ~**i dârıbeka etm.,** to pass into the next world: ~ **etm.,** to pass away, die.

irtika (··ˡ) A rising, ascending. ~ **etm.,** to rise; be promoted.

irtikâb (··ˡ) Perpetration; corruption, embezzlement. ~ **etm.,** to commit (a crime), perpetrate; to embezzle; take a bribe.

irtisam (··ˡ) Projection (map). ~**etm.,** to be delineated *or* portrayed.

irtişa (··ˡ) Corruption; the taking of bribes.

irva (·ˡ) *etm. va.* Give to drink; water; irrigate.

irza[1] (·ˡ) *etm. va.* Content; get *s.o.* to consent.

irza[2] (·ˡ) *etm. va.* Suckle *a child.*

is Soot. ~ **kokmak,** (of food) to be slightly burnt.

İsa Jesus.

isabet (·–ˡ), **–ti** A hitting the mark; a thing said or done just right. ~ **!,** well done !, capital ! : ... **de** ~ **!,** 'and a good thing too ! ' : ~**i ayn,** the evil eye: ~ **etm.,** to hit the mark; to do *or* say just the right thing; to guess rightly: ~ **oldu da (ki),** it was a good thing that ... : ⌐**beni istintak etmeseniz daha** ~ **edersiniz**⌐, 'you would be wiser not to cross-examine me': ⌐**piyangoda bana yüz lira** ~ **etti**⌐, 'I won a hundred lira in the lottery'.

is'af (·ˡ) *etm. va.* Grant (a request).

isağa (·–ˡ) *etm. va.* Cast (metals).

isal (–ˡ) *etm. va.* Cause to arrive *or* attain.

isale (·–ˡ) *etm. va.* Bring *or* divert (water).

isar (–ˡ) *etm. va.* Give in abundance.

isbat (·ˡ), **–tı** Proof; confirmation; maintenance of stg. in its present condition. ~ **etm.,** to prove, demonstrate, confirm: ~**ı vücud etm.,** to appear in person, to put in an appearance.

ise 1. *Verbal suffix forming the 3rd pers. sing. of a conditional tense, generally abbreviated to* **–se, –sa.** 2. *conj.* However; as for. ~ **de,** although: **ben** ~, as for me: ···**mekten** ~, instead of ···ing: ⌐**okudunsa okudun artık bir az dinlen**⌐, 'well, you've done your reading, now take a rest': ⌐**gittimse gittim, sana ne?**⌐, 'well, if I did go, what's that to you?'

isevî (–·ˡ) Christian. ~**lik,** Christianity.

isfenc Sponge. ~î (··⸴), spongy.

isfendan Maple-tree.

isfenks Sphinx.

isga (·⸴) *etm. va.* Listen to; comply with.

ishak, –kı Scops' owl.

ishal (·⸝), **–li** Purging; diarrhoea. ~ olm., to have diarrhoea.

isilik Heat-spots; rash.

isim, –smi Name; noun. ismini cismini bilmem, I know nothing about him: ismi fail, active participle: ismi geçen, aforesaid, above-mentioned: ismi has, proper noun: ismi mef'ul, passive participle: ⌐ismi var cismi yok¬, known by name but non-existent. ~**lendirmek**, to name, call.

isir, –sri Trace; track. ···in isrine iktifa etm., to follow in the footsteps of ... .

iska (·⸴) A watering *or* irrigating. ~ etm., to water *or* irrigate.

iskambil Playing card; *name of a card game.* ~ (kâğıdı) gibi dağıtmak, to scatter in all directions.

iskân (·⸝) A causing to settle *or* inhabit; settling in; inhabiting. ~ etm., to settle *emigrants etc.*; to inhabit, dwell.

iskandil Sounding-lead. ~ etm., to sound; to probe.

iskarça (·⸴·) Crowded, packed tight.

iskarpelâ Carpenter's chisel.

iskarpin (Woman's) shoe.

iskât (·⸴) *etm. va.* Silence; appease.

iskeç Sketch.

iskefe (·⸴·) Skull-cap. The stretching and softening of leather.

iskele (·⸴·) Landing-place; quay; port of call; ladder; scaffolding; port (*opp. to starboard*). ~ verilmek, for a gangway to be attached to a ship.

iskelet, –ti Skeleton.

iskemle Chair; stool.

İskender Alexander the Great. ~**iye** (···⸴·), Alexandria. ~**un**, Alexandretta.

iskete (·⸴·) Finch.

İskoç Scotch. ~**ya** (·⸴·), Scotland. ~**yalı**, Scotch, Scotchman.

iskonto (·⸴·) Discount.

iskorbut, –tü Scurvy.

iskorpit, –ti Scorpion fish (*scorpaena*).

islâm Islam. ~**a** gelmek, to become a Moslem: ehli ~, Moslems; a Moslem. ~**iyet, –ti**, the religion of Islam; the Moslem world.

is·lemek *va.* Blacken with soot; smoke (fish *etc.*); burn (food). ~**lenmek**, to become black with soot; smell of soot. ~**li**, sooty: ~ balık, smoked fish.

islim Steam. ~ üzerinde, with steam up: ⌐~ arkadan gelsin!¬, *used of* (i) *people who do not understand what they are talking about;* (ii) *people who enter upon an under-*

taking without proper preparation; v. App.: v. also istim.

ismen (⸴·) By name.

ismet, –ti Chastity; honour; innocence.

ismi *v.* isim. ~has, proper name.

isnad (·⸝) Imputation. ~ etm., to impute, ascribe.

İspanya (·⸴·) Spain.

ispanyol Spanish; Spaniard. ~**ca**, Spanish (language).

ispanyolet, –ti Window latch.

ispat *v.* isbat.

ispenc, ispec Bantam. ~ horoz gibi, 'cocky'.

ispenciyar Chemist, pharmacist. ~î (····⸴), pharmaceutical.

ispendik Small bass.

ispermeçet, –ti Spermaceti.

ispinoz Chaffinch.

ispir Groom.

ispirto (·⸴·) Alcohol. ~**luk**, spirit-lamp.

ispitalya (··⸴·) Hospital.

isporcu Sportsman.

israf (·⸝) Wasteful expenditure; prodigality. ~ etm., to waste, squander.

İsrafil (·—⸴) *The name of* the Archangel who will sound the Last Trump (surü ~).

İsrail (·—⸴) Israel. beni ~, the Israelites. ~**iyat, –tı**, false beliefs, superstitions.

istaka (·⸴·) Billiard cue.

istakoz Lobster.

istalâktit, –ti Stalactite; pendant (architecture).

istalya (·⸴·) Demurrage.

istalyoz (·⸴·) Awning stanchions.

istampa (·⸴·) Stamp; inking-pad.

istanbulin Kind of frock-coat *formerly worn by higher Turkish officials.*

istasyon Station.

istavrit, –ti Horse mackerel. ~ azmanı, tunny.

istek Wish; longing; appetite. ~**li**, desirous; bidder *at an auction.* ~**siz**, unwilling, reluctant; apathetic.

isteka (·⸴·) Billiard cue.

istemek *va.* Wish for, desire; ask for; require, need. istemez!, it is not necessary; arsızlık istemez!, none of your cheek!: ister ... ister..., whether ... or ...; ister gelsin ister gelmesin, whether he comes or not *or* I don't care whether he comes or not: ister inan ister inanma, believe it or not, just as you wish: ister istemez, whether he will or not, willingly or unwillingly: ⌐ister misin şimdi gelsin!¬, 'I am afraid he may come now', *but it may also mean* 'what a pleasant surprise it would be if he came now': istersen! *to one who is unwilling to do as he is asked,* 'well, have it your own way!': ⌐isteyenin bir yüzü kara, vermeyinin iki yüzü kara¹, it is more embarrassing to refuse than to ask : birinin kızını ~, to ask s.o. for the hand of his daughter : canım istemiyor !, I don't like it ! : çok zaman ister, it will require a long time.

istenmek, istenilmek vn. pass. of istemek.

ister v. istemek.

isteri Hysteria.

isterlin Pound sterling.

istetmek va. caus. of istemek.

istıktab (··⌣) Polarity.

istıtla (··⌣), **-aı** An asking for information.

istiab (··⌣) Capacity. ~ etm., to contain, to hold so much.

istiane (··—⌣) etm. va. (with abl.) Ask s.o. for help; to make use of the help of s.o. or stg.

istib'ad (··⌣) etm. va. Deem unlikely.

istibdad (··⌣) Despotism; absolute rule. ~kârane (···—⌣), despotic; in a despotic way.

istibdal (··⌣), **-li** Exchange; replacement, esp. replacement of conscripts by new recruits. ~ etm., to exchange; to release or disband conscripts.

istical (·—⌣), **-li** Haste. ~ etm., to make haste, hurry.

isticar (·—⌣) Hiring. ~ etm., to take on hire.

isticvab (··⌣) Interrogation. ~ etm., to interrogate.

istida (··⌣) Demand; petition, esp. an official request. ~ etm., to request, make a formal demand. ~name (··—⌣), formal written petition.

istidad (·—⌣) Aptitude; readiness to learn : talent. ~lı, promising, talented.

istidlâl (··⌣), **-li** Deduction, inference. ~ etm., to deduce, infer. ~en (··⌣·), by deduction.

istif Stowage; arrangement of goods in a warehouse or ship. ~ini* bozmak, to disturb, disconcert; ~ini* bozmadan, without being upset, quite unperfurbed; ~ini* bozmamak, to be quite unperturbed; to look on with indifference : ~ etm., to pack, stow : balık ~i, packed like sardines.

istifa¹ (·—⌣) Resignation from an office. ~ etm., to resign. ~name (·——⌣), letter of resignation.

istifa² (·—⌣) Full payment of a debt. ~ etm., to be paid in full; to demand full payment.

istifade (··—⌣) Profit, advantage. ···den ~ etm., to benefit by, profit by, take advantage of. ~li, profitable, advantageous : ⌐hem faydalı hem ~¬, both useful to others and profitable to oneself.

istifçi Packer; stevedore; hoarder. ~lik, stowage, packing; hoarding for profit.

istifham (··⌣) An asking for explanation; interrogation. ~ etm., to interrogate : ~ işareti (alameti), interrogation mark.

istiflemek va. Stow; pack; hoard.

istifrağ (··⌣) etm. va. Vomit.

istifraş (··⌣) Concubinage. ~ etm., to take as concubine.

istifsar (··⌣) An asking for information or explanation. ~ı hatır etm., to inquire after s.o.'s health etc.

istifta (··⌣) etm. va. Ask a mufti a decision on a point of religious law.

istiğfar (··⌣) etm. vn. Ask God's pardon.

istiğlal (··⌣), **-li** Mortgage of a house etc., the creditor receiving the rent until the mortgage is redeemed.

istiğna (··⌣) A being able to do without; independence; disdain. ~ göstermek, to show that one has no need of a thing; to be disinterested.

istiğrab (··⌣) A being surprised. ~ etm., to feel surprise or wonder.

istiğrak (··⌣), **-kı** A being immersed (fig.); a mystic's being plunged into ecstasy; transport, rapture.

istihale (··—⌣), Transformation; metamorphosis.

istihare (··—⌣) Oneiromancy; divination by dreams. ~ye yatmak, to pray and go to sleep hoping for a dream in which God will show his will.

istihbar (··⌣) An asking for information. ~ etm., to get information, to make inquiries. ~at (··—⌣), **-tı**, news : ~ hizmeti, intelligence service.

istihdaf (··⌣) etm. va. Aim at, pursue an object.

istihdam (··⌣) etm. va. Take into service, employ.

istihfaf (··⌣) Contempt. ~ etm., to despise; consider unimportant.

istihkak (··⌣), **-kı** Merit; that which is due; fee, remuneration; ration. ~ etm., to deserve, have a right to : ~ kesbetmek, to earn.

istihkâm (··⌣) Fortification; military engineering. ~ bulmak, to be consolidated : ~ subayı, engineer officer (mil.). ~at, **-tı**, fortifications. ~cılık, military engineering.

istihkar (··⌣) Scorn, contempt. ~ etm., to despise, treat with contempt : hayatını ~ etm., to scorn death, to sacrifice one's life.

istihlâf (··⌣) Succession. ~ etm., to succeed s.o.

istihlâk (··⌣), **-ki** Consumption; using up. ~ etm., to consume, use up : dahilî ~ için, for internal consumption.

istihlâl (··⌣) etm. va. Consider or make lawful.

istihlâs $(\cdots \overset{\cdot}{\cdot})$ Rescue. ~ etm., to rescue; to appropriate to oneself.

istihmam $(\cdots \overset{\cdot}{-})$ etm. *vn.* Take a bath.

istihrac $(\cdots \overset{\cdot}{\cdot})$ Deduction; divination. ~ etm., to try to get the meaning of. ~**at** $(\cdots - \overset{\cdot}{\cdot})$, –**tı**, auguries; ~**ta bulunmak**, to draw arbitrary conclusions.

istihsal $(\cdots \overset{\cdot}{\cdot})$, –**li** Act of producing *or* acquiring. ~ etm., to produce, to obtain. ~**at** $(\cdots - \overset{\cdot}{-})$, –**tı**, products.

istihsan $(\cdots \overset{\cdot}{-})$ etm. *va.* Approve, commend.

istihza $(\cdots \overset{\cdot}{-})$ Ridicule, mockery; irony, sarcasm. ···**le** ~ etm., to ridicule, mock : ~ **tarikile**, ironically : **mukadderatın** ~**sı**, the irony of fate.

istihzar $(\cdots \overset{\cdot}{-})$ etm. *va.* Prepare. ~**at** $(\cdots - \overset{\cdot}{\cdot})$, –**tı**, preparations.

istikamet $(\cdots - \overset{\cdot}{\cdot})$, –**ti** Direction; uprightness, integrity.

istikbal $(\cdots \overset{\cdot}{\cdot})$, –**li** Future; a going to meet s.o. ~**e çıkmak** *or* ~ etm., to go forth to meet s.o. *esp. as a formal ceremony.*

istiklâl $(\cdots \overset{\cdot}{\cdot})$, –**li** Independence. ~ **harbi**, the war of independence (1922) : ~ **marşı**, the Turkish National Anthem. ~**iyet, –ti,** the state of being independent.

istikmal $(\cdots \overset{\cdot}{\cdot})$, –**li** Completion. ~ etm., to complete : **esbabını** ~ etm., to take steps to, to take care that.

istiknah $(\cdots \overset{\cdot}{\cdot})$ A going deeply into stg. ~ etm., to investigate profoundly.

istikra $(\cdots \overset{\cdot}{-})$ Inductive reasoning.

istikrah $(\cdots \overset{\cdot}{\cdot})$ Aversion. ···**den** ~ etm., to loathe.

istikrar $(\cdots \overset{\cdot}{\cdot})$ A becoming established; stabilization; stability. ~ etm., to become fixed, established. ~**lı**, settled, established, stabilized. ~**sız**, unstable, unsettled; inconsistent.

istikraz $(\cdots \overset{\cdot}{\cdot})$ Loan. ~ etm., to borrow money.

istiksar $(\cdots \overset{\cdot}{-})$ etm. *va.* Deem excessive.

istikşaf $(\cdots \overset{\cdot}{\cdot})$ Reconnaissance. ~ etm., to reconnoitre; to endeavour to discover.

istilâ $(\cdots \overset{\cdot}{-})$ Invasion. ~ etm., to invade; to flood. ~**î** $(\cdots - \overset{\cdot}{-})$, invading.

istilâm $(\cdots - \overset{\cdot}{-})$ etm. *va.* Ask for information about.

istilyoz *v.* **istalyoz.**

istilzam $(\cdots \overset{\cdot}{-})$ etm. *va.* Render necessary; make inevitable; involve, entail.

istim Steam. ~**ini tutmak**, to have steam up; (*sl.*) to boil over with anger *etc.*; to be drunk. *v. also* **islim.**

istima $(\cdots \overset{\cdot}{-})$, –**aı** A hearing. ~ etm., to hear.

istimal $(\cdots \overset{\cdot}{\cdot})$, –**li** A making use of. ~ etm., to employ, make use of.

istiman $(\cdots - \overset{\cdot}{-})$ etm. *vn.* Ask for quarter, surrender.

istimar $(\cdots \overset{\cdot}{-})$ A making *a place* prosperous. ~ etm., to colonize.

istimbat *v.* **istinbat.**

istimbot, –tu Small steamboat.

istimdad $(\cdots \overset{\cdot}{\cdot})$ An asking for help. ~ etm., to ask for assistance.

istimhal $(\cdots \overset{\cdot}{-})$ etm. *vn.* Ask for delay; ask for a period of grace.

istimlâk $(\cdots \overset{\cdot}{\cdot})$, –**ki** Legal expropriation (against payment). ~ etm., to expropriate, to acquire property by force of law.

istimna $(\cdots \overset{\cdot}{-})$ Self-abuse, masturbation.

istimrar $(\cdots \overset{\cdot}{\cdot})$ Continuation. ~ etm., to proceed without interruption.

istizmac $(\cdots \overset{\cdot}{-})$ etm. *va.* Make polite inquiries of *s.o.*; ask about *s.o.*'s tastes and feelings; to inquire whether a person is *persona grata* (to another Government).

istinabe $(\cdots - \overset{\cdot}{\cdot})$ Appointment of a proxy; the taking, on commission, of the evidence of an absent witness. ~ **suretile**, by proxy.

istinad $(\cdots \overset{\cdot}{\cdot})$ A relying upon, a being supported. ···**e** ~ etm., to rely on, lean on, be supported by, be based on. ~**en** $(\cdots \overset{\cdot}{-} \cdot)$, ···**e** ~, based on, supported by. ~**gâh**, point of support.

istinaf $(\cdot - \overset{\cdot}{\cdot})$ Appeal *at law.* ~ etm., to appeal *against a legal decision* : ~ **mahkemesi**, court of appeal. ~**en** $(\cdot - \overset{\cdot}{-} \cdot)$, on appeal. ~**î** $(\cdot - - \overset{\cdot}{-})$, pertaining to an appeal.

istinare $(\cdots - \overset{\cdot}{-})$ etm. *vn.* Be enlightened.

istinas $(\cdot - \overset{\cdot}{\cdot})$ A being friendly *or* familiar; tameness; practice. ~ etm. *or* ~ **peyda** etm., to become familiar *or* tame; to have practise *in doing stg.*

istinbat $(\cdots \overset{\cdot}{\cdot})$, –**tı** A bringing a hidden matter to light. ~ etm., to deduce, infer.

istinga $(\cdot \overset{\cdot}{\cdot} \cdot)$ Brail; rope for closing a purse-seine net.

istinkâf $(\cdots \overset{\cdot}{\cdot})$ Rejection, refusal. ~ etm., to draw back, refuse, abstain.

istinsah $(\cdots \overset{\cdot}{-})$ etm. *va.* Make a copy of.

istintac $(\cdots \overset{\cdot}{-})$ etm. *va.* Conclude; infer.

istintak $(\cdots \overset{\cdot}{\cdot})$, –**kı** Interrogation; cross-examination. ~ etm., to interrogate. ~**name** $(\cdots \cdot \overset{\cdot}{-})$, official record of evidence taken by an examining magistrate from an accused person.

istirahat $(\cdots - \overset{\cdot}{\cdot})$, –**tı** Repose. ~ etm., to rest, to take one's ease.

istirdad $(\cdots \overset{\cdot}{\cdot})$ A retaking, recovery *of stg.* ~ etm., to retake, recover.

istirham $(\cdots \overset{\cdot}{\cdot})$ A begging for mercy; an asking a favour; petition. ~ etm., to beg, petition. ~**name** $(\cdots \cdot \overset{\cdot}{-})$, written petition.

istiridye $(\cdots \overset{\cdot}{\cdot} \cdot)$ Oyster.

istirkâb $(\cdots \overset{\cdot}{-})$ etmek *va.* Be jealous of; regard as a rival.

istisal $(\cdot - \overset{\cdot}{\cdot})$, –**li** Extirpation. ~ etm., to exterminate.

istisgar (··⌐) etm. va. Regard as insignificant; despise; underestimate.

istiska (··⌐) Dropsy.

istiskal (··⁴), **–li** A giving s.o. a cold reception. ~ etm., to show s.o. that he is not welcome; to be disagreeable.

istismar (··⌐) etm. va. Bring to fruition; exploit, profit by. ~cı, one who exploits something for his own ends.

istisna (··⌐) Exception. ~ etm., to except, exclude. ~î (··—⌐), exceptional.

istişare (··—ˡ) Consultation. ~ etm., to hold a consultation.

istişhad (··⌐) etm. va. Call to witness; give s.o. as a reference; cite as proof; to suffer martyrdom (esp. in fighting for Islam).

istişmam (··⌐) etm. va. Scent, smell out; get an inkling of; deduce from clues.

istitaat (··—⁴) Power; ability, capacity.

isti'taf (··⌐) etm. va. Beg as a favour.

istitale (··—ˡ) Elongation, projection.

istitrad (··⁴) Digression. ~en (··⌐·), by way of digression. ~î (··—⌐), digressive, parenthetical.

istiva (··⌐) A being equal or level. hattı ~, the Equator. ~î (··—⌐), equatorial.

istizah (··—⁴) An asking for an explanation; interpellation. ~ etm., to ask for an explanation, esp. to question a Minister.

istizan (··—⁴) An asking for permission. ~ etm., to beg for permission or authorization.

istofa (·ˡ·) Brocade.

istok, –ku Stock of goods.

istop, istoper Stop. ~ etm., to stop.

istor Roller blind. ~lu yazıhane, roll-top desk.

istralya (·ˡ·) Stay of a mast.

istromaça (··ˡ·) Twisted ropes used as a fender.

istrongilos (·ˡ··) Kind of sea-bream (Smaris vulgaris).

İsveç Sweden. ~li, Swedish.

İsviçre (·ˡ·) Switzerland. ~li, Swiss.

isyan (·⁴) Rebellion. ~ etm., to rebel. ~kâr, rebellious, refractory.

iş¹ Work; action; business; occupation, profession; affair, matter. ~imiz ~, all goes well (often ironically used to mean the opposite): ~ adamı, a business man; a businesslike man: ~im Allaha kaldı, I am done for (often jokingly): ~ten anlamak, to be an expert: sen ~ine bak!, mind your own business!: ~ başa gelmek (düşmek), for stg. to have to be done personally; ⌐~ başa gelince çaresiz katlanılır⌐, when one has to do a job oneself there's no getting out of it: ~ başında, at one's work: ~ başındakiler, those in authority: ~ başına

geçmek, to take the lead; to take control: ···in ~ini bitirmek, to finish s.o. off (kill): ~ çıkarmak, to raise unnecessary difficulties; ~i çıkarmak, to finish a job: ~ten değil or ~ deme değil, it's an easy matter, it's a mere nothing; also in such phrases as çıldırmak ~ten değil, it's enough to drive one mad: ⌐adama o kadar kızdım ki öldürmek ~ deme değil⌐, 'I was so angry with the man that I could have killed him': ···e ~i* düşmek, to be obliged to apply to s.o. for help, advice etc.; for one's business to take one to a certain place or person: ~ ~ten geçti, it's all over now, it's too late to do anything: ~ine göre, according to his work or skill; according to its workmanship or quality; 'it all depends!': ~ görmek, to work; to perform a service: ···e ~ göstermek, to give s.o. a job of work: ~ güç, v. işgüç: ~in içinde ~ var!, there's stg. behind all this!: ~ ~i olm., for things to go well with one, e.g. oraya tayin edilirse ~i ~tir, if he is appointed there, he is in luck's way: ~ ola or ~ olsun diye, used sarcastically of one who does stg. only for show or as eyewash; to do stg. unnecessarily or officiously or in order to appear busy: ~inden* olm., to lose one's job: ~im mi yok!, (as a refusal) 'not for me!'; 'I don't feel like it!': ~in mi yok, much as ~ im mi yok, but also 'what an idea!'; 'what an absurd suggestion!': ~im var, I am busy; bu adamla ~im var, I've a job with this man!; he wants a lot of looking after; he's a damned nuisance!: bunda bir ~ var!, there's stg. funny about this!: birinin başına ~ açmak (çıkarmak), to get s.o. into difficulty: bu ~ yürümez (sökmez), this sort of thing can't go on!

iş² A joyous life. v. işünüş.

işaa (·—ˡ) etm. va. Spread; publish; divulge.

iş'ar (·⁴) A making known. ~ı ahire değin, until further notice: ~ etm., to communicate, notify.

işar·et (·—ˡ), **–ti** Sign; signal; mark; punctuation mark. ~ çekmek, to hoist a signal: ~ etm., to make a sign; beckon; make a mark: ~ kolu (değneği), traffic indicator: ~ memuru, traffic policeman: ~ zamiri, demonstrative pronoun. ~leşmek, to make signs to one another, esp. in a furtive flirtation. ~î (·—⌐), conveyed by a signal, indicated: reyi ~ ile, vote by a show of hands.

işba (·⌐), **–aı** Saturation. ~ etm., to satiate, saturate.

iş·başi, –nı Head of a business; foreman; hour at which work begins; place of business. ~**bilir,** who knows his work; businesslike. ~**birliği, -ni,** co-operation. ~**bölümü, -nü,** division of labour.

işbu (¹·) This; the present (*year etc.*).

işçi Workman, labourer; workwoman. ~**lik,** occupation *or* pay of a workman.

işemek *vn.* Urinate, make water.

işgal (·⁴), **-li** A causing to be occupied; occupation. ~ *etm.,* to keep busy; engage the attention of; keep *s.o.* from his work; occupy (*mil.*).

işgüc (*Decline both words*) Occupation, employment. **bir adamın işi gücü,** a man's job, his daily work.

işgüzar Who does his work; efficient; officious. ~**lık,** officiousness.

işhad (·⁻¹) **etm.** *va.* Call to witness; cause to testify.

işit·ilmek *vn. pass. of* işitmek. be heard; be heard of by all. ~**ilmiş,** heard; hearsay.

işit·mek (işidiyorum *or* işitiyorum) *va. & vn.* Hear; listen. ⌐ağzından çıkanı kulağı işitmez¹, he speaks without weighing his words: **azar** (lâf) ~, to get a scolding. ~**memezlik** (*in dialect* işitmezlik), a not hearing: ~**ten gelmek,** to pretend not to hear, to feign deafness. ~**tirmek,** to cause to hear *or* be heard; announce; communicate.

işkâl (·⁻¹) **etm.** *va.* Hinder, make difficult.

işkampaviye (··¹··) Longboat, pinnace.

işkembe (·¹·) Paunch; tripe. ~**den** (*or* ~i kübradan) **atmak** (söylemek), to invent *a story etc.,* to exaggerate, to embroider *a tale*: ~ **çorbası hikâyesi,** one mustn't expect too much of an inferior article *or* man: ~**sini*** düşünmek, to think only of one's belly (*fig.* one's interests): ~**sini*** şişirmek, to eat greedily: ~ **suratlı,** pockmarked.

işkence Torture.

işkil Doubt, suspicion. ~**lenmek,** to be dubious; be anxious. ~**li,** suspicious, anxiously doubtful. ~**lik,** dubiousness; mistrust.

işkine *v.* eşkine.

işlek Working well and easily; good flowing *handwriting*; busy *thoroughfare*; experienced.

işleme Work, workmanship; handiwork; embroidery; carving; engraving.

işlemek *va. & vn.* Work; function; work up; manipulate; take effect; embroider; carve; engrave; be frequented; penetrate (*with dat.*); commit (crime); (of a road) to be open *or* much used; (of a ship *or* vehicle) to ply; (of a boil) to discharge; (of a dye) to penetrate. **canına*** (içine*) ~, to hurt

one's feelings, to affect one painfully: **kurşun işlemez,** bullet-proof.

işle·meli, embroidered, decorated with needlework. ~**nmek,** *pass. of* işlemek; be embroidered, worked up. ~**tme,** the working *of a railway, a mine etc.*; the running *of an hotel, a business etc.*: ~ **Bakanı,** Minister of Industry: ~ **dairesi,** the traffic department *of a railway*: ~ **malzemesi,** rolling-stock. ~**tmek,** *caus. of* işlemek; cause to work; work (a machine, railway, mine *etc.*). ~**yici,** penetrating.

işmar (·⁴) Sign; nod; wink.

işmizaz (·—¹) Grimace; look of disgust.

işporta (·¹·) Large basket. ~ **malı,** shoddy goods. ~**cı,** hawker, pedlar.

işrab (·⁴) Insinuation; imputation. ~ **etm.,** to insinuate.

işret, -ti Drinking, carousal; festival. ~ **etm.,** to drink (wine *etc.*), to make merry.

işsiz Without work, unemployed. ~**lik,** unemployment.

iştah, iştiha Appetite; desire; greed. ~ **açan,** appetizer, apéritif: ~ **açmak,** to whet the appetite: ~**ım yok,** I have no appetite. ~**lı,** having an appetite, hungry; desirous; too keen, officious. ~**sız,** without appetite; without desire.

işte Look!; here!; now; thus.

iştial (··⁴), **-li** A becoming kindled; a blazing up; conflagration. ~ **etm.,** to burst into flames.

iştibah (··⁴) Doubt. ~ **etm.,** to be doubtful. **bilâ** ~, without doubt.

iştidad (··⁴) A becoming severe *or* strong; aggravation. ~ **etm.,** to be aggravated, become heavier, more difficult.

iştigal (··⁴), **-li** An occupying oneself. ···**le** ~ **etm.,** to busy oneself with ... .

iştiha (··⁻¹) *v.* iştah.

iştihar (··⁴) A becoming famous; fame, notoriety. ~ **etm.** (bulmak), to become celebrated.

iştikâ (··⁻¹) A complaining. ~ **etm.,** to complain.

iştikak (··⁴), **-kı** Derivation; etymology. ···**den** ~ **etm.,** to be derived from ... .

iştira (··⁻¹) Purchase. ~ **etm.,** to buy.

iştirak (··⁴), **-ki** Participation. ···**e** ~ **etm.,** to share, participate in: ~ **üzere,** jointly, in participation.

iştiyak (··⁴), **-kı** Longing. ···**e** ~ **çekmek,** to long for.

işünüş (⁻··) Revel, carousal.

işve Coquetry, flirting. ~**baz,** ~**kâr,** coquettish, amorous.

it, -ti Dog. ⌐~e atsan yemez¹, a dog wouldn't eat it; very nasty: ⌐~e bulaşmaktansa çalıyı dolaşmak¹, to go out of one's way to avoid unpleasantness: ~

canlı, very tough and enduring: ⌐~ dişi domuz derisi⌐, (a dog's tooth and a pig's hide), it is pleasant to see one's enemies quarrel: ⌐~in duası kabul olunursa gökten ekmek yağar⌐, 'if wishes were horses then beggars would ride': ⌐~ ~e, ~ de kuyruğuna⌐, 'a dog asked another to do stg., the other dog asked his tail', everyone trying to get another to do the job: ⌐~ izi at izine karışmak⌐, a very involved matter: ~ nişanı, an excrescence on a horse's fetlock: ~oğlu ~, a scoundrel, foul brute: ~ sürüsü, a pack of scoundrels; a whole crowd (pej.).

ita (−·⁻) A giving or paying. ~ âmiri, the official authorized to sign an ~ emiri, an order for payment of government money: ~ etm., to give; to pay: ahzü ~, (taking and giving), commerce.

itaat (·−¹), −ti Obedience. ~ etm., to obey. ~lı, obedient. ~siz, disobedient.

itab (·⁴) Reproof, reprimand. ~ etm., to reprove, reproach.

it'ab (·⁻) etm. va. Fatigue, weary.

itboğan Meadow saffron, colchicum.

itburnu (¹··), −nu Hip of the wild rose.

itdirseği (¹···), −ni Stye.

iteklemek va. Treat roughly, manhandle.

itfa (·⁻) An extinguishing. ~ bedeli (akçesi), sinking fund : ~yı düyun, amortization : ~ etm., to extinguish (fire), pay off, redeem (debt). ~iye, fire-brigade: ~ neferi, fireman.

ithaf (·⁴) Presentation; dedication. ~ etm., to present stg. rare, to dedicate a poem etc. ~iye (·−¹), dedication (of a book).

ithal v. idhal.

itham (·⁴) Imputation; accusation. ~ etm., to suspect; to accuse. ~name (···−¹), indictment.

ithiyarı (¹···), −nı Colocynth.

itibar (−·⁴) Esteem; consideration; regard; credit; nominal value; hypothesis. ... ~ile, as regards ...: ~dan düşmek, to be discredited : ~ etm., to esteem, consider, deem: ~ görmek, to be respected; to be in demand : ~ mektubu, letter of credit: millî ~, national credit: ~ı olm., to be held in esteem: ~ı var, his credit is good: açık ~, overdraft: bu ~la, and therefore, and so: esas ~ile, essentially: nazarı ~a almak, to take into account.

itibar·en (−·⁻·), from, dating from. ~î (−·−⁻), theoretical; conventional; nominal. ~lı, esteemed, trusted. ~siz, discredited; not held in esteem.

itidal (−·⁴), −li Moderation; temperance; equilibrium; equanimity; equinox. ~ kesbetmek, to moderate (vn.). ~siz, immoderate, extreme.

itikad (−·⁴) Belief; creed. ···e ~ etm., to believe in. ~lı, believing. ~sız, unbelieving, irreligious.

itikâf (−·⁴) A going into religious seclusion for a day or two. ~a çekilmek, to go into seclusion or retirement.

itikâl (−·⁴), −li A being corroded.

itilâ (−·⁻) An ascending, a being elevated; progress to a higher standard; exaltation. ~ etm., (of a people etc.) to progress.

itilâf (−·⁴) Agreement; understanding, entente, friendship. ~ etm., to come to an agreement: Hürriyet ve ~ fırkası, the name of the party in opposition to the İttihad ve Tarakkı Cemiyeti in the years succeeding the Constitution of 1908. ~cı, a member of that party. ~giriz, uncompromising.

itimad (·−·⁴) Confidence; reliance. ···e ~ etm., to have confidence in, to rely on : ~ı nefis, self-reliance : ~ telkin etm., to inspire confidence. ~name (−···¹), letter giving credentials.

itina (−·⁻) Care; attention. ~ etm., to pay great attention, be very careful.

itiraf (−·⁴) Confession, admission. ~ etm., to confess, acknowledge, admit.

itiraz (−·⁴) Objection; (pl. ~at). ~ etm., to raise an objection, to demur.

itisaf (−·⁴) Injustice; oppression; persecution. ~ cinneti, persecution mania.

itişmek vn. Push one another; brawl; skylark. itişe kakışa, pushing and shoving one another.

itiyad (−·⁴) Habit. ~ etm., to accustom oneself to; to make a habit of: ~ üzere, habitually.

itizal (−·⁴), −li Schism. ~ etm., to secede.

itizar (−·⁴) etm. vn. Make excuses.

itlâf (·⁻) Destruction; waste. ~ etm., to destroy, waste.

itlik Quality of a dog; villainy, vileness.

itmam (·⁴) A completing, perfecting. ~ etm., to complete, finish.

itmek va. Push. itip kakmak, to push and shove, to elbow one's way.

itminan (·−⁴) Tranquillity of mind; confidence; a feeling certain.

ittırad (··⁴) Regularity; continuity; monotonous rhythm. ~sız, irregular, discontinuous.

ittiba (···⁻), −aı A following; a copying or obeying another. ~ etm., to follow, obey, copy. ~en (···⁻·), in conformity with.

ittifak (··⁻), −kı Harmony, concord; alliance; agreement; coincidence, chance. ~ı âra, unanimity: tedafüî (tecavüzî) ~, a defensive (offensive) alliance. ~sızlık, disagreement.

ittihad (··⁴) Union. İttihad ve Tarakkı Cemiyeti, the famous Party of Union and

Progress, *mainly in power after the Constitution of 1908.*

ittiham (··⁴) A being accused. ···le ~ etm., to be accused of ...; (*sometimes confused with* itham *which means 'an accusing'*).

ittihaz (··⁻) etm. *va.* Procure; take; adopt (a proposal *etc.*).

ittika (··⁻) Piety; fear of God. ~ etm., to fear God, to be devout.

ittikâ (··⁻) etm. *vn.* Lean *on stg.*

ittisa (··⁻), –aı Extension; a becoming ample *or* commodious. ~ etm., to become extensive *or* abundant.

ittisal, –li A being in contact; contiguity. ~ bulmak, to get in contact with; be joined.

itüzümü (¹···), –nü Black nightshade.

ityan (··⁻) etm. *va.* Bring forward; mention.

ityatağı (¹···), –nı Dog's bed; meeting-place of vagabonds; filthy spot.

ivaz An exchanging; thing given in exchange. bilâ ~ *or* ~sız, without anything being given in exchange; without expecting anything in return, disinterested.

ivdirmek *va.* Hasten.

ivgi Small hatchet.

ivicac (−·⁴) Crookedness.

ividi In a hurry.

ivik A kind of ski or snowshoe.

ivirmek *va.* Hasten.

iviz Gad-fly.

ivmek *vn.* Be in a hurry.

iyadet (·−¹), –ti Visit. ~ etm., to go and see, to visit (a sick man).

iye Possessor, owner.

iyi, eyi Good; well; in good health. The good; the good side of a thing. ~den ~ye, properly, thoroughly: ~ etm., to make well, to cure; to do well: ~siniz inşallah!, I hope you are well!: ~ kötü, mediocre; more or less: ~si mi, the best thing to do is ...; if I were you ...: en ~si, the best of it (*or* them) : ⌐kime rastgelsem ~ ?¹, 'guess whom I met!': pek ~ !, very good !, all right!: ⌐sizden ~ olmasın !¹, *said when praising a person to another, stg. like 'of course I don't like him as much as I do you', or 'present company excepted'.*

iyi·ce, eyi·ce (··¹), pretty well; rather good; (·¹·) thoroughly. ~leşmek, to improve, to get better; to recover from an illness. ~lik, goodness; kindness; good health; good part *or* side: ~ bilmek, to be grateful: ~ görmek, to experience kindness *or* favour: ⌐iyiliği yap, denize at, balık bilmezse Hâlik bilir¹, 'do good, throw it in the sea, if the fishes don't recognize the Creator will'; 'cast thy bread upon the waters, for thou shalt find it after many days'; a good action is never in vain. ||~mser, optimistic; eulogistic.

iyod Iodine. ~ür, iodide.

iz¹ Footprint; track; trace. ~i belirsiz olm., to disappear without leaving a trace: ~ini kaybetmek, to lose track of: ~ toz, the tracks of s.o.; ⌐ne ~i belli ne tozu¹, he disappeared without trace: ~ine uymak, to follow in the footsteps of: ⌐karda yürür de ~ini belli etmez¹, he is very cunning and cautious: tekerlek ~i, rut.

iz², –zzi Glory; power.

izaa (·−¹) Waste, loss. ~ etm., to waste.

izabe (·−¹) etm. *va.* Melt, fuse.

iz'ac etm. *va.* Vex, worry, disturb.

izafe (·−¹) An attributing, attaching. ~ etm., to attribute, attach; to join two words together. ~t, –ti, the joining of two words together by an i or ı. *e.g.* Babıâli, the Sublime Porte; izzetinefis, self-respect. ~ten (·⁻·), referring, attributing, *used in such phrases as:* Vali, Baş Vekile ~, seçimlerin Martta yapılacağını söyledi, the Vali said that, according to the Prime Minister, elections would take place in March: bu şehre kurucusu İskender adına ~ İskenderiye denilir, this town is named Alexandria after its founder Alexander.

izafî (·−⁻) Relative; extrinsic; nominal. ~ siklet, specific gravity. ~yet, –ti, relativity.

izah (−¹) Explanation; manifestation; elucidation. ~ etm., to manifest, explain, elucidate. ~en (−⁻·), in explanation, by way of elucidation. ~at, –tı, explanations: ~ vermek, to give a full explanation, give full details. ~name (−·−¹), manifesto.

izale (·−¹) A removing, a causing to disappear. ~ etm., to remove, to put an end to, to destroy: ~i bikir etm., to deflower.

izam¹, îzam (−⁴) An enlarging, exaggerating. ~ etm., to exaggerate.

izam² (−⁴) etm. *va.* Send.

izan, iz'an (·⁴) Quickness of understanding; consideration for others. ~lı, intelligent; considerate. ~sız, inconsiderate.

izaz (−⁴) etm. *va.* Honour, treat with respect; entertain, regale.

izbarço (·¹·) ~ bağı, bowline (knot).

izbe Hovel, hut; basement. Dark and dirty.

izbiro (·¹·) Sling *for lifting bulky goods.*

izci Tracker; boy-scout.

izdiham (··⁴) Crowd. seyrüsefer ~ı, congestion of traffic.

izdivac (··⁴) Mating; matrimony. ~ etm., to marry.

izdiyad (··⁴) Augmentation. ~ etm., to grow, increase.

izhar (·⁴) etm. *va.* Manifest, display.

izin, –zni Permission; leave; discharge. ~

vermek, to grant leave; give permission; dismiss. ~li, on leave; one who has inherited the gift of curing by charms or üfürük, *q.v.* ~name (··—¹), permit; licence; marriage licence. ~siz, without permission, unauthorized; 'kept in' (of school-children); school punishment of being 'kept in': ~ almak, to receive such punishment: ~ kalmak, to be 'kept in'.
izlâl (·⁻¹) etm. *va.* Lead astray, pervert.
izlemek *va.* Track, trace.

izli Leaving a trace. ~ mermi, tracer shell.
izmarit (··⁻¹), –ti Sea-bream (*Smaris alcedo*); cigarette stump.
izmavla (·¹·) Yellow raspberry.
izmihlâl (··⁴), –li Disappearance; annihilation.
izzet, –ti Might; glory, honour, dignity. ~inefis, self-respect; 'amour propre'. ~lemek, to treat with respect, honour. ~li, ~lû, honourable (*title formerly given to officers and officials of a certain rank*).

J

jaketatay (*Fr. jaquette à taille*) Morning coat.
jale (–¹) Dew.
jaluzi (*Fr. jalousie*) Venetian blind.
jant Rim.
Japon Japan; Japanese. ~ca, in Japanese. ~ya (·¹·), Japan.
jartiye Garter.

jenk Wrinkle.
jest, –ti (*Fr. geste*) Gesture.
jilet, –ti Safety-razor.
jurnal Report of a delator; diary. ~cı, denouncer, delator.
jüjkomiser (*Fr. juge-commissaire*) Official receiver in bankruptcy.
jüt, –tü Jute.

K

kâad *v.* kâğıd.
kaadir (–¹) Powerful; Almighty God; capable (of = *dat.*).
kaan Khan; ruler.
kaatı (–¹) Cutting; interrupting; deciding. Secant. ~a (–·¹), incisor tooth.
kaatibe (–·¹) The whole; all. ~i ahvalde, in all circumstances: ~i nas, everyone. ~ten (–¹··), not at all, in nowise.
kaatil (–¹) Murderer. ~lik, a being a murderer; murder.
kab Cover; envelope; vessel, receptacle; dish, portion (of food). ···e ~ geçirmek, to put a cover on; to bind (book): ~ kacak, pots and pans; ~ yok kacak yok, bare of the simplest necessities: bir ~a kotaramamak (*sometimes err.* kurtaramamak), to be unable to find a solution *to a problem etc.*: ~ına sığmamak, to be uncontrollably impatient *or* ambitious: üç ~ yemek, three portions of food.
kâb (–) Ankle; knuckle-bone; cube; dice. ···e ~ında olmamak, not to reach the standard of ... : ~ına varılmaz, unrivalled, peerless.
kaba¹ (·⁻¹) Clothing, *esp.* coat or cloak.
kaba² Large but light; puffed out; spongy; coarse; common, vulgar; rough (calculation, guess *etc.*). ~sını almak, to tidy up roughly, to get rid of the worst *of the dirt*

etc.; to trim roughly, to rough hew: ~ et› the buttocks: ~ döşek, a soft downy mattress: ~ kumpas, dead-reckoning (*naut.*): ~ saba, common, coarse: ~ sakal, a bushy beard: ~ toprak, freshly dug soil: ~ türkçe, simple Turkish *as opp. to the flowery written language of the last century.* ~ca (··¹), rather bigger *or* older; (·¹·) roughly, coarsely.
kabadayı (·¹··) Swashbuckler, bully; 'tough'; having 'guts'; the best of anything. ⌈bizim yediğimiz ne ki, en ~sı peynir ekmek⌉, 'what do we get to eat? At the most a bit of bread and cheese!: muflisin ~sı, one who spends money he can't afford, in order to show off.
kabahat, –ti Unseemly act; fault; offence. ~ etm. (işlemek), to commit an offence. ~li, guilty. ~siz, innocent.
kabail (·–¹) *pl.* of kabîle. Tribes.
kabak Pumpkin; marrow. Bald, bare; close-shaven (head); tasteless. ~ başına* patlamak, to suffer a disaster; kabağı başka yerde patlatmak, to cause trouble to break out elsewhere: ~ çekmek, to smoke hashish: ⌈~ çiçeği gibi açılmak⌉, (of a new-comer) to be too forward; suddenly to become too free-and-easy: ~ tadı vermek, to become a bore: karpuz ~ çıktı, the melon turned out to be tasteless.

kabakulak (·¹··) Mumps.

kabalak A kind of military hat, *worn by the Turkish Army in the First World War*.

kabalaşmak *vn.* Become coarse *or* vulgar.

kabalık Sponginess; bushiness; coarseness; vulgarity.

kabara (·¹·) Hob-nail; ornamental brass-headed nail.

kabarcık Bubble; pimple; pustule. kara~, carbuncle; anthrax.

kabare Cabaret.

kabarga Musk-deer.

kabarık Swollen; blistered; puffy; loose, *i.e.* not compressed nor compact. Blister; swelling. ~ deniz, high tide.

kabar·mak *vn.* Swell; be puffed out; become fluffy; blister; be raised; be increased; be puffed up, swell with importance; rise when boiling; (sea) become rough. içi* (midesi, safrası) ~, to become bilious, to feel sick: koltuğu* ~, to be puffed up with pride. ~tı, swelling; puffiness. ~tma, embossed (design); raised in relief. ~tmak, *caus. of* kabarmak: göğsünü ~, to puff out the chest with pride: kulak ~, to prick up one's ears: toprağı ~, to break up or loosen ground.

kaba·saba (·¹··) Coarse; rough; common. ~sakal, having a bushy beard. ~soğan, a 'rotter', a coward at heart. ~sorta, ~ donanımlı, square-rigged. ~taslak, roughly drawn; in outline without details. ~yel, south wind. ~yonca, lucerne.

kabayih *pl. of* kabiha. Disgraceful deeds.

Kâbe (−¹) The Kaaba, cubical temple at Mecca.

kabız¹ (−¹) Astringent.

kabız², −bzı A grasping with the hand; constipation. ~ olm., to be constipated: ~ olunmak, to be grasped or taken: kabzı mal, a receiving possession of income (*v. also* kabzımal). ~lık, constipation.

kabih Hideous; unseemly. ~a (·−¹), shameful deed.

Kabil (−¹) Cain.

Kâbil (−·) Kabul.

kabil¹ (−¹) Capable; possible. *As prefix with the izafet* = capable of ..., admitting ..., *e.g.* ~i istifade, by which one can profit, profitable; ~i tahammül, capable of being borne, tolerable. ~dir, it is possible, it may be: temyizi ~ olarak, with right to appeal (law).

kabil² (·−¹) Sort; category. ... ~inden, on the lines of, something like ...: bu ~den, of this sort.

kabile (−·¹) Midwife. ~lik, midwifery.

kabîle (·−¹) Tribe.

kabiliyet (−··¹), −ti Capability; possibility. ~li, intelligent; skilful. ~siz, incapable, unintelligent.

kabine (·¹·) Cabinet; small room; office; water-closet.

kabir, −bri Grave; tomb. ~ suali, endless questioning.

kabl- *prefix*. Before ... (*accent always on the* kabl). ~elmilâd, before Christ (B.C.). ~elvuku (¹··−), before the event: bir hissi ~, a premonition. ~eşşüru (¹··−), before beginning. ~ettarih (¹·−), prehistoric. ~ettufan (¹·−−), before the Flood; antidiluvian. ~ezzeval, before noon.

kablî (·¹) A priori.

kablo (¹·) Telegraphic cable.

kabotaj (*Fr. cabotage*) Coasting trade.

kabran Slack; without energy. Trunk (of a tree).

kabri *v.* kabir. ~stan, cemetery.

kabuk The outer covering *of anything*; bark, rind, peel, skin, shell, crust. ~ bağlamak, to form a skin *or* crust. ~lanmak, to form a skin *etc.* ~lu, having a shell, skin *etc.*

kabul, −lü Acceptance; reception; consent. ~ümdür, I accept: ~ etm., to accept, receive, consent, admit: ~ etmem, I won't accept that; I don't agree; I will not consent: ne desen ~ümüz, I'll do whatever you say: kaydü ~, admittance or entry *to a school*. ~lenmek, to seize for oneself, appropriate.

kaburga (·¹·) The ribs; a rib; frame of a ship.

kâbus (−¹) Nightmare.

kabza Handle; hilt.

kabzetmek (¹··), −eder *va.* Grasp; take.

kabzı *v.* kabız. ~mal, middleman (*esp. in fruit and vegetables*).

kaç How many?; how much? ~a?, what is the price?: ~a ~sınız?, what's the score?, how does the game stand?: ~ın kur'ası, one who 'knows a thing or two', an old hand: ayın ~ında?, on what day of the month?: bir ~, a few, some: her ~a, at whatever price: saat ~?, what is the time?

kaçaburuk Bradawl; shoemaker's awl.

kaçak Fugitive; deserter; contraband; leakage (*elect.*). Smuggled. ~ inşaat, unlicensed building: muayene kaçağı, that has escaped inspection; who has escaped medical inspection. ~çı, smuggler. ~çılık, smuggling. ~lık, desertion (*mil.*).

kaçamak Flight; evasion; subterfuge; refuge; shelter; a kind of hasty pudding of maize flour. ~ yolu, an excuse *or* subterfuge for getting out of doing stg. ~lı, evasive.

kaçan¹ When; at the time that … .

kaçan² Running away. kulağa ∼, earwig.

Kaçar¹ Kajar. ∼ hanedanı, the Kajar dynasty of Persia.

kaçar² Fugitive.

kaçar³ How many each? ∼a?, for how much each? : bu evler ∼ kattır?, how many stories has each of these houses?

kaçarula (·.¹.) Casserole.

kaçgöç *The Moslem practice of women covering their faces in the presence of men.*

kaçık Crazy; receding. Ladder *in a stocking.* sağa ∼, leaning to the right.

kaçıncı Of what number (*in a series*)? ∼ katta?, on what floor?

kaçınmak *vn.* Abstain; be reluctant. ···den ∼, to avoid, keep away from.

kaçırmak *va.* Make *or* let escape; drive away; smuggle; kidnap, elope with; hide *possessions etc. from the tax-gatherer etc.;* miss (train *etc.*); lose (an opportunity); let slip (a remark). *vn.* Go off one's head. ağzından* ∼, inadvertently to let out stg. that one did not want to: aklını* ∼, to go off one's head: altına (yatağına) ∼, (of a child) to mess its clothes (bed): fazla ∼, to have a drop too much; to let (pour) out more than one intends: ⌐gümrükten mal kaçırır gibi¬, (as though one were smuggling goods), in great hurry and confusion: kelepir ∼, to miss a golden opportunity: rahatını* ∼, to disturb the peace of, to be a source of worry to …: tadını ∼, to spoil the taste of stg.; to be very tiresome about stg.; to spoil the pleasure *of a party etc.*

kaçırmaz Tight; that cannot slip.

kaçışmak *vn.* Disperse; flee in confusion.

kaçkın Fugitive; deserter; crazy. dayak ∼ı, one who deserves a beating: medrese ∼ı, fanatic; reactionary: mekteb ∼ı, ignorant and uneducated: tımarhane ∼ı, almost a lunatic.

kaçlı Having how many? ∼sınız?, what is your year of birth (*i.e.* to which class do you belong for the military call-up?): elindeki kâğıd ∼?, what is the value of the card you hold?

kaçlık Worth how many pounds?; at which price?

kaçmak *vn.* Flee, run away; escape; desert; (of a woman) to veil herself before men; seem (rude, inopportune *etc.*); (of a stocking) to ladder. ···den ∼, to avoid: ···e ∼, to slip into: ağzından* ∼, (of a word) to slip out inadvertently: gözüme toz kaçtı, dust got into my eye: işten ∼, to avoid work: keyfi* ∼, to become dispirited or gloomy: geç oldu; ben artık kaçayım!', 'it's late, I must be going': gösterişe (lükse) ∼, to be prone to, given to ostenta-

tion (luxury): bu söz tatsız kaçtı, that remark sounded rather out of taste: tuz bir az fazla kaçtı, there was a bit too much salt. .

kaçsız *Only in* ∼ göçsüz, not respecting the rule about women veiling in the presence of men.

kad, –ddi Form, figure. ∼dükamet, stature.

kadana¹ (·¹·) Fetters *of a prisoner.*

kadana² (·¹·) Heavy horse; artillery horse; huge woman.

kadar Quantity, amount; degree. As much as; as big as; about. ···e ∼, as much as; until; up to; as far as. ⌐al benden de o ∼¬, I agree; 'same here!': anladığım ∼, as far as I understand: bu ∼, so much; to this amount *or* number: bunun ∼ büyük, as big as this: ⌐bu ∼ olur¬ *or* ⌐bu ∼ı da fazla¬, 'this is a bit too much of a good thing!': gelinceye ∼, until he comes: ne ∼, how much?; however much: o ∼, so; so much; sekiz ∼, about eight; sekize ∼, up to eight: sizin ∼ zengin değilim, I am not as rich as you: şu ∼ ki, only, but: yaşadığım ∼, as long as I live.

kadarcık A small amount. bu ∼ şeyi bilmeli idiniz!, you ought to know better!

kadastro (·¹·) Land survey.

kadavra (·¹·) Corpse; carcass.

kadayıf *Name of various kinds of sweet pastry.*

kaddükamet (···¹), –ti Stature.

kadeh Glass; cup; wine-glass.

kadem Foot; foot (measure); pace; good luck. ···e ∼ basmak, to set foot in, enter: ∼ getirmek *or* ∼i yaramak, to bring good luck: sırra ∼ basmak, to disappear. ∼e, step; stair; rung *of a ladder*: ∼ ∼ *or* ∼ nizamı, en échelon. ∼eli, en échelon. ∼hane (···¹), latrine. ∼li, lucky, auspicious: uğurlu ∼ olsun!, good luck to you! ∼siz, unlucky, inauspicious.

kader Destiny, fate; providence; worth; dignity; power. ∼i ilâhî, Divine providence: ∼ini küs!, it's a bit of bad luck!; you're not to blame!: ∼de varmış, it was inevitable; it was fated thus: hükmü ∼, the decrees of fate. ∼iye, fatalism. ∼iyeci, fatalist.

kadı Cadi; Moslem judge. ⌐bu kadar kusur ∼ kızında da bulunur¬, that's a very trifling fault.

kadın Lady; woman; matron. aşçı ∼, woman cook: bir yere ∼ atmak, to bring a woman to a place for immoral purposes. ∼budu (·¹··), –nu, meat and rice rissoles fried in egg batter. ∼cık, *only in* kadın ∼, quiet, domestically minded woman. ∼cıl, one who runs after women. ∼göbeği (·¹···), –ni, sweet dish made with semolina and eggs. ~**lık**, quality of a lady; ladylike behaviour. ~**tuzluğu** (·¹···), **–nu**, barberry.

kadırga (·¹·) Galley; ancient warship. ~**balığı**, **–nı**, cachalot.

kadib Twig; rod; penis.

kadid Skeleton; skin and bone. ~**i çıkmak**, to be all skin and bones: **kuru** ~, a mere skeleton.

kadife Velvet.

kadih (·⅟) Reproach; slander.

kadim (·⅟) Old; ancient; eternal (in the past). The olden time; bygone days. **kârı** ~, old style. ~**en**, in olden times; from the beginning of time.

kadinne (·¹·) (*For* kadın nine) grandmother; old woman.

kadir[1] (–¹) *v.* kaadir.

kadir[2], **–dri** Worth; personal value; rank, dignity. ···**in kadrini bilmek**, to know the value of, to appreciate : ~ **gecesi**, the Night of Power (the 27th of Ramazan, *when the Koran was revealed*) : **anası** ~ **gecesi doğurmuş**, very lucky. ~**naşinas** (···–¹), who does not appreciate the value of *stg. or s.o.* ~**şinas**, who appreciates value or merit; appreciative.

kadir (·⅟) All-powerful (of God only).

kadran (*Fr. cadran*) Face, dial (of a clock *etc.*).

kadril Quadrille.

kadro (¹·) (*Fr. cadre*) Staff; roll; establishment; framework. ~**da dahil**, on the permanent staff : ~ **harici**, not employed, on half-pay, 'en disponibilité'.

kadron (? *Fr. quart de rond*) Quartered timber.

kaf The Arabic letter 'kaf'; *name of a fabulous mountain.* ~**tan** ~**a**, from one end of the world to the other. *v. also* Kafdağı.

kafa Head; back of the head, nape; intelligence. (*In many idioms* kafa *and* baş *are interchangeable*). ~**sı* almamak**, not to understand; to be unable to take *stg.* in : ~**sından* ayrılmamak**, to follow *s.o.* wherever he goes : ~**sı* boş**, empty-headed, stupid : ~**yı çekmek**, to drink heavily : ~**m durdu**, my mind won't work, I am too tired : ~ **kâğıdı**, identity card : ~**sına* koymak**, to make up one's mind, to decide *to do stg.* : ~ **sallamak**, to flatter : ~**sına* söz girmez**, he is stupid *or* obstinate : ~**sı* taşa çarpmak**, to suffer for one's mistake : ~**sını* taştan taşa çarpmak**, to repent bitterly : ~ **tutmak**, to be obstinate *or* defiant : ···**e karşı** ~ **tutmak**, to resist obstinately : ~ **yormak**, to ponder, to think hard : ~ **yorucu**, head-splitting : **bu** ~**da adamlar**, these kind of people : **bu** ~**yı bırak !**, you must give up these sorts of ideas : **her** ~**dan**

bir ses, everyone expressing a different opinion.

kafa·dar, intimate friend; intimate; likeminded. ~**lı**, having *a certain* head; intelligent : **boş** ~, stupid : **eski** ~, oldfashioned; narrow-minded. ~**sız**, stupid. ~**tası** (·¹··), **–nı**, skull.

Kafdağı, **–nı** *A fabulous mountain inhabited by djinns (often used to express enormous difference, great obstacle)*; Caucasus. ~**na kadar**, to the end of the world : **burnu** ~**nda**, very conceited.

kafes Cage; lattice; grating; framework of a wooden house; (*sl.*) prison. ~ **gibi**, a mere skeleton : ~**e girmek**, to be duped : ~**e koymak**, to deceive, to take in : ~**te oturmak**, to live in solitude : ~ **tamiri**, extensive repairs to a building : **tel** ~, wire netting. ~**lemek** (*sl.*), to cheat; to get by cheating.

kâffe The whole; all; everyone. ~**ten** (¹··), wholly, entirely.

kâfi (–⅟) Sufficient, enough.

kâfil (–¹) Who guarantees *or* undertakes.

kafile (––¹) Caravan; convoy; gang.

kâfir (–¹) Misbeliever; non-Moslem; who denies. ~**i nimet**, ungrateful : **vay** ~ !, *an exclamation of surprised admiration,* 'oh!, well done!' ~**lik**, disbelief, irreligion; cruelty. **Kafiristan**, country of the infidels; Europe.

kafiye (––¹) Rhyme. ~**ci**, composer of rhymed verse. ~**li**, rhyming.

Kafkasya (·¹·) Caucasus; a dark variety of walnut wood. ~**lı**, Caucasian.

kaftan Robe of honour; robe. **biçilmiş** ~, well-suited, appropriate; 'cut out for'. ~**böceği**, **–ni**, ladybird.

kâfur (–¹) Camphor; anything very white. ~**î** (–·⅟), ~**lu**, pertaining to camphor, camphorated. ~**u**, spirits of camphor.

kağan Khan; ruler. ~**lık**, khanate.

kâğıd Paper; letter; playing-card; (*sl.*) pound note. Of paper. ~ **balığı**, Deal-fish (*Trachypterus*) : ~ **hamuru**, cellulose : ~ **helvası**, a kind of pastry in thin layers : ~ **sepeti**, waste-paper basket : ~ **üzerinde**, on paper only, theoretical. ~**cı**, stationer.

kağış, **kağıştı** Clashing, clanking noise.

kâğıthane (···–¹) Paper-mill; *the valley of the Sweet Waters of Europe, at the top of the Golden Horn.*

kâğir (–¹) Built of brick or stone (house).

kağnı Two-wheeled ox-cart.

kağşa·k Dry and crackling; about to collapse. ~**mak**, to crack with dryness; become old and wizened; be about to collapse.

kâh, **gâh** (–) A time; moment; place. At

one time; sometimes. ~ ... ~ ..., at one time ... and at another ... .

kahhar Overpowering; irresistible; all-powerful (God).

kahır, -hrı An overpowering; subjugation; anxiety, distress. ···in kahrını çekmek, to suffer anxiety or trouble on account of ...: ˹~ yüzünden lûtuf˺, good fortune arising from misfortune: kahrından* ölmek, to die of a broken heart. ~lanmak, to be grieved or distressed.

kâhi¹ (−¹) At times. ~ce, occasionally.

kâhi² A kind of three-cornered pastry puff.

kâhil (−¹) Adult; mature.

kâhin (−¹) Soothsayer; seer; oracle. ~lik, profession or quality of a soothsayer.

kahir (−¹) Overpowering; dominant; irresistible.

Kahire (−·¹) Cairo.

kahkaha Loud laughter. ~ atmak, to burst out laughing: ~ çiçeği, convolvulus: ~ ile gülmek, to roar with laughter.

kahkarî (···−¹) In precipitate retreat. ~ bir hezimet, utter rout.

kahpe Prostitute. Perfidious, deceitful. ~lik, prostitution; dirty trick; perfidious behaviour. ~oğlu, -nu, 'son of a bitch'; low-down treacherous fellow.

kahraman Hero; gallant fellow; hero (of a book etc.). ~lık, heroism.

kahren (¹·) By force, violently.

kahr·etmek (¹··), **-eder** va. Overpower, subdue. vn. Be distressed; fret. ···i Allah kahretsin !, may God curse ... . ~1, v. kahır. ~olsun, damn him !

kaht, -tı Drought; scarcity; famine. ~ü galâ, dearth and famine: ~ı rical, a dearth of able men. ~zede, famine-stricken.

kâhtane (·−¹) Paper-mill.

kahvaltı A light meal with coffee; breakfast. ikindi ~sı, light refreshment in the afternoon.

kahve Coffee; café. çekilmiş ~, ground coffee: kuru (çekirdek) ~, coffee beans: sade ~, black coffee without sugar: ~ ocağı, room where coffee is made: ~ parası, tip, pourboire: ˹buyurun da bir acı ~ içelim !˺, 'come and have a little drink in my house !': mahalle ~sine dönmek, to become disorderly and slack. ~ci, keeper of a coffee-shop or café; coffee-maker in a large establishment. ~hane (···−¹), coffee-shop; café. ~rengi, -ni, coffee-colour; brown.

kâhya Steward; major-domo; bailiff; warden of a trade-guild. ~ kadın, housekeeper: ~ kesilmek, to set oneself up as the adviser of others; to interfere in other people's affairs: ˹~sı yok˺, he can do as he likes: hazine ~sı, Keeper of the Privy

Purse: ˹keyfimin ~sı mısın?˺, what right have you to interfere in my affairs ? ~lık, office of a kâhya: ···e ~ etm., to meddle with the affairs of ... .

kaır, -a'rı Bottom of the sea etc.; profundity.

kaide (−·¹) Base; pedestal; rule, principle, custom. ~ten (−¹··), according to rule; in principle.

kail (−¹) Saying; consenting, agreeing. Speaker. ~ etm., to persuade: ···e ~ olm., to consent or agree to.

kaim (−¹) Standing; lasting; taking the place of; perpendicular; rectangular. ···le ~ olm., to exist thanks to ..., to be dependent on ...: ···in yerine ~ olm., to act for, take the place of ...: ~ zaviye, right angle. ~e (−·¹), bank-note; bill; account; right angle. ~en (⌐·¹), standing; perpendicularly.

kak Dried up; crackling. Dried fruit.

kaka (Childish language) 'gaga'; excrement. tü ~ olm., to be discredited.

kakac¹ Dried buffalo meat.

kakac² Beak. ~ına, snipe.

kakan pres. part. of kakmak.

kakao (·¹·) Cocoa.

kakavan Tiresome, peevish and old (gen. of a woman); stupid.

kakıç Fisherman's gaff.

kakılı Nailed; driven in. olduğu yerde ~ kaldı, he was rooted to the spot.

kakım Ermine, stoat.

kakımak va. Rail at, reproach.

kakır Dry and crackling. Noise of a dry crackling thing.

kakırca (·¹·) Dormouse (?).

kakır·dak Making a crackling noise. Skin of suet and sheep's fat after melting down the fat. ~damak, to rattle, rustle, crackle, make a harsh sound; become dry and hard; be without life and spirit; die. ~datmak, caus. of kakırdamak; (sl.) to kill. ~tı, crackling noise made by dry things.

kakışmak vn. Push one another about.

kakma Worked in relief; repoussé. Repoussé work. ~lı, with a decoration in relief; inlaid; encrusted with jewels etc.

kakmak va. Push; prod; tap; nail; strike metal to raise relief on the other side; inlay; encrust with jewels etc.; embroider with a raised pattern of gold or silver or mother-of-pearl. başa ~, to remind s.o. of a former kindness, twit with, taunt.

kaknem (sl.) Very ugly.

kakule (·−¹) Cardamon.

kakûle Stretcher slung between two camels.

kâkül Lock of hair, esp. a side-lock. ~lü, having pendent locks: ~ belâ, a damned nuisance.

kal¹, -i Speech; talk. ~e almak, to take into consideration: ~e gelmek, to come under discussion.

kal² Operation of refining metal.

kala Gerund of kalmak. In such phrases as: saat dokuza beş ~, five minutes to nine: üç gün ~, three days wanting to ...: ~ ~ ... kaldı, there only remains ...; all that is left is ... .

kalabalık Crowd; throng; confused mass; a mass of furniture or belongings. Crowded; bustling; thronged. ~ etm., to be in the way: kalabalığı kaldırmak, to tidy up: ağız kalabalığı, a torrent of words; ağız kalabalığına getirmek, to bewilder by many words: başı ~, who has to deal with a lot of people: kuru ~, unnecessary presence, a being present and doing nothing.

kalafat, -tı Caulking; spurious decoration to hide repairs; trick. ~çı, caulker. ~lamak, to caulk; paint; hide defects by superficial repair or paint.

kalak Nostril (of an animal).

kalakalmak (·¹··) vn. Stand petrified with fear or amazement.

kalamar Large squid, cuttle-fish.

kalamış Reed-bed.

kalantor One having the appearance of a well-to-do and important man.

kalas Beam; rafter; plank.

kalavra (·¹·) Rough leather shoe; patched shoe; old leather goods.

kalay Tin; tinsel; scolding. ~ atmak (vermek), to give a good scolding: ~ basmak, to abuse: ⌐altı alay üstü ~¬, with smart outer clothes (for ostentation, though underneath may be shabby clothes). ~cı, tinsmith; fraud (man), impostor. ~lamak, to tin; adorn superficially, cover with sham decoration; abuse. ~lı, tinned; tinsel; sham. ~sız, untinned; without sham decoration.

kalb Heart; core; kernel. ~ ~e karşıdır, friendship is mutual. ~en (¹·), from the heart, sincerely. ~gâh (·⌐), heart (fig.); centre. ~î (·⌐), cardiac; cordial. ~lı, -hearted; having a weak heart.

kalbetmek (¹··), -eder va. Transform; transpose; convert.

kalbur Sieve, riddle, screen. ~a dönmek, to be riddled: ~dan geçirmek, to sieve: ~la su taşımak, to make futile efforts: ~ üstü, 'the cream', the choicest or most distinguished: ⌐evvel zaman içinde ~ saman içinde, deve tellal iken¬ etc., formula for the beginning of a story (cf. 'once upon a time'). ~lamak va., to sieve, sift.

kalça, kalçça Hip.

kalçete (·¹·) Gasket (naut.).

kalçın Long felt hose reaching to the hip; felt boot worn inside jack boots.

kaldırım Pavement; causeway. ~ mühendisi, loafer, ne'er-do-well: ~ taşı, paving-stone: ~ yaması (kargası), loose woman. ~cı, paviour; loafer. ~cılık, picking the pockets of s.o. whose attention is distracted by an accomplice. ~lı, paved. ~sız, unpaved.

kaldırmak va. [Note: kaldırmak is one of the few exceptions in the Turkish language; it is the causative of kalkmak, not of kalmak, and therefore bears exactly the opposite meaning to that which it would appear to bear.] Raise, erect; lift; carry; remove; abolish, abrogate; tolerate; let start or sail; cause to get up; cause to recover from an illness. atı dört nala ~, to put one's horse into a gallop: ayağa ~, to cause a commotion: baş ~, to rise in rebellion: dansa ~, to invite to dance: derse ~, (of a teacher) to hear a pupil his lesson: ⌐beni erken kaldır!¬, 'call me early!': lâkırdı (söz) kaldırmamak, to be easily offended, to be unable to stand criticism: masraf ~, to bear an expense: ortadan ~, to do away with: bir malı piyasadan ~, to corner goods: tabanı ~, to take to one's heels: vergi ~, to be capable of paying so much tax: birinin vücudünü ~, to do away with s.o.

kaldırtmak va. caus. of kaldırmak.

kale¹ (-¹) v. kal¹.

kale² Fortress; castle; wall round a fortress; goal (in football etc.). ~ gibi, as firm as a castle: çift ~ oynamak, to play a proper game of football (as opp. to tek ~, using only one goal for practice). ~bent, confined in a fortress. ~ci, goalkeeper.

kalem Reed; pen; paint-brush; cutting of a plant; fine chisel, turning tool; office; style; item or entry in an account; category; vaccination tube. ~e almak, to write, to draw up, edit: ~ aşısı, graft: (üstüne) ~ çekmek, to draw the pen through, cancel: ~ efendisi, (formerly) clerk in a government office: ~e gelmez, indescribable; unreasonable: ~inden·kan damlıyor, his style is brilliant: ~ kömürü, high quality charcoal: ~ kulaklı, having small upright ears (horse): ~i mahsus, the private secretariat of a Minister: ~ oynatmak, to write; to correct; to spoil by altering: bir ~de, at one effort; instantly: eli ~ tutar, capable of expressing himself in writing: erbabı ~, literary people: taş ~, slate pencil: taşçı ~i, mason's chisel: üç ~ eşya, three items.

kalembek A yellow scented wood (aloeswood); a kind of maize.

kalem·dan Pen-case. ~en (·¹·), in writing. ~î (··⌐), shaped like a reed or pen; pertaining to writing. ~iye, office fees. ~kâr (··⌐), a painter of designs on muslin etc.;

an engraver on gold or silver. ~**kârî** (···–¹),
painted or engraved by hand. ~**lik**,
lathe tool-post. ~**traş**, penknife; pencil-
sharpener. ~**ucu** (·¹··), –**nu**, nib; steel
pen.

kalender A wandering mendicant; dervish
who has renounced the world; unconventional person. ~ **hane** (**yurdu**), a hospice
for wandering dervishes. ~**ane** (···–¹),
unconventional; unconcerned; free-and-
easy. ~**lik**, unconventionality; free-and-
easiness; a bohemian existence: **işi kalen-
derliğe vurmak,** to take things philoso-
phically.

kalensöve Peaked headgear; (*bot.*) hood,
calyptra.

kaleska (·¹·) Small open carriage.

kaleta (·¹·) A kind of biscuit.

kaletmek (¹··), –**eder** *va.* Refine *metals.*

kal'etmek (¹··), –**eder** *va.* Eradicate; extirpate.

kalevî (···–¹) Alkali; alkaline.

kalfa (¹·) Usher (of school); master builder;
qualified workman; head clerk. ~ **kadın,**
elderly domestic servant: ˹**boş gezenin boş
~sı**˺, lazy and out-of-work.

kalga Heir apparent of the ancient Khans
of the Crimea.

kalgımak *v.* **kalkımak.**

kalhane (·–¹) Metal refinery.

kalıb Mould; form; die; model; shoe-tree.
~**ının adamı olmamak,** not to come up to
appearances: ~**ını basmak,** to be certain
about, to guarantee: ~**ı dinlendirmek,** (*sl.*)
to die: ~**dan** ~**a girmek,** to keep changing
one's profession *or* one's ideas: ~ **kesilmek,**
to be petrified: ~**ı kıyafeti yerinde,** well set
up and well-dressed: **bir** ~ **sabun,** a cake
of soap: ~ **gibi yatmak,** to lie in bed *or*
elsewhere from laziness. ~**lamak,** to make
in a mould; block (a hat *etc.*).

kalık Defective; wanting. Omission; defect.

kalım *In* **ölüm** ~, life-and-death.

kalın¹ Thick; stout; coarse; dense. ~ **barsak,** the large intestine: ~ **kafa**(**lı**), thick-
headed: ~ **ses,** deep voice. ~**lık,** thickness; coarseness; stupidity.

kalın² A present or settlement given by
bride to bridegroom.

kalınmak *vn. impers. of* **kalmak**; **burada
kalınır mı?,** can one stay here?

‖**kalıntı** Remnant, remainder.

kalibre (*Fr. calibre*) Jig (*mech.*).

kaliçe (·–¹) Small carpet.

Kalikut Calcutta; calico.

kalil (·–¹) Small in quantity; few; short
(time).

kalinis Sandpiper.

kalinos A kind of bass (?).

kalite (*Fr. qualité*) Quality. ~**si bozuk,**
good-for-nothing, degenerate.

kalkan Shield. ~ **balığı,** turbot; ~ **otu,**
coltsfoot (?).

kalkık Raised; tilted, upturned (nose).

kalkımak *vn.* Give a slight jump, start;
prance, run.

kalkınma Recovery *of a nation etc.*; progress.

kalkınmak *vn.* Pick up *after an illness*; (of
a nation *etc.*) to make a material recovery.

kalkış Departure.

kalkışmak *vn.* Attempt *stg.* beyond one's
powers; pretend to be able to do *stg.*

kalkıtmak *va.* Cause to jump *or* start;
cause to prance.

kalkmak *vn.* Rise; get up; start *to do stg.*;
take it into one's head *to do stg.*; set out *on
a journey*; (steamer) sail; be annulled or
cancelled; be removed, be done away with;
stand up; rise in rebellion. **kalkıp kalkıp
oturmak,** to show one's anger by one's
movements: **kalk gidelim etm.** (*sl.*), to
pinch stg.; **âdet** ~, of a custom to fall into
disuse; **bir şeyin altından** ~, to get out of
a difficulty etc.: **yüreği*** ~, to feel sick.

kallâvi Ceremonial turban *formerly worn
by Ministers*; large coffee-cup. Huge;
weighty.

kalle A stew of meat and quinces; flour
soup.

kallem *v.* **allem.**

kalleş Untrustworthy; mean, caddish
fellow who lets one down. ~**lik,** a dirty
trick.

kalma Act of remaining; passing the night
at a place. Remaining (from); dating
(from). **babadan** ~, inherited.

kalmak, –**ır** *vn.* Remain; be left; be left
over; survive; halt; cease; be abandoned;
be postponed; stay the night; (of the wind)
to drop. [*Used as an auxiliary verb it implies the continuation of an action, e.g.* **bakakalmak,** to keep on looking]. ···**den** ~, to
be prevented from *doing stg.*: **kala kala,**
there only remains; all that is left; **kala
kala bir çocuğu kaldı,** only one child remained to him: **kala** ~, suddenly to find
oneself in a difficult position; to be disconcerted; to find oneself left in the lurch:
kaldı ki, there remains the fact that …;
there only remains to say …; and more-
over: **kalsın !,** leave it !; it doesn't matter !:
açıkta ~, to be left without employment;
to be destitute: **ağzı*** **açık** ~, to be left
gaping: **altı aya kalmaz sulh olur,** in less
than six months there will be peace: **az
kaldı,** nearly, all but: **babadan** ~, to be
inherited: **bana kalırsa** (**kalsa**), if it were
left to me, in my opinion: **bildiğinden kal-**

mamak, to go one's own way: demesine
(sormasına *etc.*) kalmadan, before he could
say (ask *etc.*): artık iş bir otomobile kaldı,
all that is needed now is a car: işinden* ~,
to be kept from one's work: bu kadarla
kalsa iyi, it would not have mattered if he
had gone no further *or* if that had been all:
nerede kaldı!, well, what about it!: nerede
kaldı ki, how much less ...; let alone the
fact that ...: uykuya ~, to fall asleep:
üstünde* ~, (of a lot at an auction) to fall
to one's bid: ⌐aman üstümde kalmasın,
size selâm söylediler⌐, *formula for conveying
s.o.'s greetings to another*, 'before I forget,
they send you their greetings': ···den kalır
yeri yok, he (it) is not much better than ... .
kalmar *v.* kalamar.
kalmaz *v.* kalmak; ⌐aman demeye ~⌐,
before I (he *etc.*) could say a word ... .
kaloma (·¹·) Slack (of a rope or anchor
chain). ~ etm., to pay out (rope).
kalorifer Stove; central heating.
kaloş Galosh.
kalp¹ *v.* kalb.
kalp² False; spurious; adulterated; blustering; insincere, untrustworthy.
kalpak *Headgear shaped like a fez but made
of fur or astrakhan.*
kalpazan False-coiner, counterfeiter; liar;
cheat. ~lık, manufacture of false coins;
lying, cheating.
kalsiyum Calcium.
kaltaban Pander; cuckold; charlatan.
kaltak Saddle-tree; saddle; whore. ~kaşı
(·¹··), -nı, the raised part in front and
behind of an eastern saddle. ~lık, dirty
trick, mean behaviour (*only of a woman*).
kalûbelâ (−··¹) *In* ~dan beri, from time
immemorial.
kalya¹ (¹··) Potash.
kalya² (¹··) Vegetable stew.
kalyon Galleon. ~cu, sailor; (*sl.*) old sea-
dog.
kam Cam.
kâm (−) Desire, wish. ···den ~ almak, to
enjoy *stg.*
kama Wedge; dagger; breech-block *of a
gun*; key (*mech.*); mark *made by the winner
on the loser's face in certain games*. ~ basmak, to win a game: ~ ~ya gelmek, to
come to blows with knives. ~cı, artillery
artificer. ~lamak, to stab.
kamara (·¹·) Ship's cabin; House *of Commons or Lords*.
kamarot, -tu Ship's steward.
kamaş·mak Be dazzled; (of teeth) to be
set on edge. ~tırmak, to dazzle; to set
the teeth on edge.
kâmbahş (−¹) Gratifying; giving enjoyment; fulfilling a desire.

kambel Hunch of a hunchback. ~i çıkmış,
doubled-up with age.
Kamber *v.* Kanber.
kambiyal, -li Bill of Exchange.
kambiyo (¹··) Foreign exchange.
kambur Hunchback(ed); round-backed;
crooked, warped. ~u* çıkmak, to become
hunchbacked: ~unu* çıkartmak, to cause
to become hunchbacked; to hunch the
shoulders, to stoop: ~ felek, cruel Fate: ~
üstüne ~, one trouble after another: ~
zambur, bumpy, uneven.
kamçı Whip. ~ bağı, rolling-hitch: ~
yemek, to get a whipping. ~lamak, to
whip; stimulate; pursue and hasten *an
affair*.
kamer Moon. ~î (··¹), lunar. ~iye,
arbour, summer-house: senei ~, lunar
year.
kamet (−¹), -ti Stature; fathom; prayer
before a Moslem service; outcry. ~i artırmak, to become presumptuous *or* bump-
tious; become more insistent.
kamış Reed; cane; fishing-rod; penis. ~
bayramı, the Jewish Feast of Tabernacles:
~ böceği, razor-shell. ~çık, jeweller's
blowpipe; nozzle of bellows. ~lı, furnished
with a reed *etc.*; large-stemmed. ~lık,
reed-bed.
kâmil (−¹) Perfect; complete; mature; of
mature years; well-educated; well-conducted. ~ce, in a quiet good-mannered
way. ~en (¹··), perfectly; fully, entirely.
kamineto (··¹·) Methylated spirit lamp.
kamis Shirt; tunic.
kâmkâr (−¹) Prosperous; successful;
august; despotic.
kamlı having a cam. ~ mil, camshaft.
kampana (·¹·) Bell.
kampanya (·¹·) Cropping-season (*esp.* of
sugar-beet).
kâmran (−¹) Successful; fortunate.
kamu All; the whole.
kamus (−¹) Lexicon.
kâmyab (−¹) Who attains his desire;
happy; successful.
kamyon Lorry.
kan Blood; bloodshed; revenge for murder.
~ ağlamak, to weep bitterly; to be in deep
distress: ~ aktarmak, to give a blood trans-
fusion: ~ almak, to let blood, bleed (*va.*):
~ boğmak, to die of cerebral haemorrhage:
~ı bozuk, suffering from unhealthy blood
or indigestion; degenerate, base: ~a boyamak, to cause bloodshed: ~a bulamak
(boyanmak), to be bloodstained: ~ dâvası,
blood-feud, vendetta: ~ına* dokunmak, to
make one's blood boil: ···in ~ına ekmek
doğramak, to torture (mentally): ~ına
girmek, to have *s.o.'s* blood on one's hands:

~ **gütmek**, to cherish a vendetta: ~ını*
içine* akıtmak, to hide one's sorrows: ~ı*
kurumak, to be beside oneself with anxiety
or suffering: ~ **olm.**, to be bloodstained;
to cause bloodshed: ~ **oturmak**, for blood
to be effused (bruise *etc.*); **elime** ~ **oturdu,**
my hand was severely bruised: ~ı* paha-
sına, at the cost of one's life: ~a **susamış,**
bloodthirsty; **kendi** ~ına susamak, to seem
anxious to sacrifice one's life: ~ **tutmak,**
(i) to faint at the sight of blood; (ii) for a
murder to haunt the mind of the murderer:
~ında* var, inborn, innate: içinden* ~
gitmek, to suffer secretly: **iki eli*** ~da, in
straits; overburdened with work.
kana¹ Waterline marks *on the stem and stern
of a ship.*
kana² *In* ~ ~, to repletion; abundantly.
kanaat (·—¹), **-tı** Contentment; conviction;
opinion. ~ındayım, I am of the opinion
that ...: ~ **etm.**, to be satisfied: ~ **getirmek,**
to be convinced *or* persuaded: ~ **sahibi,**
contented with what he has. ~**kâr** (·—·¹),
contented; satisfied with little. ~**kârlık,**
contentment.
kanad Wing; fin; leaf *of a door*; fold *of a
screen*; flap *of a tent*; sail *of a windmill*;
paddle *of a waterwheel.* ~ı altına sığınmak,
to be under *s.o.'s* protection: **emniyet** ~ı,
safety-catch *of a rifle*: **tutar kolu** ~ı
olmamak, *or* **kolu** ~ı **kırılmak,** to be helpless *or* broken. ~**lanmak,** to take wing,
fly away; be fledged. ~**lı,** winged; finned;
folded.
Kanada (·¹·) Canada. ~**lı,** Canadian.
kanadil (·—¹) *pl. of* kandil. Lamps.
kanal Canal.
kanamak *vn.* Bleed. ⌐kimsenin burnu
kanamadan¹, without hurting anyone;
bloodlessly.
kanape Sofa.
kanara Slaughter-house.
kanarya (·¹·) Canary. ~**lık,** stern-galley
on a ship. ~**otu, -nu,** groundsel.
kanata (·¹·) Small earthenware or tin
receptacle *for measuring liquids.*
kanatmak *va.* Make bleed. **burun kanat-**
mamak, to act gently, without bloodshed.
kanaviçe (··¹·), **kanava** (·¹·) Coarsely
woven linen; fine canvas.
Kanber *Name of a faithful slave of Ali.*
⌐~**siz düğün olmaz**¹, *used of s.o. who turns
up on every occasion*; 'of course he was (will
be) there!'
kanca (¹·) Large hook; meat-hook; boat-
hook. ~**yı atmak,** to make a grab at *stg.*:
~**yı takmak,** to 'have one's knife' into *s.o.*,
to 'have a down on' *s.o.* ~**lamak,** to
grapple with a hook; to put on a hook.
~**lı,** hooked: ~ **kurd,** hook-worm.

kancıga Breast-strap in front of a saddle.
kancık Bitch; any female animal; perverse
treacherous person. ~**lık,** treachery, deceit.
kan·çanağı (¹···), **-nı** Bleeding-basin; eye
red with rage or weeping. ~**çıbanı** (¹···),
-nı, boil.
kançılar Vice-Consul; consular assistant.
~**ya** (··¹·), Consular office.
kand Sugar candy.
kanda, kande Where?
kandaş One of the same blood.
kandan, kanden Whence?
kanderi Small reed (*calamagrostis*).
kandır·ıcı Convincing; satisfying. ~**mak,**
to satisfy; convince, persuade; satiate; take
in, cheat.
kandil *Old-fashioned* oil lamp. **kör** ~, very
drunk. ~ **gecesi,** the night of a Moslem
feast *when the minarets are illuminated.*
kandilisa (··¹·) Halyard.
kandil·leşmek *vn.* Greet one another on
the feast of **kandilgecesi.** ~**li,** decorated
with lamps, illuminated. ~ **geçmişi (ölüsü),**
the cursed fellow: ~ **selâm (temenna),** *old-
fashioned* very polite salutation, *raising the
hand from the ground several times*: ~ **süm-**
bül, grape-hyacinth.
kangal Coil; skein. ~ **etm.** *or* ~**lamak,** to
coil, wind in a skein.
kangı (¹·) *v.* hangi.
kanık Content; satisfied. ~**samak,**
~**sımak,** to be satiated; to become inured.
kanırık *v.* kanrık.
kanırmak *va.* Force back; bend; attempt
to force open.
kan·ısıcak Warm-hearted, friendly.
~**ısoğuk,** cold in manner; antipathetic.
~**kardeşi** (¹···), **-ni,** intimate friend.
~**kırmızı** (¹···), blood-red. ~**kurutan**
(¹···), mandrake. ~**lamak,** to stain with
blood. ~**lanmak,** (i) to be stained with
blood; (ii) to become healthy.
kani (—¹) Content; satisfied; convinced.
kanlı· Bloody; underdone (meat); guilty of
murder; full-blooded. ~ **canlı,** full of
health: ···**in** ~ **gömleğini giymek,** to be
hated by *s.o.*
kanmak *vn.* Be satiated; be content; be
persuaded. ···**e** ~, to be taken in by ...:
kana kana, to repletion: **kana** ~, to shed
blood unsparingly: **paraya kanmamak,** to
have an insatiable desire for money.
kanotye (*Fr. canotier*) Straw-hat; boater.
kanrevan Flowing with blood; sanguinary.
kanrık Perverse; very obstinate.
kansa Crop; gizzard.
kanser Cancer; canker; gall; (potato) wart
disease.
kansız Anaemic. ~**lık,** anaemia.
kantar Weighing-machine; steelyard;

weight of 40 okes (about 120 lb.). ~ı belinde, wide awake, acute : ~a çekmek, to weigh in one's mind : ~ topu, the ball of a steelyard; ~ın topunu kaçırmak, to go too far, to overdo stg.: yeni ~, modern weight of 100 kilos. ~cı, public weighing official. ~iye, fee for weighing. ~lı, in ~ küfür, violent abuse.

kantara Arch; centre (architecture).

kantarma (·¹·) Heavy curb; curb-rein. ~k, to pull up *a horse*.

kantaron Centaury.

kantaşı (¹··), -nı Agate.

kanter v. ter.

kantin Canteen.

kanto Song (in cabaret or theatre).

kanun¹ (-⁴) (*Formerly*) Military police-man.

kanun² (-⁴) Dulcimer. ~î¹, player of the dulcimer.

kanun³ (-⁴) Rule; law; code of laws. ~u esasî, Constitution : ~ hükmünde olm., to have the force of law, to be as good as a law : ~ vazetmek, to lay down a law *or* a code. ~en (-⁴·), according to law; legally. ~î² (--⁴), legal; legislative; *name given to the Sultan Suleiman I* (*the Lawgiver*). ~iyet (--·¹), -ti, legality; force of law. ~name (--·-¹), Code of laws. ceza ~si, the Criminal Code; ticaret ~si, the Commercial Code. ~şinas, jurist.

kânun (·⁴) *In* ~uevvel (birinci ~) and ~usani (ikinci ~), *old names of* December and January.

kanyak Brandy.

kanyot, -tu (*Fr. cagnotte*) Pool, pot (in gambling).

kap Cape; mantle.

kapak Cover; lid. kapağı bir yere atmak, to take refuge in a place; to succeed in getting to a place : ambar kapağı, hatch (of a ship) : dış ~, outer part of a leg of mutton : işe ~ vurmak, to hush a matter up.

kapaklanmak vn. Stumble and fall on one's face; capsize; overturn.

kapaklı Provided with a lid *or* cover; concealed; clandestine. Early breech-loading gun. gizli ~, secret and clandestine.

kapalı Shut; covered; secluded, out-of-the-world; reserved; overcast (sky); obscure. ~ kutu, a closed box; a secret; (of a man) inscrutable : ~ zarf usuliyle, by sealed tender : gözü ~, inexperienced, without knowledge of the world; thoughtless : bir noktayı ~ geçmek, to pass over a point without mention : üstü ~, sous entendu; indirectly. ~çarşı, covered market; bazaar.

kapama Act of shutting *etc.*; complete suit of ready-made clothes; stew of lamb and

onions. ~ca, *in* kapı ~, everyone in the house. ~cı, dealer in all kinds of ready-made clothing, boots *etc.*

kapamak va. Shut, close, shut up; confine; cover up; hush up (a matter); turn off (tap *etc.*); fill up (hole *etc.*); close (an account). göz ~, to close the eyes; pretend not to see; cut off the view from another's house.

kapan¹ Who seizes *or* grabs. ~ ~a, a general scramble : ~ın elinde kalmak, to be in great demand : ⌜~ da kaçan mı⌝ (*dial. for* kapar da kaçar mısın), 'nothing doing !'; 'no you don't !'

kapan² Trap; wicker covering for tobacco plants. ~a kısılmak, to be caught in a trap : ~ kurmak, to set a trap. ~ca, small trap for birds.

kapanık Shut in, confined (place); cloudy, overcast; dark; unsociable, shy; gloomy.

kapaniçe (··¹·) A kind of fur cloak *formerly worn by high State officials*.

kapanmak vn. *pass. of* kapamak. Be shut *or* closed; be shut up *or* confined; be covered; (of the weather) to be dull and cloudy; (of a subject or discussion) to be closed; shut oneself up, not go out; (of a woman) to veil herself before men; (of a factory or business) to cease work; fall down, stumble; (of a wound) to heal up; (of a family) to die out; (of a ship) to broach to. ağzı ~, to be reduced to silence : ayağa ~, to supplicate : içi* ~, to feel depressed : kitaba *etc.* ~, to be absorbed in a book *etc.* : yere ~, to prostrate oneself.

kaparo (·¹·) Earnest money.

kaparoz Illicit gain; bribe. ~a gezmek, to be on the look out for pickings. ~cu, one who picks up what he can, who lives on his wits.

kapatma Shut up, confined; acquired by underhand means at less than its value. Kept mistress.

kapatmak va. caus. of kapamak, *but usually used as* kapamak *except in the following meanings*: acquire by a trick; get stg. cheap; keep (a mistress). içini* ~, to depress s.o.: ⌜o faslı kapat !⌝, 'let's close that subject'.

kapı, kapu Door; gate; situation, employment; place of employment; point *at backgammon*; (*popularly*) 'the Government'. ~yı açmak, to open the door; to start stg.: ~yı büyük açmak, to start an expensive undertaking, to spend money prodigally : ~yı çekmek, to shut a door : ~ dışarı etm., to show s.o. the door, eject : ~ dolaşmak, to go from door to door, to have recourse to all sorts of places : ~ gibi, large, powerful (person) : ~ halkı, the household *of a great house* : ~ kâhyası, (*formerly*) agent of a provincial governor, *who transacted his business with the Sublime Porte*: ~ oğlanı, an agent of the Patriarchate *etc.*, *to conduct business with the Sublime Porte*: ~sından* **olm.**, (of a servant) to lose his job: ~ yapmak, to prepare the way for stg. one is going to say; to capture a space *at backgammon*: ~ yoldaşı, a fellow servant: ┌Allah bir ~yı kaparsa bin ~yı açar┐, if you fail in one thing there are lots more to try: aynı bir ~ya çıkar, it all leads to the same thing: ┌başka ~ya (müracaat) !┐, 'you'd better try somewhere else!': bu iş beş liranın ~sıdır, this business will cost a fiver: kırk (seksen) ~ının ipini çekmek, to knock at many doors.

kapı ağası, –nı, *formerly* the Chief White Eunuch *in the Imperial Palace.* ~cı[1], doorkeeper, porter, concierge. ~cılık, the occupation and duty of a doorkeeper. ~kulu, –nu, *formerly* a lifeguardsman of the Janissaries; palace servant. ~lanmak, to secure a situation; to enter *s.o.'s* service.

kapıc Heifer.

kapıcı[2] One who seizes; attractive. ~ kuş, bird of prey.

kapılgan Easily misled; easily carried away *by emotion etc.*

kapılmak *vn. pass. of* kapmak *q.v.* Be seized; be deceived. bu zanna kapılanlar, those who are carried away by this idea: derin bir ümidsizliğe kapılmıştık, we were seized with deep despair: söze ~, to be taken in by fair words.

kapısız Without a door; without a job.

kapış Manner of seizing; looting; scramble. ~ ~ gitmek, to sell like hot cakes: ~ ~ yemek, to eat greedily.

kapışmak *va. & vn.* Snatch *stg.* from one another; scramble for *stg.*; quarrel, wrestle. ···le ~, to get to grips with …: bu malı kapışıyorlar, there is a rush on these goods.

kapik, –ki Copeck.

kapkacak Pots and pans, household utensils.

kapkaç Snatch-thief; stealing by snatching.

kapkara (¹··) Exceedingly black; pitch dark.

kaplama Act of covering *etc.*; covering, coating; plate; crowning (tooth); skin *of a boat.* Covered; lined; faced; plated. gümüş ~, silver-plated. ~cı, silver-plater.

kaplamak *va.* Cover over; line; face; plate; bind (book); envelop, surround; include, comprise.

kaplan Tiger; (err.) leopard.

kaplayıcı Covering; surrounding. Silver-plater.

kaplı Covered; bound (book). bakır ~,

copper-sheathed: kara ~ kitab, orthodox, formal, traditional way; the law.

kaplıca[1] (·¹·) Thermal spring.

kaplıca[2] Spelt.

kaplumbağa (·¹··) Tortoise; turtle.

kapma Act of seizing. Seized.

kapmaca Puss-in-the-corner (children's game).

kapmak *va.* Snatch; seize; carry off; acquire; scramble for *stg.*; learn quickly, pick up. **kapan,** *v.* **kapan**: ağızdan ~, to learn by listening to others: ağzından* ~, to catch s.o. off his guard and learn a secret which he does not wish to divulge: hastalık ~, to catch a disease: nem ~, to get damp; to be easily offended: su ~, for a blister to form; to fester.

kapot, –tu Hood *of a car.*

kapsol Percussion cap.

kapsül Capsule.

kaptan Captain (of a ship). K~ Paşa, *formerly the title of the head of the Navy:* ~ oynamak, to play marbles: ┌gemisini kurtaran ~(dır)┐, a clever or skilful man will find his way out of a difficulty.

kaptıkaçtı A small motorbus; a kind of card game.

kaptırmak *caus. of* kapmak *q.v.* ···e gönlünü* ~, to fall in love with: kendini eğlenceye (içkiye *etc.*) ~, to give oneself up to amusement (drink *etc.*).

kapu *v.* kapı.

kapurta (·¹·) Hatchway; skylight *of a ship's cabin.*

kapuska (·¹·) Cabbage stew.

kaput, –tu Military cloak; French letter. ~ bezi, coarse calico.

kar Snow. ~ yağmak, to snow: ┌~da gezer izini belli etmez┐, 'he walks on snow without leaving footmarks' (*said of a very cunning or adroit person*): ~ tutmadı, the snow did not lie: ┌bu sıcağa (buna) ~ mı dayanır?┐, such an expenditure, or such a consumption, had obviously soon to come to an end: ┌güvendiği dağlara ~ yağdı┐, what he relied upon has failed him.

kâr Work; business; gain, profit; effect. bu iş akıl ~ı değildir, this is unreasonable, without sense: ···den ~ çıkarmak, to profit by …: ~ etmez, it's no good; it's useless: ~ı kadim, old-fashioned; of an old type: ~dan zarar, not to get all one hoped, but still to get stg.: ┌zararın neresinden dönülürse ~dır┐, any diminution of loss may be counted a profit.

–kâr (–) *Pers. suffix.* Who does …; who makes …, *e.g.* hilekâr, a trickster; sanatkâr, an artist.

kara[1] Land; mainland; shore. ~ Ataşesi, Military Attaché: ~ya çıkmak, to go ashore: ~ya düşmek (oturmak), (of a ship) to run aground, to be stranded: ~dan gitmek, to go by land: ~ suları, territorial waters: baştan ~ etm., (of a ship) to be run ashore intentionally; (of a man) to be in a fix; to take desperate measures.

kara² Black; gloomy; ill-omened. Black colour; negro. ~lar, mourning clothes: ~ çalı, an obstacle to the reconciliation of two parties; *v. also* karaçalı: ~sı elinde, a habitual backbiter: ~ et, lean and sinewy meat: ~ gün dostu, a friend in need: akla ~yı seçmek, to be in a predicament, to have great difficulty *in doing stg.*: ayağına* ~ su inmek, to be kept standing for a long time: yüzünün ~sı, a source of shame to one; yüzünü ~ çıkarmak, to let *s.o.* down. [*Note: most compounds of* kara *are written as one word, see below.*]

kara·ağac, elm: ⌐sındırğı sıyırmış ~a kandil asmış¬, brazen-faced; of ill repute. ~basan, nightmare. ~baş, monk; French lavender; Anatolian sheep-dog. ~batak, cormorant: kaz karabatağı, darter (*anhinga rufa*).

karabet (·–¹), **-ti** Near relationship.

karabiber Black pepper; dark man.

karabina (··¹·) Carbine; blunderbuss.

kara·borsa Black market. ~boya, sulphate of iron; copper sulphate; sulphuric acid; lamp-black. ~buğday, buckwheat. ~bulut, **-tu**, black rain-cloud. ~ça¹, somewhat black; swarthy: ~ ot, black hellebore, Christmas rose. Karacaahmed, *name of the largest cemetery in Istanbul.*

karaca² Roe deer.

karaca³ The upper arm. ~ kemiği, humerus.

karacı Brigand, highwayman; backbiter.

kara·ciğer Liver. ~cümle, *v.* cümle. ~çalı, gorse. ~çam, Austrian pine. ~çayır, rye-grass. K~dag, Montenegro. ~demir, wrought iron. K~deniz, Black Sea: ⌐~de gemilerin mı battı?¬, 'why so worried?' ~dut, black mulberry. ~fatma, cockroach, 'blackbeetle'. ~fik, a kind of vetch.

karağı Fire-rake.

karagöt Gadwall.

karagöz Black-eyed person; gipsy; the Turkish Punch. ~ oynatmak, to present the shadow-show of Karagöz; to play a trick, deceive. ~balığı, **-nı,** (?) black seabream.

karagül *The name of a breed of sheep from whose lambs astrakhan is obtained.*

karagümrüğü, -nü Custom-house for goods coming by land.

kara·gürgen Beech (?). ~haber, news of death or disaster. ~horasan, finest

Damascus steel. ~humma, typhus. ~iğne, small black ant.

karain (·–¹) *pl. of* karine. Inferences *etc.*

karakaçan *A community of Roumanian and Bulgarian nomads.*

kara·kafes Comfrey. ~kalem, pencil *or* charcoal drawing; having a black design (stuff, porcelain *etc.*). ~karga, carrion crow. ~kaş, black-eyebrowed. ~kavak, black poplar. ~kış, severe winter; the depth of winter.

karakol Patrol; guard; sentry; guardroom; police-station. ~ gezmek, to patrol. ~hane (····–¹), guard-room.

karakoncolos Bogy; vampire; very ugly person.

karakul *v.* karagül.

karakulak Lynx. *A noted spring of water near Istanbul. Formerly* a confidential messenger of the Grand Vizier. A kind of dagger.

kara·kurbağa Toad. ~kuş, eagle; a disease of horses' feet. ~(kuşî··–¹), despotic, arbitrary, high-handed (*from the name of a despotic ruler*): hükmü ~, despotic rule; arbitrary behaviour; might is right.

kara·lama Act of blackening *etc.*; writing exercise; copybook writing. ~lamak, to blacken; dirty; scribble; write exercises in a copybook. ~lık, blackness.

karaltı Blackness; a figure in the dark; an indistinct figure; slight stain.

Karaman *A former principality in Asia Minor; the town of that name in the Konia Vilayet; the fat-tailed sheep of that district and the mutton therefrom*; a swarthy complexioned man; a heavy sledgehammer. ⌐~ın koyunu, sonra çıkar oyunu¬, 'not so innocent as he looks'. ~lamak, (of a sail) to flap wildly about. ~oğlu, *title of the princes of Karaman.*

karamandola (··¹··) Prunella (textile).

karambol (*Fr.* carambole) Cannon *at billiards.* ~yapmak, to cannon into *s.o.*

karamelâ Caramel.

karamuk Corn-cockle.

karamürsel, karamusal *In* ⌐~ sepeti sanmak¬, to underestimate *s.o.*

karanfil Pink (flower); carnation; clove.

karanlık Darkness; a dark place. Dark. ~ olm. (basmak), to become dark, for night to fall: karanlığa çıkmak, to go out in the dark: bu nokta bir az ~, this point is rather obscure: sabah karanlığı, before daybreak.

karantina (··¹·) Quarantine. ~ vazetmek, to impose quarantine.

kara·oğlan A dark youth; gipsy. ~pazı, orach, mountain spinach. ~pelin, black wormwood.

karar Decision; resolution; agreement;

constancy; stability; firmness; customary state or degree. ~ınca, as much as is required: ~ında, moderately: ~larında, about, approximately (in time): ~ bulmak, to become settled, to be decided: bir şeyde ~kılmak, to abide by a decision; to settle down to stg.: ~ nısabı, a quorum: ~ vermek, to decide; idamına ~ verildi, he was condemned to death: bir ~da or bir ~ üzere, in an unvarying degree, in a uniform manner: göz ~iyle, judging by eye: tam ~, just right.

karar·gâh, military headquarters. ~lama, estimated; by rule of thumb. ~lamak, to estimate by eye. ~laşmak, to be agreed upon, be decided. ~laştırmak, to decide, resolve. ~lı, fixed, settled, decided.

kararmak vn. Become black; become dark; be indistinctly perceived; become overclouded or misty. gönlü* (yüreği) ~, to become pessimistic, to be tired of life: gözü* ~, for one's sight to become dim; to feel giddy; to be beside oneself with anger or despair: içi* ~, to despair: sular kararıyordu, night was falling.

karar·name (··—ı) Decree; legal decision. ~sız, unstable; undecided; changeable; restless; hesitating. ~sızlık, instability; indecision; fickleness; restlessness.

karart·ı v. karaltı. ~ma, black-out.

kara·saban Primitive plough. ~sakız, pitch. ~sevda, hypochondria, melancholy. ~sinek, common house-fly.

karasör (for karoseri = Fr. carosserie) Body-work.

kara·su Glaucoma; a disease of the legs in animals. ayaklarıma ~ indi, I have been kept waiting for a long time; I have been kept standing. ~suları, -nı, territorial waters. ~tavuk, blackbird.

karavana Flat copper pan; mess-tin, dixie; a miss in target shooting; a kind of flat diamond.

karavaş Female slave.

karavide (··ı·) Freshwater crayfish.

kara·yağız Very dark-complexioned; swarthy and sturdy boy. ~yazı, evil fate, ill luck. ~yel, north-west wind; north-west. ~yonca, (?) black medick, yellow trefoil. ~yüzlü, shameless, depraved.

kârazmude Experienced.

kardeş, kardaş Brother; sister; fellow; like; comrade. ~ten ileriyiz, we are bosom friends: ana baba bir ~, whole brother or sister: beş ~, a box-on-the-ear; ˥beş ~in tadını tatmamış˩, he wants a good smacking: din ~i, co-religionist: süt ~i, foster-brother. ~çe, brotherly, fraternal. ~kanı, -nı, dragon's-blood. ~lik, brotherhood; friendship.

kare (Fr. carré) Square; the four at cards. ~li, in squares; chequered.

kâretmek (ı··), -eder vn. Win; profit; produce an effect, tell.

karfiçe (·ı·) French nail.

karga Crow; rook. ˥~ bokunu yemeden˩, very early in the morning: ~ tulumba etm., to carry s.o. by arms and legs: alaca ~, jackdaw (?): ˥besle ~yı oysun gözünü˩, to nourish a viper in one's bosom: ekin ~sı, rook: korkak ~, a cowardly fellow: yeşil ~, roller. ~burun, -rnu, Roman nose; curved forceps. ~büken, nux vomica. ~cık, small crow; very bad writing, scrawl; ~ burgacık, little misshapen thing; scrawl. ~delen, a kind of soft-shelled almond. ~derneği, -ni, a crowd of roughs.

kargaşa, kargaşalık Confusion; disorder, tumult.

kargı Pike; javelin; lance.

kargılık Cartridge bag or belt.

kargımak va. Goad; curse.

kargın Carpenter's large plane.

kargış Cursing; vituperation.

kârgir v. kâgir.

karha Ulcer.

karhane (·—ı) Snow-pit (where snow is stored for use in summer).

kârhane (·—ı) Brothel; (originally) work-shop. ~ci, brothel-keeper, pimp.

ka'rı v. kaır.

karı Woman; wife. ~ almak, to marry: ~ koca, wife and husband, married couple; koca ~, old woman: koca ~ lâkırdısı, old wives' tale, silly nonsense. ~lık, woman-hood, wifehood: ~ etm., to play a dirty trick.

karık[1] Snow-blindness. Snow-blinded.

karık[2] Furrow.

karımak[1] va. Handle a beast to test its fatness.

karımak[2] vn. Grow old.

karın, -rnı Belly, stomach; womb; inside of anything; protuberant part; bulge of a ship's hull: karnım* aç (acıktı), I am hungry: karnı* ağrımak, to have stomach-ache: karnı karnına geçmiş, very thin: karnı geniş, easy-going, tolerant: karnım* tok, I am full, I have had enough; ˥böyle yalanlara karnım tok˩, 'I won't be taken in by this sort of lie': ˥ben senin karnındakini ne bileyim?˩, 'how am I to know what is in your mind?'

karın·ağrısı, -nı, stomach-ache; pest; tiresome child or person: ... ne ~dır, ..., or whatever the name of the thing is; or whatever the fellow calls himself.

karınca (·ı·) Ant; blow-hole in a moulding; pit caused by rust. ~ duası, 'the ant's prayer', a kind of written charm; very

karındaş illegible writing: ⌐~ kararınca (kaderince)¬, 'as a modest contribution'; 'as much as I can afford'. **~lanmak**, to have the feeling of formication, have pins-and-needles; feel benumbed; be full of blow-holes or blisters; be pitted by rust. **~lı**, infested by ants; full of blow-holes; pitted by rust.

karındaş v. **kardeş**.

karınlamak vn. (Of a ship) to come alongside.

karınlı Having a paunch; pot-bellied.

karınsa Moult of birds.

karınzarı, -nı Peritoneum.

karış¹ Span (about 9 in.); the third of an arşın. **~ ~ aramak**, to search every inch of the ground: **~ ~ bilmek**, to know every inch of a place: **~ ~ ölçmek**, to measure very carefully; to calculate very closely: **aklı başından bir ~ yukarı**, doing whatever comes into one's head without reflection: **burnu bir ~ havada**, very conceited.

karış² Confusion, turmoil. **~ ~ etm.**, to throw into utter confusion.

karışık Mixed; adulterated; confused, in disorder. **~ bir adam**, a man about whom one has one's doubts. **~lık**, confusion, disorder; tumult, riot.

karışılmak vn. impers. of **karışmak**. **buna karışılmaz**, one shouldn't interfere with this.

karışlamak va. Measure by the span. **alnını* ~**, to defy; to challenge s.o. to do stg.

karışmak vn. Mix (with = ile); become confused or disordered; interfere; ···**e ~**, interfere with, meddle with; exercise control over. **karışanı görüşeni yok**, he is free from interference, he can act independently: **araya lâkırdı karıştı**, another subject cropped up and the conversation changed: ⌐**ben karışmam!**¬, (after giving advice or warning) 'well, don't blame me if things go wrong!': **bu işe hangi daire karışır?**, what department deals with this?: **tarihe ~**, to become a matter of history, to be a thing of the past: **toprağa ~**, to be dead and buried.

karıştır·acak In diş karıştıracağı, toothpick. **~ıcı**, causing confusion or tumult.

karıştırmak va. Mix (with = ile); stir up; confuse; allow to interfere (with = dat,); add (to = dat.). **diş ~**, to pick the teeth.

kari (-¹), **-ii** Reader.

-kâri (**kâr** with possessive suffix used as a suffix). Worked in ...; work of ...; in the style of ...; **telkâri**, worked in wire, woven of gold or silver thread.

karib (·-¹) Near. Relation, kinsman.

karides (·¹·) Shrimp.

kariha (·-¹) Fertile mind; imaginative power.

karin, -rni Age; century; epoch; generation.

karîn (·-¹) Near; associated. Companion; relation. **hakikate ~**, near to the truth.

karina (·¹·) Underwater hull, bottom of a ship. **~ etm.**, or **~ya basmak**, to careen a ship.

karine (·-¹) Context; deduction. **bir ~ ile anlamak**, to infer from an accompanying circumstance.

kariye Village.

karkara Demoiselle crane (?).

kârlı Profiting; profitable, advantageous. **~ çıkmak**, to come out a gainer; to turn out profitably.

karlı Covered with snow; inclined to snow. **~k**, vessel for cooling water with snow; snow-pit.

karma Mixed.

karmak va. Make a mash of; knead; mix (cement etc.); shuffle (cards).

karmakarışık (¹····), **karmakarış**, **karmançorman** All mixed up; in utter disorder.

karmanyola (··¹·) A nocturnal aggression. **~ etm.**, to attack by night in order to rob.

karmık, karmuk Grappling iron; small dam.

karnabahar, karnabit Cauliflower.

karnaksı (Corr. of karınağrısı) Pest; tiresome child; nuisance.

karne (Fr. carnet) Book of tickets etc.; schoolboy's report and list of marks.

karnı v. **karın**. **~yarık**, seeds of fleawort; a dish of aubergines stuffed with mincemeat; snatch-block.

karni Retort.

karniye Cornea.

karo (Fr. carreau) Diamond (cards).

karola (·¹·) In **~ yakası**, tack of a sail.

karoseri (Fr. carrosserie) Coach-work; bodywork (of a car etc.).

karpit Calcium carbide.

karpuz Water-melon; anything round; globe of a lamp. ···**in ayağının altına ~ kabuğu koymak**, to lay a trap for s.o.; to cause s.o. to lose his job: ⌐**iki ~ bir koltuğa sığmaz**¬, one can't do two things at the same time.

karsak Corsac, Tartar fox.

kârsız Unprofitable.

karşı Opposite; opposed. Opposite side or direction. In any opposite way or direction. Against; towards; opposite to. **~ya**, to the opposite side or bank: **~ ~ya**, face to face; exactly opposite: **~dan ~ya**, from one side to another: **~nızda***, opposite you; against you: **ona ~**, against him: **denize ~ oturmak**, to sit facing the sea: ···**e ~ çıkmak**, to go to meet s.o.; to prepare to oppose *s.o.*: ~sına* çıkmak, to appear suddenly in front of one: ···e ~ gelmek, to oppose; to answer back (impertinently): ···e ~ komak, to make a stand against, to resist: ···e ~ söylemek, to speak against, oppose: yüzüne* ~, to his face.

karşı·lamak *va.*, to go out to meet; oppose; reply to; meet (a need *etc.*). ~lanmak, to be met; to come opposite or face to face. ~laşmak, to confront one another, meet face to face; balance, be equivalent: ···le ~, to come up against (difficulties *etc.*). ~laştırmak, to cause to meet *or* balance; to confront *one person* with *another*; to compare. ~lık, equivalent; reply, retort; recompense; allocation: ⌐~ istemez!⌐, 'no backchat!': karşılığını yapmak, to give the equivalent, recompense, reciprocate. ~lıklı, equivalent; reciprocal; corresponding; balanced; done in return; in reply; facing one another. **Karşıyaka**, *a district of Smyrna; sometimes used for* Pera.

kart¹, –tı Card.

kart² Dry; hard; tough; wizened; old. ~almak, ~lanmak, ~laşmak, to become dry, tough, shrivelled, old. ~lık, dryness; toughness; loss of the freshness of youth.

kartadak *v.* hartadak.

kartal Eagle.

karter (*Fr. carter*) Crank-case; gear-case.

karton·pat (*Fr. carton-pâte*) Millboard. ~piyer (*Fr. carton-pierre*), thick cardboard.

kartopu (¹··), **–nu** Snowball; guelder-rose.

kartuk Large rake.

karuçe (·¹·) Cart.

Karun (–¹) Korah; a very rich person, a Croesus. ⌐~ kadar malı olsa kimseye koklatmaz⌐, even if he were as rich as Croesus he wouldn't give a sou to anyone.

kârü·kisb Occupation, business. ~zarar, profit and loss.

karyağdılı 'As though it had been snowed upon', speckled; pepper-and-salt.

karyola (·¹·) Bedstead; bed.

karz Loan. ~ almak, to borrow money: ~ vermek, to lend money. ~an (¹·), as a loan.

kasa (¹·) Chest; coffer; packing-case; safe; till; cashier's office; banker *at cards*: spliced eye or loop of a rope. ~ dairesi, safe-deposit: ~ etm., to pull taut; to frap: atlama ~sı, springboard (gymnastics).

kasab Butcher. ⌐yüzü ~ süngerile silinmiş⌐, unblushing, brazen-faced.

kasaba¹ Small town. ~lı, belonging to a small town.

kasab·a² Reed; pipe; windpipe. ~at (··⸱), **–tı**, bronchial tubes. ~î (··⸜), bronchial.

kasab·iye *Formerly* a tax on slaughtered sheep; butcher's fee for slaughtering. ~lık, trade of a butcher; butcher's fee for slaughtering; butchery, massacre: fit for slaughter. ~ koyun gibi, 'like a lamb to the slaughter', mild and uncomplaining.

kasadar Cashier; treasurer.

kasara Deck-cabin. baş ~sı, fo'c'sle; kıç ~sı, quarter-deck. ~üstü, **–nü**, poopdeck.

kasatura (··¹·) Sword-bayonet.

kasavet (·–¹), **–ti** *Pop. form of* kasvet.

kasd Intention; endeavour; premeditation; attempt on s.o.'s life. ···den ~, what is meant by ...: ~a makrun olarak, of malice prepense, designedly: ⌐bana ~ın var mı?⌐, 'have you evil intentions against me?' ~en (¹··), intentionally, deliberately. ~etmek (¹··), **–eder**, to purpose, intend; have a design against s.o.; mean; express ~î (·⸜), premeditated, deliberate.

kâse Bowl; basin. ~lis, 'plate-licker', sponger, parasite, toady.

kasem Oath.

kasık Groin. ~ bağı, truss *for hernia*: ~ biti, crab-louse: ~ çatlağı (yarığı), rupture, hernia. ~otu, **–nu**, agrimony.

kasılmak *vn.* Be stretched; contract; diminish.

kasım Dividing. Divisor; 8 November (*regarded as the beginning of winter*); November.

Kasımpaşa *Name of a district of Istanbul.* ~ ağzı, 'billingsgate'. ~lı, foul-mouthed.

kasımpatı (·¹··), **–nı** Chrysanthemum.

kasın·mak *vn.* Shrink; contract. ~tı, tightness; tension; a taking in *of a dress to make it fit.*

kasır,¹ –srı Castle; palace; summer-house; pavilion. kasrı hümayun, imperial palace.

kasır² (–¹) Short; deficient; defective; incapable. ~ane (–·–¹), humble, modest: aklı ~mce, in my humble opinion.

kasırga (·¹·) Whirlwind; cyclone; waterspout.

kâsib Who gains *or* earns; merchant.

kaside (·–¹) Eulogy *or* commemorative poem *of not less than fifteen couplets.*

kasir (·¹) Short. ~ülbasar, short-sighted.

kaskatı (¹··) Very hard; rigid; benumbed; petrified.

kasket, –ti (*Fr. casquette*) Cap.

kasmak *va.* Stretch tight; curtail. ~ kavramak, to hold in with a tight rein, keep a tight hold on: kasıp kavurmak, to turn topsy-turvy; plague, torment, tyrannize: kendini ~, to draw oneself up in a superior manner.

kasnak Rim *or* hoop (of tambourine, sieve); embroidery-frame; embroidery; any contrivance for stretching tight; pulley; drum of a cupola.

kasnı A resinous gum (galbanum).

kaspeannek (¹···), **kaspannek** By force; willy-nilly; on purpose.

kassam (·⌐) *Moslem functionary, whose duty is to fix the shares of an inheritance.*

kastanyola (··¹·) Pawl.

kastarlamak *va.* Bleach.

kastor Beaver.

kasvet, –ti Depression, melancholy; gloom, oppressiveness. ~ **basmak**, to become dejected : ~ **çekmek**, to be anxious or distressed. ~**li**, oppressive, gloomy.

kaş Eyebrow; a curved thing; collet (of a ring); accolade (*mus.*). ~ **çatmak**, to frown : ~ **göz etm.**, to wink, to make a sign with the eye and eyebrow : ~**la göz arasında**, in the twinkling of an eye : ⌐~ **yapayım derken göz çıkarmak**⌐, when trying to effect an improvement to spoil the lot : **eyer** ~**ı**, the pommel of a saddle : ⌐**gözünün*** **üstünde** ~**ın var mı dememek**⌐, to raise not the slightest objection : **kalem** ~**ı**, slender eyebrows : **kılıc** ~**ı**, the guard of a sword : **samur** ~, thick and regular eyebrows.

kaşağı Currycomb. *v. also* **kaşak.** ~**lamak**, to curry, groom.

kaşak Back-scratcher. **kavga kaşağı**, mischief-maker; pretext for a quarrel.

kaşamak *va.* Curry, groom.

kaşan Urine (of a horse). ~**ı gelmek**, (of a horse) to wish to stale. ~**mak**, to stale.

kâşane (––¹) Luxurious dwelling; mansion.

kaşar, kaşer Kosher (meat lawful for Jews); a kind of flat cheese *made in the Balkans.*

kaşar·lanmak *vn.* Become old *or* worn out; become callous. ~**lanmış**, experienced; hardened, callous; cunning. ~**ıı**, old, worn-out; insensitive.

kaşe Cachet; pill; seal; stamp, mark; shade.

kaşer *v.* **kaşar.**

kaşgöz *v.* **kaş.**

kaşık Spoon; spoonful; castanet. ~ **atmak**, to eat heartily : ~ **düşmanı**, one's wife, 'the missus' : ⌐**kaşığı ile yedirip sapı ile göz çıkarmak**⌐, to feed s.o. with one's spoon and knock his eye out with the handle thereof, *i.e.* to spoil a good deed by a bad one : ···**in ağzının kaşığı olmamak**, to be too deep to be understood by ...; to be above *s.o.'s* head *or* capacity : ⌐**elinden gelse beni bir** ~ **suda boğar**⌐, he hates me like poison : ⌐**herkes** ~ **yapar ama sapanı ortaya getiremez**⌐, it's not as easy as it looks : ⌐**kısmetinde olan kaşığında çıkar**⌐, you get what Fate brings you : ⌐**suratı** ~ **kadar kaldı**⌐, emaciated.

kaşık·çı, spoonmaker. ~ **elması**, *the largest diamond in the Turkish regalia* : ~ **kuşu**, pelican. ~**çın**, shoveller duck. ~**lamak**, to eat spoonfuls *out of a dish etc.* : (*fig.*) to hasten to avail oneself of *stg.* ~**otu, –nu,** scurvy-grass.

kaşımak *va.* Scratch. **başını kaşımağa vakit bulamamak**, to be too busy *to attend to stg. else.*

kaşınma Itching.

kaşın·mak *vn.* Scratch oneself; itch. **dayak yemek için kaşınıyor**, he's just asking for a beating : **kavgaya** ~, to be itching for a quarrel. ~**tı**, itching.

kâşif (–¹) A discoverer *or* revealer. ~**i esrar**, a revealer of secrets.

kaşkariko (··¹·) Trick; deceit; buffoonery.

kaşkaval A Balkan cheese *in round cakes*; fid.

kaşkol (*Fr. cache-col*) Scarf.

kaşkorse (*Fr. cache-corset*) Camisole; under-bodice.

kaşlı Having eyebrows; having a ... as stone (ring). ~ **gözlü**, complete in every way (of a living thing); pretty : **dört** ~, with bushy eyebrows : **elmas** ~, diamond mounted (ring) : **kalem** ~, with thin eyebrows.

kaşmer Buffoon, clown. ~**lik**, buffoonery.

kaşmir Kerseymere (soft material resembling cashmere).

kat, –tı Fold; layer; coating; story *of a building*; quantity; time *of repetition*; opinion. ~ ~, in layers; time after time; many times more, much more : ~ **çıkmak**, to add a story *to a building* : ~ **etm.**, to fold; to stow in layers *or* tiers : **alt** ~, the lower story; first layer; first coat *of paint etc.* : **benim** ~**ımda**, as for me; in my opinion : **bin** ~, a thousandfold : **bir** ~ **daha**, one more of the same : **bir** ~ **elbise**, a suit of clothes : **iki** ~, double; folded double; bent double with age; two stories; two-storied; **iki** ~ **olm.**, to bow to the ground : ···**in yüksek** ~**ına sunmak**, to offer *thanks etc.* to ... (some great person).

kat'a, kat'an Absolutely; definitely.

katakulli, katakofti (··¹·) Act of cheating; hoax. ~**ye gelmek**, to be taken in : **Hacı** ~**!**, old humbug!; swindler!

katar String *or* file (of camels *etc.*); railway train. **eşya** ~**ı**, goods train : **surat** ~**ı**, express train. ~**lamak**, to make a file or train *of camels, carts etc.*

kat'etmek (¹··), **–eder** *va.* Cut; interrupt; terminate; travel over, traverse.

katı¹ Hard; violent; dry; strong. Very. Gizzard.

katı² (–¹) *v.* **kaatı.**

katı³, katı', –t'ı A cutting *or* cutting off;

interruption; a deciding; a terminating.
kat'ı alâka etm., to cease to take interest;
to discontinue relations : ~ **etm.,** *v.* **kat'-
etmek**: **kat'ı mesafe etm.,** to traverse a
distance: **kat'ı muhabere etm.,** to cease
correspondence: **kat'ı mükâfi,** parabola:
kat'ı nakıs, ellipse: **kat'ı nazar,** leaving
out of consideration; besides, apart from:
kat'ı ümid etm., to give up hope, to despair:
kat'ı zaid, hyperbola.

katıa (−·ı) *v.* **kaatıa.**

katıbe (−·ı), ~**ten** *v.* **kaatıbe.**

katık Added. Anything eaten with bread
as a relish; condiment; exaggeration. ~
etm., to eat *stg.* with bread; not to eat up
all one's **katık** before one's bread, to eke
out *one's cheese etc.* ~**sız,** unmixed, unadulterated : ~ **ekmek,** dry bread.

katı·lanmak, ~**laşmak,** to become hard
or heavy; to coagulate. ~**lık,** hardness,
dryness; severity.

katılmak[1] *vn. pass. of* **katmak.** Be added;
be mixed; be driven along; join oneself to
others. **su katılmadık bir Türk,** a pure-
blooded Turk; a Turk of the Turks.

katılmak[2] *vn. (from* **katı,** hard). Become
hard; get out of breath *from laughing or
weeping.* **katıla katıla ağlamak,** to choke
with tears : **katıla katıla** *or* **katılırcasına
gülmek,** to split one's sides with laughter:
soğuktan (içi) ~, to be chilled to the
marrow.

katıltmak *va. caus. of* **katılmak**[2]. **gülmek-
ten ~,** to make *s.o.* split his sides with
laughing.

katım An adding; a joining; a mixing.
koç ~ı, the season for putting the rams to
the ewes *and* the act of doing so.

katır[1] *In* ~ **kutur,** *v.* **hatır.**

katır[2] Mule; obstinate, ungrateful *or* malicious man; a kind of strong shoe *with iron
heel tips.* ~**boncuğu, -nu,** blue bead *often
hung round animals' necks.* ~**cı,** muleteer.
~**kuyruğu, -nu,** (?) hippocrepis. ~**tırnağı, -nı,** broom, genista. ~**yemeni,**
coarse kind of shoe with wooden soles
commonly worn by children.

katış·ık Mixed. ~**mak,** to join in; to mix
with others.

katı·yağ Oil usually found in a solid state,
e.g. paraffin wax. ~**yürekli,** hard-hearted.

kat'î (·ı) Definite; decisive; absolute.

kâtib (−ı) Clerk; secretary. ~**ane** (−·−ı),
in a correct literary manner (*iron.*). ~**iadil,**
Notary Public. ~**lik,** quality *or* profession
of a clerk *or* secretary; clerkship; secretary-
ship.

katil[1], **-tli** A killing; assassination;
murder.

katil[2] (−ı), *v.* **kaatil.**

kat'ileşmek *vn.* Become definite *or*
decisive.

kat'iy·et, -ti Definiteness; precision. ~**yen,**
~**en** (·ı·), definitely, absolutely; finally.

katlamak *va.* Fold; pleat; put layer upon
layer; repeat.

katlandırmak *va.* Bend; fold; pleat; cause
to consent *or* acquiesce; cause to cringe *or*
writhe.

katlanmak *vn.* Bend; fold; pucker; become
stratified. *va. (with dat.)* Undergo; suffer;
put up with; acquiesce in. ⌐**göz görmeyince
gönül katlanır**¬, 'what the eye does not see
the heart does not rue'; if the result is
good don't worry about the means.

katletmek (ı··), **-eder** *va.* Kill.

katliâm (··−ı) General massacre.

katma Joined on; supplementary. Addition; appendage.

katmak *va.* Add; join; mix; embroil. **bire
bin ~,** to exaggerate greatly: **biribirine ~,**
to incite one against the other: ···**e el ~,**
to interfere in : **geceyi gündüze ~,** to work
day and night, to work incessantly: ···**i
hesaba ~,** to take ... into account: **önüne*
~,** to drive in front of one: ···**i yanına* ~,**
to attach ... to *s.o. as escort or companion.*

katmer A having folds; double flower;
flaky pastry. ~**li,** having many folds;
manifold; multiplied; multiple; double
(flower); flaky (pastry).

katra Drop. ~ ~, drop by drop.

katran Tar. ~ **ağacı,** cedar tree: ~ **ruhu,**
creosote. ~**köpüğü, -nü,** a kind of
fungus (?). ~**lamak,** to tar. ~**lı,** tarred.

katrat, -tı Quadrat; quad.

kauçuk Caoutchouc, unvulcanized rubber.

kav[1] Tinder; touchwood. ~ **çakmak,** tinder
and flint: ~ **gibi,** soft; inflammable:
mantar ~ı, amadou.

kav[2] (*Fr. cave*) Pool (in a game).

kavaf Dealer in ready-made boots. ~ **işi,**
coarsely made: ~ **malı,** fraudulent rubbish:
ağız (çene) ~ı, one who tries to deceive by
talking a great deal: **ayak ~ı,** a person who
is always to be seen about: **kâğıd ~ı,** petty
official: **söz (lâkırdı) ~ı,** chatterbox. ~**iye**
(·−·ı), ready-made shoe shop; goods at
such a shop.

kavaid (·−ı) *pl. of* **kaide.** Bases; rules *etc.*;
grammar.

kavak Poplar. ⌐**balık kavağa çıktığı vakit**¬,
'when pigs have wings', 'at Greek
Kalends': ⌐**başında ~ yelleri esmek**¬, to
have childish or fantastic ideas or projects;
not to know what one is doing: ⌐**burası ~
gölgesi değil**¬, *expression used by a café-
keeper to one who sits in his café but orders
nothing.* ~**lık,** poplar wood or grove.

kaval Shepherd's pipe; any hollow pipe.

⌐(koyun) ~ dinler gibi⌐, listening without understanding: ~ kemiği, fibula: ~ tüfek, smoothbore.

kavalye (·¹·) (*Fr. cavalier*) Male partner in a dance.

kavança, kavanço (·¹·) Transhipment of goods; transfer; handing over.

kavanin (·—¹) *pl. of* kanun. Laws, rules, etc.

kavanoz Glass or earthenware jar; pot.

kavas Guard of an embassy or consulate; attendant at a court; doorkeeper of a big establishment.

kavasya (·¹·) Quassia.

kavat Wooden bowl.

kavata (·¹·) A bitter kind of tomato used for pickling.

kavelâ Dowel.

kavga Tumult; brawl, quarrel; fight; battle. ~ etm., to quarrel, to fight. ~cı, quarrelsome. ~laşmak, to quarrel. ~lı, quarrelling; angry.

kavi (·⸜) Strong; robust.

kâvi (—⸜) Caustic.

kavil, -vli Word; assertion; agreement. kavlince, according to the assertion of so-and-so: ~ etm., to agree; to promise: kavli mücerred, unwarranted assertion; mere words. ~leşmek, to come to an agreement.

kavilya (·¹·) Marlinspike.

kavim, -vmi Tribe; people; nation.

kavis, -vsi Bow; arc; curve; the constellation Sagittarius.

kaviyyen (·⸜·) Strongly.

kavla·k Having the skin or bark peeled off. ~mak, (of bark, skin etc.) to dry and fall off.

kavlen (¹·) By word, verbally; by agreement. ~ ve fiilen, by word and deed.

kavlıç Rupture; swelling.

kavl·i v. kavil. ~î (·⸜), verbal. ~iyat (··ᴗ), -tı, verbal statements; assertions.

kavmantarı (¹···), -nı Fungus from which tinder is obtained, (?) *Fomes fomentarius.*

kavm·î (·⸜) Tribal; national. ~iyet, -ti, nationality.

kavram¹ Omentum, fatty membrane covering the kidneys.

‖kavram² Conception; notion; coupling (*mech.*).

kavrama Verb. n. of kavramak. Coupling (*mech.*).

kavra·mak va. Seize; grasp; understand. ~yışlı, quick at understanding.

kavruk Scorched; dried up; stunted.

kavrulmak vn. pass. of kavurmak. Be roasted, be fried; be scorched; be withered or stunted. ···e or ... için yanıp ~, to have an obsession or to be extremely keen about ... .

kavs·i v. kavis. ~î (·⸜), pertaining to an arc; curved. ~ikuzah, rainbow.

kavşak¹ v. kavuşak.

kavşak², kavşamak v. kağşak.

kavuk Large wadded headgear formerly worn by Turks; bladder. Hollow; rotten. ⌐kavuğuma dinlet!⌐ ⌐tell that to the Marines!⌐: ~ giydirmek, to cheat, deceive: ~ sallamak, to acquiesce unhesitatingly; to toady. ~çu, toady; hypocrite. ~lu, wearing a kavuk; name of a character in the orta oyun.

kavun Melon. ~içi, -ni, flesh of the melon; dark yellow with a pinkish tinge.

kavurma Act of frying. Broiled or fried meat. Fried; roast (coffee). ~ç, parched wheat.

kavurmak va. Fry; roast (coffee, corn etc.); scorch. kasıp ~, to turn topsy-turvy; to plague, tyrannize.

kavuşak Junction.

kavuş·mak vn. Come together: ···e ~, reach; attain; obtain; join; touch; meet; meet again after a long absence. Allahına ~, to go to one's Maker: gün kavuşuyor, the sun is setting. ~turmak, to bring together; unite; join; cause two people to meet: ⌐Allah kavuştursun!⌐, 'may God bring him back to you!' (*said to one whose relative has left on a long journey*): el ~, to fold the hands on the chest in a deferential attitude: birini bir şeye ~, to enable s.o. to get a thing; to grant a thing to s.o.: kolları ~, to fold the arms: önüne ~, to button up one's coat. ~uk, joining; touching.

kavut Roasted wheat ground to flour; a gruel made of such flour.

kay¹, -yyı Vomiting.

kay² Drizzle; rainy weather.

kaya Rock; rocky cliff or hill. ~balığı, -nı, goby; dere ~, gudgeon: tatlısu ~sı, tench. ~başı, -nı, a kind of rustic song. ~cık, small rock; hop hornbeam. ~ğan, a kind of laminated rock; slate; v. also kaygan. ~keleri, -ni, chameleon. ~koruğu, -nu, stone-crop. ~lık, rocky place. ~tuzu, -nu, rock salt.

kayak Ski.

kayan Mountain torrent. Swift; violent.

kayar Horseshoe with special nails for walking on ice.

kayb·etmek (¹··), -eder va. Lose. kendini ~, to lose consciousness; to lose one's head. ~ı, v. kayıb. ~olmak, to be lost; disappear.

kayd·etmek (¹··), -eder va. Enrol; en-register; notice; note down. onun sözünü ihtiyatla kaydetmeli, what he says should be accepted with caution. ~ı, v. kayıd.

~**iye**, registration fee. ~**olmak**, ~**olunmak**, to be enrolled or enregistered.

kaydırak Flat circular stone *used in a game resembling quoits.*

kaydırmak *va. caus. of* **kaymak.** Cause to slip *etc.*; cause *s.o.* to lose his post. **birinin ayağını** ~, to cause a person to lose his job: **gözlerini** ~, to slant the eyes.

kayetmek (ˈ··), **–eder** *vn.* Vomit.

kaygan Slippery; polished; fickle, mercurial. ~**taşı, –nı,** slate.

kaygana (ˈ··) Omelette.

kaygı, kaygu Care; anxiety; grief. ⌐**kasaba yağ** ~**sı, keciye can** ~**sı**⌐, 'the butcher thinks about his suet, the goat about his life'; everyone thinks of his own interests. ~**lı,** anxious, worried; causing anxiety. ~**sız,** without care or anxiety; carefree. ~**sızlık,** freedom from care.

kaygın Polished; slippery; pregnant.

kayıb *v.* **gaib.** ~**lara karışmak,** to disappear, abscond.

kayıd, –ydı Restriction; reservation; enrolment; registration; record; a caring, a paying attention; a brooding over a thing. **kaydile,** with the reservation that; provided that: ~ **altına girememek,** to refuse to be bound by restrictions, to be independent: **kaydı hayat şartile,** for life, life *interest etc.*: **bir şeyin kaydına düşmek,** to be mainly concerned with stg.: **kaydı ihtirazî serdetmek,** to make a ⌐reservation: **kaydı ihtiyatla telakki etm.,** to accept *a rumour etc.* with reserve.

kayıd·lı, restricted; with reservation; careful; registered. ~**sız,** unregistered; careless, indifferent; carefree. ~**sızlık,** indifference, carelessness; freedom from care; a not being registered.

kayık Boat; caique. ~ **tabak,** oval dish. ~**çı,** boatman. ~**hane** (·ˈ–·), boathouse.

kayın¹ Beech.

kayın², ~birader Brother-in-law. ~**ço,** brother-in-law's child. ~**peder,** father-in-law. ~**valide,** mother-in-law.

kayıntı Crack; fissure; ebullition.

kayır Sandbank.

kayır·ıcı Protector, supporter; who looks after. ~**lık,** favouritism. ~**ma,** protection; backing : **adam** ~, favouritism.

kayırmak *va.* Look after; take care of; protect; back, support; give a job to; employ. **bir vazifeye kayırılmak,** to be given a post by favour.

kayısı Apricot. ~ **gibi,** with the yolk still liquid (of a boiled egg).

kayış¹ Act of slipping.

kayış² Strap; strop; belt. (Of meat) like leather. ~ **balığı,** Bearded Ophidium: ~**a çekmek,** to strop. ~**kıran,** rest-harrow.

kaykılmak *vn.* Lean; lean back.

kaylule Sleep in the forenoon; *also* siesta.

kaymaç Slanting (eyes).

kaymak¹ *vn.* Slip; slide; glide; skate; become awry. **gözü*** ~, (i) to squint slightly; (ii) to see by chance.

kaymak² Cream, *esp.* clotted cream; the cream *of anything*; *a Turkish dish of* sweetened clotted cream; essence; hard crust *left on the earth after rain.* Very soft and white. ~ **altı,** skim milk : ~ **tutmak,** to form cream. ~**lı,** creamy, made with cream. ~**yağı, –nı,** fresh butter.

kaymakam The governor of a **kaza** (administrative district); acting representative; *(formerly)* lieutenant-colonel. ~**lık,** office *or* district of a kaymakam.

kaynak¹ Spring, fountain; source.

kaynak² Place where two things join; where the buttocks join; welding. ~ **yapmak,** to weld. ~**çı,** welder.

kaynama Act of boiling *or* welding. Boiled.

kaynamak *vn.* Boil; be boiled; effervesce; spout up; join; (of mischief) to be brewing; swarm; be perpetually moving; be lost or ruined; (of a ship) to founder; *(sl.)* be 'pinched'. **arada** ~, to be lost in the midst of a confusion: ⌐**başından* (tepesinden) aşağı kaynar sular dökülmek**⌐, to be overcome by shame or embarrassment: **kanı*** ~, to be active and exuberant; ···**e kanı*** ~, to 'take to' s.o., to like him.

kaynana (ˈ··) Mother-in-law. ~ **zırıltısı,** child's rattle.

kaynarca (·ˈ·) Hot spring; *the treaty of Kaynardji between Russia and Turkey in 1774.*

kaynaş·mak *vn.* Unite; be welded; unite in friendship; (of a crowd) to swarm. ~**tırmak,** to cause to unite; weld together.

kaynata (ˈ··) Father-in-law.

kaynatmak *va.* Cause to boil; boil; weld; cause *a ship* to founder; plot; become friends; *(sl.)* 'pinch', pilfer.

kaypak Slippery; unreliable, shifty, fickle; stolen. ~ **mal,** stolen *or* smuggled goods. ~**çı,** thief; smuggler; receiver of stolen goods.

kaypamak, kaypımak *vn.* Slip away.

kayr·ak Shifting sandy soil; slippery spot. ~**almak,** (of a river) to become choked with sand.

kayran Clearing in a forest.

kayrı *v.* **gayrı.**

kayrılmak *vn. pass. of* **kayırmak.**

kaytan Cotton *or* silk cord; braid. ~ **bıyıklı,** having a thin curling moustache.

kaytarmak *va.* Dodge *payment*; get out of *doing stg.*

kaytaz Crest of a bird; yak; pennon of yak's hair.

kayyum, kayyım Caretaker of a mosque.

kaz Goose; silly fool. ⌐~ın ayağı öyle değil¬, the fact of the matter is really quite otherwise: ⌐~ gelen yerden tavuk esirgenmez¬, 'don't grudge a penny where you may get a pound': ~ı koz anlamak, to misunderstand out of ignorance: ⌐cevir ~ yanmasın !¬, 'don't try to get out of what you said !'

kaza (·⊥) Accident, mischance; chance; office and functions of a judge; divine judgement, fate: administrative district governed by a kaymakam; performance of a religious duty omitted at the proper time; performance of an act; payment of a debt. ~ ile, by chance, by accident: ~ kuvveti, judicial power: ~ya uğramak, to meet with an accident: görünür ~, an event which can be foreseen and prevented: görünmez ~, that cannot be seen and prevented.

kaza·en (·¹·), by chance, by accident. ~î (·—⊥), judicial.

Kazak Name of a Turkish tribe: Cossack. k~, jersey; a husband who rules his wife (opp. to kılıbık = henpecked).

kazalı (·—¹) Causing accidents; dangerous.

kazan Cauldron; boiler. ~ devirmek (kaldırmak), to overturn (remove) the kettle, both signs of mutiny among the Janissaries, hence 'to mutiny': başı* (kafası*) ~ olm., to have a buzzing in the head after a noisy environment: bir ~da kaynamak, to be in complete agreement; to get on very well together: fesad ~ını kurmak, to start a sedition.

kazanc Gain; profits; earnings.

kazan·cı Boilermaker. ~dibi, –ni, a sweet made of burnt milk stuck to the bottom of a cooking-pot.

kazanmak va. Earn; win; gain.

kazara (·⊥—) By chance.

kazasker Originally the chief military judge; later a high official in the hierarchy of the Moslem Judiciary.

kazayağı (¹···), –nı Hook with several prongs; branching halyard, three-ended rope; the herb Good King Henry; as kazın ayağı, the real truth of the matter.

kazaz v. kazzaz.

kazazede (·—·¹) Struck down by misfortune; ruined; shipwrecked.

kaz·beyinli (¹···) Stupid; idiot. ~boku (¹···), –nu, (goose dung) greenish-yellow.

kazel Dry leaf remaining on tree. ~ mevsimi, autumn.

kazemat, –tı Casemate.

kazevi Receptacle made of palm-leaves or reeds.

kazı Excavation. ~cı, excavator; engraver.

kazık Stake, peg; pile; impalement; trick, swindle. ~!, 'what a fraud !': ~ atmak (sl.), to cheat: ~ bağı, clove-hitch: ~ kakmak, to drive in a stake; to establish oneself firmly: ~ kesilmek, to be petrified: ~ kök, tap-root: kazığını koparmak, to make one's escape; (of an animal) to get loose: kazığa vurmak, to impale: ~ yemek, to be cheated: demir ~, iron stake; the Pole Star: ⌐dünyaya ~ kakacak değil ya¬, he won't live for ever: ipten ~tan kurtulmuş, a gallows-bird: sağlam ~, a secure foundation for an undertaking.

kazık·çı, swindler. ~lamak, to impale; to cheat, dupe. ~lı, having stakes; ~ humma, tetanus.

kazılı Excavated.

kazı·mak va. Erase by scraping; scratch; shave off completely; eradicate. ~nmak, scratch oneself; be scratched etc. ~ntı, scrapings; erasure: tekne ~sı, the last child of a family. ~ntılı, scraped; erased. ~tmak, caus. of kazımak.

kâzib (—¹) Who lies; false. fecri ~, the false dawn.

kaziye Question, affair; judicial decision; theorem; assertion; statement requiring proof. ~i muhkeme, 'res judicata'.

kazkanadı (¹···), –nı Name of a wrestling hold.

kazma Act of digging; pickaxe, mattock. Dug; excavated. ~ kürek, digging implements: ⌐Mart kapıdan baktırır ~ kürek yaktırır¬, March is so cold that you don't go out, but burn your tools to keep warm.

kazmak va. Dig, excavate; engrave. ···in kuyusunu ~, to dig a pit for s.o., i.e. to try to ruin him.

kazmir Kerseymere.

kazurat (·—¹), –tı Faeces.

kazzaz Silk manufacturer.

ke– Ar. prefix. As; like. **kelevvel**, as at first.

kebab Roast meat. ~ kestane, roast chestnuts: çömlek ~ı, stewed mutton with vegetables: döner ~, meat wrapped round a skewer and roasted: şiş ~ı, pieces of meat roasted on a skewer: tas ~ı, pieces of meat stewed with onions. ~cı, proprietor of a small restaurant.

kebair (·—¹) pl. of kebire. Heinous sins.

kebe Very thick kind of felt; cloak made from such felt; felt carpet. ter ~, thick horse-blanket.

kebebe Cubebs.

kebed Liver. ~î (··⊥), pertaining to the liver, hepatic.

kebeş Ram.

kebir (·–) Great; important; old. ~e (·–), heinous sin.

kebise (·–) Leap-year.

kebud(î) Blue.

kebuter Pigeon.

kebze Shoulder-blade; soothsaying. ~ci, man who foretells the future from the inspection of shoulder-blades.

keçe Felt; carpet, mat. Made of felt. koko yol ~si, coconut matting. ~külâh, conical felt hat. ~lenmek, ~leşmek, to become matted; become numb, be benumbed. ~li¹, made of felt.

keçeli² In iki ~, on both sides.

keçi Goat. Obstinate. ⌐üç ~li Kürd gibi kurulmak¹, (to be as proud as a Kurd with three goats), to give oneself airs. yaban or dağ ~si, ibex. ~boynuzu, –nu, goat's horn; carob bean : ~ gibi, insipid. ~sakalı, –nı, salsify. ~yolu, –nu, narrow path.

keder Care; grief; affliction. ~ etm., to be troubled or grieved (at = dat.). ~lenmek, to be sorrowful or anxious. ~li, sorrowful, grieved; grievous.

kedi Cat. ⌐~nin bacağını ikinci gece ayıran damad (iç güveysi)¹, taking a wise step, but too late, v. App.: ⌐~ ciğere bakar gibi¹, with intense longing: ⌐~ ne, budu ne?¹, 'well, what can you expect from such a poor creature?; sometimes 'you've nothing to fear from him!': ⌐~ye peynir ısmarlamak¹, to entrust stg. to an untrustworthy person : ⌐~ uzanamadığı ciğere pis der¹, the fox said the grapes were sour: ⌐aralarına* bir kara ~ sokmak¹, to cause bad blood between two persons; 'aranızda kara ~ mi geçti?', 'have you quarrelled?': ⌐sermayeyi ~ye yükletmek¹, to go bankrupt: ⌐süt dökmüş ~ gibi¹, keeping quiet with rather a guilty conscience.

kedi·balığı, –nı, lesser spotted dog-fish. ~otu, –nu, valerian.

keene (·⋅·) As if; as though.

keenlemyekün As though it had never been. ~ konulmak, to be considered as non-existent.

kef¹ Arabic name of the frontal k (as opp. to kaf, the guttural k; in the modern Turkish alphabet both are represented by k and called 'ke').

kef² Foam; froth.

kef³ Palm of the hand; sole of the foot.

kef⁴, –ffi A withdrawing or drawing back; abstention. ~fi yed etm., to refrain from meddling with or injuring anything.

kefafınefis (·—·) Sufficiency of food to live. ~ etm., to be satisfied with very little.

kefal Grey mullet. has ~, female grey mullet in season, from which botargo (salted fish roe) is obtained: tatlısu ~ı, chub.

kefalet (·–), –ti A being sponsor, bail or security; bail, security. ~ etm., to make oneself responsible, to stand as surety: ~e rabtetmek, to take bail or security for …: ~le salıvermek, to release on bail. ~en (·⋅··), as bail or security. ~name (·—·–), written guarantee or agreement to stand as surety.

kefaret (·–), –ti Atonement; penance; indemnity. ~ keçesi, scapegoat: hürriyetin ~i, the price one pays for liberty.

kefe¹ Scale of a balance.

kefe² Hair glove used for grooming horses. ~lemek, to groom a horse with a hair glove.

kefeki Tartar (on teeth). ~ye dönmek, to be all in holes. ~taşı, –nı, coarse sandstone.

kefen Shroud, winding-sheet. ~i yırtmak, (to tear the shroud), to cheat death; to recover from a serious illness. ~ci, maker and seller of shrouds; thief who steals grave-clothes; extortioner. ~lemek, to wrap in a shroud; cover a fowl etc. in batter before roasting. ~li, wrapped in a shroud; covered with batter.

kefere pl. of kâfir. Unbelievers.

keferet v. kefaret. ⌐~i budur¹, formula pronounced by quack healers.

keffiyed v. kef⁴.

kefgir Perforated skimmer.

kefil (·⋅) Surety; security; bail. ~ olm., to stand as surety.

kefiye Light shawl worn as head-dress by Arabs.

kefne Sailmaker's palm.

kehanet (·–), –ti Soothsaying; augury. ~ etm., to predict the future.

kehf Cave. eshabı ~, the Seven Sleepers.

kehkeşan The Milky Way.

kehle Louse. ~lenmek, to become lousy. ~li, lousy.

kehlibar, kehrübar Amber. ~ balı, clear yellow honey: kara ~, jet.

keis Calyx; wine-glass; glass of wine.

kek, –ki Cake.

kekâh Exclamation expressing a feeling of comfort.

keke Stammering. ~lemek, to stammer, stutter; be at the last gasp. ~lik, stammer. ~me, having a stammer.

kekik Thyme. ~yağı, –nı, oil of thyme.

keklik Red-legged partridge. çantadaki ~, something definitely secured.

kekre Acrid; pungent; setting the teeth on edge. ~lik, acridity. ~msi, ~si, somewhat acrid.

kel Ringworm; bald spot. Bald; bare of vegetation; mangy; poor, miserable. ⌐~

başa şimşir tarak⌐, 'a boxwood comb for a bald head', an out-of-place luxury: ~i görünmek, for a defect to be shown up: ~ kahya, busybody: ~i kızmak, to lose one's temper (of one not easily angered): ~den köseye yardım, the blind leading the blind: ~i körü toplamak, to fill an office etc. with incompetent people: ⌐~ tavuk ~ horozla⌐, ⌐birds of a feather⌐.

kelâl, -li Lassitude, weariness.

kelâm (·⸴) Word; speech; sentence; language. ilmi ~, the study of the Koran, theology. ~ıkadim (·—··⸴), the Koran. ~ullah (·—·⸴), the Word of God, the Koran.

kelb Dog. ~î, canine; cynical. ~iyun (··⸴), the Cynics.

kelebek Butterfly; gaily dressed girl; disease affecting the liver of sheep, fluke. ~ gözlük, pince-nez.

kelek¹ Raft made of inflated sheepskins.

kelek² Unripe melon. Partly bald; not properly developed, immature.

kelem Cabbage; cabbage stew.

kelempe Roots left in newly-broken ground.

kelepçe (·⸴·) Handcuffs. ···e ~ vurmak, to handcuff. ~li, handcuffed.

kelepir Something acquired for nothing or very cheaply; bargain; bad bargain, useless thing; step-child. ~ci, bargain hunter; opportunist.

kelepser Martingale.

keler Lizard; reptile. ~balığı, -nı, monk fish. ~derisi, -ni, sharkskin (used as sandpaper); shagreen.

keleş Ringwormy; bald; dirty.

kelevvel (⸴··) As before.

kelhevam (···⸴) In ⌐elavam ~⌐, 'the common people are mere reptiles'.

kelime Word (pl. kelimat).

kellâ (⸴·) Certainly not; by no means.

kelle Head; sheep's head; sugar loaf; cake of cheese. ⌐~ götürür gibi⌐, with unnecessary haste and fuss: ~sini koltuğuna almak, to take one's life in one's hands: ⌐~ kulak yerinde⌐, phrase used to describe an exceptionally well-built man or a rather ostentatiously wealthy man, 'ah! there's not much wrong with him!': ~yi vermek, to lose one's head (be killed): ⌐bu iş böyle değilse ~mi keserim⌐, 'if this is not so, I'll eat my hat': pişmiş ~ gibi sırıtmak, to grin foolishly.

kelli¹ (dial.) Since, because; as.

kelli² Affected with ringworm.

kellifelli (·⸴··) Well-dressed; serious, dignified; showy.

kellik Baldness; bare waste land.

kellim Only in ⌐~ ~ lâ yenfa⌐, I kept on saying it, but it was no use.

keloğlan (⸴··) A popular hero of Turkish folk-tales, who starts as an unknown and poor boy, but, thanks to his talents, eventually achieves success; used sometimes affectionately for a poor child adopted by a family or taken as apprentice.

kelpe Vine prop.

kelpeten v. kerpeten.

kem Few; deficient; bad ~ göz (nazar), the evil eye: ~nazarla bakmak, to look at s.o. with evil intentions.

kema- (⸴—) As; as that which. ~filevvel, as formerly. ~fissabık (⸴—·—·), ~kan (⸴——), as it used to be, as before.

kemal (·⸴), -li Perfection; maturity; cultural attainment; moral quality; worth, value, price; the most that can be said of a thing or a person. ~i beş lira, five pounds at the most: ~ini bulmak, to attain to its perfection: ~e ermek, to reach perfection, to attain maturity: ~i ihtiram, all honour and respect: ~i muhabbet, sincere affection: '~i ne?', 'well, after all it's not a great expense!': ehli ~, possessed of every excellence.

keman (·⸴) Bow (archery); violin. ~ kaşlı, with arched eyebrows. ~cı, maker of violins; violinist. ~e (·—⸴), bow for violin. ~î (·—⸴), violinist (in Oriental music). ~keş, archer.

kem·ayar Of low standard; of base alloy. ~bizaa (···⸴), having little capital; of small ability or education.

kemençe (·⸴·) Small violin with three strings; instrument for sowing artificial manures.

kemend Rope with a noose at the end; lasso; halter; snare; (poet.) tress of hair.

kemer Belt; girdle; arch. su ~i, aqueduct. ~altı, -nı, vaulted bazaar. ~e, beam under a ship's deck. ~li, belted, girdled; arched, valuted. ~lik, leather belt used by lemonade-sellers etc. for holding glasses. ~taşı, -nı, keystone of an arch.

kemha (·⸴) Brocade.

kemik Bone. ~ atmak, to throw a bone to a dog; to appease by a favour: kemiği* çıkmak, to have a bone dislocated: ~ gibi, as hard as bone: ~ hastalığı, rickets: kemiğe işlemek, (of cold) to penetrate to the very marrow: ~ kapmak, to 'get stg. out of it' (rather contemptuously): bir deri bir kemik, mere skin and bone: ⌐bıçak kemiğe dayanmak⌐, to reach the limit of endurance: ⌐dilin kemiği yok⌐, one can never be sure that people won't blab. ~li, having bones, bony; strongly built.

kemircik, kemirtlik Small cartilage.

kemirici Rodent; corrosive.

kemirmek va. Gnaw; nibble; corrode. içi* içini* ~, to be consumed by anxiety etc.

kemiyet, –ti Quantity; number (*gram.*).
~ **ve keyfiyet,** quantity and quality.
kemküm Hesitatingly; confusedly (of
speech). ~ **etm.,** to hum and haw.
kem·lik Evil; malice. ~**maye** (·–¹), evil
disposition : evilly disposed.
kemmî (·–¹) Quantitative.
kem·niyet (¹··), –**ti** Evil design. ~**söz**
(¹·), evil *or* inauspicious language.
kemter *comp. of* **kem.** Less; inferior; worse;
(*modestly*) I. ~**leri,** your humble servant.
~**ane** (···–¹), humble : **arizai** ~, my humble
letter. ~**in,** *sup. of* **kem**: least; worst;
most humble.
kemyab (·–¹) Rare.
–ken *v.* **iken.**
kenar Edge, border; bank, shore; marginal
note, postscript; retired place, nook, corner;
suburb; breast, embrace. Out of the way,
remote. ~**a atmak,** to put aside : ~**a çekilmek,** to get out of the way; to retire apart :
~ **dilberi (nazik de olsa nazenin olamaz),**
a suburban beauty (however polite she can
never be refined) : ~**da kalmak,** to remain
in an inferior job: ~**da köşede,** in unlikely
spots : ~**da oturmak,** to sit apart.
kenar·cı, shore fisherman. ~**lı,** having an
edge *or* margin; having a marginal note *or*
postscript.
kende Dug; excavated; engraved. Ditch,
moat, trench.
kendi Self. ~**m,** myself : ~**si,** himself : ~**niz,**
yourselves : ~**ler,** themselves : ~ ~**me,** to
myself; by myself : ~ ~**sine,** to himself; by
himself; all alone : ~**nden** *or* ~**sinden,** from
itself; automatically; naturally : ~ **evim,**
my own house : ~ **kitabı,** his own book :
~**ni* beğenmek,** to think a lot of oneself,
to be conceited : ~**ni* bilmek,** to be con-
scious; to have self-respect; ~**sini bilmez,**
presumptuous; one who does not know his
place; unconscious : ~**ne* etm.,** to harm
oneself; ⌐**ne ettiyse** ~**ne etti**¹, in doing this
he only harmed himself : ~**sinden* geçmek,**
to lose consciousness; to lose one's self-
control; to be in ecstasy; to become slack :
~**ne gel !,** pull yourself together! : ~ **gelen,**
a godsend : ~ **halinde,** occupied by his own
thoughts; quiet, inoffensive.
‖**kendiişler** Automatic.
kendilik One's own personality; initiative.
kendiliğinden yapmak, to do *stg.* of one's
own accord *or* by oneself.
kendir Hemp.
kene Tick. ~**göz** (·¹·), small-eyed. ~**otu,**
–nu, castor-oil plant.
kenet Metal clamp *for holding together
masonry or cracked earthenware.* ~**lemek,**
to clamp together; bind tightly. ~**li,**
clamped together; closely united.

kenevir Hemp; hempseed.
kenise (·–¹) *for* **kilise. âbaı kenisaiye,** the
Fathers of the Church.
kenker, kenger Cardoon.
kent Fort; town.
kental Quintal.
kenz Buried treasure; treasury.
kepaze (·–¹) Vile; contemptible; scoffed at.
Ridiculous *or* contemptible person.
~**lemek.** ~**letmek,** to render vile *or*
contemptible; render worthless; cheapen.
~**lik,** vileness; degradation; ignominy.
kepbastı A kind of net *used in fish-ponds.*
kepçe Skimmer; ladle; landing-net; butter-
fly-net. ⌐**İstanbul kazan, ben** ~ **araştırdım**¹,
I had Istanbul throughly searched.
~**kulak,** having large prominent ears.
~**kuyruk** (*sl.*), sponger. ~**surat,** having a
small face.
kepek Bran; scurf; dandruff.
kepenek Moth; coarse felt cape.
kepenk Large pull-down shutter; wooden
cover.
kepir Barren, bare.
kerahat (·–¹), –**tı** A being abominable;
repugnance, aversion; a lawful but blameworthy act. ~ **etm.,** to abominate, detest :
vakti ~, drinking-time.
kerake (·–¹) A kind of light cloak. ⌐**anlaşıldı Vehbinin kerrakesi**¹, now all is clear ! :
zerdeli mor ~, completely mad.
keramet (·–¹), –**ti** Miracle; a word or deed
so opportune that it appears to be divinely
inspired. ~ **buyurdunuz !,** your words are
wonderful! (*formerly used in flattery, now
only ironically*) : ~ **göstermek,** to work a
miracle : ~ **sahibi,** prophet; miracle-worker :
⌐~**im yok ya!**¹, 'how could I possibly
know!' : **birisinin** ~**ine yormak,** to attribute
stg. to s.o.'s miraculous powers : ⌐**şeyhin** ~**i
kendinden menkul**¹, 'the sheikh's miracles
are related by himself', *i.e.* I want further
confirmation before I believe it.
kerata Shoehorn; cuckold; pander; scoundrel; *also used affectionately.* ⌐**bak** ~**ya!**¹,
'look at the little rascal!' ~**lık,** quality of
a pander *etc.*; villainy.
keraviye (··¹·) Caraway.
Kerbelâ The town Kerbela in Irak. ~
sıkıntısı, lack of water.
kere A time; bracket, parenthesis. ~
içinde, in brackets : **bir** ~, once; just; let it
be said that ...; for one thing ...; to begin
with ...; ⌐**düşün bir** ~ **azizim!**¹, 'just think,
my dear chap!; **bir** ~ **daha,** once again,
once more : **bu** ~, this time; now; recently :
kaç? ~, how often ? : **üç** ~ **dört,** three times
four.
kerem Nobility, magnanimity; munificence; kindness; favour. ~ **buyurun,** be

so kind!; I beg of you. **~kâr** (··⌐), good; generous, benevolent.

kerempe Rocky spit *running out into the sea.*

keres Large bowl.

kereste (·¹·) Timber used for building; any kind of material. **~si kavi** *or* **~li,** strongly built (man).

kerevet¹, -ti Wooden bedstead; couch. ⌐**onlar ermiş muradına, biz çıkalım ~ine**⌐, 'they attained their desire, we'll to bed', *the recognized formula for finishing a story for children, cf.* 'and they lived happily ever afterwards'.

kerevet², -ti (*Fr. crevette*) Prawn.

kerevid, kerevides Crawfish.

kereviz Celery.

kerh *v.* kerahat.

kerhane (·—¹) Brothel. **~ci,** brothel-keeper, pimp.

kerhen (¹·) With repugnance; against one's will.

kerih Disgusting; detestable. **~e** (·—¹), disgusting or abominable thing.

kerim Noble; generous; honoured, illustrious. ⌐**Allah ~!** (**~in kuyusu derindir**)⌐, 'God is generous and Kerim's well is deep' (*a pun on* kerim); 'never mind, it will come all right!' **~ane** (·——¹), noble, generous (*of deeds or words*); in a generous manner. **~e** (·—¹), daughter (*as a term of respect*).

keriz¹ Drain.

keriz² *In* **~ alayı,** a troop of gipsy musicians.

kerkenes Hawk, (?) kestrel.

kerki Large axe.

kerliferli *v.* kellifelli.

kerpeten Pincers.

kerpic Sun-dried brick. Made of sun-dried bricks; hard; dry. **~ kesilmek,** to be petrified *with fear etc.*

kerrake (·—¹) *v.* kerake.

kerrat (·⁴), **-tı** *pl. of* kere. Times. **~ cedveli,** multiplication table. **~la,** repeatedly.

kerte Rhumb; one of the 32 points of the compass; point; degree; mark, sign; best state or quality, right moment. **~sini almak,** to take the bearing *of an object*: **~sini geçmek,** to pass the exact degree, to be overdone: **~sine gelmek,** to come to the right degree, to the point of perfection; **~ye gelmek,** to come to such a point or degree that ... : **o ~** (*sl.*), at that moment.

kertenkele (·¹··), **kertenkeler** Lizard.

kerteriz Bearing *of an object or star*.

kerti *v.* kerte.

kertik Notch; gash; tally; fraction *of a pound etc.* Notched. **~li,** giving fractions, *i.e. the exact sum, not just a round figure.*

kertmek *va.* Notch; scratch; gash; scrape against.

kerubi (·—¹) Cherub. **~yun,** Cherubim.

kervan Caravan. **~a katılmak,** to join the procession, to go with the rest. **~başı** (·¹··), **-nı,** *or* **~cı,** leader of a caravan. **~kıran,** the planet Venus *when a morning star.* **~saray** (···¹), caravanserai; inn with a large courtyard.

kerye Iron hoop *tightened by bolts*; connecting part of a handcuff.

kes Person, individual.

kesad A not being saleable; dullness (of a market). **~lık,** condition of dullness in a market; time of scarcity *or* unemployment.

kesafet (·—¹), **-ti** Density; thickness; opacity; coarseness.

kesan (·—¹) *pl. of* kes. Persons.

kesb Acquisition; gain; earning. **~i şiddet etm.,** to grow in violence, to be aggravated. **~etmek** (¹··), **-eder,** to earn; gain; acquire.

kese Purse; small bag; case; cyst; hairglove *for rubbing the body*; *formerly* a sum of 500 piastres; the power of the purse, wealth. **~den eklemek,** to be out of pocket: **~sine* güvenmek,** to be able to afford: **~ sürmek,** to rub the body with a hair-glove (*as in a Turkish bath*).

kese·dar, Keeper of the Purse; treasurer. **~kâğıdı, -nı,** paper bag. **~lemek,** to rub the body with a hair-glove. **~li,** having a bag *etc.*: **~ kurd,** tapeworm cyst.

kesek Clod; a turf; a turf of peat *for fuel.*

kesel Slackness; indolence.

kesenkes (·¹·) Decisive; categorical; definite.

keser Adze.

kesici That *or* who cuts; slaughterman. **~ diş,** incisor tooth: **yol ~,** highwayman.

kesif Dense; thick; opaque; thickly populated.

kesik Cut; broken; spoilt; castrated; curdled; weary. Skim-milk cheese. **~ kalmak,** to be interrupted *or* abruptly ended: **~ sulama usulü,** system of supplying irrigation for certain periods only. **~lik,** state of being cut or broken; lassitude.

kesilmek *vn. pass. of* kesmek. Be cut *etc.*; be cut off; cease; be exhausted; be turned into, become; pretend to be; be curdled. **···den ~,** to cease from, to be unable to do any longer: **ayaklarım buz kesildi,** my feet are like ice: **dizlerim kesiliyor,** my knees are giving way: **göz ~,** to be 'all eyes': **kuvvetten ~,** to be exhausted: **nefesi ~,** to be out of breath: **taş ~,** to become as hard as stone; to be petrified: **ümid kesilecek bir hal,** a hopeless state: **yağmur kesildi,**

the rain has stopped: **yemekten içmekten**
~, to lose one's appetite.

kesim Act of cutting; slaughter (of an .
(animal); cut, shape, form; make; fashion;
abstention; vacation; agreed price *or* rent.
~ **vakti**, agreed time of payment: ~**e ver-**
mek, to put up a farm for rent: **su** ~**i**,
waterline *of a ship*. ~**ci**, contractor who
undertakes to farm a branch of the revenue.
||**kesin** Definite; certain. ~ **olarak**, for cer-
tain, certainly.

kesinti Clipping; cutting; chip; deduction
from a sum. ~**ye almak** (*sl.*), secretly to
make fun of s.o.

kesîr (·-́) Much; many; frequent. *As a*
prefix, many-, multi-; poly-. (*To find mean-*
ing of compounds not given, look up the word
following the Arabic article **ül**; *e.g. in the two*
following words one would look for **elvan** *and*
eşkal). ~**ülelvan**, many-coloured. ~**üleş-**
kal, multiform, manifold.

kesir,‑sri A breaking; fracture; fragment;
fraction.

kesişmek *va.* Conclude *an agreement*; settle
an account; draw *a game*; fix *a price*. **söz** ~,
to come to an agreement.

kesitaşı (·¹··), ‑**nı** A flat stone *on a river's*
edge upon which washerwomen beat out their
washing.

kesken Small rodent; cockchafer grub.

keski Bill-hook; coulter. ~ **kalemi**, cold
chisel; parting-tool (lathe).

keskin Sharp; keen; pungent; severe;
decided; peremptory. Edge *of a cutting*
instrument. ~**lik**, sharpness; pungency;
incisiveness; shrewdness; cutting edge.
keskinliğine koymak, to set edgewise.

kesme Cut; that can be cut; decided,
definite. Shears; Turkish delight; a kind of
flat macaroni; soft rock; apostrophe; a kind
of openwork embroidery. ~ **şeker**, lump
sugar. ~**ce**, with the right to cut for
examination (*in buying a water-melon etc*);
bought in a lump lot; for a lump sum.

kesmek *va.* Cut; cut off; interrupt; inter-
cept; cut down, diminish; determine,
decide, agree upon; cut the throat of, kill;
castrate; issue (a warrant). *vn.* Cut well, be
sharp; cost; (*sl.*) talk boringly; exaggerate.
kesip atmak, to destroy root and branch;
settle offhand; settle once and for all: **aklı***
~, to understand; come to a conclusion;
realize; think possible: **ağrıyı** ~, to stop
pain: ⌐**başını kes**¬, 'duck your head!':
···**den elini** ~, to cease from doing *stg.*:
gözü* ~, to deem possible; **gözüm kes-**
miyor, I dare not: **hesabı** ~, to settle an
account; to cut off relations: **kısa** ~, to be
brief: ···**in önünü** ~, to bar the way of; to
prevent: **paha** ~, to fix a price: **para (akçe)**

~, to mint money: ⌐**sesini kes**¬ 'shut up!':
söz ~, to arrange a marriage: **sütten** ~,
to wean: **ümidini*** ~, to despair: **yol** ~, to
hold up, to rob; to bar the way: **yolunu** ~,
to stop s.o.; (of a ship) to diminish speed.

kesmelik Quarry.

kesmez Blunt.

kesmik Chaff mixed with broken straw.

kesre Arabic vowel point for i.

kesret, ‑ti Multitude; great quantity;
superabundance, excess. ~**üzere**, in abundance; frequently. ~**li**, abundant.

kesretmek (¹··), ‑**eder** *va.* Break; subdue,
defeat; abate.

kesr·î (·-́) Fractional. ~**iadı** (···-́),
vulgar fraction. ~**iaşarî** (···--́), decimal
fraction.

kestane (·-¹) Chestnut. ~ **dorusu**, chest-
nut-bay colour: ~ **kargası**, jay: ⌐~ **kabu-**
ğundan çıkmış da kabuğunu beğenmemiş¬,
'the chestnut emerged from its shell and
did not like the look of it', *said of one who*
is ashamed of his origin: **deniz** ~**si**, sea-
urchin. ~**lik**, chestnut grove.

kestirme *verb. n.* of **kestirmek**. Snooze.
Definite, decisive; approximate. ~**den**
gitmek, not to beat about the bush: ~ **yol**,
short cut.

kestirmek *va. caus.* of **kesmek**. Cause to
cut *etc.*; shorten; cause to cease; appreciate;
estimate; cause to curdle, turn *milk etc.*
sour; decide; perceive; clearly understand;
take a bearing of (*mil.*). *vn.* Have a snooze.
kestirip atmak, to destroy utterly: **gözüne***
~, *v.* **göz**: **oğlunu***~, to have one's son
circumcised.

keş¹ Skim-milk cheese; cheese made from
yaghourt. ⌐**ağzının tadı bilen** ~ **yer**¬, ''tis
caviare to the general', people like you
(him) can hardly be expected to appreciate
so good a thing.

keş² Gullible; foolish. ~**ten gelmek**, not to
care, to be indifferent.

‑keş *Pers. suffix*. Drawing, bearing, suffering, withdrawing, drinking; *e.g.* **cefakeş**,
tormented, troubled; **esrarkeş**, hashish
smoker.

keşakeş (·-¹) Conflict; quarrel; uncertainty.

‑keşan *Pers. suffix pl.* of **‑keş**.

keşf·etmek (¹··), ‑**eder** *va.* Uncover; discover; reconnoitre; examine carefully and
estimate cost or value; guess. ~**i**, *v.* **keşif**.
~**iyat** (···₄), ‑**tı**, discoveries.

keşide (·-¹) Drawn; supported; experienced; quaffed. A drawing in a lottery;
hyphen, dash. *As suffix*, bearing ..., enduring .... ~ **etm.**, to draw (line, bill,
cheque); give (feast); send (telegram);
draw (a lot in a lottery).

keşif, –şfi Exposure; discovery; scrutiny; investigation, valuation; estimate of cost; reconnaissance; forecasting, divination. ~ **kolu**, reconnoitring patrol. ~**name** (··–¹), written estimate of costs.

keşiş Christian priest or monk. ~**hane** (··–¹), monastery; convent.

Keşişdağı (·¹··), –**nı** Mount Olympus (near Brusa). **keşişleme**, South-east wind (as blowing from the Keşişdaği to Istanbul); sirocco (in the Mediterranean).

keşke, keşki Would that ...! ~ **bilsem**, would that I knew!; ~ **bilseydim**, would that I had known!

keşkek Dish of wheat boiled with minced meat.

keşkül Beggar's bowl; abb. for ~**fukara**, a sweet made of milk and pistachio nuts.

keşmekeş Great confusion.

keşşaf Investigator; discoverer; scout.

keşti (·¹) Ship.

ket¹, –ti Obstacle. ···e ~ **vurmak**, to stand in the way of ... .

ket², –ti Starch. ~**al**, starched and glazed cotton or linen stuff.

kete Cake made of rice-flour.

ketebe¹ pl. of **kâtib**. Writers; clerks.

ketebe² Diploma for excellence in calligraphy; inscription at the end of a book (taking the place of the modern title-page).

keten Flax; linen. ~ **helvası**, sweetmeat made of honey and oil: ~ **kuşu**, linnet: ~ **tohumu**, linseed. ~**cik**, grass-wrack (sea-weed).

ketim, –tmi A concealing or keeping secret. **ketmetmek** (¹··), –**eder**, to conceal; not to divulge; dissimulate.

ketum (·¹) Discreet; reticent; keeping a secret. ~**iyet, –ti** or ~**luk**, discretion; reticence; keeping one's mouth shut.

kevakib (·–¹) pl. of **kevkeb**. Stars.

kevğir Perforated skimmer.

kevkeb Star.

kevser A river in Paradise; nectar.

keyfemayesa (¹·–·–) As it pleases your fancy; arbitrarily; just anyhow.

keyf·etmek (¹··), –**eder** vn. Amuse oneself; enjoy oneself. ~**i,** v. **keyif.** ~**î** (·¹), arbitrary; capricious.

keyfiyet, –ti Condition; quality (as opp. to **kemiyet** = quantity); circumstance; affair. ⌜~ **böyle böyle!**⌝, 'well, that's how the matter stands!': ~**i hal**, the circumstances of the case.

keyif, –yfi Health; bodily and mental condition; merriment, fun, good spirits; pleasure, amusement; inclination, whim, fancy; slight intoxication. Hilarious; tipsy. **keyfince**, as he pleases, arbitrarily: ⌜~ **benim, köy Mehmed Ağanın**⌝, 'it's my con-

cern, no one else need interfere': ⌜**keyfin bilir**⌝, 'well, as you please!': ~ **çatmak**, to make merry: ~ **etm.**, to amuse or enjoy oneself: **keyfi* gelmek**, to be delighted, to feel in a good humour: ~ **halinde**, intoxicated: **keyfim iyi değil**, I am not feeling very well: **keyfi kaçtı**, he is out of spirits: **keyfiniz nasıl?**, how are you? : ~ **olmak**, to be tipsy: ~**i sıra**, arbitrarily: ~ **sormak**, to inquire after s.o.'s health, to say 'how are you?': ~ **vermek**, to intoxicate: **keyfim yerinde**, I am well: ~ **yetiştirmek**, to make merry with drink: **ehli** ~, sensualist: **gel keyfim gel rahat etm.**, to rest and enjoy oneself.

keyif·lenmek, to enjoy oneself; be tipsy. ~**li**, merry; happy; tipsy. ~**siz**, indisposed; gloomy, not cheerful. ~**sizlik**, indisposition; ailment; depression.

keylûs Chyle; half-digested food.

keymus Chyme.

kez Time. **bu** ~, this time: **her** ~, always.

keza Thus; in like manner; too. ~ **ve** ~, and so forth.

kıbal, –li Shape; manner; style.

kıbale (·–¹) Midwifery.

kıble Direction to which a Moslem turns when praying, i.e. towards Mecca; south; south wind; place or person towards which or whom everyone turns. ~**ğâh** (··¹), the direction of the kıble. ~**nüma**, compass which indicates the direction of the kıble; any compass. ~**teyn**, dual of **kıble**: Mecca and Jerusalem.

Kıbrıs Cyprus. ~**lı**, Cypriot. ···**taşı, –nı**, crystal cut like a diamond; paste.

kıcı Any bitter pungent herb.

kıcıklamak v. **gıcıklamak.**

kıç, –çı Hinder part; behind; buttocks, rump; stern of a ship. ~ **atmak**, (of a horse) to lash out with both feet: ···e ~ **attırmak** (sl.), to get the better of s.o.: ~**tan kara etm.**, to moor by the stern: ~ **üstü oturmak**, to remain helpless: **baş** ~ **yok**, there is neither leader nor led. ~**ın** ~**ın**, backwards; astern. ~**lı**, ship down by the stern.

kıdem Antiquity; priority; precedence; seniority; eternity in the past. ~**en** (·¹·), by right of priority or seniority. ~**li**, senior; earliest. ~**siz**, without seniority; junior. ~**sizlik**, juniority.

kığ, kığı Dung (of sheep, rabbits etc.).

kıhf Skull. ~**î**, cranial.

kıkır In ~ ~, giggling. ~**tı**, giggling.

kıkır·dak Cartilage; gristle; crackling. ~**damak**, to make a crackling noise; (sl.) to die.

kıl Hair; bristle; hair's-breadth. Made of hair. ~ **çadır**, hair tent: ~**ına bile dokunul-**

maz, a hair of whose head must not be touched, sacrosanct: ~ **kadar**, the smallest degree or quantity: ···e ~ **kaldı**, he (it) was within a hair's-breadth of ...: ~ **kalem**, camelhair brush: ~**ını kıpırdatmadan**, without turning a hair: ~**ı kırk yarmak**, to split hairs; ~**ı kırk yaran**, too meticulous, hairsplitting: ~ **şaşmadan**, with scrupulous care: **burnundan** ~ **aldırmaz**, *v*. **aldırmamak**.

kılağı Wire-edge. ~**sını almak**, *or* ~**lamak**, to put a fine edge *on a tool*.

kılaptan Gilt-copper wire; gold wire wound on silk; trimming of false gold thread. ~ **işleme**, worked with imitation gold thread.

kılav Disease of sheep *causing foaming at the mouth*, (?) *foot-and-mouth disease.*

kılavuz Guide; pilot; go-between *in arranging a marriage*; leader of a file of animals (*usually a donkey*); gimlet point of an auger; screw-tap; adit (*mining*); corncrake. ⌐~**u karga olanın (burnu boktan ayrılmaz)**⌐, 'who takes a crow for his guide will never have his nose far from dung'; if you take bad advice you will regret it. ~**luk**, profession of guide *or* pilot.

kılbarak A kind of Shetland pony *bred in parts of Turkey.*

kılburun Narrow promontory.

kılçık Fish-bone; awn; string *of a bean-pod.*

kılefte (*sl.*) Theft.

kılıbık Man ruled by his wife; henpecked man.

kılıc Sword. Curved. ~**ına**, on edge: ~**dan geçmek**, to be put to the sword: ~**dan geçirmek**, to put to the sword: ~**ın hakkı olarak**, by right of conquest: ~ **oynatmak**, to be the ruler, to dominate. ~**bacak**, bandy-legged. ~**balığı**, –**nı**, swordfish. ~**lama**, edgewise; set on edge; slung from the shoulder; crosswise.

kılıf, **gılâf** Case; sheath. ⌐**minareyi çalan** ~**ını hazırlar**⌐, 'he who steals a minaret will prepare a case for it'; he who undertakes a risky business will take care to provide for the consequences; the thief will take care to cover up his tracks.

kılık Shape; appearance; cut; costume; aspect. ~ **kıyafet**, one's dress: ⌐~ **kıyafet köpeklere ziyafet**⌐, very dirty and untidy. ~**lı**, having *such and such* an appearance *or* dress; well-shaped; well-dressed. **çoban** ~, dressed like a shepherd. ~**sız**, deformed; ugly; badly dressed.

kılınmak *vn. pass. of* **kılmak**. Be done *or* performed (*used as an auxiliary verb in place of* **edilmek** *in formal or official language*).

kılkıran Alopecia; baldness.

kılkuyruk Pintail duck; tatterdemalion; shifty-looking fellow.

kıllanmak *vn*. Become hairy; (of a youth) to begin to show a beard.

kıllet, –**ti** Small quantity; scarcity.

kıllı Hairy.

kılmak Do; perform. **namaz** ~, to perform the service of worship of Islam.

kılsız Hairless; beardless.

kılükal (–·‑), –**li** Tittle-tattle; gossip.

kılyakı (¹··) Seton.

kımıl An insect pest of cereals (*Aelia*).

kımılda·mak, ~**nmak** *vn*. Move. ~**tmak** *va*. Move; shake.

kımız Koumiss (fermented mare's milk).

kın Sheath (of a sword *etc.*).

kına Henna. ~ **yakmak**, to apply henna *to a part to be dyed*; to be overjoyed. ~**cık**, rust *of plants*. ~**çiçeği** (·¹···), –**ni**, a species of balsam. ~**gecesi**, –**ni**, the night two days before a wedding (*observed as a night of entertainment and on which, formerly, the bride had her fingers and toes freshly dyed with henna*). ~**lı**, dyed with henna: ~ *or* ~ **keklik**, the Greek partridge or chukor.

kınak Claw; finger-joint.

kınakına (··¹·) Cinchona bark.

kınamak *va*. Reproach; make sarcastic remarks to; taunt, mock.

kınam·sık Hypercritical; sarcastic. ~**sımak**, to find fault with everything.

kınap, **kınnap** Yarn; twine.

kıp kıp, **kıpır kıpır** *Expresses constant rapid movement.*

kıpık Half-closed eye; winking.

kıpır *v*. **kıp**. ~**damak**, ~**danmak**, to move slightly; start; quiver; vibrate. ~**datmak**, to cause to start *or* move quickly; agitate: ⌐**işleri biraz kıpırdattık**⌐, 'we've got a move on'. ~**dı**, ~**tı**, slight quick movement; start; quiver.

kıpıştırmak *va*. Only in **göz** ~, to wink.

kıp·kırmızı, ~**kızıl** Bright red; very red.

kıpma Wink; twinkling of an eye.

kıpmak *va*. Wink *or* blink *the eye*. *v*. *also* **kırpmak**.

Kıpt, **Kıptı** Copt; Coptic; gipsy. ~**ça**, the Coptic language.

kır[1] Country (*as opp. to town*); uncultivated land; wilderness. ~ **koşusu**, cross-country race.

kır[2] Grey. Greyness; grey horse. ⌐~ **atın yanında duran ya tüyünden ya huyundan**⌐, 'who stands by a grey horse (will be affected) either by his hairs or his temper', *i.e.* one is bound to be influenced by one's environment.

kıraat, –**ti** Reading; reading-lesson. ~ **kitabı**, reading-book (for teaching). ~**hane** (·–·–¹), public reading-room; coffee-house where newspapers are kept.

kırac Uncultivated land. Parched; sterile.

kıracak Nut-crackers.

kırağı Hoar-frost.

kıral (·ᵇ), kral King. ~î (·—ᵇ), royal. ~içe, queen. ~iyet (·—·ᵇ), -ti, ~lık, kingdom; kingship.

kıran¹ Edge; shore; horizon.

kıran² Breaking; destructive. Epidemic, murrain. As suffix, breaking-, destroying-, e.g. dalgakıran, breakwater. ~ girmek, for an epidemic to break out; for some kind of plague or disease to cause damage: ... kıtlığına ~ girmedi, there is no shortage of ...

kırân Conjunction of planets. sahib ~, 'lord of a fortunate conjunction', title given to a victorious monarch.

kıranta Man whose hair is beginning to turn grey. Grizzled.

kırasıya Bone-breaking; violent.

kırat, -tı Carat; quality; value.

kırba Water-skin; leather bottle; wine-bibber. ~ olm., (of a child) to be pot-bellied and rickety. ~cı, maker of water-skins; man who claims to cure rickets by incantations.

kırbaç Whip; scourge. ~lamak, to whip.

kırçıl Sprinkled with grey.

kırçıla Marline.

kırçöz (sl.) Whose hair is beginning to turn grey.

kırdonlu Having a grey coat (horse).

kırgın¹ Disappointed, hurt.

kırgın², kırçın Murrain.

kırık Broken; cracked; milder (weather). Break fracture; fragment, splinter. ~ dököük, metal scrap etc.; broken-down; odds and ends of; broken (French etc.): vücudüm ~, I am not feeling up to much: ~ numara almak, to get bad marks: ~ tahtası, splint. ~çı, bone-setter. ~lık, state of being broken; physical weariness or weakness: hayal kırıklığı, disappointment.

kırılmak vn. pass. of kırmak. Break, be broken; be ruined or killed; suffer heavy casualties; be hurt or offended; die of laughter; be mitigated, become milder. kırılıp dökülmek, to be constantly broken; (of a woman) to be coquettish: açlıktan ~, to be starved: beli* ~, to be exhausted; to be discouraged: burnunun* direği ~, to be nearly knocked down by a stench: bir işe eli ~, to be an adept at a thing: gülmeden ~, to have one's sides ache with laughter: sular kırıldı, the weather is warmer.

Kırım¹ The Crimea.

kırım² Wholesale slaughter; the end of the Lenten fast; crease in clothes; champion in single combat.

kırıntı Fragment; crumb; crushed stone; fissure.

kırışık Wrinkle; crack, small fissure.

kırış·mak vn. Become wrinkled; kill one another; mutually break. ~tırmak (sl.) (of a woman) to 'carry on' with a man.

kırıt·ış Coquetry. ~kan, coquettish; flighty. ~mak, to behave in a coquettish manner.

kırk, -kı Forty; used especially to denote a large indefinite number. ~ anahtarlı, very wealthy; a man of property: ~ı çıkmak, (of a woman) to have completed forty days after childbirth: ~ defa, countless times: ~ evin kedisi, one who is always in and out of other people's houses: ~ ikindi, the rainy season (in parts of Anatolia): ⌈~ından sonra saz çalmak⌉, to start doing stg. later in life than usual: ~ yılda bir, 'once in a blue moon', on very rare occasions: ⌈biz ~ kişiyiz, birbirimizi biliriz⌉, we know too much about him (you) to be taken in.

kırk·ambar, general store; general dealer; person of encyclopedic knowledge; ship carrying a large and varied cargo. ~ar, forty each; forty at a time. ~ayak, centi-pede; crab-louse. ~bayır, third stomach of ruminants. ~geçid, very winding river.

kırkı Shears for shearing sheep. ~cı, sheep-shearer. ~m, the shearing season; the clip of wool.

kırk·ıncı Fortieth. ~lamak, to make forty; to do stg. forty times; complete forty days after an event; reach the age of forty: hastayı ~, to cure a sick person by spells. ~lar, the Forty Saints of Islam: ~a karışmak, to disappear. ~lı, having forty parts; being born within forty days of s.o. else: onunla ~dır, he was born soon after him. ~lık, a being forty years old; coin of forty piastres etc.; forty piastres etc. worth of goods; clothes for a newly-born child.

kırkma Shearing; hair cut so as to cover the forehead.

kırkmak va. Shear; clip.

kırlağan The bubo of plague; plague.

kırlangıc Swallow; martin; gurnard; (for-merly) a light swift galley. ~ dönümü, the time of the swallows' southward migration, early October: ~ fırtınası, storms occurring about the end of March: baca ~ı, swallow: dağ ~ı, sand-martin: kılıc ~ı, the swift: pencere ~ı, house martin. ~otu, -nu, the greater celandine; turmeric.

kırma Pleat; fold; a variety of hand-writing; crushed barley; half-breed. Broken; folding (gun etc.). ~cı, seller of small grains; corn-merchant; folder (book-binding).

kırmak va. Break; split; kibble (corn); kill, destroy; offend; fold, crease; discount (bill); change (money); lower (price); mitigate, abate (cold *etc.*). **kırıp dökmek,** to destroy; to keep on breaking: **kırıp geçirmek,** to destroy; to tyrannize: **birinin burnunu ~,** to humble s.o.'s pride, to 'take him down a peg or two': **dumeni sola (sağa) ~,** to steer to port (starboard); **dumeni ~** (*sl.*), to 'make off': **koz (pot) ~,** to make a faux pas, to 'drop a brick': **maaş ~,** to borrow money on salary due but not paid: **mezadda bir şeyi ~,** to make a successful bid for a thing at an auction: **numarasını ~,** to cut off *a schoolchild's* marks, to give bad marks to him: **para ~,** to coin money (grow rich).

kırmalı Pleated; creased.

kırmız Cochineal. **~ madeni,** kermes mineral (trisulphide of antimony).

kırmızı Red. **~msı, ~mtrak,** reddish. **~lık,** redness.

kırp·ık Clipped. **~ıntı,** clippings.

kırpıştırmak *va.* Blink *the eyes.*

kırpmak *va.* Clip; trim; shear; cut down (expenses); wink. **gözünü kırpmadan,** without batting an eyelid, without turning a hair: ⌐**ben senin karanlıkta göz kırptığını ne bileyim?**¬, how was I to know?

kırtas·î (·—⌐) Pertaining to stationery. **~ işler,** office work. **~iye** (·—·⌐), office expenses; stationery; 'red tape'. **~iyeci,** stationer; bureaucrat; one given to 'red tape'. **~iyecilik,** trade of a stationer; bureaucracy, 'red tape'.

kırtipil Wearing old clothes; common; insignificant.

kıs kıs *Imitates the sound of suppressed laughter.* **~ ~ gülmek,** to laugh under one's breath; to snigger.

kısa Short. **~ geçmek,** to refer briefly to a subject: ⌐**~ günün kârı**¬, (*iron.*) it's better than nothing; what more did you expect?: **aklı ~,** of limited intelligence: **sözün ~sı,** in short. **~ca** (·⌐·), shortly, briefly. **~cık,** very short. **~lık,** shortness.

kısac Pincers; pliers; claw *of a crab.*

kısal·mak *vn.* Become short; shrink. **~tma,** abbreviation.

kısas (·⌐) Retaliation; lex talionis. **~a ~,** an eye for an eye: **~ etm.,** to put to death for manslaughter. **~en** (·⌐·), in retaliation.

kısık Pinched; squeezed up; screwed up (eyes); hoarse *or* choked (voice). Groin. **~lı,** flowing in a mere trickle.

kısılmak *vn. pass. of* kısmak. Be pinched; be squeezed; be in difficulties; (of voice) to become hoarse; (of a limb) to be cramped *or* benumbed.

kısım¹, **−smı** Part; portion; piece; kind, sort. **Arab kısmı,** the Arabs: **kadın kısmı,** the female sex, womenfolk.

kısım² Handful.

kısır Barren, sterile. **~lık,** sterility.

kısırganmak *va.* birini bir şeyden **~,** to grudge someone something.

kıskac Pair of folding steps; vice; pincers.

kıskanc Jealous; envious. **~lık,** jealousy; envy.

kıskanmak *va.* Envy; be jealous of. **gözünden ~,** to be very jealous of, to regard as the apple of one's eye.

kıskıvrak (⌐··) Tightly bound *or* squeezed; tightly coiled up; neat and tidy. **~ yakalamak,** to catch so that escape is impossible.

kısma *verb. n. of* kısmak, istim **~ cihazı,** throttle.

kısmak *va.* Squeeze; tighten; pinch; cut down, diminish; be stingy with; (of a horse or dog) to put the tail between the legs. **dilini* kısıp oturmak,** to remain silent: **kulak ~,** (of an animal) to fold back the ears.

kısmen (⌐·) Partly, partially.

kısmet, −ti Destiny; lot; fate; luck. **~ !,** perhaps!, it may be!: **~i açık,** fortunate; (of a girl) sought after: **~i* açılmak,** to be successful, to be in luck; **~i* ···den açılmak,** to have success in ...; **~i* ···den açılmamak,** to have the bad luck to ...: **~ ise,** if fate so decrees: **~ olmamak,** not to be possible; not to succeed: **kızın ~i çıktı,** the girl's luck has come, *i.e.* s.o. has asked for her hand. **~li,** fortunate, lucky.

kısm·ı *v.* kısım. **~î,** partial.

kısrak Mare. **kız ~** *in such phrases as:* 'elâlemin kızına kısrağına yan gözle bakma!', 'don't cast covetous glances on other people's womenfolk!'

kıssa Story, tale, fable. **~dan hisse,** the moral of a tale. **~han,** story-teller.

kıstas Large pair of scales; criterion.

kıstelyevm Deduction from wages *for absence or lateness.*

kıstırmak *va. caus. of* kısmak. Cause to be pinched *etc.*; crush (a finger); catch by driving into a narrow place; corner.

kış¹ Winter; winter cold. **~ı etm.,** to reach the winter; to stay *somewhere* till winter comes: **~ta kıyamette,** in the depth of winter: **kara ~,** the depth of winter: ⌐**Allah dağına göre verir ~ı**¬, 'God tempers the wind to the shorn lamb'.

kış² *Noise made to scare away birds etc.* **~alamak,** to shoo away *birds etc.*

kışın (⌐·) In the winter.

kışır, −şrı Peel, rind; skin; shell; crust.

kışkırt·mak *va.* Incite; excite. **~ı,** incitement. **~ıcı,** provocative; inciting; inciter.

kışla (⌐·) Barracks.

kış·lak Winter quarters for animals, nomads *or* an army. **~lamak,** to become wintry or cold; to pass the winter. ~**lık**, suitable for the winter: winter residence.

kışr·ı v. **kışır**. ~**î**, pertaining to skin or shell. ~**ıarz**, the crust of the Earth. ~**iye**, crustacea.

kışt v. **kış²**.

kıt, -tı Little; few; scarce; deficient; rarely. ~**ı** ~**ına hesablamak**, to cut it fine: ~**ı** ~**ına idare etm.**, just to be able to make both ends meet: ~ **kanaat**, v. **kıtkanaat**: ~**ı** ~**ına** or ~**a** ~ **yetişmek**, to be barely sufficient.

kıt'a Portion; piece; continent; district; detachment of troops; segment; size, dimension. **bir** ~ **mektub**, one letter; **üç** ~ **gemi**, three ships. ~**at, -tı**, pl. of **kıt'a.**

kıtal¹ (·⸳), **-li** A killing; battle; massacre.

kıtal² A kind of landing-net for catching fish.

kıtık Refuse of flax; tow; stuffing of a mattress etc. **saman bir** ~, straw mattress.

kıtıpiyos Common; poor, trifling, insignificant.

kıtır Maize grains cracked over a fire; a lie. ~ ~, imitates a crackling sound, the crunching of stg. by the teeth; also indicates ferocity as in gnashing the teeth: ~ **atmak**, to lie, to make an impudent exaggeration: ~ ~ **kesmek**, to kill in cold blood. ~**cı**, liar. ~**damak**, to make a crunching sound.

kıtkanaat (⸳···) Having to be satisfied with little; in scarcity. ~ **geçinmek**, barely to be able to live: ~ **yetişmek**, barely to suffice.

kıtlama Drinking tea holding a piece of sugar in the mouth (supposed to improve the flavour).

kıtlaşmak vn. Become scarce.

kıtlık Scarcity; dearth; famine. **insan kıtlığında**, in such phrases as: ⸢**insan kıtlığında bizim Ahmed müdür oldu**⸣, 'in default of anyone better our Ahmed was made director'; ⸢**insan kıtlığında buraya beni tayin ettiler**⸣, (apologetically) 'as they couldn't get anyone else they appointed me here': ⸢**söz kıtlığında asma budayım**⸣, 'in the dearth of conversation let me prune my vines', said when s.o. talks beside the point.

kıtmir The name of the dog of the Seven Sleepers; dog.

kıvam (·⸳) Proper degree of consistency or maturity; the right moment to do anything. ~**ına gelmek** or ~**ını bulmak**, to come to the right consistency or degree; to be at the best possible moment for some action: ~**ında olm.**, to be in its prime. ~**lı**, having reached the proper degree of consistency or maturity. ~**sız**, not at the proper degree of consistency etc.

||**kıvanc** Legitimate pride.

kıvanca Transhipment; change of watch on a ship.

kıvanmak Be puffed up, be legitimately proud.

kıvılcım Spark.

kıvır ~ ~, in curls, wriggling, writhing. ~**cık**, curly; crisp. A kind of small-tailed, curly-haired sheep; the mutton therefrom: ~ **lahana**, curly kale: ~ **salata**, cabbage lettuce: ~ **zıvır**, trifling, insignificant.

kıvırmak va. Curl; twist; coil; turn in an edge of cloth and sew it round; invent (a lie); put in order; execute with success; (sl.) eat greedily; earn. vn. Succeed; turn; dance gracefully. **burun** ~, to turn up one's nose.

kıvrak Supple; brisk; dexterous; agile; coquettish.

kıvranmak vn. Writhe; wriggle; be agitated.

kıvr·ık Curled, twisted; curly; hemmed; folded. Fold. **pantolonun kıvrığı**, the turn-up of trousers. ~**ılmak**, pass. of **kıvırmak**, to be twisted etc.; to be squeezed into a tight place. ~**ım**, twist; curl; fold: ~ ~ **olm.** (**kıvrılmak**), to be doubled up with pain. ~**ıntı**, coil; a winding; turn; twist.

kıyafet (·–⸳), **-ti** The general appearance and dress of a person; aspect; physiognomy. ~ **düşkünü**, wretchedly clothed: **tebdili** ~ **etm.**, to disguise oneself. ~**li**, in such-and-such a shape or dress. ~**siz**, ill-looking; untidy.

kıyak Pretty; elegant; smart; wonderful.

kıyam (·⸳) Act of rising or starting; standing up; rebellion. ~ **etm.**, to stand up: ···**e** ~ **etm.**, to prepare to, to set about: ~ **flâması**, the Blue Peter.

kıyamamak va. impotential of **kıymak**. Spare the life of; have pity on; grudge (expense); be unable to bring oneself to do stg.; not to have the heart to.

kıyamet (·–⸳), **-ti** The Resurrection of the Dead; the end of the world; great disaster; tumult. ~ **alâmeti !**, how dreadful !: ~ **gibi** (**kadar**), heaps of: ~ **koparmak**, to create an uproar, to 'raise hell': ~ **koptu**, a great disaster has occurred; hell has broken loose; ~ **mi koptu ?**, 'what the dickens has happened?'; 'what the devil does it matter!': **kış** ~, intense cold: **kızılca** ~, the 'hell of a row'.

kıyas (·⸳) Comparison, analogy; reasoning, syllogism; rule; opinion. ~ **etm.**, to compare: ~ **ile**, by analogy: ~ **kabul etmez**, incomparable: **bu** ~ **üzere**, by analogy with this; at this rate: ⸢**var** ~ **et !**⸣, 'draw your own conclusions!' ~**en** (·–⸳), by comparison; by analogy; by rule. ~**î** (·–⸳), in accordance with rule; analogous; regular.

kıyasıya Murderous; merciless.

kıyı Edge; shore; bank; corner; extremity. ~**dan** ~**dan**, '(creeping) along the shore', very cautiously: ~**da bucakta (köşede)**, in holes and corners, in out-of-the-way places: '**büyük vapuru** ~**sına bucağına kadar bilir**', 'he knows the great ship inside out': ~**ya çekilmek**, to withdraw, to get out of the way: ~**ya inmek (çıkarmak)**, to land *from a ship*: ~ **sıra**, *v.* **kıyısıra**.

kıyıcı[1] Frequenter of the shore; shore fisherman.

kıyıcı[2] Who cuts up; cruel, pitiless. Tobacco-cutter.

kıyık Minced; chopped up.

kıyılmak *vn. pass. of* **kıymak**. Be minced *etc.*; have a feeling of debility, ache. **bakmağa kıyılmaz bir manzara**, a view one is never tired of looking at, a marvellous view.

kıyım Act or manner of mincing or chopping; a single quantity of mincing. **iri** ~, heavily-built. ~**lı**, minced; chopped up: **ince** ~ **tütün**, finely cut tobacco.

kıyıntı Anything chopped up; a griping of the stomach; aching of the limbs; languor.

kıyısıra (·¹··) Along the shore; coastwise.

kıyma Minced meat. Minced, finely chopped. ~ **tahtası**, chopping-board. ~**lı**, with minced meat.

kıymak *va. (with acc.)* Mince, chop up fine; slaughter, massacre; decide on; *(with dat.)* bring oneself to do an injury; not to spare; sacrifice; *v. also* **kıyamamak**. **canına*** ~, to have no pity on and kill: **nikâh** ~, to perform the marriage ceremony.

kıymet, –ti Value; price; esteem. ~ **bilmek**, to appreciate the value of; to appreciate (show gratitude for). ~**lendirmek**, to bring into profitable use, utilize. ~**li**, valuable, precious. ~**siz**, worthless. ~**şinas**, who knows the value *of a thing or a person*.

kıymık Splinter.

kıyye Okka = 2·83 lb.

kız Girl; daughter; virgin; queen (cards). ~ **alıp vermek**, to intermarry: ⌐~**ını dövmiyen dizini döver**⌐, keep your daughter in order or you will regret it later: ~ **gibi**, new, untouched; beautiful: ~ **ismi**, maiden name: ~ **oğlan** ~, virginal; young and fresh: ~ **tarafı**, the bride's relatives: ⌐**beğenmiyen** ~**ını vermesin!**⌐, 'anyone who does not like me needn't give me his daughter', I don't care what others think; who does not like it may lump it!: **hanım** ~, a shy little girl.

kızak Sledge; slide; slipway; ways *for launching a ship*. **kızağa çekilmek**, (of a ship) to be drawn up on a slipway; (of a man) to be put on the shelf: ~**tan indirmek**,

to launch *a ship*: ~ **kaymak**, to slide on ice, to sledge: ~ **yapmak**, to slide.

kızaklık Joist.

kızalak Wild poppy.

kızamık Measles. ~ **çıkarmak**, to have measles. ~**çık**, German measles.

kızan Youth, lad; sturdy country lad. **karı** ~, wives and children; the whole population.

kızar·mak *vn.* Turn red; blush; ripen; be roasted or toasted. **kızarıp bozarmak**, to grow red and pale by turns. ~**tma**, roasted: roast meat *etc.* ~**tmak**, to make red; cause to blush; roast, grill, fry: **yüz (yüzünü*)** ~, to overcome one's natural reluctance *in asking a favour etc.*

kızdırmak *va.* Heat; anger, annoy.

kızgın Hot; red-hot; angry; excited; feverish; on heat (sexually). ~**lık**, great heat; fury; feverish activity; sexual excitement.

kızgırmak *vn.* (Of a snake) to hiss.

kızıl Red; red-hot; golden. Scarlet fever. ~ **akçe**, gold coins: ~ **buğday**, spelt: ~ **cahil**, utterly ignorant: ~**deli**, a raving madman: ~ **şap**, light purple.

kızıl·ağac, alder; *also (comm.)* Brazil wood. **K~ay**, Red Crescent (Turkish Red Cross). ~**baş**, *a religious fraternity similar to the Bektashis; a Shiite sect; a military class in the army of Shah Ismail; used to describe* a person of easy morals. ~**ca** reddish: ~**kıyamet**, a fearful uproar. ~**cık**, cornelian cherry; cornel wood: ~ **sopası**, 'a rod in pickle': ⌐**kan kussa** ~ **şerbeti içtim der**⌐, 'if he vomits blood he says he has drunk cornel sherbet (which is red)', *said of one who is too proud to reveal his real trouble.* ~**elma**, *v.* **elma**. ~**kanad**, rudd, roach. ~**lık**, redness; red colour; rouge; scarlet fever. ‖~**ötesi, –ni**, infra-red. ~**tı**, redness; red spot.

kızışmak *vn.* Get angry *or* excited; become heated; increase in fury *or* violence.

kız·kardeş Sister. **K~kulesi, -ni**, the Maiden's Tower at the entrance to the Bosphorus. ~**kuşu, -nu**, peewit. ~**laragası, -nı**, *formerly* the chief black eunuch *in the Imperial household.* ~**lık**, maidenhood; virginity. ~**memesi, –ni**, a kind of small bitter orange.

kızmak *vn.* Get hot; glow; get red-hot; get angry; get excited; (of an animal) to be on heat. **gözü*** ~, to be beside oneself *with anger or passion.*

ki That; as; in order that; *sometimes*, seeing that, since, *e.g.* **işitmedi** ~ **cevab versin**, how can he answer since he didn't hear?: *expresses surprise, e.g.* ⌐**bilmiyor mu** ~?⌐, 'doesn't he know then?'; ⌐**geldim** ~ **kimseler yok**⌐, 'I came and found there was no one there!'; 'kapağı kaldırdım ~ sandık bomboş!', 'I lifted the lid and behold! the box was empty!' : *used as a relative, e.g.* bir çoçuk ~ çalışmaz, a child who does not work: *it often expresses stg. unsaid, e.g.* öyle yağmur yağdı ~, it rained so that ...; öyle şaştım ~, I was so surprised that ...: *used with* bilmem *in such cases as* : bilmem ~ ne yapmalı, I don't know what one should do!; bilmem ~ kime sorsam!, I don't know who to ask !: ola ~, it may be that ...: ta ~ until.

-ki *suffix. When placed after a noun in the locative or genitive it forms a pronoun or adjective;* Türkiyedeki İngilizler, the English in Turkey; 'senin bıçağın keskin, benimki kesmez', 'your knife is sharp, mine is blunt'.

kibar (·⅄) *pl. of* kebir. Great ones, eminent people; *as s.,* a great man. Noble; rich; belonging to the upper class; distinguished. orman ~ı, bear; coarse, uncouth man. ~lık, greatness; nobility; gentle birth: ~ taslamak, to pretend to be a gentleman.

kibir, –bri Pride, haughtiness; contempt. ~li, proud, haughty; contemptuous.

kibrit, –ti Sulphur; match. ~ suyu, dilute sulphuric acid: hamızı ~, sulphuric acid: köküne ~ suyu dökmek (ekmek), to exterminate. ~çi, matchseller. ~î (·–⅄), sulphurous; light yellow coloured. ~iyet, –ti, sulphate.

kibriya (··⅄) The Divine Greatness; God.

kifayet (·–⅄), –ti Sufficiency; ability, capacity. ~ etm., to suffice: ···le ~ etm., to be contented with .... ~li, having sufficient capacity or ability; adequate. ~siz, inadequate.

kik, –ki Ship's gig; skiff.

kikirik *In* Con ~, John Bull.

kikla The Ballan Wrasse.

kil Fuller's earth; clay.

kilâb *pl. of* kelb. Dogs.

kile *Measure of capacity just over a bushel.* dipsiz ~, spendthrift who is always borrowing: 'dipsiz ~ boş ambar', 'it's a sheer waste of time'; 'there is no end to it'.

kiler Store-room; pantry; larder. ~ci, a kind of butler *or* housekeeper.

kilermeni Kind of red clay, *formerly used in medicine;* bole armeniac.

kilid Lock. ~ altında, under lock and key: ···e ~ vurmak, to lock: asma ~, padlock. ~lemek, to lock. ~lenmek, to be locked; (of teeth *etc.*) to be clenched. ~li, furnished with a lock; locked.

kilim Woven matting; carpet without pile. ~i kebeyi sermek, to settle in a place.

kilis *v.* kils.

kilise (·¹·) Church.

kiliz Reed. ~ balığı, tench.

killi Clayey.

kilo Kilogram. ~ almak, to put on weight.

kils Limestone. ~î, calcareous.

kilükal Gossip, tittle-tattle.

kilye Kidney. ~vî (··⅄), renal.

kim Who?; whoever. ~iniz, some of you; ~isi, some people: '~ ~e', 'nobody will notice it'; 'nobody knows anything about it': ~i ..., ~i ..., some ..., others ...: ~e ne!, what does it matter to anyone!: '~ ~inle, o da benimle', everyone has his *bête noire* and I am his: her ~, whoever: sen ~ oluyorsun?, 'who are you to *say etc.* ?': '~ vurduya gitti', so-and-so was killed, but no one knows by whom (the murderer escaped).

kimesne *Old form of* kimse.

kimse Someone; anyone; *(with neg.)* nobody, no one. ~den korkmam, I am afraid of no one: ~si yok, he has no one belonging to him, no friends: hiç bir ~, not a soul, no one. ~cikler, *only in* ~ yok, there's not a soul there. ~siz, without relations or friends; destitute. ~sizlik, a being without anyone to look after one; destitution.

kimya (·⅄) Chemistry; rare and precious thing. bil ~, chemically. ~ger, chemist. ~gerlik, science *or* profession of chemistry.

kimyevî (··⅄) Chemical.

kimyon Cummin. ~î, sage-green coloured.

kin, kine Malice; grudge; hatred. ~ini almak, to take one's revenge: ~ tutmak (bağlamak), to cherish a grudge, to nurse a hatred. ~ci, ~dar, ~li, vindictive; nourishing a grudge.

kinaye (·–¹) Allusion; hint; innuendo. ~li, allusive; sarcastic.

kinin Quinine.

kir Dirt; uncleanliness. ~ götürmek, (of a cloth *etc.*) not to show the dirt: ~ tutmak, to show the dirt.

kira (·⅄) A hiring; hire; rent. ~ ile tutmak, to rent or hire: ~ya vermek, to let out on hire, to let: 'ağzını ~ya mı verdin?', *said to one who is silent on a matter which concerns him* : ayak ~sı, payment to s.o. for going somewhere: 'ayağına ~ mı istiyorsun?', 'why can't you take the trouble to come (go) ?': diş ~sı, *v.* dişkirası: 'her gördüğünden göz ~sı istemek', to wish to imitate everything one sees.

kira·cı, who rents or hires; tenant. ~lamak, to rent, hire; let; let out on hire. ~lı, rented; let. ~lık, for hire, to let.

kiram (·⅄) *pl. of* kerim. As *adj.* Noble, honourable (*in such phrases as* ulemayı ~, azayı ~). ~en, *in* ~ kâtibin, the Recording Angels.

kiraren (·⸱·) Time and again.
kiraz, kirez Cherry. ~ ayı, May. ~ elması, a very small kind of apple.
kirde A kind of maize bread.
kirdigâr (··⸱⸻) The Creator.
kirec Lime. ~ gibi, very white: sönmemiş ~, quicklime: ~ ocağı, lime-kiln: ~ sütü, whitewash: ~ taşı, limestone. ~kaymağı, –nı, slaked lime. ~li, containing lime; whitewashed.
kiremit Tile.
kirez Cherry.
kiriş Catgut; bowstring; violin string; rafter. ~i kırmak (sl.), to run away: ~li köprü, girder bridge: kulakları ~te, all ears. ~leme, board set on edge; set on edge. ~lemek, to string (a bow).
kirizma Trenching of land. ~etm., to double-trench.
kir·lemek, ~letmek va. Dirty, soil; slander, calumniate. ~lenmek, to become dirty; to become morally soiled; (of a woman) to have her monthlies. ~li, dirty; soiled: dirty linen, the washing: ~ye atmak, to put clothes etc. aside for washing: ⌜~ çamaşırlarını ortaya çıkarmak⌝, to show up s.o.'s misdeeds '(not 'to wash one's dirty linen in public'). ~lilik, dirtiness; canonical uncleanness.
kirman Distaff; fortress.
kirpi Hedgehog.
kirpik¹ Eyelash. kirpiğimi kırpmadım (kavuşturmadım), I didn't sleep a wink.
kirpik², kerpik Carbuncle (stone).
kirş Rumen; paunch.
kisbî Acquired (as opp. to natural); who earns.
kispet, –ti Costume; wrestler's shorts.
Kisra (·⸱⸻) Chosroes; one of the Sassanian dynasty.
kisve, kisvet, –ti Garment; costume; costume of a special class; wrestler's shorts.
kiş Check! (at chess).
kişi Person; human being; indef. pron., one, you. ⌜~ bilmediğinin düşmanıdır⌝, man hates what he does not understand: ⌜~ ettiğini bulur⌝, as you sow, so will you reap. ~lik, special to so many persons; yüz ~, (stg.) for a hundred people. ~oğlu, ~zade (···⸻), of gentle birth. ~zadelik, being of a good family.
kişlemek va. Shoo away (birds).
kişmiş A small kind of raisin.
kişnemek vn. Neigh.
kişniş Coriander.
kişver Country. ~küşa (···⸺), ~sitan, conqueror.
kitab (·⸱) Book. ~a el basmak, to take an oath on a sacred book; to be quite certain about stg.: ~a uydurmak, to do stg. dis-

honest in an apparently honest way; to get round a law, an agreement etc.
kitab·cı, bookseller. ~e (··⸺), inscription on a monument etc. ~eli (·—·⸻), having an inscription; having an ornamental pattern. ~et (·—⸺), –ti, art of writing; writing lesson; essay-writing; literary style; office and duties of a clerk or secretary. ~evi, –ni, bookshop. ~hane (···⸺), library; bookshop. ~î (·—⸺), pertaining to books; bookish: librarian; believer in a sacred book. ~iyat (·—·⸺), –tı, bibliography. ~iye (·—·⸺), bast. ~siz, not possessing a book; not believing in a sacred book, pagan; hesabsız ~, without due consideration; without counting the cost.
kitakse etm. (·⸱·⸱) (sl.) va. (with dat.). Look at.
kitara (·⸱·) Guitar.
kitle v. kütle.
kit·lemek va. Lock. ~li, furnished with a lock; locked.
kitre Gum tragacanth.
kiyanus Cyanogen.
kiyaset (·—⸺), –ti Shrewdness; sagacity.
kiyotin Guillotine.
kizib, –zbi Lie.
klâkson Motor horn.
klâsör (Fr. classeur) File.
klâviye (Fr. clavier) Keyboard.
klefte (⸍·) Theft. ~ci, thief.
kliket (Fr. cliquetis) Pinking of an engine. ~leşmek, to pink, knock.
klor Chlorium.
klüb Club.
kobat Vulgar; rude; ugly.
kobay (Fr. cobaye) Guinea-pig, cavy.
koca Old, ancient; large, great; famous. Husband; old man; elder. ~ baş, cattle; v. also kocabaş: ~ya varmak, (of a woman) to marry: karı ~, a married couple; karı ~ kavgası, domestic squabble.
koca·baş, hawfinch (?); large beet. ~başı, village headman. ~karı, old woman: ~ soğuğu (= berdelacuz), cold spell at the end of March. ~lamak, ~laşmak, ~lmak, ~mak, to grow old. ~lı, having a husband. ~lık, old age; state of being a husband. ~man, huge, enormous. ~sız, unmarried (woman); widow. ~tmak, ~ltmak, to cause to grow old. ~yemişi (·⸱···), –ni, arbutus.
kocunmak vn. Take offence; sulk; be scared. ⌜(al kaşağıyı, gir ahıra) yarası olan kocunsun⌝, 'go into the stable with a curry-comb, the horse with a sore will be scared' ('let the galled jade wince'); a guilty conscience betrays itself; hence ⌜yaran yok ne kocunuyorsun?⌝, 'you've done nothing wrong, why are you scared?'

koç, -çu Ram; sturdy and plucky young man. ~ burunlu, Roman-nosed: ⌐ak ~ kara ~ o dövüşte belli olacak⌐, that fight will show who is the better man : ekmeğine ~, hospitable: yabani ~, wild sheep. ~başı (¹··), -nı, battering-ram. ~boynuzu, -nu, cleat. ~katımı, -nı, ramming season. ~kar, ram used for fighting. ~lanmak, to become a ram; to act violently or bravely.

koçak Brave; generous.

koçan Corncob; stump; heart of a vegetable; stump of counterfoils.

koçu Granary; cattle-shed; bullock-cart.

kod Code.

kodaman Large; clumsy; slow of movement; notable, influential. Magnate, 'big-wig'.

kodes (sl.) Prison, 'clink'.

kodeş, kodoş Pimp.

kof Hollow; rotten; weak; stupid; ignorant. ~luk, hollowness; ignorance.

kofana Large lüfer fish.

kofti (sl.) Lie; trick.

koğlamak, koğmak etc. v. kovlamak, kovmak etc.

koğuş, kovuş Large room; dormitory; ward. ~ağacı, -nı, baulk of timber; beam, joist.

kok, -ku Coke. ~laştırmak, to carbonize.

kokar That smells; fetid, stinking. akarı ~ı yok, in perfect order. ~ca, polecat.

kokla·mak va. Smell; nuzzle; get the wind of some coming event. koklayanın burnu düşmek, to be unpleasant. ~şmak, to smell one another; caress and kiss one another. ~tmak, caus. of koklamak q.v.; to give just a whiff of, i.e. give in very minute quantity.

kok·mak vn. Smell; stink; go bad; be at hand, give signs of being about to happen. misk gibi ~, (to smell like musk), to give very evident signs of its approach: ⌐ne kokar ne bulaşır⌐, harmless but useless. ~muş, putrid; rotten (egg etc.); very lazy; dirty (man).

kokona, kokana (·¹·) Elderly Greek woman.

kokoreç A dish of sheep's lungs.

kokoroz Ear of maize; the maize plant; any pointed ill-shaped thing. ~lamak, to be defiant or threatening.

kokoz Very poor; (sl.) hard up. ~luk, destitution.

kokteyl Cocktail.

koku Smell; scent; indication or inkling of stg. as yet unseen. ···in ~sunu almak, to perceive the smell of; to get an inkling or have a presentiment of stg.: ~su çıkmak, (of a secret) to be divulged; (of anything)

to give signs of its approach : doğru ~su da var, there is an air of truth about it : ben herkesin ağzının ~sunu çekemem, I can't put up with other people's whims or moods. koku·lu Having a certain smell; perfumed. ~tmak, to give out a smell; smell (badly) : make a place smell; cause s.o. to smell; sicken, disgust.

kol Arm; foreleg; neck; team; troupe; patrol; wing of an army; column of troops; branch, subdivision; handle; bar; strand of rope. ~ ~a, arm-in-arm : ~ atmak, to send forth branches, ramify, extend, develop : ~ emeği, manual labour : ~ gezmek, to go the rounds : ···in ~una girmek, to take s.o. by the arm : ~ kayığı, patrol-boat : ~ vurmak, to patrol : ~ yürütmek, to splice (rope).

kola Starch; starch paste. ~lamak, to starch. ~lı, starched.

kolaçan A walking about (esp. with an eye to pilfering). ~a çıkmak, to wander about seeing what can be picked up : ~ etm., to rummage about, poke about.

kolağası (¹···), -nı (Formerly) adjutant-major.

kolan¹ Broad band or belt; girth; binding round the bottom of a tent; rope of a swing. ~ vurmak, to girth a horse; to swing a swing standing. ~yeri, -ni, the part of a horse where the girth goes.

kolan² Young foal; wild ass.

kolay Easy. Easy way to do stg.; means. ~ına bakmak, to look about for the easiest way of doing stg.: ~ını bulmak, to find an easy way: ⌐~ gele!⌐, 'may it be easy!' (said to s.o. at work) : dile ~, easy to say but not so easy to do.

kolay·ca, pretty easy; quite easy. ~lamak, to facilitate; to have nearly finished (a job, money, food etc.); to 'break the back' of a task. ~laşmak, ~lanmak, to become easy; to be nearly finished. ~lık, easiness; facility in working; means; easy circumstances, comfort: ~ göstermek, to give facilities, to make things easy.

kol·cu Watchman; custom-house guard; agent for servants. ~çak, gauntlet; mitten; cuff-protector; armlet. ~daş, associate; companion; mate. ~demiri (¹···), -ni, iron bar for barring a door. ~düğmesi, -ni, cuff-link.

kolej College.

kolera (·¹·) Cholera.

kolkola (¹··) Arm-in-arm.

kollamak va. Search; keep under observation; look after, protect. sıra (fırsat) ~, to watch for an opportunity.

kollap Machine for winding gold thread on silk; hinge of a gate.

kolleksiyon Collection.

kollu Having arms *or* sleeves; having *so many* contingents (military force); having *so many* strands (rope). **dört ~ya binmek** (*sl.*), *lit.* to mount the four-handled (bier), *i.e.* to go to the grave.

kolluk Cuff.

kolon Colonist; column; colon.

kolona (·ᐟ·) Mullion.

kolonya (·ᐟ·) Eau-de-Cologne.

kolordu (ᐟ··) Army Corps.

koloridye (··ᐟ·) Young Spanish mackerel.

kolsaatı (ᐟ···), **–nı** Wrist-watch.

koltuk Armpit; arm-chair; out-of-the-way spot; small wine-shop; hawker; dealer in old clothes; flattery; *the ceremony during a wedding when the bridegroom gives his arm to the bride,* hence **koltuğa girmek,** to marry; **koltuğuna* girmek (takmak),** to give one's arm to s.o., to put one's arm through his: **~ değneği,** crutch; **~ değneğiyle,** with the help of others: **~ halatı,** mooring-rope: **koltuğu* kabarmak,** to swell with pride: **~ kapısı,** servants' entrance *in a big house*: **~ta olm.,** to be another's guest, to go to an entertainment at another's expense: ···**in koltuğuna sığınmak,** to be under the wing of ...: **~ vermek,** to flatter.

koltuk·altı (·ᐟ··), **–nı,** armpit; space under the arm. **~çu,** old-clothes man; keeper of a small out-of-the-way tavern; flatterer, hypocrite. **~lamak,** to support by the arm; to take *stg.* under the arm. **~lu,** having arms (chair); arm-chair.

kolye (*Fr. collier*) Necklace.

kolyoz Spanish mackerel.

kom Rough wayside inn *or* shelter.

koma¹ (ᐟ·) Apostrophe.

koma² Fellow wife; second wife of two.

koma³ Act of putting. Put; set down; (matter) brought forward. *Adv. expressing haste*: **~ koş !,** run hard !

komak *v.* **koymak.**

komalika (··ᐟ·) Shellac.

kombina (·ᐟ·) Combine.

komiser Superintendent of police.

komisyoncu Commission-agent.

komita (·ᐟ·) Revolutionary committee; secret society; member of such a society. **~cı,** member of a secret revolutionary society; rebel (*esp. applied to Bulgarian, Greek, and Serbian revolutionary plotters at the end of the 19th and beginning of the 20th centuries*).

kompas *v.* **kumpas.**

komplo (*Fr. complot*) Plot.

komposto (·ᐟ·) Stewed fruit.

komşu Neighbour. ⌐**~nun tavuğu ~ya kaz görünür**⌐, one always envies another's possessions: ⌐**ev alma ~ al**⌐, one's neighbours

matter more than one's house: ⌐**gülme ~na gelir başına**⌐, don't laugh at another's misfortune, it may happen to you one day. **~luk,** a being a neighbour; neighbourly deed.

‖**komuta** Command; order.

‖**komutan** Commander; commandant.

komün·ism Communism. **~ist,** communist.

konak¹ Scurf. **~lı¹,** scurfy.

konak² Halting-place; stage; day's journey; mansion; government house. **~ etm.,** to make a stop on a journey. **~çı,** billeting officer. **~lamak,** to stay for the night *when on a journey*; (*mil.*) to be billeted. **~lı²,** who lives in a big house; gentleman.

konc Leg of a boot *or* stocking.

konca Bud.

koncolos Vampire; werewolf.

kondurmak *va. caus. of* **konmak** *q.v.*; find lodgings for s.o.; quarter (troops); retort. ···**e ~,** to put or place on ...; to attribute to, to charge s.o. with *stg.*: **hastalığı kendine kondurmuyor,** he will never admit his illness: ···**e toz kondurmamak,** not to allow a word to be said against ... .

konferans Conference; lecture.

konfor Comfort.

‖**koni** Cone. **~k,** conic.

konişmento (··ᐟ·) Bill of lading.

konmak *vn.* Alight; settle; perch; camp; make a night's halt *during a journey*; have a piece of good luck. **konup göçmek,** to lead a nomadic life: **mirasa ~,** to come into an inheritance.

konser Concert.

konsey (*Fr. conseil*) Council.

konsol (*Fr. console*) Bracket; corbel.

konsolos Consul. **~hane** (···—ᐟ), consulate.

konsolto (·ᐟ·), **konsültasyon** Medical consultation.

kont, –tu Count.

kontak Contact (*elect.*); short circuit. **kafadan ~** (*sl.*), a bit touched in the head.

kontenjan (*Fr. contingent*) Quota.

kontes Countess.

kontluk County.

kontra (ᐟ·) Against. **~ flok,** flying-jib: **~lar sancaktan (iskeleden) seyretmek,** to be on the starboard (port) tack.

kontrat Contract.

kontrol Control.

‖**konu** Subject (matter).

konuk Guest. **~ lamak,** to entertain; put up (a guest); give a feast.

konukomşu The neighbours; all the neighbourhood.

konulmak *vn. impers. of* **konmak.** Be put, placed, set.

konur Swarthy; brave; proud (*in a good sense*).

konuşkan Loquacious.

konuş·mak *vn.* Converse, talk. *va.* Talk about. birisile konuşmamak, to have no more to do with a person. ~turmak *caus. of* konuşmak; to introduce *s.o. to another.*

konyak Brandy.

kopanakı (··¹·) Bobbin-lace.

koparmak *va.* Pluck; break off; take by force; get *stg.* out of *s.o.*; set up (an outcry). ⌜domuzdan kıl ~⌝, to succeed in getting stg. difficult (*e.g. money from a miser*): izin ~, to manage to get leave: kıyamet ~, to raise hell, to make a great fuss or row: ödünü ~, to terrify *s.o.*: toz ~, to raise a great dust: tuttuğunu koparır, he sees a thing through; he is resolute, dogged: zincirini ~, to become furious; to go raving mad.

kopasıca (··¹·) (*Lit. may it break off*) kafası ~ !, damn him!

kopay *v.* kopoy.

kopça Hook-and-eye. dişi ~, eye; erkek ~, hook. ~lamak, to fasten with hooks-and-eyes.

kopil Small Greek boy; rascal.

kopmak *vn.* Break in two; snap; set out or start off on an action; break out, begin (of any violent commotion or natural disturbance); ache violently; (*dial.*) run. bora koptu, the storm burst: gönülden ~ (of an act) to proceed from kindness of heart; gönülden ne koparsa, whatever one feels inclined to give: ödüm koptu, I was frightened to death: patırdı koptu, a great noise arose.

kopoy Sporting dog; hound.

kopuk Broken off, torn; penniless; vagabond.

kopuz Kind of guitar with one string.

kopya, kopye (¹·) Copy. ~cı, who copies; who cribs *at examinations.*

kor Red-hot cinder. bu kömür iyi ~ döker, this charcoal burns a long time.

koramiral (¹···), –li Vice-admiral.

kordele, kordela (·¹·) Ribbon.

kordon Cord; watch-chain; cordon; strand of rope *when separated.*

korgeneral (¹···), –li Corps Commander, Lieut.-General.

korınga Sainfoin.

korindon Corundum.

korkak Timid; cowardly. Coward. ~lık, cowardice; timidity.

korkmak *vn.* Be afraid. ···den ~, to be afraid of, to fear: ···den gözü* ~, to dread, be terrified of.

korku Fear; alarm; danger. ⌜~ dağları bekler⌝, of course he is (you *etc.* are) afraid,

can (baş) ~su, fear for one's life. ~lmak, *impers. of* korkmak: korkulur bir şey, a thing to be afraid of. ~lu, frightening, dangerous: ~ ruya, nightmare; ⌜~ ruya görmektense uyanık durmak hayırlıdır⌝, it is better to remain awake than to have a nightmare, better to be safe than sorry. ~luk, scarecrow; banister; parapet; guard of a sword-hilt; mere figurehead. ~nc, terrible, fearful. ~suz, fearless, intrepid; safe. ~suzluk, fearlessness; safety. ~tmak, to frighten, threaten.

korluk Fire of red-hot embers; brazier.

korna, korne (¹·) Motor horn.

korno (¹·) Horn; powder-horn; oil-can.

koro (¹·) Chorus.

korsan Pirate; corsair.

korse Corset.

korte Courtship.

koru Small wood, copse. ~cu, rural guard; forest watchman.

koruk Unripe grape. ~ lüferi, medium-sized lüfer, caught in August.

koru·mak *va.* Defend; watch over; cover (expenses). ~nma, defence: millî ~ mahkemesi, special tribunal set up for emergencies: pasif ~, air-raid precautions. ~nmak, to defend oneself; to take shelter: ···den ~, to avoid. ~yucu, protective: defender: ~ tababet, preventive medicine.

korunga *v.* korınga.

koskoca (¹··) Enormous; very eminent.

koskoslanmak (*sl.*) *vn.* Swagger.

koşaltı Pair of animals yoked or harnessed together.

koşma A kind of popular ballad.

koş·mak *vn.* Run. *va.* Harness; give as escort or companion; put to work; attribute; lay down (conditions). baş ~, to be obstinate, to insist: işe ~, *va.* to put to work: *vn.* to rush to work. ~turmak, *va. caus. of* koşmak, cause to run *etc.*; *also* to run about and tire oneself in *doing stg.*; to dispatch.

koşu Race. ~ atı racehorse: ~ yolu, racecourse, track: bir ~ (*pronounced* bikoşu), quickly, with a dash. ~cu, runner. ~lu, harnessed; (*mil.*) horse-drawn.

koşuk Ballad; folk-song.

koşulmak *vn. pass. and impers. of* koşmak. böyle koşulur, one runs like that.

koşum Act of harnessing; harness. ~ hayvanı, carriage-horse, draught-horse: ~ kayışı, trace.

koşuşmak *vn.* Run together; crowd in; make a concerted rush.

kota Quota.

kotarmak *va.* Dish up *food*; serve out. pişirip ~, to cook and serve up *food*; to settle *a question*; to finish off *a job*.

kotas Plume of yak's hair *used as an ornament on a horse*.

kotra (ˡˑ) Cutter (boat). Pen for small animals.

kova Bucket.

kovalamaca The game of 'touch-last' or 'catch'.

kovalamak *va.* Pursue; endeavour to obtain; wait for. **arkasından atla kovalar gibi**, 'as though pursued by horsemen', in great haste.

kovan Hive; cartridge-case; shell-case. **torpito ~ı**, torpedo-tube: **~lı anahtar**, box spanner.

kovcu Informer.

kovlamak *va.* Denounce.

kovmak, koğmak *va.* Drive away; turn back; repel; persecute; denounce, slander.

kovucu Who chases; *v. also* **kovcu.**

kovuk Hollow. Cavity. **dişinin kovuğuna bile gitmedi**, 'not enough to fill the hollow of a tooth', *i.e.* a very exiguous portion of food.

kovulamak *va.* Denounce.

kovuş *v.* **koğuş.**

‖**kovuşturma** Legal proceedings, prosecution.

koy Small bay *or* inlet; nook.

koyak Valley.

koyar Confluence of two streams.

koymak, komak *va.* Put; let go; leave; permit; suppose. ⌐**koydunsa bul!**⌐, 'I can't find it anywhere': **koyup gitmek**, to leave a thing and go away: **araya ~**, to use *s.o.* as intermediary: **bahis ~**, to lay a wager: **(bir yola) baş ~**, to be ready to sacrifice oneself for stg.: **el ~**, to requisition: **elden koymamak**, not to grudge; not to neglect: **ortaya (meydana) ~**, to produce; to bring foward *an argument etc.*; to prove: **üstüne ~**, to add: **yanına koymamak**, to leave unpunished: **yola ~**, to send *s.o.* off on a journey; **yoluna ~**, to put right; to set *a business going*.

koynu *v.* **koyun¹.**

koyu Thick; dense (liquid, darkness); deep, dark (colour); true, genuine; fervent, extreme. **~lanmak, ~laşmak**, to become dense; become dark (colour). **~lmak¹**, to become dense *etc*. **~ltmak**, to render dense; thicken (soup *etc.*); darken (colour). **~luk**, density; deepness *of colour*.

koyulmak² *vn. pass. of* **koymak.** Be put, *etc.*; be poured; **···e ~**, be busied with; set to *work etc.*, begin; fall on; attack.

koyun¹, -ynu Bosom; breast pocket. **~ koyna**, in each other's arms: **koynuna* almak**, to take to bed with one: **birinin koynuna girmek**, to go to bed with s.o.: **~ saatı**, pocket-watch: **elleri koynunda**, help-

less, not knowing what to do: **yüzü ~**, face downwards.

koyun² Sheep; mild, spiritless person; simpleton. **dağ ~u**, mouflon. **~gözü** (·ˡ··), **-nu**, feverfew; camomile. **~yılı, -nı**, 'the year of the sheep' *(the eighth year in the old Turkish cycle of years)*.

koyuvermek, koyvermek *va.* Let go; just to put down; allow. **altına ~**, to soil one's clothes involuntarily: **kahkahayı ~**, to burst into laughter: **kendini kapıp ~**, to cease to take an interest in oneself, in one's ordinary life, in one's business *etc.*; to let oneself drift; to feel quite free: **sakal ~**, to let the beard grow.

koz Walnut; trump *at cards*. **~ helvası**, nougat: **~ kabuğuna girmek**, to creep into any hole in order to hide oneself: **~ kaybetmek**, to lose one's case *at law or in an argument*: **~ kırmak**, to play a trump; to commit an indiscretion, make a *faux pas*. **~unu pay etm.**, to reach a settlement: **~ paylaşmak**, to go shares, to come to an agreement; **···le ~unu paylaşmak**, to settle accounts with …; 'sizinle paylaşacak **~um** var', 'I have a bone to pick with you'; ⌐**biz ~umuzu kendimiz paylaşırız**⌐, we'll settle our differences without your help.

koza Silk cocoon; a kind of bean; any small round thing.

kozak Cone of a coniferous tree; round thing.

kozalak Cypress cone; small stunted thing. **~lı**, coniferous.

köçek Dancing-boy; camel foal.

köfte Meat rissole.

köftehor Cunning rogue *(half affectionately)*; **~!**, lucky dog!

köftün Oil-cake.

köhne Old; worn; antiquated; secondhand.

kök¹, -kü Tuning-key of a stringed instrument. **sazı ~ etm.**, to tune a stringed instrument.

kök², -kü Root; base; fang *of a tooth*; origin; lode. **~ünden koparmak**, to eradicate: **~ünü kurutmak**, to exterminate: **~ salmak**, to be deeply rooted: **~ten sürme ressamdır**, he is an artist by descent: **işi ~ünden kesip atmak**, to reject *or* settle a matter once and for all: ⌐**hepsinin ~üne kibrit suyu!**⌐, 'to hell with the lot of them!' **kök·boyası** (ˡ···), **-nı**, madder. **~çü**, herbalist. **~lemek**, to uproot; to clear roots from the ground. **~lenmek, ~leşmek**, to take root; become firmly established. **~lü**, having roots; rooted.

köken Branch of a melon or marrow plant.

köknar Fir.

kölçer Darnel (?); smut (?).

köle Slave. **~niz**, your very humble servant: **~ doyuran**, a filling *food*.

kölemen Mameluke; *formerly* a corps of military slaves.

kömür Charcoal; *also used for* coal (*properly* maden *or* taş ~ü). Coal-black. ~ ocağı, coal-mine. ~cü, charcoal burner; coal-dealer; stoker. ~lük, coal-hole; coal-cellar; bunker (*naut.*).

köpek Dog; vile man. ~ balığı, shark. ~dişi (·¹··), **-ni**, canine tooth. ~lemek, ~leşmek, to cringe like a beaten dog. ~lik, low-down action; baseness. ~memesi, **-ni**, tumour which comes under the armpit.

köpoğlu, -nu Scoundrel. ~ köpek!, (dog son of a dog!), *term of violent abuse*. ~luk, a dirty trick.

köprü Bridge; hasp (of a lock). ~nün gözleri, the arches of a bridge.

köprücük Collar-bone.

köpük Froth; foam; scum; lather.

köpürmek *vn.* Froth; foam; foam at the mouth.

kör Blind; without foresight; careless; blunt (knife); small-meshed (net). ~ ~üne, blindly; carelessly: ~ boğaz, appetite (*contemptuously*): ~ düğüm, knot that can't be undone, tangle; deadlock: ⌐~ kadıya ~sün demek⌐, to 'call a spade a spade', *hence* ~ kadı, outspoken, downright: ~ kandil, blind drunk: ~ kaya, submerged rock: ~ünü kırmak, to humble the pride of *s.o.*: ~ kütük, dead drunk: ⌐~ ~ parmağım gözüne⌐, as plain as a pikestaff: ~ ocak, a childless family: ~ olası herif, the cursed fellow: ⌐~ ölür badem gözlü olur (kel ölür sırma saçlı olur)⌐, 'when the blind man dies, they say he had almond eyes (when the bald one dies, they say he had golden hair)', *exaggerated praise of the dead or the past*: ~ talih, bad luck, evil destiny: ~ tane, 'bunted' grain; smut-ball: ⌐~ün taşi rasgeldi⌐, 'the blind man's stone hit the mark', *said when some unlikely person has achieved success*: elinin ~ü!, you can go to hell!: ⌐kavga elinin ~ünden çıkar⌐, a mere trifle may cause a quarrel: gözün ~ olsun (olası)!, curse you!

kör·barsak, caecum, appendix. ~boğaz, gluttonous. ~döğüşü, **-nü**, confusion, muddle. ~ebe (¹··), blind man's buff; the ·blindfolded player.

köreşe Frozen crust on top of snow.

körfez Gulf.

kör·körüne (¹···) Blindly; at random; carelessly. ~lemeden, ~lemesine, blindly; at random. ~lemek, *v.* kör-letmek. ~lenmek, to become blind; become blunt; to get 'rusty' or stale (*fig.*). ~letmek, ~leştirmek, to blind; to blunt; damp, discourage; bring to nought: nef-

sini ~, to 'take the edge off' one's appetite *or* desire; to have a snack to satisfy one's hunger for the moment. ~lük, blindness; bluntness; lack of foresight; blundering.

köroğlu (¹··), **-nu** *The hero of a popular legend*; wife, 'the missus'. ~nun ayvazı, an inseparable companion: bir ~ bir ayvaz, just a wife and husband without children.

körpe Fresh; tender; very young and fresh. ~lik, freshness; tenderness; youth.

körsıçan (¹··) Mole.

körük Bellows; folding hood (of a car). yangına ~le gitmek, to add fuel to the flames. ~çü, bellows-maker; one who fans the flame, instigator, agitator. ~lemek, to fan a flame with bellows; encourage, incite. ~lü, having bellows: ~ bavul, expanding suit-case.

kör·yılan (¹··) Blind-worm. ~yol (¹·), railway branch line coming to a dead end.

kös[1] Big drum. ⌐~ dinlemiş (davulun sesi vız gelir)⌐, 'who has heard the big drum takes no notice of the sound of the kettle-drum', too sophisticated to be impressed; callous, insensitive.

kös[2] *In* ~ ~ yürümek, to walk in a pensive and dejected manner.

köse With little or no beard; sparsely timbered. ⌐her şey olur biter, ~nin sakalı bitmez⌐, (*a pun*) 'everything comes to an end (biter), but a beardless man's beard does not grow (bitmez)', all things come to an end: ⌐vay benim ~ sakalım!⌐, I am non-plussed. ~lik, scantiness of beard.

köseğen Sensitive plant (a kind of mimosa).

köseği Poker; piece of wood burnt at the end.

kösele (·¹·) Stout leather *used for soles*. ~ suratlı, shameless. ~taşı, **-nı**, sandstone *used for polishing marble*.

kösem, kösemen Ram or goat that leads the flock; bell wether; ram trained to fight; daredevil.

köskötürüm (¹···) Completely paralysed.

kösmek *vn.* Become slack and languid.

kösnü Lust; sensuality. ~k, lustful; on heat. ~mek, to be on heat.

köstebek Mole. ~ illeti, a kind of scrofula *which a mole was supposed to cure*.

köstek Watch-chain; fetter, hobble; brake. kösteği kırmak, to break one's fetters, run away.

kösümek, kösünmek *vn.* Be on heat.

köşe Corner; angle; nook; retreat. ~ ~ *or* ~ bucak, every hole and corner: ~ başı, street-corner: ~ kadısı, stay-at-home: ~ye oturmak, (of a girl) to get married: ~ sarrafı, street-corner money-changer: baş (üst) ~ye çıkmak, to place oneself at the top of the table, *i.e.* in the post of honour:

bir ~ye çekilmek, to go into retirement, to withdraw from public life.

köşebent Angle-tie.

köşek Camel foal.

köşe·kapmaca Puss-in-the-corner. ~**leme**, angular; having angles *or* corners. ~**li**, having corners *or* angles: üç ~, three-cornered, triangular. ~**taşı, –nı**, corner-stone.

kösk, –kü Pavilion; summer-house; villa; after deck-cabin. ~**lü**, *a man formerly employed to give warning of a fire.*

kötek[1] A beating. ~ **atmak** (çekmek), to give a beating: ~ **yemek**, to get a beating.

kötek[2] The Umbra (fish) (*Umbrina cirrhosa*).

kötü Bad. ~ **kadın**, prostitute: ~ **kişi olm.**, to become a bad man in the eyes of s.o. ~**lemek** *va.*, to speak ill of, slander: *vn.* to become a wreck *from illness.* ~**leşmek**, to become bad; deteriorate. ~**lük**, badness; bad action; harm.

‖**kötüm·semek** *va.* Think ill of. ‖~**ser**, pessimistic; derogatory.

kötürüm Paralysed; crippled. ~**lük**, paralysis.

köy Village; country (*as opp. to town*). ~**lü**, belonging to a village; peasant; fellow villager; rough, bucolic. ~**lülük**, a being born in *or* belonging to a village.

köymek *va.* Burn; brand.

köz Embers.

kral *v.* **kıral**.

krank *In* ~ **mili**, crankshaft.

kredi Credit.

kremayer (*Fr. cremaillère*) Rack (*mech.*).

krep Crêpe; pancake. ~**döşin**, crêpe-de-Chine.

kriko (¹·) Jack (for lifting).

kriz (*Fr. crise*) Crisis.

kroki (*Fr. croquis*) Sketch.

krom Chromium.

kron Crown (coin).

kropi *In* ~ **bağı**, figure-of-eight knot.

kruvazör Cruiser.

kubat Vulgar, coarse; common (accent or way of speaking).

kubbe Dome; cupola; vault *of heaven.* ~**leri çınlatmak**, to make the welkin ring: habbeyi ~ **yapmak**, to make a mountain out of a molehill: bir yalanın ~**sini yapmak**, to make a lie seem true by telling another.

kubuh, –bhu Ugliness; unseemliness; defect. **kubhiyat, –tı**, shameful acts.

kubur[1] *pl. of* **kabir**. Graves.

kubur[2] Holster; quiver; horse pistol; hole in old-fashioned latrine. ~**luk**, quiver.

kucak Breast; embrace; armful; lap. ~ ~, by armfuls: ~ **kucağa**, in one another's arms: kucağına almak, to embrace; to take on one's lap: ~(ta) çocuk, a child in arms.

~**lamak**, to embrace; surround; include. ~**laşmak**, to embrace one another.

kuçu kuçu Bow-wow; *call to a dog.*

kuddas Mass; Holy Communion.

kudema (··⌐) *pl. of* **kadim**. The ancients; eminent people; elders.

kudret, –ti Power; strength; capacity; the omnipotence of God; wealth; nature. ~**ten**, natural *phenomena etc.*: ~ **hamamı**, thermal spring: ~**im yetişmez**, I am not strong enough; I can't afford it: yedi ~, (the hand of power) Providence: yedi ~**inde*** olm., to be within one's power. ~**helvası, –nı**, manna. ~**li**, powerful; capable. ~**siz**, powerless; feeble; incapable.

kud·sal *v.* **kutsal**. ~**sî** (··⌐), sacred; divine. ~**siyat, –tı**, sacred things. ~**siyet, –ti**, sanctity.

kudum (·⌐) Arrival.

kudur·mak *vn.* Be attacked by rabies; go mad. ~**muş**, mad (dog): ⌐alışmış ~**tan** beterdir⌐, a habit is a curse. ~**tmak**, to infuriate.

kuduz Hydrophobia, rabies. Suffering from hydrophobia; furious. ~**böceği, –ni**, cantharides.

Kudüs Jerusalem.

kufa Round wickerwork coracle *used on the Tigris.*

kûfî (−⌐) Cufic characters for Arabic writing.

kuğu Swan.

kuğurmak *vn.* Coo.

kûhi Tumble-down.

kuka Ball (of wool *etc.*); coconut-wood.

kukla (¹·) Doll; puppet; very small man.

kuku Cuckoo.

kukulete (··¹·) Hood; cowl.

kukulya (·¹·) Silkworm cocoon. ~**cı**, gipsy fortune-teller: ~ **fırtınası**, storm occurring in mid-April.

kukumav The Little Owl. ~ **gibi**, sitting apart by himself.

kul Slave; creature; man (*in relation to God*); (*formerly*) Janissary. ~**unuz**, your servant, I: ~ **hakkı**, one's duty to one's neighbour (*as opp. to one's duty to God*): ···e ~ **kurban olm.**, to be devoted to ...: ~ olm., to be the slave of s.o., to do everything asked of one: ~ **yapısı**, man-made, perishable: Allahın ~**u**, human being: ⌐Allahın bildiğini ~**dan ne saklıyalım**⌐, I may as well say it: ⌐Allah birine 'yürü ~**um deyince**'⌐, 'when God says to s.o. 'progress, my slave!'', *used about one who has made rapid progress in his career*: ⌐Allah ne verir de ~ **kaldırmaz** (götürmez)⌐, human beings can bear whatever burdens Fate decrees.

kula (¹·) Russet; dun (horse).

kulaç Fathom. ~ ~, in full measure, freely: ~ **atmak**, to take soundings; to swim over-arm: **çift ~ yüzmek**, to swim double over-arm. ~**lamak**, to fathom; to measure with the extended arms; to walk swiftly.

kulağakaçan Earwig.

kulak Ear; attention; ear-shaped projec-tion *or* handle; flap; peg *of a violin*; mould-board (plough); guard *round a key-hole etc.*; slip of paper *attached to a letter*; branch pipe; small ball of forcemeat *put in soup*. ~**tan kulağa**, (news *etc.*) secretly passed on: **kulağı* ağır**, hard of hearing: ~ **asmak**, to lend an ear, to pay attention; '~ **asma!**', 'pay no heed!': **kulağını* bükmek**, to warn *s.o.* secretly about stg.: **kulağı delik**, alert, intelligent: ~ **demiri**, mouldboard *of a plough*: **kulağını* doldurmak**, to persuade *or* prime *s.o.*: ~ **dolgunⁱuğu**, hearsay; know-ledge acquired by listening to others: ~**tan dolma**, hearsay: ⌐**kulağını ensesinden gös-termek**⌐ *or* ⌐**sağ kulağını sol el ile göstermek**⌐, to point to the right ear with the left hand, *i.e.* to do stg. in a clumsy way: **kulağına girmedi**, he paid no attention: ~ **kesilmek**, to be all ears, to listen attentively: ~ **kiri**, ear-wax: **kulağına* koymak**, to prime *s.o.*, to drop him a hint: ~ **memesi**, lobe of the ear: ~ **misafiri**, one who overhears: **bir kulağı sağır olm.**, to shut one's eyes to stg., to wink at it: **kulağına* sokmak**, to force *stg.* on *s.o.'s* attention: ~ **tozu**, the sensitive spot behind the ear; *also sometimes used for* ear-drum: ~ **yumşağı**, lobe of the ear: ~ **zarı**, ear-drum: **eli kulağında**, stg. that may happen any moment, imminent, *v. App.*: **eli kulağa atıp gazeli başladi**, 'putting his hand to his ear he started to sing' (*describes the attitude of oriental singers*): **can kulağı ile dinlemek**, to listen with rapt attention: **göz ~ olm.**, to be all eyes and ears.

kulak·çın Ear-flap. ~**lık**, ear-flap; head-phone.

kulampara Pederast. ~**lık**, pederasty.

kule Tower; turret.

kulis Coulisse.

kullanış Method of using. ~**lı**, serviceable; handy. ~**sız**, unhandy; not practical.

kullanmak *va.* Use; employ; treat; deal tactfully with, humour: direct; drive (a car *etc.*); take habitually (a food, drink, tobacco *etc.*); appoint (to an office *etc.*).

kulluk Slavery, servitude; worship.

kullukçu (*Formerly*) Janissary stationed at a guard-house; subaltern in the Janissaries.

kuloğlu (ⁱ··), –**nu** (*Formerly*) member of a military force consisting of the sons of slaves.

kulp, –pu Handle (of a jug *etc.*); pretext. **bir ~una getirmek**, to seize an opportunity *to say stg.*: ~**takmak**, to invent a pretext;

to find an excuse *for blame or ridicule*: (ucunu) ~**unu bulmak**, to find a way of settling a matter: (ucunu) ~**unu kaybet-mek**, to be at a loss to know what to do: **yumurtaya ~ takmak**, to give the most absurd pretexts.

kulplu Having a handle.

kulûb *pl. of* **kalb**. Hearts.

kuluçka Broody hen. ~**devri**, incubation period (*also of a disease*): ~ **makinesi**, in-cubator: ~**ya oturmak**, (of a bird) to sit: ~**ya yatmak**, to incubate.

kulumbur Swivel-gun; carronade.

kulun New-born foal. ~ **atmak**, (of a mare) to abort.

kulunc Colic; cramp; lumbago. ~ **kırmak**, to cure lumbago by massage.

kulüb, klüb Club.

kulübe Hut; shed; sentry-box.

kum Sand; gravel; gravel (disease). ~ **balığı**, sand-eel: ~ **gibi kaynamak**, to swarm in countless numbers: ~**a oturmak**, (of a ship) to run on to a sandbank: ⌐~**da oyna da kıçına çöp batmasın**⌐, *means stg. like* 'you could hardly have done this with-out help': ~ **saatı**, hour-glass: ⌐**denizde ~ onda para**⌐, he is immensely wealthy.

kuma The second wife (of two).

kumanda Military command (order); com-mand (authority). ~ **etm.**, to command; to give a command. ~**n**, military com-mander; major (in some armies).

kumandarya (··ⁱ··) The Comanderia wine of Cyprus.

kumanya (·ⁱ·) Ship's provisions; portable rations *of a soldier*; small stern locker of a boat.

kumar Gambling. ~**baz**, ~**cı**, gambler. ~**bazlık**, gambling. ~**hane** (··–ⁱ), gambling-den.

kumaş Tissue; fabric, stuff; cloth; texture; quality.

kumbar Large lüfer.

kumbara (ⁱ··) Bomb; money-box. ~ **çivisi**, hobnail: **el ~sı**, hand-grenade. ~**cı**, bombardier.

kumkuma (·ⁱ·) Narrow-necked vase *or* bottle; ink-bottle; *used in such expressions as:* **esrar ~sı**, one full of secrets; **malûmat ~sı**, a mine of information.

kum·lu Sandy; gravelly; gritty; speckled with small spots (cloth *etc.*). ~**luk**, sandy place; sands; sandy.

kumpanya (·ⁱ·) Company.

kumpas Callipers; composing-stick; con-sideration and calculation; trick, plot. ~ **kurmak**, to calculate, plot, take counsel: ~**ı iyi kurdu**, he laid his plans well. ~**lı**, arranged; concerted; plotted; secretly *or* treacherously planned.

kumral Reddish-yellow; light-brown (hair); light chestnut (horse); darkish (complexion).

kumru Turtle-dove.

kumsal Sandy. Sandy place; sand beach. ~**lık**, sand-pit; gravel-pit.

kunda A kind of large poisonous spider.

kundak Bundle of rags; swaddling clothes; bun *of hair*; bundle of oily rags for incendiary purposes; stock *of a gun*; gun-carriage. ~**tan beri**, from the cradle: ~**taki çocuk**, a baby in arms: ···**e** ~ **sokmak**, to set fire to; sabotage. ~**çı**, gun-stock maker; incendiary; one who wrecks *a project etc.* ~**çılık**, arson; wrecking (*fig.*). ~**lamak**, to swaddle; set fire to; wreck (*fig.*), sabotage; to do the hair up in a bun. ~**lı**, swaddled; filled with combustibles.

kundura (¹··) Shoe. ~**cı**, shoemaker.

kunduz Beaver; (*err.*) otter. ~ **böceği**, cantharides.

kunt Strong; thick; solid.

kuntrat, kunturat, -tı Contract. ~**lı**, let *or* sold by contract.

kupa (¹·) Cup; wine-glass; cupful; hearts (cards); coupé.

kupes Bogue (*a kind of sea-bream, Box vulgaris*).

kupkuru (¹··) Bone-dry.

kupon Coupon; sufficient cloth to make a suit.

kur¹ (*Fr. cours*) Course *of studies etc.*; rate of exchange.

kur² (*Fr. cour*) Courtship.

kura kura *v.* **kurmak.**

kura (·¹) *pl. of* **kariye.** Villages.

kur'a The drawing of lots; military conscription; year (class) of conscripts. ~ **çekmek**, to draw lots: ~ **isabet etm.**, for the lot to fall to one; to be recruited by drawing lots: ~**ya girmek**, to reach military age: ~ **neferi**, conscript: ⌐**kaçın ~sıyız**⌐, 'I'm too old a bird to be caught by chaff'. ~**cı**, officer or committee charged with the drawing of lots for military service.

kurabiye (·—·¹) Cake made with almonds or nuts.

kurada Shrivelled; decrepit; worn out.

kurak Dry, arid. ~**lık**, drought.

Kur'an (·⸰) The Koran.

kuran (*Fr. courant*) Current *of air etc.* ~**der** (*Fr. courant d'air*), draught.

kurb, -bü Proximity; neighbourhood.

kurbağa Frog; the Star-gazer (*Uranoscopus scaber*). **kara** ~, toad. ⌐**yaptığı hayır ürkütüğü ~ya değmez**⌐, 'the good done will not make up for the frog which was frightened', *said about doing stg. which entails more fuss than it is worth.* ~**cık**, little frog; tumour on the tongue; handle

of a window-frame; wire-cutters. ~**lama**, frogwise: the breast stroke in swimming.

kurban (·⸰) Sacrifice; victim. ~ **bayramı**, the Moslem Festival of Sacrifices: ~ **kesmek**, to kill as a sacrifice: ~ **olm.**, to sacrifice oneself, to be a victim: ⌐~ **olayım!**⌐, 'I beseech you!': ~ **payı**, part of the sheep sacrificed given to the poor: **can** ~, (i) a thing one would give one's life for; (ii) 'I'd be only too glad!' ~**lık**, animal destined for sacrifice: ~ **koyun**, sheep for sacrifice; mild uncomplaining man.

kurbiyet, -ti Proximity.

kurca Irritation; itching. ~ **çıbanı**, an irritable ulcer.

kurcalamak *va.* Scratch; rub; irritate; meddle with; fiddle about with, tamper with. **mazıyı** ~, to rake up the past: **zihnini*** ~, to cause one to 'scratch one's head', to worry.

kurcata Crosstrees (*naut.*).

kurd *v.* **kurt.** ~**ağzı** (¹··), **-nı**, dovetail; (*naut.*) fairlead. ~**ayağı**, **-nı**, club-moss.

kurdela (·¹·) Ribbon.

kurdeşen Rash (measles, nettle-rash, harvest-bug bites).

kurena (··—¹) *pl. of* **karin.** Associates, companions; *as sing.* a chamberlain of the Sultan.

Kureyş The Koreish (the Prophet's tribe).

kurgan Castle; fortress.

kuriye Courier.

kurlağan Whitlow.

kurma An erecting *etc.* Portable; *toy etc.* that winds up.

kurmak *va.* Set up; establish; organize; plan, meditate; set (trap); cock (gun); pitch (tent); wind (clock *etc.*); prime (a person); make (a pickle). *vn.* Brood over *stg.* **kura kura**, by brooding over *stg.*: **bağdaş** ~, to sit cross-legged in oriental fashion: **sofra** ~, to lay a table.

‖**kurmay** Staff (*mil.*). **Genel** ~ **Başkanı**, Chief of the General Staff.

kurna Basin of a bath *or* fountain; sink.

kurnaz Cunning; shrewd. ~**lık**, cunning, shrewdness.

kuron (*Fr. couronne*) Crown *of a tooth*; crown, kroner (coin).

kurra (·¹) *pl. of* **kari.** Readers (*esp.* of the Koran).

kurs¹ (*Fr. cours*) Course *of lessons etc.*

kurs² Disk; lozenge; pastille of incense.

kursak Crop *of a bird*; stomach; dried bladder *or* its membrane. **varakçı kursağı**, goldbeaters' skin. ~**lı**, greedy; 'full of guts'; goitrous person.

kurşun Lead; bullet; lead seal. ~ **atmak**, to fire a rifle *etc.*; ~**a dizmek**, to execute by shooting: ~ **dökmek**, *to perform the* *superstitious custom of melting lead and pour-ing it into cold water over the head of a sick person*; ~cu kadın, the woman who per-forms this ceremony: ~ kâğıdı, tinfoil: ~ sirkesi, solution of subacetate of lead. Goulard water: ~ tavası, ladle for melting lead: ~ tuzu, subacetate of lead: ⌐şeytan kulağına ~!⌐, (may the Devil's ears be plugged with lead!), 'touch wood!' **kurşun·î** (··⸏), lead-coloured. **~kalem,** lead pencil. **~lamak,** to cover *or* seal with lead.

kurt Wolf; worm, maggot. ~ dökmek, to pass a worm; ~larını* dökmek, (i) to sow one's wild oats; (ii) to achieve a long desired object: ~ kapanı, pit for trapping wolves; a wrestling trick: kurdunu* kırmak, to satisfy one's whims: ⌐~ kuş yuvasına döndü⌐, everybody has gone home: ~ masalı, *v.* kurtmasalı: ···in kurdu olm., to be an old hand at ...; to be a hard-bitten ...: eski ~, old hand, old stager: ⌐hangi dağda ~ öldü?⌐, *said when stg. pleasant happens unexpectedly*: içine* ~ düşmek, to have a misgiving; içini* ~ gibi yemek, to be consumed by anxiety, to be very worried: kafasına* ~ sokmak, to put an idea into *s.o.'s* head.

kurt·ağzı (⸏··), –nı Dovetail; (*naut.*) fair-lead. **~bağrı, –nı,** privet. **~boğan,** aconite. **~çuk,** grub. **~lanmak,** to be-come maggoty *or* worm-eaten; become agitated *or* impatient; fidget. **~lu,** mag-goty, wormy; uneasy, suspicious; fidgety: ~ kaşar (peynir), a fidgety child. **~man-tarı, –nı,** puff-ball. **~masalı, –nı,** a story told to explain away stg.; 'the same old story': ~ okumak, to invent all sorts of pretexts in order to get out of doing stg. **~pençesi, –ni, ~tırnağı, –nı,** bistort. **~yeniği, –ni,** worm-hole in wood; *also used for* bityeniği, stg. 'fishy'.

kurtarmak *va.* Save, rescue; redeem *stg. pawned;* recover *one's losses at a game; also used err. for* kotarmak *q.v.* ⌐daha (bundan) aşağısı kurtarmaz⌐, (i) I can't sell it for less; (ii) nothing less will do for him, he must always have the best (*iron.*).

kurtul·mak *vn.* Escape; be saved; slip out; (of a pregnant woman) to be delivered; ···den ~, to be rid of, be free from; get out of; lose one's grip of. **~uş,** liberation; escape; way of escape.

kuru Dry; dried; withered; emaciated; bare; mere. Dry land; dry part *of anything.* ~ ~ya, uselessly, in vain; without good reason; mere: ~ çaylarda boğulmak, to toil without reward: ~ ekmek, dry bread (bread and nothing else): ~ gürültü, mere clamour; just rumour: ~ iftira, sheer

calumny: ~ kafa, skull; stupid; bir ~ kafa kalmak, (of a widow *etc.*) to be left all alone: ~ kahve, roasted *or* ground coffee-beans: ~ kalabalık, an aimless crowd; ~ kalabalık etm., to hang around and do nothing: ~ oda, unfurnished room: ~ sandalye, non-upholstered arm-chair: ~ sıkı, blank shot; empty threat; ~ sıkı atmak, to fire a blank shot; to utter empty threats: ~ tahtada kalmak, to lose one's furniture; to be destitute: ⌐~ yanında yaş ta yanar⌐, 'the green burns along with the dry', *i.e.* the innocent suffer with the guilty: ~ yerde (toprakta), on the bare earth: dut ~su, dried mulberries: kara ~, dark and skinny: piç ~su, a tiresome naughty child.

kurucu Founder.

kuruk Green grapes; sour wine.

kurulamak *va.* Wipe dry; dry.

kurulmak *vn. pass. of* kurmak. Be founded *etc.*; pose; swagger; settle oneself com-fortably. dünya kurulalıdan beri, since the beginning of the world.

kurultay Assembly; congress.

kurulu Established; set up; strung (bow); ready to fire (gun).

kuruluk Dryness.

kuruluş Foundation; structure; (*mil.*) dis-tribution of forces.

kurum[1] Soot. ~ tutmak, to be full of soot.

kurum[2] Pose; conceit. ~undan geçilmiyor, his conceit is intolerable: ~ ~ kurulmak, to be exceedingly puffed-up: ~ satmak, to give oneself airs.

‖**kurum**[3] Association; society.

kurumak *vn.* Dry; wither up; become thin; become paralysed. ⌐dilin kurusun!⌐, 'may your tongue be withered!' (*a curse*): kanı* ~, to be worried out of one's life.

kurum·lanmak *vn.* Be puffed-up, give oneself airs. **~lu,** conceited, puffed-up. **~suz,** without conceit; modest.

kurun (·⸏) *pl. of* karin. Ages. ~u ûlâ, ancient times: ~u vusta, the Middle Ages: ~u vustaî, medieval.

kurunmak *vn.* Dry oneself.

kuruntu Strange fancy; unfounded suspicion; illusion; melancholy. **~lu,** afflicted with unfounded fears or suspicions.

kuruş Piastre. **~luk,** piastre piece; piastre's worth.

kurut Dried milk product.

kurutma Action of drying. ~ kâğıdı, blotting-paper.

kurutmak *va.* Dry; cause to shrivel. kanını* ~, to persecute, vex, exasperate: kökünü* ~, to eradicate, utterly destroy.

kuruyası *Optative form of* kurumak. ⌐ağzı ~⌐, may his tongue be withered!' (*a curse*).

kuskun Crupper; stern-cable. ~u düşük,

broken-down (horse); down and out, too wretched to bother about his dress. **~suz**, without a crupper; free, unbridled; neglected, broken-down.

kuskus Dough in small pellets *used for pilaf*; semolina.

kusmak *va. & vn.* Vomit; (of cloth after being dyed or cleaned) to show up an old stain. **kusacağım geliyor**, I feel like being sick; I am utterly disgusted: **kan ~**, to be in great pain, to suffer greatly: ⌐**altın tasa kan ~**¹, 'to vomit blood into a golden bowl', *used of a rich man who is in bad health or otherwise unhappy.*

kus·muk, –uk, –untu Vomit. **~turucu**, emetic.

kusur (·⸱) Failure to do one's duty; defect, fault; remainder *of a sum of money.* **~a bakmamak**, to overlook an offence, to forgive: **~ etmemek**, to spare no effort: **analar ~u**, a poor sort of mother, a parody of a mother. **~lu**, faulty; incomplete, defective. **~suz**, without defect; complete; innocent.

kusva (·⸱) Very far; extreme. Extreme limit.

kuş Bird. **~a benzetmek**, to spoil *stg.* by trying to improve it (*v.* **~a dönmek** *and* *App.*): **~ beyinli**, of limited intelligence: **~a dönmek**, to look 'something like' (*iron.*), *v. App.*: **~ gibi**, very light *or* agile: ⌐**~ uçmaz, kervan geçmez**¹, a desolate, deserted spot: **~ uçurmaz**, very alert and capable: **~ uykusu**, a sleep from which one awakes at the slightest sound: ⌐**ağzıyle* ~ tutsa* faidesi yok**¹, even if he were to perform a miracle it would be no use now: ⌐**her ~un eti yenmez**¹, everyone is not at your service: **ona ~um kondu**, I took to him.

kuşak Sash; girdle; cummerbund; supporting beam; generation. **ipten ~ kuşanmak**, to be very poor: **ipsiz ~sız**, vagabond. **~lama**, diagonally. **~lamak**, to brace *or* tie (a wall *etc.*). **~lık**, *in such phrases as*: **üç ~ şehid çocuk**, a boy whose forefathers for three generations had died in battle.

kuşam *In* **giyim ~**, dress: **giyimli ~lı**, smartly dressed.

kuşane *v.* **kuşhane**.

kuşan·mak *vn. & va.* Gird oneself; put on a sash; gird on *a sword*; dress. **giyinmiş kuşanmış**, all dressed up: ⌐**iş becerenin, kılıç kuşananın**¹, success comes to those who know their job. **~tı**, *in* **giyinti ~**, clothes.

kuşatmak *va.* Wind round the waist; gird on; surround, envelop; besiege.

kuş·bakışı (¹···), **–nı** Bird's-eye view. **~başı**, in small pieces; (of snow) in big flakes: **~ et**, pieces of meat the size of a walnut. **~baz**, bird-fancier; bird-catcher. **~burnu, –nu**, beak; hip *of the dog-rose.* **~çu**, falconer; bird-fancier., **~dili, –ni**, thieves' slang; childish language *with an f or other letter added to each syllable.* **~gömü**, *in* **~ et**, the fillet of meat on each side of the back-bone. **~hane** (·–¹), place where hawks used to be kept; small saucepan. **~konmaz**, asparagus.

kuşe (*Fr. couché*) *In* **~ kâğıd**, art paper.

kuşku Suspicion. **~lanmak**, to feel nervous *or* suspicious.

kuş·lokumu (¹···), **–nu** Kind of sweet cake *sold in the street to children.* **~luk**, aviary; forenoon; lunch. **~palazı, –nı**, diphtheria. **~sütü, ~südü, –nü**, (*lit.* bird's milk); a non-existent or unobtainable thing. ⌐**~nden gayri her şey vardı**¹, there was every conceivable thing to eat: ⌐**~ ile beslemek**¹, to look after *s.o.* with every possible care. **~tüyü, –nü**, feather: **~ yatak**, feather-bed. **~üzümü, –nü**, dried currants. **~yemi, –ni**, canary seed; bird-seed.

kut¹ (–), **–tu** Food. **~u lâyemut**, just enough food to keep alive: **~u lâyemut geçinmek**, to live in utter poverty.

kut², **–tu** Luck; prosperity.

kût, –tü Fortress.

kûtah Short.

kutan Large plough.

kutb·î (·⸱) Polar. **~iyet, –ti**, polarity. **~u**, *v.* **kutub**.

kûtehbin Short-sighted.

kut·lamak *va.* Celebrate; congratulate. **~lu**, lucky; auspicious; happy. **~lulamak**, to offer congratulations to *s.o. on a feast-day etc.*

kutnu Kind of silk and cotton cloth. **Mısır ~su**, fustian.

‖**kut·sal** *Invented word to replace* **kutsî** (*properly* **kudsî** *q.v.*); sacred. **kutsuz** Unlucky. **~luk**, bad luck.

kuttaıtarik (·–·¹), **–ki** *pl. used also as sing.* Brigands; highwayman.

kutub, –tbu Pole (of the Earth); pole (*elect.*); most eminent person; the axis around which a business revolves. **kutbu şimalî (cenubî)**, North (South) Pole. **~eyn**, the two poles. **~yıldızı, –nı**, the Pole Star.

kutulâyemut (·–·⸱) *v.* **kut**.

kutur, –tru Region; diameter.

kuud (·⸱) Act of sitting; the sitting posture *in Moslem praying.*

kuva *pl. of* **kuvvet**. Powers; forces. **~yı külliye**, (*mil.*) main force.

kuvafür (*Fr. coiffeur*) Hairdresser.

kuvars Quartz.

kuvve *As* **kuvvet** *q.v.*; *also* faculty; quality;

potency; possibility. ~**den fiile getirmek** (**çıkarmak**), to put a project into execution : ~**de kalmak**, to remain merely as a project, not put into execution : ~**de olm.**, to be a possibility, to exist as a project; ~**de olarak**, potentially : ~**i samia**, the faculty of hearing.

kuvvet, –ti Strength; force; power; vigour. ~**le**, strongly : ~**ten düşmek**, to weaken, to lose strength : **paraya ~ muvaffak oldu**, he succeeded thanks to money : **var ~i ile**, with all his might. ~**lenmek**, to become strong; to be strengthened. ~**li**, strong, powerful. ~**siz**, weak, without strength. ~**sizlik**, weakness.

kuyd *Only used to emphasize* **kayıd**.

kuyruk Tail; appendix; follower; queue; train (of a dress or a great personage); corner or tail *of the eye*; breech *of a gun*. **kuyruğuna baka baka**, very dejectedly : **kuyruğuna basmak**, to provoke *s.o.* : **kuyruğu*** (**kapana**) **kısılmak** *or* **ele vermek**, to be caught by the tail, to be in great straits : **kuyruğunu* kısmak**, to put the tail between the legs (*also fig.*) : ~ **sallamak**, to wag the tail; to fawn and flatter : **kuyruğunu* tava sapına çevirmek**, to thrash *s.o.* : **kuyruğuna* teneke bağlamak**, to make a laughing-stock of *s.o.* : **kuyruğu titretmek** (*sl.*), to die : **çekiver kuyruğunu!**, forget about him! he's not worth worrying about : **o, bu adamın kuyruğudır**, he follows that man about like his shadow.

kuyruk·acısı, –nı, rancour; desire for vengeance for some wrong suffered. ~**lu**, having a tail : ~ **piyano**, grand piano : ~ **saat**, grandfather clock : ~ **sürme**, eyelid stain (antimony) slightly overdone : ~ **yalan**, a 'whopping' lie : ~ **yıldız**, comet. ~**sallıyan**, wagtail. ~**sokumu, –nu**, coccyx. ~**yağı, –nı**, fat melted down from the tail of the fat-tailed sheep.

kuytu Sheltered from the wind; snug; dark; hidden. Sheltered nook; remote spot.

kuyu Well; pit; borehole; mine-shaft. ~ **fındığı**, a kind of hazelnut *which is buried to give it a special flavour* : ···**in ~sunu kazmak**, to lay a trap for *s.o.* : **kar ~su**, snow-pit *for keeping snow for summer use.* ~**cu**, well-sinker.

kuyud (·**ᴗ**) *pl. of* **kayıd**. Bonds *etc.* ~**at, –tı**, registrations.

kuyum Gold *or* silver trinkets. ~**cu**, jeweller; goldsmith.

kuzahiye Iris *of the eye.*

kuzey Sunless side of a mountain; ‖north.

kuzgun Raven. ⌐~**a yavrusu şahin görünür**⌐, 'all his geese are swans' : ⌐**ya devlet başa ya ~ leşe**⌐, either good fortune or a miserable death; there is no saying what

may happen to one; ⌐neck or nothing⌐. ~**cuk**, grille in a prison door. **K~denizi, –ni**, the Caspian Sea. ~**î** (··ᴗ), black as a raven.

kuzu Lamb; mild man. ~**m**, my dear chap! : ~ **sarması**, lamb chitterlings, *v.* **canciğer** : **anasının körpe ~su**, mother's little darling. ~**cuk**, little *or* pet lamb. ~**çıbanı, –nı**, small boil. ~**dişi, –ni**, milk-tooth. ~**kestanesi, –ni**, a small variety of chestnut *eaten raw*. ~**kulağı, –nı**, sheep's-sorrel : ~ **tozu**, potassium oxalate. ~**lamak**, to lamb. ~**laşmak**, to become as mild as a lamb. ~**lu**, big with young *or* with a lamb at side. ~**mantarı, –nı**, morel.

kübik Cubic.

kübra (·ᴗ) *fem. of* **ekber**. Greater, greatest. Major premise.

küçücük (ᴗ··) Tiny; darling.

küçük Small; young; insignificant. Child; young animal. ~**ten beri**, from childhood : ~ **düşmek**, to look small, to feel ashamed : ~ **düşürmek**, to make *s.o.* feel small : **kendimizi ~ düşürmiyelim**, do not let us demean ourselves : ⌐~ **köyün büyük ağası**⌐, *said of a self-important man* : ~ **zabıt**, non-commissioned officer.

küçük·dil, uvula; *v.* **dil¹**. ~**lemek**, to despise; to slight. ~**lü**, intermixed with small : ~ **büyüklü**, some large, some small; young and old. ~**lük**, smallness; childhood; pettiness; indignity. ~**semek**, to despise; belittle.

küçül·mek *vn.* Become small; be reduced; wane; feel insignificant. ~**tmek**, to make small; diminish; reduce; belittle. ~**tücü**, humiliating.

küçümsemek *va.* Belittle.

küçürek Rather small.

küduret (·–ᴗ), **–ti** Grief, sadness.

küf Mould, mouldiness. ~ **bağlamak** (**tut-mak**), to become mouldy : ~ **tadı**, mouldy taste.

küfe Large deep basket *usually carried on the back*. ~ **ile getirilmek**, to be so drunk that one has to be carried home in a basket : ⌐**arkasında yumurta ~si yok ya, dönüverir**⌐, there's nothing to stop him changing his mind, his plans *etc.* ~**ci**, basket-maker; porter *who carries goods in a large basket on his back*. ~**li**, who carries goods in a küfe. ~**lik**, basketful; a man so drunk that he has to be carried home in a basket.

küfeki *v.* **kefeki**.

küffar *pl. of* **kâfir**. Unbelievers.

küf·lenmek *vn.* Turn mouldy; suffer from neglect. ~**lü**, mouldy; perished from neglect; out-of-date : ~ **para**, hoarded money.

küfran (·ﺣ) Ingratitude (*also* ∼ı nimet).

küfür, -frü Unbelief; blasphemy; cursing, swearing. ∼ **etm.**, to curse and swear. ∼**baz**, swearing; foul-mouthed.

küfür küfür *Imitates the rustling of the wind.*

küfüv, -fvü An equal in rank or social status (*mainly in connexion with marriage*).

küheylân Pure-bred Arab horse.

kükremek *vn.* Become infuriated with rage *or* sexual desire; foam at the mouth; (lion) roar.

kükürt Sulphur. ∼**lü**, sulphurous.

kül¹ Ashes. Ash-coloured; ruined. ∼ **etm.**, to ruin: ∼ **kedisi**, one who feels the cold, who likes the fire: ∼ **kesilmek**, to turn pale: ∼ **(kömür) olm.**, to be utterly ruined: ···**in** ∼**ünü savurmak**, to ruin *s.o.*: ∼ **yutmak**, to be duped.

kül², -llü The whole; all. ∼ **halinde**, as a whole: ∼**le yevmin**, every day, always.

külâh Conical hat; anything of that shape; trick, deceit. ∼ **giydirmek**, to play a trick on *s.o.*: ∼**ını* havaya atmak**, to throw one's hat in the air for joy: ∼ **kapmak**, to secure some advantage for oneself by cunning: ∼ **sallamak**, to flatter, toady: ⌐**Alinin** ∼**ını Veliye, Velinin** ∼**ını Aliye giydirmek**⌐, to make one's way or earn one's living by little tricks: ⌐**bunu (gecelik)** ∼**ıma anlat!**⌐, 'tell me another!': ⌐**sonra** ∼**ları değişiriz**⌐, *do this or* we shall fall out: ⌐**şeytana** ∼**ını ters giydirmek**⌐, to be very cunning.

külâhçı Trickster.

külbastı Grilled cutlet.

külbütör (*Fr. culbuteur*) Rocker-arm.

külçe Metal ingot; heap; pile; bunch *of keys.* ∼ **gibi oturmak**, to collapse from fatigue.

küldür *v.* paldır.

külek Tub *with handles.*

külfet, -ti Trouble; inconvenience; great expense; ceremonious behaviour. ∼ **etm.**, to put oneself to inconvenience. ∼**li**, troublesome; laborious; expensive; ceremonious; forced, unnatural. ∼**siz**, easy; without inconvenience; unceremonious; natural; spontaneous; informal; not involving great expense.

külhan Stoke-hole of a bath. ∼**beyi** (·ﺣ···), **-ni**, a rough, a rowdy; a young blood of the lower classes. ∼**ı** (·—ﺣ), urchin; young scamp; merry fellow.

külkedisi *v.* kül.

külleme Mildew of vines.

kül·lemek *va.* Cover with ashes. ∼**lenmek**, to be turned to ashes; smoulder; cool down, die down.

küll-î (·—ﺣ) Total; universal; abundant. ∼**iyat, -tı**, complete works of an author. ∼**iyen** (·ﺣ·), totally; entirely; (*with neg.*)

not at all, absolutely not. ∼**iyet, -ti**, totality; entirety; abundance: ∼**le**, in great quantity. ∼**iyetli**, abundant.

küllü¹ Containing *or* mixed with ashes. ∼ **su**, lye.

küllü² *v.* küllî.

külot, -tu (*Fr. culotte*) Knickerbockers; riding-breeches.

külrengi (ﺣ··) Ash-coloured.

kültür Culture.

külünk Pick; mace; crow-bar.

külüstür Shabby; out-of-date; poor in quality.

kümbet, -ti Vault; dome; projection; (*sl.*) the behind. ∼**li**, projecting.

küme Heap; mass; mound; hill; straw or reed hut; hide *for shooting.*

kümeç *v.* gümeç.

kümes Poultry-house; coop; hut. ∼ **hayvanları**, poultry.

kümültü Small hut *for keepers or huntsmen.*

künbed *v.* kümbet.

künde Fetter, hobble; trap; ambush. ∼**ye almak** (düşürmek), to throw by a trick *in wrestling*: ∼**den atmak**, to trip s.o. up (*fig.*).

künfeyekûn (ﺣ···) (Be and it is!); Divine creation out of chaos.

küngürlemek *vn.* Be drowsy.

künh Essence; reality. ∼**üne varmak**, to get to the bottom of a matter, to learn thoroughly.

künk Earthenware water-pipe. ∼ **döşemek**, to lay down water *or* drainage pipes.

künke Chip *or* splinter of wood.

künuz *pl.* of kenz. Treasures.

künye Patronymic. ∼ **(defteri)** register of names, *esp.* Army list: ∼**si bozuk**, who has a bad record.

küp, -pü Large earthenware jar. ∼**lere binmek**, to get into a rage: ∼ **gibi**, enormously stout: **altın** ∼**ü**, a Croesus: ∼**ünü doldurmak**, to grow rich; to feather one's nest.

küpe Ear-ring; dewlap. ⌐**kulağında*** ∼ **olsun**⌐, take that piece of advice, let that be a warning to you; **bu benim kulağıma** ∼ **oldu**, that was a lesson to me; I never forgot it. ∼**çiçeği** (·ﺣ···), **-ni**, fuchsia. ∼**li**, wearing ear-rings; having a dewlap.

küpeste (·ﺣ) Gunwale (boat); bulwarks (ship); rail *of banisters.*

kür Health cure.

Kürd Kurd; Kurdish.

kürdan (*Fr. cure-dents*) Tooth-pick.

küre Globe; sphere. ∼**i mücesseme**, globe (terrestrial or celestial). ∼**iarz**, terrestrial sphere; the Earth.

kürek Shovel; oar; hard labour, penal servitude. ∼**çekmek**, to row: **akıntıya** ∼ **çekmek**, to row against the current, to struggle in vain: on sene küreğe mahkûm oldu, he was sentenced to ten years' hard labour: ⌈tek ~le mehtaba çıkmak⌉, (to go for a moonlight row with only one oar), (i) to undertake stg. with insufficient means; (ii) to make a feeble attempt at mocking s.o. ~çi, oarsman, rower. ~kemiği, -ni, shoulder-blade. ~li, having *so many* oars; iki çifte ~ sandal, a two pair-oar boat.

kürelemek, küremek *va.* Shovel up; clear away.

kürevî (··⌐) Spherical. ~yat (···⸜), -tı, spherical trigonometry.

kürey·vat, -tı Globules; corpuscles. ~ı beyza (hamra), white (red) corpuscles. ~ve, globule.

kürk, -kü Fur; fur-coat. ⌈ye ~üm, ye!⌉ *or* ⌈buyurun ~üm!⌉, *used when s.o. is judged by his outward appearance only, v. App.* ~çü, furrier. ~lü, of fur; adorned with fur; fur-bearing (animal); wearing a fur-coat.

kürsü Throne; sofa; chair; footstool; pulpit; dais; tribune; the upper heaven supporting the throne of God. ~ taşı, pedestal stone.

kürtaj Curetting.

kürtün Large and clumsy pack-saddle.

küs Easily offended; sulky.

küskü Crow-bar; fire-dog; iron wedge; half-burnt piece of wood.

küskün Disgruntled; offended. talih ~ü, unlucky. ~lük, vexation; a being in the sulks.

küşkütük Helplessly drunk.

küsmek *vn.* Be offended; sulk. ⌈bahtina (talihina) küssün⌉, it's just a bit of bad luck: talihe (tecelliye) ~, to be tired of life; to curse one's fate: ⌈tavşan dağa küsmüş, dağın haberi olmamış⌉, the hare was offended with the mountain, but the mountain never noticed it.

küspe Residue of crushed seeds; oilcake.

küstah Insolent. ~lık, insolence, effrontery.

küstere Jack-plane; grindstone. ~ye tutmak, to sharpen on a grindstone.

küstümotu (·⸜··), -nu Mimosa.

küsuf Solar eclipse.

küsur *pl. of* kesir. Fractions. iki bin ~, two thousand odd: bir ~ yıldır, it's a year and a bit since .... ~at (··⌐), -tı, *pl. of pl. of* kesir: groups of fractions; fractions (*arith.*).

-küşa (·⌐) *Pers. suffix.* Opening ...; expanding ...; conquering ...; *e.g.* kişverküşa, conquering lands, conqueror.

küşad Opening; inauguration; opening *at chess or backgammon.* ~ etm., to open (exhibition, hospital *etc.*): resmi ~, official opening or inauguration. ~e (·−⌐), open; cheerful.

küşayiş (·−⌐) Cheerfulness.

küşne A kind of vetch.

küt¹ Blunt; not pointed; paralysed.

küt² *Imitates the noise of knocking on a door or of the heart beating etc.* ~ diye vurdu, he gave it a sharp blow: para ~ cebe, he popped the money into his pocket.

kütah (·⌐) *Vulg. form of* kûtah *only used in* ömrünü (gencliğini) ~ etm., not to have enjoyed one's life (youth).

kütle Heap; block; mass; great quantity; aggregate. ~vî (··⌐), massive; in the bulk or mass.

kütlemek *vn.* Give out a thudding noise.

kütlü *Cotton* with the seed in it.

küttab *pl. of* kâtib. Writers.

küttedek (⸜··) With a bang.

kütüb *pl. of* kitab. Books. ~hane, ~ane (···−⌐), library; book-shop.

kütük Tree-stump; baulk; log; stock *of a vine*; ledger, register; cartridge pouch. ~ gibi, dead drunk: cehennem kütüğü, a hardened sinner: eski ~, a seasoned log; an experienced old man. ~lük, belt with cartridge pouches attached.

kütür Crisp, fresh (fruit). ~ ~, the noise made when eating such; a crunching sound. ~demek, to give out a crashing *or* crunching sound. ~dü, the sound of stg. cracking *or* of an apple or a cucumber being eaten.

küul, -lü Alcohol. ~î (··⌐), alcoholic.

küvet, -ti (*Fr. cuvette*) Wash-hand basin; developing dish.

küzaz Tetanus.

L

lâ- (−) *Arabic neg. particle used only in Arabic compounds or phrases, e.g.* lâübali (I care not), free-and-easy; lâyemut (he dies not), immortal.

lâakal (⌐··) At least; not less than.

lâalettayin (⌐··−·) At random; whosoever; whatsoever.

lâbada Dock (plant).

lâbirent, -ti Labyrinth.

lâbis (−⌐) Wearing, dressed in (*acc.*).

lâbüd (−⌐) Indispensable; inevitable; necessarily.

lâçin Peregrine. Severe; determined.

lâçiverd (−·⌐) Lapis-lazuli; dark-blue colour. ~î (−−·⌐), dark-blue.

lâçka (⌐·) Let go!; slacken off (rope)! Play

or slack *in machinery*. ~ etm., to slacken *or* cast off *a rope*; to get slack: demiri ~ etm., to let go the anchor.

lâden (−¹) Ladanum; resin of Cistus plants.

lâdes (−¹) A game *or* bet with the wishbone of a fowl. ~ tutuşmak, to pull a wishbone with one another: ⌐bile bile ~l¬, 'I know I shall be worsted', *said when one is obviously going to be cheated*.

lâdin Spruce.

lâdinga (·¹·) Cartridge-belt.

lâdinî (−−¹) Not connected with religion; lay.

lâedri (−¹·) (*Lit.* I do not know); anonymous author; anon.

lâf Word; talk; empty words; boasting; [*in many phrases* lâf *is interchangeable with* söz *q.v.*]. ~ ~fı açar, one topic leads to another: ~ altında kalmamak, to be quick to retort, to give as good as one gets: ⌐~ anlayan beri gelsin¬, no one seems to see the point *of what I am saying*: ~ atmak, to chatter; to make insolent remarks to a woman in the streets: ~ını bilmek, to weigh one's words: ~ değil, it's no trifle, it's important: ~ ebesi, a great talker; quick at repartee: ···i ~ etm., to gossip about (unfavourably); ···in ~ını etm., to talk about *s.o. or stg.*: ~ü güzaf, empty words, brag: ~ işitmek, to be rebuked: ⌐~kıtlığında asmalar budayım¬ *or* ⌐~ söyledi balkabağı¬, 'what's that got to do with it?; 'don't talk rot!': ⌐~ ola beri gele¬, that's nothing to do with the question; that is beside the mark; ~ olsun (*or* ola) diye, just for stg. to say: 'Ahmedin yanında onun ~ı olur mu?', he cannot be spoken of in the same breath with Ahmed: 'böyle yapmıyalım, ~ olur', 'don't let's do this or people will talk': ~a tutmak, to engage *s.o.* in conversation *thereby preventing him from working etc.*: uzun ~ın kısası, in short.

lâfazan Braggart; windbag. ~lık, chatter; boasting.

lâfetmek (¹··), **−eder** *vn.* Speak, talk; gossip; grumble.

lâfız, −fzı Word. lâfzı murad, (i) said but not meant; (ii) person *or* thing of no account.

lâf·zan (¹·) Literally; *v. also* **lâfazan.** ~î (·¹), literal.

lâğar (−¹) Thin and weak; weedy (*of animals only*).

lâğım, −ğmı Underground tunnel; sewer; explosive mine; adit. ~ açmak, to dig a drain; to tunnel for a mine: ~ atmak, to fire a mine. ~cı, sewerman; sapper.

lâğıv, −ğvı Cancellation, annulment; suppression. **lağvetmek** (¹··), **−eder**, to abrogate, cancel; abolish.

lahana (·¹·) Cabbage. ~ turşusu, pickled cabbage: ⌐bu ne perhiz, bu ne ~ turşusu?¬, *said of two opposite extremes*: frenk ~sı, Brussels sprouts.

lâhavle (−¹·) *The use of the expression* 'lâ havle ve lâ kuvvete illâ billâh' (there is no power nor strength but in God) *used to express boredom or impatience*: ~ çekmek, to use this expression.

Lahey The Hague.

lâhid, −hdi Tomb.

lâhik¹ (·¹), **−hki** Alluvial soil.

lâhik² (−¹), **−ki** Joined on to; added; succeeding to *or* newly appointed to a post; present holder of an office. ~a (−−¹), appendix; suffix; codicil; additional note.

lâhim (·¹), **−hmi** Meat; pulp *of a fruit*; ~ *or* lâhmi zaid, sarcoma. ~ (−¹), carnivorous.

lâhin, −hni Note; tone; melody.

lâhm·i *v.* lâhim. ~î (·¹), fleshy; sarcomatous.

lâhur·aki (··¹·) A fine merino *imitating Lahore shawls*. ~î (··¹), the stuff of which Lahore shawls are made.

lâhut (−¹), **−tu** Divinity. âlemi ~, the spiritual world, the eternal life. ~tî (−−¹), divine; spiritual.

lâhza, lâhze The twinkling of an eye; instant.

lâik (*Fr. laïque*) Lay, secular.

lâin (−¹) Who curses. ~ (·¹), accursed; godforsaken; execrable.

lâk, lâka Lacquer.

lâkab Family name; cognomen; nickname.

lâkayd (−¹) Indifferent; nonchalant. ~î (−·¹), nonchalance; indifference.

lâke Lacquered.

lâken *v.* leken.

lâkerda (·¹·) Salted tunny.

lâkırdı Word; talk; promise. ~ ağzından* dökülmek, to talk unwillingly: ~ altında kalmamak, to give as good as one gets, to be quick to retort: ~ya boğmak, purposely to obscure or divert the conversation by a lot of irrelevant talk: ~ etm., to talk; to gossip; ···in ~sını etm., to mention: ~ karıştırmak, to draw a red herring across the trail: ~ taşımak, to repeat to s.o. other people's gossip about him: bu çocuk ~ anlamıyor, this child is incorrigible. ~cı, loquacious; chatterbox.

lâkin (−¹) But; nevertheless.

lâklâk, ~a The clacking noise made by storks; senseless chatter. ⌐leyleğin ömrü ~ ile geçer¬, *said of people who just talk and do nothing*. ~ıyat, **−tı**, twaddle.

lâl¹ (·) Mute.

lâl² (−), **−lı** Ruby; garnet; ruby lips; red ink.

lâla (¹·) Servant placed in charge of a boy; tutor; pedagogue. ⸢~ **paşa eğlencesi değilim**⸣, 'it's not my job to keep people amused *or* flattered'.

lâlanga (·¹·) Kind of pancake.

lâle¹ (−¹) Iron ring *formerly put round the neck of convicts and lunatics*; forked stick *for picking figs*.

lâle² (−¹) Tulip. ~ **devri**, the early eighteenth century (*when tulips were greatly in vogue*). ~**gün**, red. ~**zar**, tulip garden: ⸢**mangal kenarı kış gününün ~ıdır**⸣, 'the fireside is the tulip garden of winter', *i.e.* the best place.

lâm¹ The Arabic letter L. ~ **elif çevirmek**, to take a stroll: ~ **cim istemez**, *or* ~**ı cimi yok**, it must be done; there's no question about it!; *also used of a very critical situation*, 'it's all up!'

lâm² (*Fr. lame*) Thin plate; microscope slide.

lâma Sheet of metal. ~ **demiri**, sheet-iron.

lâmba¹ (¹·) Cornice; mortise; rebate.

lâmba² (¹·) Lamp; radio valve. ~ **gömleği**, incandescent mantle.

lâmekân (−·¹) That which is without place; infinity; God.

lâmel (*Fr. lamelle*) Cover-glass (microscope).

lâmı (−¹) Shining.

lâmis (−¹) Feeling; touching. ~**e**, the sense of touch.

lâmpasa (·¹·) Large and untidy; uncouth. Untidy, long and loose garment.

lândo, lândon Landau.

lâne (−¹) Nest.

lânet (⸣·), −**ti** Curse, imprecation. Damnable; peevish, cross-grained. ~ **etm.**, to curse: ~ **olsun!**, a curse upon him (it *etc.*). ~**leme**, act of cursing *or* of pronouncing an anthema against s.o.: accursed, anathematized. ~**lemek**, to curse; to pronounce a formal anathema against *s.o.*

lângır lûngur Who speaks in a loud voice and with a vulgar accent; random and tactless (talk); lumbering along.

lâp lâp Flop! flap! ~ ~ **yemek**, to eat greedily, smacking the lips.

lâpa Rice pudding; any moist dish; poultice. Soft, flabby. ~ ~ **kar yağmak**, to snow in large flakes. ~**cı**, fond of sloppy dishes; languid, flabby (person); milksop. ~**msı**, flabby.

lâpçin Sort of indoor boot *laced at the side*. ~ **ağızlı**, windbag.

lâpina (·¹·) Wrasse.

Lâpon Laplander. ~**ya** (·¹·), Lapland.

lâppadak, lârpadak (¹··) Suddenly; with a flop.

lârmo (¹·) *In* ~ **yakası**, luff *of a sail*.

lâsta (¹·) Maximum load a ship can carry.

lâstik Rubber; galoshes; tyre. ~**li**, made of rubber; elastic.

lâşe Corpse, carcass; putrid thing; thing no no longer fit for use and past repair.

lâşek (−¹) Without doubt.

lâşey (−¹) A thing of no account.

lâşka (¹·) *v.* **lâçka**.

lâta (¹·) Lath; gown *formerly worn by ulema*; frock *of a priest*.

lâtarna, lâterna (·¹·) Barrel-organ.

lâteşbih (⸣··) Anything but ...; far from being ... .

lâtif Fine; slender; pleasant; elegant; light; subtle; witty. ~**e** (·−¹), Joke, witticism; anecdote: ⸢~ **lâtif gerek**⸣, a joke should be refined. ~**eci**, ~**egû** (·−·¹), fond of making jokes or telling stories.

lâtilokum Turkish delight.

lâtin¹ (¹·) Eastern Catholic; Latin. ~ **çiçeği**, nasturtium. ~**ce**, Latin language.

lâtin² (⸣·) Lateen sail.

lâübali (−·−⸣) (*Lit.* 'I don't care'); free-and-easy; too familiar or intimate; careless; offhand. ~**leşmek**, to be too free-and-easy; to take liberties. ~**lik**, too free-and-easy behaviour; an offhand manner.

lâv Lava.

lâva (¹·) Pull!; hoist away! ~**etm.**, to pull a boat *etc.*

lâvanta (·¹·) Lavender water; perfume. ~ **çiçeği**, lavender (flower).

lâvha *v.* **levha**.

lâvta¹ (¹·) Obstetric forceps; doctor *or* midwife.

lâvta² (¹·) Lute.

lâyakil (−·¹) Beside oneself; unconscious; blind drunk.

lâyemut (−·⸣) Undying; immortal. **kutu** ~, food just sufficient to keep body and soul together.

lâyenkati (−··¹) Incessantly, without interruption.

lâyetecezza (⸣···−) Indivisible. **cüz'ü** ~, indivisible fraction, atom.

lâyetegayyer (⸣····) Immutable.

lâyezal (−·⸣) Permanent; eternal.

lâyık (−¹), −**kı**, −**ğı** Suitable; worthy. That which one deserves. ~**ile**, as it should be; in a worthy manner: ~**ını bulmak**, to get one's deserts: ~ **görmek**, to deem worthy or suitable: ···**e** ~ **olm.**, to be worthy of, to merit: ~**ı vechile**, properly, adequately: ⸢**ağzına** ~⸣, (worthy of your palate); that was a really good meal; I wish you could have been there.

lâyiha (−·¹) Explanatory document; project; bill (proposed law).

lâyuad (−·¹), −**ddi** Innumerable.

lâyuhsa (−·⸣) Countless.

lâyuhti (–·$\overset{\backslash}{·}$) Infallible.

lâyüflühun (–··$\overset{\backslash}{·}$) Incorrigible.

lâyüs'el (–·$\overset{\backslash}{·}$) Not liable to be called to account; not responsible.

Lâz The Laz people *of the SE. coast of the Black Sea.* ~**ca** ($\overset{\backslash}{·}·$), in the Laz way; the Laz language.

lâza Tray *or* small trough.

lâzım (–$\overset{\backslash}{·}$) Necessary; requisite; neuter (verb). ~ **gelmek**, to be necessary; to be a necessary consequence; ~ **gelenlere**, to whom it concerns: ~ **olm.**, to be necessary; to be needed: **neme (nesine, nenize)** ~**?**, what's that to me (him, you)?; *also sometimes*: but still; all the same: **senin ne üstüne** ~**?**, what's that got to do with you? ~**lı**, necessary; unavoidable. ~**lık**, chamber-pot.

lâzime (–·$\overset{\backslash}{·}$) A necessary thing; natural consequence; corollary; obligation; requisite *for a journey etc.*; ship's stores. ~**ci**, ship-chandler.

leb Lip; edge. ~**i derya**, sea-shore. ~**aleb** ($\overset{\backslash}{·}·$), brimful.

lebbeyk, lebbey Sir!; at your service!

leblebi Roasted chick-peas; bullet. **demir** ~, a very difficult task; a hard nut to crack; stg. hard to stomach: ⌐**leb demeden** ~**yi anlamak**⌐, to understand instantly. ~**ci**, seller of roasted chick-peas.

ledel- ($\overset{\backslash}{·}·$) *Prefix forming an adverb with Arabic nouns*: at the time of ...; on (on the occurrence of ...): ~**vusul**, on its arrival: **ledessual**, on being questioned. ~**hace** ($\overset{\backslash}{·}$–·), in case of necessity. ~**icab**, when required. ~**istintak**, after interrogation. ~**muayene** ($\overset{\backslash}{·}$··–··), on inspection. ~**tahkik**, on investigation.

ledün Consciousness of God. **ilmi** ~, the knowledge of Divine Providence. ~**î** (··$\overset{\backslash}{·}$), derived from *or* existing in God. ~**iyat** (···$\overset{\backslash}{·}$), **–tı**, the mysteries of the Divine Nature; the real truth or inner secrets of a thing.

lef, –ffi A wrapping up; an enclosing. ~**fen** ($\overset{\backslash}{·}·$), enclosed (in a letter or parcel). ~**fetmek** ($\overset{\backslash}{·}·$), **–eder**, to wrap up; to enclose *in a letter etc.*

leğen, liğen Bowl, basin. ~ **ibrik**, bowl and ewer (*formerly handed round after a meal for washing the hands*): ⌐**her şey bitti, işimiz bir ~ örtüsüne kaldı**⌐, 'all is complete save for a covering for the basin', *said ironically when an unnecessary thing is provided while essentials are missing.*

leh For him *or* it; in favour of him. ~**imde**, in my favour: ~ **ve aleyh**, for and against.

Leh Pole; Polish. ~**çe¹** ($\overset{\backslash}{·}·$), Polish (language). ~**istan**, Poland. ~**li**, Polish, Pole.

lehçe² (·$\overset{\backslash}{·}$) Dialect.

lehim Solder. ~**lemek**, to solder. ~**li**, soldered.

leh·tar Supporter; in favour of. ~**te**, in his (its) favour: ~ **ve aleyhte**, pro and con.

lehülhamd ($\overset{\backslash}{·}$··) Thank God!

leim (·$\overset{\backslash}{·}$) Abject; base.

leke Spot of dirt; stain; mark. ~ **çıkarmak**, to remove a stain: ···**e ~ getirmek**, to dishonour, to stain the character of: ~ **olm.**, to become stained *or* spotted: ~ **sürmek**, to besmirch *s.o.'s name.* ~**ci**, a cleaner of clothes: ~ **toprağı**, fuller's earth. ~**dar** (··$\overset{\backslash}{·}$), whose honour is stained, dishonoured. ~**lemek**, to spot, stain; cast aspersions upon. ~**li**, spotted, stained; dishonoured: ~ **humma**, typhus fever; spotted fever. ~**siz**, spotless; immaculate.

leken A kind of snowshoe.

lem·'a Gleam; flash. ~**ean** (··$\overset{\backslash}{·}$), a shining *or* flashing; luminescence.

lemha Furtive glance; flash.

lemis, –msi A touching *or* feeling. **lemsetmek** ($\overset{\backslash}{·}·$), **–eder,** to touch, handle, feel. **lemsî** (·$\overset{\backslash}{·}$), tactile.

lemyezel Who declines not (God).

lenduha (·–$\overset{\backslash}{·}$) Enormous; clumsy.

lenf, ~a (·$\overset{\backslash}{·}$) Lymph. ~**avî** (·–$\overset{\backslash}{·}$), lymphatic; sluggish.

lenger Anchor; large deep copper dish. ~**endaz** (···$\overset{\backslash}{·}$), anchored.

lenk Lame.

lento Lintel.

lep *v.* leb.

lepiska (·$\overset{\backslash}{·}·$) Flaxen (hair).

lerci Musk-deer (?).

lermo *v.* lârmo.

lerz, ~e A tremble; shiver. ~**an, ~enak**, trembling; shivering.

leş Carcass. ~ **bağı**, running bowline: **gemi ~i**, wreck.

leşger Army; troops.

letafet (··$\overset{\backslash}{·}$), **–ti** Charm; grace; elegance; amiability.

letaif (·$\overset{\backslash}{·}·$) *pl. of* lâtife. Jokes; witticisms.

levahik (·–$\overset{\backslash}{·}$), **–kı** *pl. of* lâhika. Appendices *etc.*

levaih (·–$\overset{\backslash}{·}$) *pl. of* lâyiha. Projects *etc.*

levanten Levantine.

levazım (··$\overset{\backslash}{·}$), **levazımat, –tı** *pl. of* lâzime. Necessities; materials; munitions; supplies, provisions; commissariat department, Quartermaster-General's department.

leve (*Fr. levée*) Trick (at cards).

levend *Formerly* an irregular military force; a gay young spark; a fine well-set-up lad.

levha Signboard; inscribed card; framed inscription; metal plate; slab; picture.

levhimahfuz The tablet preserved in Heaven, *containing God's decrees and the destiny of everyone.*

levin, –vni Colour; sort; variety.

levis, –vsi Dirt; filth.

leviye (*Fr. levier*) Gear lever.

levm Reproach; censure. **~etmek** (¹··), **–eder,** to blame *or* reproach.

levrek Bass (fish). **tatlı su ~,** perch.

leyâl (·¹·), **–li** *pl. of* **leyl.** Nights.

leyl, leyle Night. **~en** (¹··), at night, by night. **~î** (·¹·), nocturnal; boarder *at a school*: **~ mekteb,** boarding-school.

leylâk Lilac. **~î** (··¹·), lilac-coloured.

leylek Stork.

leytelealle (···¹·) *and various other forms of* **leyte ve lâalle.** Shilly-shally; needless delays; futile pretexts.

leyyin Soft; mild.

lezaiz (·¹·) *pl. of* **lezize.** Delights.

leziz Tasty; delicious; delightful.

lezzet, –ti Taste; flavour; pleasure, enjoyment. **~ duymak (almak),** to enjoy the taste of a thing; to find pleasure in *stg.* **~lenmek,** to become tasty *or* enjoyable. **~li,** pleasant to the taste; delightful. **~siz,** tasteless; insipid.

lık·ırdamak *vn.* Gurgle. **~lık,** gurgling.

li– *Ar. prep.* For; in favour of; on. **liecli,** for the purpose of, on the score of: **lieb,** on the father's side, paternal.

libade (·—¹) Short quilted coat.

libas (·¹) Garment.

libre (¹·) Pound (weight).

lider (¹·) Leader. **~lik,** leadership.

liecli (·¹·) For the purpose of; on the score of.

lif Fibre; loofah; bunch of palm fibres *used for scrubbing oneself in a bath.* **~ gibi,** rough, scratchy. **~î** (—¹), fibrous.

lifti Mortise chisel.

liftinuskuru (¹····) (Lifting screw); turnbuckle.

lig League; union.

liğen *v.* **leğen.**

lihye Beard.

lika¹ (¹·) Crude silk *used to hold the ink in an inkstand for Arabic writing.*

lika² (·¹) Face; aspect.

liken Lichen.

likorinos (··¹·) Smoked mullet.

liman Harbour. **~ odası,** harbour-master's office: **~ reisi,** harbour-master. **~lamak,** to come into harbour; (of the wind or sea) to die down. **~lık,** place serving as a harbour; calm sea: calm (sea); suitable for a harbour: **süt ~,** dead calm; absolute quiet.

limba A kind of barge.

limbo¹ (¹·) Mortise.

limbo² (¹·) Salvage.

lime (—¹) Strip. **~ ~,** in strips; in tatters.

limon Lemon. Lemon-coloured; made of lemon-tree wood. **~ gibi sararmak,** to turn

pale: **~ küfü,** bluish-green. **~ata** (··¹·), fresh lemonade. **~atacı,** lemonade seller. **~î** (··¹), pale yellow; capricious, touchy. **~lu,** flavoured with lemon juice; sour. **~luk,** conservatory. **~tuzu** (·¹··), **–nu,** citric acid.

linç Lynching. **~ usulü,** lynch law. **~etmek** (¹··), **–eder,** to lynch.

link, –ki Trot. **~ etm.,** to trot.

linyit, –ti Lignite.

lipari (¹··) A species of mackerel (?).

lipsos A species of sea scorpion.

lira (¹·) Lira; pound; Turkish lira of 100 piastres. **~lık,** of the value of a lira.

liret, –ti Italian lira.

lisa (¹·) Sheet of a sail. **~ etm.,** to hoist sail.

lisan (·¹) Tongue; language; dialect; talk. **~a almak,** to talk about *stg.*: **~a gelmek,** (i) to become talked about; (ii) (of stg. that does not usually talk) to start talking. **~aşina** (·—·¹), linguist. **~en** (·¹·), by word of mouth, verbally. **~ıhal** (·—·¹), the conveyance of meaning without words; a giving to understand stg. without saying it. **~î** (·—¹), lingual; linguistic. **~iyat** (·—·¹), **–tı,** the study of language; philology; linguistics. **~iyun** (·—·¹), linguists; philologists.

lisans (*Fr. licence*) Diploma or examination *for passing out of High School or University*; licence. **~iye,** one who holds a degree or diploma from a University or High School.

lise (¹·) (*Fr. lycée*) Grammar School; High School. **~li,** student at a Grammar or High School.

lisebebin (·¹··) For some reason; not without reason.

liste (¹·) List.

litre (¹·) Litre (= 1¾ pints). **~lik,** holding *or* amounting to one litre.

liva (·¹) Flag; brigade (*mil.*); *formerly an administrative district governed by a Mutessarif.*

livar Enclosure connected with the sea *for keeping fishes alive.*

livata (·—¹) Sodomy.

livre Livery.

liyakat (·—¹), **–tı** Merit; suitability; capacity.

liyme *v.* **lime.**

liynet, –ti Looseness of the bowels; mild diarrhoea.

lobut, –tu Cudgel; Indian clubs.

loca (¹·) Box *at the theatre*; Masonic lodge; small room, cell.

loça (¹·) Hawse-pipe.

loda (¹·) Heap of straw *etc.* covered with earth.

lodos South-west wind; south-west; southwesterly gale. ~ **poyraz**, blowing hot and cold : ~a tutulmak, to sway about like a drunken man. ~**lamak**, (of the wind) to blow from the south-west; (of the weather) to become mild. ~**luk**, exposed to the south-west.

lofça Very large nail *used in building construction.*

loğ Stone roller.

loğusa, lohusa Woman after childbirth. ~ **otu**, aristolochia : ~ **şekeri**, a red-coloured sugar *used in* ~ **şerbeti**, a drink offered to visitors to a newly confined woman.

loka (ˈ·) Untidy.

lokanta (·ˈ·) Restaurant. ~**cı**, restaurant keeper.

lokavut, lokavt Lock-out.

lokma Mouthful; morsel; a kind of sweet fritter *distributed to the poor on the death of a relation*; rounded head of a bone, condyle; screw-die. ~ ~, piece by piece : ~ **dökmek**, to distribute lokma : ~ **göz**, pop-eyed : ˹**ağzına vur ~sını al!**˺, 'you can take the very bread out of his mouth', *said of a very mild person*: ağzından ~sını almak, to take from s.o. what rightfully belongs to him : ˹**büyük ~ yüt, büyük söz söyleme !**˺, 'don't boast about the future !': gözleri ~ gibi fırlamış, his eyes started out of his head.

lokmacı, a maker of lokma; sponger.

Lokman *Name of two legendary sages, one regarded as the father of medicine, the other as a famous storyteller.* ˹~ **hekimin ye dediği**˺, 'advised by the doctor as good to eat', *said of an attractive woman or delicious food.* ~**ruhu** (·ˈ··), –**nu**, sulphuric ether.

lokum Turkish Delight; diamonds (cards).

lololo Nonsense; empty words *used to deceive or put off s.o.* ˹**bize de mi ~?**˺, 'do you really think I can be taken in by that?'

lombar Port *in a ship's side.*

lomboz Port-hole; dead-light; scuttle for air.

lonca Tradesmen's guild or corporation; meeting-place of such.

lop Round and soft (that can be swallowed at a mouthful). ~ ~, *describes the falling of a soft round thing or the swallowing of such*: ~ **et**, boneless meat : ~ ~ **yutmak** *or* ~**latmak**, to bolt (food).

loppadak (ˈ··) *v.* lop lop.

lopur lopur *In* ~ ~ **yutmak (yemek)**, to swallow greedily in large mouthfuls.

Lor[1] The Lur people (Kurds of S. Persia).

lor[2] Curd of goat's milk. ~**peyniri** (ˈ··), –**ni**, cheese of goat's milk.

lord, lort Lord. ~**lar Kamarası**, the House of Lords.

lorta (ˈ·) Shoemaker's last.

lostarya (·ˈ·) Small tavern.

lostra (ˈ·) Shoe polish. ~**cı**, bootblack.

lostromo (·ˈ·) Boatswain.

losyon (*Fr. lotion*) Eau de Cologne; scent.

loş Dark, gloomy; slack, weak. ~**luk**, darkness; slackness.

lotarya (·ˈ·) Lottery.

löğusa *v.* loğusa.

lök Awkward; clumsy; sluggish. Male camel. ~ **gibi oturmak**, to sit in an awkward and lazy manner.

lökece, lökeşe Woodcock.

lökün Putty.

lu'ab Saliva; mucilage.

lûbiyat (··ˋ), –**tı** Games; amusements.

lûgat, –**tı** Word; dictionary. ~ **paralamak**, to use learned *or* pedantic language. –**çe**, vocabulary; glossary.

lûgavî (··ˊ) Pertaining to words. Lexicologist.

lukata A thing found, which, after an interval, becomes the property of the finder.

lululu *v.* lololo.

lûmbar, lûmboz *v.* lombar, lomboz.

lûtf·en (ˈ·) As a favour; please ! ~**etmek** (ˈ··), –**eder**, to do the favour; to have the kindness; to kindly send.

lûtî (–ˊ) Pederast.

lûtuf, –**tfu** Kindness, goodness; favour. ···**mek lûtfunda bulunmak**, to be so kind as to .... ~**dide** (··–ˋ), who has received a favour. ~**kâr** (··ˊ), kind; gracious. ~**name** (···ˋ), *polite form for* your letter.

lüb, –**bbü** Kernel; marrow; essence; heart; mind, understanding. ~**bî** (·ˊ), pertaining to the kernel *or* marrow.

Lübnan (ˈ·) Lebanon.

lücce The high sea; the ocean.

lüfer *Name of a delicious fish caught in the Bosphorus*, blue-fish (*Temnodon saltator*).

lüks ¬(*Fr. luxe*) Luxury. ~ **lâmbası**, vaporized oil lamp.

lüle Pipe; bowl of a tobacco pipe; spout; paper cone; curl; fold; a kind of water measure. ~**cı**, maker of pipe-bowls : ~ **çamuru**, red clay from which pipe-bowls are made. ~**taşı** (·ˈ··), –**nı**, meerschaum.

lüp[1] *v.* lüb.

lüp[2], –**pü** Stg. got without cost or trouble. ~ **diye yutmak**, to gulp down : ~**e konmak**, to get stg. gratis or without effort. ~**çü**, one who lives by his wits; parasite.

lüzucet (·–ˋ), –**ti** Viscosity. –**li**, viscous.

lüzum Necessity; need. ~**lu**, necessary; needed; useful : ~ **lüzumsuz yere**, even when not needed. ~**suz**, unnecessary; useless.

M

ma Water. ~**i mahrec**, displacement of a ship: ~**i mukattar**, distilled water.

maa (¹·), **ma** *Arabic prep.* With (*generally joined to following word*). ~**takım**, with all accessories.

maabahçe (¹···) With garden.

maabid (·−¹) *pl. of* **mabed**. Places of worship.

maabir (·−¹) *pl. of* **maber**. Fords; passes; roads; bridges.

maada (−·−⁻ *or* −−⁻) Besides; in addition to; except. Rest; remainder. **bundan** ~, furthermore, besides this: ~**sı**, the rest of it.

maadin (·−¹) *pl. of* **maden**. Metals.

maahaza (¹···−) In spite of this; nevertheless.

maaile (¹···) Together with the family.

maal *v.* **meal**.

maalesef (¹···) Unfortunately; with regret.

maali (·−⁻) Great affairs; high qualities.

maal·iftihar (¹····) With pride; with pleasure. ~**kasem**, under oath. ~**kerahe** (¹···−·), with repugnance; against one's will. ~**memnuniye** (¹···−··), with pleasure.

maamafih (¹···) Nevertheless.

maan (¹·) Together; in company.

maani (·−¹) *pl. of* **mana**.

maarif (·−¹) *pl. of* **marifet**. Branches of science; education. ~ **Vekâleti**, Ministry of Education (*now* ‖**Eğitim** ‖**Bakanlığı**!). ~**çi**, educationalist.

maaş (·⁺) Salary; allowance *to widows etc.* **açık** ~, half-pay, payment while unemployed. ~**at** (·−⁺), −**tı**, *pl. of* **maaş**. ~**lı**, receiving a salary *etc.*

maattessüf (¹····) With regret, unfortunately.

maazalik (¹·−·) All the same, nevertheless.

maazallah (·−⁺··) God preserve us !; Heaven forfend !

maaziyadeten (¹···−··) Abundantly; amply.

mabadüttabia (·−··−¹) Metaphysics.

mabaid (−·¹), −**badi** Sequence, continuation; remainder. **mabadi var**, to be continued.

mabaki (−−¹) The remainder.

mâbed (−¹) Place of worship, temple.

mabeyin, −**yni** Interval; room between the women's quarters and the men's quarters *in a large house*; the private apartments of the Palace, *where the Sultan usually received*; relations between two people. **mabeynde**, between them; **mabeynimizde**, between us: **mabeynleri bozuk**, they are on bad terms. ~**ci**, Court chamberlain.

mabih− *Prefix.* The thing of which there is

...; cause; motive. ~**ülihtiyac**, what is necessary: ~**üliftihar**, cause of pride: ~**ülihticac**, the basis of an argument.

mablak Spatula; putty knife.

mabud (−⁺) Worshipped. God; idol. ⌈**vermedi** ~, **ne yapsın Mahmud ?**⌉, 'man proposes, God disposes'; it can't be helped. ~**e** (−−¹), Goddess.

macar Hungarian; (*sl.*) louse. ~**ca**, Hungarian language. **M~istan**, Hungary. ~**lı**, Hungarian.

macera (−·−⁻) Event; adventure. ~**lı**, adventurous; hazardous. ~**perest**, adventurous.

macid (−¹) Illustrious.

macun (−¹) Putty; paste; cement; electuary; fruit paste. **diş** ~**u**, tooth-paste. ~**lamak**, to stop up with putty or cement.

maç, −**çı** Match (football *etc.*).

maça (¹·) Spade *at cards*; core *of a moulding.* ~ **bey**, the knave of spades; ostentatious and conceited person.

Maçin (−¹) Southern China.

maçuna (·¹·) Crane (machine).

madalya (·¹·) Medal.

madam Madame; Mrs. (*only of non-Turkish women*).

madampol, −**lü** Madapollam; calico.

madd·e Matter; substance; material; subject; article or paragraph *of a regulation or law.* ~**eci**, materialist. ~**ecilik**, materialism. ~**eten** (¹··), materially. ~**î** (·⁻), *a.* material. ~**iyat**, −**tı**, material things; *as sing.* materialism. ~**iyun** (···⁻), materialists.

mâdelet (−·¹), −**ti** Justice.

madem (−¹), **mademki** While; since; as.

maden (−¹) Mine; mineral; metal; a mine *of learning etc.* ~ **direği**, pit-prop: ~ **kömürü**, coal: ~ **ocağı**, mine (coal *etc.*): ~ **suyu**, mineral water. ~**ci**, miner; mining expert; metallurgist; mine owner. ~**î** (−·⁻), *a.* metal, mineral. ~**iyat**, −**tı**, *as sing.* mineralogy; mining: ~ **mektebi**, school of mining.

mader (−¹) Mother. ~**ane** (−·−¹), maternal; in a maternal manner. ~**î** (−·⁻), motherly; maternal. ~**şahi** (−·−¹), matriarchal. ~**zat** (−·⁻), innate, congenital; mother (tongue *etc.*).

madik Trick, ruse. ~ **atmak**, to cheat.

madrabaz Middleman; cheat, impostor.

madrub *v.* **mazrub**.

madud (−¹) Counted; limited. ···**den** ~, comprised in ...; considered as ... .

madum (−⁺) Non-existent; *in compounds*

without ..., *e.g.* ~ülfıkarat, invertebrates.
~iyet, –ti, non-existence; absence.
madun (–⏑) Inferior; subordinate. ~da, below.
madükkân (⏑··) *Err. for* maadükkân. With shop.
mafa (⏑·) Bolt *or* screw with a ring at the end.
mafat (–⏑), –tı That which is lost; missed opportunity. telâfii ~, a regaining stg. lost, a making up for lost time.
mafe *v.* mahfe.
mafevk (–⏑), –kı That which is above; a superior. ~ınde, above him *or* it. ~attabia (–····–⏑), a supernatural thing.
mafiş (–⏑) Finished!; nothing left! A kind of very light fritter.
mafizzamir (–···⏑) Secret thought; hidden intention.
mafsal Joint; articulation.
mafu (–⏑) Pardoned; amnestied.
mağ A kind of pigeon.
mağara (·⏑·) Cave; pit.
mağaza Large store; storehouse.
mağdur (·⏑) Unjustly treated; wronged. Sufferer, victim. ~iyet (·–·⏑), –ti, a being unjustly treated; oppression; a suffering loss.
mağf·iret, –ti Remission of sins, forgiveness; grace. ~ur, whose sins are forgiven; deceased.
mağlata Fallacious argument; sophistry.
mağlûb (·⏑) Defeated, overcome. hırsına ~ olarak, losing his temper. ~iyet, (·–·⏑), –ti, defeat.
mağmum (·⏑) Sad; anxious; gloomy; overclouded. ~iyet (·–··), –ti, ~luk, sadness, gloominess.
magnez·ya (·⏑·) Magnesia. ~yum (·⏑·), magnesium.
mağrı Conger eel.
mağrib West; sunset. Mağrıb, Morocco. ~î (··⏑), Moroccan; Moor: ⌐mal bulmuş ~ye dönmek⌐, to be overjoyed.
mağruk (·⏑) Drowned; submerged; inundated; sunk, foundered (ship).
mağrur (·⏑) Self-confident; proud, conceited. ~en (·–·), proudly; confidently; ···e ~, trusting in ... . ~iyet (·–··), –ti, ~luk, conceit, over-confidence.
mağşuş (·⏑) Alloyed; adulterated; base (coin).
mağz Brain; marrow; kernel.
mah Month; moon. ~ gelmemek, to be insufficient, to have no effect.
mahafil (·–⏑) *pl. of* mahfil. Resorts *etc.*
mahakim (·–⏑) *pl. of* mahkeme. Courts.
mahal, –lli Place; post; occasion. ~linde, at his post; opportune: ···e ~ bırakmamak *or* vermemek, not to give occasion for ...:

~line masruf (emek, para), (efforts, money) well spent: ~li vaka, the scene of action: bu sözlere ~ yoktur, there is no occasion for using such words.
mahalâkallah (–⏑····) 'What God has created', (all creation); very crowded; a great crowd.
mahall·ât, –tı *pl. of* mahalle. ~e, quarter *of a town*; ward. ~ çocuğu, street urchin, guttersnipe: ~ karıları, common women: ~ tavrı, vulgar manners. ~eli, person belonging to a quarter or ward; neighbour. ~î, local.
mahallebi Sweet dish made with rice and milk. ~ci, maker and seller of milk dishes: ~ çocuğu, mother's darling; milksop.
mahalsiz Inopportune; out-of-place.
maharet (·–⏑), –ti Skill, proficiency. ~li, skilful, proficient. ~siz, unskilful; clumsy.
mahasin (·–⏑) Good actions *or* qualities; good results.
mahaşerallah (–⏑····) (Whom God has assembled together), very crowded.
mahazir (·–⏑) *pl. of* mahzur. Objections.
mahbemah (⏑··) Month by month.
mahbes Prison.
mahbub (·⏑) Beloved; catamite.
mahbus (·⏑) Imprisoned; prisoner.
mahcub (·⏑) Ashamed; bashful. ~iyet (·–·⏑), –ti, bashfulness; shame; modesty.
mahcur (·⏑) Under interdiction; not allowed to dispose of his property.
mahcuz (·⏑) Sequestrated.
mahdud (·⏑) Limited; definite; bounded.
mahdum (·⏑) Son.
mahfaza Case; casket; sheath. ~lı, having a case; kept in a case.
mahfe A frame across a camel's back with seats on either side.
mahfi (·⏑) Hidden; secret; clandestine. ~ce (·⏑·), secretly.
mahfil Place of resort; circle; club; private pew in a mosque; masonic lodge.
mahfuz (·⏑) Protected; looked after; committed to memory; reserved. ~en (·⏑·), under guard *or* protection; in custody ~iyet (·–·⏑), –ti, protection; conservation; safeguard; reservation.
mahıv, –hvı Destruction; annihilation; abolition.
mâhi Fish. ⌐o ~ler ki derya içredir deryayı bilmezler⌐, 'the fish that are in the sea know not the sea'; some people can't see what is right under their nose.
mahir (–⏑) Skilful. ~lik, skill.
mahitab (–·⏑), mahtab *v.* mehtab.
mahiyet (–··⏑), –ti Reality; the true nature of a thing; character. hayatî bir ~, a matter of vital concern: ... bir ~ almak, to assume *such and such* a character *or* form.

~li, having the character of : ultimatom ~ bir nota, a note bearing the character of an ultimatum.

mahkeme Court of Justice. bidayet ~si *or* ~i asliye, Court of First Instance : ceza ~si, Criminal Court : hukuk ~si, Civil Court : sulh ~si, court of summary jurisdiction, Police Court. ~lik, a matter for the courts : ~ olm., to have a dispute which can only be settled in a court of law.

mahkûk (·≀), –kü Engraved ; scratched ; erased. Erasure. ~ât (·–≀), –tı, engravings ; inscriptions.

mahkûm (·≀) Sentenced ; condemned ; judged ; subject to. The condemned. ~iyet (·—·≀), –ti, condemnation ; sentence.

mahlâs Surname ; pseudonym.

mahleb Mahaleb (cherry).

mahlû (·≀) Dethroned, deposed.

mahlûk (·≀), –ku Created. Creature. ~at, –tı, created things ; creatures.

mahlûl (·≀), –lü Dissolved ; vacant ; escheated (property). Solution, lotion. ~at (·–≀), –tı, property lapsing to the State on the owner's death because there are no heirs.

mahlût (·≀), –tu Mixed ; adulterated. Mixture.

mahmi (·–⁻) Guarded ; protected ; protégé ; vassal.

mahmude (·—⁻) Scammony (purgative).

mahmudiye (·—·⁻) Gold coin of 25 piastres, *coined in the reign of Mahmud II.*

mahmul (·≀) Borne ; loaded *on an animal* ; attributed, imputed ; heavy (style).

mahmum (·≀) Feverish.

mahmur (·≀) Heavy after a drunken sleep ; pleasantly torpid (*as a baby after a good sleep*) ; sleepy, languid (eye) ; lackadaisical. ~ bakış, a soft, tender look. ~luk, heaviness after a drunken sleep, 'hang-over' ; *also* a pleasant sleepy feeling ; dreaminess *or* tenderness of look : ~ bozmak, to take a pick-me-up to cure a 'hangover' (a hair of the dog that bit one).

mahmuz (·≀) Spur ; ram *of a ship.* cavdar ~u, ergot : direk ~ları, climbing irons. ~lamak, to spur.

mahnuk (·≀) Strangled ; choked. ~an (·⁻·), by strangling.

mahrama *v.* makrama.

mahrec Outlet ; origin, source ; vocal organs ; pronunciation of a letter *or* sound ; denominator (*arith.*) ; specialized school for a profession *or* trade.

mahrek, –ki Orbit *of a planet etc.* ; trajectory.

mahrem Confidential ; secret ; intimate ; within the degrees of relationship forbidden for marriage, *thus permitted, though of differ-*

ent sexes, to be intimate and to have access to the harem. ~ane (···⁻), confidential (speech *etc.*) ; confidentially, as a secret. ~iyet, –ti, the condition of being mahrem ; a being a confidant.

mahruk (·≀) Burnt. Fuel ; combustible. ~at (·–≀), –tı Combustibles ; fuel.

mahrum (·≀) Deprived ; disappointed. ~ kalmak, to be disappointed ; to remain deprived (of = ···den). ~iyet (·—·≀), –ti, deprivation ; destitution : ~e katlanmak, to suffer privation ; to do without.

mahrusa (·—⁻) City ; capital. memaliki ~, (*formerly*) the Ottoman Empire.

mahrut (·≀), –tu Cone. kara ~u subay, a naval officer on shore duty *or* an air-force officer on ground duty. ~î (·—⁻), conical : ~ çadır, bell tent. ~iyet, –ti, a being conical.

mahsub (·≀) Counted ; calculated. ~ etm., to count, to reckon in an account. ~en (·⁻·), on account ; to the account of (= *dat.*).

mahsud (·≀) Envied.

mahsul (·≀), –lü Product ; produce ; crop ; result. ~at (·–≀), –tı, *pl. of* mahsul. ~dar (··), –lü, productive, fertile.

mahsur (·≀) Confined ; limited ; besieged ; cut off *by floods etc.*

mahsus (·≀) Special ; peculiar to ; proper ; particular ; private ; reserved ; not seriously meant. (⁻·), specially, expressly, on purpose.

mahsûs (·≀) Felt ; perceived. ~ bir surette, perceptibly. ~at (·–≀), –tı, perceptible things ; sensations ; the visible world.

mahşer The Last Judgement ; great crowd ; great confusion. ~î (···⁻), crowded.

mahud (·≀) Well-known, notorious ; (*contemptuously*) your.

mahuf (·≀) Fearful, terrible.

mahun Mahogany.

mahunya (·≀·) Barberry (*Berberis*).

mâhur (–⁻) A mode of Oriental music.

mahv·etmek (≀··), –eder *va.* Destroy ; abolish. ~olmak (≀··), to be destroyed, ruined, abolished. ~üharab, utterly destroyed.

mahviyet, –ti Modesty ; unobtrusiveness.

mahya Texts or figures made by lamps suspended between minarets during Ramazan ; festoon.

mahz Pure ; unmixed ; mere. ~ı riya, sheer hypocrisy. ~a (⁻–), merely ; only ; entirely.

mahzen Underground store-house ; granary ; cellar.

mahzuf (·≀) Cut off ; curtailed ; elided.

mahzun (·≀) Sad, grieved. ~iyet (·—·≀), –ti, grief, sadness.

mahzur (·≀) Something to be guarded

against; objection; inconvenience; danger. ~u şer'î, a religious objection; ⌈her hangi bir ~u şer'î var mı?⌉, 'is there any real objection?' ~at (·–⸗), –tı, forbidden, illicit things.

mahzuz (·⸗) Pleased, happy. ~iyet (·–·¹), –ti, joy; pleasure.

mai (–¹) Light blue. v. also ma.

maî (–⸗) Aqueous, aquatic.

maide (–·¹) A laid table; feast.

mail (–¹) Leaning; inclined; oblique; inclined to; tending towards. ~i inhidam, likely to collapse, in a dangerous condition (of a building). ~e, slope. ~iyet, –ti, inclination.

maimukattar (–···¹) Distilled water.

main Rhombus; lozenge.

maişet (·–·¹), –ti Means of subsistence; livelihood.

maiyet, –ti Suite; following. ~inde, in his suite; accompanying him: ~ vapuru, stationnaire of an ambassador.

makabil (–·¹), –bli That which goes before. makabline şamil olm., (of a law etc.) to be retrospective.

makabir (·–¹) pl. of makbĕr. Tombs.

makad Covering (of a sofa etc.); cushion; the behind.

makadir (·–¹) pl. of mikdar. Quantities.

makal (·⸗), –li Saying; word.

makale (·–¹) Article in a newspaper.

makam (·⸗) Place; abode; post; rank; office; executive; tomb of a saint; tune. ~ında, in token of, after the manner of, e.g. tezyif ~ında, by way of derision, in contempt: ~ otomobili, car allotted to an official or to a particular post: ~ tutturmak, to strike up a tune; to annoy by constant repetition: alâkalı ~, the competent authority: her ~dan söylemek, to talk on all kinds of subjects. ~at, –tı, high offices; authorities. ~lı, harmonious. ~sız, inharmonious, discordant.

makar, –rrı Seat; centre. ~rı sultanat, the Capital.

makara (·¹·) Pulley; reel; spool; drum. ~ gibi söylemek, to chatter incessantly: ~ları salıvermek or koyuvermek, to burst into roars of laughter: üç dilli ~, a three-sheaved block.

makarna (·¹·) Macaroni. ~cı, a macaroni maker or seller; an Italian.

makas Scissors; shears; claw of a lobster etc.; switch or points of a railway; steering-rods; anything in the form of scissors; a cross-leg throw in wrestling. ~ ateşi, cross-fire: ~ gülle, chain-shot: ~ hakkı, cuttings left over after cutting out a suit: ~ı kapa! (sl.), shut up!; fiatlar arasındaki ~ ağzı, a very small difference in price. ~çı, a rail-

way pointsman. ~lamak, to cut with scissors; to tweak with the first and second fingers; to rob; plagiarize. ~lı, having the form of scissors: ~ dürbün, stereo-telescope. ~tar, tailor's cutter.

makasıd (·–¹) pl. of maksad. Purposes, intentions.

makber, makbere Tomb; cemetery.

makbul (·⸗) Accepted; acceptable; liked. ~e geçmek, to be received with pleasure: ~ümdür, I accept gladly.

makbuz (·⸗) Received. Receipt for payment. yüz lira ~um olmuştur, I acknowledge receipt of 100 lira. ~at (·–⸗), –tı, receipts.

makduh (·⸗) Ill-spoken of; reviled.

mâkes (–¹) Reflector. bu hatib halkın fikirlerine ~ oldu, this speaker reflected public opinion.

maket, –ti (Fr. maquette) Sketch; outline; model.

makferlân (·¹·) (Macfarlane) Inverness cape (woman's cloak with cape).

makhur (·⸗) Overwhelmed; defeated.

maki Lemur.

Makidonya (···¹·) Macedonia.

makina, makine (¹··) Machine; engine. ~ye verilerken, 'Stop Press' (in a newspaper): ~ zabıtı, engineer officer (naut.): yazı ~si, typewriter. ~ci, mechanic; engine-driver. ~li (·¹··), driven by or fitted with a machine: ~ tüfek, machine-gun.

makinist, –ti Engine-driver; engineer; mechanic.

makis Comparable. ~ünaleyh (·–···¹), serving as a basis for comparison.

makiyaj (Fr. maquillage) Making-up, painting the face.

makkab For matkab. Drill.

maklûb (·⸗) Overturned; inverted; reversed.

makrama Napkin; kerchief; handkerchief; bedspread; face-towel.

makrun (·⸗) Joined; near. sıhhate ~, joined to truth, i.e. true. ~iyet (·–·¹), –ti, proximity; a being joined.

makruz (·⸗) Lent.

maksad Aim, purpose, intention. ~ile, with a view to, with the intention of: ... demekten ~, ... means ... .

maksud (·⸗) Intended; wished for. Aim, intention. ⌈herkesin ~u bir, amma rivayet muhtelif⌉, everyone has the same aim, but their approach is different.

maksum (·⸗) Divided. Dividend (arith.). rızkı ~, one's daily bread, as supplied by Providence. ~unaleyh, divisor (arith.).

maksur (·⸗) Shortened; limited; reduced (military service). ~e (·–·¹), private pew in a mosque; private grounds. hizmeti ~, reduced military service.

makta (·⸜), **-aı** Place of cutting; section; pause; cutting (in a wood).

maktel Place of execution *or* murder.

maktu (·⸜), **-uu** Cut off; interrupted; fixed (price). **~a**, cutting *of a newspaper etc.* **~an** (·⸜·), at a fixed price; in the lump.

maktul (·⸜) Killed.

mâkul (−⸜) Reasonable; wise; prudent. **~ görmek**, to deem reasonable, to approve. **~ât** (−−⸜), **-tı**, conceivable and comprehensible things; a thing based on reason. **~iyet** (·−·⸜), **-ti**, reasonableness.

makule (·−⸜) Kind, sort; category. **bu ~ adamlar**, these sort of men.

makûs (−⸜) Inverted; inverse; reversed; reflected; opposed; perverse (fate *etc.*); unlucky. **~en** (−⸜·), inversely.

mal Property; possession; wealth; goods; an animal owned (sheep, cows *etc.*); scamp, scoundrel; loose woman. **~ buluşa dönmek**, *v.* **mağribî**: **~ canlısı**, covetous, avaricious: **~ edinmek**, to become rich; to appropriate; *v. also* **maletmek**: **~ edinmemek** *or* **üzerine ~ etmemek**, to take no account of, not to worry about: **~ etm.**, *v.* **maletmek**: **~ın gözü**, rascal, ne'er-do-weel: **~ meydanda**, the proof is here, *i.e.* it's obviously bad: **~ mülk** *or* **~ menal**, property; goods: **~ olm.**, *v.* **malolmak**: **baba ~ı**, patrimony: **hepsi bir ~**, one's as bad as the other: **ne ~ olduğu anlaşıldı**, it is clear now what a scoundrel he is.

mala (⸜·) Bricklayer's trowel. **~lamak**, to work or smooth with a trowel.

malafa Arbor; mandrel.

malakof Crinoline.

malak Buffalo calf.

malâmal Brimful.

malârya (·⸜·) Malaria.

malâyani (−−−⸜) Meaningless; useless. Nonsense; futile thing.

malayî (·−⸜) Malay.

malâyutak (−−·⸜) Impracticable; not feasible.

mal·dar Wealthy. **~edilmek** (⸜···), *pass. of* **maletmek**, to be appropriated *etc.*; to belong. **~en** (⸜·), in goods; financially.

maletmek (⸜···), **-eder** *va.* Take possession of, appropriate; attribute to, ascribe to. **bir şeyi üstüne** *or* **kendine ~**, to appropriate stg. that does not belong to one; **üstüne ~**, to enter as a debit against: **···i ucuza ~**, to get *stg.* cheap.

malgama Amalgam.

malıtaşı, **-nı** Large stone used as an anchor.

malî¹ (−⸜) Pertaining to property; financial.

malî² (−⸜) Full.

malihulya (····⸜) Melancholy; whim, fancy.

malik (−⸜), **-ki** Owning, possessing; (*with dat.*) owner of. **···e ~ olm.**, to possess: **kendine ~ olmamak**, to lose one's self-control; to be unconscious. **~âne** (−·−⸜), State lands held in fief by a private owner; large estate. **~iyet**, **-ti**, ownership; rights of ownership.

maliye (−·⸜) *Fem. of* **malî**. Financial. Finance; Ministry of Finance. **~ci**, financier.

maliyet (−·⸜), **-ti** Cost; **~ fiati**, cost price.

malkoç *The nickname of a famous Akinji leader.* **~ oğlu**, swindler.

malmüdürü (⸜···), **-nü** Financial officer of a district.

malolmak (⸜··) *vn.* (*with dat.*). Cost. **kaça maloldu ?**, how much did it cost ?

mal·perest Who worships money. **~sahibi** (⸜···), **-ni**, proprietor. **~sandığı** (⸜···), **-nı**, government financial department.

Malta (⸜·) Malta. **~ eriği (muşmulası)**, loquat. **~ palamudu**, the Pilot Fish (*Naucrates Ductor*). **~taşı** (⸜···), **-nı**, a soft building stone.

maltiz Maltese; a kind of brazier; a kind of goat.

malûl (−⸜), **-lü** Ill; invalid; defective. **~ gazi**, disabled soldier: **···le ~**, tainted with. **~in** (−−⸜), disabled soldiers; war victims. **~iyet** (−⸜··), **-ti**, infirmity; defect.

malûm (−⸜) Known; active (verb). Yes; true ! **~u ilâm**, a telling stg. that is known to all: **~unuzdur ki**, you know that.

malûmat (−−⸜), **-tı** Information; knowledge. **~ına müracaat etm.**, to ask for information about: **~ sahibi**, a man of learning: **ondan ~ım yok**, I have no knowledge of, *or* no information about that. **~furuş**, who poses as learned; pedant. **~lı**, learned; educated; well-informed. **~sız**, ignorant; uneducated. **~tar**, informed.

malûmiyet (−−·⸜), **-ti** A being known.

malzeme Necessaries; materials.

mama (*inf.*) Food. **~ bezi**, bib.

mamaliga Maize girdle-cake.

mamelek (−·⸜) All that one possesses.

mamul (−⸜) Made; manufactured. **···den ~**, made of ... . **~ât** (−−⸜), **-tı**, manufactures; manufactured goods.

mamur (−⸜) Prosperous, flourishing. **dört başı ~**, flourishing in every way; first-class. **~e** (−−⸜), a prosperous and cultivated place. **~iyet** (−−·⸜), **-ti**. **~luk** (−−⸜), a flourishing condition; prosperity.

mamut, **-tu** Mammoth.

mâna (−⸜) Meaning; sense; motive; essence; dream; reason. **···den ~ çıkarmak**, to put a false interpretation on ...; to read into *a remark* an insinuation which was not there: ~ **vermek**, to interpret, to translate (orally); ···e ~ **vermemek**, to be unable to explain *stg.*; to be rather suspicious about it: âlemi ~da görmek, to see in a dream: ismi ~, abstract noun: tam ~sile, in the fullest sense of the word.

mâna·lı (—-ᵛ), significant; having the meaning of; suggestive; allusive. **~sız** (—-ᵛ), senseless; without significance.

manastır Monastery.

manav Fruiterer.

manazır (·-ᵛ) *pl. of* **manzara**. Aspects; *as sing.* perspective.

manca (ᵛ·) (*vulg.*) Food.

mancana (·ᵛ·) Large water-cask *on board ship*.

mancınık Catapult; ballista.

manda¹ Water buffalo; very fat person.

manda² (*Fr. mandat*) Mandate.

mandal Latch; catch; tumbler, pawl; cleat; clothes-peg; tuning-peg *of violin etc.* dış kapının ~ı, a distant relative: kırk kapının ~ı, one who goes everywhere and pokes his nose into everything. **~lamak**, to shut with a latch; to hang up washing with clothes-pegs.

mandapost, –tu Postal money-order.

mandar Small pulley-block.

mandater (*Fr. mandataire*) Mandatory.

mandepsi *In* ~ya basmak (gelmek), to be taken in, to be cheated.

mandıra (ᵛ··) Small cow-shed; sheep-pen; cheese dairy. ~ köpeği, cattle dog; a brutal man *in the service of others*.

mandoz Block; pulley.

mandren (Drill) chuck.

mânen (⁻·) In sense; as regards the meaning; virtually; indirectly; in so many words; morally (*as opp. to* materially).

manend (⁻ᵛ), **menend** Resembling; similar.

maneska (·ᵛ·) A pulley with two double blocks.

manevî (—-⁻) Moral (*as opp. to* material); spiritual. ~ evlâd, another's child who is, to all intents and purposes, a son: şahsi ~, juridical person. **~yat, –tı**, spiritual and moral matters; morale.

manevra (·ᵛ·) Manœuvres; a manœuvre, trick. ~ çevirmek, to manœuvre: ~ fişeği, blank cartridge: ~ yapmak, to manœuvre; to shunt *a train*. **~lı**, (*sl.*) foul, diabolic: ~ iş, stratagem, ruse.

manga (ᵛ·) Squad (*mil.*); mess (*mil.*).

mangal Brazier.

mangır *An obsolete* copper coin; money; small disk of charcoal dust *placed on the bowl of a narghile to keep it alight*.

mangiz (*sl.*) Money.

manık (*sl.*) Puppy.

5798

mani¹ (⁻ᵛ) Song; ballad.

mani² (⁻ᵛ) (*Fr. manie*) Mania.

mâni (⁻⁻), **–ii** Preventing; hindering. Obstacle; impediment. ~ olm., to prevent, hinder.

mania (—·ᵛ) Obstacle; difficulty. **~lı**, presenting obstacles *or* difficulties: ~ yarış, obstacle race.

manidar (—-ᵛ) Significant; expressive.

manifatura (··ᵛ··) Textiles. **~cı**, draper.

manika (·ᵛ·) Windsail *for ventilating a ship*.

manipülatör Signalling-key.

manita Swindle.

manivela (··ᵛ·) Lever; crank.

mankafa (ᵛ··) Stupid; dazed; awkward; big; suffering from chronic glanders (horse). **~lık**, stupidity, thick-headedness; glanders.

manke (*Fr. manqué*) Miss.

manken Mannequin; scarecrow; ninny.

manolya (·ᵛ·) Magnolia.

mansab River-mouth.

mansıb High office.

mansub (·ᵛ) Appointed to an office; set up, erected.

mansur (·ᵛ) Aided by God; victorious.

Manş (*Fr. Manche*) The English Channel.

manşet, –ti (*Fr. manchette*) Cuff; headline.

mantar Mushroom; cork; inner sole of a shoe: lie, invention. ~ atmak, to tell lies: ~a basmak, to be duped: ~ meşesi, cork-oak: ~ pabuc, shoe with cork soles *or* high cork heels. **~cı**, mushroom-seller; liar.

mantı¹ Large pulley-block (on a ship).

mantı² A kind of meat pasty.

mantık Logic. **~î** (··⁻), logical. **~ıyun** (···⁻), logicians.

mantin A thick silk tissue.

mantinato (··ᵛ·) A kept woman; mistress.

manto (*Fr. manteau*) Cloak; mantle.

mantol Menthol.

manya (ᵛ·) Mania.

manyat A kind of fishing-net.

manyet·ize Magnetized; mesmerized. **~izma** (··ᵛ·), magnetism; mesmerism. **~o** (·ᵛ·), magneto.

manyezi Magnesia.

manzar Aspect; appearance; look-out. ~ olm., to be the object of: ~ı inayet olm., to be the object of kindness. **~a**, view; spectacle; panorama; perspective. **~alı**, having a fine view.

manzum (·ᵛ) Written in rhyme and metre. **~e** (·⁻ᵛ), row; series; poem. **~i şemsiye** *or* güneş ~si, the solar system.

manzur (·ᵛ) Seen; considered. ... **~unuz** oldu mu?, have you seen ... ?

mapa eye-bolt.

mar Snake. **~ı sermadide**, a torpid snake.

Q

maraba Shepherd's assistant.
marabet, -ti Marabout.
maral Doe.
marangoz Joiner; cabinet-maker. ~ balığı, saw-fish. ~luk, joinery; cabinet-making.
mâraz Place of an occurrence; occasion.
maraz Disease, illness; worry; pain; evil. ⌐merhametten ~ çıkar¬, misplaced pity may be the cause of evil. ~î (··⌐·), pertaining to disease; pathological; morbid.
maraza *Vulg. for* muaraza. Controversy; tumult.
marda Discarded goods; rubbish.
mâreke (−·¹) Battle; battlefield.
mareşal Marshal (*mil.*).
margarita (··¹·) Sheepshank (knot).
marife (−·¹) Definite noun (*Ar. gram.*).
marifet (−·¹), **-ti** Knowledge; skill; talent; craft, skilled trade; clever thing; contrivance; curiosity; means; intervention. onun ~iyle oldu, it happened by means of him, *i.e.* he did it *or* it occurred with his knowledge: ehli ~, talented, able: 'gördün mü yaptığın ~i?', 'see what a mess you've made of it!' ~li, skilful; talented; cleverly made.
marin (−·⸴) *In* ~ ve âbirin, the passerby.
mariz¹ (·⸴) Sick, ailing; depressed.
mariz² A beating.
marka (¹·) Mark; trademark; initials on clothing. ~lı (¹··), marked; bearing the mark of.
markacı (*sl.*) Swindler.
marki Marquess. ~z, marchioness.
Marko *Prop. n.* ~ Paşa, *Abdul Hamid's chief physician, renowned for his patience in listening to his patients, hence:* ⌐derdini ~ Paşaya anlat!¬, 'nobody wants to hear about your troubles!'
maroken Morocco leather.
marpuc Tube of a narghile.
mars Grand slam; (at backgammon) a game lost without taking a piece. ~ olm., to be badly beaten; to be dumbfounded.
marsık Imperfectly burnt charcoal *giving off poisonous fumes.* ~ gibi, black and ugly (woman).
marsıvan (eşeği) Ass.
marş March (tune); treadle *of a loom etc.* March! ~ motörü, (car) starter.
marşandiz Goods train.
mart, -tı March (month). ~ havası, changeable weather.
martaval Nonsense; lies. ~ okumak, to talk nonsense; to tell lies.
martı Gull.
martika (·¹·) A kind of two-masted sailing-vessel used along the Black Sea coast.

martin Martini rifle. at ~i!, *v.* Debreli.
martoloz Sailor from the Danube in the pay of the Turks.
mâruf (−⸴) Known; well known; proper, usual. ... demekle ~, *or* ... namile ~, known as ...: emir bil~, religious injunction to act kindly and righteously. ~iyet (−−·¹), **-ti**, notoriety; reputation.
marul Cos lettuce. ~cuk, Christmas rose.
mâruz (−⸴) Exposed to (*with dat.*); presented; submitted. ~at (−−⸴), **-tı**, representations; matters submitted *by an inferior to a superior.*
marüzzikir Aforementioned.
marya (¹··) Ewe; female animal; young fish, fry.
mas, -ssı Act of sucking *or* absorbing. ~setmek, to absorb.
masa (¹·) Table; office desk; department in a government office; bankrupt's effects.
masad Steel *for sharpening knives.*
masadak (−·¹) That which confirms *or* conforms; confirmatory; conforming.
masal Story, tale; myth; silly tale. ~ kabilinden, fabulous: ~ okumak, to read *or* tell a tale; to romance: ~ söylemek, to tell idle tales. ~cı, story-teller.
mâsara Oil *or* wine press.
masarif (·−¹) *pl. of* masraf. Expenses; disbursements.
masdar Source, origin; verbal noun.
mâsebak (−·¹), **-kı** That which has gone before; the past; precedent.
masiyet (−·¹), **-ti** Disobedience; sin.
mâsiva (−·⸴) Everything except ...; everything else; the vanities of this world. ~dan geçmek, to renounce all but God.
maskara Buffoon; laughing-stock; droll child. Ridiculous; dishonoured. ~ etm. *or* ~ya almak, to make a laughing-stock of. ~lanmak, to make oneself a laughing-stock; to play the buffoon. ~lık, buffoonery; making oneself ridiculous; shame; dishonour: ~ etm., to play the fool.
maskatıreis, -re'si Birthplace.
maske (¹·) Mask. ~yi indirmek *or* atmak, to throw off the mask: ~sini* indirmek, to unmask *s.o.* ~lemek, to mask; to camouflage. ~li, masked.
maslahat, -tı Business; affair; the proper course. idarei ~ etm., to manage with what one has. ~güzar, Chargé d'Affaires.
maslak Stone trough *for watering animals;* running tap; water tower.
maslub (·⸴) Hanged. ~en (·⸴·), by hanging.
masmavı (¹··) Very blue.
masnu (·⸴) Manufactured; artificial, false. ~at (·−⸴), **-tı**, things made by skill; manufactures; created things; false news.

masraf Expense; outlay. ~ını çıkarmak, to pay for itself: ~ kapısı, the expenditure side of an account; ~ kapısını açmak, to cause expense: ···i ~a sokmak, to put *s.o.* to expense. ~lı, expensive.

masruf (·⊥) Spent; expended. Expense.

mass·edici Absorbent. ~etmek (¹··), –eder, to suck; to absorb.

mastaba Bench.

mastar *v.* masdar.

mastara (·¹·) Index (of a sextant *etc.*); cursor.

mastelâ Small tub.

mastı Small short-legged dog. ~bacak, *v.* bastıbacak.

mastika (·⊥·) Resin; raki with resin in it.

mastur (*sl.*) Drunk; drowsy.

masturi The broadest part of a ship.

mâsum (–⅟) Innocent. Child. ~iyet (––·¹), –ti, innocence; infancy.

masun (·⅟) Preserved, guarded; safe; inviolable. ~iyet (·–·¹). –ti, security; inviolability; immunity.

masura (·¹·) Small reed; weaver's shuttle; bobbin; spout; measure of water (= ¼ of a lûle).

maş Indian pulse.

maşa Tongs; pincers. ⌜~ varken elini yakmak⌝, to burn one's hand when tongs are available, *i.e.* to do sth. in an unnecessarily difficult way: emniyet ~sı, split-pin. ~lı, having pincers *or* tongs: eli ~, truculent, malevolent: ~ gözlük, pincenez. ~lık, a being the tool of *s.o.*; ···e ~ etm., to be the catspaw of ... .

maşallah (⊥·–) (*Lit.* what (wonders) God hath willed!); wonderful!; *used to express admiration or wonder; to admire a child etc. without saying it would incur the risk of the evil eye.* Charm *worn by children to avert the evil eye.* ~ı var! *has much the same meaning as* maşallah : kirk bir kere ~, to say ~ over and over again in admiration.

maşatlık Non-Moslem (*esp.* Jewish) cemetery.

mâşer (–¹) Company, community; assembly. ~î (–·⊥), collective.

maşiyen (⊥··) On foot.

maşlah A loose open-fronted cloak without sleeves.

maşraba Metal pot *or* mug.

maşrık, –kı The place where the sun rises on any particular day; the East. ~ı âzam, Grand Lodge (Freemasonry).

mâşuk (–⅟), –ku (*fem.* ~a) Beloved.

mat¹, –tı Checkmate (chess).

mat² Matt.

matafora (··¹·) Davit.

matafyon Eyelet.

matah *A form of* meta, goods, *only used*

contemptuously. 'bu ~ değil ya!', it's not as precious as all that!

matara (·¹·) Leather *or* tin waterbottle. ~cı, water-carrier attached to caravans.

matbaa Printing-press. ~cı, printer.

matbah, mutfak Kitchen.

matbu (·⊥) Printed; natural; good-natured. ~a (·–¹), printed form. ~at (·–⅟), –tı, the papers; the Press.

matem (–¹) Mourning. ~ etm., *or* ~ tutmak, to mourn; to go into mourning: ~ havası *or* marşı, funeral march. ~li, *a.* mourning; in mourning. ~zede, *a.* mourning.

matetmek (¹··), –eder Checkmate; defeat.

matiz¹ Drunk.

matiz² Long splice.

matkab Drill; auger.

matla (·⊥), –aı Place *or* time of the rising of a star; opening distich of a poem.

matlab Demand; wish; question.

matlub (·⊥) Desired; demanded. Debt due; desideratum. ~a kaydetmek, to pass to s.o.'s credit: ~a muvafık çıkmadı, it was not up to standard, not up to expectation: ~ vechile, as desired; as it should be: bakiyei ~, what remains due. ~at, –tı, demands; debts due.

matma (·⊥), –aı A desired thing; lure.

matmah Object looked at *or* coveted. ~ı nazar, the object of one's desires.

matmazel Mademoiselle.

matolmak (¹··) *vn.* Be checkmated *or* defeated.

matrah Category of taxed goods *or* of taxpayers; standard by which a tax is assessed.

matrak, –kı Mace; cudgel.

matrud (·⊥) Driven away; banished; expelled.

matruh (·⅟) Imposed (tax); subtractive.

matruş (·⊥) Shaven.

mâtuf (–⅟) Directed; imputed; aiming at (= dat.).

mâtuh (·⅟) Doddering; in one's dotage.

maun Mahogany.

mavaka (–·⊥), –aı Occurrence, event.

maval Lie; story.

mavera (–·⊥) That which is beyond. ~yı Erdün, Transjordania; ~yı tabiat, metaphysics. ~î (–·–⊥), which lies beyond; transcendental. ~ünnehir, Transoxiana.

mavi (–¹) Blue. ~lik, blue colour. ~msi, ~mtrak, bluish. ~ş, blue-eyed; blond.

mavna (¹·), **mavuna** (·¹·) Barge; lighter. ~cı, lighterman; bargee.

mavzer (¹·) Mauser.

maya Ferment; yeast; essence, essential; origin; stock; talent; brood mare *or other female animal.* bu ~daki ..., this sort of ...; ~sı bozuk, a 'bad lot'. ~lanmak, to ferment; increase; be accumulated. ~**lı,** fermented, leavened. ~**lık,** anything serving as a ferment.

mayasıl Chilblain; (*pop.*) piles. ~**otu** (··²··), **-nu,** scrofularia (?); *name given to various medicinal plants.*

mayasız Unfermented; unleavened; worthless (person).

maydonoz Parsley. ⌐**neler neler de** ~**lu köfteler**⌐, 'ah, I could tell you a lot of stories' *or* 'wouldn't you like to know!'

mayhoş Slightly acid; tart; bitter-sweet. ~**luk,** a slightly sour taste.

mayın Floating mine.

mayıs[1] May (month). ~**böceği, -ni,** cockchafer.

mayıs[2] Fresh cow *or* sheep dung; dried cow-dung *used as a fuel.*

mayi (−²) Liquid; fluid. ~ **mahruk,** liquid fuel. ~**at** (−·²), **-tı,** liquids. ~**iyet, -ti,** liquidity.

mayistra (·²·) Mainsail. ~ **sereni,** mainyard.

maymun Monkey. ⌐~ **gözünü açtı**⌐, 'we shan't be caught napping again!': ~ **iştahlı,** inconstant, capricious: ~ **suratlı,** hideous, repulsive. ~**cuk,** little monkey; picklock. ~**luk,** drollery.

mayn Floating mine.

mayna (²·) Down sails! ~ **etm.,** to down sails; to cease work: ~ **olm.,** to come to a stop; to calm down.

mayo (*Fr. maillot*) Bathing costume. ~**lu,** wearing a bathing costume.

maytab (*corr. of* mehtab *q.v.*) Small firework; Bengal fire. ~**a atmak,** *or* ~ **etm.,** to make fun of: **çanak** ~**ı,** Bengal fire.

mayub (−²) Shameful; defective; vicious; found fault with.

mazak The Streaked Gurnard (*Trigla lineata*).

mazanne Person *or* place giving rise to suspicion. ~**den,** a saint. ~**isu** (·····²), suspected person.

mazarrat, -tı Injury, harm; detriment. ~**ı dokunmak,** to harm, to be detrimental: ···**e isalı** (irası) ~ **etm.,** to do harm to *or* inflict an injury on.

mazbata (·²·) Official report; protocol; minutes *of a meeting.*

mazbut (·²) Recorded; well protected *against rain etc.*; solid, well-built (house); fixed *in the mind*; decided; neat, compact; correct (style *etc.*); level-headed; decent; (of pious foundations) administered by the State.

mazeret (−·²), **-ti** Excuse; apology. ~**i şeriye,** a valid legal reason.

mazgal Embrasure; loop-hole; slit in a machine-gun shield; *err. for* mıskal *q.v.*

mazhar Who acquires; honoured; distinguished; the object of (favours, honour *etc.*). ~**iyet, -ti,** attainment; distinction; acquisition; success.

mazı Gall-nut; gall-bearing oak; arbor vitae; thuja.

mazi (−²) Past; bygone. The past; the past tense. ~**ye karışmak,** to belong to bygone days, to be a thing of the past. ~**perest,** who worships the past, 'laudator temporis acti'.

mazlum (·²) Victim of cruelty; oppressed; mild, inoffensive. ⌐**alma** ~**un âhını çıkar aheste aheste**⌐, don't provoke the curse of the oppressed, it will take effect sooner or later. ~**iyet** (·−·²), **-ti,** ~**luk,** mildness; tractability.

mazmaza A rinsing the mouth.

mazmum (·²) Marked with the Arabic vowel point for 'u'.

mazmun (·²) Signification; implication; tenor.

maznun (·²) Suspected; accused (of = ile *or* ···den).

mazot, mazut, -tu Crude oil.

mazrub (·²) Multiplicand.

mazruf (·²) Enclosed in an envelope. ~**en** (·²·), under cover; enclosed (letter *etc.*).

mazul (−²) Dismissed *from a post*; out of office. ~**en** (−²·), *adv.* in retirement; discharged. ~**in** (−−²), dismissed officials. ~**iyet** (−−·²), **-ti,** condition of being dismissed: ~ **maaşı,** salary paid to an official dismissed from his post.

mazur (−²) Excused; excusable. ···**in bir şeyini** ~ **görmek,** to pardon *s.o.* for stg.: ~ **tutmak,** to hold *s.o.* excused.

mazut *v.* mazot.

mea (·²) (*pl.* em'a) Intestine.

meabir (·−²) Fords; passages; roads; bridges.

meadin (.−²) *v.* maadin.

meahiz (·−²) *pl. of* mehaz. Sources *of information.*

meal (·²), **-li** Meaning, purport. **şu** ~**de bir şayia,** a rumour to this effect. ~**en** (·²·), having regard to the meaning.

mebadi (·−²) *pl. of* mebde. Beginnings; first principles.

mebahis (·−²) *pl. of* mebhas. Subjects of investigation.

mebaliğ (·−²) *pl. of* meblâğ. Sums.

mebani (·−²) Buildings; *as sing.* base; foundation.

mebde, -ei Beginning; origin; first principle; starting-point.

mebhas Subject of investigation *or* discussion; treatise; chapter.

mebhus (·²) Above-mentioned; the said.

mebhut (·◌), **-tu** Bewildered; dumb-founded.

mebiz Ovary.

meblâğ Sum of money; amount.

mebni (·⌐) Built, erected. ···e ~, based on.

mebsut (·◌) Spread out; dilated; detailed. ~en (·⌐·), in ~ mütenasib, directly proportional.

mebus (·◌) Deputy; member of Parliament. ~an (·—⌐), obs. pl. of mebus. ~luk, quality of a deputy.

mebzul (·◌) Abundant, lavish; cheap. ~iyet (·—·⌐), -ti, abundance; lavishness.

mecal (·⌐), **-li** Power; ability; possibility. ~i* kalmamak, to have no power left, to be no longer able. ~siz, powerless, exhausted.

mecalis (·—⌐) pl. of meclis. Assemblies.

mecaz (·⌐) Metaphor; figurative expression. ~en (·⌐·), figuratively. ~î (·—⌐), figurative; metaphorical.

mecbul (·⌐) Innate; natural; naturally endowed.

mecbur (·◌) Compelled. ~ etm., to compel. ~en (·⌐·), by force, compulsorily. ~î (·—⌐), obligatory; forced. ~iyet (·—·⌐), -ti, compulsion; obligation; necessity.

meccan·en (·⌐·) Gratis; gratuitously. ~î (·—⌐), gratuitous.

mecelle Volume; book; the old Turkish Civil Code.

mechul (·◌) Unknown; passive (verb). Unknown quantity, 'x' (math.). ~iyet (·—·⌐), -ti, a being unknown.

mecid Illustrious, glorious. ~î (··⌐), pertaining to the Sultan Abdulmejid. ~iye, Order of the Mejidieh; silver coin of 20 piastres.

meclis Sitting; assembly; council; scene of a play; social gathering. Millet ~i or ~i millî, the National Assembly, Chamber of Deputies. ~ kurmak, to sit in council: sözüm ~ten dışarı, excuse the term! ~ara (···—⌐), who is good company, amusing.

meclûb (·⌐) Drawn, attracted; brought; won over to a cause; ···e ~, delighted by, enthusiastic about. ~iyet (·—·⌐), -ti, a being drawn or attracted.

mecma (·⌐), **-aı** Place of assembly; place of junction; reunion.

mecmer Censer; chafing-pan.

mecmu (·⌐), **-uu** Assembled, gathered together. Collection; heap; total. ···in ~u, all of ... . ~a, fem. of mecmu; collection; review, periodical, magazine. ~an (·⌐·), in all; wholly, totally.

mecnun (·◌) Mad; madly in love. M~, name of the hero of Eastern romance, the lover of Leyla. ~iyet (·—·⌐), -ti, ~luk, madness; passion.

mecra (·⌐) Watercourse, conduit, canal; course.

mecruh (·◌) Wounded; confuted, untenable.

Mecuc (—⌐) Magog; fabulous race of dwarfs. Yecuc ve ~, Gog and Magog.

mecus, mecusî (·—⌐) Magians; fire-worshippers. Pertaining to fire-worshippers; pagan; also loosely used for Hindu. ~ilik (·——⌐), ~iyet, -ti, fire-worship; Zoroastrianism; paganism.

meczub (·◌) Attracted; crazy. One possessed by devils; ecstatic dervish; crazy fellow.

meç, -çi Rapier; foil.

med, -ddi Prolongation, extension; flow of the tide; high tide; Arabic sign for the prolongation of the vowel ' a '.

medar (·◌) Centre of movement; orbit; tropic; point on which a question turns; means; help. ~ı kelâm, subject of conversation : ~ı maişet, means of subsistence : ···e ~ olm., to help. ~î (·—⌐), tropical.

meddah Who praises; eulogist; public story-teller or mimic. ~lık, quality and occupation of such a story-teller; sycophancy, toadying.

medd·e Arabic sign showing the long ' a '. ~i, v. med. ~ücezir, ebb and flow, the tide.

meded Help, aid. ~ !, help ! : ~ Allah, 'only God can help!' (used about a desperate situation or terrible event). ~hah (···⌐), who asks for aid.

medenî (···⌐) Civilized; civil; civic. ~ cesaret, moral courage. ~ye, fem. of medenî. ~yet, -ti, civilization.

medfen Tomb, cemetery.

medfuat (·—◌), **-tı** Disbursements; payments.

medfun (·◌) Buried.

medhal, -li Entrance; beginning; introductory principles; connexion, influence. ~i olmamak, to have no connexion with, to have nothing to do with. ~dar, participating; involved in.

medh·etmek (⌐··), **-eder** va. Praise. ~i, v. medih. ~iye, eulogy. ~üsena (···⌐), ~ etm., to praise and extol.

medid (·⌐) Lengthy; extended.

medih, -dhi Praise.

medine (·⌐·) Town, city. **Medine**, Medina; ~ fıkarası, in rags and tatters.

medlûl (·◌), **-lü** Inferred; understood. Sense, meaning.

medrese (·⌐·) Formerly Moslem theological school; high school; faculty of a university. ~li, educated at a Moslem school.

med'uv (·⌐) (pl. med'uvin) Invited.

medyun (·◌) Indebted; in debt. Debtor. (with acc.) Owing ... .

mefahir ($\cdot-^\backprime$) *pl. of* **mefharet.**

mefasid ($\cdot-^\backprime$) *pl. of* **mefsedet.**

mefer, –rri Refuge, asylum.

mefhar Glory. ∼ı kâinat, (the Glory of the Universe), Mohammed. ∼et, –ti, cause *or* object of glory; pride.

mefhum ($\cdot\cdot$) Understood. Sense; significance; concept, idea.

mefkud ($\cdot\cdot$) Non-existent; missing, lost. ∼iyet ($\cdot-\cdot$), –ti, non-existence; absence; lack.

mefkûre ($\cdot-^\backprime$) Ideal. ∼ci, idealist. ∼vî ($\cdot-\cdot$), ideal.

meflûc ($\cdot\cdot$) Paralysed.

mefruğ ($\cdot\overset{\backprime}{-}$) Vacated; assigned; ceded.

mefruk ($\cdot\overset{\backprime}{-}$) Separated; disjoined.

mefruş ($\cdot\cdot$) Spread (carpet *etc.*); furnished. ∼at ($\cdot-\cdot$), –tı, carpets, mats *etc.*; furniture.

mefruz[1] ($\cdot\overset{\backprime}{-}$) Separated; divided into plots (land).

mefruz[2] ($\cdot\overset{\backprime}{-}$) Incumbent; obligatory; hypothetical.

mefsedet, –ti Mischief; intrigue; villainy; seditious act.

mefsuh ($\cdot\overset{\backprime}{-}$) Annulled; abrogated.

meftuh ($\cdot\overset{\backprime}{-}$) Opened; conquered.

meftun ($\cdot\overset{\backprime}{-}$) (*with dat.*) Madly in love with; admiring. ∼iyet, –ti, a being madly in love; intense admiration.

meftûr ($\cdot\cdot$) Languid; lukewarm.

mef'ul, meful ($\cdot\cdot$) Made; done; passive. ismi ∼, passive participle. ∼ü(n)anh ($\cdot-\cdot$), ablative. ∼ü(n)bih, accusative. ∼ü(n)fih, locative. ∼ü(n)ileyh, dative. ∼ü(n)maah, instrumental (*gram.*).

meğer ($^\backprime\cdot$), **meğerse** ($\cdot^\backprime\cdot$) But; however; only; it seems that. ∼ki ($^\backprime\cdot\cdot$), provided that.

meh *v.* **mah.**

mehabet ($\cdot-^\backprime$), –ti Awe; majesty. ∼li, majestic; awe-inspiring.

mehalik ($\cdot-^\backprime$), –ki *pl. of* **mehleke.** Dangers.

meham ($\cdot\overset{\backprime}{-}$), –mmi *pl. of* **mühimme.** Important matters.

meharet ($\cdot-^\backprime$), –ti Skill; proficiency.

mehasin ($\cdot-^\backprime$) *pl. of* **hüsün.** Good qualities.

mehaz ($-^\backprime$) Source from which something is taken; authorities *used in writing a book.*

mehbil Vagina. ∼î ($\cdot\cdot\overset{\backprime}{-}$), vaginal.

mehcur ($\cdot\overset{\backprime}{-}$) Forsaken, deserted; separated. ∼iyet, –ti, a being separated *or* abandoned.

mehçe Small crescent.

mehd Cradle. ∼i zuhur, place of origin (of a movement, a religion *etc.*).

Mehdi The Moslem Messiah, *who will appear in due time to deliver the faithful;* Mahdi.

mehel *For* mahal *in* ∼dir, it serves him right. sana ∼dir, it serves you right.

mehengir Carpenter's gauge; surface gauge. mafsallı ∼, scribing-block.

mehenk *v.* **mihenk.**

mehib ($\cdot\overset{\backprime}{-}$) Dreadful; awful; venerable.

mehil Term; permitted delay; days of grace.

mehlika ($\cdot\cdot\overset{\backprime}{-}$) Moon-faced; beautiful.

mehlike Dangerous place *or* work.

mehmaemken ($\cdot\overset{\backprime}{-}\cdot\cdot$) As far as possible.

Mehmedcik The Turkish 'Tommy Atkins'.

mehpare ($\cdot-^\backprime$) Very beautiful person.

mehr Marriage settlement or dowry, *part of which is paid by the husband to the wife at marriage* (mehri muaccel), *and part in case of divorce or widowhood* (mehri müeccel).

mehtab Moonlight; *v. also* **maytab.**

mehter (*Formerly*) a doorkeeper at the Sublime Porte; official who announced the award of promotions or decorations; band which played to a great man. ∼hane ($\cdot\cdot\cdot-^\backprime$), a military band in the suite of a Vizier *and* the place where that band lived.

mehuz ($-^\backprime$) Taken, obtained; quoted (from); borrowed.

mekabir ($\cdot-^\backprime$) *pl. of* **makber.** Tombs, graves.

mekadir ($\cdot-^\backprime$) *pl. of* **mikdar.** Amounts, quantities; value, worth.

mekân ($\cdot\overset{\backprime}{-}$) Place; site; abode. ∼ tutmak, to establish oneself.

mekanik Mechanics.

mekârim ($\cdot-^\backprime$) *pl. of* **mekremet.** ∼i ahlâk, moral virtues.

mekâtib ($\cdot-^\backprime$) *pl. of* **mekteb.** Schools.

meke A kind of thorny plant; coot.

mekel That which can be eaten; a profitable affair. ∼ ittihaz etm., to think only of what one can personally get out of stg.

mekful ($\cdot\overset{\backprime}{-}$) Guaranteed; pledged.

mekik Weaver's shuttle. ∼ dokumak, to be moved about from pillar to post.

mekin ($\cdot\overset{\backprime}{-}$) Firmly established; solid; influential.

mekkâr ($\cdot\overset{\backprime}{-}$) Deceitful.

mekkâre ($\cdot-^\backprime$) Animal let out on hire; goods carried by hired pack-animals; pack-horses of an army. ∼ci, man who hires out pack-animals and looks after them; soldier in charge of military pack-animals.

Mekke ($^\backprime\cdot$) Mecca.

meknî ($\cdot\overset{\backprime}{-}$) Latent.

meknun ($\cdot\overset{\backprime}{-}$) Veiled; concealed; put away.

meknuz ($\cdot\cdot$) Stored away; hidden; buried (treasure); understood (meaning).

mekremet, –ti Magnanimity; benevolence; honour.

mekruh ($\cdot\cdot$) Abominable, disgusting; not prohibited but frowned upon by religious law. ∼at ($\cdot-\cdot$), –tı, disgusting things.

mekseb Earning; gain; livelihood.

meksetmek ($^\backprime\cdot\cdot$), –eder *vn.* Pause; halt.

meksub ($\cdot\cdot$) Gained; earned.

meksur (·ᵼ) Broken; having the vowel point **kesre**, *i.e.* with the sound of 'i'.

mekşuf (·ᵼ) Uncovered; discovered; manifest.

mekteb School. ~**i asmak**, to play truant: ~ **görmüş**, who has been educated at a school: **ana** ~**i**, kindergarten. ~**li**, schoolchild; who has a school diploma; officer who has been at a military school.

mektub (·ᵼ) Written. Letter. ~**cu**, Chief Secretary of a Ministry. ~**laşmak**, to correspond by letter.

mektum (·ᵼ) Kept secret; not divulged *or* denounced; undisclosed.

mekûlât (——ᵼ), -**tı** Comestibles.

mel'abe Game; toy.

melâhat (·—ᵌ), -**tı** Beauty; sweetness.

melâike (·—·ᵌ) *pl. of* **melek.** Angels; *as sing.* angel.

melâl (·ᵳ), -**li** Melancholy; depression.

melâl (·ᵳ) *In* **mal** ~, goods and chattels.

melâmet (·—ᵌ), -**ti** Blame, censure.

melâmî (·—ᵳ) *Member of a sect of dervishes who disregard the outward rites of religion.*

mel'anet, -ti An execrable act. ~**kârane** (····—ᵌ), execrable; diabolical.

melâs Molasses.

melâz (·ᵳ) Asylum, refuge.

melbus (·ᵼ) Clothed. ~**at** (·—ᵼ), -**tı**, clothes.

melce, -ei Refuge, asylum.

melek Angel. ~ **otu**, angelica. ~**sima** (····ᵳ), of angelic countenance (*epithet of the Sultan*). ~**üssiyane** (·····ᵌ), guardian angel.

melek·ât (··ᵼ), -**tı** *pl. of* **meleke.** Innate faculties; *as sing.* natural capacity. ~**e**, proficiency, skill; natural faculty.

melekût, -tu God's spiritual dominion; creation.

melemek *vn.* Bleat.

melengeç *v.* merlengeç.

melez Cross-bred; half-bred. Mulatto; a cross (in breeding). ~ **ağacı**, larch. ~**lemek**, to cross *in breeding*: **ilk melezleme**, first cross.

melfuf (·ᵼ) Wrapped up; enclosed *in a letter.* Enclosure. ~**at** (·—ᵼ), -**tı**, enclosures. ~**en** (·ᵳ·), as an enclosure.

melhame Battle; carnage.

melhem Ointment; salve. ⌐**kelin** ~**i olsa kendi başına sürer**⌐, 'don't expect help from one who needs help himself'.

melhuz (·ᵼ) Anticipated; probable. ~**at** (·—ᵼ), -**tı**, things occurring to the mind; anticipated *or* probable events.

melih Pretty; sweet.

melik, -ki King. ~**âne** (··—ᵌ), kingly, royal; in a regal manner. ~**e** (·—ᵌ), queen.

melisa Lemon verbena.

mellâh Seaman, sailor.

melon Bowler-hat.

meltem Breeze that blows every day in summer off the shore.

melûf (—ᵳ) Usual; accustomed.

melûl (·ᵳ) Low-spirited; vexed. ~ ~ **bakmak**, to wear a piteous expression.

mel'un (·ᵳ) Accursed. Accursed man.

melzum (·ᵼ) Inseparably accompanied.

memalik (·—ᵌ), -**ki** *pl. of* **memleket.** Countries.

memat (·ᵼ), -**tı** Death. **hayat** ~ **meselesi**, a matter of life or death.

memba (·ᵳ), -**aı** Spring; source; origin.

memdud (·ᵼ) Prolonged; extended; with a long vowel.

memduh (·ᵼ) Praised; praiseworthy.

meme Teat; nipple; lobe *of the ear*; tumour; burner *of a lamp.* ~**den kesmek**, to wean: **köpek** ~**si**, a tumour in the armpit. ~**li**, having teats; mammiferous: ~ **hayvan**, mammal. ~**lik**, cover to protect a sore teat *or* to prevent sucking.

memer, -rri Passage. ~**i nas**, thoroughfare.

memeş Saliva dripping from an ox's mouth.

memhur (·ᵼ) Sealed; signed with a seal.

memişhane (···ᵌ) Privy.

memleha Salt-pit; saltworks.

memleket, -ti Dominion; country; town; a man's home district. ~**li**, inhabitant; fellow countryman.

memlû (·ᵼ) Full; filled.

memlûh (·ᵼ) Salted; pickled.

memlûk (·ᵼ), -**kü** Possessed. Slave; Mameluke. ~**iyet** (·—·ᵌ), -**ti**, slavery.

memnu (·ᵳ) Forbidden. ~**at**, -**tı**, forbidden things. ~**iyet, -ti,** prohibition.

memnun (·ᵼ) Pleased; glad; happy; grateful; under an obligation. ~ **etm.**, to please; to make happy. ~**en** (·ᵳ·), gladly, with pleasure. ~**iyet** (·—·ᵌ), -**ti**, pleasure; gratitude.

memşa (·ᵳ), **memşane** Privy.

memul (—ᵼ), -**lü** Hoped; expected; desired. Thing hoped for; a hope. ~ **etm.**, to hope, expect.

memun (—ᵼ) Secure; trusted.

memur (—ᵼ) (*with dat.*) Charged with; ordered to. Official; agent; employee. ~ **olm.**, to be charged with *some duty*: **devlet** ~**u**, a government official: **sıhhiye** ~**u**, health officer. ~**e** (——ᵌ), *fem. of* **memur**: **umuru** ~**si**, his official duties. ~**en** (—ᵳ·), officially. ~**in** (——ᵳ), officials. ~**iyet** (——·ᵌ), -**ti**, official duty; appointment; office; charge; post. ~**luk** (——ᵌ), quality and duties of an official; official post.

memzuc (·ᵼ) Incorporated; blended.

men, –n'i A preventing *or* prohibiting; prohibition.

menaat (·–≀), **–ti** Inaccessibility; impregnability.

menabi (·–≀), **–ii** *pl. of* memba. Sources.

menafi (·–≀), **–ii** *pl. of* menfaat. Benefits *etc.*

menakib (·–≀) *pl. of* menkibe. Eulogies; legends; epic deeds. **~name,** life of a saint.

menal (·≀), **–li** Goods; chattels.

menam Sleep; dream.

menasıb (·–≀) *pl. of* mansıb. High offices.

menasik (·–≀), **–ki** *pl. of* mensek. Rites and ceremonies of the pilgrimage to Mecca.

menatık (·–≀), **–kı** *pl. of* mıntaka. Zones.

menazır (·–≀) *pl. of* manzara. Spectacles; *as sing.* perspective. **~î** (·–·≀), in perspective.

menba *v.* memba.

mendebur Idle; good-for-nothing; disagreeable, disgusting.

Menderes The Meander; any winding river.

mendil Handkerchief.

mendirek Breakwater; artificial harbour.

Mendires *v.* Menderes.

mendub (·≀) Licit; approved.

menekşe (·≀·) Violet.

menend Resembling, like. **misli ~i yok,** he has no peer.

menengüş *v.* merlengec.

menetmek (≀··), **–eder** *va.* Forbid; prevent.

menevî (··≀) Seminal.

meneviş Fruit of the terebinth; wavy appearance of shot silk; blueing of steel. **~li,** wavy; watered (silk); blued (steel).

menfa (·≀) Place of exile.

menfaat, –ti Use; advantage; profit. **~ görmek,** to experience a benefit. **~bahş, ~li,** useful; advantageous; beneficial. **~perest,** self-seeking; always looking for gain.

menfez, menfes Hole; air-hole; vent.

menfi (·≀) Exiled, banished; negative; contrary, perverse, antagonistic; adverse. **~lik,** negation; denying; contrariness. **~yen** (·≀·), in exile; negatively; perversely.

menfur (·≀) Loathed, abhorred. **herkesin ~u,** detested by everyone.

mengec Large shuttle for wool.

mengel Bangle.

mengene (≀··) Press; vice; clamp; mangle.

menhiyat (··≀), **–tı** Forbidden things.

menhus (·≀) Ill-omened, inauspicious; cursed.

menî Semen.

men'i (≀·) *v.* men.

menkibe, menkabe Epic; panegyric; recital of a great man's deeds or virtues; legend. **~vî** (···≀), legendary.

menku (·≀), **–uu** Infused; macerated. Infusion.

menkub (·≀) Unfortunate; disgraced. **~iyet** (·–·≀), **–ti,** a being disgraced.

menkûha (·–≀) Wife.

menkul (·≀) Transported, conveyed; traditional. **~dur ki,** it is traditionally related that: **kendinden ~,** that which, according to himself, he possesses: **gayri ~,** real (estate). **~ât, –tı,** movables; traditions.

menkuş (·≀) Drawn as a picture; ornamented; impressed on the memory.

menolunmak (≀···) *vn.* Be prevented *or* forbidden.

mensi (·≀) Forgotten.

mensub (·≀) Related to, connected with. **~at** (·–≀), **–tı,** things belonging *or* attributed; one's relatives. **~iyet** (·–·≀), **–ti,** relationship; connexion; membership (of a society *etc.*).

mensuc (·≀) Woven. **~at** (·–≀), **–tı,** textiles.

mensuh (·≀) Cancelled; annulled.

mensur (·≀) In prose. **~e** (·–≀), prose.

menşe Place of origin. **~li,** originating from; exported from.

menşur Prism; Royal patent. ... **~undan geçirmek,** to see *stg.* in the light of ... .

menteşe (≀··) Hinge.

menus (–≀) To which one is accustomed; familiar; in common use, current.

menut (·≀), **–tu** (*with dat.*) Suspended from; depending on.

menzil Halting-place; stage, day's journey; house; inn; range (of a gun); transport branch of an army; lines of communication. **~ beygiri,** post-horse: **~i maksuda ermek,** to attain one's object. **~ci,** courier; postman travelling with relays of horses. **~e,** degree; rank; social status. **~hane** (···≀), posting-house for horses. **~li,** having a range of ... : **uzun ~,** long-range (gun *etc.*).

menzul (·≀), **–lü** Stricken with apoplexy; paralysed.

menzur (·≀) Vowed; votive.

mephas *etc. v.* mebhas *etc.*

mer'a Pasture.

merahil (·–≀) *pl. of* merhale. Stages of a journey.

merak, –kı, –ğı Curiosity; whim; passion *for stg.,* great interest; anxiety; depression, melancholy. **birini ~ta bırakmak,** to cause anxiety to s.o.: **birinin ~ına dokunmak,** (of a matter) to make s.o. uneasy: **···e ~ etm.,** to have a passion for, *or* to be very interested in *stg.*; **bir şeyi ~ etm.,** to be curious about a thing: **birini ~ etm.,** to be anxious about a person: ~ **halini almak**, (of stg.) to become a passion: **bir şeye ~ı* olm.**, to have a passion for, to make a hobby of stg. ~**aver** (··—¹), causing anxiety. ~**lanmak**, to be anxious: ···e ~, to be curious about *or* have an interest in *stg.* ~**lı**, curious; interested in, fond of; anxious: **futbol ~sı**, a football devotee. ~**sız**, free from anxiety; uninterested, indifferent.

merakib (·—¹) *pl. of* **merkeb**. Ships.

merakiz (·—¹) *pl. of* **merkez**. Centres *etc.*

meral, –li Roe; doe.

mer'alık (·—¹) Well-pastured. Pasturage.

meram Desire; intention; aim. ~ **etm.**, to wish, intend, strive: ~ **anlamaz**, unreasonable; who can't be made to understand: ~**ını* anlatmak**, to be able to express what one wants: ⌜~ **anlıyan beri gelsin**⌝, what's the good of talking; nobody takes any notice!: ⌜~**ın elinden bir şey kurtulmaz**⌝, 'where there's a will there's a way': ⌜~ **etmiye görsün**⌝, if he wants a thing he gets it: ~**ına* nail olm.**, to attain one's object.

meramet (·—¹), **–ti** Temporary repair. ~ **etm.**, to repair temporarily, to patch up. ~**çi**, mender, tinker, cobbler.

meranet (·—¹), **–ti** Ductility.

meraret (·—¹), **–ti** Bitterness.

merasim (·—¹) Ceremonies; established usages; *as sing.* ceremony; commemoration. ~ **geçişi**, ceremonial march-past: ~**le karşılamak**, to give a ceremonious welcome to ... .

meratib (·—¹) *pl. of* **mertebe**. Ranks; degrees.

merbut (·⸱) Attached; appended; dependent; captive (balloon), ~**at** (·—⸱), **–tı**, attached documents; attachments. ~**en** (·⸱—·), as an attachment *or* appendage. ~**iyet** (·—·¹), **–ti**, dependence; devotion.

mercan Coral. ~ **balığı**, red sea-bream: ~ **kayaları**, coral reef, atoll: ~ **terlikleri**, red leather slippers. ~**köşk**, marjoram.

merci (·⸱), **–ii** Place to which recourse is had; source to which a thing is referred; recourse; reference; competent authority.

mercimek Lentil. ···**le mercimeği fırına vermek**, to flirt with; to come to terms with: **su mercimeği**, duckweed.

mercu (·⸱) Requested.

merd Man; brave; manly man. Manly; brave; fine *in character*. ~**ane¹** (·—·), manly, virile: in a manly way. ~**ce** (⸱·), bravely; as becomes a man. ~**lik**, manliness, courage.

merdane² (·—¹) Inking cylinder; rolling-pin; roller.

merdiven Ladder; steps; stairs. **kırkına ~ dayamak**, to be nearing forty *years of age.*

merdud (·⸱) Rejected; returned; cursed.

merdüm Man; human being. ~**ek**, little man; manikin; pupil of the eye. ~**giriz**, misanthropic; unsociable. ~**perest, –ti**, hero-worshipper.

meremet *v.* **meramet**.

meret, –ti The damned fellow!; the cursed thing!

merfu (·⸱) Elevated; removed; abolished.

mergub (·⸱) Longed for; sought after; desirable.

merhaba (¹·· *or* ¹·—) Good-day!; how are you? ~**laşmak**, to greet one another.

merhale A day's journey; stage. ~ ~, by stages.

merhamet, –ti Mercy, pity; ~**li**, merciful; tender-hearted. ~**siz**, merciless; cruel.

merhem Ointment; salve.

merhum (·⸱) Deceased; 'the late ...' (*correctly only used of Moslems*). ~ **olm.**, to die.

merhun (·⸱) Pledged; pawned; contingent.

meri¹ (·⸱) Visible.

meri² (·⸱) Gullet; oesophagus.

mer'i (·⸱) Observed; in force (of a law *etc.*).

Meriç (¹·) The river Maritza.

Merih Mars.

merinos Merino.

mer'iülicra In force, observed (law *etc.*).

meriyat (··⸱), **–tı** Visible objects; the visible world.

mer'iyet, –ti A being valid *or* in force; validity. ~**e geçmek**, to come into force.

mer'iyülhatır (·—·—¹) To whom respect is paid; distinguished; of some standing.

merkad Resting-place; bed; grave.

merkeb Mount (horse *etc.*); donkey; ship. ~**ci**, donkeyman.

merkez Centre; administrative centre; central office; condition, manner. **polis ~i**, police-station: **siklet ~i**, centre of gravity: '**düşünceniz ne ~dedir?**', 'what do you think about it?' ~**î** (··⸱), central. ~**iyet, –ti**, centralization; a being central. ~**lenmek**, ~**ileşmek**, to be centralized.

merkum (·⸱) The said (person), the above-mentioned (*contemptuously*).

merkûz (·⸱) Set up; planted.

merlanos Whiting.

merlengec Mastic-tree (Lentiscus).

mermer Marble. ~ **kaymağı** *or* **su ~i**, alabaster: ~ **kireci**, lime from burnt marble. ~**lik**, marble paving. ~**şahi** (··—¹), book muslin.

mermi Projectile; shell.

mersa (·⸱) Anchorage; port.

mersad *v.* **mirsad**.

mersin Myrtle. ~ **balığı**, sturgeon: ~ **morinası**, the largest of the sturgeons (*Acipenser huso*): **çiga (çuka) ~**, sterlet (*Acipenser ruthenus*).

mersiye Elegy.

mersörize Mercerized.

mersum (·⸺) Drawn; designed; above-mentioned; usual.

mert *v.* merd.

mertebani A bluish-green pottery *formerly made at Martaban*; bluish-green colour.

mertebe Degree; rank; grade. mümkün ~, as far as possible.

mertek Squared baulk of timber; beam. elifi ~ zannetmek, to be very ignorant.

mervarit (·—ͺ) Pearl.

mervi (·⸺) Narrated; traditional.

Meryem Miriam; Mary. ~ana (·ͺ··), the Virgin Mary.

meryemiye Salvia.

merzagî (···⸺) Marshy.

merzengûş Marjoram.

merzuk (·ᵛ) Fed; rationed. ~iye (·—·ͺ), food ration.

mes¹, –ssi Contact; touch. ~i hacet, an occasion of need.

mes² (*Fr. messe*) Mass (religious).

mes³ *v.* mest².

mesa (·⸺) Evening.

mesabe (·—ͺ) Degree; quality; nature. ... ~sinde, of the nature of ..., like ... .

mes'adet (·—ͺ), –ti Happiness.

mesafe (·—ͺ) Distance; space. kat'ı ~ etm., to traverse a distance.

mesağ (·⸺) Sanction; lawfulness.

mesaha (·—ͺ) The measurement of land; the measure *of a field etc.* ~ı sathiye, super-ficial measurement: ~ şeridi, tape-measure: ~ zinciri, measuring-chain: ilmi ~, the science of surveying.

mesai (·—ͺ) Efforts; pains. ···e sarfı ~ etm., to strive to ... .

mesaib (·—ͺ) *pl. of* musibet. Calamities.

mesail (·—ͺ) *pl. of* mesele. Questions.

mesakin (·—ͺ) *pl. of* mesken. Dwellings.

mesakîn (·—ͺ) *pl. of* miskin. Lepers; paupers.

mesalih (·—ͺ) *pl. of* maslahat. Affairs.

mesalik (·—ͺ), –ki *pl. of* meslek. Careers; professions.

mesam·e (·—ͺ) (*pl.* ~at) Pore. ~î (·—⸺), porous.

mesane (·—ͺ) Bladder.

mesar (·⸺) *pl. of* meserret. *As sing.* Joy, rejoicing.

mesavi (·—⸺) Evil conditions *or* acts; mis-deeds, vices.

mesbuk (·ᵛ) Preceded; surpassed; having a precedent. ~ulemsal, having precedents: ~ hizmetlerine, for services rendered: gayri ~, unprecedented.

mescid Mosque (*esp.* a small mosque).

mesdud (·ᵛ) Barred; shut; plugged up.

mesel Proverb; parable; instance. ~â (ͺ·—), for instance, for example.

mesele Question; problem; thesis; a matter of concern. hiçten bir ~ çıkarmak, to make a fuss about nothing: bir şeyi ~ yapmak, to make a to-do about stg.

meserret, –ti Joy; rejoicing. ~aver (····—ͺ), ~bahş, causing joy; joyful.

meshetmek (ͺ··), –eder *va.* Stroke; rub lightly; wipe the shoes with the palm of the hand to replace ritual ablution.

meshuf (·ᵛ) Having an unquenchable thirst *or* an unsatisfied passion.

meshur (·ᵛ) Bewitched.

mesih¹, –shi A touching lightly with the hand.

Mesih² (·⸺), ~a The Messiah. ~adem (·——ͺ), having a healing breath like Christ. ~î (·—⸺), Christian.

mesina (·ͺ·) Silkworm gut.

mesire (·—ͺ) Promenade; excursion spot.

mesken Dwelling.

meskenet, –ti Lack of spirit; sluggishness.

meskûkât (·—ᵛ), –tı Coins.

meskûn (·ᵛ) Inhabited.

meskût (·ᵛ) Silenced; passed over in silence.

meslek, –ki, –ği Career, profession; mode of acting *or* thinking; moral character; principle. ~ten, by profession: ~ sahibi, who has a profession; a man of sound prin-ciples: ~ten yetişme, professional, ' de carrière'. ~daş, one of the same profes-sion; colleague. ~î (···⸺), professional. ~siz, without a career; unprincipled.

mesmu (·⸺) Heard, audible; valid. ~at (·—ᵛ), –tı, rumours; hearsay.

mesmum (·ᵛ) Poisoned. ~en (·⸺·), by poison.

mesned Place of support; fulcrum; post, office of dignity.

mesnevi (···⸺) A poem in rhymed couplets.

mesrud (·⸺) Mentioned; above-mentioned.

mesruk (·ᵛ) Stolen.

mesrur (·ᵛ) Glad; contented. ~iyet (·—·ͺ), –ti, happiness.

messetmek (ͺ··), –eder *va.* (*with dat.*) Touch. *vn.* Arise; happen. hacet *or* ihtiyac ~, to become necessary.

mest¹, –ti Light soleless boot, *worn in the house or with overshoes.*

mest² Drunk. ~ etm., to intoxicate; to enchant: ~ olm., to be intoxicated; to be enraptured. ~ane (·—ͺ), in a drunken manner. ~edici (ͺ···), intoxicating.

mestur¹ (·ᵛ) Covered; veiled; secret. ~ endaht, indirect fire (*mil.*). ~e (·—ͺ), *for* tahsisatı ~, secret funds.

mestur² Written.

mes'ud (·ᵛ) Happy; fortunate. ~iyet (·—·ͺ), –ti, happiness.

mesul (·ᵛ) Responsible, answerable (for =

···den). ~**iyet** (·−·¹), **-ti**, responsibility. ~**iyetli**, involving responsibility.

meşacir (·−¹) *pl. of* **meşcere**. Wooded places.

meşagil (·−¹) *pl. of* **meşgale**. Preoccupations *etc.*

meşahir (·−¹) *pl. of* **meşhur**. Famous men.

meşak (·−¹), **-kkı** *pl. of* ~**kat, -tı**, hardship; trouble. ~**katlı**, troublesome; exhausting, wearisome.

meşale Torch. ~**ci**, torch-bearer.

meşayih (·−¹) *pl. of* **şeyh**. Elders; doctors of law.

meşbu (·−¹) Satiated; saturated.

meşcere Wooded place.

meşe Oak. Oaken. ~ **odunu**, blockhead. ~**cik**, germander. ~**lik**, wood of oak trees.

meşgale Business; occupation; preoccupation; pastime.

meşgul (·ⁱ) Occupied; busy; preoccupied. ~**iyet** (·−·¹), **-ti**, preoccupation; occupation; a being busy.

meşhed Place of martyrdom; battlefield; tomb of a **şehid**, *q.v.* ~**i**, inhabitant of Meshed: ~ **mubalâğası**, a gross exaggeration.

meşher Exhibition.

meşhud (·ⁱ) Seen, witnessed.

meşhun (·ⁱ) Filled.

meşhur (·ⁱ) Famous; well-known.

meşihat (·−ⁱ), **-tı** Office of a sheikh, *esp.* of the Sheikh-ul-Islam.

meşime (·−¹) Womb; placenta, afterbirth. ⌜**gün doğmadan** ~**i şebden neler doğar**⌝, before the day is born what strange things may be born in the womb of the night' (*v. under* **gebe** 'geceler gebedir').

meşin Leather. ~ **suratlı**, thick-skinned.

meşiy, -şyi A walking. ~**et, -ti**, gait.

meşk, -ki Model for writing; copy-book; musical exercise. ~ **olm.**, to serve as a model. ~**etmek** (¹··), **-eder**, *va.* to take as a model; *vn.* to practise writing; to practise music.

meşkûk (·ⁱ) Doubted; doubtful.

meşkûr (·ⁱ) Acknowledged with thanks; deserving thanks.

meşreb Natural disposition; character. (*As a compound*) having *such and such* a character, *e.g.* **hafif**~, flighty, frivolous.

meşru (·ⁱ) Legal; legitimate. ~**iyet** (·−·¹), **-ti**, ~**luk**, legitimacy; legality.

meşrub (·ⁱ) Drinkable. Beverage. ~**at** (·−ⁱ), **-tı**, drinks.

meşruh (·ⁱ) Commented on; explained. ~**at** (·−ⁱ), **-tı**, marginal notes; written comments: ~**ta bulunmak**, to add comments or explanations.

meşrut (·ⁱ) Stipulated; bound by conditions. ~**a** (·−¹), property left by will with conditions attached. ~**e** (·−¹), *fem. of* **meşrut**; **hükûmeti** ~, constitutional government. ~**i** (·−¹), constitutional. ~**iyet** (·−·¹), **-ti**, constitutional government.

meşşate (·−¹) Coiffeuse.

meşum (·ⁱ) Inauspicious, ill-omened; sinister.

meşveret, -ti Consultation; council. **ehli** ~, member of a council; competent adviser.

meta (·ⁱ), **-ai** Merchandise; goods. **ne** ~ **olduğunu öğrendik**, we know now what sort of fellow he is (*i.e.* a scoundrel).

metafora (··¹·) Davit. **borda** ~**sı**, boat-boom.

metalib (·−¹) *pl. of* **matlab**. Requests; things demanded.

metanet (·−¹), **-ti** Firmness; solidity; tenacity; toughness.

metazori (··¹·) (*sl.*) By force and threats.

metbu (·ⁱ), **-uu** Obeyed. Sovereign. **devlet** ~**ası**, the state of which he is a subject. ~**iyet** (·−·¹), **-ti**, sovereignty.

metelik Obsolete coin of 10 paras. ~ **etmez**, not worth a sou: **meteliğe kurşun atmak**, to be penniless: ···**e** ~ **vermemek**, not to care a damn for ···. ~**siz**, without a sou, penniless.

meteris Trench (*mil.*).

metfen, methal *etc. v.* **medfen, medhal** *etc.*

metin, -tni Text.

metîn (·ⁱ) Solid; firm; tough; trustworthy; strong (in character).

metot Method.

metre (¹·) Metre. ~ **kare**, square metre: ~ **küp**, cubic metre.

metres (*Fr.* **maîtresse**) Mistress; kept woman.

metris Trench (*mil.*).

metropolit Greek bishop; Metropolitan. ~**lik**, title or office of a Metropolitan.

metruk (·ⁱ) Left; abandoned; deserted; neglected; obsolete. ~**ât** (·−ⁱ), **-tı**, effects left by a deceased person. ~**e** (·−¹) *fem. of* **metruk**; divorced woman: **arazii** ~, lands given up to public use: **asarı** ~, posthumous works. ~**iyet** (·−·¹), **-ti**, a being abandoned: ~ **halinde**, in a neglected condition.

me'va (·ⁱ) Home; shelter.

mevacib (·−¹) Salary; appropriations.

mevad (·ⁱ), **-ddı** *pl. of* **madde**. Matters; materials; objects; articles, paragraphs.

mevaid (·−¹) *pl. of* **mev'id**. Places *or* times agreed upon; appointments; promises.

mevaki (·−·¹), **-ii** *pl. of* **mevki**. Places.

mevakif (·−¹) *pl. of* **mevkif**. Halting-places.

mevali (·−·¹) *pl. of* **mevlâ**. Masters.

mevalid (·−¹) *pl. of* **mevlûd**. Births; the 'kingdoms' of nature (animal, vegetable, and mineral).

mevani ($\cdot-\stackrel{\text{\tiny$\perp$}}{}$), **–ii** *pl. of* **mâni.** Impediments.

mevasim ($\cdot-\stackrel{\text{\tiny$1$}}{}$) *pl. of* **mevsim.** Seasons.

mevaşi ($\cdot-\stackrel{\text{\tiny$\perp$}}{}$) Cattle; livestock.

mevazi ($\cdot-\stackrel{\text{\tiny$\perp$}}{}$), **–ii** *pl. of* **mevzi.** Places; situations.

mevc Wave. ~e, a single wave *or* ripple.

mevcud ($\cdot\stackrel{\text{\tiny$\cdot$}}{}$) Existing; present. The number present (at a meeting *etc.*); stock; available force (*mil.*). ~at ($\cdot-\stackrel{\text{\tiny$\cdot$}}{}$), **–tı,** all existing things; creation. ~iyet ($\cdot-\cdot\stackrel{\text{\tiny$1$}}{}$), **–ti,** existence; presence: bir ~ göstermek, to make oneself noticed.

mevdu ($\cdot\stackrel{\text{\tiny$\perp$}}{}$) Entrusted. ~at ($\cdot-\stackrel{\text{\tiny$\cdot$}}{}$), **–tı,** things entrusted; deposits (with a bank *etc.*).

meveddet, –ti Affection, love.

mevhibe Gift; talent.

mevhub ($\cdot\stackrel{\text{\tiny$\cdot$}}{}$) Given; God-given, inborn.

mevhum ($\cdot\stackrel{\text{\tiny$\cdot$}}{}$) Imaginary, fancied; fictitious. ~at ($\cdot-\stackrel{\text{\tiny$\cdot$}}{}$), **–tı,** imaginations; imaginary fears.

mev'id Place *or* time agreed upon; appointment. ~i mülâkat, rendezvous.

mev'iza Exhortation; homily.

mevki, –ii Place; position; situation; post; seat *in a theatre etc.*; class *on a train etc.* ~ine göre, according to circumstances. ~î ($\cdot\cdot\stackrel{\text{\tiny$\perp$}}{}$), local. ~li, having a first-class compartment, seat *etc.*

mevkib Procession.

mevkif Halting-place; station.

mevkuf ($\cdot\stackrel{\text{\tiny$\cdot$}}{}$) Stopped; arrested; detained; dependent; *property* in trust for some pious use. Arrested person, prisoner. ona ~dur, it depends on him: bir şeye ~, given up to a thing. ~at ($\cdot-\stackrel{\text{\tiny$\cdot$}}{}$), **–tı,** properties held in mortmain. ~en ($\cdot\stackrel{\text{\tiny$\perp$}}{}\cdot$), under arrest. ~iyet ($\cdot-\cdot\stackrel{\text{\tiny$\cdot$}}{}$), **–ti,** arrest; detention; a being held in mortmain.

mevkûl ($\cdot\stackrel{\text{\tiny$\cdot$}}{}$) Entrusted to a representative *or* deputy.

mevkut ($\cdot\stackrel{\text{\tiny$\cdot$}}{}$) Fixed for a certain period; periodical.

Mevlâ ($\cdot\stackrel{\text{\tiny$\perp$}}{}$) The Lord God. **mevlâ,** master. ~sını* bulmak, to get what one deserves: ⌜arayan ~sını da bulur belâsını da⌝, he got what he was asking for; it serves him right. ~na ($\cdot-\stackrel{\text{\tiny$\perp$}}{}$), 'our lord', *title formerly given to great religious personages; dervishes' mode of addressing a man.*

mevlevî ($\cdot\cdot\stackrel{\text{\tiny$\perp$}}{}$) *A member of the order of Dervishes founded by Mevlana Jelaluddin-i-Rumi, esp. the order of 'Whirling Dervishes'.*

mevlid Time *or* place of birth; birthday.

mevlûd Born. Child; birthday of Mohammed; poems in honour of that birthday; funeral ceremony held forty days after a death; one of the natural 'kingdoms' (animal, vegetable, or mineral). ~ kandili,

evening of the Feast of the Prophet's birthday.

mevrid Place of arrival.

mevrud ($\cdot\stackrel{\text{\tiny$\cdot$}}{}$) Arrived; touched upon. ~at ($\cdot-\stackrel{\text{\tiny$\cdot$}}{}$), **–tı,** things arrived (letters *etc.*).

mevrus ($\cdot\stackrel{\text{\tiny$\cdot$}}{}$) Inherited; hereditary.

mevsim Season; proper time *for anything*; the between seasons, spring and autumn. ~lik, suitable for spring or autumn; seasonal. ~siz, unseasonable; premature; out-of-place.

mevsuf ($\cdot\stackrel{\text{\tiny$\cdot$}}{}$) Endowed; qualified by *such and such an adjective.* Substantive.

mevsuk ($\cdot\stackrel{\text{\tiny$\cdot$}}{}$) Trusted; reliable; authentic; documented. ~an ($\cdot\stackrel{\text{\tiny$\perp$}}{}\cdot$), authentically, reliably. ~iyet ($\cdot-\cdot\stackrel{\text{\tiny$1$}}{}$), **–ti,** authenticity; reliability.

mevsul ($\cdot\stackrel{\text{\tiny$\cdot$}}{}$) Joined; united. ismi ~, relative pronoun.

mevt, –ti Death. ~a ($\cdot\stackrel{\text{\tiny$\perp$}}{}$), *pl. of* **meyyit,** the dead. ~aî ($\cdot-\stackrel{\text{\tiny$\perp$}}{}$), pertaining to the dead; sepulchral (voice *etc.*).

mev'ud ($\cdot\stackrel{\text{\tiny$\cdot$}}{}$) Promised; appointed; predestined. eceli ~, the appointed time of death.

mevvac With waves; rough (sea).

mevzi ($\cdot\stackrel{\text{\tiny$\perp$}}{}$), **–ii** Place; position. ~î ($\cdot\cdot\stackrel{\text{\tiny$\perp$}}{}$), local.

mevzu ($\cdot\stackrel{\text{\tiny$\perp$}}{}$), **–uu** Placed; laid; situated; instituted; subject (to); conventional; customary. Subject; proposition. bahis ~u *or* ~ubahis, **–hsi,** in question; subject under discussion: para ~ değildir, it is not a question of money. ~a ($\cdot-\stackrel{\text{\tiny$1$}}{}$), *fem. of* **mevzu:** postulate; convention. ~at ($\cdot-\stackrel{\text{\tiny$\cdot$}}{}$), **–tı,** subjects; rules, dispositions, regulations; conventions; legislation.

mevzun ($\cdot\stackrel{\text{\tiny$\cdot$}}{}$) Weighted; balanced; symmetrical.

mey Wine.

meyal *In* hayal ~, *v.* hayalmeyal.

meyan[1] *n.* Middle; midst; interval. ~larında, in the midst of them; between them: bu ~da, amongst these; including ...; in the meantime.

meyan[2] Liquorice. ~balı ($\cdot\stackrel{\text{\tiny$1$}}{}\cdot\cdot$), **–nı,** liquorice (sweet, medicine). ~kökü, **–nü,** liquorice root.

meyane ($\cdot-\stackrel{\text{\tiny$1$}}{}$) Middle; interval; correct degree of cooking (jam *etc.*). Middling, moderate. ~de, between us (them *etc.*): ~sini bulmak, to find the means; to reconcile; to reach just the right moment *for stg. to be done:* ~si gelmek, to reach the right moment; (of a dish) to reach the right consistency: ~ye girmek, to get between, as an obstacle *or* as mediator. ~ci, middleman.

meydan Open space; public square; arena, ring, ground; the open; opportunity. ~da, in the open; houseless; exposed; manifest, obvious; 'evidently': ~ aramak, to seek space; to seek an opportunity: ~a atmak, to put forward, to suggest: ~ bulmak, to find an opportunity: ~a çıkmak, to come forth, to show oneself; (of a child) to grow up: ~a çıkarmak, to expose to view, publish, discover; to bring up *a child* to maturity: ~a gelmek, to come into the open; to become celebrated; to reach maturity: ~a getirmek, to bring into view; to form *or* create: ~ı harb, battlefield: ~ muharebesi, pitched battle: ~ okumak, to challenge: ~ vermek, to give an opportunity; to give encouragement: At ~ı, the Hippodrome in Istanbul: 'vaziyet ~da!', 'you know very well what the situation is!' **meydan·cı**, man employed to clean public places; caretaker. ~**lık**, open flat space.

meyelân Inclination; affection.

meyhane (·–¹) Wine-shop, tavern. ~**ci**, tavern-keeper, publican.

meyil, –yli Inclination; slope; propensity; affection, liking. ···e ~ **göstermek**, to have an inclination for ..., to desire. ~**li**, inclined.

meyl·etmek (¹··), **–eder** *vn.* Be inclined. ···e ~, to have a propensity *or* liking for. ~**i**, *v.* meyil.

meymenet, –ti A being lucky or auspicious. ~**li**, auspicious, lucky; prosperous. ~**siz**, unlucky; inauspicious; unsympathetic, disagreeable (person).

meyus (–⁴) Hopeless, despairing. ~**iyet** (––·¹), **–ti**, hopelessness, despair.

meyva Fruit. ~ **yaprağı**, fruit-bud. ~**cı**, fruiterer. ~**dar**, fruit-yielding, fruitful. ~**hoş**, fruit market (*name of a district of Istanbul*). ~**lı**, made of fruit. ~**lık**, fruit-garden; receptacle for fruit.

meyyal (*with dat.*) Very inclined towards; very fond of.

meyyit, –ti Dead. Dead man; corpse.

meyzin *v.* müezzin.

mezad Auction; auction-place. ~**a koymak** (vermek, çıkarmak), to sell by auction: ~ **malı**, goods bought at an auction; cheap trifles; bargain; cheap, tawdry: ~ **olm.**, to be sold by auction. ~**cı**, auctioneer.

mezahib (·–¹) *pl. of* mezheb. Beliefs; religions.

mezahim *pl. of* zahmet. Troubles, obstacles.

mezalim (·–¹) *pl. of* mazleme. Cruelties.

mezamir (·–¹) Flutes; psalms.

mezar Grave, tomb. ~ **kaçkını**, a person with one foot in the grave: ~ **kitabesi**, inscription on a tombstone. ~**cı**, grave-digger. ~**ıstan** (·–·¹), ~**lık**, cemetery. ~**taşı** (·¹··), **–nı**, tombstone.

mezarna (·¹·) Coaming.

mezaya (·–⁴) *pl. of* meziyet. Good qualities, *esp.* excellent points in literary composition.

mezbaha Slaughterhouse.

mezbele Refuse-heap.

mezbuhane (·––¹) Desperate; homicidal; suicidal; with one's back to the wall.

mezbur (·⁴) Aforesaid.

mezc A mixing *or* blending. ~**etmek** (¹··), **–eder**, to mix, combine, blend.

meze Appetizer; snack; hors-d'œuvre. ~**ci**, seller of snacks. ~**lik**, anything used as an appetizer or to accompany a drink.

mezeborda (·¹··) Broadside.

mezellet, –ti Abjectness; baseness.

mezestre Half-mast.

mezevolta Half-hitch.

mezgerdek, mezgeldek The Little Bustard.

mezgid *v.* mezit.

mezheb Religion, creed; doctrine; sect; school of thought. ~**i geniş**, too tolerant in matters of morals.

mezid Increased; abundant. Increase.

mezin *v.* müezzin.

mezit, –ti, mezitbalığı, –nı Whiting.

meziyet, –ti Excellence; virtue; talent, ability; value.

mezkûr (·⁴) Mentioned; aforementioned; the said ... .

mezmum (·⁴) Blamed; blameworthy; ill-spoken of.

mezmur Psalm.

mezraa Arable field.

mezru (·–⁴) Sown. ~**at** (·–⁴), **–tı**, sowings; seeded fields; crops.

mezun (–⁴) Authorized; on leave; having a school diploma; graduate; excused *from performing some duty.* ~**en** (–⁴·), *adv.* on leave. ~**iyet** (–––¹), **–ti**, leave, furlough; permission, authorization.

mıcır Grit used in road surfacing; coal-dust; small ashes. ~**ık**, crushed, squashed.

mıh Nail. ~ **gibi kapalı**, tightly shut: ᴴhem nalına hem ~**ına**ᴴ, regardless; without respect of persons; impartially. ~**î** (·⁴), nail-shaped: **hattı** ~ *or* ~ **yazı**, cuneiform writing. ~**lamak**, to nail. ~**lanmak**, to be nailed; to be nailed to the spot. ~**lı**, nailed.

mıhladız *v.* mıknatıs.

mıknatıs Magnet. ~**î** (·––⁴), magnetic. ~**iyet, –ti**, magnetism.

mıncık *v.* cıcık.

mıncıklamak *va.* Claw about (as a cat); ill-treat; tease apart.

mıntaka Zone; district. ~**i baride** (mahruka, mutedile), the frigid (torrid, temperate) zone. ~**vî** (····⁴), regional.

mırdar *v.* murdar.

mırıl·damak, ~danmak *vn.* Mutter to

oneself; grumble. ~tı, muttering; grumbling.

mırın *Only in* ~ kırın etm., to show vague disapproval; to appear unwilling; to boggle.

mırmır *Imitates the sound of muttering.*

mırnav Miaow.

mısdak, -kkı Criterion; proof; authority. ... ~ınca, according to the sense of ... .

Mısır[1] (⌣·) Egypt. mısırlı, Egyptian.

mısır[2] Maize; parched maize.

mıskal Burnisher. ~a vurmak, to burnish.

mısra (·⌣), -aı Hemistich; line of poetry.

mısrî (·⌣) Egyptian.

mıstak *v.* mısdak.

mışıl mışıl *Imitates the sound of heavy breathing.* ~ ~ uyumak, to sleep soundly.

mıymıntı Weak; slack; useless (man).

mızık Shilly-shallying, indecision; a not obeying the rules of a game. ~çı, an untrustworthy, querulous, dithering sort of fellow; one who does not obey the rules of a game. ~lanmak, to spoil a game by not obeying the rules.

mızıka (·⌣·) Military band. ağız ~sı, mouthorgan.

mızmız Hesitant, unable to make up his mind; lazy, slow; querulous.

mızrab Instrument for striking; plectrum

mızrak, -kı Lance. ⌜~ çuvala sığmaz⌝, 'the spear will not go into the sack', *used to deride an obvious falsehood*: ⌜suyu ~la delmek⌝, (to pierce water with a lance), to make useless efforts: ⌜tek (yek) at tek mızrağı⌝, all alone; without family. ~lı, armed with a lance; lancer: ~ ilmihal, *(formerly)* a standard elementary school-book.

mi, mı, mu, mü 1. *Interrogative particle.* 2. *Adds emphasis.* geldi mi?, has he come?: o mu geldi?, is it he who has come?: mektub yazıyor musunuz?, are you writing a letter?: mektub mu yazıyorsunuz?, is it a letter that you are writing?: cahil mi cahil, ignorant beyond words: yapar mı yapar!, he's quite capable of doing that; of course he will do that: ne mi var?, *(really in reply to* ne var? = what's the matter), is there any need to ask what's the matter?

mia Intestine. ~î (·—⌣), intestinal.

miad (-⌣) Fixed place *or* time; rendezvous; the Last Day; fixed period *for the renewal of clothes etc. issued to soldiers or pupils, or for the renewal of tyres on a car etc.*

miat (-⌣), -tı Hundreds.

mibzer Drill for sowing.

micmer Censer.

miço (⌣·) Cabin-boy; boy waiter.

mide (-⌣) Stomach; good taste. ~ bulanmak, to be nauseated; to feel suspicious: ~si kaldırmak (kabul etm,) to feel like eating stg.; to swallow an insult: ~ye

oturmak, to lie heavy on the stomach, be indigestible. ~ci, who thinks only of his belly; self-seeker. ~siz, having bad taste; eating anything: ne ~lik!, what bad taste! ~vî (-·⌣), good for the stomach; pertaining to the stomach.

Midilli (·⌣·) Mitylene. midilli, small shaggy pony: mahşer ~si, short person; mischief-maker.

midye (⌣·) Mussel.

miftah Key.

miğfer Helmet.

miğra, miğri (⌣·) Conger eel.

miğren Migraine, headache.

mihanik Mechanics. ~î, mechanical.

mihber Test-tube.

mihenk, mihek Touchstone; test; standard. mihenge vurmak, to test: ⌜içki insanın mihengidir⌝, a man's true nature is shown when in his cups; 'in vino veritas'. ~çi, silversmith who tests metals; a man who quickly weighs up a matter or a man.

mihir[1], -hri *v.* mehr.

mihir[2], -hri Sun; affection, love. ⌜varakı mihri vefayı kim okur kim dinler?⌝, (who reads or listens to the letter protesting affection and loyalty?), who listens!, who cares!

mihman Guest. ~dar, host; official charged with offering hospitality to distinguished visitors. ~nüvaz, hospitable.

mihnet, -ti Trouble; affliction. ~keş, ~zede, afflicted; disconsolate.

mihrab Niche in a mosque indicating the position of Mecca (and corresponding to the altar in a church). ⌜cami yıkılmış amma ~ yerinde⌝, (the mosque has fallen down but the mihrab is in its place), in spite of damage the essential part is unharmed; a woman still beautiful though no longer young.

Mihrace (·—⌣) Maharajah.

mihriban Kind; affectionate. Sincere friend.

mihver Pivot; axle; axis.

mika (⌣·) Mica.

mikâb Cube.

mikat, -tı Appointed time or place.

mikdar Quantity; amount; value. bir ~, a small amount.

mikrob Microbe; evil person.

mikta (·⌣), -aı Any cutting instrument.

mikyas (·⌣) Measuring instrument; proportion; scale; standard. altın ~ından ayrılmak, to come off the Gold Standard: vâsi ~ta, on a large scale. ~ımatar (·—··⌣), rain-gauge. ~ülma (·—·⌣), -aı, water meter.

mil[1] Style; probe; obelisk; pivot. ana ~i, lead-screw of a lathe: menteşe ~i, gudgeon: **piston** ~i, gudgeon-pin: **göze** ~ **çekmek**, to blind *with an instrument*.

mil³ Silt.

mil³ Mile.

milâd (–⌐) Birthday; birth of Christ; Christmas Day. ~**î** (––⌐), connected with the birth of Christ; Anno Domini, A.D.

mildiyu Mildew. **patates** ~su, the potato disease (late blight).

milel *pl. of* millet. Peoples; nations.

milh Salt.

milim Thousandth; millième.

milis Militia.

millet, –ti Nation; people; people united by a common faith; a class of people; crowd. **Millet Meclisi,** the National Assembly. ~**vekili** (·¹···), –ni, deputy; member of the Turkish Parliament.

millî (·⌐) National. ~**leştirmek**, to nationalize. ~**yet, –ti,** nationality; religious community. ~**yetçi,** ~**yetperver,** nationalist.

milyar Thousand million.

milyon Million.

mim The Arabic letter mim (m); tick, mark. ~ **koymak**, to tick off, to make a mark against *stg*.

mimar (–⌐) Architect. ~**i** (––⌐), ~**lık,** architecture. ~**î** (––⌐), architectural.

mimber Pulpit in a mosque.

mimik Mimic.

mim·lemek *va*. To mark off with a tick; to mark down (as suspect *etc.*). ~**li,** marked off; politically suspect; a marked man.

min- *Ar. prep.* From; by means of; among.

mina¹ (–⌐) Harbour.

mina² (⌐–) Enamel; glass; sky. Blue.

minakop The Umbra (fish) (*Umbrina cirrhosa*).

minare (·–¹) Minaret. ~ **boyu**, 30 or 40 feet high: **şeytan** ~si, whelk.

mincihetin (·¹··) From one point of view, in one respect.

minder Cushion; mattress; wrestling ring. ~ **çürütmek**, (of a visitor *etc.*) to show no signs of going away.

mine (⌐·) Enamel; dial (of a clock). ~**çiçeği** (⌐····), –ni, verbena. ~**lemek,** to enamel. ~**li** (⌐··), enamelled.

minelgaraib *In* ve ~, how odd!

mingayrihaddin (·¹···) Although it is not for me to say; without wishing to lay down the law.

minha (¹·) *In* anha ~, *in such expressions as* anha ~ razı oldu, after much humming and hawing he agreed.

minhac Highway; method, way.

minhayselmecmu (·¹···) 'In toto'; in all.

mini·cik Tiny. ~**k,** small and sweet ~**mini** (·¹··), tiny.

minimom Minimum.

minkale Protractor.

minkar Beak.

minküllilvücuh In every way.

minnacık (¹··) Tiny.

minnet, –ti Obligation *for a favour received*; taunt *about a former kindness*. ~ **etm.**, to put oneself under an obligation *to s.o.*; to ask a favour; to bow: **canına*** ~ (**bilmek**), *expresses great pleasure, especially a pleasure mingled with relief*; **o içi sıkıldığı için bu daveti canına** ~ **bildi**, in his boredom he gratefully accepted this invitation; **canıma** ~ **!**, so much the better! *or* I accept with pleasure (and relief): ⌐**ne sakala** ~ **ne bıyığa¹**, avoid being under an obligation to anyone.

minnettar, grateful; indebted. ~**lık,** gratitude.

minşar Saw.

mintan Sort of waistcoat with sleeves; shirt.

mintarafillah (¹····) By divine dispensation; fortunately; thank Heaven!

minval, –li Method; manner. **bir** ~ **üzere,** in the same way, regularly, uniformly: **bu** ~ **üzere**, in this manner.

mir Chief; commander.

mira (¹·) Surveyor's rod.

mirac (–¹) Mohammed's ascent to heaven.

mirahor (*Formerly*) Master of the Horse.

miralay (*Formerly*) Colonel; Captain (Navy).

miras Inheritance. ~**a konmak (yemek),** to come into an inheritance: ⌐**ölüm hak,** ~ **helâl¹**, there is nothing wrong in coming into an inheritance. ~**çı**, inheritor. ~**yedi,** spendthrift. ~**yedilik,** extravagance, squandering.

mir'at, –tı Mirror; aspect.

mirî (–⌐) Belonging to the State. The State treasury. ~ **ambarı,** a government storehouse: ~ **için**, on government account: ~ **malı**, public money or property.

mirikelâm (–···⌐) Eloquent man; good orator.

mirim (–¹) My dear!

mirliva (··⌐) (*Formerly*) Brigadier-general.

mirsad Look-out; ambush; observatory.

mis Musk. ~ **gibi**, sweetly scented; delicious; in a perfect manner: **kavga** ~ **gibi kokar**, a quarrel seems certain.

misafir (·–¹) Guest; visitor; company; traveller; a speck in the eye. ~ **konağı**, guest-house for travellers in a village: ~ **odası**, guest-chamber, reception room: ~ **tohumu**, natural child. ~**eten** (·–¹··), as a guest. ~**hane** (·–·¹), public guest-house for travellers. ~**lik**, ~**et**, **–ti**, a being a guest; visit: misafirliğe gitmek, to pay a visit. ~**perver**, hospitable. ~**perverlik**, hospitality.

misak (–ᴗ), **–kı** Compact; solemn promise; pact.

misal (·ᴗ), **–li** Model; precedent; like, match. ~ **getirmek**, to give an example.

misbah (·ᴗ) Fin; bladder; float.

misil, –sli A similar; an equal amount; as much again. iki misli, the double: âzaların sayısı hemen bir misli artmıştır, the number of members has practically doubled: misli müştereki asgar, the lowest common multiple: misli yok, matchless. ~**li**, ~**lü**, like, similar: bu ~ adamlar, these sort of people: o ~, like that, similar.

misina (ᴗ··) Gut (trace).

misk, –ki v. mis.

miskab Drill; augur.

miskal[1] (·ᴗ), **–li** Weight of 1½ drams (for precious stones). ~ **ile**, a tiny quantity: ⌐alışveriş ~le⌐, 'business is business'.

miskal[2] (·ᴗ), **–li** Pan-pipe.

misket[1], **–ti** Scented fruit; muscatel grape; Lady apple; grape-shot.

misket[2], **–ti** Musket.

miskin Poor; wretched; lazy; abject; poor-spirited; leprous. ~ **illeti**, leprosy. ~**hane** (···ᴗ), leper hospital. ~**lenmek**, to become poor or wretched; become indolent. ~**lik**, poverty; abjectness; incompetence; leprosy.

misli v. misil.

misma (·ᴗ), **–aı** Stethoscope.

mismar Nail. ~**î** (··ᴗ), cuneiform.

mistar Ruler (for lines).

misvak, –kı Piece of wood beaten into fibres at one end for use as a toothbrush. başı ~**lı**, fanatic.

mişvar Manner of going or acting; course (of events).

mit, –ti Myth.

mitil A kind of light quilt.

miting Meeting.

miyah (·ᴗ) pl. of ma. Waters.

miyan Middle; midst; interval; loins. ~**larında**, in the midst of them; between them. ~**beste**, with loins girded, ready for the fray. ~**cı**, go-between; intercessor.

miyane v. meyane.

miyar (·ᴗ) Standard of weight or measure; chemical reagent.

miyavlamak vn. Miaow.

miyop Short-sighted.

mizac, –cı Temperament; disposition; state of health; constitution; mood, whim. ~**gir**, obsequious; sycophantic. ~**li**, having such and such a temperament or constitution: tez ~, hasty, passionate:

zayıf ~, of weak constitution. ~**siz**, unwell. ~**sizlik**, indisposition.

mizah (·ᴗ) Jest, joke. ~**î** (·—ᴗ), humorous.

mizan (–ᴗ) Balance; pair of scales; proof of an arithmetical computation; mind, judgement. In compounds, -meter, e.g. ~**ülharare**, thermometer; ~**ülhava**, barometer.

mizana (·ᴗ·) Mizzen.

mizansen (Fr. mise en scène) Staging of a play (also fig.).

mizitra (·ᴗ·) Fresh cheese from goat's milk.

mizmar (·ᴗ) Pipe, flute; windpipe.

mobilya (·ᴗ·) Furniture.

moda (ᴗ·) Fashion.

model Pattern; model. ~**ci**, pattern-maker.

Moğol Mongolian. ~**istan**, Mongolia.

mola (ᴗ·) Rest; pause; act of letting go or slacking off. ~ **etm.**, to ease off, to slacken; to rest oneself: ~ **taşı**, stone on which hammals can rest their loads while taking a breather.

molada Aged female slave.

molla Theological student; chief judge; doctor of Moslem law.

moloz Rough stone; rubble. Useless. ~ **duvarı**, wall of rough stones.

monden (Fr. mondain) Mundane; worldly.

montaj (Fr. montage) Mounting; fitting.

mor Purple, violet. ⌐alı alına ~**u** ~**una**⌐, flushed and out-of-breath: ~ **salkım**, wistaria: ~ **tavuk**, Purple Gallinule. ~**armak**, to become purple; become bruised; be red with weeping. ~**luk**, a being purple or violet. ~**umtrak**, ~**umsu**, purplish.

morg (Fr. morgue) Mortuary.

morina (·ᴗ·) Cod. mersin ~**sı**, the largest sturgeon or beluga.

morto (sl.) Dead. ~**yu çekmek**, to die.

moruk (sl.) Dotard; old fogey; 'the old man', 'the governor'.

moskof Russian; ruthless. ~**toprağı**, holystone.

mosmor (ᴗ··) Bright purple.

mostra (ᴗ·) Pattern; sample. ~ **olm.** (sl.), to make an exhibition of oneself. ~**lık**, a thing that is a sample only and not for sale, hence a person who puts in an appearance but does nothing.

motör Motor; (generally) motor-boat. ~**lü**, having a motor; motorized.

motris (Fr. motrice) Electric locomotive.

mozalak Stunted.

muabbir Interpreter of dream; soothsayer.

muaccel Paid down; paid in ready money. ~**e**, sum of money paid on conclusion of a bargain; part purchase price paid in advance.

muacciz Importunate; annoying.

muadd·el Corrected; modified. ~il, adjusting; modifying.

muad·ele (·—·¹) Equation. ~elet, –ti, a being equivalent. ~il (·—¹), equivalent: an equivalent, a similar one.

muaf Pardoned; excused; exempt; immune (to = den). ···den ~ tutulmak, to be exempted from .... ~iyet (·—·¹), –ti, a being excused; exemption; immunity.

muahede (·—·¹) Pact; treaty. ~name (·—·—·¹), document containing an agreement or treaty.

muaheze (·—·¹) Censure; criticism. ~ etm., to blame *or* criticize.

muahhar Posterior; deferred; subsequent. ~en (·¹··), subsequently.

muahid (·—¹) Contracting. Signatory *of a treaty etc.* ~eyn, *dual of* muahid, the two contracting parties to an agreement.

muakkib Follower; pursuer.

mualece (·—·¹) Medical treatment.

muallâ (··—¹) Exalted; sublime.

muallâk Suspended; in suspense. ~ta kalan meseleler, outstanding questions, matters in suspense.

muallel Having a motive; for which there is a cause.

muall·em Taught; trained. ~im, teacher, professor. ~ime, female teacher.

muamele (·—·¹) (*pl.* muamelât) A dealing with another; treatment; conduct; transaction; procedure; interest on money; sexual relations. ···e fena (iyi) ~ etm., to treat *s.o.* badly (well): ~ görmüş, approved and marked 'for action' (of an application or decision): ···i ~ye koymak, to take the necessary official steps to carry out *an approved application etc.*: ~ vergisi, tax on business transactions: ···le ~ yapmak, to have dealings with ... .

muamele·ci (·—·¹), broker. ~li, which is under consideration: (of an application *etc.*) approved and marked 'for action'.

muamma (··—¹) Enigma.

muammer Long-lived.

muanaka (·—·¹) Mutual embrace.

muannid Obstinate, unyielding.

muaraza (·—·¹) Controversy.

muarefe (·—·¹) A being acquainted. onunla ~m var, hukukum yok, I am acquainted but not on terms of friendship with him.

muareke (·—·¹) Combat, battle.

muariz (·—¹) Opposing; hostile; objecting. Opponent, antagonist.

muarra (··—¹) Nude; void. ···den ~, denuded of; exempt from.

muarreb Arabicized.

muarr·ef Explained; made known; definite. ~if, explaining; defining; making known.

muasir (·—¹) Contemporary.

muaşaka (·—·¹) A loving one another; love-making.

muaşeret (·—·¹), –ti Social intercourse. ~ etm., to live together: adabı ~, the rules of social behaviour, code of manners.

muateb (·—¹) Reproved.

muattal Vacant; abandoned; disused; (factory) idle.

muattar Perfumed.

muavaza (·—·¹) Exchange; compensation.

muavedet (·—·¹), –ti Return.

muavenet (·—·¹), –ti Help, assistance. ···e ~ etm., to help.

muavin (·—¹) Assistant, *esp.* an assistant official, assistant headmaster *etc.*; halfback (football). ~lik, post of an assistant official.

muavvec Bent; crooked.

muayede (·—·¹) Reciprocal visit of congratulation on a feast-day; wishing one another the compliments of the day.

muayene (·—·¹) Inspection; examination; scrutiny. ~ etm., to inspect, examine, scrutinize. ~ci, custom-house inspector. ~hane (·—·—·¹), doctor's consulting-room.

muayyeb, muayyıb Vicious; immoral. ~at (···¼), –tı, shameful things.

muayyen Definite; determined; known.

muazzam Great; esteemed; important. düveli ~a, the Great Powers.

muazzeb Tormented, pained.

muazzez Cherished; esteemed; honoured. ~en (·¹··), in an honoured way; with great honours.

mubah Neither commanded nor forbidden by religious law; lawful, permissible.

mubassır Superintendent; usher at a school.

mubayaa (·—·¹) (*pl.* ~t) Purchase; commercial transaction; wholesale buying. ~ etm., to buy wholesale. ~cı, stockbroker; (*formerly*) an agent for the wholesale purchase of grain *etc.*, and especially of old, obsolete coins for the Mint.

mûbed, mûbid (—¹) Zoroastrian High Priest.

mucib (—¹) Rendering necessary, causing. Cause; motive; requirement; necessary consequence. bir ~ çekmek, to pass a petition *etc.* as 'approved' (*v.* mucibince): ~den çıkmak, (of a decree *etc.*) to be approved: ~i ibret, a means of warning to others, an example: ~ olm., to cause: esbabı ~e, determining cause, preamble to a Bill. ~ince (··¹··), according to requirements; as necessary; (*formula used by a superior official to denote that stg. is approved and passed for action*).

mucid (—¹) Inventor. Inventing.

mucir (—¹) Who lets or hires out.

muciz (–ᵛ) Laconic, concise.

mûciz (–ᵛ) Overpowering; perplexing.

mucize (–·ᵛ) Miracle; wonder. ~ kabîlinden, by a miracle. ~vî (–··ᴸ), miraculous.

mucur Scoriae; dross; slag.

muçik Scraper *attached to one end of a goad for cleaning the mud off a plough.*

muço (ᵛ·) Cabin-boy; boy waiter.

mudalla Polygon. Polygonal.

mudarebe (·–·ᵛ) Strife; struggle.

mudhik Comic. ~e, comedy, farce. ~ât, –tı, drolleries; comedies.

mudi (–ᵛ) Depositor; investor.

mudil (–ᵛ) Difficult; arduous. ~e (*pl.* ~at), difficult, complicated matter.

mufad (·ᴸ) Purport; contents. ~ınca, by virtue of, in accordance with.

mufarakat (·–·ᵛ), –tı Separation. ~ etm., to part; to say goodbye to one another.

mufarik (·–ᵛ) Separate; separable. lâzımı gayri ~, indispensable.

mufassal Detailed; lengthy. ~an (·ᵛ··), at length and in detail.

muğ Magian; fire-worshipper; tavern-keeper.

muğaddi (··ᴸ) Nutritious.

muğalâta (·–·ᵛ), **mağlata** Misleading argument; sophistry; fallacy.

muğanni (··ᴸ) Singer. ~ye, female singer.

muğayeret (·–·ᵛ), –ti A not conforming; difference; opposition.

muğayir (·–ᵛ) Opposed; contrary; adverse. ~i edeb, contrary to good manners; uncivil.

muğaylan (··ᴸ) Camel-thorn.

muğayyebat (···ᵛ), –tı Invisible things; mysteries.

muğayyer Changed, altered.

muğbeçe *v.* muğpeçe.

muğber Hurt, offended.

muğfil Deceitful; deceptive.

muğlâk Abstruse; obscure; complicated; confused.

muğpeçe Boy waiter *at a tavern*; attractive youth.

muh, –hhu Marrow.

muhabbet, –ti Love; affection; friendship; friendly chat. ~ çiçeği, mignonette: ~ etm., to have a friendly chat. ~li, friendly; affectionate. ~name, friendly letter.

muhab·ere (·–·ᵛ) Correspondence by letter *etc.*; signals service (*mil.*). ~erat (·–·ᵛ), –tı, correspondence; communication. ~ir, correspondent.

muhaceme (·–·ᵛ) Concerted attack; sudden onslaught.

muhaceret (·–·ᵛ), –ti Emigration.

muhacim (·–ᵛ) Assailant; raider; forward (football).

muhacir (·–ᵛ) Emigrant; refugee (*esp.* Moslem).

muhaddeb Convex.

muhadder Veiled, concealed; read or recited rapidly. ~at, –tı, devout and virtuous women.

muhaddis One who studies and hands on the traditions of Islam.

muhadenet (·–·ᵛ), –ti Mutual friendship.

muhafaza (·–·ᵛ) Protection; conservation; preservation. ~ etm., to protect, take care of, keep. ~kâr (·–··ᴸ), conservative.

muhaff·ef Lightened; alleviated. ~if, lightening, alleviating: esbabı ~e, extenuating circumstances.

muhafiz (·–ᵛ) Guarding. Guard; defender; commander of a fort. ~ kıtası, bodyguard.

muhakeme (·–·ᵛ) Hearing of a case in court; trial; judgement, discernment. ~ etm., to judge, decide. ~li, of sound judgement.

muhakk·ak Certain; well-known. Without doubt, certainly. ~ik, –kı, who verifies *or* scrutinizes.

muhakkar Contemptible.

muhal (·ᴸ) Impossible; inconceivable. farzı ~, if the impossible were to happen; in the unlikely event of.

muhalefet (·–·ᵛ), –ti Opposition; contrariness. ···e ~ etm., to oppose; to disagree with: ···e ~ten dolayı, for contravention of ... : havanın ~i yüzünden, on account of unfavourable weather.

muhalesat, –tı Sincerity; sincere friendship.

muhalif (·–ᵛ) Opposing; contrary; contradictory.

muhalled Eternal. ~at, –tı, immortal works; classics.

muhallef Left (by deceased person). ~at, –tı, things left to his heirs by a dead man; inheritance.

muhallil Solvent; disintegrating.

muhami (·–ᵛ) Defender; advocate.

Muhammed Mohammed. ~î (···ᴸ), pertaining to Mohammed; Moslem.

muhammen Estimated. ~ fiat, estimated price. ~at, –tı, estimates.

muhammes Pentagon. Pentagonal; having five (verses *etc.*).

muhammin Who estimates. Valuer.

muhanat, muhanet (·–ᵛ) Cowardly; abject.

muhannes Effeminate. Catamite.

muhar·ebe (·–·ᵛ) Battle; war. ~ib (·–ᵛ), belligerent; warrior; combatant.

muharref Altered; falsified.

muharrem The month Muharrem, the first month of the Arabic lunar year.

muharrer Written. ~at, -tı, writings; correspondence.

muharrib Ruining; destroying.

muharrif Who alters *or* falsifies a written thing.

muharrik, -ki Causing to move; motive; stirring up. Motor; instigator, agitator.

muharrir Writer; editor; author.

muharriş Irritating; itching.

muhasama (·—·ᵌ) Hostility; contention; dispute. ~at, -tı, hostilities; war.

muhasara (·—·ᵌ) Siege. ~ etm., to besiege.

muhaseb·at (·—·—ᵌ), -tı Accounts. ~e, accountancy, book-keeping; the accounts office of a business : ~ görmek, to audit the accounts. ~eci, accountant; Chief Accountant; auditor.

muhasım (·—ᵌ) Hostile; opponent, adversary.

muhasır (·—ᵌ) Besieging, investing.

muhasib (·—ᵌ) Who reckons. Accountant. ~lik, book-keeping; accountant's office.

muhassala Resultant.

muhassas Assigned *or* appropriated *to.* ~at, -tı, appropriations; salary.

muhassenat, -tı Good *or* beautiful things; virtues; advantages.

muhassıl Who produces; productive.

muhat¹ (·—ᵌ), -tı Surrounded; contained. ~ı ilm, within the bounds of knowledge, known.

muhat² (·—ᵌ), -tı Mucus.

muhatab (·—ᵌ) One addressed in speech; second person (*gram.*).

muhatara (·—·ᵌ) Danger. ~lı, dangerous.

muhatî (·—ᵌ) Mucous.

muhavere (·—·ᵌ) Conversation; dialogue. ~ etm., to converse together.

muhavv·el Changed; transformed; turned over to. ~ile, transformer.

muhayyel Imagined; imaginary. ~ât, -tı, imaginations; fancies.

muhayyer Who has a choice or option; optional; on approval.

muhayyile Imagination; fancy.

muhayyir Bewildering.

muhbir Who gives information; newspaper correspondent, reporter.

muhdes Invented; created; newly created (post *etc.*); added (parts).

muhib, -bbi Who loves; friend.

muhik, -kki True, right; justifiable.

muhil, -lli Who troubles *or* spoils. ~i asayiş, disturber of the peace.

muhit (·ᵌ), -ti Surrounding; comprehending. Circumference; surroundings; the circle in which one moves, milieu; doctor's practice. ~i daire, periphery. ~ülmaarif (·—·—·ᵌ), encyclopaedia.

muhkem Firm; sound; strong; tight.

muhlis Sincere. Sincere friend. halis ~, unadulterated; pure-blooded.

muhnik Throttling; asphyxiating.

muhrib Destructive. Destroyer (*naut.*).

muhrik Burning; heart-rending.

muhsin Beneficent.

muhtac (·ᵌ) In want; indigent; in need. ···e ~ olm., to be in need of. ~ı beyan, needing explanation. ~iyet (·—·ᵌ), -ti, ~lık, a being in need, neediness, poverty.

muhtar Chosen, elected; free to choose, independent, autonomous. Headman *of a village or quarter.* faili~, a free agent. ~iyet (·—·ᵌ), -ti, freedom of action, autonomy. ~lık, the post and duties of a headman.

muhtas, -ssı Special; exclusively used for (= *dat.*).

muhtasar Shortened, abridged; frugal, unpretentious. ~ ve müfid, brief but to the point; pithy. ~an (·ᵌ··), in brief; concisely.

muhtazır Dying.

muhtecib Hidden; veiled.

muhtefi (··ᵌ) Concealed; clandestine.

muhtekir Who hoards or corners *foods etc. in order to make a profit*; profiteer.

muhtel, -lli Spoilt; injured; disturbed. şuuru ~, mentally afflicted.

muhtelefünfih Controversial.

muhtelic Shaking, quivering; troubled.

muhtelif Diverse, various. ~üccins, of various kinds.

muhtelis Embezzler; pilferer.

muhtelişşuur (·ᵌ···) Mentally afflicted, insane.

muhtelit Mixed; composite. ~ tedrisat, co-education.

muhtemel Possible; probable; (*implies possibility more than probability*; *'probable' is best rendered by* kuvvetle ~). ~ât, -ti, possibilities; probabilities.

muhtemir Leavened; fermenting.

muhterem Respected; honoured.

muhteri (··ᵌ), -ii Who invents. Inventor.

muhteris Covetous; desirous.

muhteriz Cautious; reserved; timid, hesitating.

muhteşem Magnificent; majestic.

muhtev·a (···ᵌ) Contents. ~ı (··ᵌ), containing. ~iyat (··—ᵌ), -tı, contents.

muhtıra Note; memorandum. ~ defteri, note-book; diary.

muhti (·ᵌ) Erring; culpable.

muhuşevkî (···ᵌ) Spinal marrow.

muhyi (·ᵌ) Giving life; reanimating.

muhzir Process-server; bailiff *of a court.*

muin Who helps; assisting. Allah ~in olsun, God help you!

muit (*Formerly*) Usher or supervisor in a school.

mukaar Concave.

mukabele (·—·¹) A confronting; a reciprocating; reward; retaliation; retort, reply; a collating or comparing; recitation of the Koran. ~ etm., to confront; collate; retaliate; retort; reciprocate; resist : ···le ~ görmek, to be received with (applause *etc.*) : ~ okumak, to recite the Koran by heart. ~bilmisil, **–sli**, reprisal, tit-for-tat. ~ci, an official who collates documents; reciter of the Koran. ~ten (·—¹··), in return; reciprocally.

mukabil (·—¹) Facing, opposite; corresponding; equivalent. The opposite; equivalent; thing given in return; in return; in compensation. In return for (= *dat.*). ~inde, opposite; in return : ~ hücum, counter-attack : **buna** ~, on the other hand.

mukaddem In front; previous; preferable; first. Before, ago. **ondan** ~, before that: **bir ay** ~, a month before; a month ago. ~a (·¹·—), previously, in the past. ~e (*pl.* ~at, **–tı**), preface; introduction; preliminary; forerunner of an event; rudiment, first principle; premiss.

mukadder Decreed by Providence; predestined, fated; inevitable. Fate. ~at, **–tı**, preordained things; destiny, fate.

mukaddes Sacred, holy. ~at, **–tı**, sacred things.

mukaffa (···²) Rhymed.

mukallib Changing, transforming.

mukallid Mimicking. Mimic.

mukannen Fixed; regular.

mukarebet (·—·¹), **–ti** An approaching one enother; proximity; relationship.

mukarenet (·—·¹), **–ti** A drawing nearer; *rapprochement*; association; conjunction *of stars*.

mukarin (·—¹) Joined; associated. ~i **hakikat**, close to the truth, true.

mukarreb Intimate; allowed access to God *or* to a royal presence.

mukarrer Established, fixed; decided; certain. ~at, **–tı**, decisions.

mukarrib Who allows to approach; bringing nearer; adductor.

mukaseme (·—·¹) A sharing out; apportionment.

mukassat Paid *or* supplied in instalments. ~an (·¹··), by instalments.

mukassi Oppressive, stuffy.

mukassim Who divides *or* distributes.

mukataa A farming out of public revenue; sale of a business for a lump sum; rent paid to the **evkaf** for cultivated land turned into building land or gardens. ~lı, subject to the mukataa rent.

mukatele (·—·¹) Mutual slaughter; battle.

mukatta Broken off; cut; interrupted.

mukattar Distilled. **mai** ~, distilled water.

mukavele (·—·¹) Agreement; contract. ~ etm., to agree mutually to do *stg*. ~li, that has been settled by an agreement. ~name (·—···—¹), written agreement; pact.

mukav·emet (·—·¹), **–ti** Resistance; endurance. ~koşusu, long-distance race: **yarı** ~ koşusu, medium distance race. ~im (·—¹), resisting; resistant; strong; enduring.

mukavva (·¹·) Cardboard.

mukavves Curved; arched.

mukavvi (·—²) Strengthening; tonic.

mukayese (·—·¹) Comparison. ~ etm., to compare.

mukayyed Bound; restricted; registered; diligent, attentive. ~ olm., to be registered; to attend diligently (to *stg*.).

mukayyi (··²), **–ii** Emetic.

mukayyid Registrar.

mukbil Favoured by fortune, prosperous.

mukdim Diligent; persevering.

mukim Who dwells *or* stays; stationary.

mukni (·²) Satisfying; convincing. **delaili** ~a, convincing proofs.

mukriz Who lends money.

muktataf Gathered; culled.

muktaza (··²) Required; necessary. Need; exigency; requirement. ~sınca, as required by, according to the requirements of .... .

muktazi (··²) Necessary. ~yat, **–tı**, requirements; requisites.

muktebes Acquired from another; quoted.

mukteda (··²) Imitated; taken as a model; who presides *or* guides. Model.

muktedir Capable; powerful. ···e ~ olm., to be able to, be capable of.

muktesid Economical; careful in spending.

mum Wax; candle. ~la aramak, to search for *stg*. very difficult to find; to search very diligently; to crave for; to miss bitterly : ~a çevirmek, to render disciplined and obedient : ⌈~ dibine ışık vermez⌉, 'a candle does not light its own bottom', sometimes one does not think sufficiently about one's own interests; helping others without helping oneself : ~ gibi, (i) very upright; stiff; like new; (ii) docile : ~ hala gibi, (i) awake; (ii) restless, always on the move : ~ olm. *or* ~a dönmek, to become disciplined *or* compliant : ⌈~ söndü⌉, 'the candle was extinguished', *alluding to a Bektashi ceremony, in which the lights were put out and which was popularly supposed to be immoral, hence* immoral, improper.

mumaileyh (²—··) Afore-mentioned (*fem.* ~a, *pl.* ~im).

mumbasit *v.* münbasit.

mum·cu Tallow-chandler. ~hala *v.* mum. ~lamak, to wax; to attach a seal to.

~luk, candle-power. **~yağı** ($\cdot\cdot$), **–nı**, tallow.

mumya ($\cdot\cdot$) Mummy; a shrivelled sallow man.

munakkid v. münekkid.

mundar Dirty; v. murdar.

munfasıl Separated; disjoined; removed from office.

munhasır Restricted; limited. ···**e ~**, limited to, exclusively for the use of. **~an** ($\cdot\cdot\cdot$), exclusively.

munis (–$\cdot$) Companionable, sociable; tame; friendly; familiar.

munkabız Constipated; shrivelled; uncomfortable, tongue-tied.

munkalib Changed; transformed. **hakikate ~ olm.**, to prove true.

munkatı Cut off; interrupted; come to an end; separated.

munsab Poured; flowing. ···**e ~ olm.**, to flow into. (*err. for* **mansab**) Estuary.

munsarif Turning away; declinable (*gram.*).

munsif Just, equitable, fair. **~ane** ($\cdot\cdot$–$\cdot$), just, reasonable (act); in an equitable manner, fairly.

muntabı, –ıı Stamped, printed; docile.

muntabık Fitting together; coincident; adapted.

muntafi Extinguished.

muntazam In a line; regular; well-arranged, tidy, orderly; regular (army). **~an** ($\cdot\cdot\cdot$), in an orderly manner; regularly.

muntaz·ar Awaited, expected. **~ır**, who waits expectantly. **~ olm.**, to be ready and waiting; to await (*with dat.*).

munzam Added, extra, additional; appended.

mûr Ant.

murabaha ($\cdot$–$\cdot$) Usury. **~cı**, usurer.

murabba¹ ($\cdot\cdot$), **–aı** Square; squared. **metre ~ı**, square metre.

murabba² ($\cdot\cdot$) Preserve of fruit; jam; marmalade.

murabit ($\cdot$–$\cdot$), **–ti** Moslem hermit, marabout.

murad Wish; intention, aim. **~ da o!**, that's exactly what's wanted: **~ edinmek**, to hope, desire: **~ına ermek**, to attain one's desire: **~ etm.**, to desire, to propose to oneself: **bunu demekten ~**, by that is meant.

murafaa Recourse to a court; a pleading before a court; a summoning s. o. to appear in court.

murahhas Delegated. Delegate; plenipotentiary. **heyeti ~a**, delegation with full powers.

murahhasa ($\cdot$–$\cdot$) Armenian bishop.

murak·abe ($\cdot$–$\cdot$) Vigilance; control; super-

vision; religious meditation. ···**i ~ altında bulundurmak**, to put under control. **~ıb**, controller; auditor.

murakkam Numbered.

murassa ($\cdot\cdot$), **–aı** Bejewelled.

murdar, mırdar Dirty; unclean. **~ ilik**, spinal marrow. **~lık**, dirt, filth.

muris (–$\cdot$) Who makes s. o. his heir; who bequeaths. Testator.

murtad v. mürted.

Musa Moses.

musab ($\cdot$) Stricken by illness *or* calamity. Victim. **~iyet** ($\cdot$–$\cdot$), **–ti**, a being afflicted by a calamity *or* illness.

musadakat ($\cdot$–$\cdot$), **–tı** Sincere friendship.

musadd·ak Confirmed; certified. **~ik**, who confirms *or* certifies.

musademe ($\cdot$–$\cdot$) Collision; encounter; skirmish; percussion (*mil.*). **~ iğnesi**, firing-pin: **~ kıtası**, detachment of shock troops: **~ tapası**, percussion fuse; **tavikli ~ tapası**, delayed percussion fuse: ···**le ~ etm.**, to collide with, to encounter.

musadere ($\cdot$–$\cdot$) Confiscation. **~ etm.**, to confiscate.

musadif ($\cdot$–$\cdot$) Who meets by chance; coinciding. ···**e ~ olm.**, to meet by chance; to coincide with.

musaf v. Mushaf.

musafaha ($\cdot$–$\cdot$) A shaking hands.

musaffa ($\cdot\cdot$) Purified; clarified; pure.

musahabe, musahabet ($\cdot$–$\cdot$), **–ti** Company; conversation. **~ etm.**, to associate *or* to have conversation with another.

musahh·ah Corrected. **~ih**, corrector; proof-reader.

musahib ($\cdot$–$\cdot$) Companion; gentleman-in-waiting.

musalâha ($\cdot$–$\cdot$) A making peace with another; reconciliation.

musalla ($\cdot\cdot$) Public place for prayer. **~ taşı**, stone on which the coffin is placed during the funeral service: ⌐**kadrini sengi ~da bilmek**⌐, to recognize a person's worth only after his death.

musallat, –tı Worrying; attacking. ···**e ~ olm.**, to worry, pester, fall upon; (of robbers *etc.*) to haunt a place.

musalli ($\cdot\cdot$) Engaged in prayer; who says his prayers regularly; devout.

musammem Decided upon; intended.

musandıra ($\cdot\cdot\cdot$) Large wardrobe for storing mattresses *etc.*; fixed slab at the the end of a sofa frame; sideboard. ⌐**çingene evinde ~ olur mu?**⌐, can one expect to find luxury in a poor man's house?

musanna ($\cdot\cdot$), **–aı** Skilfully or artistically made.

musann·efat ($\cdot\cdot\cdot$), **–tı** Literary works. **~if**, compiler of a book; classifier.

musaraa Wrestling.

musarrah Openly and clearly set forth. ~an (·¹··), clearly and explicitly.

musavv·er Imagined; depicted, illustrated. ~ir, who depicts; artist, designer.

Musevi (─··─́) Jew.

Mushaf The Koran.

musır, –rrı Persevering; persistent. ~rane (···─́), pertinacious, insistent (acts); in a persistent manner.

musib (·─́) That hits the mark; right, appropriate.

musibet (·─́), –ti Calamity, evil; tiresome person. Ill-omened, foul. ~ !, you pest!: ⌐bir ~ bin nasihattan yeğdir¹, one misfortune is better than a thousand pieces of advice; experience is the best teacher. ~li, disastrous; ill-omened.

musik·ar (─·¹) Pandean pipe; a fabulous bird *with holes in its beak, through which the wind blew and produced music.* ~i (─··─́), music (*in general*); (müzik *is European music as opp. to* saz, *Oriental music, while* mızıka *is a military band*). ~işinas, lover of music; musician.

muska Amulet; charm. şirinlik ~sı, a charm worn by women to gain the affections of a man.

muslih Who puts right; conciliatory. ~ane (···─́), improving, setting right, peaceable (*not used of persons*); in a conciliatory manner.

muslin Muslin.

musluk Tap; spigot. ~taşı (·¹··), –nı, stone basin under a tap.

muson (*Fr. mousson*) Monsoon.

mussaka (·¹··) Moussaka (a Roumanian dish of mutton, aubergines, and onions).

mustalah Too technical and pedantic.

mustatil (··─́) Rectangle.

muş¹ Mouse; rat.

muş² (*Fr. mouche*) Steam launch.

muşabak (*For* müşebbek) Open-work embroidery.

muşamba (·¹··) Oiled silk; tarpaulin; linoleum; mackintosh, waterproof. ~ gibi, very dirty (clothes *etc.*).

muşer Curved saw.

muşikâf (─·─́) Who splits hairs.

muşmula (¹··) Medlar; any shrivelled thing; 'old fogey'.

muşta Fist; blow with the fist; iron ball *used by shoemakers for pounding seams.* ~lamak, to thump, pound.

mut, –tu Luck; fortune; happiness.

mutâ (·─́), –aı Obeyed.

muta Robin.

mûta (─́) Given. Datum.

mutaassıb Fanatical; bigoted. Fanatic.

mutaazzım Proud, arrogant.

mutab·akat (·─·⅄), –tı Conformity; agreement. ···le ~ etm., to agree with. ~ık (·─́), conforming; agreeing.

mûtad (─́) Customary; habitual. Custom, habit. ~ım değil, it is not my habit: ~ hilafına, contrary to custom.

mutaf Things made of woven goat-hair; maker of such things.

mutahhar Canonically clean; purified; sacred.

mutalebat (·─·─́), –tı Things demanded; demands.

mutallâ Gilded.

mutallâka Divorced woman.

mutantan Accompanied by noise and pomp; ostentatious; gorgeous.

mutarıza Bracket; parenthesis.

mutarra (··─́) Juicy; fresh; fragrant.

mutasaddi (···─́) Who sets about a task; venturesome; audacious. ···e ~ olm., to venture upon, dare to do, perpetrate.

mutasallif Boastful; pretentious; conceited; presumptuous.

mutasarrıf Owning; having the disposal of *a thing*; (*formerly*) governor of a sanjak (province). ···e ~ olm., to be absolute master or owner of ... . ~lık, post and jurisdiction of a mutasarrıf.

mutasavver Imagined; contemplated; projected.

mutasavvıf Who becomes a Sufi; who studies mysticism.

mutatabbib Quack (doctor).

mutavaat (·─·─́), –tı Submission; obedience; compliance; reflexive form of a verb.

mutavvel Elongated; detailed; prolix.

mutazallim Who complains of injustice.

mutazammin Comprising, containing. ···i ~ olm., to comprise, contain.

mutazarrır Injured; suffering loss.

mutbah Kitchen.

muteber (─·¹) Esteemed; of good repute; solvent; enjoying credit; valid. Notable (*pl.* ~an (···─́)).

mutedil (─·¹) Temperate; moderate; mild.

mutekadat (─́···─), –tı Points of belief; religious convictions.

mutekid (─·¹) Who firmly believes; religious.

mutekif (─·¹) Who retires for fasting and prayer.

mutemed (─·¹) Relied on; reliable. Fiduciary; man entrusted with the finances of a department.

mutena (─·─́) Important; carefully attended to; select, refined, 'distingué'.

muterif (─·¹) Confessing, acknowledging.

muteriz (─·¹) Opposing; objecting. ~ olm., to make objections.

mutesif (─·¹) Harsh; oppressive.

mutezil (–·ᴵ) Seceding; schismatic. Dissenter. ~e, *name of* a schismatic Moslem sect.

mutfak Kitchen; cuisine.

muthik *v.* mudhik.

muti (·⸛) Obedient.

mûti (–⸛) Who gives. God *as the giver of all.*

mutlak, –kı Absolute; autocratic; unconditional. Absolutely; certainly. ~ gelecek, he is sure to come: ~ gelmeli, he *must* come: vekili ~, a plenipotentiary. ~a (ᴵ·–), absolutely; without fail; certainly. ~iyet, –ti, absolutism; autocracy.

mutlu Lucky, fortunate. ne ~ !, what luck ! how fortunate! : ne ~ ona!, how lucky for him! ~luk, luck, good fortune.

mutmain Tranquil; contented; satisfied, assured.

muttaki Pious; devout.

muttali (··⸛) Informed; aware. ···e ~ olm., to become aware of ... .

muttarid In succession; regular; uniform. ~en (·ᴵ··), regularly; in regular succession.

muttasıf Endowed (with = ile); having the quality of ... .

muttasıl (··ᴵ) Joined to another; continuous. (ᴵ··); continuously; all the time.

muvac·ehe (·–·ᴵ) A being face to face; confrontation. ···in ~sinde, in the presence of, vis-à-vis ...; with regard to ... : ~ etm., to confront. ~eheten (·–ᴵ··), face to face; in each other's presence. ~ih, facing; in the presence of.

muvafakat (·–·ᴵ). –tı Agreement, consent. ~ etm., to agree, consent.

muvaffak Successful. ~ olm., to succeed : bunu yapmağa ~ oldu, he succeeded in doing this. ~iyet, –ti, success; victory (*pl.* ~iyat). ~iyetli, successful. ~iyetsizlik, lack of success, failure.

muvafık (·–ᴵ) Agreeable; suitable; conformable; favourable.

muvahh·ad Unified; unique (of God). ~id, monotheist.

muvahhiş Frightening; dreadful.

muvakkar Honoured; reverenced.

muvakkat Temporary; provisory. ~en (·ᴵ··), temporarily.

muvakkit, –ti Time-keeper at a mosque; chronometer. ~ane (····–ᴵ), clock-room of the muvakkit.

muvaneset (·–·ᴵ), –ti Familiarity; friendly association; taming of animals.

muvared·at (·–·⸛), –tı Arrivals (of things or persons). ~e, arrival.

muvasala (·–·ᴵ) Communication. ~ hatları, lines of communication. ~t, –tı, arrival.

muvaşşah Adorned.

muvazaa (·–·ᴵ) Collusion; a pretending to agree with one another for some ulterior motive; dissimulation. ~tan (·–ᴵ··), in pretence, in collusion.

muvazat (·–⸛), –tı A being parallel; a drawing a parallel.

muvazene, muvazenet (·–·ᴵ), –ti Equilibrium, balance. umumî ~, general budget (of a government). ~li, in equilibrium; balanced; level-headed; well-judged. ~siz, unbalanced.

muvazi (·–·⸛) Parallel.

muvazin (·–ᴵ) Equal in weight; well-balanced.

muvazzaf Having a duty; charged with; salaried; regular (army); on the active list (officer).

muvazzah Explained; clear. ~an (·ᴵ··), clearly.

muylu Trunnion *of a cannon;* hub *of a car.*

muz Banana.

muzaaf (·–ᴵ) Double; multiple. usulü ~a, book-keeping by double entry.

muzad, –ddı Opposing, contrary. ~dı taaffün, disinfectant.

muzaf Added; appended to. Noun depending on one in the genitive. ~ünileyh (·–··ᴵ), noun in the genitive governing another noun; genitive.

muzaffer Victorious. ~en (·ᴵ··), victoriously. ~iyet, –ti, victory, triumph.

muzari (·–ᴵ), –ii Aorist tense.

muzıka *v.* mızıka.

muzır Harmful, detrimental.

muzib (–ᴵ) Plaguing, tormenting, teasing ; mischievous. ~lik, teasing; mischievous behaviour; practical joke.

muzlim Dark, gloomy; sinister.

muzmahil Dispersed; annihilated. ~ olm., to come to nought; to be annihilated.

muzmer Secret (thought, intention); implied but not expressed; understood (*sous-entendu*). ~at, –tı, hidden thoughts *or* desires.

muztar Forced, compelled.

muztarib Agitated, worried, disturbed; suffering (from = ···dan).

mübad·ele (·–·ᴵ) Exchange; barter. ~il (·–ᴵ), exchanging; subject to exchange (of a population *etc.*) : Turkish immigrant from Greece after the 1921-2 war, settled on land of an exchanged Greek.

mübahase (·–·ᴵ) Discussion. ~ etm., to discuss.

mübahat (·–ᴵ), –tı A vaunting *or* glorying. ~ etm., to glory, to boast with a just pride.

mübalâga (·–·ᴵ) Exaggeration. ~ etm., to exaggerate: ismi ~, the superlative adjective. ~cı, given to exaggeration. ~lı, exaggerated.

mübalât (·—⸱), **-tı** Heed; careful attention. ~**sız**, careless; free-and-easy, too familiar.

mübarek (·—⸱) Blessed; sacred; bountiful; auspicious. ~!, bless it!: ~ **herif**, the blessed fellow (*iron.*): ~ **ağzını* açmak**, to start speaking evil.

mübar·eze (·—·⸱) Combat between champions; contest; duel. ~**iz**, champion; duellist; wrestler.

mübaşeret (·—·⸱), **-ti** A setting about doing stg.; beginning; sexual act. ~ **etm.**, to set about *stg.*

mübaşir (·—⸱) Process-server; official who conveys the order of a department; agent.

mübay·enet (·—·⸱), **-ti** Divergence; conflict (of statements *etc.*). ~**in** (·—⸱), opposed; different.

mübdi (·⸱), **-ii** Innovator; creator (aesthetically).

mübeccel Honoured; reverenced.

müberra (··⸱) Absolved; free.

müberrid Cooling. Refrigerator.

mübeşş·er Who receives good news. ~**ir**, announcing good news.

mübeyyin Declaring, stating, certifying; making clear.

mübeyyiz Clerk who makes a fair copy from a draft.

mübhem Vague, indefinite. ~**iyet**, **-ti**, vagueness; lack of precision.

mübin Evident, manifest. **dini** ~, Islam.

mübrem Inexorable (decree *etc.*); inevitable; urgent.

mübriz Who presents *or* displays.

mübted·a (··⸱) Beginning; subject (*gram.*). ~**i** (··⸱), who begins; beginner, novice.

mübtelâ (··⸱) (*with dat.*) Subject to; suffering from; addicted to; having a passion for; in love with. **kumara** ~ *or* **kumar** ~**sı**, addicted to gambling.

mübteni (··⸱) Founded, built; established; based (on = *dat.*).

mübtezel Abundant; common; of no account.

mücadele (·—·⸱) Dispute; struggle.

mücah·ede (·—·⸱) Endeavour; a fighting for Islam. ~**id** (·—⸱), champion (of Islam *or* of some ideal).

mücamaa (·—·⸱) Copulation.

mücamele (·—·⸱) Kindness; courtesy; consideration.

mücanebet (·—·⸱), **-ti** A keeping apart; abstention. ~ **etm.**, to keep aloof; to abstain.

mücaneset (·—·⸱), **-ti** Homogeneity; uniformity.

mücaseret (·—·⸱), **-ti** A daring. ···**meğe** ~ **etm.**, to dare to ... .

mücav·eret (·—·⸱), **-ti** A being a neigh-

bour; a retiring to a religious place for meditation and prayer. ~**ir** (·—⸱), neighbouring: neighbour; who dwells near a religious place for pious meditation.

mücazat (·—⸱), **-tı** Punishment; retribution. ···**e** ~ **etm.**, to punish.

mücbir Compelling; coercive. **kuvvei** ~**e**, 'force majeur'.

mücedd·ed Renewed; new. ~**en** (·⸱··), newly, recently; afresh, anew. ~**id**, who renews, renovates *or* innovates.

mücef, **-ffi** (*for* **mücevvef**) Hollow. A hollow part, cavity; bore of a gun.

mücehh·ez Equipped; furnished. ~**iz**, who equips; shipowner.

mücellâ (··⸱) Polished; shining.

mücell·ed Bound (book). Volume. ~**id**, bookbinder.

mücerreb Proved; tested. ~**at**, **-tı**, things proved by experience.

mücerr·ed Stripped; bare; isolated; simple, mere; pure; abstract; incorporeal; unmarried. Merely, simply. ~**at** (··⸱), **-tı**, spiritual, abstract things; things hard to understand. ~**id**, isolating; insulating; insulator.

mücessem Having a body; corporeal; solid; personified. **kurei** ~**e**, globe: **namusu** ~, honour personified.

mücevher Bejewelled. Jewel. ~**at**, **-tı**, jewellery.

mücmel Succinct, concise. Summary. ~**en** (⸱··), concisely, summarily.

mücrim Culpable, guilty. Culprit; criminal; (*pl.* **mücrimin**; **iadei** ~, extradition). ~**iyet**, **-ti**, guilt, culpability.

müctehid Expounder of Islamic laws.

müctemi Gathered together; collected. ~**an** (·⸱··), collectively; in a united manner.

müctenib Abstaining; avoiding; aloof.

mücver Croquette.

müdaf·aa (·—·⸱) Defence; resistance. ~**i** (·—⸱), **-ii**, defender; back (football).

müdah·ele (·—·⸱) Interference; intervention. ~ **etm.**, to meddle, interfere (in *or* with = *dat.*). ~**il** (·—⸱), intervening; intervener.

müdah·ene (·—·⸱) Flattery; sycophancy. ~**eneci**, ~**in** (·—⸱), flatterer; sycophant.

müdara (·—⸱) Dissimulation; feigned friendship.

müdavat (·—⸱), **-tı** Medical treatment. **ilk** ~, first aid.

müdavele (·—·⸱) A causing to circulate. ~**i efkâr.** exchange of views.

müdavemet (·—·⸱), **-ti** Assiduity; unremitting attention (to work); a frequenting (school *etc.*). ···**e** ~ **etm.**, to be assiduous in, to frequent.

müdavi (·—⸱) Who treats or cures.

müdavim (·–¹) Who frequents; assiduous, persevering. Habitué, regular visitor, customer *etc.*

müddea (··¹) Claim; accusation; thesis; subject of a claim before a court (*pl.* ~at, –ti). ~aleyh, defendant.

müddei (··¹) Who asserts *or* claims; claimant; plaintiff; prosecutor. ~umumi (··–·–¹), Public Prosecutor.

müddet, –ti Space of time; period; interval. ~i ömür, lifetime: ~ tayin etm., to fix a time or period of delay: ~siz olarak, indefinitely.

müdebbir Prudent; far-sighted. Efficient manager.

müdebdeb Magnificent; pompous; gorgeous.

müdekkik, –ki Who investigates minutely; research student. ~ane (···–¹), minute (researches *etc.*): minutely, meticulously.

müdellel Proved; supported by evidence.

müderris Professor; *a grade in the hierarchy of the* ulema.

müdevven Collected into a book. Book; collection of writings. ~at, –tı, collected writings; complete works.

müdevver Round, circular, spherical; transferred (to a new balance sheet).

müdhiş Terrible, fearful; enormous; extraordinary; excessive.

müdir *v.* müdür. ~an, *pl. of* müdir.

müdrik Perceiving, comprehending. ~e, the intellect: kuvvei ~, the intellectual faculty.

müdrir Diuretic.

müdür Who manages *or* superintends. Director; administrator; official governing a nahiye (sub-district). ~lük, ~iyet, –ti, office and functions of a müdür; directorate; head office.

müebbed Eternal; perpetual. ~en (·¹··), eternally; in perpetuity.

müeccel Fixed for a future date; adjourned, put off; *v.* mehr.

müedda (··¹) Meaning, tenor; contents (of a document *etc.*). ~sınca, as is meant by (a proverb *etc.*).

müeddi (··¹) Causing; performing.

müekk·ed Strengthened; corroborated; reiterated; warned afresh. ~id, who strengthens, reiterates, warns again.

müekk·el Appointed representative; charged (with = *dat.*). ~il, who appoints a representative; client *of a lawyer.*

müell·ef Composed, compiled. ~at, –tı, written works; literary compositions. ~if, author: ~ hakkı, author's rights.

müellim Painful; grievous.

müemmen Assured, safeguarded.

müennes Female; feminine.

müesses Founded; established. ~e, foundation; establishment; institution (*pl.* ~at, –tı; ~ı hayriye, pious foundations, benevolent institutions).

müessif Sad; regrettable.

müessir Effective; influential; touching. ~ fiili, assault and battery: ibreti ~e, an effective warning.

müessis Who establishes; founder (*pl.* ~in, ~an).

müeyy·ed Strengthened; corroborated; aided. ~id, strengthening; corroborating. ~ide, corroborative or confirming statement or action; sanction (*jur.*): ~ cezaî, penalty.

müezzin, meyzin Muezzin; he who calls Moslems to prayer.

müfahham Illustrious; august.

müfekkire Thought; the power of thinking. kuvvei ~, the faculty of thought.

müferrih Gladdening; exhilarating. An exhilarating drug; exhilarant.

müfessir Who expounds. Commentator of the Koran.

müfettiş Who examines or investigates. Inspector. ~lik, inspectorship; inspectorate.

müfid Useful; advantageous.

müflis Bankrupt; penniless.

müfred Separate; single; isolated. Singular (*gram.*). ~at (··◊), –tı, details; particulars; enumeration; detailed inventory. ~ programı, programme giving items (of a school course *etc.*); ~ı tıb, materia medica.

müfrez Separated; detached. ~e, detachment of troops.

müfrit Excessive; beyond bounds; exaggerated. Extremist.

müfsid Disturber of the peace. Seditious; mischief-making; subversive.

müftakir Needy. ···e ~ olm., to be in need of.

müftehir (*with* ile) Who glories in; who is proud of.

müftekir¹ *Err. for* müftakir.

müftekir² Who ponders.

müfteri (··¹) Calumniator, slanderer. ~yat, –tı, calumnies.

müfteris Predatory; rapacious; that tears its prey.

müfti, müftü Moslem jurist; mufti, senior Moslem priest. ~lik, office and rank of a mufti.

mühendis Engineer. ~hane (···–¹), school of engineering; (*formerly*) school of gunnery. ~lik, profession of engineering.

müheykel Giant; huge; clumsily built.

müheyya (··¹) Ready, prepared.

müheyyic Stirring, exciting, rousing.

mühib *v.* mehib.

mühim Important; urgent. ~**mat** (··̇), –**tı**, munitions of war; ammunition; important matters. ~**me**, important or urgent affair.

mühlet, –**ti** Respite; delay; grace. ~ **vermek**, to grant a delay.

mühlik Dangerous; destructive; deadly.

mühm·el Neglected; abandoned; meaningless. ~**at**, –**tı**, meaningless words. ~**il**, negligent.

mühre Burnisher; glass ball or cowry shell or agate *used for polishing paper or parchment*; a vertebra; bead; artificial bird, decoy (shooting). ~**lemek,** to polish with a mühre. ~**li**, polished (paper).

mührühas Keeper of the Privy Seal.

mühtedi (··̲‿) Converted to Islam.

mühtez Trembling; vibrating.

mühür, –**hrü** Seal; signet-ring; impression of a seal; the whorl of hair at the top of the head. ~**ünu* basmak**, to put one's seal to stg.; to guarantee the truth of stg., to be absolutely certain about it: ~**ünü* yalamak**, to go back on one's word, not to abide by an agreement. ~**dar**, seal-keeper; private secretary to a Minister. ~**lemek**, to stamp with a seal. ~**lü**, sealed : ağzı ~, who may not *or* will not divulge what he knows, whose lips are sealed.

müjde Good news; present given to a bearer of good news. ~ etm., *or* ~**lemek**, to bring good news. ~**ci**, who brings or announces good news. ~**lik**, gift to the bringer of good news.

mükâfat (·‿̇), –**tı** Recompense, reward; prize. ~ etm., to reward. ~**en** (·̲‿·), as a reward.

mükâfi (·‿̲) Alike; equal; equivalent.

mükâleme (·‿·̇) Conversation; dialogue; conference; (pl. ~**at**, *diplomatic* negotiations).

mükâtebe (·‿·̇) Correspondence (in writing).

mükedder Sad, grieved; turbid.

mükellef Charged; bound; obliged; liable; taxed; conscripted; highly adorned, sumptuous. **beden terbiyesi** ~**leri**, people who are called up for compulsory physical training. ~**iyet**, –**ti**, obligation (to pay taxes, perform services *etc.*), liability.

mükemmel Complete; perfect; excellent. ~ !, splendid ! ~**en** (·̇·̇·), perfectly.

mükerrem Honoured; revered. ~**en** (·̇·̇·), with great honours.

mükerrer Repeated. ~**en** (·̇·̇·), repeatedly.

mükesser Broken; fractional; broken (Arabic plural).

mükessif Condensing. ~**e**, condenser.

mükevv·en Created; produced. ~**enat**,

–**tı**, creatures; productions. ~**in**, producing; creating.

mükeyyifat (···̇), –**tı** Intoxicants; stimulants; narcotics.

mükrim Who treats with honour; hospitable; kind.

müktes·eb Acquired; earned. ~ **hak**, vested interest. ~**at**, –**tı**, acquisitions; attainments. ~**ib**, who acquires or earns.

mülâabe (·‿·̇) An amusing oneself; a playing about or joking with another.

mülâbese (·‿·̇) Intercourse; meddling; relations. ~**sile**, in connexion with; having regard to; in the fear that.

mülâhaza (·‿·̇) Consideration; observation; reflection. ... ~**sile**, in consideration of ...: ... ~**sındayım**, I am of the opinion that ...: ~ etm., to observe; to consider: (*pl.* ~**at**,–**tı**, ~ **hanesi**, column for remarks). ~**sızlık**, thoughtlessness; rashness.

mülâham Fleshy; corpulent.

mülâk·at (·‿̇), –**tı** Meeting; interview; audience. ~ etm., to have an audience or interview. ~**î** (·‿̲), who meets or interviews: ···e ~ olm., to meet with ..., to have an interview with ....

mülâkkab Designated; surnamed; nicknamed.

mülâsık Contiguous; in contact (with = *dat.*).

mülâtafa (·‿·̇) A joking with another; affability; courtesy.

mülây·emet (·‿·̇), –**ti** A suiting or fitting; mildness, gentleness; softness; freedom of the bowels. ~**im**, suitable; mild, gentle; soft, pliant; free in the bowels : ~ **gelmek**, to seem reasonable, to appeal *to* one.

mülâz·emet (·‿·̇), –**ti** A holding tenaciously to stg.; persistence, assiduity; a serving as an unpaid beginner in an official post; novitiate. ~ etm., to serve as a novice or candidate for a post. ~**im**, novice; assistant functionary; (*formerly*) lieutenant.

mülemma (···̲) Soiled, smeared; variegated. Poem written in two languages.

mülevv·en Coloured. ~**in**, who colours.

mülevves Soiled, dirty.

müleyyin Softening; laxative.

mülga (·̲·) Suppressed; abolished.

mülhak Added, appended; annexed; attached; dependent (on = *dat.*). ~**at**, –**tı**, added things; places subordinate *to a centre of government*.

mülhem Inspired; suggested. ···den ~ olm., to be inspired by ....

mülhid Atheist. Irreligious; heretic. ~**lik**, unbelief; irreligion.

mülk, –**kü** Possession; property; dominion. ~ **almak**, to acquire landed property: ~

sahibi, landed proprietor. ~i (·-͜·), belonging to the state; civil; civilian. ~iye, civil service; school for civil servants. ~iyeli, qualified as a civil servant. ~iyet, –ti, the quality of being freehold.

mülsak Adjoining; adhering.

mültec·a (··-͜·) Refuge; asylum. ~i (··-͜·), refugee.

mültefit Attentive, courteous, kind.

mülteka (··-͜·) Junctions (of rivers or roads); place of meeting.

mültem·es Asked for as a favour; solicited; protected; backed; protégé. ~is, who asks a favour.

mültesık Contiguous, adjoining.

mültez·em Favoured; considered necessary. ~im, one who farms a branch of the revenue: regarding as necessary; favouring.

mülûkâne (·—·) Royal, regal.

mülz·em Beaten in an argument; reduced to silence. ~im, who convinces and reduces to silence.

mümanaat (·—·), –ti Opposition; prevention. ~ etm., to oppose, prevent.

mümarese (·—·) Skill acquired by practice; dexterity; practice, training.

mümas (·-͜·), –ssı Touching. Tangent.

mümas·elet (·—·), –ti Similarity. ~il, similar.

mümaşat (·—·), –tı A going together; a complying; feigned approval; flattery: ···e ~ etm., to make concession to ...; to approve in order to flatter.

mümbais Caused; resulting; due (to = abl.).

mümbit Fertile; productive.

mümessil Representative; editor; actor.

mümeyyiz (Legally) capable of distinguishing between right and wrong; distinguishing; distinctive. Chief clerk; examining official at a school. kuvvei ~e, discernment: vasfı ~, distinguishing quality.

mümin (–·) Believer in Islam (pl. ~in).

mümkün Possible. ~ olduğu kadar or ~ mertebe, as far as possible: sürati ~e ile, with the greatest possible speed. ~at (··ƨ̇), –tı, possibilities.

mümsik Abstemious; sober; reticent; close-fisted.

mümtaz (·ƨ̇) Distinguished; privileged; autonomous. ~iyet (·—·), –ti, ~lık, a being distinguished or privileged; autonomous.

mümted, –ddi Extending; protracted. ~olm., to be extended, be protracted, continue.

mümteli (··-͜·) Full; filled.

mümteni (··-͜·) Who refuses; standing aloof; unattainable.

mümtezic Accommodating; fitting in with; compatible.

mümzi (·-͜·) Signing. Signatory.

münacat (·-͜·), –tı Prayer to God; inward prayer; prayer in poetry.

münadi (·-͜·) Herald; public crier.

münaferet (·—·), –ti Mutual aversion.

münafese (·—·) Rivalry; animosity.

münafi (·-͜·) (with dat.) Incompatible; irreconcilable; opposed or contrary to.

münafık (·-͜·), –kkı Hypocrite; mischief-maker; double-dealing; tell-tale.

münakale (·—·) Transport; transfer; (pl. münakalat, transport; communications).

münakasa (·—·) A giving of a contract to the lowest bidder; a putting up to tender; adjudication. ~ya konulmak, to be put up to tender.

münakaşa (·—·) Dispute. ~ etm., to dispute, to wrangle: ~ götürmez, indisputable.

münakeha (·—·) A being betrothed or married.

mün'akid Concluded; ratified; assembled, convoked.

mün'akis Reflected; inverted; reflex.

münakkah Trimmed; cleaned; corrected; polished (poem); carefully revised.

münakkaş Ornamented, decorated.

münakkid Critic. Criticizing.

münasaf·a A dividing in half. ~eten (··ƨ̇··), in two equal parts.

münasebet (·—·), –ti Fitness; proportion; reason; relation, connexion; pretext, motive; opportunity; (pl. münasebat, relations between nations or people). ... ~iyle, in connexion with ...: ~ almaz, it is not seemly: ~ aramak, to seek an opportunity: bir ~ düşürmek, to find a suitable occasion: bir ~ ile, on a fitting occasion; under a suitable pretext: bu ~le, in this connexion: 'ne ~!', 'by no means!'; 'not a bit of it!'; 'not likely!'; 'what's that got to do with it?'

münasebet·li, reasonable; suitable; opportune. ~siz, inopportune; unsuitable; unseemly; unreasonable. ~sizlik, unseemly action; silly act; stg. done at the wrong moment. ~tar, connected with.

münasib (·–·) Suitable; proper; opportune. ~ görmek, to think proper or opportune.

mün'atıf Bent; turned (towards = dat.).

münavebe (·—·) Alternation; a taking turns; rotation. ~ten (·—···), in turns, alternately.

münazaa (·—·) Dispute; quarrel. ~lı or münazaunfih, about which there is a dispute; controversial.

münazara (·—·) Discussion; argument; debate.

münazil Dismissed from office.
münbais Caused; resulting.
münbasit Extended; dilated; joyful; expansive. ~ olm., to be happy, to be at ease.
münbit Fertile.
münceli (··⸌) Manifest; come to light.
müncemid Frozen; congealed. bahri ~, the Arctic Ocean.
müncer Drawn; attracted; ···e ~, resulting in, leading to. ~ olm., to be drawn or attracted; to result in; to have as consequence.
müncezib Attracted.
münci (·⸌) Saving. Rescuer, deliverer.
mündefi (··⸌) Repulsed, driven away; removed.
mündemic Entering in; contained in. Almanların muvaffakiyetsizliği ... olmalarında ~dir, the failure of the Germans is to be found in the fact that they are ....
münderic Inserted; written; published. ~at, -tı, contents (of a letter or book).
münderis In utter ruin; obliterated.
münebbih Rousing; awakening. Stimulant; excitant (coffee etc.).
müneccim Astronomer; astrologer.
münekkid Criticizing. Critic.
münevv·er Enlightened; educated. Educated person, intellectual. ~ir, illuminating; enlightening.
münevvim Soporific; narcotic.
münezzeh Kept free (from= den); exempt; pure.
münfail Annoyed; offended.
münfek Severed; separated; dislocated.
münferic Wide apart. zaviyei ~e, obtuse angle.
münferid Separated; isolated; insulated. ~en (·⸌··), separately; singly; alone.
münfesih Abrogated, annulled; abolished.
münhal Loosened; solved; dissolved; vacant.
münhani Bent, curved. Curve; arc.
münharif Deviating; leaning; indisposed. Trapezium.
münhasif Eclipsed (of the moon); put into the shade by stg. better.
münhat Fallen down; depressed, low-lying (place); low; degraded.
münhedim Fallen down; in ruins.
münhemik (with dat.) Given up to; absorbed in; indulging in.
münhezim Routed, defeated. ~en (·⸌··), in rout, in disorderly flight.
münif (·⸌) Exalted; illustrious.
mün'im Benevolent; charitable. Philanthropist.
münir Luminous; bright.
münkad (·⸌) Docile, submissive, obedient.
münkalib Transformed.

münkariz Extinct (of a dynasty etc.); exterminated; perished.
münkasim Divided into parts.
münkazi (··⸌) Finished; expired (period).
münker Denied; unacceptable; not allowed by religious law. Name of one of the two angels who question the dead.
münkesif Eclipsed (of the sun).
münkesir Broken; annoyed; brokenhearted.
münkeşif Revealed; brought to light; discovered; developed.
münkir Who denies or disbelieves.
münselib Carried off; stolen; removed; non-exstent. ~ olm., to be carried off; to cease to exist.
münşeat (··⸌), -tı Literary compositions; letters; sets of examples of letters, guide to letter-writing.
münşerih Cheerful, in good humour.
münşi (·⸌) Letter-writer; secretary. ~ane (·—⸌), written in a bombastic style.
müntah·ab Selected; chosen; elected; privileged. ~at, -tı, selected passages (of an author); anthology. ~ib, who selects; elector.
müntahil Who plagiarizes. Plagiarist.
müntahir Who commits suicide, suicide (person).
müntakil Migrating; transferred; passed on, inherited.
müntakim Avenging.
müntefi (··⸌) Who profits or gains an advantage (by = den).
münteha (··⸌) Limit; extreme. Final.
müntehab etc. v. müntahab etc.
müntehi (··⸌) Final; last. ~ olm., to end (in = dat.).
müntehir Suicide (person).
müntesib (with dat.) Connected with; having relations with; belonging to.
münteşir Disseminated; diffused; published.
müntic (with acc.) Resulting in, causing. ···i ~ olm., to produce as result, to cause.
münzevi (··⸌) Retiring to a solitary place. Recluse, hermit. ~ yaşamak, to live a secluded life.
müphem v. mübhem.
müpteda, müptelâ etc. v. mübteda etc.
mür, -rrü Myrrh.
müracaat (·—·⸌). -tı, (pl. ·—·⸌) Recourse; application; reference. ···e ~ etm., to have recourse to, refer to, consult. ~gâh (·—··⸌), place or authority to which recourse must be had.
müradif (·—⸌) Synonymous. Synonym.
mürahik (·—⸌) On the verge of puberty.
mürai (·—⸌) Hypocritical. Hypocrite. ~lik, hypocrisy.

mürasele (·—·¹) Correspondence.

mürd Dead (of animals).

mürdesenk Litharge, peroxide of lead.

mürdüm, ~eriği Damson.

mürebbi (··¹) Who brings up or educates. Tutor; trainer. **~ye,** governess.

müreccah Preferable; preferred.

müreffeh Prosperous; well-to-do. **~en** (·¹··), comfortably; in easy circumstances.

mürekkeb Compound; composed (of = den). Ink. **cehli ~,** the ignorance of one who is sure he knows: **oldukça ~ yalamiş,** somewhat educated. **~balığı, –nı,** squid, cuttle-fish. **~lemek,** to ink in; to cover with ink. **~li,** inky; filled with ink: **~ kalem,** fountain-pen.

müressem Designed; decorated with designs or illustrations.

müretteb Set in order, arranged; prepared; invented, concocted; incumbent (duty); allotted; destined for; 'ear-marked' for. **~at, –tı,** pl. used as sing., appropriation; crew (of a ship); troops allotted to or destined for some place or duty.

mürettib Compositor. **~ hatası,** misprint.

mürevvic Giving currency to; propagating (ideas etc.); who pushes or facilitates stg.

mürid Novice in an order of dervishes; disciple. ⌈**şeyh uçmamış ~i uçurmuş**⌉, the sheikh could not fly but his disciple said he did; the prodigies of a great man are often only the invention of his admirers.

mürnel Three-stranded twine.

mürs·el Sent. Envoy; apostle. **~ileyh,** to whom a thing or person is sent, addressee. **~il,** who sends. **~ile,** transmitter, transmitting station.

mürşid Who shows the right way; guide; spiritual teacher.

mürt v. **mürd.**

mürteci, –ii Reactionary.

mürted, –ddi Apostate, renegade.

mürtefi (··¹) Elevated; raised; removed.

mürtekib Corrupt; taking bribes; who commits a sin.

mürtesem Delineated. Projection.

mürteşi (··¹) Who accepts bribes, corrupt.

mürur (·¹) Passage (of a person); lapse of time. **~ tezkeresi,** permit to pass, pass. **~iye,** toll; permit to pass. **~uzaman,** prescription, limitation (time after which an action cannot be taken): **~la sakıt olm.,** (of an action at law) to fail under the Statute of Limitations.

mürüvvet, –ti Generosity; munificence; blessing; family feast for a birth, marriage etc. **evlâdının ~ini görmek,** to see one's child grow up and get married. '**~e endaze olmaz**', 'there is no limit to generosity', give all you can! **~li, ~mend,**

generous; considerate. **~siz,** ungenerous; inconsiderate.

mürver Elder (tree).

müsaade (·—·¹) Permission; favour; (pl. müsaadat, favours; facilities). **···e ~ etm.,** to permit, consent to: **en ziyade mazharı ~ millet muamelesi kaydı,** the most-favoured-nation clause. **~kâr,** tolerant.

müsab·aka (·—·¹) Competition; race. **~ya girmek,** to compete: **~ imtihanı,** competitive examination. **~ık** (·—¹), competitor.

müsademe, müsadere, müsadıf v. **musademe** etc.

müsaferet (·—·¹), **–ti** A being a guest.

müsahele (·—·¹) A being obliging; indulgence; lenience. **~kâr,** tolerant.

müsaid (·—¹) Permitting; favourable; convenient. **~ davranmak,** to show oneself favourably disposed.

müsakkafat (··¹), **–tı** Roofed buildings; house property; Vakıf income derived from house property.

müsalâha (·—·¹) A making peace, reconciliation.

müsalemet (·—·¹), **–ti** Tranquillity; a living in peace, harmony.

müsamaha (·—·¹) Indulgence; tolerance; forbearance; negligence. **~ etm.,** to shut one's eyes to an impropriety. **~kâr, ~cı,** indulgent; non-censorious; tolerant.

müsamere (·—·¹) Evening entertainment; soirée; concert.

müsanede (·—·¹) Support; aid.

müsaraat (·—·¹), **–tı** Haste.

müsattah Levelled; on a plane; superficial.

müsav·at (·—¹), **–tı** Equality. **~i** (·—·¹), equal: equivalent; the sign =.

müsb·et Proved; established; positive; positive (elect.). The positive sign (elect.). **~ cevab,** an answer in the affirmative: **~ kafalı,** realistic, hard-headed. **~it,** proving: **evrakı ~e,** documents in proof of stg.

müsebba, –aı Of seven parts; heptagon; stanza of seven lines.

müsebb·eb Caused, brought about. **~ib,** causing; producing: cause, motive; author, instigator.

müsecca (··¹) Rhymed (prose).

müseccel Officially registered; matriculated; notorious (thief etc.).

müseddes Having six parts; hexagon; stanza of six lines.

müsekkin Quieting, calming. Anodyne, sedative.

müsellâh Armed. **gayri ~,** unfit to bear arms, fit only for non-combatant duties (mil.): **kafadan gayri ~,** off his head, having 'a screw loose'. **~an** (·¹··), with arms in their hands.

müsellem Admitted by all, incontestable. ~at, –tı, admitted truths, truisms.

müselles Triple; triangular. Triangle; a syrup or wine reduced to a third by boiling. ~at, –tı, trigonometry.

müselsel Connected; consecutive; linked.

müsemma (··⸱) Named, called.

müsevvid Secretary who drafts letters etc.

müseyyeb Feckless; reckless; negligent; untidy. ~ane (····⸱), in a negligent, take-it-easy manner. ~lik, negligence, taking it easy; untidiness.

müshil Purgative.

müsin Aged.

müskir Intoxicating. ~at, –tı, intoxicants.

müskit Who silences; who reduces to silence by his arguments, persuasive.

müslim Moslem.

müslüman Moslem; pious; honest. ~ca (··⸱·), in a Moslem way; honestly; honourably.

müsmir Fruitful; productive; successful.

müsned Leaning against; supported. Predicate (gram.). ~ünileyh, subject (gram.).

müspet v. müsbet.

müsrif Spendthrift; extravagant; prodigal.

müstacel (·–⸱) Urgent. ~en (·⸱··), urgently, in haste. ~iyet, –ti, urgency.

müstafi (·–⸱) Who resigns.

müstağallât (····⸱), –tı Landed property (as opp. to müsakkafat, house property), the income of which goes to a trust.

müstağfir Who asks pardon; penitent.

müstağni (··⸱) Having no need (of = den); independent; satisfied; disdainful. bir şeyden ~ olmamak, to be unable to do without a thing: izahtan ~dir, it has no need of explanation.

müstağrak Submerged; overwhelmed. ··e ~, plunged into; inundated by.

müstahak, –kkı Due; merited; (also used for müstahik, who merits, who asks or is entitled to). Deserts; due reward or punishment. ~kını bulmak, to get one's deserts: ··e ~ olm., to deserve, to be entitled to: 'Allah ~kını versin!', 'may Heaven punish him!'

müstahber Learnt; heard; announced. Information received; (pl. ~at, news or information received). ~dir, information has been received that.

müstahdem Employed. Employee, servant. ~in, employees, personnel: ~ idarehanesi, employment bureau.

müstahfız Reservist (mil.). ~lık, service in the reserve.

müstahik Who deserves; who is entitled to; v. müstahak.

mustahil (··⸱) Absurd; impossible.

müstahkar Despised; contemptible.

müstahkem Fortified.

müstahrec Extracted; deducted, inferred.

müstahsalat (···⸱), –tı Products.

müstahsen Admired; approved.

müstahsil Productive. Producer. kuvvei ~e, productive capacity.

müstahzar Made ready, prepared. Ready-made drug. ~at, –tı, prepared drugs, medicinal preparations.

müstaid Clever, capable. ···e ~, clever at; capable of; inclined, disposed to (an illness).

müstakar, –rrı Settled place or time; used for müstakır q.v.

müstakbel Future. The future; the future tense.

müstakır Settled; stationary; stable. ~an (··⸱·), firmly; steadily.

müstakil Independent; apart. Absolutely; solely; expressly. ~len (··⸱·), independently; absolutely; solely; expressly.

müstakim Straight; upright, honest.

müstakriz Who borrows money.

müstamel (·–⸱) Used; employed; not new.

müstam·er (·–⸱) Colonized. ~ere (pl. ~erat), colony. ~ir, colonizing: colonist.

müstantık Examining magistrate, 'juge d'instruction' (no English equivalent).

müstâraz Transverse.

müstareb (·–⸱) Who becomes an Arab; arabicized.

müstashiben (·⸱··) Carrying on him, having with him.

müstatil Oblong.

müstear (··⸱) Temporarily borrowed; temporary. namı ~, pseudonym.

müsteb'ad Remote; improbable; far-fetched.

müsteban (··⸱) Clearly explained; evident.

müstebid Despotic, tyrannical. Despot, tyrant. ~ane (····⸱), despotic (action etc.); despotically, tyrannically.

müstecab (··⸱) Answered; granted.

müstecir (·–⸱) Who rents; tenant. ~en (·⸱··), on lease; as a tenant.

müstecvib Who or that necessitates; requiring.

müsted'a (··⸱) Asked for. Request; (pl. ~yat).

müstedam (··⸱) Continuous; perpetual.

müstedel Deduced; inferred.

müsted'i (··⸱) Who requests. Petitioner.

müstefad (··⸱) Inferred; understood; gained.

müstefid (··⸱) Who profits. ···den ~ olm., to profit by; to learn from; to enjoy (rights etc.).

müstefiz (··⸱) Benefited. ~ olm., to profit; to learn.

müstefreşe Concubine.

müstehab Laudable; recommended but

not enjoined by religious law.
müstehase (···-ı) Fossil (*pl.* müstehasat).
müstehcen Loathsome; obscene.
müstehlik, -ki Consuming. Consumer.
müstehzi (··-ı) Jeering, mocking; sarcastic, ironical.
müstekim Straight; upright, honest.
müstekreh Loathed; disgusting.
müstelzim Necessitating; involving; implying.
müstemi (··-ı), **-ii** Who listens. One who learns by oral instruction.
müstemir Continuous; unbroken; firm; solid. **âdeti ~e**, an unbroken custom. **~ren** (··ı··), perpetually.
müstemleke Colony (*pl.* müstemlekât).
müstenbat (··-ı) Inferred.
müstenid (*with dat.*) Relying *or* based on. **~en** (·ı··), based on, relying on.
müstenkif Who abstains *or* refuses.
müstensih Who makes a copy. Copying press; hectograph.
müsterham Implored, begged.
müsterih (··-ı) At rest; at ease. **~ etm.**, to set at ease.
müsteskal Regarded as disagreeable; coldly received.
müsteskî (··-ı) Dropsical.
müstesna (·· ı) Excluded, exceptional; extraordinary. **~lık**, a being exceptional.
müsteşar Councillor; Secretary of State. **~lık**, under-secretaryship.
müsteşfi (··-ı) Who seeks a cure.
müsteşrik, -ki Orientalist.
müstetab (··-ı) Approved; pleasant, agreeable.
müstetir Veiled; hidden. **tahtında ~**, implied but not expressed, 'sous-entendu'.
müstevdi (··-ı) Who entrusts for safe keeping; depositor; (*also* depositary).
müstevi (··-ı) Level; uniform; plane. Plane (in geometry).
müstevli (··-ı) Invading; predominant; prevalent; epidemic. **···e ~ olm.**, to invade.
müstezad (··-ı), **-dı** Increased; supplemented. Poem having a rhymed supplement to each hemistitch.
müsvedde Draft, rough copy. **~lik**, paper for rough copies.
müşaare (·-·ı) Poetic contest.
müşab·ehet (·-·ı), **-ti** Resemblance. **~ih** (·-ı), resembling: **~ olm.**, to resemble.
müşahede (·-·ı) A seeing or witnessing; observation (*med.*). **~ altına alınmak**, to be placed under observation: **~ etm.**, to see, witness. (*pl.* müşahedat, things witnessed, observations; visions).
müşahhas Personified; identified; concrete (*as opp. to* mücerred, abstract).
müşahid (·-ı) Observer.

müşareket (·-·ı), **-ti** Participation; partnership; association; reciprocal form of the verb.
müşarileyh (·-·ı), **müşarünileyh** Aforementioned; the said; (*fem.* **~a,** *pl.* **~im**).
müşaşa (·-ı) Shining; splendid; gorgeous.
müşateme (·-·ı) Mutual abuse.
müşav·ere (·-·ı) Consultation; deliberation. **~ir** (·-ı), who consults *or* is consulted; counsellor; consultant (*med.*): **hukuk ~i**, legal adviser.
müşebbeh Compared. Object of comparison; the thing which, in a simile, is likened to stg. else. **~ünfih**, that to which a thing is likened in a simile.
müşebbek Reticulated.
müşedd·ed Made strong; increased in violence; doubled (consonant). **~id**, increasing the violence; reinforcing; aggravating: **esbabı ~e**, aggravating circumstances.
müşekkel Of imposing form; huge.
müşerref Honoured. **~ olm.**, to be honoured, to feel it an honour: **~ oldum,** I am glad to meet you.
müşerrih Anatomist; commentator.
müşevves Confused; dubious.
müşevvik, -ki Inciting; encouraging. Instigator.
müşfik Tender; compassionate.
müşir *v.* müşür.
müş'ir Marking; pointing out; informing. Index, pointer. **~e**, dial *or* scale (of a pressure gauge *etc.*).
müşiriyet, -ti Rank of a field-marshal.
müşkül Difficult. Difficulty; doubt; (*pl.* müşkülât, **-tı**: **~ çıkarmak**, to raise difficulties: **~ çekmek** *or* **düçarı ~ olm.**, to meet with difficulties). **~pesend,** hard to please; fastidious; exacting.
müşrif Overlooking; overhanging; on the point of. **~i harab**, on the point of falling down.
müşrik, -ki Polytheist; pagan; (*pl.* **~in**, people who do not believe in the unity of God).
müştagil Busy; occupied.
müştail Inflammable.
müştak, -kkı Derived. Derivative; (*pl.* **~kat, -tı**).
müştâk (··-ı) Filled with desire (of, to = *dat.*).
müştehi (··-ı) Having an appetite; longing for; (*err. for* müşteha) appetizing.
müştehir Well-known; renowned.
müşteil *v.* müştail.
müşteki (··-ı) Who complains. Complainant.
müştemelat (··-ı), **-tı** Contents; things of which a thing consists; annexes; outhouses.

müştemil Containing; comprising; (*err. for* müştemel) contained.

müşterek Common; shared; collective; joint. faslı ~, ratio, intersection (*math.*). ~en (·¹··), in common; jointly.

müşteri[1] Customer; purchaser; client.

Müşteri[2] (··⸜) The planet Jupiter.

müşür Field-marshal. ~lük, rank and position of a field-marshal.

müt'a Advantage, benefit; temporary marriage (*practised by Shiites*).

mütaa- *v.* mütea-.

mütabaat (·—·¹), –tı A conforming *or* following; conformity; obedience. ~ etm., to follow, conform.

mütalâa (·—·¹) A studying; observation, remark; opinion. ... ~sında bulunmak, to be of the opinion that ...: ~ etm., to read, study.

mütareke (·—·¹) Armistice.

müteaccib Astonished, amazed.

müteaddi (···⸜) Aggressive; transitive (verb).

müteaddid Numerous; several.

müteaffin Putrid; stinking.

müteahhid Contractor; purveyor.

müteahhir Subsequent; latest, last; modern; (*pl.* ~in, the moderns *or, as sing.*, a modern man).

müteakıb (···—¹) Successive; subsequent. birbirini ~, one after the other. ~en (··⸜··), subséquently; successively.

müteakkıd Agreed to.

müteallik (*with dat.*) Dependent on; relative to; concerning; connected with.

müteammid Acting deliberately *or* with premeditation. ~en (··¹··), with premeditation; deliberately.

müteammim General; in common use.

müteannid Obstinate.

mütearife (···—·¹) Axiom.

mütearrız Attacking; aggressive. Aggressor.

müteassir Difficult; arduous.

müteayyin Fixed; determined; designated; distinguished.

müteazzi (···⸜) Organic; having organs.

müteazzım Proud, arrogant.

mütebadil (···—¹) Taking each other's place; interchangeable; alternate.

mütebahhir Very erudite. Learned scholar.

mütebaid (···—¹) Divergent; becoming distant.

mütebaki (···—⸜) Remaining; outstanding. Remainder; balance; surplus.

mütebariz (···—¹) Prominent; outstanding.

mütebasbıs Fawning; cringing.

mütebayin (···—¹) Distinct; contrasting; incommensurable (*arith.*).

mütebeddil Changed, altered.

mütebellir Crystallized; as clear as crystal; very evident.

mütebessim Smiling.

mütebeyyin Manifest; proved.

mütecahil (···—¹) Who feigns ignorance.

mütecanis (···—¹) Homogeneous; of the same kind.

mütecasir (···—¹) Audacious; presumptuous. ~ olm., to dare (impudently).

mütecavir (···—¹) Neighbouring; adjacent.

mütecaviz (···—¹) Exceeding; transgressing; exorbitant; presumptuous. Aggressor. bini *or* binden ~, exceeding a thousand.

müteceddid Innovator; modernist; following the latest fashion.

mütecelli (···—⸜) Becoming manifest. ~ olm., to become manifest; to show oneself.

mütecellid Daring, courageous; challenging. ~ane bir hareket, a brave defiant action.

mütecemmi Collected together, assembled.

mütecessim Appearing solid; corporeal; personified.

mütecessis Inquisitive, curious.

mütecezzi (···—⸜) Divided; divisible.

mütedahil (···—¹) Entering each other; intermixed; overlapping; commensurable (*arith.*); in arrears (of payments *etc.*).

mütedair (···—¹) Concerning, relative.

mütedavil (···—¹) Current; in common use. ~ sermaye, working capital.

mütedenni (···—⸜) Retrograde; decadent; degenerate.

mütedeyyin Religious.

müteehhil Married.

müteellim Suffering; grieved.

müteemmil Reflecting; meditative.

müteenni Slow and cautious; circumspect.

müteessif Grieved, sorry, regretful.

müteessir Hurt; grieved; touched; affected. ~ olm., to be grieved, touched, affected, impressed. ~en (··¹··), ···den ~, grieving that ..., in sorrow for ....

müteezzi (···—⸜) Vexed; oppressed.

mütefavit Dissimilar; various.

mütefekkir Thoughtful, pensive. Thinker. kuvvei ~e, the thinking faculty.

mütefennin Versed in science or art. Scientist.

müteferri (···—⸜), –ii Having ramifications; derived; accessory; subordinate. ~yat, –tı, offshoots; ramifications; derivatives.

müteferrid Isolated; sole, unique.

müteferrik Separated; dispersed; various, miscellaneous. ~a, money for miscellaneous expenses; petty cash; sundries; the department of a police station dealing with petty offences, licences *etc.*

mütefessih Putrified; degenerate.

mütefevvik Superior.

mütegallib Usurping; tyrannical. Tyrant. ~ane (·····¹), tyrannically; in a cruel and violent manner. ~e, oppressors; usurpers.

mütegayyir Changed; spoilt.

mütehab (··⸽) Friendly. düveli ~be, friendly Powers.

mütehaccir Petrified.

mütehaddis Coming to pass, occurring; arising *from*; due *to*.

mütehakkim Despotic; domineering.

mütehalif (···¹) Diverse; mutually opposed.

mütehalik (···¹) Precipitate; enthusiastic.

mütehalli (···⸽) Embellished, adorned.

mütehallik (*with* ile) Endowed with; possessing.

mütehammil (*with dat.*) Supporting; enduring; capable of.

müteharrik Moving; movable; portable.

mütehassıl Produced; resulting.

mütehassıs Specialist.

mütehassir Who regrets an absent person *or* thing desired; longing; disappointed.

mütehassis Moved (by emotion). ···le ~, animated by (a désire *etc.*).

mütehaşi (···⸽) Shrinking; abstaining, refraining.

mütehaşşid Concentrated; mobilized.

mütehavvil Changing; variable.

mütehayyil Imagining; fanciful. **kuvvei** ~e, the imaginative faculty.

mütehayyir Amazed; bewildered.

mütehayyiz Occupying a special place; distinguished.

mütehevvir Impetuous; rash; furious.

müteheyyi (····⸽) Ready; in readiness.

müteheyyic Excited.

mütekabil (···¹) Opposite each other; reciprocal; mutual. ~en (··⸽··), mutually; reciprocally. ~iyet, ~ti, reciprocity.

mütekaddim Preceding; former; ancient; (*pl.* ~in, the ancients; men of old).

mütekaid (···¹) Retired on a pension. Pensioner (*pl.* ~in).

mütekallis Shrunken; contracted.

mütekâmil (···¹) Arrived at perfection, perfected; developed by evolution.

mütekarib (···¹) Approaching one another; convergent.

mütekarrib Approaching; attempting to approach; near.

mütekâsif (···¹) Thick; condensed; concentrated.

mütekatı (···¹) Intersecting.

mütekebbir Proud, haughty.

mütekeffil (*with acc.*) Standing surety for; responsible for; guaranteeing.

mütekellim Speaking. Speaker; first person (*gram.*).

mütelâki (···⸽) Meeting *or* joining together.

mütelaşi (···⸽) Flurried.

mütelâtım (···¹) Dashing together (of waves); rough (sea).

mütelehhif Sighing; lamenting.

mütelevvin Of various colours; variegated; fickle.

mütelezziz Enjoying the taste; relishing. ···den ~ olm., to relish, to enjoy.

mütelif (−·¹) In agreement; in accord; familiar *with*; accustomed *to*. düveli ~e, the Entente Powers.

mütemadi (···⸽) Continuing; continuous. ~iyen (··⸽··), continuously; continually.

mütemarız (···¹) Feigning illness, malingering.

mütemayil (···¹) Inclined; leaning.

mütemayiz (···¹) Distinguished (for = ile).

mütemeddin Civilized.

mütemekkin Settled (in a place); established.

mütemenna Desired; asked for. Wish; request.

mütemerrid Obstinate; rebellious; recalcitrant.

mütemevvic With waves; billowy; wavy; rough (sea); fluctuating.

mütemmim Completing, perfecting; supplementary. Supplement. cüz'i ~, integral part.

mütenahi (···⸽) Reaching a limit; ending; finite.

mütena'im (···¹) Loaded with favours; living in comfort.

mütenakıs (··−¹) Diminishing; dwindling.

mütenakız (···¹) Contradictory.

mütenasib (···¹) Proportional; symmetrical; well-proportioned; well-built. mebsuten (makûsen) ~, directly (indirectly) proportional.

mütenavib (···¹) Happening· *or* acting alternately; alternating.

mütenazır (···¹) Facing one another; corresponding; symmetrical.

mütenebbi (····⸽) Falsely claiming to be a prophet.

mütenebbih Warned; vigilant; on his guard *as the result of unpleasant experience*.

müteneffir Feeling aversion (*for* = den).

müteneffiz Influential; (*pl.* ~an, influential people).

mütenekkir Disguised; unrecognizable; incognito. ~en (··⸽··), incognito (*adv.*).

mütenevvi (····⸽) Of various kinds; diverse.

mütenezzih Who goes for a walk or ride for amusement; excursionist.

müteradif (···¹) Synonymous.

müterafik [262] **müttekâ**

müterafik Mutually associating; concurrent (*with* = ile).

müterakim (··–ʾ) Accumulated.

müterakki (···–ʾ) Progressive.

müterakkib Hoping for; expecting.

müterassıd Observing; lying in wait.

müterc·em Translated. ~im, translating; translator.

mütereddi (···–ʾ) Depraved; degenerate.

mütereddid Hesitating; undecided.

müterekkib Consisting of parts; composed (of = den).

müterennim Singing; trilling.

müteressib Precipitated; deposited a a sediment.

müteresşih Oozing out.

müterettib Arranged in order. ···den ~, resulting from : ···e ~, requiring : uhdemize ~ vazife, the duty which it falls on us to perform.

mütesaddi (···–ʾ) Who dares *or* sets out to do.

mütesadif (···–ʾ) Meeting by chance; happening by chance; coincident.

mütesanid (···–ʾ) Mutually supporting; solidary; joint (responsibility).

mütesavi (·–·ʾ) Equal to one another.

müteselli (···–ʾ) Who consoles himself; comforted.

mütesellim Who takes delivery of stg. from another; (*formerly*) a deputy lieutenant-governor and collector of taxes.

müteselsil Forming a chain; in continuous succession; uninterrupted (sequence). ~ mesuliyet, joint liability. ~en (··ʾ··), in continuous succession; one after the other.

mütesabih (···–ʾ) Resembling one another; similar.

müteşair (··–ʾ) Who professes to be a poet; poetaster.

müteşebbis Who has initiative; enterprising; who starts an enterprise. ···e ~ olm., to set to work on.

müteşekki (···–ʾ) Who complains. ···den ~ olm., to complain of.

müteşekkil Formed. ···den ~, formed *or* composed of.

müteşekkir Thankful; grateful.

müteşerri (···–ʾ) Conforming to the religious law. Canonical jurist.

mütetabbib A tyro in medicine; quack.

mütetebbi (···–ʾ) Who investigates *or* researches.

mütevafık (···–ʾ) In accord with one another; congruous; commensurable (*arith.*).

mütevahhiş Frightened; scared.

mütevakkıf At a stop, standing still; dependent (on = *dat.*).

mütevali (···–ʾ) Consecutive; successive;

continuous. ~yen (··–ʾ··), successively, consecutively, continuously.

mütevarid (···–ʾ) Arriving.

mütevaris (···–ʾ) Inherited; hereditary.

mütevasıl (···–ʾ) Joined together.

mütevassıt Medium, intermediary; mean.

mütevatir (···–ʾ) Spread from mouth to mouth; well-known. A generally admitted truth. ~en (··–ʾ··), by general report; by general admission; as rumoured.

mütevattın Who settles in a place; resident.

mütevazı (···–ʾ) Humble; modest.

mütevazi (···–ʾ) Parallel. ~yüladla (··–··–ʾ), parallelogram.

mütevazin (···–ʾ) Equal in weight; balancing one another.

müteveccih (*with dat.*) Turned towards; facing; aimed at; favourably disposed to. ~en (··ʾ··), in the direction of.

müteveffa (···–ʾ) Deceased; the late.

mütevehhim Who has imaginary fears or suspicions.

mütevekkil Who puts his trust in God; resigned.

mütevelli (···–ʾ) Administrator, *esp.* the trustee of a pious foundation.

mütevellid Born; caused; resulting.

müteverrim Consumptive.

müteyakkız Wide awake, vigilant.

müteyemm·en Auspicious; fortunate. ~inen (··ʾ··), auspiciously.

mütezad (··–ʾ) Mutually opposed; contrasting.

mütezahir (···–ʾ) Visible; manifest. ~ olm., to show oneself, to appear.

mütezaif (···–ʾ) Redoubled.

mütezayid (···–ʾ) Increasing.

mütezebzib Tossed about; wavering; capricious; agitated, confused, restless.

mütezellil Humiliated; debased; mean, contemptible, servile.

mütezelzil Shaken; convulsed; vacillating.

mütezevvic Married.

müthiş v. müdhiş.

müttakî (··–ʾ) God-fearing; devout.

müttefik, –ki Agreeing; unanimous; allied. Ally. ~an (·ʾ··), unanimously; in agreement. ~ürrey, of the unanimous opinion.

müttehaz Adopted, accepted; current, in use.

müttehem Accused *or* suspected (of = ile).

müttehid United; unanimous. Amerika ~ devletleri, the United States of America (*obs.*). ~en (·ʾ··), unanimously; unitedly. ~ülmeal, having the same purport.

müttehim Accusing; *used also err. for* müttehem.

müttekâ (··–ʾ) Anything leaned upon; bolster, cushion.

müvacehe (·−·ᵎ) A being face to face. ~sinde, in the presence of.

müvaneset (·−·ᵎ), **-ti** Familiarity; tameness.

müvelled Born; begotten; hybrid. ~at, **-tı**, creatures born; births.

müvellid Generating; begetting; who *or* that causes to be born. Midwife. ~ülhumuza, oxygen. ~ülma (····ᵎ), hydrogen.

müverrih Historian; chronicler; (*pl.* ~in).

müvesvis Apprehensive; suspicious; troubled by scruples.

müvezzi (···ᵎ), **-ii** Distributing. News-vendor; paper boy; postman.

müyesser Facilitated; practicable; helped by God. ~ olm., to be granted by God.

müzab Melted; fused.

müzaheme (·−·ᵎ) A thronging or crowding together.

müzah·eret (·−·ᵎ), **-ti** Help, support. ~ir (·−ᵎ), who supports or assists.

müzahrefat (···ᵎ), **-tı** Excrement; filth.

müzakere (·−·ᵎ) Discussion; conference; negotiation; the rehearsing of their lesson by schoolboys amongst themselves; (*pl.* müzakerat, negotiations; ruznamei ~, agenda *of a meeting etc.*). ~ etm., to talk

over, discuss *stg.* ~ci, master who hears boys their lessons; tutor.

müzayaka (·−·ᵎ) Hardship; straits. ~ ile geçinmek, to subsist with difficulty.

müzayede (·−·ᵎ) Auction.

müzdad (·ᵎ) Increased, augmented. ~ etm., to augment.

müzdahim Crowded.

müze (ᵎ·) Museum.

müzebzeb In utter confusion.

müzehh·eb Gilded, gilt. ~ib, gilder.

müzehher In flower.

müzekker Male; masculine.

müzekkere Memorandum; note; warrant. tevkif ~si, warrant of arrest.

müzevvir Who falsifies; trickster; sneak; mischief-maker. ~lik, tale-telling; knavery.

müzeyyel Having an appendix or addendum *or* postscript; (document) having an answer appended below. ~en (·ᵎ··), as an appendix *or* addendum.

müzeyyen Embellished; decorated.

müzeyyif Derisive.

müz'ic Annoying; vexatious.

müzik Music (*European as opp. to* saz, *oriental music*).

müzmin Chronic. emrazı ~e, chronic illnesses. ~leşmek, to become chronic.

N

na There!; there it is!; take it! ~ kafal, what a fool I (he) was!; what am I thinking about!: ~ sanal, so much for you!; there, take that!

na-, nâ- (−) *Pers. negative prefix, e.g.* durust, honest; nadurust, dishonest.

nabeca (·−ᵎ) Out-of-place; inopportune.

nabedid (−·ᵎ) Disappeared; invisible. ~ olm., to disappear.

nabehengâm (···ᵎ) Untimely; unseasonable.

nabekâr (−·ᵎ) Good-for-nothing; useless.

nabemahal (−··ᵎ) Out-of-place; untimely.

nabemevsim (−··ᵎ) Premature; out-of-season.

nabız, -bzı Pulse. nabzına bakmak *or* nabzını yoklamak, to feel s.o.'s pulse: ⌐nabza göre şerbet vermek⌐, to use tact with a person. ~gir, tactful, diplomatic.

nabit (−ᵎ) Growing. ~ olm., to grow (as a plant).

nabud (−ᵎ) Non-existent; disappeared. ~ etm., to annihilate.

nabzı *v.* nabız.

nacak Large axe with a hammer at the back. ⌐oldu olacak kırıldı ~⌐, there's

nothing more to be done about it; the die is cast.

nacar Carpenter.

naçar (−ᵎ) Who has no remedy; forced by necessity; helpless, in distress. Reluctantly; of necessity.

naçiz (−ᵎ) Of no account, insignificant; modest, humble. ~ane (−−ᵎ), humble (petition *etc.*) belonging to one's humble self: humbly.

nadan (−ᵎ) Tactless; unmannerly; uneducated.

nadas The preliminary ploughing of land for cleaning before preparing the seed-bed; fallowing: yeşil ~, green manuring of land.

nadide (−−ᵎ) Never seen before; curious; rare.

nadim (−ᵎ) Regretful; contrite. ···e ~ olm., to regret, to be sorry for having done.

nadir (−ᵎ) Rare; unusual. ~at,-tı, rarities; rarity. ~e (−··ᵎ), rarity; amusing anecdote. ~en (ᵎ··), rarely.

naehil (−·ᵎ) Unworthy; incapable; inexpert, unqualified.

nafaka Means of subsistence, livelihood; maintenance allowance; alimony. ···e ~

bağlamak, to assign a subsistence allowance to : ~sını temin etm., to earn one's living.

nafe (-ⁱ) Perfume obtained from the muskdeer; hair of the beloved; fur from the belly of an animal.

nafi (-ⁱ) Useful; profitable; beneficial. ~a (-·ⁱ), Public Works; Ministry of Public Works.

nafile (-·ⁱ) Useless; in vain. A supererogatory act (of prayer *etc.*). ~!, it's no use!; don't persist ! : ~ yere, uselessly, in vain.

nafiz (-ⁱ) Penetrating; influential.

nagâh (-ⁱ) Unexpected.

nagant An old-fashioned kind of pistol.

nagehani (-·-ⁱ) Sudden, unexpected; unawares.

nagezuhur (-··ⁱ) Sudden, unexpected.

nagış *v.* nakış.

nağme Tune; song. ~yi değiştirmek, to change one's tune : ara ~si, intermezzo, interlude.

nah *v.* na.

nahâh (-ⁱ) Unwillingly, involuntarily.

nahak (-ⁱ) Unjust; iniquitous. ~ yere, unjustly, unfairly.

nahif Thin, emaciated; weak, fragile.

nahil, -hli Date palm.

nahiv, -hvi Syntax.

nahiye (-·ⁱ) Region; sub-district *of one or more villages, forming an administrative unit under a* müdür. ~vî (-··ⁱ), regional; local (*med.*).

nahoş (-ⁱ) Disagreeable; unpleasant; unwell. ~luk, unpleasantness; indisposition.

nahvet, -ti Pride; conceit.

nahvî (·ⁱ) Connected with syntax. ~yun (··ⁱ), teachers of syntax; grammarians.

naib (-ⁱ) One who acts for others; substitute; judge; regent; vice-regent.

nail (-ⁱ) Who obtains. ··e ~ olm., to obtain, attain. ~iyet, -ti, acquisition; attainment (of an object *etc.*).

naim¹ (-ⁱ) Sleeping.

naim² (·ⁱ) *Only in* nazü ~ içinde, in comfort and luxury.

naime (-·ⁱ) Molluscs.

nakabil (--ⁱ) Incapable; impossible. ~i icra, impossible to carry out, impracticable.

nakâm (-ⁱ) Unsuccessful; disappointed.

nakarat, -tı Refrain; tiresome repetition; harping.

nakavt (ⁱ·) Knock-out.

nakd·en (ⁱ·) In cash; for ready money. ~î (·ⁱ), cash, in ready money.

nakes (-ⁱ) Mean, despicable (*of persons only*).

nakıl *corr. of* nahil. Palm branch. ~ çiçeği, phlox.

nâkıl (-ⁱ) *v.* nâkil.

nakır, -krı Sculpture; carving.

nâkıs (-ⁱ) Deficient; defective; minus; below zero.

nakıs, -ksı Deficiency; the minus sign (-).

nakış, -kşı Design; drawing; picture; embroidery; decoration. ~ işlemek, to embroider.

nakız, -kzı Annulment; violation (of a treaty *etc.*).

nâkız (-ⁱ) Abrogating; violating. yekdiğerini ~ havadisler, items of news that contradict each other.

nakibuleşraf (*Formerly*) The representative at Istanbul of the Sherif of Mecca.

nakid, -kdi Cash; money; ready money.

nâkil (-ⁱ) Transporting; transferring; narrating. Narrator; conductor (*elect.*). ~iyet, ~ti, a being a transporter; conductivity.

nakil, -kli Transport; removal; transfer; narration; translation. ~ vasıtaları, means of transport.

nakisa (·-ⁱ) Defect; shame. ···e ~ getirmek, to bring dishonour upon.

nakiz (·ⁱ) Contradictory; opposite. ~a (·-ⁱ), contradictory thing; converse.

nakkar·e (·-ⁱ) Large kettle-drum. ~hane (·--ⁱ), (*formerly*) the military band of a sovereign or vizier.

nakkaş Artist (*esp.* an illuminator of manuscripts); decorator.

naklen (ⁱ·) By tradition; by transfer.

nakletmek (ⁱ··), -eder *va.* Transport; transfer; relate; narrate; translate. *vn.* Move, change one's abode.

nakl·i *v.* nakil. ~î (·ⁱ), pertaining to transport; traditional. ~iyat, -tı, things handed down by tradition; means of transport; transport (*mil.*). ~iye, transport expenses; means of transport : ~ gemisi (tayyaresi), transport ship, (plane).

nakris Gout.

nakş *v.* nakış. ~berâb, writing on water, building on sand. ~etmek (ⁱ··), -eder, to decorate; to design.

nakten, naktî *v.* nakden, nakdî.

nakus (-ⁱ) Church bell.

nakz·en (ⁱ·) By annulment; in violation. ~etmek (ⁱ··), -eder, to annul, quash; violate; contradict. ~ı, *v.* nakız.

nal Horseshoe. ~ları dikmek, (of a horse and contemptuously of a man) to die : ~ döken, stony road : dört ~a gitmek, to gallop at full speed: ⌐hem ~ına hem mıhına¬, to act impartially, to try to please both parties; to hit out right and left regardless of persons: ⌐iş üç ~la bir ata kaldı¬, 'all that is wanted now is three shoes and a horse', *said ironically of stg. that has only just begun.*

nalân (-ⁱ) Moaning, lamenting. ~ olm., to moan *or* lament.

nalâyık (‒‒¹) Unworthy; unsuitable.

nalband Shoeing-smith, farrier; horse-doctor. ~**lık**, horse-shoeing, farriery.

nalbur Man who makes or sells horseshoes or small articles of hardware, ironmonger.

nalça Iron tip or heel on a boot.

nâle, nâliş (‒¹) Moan, groan.

nâlet (*corr. of* lânet) Cross-grained, peevish. ~ olsun !, damn the fellow !

nalın Pair of pattens *or* clogs. ~**cı**, clog-maker: ~ keseri, clog-maker's adze; egoist; ⌐~ keseri gibi kendine yontmak⌐, to think only of one's own advantage.

nallamak *va.* Shoe (a horse).

nam (‒) Name; renown; reputation; quality. Named. ~**ına**, in the name of; by way of *in such phrases as* : akraba ~ kimsesi yok, he has nothing in the way of relations; para ~ bir şey yok, there isn't a farthing, I haven't a sou : ~ında, of the name of : ~ ile, under the name of : ~ kazanmak, to make a name for oneself : ~ ve hesabına, for, on behalf of : ~ ve nişanı kalmadı, it has left no trace, it has perished utterly : bi ~ ve nişan, void of name or trace, unknown : dünyaya ~ vermek (salmak), to acquire a world-wide reputation.

namağlûb (‒·¹) Unconquered; invincible.

namahdud (‒·¹) Boundless; unlimited.

namahrem (‒·¹) Not related *or* intimate; not having access to the harem.

namakul (‒·¹) Unwise; unreasonable.

namalûm (‒‒¹) Unknown.

namaz (·⁴) Ritual worship; prayer. ~ **kılmak**, to perform the ritual prayers of Islam; ~**ı kılındı**, his burial service has been read; (*sl.*) he's as good as dead. ~**gâh**, open space devoted to prayer.

namdar (‒·¹) Famous, celebrated.

name (‒¹) Letter; love-letter; document; *used in compounds for any written agreement or document, e.g.* kanunname, code of laws; nizamname, regulations; sulhname, treaty of peace.

namerd (‒¹) Unmanly; cruel; cowardly; vile. Vile, despicable person. ~**e muhtac olm.**, to be obliged to ask help from one whom one despises : ~**e muhtac olmamak**, to depend on no one for one's living, to be under obligation to no one. ~**ce**, cowardly; unmanly; contemptible. ~**lik**, cruelty; cowardice; vileness.

nameri (‒·¹) Invisible.

namer'i (‒·¹) Not observed; not in force; obsolete.

nami (‒¹) Germinating, growing. ~**ye** *or* kuvvei ~, the vegetative force.

namizac (‒·¹) Indisposed; ill.

namkör *v.* nankör.

namlı Renowned, famous.

namlu Barrel (of a gun); blade (of a sword). ~ matkabı, D-bit.

namurad (‒·¹) Dissatisfied; disappointed.

namus (‒⁴) Honour; good name; rectitude, honesty. ~**una dokunmak**, to affect one's honour; to hurt one's pride: eshabı ~, honourable men. ~**kâr**, ~**lu**, honourable; honest, upright. ~**suz**, without honour; shameless; dishonest.

namüsaid (‒·‒¹) Unfavourable.

namütenahi (‒··‒¹) Unending; infinite.

namzed Nominated, designated; betrothed. Candidate; betrothed person; military cadet. ~**lik**, candidature.

nan Bread; livelihood. ~**ı aziz**, one's daily bread : ~**ü nemek**, bread and salt, hospitality; gratitude for hospitality : ~**ü nimet**, benevolence, generosity.

nane (‒¹) Mint; peppermint. ~ **yemek**, to commit a blunder; to say stg. silly : ⌐bak yediği ~ !⌐, what a silly thing to say (do)!

nanemolla (‒¹··) A timid and useless fop.

nanik Long nose, snook. ~ **yapmak**, to cock a snook.

nankör Ungrateful. ~**luk**, ingratitude.

nanpare (·‒¹) A piece of bread; livelihood. ~**ye muhtac olm.**, to be destitute.

napak (‒¹) Unclean; foul.

nar Pomegranate.

nâr (‒) Fire; hell-fire; pain, injury. ~**ı beyza**, white heat : ~**a yakmak**, to injure : birinin ~**ına yanmak**, to suffer for another's misdeeds : başı ~**a yandı**, he has burnt his fingers : ehli ~, the damned.

nara (‒¹) Cry, shout. ~ **atmak**, to yell at the top of the voice.

narcıl Coconut.

nardenk Syrup made of pomegranate or damson juice.

narenc (‒¹) Orange. ~**iye**, the Citrus family.

nareva (‒·¹) Undeserved; unjust.

nargile Water-pipe, hookah, narghile.

narh Price officially fixed.

nârıbeyza (‒··¹) White heat, incandescence.

narî (‒¹) Pertaining to fire. eslihai ~**ye**, firearms.

narin (‒¹) Slim, slender; tender; delicate.

nark, ‒kı *v.* narh.

nas, ‒ssı A text of the Koran giving a decisive ruling on a point of canon law. ~**sı kat'i**, dogma; incontrovertible proof.

nâs (‒) People, men; mankind; the public.

nasaz (‒¹) Discordant; improper; not in order; untoward.

nasb Nomination; appointment. ~**etmek** (¹··), ‒**eder**, to nominate, appoint.

naseza (‒·¹) Unseemly.

nâsıh (−¹) Adviser, counsellor.

nasıl (¹·) How?; what sort?; whatever sort. ~sınız?, how are you?: ~sa, in any case; somehow or other: her ~sa, in whatever way; somehow or other: ~ ki, just as; as a matter of fact; ~ ki kimse ona ehemmiyet vermiyorsa o da başkalarına aldırış etmiyordu, just as nobody attached any importance to him, so he took no notice of others: hem de ~!, *emphasizes what has gone before, e.g.* çocuk isterdim ... hem de ~ !, I longed for a child—oh! how I longed!; şimdi nezle oldum ... hem de ~ !, now I've got a cold, and what a cold!

nasır Wart; corn; callosity. ~lanmak, to get warts *or* corns; to become calloused *or* callous. ~lı, warty; with corns; calloused; callous.

nâsır (−¹) Who helps.

nasıye (−·¹) Forehead. ~i hal, the first appearance of a situation: ~de mestur olan, written on the forehead (by the finger of destiny): ⌜kaç ~ vardır çıkacak pâkü dırahşan?⌝, 'how many men are really honest?'

nasib (·⁴) Lot, share, portion; one's lot in life. ~ almak, to be initiated *into a dervish order*: ···den ~ almak, to enjoy: ... ~im olmadı, ... did not fall to my lot; it was not vouchsafed to me to ...: ~ olursa, if destiny should will it: insanlıktan ~i yok, there is nothing human about him.

nasibedar (·−·¹) Who enjoys; to whose lot *a thing* has fallen.

nâsih (−¹) Effacing, cancelling; who copies.

nasihat (·−¹), **−ti** Advice; admonition. ~ etm., to advise: birinin ~ini tutmak, to follow s.o.'s advice.

nasir (−¹) Prose-writer.

nasiye *v.* nasıye.

nasrani (·−¹) Christian.

Nasreddin Hoca *The semi-mythical hero of countless Turkish humorous stories.* ⌜~ ~ türbesi gibi⌝, 'like N.H.'s tomb', *which was surrounded by an iron railing, the gate of which was locked with a heavy padlock; but some of the railing was missing.*

nassı *v.* nas.

nasuh *In* ~ nusuh tövbesi, never again !

nasut (−¹), **−tu** Humanity; human nature.

naş (−) Bier *or* coffin with a corpse; corpse.

naşad (−¹) Unhappy.

naşenide (−·−¹) Unheard of; original. ~lik, originality.

naşi (−¹) Springing from; originating. ~ olm., to originate: bundan ~, arising out of this, hence.

nâşir (−¹) Spreading, diffusing; divulging. Publisher.

natamam (−·¹) Incomplete.

natık (−¹) Speaking; expressing *or* setting forth. hayvanı ~, the speaking animal, man: hayvanı gayri ~, one of the brute creation. ~a, the faculty of speech; eloquence. ~alı, eloquent.

natır Servant in a women's bath; watchman *of a garden or vineyard.*

natuk (·−¹) Eloquent.

natura (·¹·) Nature; constitution.

natüvan (−·¹) Weak.

navlun Sum paid for chartering a ship; freight. ~ mukavelesi, charter-party.

nay, nayzen *v.* ney, neyzen.

naz Mincing air; coquetry; coyness; whims; disdain; smirking; endearments. ~ etm., ~yapmak *or* ~a çekmek, to show coyness *about doing stg.*; to pretend not to be keen *about stg. when one really is*: ~ını* çekmek, to tolerate s.o., to put up with his peculiarities: ~ı* geçmek, for one's whims to be tolerated; to be a 'persona grata': ~u nimet içinde büyümek, to grow up amid fondlings and favours; to be spoilt: ⌜bu ne ~?⌝, why this coyness?; why so reluctant?: ⌜çok ~ âşık usandırır⌝, excessive coyness anoys the lover; 'oh well! if you don't want to, don't!'

nazar Look; regard; consideration; the evil eye. ~ımda, in my view, as for me: ~ında, according to him, in his view: ~a atmak, to take into account: ~ atmak (atfetmek), to glance (at = *dat.*): ... ~iyle bakmak, to regard as ...: ~ boncuğu, bead worn to avert the evil eye: birisine ~ı değmek, to overlook s.o., to cause illness *etc.* by the evil eye: çocuğa ~ değdi *or* çocuk ~a geldi, the evil eye has been cast upon the child, he has been overlooked: ···in ~ı dikkatini celbetmek, to attract the attention of: ~dan düşmek, to fall from favour: ~ı itibara almak, to take into consideration: ~da olm., to be in favour: sarfı ~ etm., to give up, to renounce.

nazaran (¹··) (*with dat.*) According to; in respect of, with regard to; in proportion to; seeing that.

nazare *In* ~ye almak, to make fun of.

nazari (··¹) Theoretical; visual. ~yat (···⁴), **−tı**, *pl. of* nazariye. ~yatçı, theorist. ~ye (···¹), theory.

nazarlık Charm against the evil eye.

nazenin (−·¹), **nazende** Graceful; delicate; amiable, nice; petted, spoilt; (*sarcastically*) whippersnapper.

nazım (·¹), **−zmı** Versification, verse.

nâzım (−¹) Regulator (*mech.*); who arranges; versifier.

nazır (−¹) Who watches; overlooking, facing. Minister; spectator. **denize** ~, overlooking the sea: **Hariciye** ~ı, Minister for Foreign Affairs: hazır ve ~, all-present and all-seeing (*an attribute of the Almighty*). ~lık, Ministry.

nazif (·⸋) Clean; neat.

nazik (–⸌) Delicate; agreeable; polished, refined, courteous. ~**lik**, delicacy; refinement; polished manner; courtesy.

nazil (–⸌) Descending; alighting. ~ **olm.**, to descend, alight.

nazir (·⸋) Anything opposite *or* parallel; match, like. ~**e** (·–⸌), a similar thing; a poem written to resemble another poem in form and subject.

nazlanmak *vn.* Behave coquettishly; be coy; show contempt or disdain; feign reluctance; behave in an affected manner.

nazlı Coquettish; coy; wayward; petted, spoilt; reluctant; ticklish (job *etc.*).

nazm·en (⸌·) In verse. ~**ı**, *v.* nazım.

ne[1] ~ ... ~ ..., neither ... nor ... .

ne[2] What?; what; whatever; how. ~**den**, for what reason?, why?: ~**ye**, what for?, why?: ~**yin nesi?**, *lit.* what relation to who?, *i.e.* who on earth is that person?: **o adam sizin** ~**niz?**, what relation to you is that man?: ~**yleyim** *etc. v.* neyleyim: ~ **de olsa**, still; all the same; after all: ~ **demek?**, what does it mean?; *v.* demek: ~**ler gördüm!**, what didn't I see!; I saw all sorts of things: ~ **güzel!**, how nice!: ~ **ise!**, fortunately; well never mind; anyway: ~ ... **ise**, whatever, *e.g.* ~ **işitse inanır**, he believes whatever he hears: ~**me lâzım**, *v.* lâzım: ~ **olur** ~ **olmaz**, just in case: ~**den sonra**, shortly afterwards: ~ **vakit (zaman)?**, when?: ~ **var** ~ **yok?**, what's the news?, how are things getting on?: **bu** ~ **hal!**, what's all this?: **hususî tren** ~**sine*?**, who is *he* to have a special train?

nebat (·⸋), –**tı** Vegetation; plant (*pl.* ~**at**; ilmi ~, botany; ~ **bağçesi**, botanical garden). ~**î** (·–⸌), vegetable; botanical.

nebbaş Despoiler of graves.

nebevî (··⸋) Pertaining to a prophet; prophetic.

nebi (·⸋) Prophet. ˹**bazıları** ~ **bazıları veli dediler**˼, it's not quite certain what is meant.

nebil Noble and talented.

nebiz (·⸋) Treacle of date juice; date wine.

nebze Particle; bit. **bir** ~, a little bit.

necabet (·–⸌), –**ti** Nobility. ~**li**, noble.

necah Success; victory.

necaset (·–⸌), –**ti** Impurity, canonical uncleanness; excrement.

Necaşi (·–⸌) Negus; Emperor of Abyssinia.

necat (·⸋), –**tı** Salvation; safety. ~ **bulmak**, to escape.

nece (⸌·) In what language?

Necef Nejef. ~ **taşı**, rock-crystal.

neci Of what trade? ~**dir?**, what is his trade?, what does he do?

necib Noble, of high lineage.

Necid, ~**cdi** Nejd.

necim, –**cmi** Star.

necis Impure, unclean. Dirt; excrement.

nedamet (·–⸌), –**ti** Regret; remorse. ~ **etm.**, (getirmek), to regret.

nedbe Scar; cicatrice.

nedense (·⸋·) ~ **or her** ~, somehow or other; for some reason or other.

nedim (·⸋) Boon companion; courtier; court buffoon. ~**e** (·–⸌), Lady of the Court.

nedret, –**ti** Rarity.

nefais (·–⸌) *pl. of* nefise. Rare and exquisite things.

nefaset (·–⸌), –**ti** A being exquisite, beautiful *or* rare.

nefer Individual; person; private soldier.

nefes Breath; moment; spell. ~ **aldırmamak**, to give no rest, not to give any respite: ~ **almak**, to breathe, to take a breath; to breathe freely again: ~ **çekmek**, (i) to take a whiff (of tobacco *etc.*); (ii) to smoke hashish: ~ **darlığı**, asthma: ~ **etm.**, to cure by breathing on s. o. and casting a spell: ~ ~**e olm.**, to be out of breath: ~**i*** **tutulmak**, to be unable to breathe; to have an attack of asthma: ~ **tüketmek**, to talk oneself hoarse: ~ **vermek**, to breathe out: **geniş** ~ **almak**, to breathe freely again.

nefes·darlığı, –**nı**, asthma. ~**lenmek**, to breathe; take a short rest; breathe again (with relief). ~**lik**, ventilator; vent-hole; the time passed in taking a breath: **bir** ~ **canı kalmış**, he's quite worn out; he looks wretched.

nefh·a Puff; breath; blast *of a trumpet*; distention, puffiness. ~**etmek** (⸌··), –**eder**, to blow; to blow out. ~**i**, *v.* nefih.

nefi, –**f'i** Advantage; profit. **nef'ine**, to one's own advantage: ~ **hazine**, the maxim that the first consideration in official matters must be the Public Purse.

nefih, –**fhi** A blowing (of the wind or of a trumpet); a (smell) diffusing itself.

nefir (·⸋) Trumpet, horn; tube (*med.*). ~**iâm** (···⸌), a mass rising of the people; 'levée en masse'. ~**zen**, trumpeter.

nefis, –**fsi** Soul; life; self; essence; concupiscence; seminal fluid. **nefsine**, in himself (itself): **nefsi Londra**, London proper (*i.e. not its suburbs*): **nefsini* beğenmek**, to think a lot of oneself: **nefsine düşkün**, self-indulgent: **nefsi emare**, concupiscence: **nefsine* mağlûb olm.**, to be overcome by one's desires: **nefsine* yedirememek**, to be unable to bring oneself *to do stg.*: **nefsini* yenmek**, to master oneself. ~**perest**, selfish.

nefîs (·⸋) Excellent; exquisite; rare.

sanayii ~e, the fine arts. ~e (·–¹), an exquisite or beautiful object.

nefiy, –fyi Banishment; exile; negation. ~ edatı, the negative particle.

nefret, –ti Disgust; loathing. ···den ~ etm., to detest, to feel an aversion for.

nefrin (·–¹) Curse, imprecation; horror.

nefrit, –ti Nephritis.

nefsan·î (·–¹) Sensual, carnal; rancorous, malignant. şehvatı ~iye, carnal lusts. ~iyet, –ti, sensuality; spite. ~iyetçi, one who bears malice, a spiteful man. ~iyetli, spiteful.

nefsî· (·–¹) Pertaining to the soul *or* to self; sensual. ~i, v. nefis. ~ülemirde, in essence; in reality.

neft, –ti Naphtha. ~î, of a dark brownish-green colour. ~yağı (¹··), –nı, naphtha oil.

nefy·etmek (¹···), –eder va. Banish, exile; deny. ~i, v. nefiy.

nehafet (·–¹), –ti Leanness.

nehale (·–¹) Mat *to put under plates*.

nehar (·⁴) Day; daytime. ~en (·–·), by day. ~i (·–¹), pertaining to the day, diurnal; who is a day pupil, home boarder.

nehib, –hbi *In* nehbü garet, plunder.

nehir, –hri River.

nehiy, –hyi Prohibition; negative imperative. ~ gaib, third person of the negative imperative: ~ hazır, second person of the same.

nehy·etmek (¹··), –eder va. Prohibit. ~i, v. nehiy.

nejat (·⁴), –tı Family; lineage.

nekadar (¹··) How much?; what a lot; however much. ~ olsa, after all.

nekahet (·–¹), –ti Convalescence.

nekais (·–¹) *pl. of* nakisa. Defects.

nekes Mean, stingy. ~lik, stinginess.

Nekir *One of the angels who question men in their graves (the other is* Münker).

nekre, nekregû Who makes odd and witty remarks.

nelik (¹·) The character or nature *of a thing*.

nem Moisture; damp. ~ kapmak, to absorb damp: buluttan ~ kapmak, to see an insult where none is meant, to be unduly touchy or suspicious.

nema (·–¹) Growth, increase; interest on money; profit. ~landırmak, to make profitable.

Nemçe (¹·) Austria; Austrian.

nemelâzımlık *The attitude of one who says* neme lâzım, '*what's that to do with me?*'; indifference, unconcern.

nem·lenmek *vn.* Become damp. ~li, ~nâk, damp, humid.

nemrud Nimrod (*an impious Chaldean king, who cast Abraham into the flames*); cruel;

very obstinate; very contrary; unmanageable. ~luk, cruelty, tyranny; obstinacy: ~luğu* tutmak, to have a fit of obstinacy.

Nemse (¹·) *Old word for* Austria. ~ arpası, pearl barley: ~ böreği, a kind of meat patty.

nerde, nerden v. nerede, nereden *under* nere.

nere (¹·) What place?; what part?; whatsoever place. ~m?, what part of me?: ~n?, what part of you?: burası ~si?, what place is this? ~de (¹··), where?; wherever: ~ ise, before long: ~ kaldı ki ..., how much less ...; let alone that ...: bu ~, o ~ !, there is no comparison between the two. ~den (¹··), from where?; whence?; wheresoever: ~ geldi ?, where did he come from?; *also* ~ geldi !, I wish to goodness he hadn't come !: ~ söyledim!, why on earth did I say that !: ~ nereye, for some reason or other; I don't quite know why. ~deyse (¹····), before long. ~li (¹··), coming from what place?: ~siniz?, where do you hail from? ~ye (¹··), to what place?, whither?; to whatever place: ~ giderse gitsin, let him go where he will; wherever he goes.

nergis Narcissus; the eye of a beauty.

nerh v. narh.

nerm (*In compounds*) Soft, mild. ~i (·–¹), softness, mildness. ~in (·–¹), soft; gentle; mild.

nesayih (·–¹) *pl. of* nasihat. Admonitions.

nesc·etmek (¹··), –eder va. Weave. ~i, v. nesic.

neseb Family; genealogy. ~i sahih olmıyan çocuk, a child of uncertain parentage, illegitimate child. ~en (¹··), by descent; by family. ~î (·–¹), relating to one's family; genealogical.

nesh·etmek (¹··), –eder va. Abolish; abrogate. ~i, v. nesih.

nesic, –sci Weaving; web; tissue.

nesih, –shi Abolition; abrogation; effacement; a kind of Arabic script.

nesil, –sli Descendants; generation; family. ~i münkarız oldu, his race is extinct.

nesim (·–¹) Gentle breeze. ~î (·–¹), atmospheric.

nesir¹, –sri Prose. ~ ci, prose-writer.

nesir², –sri Vulture.

nesnas (·–¹) Anthropoid ape; gorilla.

nesne Thing; anything.

nesr·en (¹·) In prose. ~i, v. nesir.

nesrin (·–¹) The wild rose.

nesturi (·–¹) Nestorian.

neşat, –tı Cheerfulness, gaiety; alacrity. ~lı, in good spirits.

neş'e Slight intoxication; gaiety, merriment; joy. ~si yerinde, he is in good humour. ~lendirmek, to render merry;

put in a good humour; intoxicate slightly.
~**lenmek,** grow merry; become slightly
drunk. ~**li,** merry; in good humour. ~**siz,**
in bad humour; sad.

nes'et, -ti A coming into existence; origin;
adolescence. ~ **etm.,** to originate; to grow
up; to pass out of a school.

neşide A popularly recited poem.

neşir, -şri A spreading broadcast; a publishing; publication; promulgation.

neşr'etmek (ᵕ··), **-eder** va. Spread abroad;
publish; diffuse. ~**iyat, -tı,** publications.

neşter Lancet.

neşve Smell; intoxication; exhilaration.

neşvünema (···ᴗ̱) Growth. ~ **bulmak,** to
grow and flourish.

neta (naut.) Clear; properly stowed; shipshape

netameli Ill-omened; sinister; thing or
person best avoided.

netayic (·–ᵕ) pl. of netice.

netekim, neteki v. nitekim.

netice (·–ᵕ) Consequence; effect; result;
conclusion. ... ~**si,** as the result of ...: ~**i
kelâm,** in short; in conclusion. ~**bahş,**
~**pezir** (·–··ᴗ̱), producing a result.

neuzübillah (·ᴗ̱··) Lit. 'we take refuge
with God'; God help us! ⌐dışardan baktım
bir yeşil türbe, içeri girdim; ~ !¬, 'from the
outside it looked like a saint's tomb, but
oh! my God! the inside!', used when speaking of an institution, the outer appearance of
which belies its true nature.

nev New, recent. ~ **arus,** newly-married
bride.

neva (·ᴗ̱) Tune, melody; means, food, provisions. **soğuk** ~, antipathetic, dour.

nevahi (·–ᴗ̱) pl. of nahiye, q.v.

nevakıs (·–ᵕ) err. pl. of nakisa. Defects.

nevale (·–ᵕ) Portion; food; meal. ~ **düzmek,** to provide food. ~**çin olm.,** to take
a light meal; to get 'pickings' out of stg.
~**lenmek,** to take a taste (of = abl.).

nev'·ama (··ᴗ̱) In a certain manner; to a
certain extent; a kind of; so to speak. ~**an**
(ᵕ·), as to its species or kind; in a way.

nevazil (·–ᵕ) Cold in the head. ~ **olm.,** to
have a cold.

nevbahar Spring.

nevbet v. nöbet.

nevcivan Youth; young man.

nevha Lament; wail for the dead. ~**ger,**
woman who wails for the dead; hired
woman mourner.

nevheves Who shows fresh enthusiasm for
a thing; who starts off on a thing enthusiastically; who has a new desire every
day; frivolous; capricious.

nev'·i, -v'i Species; sort, variety, kind. ~ ~,
of various kinds: ~ **beşer,** the human race:

nev'i şahsına münhasır, of its own kind;
'sui generis': **cins ve** ~, genus and species.
~**'i** (·ᴗ̱), specific.

nevicad (ᵕ··) Newly invented.

nevim, -vmi Sleep.

nev'ima v. nevama.

nevmî (·ᴗ̱) Pertaining to sleep.

nevmid Without hope; in despair. ~**ane**
(···ᵕ), desperate. ~**i** (·–ᵕ), despair, hopelessness.

nevr In ~**i*** **dönmek,** for one's mood to
change; to become moody or angry.

nevralji Neuralgia.

nevruz The Persian New Year's Day (22
March). ~**iye** (··–ᵕ), a kind of sweetmeat
offered as a present on the Persian New Year's
Day. ~**otu, -nu,** toad-flax.

nevzad Newly-born (child).

ney Reed; flute. ~**zen,** flute player.

neyleyim (ᵕ··) etc. for ne eyleyim etc. What
can I do? **neylersiniz?,** what is one to do
about it?

nezafet (·–ᵕ), **-ti** Cleanliness. ~**i fenniye,**
the Hygiene Department.

nezahet (·–ᵕ), **-ti** Purity; cleanness;
decency, decorum.

nezaket (·–ᵕ), **-ti** Delicacy; refinement;
good breeding; a matter requiring delicacy
in its treatment. ~**li,** refined, delicate.

nezamandır (ᵕ···) For a long time past.

nezaret (·–ᵕ), **-ti** Prospect, view; inspection; supervision, superintendence; administration; direction; Ministry. ···**e** ~
etm., to superintend, direct, inspect: Hariciye N~**i,** Ministry of Foreign Affairs.

nezd Vicinity of a person. ~**inizde,** near
you; in your opinion: **hükûmet** ~**inde,** in
the view of the Government; with the
Government; 'auprès du gouvernement'.

nezetmek (ᵕ··), **-eder** va. Tear away;
remove.

nezf·î (·ᴗ̱) Haemorrhagic. ~**i,** v. nezif.

nezi (·ᴗ̱), **-z'i** A pulling or tearing away;
removal. **haleti** ~, the death agony.

nezif, -zfi Haemorrhage. **nezfi dimagî,**
cerebral haemorrhage.

nezih (·ᴗ̱) Pure in life and character; quiet,
pleasant (place).

nezir, -zri A vowing or devoting; vow;
thing vowed.

nezle Cold in the head. ~ **olm.,** to get a
cold in the head.

nezolunmak (ᵕ···) vn. Be removed.

nezretmek (ᵕ··), **-eder** va. Vow; promise
to give (as a vow).

nıkat (.ᴗ̱), **-tı** pl. of nokta. Points.

nıkrıs Gout.

nısab (·ᴗ̱) The minimum income above which
the Moslem tax of **zekât** becomes payable; the
number necessary for a quorum; the proper

condition of a thing. ~ını bulmak, to acquire the proper degree or condition.

nısf·en (¹·) Half; in half. ~ı, v. nısıf.

nısfet, -ti Equity.

nısf·ılleyl Midnight. ~ınnehar, midday; meridian.

nısfıye Small flute.

nısıf, -sfı A half. ~ daire, semicircle : ~ küre, hemisphere : ~ kutur, radius.

nışadır Salammoniac; ammonia.

nışasta (·¹·) Starch.

niam *pl. of* nimet. Benefits *etc.*

nice (¹·) How many!; many a ...; how?; however many; howsoever. ~ adamlar, how many men ...!; many a man : ~ olur?, how will it be?; what will happen? : ⌐~ senelere!⌐, *a formal greeting on feast-days like 'many happy returns of the day!'*

nicelik (¹··) State; quantity.

niçin (¹·) Why?

nida (·⁻) Cry; shout. ~ etm., to shout, proclaim : harfi ~, interjection (*gram.*).

nifak (·⁴), -kı Discord, enmity, strife.

nifas (·⁴) The period of forty days after childbirth; confinement. ~î (·—⁻), puerperal; lochial.

nigâh (·⁴) Glance; look.

nigâr (⁴) Picture; figure; beautiful person.

nigehban (··⁴) Watcher; guardian.

nihaî (·—⁻) Final.

nihal (·⁴), -li Twig; sapling.

nihale v. nehale.

nihan (·¹) Concealed; treasured up. gözden ~ olm., to disappear.

nihavend *A motif in oriental music.*

nihayet (·—¹), -ti End; extremity; extreme. (¹—·) At last; at most. ~ bulmak, to come to an end : ~ derecede, extremely : ···e ~ vermek, to bring to an end, to put an end to. ~siz, endless; infinite; countless. ~ülemir (·⁻····), in the end; at length. ~ünnihaye (·⁻····—·), after all, when all is said and done.

nikâb (·⁴) Veil with two holes for the eyes; mask.

nikâh Betrothal; marriage; marriage portion *paid by the bridegroom to the bride.* [nikâh is the legal and religious ceremony before the düğün, the wedding-party; after nikâh one is legally married, but socially the marriage is not usually regarded as complete until after the düğün; before the düğün the couple are nikâhlı, but afterwards evli]. ~ düşmek, for a marriage to be possible, *i.e. for the parties not to be within the prohibited degrees of relationship* : ~ etm., to betroth, to marry : ~ kıymak *or* akdi ~ etm., to perform the ceremony of marriage : ⌐anasının ~ını istemek⌐, to ask an absurd price for a thing.

nikâh·lanmak, to become betrothed or married. ~lı, betrothed; married (*v.* nikâh). ~sız, unmarried. ~ yaşamak, to live together without being married.

nikbet, -ti Misfortune; disgrace.

nikbin (·⁴) Optimistic. Optimist. ~lik, optimism.

nikel Nickel.

nil Indigo.

nilüfer Water-lily.

nim (–) Half.

nimet (–¹), -ti Blessing; good fortune; benefaction; favour; food (*esp.* bread). ~i ayağiyle tapmek, to spurn a piece of luck. ~şinas (—··¹), grateful.

nimresmî (⁻·—) Semi-official.

nine (¹·) Granny; mummy.

ninni Lullaby.

nirengi (—·⁻) Triangulation. ~ noktası, trigonometrical point; landmark, reference mark, guide mark.

nisa (·⁻) Women; womankind. ~î (·—⁻), pertaining to women; womanish. ~iye (·—·¹), gynaecology.

nisan (–¹) April.

nisb·et, -ti Relation; proportion, ratio; comparison; relationship; spite. ~ine, out of spite; in defiance : ~ etm., to attribute; to compare; to act spitefully : ~ tutmak, to compare : ~ vermek, to say stg. out of spite : imkân ~inde, within the limits of possibility. ~etçi, spiteful; defiant. ~eten (¹··), relatively; in comparison; in proportion; in order to spite, spitefully. ~î (·⁻), proportionate; proportional. ~iyet, -ti, relativity.

nisevî (··⁻) Pertaining to women.

nisv·an (·⁴) Women. ~î (·⁻), pertaining to women. ~iyet, -ti, femininity.

nisyan (·⁴) Forgetfulness; oblivion.

nişadır v. nışadır.

nişan (·⁴) Sign; mark; indication; scar; target; order, decoration; engagement, betrothal; token given on betrothal. ~ almak, to take aim *at* stg. : ~a atmak, to shoot at a target : ~dan dönmek, to break off an engagement (of marriage) : ~ koymak, to make a mark : ···den ~ vermek, to bear a resemblance to : ~ yapmak, to arrange an engagement : ~ yüzüğü, engagement ring : namü ~ı kalmadı, no trace of him remains : meziyet ~ı, Order of Merit.

nişan·cı, marksman. ~e (··¹), sign, mark. ~gâh (··¹), butt, target; backsight (of a gun) : ~ dürbünü, telescopic sight. ~lamak, to sign; to aim at; to become engaged to, betroth. ~lı, engaged to be married.

nişasta (·¹·) Starch.

nitekım (¹··), **niteki** Even as; just as; thus; e.g.; as a matter of fact.

‖nitelik Quality.

niyabet (·–¹), **–ti** An acting as substitute; office and functions of a naib *q.v.* ~i **saltanat**, regency.

niyaz (·⁴) Entreaty, supplication. ~ **etm.**, to ask as a favour, to entreat for: **naz** ~ile **yapmak**, to do *stg.* only after much entreaty. ~**kâr**, ~**mend**, supplicant.

niye Why?

niyet, **–ti** Resolve; intention; formal resolve to perform some religious act. ... ~ **ile**, with the intention of ...: ~**i bozmak**, to change one's mind: ~ **çekmek**, to have one's fortune told *by drawing slips of paper bearing various possible (or impossible) prophecies*: ~ **etm.**, to resolve: ~ **kuyusu**, well at which vows are made: ~ **tutmak**, when consulting a fortune-teller to think of the matter about which you are inquiring.

niyetli, who has an intention; who has resolved to fast: **bu gün** ~yim, I am fasting today.

niza (·⁻¹), **–aı** Quarrel; dispute. ~ **etm.**, to contend, dispute. ~**cı**, contentious, quarrelsome. ~**lı**, about which there is a dispute.

nizam (·⁴) (*pl.* ~at) Order; regularity; law; regulation; system. ~**a koymak** (**getirmek**), to put in order. ~**en** (·⁻·), according to law; legally. ~**î** (·–⁻), legal; regularized. ~**iye** (·–·¹), the Regular Army: ~ **kapısı**, the main entrance to a barracks. ~**lı**, in order; regular; legal. ~**name** (···¹), regulation. ~**sız**, in disorder; irregular; illegal. ~**sızlık**, disorder; irregularity; illegality.

nobran Arrogant; discourteous, churlish, ill-bred.

noelbaba (·¹··) Father Christmas.

nohut Chick-pea. ⌐~ **oda bakla sofa**⌐, *said of a small-roomed house.*

nokat (·⁴), **–tı** *pl. of* nokta.

noksan Deficient; defective; missing. Deficiency, defect, shortcoming. ~ **görmek**, to suffer a falling-off. ~**lık**, deficiency, defect.

nokta Point, dot; spot; speck; full stop; centre punch; dot *in Morse* (*dash* = çizgi); isolated sentry; military *or* police post. ~**i nazar**, point of view: ~**sı** ~**sına**, exactly, in every way. ~**lamak**, to dot, punctuate, mark with a centre punch. ~**lı**, dotted; punctuated.

Norveç (¹·) Norway.

not, **–tu** Note; memorandum; mark (in school). ~**etm.**, to make a note: ~ **tutmak**, to take notes: ···e ~ **vermek**, to give marks to; to pass judgement on; **bu adama fena** ~ **verdim**, I don't think much of this man.

nota (¹·) Note (musical, diplomatic); bill; memorandum; music (book or score).

noter Notary.

nöbet, **–ti** Turn (of duty *etc.*); watch (of a sentry *etc.*); access *of fever*; set performance of a military band. ~**le**, in turn, by turns. ~ **beklemek**, to mount guard; to await one's turn: ~ **çalmak**, (of a band) to play before a sovereign or governor: ~**e çıkmak** (**girmek**), to mount guard; to go on sentry duty: ~ **şekeri**, sugar candy: **bir isteri** ~**i**, an attack of hysterics.

nöbet·çi, on guard; on duty; sentry; watchman: ~ **eczane**, pharmacy whose turn it is to be open at night: ~ **zabiti**, officer of the watch; orderly officer. ~**leşme**, a taking turns; rotation of crops. ~**leşmek**, to take turns; to take turn and turn about.

nufus *v.* nüfus.

Nuh Noah. ~'un **gemisi** *or* sefinesi, Noah's Ark: ~ **nebiden kalma**, antidiluvian: ⌐~ **der peygamber demez**⌐, he is very obstinate: ~ **teknesi**, merrythought.

nuhuset (·–¹), **–ti** A being unlucky; evil omen.

nukra The swelling and hole in the skin made by the warble-fly.

nukre Ingot of silver.

nukud (·⁻) *pl. of* nakıd. Moneys.

nukul (·⁻) *pl. of* nakil. Traditions; narrations; transfers.

nukuş (·⁻) *pl. of* nakış. Designs *etc.*

numara (¹··) Number; marks; trick; performance; item, event (in an entertainment). ~ **on**, full marks: ~ **yapmak**, to play a part, to act: **iyi** (**fena**) ~ **vermek**, to give good (bad) marks *to s.o.*, *i.e.* to think well (ill) of him; **adamı görür görmez** ~**sını verdim**, I sized the man up as soon as I saw him: **o** ~**lar bize geçmez**, it's no good spinning those yarns to me: **tam** ~ **almak**, to get full marks: **100** (**yüz**) ~, W.C.: ~**cı**, tall-talker; charlatan. ~**lı**, numbered.

numune *v.* nümune.

nur (–) Light; brilliance; halo, the spiritual light of saintliness; glory. ~**u âlem**, 'the light of the world', *i.e.* Mohammed: ~**u çeşm** (**dide**), 'light of the eyes', darling: ~ **topu** (**damlası**), a lovely child: ⌐~ **içinde yatsın**!⌐, *said when mentioning a beloved dead one*: ~ **yüzlü**, benevolent looking (old man): **göz** ~**u dökmek**, to try one's eyes with work: **gözümün** ~**u**, my darling: **mezarına** ~ **inmek** (**yağmak**), for a light to descend upon his tomb, *i.e.* to be very holy.

nura (·⁻) Place for storing straw.

nuranî (––⁻), **nurlu** Luminous, shining; majestic; of blessed aspect. ~**yet**, **–ti**, a having a saintly aspect.

nusayri (··॒) Of the Nusayriyye sect (inhabiting North Syria).

nush Advice, admonition.

nusha, nuska (*corr. of* **muska**). Amulet, charm.

nusret, –ti, nusrat Help, *esp.* Divine help; victory.

nuş (–) A drinking; carouse. **~etmek** (¹··), **–eder**, to carouse.

nutfe Seminal fluid.

nutkî (·॒) Pertaining to speech.

nutuk, –tku The faculty of speech; speech; discourse. **nutka gelmek**, to begin to speak: **nutku* tutulmak**, to be tongue-tied, to be confused and silent.

nuzzar (·॒) *pl. of* **nazır**. Ministers *etc.*

nübüvvet, –ti Quality of a prophet; the gift of prophecy.

nücum (·ॱ) *pl. of* **necim**. Stars.

nüdbe A mourner's reciting the virtues of the dead.

nüdema (··॒) *pl. of* **nedim**. Boon companions *etc.*

nüfus (·ॱ) *pl. of* **nefis**. People; souls; inhabitants; *as sing.* person; inhabitant; (*for* ~ **tezkeresi**) identity papers. ~ **cüzdanı** (**kâğıdı**), identity book: ~ **kütüğü**, state register of persons: ~ **memurluğu**, Registry of Births *etc.*: ~ **tahriri** (**sayımı**), census: **beher ~a**, for each inhabitant, per head.

nüfus·ca (·॒·), as regards persons: ~ **zayiat yokmuş**, there was no loss of life. **~lu**, having ... inhabitants: **otuz milyon** ~ **bir devlet**, a country of 30 million inhabitants.

nüfuz (·ॱ) Penetration; permeation; insight; influence. ~ **etm.**, to penetrate; to go into; to influence. ~ **sahibi**, an influential person: **~u nazar sahibi**, a person of insight. **~iyet** (·—·¹), **–ti**, permeability. **~lu**, influential. **~suz**, without influence.

nüha (·॒), **–aı** Marrow. **~işevki** (·—··॒), spinal cord.

nühas (·ॱ) Copper; copper coin. **~î** (·—॒) *a.*, copper.

nüks·etmek (¹··), **–eder** *vn.* (Of a disease) to return and cause a relapse. **~ü**, *v.* **nüküs**.

nükte Subtle point; nicety *of language*; witty remark; epigram. ~ **saçmak**, to make witty remarks. **~ci**, witty; witty person. **~dan**, witty; who appreciates niceties of language or argument. **~li**, witty; subtle (of speech).

nükûl (·ॱ), **–lü** A withdrawing *or* abstaining; withdrawal. ~ **etm.**, to withdraw, retract, recant.

nüküs, –ksü Relapse (in illness).

nümayan (·—॒) Apparent, manifest.

nümayiş (·—¹) Show; pomp; simulation; demonstration (political *etc.*). **~çi**, demonstrator. **~kâr**, who demonstrates or makes a show; who simulates. **~kârane** (·—·—¹), demonstrative (act *etc.*); done to make a show; affected (manner *etc.*).

nümune (—·¹) Sample; pattern; instance, example; model. ~ **çiftliği**, model farm: **~i imtisal**, an example to be followed. **~lik**, pattern, sample; (*sl.*) ridiculous, absurd.

nüsug, –sgü Sap.

nüvaziş (·—¹) A caressing or petting; kind treatment. ~ **etm.**, to caress, to show kindness. **~kâr** (·—·॒), caressing; kindly, attentive.

nüve Focus; centre; nucleus.

nüzul (·ॱ), **–lü** A descending or alighting; apoplexy. **~etm.**, to descend, alight: **ona** ~ **isabet etti**, he had an apoplectic stroke.

O

o¹ That; those. ~ **adam**, that man: ~ **çocuklar**, those children: ~ **bir**, that other one, the other: ~ **bir gün**, the other day, several days ago: **yarın değil** ~ **bir gün**, the day after tomorrow: ~ **bu**, whether this or that: ~ **gün bu gün**, from that day onwards.

o², **–nu** (**onun, ona, ondan**, *pl.* **onlar**). He; she; it.

oba Large nomad tent *in several compartments*; nomad family.

obruk Steep; precipitous; broken (ground). Pit.

obur Gluttonous, greedy. **~luk**, gluttony.

obüs Shell; howitzer.

‖**ocak¹** January.

ocak² Furnace, kiln, hearth, fire-place, oven, range; quarry, mine: bed (garden); fraternity, guild, club; family, dynasty; home. ~ **bucak**, every corner of the house, the whole house: ~ **çekirgesi**, cricket: **ocağı daim yanan**, a family or dynasty that will never die out: ···**in ocağına düşmek**, to seek the protection of; to implore; to be at the mercy of: ~ **kaşı**, stone stand for saucepans *etc.* in front of a fire-place: **ocağı söndü**, his line has died out: ···**in ocağını söndürmek**, to destroy the family of, to ruin: **ev** ~ **kurmak**, to set up house, to start a family: **kömür ocağı**, coal-mine: **yeniçeri ocağı** *or* ~ **halkı**, the Corps of

Janissaries: **Türk Ocağı**, the Turkish Nationalist Club.

ocak·çı, chimney-sweep; stoker; member of the Türk Ocağı. **~çılık**, profession of a chimney-sweep. **~lı**, having a fire-place; belonging to the Türk Ocağı. **~lık**, fireplace; hearth-stone; chimney; (*formerly*) a family estate given by the sovereign; baulk of timber *serving as base for a superstructure*: ~ **demiri**, sheet-anchor.

od Fire; poison; a depilatory. ~ **taşı**, a kind of coarse sandstone: ~ **ocak temin etm.**, to secure a home: ⌐~ **yok ocak yok**⌐, no fire, no hearth', *used to imply great poverty*: **yüreğine*** ~ **düşmek**, to be deeply grieved.

oda Room; office; (*formerly*) Janissary barracks. **ticaret** ~**sı**, Chamber of Commerce: **yatak** ~**sı**, bedroom; **yemek** ~**sı**, dining-room. **~başı** (·¹··), **–nı**, man in charge of the rooms of an inn or caravanserai. **~cı**, man employed to clean and watch the rooms of a public building or an office; servant at an inn.

odalık Concubine; odalisque.

odun Firewood; log; cudgel; stupid coarse fellow. ~ **ağa**, blockhead. **~cu**, woodcutter; seller of firewood. **~luk**, woodshed; forest or tree suitable for cutting for firewood.

of! *Interjection expressing disgust, grief, or annoyance.* **~karmak**, (of an animal) to draw a deep breath or sigh from pain. **~lamak**, to ejaculate 'ugh!': **oflayıp poflamak**, to say 'ugh!' from heat and weariness.

ofsayd Offside (football *etc.*).

oğalamak *va.* Rub and press with the hand; crumble.

Oğan The Almighty.

oğlak Kid.

oğlan Boy; servant; catamite; tongue (carpentry). **kız** ~ **kız**, young virgin. **~cı**, pederast. **~cık**, little boy.

oğlu *v.* **oğul**. *Also in such expressions as*: **yok** ~ **yok**, it simply wasn't there: **varoğlu var**, everything was there.

oğmaç, oğmak¹ Freshly made **tarhana** (curd soup).

oğmak² *va.* Rub and press with the hand; massage; polish.

oğul, –ğlu Son; swarm of bees. **~dan oğla**, from father to son: ~ **arısı**, young bee: **er oğlu er**, a fine man. **~balı** (·¹··), **–nı**, honey from a fresh swarm. **~duruk**, womb. **~luk**, sonship; duty of a son; adopted son. **~otu, –nu**, Lemon verbena.

oğulmak *vn.* Be rubbed, massaged, polished.

oğuşturmak *va.* Rub against each other.

oğuz *Name of a legendary Turkish king;*

name given to that part of the Turkish race inhabiting SW. Asia; robust lad; simple fellow; peasant; good fellow.

oh! *Interjection expressing satisfaction etc.* ~ **olsun!**, serve you right!; I'm so glad! (*malignantly*): ~ **çekmek**, to gloat over another's misfortunes: ~ **demek**, (i) to breathe a sigh of satisfaction; (ii) to rest: ⌐**ah deme düşmanın** ~ **demesin**⌐, 'say not "alas!" lest your enemy say "good!".'

ok, –ku Arrow; pole *of a carriage*; *any long straight piece of wood at right angles to another part.* ⌐~ **yayından fırlamış**⌐, 'the arrow has sped from the bow', *i.e.* the deed is done and can't be undone: **tatar** ~**u**, crossbow. **~çu**, bowman, archer; bow-maker.

okadar *v.* **kadar**.

okka Oke (*a measure of weight* = *400 dirhems* = *2·8 lb.*). ~ **altına gitmek**, to bear the brunt, to be the chief victim: ~ **çekmek**, to weigh heavy: ~ **tutmak**, to be heavy: **kara** ~, the old **okka** *as opposed to the modern use* = *kilogram*: ⌐**nereye gitsen** ~ **dörtyüz dirhem**⌐, men are the same everywhere: ⌐**tam** ~ **dörtyüz dirhem bir adam**⌐, a first-class thoroughly reliable man: **yeni** ~, 1 kilogram.

okka·lı, weighing *so many* okes; heavy, weighty, important: ~ **kahve**, large cup of coffee. **~lık**, an oke of *stg.*

oklava Rolling-pin.

okluk Quiver.

oksijen Oxygen.

okşamak *va.* Caress, fondle; flatter; faintly resemble, remind one of. **zevkini*** ~, to be to one's taste.

okşaş Like, resembling. Resemblance.

okşayış Caress; petting.

oktruva Octroi.

‖**okul** School. **ilk** ~, primary school. **~lu**, who has been to school.

okumak *va.* Read; learn; study; sing; recite; say a prayer; invite; call; exorcize; (*sl.*) curse. **kendi bildiğini** ~, to go one's own way: ···**in canına** ~, to harass, ruin: **düğüne** ~, to invite to a wedding-feast: ···**e lânet** ~, to curse *s.o.*: **masal** ~, to romance: **meydan** ~, to defy, to challenge: **pek** ~, to read aloud; to sing loudly: ···**e rahmet** ~, to pray for the soul of, to bless.

okumamışlık Illiteracy.

okumuş Educated; learned.

okun·aklı Legible. **~mak**, *pass. of* **okumak** *q.v.* Be prayed over *or* exorcized. **okunmuş su**, holy water.

okut·mak *va. caus. of* **okumak**. Cause to read *or* learn; instruct; educate; sell. **başını*** ~, to get oneself exorcized; ⌐**kendini okut!**⌐, go and get yourself exorcized!, *i.e.* you're crazy!: ⌐**gelen gidene rahmet**

okuttu[1], the new-comer caused his predecessor to be blessed, *i.e.*. regretted. **~turmak**, *caus. of* okutmak: cause to be taught; have educated; cause to be sold.

okuyucu Reader; singer; exorcist; one who recites incantations.

okyanus Ocean. **~ya** (··¹·), Oceania.

okyılanı (¹···), **–nı** A small poisonous snake.

ol That. **~ babda**, in that respect; in this connexion.

ola *3rd pers. sing. opt. of* olmak. **~ ki**, it may be *or* happen that: **geçmiş ~**, (i) *said to one who has just been ill or met with an accident*, 'I hope you are all right now' *or* 'I'm glad you're better!'; (ii) 'it's too late, you've missed your chance!'

olabilir Possible; it may be.

olacak *3rd pers. sing. fut. and fut. part. of* olmak. Which may *or* will happen; **~!**, so Fate has willed!: **~ olur**, what is fated will happen: **~ iş değil!**, that's impossible!; it's absurd!: **olacağı nedir?**, what's its lowest price?: **iş olacağına varır**, things must take their course: **o kâtib ~ adam**, that confounded clerk.

olağan That commonly happens; frequent; possible; probable; everyday. ‖**~üstü** (··¹··), extraordinary.

olagelmek (·¹··) *vn.* Happen now and again; happen frequently.

olamak *va.* Remove the suckers of *a vine*.

olan *pres. part. of* olmak. Being; becoming; that which is *or* happens. **~ biten**, event: **~ oldu**, what's done is done; it's too late now!: **insan ~**, a decent fellow, a real man: ⌜**sana ~ olmuş**⌝, 'what's come over you?'; you must be mad *to do or speak thus!*: ⌜**vay bize ~lar!**⌝, how disappointing!; what a nuisance!

olanca (·¹·) Utmost; all possible. **~ kuvvetiyle**, with all his strength.

olarak (·¹·) *gerund of* olmak. Being; *often used to make an adverb from an adjective*, *e.g.* **mevkiî ~**, locally; **kat'î ~ yasak**, definitely forbidden; *other uses can best be shown by examples*: **ilk defa ~**, for the first time; **bunun neticesi ~**, as the result of this; **sarhoş ~**, in a drunken condition.

olası *optative form of* olmak. May it be!; which may be, possible, probable. **gözü kör ~ (olasıca)**, 'may his eye be blind!', 'curse the fellow!': **oldum ~ya**, ever since I can remember.

‖**olay**, Event.

olaydım, olaydı (·¹·) *etc. In such phrases as*: **söylemez olaydım!**, would to God I hadn't said it!; **gelmez olaydı!**, I wish to Heaven he hadn't come!

oldu *3rd pers. sing. perf. of* olmak. olan **~**,

what's done is done; it's too late now!: **~ bitti**, 'fait accompli': ⌜**~ da bitti maşallah!**⌝, 'well, that's done the trick!', *said of stg. done hastily in order to trick s.o. into doing stg. willy-nilly, or of a thing rushed through,* e.g. *of a hasty trial in order to get s.o. executed with a semblance of reality*: ⌜**ne ~ ne olmaz**⌝, just in case: **~ olacak**, 'the inevitable has happened, *or* (*since one has got so far or things have taken this turn*) one may as well ...*, or* it's no use worrying any more about it.

oldukça (·¹·) Rather. **~ zengin**, pretty rich.

oldurmak *va. caus. of* olmak. Cause to be *or* become; cause to ripen; bring to perfection; raise (plants).

olduyse *3rd pers. sing. past cond. of* olmak. *In such phrases as*: **bu işte ne ~ bana oldu**, it is I who have had to bear the brunt; I am the one who suffered most.

olgun Ripe; mature. **~luk**, ripeness; maturity: **~ imtihan**, examination *corresponding to the Higher School Certificate*.

olmadık (¹··) *neg. past part. of* olmak. That has not happened; without precedent; inacceptable. **~ bahaneler ileri sürürek**, putting forward all sorts of pretexts: **~ bir şey değil**, it may well happen; it is not out of the common: **~ olmaz**, anything may happen; nothing is impossible.

olmak, olur [*This verb is so important and its many parts so frequently used in idiomatic ways that these have been largely put under special headings, v.* ola, olacak *etc., etc.*] *vn.* Be; become; happen; be suitable; fit; ripen, mature; be cooked *or* prepared; (*sl.*) get drunk. ···**den ~**, to lose *stg.*; **işinden oldu**, it cost him his job: **~ bitmek**, (*both verbs declined*) to happen, *e.g.* **oldu bitti**, it happened; **olup bitenler**, events; **ne olup bitiyor?**, what is happening?: **bana her şeyi olduğu gibi söyle**, tell me everything as it is, *i.e.* the whole truth: **çocuğu olmuyor**, she can't have a child.

olmamış (¹··) *past part. neg. of* olmak. That did not happen *etc.* Not ripe, immature.

olmasına *In such phrases as*: 'genc **~** genc, amma tembel', 'yes, he's young, it's true, but he's lazy' (*in reply to a question*).

olmaz *3rd pers. sing. aor. neg. of* olmak. That does not happen; impossible; wrong; unsuitable. **~!**, it's impossible; you mustn't do it!: **~ ~**, there is nothing that does not happen, *i.e.* anything may happen: **hiç olmazsa**, at least, at any rate: **ne oldu (olur) ne ~**, just in case.

olmıya (¹··) *In ~* ki ..., beware lest ....

olmıyacak *fut. part. of* olmak. Unlikely; unseemly; unsuitable.

olmıyarak *neg. gerund of* olmak. kendisinde ~, beside himself (with anger, joy, *etc.*).

olmuş *past part. of* olmak. That has happened; completed; ripe, mature. ~ bitmiş iş, 'fait accompli'.

olsa *3rd pers. sing. cond. of* olmak. ~ ~, at the very most; in the last resort; ~ ~ olabilir, the worst that can happen is ...: ⌐~ da olur, olmasa da⌐, it's all the same whatever happens.

olsun *3rd pers. sing. imperative of* olmak. So be it!; even; if only. ~!, all right!, so be it!, I don't mind : ~ ~, at the very most : bir kuruş ~, even a piastre; if only one piastre : iyi saatte ~lar, spirits, the unseen : iş diye ~ , *v.* iş : oh ~ !, *v.* oh.

olta¹ Fishing-line. ~ iğnesi, fish-hook : ~ yemi, bait.

olta² *v.* volta.

oluk Gutter pipe; groove. ~ ~, in streams. ~lu, grooved : ~ kalem, gouge : ~ sac, corrugated iron.

olunmak *vn. As an auxiliary verb with Arabic verbal nouns it forms the passive of verbs, the active forms of which are formed with* etmek, *e.g.* zikrolunmak, *pass. of* zikretmek; tatbik ~, *pass. of* tatbik etmek.

olupbitti (·¹··) 'Fait accompli'.

olur *3rd pers. sing. aor. of* olmak. It is; it becomes *etc.* Possible; it may be; permissible. ~!, all right!; you may do it! : ~mu ~, of course it's possible!; it may happen so; one never knows: ~una bağlamak, to make the best of a matter: ~u ile iktifa etm., to make the best of things: ~ olmaz, any, whatever; anybody; whoever: ~ şey değil!, it's incredible!: bir gün ~ ki, the day will come that ... : hiç ~ mu?, can such a thing be!; can such a thing be done!: işi ~una bırakmak, to leave things to take their own course: ne ~ ne olmaz, just in case.

oluş *verbal noun of* olmak. State *or* manner of being *or* becoming. Nature; condition; event. ~unda, in itself, in reality.

om, oma A rounded prominence (*like the head of a bone*).

omaca Stump of a tree.

omaç *v.* oğmaç.

ombra (¹·) Umber.

omlet, -ti Omelette.

omurga (·¹·) Backbone; keel. iç ~, keelson. ~lı, vertebrate.

omuz Shoulder. ~una almak, to shoulder; to undertake: ···e ~ çevirmek, to give the cold shoulder to: ~ ile öpüşmek, to be almost equal to; to be neck and neck with: ~ silkmek (kaldırmak), to shrug the shoulders: ~da taşımak, to honour, to hold in high esteem: ~ vermek, to push or hold

with the shoulder: ···e ~ vermek, to give *s.o.* a shoulder up: bir lâfa ~ vermemek, to ignore what s.o. says: ~a vurmak, to shoulder: ~ ~a yürümek, to walk shoulder to shoulder.

omuz·başı, -nı, point of the shoulder. ~daş, companion, pal; fellow tulumbacı (*q.v.*) : ~ pantolonu, bell-bottomed trousers. ~lamak, to shoulder, give a shoulder to, assist. ~lu, having *such-and-such* shoulders. ~luk, epaulet; quarter (*naut.*).

on Ten. ~ bir, eleven; ~ iki, twelve, *etc. etc.* : ~ numara, full marks.

ona *dat. of* o. To him, her, it.

onamak *va.* Like; prefer; choose.

onar Ten each; ten at a time.

onarmak *va.* Repair; put in order.

onbaşı (¹··), -nı Corporal.

onbeş (¹·) Fifteen. ~ gün, fortnight.

onca According to him (her); in his (her) opinion; as far as he (she) is concerned.

oncuk *Only in* ~ boncuk, trashy jewellery.

ondabir A tenth.

ondalık A tenth; tithe; ten per cent. ~çı, one who works on a ten per cent. commission.

ondan *abl. of* o. From him, her, it.

ondurmak *va. caus. of* onmak. Cure, heal; improve; better the condition of. ⌐ne öldürür ne ondurur⌐, 'he neither kills nor heals', *said of a rather half-hearted man, who is unwilling to do what is expected of him*.

ongun Flourishing, prosperous.

oniki Twelve. O~ ada, the Dodecanese. ~parmak, duodenum. ~telli, a 12-stringed guitar.

onlar *pl. of* o. They.

onlu Having ten parts. The ten *of a suit of cards*. ~k, of ten parts; worth ten (piastres *etc.*); ten piastre *or* ten para piece.

on·madık (¹··) Not cured; not healed; unfortunate. ~maz, that will not heal. ~mak *vn.*, heal up; mend, improve.

ons Ounce.

onsuz Without him, her, it.

onul·mak *vn.* Be healed; be cured. ~maz, incurable.

onun *gen. of* o. Of him, her, it; his, hers, its. ~la beraber, together with him, her, it; for all that; at the same time.

onuncu Tenth.

onur Dignity; honour; self-respect. ~una* dokunmak, to hurt *a person's* pride. ~lamak, to do honour to.

operatör Surgeon.

or Dyke; earthwork protected by a ditch.

ora (¹·) That place (*only used with suffixes*). ~sı, that place; that affair: ~sı öyle, that is so: ~ları, those places; those circumstances : ⌐~sı sizin, burası benim dolaşmak⌐, to saunter about. ~**da** (ˈ··), there. ~**dan** (ˈ··), from there, thence. ~**ya** (ˈ··), to that place, thither, there.

orak Sickle, reap-hook; harvest. ~**böceği, -ni,** grasshopper. ~**çı,** reaper. ~**lamak,** to reap.

oralı Of that place; native of that place. ~ **olmamak,** to pay no attention; to feign indifference.

‖**oramiral** Vice-admiral.

oran Measure; scale; proportion; symmetry; estimate. ~**lamak,** to measure; estimate; plan; contrive. ~**lı,** proportioned; symmetrical; suitable. ~**sız,** badly proportioned; unsymmetrical; clumsy.

‖**orantı** Ratio.

orası v. **ora.**

oratmak va. Cause to be reaped; clean up, eat up, devour.

oraya (ˈ··) To that place, thither, there.

ordinaryüs (··ˈ·) Senior professor holding a 'chair' in a university.

ordino (ˈ··) Certificate of ownership; delivery order; licence; order.

ordu Army; camp. ~ **kurmak,** to encamp. ~**bozan,** spoil-sport, marplot; varicose veins. ~**gâh,** military camp: **açık** ~, bivouack.

org Organ.

orgeneral (ˈ···) Full general; Army Commander.

orkinos (ˈ··) Large tunny-fish.

orman Forest; wood. ~ **dağ ezmek,** to walk over hill and dale, to walk straight across country : ~ **horozu,** blackcock. ~**cı,** forester; forest-guard. ~**cık,** little wood, copse. ~**lık,** thickly wooded; woodland.

orospu Prostitute, whore.

orostopoğlu (··ˈ··), **-nu** Son of a bitch; scoundrel.

orsa (ˈ·) Direction of the wind as regards a ship's sailing. ~ **alabanda!,** down with the helm !; ~ **alabanda yatmak (eğlendirmek),** to be hove to : ~ **boca etm.,** to tack and veer, to cruise about; to struggle along : ~ **etm.,** to luff : ~**sına seyretmek (gitmek),** to be close-hauled, to hug the wind. ~**lamak,** to hug the wind.

orta Middle; centre; mean; the space around one; the high sea; a regiment of the Janissaries. Middle; central; medium; middling; public. ~**da,** in the middle; in sight; ~**da bir şey yok,** there is nothing to be seen; ~**da bir çok sözler geçti,** many words passed between those present : ~**ya almak,** to put in the middle, to set in the midst : ~**da bırakmak,** to leave in the lurch : ~ **boylu,** of medium height : ~**sını bulmak,** to find a middle course, to come to a compromise : ~**ya çıkmak,** to arise, to

come into being : ~**ya dökülmek,** (of a secret) to be revealed : ~**dan gidermek (kaldırmak),** to remove, to do away with : ~ **hizmetçisi,** housemaid : ~ **işi,** housework : ~**dan kalkmak,** to be removed, to disappear, to be destroyed : ~**dan kaybolmak,** to be lost to view, to disappear : ~**ya koymak,** to produce; to put forward; **canı*** ~**ya koymak,** to stake one's life : ~ **malı,** common to all; common possession : prostitute : **ikisi** ~**sı,** the middle or mean between the two; **ikisi** ~**sı yok,** there is no middle course : **varını* yoğunu*** ~**ya atmak,** to be ready to sacrifice one's all.

orta·çağ, the Middle Ages. ~**elçi,** Minister Plenipotentiary. ~**halli,** of moderate means; moderate.

ortak Partner; associate; accomplice; fellow wife in a polygamous household. ~ **olm.,** to be a partner. ~**laşa,** as a partner; in common. ~**laşmak,** to enter into partnership with one another. ~**lık,** partnership; being a wife in a polygamous family : ⌜**öküz öldü** ~ **ayrıldı**⌝, 'the ox has died, the partnership is dissolved', i.e. the reason which united the two parties no longer exists.

ortalama Medium; average. ~ **bir hesabla,** on an average. ~**k,** to divide in the middle; split the difference; put in the midst; reach the middle.

ortalık One's immediate surroundings; the world around; the face of nature; people, the public. ~ **ağarmak,** for the dawn to break : **ortalığı birbirine katmak,** to make a mess, to turn the place upside down; to cause alarm and confusion : ~ **hizmetçisi,** housemaid : ~ **kararmak,** for night to fall : ~ **karışmak,** for rebellion or disturbances to break out : ~**ta kimse yok,** there is no one about : '~ **pahalılık!',** everything is dear!: ~ **süpürmek,** to sweep up; **gayet iyi** ~ **süpürür,** she is a good housemaid : **ortalığı toplamak,** to tidy up, to put a room straight.

orta·malı v. **orta malı.** ~**mekteb,** secondary school. ~**oyunu, -nu,** the old Turkish theatrical show. ~**zaman** (·ˈ···), the Middle Ages.

ortanca¹ Middle; middling; middle son of three.

ortanca² (·ˈ·), **ortanea, ortansiya** Hydrangea.

ortıkolana Water-rail.

ortodoks Greek Orthodox (Christian).

oruc Fasting; fast. ~ **açmak (bozmak),** to break or violate the fast : ~ **tutmak,** to fast : ~ **yemek,** purposely not to observe the fast : ⌜**gavura (papaza) kızıp** ~ **bozmak**⌝, 'to quarrel with a Christian and break the fast (to spite him)', i.e. ⌜to cut off one's nose to spite one's face[1]. **~lu,** fasting. **~suz,** not fasting.

orun Place; post, employment.

osmanlı Ottoman. **~ca** (··¹·), the Ottoman Turkish language, *i.e.* Turkish before the Revolution (*although of course the Turks of Turkey are still Ottoman Turks !*).

osur·mak *vn.* Break wind, fart. **~uk,** fart.

oş, oşt *Cry used to drive away a dog.*

ot¹ *v.* **od.**

ot², **-tu** Grass; any small plant or herb; weed; fodder. **~ tutunmak,** to remove hair by means of a depilatory.

ot³, **-tu** Ox, bull, buffalo.

otak, otağ Large nomad tent. **otağı hümayun,** the Imperial tent.

otarmak *va.* Pasture.

otel Hotel. **~çi,** hotel-keeper.

otlak Grassland, pasture. **~ lüferi,** medium-sized lüfer, caught in August. **~çı,** sponger. **~iye,** pasture tax; rent on pasture.

otla·mak *vn.* Be out to pasture; graze; lead a bovine existence, vegetate; (*sl.*) sponge. **hala koyduğum yerde otluyor,** he is just where he was; he's made no progress. **~nmak,** be at pasture; be fed off by beasts; be overgrown with grass.

otlubağa (·¹··) Toad.

otluk Pasture; hayrick; hay-barn; priming powder.

oto Motor-car. **~büs,** motor-bus. **~kar,** large motor-car. **~mobil,** motor-car. **~ idare etm.,** *or* **kullanmak,** to drive a car.

oto- Auto-.

oturak Seat; thwart; residence; halting-place; place on which a thing stands (foot, stand, bottom); the posterior; chamber-pot. Seated; resting; halting; sedentary (*as opp. to nomadic*). **~ âlemi,** a drinking-party with dancing women: **yarım ~,** stretcher (in a rowing-boat). **~lı,** well settled; solidly based; sound solid (man); imposing looking (man); suitable, well-chosen, dignified (language).

oturmak *vn.* Sit; sit and enjoy oneself; rest; fit well; (of a ship) to be stranded, to run aground; (of a building) to settle or sink; (of a liquid) to settle. ⌜**otur oturduğun yerde!**⌝ *or* ⌜**otur oturmana bak!**⌝, 'don't meddle!'; 'mind your own business!': **bir pazarlığa ~,** to agree to a bargain: **tahta ~,** to ascend the throne: ···**in üstüne ~,** to appropriate what does not belong to one; to embezzle: ···**in üzerine ~,** not to restore *a borrowed thing,* to stick to *it*: **yerine ~,** to sit down; to fit into its place.

oturtma Set, mounted (gem). A dish of minced meat with vegetables.

oturtmak *va. caus. of* **oturmak.** Cause or

allow to sit *etc.*; seat; place; run *a ship* aground; set, mount (jewel).

oturulmak *impers. of* **oturmak. bu evde oturulmaz,** one can't live in this house.

‖**oturum** Sitting (of a court *etc.*).

oturuşmak *vn.* Become calm *or* pacified.

otuz Thirty. **~ar,** thirty each; thirty at a time. **~luk,** of thirty ...; worth thirty *piastres etc.*; thirty years old. **~uncu,** thirtieth.

ova Grassy plain; meadow. **~lık,** level country, plain.

ovalamak, ovmak *etc. v.* **oğalamak** *etc.*

oy Opinion; ‖vote. **beyaz ~,** vote in favour; **kırmızı ~,** vote against; **yeşil ~,** neutral vote.

oya Pinking; embroidery on the edges of a garment. **~lamak,** to pink *or* embroider, *v.* **oya;** put *s.o.* off to gain time; distract *s.o.*'s attention; make *one* waste one's time; keep *a child* quiet by amusing it. **~landır-mak,** to put *s.o.* off by false promises. **~lanmak,** to loiter; waste time; be put off by frivolous pretexts; distract oneself; do *stg.* to take one's mind off troubles. **~lı,** pinked; embroidered on the edge.

oydu (¹··) It was he.

oygalamak *v.* **oyulgalamak.**

oyluk Thigh.

oylum Excavation; pit; pock-mark. Hollowed out; holed; carved. **~ ~,** (of smoke *etc.*) curling.

oyma Decoration by hollowing out; sculpture, carving, engraving *etc.* **~cı,** sculptor, engraver. **~lı,** carved, sculptured *etc.*

oymak¹ *va.* Excavate; scoop out; engrave; carve; cut out *paper etc.* in decorative designs.

oymak² Subdivision of a people; tribe; troop of boy-scouts.

oynak Playful; frisky; mobile; unstable; flirtatious; loose, having much play, shifting (*mech.*); handy (airplane). **~lık,** playfulness, friskiness; lightness of character, frivolity; looseness, play (*mech.*). **~yeri,** **-ni,** articulation.

oynamak *vn. & va.* Play; move; dance; skip; jump about; be loose, have too much play (*mech.*); palpitate; dawdle; slip (of the ground in a landslide). **oynama!,** don't joke!, be serious! *or* don't dawdle!: **oynıya oynıya,** joyfully: **aklı* ~,** to go off one's head: **içe ~,** to keep losing *in a game*: **yerinden bile oynamıyor,** he does not even budge from his position: **yüreği* ~,** to be startled: **zilsiz ~,** to be overflowing with joy: **yer yerinden oynasa,** if the heavens fall, come what may.

oynanılmak *impers. of* **oynamak. burada oynanılmaz,** no playing here.

oynaş Playfellow; sweetheart, lover. ~**mak,** to play with one another; joke together.

oynatmak *va. caus. of* **oynamak.** Cause to play, dance *etc.*; move; perform (a play); dupe; trifle with. **aklını*** ~, to go off one's head: **at** ~, to be of some account, to have a say in matters: **yüzünü gözünü** ~, to make a wry face.

oysaki Yet; however.

oyuk Hollowed out; gouged out. Hollow part of a thing; grotto, cave; run *of a mole etc.*

oyulga Tacking; sewing loosely together. ~**lamak,** to tack *cloth etc.* together; baste. ~**nmak,** to be tacked: **oyulgana oyulgana gelmek,** to creep up in a toadying and hypocritical manner.

oyum[1] A scooping *or* digging out; pit; hollow; tap-root. ~**lamak,** to take root.

oyum[2] (¹˙) I am he.

oyun Game; play; spectacle; jest; dance. ~ **almak,** to win a game: ~ **etm. (yapmak),** to play a trick, deceive: ~**a gelmek,** to be deceived: ~ **oyuncak,** an easy matter, a mere trifle: ~ **vermek,** to lose a game: **can** ~**u,** a venture where life is at stake.

oyun·baz, playful; deceitful; swindler. ~**bozan,** spoil-sport, kill-joy; quarrelsome; who keeps making fresh difficulties; who goes back on his word at the last minute. ~**cak,** toy, plaything; trifle, easy job; laughing-stock. ~**cu,** player; actor; gambler; dancer; comedian; trickster.

ozan Wandering minstrel.

Ö

öbek Heap; mound; group. ~ ~, scattered groups.

öbür The other. ~**ü,** the other one; that one.

öc Revenge; bet. ···**den** ~ **almak,** to take revenge on; ~**ünü almak,** to avenge: ~ **tutmak,** to lay a wager.

öceşmek, öcüşmek, öcürmek *vn.* Bet with s.o.; pull the merrythought of a fowl with s.o.

öd Gall; bile; courage, 'guts'. ~**ü* kopmak (patlamak),** to be frightened to death.

ödağacı (¹···), **-nı** Aloe wood.

ödek Indemnity; compensation.

öde·mek *va.* Pay; indemnify. ~**şmek,** to pay one another; settle accounts.

‖**ödev** Duty.

ödlek Cowardly.

ödül Reward; prize.

ödünc Loan. ~ **almak,** to borrow: ~ **vermek,** to lend: **deniz** ~**ü,** bottomry.

öf! *Expresses disgust*; 'ugh!'

öfke Anger, rage. ~ **topuklarına çıkmak,** to fly into a rage. ~**ci,** irascible. ~**lenmek,** to grow angry, get into a rage. ~**li,** choleric; hot-headed; impetuous.

öğle, öğlen Noon. ~**den sonra,** afternoon: ~ **yemeği,** the midday meal. ~**yin** (·¹·), at noon, about midday.

öğmek, övmek *va.* Praise; commend.

‖**öğren·ci** Pupil, student. ‖~**im,** education.

öğrenmek *va.* Learn; become accustomed to *or* familiar with.

öğret·ici Apt at teaching; teacher. ‖~**im,** instruction; lessons.

öğretmek *va.* Teach (a thing); suggest; admonish, punish. **söz** ~, to put words into the mouth, to prompt.

‖**öğretmen** Teacher; instructor.

ögü[1] Hole in the ice *to obtain water.*

ögü[2] Great owl.

ögü[3] Obstinacy; perversity.

öğücü, övücü Who praises.

öğün, övün Share; portion; meal. ~**lük,** enough for *so many* meals.

öğüngen, övüngen Boastful, vainglorious.

öğünmek, övünmek *vn.* Praise onself; boast. ~ **olmasın,** without wishing to boast.

öğür, övür Of the same age; broken in, quiet (horse); used to, accustomed to.

öğür·demek *vn.* Retch; sob. ~**mek,** to low, bellow; retch; belch. ~**tmek,** to cause to bellow *etc.*; break in (an animal). ~**tü,** a lowing *or* bellowing; a retching; belch.

öğüş, övüş Praise, commendation.

öğüt Advice. ~**lemek,** to advise.

ogüt·mek, övütmek *va.* Grind; eat heartily. ~**ücü,** that grinds; molar (tooth).

öhö *Expresses contempt or derision.*

ökçe Heel *of a boot.* ~**li,** having heels: **yüksek** ~, high-heeled. ~**siz,** without heels (shoe).

ökse Birdlime. ~**ye basmak,** to fall into a trap. ~**otu** (·¹·˙), **-nu,** mistletoe.

öksemek, öksümek *va.* Long for; miss.

öksü Half-burnt piece of wood.

öksür·mek *vn.* Cough; be at the last gasp. ~**ük,** cough. ~**otu,** coltsfoot.

öksüz Orphan (without mother); without relations or friends; the Piper fish (*Trigla lyra*). ~ **babası,** charitable man: ~ **sevindiren,** a common tawdry thing: **kül** ~, completely orphaned, *i.e.* without father or mother: ⌜~ oğlan kırk yılda bir hırsızlığa çıkmış, ay akşamdan doğmuş⌝, 'an unlucky (*lit.* orphan) boy once in his life set out to steal and the moon rose early', *i.e.* if you are born unlucky there is nothing to be done about it.

öküz Ox; heavy, stupid person. ⌜~ün altında buzağı aramak⌝, 'to search for a calf under an ox', *i.e.* to hunt for stg. in the most unlikely place: ⌜~ü bacaya çıkarmak⌝, to undertake an impossibility: ⌜~ü bıçağın yanına götürmek⌝, to make things unduly difficult: ~ damı, ox-stall, cow-shed. **öküz·gözü, –nü,** leopard's bane, arnica. ~**lük,** a being bovine; dullness, stupidity.

ölçek *A measure of capacity for grain* = ¼ of a kile; measure; scale.

ölçer Poker; fire-rake.

ölç·mek *va.* Measure. ölçüp biçmek (tartmak), to decide after full consideration; to plan carefully: yeri ~, to measure one's length, fall prostrate. ~**ü,** a measure; dimensions; quantity: ~ vermek, to be measured *for a suit of clothes*: ağzının* ~sünü vermek, to put s.o. in his place with a snub or reproof: boyunun* ~sünü almak, to learn one's lesson: göz ~sü, an estimate made by eye. ~**ülü,** temperate, moderate, well-balanced. ~**üm,** the measure of a thing; apprisal, estimate; air, manner: ~ünü bozmak, to alter one's behaviour for the worse: ~ etm., to give oneself airs. ~**üsüz,** unmeasured; unmeasurable; immoderate, excessive. ~**üşmek,** *only in* ···le boy ~, to measure oneself against *s.o.*

öldüresiye With the intention of killing; ruthlessly; to death.

öldür·mek *va. caus. of* ölmek. Kill; kill time; render soft or tender. körünü (nefsini) öldürmez, he will not give way. ~**ücü,** mortal, fatal, deadly.

ölgün Faded; withered; enervated; calm (sea).

ölker Nap, pile; down *on fruit.* ~**siz** şeftalı, nectarine.

öllük Child's diaper.

ölmek, –ür *vn.* Die; fade, wither, lose freshness; suffer great grief or anxiety. ⌜ölür müsün öldürür müsün⌝, *said when very angry with s.o., but unable to do anything about it*: ⌜~ var dönmek yoktur⌝, he has (we *etc.* have) burnt his (our *etc.*) boats.

ölmez He *etc.* does not die. Undying, immortal; hard-wearing, resistant. ~**leştirmek,** to immortalize. ~**oğlu,** hard-wearing, resistant.

ölmüş Dead.

ölü, ölük Dead; feeble, lifeless; faded, withered. Corpse. ~ deniz, swell: yarın

gelmezse ~mü öp!, I'll eat my hat if he doesn't come tomorrow!, *but* oraya gidersen ~mü öp!, I adjure you not to go there.

ölücü Mortal.

ölüm Death. ~ dirim, life-and-death: ~ döşeği, death-bed: ⌜~ün ötesi kolay⌝, the next life will be easy (compared with this one); it's a hard world!: ⌜~ var dirim var⌝, one must be prepared for all eventualities: bu ~lü dünya, this transitory world. ~**lük,** *in such phrases as*: ~, dirimlik, 50 liram var, all I have in the world is 50 liras.

ömür, –mrü Life; existence; enjoyment of life, happiness; age. Odd, amusing. ömrü* oldukça, for the rest of one's life, as long as one lives: ⌜ömrünüz çok olsun!⌝, 'may your life be long', *i.e.* may you be rewarded!: ~ sürmek, to live happily: ömrü yokmuş, said of one who died when very young: ⌜Allah ~ler versin!⌝, 'may God prolong your life' (*an expression of gratitude*): çok ~ adamdır, he's an odd fellow (but one can't help liking him): ne ~ şey!, how wonderful!; how beautiful!: sizlere ~!, may you live!, *euphemism for* 'he is dead'.

ömür·lü, having a ... life; kısa ~, short-lived. ~**süz,** short-lived.

ön Front; space in front; breast, chest; the future. Front; foremost; *as prefix*, fore-, front-. ~**ümde, ~ümüzde, ~lerinde** *etc.*, in front of me, us, them *etc.*: ~ümüzdeki hafta, the coming week: ···in ~ünü almak, to prevent, to avoid: ~ü ardı, the beginning and the end: ···ünü ardını bilmek, to be tactful and considerate; ~ünü ardını düşünmek, to think well before acting, to act circumspectly: ~üne arkasına bakmadan, thoughtlessly, without regard for the consequences: ~üne bak!, look out!, mind!, *or* mind your own business!: ~üne bakmak, to hang one's head: ···in ~üne düşmek, to place oneself at the head or in front of ...; düş ~üme!, come along with me!: ···in ~üne geçmek, to avoid, to take measures against, to combat: ···in ~üne gelmek, to come before ..., to present oneself to ...: ~üne gelene kavga eder, he quarrels with everyone he meets: ···in ~ünü kesmek, to bar the way of, to waylay: ~ünde sonunda, sooner or later: başı ~ünde, quiet, unassuming: göz ~ünde tutmak, not to lose sight of, to take into consideration.

önayak Pioneer; the first to do stg.; promoter; ringleader.

önce A little in front; first: ···den ~, before. ~**den,** beforehand; first of all: ~**leri,** at the beginning; at first; formerly: ilk ~, first of all; in the very first place.

öncü Vanguard.

||önder Leader. ~lik, leadership.

||önem Importance. ~li, important; notable.

||önerge Proposal; motion.

önle·mek va. Resist; face; stop, prevent. ~yici, preventive.

önlü Pertaining to the front. ~ ve arkalı bir sahife, a page written both on the back and the front.

önlük Apron.

||önsöz (¹·) Preface.

önüsıra (·¹··) Before him.

öpmek va. Kiss. ⌐öp babanın elini!⌐, 'well, this is a mess!'; 'what's to be done now?': ⌐öp de başına koy!⌐, 'be thankful for small mercies!': ⌐annemin ölüsünü öpeyim ki⌐, (an oath) 'may my mother die if ...': ⌐ağzını öpeyim!⌐, said to one who has given good news: el etek ~, humbly to beg a favour: gözlerinizden öperim, (in a letter) I send you my love: 'sen bu evi elini öpene beş bin lira satarsın', 'you could sell this house for £5,000 and the buyer would be grateful to you'; 'many would be only too glad to give you £5,000 for it'.

öp·ücük Kiss. ~üş, act or manner of kissing; kiss. ~üşmek, to kiss one another; be reconciled.

ör Fence; artificial barrier.

örçin Rope ladder.

ördek Duck; urinal for use in bed. ~ balığı, striped wrasse. ~başı, greenish-blue.

örek Network of a tissue; build of a wall.

öreke Distaff; midwife's stool.

ören Ruined building.

örf Common usage; extra-judicial civil usage; sovereign right; tyranny, oppression; turban formerly worn by sultans and judges. ~en (¹·), according to common usage; by sovereign right; extra-judicial, arbitrary. ~î, conventional, customary; extra-judicial, arbitrary: kanunu ~, martial law: idarei ~ye, state of siege.

örgü Plaited or knitted thing; plait; tress of hair; rush mat; || tissue.

örgüc v. hörguc.

örme Plaiting; knitting; darning. Plaited; knitted; interwoven; darned; built with mortar.

örmek va. Plait; knit; interlace; darn; build; lay bricks or stones in building.

örnek Specimen, sample; model; pattern. tıpkı örneğini yapmış, he has copied the model exactly. ~lik, model; sample: serving as a model or sample.

örs Anvil.

örselemek va. Handle roughly, misuse; wear out; spoil; rumple; exhaust, weaken.

örtbas A hushing up or concealment. ~ etm., to hush up, to endeavour to conceal some unpleasant fact or defect.

ört·mek va. Cover; wrap; veil; conceal; shut. ~türmek, caus. of örtmek.

örtü Cover; wrap; roof; blanket. masa ~sü, tablecloth: baş ~sü, scarf worn over the head. ~cü, covering, concealing. ~lü, covered; wrapped up; concealed; shut; roofed; obscure (of speech): üstü ~ söz, equivocal, dubious speech; words implying more than they say. ~nmek vn., to cover oneself; to veil oneself: va. to cover oneself with. ~süz, uncovered; open; bare.

örü¹ Upright; standing.

örü² Texture; web; darn; wall, building; barrier, division; enclosed space. ~cü, mender, darner. ~lü, plaited, knitted; enclosed by a wall or hurdles.

örümcek Spider; cobweb. ~ almak, to sweep away cobwebs: ~ kafalı, old-fashioned, incapable of accepting new ideas: ~ kuşu, shrike: ~ tutmak, to be covered with cobwebs: şeytan örümceği, gossamer. ~ağı, ~nı, spider's web; cobweb. ~lenmek, to become covered with cobwebs.

öşür v. üşür.

öte The farther side; what is on the farther side. Other; farther; being farther away or on the other side. ~de, ~ye, over there, farther on: ~si, the rest; what follows; ~si berisi, this side and that; here and there: ~sini beri etm., to look at a matter from all sides; to do all that is possible: ~sine varmak, to surpass, to exceed what is usual: daha ~, farther still: denizin ~si, overseas: bir kaç adım ~si, a few paces away: bundan ~sine karışmam, further than that I am not concerned.

öte·beri (both öte and beri are declined, v. öte), this and that; various things; this side and that side; here and there. ~deberide, here and there: ~denberi (··¹··), from of old; heretofore. ~ki, the other; the farther; farther away: ~ beriki, this one and that, the one and the other. ~yanda, on the other side.

ötleğen Warbler.

ötlegü Lammergeier.

ötlek Cowardly; timid.

ötmek vn. Sing (of birds); resound, echo; crow (of a cock); talk foolishly, chatter. borusu* ~, to have a say in a matter; for one's words to carry weight.

ötre Name of the Arabic vowel sign for 'u'.

öttürmek va. caus. of ötmek. Cause to sing etc.; talk airily; swank. öttürme!, don't talk through your hat!: onun yapacağı yok,

sade öttürüyor, he can't do anything, he's only swanking.
ötürü *(with abl.)* By reason of, on account of.
ötüş Singing (of birds); resonance. **~mek,** (of birds) to sing together; sound together.
övmek, övücü, övünmek *etc. v.* **öğmek** *etc.*
övünc Boasting.
övüş, övütmek *etc. v.* **öğüş** *etc.*
öyle So; in that manner. Such; like that. **~mi?,** is that so? : **~ ya!,** isn't it so! **~ ise, öyleyse,** if so, in that case: **~ bir adam,** such a man: ⌐**~ de battık, böyle de**⌐, we're done for anyhow: **bana ~ geliyor ki,** it seems to me that: **içime ~ geldi ki kafasına vurayım,** I felt like hitting him on the head. **öyle·ce,** in that manner; somewhat so. **~lik,** that manner; such a way: **~le,** in such a manner. **~si,** such. **~yse,** if so, in that case.
öyük¹ Scarecrow.
öyük², höyük Artificial hill; mound.
öyün *v.* **öğün.**
öz Own; real; genuine; essential. Marrow; kernel; essence; pith; cream; self. **~ü sözü bir,** genuine, sincere: **~ türkçe,** pure Turkish: **az konuştu fakat ~ konuştu,** he spoke little but to the point: ⌐**açık ~ tok söz**⌐, sincerely and frankly: **sözü ~üne uymak,** to be sincere; to be consistent: ⌐**az olsun ~ olsun**⌐, it's not the quantity but the quality that matters.
Özbek The Uzbek tribe *of Central Asia.*
özbeöz (ˡ··) Essentially. Real, true.
özdek Stem, trunk; matter.
özden Ear-ring; pendant.

‖**özel** Personal; private; special. **~ ad,** proper name. **~lik,** peculiarity.
özen Pains; a taking pains. **~ bezen,** trinkets, ornaments; ceremony; ruse: **~e bezene,** painstaking, with particular care.
özengi *v.* **üzengi.**
özen·mek *vn.* Take pains, be painstaking, try hard; *(with dat.)* take pains about *stg.*; desire ardently; try to imitate *others*; have a passing fancy *to do stg.* : **özenip bezenmek,** to go to great trouble, take great pains. **~siz,** careless; not elaborate; superficial. **~ti,** aping; pseudo-, counterfeit; mock; swanking: **~ şair,** a pseudo poet.
özge Other; another; different; peculiar, uncommon; stranger.
özle·mek *va.* Wish for; long for. **~nmek¹,** *pass. of* özlemek.
özlenmek², özleşmek *vn.* Become of a pasty consistency; acquire pith, kernel *etc.*
özleştirmek *va.* Purify (a language); render authentic and unadulterated.
özleyiş Longing; home-sickness.
özlü Having a kernel, pith *etc. v.* öz; sappy, pulpy; of a sticky *or* pasty consistency; pithy, terse; substantial; fertile. **~ toprak,** potter's clay.
özlük Egoism; selfishness; pride; essence; pith; substance of a thing; stickiness.
özür, ~zrü Defect; impediment; apology, pardon. **~ dilemek,** to ask pardon: **özrü meşru,** a legitimate excuse: ⌐**özrü kabahatından büyük**⌐, his excuse is worse than his fault. **~lü,** defective; having an excuse. **~süz pürüzsüz,** free from any defect.

P

pa (–) Foot; leg.
pabuç, papuç Shoe; slipper; tag (of an electric wire). ⌐**pabucumu alırsın!**⌐, 'nothing doing!': **~tan aşağı,** contemptible: ···**in ayağının papucu olmamak,** not to be fit to hold a candle to ... : ⌐**pabucu başına* giydirmek**⌐, to make *s.o.* do the wrong thing: ⌐···**e ~ bırakmamak**⌐, not to be intimidated by ... : **~larını çevirmek,** to give *s.o.* a hint that it is time he went: ⌐**pabucu dama atılmak**⌐, to fall into discredit: ···**in ~larını eline vermek,** to send *s.o.* away; to give the sack *to s.o.*: **~ eskitmek (paralamak),** to display great energy in following up a matter: **~suz kaçmak,** to flee in haste; to be very frightened: ⌐**~ kader dili var**⌐, 'his tongue is as long as a shoe's', *said of one who*

answers back rudely: ⌐**~ pahalı**⌐, *(on recognizing that s.o. is too much for one)* 'time to quit', 'time to throw up the sponge!': ⌐···**e pabucunu ters giydirmek**⌐, (i) to teach *s.o.* a lesson; (ii) to play a trick on *s.o.*; (iii) to cause *s.o.* to escape hurriedly: ⌐**iki ayağı bir ~ta**⌐, hustled, perplexed: ⌐···**in iki ayağını* bir pabuca sokmak**⌐, to hustle or confuse *s.o.*: ⌐**sen kendini pabucu büyüğe okut!**⌐, 'get yourself exorcized by one with big shoes (a hodja)!', *i.e.* you must be crazy *to do such a thing!*
pabuççu Shoemaker; attendant who looks after people's shoes in a public building. **~ kölesi,** a shoemaker's iron last.
paça Sheep's or pig's trotters; dish made from trotters; lower part of the leg; lower part of the trouser leg. **~sını çekecek hali olmamak,** to be hopelessly clumsy and

incapable: ~sı düşük, slovenly, untidy: ~ günü, the day after a wedding *when a dish of trotters is eaten*: ~sını kurtarmak, to escape: ~ları sıvamak, to tuck up one's trousers; to 'roll up one's sleeves', to get down to a job; ⌐çayı görmeden ~ları sıvamak¬, to tuck up one's trousers (and prepare to cool one's legs) before seeing a stream, *i.e.* to count one's chickens before they are hatched; *also* 'there's many a slip 'twixt the cup and the lip': baş ~sı, jelly made of sheep's head: yaka ~ götürmek, to collar s.o. and take him away: yaka ~ olm., to be in a confused scuffle.

paçal The proportion of various grains legally permitted in bread.

paçalı Having trouser legs; made of trotter jelly; (fowl *etc.*) having feathered legs. **dar ~,** having narrow trousers.

paçarız Crosswise; intricate. **~ düşmek,** to fall foul of a thing and get entangled in it.

paçavra (·¹·) Rag; miserable rag (of a newspaper). **~ etm.** *or* **~ya çevirmek,** to botch, to make a mess of *stg.*: **~ hastalığı,** influenza. **~cı,** ragman.

paçuz, paçoz Small grey mullet; (*sl.*) prostitute.

padavra (·¹·) Shingle; thin board *used under tiles.* **~ gibi** *or* **~sı çıkmış,** so thin that his ribs show.

padişah Ruler, sovereign, *esp.* the Sultan of Turkey. **~lık,** Sultanate.

pafta (¹·) Metal decoration on horses' harness; screw-plate; each section of a large map; large coloured spot. **~ ~,** decorated with metal plates; covered with spots: **~ kolu,** die stock: **~ lokması,** screw-die.

pağurya Crab.

pah Bevel. **~lamak,** to bevel.

paha, baha Price. **~ biçilmez,** priceless: **~ya çıkarmak,** to raise in price: **~ya çıkmak,** to rise in price: **~dan düşmek,** to fall in price: her ne **~sına olursa olsun,** at whatever cost: yok **~sına,** for a mere nothing. **~cı,** who sells at a high price. **~lanmak,** to become dear. **~lı,** dear, high-priced: **~ya oturmak,** to be very expensive.

pahıl Uncharitable; disobliging; dog-in-the-manger.

pak (–) Clean, pure, untarnished; holy. pirü **~,** spotlessly clean.

paket, –ti Packet; parcel. **~lemek,** to make into a parcel; pack up.

pak·lamak *va.* Clean; clear *of an accusation,* acquit; take away; use up; kill. **~lık,** purity, cleanliness

pakt, –tı Pact.

pala Scimitar; blade of an oar *or* similarly shaped thing, paddle; thin wide plank set on edge. **~ çalmak,** to brandish a scimitar; to swagger about; to strive; kırk yıllık **~ çalmış kalem,** the pen I have wielded for forty years. **~bıyık,** large curved moustache.

palaçka Loot.

palalık Edge of a rafter. **palalığına koymak,** to set up on edge.

palamar Hawser. **~ı çözmek (koparmak),** to slip the cable; to make off. **~gözü, –nü,** hawse-hole.

palamut¹ The Short-finned Tunny *or* Pelamid (*Pelamys Sarda*).

palamut² Valonia (dried acorns of *Quercus aegilops*).

palan Broad soft saddle without frame.

palandız Stone in which the tap of a public fountain is fixed.

palanga, palanko (·¹·) Tackle, pulley-block.

palanka (·¹·) Redoubt of a fortress.

palas Coarse textile; rag.

palaska (·¹·) Cartridge-belt; bandolier.

palas pandıras Hastily; abruptly; brusquely.

palaspare (··–¹) Rags.

palavra (·¹·) Main-deck; idle talk, boast. **~cı,** braggart, boasting.

palaz Duckling, gosling *etc.* Fat. **~lamak,** to grow plump; (of a child) to grow up; to become noticeably better off.

paldım Crupper.

paldırküldür (·¹··) With great noise.

palet, –ti (*Fr. palette*) Mat; palette; articulated track of a caterpillar vehicle. **~li,** tracked (vehicle).

palikarya (··¹·) Greek youth; Greek rowdy.

palto (¹·) Overcoat.

palûze (––¹) *A kind of blancmange or jelly made of starch and sugar.*

palyaço (·¹·) Harlequin; buffoon.

palyos Short sword; dagger.

pamuk Cotton. **~ atmak,** to card cotton; **~ gibi atmak,** to throw into utter confusion. **~ balı,** white honey: **~ balığı,** Blue shark: **~ barutu,** guncotton: **~ ipliği,** cotton thread; **~ ipliğile bağlamak,** to make a temporary or unsatisfactory arrangement: kulaktan pamuğunu çıkarmak, to become attentive; to listen to advice.

pamuk·akı (··¹·), *a kind of* cotton thread *used for embroidery.* **~çuk,** aphtha, thrush (*med.*). **~lu,** of cotton; wadded.

pan (*Fr. panne*) Breakdown (of a car).

panayır Fair.

pancar Beet. **~ kesilmek,** to turn red in the face.

pancur Outside shutter, *esp.* slatted shutter.

pandantif Pendant (necklace).

pandispanya (··¹·) *A kind of cake resembling Bath Bun.*

pandomima (··¹·) Pantomime.

pansiyon Pension, boarding-house.

pantolon Trousers.

pantufla (·¹·) Felt slipper.

panya (¹·) Stern painter of a boat.

panzehir Antidote.

Papa (¹·) Pope. **~lık,** papacy.

papağan Parrot.

papak High Persian lambskin cap.

papara (·¹·) Cheese soup; any insipid thing. **~ yemek,** to get a severe scolding.

papatya (·¹·) Camomile; daisy.

papaz Priest; monk; king (cards). **~a dönmüş,** in need of a hair-cut: **~ kaçtı (üçtü),** *a kind of card game*: ⌐**a kızıp perhiz bozmak**⌐, 'to get angry with the priest and break one's fast', *i.e.* to ⌐cut off one's nose to spite one's face⌐: **~ uçurmak,** to have a drinking party: **~ yahnisi,** fish or meat stewed with vegetables: ⌐**her gün ~ pilav yemez**⌐, you can't expect a good thing to go on for ever; one mustn't take things for granted. **~lık,** office and duties of a priest, priesthood.

papazi (·—¹) A kind of gauze.

papel (*sl.*) A Turkish pound note. **~ci,** cardsharper.

papiyon (*Fr. papillon*) Bow-tie. **~ somunu,** winged nut: **~ vidası,** thumb screw.

papuç v. pabuç.

papura (·¹·) Heavy plough *drawn by two yoke of oxen.*

papye·büvar (*Fr. papier buvard*) Blotting-paper. **~kuşe** (*Fr. papier couché*), surface-coated paper, art paper.

para Money; a para (the fortieth part of a piastre). **~ bozmak,** to change money: **~ çekmek,** (i) to withdraw money *from a bank etc.*; (ii) to squeeze money *out of s.o.*; **~ ~yı çeker,** money breeds money: **~dan çıkmak,** to be obliged to spend money: **~ ile değil,** very cheap: **~ etm.,** to be worth stg.: **~ etmemek,** to be worthless; to be in vain, to have no effect: **para farkı,** rate of exchange: ⌐**~na geçer hükmün**⌐, 'your jurisdiction goes with your money', *said to one who has been paid for stg. but still wishes to concern himself with it*: **~yı sokağa atmak,** to throw money away: **~ tutmak,** to have money; to save money: **~ yemek,** to spend money on pleasure: ⌐**beş ~ ver şöylet, on ~ ver sustur!**⌐, 'pay him a penny to talk and twopence to hold his tongue', *said of a tiresome talkative man*: **dünyanın ~sı,** a 'mint of money': **kaç**

para?, what's it worth?; what's the use!, it's in vain, it's too late.

paraçol A one-horse light carriage without springs; knee *of timber*; bracket.

paradi Paradise; gallery (theatre).

paraf Flourish *at the end of a signature.* **~e etmek,** to initial (agreement *etc.*).

parafin Paraffin wax.

parafudr (*Fr. parafoudre*) Spark-gap arrester.

paragöz(lü) Money-grubber.

parakete (··¹·), **parageta, paragat** Ship's log (instrument); fishing-line with several hooks. **~ hesabı,** dead reckoning.

para·lamak *va.* Tear *or* cut to pieces. **lûgat ~,** to use learned words *in order to show off.* **~lanmak,** to be torn *or* broken to pieces; become rich; strain every nerve; to do everything possible to help s.o. **~latmak,** *caus. of* paralamak.

paralel Parallel. **~ bağlanmış,** shunt (motor *etc*), connected in parallel.

paralı Having money; rich; requiring payment.

paralık Of *so many* paras. **bir ~ etm.,** to vilify, to ruin *s.o.'s* reputation.

paramparça (·¹··) All in bits. **~ etm.,** to tear to pieces, to break to bits.

parantez Parenthesis; inverted commas.

parasız Without money; penniless; gratis. **~ tellal,** one who blazes abroad news that is no concern of his.

parasvana v. prazvana.

paraşol v. paraçol.

paraşüt Parachute. **~çü,** parachutist.

paratoner (*Fr. paratonnerre*) Lightning-conductor.

paravana (··¹·) Folding screen.

parazit Parasite; atmospherics (W/T.).

parça Piece; bit; segment; length *of cloth.* ... **~sı,** *used contemptuously of a person of a certain category, e.g.* **kâtib ~sı,** a very ordinary clerk, some sort of clerk: **~ ~,** in bits, in pieces; by instalments; **~ ~ etm.,** to break *or* tear to pieces; **~ ~ olm.,** to be broken to bits, be torn to pieces: **~ başına,** per piece; piecework: **~ tesiri bomba,** fragmentation bomb: **bir ~,** a bit, a little, a moment: **elmas ~sı,** enchanting (child *etc.*).

parça·cı, seller of piece goods. **~k pur-çak,** in rags and tatters. **~lamak,** to break *or* cut into pieces. **~lanmak,** as paralanmak.

pardı Half-burnt piece of wood.

pare (—¹) Piece. **~ ~,** all in pieces: **101 ~,** salute of 101 guns.

parele (·¹·) Mortise-joint.

parıl ~ ~, very brightly, brilliantly, flashing. **~damak,** to gleam, glitter, twinkle. **~tı,** glitter, gleam, flash.

parke Parquet; small paving stones.

parlak Bright; brilliant; shining; successful, influential. ~lık, brilliance; beauty; influence; ability.

parla·mak vn. Shine; burn and flare up; flare up in anger; acquire influence, become distinguished. va. Fly a falcon at its quarry. ~tmak, caus. of parlamak, to cause to shine etc.; (sl.) to drink. ~yış, brilliance; a shining.

parmak Finger; toe; spoke of a wheel; bar, rod, single piece of a railing etc. (v. parmaklık); peak of a hill; measure = about 1¼ in.; a touch or taste of stg. **parmağı* ağzında kalmak,** to be lost in admiration; to be astounded: **parmağımı basıyorum,** I'll take my oath on it: ~la gösterilmek, to be a person of distinction : ~ hesabı, counting on the fingers; syllabic metre in Turkish poetry: parmağı içinde, he has a finger in the pie: ~ izi, finger-print: ~ kader çocuk, a tiny child: ~ karıştırmak, to meddle: ···e parmağını* koymak, to take a hand in a matter: ···i parmağında* oynatmak, to twist s.o. round one's little finger: ···i parmağına sarmak (dolamak), to have 'bee in one's bonnet' about stg.: ~la sayılmak, to be counted on one's fingers, to be rare: ···e parmağını* sokmak, to meddle with stg.: ~ üzümü, a long kind of grape: ~larını yemek, to find a dish delicious: baş ~, thumb, big toe: ⌐beş ~ bir değil⌐, everyone is different: ⌐on parmağında on kara⌐, said of one who calumniates everyone: ⌐on parmağında on hüner (marifet)⌐, he is very skilful or versatile.

parmak·çı, maker of banisters, spokes etc. ~lamak, to finger; meddle with; stir up, incite. ~lık, railing; balustrade; banisters; grating; grill.

parmıcan Parmesan cheese.

parola (·¹·) Password.

parpa (¹·) Young turbot.

parpar Brightly; gleamingly.

pars Leopard; cheetah.

Pars Persia proper with the province of Tabriz; the province of Shiraz.

parsa (¹·) Collection of money. ~ toplamak, to make a collection, to hand the hat round: ~yı başkası topladı, s.o. else got the benefit: ···den ~ toplamak, to profit by ..., to exploit.

parsal, partal Old, worn clothes. In tatters.

parsel (Fr. parcelle) Plot of land.

parşömen Parchment.

parti Political party; party (social); game, match; consignment of goods. ~yi vurmak, to do a good stroke of business.

parya (¹·) Pariah; outcast.

pas¹ Rust; tarnish, dirt. ~ açmak, to clean off rust; (sl.), to have a drink: ~ tutmak, to rust: buğday ~ı, rust of wheat: dil ~ı, fur on the tongue: kulakların ~ını gidermek, to hear good music after having been deprived of it, v. paslanmak.

pas² Stake (at cards); pass! (at bridge); pass (football).

pasak Dirty and untidy clothes. ~lı, dirty or untidy in dress, slovenly.

pasaparola (···¹·) Verbal command passed along the ranks (mil.).

pasaport, –tu Passport.

pasban v. pazvant.

paskal Comic. Buffoon.

paskalya (·¹·) Easter. ~ yumurtası gibi, very much made-up woman.

pas·lanmak vn. Become rusty; (of the tongue) to be furred. kulakları* ~, not to have heard good music for some time. ~lı, rusty; dirty; pale, faded.

paso (¹·) Pass (on a railway etc.). benden ~!, 'I've had enough of it!'; 'don't count on me!'

paspas Doormat. koko ~, coconut doormat.

pasta (¹·) Sweet cake; pastry; tart; fold, pleat. ~hane (···¹), pastry-shop.

pastal, pastav Bundle of tobacco leaves.

pastırma Preserve of dried salt meat. ~sını* çıkarmak, to give s.o. a good thrashing: balık ~sı, dried or salted fish: domuz ~sı, ham or bacon: ~ yazı, a spell of warm sunny weather early in December.

paşa Pasha (formerly the highest title of Turkish civil and military officials, now reserved for generals). **Paşa eli,** (formerly) European Turkey: ~ kapısı, government office in the provinces. ~lık, title and rank of pasha. ~zade (···¹), son of a pasha.

paşmak Shoe, slipper.

pat¹, –tı Aster; diamond star.

pat² Suddenly. Onom. expressing the noise of a blow with a flat thing.

pat³ Flat; snub (nose).

pata¹ A drawn game; stalemate; deadlock. 'All square'.

pata² Cringle (naut.).

patadak, patadan (¹··) All of a sudden.

patak A whacking. ~lamak, to give a whacking to s.o.; beat a carpet or washing.

patalya (·¹·) Small ship's-boat.

patates (·¹·) Potato.

patavatsız Who talks at random without reflection; tactless.

paten Skate.

patenta (·¹·) Patent; licence; bill of health; letters of naturalization. ~lı, possessing papers of naturalization; having a patent or licence.

patır A tapping sound. ~ ~, *imitates the noise of footsteps*: ~ **kütür**, with the noise of footsteps; noisily. ~**damak**, to make a knocking noise; make the noise of footsteps. ~**dı**, noise; row: ~ **çıkarmak**, to make a row, to cause a commotion: **ayak** ~**sı**, the noise of footsteps; a mere threat; a false alarm. ~**dılı**, noisy; rowdy.

patik Child's shoe.

patika (·⌐·) Foot-path; track.

patinaj ~ **yapmak**, to slip, to skid.

patiska (·⌐·) Cambric.

patka Tufted duck.

patküt (⌐·) Noise of repeated blows.

patlak¹ Explosion; bursting. Burst; torn open. ~ **gözlü**, goggle-eyed: ~ **vermek**, to burst; to burst out (rebellion *etc.*); to be discovered *or* divulged.

patlak² Pallas' sand-grouse.

patla·mak *vn.* Burst; explode; burst open; (of winter *etc.*) to arrive suddenly. **patlama!**, keep calm!; wait a moment!: **beş yüz lira patladı**, it cost 500 lira: **tabanları*** ~, for the feet to become blistered, to be very tired from walking. ~**ngıç**, pop-gun; cracker; paper bag blown up and burst. ~**tmak**, to cause to burst *or* explode: make *s.o.* furious: **kafa** ~, to work very hard (mentally); to rack one's brains to try to understand stg.; to give s.o. a headache by noise or worrying.

patlıcan Aubergine, egg-plant. ⌐~**sız tarafından olsun!**⌐, 'for goodness' sake let's have a change!': ⌐**acı** ~**ı kırağı çalmaz**⌐, the bad one escapes; *or* you can't spoil what is already spoilt: ⌐**ben** ~**ın dalkavuğu değilim**⌐, *said of one who changes his opinions in order to serve his interests*: ⌐**seninki (onunki) can da herkesinki** ~ **mı ?**⌐, 'why should you (he) be the only one ?', 'why should you be treated differently from others ?' ~**giller**, solanaceae.

patra *v.* **çatra**.

patrik Patriarch. ~**hane** (···⌐), Patriarchate (house). ~**lik**, patriarchate, the office of a patriarch.

patron Head *of a firm or business*; model, pattern.

patrona (·⌐·) (*Formerly*) Vice-Admiral.

pattadak *v.* **patadak**.

Pavlina *In* ⌐**kabahat kimde ?** ~**da**⌐, to give an unknown name as that of the culprit in order to escape the blame oneself.

pavurya (·⌐·) Large edible crab. **ayı** ~**sı**, spider crab.

pay¹ Share; lot, portion; reproach, blame; margin, tolerance (*mech.*). ···**den** ~ **biçmek**, to take as an example, to judge or deduce from; ⌐**kendinden** ~ **biç!**⌐, what would *you* do in the circumstances?; put yourself in his place!; ~ **etm.**, to share, to go shares: **ağzının*** ~**ını almak**, to get snubbed in return for an insolent remark: **ağzının*** ~**ını vermek**, to snub s.o. severely, to give s.o. 'what for' for insolence: **bu sözlerin bir kısmını nezaket** ~**ı olarak çıkarsak bile**, even if we discount some of these words as being said merely out of politeness: **ihtiyat** ~**ı bırakmak**, to leave a margin for safety: **kardeş** ~**ı**, equally, half and half: **kedi** ~**ı**, cat's-meat.

pay² Foot. ~**a** ~, completely.

pâyan (−⌐) End, extremity; margin; result. **neş'esine** ~ **yoktu**, his joy was unbounded. ~**sız**, unending; unlimited.

payanda (·⌐·) Prop, support. ···**e** ~ **vermek**, to prop up.

paybend *v.* **payvant**.

paydos *Cry given to workmen to knock off work* (*from the Greek* φάγετος, feeding-time); cessation from work; break, rest. ~ **!**, enough!, pax!: ~**etm.**, to cease work, to knock off.

pâye (−⌐) Grade, rank; degree; dignity. ···**e** ~ **vermek**, to show deference to, to esteem unduly.

payi·dar (··⌐) Firm, stable; enduring. ~**mal**, trodden under foot, oppressed, despised: ~ **etm.**, to trample on; destroy; despise. ~**taht**, −**tı**, (*lit.* the foot of the throne), residence of the sovereign; capital.

pay·lamak *va.* Assign a share *to*; give one his due, scold. ~**laşmak**, to share, divide up; go shares. ~**latmak**, to scold, reprove.

paytak Knock-kneed; bandy-legged. Pawn (chess).

payvant Fetter; hobble.

pazar¹ Sunday.

pazar² Bazaar; market; market-place; bargaining. ~ **etm.**, to bargain: ~ **kesmek**, to conclude a bargain; to settle a price: **can** ~**ı**, situation where life is at stake: ⌐**evdeki** ~ **çarşıya uymaz**⌐, things don't turn out as one expects: 'counting one's chickens before they are hatched'.

pazar·cı, dealer in a market. ~**laşmak**, to bargain, chaffer; settle a price. ~**lık**, bargaining; deal; agreement as to price: **pazarlığını bozmak**, to break one's bargain or agreement: ~**etm.**, to bargain, to do a deal: ~ **uymamak**, for no agreement to be reached in bargaining: **içten** ~, mental reservation. ~**lıklı**, clever at bargaining: **içten (içinden)** ~, cunning, insincere, hypocritical.

pazartesi (·⌐··) Monday.

pazen *v.* **bazen**.

pazı¹ Mountain spinach (?); wild beet (?).

pazı², bazu Arm; muscle; strength. ~**bend**, armlet; amulet worn round the arm.

pazvant Watchman.

peç *v.* beç.

peçe Black veil *worn by Moslem women.* ~li, veiled.

peçeta (·¹·) Peseta.

peçete (·¹·) Napkin.

peçiç *A game in which sea-shells are used in place of dice.*

peçuta, peçota (·¹·) Largest sized bonito (palamut).

pedavra *v.* padavra.

peder Father. ~ane (···—¹), fatherly, paternal. ~şahî (···—⁻¹), patriarchal.

pehlivan Wrestler; hero. yalancı ~, not quite such a fine fellow as he makes out. ~lık, wrestling; bravery.

pehpeh Bravo! ~lemek, to applaud; flatter.

pehriz, perhiz Abstinence; continence; diet (*med.*). ~ tutmak, to fast; to observe a diet: *v.* lahana. ~li, ~kâr, fasting; on a diet.

pejmürde Withered, faded; decayed; shabby.

pek¹ Hard; firm; unyielding; violent; tight. ~ gözlü *or* gözü ~, bold, courageous: ~ yürekli, hard-hearted: ~ yüzlü *or* yüzü ~ brazen-faced; thick-skinned; callous; blunt; with no respect for the feelings of others: ağzı ~, who can keep a secret, discreet: başı ~, stupid; obstinate: canı ~, stoical: eli ~, stingy: ⌐karnı tok, sırtı ~¬, well-fed, well set-up, one who leads a happy life: 'yumuşak huylu atın çiftesi ~tir', the quiet man's anger is the most dangerous.

pek² Very; very much; very often; violently; loudly. ~ ~, at most: ~ iyi, very good; very well; all right! ~âlâ (¹——), very good; all right! ~i, *v.* pek iyi.

pekçe *dim. of* pek¹. Rather hard *etc.*; somewhat loudly *or* violently. ~ koşmak, to run rather quickly.

pekgözlü *v.* pek¹.

pek·işmek *vn.* Become hard *or* firm *or* tight. ~iştirmek, *caus. of* pekişmek, yüzü ~, to become pek yüzlü, *v.* pek¹. ~itmek, to make hard *or* firm; strengthen. ~leştirmek, *v.* pekiştirmek. ~lik, hardness; firmness; stinginess; constipation.

pekmez Boiled grape-juice. şeker ~i, molasses: ⌐~in olsun, sineği Bağdad'dan gelir¬, parasites soon gather round one who has money.

peksimet Hard biscuit; ship's biscuit.

pek·yürekli, ~yüzlü *v.* pek.

pelenk Leopard.

pelesenk¹ Balsam; balm.

pelesenk² Common bittern; *v. also* persenk.

pelin Wormwood; absinthe.

pelit Acorn; valonia.

pelte Jelly. Jelly-like, flabby. ~lenmek, ~leşmek, to become jellified *or* flabby.

peltek Lisp. ~lemek, to lisp. ~lik, lisping.

pelüş Plush.

pembe Rose colour. Rosy, pink. toz ~si, light pink; dünyayı toz ~ görmek, to see the world through rose-coloured spectacles: kepazeliğin düz (toz) ~si! (*sl.*), this is absolutely scandalous! ~lik, rose colour, rosiness. ~msi, rather rosy, pinkish. ~zar, a kind of fine silk tissue.

penah Asylum; refuge; protector. Risalet ~, the Prophet: Âlem~, the Sultan.

penc *In* ~ tavuğu, guinea-fowl.

pencere (¹··) Window.

pencik Title-deed to a slave. ~li, (slave) sold with a title-deed.

pençe The whole hand; paw; talon; strength; violence; ancient official signature of the Sultans; large stain; sole *for shoe repair*; tuber, crown (of asparagus *etc.*). ···e ~ atmak, to lay hands on, seize: ~ vurmak, to re-sole (a shoe): ~ ~ yanakları, fresh pink cheeks (as though they had just been slapped): el ~ durmak, to stand in an attitude of respect *with the right hand grasping the left.*

pençe·lemek, to grasp, seize; claw. ~leş-mek, to lock fingers with another and have a test of strength; be at grips with (= ile); engage in contest. ~li, having claws; formidable; repaired, re-soled (boots).

peni Penny.

pens (*Fr.* pince) Pincers; pleat.

pepe, pepeme Stammer. Stammerer. ~lemek, to stammer, stutter. ~lik, ~melik, a stammering.

perakende (·—·¹) Dispersed, scattered; disjoined; confused; retail. ~ci, retailer.

perçem Tuft of hair; long lock on the top of the head; forelock (of a horse). ⌐tut kelin ~inden¬, 'it's like trying to hold a bald man by his hair', *said of one from whom due reparation for a wrong cannot be expected or who cannot be held responsible.*

perçin Clenching of a nail; riveting a bolt; putting a nut on the protruding end of a bolt; rivet. ~ etm. *or* ~lemek, to rivet, clench. ~li, riveted.

perdah Polish; gloss; finishing shave. ~lamak, to polish, burnish; shave a second time. ~lı, polished; shining. ~sız, unpolished; dull; matt.

perde Curtain; screen; partition shutting off the women's quarters; veil; membrane; cataract (eye); act (of a play); fret of a stringed instrument: musical note, pitch of the voice; modesty, chastity. ···e ~ çekmek, to veil: ~si* yırtılmak, to be shameless: **göz** ~**si**, cataract: **tiz** ~**den**, on a high note; violently: **üst (yüksek)** ~**den**, on a high note, in a high pitch: **üst** ~**den başlamak,** to start threatening *or* cursing; **üst** ~**den atıp tutmak,** to talk big, to give oneself airs.

perde·birun (··–ʲ), impudent; indecent. ~**ci,** doorkeeper. ~**dar,** curtained, veiled; doorkeeper. ~**lenmek,** to be veiled *or* curtailed; (eye) to have cataract. ~**li,** veiled, curtained; webbed; membraneous; having cataract; modest, chaste. ~**siz,** without veil; unscreened; shameless, immodest. ~**sizlik,** immodesty, unchastity.

pereme Greek two-oared boat.

perende (·ʲ·) Somersault. ~ **atmak,** to turn a somersault: ···**in önünde** ~ **atmak,** to dupe, to play tricks on. ~**baz,** acrobat, tumbler.

perese Mason's plumb-line; level; direction, bearing; state, condition. ···**i** ~**ya almak,** to weigh (a matter *etc.*): **bir** ~**ye geldi ki,** it came to such a point that: ···**i** ~**sine getirmek,** to choose the right moment for *stg.*

-perest *Pers. suffix.* Worshipping ..., *e.g.* **zevk**~, a worshipper of pleasure; **put**~, an idolator. ~**ide** (··–ʲ), worshipped. ~**iş,** a worshipping, adoration: ···**e** ~ **etm.,** to worship. ~**kâr,** adoring, worshipping; adorer.

pergel Pair of compasses. **iğneli** ~, dividers. ~**lemek,** to measure *or* scribe with compasses; think out.

perhiz *v.* **pehriz.**

peri Fairy; good genius; beautiful person. **Ahmed'in perisi Mehmed'den hoşlanmamış,** Ahmed dislikes Mehmed: ~ **illeti,** epilepsy; hysteria: ~**si pis,** he likes dirt, he is never clean. ~**cik,** little fairy; bolt of a door; epilepsy. ~**li,** haunted; sinister; possessed.

perişan Scattered; disordered, in confusion; routed; perplexed; wretched, ruined. ~ **etm.,** to scatter, to ruin, to rout. ~ **olm.,** to be scattered, routed; to be in a state of misery or ruin. ~**lık,** a state of disorder, ruin *or* wretchedness.

perki A voracious freshwater fish.

perkitmek, perkişmek *etc. v.* **pekitmek** *etc.*

permeçe (·ʲ·) Small hawser; tow-rope.

persenk Refrain; word continually repeated *like* '*you know*', '*you see*'.

perşembe Thursday. ⌐~**nin gelişi çarşambadan belli olur**⌐, 'it's as clear as that night follows day', *or* 'one can feel it coming'.

pertav Jump; run taken before a jump; bowshot. ~ **almak,** to take a run before a jump: ~ **etm.,** to shoot (an arrow *etc.*).

pertavsız Magnifying-glass; burning-glass.

peru A single pear-shaped gem.

peruka (·ʲ·) Wig. **perukâr,** hairdresser.

perva (·–ʲ) Heed, attention; fear, anxiety; restraint. ~**sız,** fearless; caring for no one; free from concern; without restraint. ~**sızlık,** fearlessness; a not caring for anyone.

pervane (·–ʲ) Moth; fly-wheel; propeller; paddle-wheel; sails of a windmill; sun-fish. **üstüne** ~ **olm.,** to look after and protect.

pervaz[1] Ornamental border; cornice; moulding; fringe. ~**lık,** anything suitable or sufficient for a border.

pervaz[2] Flight. (*in compounds*) Flying, *e.g.* **bülend**~, high-flying, soaring.

-perver *Pers. suffix.* Nourishing ...; caring for ..., *e.g.* **misafir**~, hospitable; **hayâl**~, nourishing vain hopes.

perverde Nourished, brought up, educated. ~ **etm.,** to maintain and care for.

pes[1] Low, soft (voice).

pes[2] *In such phrases as:* ~ **dedir(t)mek,** to make *s.o.* cry small, give in: ~ **demek,** to submit, to give in: ~ **etm.,** to cry small: **yanında** ~ **demek,** to recognize the superiority of, to give in to: **buna** ~ **!,** 'it's beyond me!', *i.e.* it passes my comprehension; *or* 'it's the limit!' (of s.o.'s behaviour or speech).

pesek Tartar *of the teeth.*

pesendide (··–ʲ) Approved; pleasing.

pespase *v.* **besbase.**

pespaye (·–ʲ) Common, vulgar.

pest *v.* **pes.**

pestenkerani (···–ʲ) Idiotic; nonsensical.

pestil Fruit pulp pressed into thin layers and dried. ~**ini*** **çıkarmak,** to beat *s.o.* to a jelly: ~**i*** **çıkmak,** to be beaten *or* crushed: ~ **gibi yatmak,** to lie exhausted.

peş The space behind; edging *of a garment.* ~**imde,** ~**inde** *etc.,* after *or* behind me, him *etc.*: ~**inden,** following ..., in company with ...: ~**ini bırakmak,** to cease following: ~ **inde dolaşmak (gezmek),** to go around with s.o.; to pursue *a matter*: ~**ine düşmek,** to follow: ~**inden koşmak,** to run after: ~**i sıra,** behind him, following him, with him; afterwards: ···**i** ~**ine*** **takmak,** to bring along with one; ···**in** ~**ine takılmak,** to tack oneself on to *s.o.*

peşekâr A kind of clown *in the old Turkish plays.*

peşiman (··–ʲ) *v.* **pişman.**

peşin Former; first; paid in advance, ready (money). First, in the first place; in advance. ~ **almak,** to buy for cash: ~ **söylemek,** to tell in advance, prognosticate: **berveçhi** ~, in anticipation; ready money being paid down. ~**ci,** one who deals for cash.

peşisıra *v.* peş.

peşkeş Gift. ~ çekmek, to make a present of a thing that does not belong to one.

peşkir Napkin.

peşrev Overture, prelude (*mus.*);ʼ grape-shot; preliminary movements of wrestlers. ⸢zurnada ~ olmaz (ne çıkarsa bahtına)⸣, you mustn't expect too much: *v. also* pişrev.

peştahta Small desk; counter; money-changer's board.

peştamal Large bath-towel. ~ küşanmak, to finish one's apprenticeship and become a master workman. ~cı, dealer in bath-towels. ~iye, (*formerly*) a fee paid by an apprentice to his master on leaving his apprenticeship to work on his own. ~lık, money paid for the goodwill of a business: ~ vermek, to buy the goodwill.

petalides (··¹·) Limpet.

petek Honeycomb; any circular disk; jar made of clay. ~ gözü, cell in honeycomb. ~göz, compound or mosaic eye *of insects.*

petkir Hair sieve.

petrol Petroleum (*not* petrol, *which is* benzin).

pey Earnest-money; money on account; deposit; bid *at an auction.* ~ sürmek, to run up the bidding: ~ tutulmaz, that cannot be taken as serious, not to be relied upon: ~ vermek, to pay a deposit: ~ vurmak, to make a bid.

peyam Message; tidings; divine revelation.

peyapey (¹—·) Gradually; incessantly.

peyda (·¹) Existent; produced; manifest; born. ~ etm., to procure, beget, create; acquire (a habit *etc.*): ~ olm., to come into being, be manifested, appear.

peydahlamak *va. v.* peyda etm., çocuk ~, (of an unmarried woman) to be with child.

peyderpey (¹··) One after the other; in succession; step by step.

peygamber Prophet *esp.* the prophet Mohammed. ~ ağacı, guaiacum, lignum vitae: ~ çiçeği, cornflower: ~ devesi, the praying mantis: ~ kuşu, wagtail.

peyk, –ki Lackey; messenger; follower; satellite.

peyke (¹·) Wooden bench.

peyker Form, figure; face.

pey·lemek *va.* Pay a deposit on *stg.* (to seal a bargain); make sure of getting *stg.*; book, engage. ~leşmek, to conclude a bargain by paying a deposit.

peyman Oath.

peynir Cheese. ~ dişi, the last remaining tooth of an old man; ~ dişli, toothless: ~ ekmekle yemek, to do stg. easily, as a matter of course; ⸢aklını ~ ekmekle mi

yedin?⸣, 'have you gone out of your senses?': kirli hanım ~i, a soft rich white cheese: ⸢lafla ~ gemisi yürümez⸣, 'fine words butter no parsnips'. ~ci, cheese-monger. ~lenmek, to become cheesy; (of milk) to coagulate; to be flavoured *or* sprinkled with cheese.

peyrev Who follows in another's footsteps; subordinate; follower, imitator.

pezevenk Pimp; *a term of general abuse.*

pıhtı Coagulated liquid. Coagulated, clotted. kan ~sı, clot of blood. ~lanmak, ~laşmak, to become coagulated, to clot. ~latmak, to cause to coagulate.

pılıpırtı (*pl.* ~lar, *but acc.* pılıyı pırtıyı). Old rubbish; belongings. pılıyı pırtıyı toplamak, to pack up one's belongings.

pınar Spring, source göz ~ı, inner corner of the eye.

pır A whizzing *or* whirring. ~ ~ etm., to whiz, to whirr: lâmba ~ ~ edip söndü, the lamp spluttered and went out.

pırasa, pırazvana *etc. v.* prasa *etc.*

pırıl *etc. v.* parıl *etc.*

pırlak Lure, decoy.

pırlamak *vn.* Flutter. *v. also* parlamak. pırlayıp gitmek, to fly away.

pırlangıç Musical top.

pırlanmak (Of a young bird) to flutter and try to fly.

pırlanta (·¹·) A brilliant. Set with brilliants.

pırnal, pırnar Ilex, holm-oak (*Quercus ilex* not *Ilex aquifolium,* holly, which is çoban püskülü).

pırpı *A kind of stone used as an antidote to snake-bites;* monkshood.

pırpırı Shabbily dressed. A dissolute rake; (*formerly*) a cloak of red felt *worn by constables.*

pırpıt Coarse homemade cloth. Old, worn-out, shabby.

pırtı *v.* pılıpırtı.

pırtık Torn; ragged; in rags.

pırt·lak Bulging. ~lamak, to bulge out.

pısırık Shy, diffident; weak, incapable.

pıt *In* ~ yok, there's not a sound.

pıtır ~ ~, *imitates the sound of rapid footsteps.* ~damak, to make a tapping sound, to crackle. ~dı, light tapping *or* crackling sound.

pıtrak Plant bearing innumerable burrs (such as burdock). ~ gibi, covered with fruit.

piç¹ Bastard; offshoot, sucker; cuticle of the nail; the small, incomplete or deficient replica of anything. ~ etm., to spoil (sleep *etc.*) by frequent interruption: ~ kurusu, tiresome, naughty child.

piç² Pitch *of a propeller.*

pîç³ Twist; curl; distortion. ~**apiç** (−·−́),
full of twists and turns; involved.

piçota Largest sized palamut (bonito).

pide *Kind of* bread *baked in thin flat strips.*

pikap, -pı Pick-up (gramophone).

pike¹ *The cotton material* piqué, quilting.

pike² (*Fr. piqué*) ~ uçağı, dive-bomber: ~
etm., (of an aircraft) to dive.

pil (*Fr. pile*) Electric battery.

pilâki Stew *of fish or beans with oil and
onion, eaten cold.*

pilâv Pilaf (rice with bits of meat, pine
kernels, raisins *etc.*) ⌐~**dan dönenin kaşığı
kırılsın**⌐, 'one does not refuse a good offer',
also 'I won't fail', 'I'll abide by my
decision': **iç** ~, pilaf with meat and
raisins.

piliç Chick. ~ **çıkarmak,** to hatch eggs.

pineklemek *vn.* Slumber; doze.

pines A kind of sea mollusc, pinna.

pinpon Dotard.

pinti Miserly, stingy; shabby. ~**lemek,** to
become dirty and shabby from miserliness.
~**lik,** stinginess, meanness; shabbiness.

pipo Tobacco pipe.

pir Old man; founder of an order of dervishes; patron saint. ~ **aşkına,** just 'for
love', without expecting anything in re-
turn : ~**i fani,** a decrepit old man : ⌐~ **ol !**⌐,
'bravo !' : ⌐**bir oldu amma ~ oldu**⌐, it was a
great success: **bir kızarsa ~ kızar,** he
doesn't often lose his temper, but when he
does ...!

pirahen (−−́) Shirt; chemise.

pirane (−−́) Suitable to an old man;
senile.

pira·ste (−−́) Adorned, decked out. ~**ye,**
ornament, embellishment. ~**yiş,** act of
adorning; decoration.

pire Flea; aphis. ⌐~**yi deve yapmak**⌐, to
exaggerate grossly : ~ **gibi,** very agile,
lively : ⌐~ **için yorgan yakmak**⌐, 'to burn a
blanket to get rid of a flea', *i.e.* to cause
great damage to oneself in order to avenge
a trifle : ⌐~**yi nallamak**⌐, 'to shoe a flea', to
attempt the impossible, *but it sometimes
means* 'to be very cunning'.

pire·lenmek, to become infested with
fleas; to hunt for fleas on oneself; to be
worried by suspicion; to feel uneasy; to be
in a bad temper. ~**li,** full of fleas; suspicious; uneasy. ~**otu, -nu,** pyrethrum;
insect powder.

piri (−́) Old age; senility. **hırsı ~,** senile
avarice.

pirina (·¹·), **pirin** Cake of crushed olives
from which the oil has been extracted.

pirinc¹ Rice. ~ **örgüsü,** moss-stitch (knitting) : ~ **su kaldırmamak,** (of rice) to be
unable to absorb much water; ~**i su**

kaldırmaz, he is very touchy : ⌐**ayıkla ~in
taşını !**⌐, 'pick out the stones from the rice !',
'here's a pretty mess !'; 'this is a difficult
and tiresome job !'

pirinc² Brass.

pirohu, piruhi *A dish of* stewed dough
with cheese.

pirüpak (−·−́) Spotlessly clean.

piryol Cask wide at the bottom and narrow
at the top; cylindrical iron vessel; 'turnip'
watch.

pirzola (·¹· *or* ¹··) Cutlet, chop.

pis Dirty; foul; obscene. ~**i ~ine,** uselessly,
in vain : ~ ~ **düşünmek,** to brood, to appear
distraught and worried : ~ ~ **gülmek,** to
laugh in a scoffing manner. ~**boğaz,**
greedy; so greedy that he eats anything at
any time.

pisi (*Childish language*) Cat; pussy-cat.
~ ~ !, **puss ! puss !** : ~ **balığı,** plaice; **dere ~
balığı,** flounder.

pisi pisine *v.* **pis.**

pisin (*Fr. piscine*) Fish-pond; bathing-pool.

piskopos Bishop. ~**luk,** bishopric; rank
of bishop; bishop's house.

pis·lemek *va.* Dirty; soil; spoil; relieve
oneself : make a mess of; (of an animal or
baby) to make a mess on *stg.* ~**lenmek,**
~**leşmek,** to become dirty; to be soiled.
~**letmek,** to make dirty, to soil. ~**lik,**
dirtiness; dirt; mess; obscenity.

pist¹ *Noise made to drive away cats.*

pist² (*Fr. piste*) Running track; runway.

piston Piston; (*sl.*) backing, influence.

pişdar Vanguard.

pişekâr *v.* **peşekâr.**

pişik Inflamed sore *in the groin or armpit
resulting from heat or sweat.*

pişim Act of being cooked; amount cooked
at one time.

pişirim Act of cooking; amount that one
will cook at one time.

pişirmek *va.* Cook; bake; ripen; plan (a
course of action); hatch (a plot); (of sweat)
to cause a sore, *v.* **pişik;** to learn *stg.* extremely well. **işi ~,** to concoct a plan; to
have an amorous adventure.

pişkin Well-cooked; well-baked; ripe,
mature; 'hard-baked', hardened, experienced. ~**lik,** a being well cooked *or*
ripened; maturity; experience, knowledge
of the world.

pişman Sorry (for = *dat.*); regretful; penitent. ⌐**geldiğine geleceğine ~ etm.**⌐, to give
s.o. a hot reception. ~**lik,** regret; penitence.

piş·mek *vn.* Be cooked *or* baked; ripen,
mature; be perfected; become experienced;
be overcome by the heat; (of the skin) to
be chafed or inflamed by heat or sweat.

~**memiş,** uncooked; immature; inexperienced.

pişrev Scout; forerunner; prelude; preamble. **el** ~**i,** feints made by wrestlers before coming to grips. *v. also* **peşrev.**

pişti *A kind of* ball game.

piştov Pistol.

pişüva (—·⸴), **pişva** Leader; guide; pattern.

pitalinez *corr. of* **petalides.** Limpet.

piyade (·—⸴) Foot-soldier; infantry; pedestrian; pawn (chess); a single-pair boat; a man of small capacity *or* knowledge. **deniz** ~**leri,** marines.

piyale (·—⸴) Cup; cup of wine.

piyan Seizing (of a rope).

piyango (·⸴·) Lottery; raffle. ~**su çıkmak,** to win a lottery.

piyano (·⸴·) Piano.

piyasa (·⸴·) Place of passage; public place; open space; rate of exchange; current price. ~**ya çıkmak,** to go out for a walk: ~**ya düşmek,** (of a woman) to go on the streets: ~ **etm.,** to walk about.

piyastos olm. (*sl.*) (Of a culprit) to be caught.

piyata (·⸴·) Plate.

piyaz Stew with onions. **fasulye** ~**ı,** salad of beans cooked with onions, oil, vinegar, eggs *etc.* : ~**ı vermek** *or* ~**ları basmak,** to applaud, to flatter. ~**cı,** flatterer. ~**lamak,** to marinade; to sing the praises of, to flatter.

piyes (*Fr. pièce*) Piece, theatrical play.

plâçka (⸴·) Spoil, booty. ~**cı,** raider, free-booter.

plâk (*Fr. plaque*) Plate; disk; gramophone record; clay pigeon. ···**i** ~**a almak** *or* **imlâ ettirmek,** to make a record of (song *etc.*).

plâka Plate; name-plate.

plân Plan. **arka** ~, background; **ön** ~, foreground.

plânçete (·⸴·) Plane-table.

plânör (*Fr. planeur*) Glider.

plânya (⸴·) Carpenter's plane.

plâsiye (*Fr. placier*) Commercial traveller, agent.

plâsman (*Fr. placement*) Investment *of money.*

plâtin Platinum.

podösüet (*Fr. peau de suède*) Suede leather.

pof *Imitates a popping noise.*

poğaça (·⸴·) Flaky pastry.

poğama (·⸴·) Crane; derrick.

pohpoh Bravo! Applause; flattery. ~**lamak,** to applaud; to flatter.

poliçe (·⸴·) Bill of exchange; insurance policy.

poligon (*Fr. polygon*) Artillery range.

polis Police.

politika (··⸴·) Politics; policy; cunning or

flattery in conversation. ~**cı,** politician; one who knows when to use flattery or cunning in his talk.

Polon·ya (·⸴·) Poland. ~**yalı,** ~**ez,** Polish.

Pomak Moslem inhabitant of Bulgaria.

pomata (·⸴·) Pomade.

pompa (⸴·) Pump.

ponza (⸴·) Pounce, pumice; rotten-stone.

porselen Porcelain; porcelain insulator.

porsuk Badger. ~ **ağacı,** yew.

porsuk, porsumak *v.* **pörsük, pörsümek.**

porsun Boatswain.

portakal Orange.

Portekiz (⸴··) Portugal. ~**li,** Portuguese.

portmanto (·⸴·) Coat-stand; coat-hanger; (*not* portmanteau *which is* **bavul**).

portolon Chart; plan.

posa (⸴·) Sediment; dregs. ~**lanmak,** to deposit a sediment; to settle as dregs.

posbıyık (⸴··) Large bushy moustache; having such a moustache.

post, –tu Skin; hide; tanned skin with the fur on, *esp. when used as a rug*; rind, shell; office, post; *v. App.* ~ **elden gitmek,** to lose one's skin (life); to lose one's post: ~ **kalpak,** sheepskin cap: ~ **kapmak,** to get an office (*with a suggestion of fraud or cunning*) : ~ **kavgası,** a quarrel about getting a post: ~**u kurtarmak,** to save one's skin (life) : ~**una oturmak,** to take possession of one's official post; to assume airs: ~**u sermek,** to settle oneself down in a place or a post *with the intention of staying*: ⸢(inanma dostuna) saman doldurur postuna⸣, *said when a friend has betrayed one.*

posta (⸴·) The post (letters); postal service; mail steamer; mail train; military post; shift, gang, relay. ~ **etm.,** (of a policeman) to take *s.o.* up, to take to the police-station : ~**yı kesmek,** to cease frequenting a place *or* doing stg. ~ **polisi,** policeman on a beat.

posta·cı, postman. ~**hane** (···—⸴), post-office. ~**l¹,** postal; ~**ne** (·—⸴), post-office. ~**pulu,** postage stamp.

postal² Heavy army shoe; loose woman.

postnişin Established in an office of dignity, *esp.* as head of a religious order.

poşu *v.* **puşu.**

pot, –tu Crease, fold, pleat; punt, raft; wooden floor of a cattle-shed. Puckered; too full (dress). ~ **gelmek,** to go wrong, to turn out badly : ~ **kırmak,** to make a faux pas, to 'drop a brick' : ~ **yeri,** defect.

pota (⸴·) Crucible.

potin Boot.

pot·lanmak *vn.* Be creased *or* puckered. ·~**lu,** puckered; in folds. ~**uk,** puckered; full (dress); in pleats: young camel.

potur Pleat; fold; corrugation; full pleated knee-breeches. Puckered; pleated. ~**lu,**

wearing the breeches known as **potur**: peasant.

poyra (¹·) Hub; axle-end (of a car). **~luk,** log of hard wood out of which hubs are made.

poyraz North-East wind; NE. point of the compass. **~ kuşu,** oyster-catcher: **ağzını* ~a açmak,** to be disappointed; to get nothing.

poz (*Fr. pose*) Pose; exposure (photography).

pörçük pörçük In bits and pieces.

pörs·ük Shrivelled up; withered. **~ümek,** to shrivel up, become withered *or* wrinkled.

pösteki Sheepskin; sheepskin rug used to sit on. **~ olm.,** to become limp: **~ saymak,** (to count the hairs of a sheepskin), to be engaged on a useless and tedious task: **~sini* sermek,** to flay *s.o.,* to give *s.o.* a severe thrashing: **deliye ~ saydırmak,** to give *s.o.* a tiresome but useless job.

prafa (¹·) **~ oyunu,** a card game for three people.

pranga (¹·) Fetters attached to the legs of criminals; penal servitude.

prasa (¹·) Leek. **~ bıyıklı,** with a very long moustache: ⌜**~ olsa yemem**⌝, 'thank you, I'm not hungry'; 'I couldn't eat anything', *v. App.*

pratik Practical. Practice.

pratika (·¹·) Pratique, clean bill of health.

prazvana (·¹·) Shank *of a blade*; metal socket; ferrule.

prens Prince. **~lik,** principality. **~es,** princess.

prese (¹·), **preze** *v.* perese.

prevantoryum Sanatorium for the treatment of tuberculosis in its early stage.

prim Premium; prize.

priz (*Fr. prise*) Electric connexion, plug; drive (*mech.*).

profilli Sectional (iron).

prostela (·¹·) Apron.

protesto (·¹·) Protest. **~ etm.,** to protest: **~ çekmek,** (of a government) to make a formal protest.

prova¹ (¹·) Trial; printer's proof. **~ etm.,** to try on (a dress).

prova² (¹·) Prow, bow *of a ship*.

provadifortuna (¹···¹·) Protest of average (*comm.*).

Prusya Prussia. **~lı,** Prussian.

pruva *v.* prova².

puç¹ Cleft between the buttocks.

puç² Useless; good-for-nothing.

pud Warp, woof.

puding Pudding; conglomerate (*geol.*).

puduk Newly-born camel foal.

puf Puff. **~böreği, -ni** (¹···), pastry puff stuffed with meat and cheese. **~la** (¹·),

puffed out; soft: down (eiderdown). **~lamak,** to blow, to puff; to become puffed out *or* soft: **oflayıp ~,** to puff and blow, pant.

puhu Eagle owl.

pul Thin round disk; scale (*as* fish scale); spangle; washer; stamp (postage *etc.*); piece (in draughts and backgammon); nut (of a bolt); small coin, mite. **bir ~ etmemek,** to be worthless: **para ~,** money; **parası ~u yok,** he has no money.

pulad Steel.

pul·lamak *va.* Stamp. **allayıp ~,** to ornament with spangles; to over-decorate. **~lu,** scaly; spangled; bearing stamps; spotted.

pulluk Heavy plough.

punar *v.* pınar.

pund Position of a ship. **~unu bulmak** *or* **~una getirmek,** to find a suitable opportunity *to do stg.*: **~ tâyini,** finding a ship's position by astronomical calculations.

punta (¹·) (Lathe) centre. **fener ~,** live centre: **gezer ~,** back centre; **gezer ~ gövdesi,** tailstock, poppet.

puntal Stanchion.

punto (¹·) Size of type.

pupa (¹·) Stern *of a ship*; following wind. **~ gitmek,** to sail before the wind: **···e ~ yelken açmak,** to take advantage of ..., to profit by ... .

puro Cigar.

pus¹ Mist, haze; condensation (on a cold glass); bloom *on fruit*; blight, mildew; moss *on trees and plants*; web *made by insects on leaves*; crust *formed on the nipples of ewes*.

pus² (*Fr. pouce*) Inch.

pusarık Haze; hazy weather; mirage.

pusat, -tı Arms; equipment; instruments of war. **~çı,** clown in the **ortaoyunu** having a slapstick or wooden sword. **~lanmak,** to be armed; to put on armour. **~lı,** armed; clad in armour.

puse (−¹) Kiss.

pusla¹ (¹·), **pusula** Note; memorandum; list. **~ etm.,** to make a note of, to make a list.

pusla² (¹·), **pusula** *v.* pusula².

pus·lanmak *vn.* (Of a cold glass) to be misty with condensation; (of fruit) to have the bloom on it. **~lu,** hazy, misty; having the bloom on it.

puslu *In* uslu **~,** quiet and shy.

pusmak *vn.* Crouch down; lie in ambush; descend; become misty; be grieved *or* offended.

pusu Ambush. **~ kurmak,** to lay an ambush: **~ya yatmak,** to lie in wait.

pusula¹ *v.* pusla¹.

pusula² (¹··) Compass. **~yı şaşırmak,** to lose one's bearings; to be bewildered.

puşide (−−¹) Covered; hidden. Covering; quilt; a kind of scarf worn round the head.

puşt, -tu Catamite.

puşu Light turban *formerly worn by soldiers*; kerchief worn round the head.

put, -tu Idol; beautiful boy *or* girl. ~ gibi durmak, to stand like a graven image. ~kıran, iconoclast. ~laştırmak, to idolize. ~perest, idolater. ~perestlik, idolatry.

putlamak *vn.* (Of a camel) to foal.

putrel (*Fr. poutrelle*) Iron beam *or* post *used in building.*

puvan Point; score.

puyan (−¹) Wandering about; (*with dat.*) immersed in; full of.

püf *Imitates a puff of wind or breath.* ~ noktası, a weak spot. ~etmek (¹··), -eder, ~lemek, ~kürmek, to blow out, blow on; puff.

püfteri Decoy whistle.

püfür püfür *Imitates the noise of a gentle breeze.*

pünez (*Fr. punaise*) Drawing-pin.

pür- *Pers. prefix.* Full of ..., *e.g.* pürhiddet, full of fury; pürümid, full of hope.

pürçek Curl.

pürçük *In* bölük ~, in fragments; incomplete.

pürmelâl *In* hali ~, a hopeless state.

pürnakıl Full of ..., covered with ... .

pürtük Uneven, rough, knobbly. Knob, small protuberance.

püruz Shagginess; roughness; unevenness, irregularity; roughness on the surface of castings; fluff; hitch, difficulty. ~ ayıklamak *or* temizlemek, to settle a matter; to clear away difficulties. ~lenmek, to become rough *or* shaggy; to be beset with difficulties. ~lü, rough, shaggy; covered with ink stains *or* splashes of paint; uneven, irregular; beset with difficulties. ~süz, even, smooth; without defects: türkçe ~ konuşmak, to talk Turkish fluently.

püskü *v.* eskipüskü.

püskül Tuft; tassel; difficulties. ~lendirmek, to tease out into a tassel; to attach a tassel; to cause to become difficult or complicated. ~lü, tasselled; difficult, complicated: ~ belâ, a serious calamity; a damnable nuisance.

püskür·geç Atomizer. ~me, scattered about (of water *etc.*): anything splashed about: ~ ben, beauty spots scattered about over the face: ~ memesi, injection nozzle: ~ pompa, fuel-pump (Diesel). ~mek, to blow out water from the mouth; to spray (liquid); to foam at the mouth; splutter; scatter, drive away: ateş ~, to be furiously angry. ~tmek, *caus. of* püskürmek; to scatter (an enemy).

püsür *Used in conjunction with words expressing filth*; unpleasant additions and accessories. bu işin bir çok boku ~ü var, there are a lot of complications in this business.

R

Rab, -bbi The Lord God. **Rabbim!**, my God!: **Rabbena,** our Lord, God: ya Rabbi!, oh! my God! ~bani (··−¹), divine: ilhamı ~, divine inspiration.

rabıt¹, -btı A binding; bond; connexion; grammatical construction. rabtı kelâm, grammatical construction of sentences: ···e ~ı kalb etm., to set one's heart on.

rabıt² (−¹) Binding, connecting. ~a (−·¹), tie, bond; connexion; orderly arrangement; copula; logical *or* grammatical conformity. ~alı, in good order; regular; decorous, well-conducted, decent. ~asız, disordered; irregular; incoherent; rambling; disorderly. ~asızlık, disorder; irregularity; bad behaviour.

râbı Fourth. ~an (¹··), fourthly.

rabt·etmek *va.* Bind; fasten; connect. bir karara ~, to decide or settle *a question etc.* ~iye, tether, tie, bond; fastener.

raca (¹·) Rajah.

raci (−¹) Returning; concerning, relating to. ···e ~ olm., to concern, to fall on.

racih (−¹) Preponderant; preferable.

racon (*sl.*) Custom, rule.

ra'd Thunder.

radansa (·¹·) Thimble *or* cringle *of a rope.*

radde Degree. ~sinde, approximately: saat on ~lerinde, about ten o'clock: bayılma ~ lerine gelmiştim, I came near to fainting.

radike Dandelion.

radyo (¹·) Radio, wireless.

raf Shelf. ~a koymak, to shelve *a matter.* ⌐~tan sünger düştü başı yarıldı⌐, a sponge fell off the shelf and cracked his skull; (an absurd exaggeration; much to-do about nothing).

rafadan Very lightly boiled egg.

rafızî (−·¹) Heretic; Shiite.

rafi (−¹) Raising, erecting. Erector (muscle).

rağbet, -ti Desire, inclination. ···e ~, wish for *stg.*; demand for *goods.* ~ten düşmek, to be no longer in demand, to be out of favour: ···e ~ etm., to wish for, to esteem: ~ görmek, to be in demand, to be esteemed: ···e ~i var, he has an inclination for: ~e ~i yok, he has no inclination for.

rağbet·li, desirous; having an inclination *for stg.*; in demand, sought after, liked: ~si çok, there is a great demand *for some kind of goods*: ~si yok, there is no demand for it. ~siz, who feels no inclination *for stg.*; unesteemed, not sought after. ~siz·lik, a being without inclination; lack of esteem, a not being in demand.

rağm Spite. ~ına, out of spite: ···in ~ına, to spite ... . ~en (¹·), in spite of (*dat.*).

rah, reh Road, way; course, rule, system.

rahat, -tı Rest; ease; comfort; quiet. At ease; tranquil; comfortable; easy. ~ına bakmak, to look after one's own comfort; ~ınıza bakın !, (i) please don't worry; it really doesn't matter; (ii) don't bring trouble upon yourself by unnecessary interference: ~ mı battı ?, *lit.* 'did comfort disturb you ?', *i.e.* 'why did you give up your comfortable job ?': ~ etm., to be at ease, to make oneself comfortable, to rest: ~ durmak, to keep quiet, not to fidget; ~ dur !, don't fidget !; (*mil.*) order arms !: bir gün ~ yüzü görmedim, I have not had a day's peace.

rahat·lanmak, to rest; take one's ease; calm oneself. ~lık, ease; comfort; quiet: Allah ~ versin, sleep well ! ~sız, unquiet; uneasy; indisposed; uncomfortable : ~etm., to disturb: ~ olmayınız !, don't be uneasy, don't worry ! ~sızlık, uneasiness; discomfort; indisposition.

rahib (−¹) Monk; ~e, nun.

rahim, -hmi Womb.

râhim (−¹) Merciful.

rahle Low reading-desk.

rahman Compassionate, merciful (of God). ~î (·−−¹), pertaining to the All-compassionate God; bestowed by God; divine.

rahmet, -ti Mercy; God's compassion; rain. ···e ~ okumak, to pray for the soul of ...; to regret *stg. lost*: ···e ~ okutmak, to cause one to regret ...; to make one long for ... (in place of stg. else): ···e Allah ~ eylesin !, God's blessing on ... !: Hakkın ~ine kavuşanlar, those who have obtained God's mercy, *i.e.* the dead. ~li, ~lik, the deceased, the late.

rahmetmek (¹··), **-eder** (*with dat.*) Have mercy on.

rahmî (·−¹) Uterine.

rahne Rent; breach, fissure; damage. ~dar, cracked; damaged.

raht, -tı Luggage; household effects; furniture; harness; hinge *of a window or door*.

rahvan Amble; ambling horse. Ambling.

raiyye (−·¹) Flock at pasture; subject community, people under a ruler.

rakam Figure; arithmetic.

rakı Raki, arrack. **Alman** ~sı, a drug consisting of brandy mixed with purgatives: **sakız** ~sı, raki with mastic in it. ~cı, maker *or* seller of raki; raki addict.

râkım (−¹) Who writes *or* marks. Altitude above the sea-level. ~ül huruf, the writer of this.

rakîb (·−¹) Rival. ~siz, unrivalled.

râkib (−¹) Mounted; riding; travelling on (a ship). ···e ~ olm., to mount, ride on, travel in (ship). ~en (−¹··), (*with dat.*) riding on, on board ... .

rakik (·−¹) Slender, fine; tender, soft-hearted.

rakkas Dancer; pendulum. ~ çarkı, balance-wheel of a watch.

raks Dance, dancing. ~an *a.*, dancing. ~etmek (¹··), **-eder,** to dance; oscillate.

râm Tame, gentle, submissive. ~ etm., to subjugate, to cause to yield.

ramak, -kı The last spark of life in a dying man; the minimum of food sufficient to keep life going; smallest possible quantity of anything. **bu kazanın hayatına mal olmasına** ~ **kaldı,** this accident all but cost him his life.

ramazan Ramazan, *the ninth month of the Moslem year, during which Moslems fast between dawn and sunset.* ~ tiryakisi, a quick-tempered man (*orig. from the bad temper caused by fasting*). ~lık, suitable for Ramazan.

rami (−¹) Who throws *or* shoots; archer; the constellation Sagittarius.

rampa (¹·) Boarding (*naut.*); a ship's going alongside another or a wharf; incline; loading-platform. ~ etm., to board *an enemy's ship*; (*sl.*) to accost (a woman); to join *a party* uninvited.

râna (−−¹) Pretty, exquisite. ~ bilmek, to know perfectly.

randa (¹·) Spanker (*naut.*).

randevu (¹··) Rendezvous.

randıman (*Fr. rendement*) Yield; profit; output. ~lı, profitable.

ranza (¹·) Bunk (*naut.*).

rap *Imitates the sound of marching.*

rapor Report; medical certificate.

rapt- *v.* rabt-.

ras *v.* rast.

rasad A watching; astronomical *or* meteorological observation. ~hane (··−¹), observatory; meteorological station.

ras·gele, rastgele Chance, met by hazard. By chance; at random. **rasgele !,** good luck ! ~gelmek (¹··) (*with dat.*), to meet by chance, come across; hit *the mark*; turn out right, succeed. ~**getirmek** (¹···), to succeed in meeting; to cause to succeed; cause to hit the mark: Allah işinizi rasgetirsin!, may God grant you success! ~**gitmek**, *in* iş ~, (of an affair) to succeed.

râsıd (−¹) Observer.

râsime (−·¹) Ceremony; pageant; custom.

rasîn (·−¹) Firm; solid; grave.

raslamak, rastlamak (*with dat.*) Meet by chance; coincide with.

raspa (¹·) Scraper; grater. ~ **etm.**, to scrape: ~ **taşı**, pumice-stone, holystone.

rast, −tı, ras Straight; right; proper; straightforward; in order; successful. ~ **gitmek**, to turn out well, prosper: ~ **makamı**, *a mode in Oriental music.*

rastık Cosmetic used for blackening the eyebrows; bunt or stinking smut of wheat. ~ **çekmek**, to blacken the eyebrows: ~ **mürekkeb**, black indelible ink: ~ **taşı**, antimony.

râşe (−¹) Tremor; shudder. ~**dar** (−·¹), trembling.

râşi (−¹) Who bribes.

raşid (−¹) Well-directed; well-guided; of age. **hulefai raşidin**, the first four Caliphs.

raşit·ik Rachitic, rickety. ~**ism**, rickets.

râtıb (−¹) Damp.

râtib (−¹) Firm; constant.

ravak Run honey.

râvend Rhubarb.

ravi (−¹) Narrator.

ravnt Round (boxing *etc.*).

ravza Garden; tomb of a saint, *esp.* the tomb of the Prophet.

ray Rail (railway *etc.*).

râya (−¹), **reaya** *pl. of* **raiyye**. Subjects, *esp.* the non-Moslem subjects of the Ottoman Empire.

rayba Reamer. ~**lamak**, to ream.

rayegân (−−¹) Gratis; abundant; current.

rayet (−¹), −**ti** Flag.

rayetmek (¹−·), −**eder** *va.* Pasture.

rayic (−¹) Current; in demand; saleable; in common use. Market price; current value. ~ **usulü**, ad valorem.

rayiha (−·¹) Smell, odour. ~**lı**, scented.

raz (−) Secret; mystery.

razaki *A variety of* white grape, *from which the best raisins are made.*

razı (−¹) Satisfied, contented; willing; pleased. ~ **etm.**, to satisfy (a person), to obtain the acquiescence of: ~ **olm.**, to be willing, to consent; to approve; to be pleased. ⌈**alan** ~, **satan** ~⌉, the buyer satisfied, the seller satisfied; since those concerned are content, no one else should interfere: **Allah** ~ **olsun**, may God reward you (him *etc.*).

raziyane Fennel.

reaya (·−¹) *v.* **raya**.

rebab A sort of guitar. ~**î**, lyrical.

rebi (·¹), −**ii** Spring. ~**î** (·−¹), pertaining to spring, vernal. ~**yülâhır**, *fourth month of the Moslem year.* ~**yülevvel**, *third month of the Moslem year.*

receb *Seventh month of the Moslem year.*

recim, −cmi A pelting; a stoning to death. **recmetmek** (¹··), −**eder**, to pelt; stone to death.

recül A man. ~**ü devlet**, statesman. ~**iyet**, −**ti**, virility; manliness.

reçel Fruit preserve; jam.

reçete (·¹·) Prescription; recipe.

reçina, reçine (·¹·) Resin.

red, −ddi A repelling *or* rejecting; expulsion; refutation; repudiation. ~**di cevab etm.**, to return an answer; ~**dile cevab vermek**, to answer with a refusal: ~**di hükkâm talebi**, a demand for other judges. ~**detmek** (¹··), −**eder**, to reject; repel; return (an answer); repudiate; refute.

redaet (·¹·), −**ti** Worthlessness; viciousness.

redif (·¹) Reserve. Reservist; word repeated at the end of every line of a poem.

refah (·⁴) Easy circumstances; comfort; luxury.

refakat (·−¹), −**ti** Accompaniment; companionship. ···**in** ~**inde**, accompanied by, in the company of ...: ···**e** ~ **etm.**, to accompany *s.o.*

ref'etmek (¹··), −**eder** *va.* Raise, heighten; promote; remove; annul.

ref·i, −f'i A raising *or* elevating; removal; abolition. ~**î**, high; eminent.

refik (·⁴), −**ki** Companion, associate; husband. ⌈**kişi** ~**inden azar**⌉, 'evil communications corrupt good manners'. ~**a** (·−¹), female companion; wife.

reftar Gait; conduct.

refte refte Little by little.

reftiye Export duty.

regaib (·−¹) Gifts. **leylei** ~, the 12th of Rejeb, *anniversary of the conception of Mohammed.*

reh *v.* **rah**.

reha (·¹) Escape; preservation. ~ **bulmak**, to escape. ~**kâr**, who liberates; liberator.

rehavet (·−¹), −**ti** Softness; limpness; slackness, lethargy.

rehavî (·−¹) *Name of a musical mode;* musical-box.

rehayab (·−¹) Who escapes; who recovers from an illness.

rehber Guide; guide-book. ~**lik**, a guiding: ~ **etm.**, to guide.

rehgüzar (···¹) Place through which a road passes; frequented place.

rehin, –hni Pawn, pledge, security; hostage. **rehne koymak** *or* **bırakmak,** to pawn or pledge, to give as security. **rehîn** (··), pawned, pledged, deposited as security, given as hostage: ~**i iz'an,** understood. ~**e** (··-), object given as pledge; hostage.

rehnüma (···-) Guide; guide-book.

reis Head; chief; president; captain (of a merchant ship). *a.* Principal, chief. ~ **vekili,** Vice-president: *v. also* **re's.** ~**icumhur,** President of the Republic (*now* **Cumhurbaşkanı**). ~**ülküttab,** (*formerly*) Minister of Foreign Affairs.

reji (¹·) Regie (former administration of the Tobacco Monopoly).

rejisör (*Fr. regisseur*) Stage-manager.

rekabet (·–¹), **–ti** Rivalry; competition.

rekâket (·–¹), **–ti** Defect in speech; stammer; incoherence; defect in style.

rekât, –tı Complete act of worship with the prescribed postures.

reklâm (*Fr. réclame*) Advertisement.

rekolta, rekolte (·¹·) Harvest; crop.

rekor Record. ~**cu,** ~**tmen,** record-breaker.

rekz A setting up *or* planting; erection. ~**etmek** (¹··), **–eder,** to set up, erect; plant.

remad (·-) Ashes.

remed Ophthalmia.

remel *Name of a poetical metre.*

remide (·–¹) Scared; put to flight.

remil, –mli Sand; geomancy. ~ **atmak,** to tell the future by geomancy.

remiz, –mzi Sign; nod; wink; allusion; symbol. ~**lendirmek,** to symbolize.

remmal (·-) Geomancer.

remz·etmek (¹··), **–eder** *vn. & va.* Make a sign; allude, hint; symbolize, typify. ~**î** (·-), allusive; symbolical.

Ren¹ The Rhine.

ren² (*Fr. renne*) Reindeer.

rencber Labourer; workman; farm-hand; day-labourer. ~**başı, –nı,** labourers' foreman. ~**lik,** occupation of labourer *or* farm-hand.

rencide (·–¹) Pained, hurt; annoyed. ~ **etm.,** to hurt; annoy.

rende Carpenter's plane; grater. ~**lemek,** to plane; shave; grate.

reng·ârenk Multi-coloured; variegated. ~**in,** coloured; brightly coloured; beautiful; ornate.

renk Colour; colour *or* complexion of a thing. ~ **atmak,** to lose colour, fade: ~**ten renge girmek,** to change colour; to be inconstant; to blush with shame: **rengi* kaçmak,** to turn pale: ~ ~ **olm.,** to change colour *from emotion*: ~ **vermemek,** to appear unmoved, to conceal one's feelings: **rengi yok,** colourless; unreliable: **bin renge girmek,** to keep changing colour; to be inconstant; to use every kind of subterfuge.

renk·lemek, to colour. ~**li,** coloured; of *such and such* a colour. ~**siz,** colourless; pale; without personality.

re's Summit; promontory; head *of cattle; v. also* **reis.**

resanet (·–¹), **–ti** Firmness; solidity; gravity. ~**li,** firm; solid.

resas (·-) Lead.

resçekmek *v.* **rest.**

re'sen (¹·) On one's own account *or* initiative; directly; as a principal.

resen Cord; halter.

resif (*Fr. recif*) Reef.

re'sikâr Supreme direction *of a business etc.*; highest post.

resim, –smi Design; drawing; picture; ceremony; due, tax, toll. ~ **çekmek,** to take a photograph: **resmini* çıkarmak,** to have one's photo taken: **resmi geçid,** military review: **resmi kabul,** official reception: **resmi küşad,** inauguration: **mahvolduğumuzun resmidir,** our ruin is certain.

resim·ci, draughtsman; artist; photographer; picture-dealer. ~**li,** illustrated.

resm·en (¹·) Officially; ceremoniously; as a mere matter of form. ~**etmek** (¹··), **–eder,** to draw; describe (a circle *etc.*). ~**i,** *v.* **resim.** ~**î** (·-), official; ceremonious; formal; done as a matter of form. ~**iyet, –ti,** official character *of stg.*; formality: **işe** ~**e dökmek,** to become formal, to adopt an official manner.

ressam Designer; artist. ~**lık,** the art *or* profession of painting.

rest (*Fr. reste*) *In* ~ **çekmek,** to stake all; to act boldly, to dare to do stg.: **bir şeye** ~ **çekmek,** to stake a thing: **şerefine** ~ **çekti,** he staked his honour.

resto (¹·) *Cry used by waiters to cancel an order.*

resul, –lü Envoy; apostle; prophet.

resülmal (¹··) Capital (*finance*).

reşadet (·–¹), **–ti** A doing what is right; good conduct. ~**lû,** *title formerly given to the head of a Dervish convent.*

reşid Who follows the right road; well-conducted; orthodox; capable and careful; who has attained his majority (18 years old).

reşme Chain *or* leather noseband *for a horse.*

ret *v.* **red.**

retuş (*Fr. retouche*) Retouch.

reva (·-) Lawful; permissible; proper, suitable. ~ **görmek,** to deem lawful *or* proper.

revabıt (·–ı), –tı *pl. of* rabıta. Bonds *etc.*

revac A being in demand; a being current.
~landırmak, to cause *stg.* to be in demand.
~lı, in demand; current. ~sız, not in
demand; not current.

revak, –kı Porch; pavilion; arbour. ~î
(·–ᵘ), stoic.

revan Going; flowing; current. Soul, spirit.
~ olm., to go, to flow; to pass as current.

revani (·–ı) *A kind of sweet made with
semolina.*

revanş (*Fr. revanche*) ~ maçı, return match.

revir Small military hospital; infirmary *at
a factory or school*; sick-bay. ~ âmiri,
district inspector.

reviş A going; gait; trend; conduct.

reviyet, –ti Careful consideration; reflection; vigilance; ability.

revnak, –kı Brightness, splendour; brilliance; sparkle; beauty. ~lı, brilliant;
splendid; beautiful; in full prime. ~sız,
lustreless, dull.

rey Opinion; judgement; vote. ~ beyan
etm., to set forth one's opinion: ~e koymak, to put to the vote: ~ vermek, to
vote: ehli ~, a man of sound judgement.
~iâm (ı·–), plebiscite; general vote; universal suffrage.

reyb Doubt, suspicion. ~î (·–ᵘ), sceptical;
sceptic. ~iye, scepticism. ~iyun, the
sceptics.

rey'elayn (ı··), reyülayn *In* ~ görmek *or*
müşahede etm., to see with one's own eyes,
to see for oneself.

reyyan Full of sap; juicy; vigorous; having
the thirst quenched, refreshed.

rezail (·–ı) *pl. of* rezalet.

rezakı *v.* razakı.

rezalet (·–ı), –ti Vileness, baseness; scandal; scandalous behaviour. ~ çekmek, to
suffer disgrace: ~ çıkarmak, to cause a
scandal.

reze Hinge.

rezene Fennel.

rezil Vile, base; disreputable; disgraced.
Scoundrel. ~ etm., to hold up to scorn, to
disgrace: ~ olm., to be disgraced.

rezzak God the Provider of all; one who
provides extravagantly.

rıdvan Satisfaction, contentment; Paradise.

rıfk, –kı Gentleness; suavity.

rıh Sand *used to dry writing.* ~dan, sand-
box.

rıhtım Quay, wharf.

rıtıl, –tlı *An old liquid measure*; goblet.

rıza (·–ᵘ) Consent, acquiescence; resignation. ~sı oluyor, he gives his consent, he
approves: Allah ~sı için, for the love of
God!: kazaya ~!, it can't be helped!:

kazaya ~ göstermek, to resign oneself to
one's fate.

rızk, –kı One's daily food; sustenance; the
necessaries of life.

riayet (·–ı), –ti A respecting; observance;
respect, esteem; respectful treatment; consideration, regard, kind attention. ···e ~
etm., to treat with respect, to pay attention
to. ~en (·–ᵘ·), (*with dat.*) out of respect
for ...; in consideration of .... ~kâr,
respectful; considerate. ~siz, disrespectful;
irreverent. ~sizlik, disrespect; irreverence.

rica (·–ᵘ) Request, prayer. ~ etm., to request, to desire: size bir ~m var *or* sizden
bir ~da bulunacağım, I have a request to
make of you: ~ minnet, after much be-
seeching. ~cı, who makes a request:
intercessor. ~kâr, containing *or* making a
request.

rical, –li *pl. of* recül. Men; men of importance, high officials.

ricat, –ti Return; retreat. ~ etm., to
retreat.

ricî Retrogressive.

rida (·–ᵘ) Woollen cloak.

rie Lung. ~vî, pulmonary.

rifat, –ti Eminence; high rank. ~lû,
eminent (*formerly the official address of a
major or civil functionary of similar rank*).

rihlet, –ti Change of abode; migration;
death.

rik'a Cursive Arabic script *formerly used
chiefly by Turks.*

rikâb Stirrup; retinue *of a prince*; the
Royal Presence.

rikkat, –ti Slenderness; delicacy; tenderness, compassion. ~amiz (···–ı), ~engiz,
piteous, deplorable. ~li, compassionate,
pitiful.

rimel A cosmetic for the eyelashes.

rind *Originally a mystic, whose philosophy
consisted in living in an unconventional,
happy, and convivial manner; hence* : a jolly,
unconventional, humorous man. ⌐dökülen
mey, kırılan şişei rindan olsun¬, 'never
mind the spilt wine and the drinker's
broken glass!', *i.e.* whatever may happen
we are enjoying ourselves. ~ane (·–ı), in
the manner of a rind. ~lik, the quality of
a rind. ~meşreb, having the temperament of a rind.

ringa (ı·) Herring.

risale (·–ı) Treatise; pamphlet. ~i mah-
suse, monograph.

risalet (·–ı), –ti Mission of a prophet;
apostleship.

riş Beard; plumage; wound, sore.

rişe (–ı) Tendril; fibre; fibrous roots;
feather.

rişte Yarn, twine; clue; link; guinea-worm, worm, jigger.

rivayet (·–¹), **–ti** Narrative, tale; rumour. ~ **etm.**, to tell, relate: ~ **olunmak**, to be narrated, to be rumoured.

riya (·–¹) Hypocrisy. ~**kâr** (·–—¹), hypocritical. ~**kârlık**, hypocrisy. ~**kârane** (·—–¹), hypocritical (conduct *etc.*): in a hypocritical manner.

riyal Silver dollar.

riyaset (·–¹), **–ti** Presidency; chairmanship. ~**icumhur**, Presidency of the Republic.

riyasız (·–¹) Without hypocrisy, genuine, sincere.

riyazet (·–¹), **–ti** Asceticism; mortification of the flesh; prison punishment *with only dry bread for food and no smoking or reading.*

riyazî (·–—¹) Mathematical. **ulümu** ~**ye** (~ **ilimler**), the mathematical sciences. ~**yat**, **–tı**, mathematics. ~**iyun**, mathematicians.

rizofora Mangrove.

robdöşambr (*Fr. robe de chambre*) (Woman's) dressing-gown.

roda (¹·) Coil of rope.

rodaj (*Fr. rodage*) ~ **yapmak**, to grind in (a valve).

roka (¹·) Rocket (plant used for salad).

roket, **–ti** Rocket.

rol, **–lü** Role, part.

rom Rum.

Romalı (¹··) Roman.

roman Novel. ~**cı**, novelist.

Romanyalı (·¹··) Roumanian.

romatizma (··¹·) Rheumatism. ~**lı**, rheumatic.

rondelâ Washer.

rosto (¹·) Roasted. Roast meat.

rota (¹·) Ship's course.

roza (¹·) Rose diamond.

rozet, **–ti** Rosette.

römork, **–ku** (*Fr. remorque*) Trailer (vehicle). ~**ör** (*remorqueur*), tug.

Rönesans Renaissance.

rönons (*Fr. renonce*) Revoke (cards).

rötar (*Fr. retard*) Delay.

ru (–), **ruy** (–·) Face; surface. ~**yu kabul görmek**, to have a good reception.

ruam Glanders.

ruba (·–) Clothing, clothes. ~**lık** (¹··), suitable for making clothes.

rubab *v.* rebab.

ruberu (–·–) Face to face; opposite.

rub'iye Gold ¼ lira piece; Batchelor's-button (?).

rubu (·–), **–b'u** Quarter; quarter of a piastre; eighth of a cubit (*i.e. about 14 cm.*). **rub'u daire**, quadrant: **rub'u meskûn**, the inhabited quarter of the globe.

rubya (¹·) Rupee.

rugan Varnish; grease; patent leather. ~**lamak**, to varnish; polish. ~**lı**, varnished; polished; patent leather.

ruh¹ (·) The breath of life; soul; spirit; essence; energy, activity. ~ **haleti**, psychological condition; morale; mood: ~**u bile duymadı**, he didn't even notice: **ilmi** ~, psychology.

ruh² Cheek.

ruh³ Rook *or* castle (chess).

ruhan·î (––·) Spiritual; clerical; immaterial. Angel; ghost. ~**iyet**, **–ti**, spirituality; saintliness.

ruhban *pl. of* rahib. Clergy. ~**iyet** (·–·¹), **–ti**, monastic life.

ruh·î (–·) Psychic; psychological. ···**in ahvali** ~**ye**, the psychology of ...: **haleti** ~**ye**, the psychological condition. ~**iyat** (–·¹), **–tı**, spiritual matters; psychology. ~**iyet**, **–ti**, spiritual state; temperament.

ruh·lanmak *vn.* Become animated; revive. ~**lu**, animated; having *such and such* a spirit; lively; vivid, full of feeling; spirituous (liquor). Spirit level. ~**nüvaz** (··–), charming. ~**perver**, animating; exhilarating.

ruhsar Face; cheek.

ruhsat, **–tı** Permission; permit; leave; dismissal. ~ **vermek**, to give leave; to dismiss. ~**iye**, licence. ~**lı**, authorized; on leave. ~**name** (···–¹), permit; credentials.

ruhsuz Inanimate, lifeless; spiritless. ~**luk**, lifelessness; lack of spirit.

Ruhulkudüs (*To Moslems*) the Angel Gabriel; (*to Christians*) the Holy Ghost.

rulo (*Fr. rouleau*) Roller; roll.

Rum Byzantine Greek; Greek of Turkish nationality. (*Formerly*) Turkey, *hence* **Sultani** ~, the Sultan of Turkey; **iklimi** ~, Turkey. ~**ca** (¹·), modern Greek language. ~**î** (–·), belonging to the ancient Romans *or* to the Byzantine Greeks; Gregorian (calendar). ~**laşmak**, to become a Greek of Turkish nationality. ~**luk**, place inhabited by Turkish subjects of Greek race; condition of being a Greek under Turkish rule.

rumuz *pl. of* remiz. Signs, nods *etc.*; *as sing.* symbol; abbreviation; initial. ~**at** (·–·), **–tı**, formulae.

rupye Rupee.

Rus Russian. ~**ça**, the Russian language. ~**laşmak**, to become Russian.

rusta (·–) Village; peasant. ~**yî** (·–·), peasant; boorish; rustic, pastoral.

Rusya (¹·) Russia. ~**lı** (¹··) Russian.

ruşen (–¹) Shining; bright; evident.

rutubet (·–¹), **–ti** Dampness, humidity. ~**li**, damp.

ruy *v.* ru.

ruya (−⊥) Dream. ~ görmek, to have a dream: ~ tabiri, the interpretation of dreams.

ruz Day. ~u ceza *or* ~u hesab, the Day of Judgement.

ruze (−ι) Fast.

ruzmerre Daily; everyday, common.

ruznamçe (*Formerly*) rough day-book of financial transactions in a government office. ~cı, clerk in charge of foregoing.

ruzname (·−ι) Calendar; journal; daily cash-book; daily paper; agenda.

rüchan Preponderance; preference; advantage. ~ hakkı, priority. ~ıyet (·−·ι), −tı, a being preferable; a having priority.

rücu (·⊥), −uu Return; a going on one's word. ~ etm., to return; to go back on *one's word etc.*

rüesa (··⊥) *pl. of* reis. Heads; chiefs.

rüfai (·−ι) *A sect of dervishes, renowned for their spectacular performances.* ⌐bu işe ~ler karışır⌐, what happens next is beyond our ken.

rüfeka (··⊥) *pl. of* refik. Companions; partners.

rükû, −ûu A bowing down in prayer.

rüküb etmek *va.* Mount; ride upon *or* in.

rükûd (·⊥), **rükûdet, −ti** Stagnation; calm.

rükün, −knü Pillar, column; prop, support; basis; fundamental principle; influential person.

rüküş (hanım) A comically dressed, helpless little woman.

rüsgulkadem Tarsus.

rüsub (·⅄) Dregs; sediment. ~î (·−⊥), sedimentary.

rüsuh A being well-versed *in a subject.*

rüsum (·⅄) *pl. of* resim. Usages; rites; dues,

taxes. **belediye** ~u, municipal taxes: 80 ~ tonluk motörü, a motor-boat of 80 tons registered tonnage. ~at (·−⅄), −tı, dues, taxes; *as sing.* Customs Administration.

rüsvay Publicly disgraced; object of scorn. ~ı âlem, the object of universal scorn.

rüşd Orthodoxy; rectitude; right judgement; majority, coming of age. ~ünü* isbat etm., to come of age: sinni ~, the age of reason, majority. ~iye, high school, secondary school.

rüşeym Embryo, germ.

rüşvet, −ti Bribe; ship's spare rigging stores; place where these are kept. ~i kelâm, complimentary words before criticizing: ~ yemek, to accept a bribe: ~ yedirmek (vermek), to give a bribe. ~çi, taker of bribes.

rütbe Degree; grade; rank. ~ almak, to rise in rank: eshabı ~, persons of rank: o ~de, to such a degree. ~li, having high rank.

rütbetlû Of high rank (*title given to high ecclesiastics*).

rüteb *pl. of* rütbe. Ranks *etc.* ~î (··⊥), pertaining to rank.

rüus *pl. of* re's. Heads; *a grade of the* ulema; diploma in theology.

rüya *v.* ruya.

rüyet, −ti A seeing; visibility; perception; examination; supervision. ~ etm., to examine (a disputed question *or* accounts): dâvayı ~ etm., to hear a case *at law*: derdesti ~, in the course of being examined.

rüzgâr Wind. ~ ile gitmek, to sail with the wind; to trim one's sails to suit the occasion: ~ gülü, compass rose: ~ payı, wind allowance in shooting: ~ üstü, the windward side. ~altı, the lee: ~ya düşme, leeway: ~ yakası, the leech of a sail.

S

−sa *v.* ise.

saadet (·−ι), −ti Happiness; prosperity. ~le, good-bye! : der ~, (the gate of felicity), old official name of Istanbul. ~li, ~lû, happy; fortunate; *official title formerly given to generals etc.*

saat, −ti Hour; time; time of day; one hour's journey on foot; watch, clock. ~ altıda, at six o'clock : ~ besaat, from hour to hour: ~ kaç?, what's the time? : ~ler olsun !, *popular form of* sıhhatler olsun !, *q.v.*: ~ tutmak, to time (a race *etc.*): ~ vurmak, to strike the hour: bir ~ evvel, as soon as possible: iyi ~te olsunlar, djinns,

evil spirits: o ~, at that moment; at once. **saat·başı, −nı,** the end of an hour; a general pause in the conversation. ~çi, watchmaker. ~çilik, the trade of a maker, seller *or* repairer of watches. ~lik, lasting *so many* hours.

saba (·⊥) Gentle wind from the east.

Saba *v.* Seba.

sabah Morning. In the morning; tomorrow morning: ~ları, in the morning; every morning: ~tan, from early morning; from tomorrow: ~ı bulmak (etmek), to stay awake all night, to work *etc.* through the night: ~a çıkmak, (of a sick person) to live till the morning: ~ınız hayır olsun!, good morning!: ~ yıldızı, the planet Venus *as a morning star*.

sabahat, -tı Beauty.

sabah·çı Early riser; working *or* remaining till daybreak. ~**ki**, this morning's .... ~**lamak**, to sit up all night; to become morning. ~**leyin** (·ˡ··), in the morning, early. ~**lık**, woman's morning dress.

saban Plough. ~ **bıçağı (keskisi, kılıcı)**, coulter: ~ **kulağı**, mould-board: ~ **oku**, pole of a plough: ~ **ökçesi**, heel of a plough: ~ **uc demiri**, ploughshare. ~**kıran**, restharrow.

sabavet (·—ˡ), **-ti** Infancy.

sabık (—ˡ) Former, previous, preceding; foregoing. ~**a** (—·ˡ), former misdeed; previous conviction. **on ~sı bulunan bir yankesici**, a pickpocket with ten previous convictions. ~**kalı**, previously convicted; recidivist. ~**an** (—ˣ··), formerly; previously.

sabır, -brı Patience; aloes; *v. also* **sabur**. ~**lı**, patient. ~**sız**, impatient. ~**sızlanmak**, to grow impatient.

sabi (·ˣ) Male child, boy.

sâbi (—ˣ) Seventh. ~**an** (—ˣ··), seventhly.

sâbih Swimming; floating. ~ **havuz**, floating dock.

sabit (—ˡ) Fixed; stationary; firm, enduring; proved, sure; valid. ~ **kadem**, steadfast: ~ **mürekkeb**, indelible ink: ~ **olm.**, to be fixed *or* firm; to be proved *or* confirmed: ~ **seviye kabı**, float-chamber (carburettor). ~**e** (—·ˡ), fixed star; constant (*math.*).

sabretmek (ˡ··), **-eder** *vn.* Be patient; (*with dat.*) endure *stg.*

sabuk Astray; senseless. **abuk ~ söylemek**, to talk nonsense.

sabun Soap. ⌐**suya ~a dokunmamak**⌐, to avoid anything likely to cause trouble. ~**cu**, soap-maker, soap-seller. ~**hane** (···ˡ) Soap factory. ~**lamak**, to soap. ~**lu**, soapy.

sabur Patient. **ya ~ çekmek**, to call on God (the Patient One) *to give one patience*, to grow angry and impatient.

sabura (·ˣ·) Ballast.

sac¹ Sheet-iron; iron plate; thin iron plate for cooking, girdle. Made of sheet-iron.

sac² Teak.

sacayağı (ˡ···), **-nı** Trivet; trio. ~ **yürümek**, to march with one company in front and two in the rear separated by an interval.

saç¹, -çı Hair. ~ ~**a baş başa gelmek**, to come to blows: ⌐~ı **bitmedik yetim**⌐, an orphan while still a baby: ⌐~**ına sakalına bakmadan**⌐, forgetting his age: ⌐~ **sakal biribirine karışmış**⌐, dishevelled and upset.

saç² *v.* **sac.¹**

saçak Eaves of a house; fringe. ⌐**alev saçağı sardı**⌐, 'the flames have reached the eaves', the matter has got out of control: **salkım ~**, hanging about in disorder or in rags. ~**lı**, having eaves; fringed; dishevelled, untidily dressed.

saçbağı (ˡ··), **-nı** Hair ribbon.

saçı (*Formerly*) wedding present given to a bride; coins, sweets, rice *etc.* thrown over a bride. ~ **kılmak**, to scatter such things.

saçık Disordered; scattered. **açık ~**, untidily dressed; immodest, indecent.

saçılmak *vn. pass. of* **saçmak**. Be scattered; be sprinkled. **açılıp ~**, to be scattered; to dissipate one's forces; to be immodestly dressed (*also* **dökülüp ~**): **dökülüp ~**, to spend lavishly.

saçıntı Things thrown and scattered about.

saçıştırmak *va.* Sprinkle; dredge; sow.

saçkıran Baldness; alopecia.

saçlı Having hair; hairy. ~ **sakallı**, of mature age.

saçma Act of scattering; anything scattered *or* sprinkled; small shot; cast-net; nonsense. Nonsensical.

saçmak *va.* Scatter; sprinkle, dredge; sow broadcast. **saçıp savurmak**, to spend money prodigally: **ateş ~**, to fire in all directions; to be in a furious rage: **yaraya tuz ~**, (to sprinkle salt on the wound), to add fuel to the flames: **yaş ~**, to weep copiously.

saçma·lamak *vn.* Talk nonsense; say incongruous things. ~**sapan**, incongruous nonsense.

saçula (·ˡ·) Wooden mould *for casting metals*.

sada, seda (·ˣ) Echo; sound; voice.

sadaka Alms; charity. ~**ya muhtac olm.**, to be reduced to penury: **baş* göz* ~sı**, an involuntary sacrifice *made to avert some mishap*; a thank-offering *grudgingly given after recovery from an illness and so forth* (*with a semi-religious idea that one will be compensated for it in some way*): ⌐**verilmiş ~dan varmış**⌐, you've had a lucky escape!

sadakat (·—ˡ), **-ti** Faithful friendship; fidelity; devotion; *also* hypocritical friendship, flattering those in power. ~**lı**, faithful; devoted.

sadakor Raw silk.

sadalı (·—ˡ) Sounding; with a voice; talking (film). ~ **harf**, vowel.

sadaret (·—ˡ), **-ti** Grand Vizierate.

sadasız (·—ˡ) Without sound; silent. ~ **harf**, consonant.

sadberk Hundred-leaved (rose).

sade (—ˡ) Mere; simple; ummixed; pure; simple-minded; ingenuous; single (flower); plain, unadorned; unsweetened (coffee); unstuffed (pastry). Simply, merely, just.

~ **güzel**, beautiful in itself without ornament: ~ **suya çorba**, soup made without fat, *hence* ~ **suya**, mere, plain; unimportant. ~**ce** ($\overset{\perp}{\cdot\cdot}$), simply, merely.

saded Point *or* object in view; intention; scope. ... ~**inde**, within the scope of ...: ... ~**inde bulunmak**, to have the intention of ...: ~**im dahilinde değil**, it is not within the scope of my article (my lecture *etc.*): ~**e gelelim**, let us come to the point under discussion: ~**den haric**, extraneous to the question, off the point.

sadedil ($-\cdot\overset{1}{}$) Ingenuous; guileless; naïve. ~**lik**, ingenuousness, simpleness of heart.

sadef *v.* **sedef**.

sadefe A mother-of-pearl shell; the external ear, concha.

sade·gi ($-\cdot\overset{\perp}{}$) Simplicity; purity. ~**leştirmek**, to simplify. ~**lik**, simplicity, plainness. ~**yağ**, butter.

sadık ($-\overset{1}{}$) True; sincere; faithful; honest; devoted.

sadır, -drı Breast, chest; heart; front; prominence; post of honour; most important person. **sadra geçmek**, to take the chief seat in an assembly; to become Grand Vizier: **sadra şifa verecek**, satisfactory.

sâdır ($-\overset{1}{}$) Emanating. ~ **olm.**, to emanate (of a decree *etc.*); to happen.

sâdis ($-\overset{1}{}$) Sixth. ~**en** ($\overset{\perp}{\cdot\cdot}$), sixthly.

sadme Collision; sudden blow *or* misfortune; explosion.

sadra *v.* **sadır**.

sadrazam ($\cdot-\overset{1}{}$) Grand Vizier.

sadrî ($\cdot\overset{\perp}{}$) Pectoral.

saf, -ffı Row; line; rank. ~ ~, in rows *or* ranks: ~ **düzmek**, to draw up a line of battle: ~**fı harb**, line of battle: ~**tan haric**, hors de combat.

sâf (-) Pure; unadulterated; limpid; sincere, unfeigned; ingenuous, simple, naïve.

safa, sefa ($\cdot\overset{\perp}{}$) Freedom from anxiety; peace, ease; enjoyment, pleasure. ~ **geldiniz!** (*the reply to which is* ~ **bulduk**): ~**yı hatır**, peace and quiet, ease and comfort: ~**yı hatırla kullanınız!**, 'may you enjoy the use of it!', *said to one who has acquired stg.*: ~ **olm.**, to enjoy *or* amuse oneself: ~ **sürmek**, to live a quiet and happy life; to enjoy oneself: ~ **vermek**, to give pleasure: **ehli** ~, one given to self-indulgence. ~**bahş** ($\cdot-\overset{1}{}$), pleasant, delightful.

safahat ($\cdot\cdot\overset{\cdot}{}$), **-tı** *pl. of* **safha**. Phases.

saf·derun Simple; sincere; silly. ~**derunluk**, simplicity; good nature; credulity. ~**dil**, simple-hearted, ingenuous, naïve, credulous.

safer *Second month of the Moslem year*.

saffet, -ti Purity; sincerity; ingenuousness.

saffıharb Line of battle. ~ **gemisi**, capital ship.

safha Surface, face; plate; leaf, page; phase.

sâfi ($\overset{\perp}{\cdot}$) Clear; pure; sincere; net. ~ **su**, mere water and nothing else: **gayri** ~, gross (profits *etc.*).

safiha Thin leaf *or* sheet; plate, plaque; surface.

safir[1] Sapphire.

safir[2] Whistling noise; hiss. ~**î** ($\cdot\cdot\overset{\perp}{}$), sibilant.

saflık Simplicity; ingenuousness.

safra[1] Ballast. ~ **atmak**, to get rid of useless persons *or* things.

safra[2] Bile; gall. ~ **bastırmak**, to have a snack: ~**sı bulanmak**, to be nauseated: ~**m kabarıyor**, I feel like being sick: ~ **galib**, bilious. ~**lı**, bilious; feeling sick *or* giddy. ~**vî** ($\cdot-\overset{\perp}{}$), biliary; bilious.

safran Saffron.

safsata False reasoning; sophistry; quibbling. ~**ya düşmek**, to use silly arguments. ~**cı**, sophist. ~**lamak**, to use sophistry, to quibble, to argue falsely.

safşiken, safzen Who breaks the enemy's ranks; valiant.

sağ[1] Alive; safe; sound in body; trustworthy; strong. ~ **akçe (para)**, good money, genuine coin: ~ **kalanlar**, the survivors (after a disaster *or* battle): ~ **kurulmak**, to escape with one's life; to come out safe and sound: ~ **ol!** (**olsun!**), *a phrase for thanking*: ~ **salim** *or* **selâmet**, safe and sound: ⌈**başınız** ~ **olsun!**⌉, *formal phrase for offering condolences on the loss of a relative*; **başın** ~ **olsuna gitmek**, to pay a visit of condolence: ⌈**sen** ~ **ben selâmet**⌉, 'well, there's none left' (*regretfully and perhaps reproachfully*); *also in such phrases as*: '**bu işi bir ayda bitirdik mi, sen** ~ **ben selâmet!**', 'if we get this job done in a month, we shall have seen the last of it, thank Goodness!': **siz** ~ **olun!**, it doesn't matter, don't worry!

sağ[2] Right, right-hand. The right-hand side. ~**a bak!**, eyes right!: ~**ına soluna bakmak**, to look about one: ~**ına soluna bakmamak**, to act without consideration: ~**ı solu yok**, tactless; eccentric; devil-may-care; unpredictable: ~**ını soluna şaşırmak**, to be bewildered, not to know what to do.

sağaçık Outside right (football).

sağalmak *vn.* Be cured, become well.

sağanak, sağnak Heavy rainstorm, downpour; squall; sudden loss *or* damage.

sağcı Right-wing sympathizer.

sağdıç Intimate friend of the bride *or* bridegroom; intimate friend *in general*; godfather. ~ **emeği**, useless efforts.

sağı Bird excrement; fowl dung.

sağılmak *vn. pass. of* **sağmak.** Be milked *etc.*; be frayed; (of a snake) to uncoil itself.

sağım Single act of milking; quantity milked; quantity of honey taken. ~**lı,** kept for milking; in milk. ~**lık,** beast kept for milking.

sağır Deaf; giving out a dull sound (*as a full cask*); opaque (glass); closed-up, sham (door *etc.*); having a low conductivity of heat (kettle *etc.*); sound-proof. ⌐~ sultanın bile duyup bildiği⌐, a thing that is known and obvious to all: bir kulağı ~ olm., to condone, to take no notice of *a fault*: hem ~ hem sığır, stupid and obstinate. ~**lık,** deafness.

sağış *n.* Milking.

sağıtmak *va.* Cure.

sağiç (¹·) Inside right (football).

sağlam Sound; whole; healthy; trustworthy; wholesome. ~**a** *or* ~ kazığa bağlamak, to make safe *or* sure: ~ rüzgâr, a steady wind. ~**lamak, sağlamak,** to make safe, secure *or* certain; put in working order; secure, ensure. ~**laşmak,** to become sound *or* firm; be put right (broken machine *etc.*); prove to be true; become safe, escape from danger. ~**lık,** soundness, wholeness; safety; health; trustworthiness; wholesomeness; truthfulness (being true).

sağlı Connected with the right hand; having a right-hand side. ~ sollu, ambidextrous.

sağlıcak *Used in expressions like* ~**la** gidiniz !, go in good health !, good journey !

sağlık A being alive; life; good health; health in general (*instead of the proper Turkish* sıhhat). ~ !, all is well !: sağlığında, in his lifetime, while he was alive : ~ almak, to ask the way; to have *stg.* recommended : ~ olsun !, never mind ! : ~ selâmetle, in health and safety : ~ vermek, to recommend (a shop, a doctor *etc.*): can sağlığı, health; ⌐her şeyin başı ~ (can sağlığı)⌐, health above all !; bundan iyisi ~ (can sağlığı), the best one can have : eline ~ !, well done !; thank you !: ⌐üstüme iyilik ~ !⌐, (i) that's the limit !; (ii) I've never heard of such a thing !; (iii) God forbid !

sağmak *va.* Milk; fleece (*fig.*); take honey; (of a cloud) to pour out rain; unwind.

sağmal (Cow *etc.*) kept for milking.

sağnak *v.* sağanak.

sağrı Rump; leather made from the rump of a horse; mountain ridge.

sağu Eulogy of the dead; lamentation. ~**cu,** professional mourner.

sağyağ (¹·) Cooking butter.

sah, -hhı Official flourish on a document *to show that it has been examined or registered.*

saha (–¹) Open space; courtyard; field (*also fig.*); area; ground (football *etc.*). hayat ~sı, 'Lebensraum'.

sahâ (·¹) *v.* sahavet.

sahabe (·–¹) The disciples of Mohammed.

sahabet (·–¹), –**ti** Support, protection; patronage. ···e ~ etm., to support and protect.

sahaf Seller of secondhand books.

sahaif (·–¹) *pl. of* sahife. Pages.

sahan Large copper food dish; a dish of food. ~**lık,** marble-topped stand *to put dishes on*; landing *on a staircase*; platform *of a tram etc.*; amount of food in a **sahan.**

sahavet (·–¹), –**ti** Generosity, munificence.

sahhaf *v.* sahaf.

sahi¹, sahî (·¹) Generous, open-handed.

sahi² (–¹) *v.* sahih.

sahib (–¹) Possessing; endowed with. Owner, possessor; master; protector. ···e ~ çıkmak, to claim ownership of *stg.*; to stand as protector *or* patron of *s.o.*: ~**i** itibar, one who enjoys general esteem *or* credit : namus ~**i,** a man of honour : mal ~**i,** owner of a property, rich man : tabiat ~**i,** a man of good taste : ev ~**i,** the master *or* the owner of a house.

sahib·e, female owner *etc.* ~**lik,** ownership; protection. ···e ~ etm., to protect, to champion. ~**siz,** unowned, ownerless; without a protector; abandoned.

sahi·ci (¹··) Real, genuine, true. ~**den** (–·¹), really, truly.

sahif (·⸜) Thin; flimsy; weak; silly.

sahife (··¹) Page; leaf.

sahih (·⸜) Sound; true, correct. ~ mi ?, is that really so ? ~**an** (··¹·), truly.

sahil (–¹) Shore; coast; bank. ~**i** selâmet, safety from danger; ~**i** selâmete vasıl olm., to reach safety; to come to a successful conclusion. ~**hane** (–·–¹), house on the sea-shore *or* the bank of a river. ~**topu** (–¹··), -**nu,** coastal gun.

sahileş·mek *vn.* Turn out to be true; be confirmed. ~**tirmek,** to verify, show to be true; fulfil.

sahne Scene (theatre); stage.

sahra (·¹) Open plain; open country; wilderness, desert: field (*mil.*). ~**ı** kebir, the Sahara: ~ topu, field-gun. ~**î** (·–¹), pertaining to the country *or* desert; rural.

sahre Boulder, rock.

sahrınc *v.* sarnıç.

sahte False; spurious; counterfeit, sham. ~**kâr,** who counterfeits *or* forges. ~**kârlık,** forgery; counterfeiting, false coining. ~**lik,** falsity, spuriousness. ~**vakar,** who assumes an air of dignity; who pretends to be imposing.

sahtiyan Morocco leather.

sahur Meal before dawn during the Ramazan fast.

sai (–⸜) Courier, messenger.

saib (–⸜) That hits the mark; right; sound.

said (–⸜) Ascending.

sâid (–⸜) Forearm.

saîd (·⸜) Auspicious.

saik (–⸜), **–ki** Driving, impelling. Factor. ···e ~ olm., to cause, to induce. **~a¹** (–·⸜), cause, motive, incentive. **~ane** (–·–⸜), exciting desire, lascivious.

saika² (–·⸜) Lightning; thunderbolt.

sail¹ (–⸜) Beggar. **~lik** (–·⸜), begging.

sail² (–⸜) Flowing; fluid; molten. **~iyet** (–···⸜), **–ti**, liquidity.

sair (–⸜) That remains; the rest of; other; that walks or goes; well-known, current. **ve ~e** (*abb. to* v.s.) etcetera. **~filmenam**, somnambulist.

sâit (–⸜), **–ti** Vowel. Sounding. *v. also* sâid.

sak, **–kki** Legal document; book of legal formulas.

sâk (–), **–kı** Shank; stem; trunk.

saka Water-carrier. **~kuşu**, **–nu**, goldfinch.

sakağı Glanders; farcy.

sakak Double chin; dewlap.

sakal Beard; whiskers. **~ bırakmak** *or* **salıvermek**, to let the beard grow: **~ı ele vermek**, to allow oneself to be led by the nose; to allow all one's secrets to be guessed: ···**in ~ına gülmek**, to make a fool of ...; to ridicule, to deceive: **~ı saydırmak**, to be no longer respected, to cease to be important: **işin ~ı bitti**, the matter is getting tedious: **~ımı uzatsam değecek**, very close: **ak ~ kara ~**, high and low, rich and poor: **ak ~dan yok ~a kadar**, old and young alike.

sakal·lanmak *vn.*, to grow a beard. **~lı**, bearded: ⸢**her ~yı baban mı sandın?**⸥, people are not always what you think they are.

sakamet (·–⸜), **–ti** Defect; fault; harm.

sakamonya (··⸜·) Scammony (*a purgative*).

sakangur Skink; coarse book-muslin.

sakar White blaze on a horse's forehead. Ill-omened, unlucky; sinister; (servant *etc.*) who always breaks things. **~ meki**, coot. **~ca**, white-fronted goose. **~lı**, having a white blaze (horse); unlucky, ill-omened. **~lık**, clumsiness.

sakat, **–tı** Unsound, defective; disabled, invalid; broken, damaged. Offals. **~at**, **–tı**, offals. **~çı**, seller of offals. **~lamak**, to injure, damage, mutilate. **~lık**, infirmity; defect; mistake.

sakıb, **–kbı** A boring *or* puncturing; perforation. **sâkıb** (–⸜), perforating; penetrating.

sakıf, **–kfı** Roof.

sakın Beware !, take care !, mind!; don't! **~gan**, timid; cautious; retiring. **~ıcı**, cautious man who avoids risks. **~ma**, a looking after oneself; an avoidance of risks: **~sı olmamak**, not to care a straw for anyone.

sakınmak *vn.* Take care of oneself; be cautious. *va.* Protect *oneself or one's property.* ···**den ~**, to guard oneself from ..., be on one's guard against ...: ⸢**sakınan göze çöp batar**⸥, being over-careful invites misfortune: **gözünü budaktan sakınmaz**, dare-devil: **sözünü sakınmaz**, he doesn't mince words: **yankesicilerden sakınınız !**, beware of pickpockets !

sakır ~, shivering *or* trembling. **~damak**, to shiver with cold *or* fear. **~dı**, a shivering with cold *or* fear.

sakırga Tick.

sakıt (–⸜) Falling; dropping down; fallen in esteem; become of no account; aborted. **~ olm.**, to fall, to lapse, to become of no effect.

sakız Mastic; chewing-gum; **~ or ~ gibi**, very white and clean: **âlemin ağzında ~ olm.**, to be a matter of common talk: **birinin ağzının ~ı olm.**, to be an object of s.o.'s ill-natured gossip; stg. that s.o. never ceases talking about: ⸢**her kes ~ çiğner amma çatlamasını beceremez**⸥, 'anyone can chew gum but not everyone can make it crack', *i.e.* anyone can do this but few can do it properly.

sâki (–⸜) Cupbearer; distributer of water.

sakil Heavy, ponderous; wearisome; unwholesome; harsh (word or sound); ugly.

sakim Faulty, defective; harmful; wrong.

sakin (–⸜) Quiet; motionless; stationary; calm; allayed; quiescent (letter); who inhabits *or* dwells.

sakiname (– – –⸜) Lyric addressed to a cupbearer.

sâkit (–⸜) Silent; taciturn.

sakiye Female cupbearer.

saklamak *va.* Hide; keep secret; keep, store, save for future use; preserve from danger. **Allah saklasın !** *or* **Hak saklıya !**, God preserve us !, Heaven forfend !; **halktan ~**, to keep a secret from the people; to preserve from the rabble.

saklambac Hide-and-seek.

sakla·nmak *vn.* Hide oneself; be concealed; be kept *or* stored; be preserved from harm. **~yıcı**, protecting, preserving; concealing, secretive.

saklı Hidden; secret; put aside; preserved.

saklıya *v.* saklamak.

saksağan Magpie. ⸢**dam üstünde ~ beline**

vurdum kazmayı[1] (*a nonsensical rhyme*), 'what's that got to do with it?'; 'what rot you are talking!'

saksı Flower-pot; vase. **~lık**, shelf for flower-pots; place for keeping flowers in pots during the winter.

Saksunya (·¹·) Saxony. **s~**, Dresden china.

sakulta (·¹·) Case-shot.

sal[1] (*Fr. salle*) Hall.

sal[2], **sâl** (–), **–li** Year.

sal[3], **–lı** Raft; stretcher; bier.

salâ Call to prayer *or* to a funeral; challenge; a fight with stones between two parties of boys; *interjection used to call attention or to issue a challenge, cf. 'oyez!'* **~ etm.**, to proclaim publicly.

salâbet (·–¹), **–ti** Hardness, toughness; firmness; solidity. **~li**, firm; rigid; tough; strong *in faith or character*.

salacak Slab on which corpses are placed for washing.

salâh Goodness, righteousness; improvement. **~a doğru**, improving, getting better. **~ kesbetmek**, (of conditions) to improve: **sulhu ~**, peace and amity.

salâhiyet (·–·¹), **–ti** Authority *or* right to do stg.; competence. **~i tamme**, full powers: **bunu yapmaga ~i yok**, he has no right *or* authority to do this: **dairei ~**, the limits of one's authority, the sphere of one's competence. **~li**, authorized; competent; (the department or authority) concerned. **~name**, credentials; written authority. **~tar**, authoritative; competent.

salahur *Ancient title like the old English 'esquire'; a knight, free from taxes, but charged with the safety of a fortress.*

salak[1] Silly, doltish.

salak[2] *Ancient weapon consisting of a pole with chains attached to iron balls at the end.*

salam *A kind of* sausage.

salamandra (··¹·) Salamander.

Salamon Solomon *when used to mean Jews in general (cf. our 'Moses'); (King Solomon is* **Süleyman peygamber**).

salamura (··¹·) Brine for pickling; anything pickled in brine.

salapurya (··¹·) Small lighter.

salâr Leader, chief.

salaş Booth; market stall; temporary shed.

salaşpur A loosely woven cotton fabric *used for linings*.

salât (·¹), **–tı** Moslem ritual prayer. **~ü selâm getirmek**, to pronounce the formula calling God's benediction on the Prophet (*during prayer or in times of peril*).

salata (·¹·) Salad; lettuce. **frenk ~sı**, endive. **~lık** (·¹··), cucumber.

salâtüselâm (·–···¹) Prayer in moments of danger, *v.* **salât**.

salâvat (··¹), **–tı** *pl. of* **salât**. Prayers. **yanına ~la varılır**, approached only with fear and trembling (*said of a proud inaccessible man or a cruel or angry man*).

salb, **–bi** Execution by hanging; crucifixion; impaling. **~etmek** (¹··), **–eder**, to hang, crucify. **~en** (¹·), by hanging.

salça (¹·) Sauce; tomato sauce.

saldır·gan Aggressor. Aggressive. **~ım**, aggression, attack. **~ma**, act of attacking; large knife.

saldır·mak *va. caus. of* **salmak**, *q.v.*; rush *s.o.* to a place. *vn.* Hurl oneself; make an attack (on = *dat.*) ‖**~mazlık**, non-aggression.

saldide (·–¹) Full of years.

salep (–¹) Salep (*root of Orchis mascula*); the hot drink made of this root.

salgın Aggressive; savage (animal); contagious. Epidemic (*also fig.*); contagion; general tax levied on a community; annual tribute. **sinema ~ına kapılmak**, to be caught by the general craze for the cinema.

salhane (·–¹) Slaughter-house.

salhurde Aged.

salı Tuesday.

salık Information; indication as to one's way. **~ vermek**, to give directions as to route.

salıncak Swing; hammock. **~ sandalye**, rocking-chair: **kayık ~**, swing-boat.

salınmak[1] *vn. pass. of* **salmak**. Be thrown *etc.*; (of water, electricity) to be turned on. 'onun suyuna pirinç salınmaz', he is not to be relied upon.

salın·mak[2] *vn.* Sway; oscillate; loiter along, swaying from side to side. **~tı**, swell (at (sea); a swaying about. **~tılı**, running with a swell (sea); swaying; tottering.

salıvermek (·¹··) *va.* Let go; set free; release; allow to grow (beard *etc.*). **kahkaha ~**, to burst out laughing.

salib Cross. **~iahmer** (·–··¹), the Red Cross.

salif (–¹) Preceding. **~üzzikir**, above-mentioned.

salih (–¹) Good; serviceable; suitable, proper; pious. **şarab imaline ~ üzüm**, grapes suitable for wine-making.

sâlik (–¹), **–ki** Who follows *a profession*. Class of dervishes above the novitiate; devotee.

salim (¹) Safe, sound; free from (defects *etc.*). **···en** (¹···), safely and soundly.

salis (–¹) Third. **~e**, a third; one-sixtieth of a second; **bir ~de**, in a flash. **~en** (¹··), thirdly.

salkı Hanging; relaxed; defective, deformed, paralysed.

salkım Hanging bunch *of grapes or flowers*; any tree bearing hanging flowers (acacia, wistaria *etc.*); cluster. Hanging, pendent. ~ **ateş**, firework ending in a shower of stars: ~ **saçak**, hanging about untidily or in rags: ~ **söğüt**, weeping-willow. ⌜**halka verir talkını, kendi yutar ~ı**⌝, he preaches one thing and practises another.

salkımak *vn.* Hang loosely.

sallabaş Afflicted with an involuntary shaking of the head.

sallamak *va.* Swing; rock; shake; wag; put off; leave in suspense. **baş ~**, to nod the head; to listen without paying attention; **her şeye baş ~**, to agree to everything, to raise no objection; **el ~**, to wave the hand; ⌜**elini sallasan ellisi, kolunu sallasan çifte tellisi**⌝, you have only to wave your hand and people will come in crowds; no dearth of candidates: **hiç sallamamak** (*sl.*), to pay no attention; not to care a brass farthing: ···**e kuyruk ~**, to flatter.

sallan·dirmak *va.* Swing; shake; hang (execute); put off, delay; put off by false promises. **~mak** *vn.*, swing about; rock; oscillate; totter; be about to fall; loiter, lounge about, waste time.

sallapatı Without reflection; suddenly. Careless; tactless.

sallasırt etm. *va.* Hoist on the shoulders, shoulder.

sallı Large and wide; open-mouthed; straggling.

salma *verb. n. of* **salmak**. Untethered, let out to pasture; running continuously (water). Local rate levied on villages; (formerly) a kind of police force; long hanging sleeve; a kind of stew containing rice. ~ **tomruğu**, (*formerly*) a police cell: **güvercin ~sı**, pigeon-loft.

salmak *va.* Throw; let go; send in haste; insert; spread out; let hang down; send forth (shoots, smoke); postpone; impose (tax); give out (shade); cast (shadow); lay (foundation); throw into a saucepan. *va.* Be aggressive; (*with dat.*) hurl oneself at, attack. **ah ~**, to heave a sigh: **atını ~**, to let one's horse go at full speed: **boy ~**, (of young trees *etc.*) to grow: **su ~**, to add water to *a thing when cooking*; **suya ~**, to waste: **yatak ~**, to spread a bed.

salmastra (·⌐·) Cord wound round anything to protect it against chafing; gasket; packing. ~ **kutusu**, stuffing-box.

salname (——ᴵ) Almanac.

salon Guest-room; dining-room; hall.

sâlp *v.* **salb**.

salpa Loose; slack; untidy; slovenly dressed; up and down (anchor).

salt Mere, simple. Merely, solely.

salta[1] *A kind of* short jacket.

salta[2] (ᴵ·) **etm.** *vn.* Stand on the hind legs (dog *etc.*). *va.* Slacken off (a tight rope).

salta[3] (ᴵ·) Sovereignty, dominion.

saltanat, –tı Sovereignty, dominion; authority, rule; pomp, magnificence. ~ **seniye**, the Ottoman Government: ~ **sürmek**, to rule as Sultan; to live in great splendour. **~lı**, regal, pompous, magnificent.

salya (ᴵ·) Saliva.

salyana (ᴵ··) Annual tribute; tax levied on a community.

salyangoz Snail. ⌜**Müslüman mahallesinde ~ satmak**⌝, 'to sell snails in the Moslem quarter', to do stg. that 'isn't done'.

Sam[1] Shem.

sam[2], **–mmi** Poisonous. Poisonous wind, simoon; blight. ~ **vermek** (**çalmak**), for the wind to scorch *or* the blight to injure.

samame (·—ᴵ) Embolism.

sâman (—ᴵ) Wealth; well-being.

saman Straw. ⌜~ **altından su yürütmek**⌝, to do stg. in an underhand way, to intrigue covertly: ~ **gibi**, insipid· ~ **tozu** (**çöpü**), chaff: ⌜**sakla –ı, gelir zamanı!**⌝, don't waste anything, it may come in useful some day. **saman·i** (·—ᴵ), straw-coloured. **~kâğıdı**, **–ni**, tracing-paper. **~kapan**, amber. **~lık**, straw-rick; place for storing straw: ⌜**iki gönül bir olunca ~ seyran olur**⌝, where two hearts beat as one the surroundings make no difference. **~uğrusu**, **–nu**, **~yolu**, **–nu**, the Milky Way.

samedan·î (···—ᴸ) Divine. **~iyet**, **–ti**, divinity.

sâmi (—ᴵ) High; illustrious. **emri ~**, an order emanating from the Grand Vizier: **zatı ~leri**, Your Highness.

Samî (—ᴸ) Semitic.

sami (—ᴵ), **–ii** Who hears. Listener; one who attends lessons at a school without being a regular pupil. **~a** (—·ᴵ), the sense of hearing. **~in** (—·ᴵ), listeners, the audience.

samim (·⅃) Inmost *or* essential part of a thing; essence. **an ~ül kalb**, from the bottom of the heart, sincerely. **~î** (·—ᴸ) sincere; cordial. **~iyet** (·—·ᴵ), **–ti**, sincerity.

samin (—ᴵ) Eighth. **~en** (ᴸ··), eighthly.

samit, **–ti** Silent; mute (letter); passive (capital or wealth). Consonant.

samsa *A kind of* pastry *sweetened with syrup.*

samsun Mastiff. **~cu**, soldier in charge of mastiffs, *formerly used against the enemy.*

samur Sable. ~ **kürk**, sable skin coat; ~ **kürkü sırtına almak**, to take the blame, to bear the responsibility; ~ **kürkü** ···**in**

sırtına giydirmek, to lay the blame on ...:
~ kaş, thick black eyebrows: sarı ~, pine-marten: su ~u, otter.

samyeli (ˈ··), **–ni** Hot poisonous wind, simoom.

san[1] Reputation, esteem; surname. adı ~ı
yok, he is of no account, of no repute:
adımız ~ımız, our good name.

san[2] A disease of corn crops, *causing yellow-ness.*

sana *dat. of* sen. To you. o ~ ne?, what's
that to you?

san'at, **–ti** *or* **–tı** Trade, calling, craft;
industry; art; skill, ability. ~le, artistically. ~çı, artisan, craftsman. ~kâr,
artisan; artist; actor. ~kârlık, profession
of an artisan; profession of art; skill,
artistic ability.

sanavber Pine; conifer; fir-cone. ~iye,
conifers; coniferous.

sanayi (·–ˈ), **–ii** *pl. of* san'at. Industries
etc. ~ci, industrialist. ~leştirmek, to
industrialize.

sancak Flag, standard; starboard side;
(formerly) a subdivision of a vilayet.
sancağı şerif, the flag of the Prophet, *only
unfurled for a Holy War.* ~tar, standard-bearer.

sancı Stomach-ache, colic, gripes, stitch.
~lanmak, to have a stomach-ache *or*
similar internal pain. ~lı, having a
stomach-ache. ~mak, to ache, to be
griped.

sancılmak *vn. pass. of* sançmak.

sançmak *va.* Thrust into; set up in the
ground; plant.

sandal[1] Rowing-boat. ~cı, boatman.

sandal[2] Sandalwood.

sandal[3] Sandal (shoe).

sandal[4] Brocade. **Sandal Bedestini,** the
Municipal Auction-rooms at Istanbul.

sandalye (·ˈ·) Chair; office, post. ~
kavgası, struggle for a post: ~siz nazır,
Minister without portfolio: koltuklu ~,
arm-chair.

sandık Chest, coffer, box; coffer-dam;
cash-box; cash department *of a government
or business;* old-fashioned fire-pump; box
for measuring sand *etc.* ~ emini, cashier:
~ eşyası, clothes *etc.* forming part of a
bride's dowry. ~ sepet, bag and baggage:
tasarruf sandığı, Savings Bank. ~çe,
small box. ~kâr, cashier. ~lı, furnished
with a box: thin board *used for veneer:* ~
saat, grandfather clock.

sanduka (·ˈ·) Sarcophagus.

sandviç Sandwich.

sanem Idol; idol of one's heart.

sangı Confused, stupefied, dizzy. ~lamak,
to be stupefied *or* confused.

sanı Idea; imagination; surmise. ~cı,
who thinks *or* meditates; who imagines *or*
surmises.

‖ **sanık** Suspected; accused.

sani[1](–ˉ) *a.* Second.

sani[2] (–ˈ), **–ii** Worker; maker, creator; the
Creator. ~a (·–ˈ), invention, ruse.

sanih (–ˈ) Occurring to the mind. ~ olm.,
to occur to one; for an inspiration to come
to one. ~a (–·ˈ), sudden thought; inspiration.

saniye (–·ˈ) Second, moment; seconds-hand;
(formerly) second grade of officials. ~si
~sine, dead on time, to the very second:
tabiatı ~, second nature. ~li, (watch)
with seconds-hand: ~ tapa, time-fuse.
~n (ˉ··), secondly.

sank, sankı Bird excrement.

sanki (ˈ·) As if, as though; supposing that.

sanlı Well-known; esteemed. adlı ~, well-
known and talked about.

sanmak, **–ır** *va. & vn.* Think, suppose;
deem. hayır ~, to think well of: kem ~,
to think ill of.

sansar Pine-marten; polecat. ~ gibi,
stealthy, sly.

sansür (*Fr. censure*) Censorship.

santimetre Centimetre.

santral, **–li** (*Fr. centrale*) Telephone exchange; power-house.

santur Dulcimer.

santurlu Splendid, magnificent.

sanzatu (*Fr. sans atout*) No trumps.

sap Thread; stem; handle; stalk. ⌐~ derken
saman demek⌐, to talk twaddle: ⌐~ demeden samanı anlamak⌐, to be very 'quick in
the uptake': ~ına kadar, to the core,
utterly: ~ı silik, vagabond, tramp.

sapa Off the road; out-of-the-way, secluded. ~ düşmek, to be off the main road;
to be remote *or* inaccessible: ~ yol, by-
road, side-street.

sapan Sling; catapult; sling *for hoisting
heavy articles.* direk ~ı, strop (*naut.*):
⌐peşinden ~ taşı yetişmez⌐, 'a stone from
a sling couldn't catch him up', *said of one
running away very hard.* ~balığı, **–nı,**
thresher shark.

saparna (·ˈ·) Sarsaparilla.

saparta (·ˈ·) Broadside; severe scolding.

sapasağlam (ˈ···) *v.* sapsağlam.

sapık Gone astray; perverted; eccentric;
crazy. Harmless lunatic.

sapılmak *vn. impers. of* sapmak. buradan
sapılır, here one turns off *in another direction.*

sapır sapır *Imitates the noise of continuously falling things.* ~ ~ dökülmek, to fall
continuously (*e.g.* grass being mown).

sapıtmak *va.* Cause to go astray. *vn.* Go

off one's head; talk nonsense. **gemiyi ~,** to alter the course of a ship: **sözü ~,** to lose the thread of an argument; to change the discourse: **yolu ~,** to take the wrong turning, to turn into another road.
sapkın¹ Astray; off the right road.
sapkın² Harpoon; fish-spear.
saplama Stud (*mech.*).
sapla·mak *va.* Thrust into; pierce; skewer. **~nmak,** (*with dat.*) to sink into, penetrate; get an idea fixed into the mind : get a handle *or* stem.
saplı Having a handle *or* stem; sticking into a thing. Bowl or pot with a handle; scoop, ladle. **eski politikaya ~ kaldılar,** they stuck to their old policy.
sapmak *vn.* Swerve; deviate; diverge; turn off into a different direction; go astray; fall into error. **çıkmaza ~,** to get into a blind alley : **yalana ~,** to have recourse to lying.
sapsarı (¹··) Bright yellow; very pale.
sapsız Without a handle *or* stem. **~ balta,** one without backing or influence : **ipsiz ~,** without a tie, vagabond; disconnected; incoherent.
saptırmak *va. caus. of* **sapmak,** *q.v.*
sar'a Epileptic fit. **~sı var (tutuyor),** he is in a fit.
sarac Saddler; leather-worker. **~lık,** the trade of a saddler, saddlery. **~hane, ~ane** (···–¹), saddlery market; saddlery workshop.
sarahat (·–¹), **-ti** Clearness; explicitness. **~en** (·˻··), clearly, explicitly.
saraka Pillory; ridicule. **~ya almak (sarmak),** to deride, ridicule.
saralı Subject to epileptic fits.
sararmak *vn.* Turn yellow *or* pale.
sarasker *v.* **serasker.**
saray Palace; mansion; government house *or* office. **~ Burnu,** Seraglio Point: **~ lokması,** a sweetmeat *made of dough, eggs and sugar.* **~lı,** attached to a palace; brought up in a palace *or* mansion : palace servant *or* slave. **~patı,** China Aster.
sardalya (·¹·) Sardine, pilchard; packed like sardines.
sardırmak *va. caus. of* **sarmak,** *q.v.* **~ or merak ~,** to start to have a passion for ... .
sardoğan A kind of hawk, (? ?) hobby.
Sardunya (·¹·) Sardinia; geranium (pelargonium).
sarf Expenditure; use; grammar. **~ı gayret etm.,** to make great efforts. **~etmek** (¹··), **-eder,** to spend, expend. **~î** (·˻·), grammatical. **~iyat** (··˻·), **-tı,** expenses.

sarfınazar Putting aside. **her şeyden ~,** apart from everything else : **~ etm.,** to disregard; to relinquish.
sargı Bandage.
sarhoş Drunk. **içmeden ~,** 'drunk without drinking', *said of one who behaves oddly.* **~luk,** drunkenness.
sarı Yellow; fair-haired; pale; haggard. Yellow colour; yolk. **~ altın,** pure gold; a Turkish lira piece : **~ çam,** Scotch pine : ⌐(orduda) **~ çizmeli (Mehmed Ağa)¹,** an unknown person; just anybody; a nobody; *said also of an incomplete address.*
sarı·ağız, the Meagre (*Sciaena aquila*). **~asma,** golden oriole. **~ca,** yellowish : **~ arı,** wasp. **~çalı,** barberry. **~göz,** a kind of sea-bream.
sarığıburma A kind of sweet pastry.
sarık Turban. **~ sarmak,** to put on *or* wear a turban. **~lı,** wearing a turban.
sarı·kanad Medium-sized **Lüfer** (fish). **~lı¹,** coloured yellow. **~lık,** yellowness; jaundice; blight.
sarılı² Wound; fastened; surrounded.
sarılmak *vn. pass. of* **sarmak.** Be surrounded; be enveloped; be entangled; be bandaged; (*with dat.*) be wound *or* wrapped round; be wound *or* wrapped up in; clasp; embrace; throw oneself upon; be absorbed in; give oneself up to *work etc.*; (of a plant) to entwine itself round, to climb. **ayağa ~,** to clasp the legs in entreaty : **boynuna* ~,** to throw one's arms round the neck of *s.o.* : ⌐**denize düşen yılana sarılır¹,** a desperate man will face any risk: ···**e dört elle ~,** to give one's utmost to ..., to show the greatest zeal in ...: **silâha ~,** to take up arms; to seize a weapon *with the intention of using it.*
sarım¹ Sharp; trenchant; decided.
sarım² Bandage; turn of winding (of elect. coil *etc.*).
sarımsak *v.* **sarmısak.**
sarımsı, sarımtrak Yellowish.
sarınmak *va. & vn.* Wrap oneself (in = *dat.*); gird oneself.
sarıot (·¹·) Small pine plank.
sarısabır (·¹··), **-brı** The finest quality of aloes.
sarısalkım (·¹··) Laburnum.
sarışın Fair-haired, blond.
sari (–¹) Contagious. **emrazi ~ye or ~ hastalıklar,** contagious diseases.
sarih Clear; explicit.
sarik (–¹) Thieving. Thief.
sark·ık Pendulous; hanging loosely; flabby. **~ılmak,** to hang down; be suspended. **~ınmak,** to hang down; lean over; (*with dat.*) molest, worry.
sarkıntı Robbery, spoliation; molesta-

tion. ~lık, act of robbery *or* molestation; importunate or insulting behaviour to a woman.

sarkıtmak *va.* Let hang down; suspend; hang. **dudak ~,** to pout, sulk.

sarkmak *va.* Hang down; lean out (of a window *etc.*); (*with dat.*) come down on, attack suddenly. **bir yere kadar ~,** to go as far as a place.

sarma Act of winding *or* enveloping; embrace; a thing wrapped up in stg. else; meat and rice wrapped up in vine leaves (**yaprakdolması**); trip (with the leg). **~ya almak,** to get a hold round one's adversary's leg in wrestling: **kuzu ~sı,** lamb chitterlings; ˹**can ciğer kuzu ~sı**˺, a very intimate friendship: **hedefi ~ kabiliyeti,** the pattern made by a shot-gun.

sarmak *va.* Wind *or* wrap round; bandage; embrace; cling to; surround; wind (wool *etc.*); comprehend, take in; captivate, interest. *vn.* (Of a vine *etc.*) to climb; busy oneself about *stg.* ˹**ateş sacağı** (*or* **bacayı**) **sardı**˺, the fire has got a hold on the eaves, *i.e.* things are pretty desperate: **başına* ~,** to wind *stg.* round the head; (of wine *etc.*) to go to the head; **bu işi (adamı) nereden başıma sardın?,** why did you saddle me with this matter (man)?: **işe ~,** to go to work assiduously on a matter: **bu adam beni hiç sarmadı,** I didn't take to that man at all.

sarmalamak *va. Only in* **sarıp ~,** to pack tightly.

sarman Huge.

sarmaşdolaş (·˺··) Close embrace. In a close embrace; inextricably intertwined. **~ olm.,** to embrace one another; to be very close friends.

sarmaşık Intertwined. Ivy. **çit sarmaşığı,** the Greater Bindweed.

sarmaşmak *vn.* Embrace one another; be intertwined.

sarmısak Garlic. **bir diş ~,** a clove of garlic: ˹**balla ~ yemesini icad etmek**˺, to think of stg. original but useless, *v. App.*

sarnıc Cistern; tank; **~lı vapur** *or* **~ gemisi,** tanker.

sarp, -pı Steep; hard, difficult; inaccessible; intractable. **iş ~a sarıyor,** the matter becomes very complicated or serious. **~laşmak,** to become steep; become difficult or impracticable.

sarpa (¹·) Sea-bream.

sarpon Pit for storing grain; silo; baker's dough-tub.

sarraf Money-changer; banker. **insan ~ı,** a good judge of men: **koltuk (köşe) ~ı,** street money-changer. **~iye** (·—·¹), rate of exchange; money-changer's charge.

~lık, profession of money-changer; money-changer's fee.

sarsak Palsied; shaking from feebleness; quivering; idiot. **~lık,** palsy; clumsiness.

sarsar Violent bitter wind.

sarsık Walking with a quivering gait; shaky.

sars·ılış A being shaken; shock; jolt; loss of balance; earthquake. **~ıntı,** a being shaken; shock; concussion; earthquake; disaster. **~ma,** a shaking (*active*); shake; joggle.

sarsmak *va.* Shake; agitate; joggle; give a shock to; upset.

sart, -tı Rope made of reeds.

sası Mouldy smell. Smelling mouldy.

sataşmak *vn.* Become aggressive; seek a quarrel; (*with dat.*) annoy; interfere with; tease.

saten Satin.

sath·an (¹·) Superficially. **~ı,** *v.* **satıh. ~î** (·˜), superficial. **~ice** (·˜·), superficially.

satı Sale. **~cı,** salesman, seller; hawker. **ayak ~sı,** street hawker.

satıh, -thı Upper surface of a thing; face; superficies; plane. **sathı mail,** inclined plane.

satılık On sale; for sale.

satım Sale. **alım ~,** purchase and sale, business. **~lık,** commission on sale.

satın Sale. **~ almak,** to buy. **~alıcı,** purchaser.

satır[1] Large knife *for cutting meat*; tobacco cutter; executioner's sword. **~ atmak,** to exterminate. **~cı,** butcher's assistant *who cuts up meat*; (*formerly*) soldier armed with a short sword.

satır[2] Line *of writing*. **~ başı,** paragraph. **~lık,** containing *so many* lines.

satış Manner of selling; sale.

satlıcan (*for* **zatülcenb**) Pleurisy.

satmak *va.* Sell; make a false show of; pretend to be; (*sl.*) get rid of *s.o.* **ağız ~,** to boast; to blow one's own trumpet: **kendini ~,** to give oneself airs; **kendini büyük devlet satan Italya,** Italy, who sets up to be a Great Power; **kendini satmasını bilmek,** to know how to make the best of oneself, to be able to display one's abilities: **ne satıyorsun?,** what are you prating about?: ˹**suda balık ~**˺, to promise what cannot be fulfilled: **ustalık ~,** to pretend to ability.

satranc Chess; a check pattern; chequered. **~lı,** with a check pattern.

satvet, -ti Spring, rush; attack; force, vigour.

savab Right action; correct judgement;

also used for **sevab** *q.v.* **hata** ~ **cedveli**, list of corrections, errata.

savak Cistern from which water is distributed; hatch to a mill-pond; sluice.

savaş Struggle, fight; battle; ‖ war. ~**çı,** combatant. ~**mak,** to struggle, fight; dispute. ···**meğe** ~, to struggle to do ..., to work hard to ... .

savat¹, -tı Engraving in black on silver; niello, Tula work. ~**lamak,** to engrave thus. ~**lı,** engraved with black.

savat², -tı Watering-place for cattle; place for fattening cattle. ~**lamak,** ~**mak,** to fatten cattle at pasture.

savla (¹·) Signal-halyards.

savlecan Curved stick *used in the game of jerid to carry the ball along.*

savlet, -ti Impetuous assault; dash.

savma *verb. noun of* **savmak.** Sent away; got rid of. **baştan** ~, superficial, careless, perfunctory: **baştan** ~ **cevab,** evasive answer.

savmaa Hermit's cell; monastery.

savmak *va.* Drive away; dismiss; get rid of; avoid, escape from; get over (an illness). *vn.* Pass away, come to an end. **başından*** ~, to get rid of *s.o.* : **baştan** ~, to do *stg.* superficially *or* carelessly: **kaza belâ** ~ **kabilinden,** as a wise precaution: **sata** (*or* **satıp**)~, to sell all one has; **sata sava geçinmek,** to be reduced to such straits that one has to sell one's belongings to live: **sırasını*** (**nöbetini**) ~, to have done one's turn; to have 'done one's bit'.

savmış Gone; come to an end; lost; past use.

savruk Awkward, clumsy; too hasty. **eteği** ~, very untidy.

savrulmak *vn. pass. of* **savurmak.**

savsa Slow.

savsak Negligent, dilatory. ~ ~, prowling about. ~**lamak,** to put *s.o.* off with excuses or pretexts; to put off doing *stg.*

savt, -tı Sound; voice; cry. ~**î** (·¹), pertaining to sound; phonetic. **harfi** ~, vowel.

savulmak *vn.* Stand aside; get out of the way. **savul!,** stand clear!, get out of the way!

‖ **savunma** Defence. **Millî** ~ **Bakanlığı,** Ministry of National Defence. ~**k,** to defend oneself.

savurmak *va.* Toss about; throw into the air; blow about; winnow; brandish (a sword). *vn.* Blow violently; bluster, brag. **atıp** ~, to bluster: **küfür** ~, to let out an oath: ···**in külünü** ~, to vow vengeance on ...: **sirkeyi** ~, to brew vinegar.

savuş·mak *vn.* Pass; cease; slip away. ~**maz,** that will not go away; incurable.

~**turmak,** to cause to go away *or* cease; ward off; escape *or* avoid *some disagreeable thing or person.*

sây Endeavour; effort; exertion.

saya¹ *Name formerly given to* a collector of the sheep tax.

saya² Upper part of a shoe.

sayd The chase; fishing. ~**î** (·¹), pertaining to the chase *or* fishing.

saydırmak *va. caus. of* **saymak.** ···**i yerinde** ~, to make *s.o.* mark time, to prevent *s.o.* making any progress.

saye (−¹) Shadow; shade; protection; favour. ... ~**sinde,** thanks to ..., under the auspices of ...; ~**nizde,** thanks to you; **bu** ~**de,** in this manner. ~**ban** (−·¹), canopy, tent; covered litter: ~ **salmak,** to give shade; to protect: **sayenizde** ~ **oluyorum,** thanks to you I am all right (*slightly ironical*). ~**dar** (−·¹), shady; affording protection.

sâyetmek (¹··), −**eder** *vn.* Endeavour; exert oneself.

sayf Summer. ~**î,** summer (*a.*). ~**iye,** summer house; villa; country house; villages near a large town: ~**ye gitmek,** to go into the country.

sayfa *v.* sahife.

saygı Respect, esteem; thoughtfulness, consideration. ~**larımı sunarım,** I present my respects. ~**lı,** respectful; considerate; well-mannered. ~**sız,** without regard or respect; inconsiderate; disrespectful. −**sızlık,** disrespect; lack of consideration.

sayha Cry; clamour.

sayı Number; reckoning. ~**ya gelmez,** innumerable: ⌜~**m suyum yok**⌝- (*orig. from a children's game*) 'pax!'; I'm not in this; I'm taking no part! ~**cı,** official teller of sheep for taxation.

sayıklama Delirium; talking in one's sleep; dreaming of stg. longed for.

sayıklamak *vn.* Talk in one's sleep *or* in delirium; rave; dream of stg. longed for.

sayılı Counted; limited in number; numbered; marked, special. ~ **gün,** a red-letter day.

sayılmak *vn. pass. of* **saymak.** Be counted *or* numbered; be esteemed; be taken into account. **hatırı sayılır,** who counts, respected; considerable.

sayım. A counting; census. ~ **vergisi,** tax on the number of animals.

‖ **sayın** Esteemed; excellent. ~ **Bay ...,** Dear Mr. ... (*in a letter*).

sayısız Innumerable.

sayışmak *vn.* Settle accounts with one another. **sövüşüp** ~, to swear at one another.

‖ **Sayıştay** *The new name of the old* **Divanı**

muhasebat: the Exchequer and Audit Department.

saykal Polisher; burnisher; polish, burnish.

saymak *va.* Count; number, enumerate; regard, count as; esteem, respect; deem, suppose. **sayıp dökmek**, to recount at length: 'bunu saymayız, sizi yine bekleriz', 'I don't call this a visit, you must come again': ···in hatırını ~, to have consideration for, to respect: hiçe ~, to account as nothing, to hold of no account: ···e sövüp ~, to swear at: yerinde ~, to mark time; to make no progress.

saymamazlık Disrespect; irreverence.

sayrı *a.* Ill.

sayvan Flounce, fringe; umbel; the external ear; tent.

sayyad Hunter.

saz¹ Rush; reed. ~ benizli, pale.

saz² Musical instrument; band; Oriental music. ~ söz, music and conversation; party; ~a söze düşkün, fond of parties: ~ şairi, minstrel; one who improvises songs and music: ince ~, Turkish orchestra of stringed instruments: meydan ~ı, a kind of large guitar. ~cı, player of a musical instrument; musician.

–saz *Pers. suffix.* Doing ...; making ....

sazan Carp. yeşil ~, tench.

sazende (–·ˡ) Player of a musical instrument; lute player.

sazlık Reed-bed; place covered with rushes.

se Three (at dice).

–se *v.* ise.

seb, –bbi Vituperation.

Seba Saba (ancient town in Arabia). ~ kraliçesi, the Queen of Sheba.

sebat (·ˣ), –tı Stability; firmness; perseverance; constancy. ~kâr, enduring; persistent. ~lı, enduring; stable; persevering. ~sız, unstable, fickle; lacking perseverance.

sebb·etmek (·ˡ·), –eder *va. & vn.* Curse; vituperate. ~i, *v.* seb.

sebeb Cause, reason; source; means; occasion. ... ~ile, on account of ..., owing to ...: ~ aramak, to search for a pretext: ···e ~ olm., to cause, to occasion: bilâ ~, without a cause *or* reason: bu ~le, for this reason, therefore: her hangi bir ~le, for some reason or other.

sebeb·iyet,–ti, a being the cause *or* motive; ···e ~ vermek, to cause. ~lenmek, to earn one's living; to get a small profit *out of stg.*; to get stg. out of *a thing.* ~li, having a reason *or* excuse: ~ sebebsiz, without any reason. ~siz, without a cause *or* reason: ⌐sebeb olanlar ~ kalsın¬ (*a curse*) 'may those responsible suffer for it!'

sebel Opaque patch on the eye, nebula.

sebil (·ˣ) Road; public fountain; free distribution of water. ~ etm., to spend lavishly, squander: ~ini tahliye etm., to set free *a prisoner*. ~ci, man who distributes water gratis *but generally begs.* ~hane (···–ˡ), public fountain: ~ bardağı gibi, all in a row (*slightly derogatory*).

sebk¹, –kı, sebkat, –tı A going before; precedence; an anticipating another; a predeceasing another. ~etmek¹ (ˡ··), –eder *vn.*, to go before, precede, happen before; predecease.

sebk², –ki Casting *of metals*; moulding *of phrases.* ~etmek² (ˡ··), –eder, to cast metal. ~ürabt, –tı, co-ordination of phrases; coherence; grammatical construction.

sebük Light; flighty. ~bar, lightly laden. ~mağz, stupid; frivolous. ~mizac, flighty, inconstant. ~pay, nimble, swift-footed. ~pervaz, swift in flight. ~rev, swift-footed, nimble. ~ruh, light-hearted, gay.

sebze Green plant; vegetable. kuru ~, pulse. ~vat, –tı, *pl. of* sebze.

secaya (·–ˡ) *pl. of* seciye. Moral qualities.

seccade (·–ˡ) Prayer rug. ~ci, maker *or* seller of prayer rugs; servant whose duty it is to look after the prayer rug of a great man.

secde Act of prostrating oneself in worship. ~ etm., *or* ~ye varmak, to perform the ritual prostrations in prayer: ~ye yatmak, to prostrate oneself, to fall down and worship (*dat.*).

seci, –c'i Rhyme in prose.

seciye Moral quality; character; natural disposition. ~li, of high moral character, good. ~siz, untrustworthy; vicious.

seçici Who chooses *or* distinguishes.

‖ **seçik** Clear; distinct.

seç·ilmek *vn. pass. of* seçmek. ~ilmiş, picked, choice; what is left after the best has been taken. ~im, choice; election; perception: göz ~i, the distance at which the eye can discern things. ~kin, choice; outstanding. ~me, a choosing; choice; election; perception: selected, choice. ~mece, allowing the purchaser to pick and choose (of a commercial transaction).

seçmek *va.* Choose, select; elect; perceive; distinguish, make out. yemek ~, to be particular about one's food.

sed, –ddi Barrier; obstacle; dam; bank; fence; rampart; obstruction *to an action.* Seddi Çin, the Great Wall of China. ~detmek (ˡ··), –eder, to bar, obstruct, barricade.

seda (·ˣ) *v.* sada.

sedef Mother-of-pearl; shell producing mother-of-pearl. Made of mother-of-pearl. ~ **hastalığı,** psoriasis. ~**li,** made of *or* decorated with mother-of-pearl. ~**otu,** **-nu,** rue.

sedir[1] Platform at the top of a room with a divan on it; divan, sofa. **baş** ~**e geçmek,** to take the top seat; to take the first place, to be very important: **erkân** ~**i,** a kind of high sofa.

sedir[2] Cedar.

sedye (¹·) Sedan-chair; stretcher. ~**ci,** stretcher-bearer. ~**lik,** a stretcher case.

sefa (·–¹) *v.* **safa.**

sefahet (·–¹), **-ti** Foolish squandering; dissipation.

sefain (·–¹) *pl. of* **sefine.** Ships.

sefalet (·–¹), **-ti** Poverty; misery. ~ **çekmek,** to suffer privation: ~**e düşmek,** to be reduced to poverty.

sefaret (·–¹), **-ti** Ambassadorship; embassy, legation. ~**hane** (·–·–¹), embassy (building), legation.

sefer Journey; voyage; campaign; state of war; time, occurrence. ~ **açmak,** to start hostilities : ~ **etm.,** to go on a journey : ~**e gitmek,** to go to war, to start a campaign : **bu** ~, this time.

sefer·ber, mobilized for war. ~**berlik,** mobilization. ~**î,** pertaining to travel *or* to a campaign : **heyeti** ~**ye,** expeditionary corps : **ordunun** ~ **mevcudu,** the war strength of an army. ~**lik,** state of travel *or* warfare; special to travel *or* campaigning. ~**tası, -nı,** travelling food box *with several metal dishes fastened together.*

sefih (·⁴) Spendthrift, prodigal; dissolute.

sefil (·⁴) Poor; miserable; destitute.

sefine (·–¹) Ship.

sefir (·⁴) Ambassador.

sefkidima (···–¹) Bloodshed.

segâh *Name of a musical cadence.*

seğirdim Recoil *of a gun;* distance run in a race. ~ **yapmak,** to recoil.

seğirme Vibration; tremor; nervous twitch. ~**k,** to tremble; to twitch nervously : **gözü** ~, for the eye to twitch (*supposed to be a good omen*).

seğirtmek *vn.* Run; hasten.

segman (*Fr. segment*) Piston-ring.

seğmen *Formerly a division of soldiers incorporated with the Janissaries;* servant in charge of dogs; young men, armed and in national costume, *who take part in a procession.*

seğrek *v.* **seyrek.**

seha (·–¹), **sehavet** (·–¹), **-ti** Generosity.

sehab Cloud. ~**ı muzî,** nebula.

seham *pl. of* **sehim.**

seher[1] Insomnia.

seher[2] Time just before dawn; early morning. ~**î** (···–¹), pertaining to the early dawn.

sehhar Enchanting; fascinating; magical.

sehil Easy, simple. **sehli mümteni,** a piece of writing, seemingly simple, but really difficult to achieve (*ars est celare artem*).

sehim, -hmi Arrow; lot, share, portion; Treasury bond; the sinking of any part of a building on account of pressure.

sehiv, -hvi Mistake; inadvertence. **sehvi kalem,** a slip of the pen.

sehli *v.* **sehil.**

sehmi *v.* **sehim.**

sehpa (·–¹) Tripod; three-legged stool *or* table; easel; gallows. **atlama** ~**sı,** vaulting-horse.

sehv·en (¹·) Inadvertently. ~**etmek** (¹··), **-eder,** to make a slip. ~**vi,** *v.* **sehiv.**

sek (*Fr. sec*). Dry (wine); champagne.

sekalet (·–¹), **-ti** Ugliness; eyesore.

sekban *v.* **seğmen.**

sekenat, -tı Quiescence; cessation of movement.

sekene *pl. of* **sakin.** Inhabitants.

sekerat, -tı Drunkenness; death agony. ~**ülmevt, -ti,** death agony.

seki Pedestal; stone seat; white sock on a horse.

sekinet, -ti Serenity.

sekir, -kri Intoxication.

sekiz Eight. ⌐**Allah** ~**de verdiğini dokuzda almaz**⌐, what is fated will happen. ~**er,** eight each; eight at a time. ~**inci,** eighth. ~**li,** having eight: the eight *of a suit of cards.* ~**lik,** worth *or* containing eight ... .

sek·me Hop; ricochet. ~**mek,** to hop; to run in a series of jumps; to ricochet; to miss; **bir gün bile sekmez (sektirmez),** he never misses a single day. ~**sek,** hop-scotch.

seksen Eighty. ~**er,** eighty each; eighty at a time. ~**inci,** eightieth. ~**lik,** worth *or* containing eighty; . . .; octogenarian.

sekte Pause; interval; stoppage; interruption; stagnation; apoplexy. ~ **vermek,** to relax, to give a respite : **kalb** ~**si,** heart failure. ~**dar,** defective; disturbed, interrupted; prejudiced. ~**lenmek,** to be hindered *or* interrupted.

sektir·me A causing to rebound *or* ricochet. ~**mek,** to cause to hop, rebound, ricochet; *v.* **sekmek.**

sel[1] Torrent; inundation; flood.

sel[2], **-lli** A drawing forth. ~**li seyif etm.,** to draw the sword.

selâ Saddle *of a bicycle.*

Selaçika The Seljuks.

selâm Salutation; greeting; salute. ~ **almak,** to acknowledge a salute *or* another's

bow: ~ (*or* ~a) **durmak,** to rise respectfully to receive the salute of a superior; to present arms; ~ **dur!,** (*formerly*) present arms!: ~ **etm.,** to send one's compliments: ···le ~ı **sabahı kesmek,** to cease relations with ..., to ignore *s.o.* completely: ~ **vermek,** to greet, to salute: ⌐**ne ~ ne sabah**⌐, without as much as saying good-morning; ignoring everyone: **resmî ~,** military salute: ···in size ~ı **var,** ... sends you his greetings: **yerden ~,** a very deferential bow.
selâmet (·−¹), **-ti** Safety; security; freedom from danger *or* illness; soundness; liberation; successful result; (sentence) free from defect or error. ~**le!,** good-bye and good luck!: ~ **bulmak** *or* ~**e çıkmak,** to gain safety; to turn out well: **Allah ~ versin!** *said when mentioning an absent friend (often when criticizing him):* **sahili ~,** the shore of safety, *i.e.* escape from danger: ⌐**(şuradan şuraya) ~le çıkmayayım**⌐, (*an oath*) 'if it be not true may I die!'
selâmetlemek, to see *s.o.* off; to wish *s.o.* God-speed.
selâm·lamak *va.* Salute; greet. ~**lık,** the part of a large Moslem house reserved for males; (*formerly*) the public procession of the Sultan to a mosque at noon on Fridays. ~**ünaleyküm,** 'peace be on you' (*the formal greeting of Moslems to each other, the reply being* **aleyküm selâm**): ~ **demeden,** without so much as by your leave; brusquely and tactlessly. ~**ünkavlen,** *euphemism for* paralysis, stroke.
Selânik (·¹·) Salonica; a Salonica Jew. ⌐**kalıb, kıyafet yerinde amma yürek ~**⌐, his outward appearance is all right, but at heart he is a coward.
selâset (·−¹), **-ti** Fluency of speech; smoothness of style. ~**le,** fluently.
selâtin *pl. of* **sultan.** Sovereigns. Imperial; grand.
selb A taking by force; a depriving; negation. ~**etmek** (¹··), **-eder,** to carry off; take by force; deprive forcibly; deny, negative. ~**î,** negative; privative.
Selçuk Seljuk. ~**î** (···⁻), ~**lu,** Seljukian.
sele Flattish wicker basket.
selef Predecessor; ancestor; man of old.
seleserpe *v.* **sereserpe.**
selika (·−¹) Natural ability to speak *or* write; good taste.
selim Free from defect; safe, sound; benignant (tumour). **aklı ~,** common sense.
selinti Small torrent caused by rain; the bed made by such a torrent.
selis Fluent; easy-flowing (style *etc.*).
sellemehüsselâm Without ceremony; without being announced; unexpectedly; rudely.

selliseyf etm. *va.* Draw the sword.
sellüloit Celluloid.
selpik Languid, lazy.
selsebil A spring in Paradise; ornamental fountain.
selvi Cypress. ~**lik,** place abounding in cypresses.
selviçe (·¹·) Running rigging.
sem, -mmi Poison.
sema¹ (·⁻) Sky; heaven.
sema², -aı Hearing; mention; dervishes' dance. ~**hane** (·−−¹), dervish conventicle for religious music and dancing.
semahat (·−¹), **-ti** Generosity, munificence. ~**lû,** bountiful, munificent; *ancient title of honour for judges.*
semaî (·−⁻) Based upon what has been heard; founded on custom, traditional. A solemn dance tune.
semav·at (·−⁻), **-tı** *pl. of* **sema.** ~**î** (·−⁻), celestial; heavenly: **ecramı ~ye,** heavenly bodies: **kütübi ~ye,** divinely inspired books, holy scripture.
sembol, -lü Symbol.
semdar Poisonous.
semek, -mki Fish.
semen Fatness. ~ **bağlamak (peyda etm.),** to grow stout.
semender Salamander.
semer Pack-saddle; pad *used by porters for carrying heavy weights.* ~**ci,** maker of pack-saddles. ~**li,** having a pack-saddle (animal); wearing a pad (porter); having a hump; coarse, vulgar.
semere Fruit; profit; result. ~**dar,** fruitful.
sem·i, -m'i Sense of hearing; act of listening *or* obeying; ear. ~**'î** (·⁻), pertaining to hearing; acoustic.
semih Liberal; generous.
semir·gin Fat because he is lazy and lazy because he is fat. ~**mek,** to grow fat. ~**tmek,** to fatten; to manure (the ground).
semiye Clan.
semiz Fat; fleshy. ~**ce,** rather fat; ~**lik,** fatness. ~**otu** (·¹··), **-nu,** purslane.
semmî (·⁻) Poisonous.
semmur (·⁻) *v.* **samur.**
sempati Sympathy.
semt, -ti Direction; region, neighbourhood; quarter in which one lives. ~ **~,** in certain places; in every quarter: ~**e gitmek,** to go in *some* direction; to go home. ~**ikadem,** nadir. ~**ürres,** zenith.
semum (·⁴) Simoom.
sen Thou, you. ~ **~ ol!,** (*a warning*) *in such phrases as:* ~ **~ ol, bir daha bunu yapma!,** now don't forget, you mustn't do this again!: ~ **misin,** *v.* **senmisin:** 'biz bu işi gizli tutmağa çalışırken ~ git her

kese söyle!', 'just when we were trying to keep the matter quiet, what must you (he) do but go and tell everyone!'

sena (·⸛) Praise; eulogy. ~ etm., to praise: ···in ~sında bulunmak, to speak highly of ... . ~kâr, ~han, ~ver, who praises; your humble servant. ~kâri (·—·⸛), (in a letter) sincere; my; your humble servant's. ~verane (·—·—⸜), (in a letter) my; tarafı ~mden, for my part (from an inferior to a superior).

sendelemek vn. Totter; stagger.

sendere Thin board; shingle.

sendika Trade union.

sene Year. kırk ~, forty years; a very long time: ~i kebise, leap-year. ~lik, lasting so many years; of so many years.

sened Written proof of a transaction etc.; document; title-deed; voucher; receipt. ~ etm., to hold or put forward as proof; ···i ~ ittihaz etm., to record stg.: ~siz sepetsiz, without giving or demanding any written proof: hatır ~i, accommodation bill: nakliye ~i, bill-of-lading, way-bill: tasarruf ~i, title-deed: 'yağmur yağacağına ~iniz var mı?', do you possess positive proof that it will rain?

sened·leşmek, to give one another written proofs etc.; to exchange documents of proof. ~li, based on written proof; accompanied by a written proof etc.

senevî¹ (··⸛) Annual.

senevî² (··⸛) Believing in two creators, one of good, the other of evil; dualist.

senfoni Symphony.

seni acc. of sen. Thee; you; sometimes used as a term of abuse usually in conjunction with gidi q.v.

senin gen. of sen. Thine, your, of you. In such phrases as: o sokak ~ bu sokak benim gezip duruyor, he spends all his time wandering about this street and that (the streets generally). ~ki, yours.

senk, –ki, –gi Stone. ⸢atarlar seng–i târizi draht–ı meyvedar üzre⸣, 'they throw the stone of reproach at the fruitful tree', i.e. people of worth must expect criticism. ~dil, stony-hearted, cruel.

senli In ~ benli, hail-fellow-well-met; unpretentious, free-and-easy. ~ benli konuşmak, to have a confidential talk; to be intimate.

senmisin (⸜··) Lit. 'is it you?'; when used with a present participle it forms an almost untranslatable idiom, implying an unexpected and unpleasant development; can often be translated by 'to teach him not to' or 'it serves you right for doing so-and-so if ...', e.g. 'Türkiye'de harbden evvel, her kes hayat pahalılığından şikâyet ediyordu.

Senmisin şikâyet eden, harbde pahalılık beş misli arttı', 'in Turkey, before the war, everyone was complaining of the cost of living; so (just to teach them not to complain) the cost of living increased five times during the war' (the idea is: 'so it's you who are complaining, is it?—well, take that!).

sentetik Synthetic.

sepek Pivot of a millstone.

sepet, –ti Basket; anything made of wickerwork; basketful. Wickerwork. ~ havası çalmak, to show a person that his room is preferable to his company, v. sepetlemek: sandığı ~i kaldırmak, to remove all one's belongings. ~kulpu, –nu, broad arch. ~leme, woven like a basket. ~lemek, to get rid of a tiresome person; to sack, dismiss. ~li, having a basket; ~ motosiklet, motor-cycle having a side-car. ~lik, substance suitable for making baskets; front part of the abdomen.

sepi Dressing for hides; tanning; dyeing of furs. ~ci, tanner. ~lemek, to tan; to prepare furs. ~li, tanned (hide); dyed and prepared (fur).

sepk, sepketmek v. sebk.

sepken Anything sprinkled; shower of rain; slight fall of snow.

sepmek va. Sip noisily; gobble; sprinkle. vn. Drizzle.

septik Sceptical.

sepya Sepia.

ser¹ Head; chief; top; end. ⸢~den mi geçmeli yardan mı?⸣, 'must one give up one's life or one's love?', i.e. which of two difficult alternatives?: ~de gençlik var!, what else do you expect of a young man?; ~de müdürlük var!, well, after all he is the manager: ~ vermek, to devote one's life to a cause: ⸢~ vermek sır vermemek⸣, better die than give away a secret.

ser² (Fr. serre) Greenhouse; hothouse.

serab (·⸛) Mirage.

serair (·—⸜) pl. of serire. Secrets.

serapa (·—⸛) From head to foot; utterly, entirely.

serasker (Formerly) Commander-in-chief; Minister of War. ~ kapısı, offices of the Minister of War. ~lik, office and duties of the above.

serazad (·—⸛) Free; independent.

serb¹ Fat surrounding the intestines.

serb² Flock, herd; a man's household.

serbest, serbes Free; independent; unreserved, frank. ~çe (·⸜·), freely. ~î, liberty. ~lik, freedom; independence; frankness.

serbeste Attached to some service; veiled, covert.

serçe Sparrow. ‖~giller, passeres. ~parmak, little finger *or* toe.

serçin Wire holding the reel in a shuttle; the best of anything selected.

serd A setting forth consecutively; proper arrangement of a discourse; exposition *of a subject.*

serdab Cellar; underground reservoir; underground room *used in hot weather.*

serdar (·ᵎ) Military chief; general. ~iekrem (·ᵎ···), commander-in-chief.

serdengeçti Troops selected for a desperate enterprise, forlorn hope, suicide squad. ~lik, mad enterprise; foolhardiness.

serdetmek (ᵎ··), –eder va. Set forth; expound.

serdümen Quartermaster (*naut.*).

sere Span between the thumb and first finger.

serefraz (··ᵎ) Holding the head high; stately; eminent.

seren Yard (*naut.*); boom, spar.

serencam Result; end; event.

Serendib Ceylon.

sereserpe (·ᵎ··) Free and unrestrained; nonchalant; with disordered clothing.

seretan Cancer (constellation); cancer (*med.*).

serfüru (··ᵎ) etm. *vn.* Abase oneself; yield, submit.

sergedan Dizzy; bewildered.

sergerde Chief; leader of a band *of bandits or irregulars.*

sergi Anything spread; mat *or* carpet *on which goods are exposed for sale*; temporary stall; shop-front; exhibition; (*formerly*) order for payment of money from a public office.

sergüzeşt, –ti Adventure.

serhad, –ddi Frontier. ~ narası, war-cry.

serhademe Head servant *in an office etc.*

serhas Fern. büyük ~, bracken.

seri¹ Series. ~ halinde imal, mass production.

seri² (·ᵎ) Quick, swift. ~ ateşli top, quick-firing gun. ~an (·ᵎ·), quickly.

serikâr Supervisor; head of a business; direction of public affairs.

seril·i Stretched out *or* spread on the ground. ~mek *vn. pass. of* sermek; to lie at full length on the ground; fall ill; drop in a faint: yatağa ~, to be seriously ill.

serin Cool. Cool weather *or* air. ~lemek, ~lenmek, ~leşmek, to become cool; to cool oneself. ~lik, coolness.

serir (·ᵎ) Couch. ~î (·—ᵎ), clinical. ~iyat (·—ᵎ), –tı, clinical instruction; clinical hospital.

serire (·—ᵎ) Secret, mystery; hidden thought.

seri·ülinfial Quick to take offence. ~ülintikal, quick-witted. ~üzzeval, transient, ephemeral.

serkâtib (ᵎ··) First secretary.

serkeş Unruly, rebellious. ~lik, disobedience, rebelliousness.

serlâvha, serlevha Title, heading.

sermadide (·——ᵎ) Torpid from the cold (snake *etc.*).

sermaye (·—ᵎ) Capital; stock; first cost; acquired knowledge; (*sl.*) prostitute. ~yi kediye yükletmek, (to be able to put'one's capital on the back of a cat), to be bankrupt: ~ komak, to invest capital: şirket ~si, the capital of a company. ~dar, capitalist. ~li, having a capital of …: ~siz, without capital; without attainments.

sermedî (··ᵎ) Eternal.

sermek va. Spread out on the ground; beat down to the ground; spread over; neglect *one's job.* haki helâke ~, to exterminate: ipe un ~, to plead vain excuses; to offer empty assurances, v. *App.* (ip): sere serpe, v. sereserpe.

sermest, –ti Drunk; intoxicated *with joy etc.* ~i (··ᵎ), intoxication.

ser·muharrir Editor-in-chief. ~mürettib, chief composition. ~name (·—ᵎ), heading, superscription. ~nigün, head downwards, inverted; overthrown, ruined. ~nüvişt, –ti, (written on the forehead), destiny.

serpantin (*Fr. serpentin*) Paper streamer.

serpenk Helmet.

serp·ilmek *vn. pass. of* serpmek. Fall as if sprinkled; stretch oneself out to rest; (of a child) to grow apace. yüreğine* su ~, to be relieved *or* comforted. ~inti, drizzle; spray from a falling liquid; traces left behind of a thing; repercussion: ~sine uğramak, to feel the effects of some remote cause. ~iştirmek, to sprinkle in small quantities; distribute *or* scatter small amounts of money; (of rain) just to begin to drop. ~me, sprinkled about; sprinkled with: a sprinkling; cast-net.

serpmek va. Sprinkle slightly; scatter with the hand. *vn.* Fall in a sprinkle. saçlarına* kır ~, for one's hair to have a sprinkling of grey.

serpuş Headgear.

serrişte Clue; pretext; occasion.

sersem Stunned; bewildered; scatter-brained; foolish. ~ sepet, stupid; stupidly. ~lemek, to be stunned *or* stupefied; to lose one's head; become silly *or* absent-minded *or* forgetful. ~lik, stupefaction; confusion; stupidity; wool-gathering.

serseri (··ᵎ) Vagabond; tramp. Loose

(mine *etc.*). ~ce (··⸓·), in the manner of a vagabond. ~lik, vagabondage, vagrancy.

sert Hard; harsh, severe; violent; potent. ~lenmek, ~leşmek, to become hard, severe, violent. ~lik, hardness; harshness; violence; potency.

serteser (¹··) Utterly, entirely.

|| **serüven** *v.* sergüzeşt.

servet, -ti. Riches, wealth. ~li, wealthy.

servi Cypress. ~ boylu, of a slender and graceful build. Lübnan ~si, cedar.

servis Service.

serzeniş Reproach; reprimand. ~kâr, reproachful.

ses Sound; noise; voice; cry. ~ çıkarmak, to speak; to blab: ~ çıkarmamak, to say nothing; to condone (*with dat.*): ~ çıkmak, to be heard; to become known; to be rumoured : ~i çıkmaz, taciturn : ~ini* kesmek or ~i* kesilmek, to cease speaking; to be reduced to silence; ~ini kes!, shut up!: ~ seda yok, not a sound to be heard : ~ vermek, to give out a sound; to say stg.; ~ vermemek, not to answer *when called.*

ses·lemek, to hearken, to give ear. ~lenmek, to call out to *s.o.* (*dat.*); to reply to one calling. ~li, having *such and such* a voice; noisy; talking (film) : kaba ~, gruff-voiced. ~siz, voiceless; quiet; silent; meek; having a poor tone (mus. instrument). ~ sizlik, quietness, silence; meekness.

set, -ti *coll. form of* sed *q.v.*

seten Satin.

setir, -tri A covering, veiling *or* hiding.

setre Old-fashioned form of frock-coat.

setretmek (¹··), -eder *va.* Cover; hide.

sevab (·⸓) God's reward for a pious act or good conduct on earth; good deed, meritorious action. ~a girmek (nail olm.), to acquire merit in God's sight : ~ etm., to do a good deed; to live virtuously. ~li, meritorious.

sevabık (·—¹), -kı *pl. of* sabıka. Precedents; antecedents; previous convictions.

sevahil (·—¹) *pl. of* sahil. Shores.

sevda (·⸓) Melancholy; spleen; passion, love; intense longing; scheme, project. bu ~dan vazgeç!, give up this idea! : kara ~, hypochondria. ~lı, madly in love; enamoured. ~vî (·—¹), atrabilious; melancholic; amorous. ~zede, stricken with passion; smitten with desire.

sevgi Love; affection; compassion. ~li, lovable; beloved; darling.

sevici Lesbian. ~lik, lesbianism.

sevil·ir Lovable; amiable; desirable.

~mek, *pass. of* sevmek *q.v.*; be lovable *or* amiable.

sevim Love; affection; affability. ~li, lovable; genial. ~siz, unattractive; unsympathetic (not likeable).

sevin·c Joy; delight. ~cli, joyful. ~mek, to be pleased *or* happy.

sevir, -vri Bull; the constellation Taurus.

sevişmek *vn.* Love *or* caress one another.

seviye Equality; level; rank; degree. yaşayış ~si, the standard of living.

sevk, -kı A driving, urging, inciting; dispatch (of troops *etc.*). ~etmek (¹··), -eder, to drive, impel; urge, incite; send : tekaüde ~, to pension off. ~itabiî, instinct. ~ıyat, -tı, dispatch of troops; consignments *of goods.* ~uidare, management, control; (*mil.*) the leadership and administration of an army. ~ulceyş, strategy. ~ulceyşî, strategic.

sevmek *va.* Love; like; fondle. yerini ~, (of plants) to prosper, to grow well.

seyahat (·—¹), -ti Journey; travelling; expedition (polar, scientific). ~name (·—·—¹), book of travels.

seyelân A flowing; flood. ~ etm., to stream, pour. ~ıdem (···—¹) haemorrhage. ~ımeni, spermatorrhoea.

seyid Master, lord, chief; Seyyid (descendant of the Prophet).

seyif, -yfi Sword.

seyir, -yri Movement; progress; travel; excursion; voyage; a looking on at a thing; spectacle. ~e çıkmak, to go for a walk or ride, to make an excursion : ~ jurnalı, log-book : ~ kılavuz kitabı, sailing-directions : ~ tecrübesi, trial trip *of a ship* : piston seyri, piston stroke. ~ci, spectator; one who merely looks on.

seyirmek *etc. v.* seğirmek *etc.*

seyis Groom.

Seylân Ceylon. ~î *or* ~ taşı, garnet.

seylâb Flood; torrent.

seyran Outing; pleasure trip; excursion. ~ etm. *or* ~a çıkmak, to go for a trip, to make an excursion. ~gâh, pleasure spot; promenade.

seyrek Wide apart; few and far between; at infrequent intervals *of space or time*; rare; rarely; loosely woven; sparse. ~çe, somewhat infrequent. ~leşmek, to become infrequent; to be at wide intervals. ~lik, distance of intervals; rarity of occurrence, infrequency; looseness of texture.

seyrelmek *v.* seyrekleşmek.

seyretmek (¹··), -eder *vn.* Move; go along; behave; look on. *va.* Look at; look on at (without interfering). seyret!, now you'll see (what's going to happen).

seyr·gâh v. seyrangâh. **~isefain** (··—¹), navigation. **~üsefer**, traffic (*movement of people and vehicles*): ~ **memuru**, traffic policeman.

seyyah Traveller. ~ **şehri**, city much visited by travellers: ~ **vapuru**, passenger ship. **~in** (··⁻), *pl. of* seyyah.

seyyal, –li a. Fluid; liquid. **~e** (·–¹) n., fluid. **~iyet** (·—¹), **–ti**, fluidity.

seyyan dual. Two equals. ~ **tutmak**, to make no distinction between two things *or* persons. **~en** (·⁻·), in equal parts; share and share alike.

seyyar Habitually moving; mobile; portable. ~ **satıcı**, street hawker. **~e** (·—·), planet (*pl.* ~at).

seyyiat, –tı *pl. of* seyyie.

seyyibe No longer a virgin; married woman; widow.

seyyie Evil thing; evil deed; vice; evil consequence. **~sini çekmek**, to suffer the consequences of an evil act.

seza (·⁻) Meet, fit, suitable; worthy (of = *dat.*). Merited punishment or reward. **~sını vermek**, to mete out deserved punishment. **~var**, worthy of, deserving (*with iz.*). **~varî** (·—⁻), a being worthy of *or* deserving.

sezaryen Caesarian (operation).

sez·i Feeling; intuition. **~inlemek, ~inmek, ~insemek**, to be aware of, be conscious of; have an inkling of. **~inti**, perception; inkling.

sezmek va. Perceive; feel; discern, make out. **evvelden ~**, to have a presentiment of.

sezü Cork oak.

sıbyan *pl. of* sabi. Boys.

sıcacık Warm; pleasantly hot.

sıcak Hot. Heat; hot place; hot bath. **sıçağı sıcağına**, 'while the iron is hot', at once: ~ **kanlı**, warm-hearted; amiable (*not* hot-blooded): ⌐**elini ~ sudan soğuk suya sokmamak**¬, (of a woman) to be unwilling to do housework. **~lık**, heat.

sıçan Rat; mouse. **~dişi** (·¹··), **–ni**, a kind of fine edging to linen. **~kırı, –nı**, mouse-coloured horse. **~kulağı, –nı**, chickweed. **~kuyruğu, –nu**, rat-tailed file. **~otu, –nu**, arsenic. **~yolu, –nu**, underground passage, *esp.* a gallery for a landmine.

sıç·ılmak vn. Be fouled with one's own excrement; be filthy; (of a thing) to be damaged. **~ırtkan**, unable to contain one's faeces or urine. **~ırtmak**, v. sıçtırmak. **~mak**, to open the bowels; to go to the rear; shit; befoul *or* spoil stg.

sıçra·ma Act of jumping. ~ **tahtası**, spring-board. **~mak**, to jump; spring;

start; spurt out. **~yış**, a jumping *or* springing.

sıçtırmak va. caus. of sıçmak. Cause to shit; frighten severely.

sıdık, –dkı Truth; sincerity. **~ile çalışmak**, to put one's heart into one's work.

sıfat, –tı Quality; attribute; adjective; mien, aspect. ... **~ile**, in the capacity of ...: **~ından anladım**, I could see from his expression. **sıfât** (·⁻), **–tı**, *pl. of* sıfat.

sıfır Zero; nought; cipher. ⌐**~a ~ elde var bir**¬, nought and carry one (*arith.*), *i.e.* the barest minimum: ~ **numara makine**, No. o hairdresser's clipper, *to cut as closely as possible*: **~ı tüketmek**, to exhaust one's means, to be reduced to the last extremity: **solda ~**, 'a nought on the left-hand side', a mere cypher.

sığ Shallow. Shoal; sandbank. **~a oturmak**, (of a ship) to go aground.

sığamak va. Tuck *or* roll up (skirts, shirtsleeves *etc.*); rub with the hand; smooth; massage; v. *also* sıvamak. **paçaları ~**, to tuck up one's trousers, to set to work with a will; v. **paça**.

sığanmak v. sıvanmak.

sığın *Probably originally* Bos primigenius; moose, elk.

‖ **sığınak** Shelter (alpine, air-raid *etc.*).

sığın·mak vn. Squeeze into *a narrow place*; take shelter *or* refuge. **Allaha sığındık**, I trust in God. **~tı**, one who takes refuge *or* to whom shelter has been given (*derogatory*); parasite.

sığır Ox; bull; cow; buffalo. ~ **eti**, beef: **kara ~**, buffalo: **su ~ı**, water buffalo: ⌐**ben ~ yüreği yutmadım**¬, 'I haven't eaten an ox's heart (and acquired his patience)', I'm sick of telling you! **~cık**, starling. **~dili, ~ni**, ox-tongue; bugloss. **~gözü, –nü**, corn marigold. **~kuyruğu, –nu**, mullein. **~lık**, bovine stupidity; boorishness. **~tmaç**, herdsman, drover.

sığışmak vn. Go *or* fit into a confined space with difficulty.

sığla Liquidambar tree (*L. orientalis*).

sığlık Shallow; sandbank.

sığmak vn. (*with dat.*) Go into; be contained by. **akla sığar**, plausible; admissible: **ele avuca sığmaz bir çocuk**, an unruly child: **ele avuca sığar bir mesele değil**, it is not an easily understood matter: **içi içine sığmamak**, to be unable to contain oneself *from joy etc.*: **kabına sığmamak**, to be uncontrollably impatient: ⌐**mızrak çuvala sığmaz**¬, 'the spear will not go into the sack', *said of a patently false statement.*

sıhhat, –ti Health; truth. **~te bulunmak**, to be in good health: **~ler olsun!**, 'good health to you!', *said to one having had a bath* *or a shave*: ~ini tahkik etm., to ascertain the truth of it.

sıhhî (·-̣) Pertaining to health; hygienic. umuru ~ye, sanitary matters. ~ye, Health Department.

sık Close together; dense; closely woven; frequent; tight. Frequently, often. ~ ~, at very frequent intervals. ~boğaz, urgently: ~ etm., to take by the throat; to force *s.o.* to give up stg.

sıkı[1] *a.* Tight; firmly driven in; strict, severe; hurried; heavy (gale); tight-fisted. ~ bas!, hold tight!; stand firm!: ~ durmak, to 'sit tight', to stick fast: ~ esmek, to blow a gale: ‖ ~ yönetim, martial law: ~ yürümek, to walk briskly: ağzı ~, taciturn, secretive: ayağına ~, a good walker.

sıkı[2] *n.* Pressing necessity; trouble, straits; severe menace *or* reprimand; wad *for a firearm.* ~ya dayanmak, to stand hard work, to brave trouble: ~ya gelmek, to meet with great difficulty, to be hard put to it: ~yı görünce, when pressed, compelled *or* threatened: ~ya koymak, to press *s.o.* hard, to try to force *s.o.* to do stg.: ~yı yemek, to receive a severe threat *or* reprimand: kuru ~, a blank cartridge; kuru ~ tehdid, an empty threat. **sıkı·fıkı**, close together; intimate: ~ konuşmak, to have a confidential chat. ~lamak, to tighten; to press with questions.

sıkıcı Tiresome; boring.

sıkılgan Easily embarrassed; awkward; shy. ~ olmıyan, unconstrained.

sıkılma *verb. noun of* sıkılmak. A being bored *etc.*; a being ashamed. bu adamda hiç ~ yok, this man has no sense of shame; his cheek is astounding; he is very thick-skinned: ~ya gelmemek, to dislike hardship *or* taking trouble.

sıkılmak *vn. pass. of* sıkmak. Be pressed *or* squeezed; be in difficulties; be bored, annoyed, uneasy, ashamed. başı* ~, to be in straits: canı* sıkılmak, to be bored.

sıkımlık *In* ⌐bir ~ canı var¬, you could knock him down with a feather (of a very weak person).

sıkıntı Annoyance; boredom; embarrassment; discomfort; distress; weariness; worry; financial straits. ~ çekmek, to suffer annoyance *or* inconvenience: ~da olm., to be in straits: ~ vermek, to cause vexation *or* inconvenience.

sıkış·ık Closely pressed together; crowded; congested. ~mak, to be closely pressed together; be crowded together; be in straits; become urgent; be 'taken short'. ~tırmak, to press, squeeze; tighten;

force; oppress; question closely; press *money etc.* into another's hand.

sıkıt, –ktı Miscarriage.

sıkkın Annoyed, disgusted; in difficulty, in need.

sıklamak *vn. In* ağlamak ~, to weep and lament.

sık·lanmak, ~laşmak *vn.* Be frequent (in time or space); be closely woven; be close together. ~laştırmak, ~latmak, to bring close together; render frequent: adımlarını* ~, to hasten one's pace.

sıklet, –ti Heaviness, weight; uneasiness, languor. ~ çekmek, to be bored: ~ vermek, to annoy, bore: merkezi ~, centre of gravity.

sıklık Density of texture; frequency. Densely populated.

sıkma *verb. noun of* sıkmak. Act of squeezing *etc.*; a kind of tightly fitting trousers.

sıkmak *va.* Press; squeeze; tighten; put pressure on; dun *for money*; cause annoyance, embarrassment *or* discomfort; discharge (firearm). ···in canını* ~, to annoy *or* bore: diş ~, to set the teeth *for perseverance or endurance.*

sıksık *v.* sık.

sıla Reunion with friends or family; visit to one's native country; relative pronoun. ···in ~sını çekmek, to feel homesick for ...: ~ya gitmek (varmak), to visit one's native country, to go home: ~ hastalığı, homesickness. ~cı, who sets off to visit his home; (soldier) on leave.

sımah (·⸱) Ear-hole; ear.

sımak *va.* Break; demolish; annihilate.

sımsıkı Very tight; squeezed; narrow.

sınaat (·–¹), **–tı** *v.* san'at.

sınai (·–¹) Pertaining to craftsmanship; industrial; artificial.

sınamak *va.* Smell in order to recognize; try, test.

‖ **sınav** Examination.

sıncan Box-thorn, tea-plant.

sındı Large cutting-out scissors.

sınd·ık, ~ırgı Scene of a defeat. ~ırık, defeat, rout. ~ırmak, to defeat utterly, rout.

sıngın Broken; defeated, routed.

sınıf Class; sort; category. ~ı(nı) geçmek, to be promoted to another class: ~ta kalmak, to fail to get promotion (in a school).

sınık *v.* sıngın.

sınır Frontier. ~ dışından, from abroad. ~daş, having a common frontier; bordering. ~lamak, to limit, determine.

sınmak *vn.* Break; be routed; be scattered; be broke (bankrupt).

sıpâ (·-̣) *v.* sehpa.

sıpa Year-old donkey foal; year-old fawn.

sır[1] Glaze (of pottery); silvering (mirror). ~ **vermek,** to give *pottery* a glaze, *v. also* **sır**[2].

sır[2], **-rrı** Secret; mystery. ~ **açmak,** to reveal *or* confide a secret: ~**ra kadem basmak** *or* ~ **olup gitmek,** to disappear: ~ **saklamak,** to keep secret: ~ **tutmak,** to keep secret; to keep a secret: ~ **vermek,** to betray a secret, *v. also* **sır**[1]: **akıl** ~ **erecek gibi değil,** unintelligible, inexplicable, mysterious.

sıra Row; file; rank; order, sequence; series; regularity; turn; opportune moment; bench; desk; line *of writing.* In a row *or* line *or* layer. Along; by. ~ ~, in rows, courses, *or* layers: ~**da,** in a row; ... ~**da,** just at the moment that ..., as ...: ~**sında,** in his (its) turn; when necessary: ~ **ile,** in rows; in turn; in order: ~**sı ile,** respectively: ~**dan bir adam,** any ordinary man (*i.e.* not specially selected): ~**ya bakmak,** to pay attention to time *or* turn: ~ **beklemek,** to await one's turn, to queue: ~**sı düştü,** the right moment for it has come: ~ **düşürmek,** to find a favourable opportunity: ~ **evler,** houses in a row: ~**sı gelmişken,** by the way, apropos: ~**sına getirmek,** to await a favourable opportunity: ~**sına göre,** according to circumstances: ~ **gözetmek,** to wait for a suitable moment; to pay regard to s.o.'s turn *or* seniority: ~ **karpuzu,** melons large and small just as they come (not picking and choosing): ~**sına koymak,** to put into its proper place; to set to rights: ~ **malı,** ordinary goods (not specially made): **aklı** ~, according to him (*implying disbelief or contempt*): **arada** ~**da,** here and there: **kıyı** ~, along the shore: **sözün** ~**sı,** the context of a word; the course of a discourse: **söz** ~**sı bende,** now it's my turn to speak: **yanı** ~, by his side; together with him.

-sıra *Suffix forming an adverb of place or time.* **ardısıra,** after him; one after the other: **önüsıra,** in front of him.

sıraca Scrofula. ~ **otu,** mullein; (?) scrophularia. ~**lı,** scrofulous.

sıra·dağ Mountain chain. ~**lamak,** to arrange in a row; set up in order; enumerate a series (of complaints *etc.*); (of a child) to begin to walk holding on to one thing after another. ~**lanmak,** to queue up. ~**lı,** in a row; in due order; at the right moment: ~ **sırasız,** in and out of season, at all sorts of times. ~**sız,** out of order; ill-timed; improper.

sırat (·⸴) **-tı** Road; path. ~**ımüstakim,** direct road. ~**köprüsü, -nü,** a bridge on the road to heaven *very narrow and difficult to pass*; a steep and dangerous road.

sıravari (··—⸴) In a line *or* row.

Sırbistan, Sırbiya Serbia.

sırça Glass; paste (false diamond); spun glass; glass bead; rock crystal; long glossy hairs *in some furs.*

sırdaş Fellow holder of a secret; confidant, intimate. ~**lık,** intimate friendship.

sırf Pure; mere; sheer.

sırık Pole; stick *for climbing plants.* ~**la atlama,** pole-jump: ~ **gibi boy büyütmek,** to grow in size but not in sense: ~ **gibi durmak,** to stand aside and do nothing.

sırıklamak *va.* Carry off, steal.

sırım Leathern thong; strap. ~ **gibi,** wiry (person).

sırıt·kan Given to grinning. ~**mak,** to show the teeth; grin; be frozen; (of a defect) to show up, to show through, to become manifest; be a fiasco. **sırıta kalmak,** to remain grinning like a dead person.

sır·lamak *va.* Glaze (pottery); silver (mirror). ~**lı,** glazed; silvered (mirror).

sırma Lace *or* embroidery of silver or silver-gilt thread. Golden (hair *etc.*). **sarı** ~, gold-thread; gold-lace. ~**lı,** embroidered with gold or silver thread. ~**keş,** maker of gold or silver thread; embroiderer in same.

sırnaş·ık Worrying, tiresome; pertinacious, importunate. ~**mak,** to worry, annoy.

Sırp, ~**lı** Serb, Serbian. ~**ça,** Serbian (language).

sırr·a, ~**ı** *v.* **sır.** ~**en** (⸴·), secretly. ~**olmak,** to disappear.

sırsıklam (⸴··) Very wet; wet to the skin.

sırt, -tı Back; ridge. ~**a almak,** to shoulder; to undertake: ~**ından* atmak,** to get rid of, free oneself from: ~**ından* çıkarmak,** to get *stg.* at another's expense: ···**in** ~**ından geçinmek,** to live at *s.o.'s* expense: ~**ı* kaşınıyor,** he's itching for a beating: ···**in** ~**ını yere getirmek,** to overcome, get the better of: **bıçak** ~**ı kadar,** very little difference: ⌐**karnı tok** ~**ı pek⌐,** well fed and well clad, in easy circumstances.

sırtar A kind of lizard *with thick skin on the back.* ~**balığı, -nı,** freshwater bream.

sırtarmak[1] *vn.* Grin.

sırtarmak[2] *vn.* (Of a cat) to arch its back; to set oneself up in opposition; (of clouds) to pile up.

sırtlamak *va.* Take on one's back; back, support.

sırtlan Hyaena.

sıska Dropsical; rickety; thin and weak, puny. ~**lık,** dropsy; rickets.

sıtkı v. **sıdık.**

sıtma Fever; malaria. ~ **görmemiş ses,** a rich deep voice: **gizli ~,** masked or intermittent fever; underhand intriguer. ~**lı,** malarial.

sıva Plaster (building). ~ **harcı,** stucco. ~**cı,** plasterer: ~ **kuşu,** nuthatch. ~**lı¹,** plastered, stuccoed. ~**lı²,** with sleeves rolled up. ~**ma,** laid on like plaster; covered with; washed over with: ~ **kel,** bald all over. ~**mak¹,** to plaster; daub; cover over with; soil. ~**mak²,** v. **sığamak.** ~**nmak¹,** pass. of **sıvamak¹**: to be plastered with: ⌈**güneş balçıkla sıvanmaz**⌉, 'the sun can't be plastered over with clay', truth will out; it's so obvious that it can't be hidden. ~**nmak²,** to roll up one's trousers or sleeves; to get to work.

sıvaşmak vn. Become sticky; adhere, stick to; be dirtied with some sticky thing.

sıvazlamak va. Stroke; caress.

‖ **sıvı** Liquid.

sıvık, sıvış Semi-fluid; sticky; bedaubed.

sıvırya (·¹·) Continually; one after the other; in full swing.

sıvışık, sıvışkan Sticky; importunate, boring (person). ~**lık,** stickiness; importunity.

sıvışmak v. **sıvaşmak** or **sivişmek.**

sıyanet (·—¹), -**ti** Preservation; protection. ~ **etm.,** to preserve, protect. **evlilik birliğinin ~i,** the preservation of married unity.

sıyga Form taken by metal when cast in a mould; form taken by a word when conjugated, mood, tense. ~**ya çekmek,** to cross-examine s.o.

sıyır·mak va. Tear or peel off; strip off; skim off; graze; draw a sword etc.; polish off (finish up). ···**den yakasını* ~,** to get out of (a difficulty etc.); to escape from ... .

sıyrık Peeled; skinned; abraded; brazen-faced. Abrasion.

sıyr·ılmak vn. pass. of **sıyırmak.** Be skinned or peeled; be scraped or rubbed off; slip off, sneak away; get out of a difficulty. ···**den ~,** to be stripped of; to get rid of ...: **ondan sıdkım sıyrıldı,** I've lost all confidence in him. ~**ıntı,** scrapings (from a kitchen utensil etc.); peelings; scratch.

sızdır·mak va. caus. of **sızmak.** Cause to ooze out; squeeze (money) out of; cause to drop into a drunken sleep. ~**maz,** (water-) tight.

sızı Ache, pain; grief.

sızıltı Lamentation; complaint; discontent. ~ **çıkarmak,** to utter murmurings of discontent; to give rise to murmurings of discontent: ~**ya meydan vermemek,** not to give anybody cause to complain.

sızıntı Oozings, tricklings; an oozing out of secrets, information etc.

sızırmak v. **sızdırmak.**

sızla·mak vn. Suffer sharp pain. **burnunun* direği ~,** to suffer acute pain (also fig.). ~**nmak,** to moan with pain; lament; complain. ~**tmak,** to pain; cause to groan or lament: **Halicin yürekler sızlatıcı hali,** the heart-breaking state of the Golden Horn.

sızmak vn. Ooze; trickle; leak; (of a secret) to leak out; infiltrate (mil.); drop into a drunken slumber. **aralarından su sızmamak,** to be closely tied by mutual interest etc.; to be very close friends.

-**si¹,** -**sı** Suffix of 3rd pers. sing. possessive pronoun after a vowel; **babası,** his father; **dedesi,** his grandfather.

-**si²** Suffix used after certain nouns to denote similarity; **erkeksi,** like a man, virile; the same particle in the form of **se** is used with verbs to denote similarity, e.g. **kücüksemek,** to think little, to underestimate, to despise; **gülümsemek,** to be like laughing, to smile.

sia Capacity, power.

sibak (·¹), -**kı** Preceding context. **siyaku ~,** the context after and before, i.e. the sequence or tenor of a discourse.

sicil, -**lli** Register; judicial record. ~**li ahval,** register of service etc. of an employee: ~ **etm.** or ~**le kaydetmek,** to enter into the register of a court of record. ~**li,** registered; previously convicted.

sicim String; cord. ~ **gibi yağmur,** pelting rain.

sidik Urine. ~ **damlaması,** incontinence of urine: ~ **tutulması,** retention of urine: ~ **yarışı,** futile rivalry; dispute about trifles, but ⌈**sen onunla ~ yarışına çıkamazsın**⌉, it's hopeless for you to think of competing with him: ~ **zoru,** difficulty in passing water.

sidik·kavuğu, -**nu,** bladder. ~**li,** soiled with urine; suffering from incontinence of urine. ~**şekeri,** -**ni,** diabetes. ~**yolu,** -**nu,** urethra.

sidre Lotus tree.

sif C.i.f. (comm.).

sifon Siphon.

siftah First stroke of business; first sale of a new commodity. For the first time. ~ **etm.,** to do the first stroke of business of the day; to begin: ···**e ~ etm.,** to eat stg. for the first time in the season: ⌈**~ senden bereketi Allahtan**⌉, I hope you will bring me good luck!, said to the first customer, but also used figuratively. ~**lamak,** to make the first sale of the day; to begin.

siftinmek *vn.* Wriggle about and scratch oneself; approach a person in a cringing, fawning manner; guzzle.

siga *v.* **sıyga.**

sigar Cigar. ∼**a** (·¹·), cigarette: ∼ **iskemlesi,** small three-legged table *or* stand. ∼**alık** (·¹··), cigarette case.

siğil Wart; green scum on water.

sigorta (·¹·) Insurance; insurance company. ∼**ya yatırmak,** to cover by insurance. ∼**cı,** insurance agent. ∼**lı,** insured.

siham (·⁴) *pl. of* **sehim.** Arrows. ∼**i kaza,** the buffetings of fate.

sihan Thickness.

sihir, –hri Magic; sorcery, witchcraft; charm; fascination. ∼**baz,** who practises magic; magician, sorcerer. ∼**bazlık,** magic, sorcery. ∼**lemek,** to bewitch, enchant. ∼**li,** bewitched.

sihrî (·⁻) Magical.

sik Penis. ∼**işmek,** to copulate.

sikke¹ Design on a coin *or* medal; coin; level road. ∼**zen,** coiner in a mint.

sikke² Dervish's cap.

siklon Cyclone.

sik·mek *va.* Have sexual intercourse with; injure, deceive. ∼**tirmek,** *caus. of* sikmek; clear out, send off.

sil Tuberculosis.

silâh Weapon, arm. ∼ **başı,** call to arms, alarm; ∼ **başına!,** to arms!: ∼**a davranmak,** to take up and prepare to use a weapon. ∼**çı,** armourer. ∼**endaz,** common soldier; fusilier; marine. ∼**hane** (···⁻), armoury; arsenal. ∼**lamak,** to arm. ∼**lı,** armed. ∼**lık,** belt for carrying weapons. ∼**sız,** unarmed: ∼**a ayırmak,** to allot to non-combatant duties. ∼**sızlanma,** disarmament. ∼**şor,** warrior; knight; musketeer; armed guards of a palace. ∼**şorluk,** knighthood, skill in the use of arms. ∼**tar,** sword-bearer; lifeguards of the Janissaries; custodian of the arms of a *great personage.*

silecek Large bath-towel.

silgi Duster for cleaning a blackboard; sponge for wiping a slate; eraser.

silici Professional cleaner *or* polisher; one who planes boards for building.

silik Rubbed out; worn; indistinct; insignificant; second-rate.

silindir Cylinder; roller. ∼ **şapka,** top-hat: el ∼**i,** garden roller.

silinmek *vn. pass. of* silmek. Be scraped *or* rubbed down *for polishing.*

silinti Wipings; anything wiped off.

silk, –ki Career, profession. ∼**i askerî,** military career.

silk·elemek *va.* Shake off (dust *etc.*).

∼**inmek,** to shake oneself; shake off the effects of stg.; shake oneself free. ∼**inti,** shake; a shaking *or* trembling; anything shaken off.

silkme *Dish of finely chopped aubergines or gourds and meat.*

silkmek *va.* Shake; shake off; pounce (make a copy of a drawing *etc.* by perforating holes in it and shaking through a coloured powder). **toz** ∼, to shake off dust, to beat: **yaka** ∼, to shake the collar *as a sign of disgust.*

sille Box on the ear; slap.

silme *verb. noun of* silmek. Wiped; scrubbed; planed; shaven; levelled to the brim (of a measure of corn). ∼ **tahtası,** board for levelling off a measure of grain.

silmek *va.* Wipe; scrub; plane; rub down; polish; erase; remove the excess of anything (skim foam off beer, level off a heap of grain *and so forth*). **silip süpürmek,** to make a clean sweep of: **burnunu*** ∼, to blow the nose.

silsile Chain; line, series; pedigree; dynasty; a chain of promotions through seniority. ∼**i meratib,** a hierarchy: ∼ **yürümek,** for such a chain to take effect. ∼**name** (····¹), pedigree, genealogical tree.

silyon *In* ∼ **feneri,** navigation light on mast.

sim¹ (· *but in old texts* –) Silver; money; silvering *on mirrors etc.*; imitation silver, electro-plate. ∼ **şerid,** imitation silver braid.

sim² Sign; symbol.

sima (–⁻) Face, features; figure, personage.

simab (–⁻) Quicksilver.

simin (–¹) Made of silver.

simit Roll of bread in the shape of a ring; lifebuoy.

simsar (·⁴) Broker; middleman; commission agent. ∼**lık,** profession of broker; brokerage. ∼**iye** (·–·¹), brokerage, commission.

simsiyah (¹··) Jet black.

simya Alchemy.

sin¹, –nni Tooth; age.

sin² Grave, sepulchre.

sina (·⁻), ∼**meki** Senna.

sinan Spear-head.

sinare (·⁻·) Large fish-hook.

sinarit, –ti, sinagrid A kind of sea-perch (*Dentex vulgaris*).

sincab (·⁴) Grey squirrel; fur of grey squirrel. ∼**i** (·–⁻), of grey squirrel fur; dark grey: **cevheri** ∼, grey matter *of the brain.*

since (¹·) As regards age.

sinderus Gum sandarac.

sindik Receiver in bankruptcy.

sindirmek *va. caus. of* **sinmek.** Digest; swallow; assimilate; terrify, cow. **sindire sindire,** permeating; very thoroughly: içine* sindirmemek, to spoil one's pleasure, *v.* sinmek.

sine¹ (−ˋ) Bosom, breast; projection. ~ye çekmek, to put up with, to resign oneself to.

sine², sinece *gerund of* **sinmek.** ~ ~, so as to sink into; ~ ~ yağmur yağmak, to rain in a soaking manner.

sinek Fly. ~ avlamak, to potter about, idle: ~ kaydı tıraş, 'a shave on which the fly slipped', a very smooth shave. ~kâğıdı (·ˋ····), −nı, fly-paper. ~lik, fly-whisk.

sinema Cinema. ~sı oynanmak, (of a book or play) to be filmed.

sinezenlik A beating the breast (*the self-imposed torture of the Persian Muharrem ceremony*).

sini Round metal tray, *used as a small table.*

sinin (·ˋ) *pl. of* **sene.** Years.

sinir Sinew; nerve; fibre; rib (*bot.*). ~leri* ayakta olmak, for one's nerves to be on edge. ~ hastalığı, neuralgia: ~ tutulması, cramp. ~lemek, to free from sinews, to hamstring. ~lenmek, to become irritated; to have one's nerves set on edge; to be hamstrung. ~li, on edge, irritable; sinewy, wiry. ~lilik, a state of nerves, irritability; wiriness.

sinmek *vn.* Be absorbed, swallowed, digested; sink into the ground; penetrate; be hidden; crouch down *to hide oneself;* 'sing small', be humiliated; be cowed. içime* sinmiyor, my pleasure is spoilt, *used when one is not enjoying oneself at a party etc., because s.o. is not there, or because that one should have been doing stg. else.*

sinmez Indigestible.

sinn·en (ˋ·) In point of view of age. ~i, *v.* sin. ~î (·ˋ), pertaining to age; dental.

sinsi Stealthy; slinking; sneaking; insidious. ~lik, stealthiness, subtlety; underhand dealing.

sintine (·ˋ·) Bilge *of a ship.*

sinyal Signal.

sipah (·ˋ) Troops; army. ~i (·−ˋ), belonging to the army: (*formerly*) cavalry soldier: ~ oğlanı, special cavalry corps in the ancient Turkish army: ~ Ocağı, *the name of a fashionable riding-school in Istanbul.*

sipariş (·−ˋ) Order (*comm.*); commission; allotment of pay *made by a soldier etc. to relatives.*

sipehdar, sipehsalar (···−ˋ) Commander of an army.

siper Shield; shelter; trench; rampart; peak of a cap; anything acting as a protection or guard; top-slide (lathe). ~ almak, to parry a blow; to take shelter behind stg.; ~e almak, to take under one's protection: ~ olm., to shield with one's own body: elini ~ etm., to shade the eyes with one's hand; elini kulağının arkasına ~ etm., to put the hand behind the ear *in order to hear better.*

siper·isaika (ˋ···−·ˋ), lightning-conductor. ~lenmek, to take shelter.

sipihr Sky; the heavens; destiny.

sipsi Boatswain's pipe; reed *of a clarinet etc.*

sipsivri (ˋ··) *In* ~ kalmak, to be suddenly deserted by everyone; to be destitute: ~ çıkagelmek, to appear unexpectedly (when not wanted).

sirayet (·−ˋ), −ti A spreading *or* propagating itself; contagion, infection. ~ etm., (of a disease) to spread.

siret (−ˋ), −ti Moral quality; conduct; character. ~i suretine uymaz, whose appearance belies his character. *v.* siyer.

sirk, −ki Circus.

sirkat, −ti Theft. ~ etm., to steal.

sirke¹ Vinegar. ⌜bedava ~ baldan tatlıdır⌝, free vinegar is sweeter than honey; a gift or an undeserved honour will often work wonders: ⌜keskin ~ küpüne zarar verir⌝, sour vinegar harms its jar, *said of one whose bad temper does him harm*: talaş ~si, wood-vinegar (acetic acid).

sirke² Nit.

sirkek Insomnia.

sirkengebin, sirkencebin (····ˋ) Drink made of vinegar and honey; oxymel.

sirküler Circular.

siroko (·ˋ·) Sirocco.

sirto (ˋ·) A kind of dance.

sis Fog, mist. ~lenmek, to become damp *or* foggy; (of a glass *etc.*) to be covered with dew. ~li, foggy, misty, hazy.

Sisam Samos.

sistire (·ˋ·) Instrument for scraping the dough off a kneading-trough; carpenter's scraper.

sitayiş (·−ˋ) Eulogy. ~ etm., to eulogize.

sitem Reproach. ~dide (···−ˋ), unjustly treated; ill-treated. ~kâr, reproachful.

sitil Large metal bucket *for watering horses;* silver brazier *for incense or coffee;* old-fashioned barber's hanging basin with tap; pot for boiling pitch.

sitteisevir 'The six of the Ox'; (*six days in April when the sun is in Taurus, reputed to be a time of bad weather*).

sittin Sixty. ~sene (·ˋ··), for sixty years; for a very long time.

Sivas Sivas. ⌜göründü ~ın bağları⌝, 'the vineyards of Sivas appeared', an unexpected and unpleasant situation.

sivil Civilian; in mufti; plain-clothes policeman; (sl.) naked.

sivilce Pimple.

sivişik v. sıvışık.

sivişmek vn. Disappear, decamp.

sivri Sharp-pointed; tapering; tall and slim. ~ akıllı, eccentric, odd and self-opinionated: ~ kafalı, obstinate. ~burun, with a pointed nose. ~lmek, to become pointed or prominent; to make rapid progress in one's career. ~ltmek ~tmek, to make pointed or sharp at the end. ~sinek, mosquito: ⌜anlayana ~ saz, anlamayana davul zurna az⌝, 'to the intelligent a mosquito is as good as an orchestra, to the fool a brass band is insufficient', a whisper is enough for a wise man, a shout won't make a fool understand.

siya (¹·) Reversing oars and rowing backwards. ~ !, back oars !

siyah Black. ~i (·—⌐), negro. ~lık, blackness; a figure in the dark.

siyak (·⸾), -kı The after context of a word; arrangement of ideas; methods of expression; logical sequence; manner, style.

siyanen (·⸝·) v. seyyanen.

siyaset (·—¹), -ti Politics; policy; diplomacy; capital punishment. erbabı ~, politicians, statesmen, diplomatists. ~en (·⸝·⸱), politically; diplomatically. ~gâh, place of execution.

siyasi (·—⸍) Political; diplomatic. ~yat (·—·⸾), -tı, diplomacy; politics. ~yun (·—·⸍), politicians; diplomats.

siyer pl. of siyret. Rules of Moslem conduct; the Canon laws of Islam; biography. ~i nebi, biography of Muhammed.

siymek vn. (Of a dog) to urinate against a wall; (of a male animal) to be sexually excited; v. cami.

siyret v. siret.

siz pron. 2nd pers. sing. pl. You (also used politely for sing.).

-siz, sız, suz, süz suffix. Without ...; ···less. sensiz, without you; parasız, without money; tüysüz, hairless; susuz, without water.

-sizin, -sızın suffix used with the infinitive. Without ..., before ...; görmeksizin, without seeing; yazmaksızın, without or before writing.

sizinki Yours.

-sizlik Suffix forming a noun of the adjective formed with -siz (with due alteration of vowels for euphony); parasızlık, lack of money; susuzluk, thirst, aridity.

smokin Dinner-jacket.

soba (¹·) Stove; hothouse. ~cı, maker or installer of stoves.

sodyum (¹·) Sodium.

sof Wool; cloth made from the hair of goats, camels etc.; camlet; mohair; alpaca.

sofa (¹·) Hall; ante-room; stone bench; sofa. ⌜nuhut oda bakla ~⌝, a very small house.

sofî Sufi, mystic; devotee.

sofra Dining-table; portable leather mat serving as a table for meals for travellers; meal. ~ başına geçmek, to sit down to a meal: ~ bezi, tablecloth: ~yı kaldırmak, to clear away (after a meal): ~ kurmak, to lay the table: ~ takımı, a table service: yer ~sı, tray laid on a low stool to serve as table. ~cı, butler; parlourman.

softa Moslem theological student; bigot, fanatic. Behind the times, old-fashioned.

sofu Religious, devout; fanatic. kaba (ham) ~, an intolerant bigot. ~luk, religious devotion; punctiliousness in observance of religious duties.

soğan Onion; bulb. kaba ~, a 'rotter', a coward: ⌜sonrasını ~ doğra⌝, don't pursue the subject!: soyup ~a çevirmek, to pillage, to strip. ~cık, pickling-onion; shallot. ~lı, prepared with onions. ~lık, onion bed or garden; place for storing onions. ~zarı (·¹··), -nı, onion-skin.

soğuk Cold; frigid, unfriendly; out-of-place, in bad taste. Cold weather. ~lar, the cold weather, winter: ~ algınlığı, a cold, chill: ~ almak, to catch cold: ~ bastı, cold weather has set in: ~ damga, embossed stamp: ~ davranmak, to behave coldly: ~ durmak, to look on coldly: ~ kaçmak (düşmek), (of a deed or word) to be out-of-place, in bad taste: ~ söz, an unfriendly word.

soğuk·bez, cotton cloth, jaconet. ~ ça, somewhat cold. ~kanlı (·¹··), calm, coolheaded; cold, unsympathetic; (not cold-blooded = merhametsiz or hissiz). ~lamak, to catch a chill. ~luk, cold, coldness; chilliness of manner; cooling room in a hammam; cold sweet: ~ etm., to act stupidly or in bad taste.

soğumak vn. Become cold; catch cold; be chilly in one's relations; cease to care for (= den). araları ~, for the relations between two people to be strained: arası ~, for an interval to pass and interest in stg. to be lost, or it forgotten: ···den buz gibi ~, to take a great dislike to ... .

soğutmak va. caus. of soğumak. Render cold; cool; alienate. bir işin arasını –, to neglect an affair: iki kişinin arasını ~, to sow discord between two people: ziyaretlerin arasını ~, to curtail their visits to one another.

sohbet, –ti Friendly intercourse; chat, conversation. ~ etm., to have a chat: helva ~i, an evening party where the guests make and eat helva together.

sok (*Fr. soc*) Ploughshare. üç ~lu pulluk, three-furrow plough.

sokak Road, street; *often means* 'not in the house, outside', *e.g.* sokağa çıktı, he went out; he is not at home: yemeği ~ta yemek, to eat out (at a restaurant *etc.*): ⌐ben canımı ~ta bulmadım⌐, 'I didn't pick up my life in the street', *i.e.* it is precious to me: bu yüzük sokağa atsan yüz lira eder, this ring is worth 100 lira anywhere: ~ süpürgesi, a loose woman: ⌐alt yanı (tarafı) çıkmaz ~⌐, 'this leads nowhere' (of a discussion *etc.*).

sokma *verb. noun of* sokmak. Introduced from outside; imported.

sokmak *va.* Thrust into, insert; introduce; involve, entail; drive into; let in; (of an insect or snake) to sting *or* bite; injure; calumniate. başını* sokacak bir yer, a place to lay one's head, a dwelling however modest: ···e burnunu* ~, to poke one's nose into …: canına* (*or* canının* içine) sokacağı* gelmek, to be extremely fond of, to adore: birinin gözüne ~, to show *a thing* in a rude or reproachful manner: … haline ~, to bring to *such and such* a condition, to make …: parayı mülk haline ~, to invest money in real property: birini işe ~, to put s.o. into a job: bir işe parmak ~, to meddle with a matter: ···i yola ~, to put *stg.* to rights.

sokman A kind of long coarse boot.

sokra Butt end *of a plank joining it to another*.

sokulgan Who insinuates himself everywhere; sociable, quick to make friends.

sokulmak *vn. pass. of* sokmak. ···e ~, to insinuate oneself into; push into; cultivate friendly relations with.

sokum Act of inserting; place where a thing is inserted; a kind of cheese sandwich made with yufka *q.v.* kuyruk ~u, where the tail of an animal joins the body; coccyx.

sokur Mole. Blind; one-eyed. ~luk, blindness; a having only one eye.

sokuş·mak *vn.* Push oneself gently *into a place or amongst others*. ~turmak, to push gently *or* secretly *into stg.* ···in eline ~, to slip (a tip *etc.*) into *s.o.'s* hand: araya ~, to try to find time for *some job* amid other occupations.

sol Left. Left-hand side. ~dan geri dönmek, to turn left about, to retire: ~

tarafından kalmak, to get out of bed the wrong side. ~ak, left-handed. ~cu, left-winger (politician). ~iç (¹·), inside left (football *etc.*).

solgun Pale; faded; withered.

solmak *vn.* Fade; wither; become pale.

solucan Worm; ascaris, round worm. ~ gibi, pale and thin; unpleasant (person).

soluğan Short of breath; asthmatic. Shortness of breath; asthma.

soluk¹ Faded; withered; pale.

soluk² Breath; breathing; panting. ~ soluğa, panting, out-of-breath: ~ almak, to take breath, to recover oneself; derhal soluğu telefonda almıştı, he at once hurried off to the telephone; soluğu Bagdadda almak, 'to hasten to Baghdad', to fly the country, to escape: soluğu dar almak, hardly to be able to breathe; to escape narrowly: ~ aldırmak, to give one time to take breath, to give a respite: bir ~ta, in a flash.

soluk·lanmak, to take a long and easy breath; take a 'breather'; have a rest. ~suz, without breath; without respite.

solumak *vn.* Breathe heavily; pant. burundan ~, to snort with anger; to pant heavily.

som¹ Solid, not hollow; massive.

som² Ivory from a fish's tooth, rhinoceros horn *etc.*

som³ ~ balığı, salmon.

somak Sumach.

somaki Porphyry.

somun Loaf; a large soft thing (*such as a camel's foot*); nut (female screw).

somur·mak, ~tmak *vn.* Pout; frown; sulk. ~tkan, sulky.

somye (¹·) (*Fr. sommier*) Spring mattress.

son End; result; afterbirth. Last; latter; final. ~unda, in the end, finally: ~dan bir evvelki (ikinci), penultimate, last but one. ~ defa, the last time: ~ derece, (to) the last degree; the uttermost: ~unu düşünmek, to think of the result (of an action): ~unu getirememek, to fail to achieve *stg.*: ⌐~a kalan dona kalır⌐, 'the Devil take the hindmost': eni ~u, the ultimate end, the long and the short of it: bunun ~u yoktur, no good will come of this.

sonbahar (¹··) Autumn.

sonda (¹·) Probe; bore; catheter.

sondaj (*Fr. sondage*) Sounding.

sondurmak *va.* Stretch.

‖ **sonek** Suffix.

sonra In future; afterwards; by and by. The future; a later time; consequence. ···dan ~, after …; bundan ~, after this; ondan ~, after him (it), after that; then:

~dan, ~ları, later; recently: ~sı, its result, its sequel: ~ya bırakmak, to put off till another time: ~dan görme, a parvenu, an upstart: ~dan görmemiş, who is not a parvenu or upstart: ~dan olma, comparatively recent: en ~, at the very end, last of all: aklı* ~dan gelmek, to think of stg. too late.

sonra·cık, *only in* ondan sonracığına, after that. ~ki (¹··), who comes later; that happens later: ~ler, successors; posterity; those who come later. ‖ ~sız, eternal.

sonsuz Endless; eternal; infinite; useless, without results.

sontraş Farrier's clippers for paring hoofs. ‖ sonuç End; result.

sonuk Dull; lustreless; tarnished; dim.

sonuncu Last; final.

sop, -pu *Only in* soy ~, family and relations, *v.* soy.

sopa (¹·) Thick stick, cudgel; beating; stripe *in cloth*. ···e ~ atmak, to give a beating to: ~ düşkünü, deserving a beating: ~ yemek, to get a beating. ~lı, armed with a stick; having broad stripes (cloth *etc.*): eli ~, a man of violence, bully.

sorgu Question; interrogation. ~ hâkimi, interrogating magistrate ('juge d'instruction'): ···i ~ya çekmek, to cross-examine.

sorguç Plume; crest; aigrette.

sorgun Ben-tree; moringa.

sormak¹ *va.* Ask; inquire; inquire about. sora sora, by dint of repeated questions: ···i *or* ···in hatırını ~, to inquire about a person's health, to ask news of *s.o.*: ⸢ne sen sor ne de ben söyleyim⸣, 'I think we had better not go into that'; 'ask no questions and you'll be told no lies⸣, *v. App.*

sormak² *va.* Suck.

sorti (*Fr. sortie*) Point (*elec.*).

soru Question; interrogation. ~ günü, the Day of Judgement.

sorulmak *vn. pass. of* sormak. soruluyor, it is asked: benden sorulmaz, it is not asked of me, I am not responsible.

sorumak *va.* Suck noisily. ‖ sorumlu. Responsible.

soruş·mak *vn.* Question one another. ~turmak, to make investigations; birine bir şeyi ~, to ask s.o. about stg.

sorut·kan Sulky, peevish; disdainful. ~mak, to be cross, sulky *or* disdainful.

soy Family; race; lineage; ancestors; descendants; kind, sort. Pure-blooded; noble. ~a çekmek, to take after one's family: ⸢~dur (*or* ~ ~a) çeker⸣, heredity is strong: ~ sop (*acc.* soyu sopu), one's family and relations; ~u sopu belli, he comes of a good family. ~adı (¹··), -nı, family name; surname: ~ kanunu, the law requiring every Turk to have a surname. ~ca (¹·) as a family; as regards family. ~lu, purebred; of good family.

soygun Pillage, spoliation. Undressed; stripped; robbed. ~ vermek, to be plundered. ~cu, plunderer, pillager. ~culuk, plundering; fleecing.

soymak *va.* Strip; undress; peel; flay; rob; sack.

soymuk The edible inner bark of the pine.

soysop *v.* soy.

soysuz Of bad race; degenerate; good-for-nothing. ~luk, degeneracy; worthlessness. ~laşmak, to degenerate.

soytarı Clown, buffoon. ~lık, buffoonery.

soyucu Footpad; brigand.

soyun·mak *vn.* Undress oneself; change one's clothes; take off clothes (in order to work). soyunup dökünmek, to change into comfortable clothes. ~tu, peel; bark; anything stripped off.

söbü Oval; conical; cylindrical.

söğmek *v.* sövmek.

söğüş Boiled meat; cold meat.

söğüt Willow. ~ yaprağı, willow leaf; a very thin kind of dagger.

söke *v.* söve.

sökmek *va.* Pull up; tear down; rip open; dismantle; undo; break through (an obstacle); surmount (a difficulty); break up (land); decipher. *vn.* Succeed; (of a purge) to take effect; appear, come out; (of mucus) to flow; (of dawn) to break. bu böyle sökmez, you won't get any further like this; this won't do: burada zorbalık sökmez, if you think you can succeed by force, you're wrong: ···in dişini ~, to draw the teeth of ...; to render harmless: bir motörü ~, to dismantle or take to pieces a motor: çocuk yazıyı sökemedi, the child could not read.

sökük Unstitched; unravelled. Dropped stitch *in knitting*; rent. ~ örmek, to repair a rent: çorab söküğü, *v.* çorab.

sökülmek *vn. pass. of* sökmek. (*sl.*) be forced to give *or* pay. sökülüp atılmak, to be utterly eradicated.

sökün etm. *vn.* Appear suddenly; burst in suddenly in a crowd; crop up; come one after the other.

söküntü Rent in a seam; place where knitting has unravelled; sudden rush of a crowd.

söküotu (·¹··), -nu Bird's-foot trefoil.

sölpü·k Lax; flabby. ~mek, to hang flabbily; to be flabby *or* sluggish. ‖ sömürge Colony.

sömürmek *va.* Gobble down; devour; nose about and eat (as a cow).

söndürmek *va.* Extinguish; slake; deflate.

sönmek *vn.* Be extinguished, go out (of a fire); (of a sail) to become slack, to flap; be deflated.

sönük Extinguished; dim; tarnished; slack (sail); washed out; deflated; obscure, undistinguished.

sör (*Fr. sœur*) Nun, sister *in a hospital*.

söve Door *or* window frame; posts on a wagon for holding up the load.

söv·mek *vn.* Curse and swear (at = *dat.*). ···e **sövüp saymak**, to swear at *s.o.* ~**üş**, cursing, vituperation. ~**üşmek**, to swear at one another.

söylemek *va. & vn.* Speak; say; tell; explain. **arkasından** ~ **gibi olmasın amma** ..., I don't like to say it behind his back, but ...: **benden söylemesi**, well, I've warned you!, *or* I felt I ought to say stg. (but I needn't go any further): **büyük** ~, to boast: **ingilizce** ~, to say *stg.* in English: **iyiliğini** ~, to speak well of: **pek** ~, to speak out, to speak loudly: **şarkı** ~, to sing a song: **yalan** ~, to lie.

söyle·nilmek, to be said; to be pronounced. ~**nmek**, to be spoken or said; to speak to oneself; mutter; grumble: **söylendiğine göre**, according to what is said. ‖ ~**nti**, rumour. ~**şmek**, to talk over, discuss *stg.*; to converse; to consult with one another. ~**tmek**, *va. caus. of* **söylemek**; ⌜**beş para ver söylet on para ver sustur**⌝, 'if you pay him five paras to talk you will give him ten to shut up' (*said of a bore*). ~**yiş**, manner of speaking: ~**ine göre**, according to what he said; from his manner of speaking.

söz Word; speech; talk; rumour; gossip; promise; agreement. ~**de**, in word only; so-called; as though, as if; supposing that: ~ **açmak**, to start a conversation about stg.; ~ ~**ü açar**, one topic leads to another: ~ **altında kalmamak**, not to remain silent when attacked or insulted: ~ **anlamak**, *v.* anlamak: ~ **anlatmak**, to persuade: ~ **aramızda**, between ourselves: ~ **arasında**, in the course of conversation; by the way: ~ **atmak**, to make a biting *or* insulting remark *to s.o.*; to make improper remarks *to a girl*: ~**ünü bilmek**, to be tactful and considerate in one's talk: ⌜~ **bir Allah bir**⌝, I am a man of my word: ~ **bir etm.**, to unite with others *against s.o. or stg.*: ···**in** ~**ünden çıkmak**, to disregard the advice of ...: ~**ünü* değiştirmek**, to change one's tone: ~**ünden* dönmek**, to go back on one's word: ~**ünde* durmak**, to keep one's word: ~ **ebesi**, quick at repartee; a good talker: ~ **ehli**, eloquent: ~ **eri**, (i) a good talker; (ii) influential, whose word 'goes'; ~**ünün eri**, a man of his word: ~ **etm.**, to

talk, gossip *unfavourably about s.o.*: ~**ü geçen**, aforesaid; ~**ü geçer**, what he says 'goes', influential; ···**in** ~**ü geçti**, mention was made of ...: ~ **geçirmek**, to make *s.o.* listen to one, to make one's influence felt: ~ **gelişi**, for example; supposing that, let's say for the sake of argument: ~**ün gelişi**, in the course of conversation: ···**e** ~ **gelmek**, to be gossiped about: ~ **götürmez**, it admits of no discussion, it is beyond question: ~ **işitmek**, to be admonished, to 'be told off': ~ **kaldırmak**, not to take offence at a joke *or* a contradiction; ~ **kaldırmaz**, who cannot stand being contradicted; who cannot take a joke against himself: ~ **kesmek**, to decide *or* agree; to conclude a marriage agreement: ~**ünü* kesmek**, to cut *s.o.* short, to interrupt him: ~ **kesimi**, agreement to marry, engagement: ~ **olsun diye**, just for stg. to say; without meaning it: ~ **olur**, people will talk about it: ~**üm ona**, so-called, alleged; ~**üm ona mühendis**, a so-called engineer; ~**üm ona gelecekti**, he was supposed to be coming (but he didn't): ~ **onun**, what he says is right; it is his turn to speak: ~ **sahibi**, a master of words, eloquent; who has a say *in a matter*: ~ **satmak**, to boast: ~**ünü* tutmak**, to keep one's word; ···**in** ~**ünü tutmak**, to take the advice of, to obey: ~ **vermek**, to give one's word, to promise: ~ **yok**, there's nothing to say to that; quite true!; ... **âlâ**, ~**üm yok**, ... well and good, I should have nothing to say against it: ~**üm yabana**, *as* ~**üm ona**; *also* 'pardon the expression!'; *v. also* yaban.

söz·başı, **-nı**, heading *of a chapter etc.* ~**birliği**, **-ni**, unanimity, agreement. ~**cü**, spokesman. ~**leşmek**, to agree together. ~**lü**, agreed together; having promised; engaged to be married; in words, verbal: ~ **sınav**, oral examination. ‖ ~**lük**, dictionary.

spiker Announcer (radio).

spor Sports; games; (*not quite the English* 'sport'). ~**cu**, ~**tmen**, athlete, games player, sportsman.

staj (*Fr. stage*) Apprenticeship; course of instruction; probation. ~**yer** (*Fr. stagiaire*), apprentice; probationer.

stepne (Stepney) Spare wheel *for car*.

stok, **-ku** Stock.

stor (*Fr. store*) Blind.

su¹, **-yu** Water; fluid; stream; sap; broth; temper *of steel*; running pattern *or* decoration. ~**dan**, worthless; insignificant: ~ **almak**, (of a ship) to make water, leak: ~ **aygırı**, hippopotamus: ~ **başı**, source; spring; fountain; waterside; *v. also* subaşı; ~**yun başı**, source; centre; most important part *of a business, etc.*; ~yu başından kesmek, to cut off at its source; to nip in the bud : ~ bendi, reservoir : ~ böreği, a kind of pastry with flaked crust : ~unu çekmek, to be exhausted, to be used up; para ~yunu çekti, the money is exhausted : bu şehrin ~yu mu çıktı?, what's wrong with this town, why don't you like it? : ~ ~ dökmek, to make water, to pump ship : ~ya düşmek, to fail, to come to nought : ~ etm., (yapmak), (of a ship) to make water, to leak : ~geçmez (geçirmez), waterproof : ⌐~ gibi aziz ol!⌐, *a form of thanks to one who offers water* : ~ gibi bilmek, to know perfectly; ~ gibi okumak, to read fluently : ···in ~yuna (~yunca) gitmek, not to go counter to *s.o.*, to treat with tact, to flatter when necessary : ~ya göstermek, to wash *stg.* lightly : ~ götürür, that will bear further inspection; ~ götürmez, indisputable : ~ içinde, easily; certainly; bu gerdanlık ~ içinde elli lira eder, this necklace is worth fifty lira at the very least : ~ kaldırmak, to absorb water : ~lar kararmak, for darkness to fall : ~ katılmamış, unadulterated : ~yu (tokmakla) kesiyor, (of a knife) it is very blunt : ~yu sert, hard-tempered (steel); harsh (man) : ~ vermek, to temper *steel* : ⌐bunun üstünde bir bardak soğuk ~ iç!⌐, you can write that off! you'll never see it again! : bir geminin çektiği ~, the water a ship draws : ⌐elini sıcak ~dan soğuk ~ya sokmamak⌐, (of a woman) to be unwilling to do any housework : ne ~larda?, in what condition?; mesele ne ~larda?, how does the matter stand? : saat iki ~larında, about two o'clock : ~yunun suyu, a distant relationship; only a remote connexion, *v. App.* (tavşan) : (ağaclara) ~ yürümek, for the sap of trees to begin to rise, for them to begin to shoot.

su² Evil (*usually in compounds* sui-, *e.g.* suikasd).

sual, –li Question; inquiry; request. ~ etm., to ask : kabir (ahret) ~i, endless interrogation. ~li, containing a question : ~ cevablı, in the form of question and answer.

sualtı (¹··) Underwater.

subaşı (¹···), –nı Farm bailiff; (*formerly*) police superintendent; *v. also* su başı.

‖ **subay** Officer.

subye (¹··) (*Fr. sous-pieds*) Trouser-straps.

sucu Water-seller.

sucuk Sausage; sweetmeat made of grape-juice and nuts. sucuğunu çıkarmak, to give a good thrashing to; to tire out *or* exhaust : ~ gibi ıslanmak, *or* ~ olm. *or* ~ kesilmek, to be wet through.

suç, –çu Fault; offence; crime; sin. ···e ~ atmak, to attribute an offence to ... : ~ etm., to commit an offence, to sin : suçundan geçmek, to overlook *s.o.'s* offence : ···e ~ yükletmek, to lay the blame on ... .

suçiçeği (¹···), –ni Chicken-pox.

suç·lamak *va.* Accuse. ~landırmak, to find guilty. ~lu, guilty : ···den ~, charged with ... : ~ çıkarmak, to find guilty : ~ durmak, to stand with the air of a guilty person. ~suz, not guilty, innocent. ~üstü (¹··), red-handed, 'in flagrante delicto' : onu ~ yakaladım, I caught him in the act.

sudak Pike-perch (*Lucioperca*).

sudan¹ *abl. of* su. Insignificant; worthless.

Sudan² (⌐·⌐) Sudan. ~lı, Sudanese.

sudolabı (¹···), –nı Wheel for raising water.

sudur¹ (·⌐) *pl. of* sadır. Breasts *etc.*

sudur² (·⌐) Emanation; issuing (of a decree *etc.*). ~ etm., to be issued; to take place.

sufî (–⌐) Moslem mystic.

suflör (*Fr. souffleur*) Prompter (theatre).

sugeçirmez Waterproof.

suğra (·⌐) Minor. Minor premise.

sui– (–·) *prefix.* Evil–. ~ahlâk (–··⌐). –kı, immorality; vice. ~hareket, –ti, evil action; misconduct. ~idare (–··–¹). misgovernment; maladministration. ~istimal (–··–¹), abuse; misuse. ~ etm., to misuse, abuse; emniyeti ~, breach of confidence. ~kasd, criminal attempt; malice aforethought. ~kasdcı, one who makes an attempt upon life; conspirator. ~misal, –li, bad example. ~muamele (–··–¹), bad treatment. ~niyet, –ti, evil intention. ~tefehhüm, misunderstanding. ~tefsir, misinterpretation. ~talih (–·–¹), misadventure; ill fortune. ~telâkki (–··· ⌐), misconception. ~zan, –nnı, suspicion, distrust.

su·kabağı, (¹···) –nı Gourd *used for holding water.* ~kamışı, –nı, bulrush.

sukbe Small hole; puncture.

su·kerevizi (¹····), –ni Water-hemlock. ~kesimi, ~ni, waterline *of a ship.* ~kuşu, –nu, moorhen.

sukut (·⌐) –tu Fall; lapse; abortion. hayal ~u, disappointment.

sulak Watery; marshy. Water-trough; water-bowl.

sula·mak *va.* Water; dilute with water; irrigate; pay cash, pay in advance. ~ndırmak, *caus. of* sulanmak; ağzını* ~, to make one's mouth water. ~nmak, to become wet *or* watery; be provided with water; be irrigated; flirt; become silly *or* too familar : ···e ~, to manifest interest in stg. one hopes to get; to envy : ağzım

sulandı, my mouth watered: **beyni* ~,** to have a softening of the brain, to become senile: **kanı* ~,** to be anaemic.

sulb¹ The loins; vertebral column; off-spring of one's loins, descendants. **~î** (·-\·), sprung from one's loins, legitimate (son).

sulb² Hard; solid; firm; tough. **~iyet, -ti,** hardness; solidity; toughness.

suleha (··-\·) *pl. of* **salih.** Pious people.

sulh Peace; reconciliation; accord. **~ etm.,** to make peace; be reconciled : **~ hakimi,** justice of the peace, police-court magi-strate: **~ mahkemesi,** minor court for petty offences (= *our petty sessions or magistrate's police-court*) : **~ olm.,** to come to an amicable agreement : **~a sübhana yatmak,** to become docile or amenable.

sulh·cu, peace-loving; pacifist. **~en** (¹·), peaceably. **~î** (·-\·), pertaining to peace, peaceable. **~name** (·-¹), treaty of peace. **~perver,** peace-loving, pacific.

sulta Sovereignty; power; authority.

sultan Ruler, sovereign; sultan; Sultan's daughter, Sultana. **~î** (·-·-\·), pertaining to a sultan; imperial; of fine quality (fruit *etc.*) : (*formerly*) secondary school; a kind of pipless grape. **~lık,** sovereignty; office of sultan; sultanate, country ruled by a sultan; great happiness.

sulu Watery; moist; juicy; silly; importu-nate; too familiar. **~ boya,** water-colour (paint): **~ sepken,** sleet. **~ca,** somewhat watery; rather too familiar. **~luk,** a being importunate, silly, too familiar.

suluk Skin disease affecting a baby's head; aigrette; water-bowl *in a bird-cage.* **~ zinciri,** curb-chain.

sumak Sumach.

sumen (*Fr. sous-main*) Writing-pad; blotting-pad.

sumercimeği (¹····), **-ni** Duckweed.

sundurma Open shed; lean-to roof.

sungur Falcon.

sun'î (·-\·) Artificial; false; affected.

sunmak *va.* Put forward; offer; present.

suntur Dulcimer; hilarious noise. **~lu,** severe (scolding); resounding (oath).

sunu (·-\·), **-n'u** A making *or* manufactur-ing; act; creation. **bunda ne ~m var?,** what part have I played in this?, how am I to blame?

sunuf (·-\·) *pl. of* **sınıf.** Classes *etc.*

supap, -pı (*Fr. soupape*) Valve.

supara Reading-book for children.

sûr City wall, rampart. **~ dahilinde,** within the city's walls.

sur¹ (-) Trumpet, *esp.* the trumpet of the Day of Judgement.

sur² (-) Wedding; wedding *or* circumci-sion feast.

sura A kind of soft silk fabric.

surat, -tı Face; mien; sour face. **~ asmak,** to frown, to make a sour face: ⌐**~ına bak süngüye davran¬,** 'look at his face and get your bayonet ready', *said when speaking of a very ugly or disagreeable looking man :* ⌐**~ından düşen bin parça olur¬,** very bad-tempered : **~ düşkünü,** very ugly : **~ etm.,** to look sulky: **yüz ~ davul derisi (hak getire, mahkeme duvarı),** brazen-faced, shameless.

surat·lı Sulky; sullen; frowning. **~sız,** sulky; ugly.

sure (-¹) Chapter of the Koran.

suret (-¹), **-ti** Form, shape; aspect; manner; picture; copy; case; supposition. **~ çıkarmak,** to take a likeness; to make a copy : **~ine girmek,** to assume the form of : **~i haktan görünmek,** to appear sincere : **bir ~le,** in some way or other; to such a degree that: **bu ~le,** in this way: **hüsnü ~le,** in a proper manner.

sureta (-·-) Outwardly, in appearance; simulated; as a matter of form.

surî (-\·) Apparent; feigned.

Suriye (-·-·) Syria. **~li,** Syrian.

sus¹ *imperative of* **susmak.** Shut up !; hush !

sus² Liquorice.

susak Thirsty; stupid. Wooden drinking cup.

susam Sesame; (*for* **süsen**) iris.

susa·mak *vn.* Be thirsty. ···**e ~,** to thirst for, long for: **canına (ölümüne) ~,** to be extremely foolhardy; to court death: ···**in canına ~,** to act without pity towards: **dayağa ~,** to 'ask for' a beating. **~mış,** thirsty; longing for (*dat.*).

susamuru (¹····), **-nu** Otter.

susa·nmak *impers. of* **susamak. susanınca su içilir,** when one is thirsty one drinks water. **~tmak** *caus. of* **susamak,** to make thirsty, to cause to long for.

susığırı (¹····), **-nı** Water-buffalo.

susmak *vn.* Be silent; cease speaking.

suspus Reduced to silence; silent and cowering.

susta¹ (¹·) Safety-catch. **~lı çakı,** clasp-knife.

susta² (¹·) *In* **~ durmak,** (of a dog *etc.*) to stand on its hind legs; to be very obse-quious.

susuz Waterless; arid; thirsty. ⌐**birini suya götürüp ~ getirmek¬,** to out-do s.o., to make short work of s.o.

sutaş (*Fr. soutache*) Braid. **~lı,** braided.

suterazisi (¹····), **-ni** Water balance (*device used in Constantinople aqueducts for maintaining a head of water and for distri-buting it*).

suteresi (¹···), **-ni** Watercress.

sutyen (*Fr. soustien*) Brassière.
suubet (·–¹), **-ti** Difficulty. ~**li**, difficult.
suud Ascent; elevation. ~**etmek** (·–¹··), **-eder**, to ascend, climb.
suüstü (¹··) Above-water. **bir denizaltının** ~ **sürati**, a submarine's surface speed.
suvare (*Fr. soirée*) Evening party.
suvar·ım Manner of watering; amount of water given at one irrigation. ~**mak**, to water (an animal).
suyol·cu (¹··) Man responsible for upkeep and repair of water conduits. ~**u, –nu**, water conduit; aqueduct; urinary passage; watermark *in paper.*
suyunca *v.* su.
suz·inak (–·–¹), ~**nak** Burning; pained, grieved. *Name of a sad mode of music.* ~**iş** (–¹), a burning; suffering; great sorrow.
sübek Urinal attached to a baby's cradle.
sübhan (·–¹) *In* ⌐**sulha** ~**a yatmaz**⌐, 'he is adamant, uncompromising'. ~ **Allah**, *lit.* 'glory be to God'; oh, my God!
sübut (·–¹), **-tu** A being proved; certainty; a being existent; reality. ~ **bulmak**, to be proved; ~ **delili**, certain proof. ~**î** (·–¹), positive; incontestable.
sübyan *v.* sıbyan.
sübye¹ (¹·) Emulsion; sweet drink *made with pounded almonds and melon or cucumber seeds.* ~**leştirmek**, to emulsify.
sübye² (¹·) Cuttle-fish.
sübye³ *In* ~ **armalı**, fore-and-aft rigged *ship.*
sücud (·⁴) A prostrating oneself in worship *or* entreaty. ~**a varmak**, to prostrate oneself. ~**etmek** (·–¹··), **-eder**, to prostrate oneself in worship.
sücü Wine.
südde Threshold; obstruction or stoppage *in a passage of the body.* ~**i saadet** *or* ~**i seniye**, the entrance to the Sultan's court.
südüs A sixth.
süfera (··–¹) *pl. of* sefir. Ambassadors.
süflî Low, inferior; common, low-down; menial; shabby. ~**yet, –ti**, ~**lik**, lowness, baseness, meanness; shabbiness.
Süha (·–¹) *A small star in Ursa Major.*
Süheyl Canopus (star).
sühulet (·–¹), **-ti** Facility, ease; gentleness; easy circumstances. ~ **göstermek**, to offer facilities. ~**li**, easy.
sühunet (·–¹), **-ti** Heat; fever; temperature.
sükkân *pl. of* sakin. Inhabitants.
süklüm püklüm In a crestfallen manner; hanging the head; sheepishly.
sükna (·–¹) Habitation; quarters.
sükûn (·⁴) Calm, quiet; repose. ~**et** (·–¹), **-ti**, quiet, calm; rest. **kesbi** ~ **etm.**, to be calmed. ~**etli**, quiet, peaceful; calm.

sükût (·⁴), **-tu** Silence. ~ **etm.**, to be silent. ~ **hakkı**, hush-money. ~**î** (·–¹), taciturn.
sülale (·–¹) Family; line; descendants.
Süleyman Suleyman; Solomon. ~ **Peygamber**, King Solomon: ⌐**mühür kimdeyse** ~ **odur**⌐, 'who holds the seal is Solomon', *i.e.* he who can prove his authority is the rightful person.
süline (·¹·) Razor-fish, solen.
sülûk (·⁴), **-kü** A following a road; a following a career; a belonging to a religious order; contemplative life. ···**e** ~ **etm.**, to follow the career of ...: **ehli** ~ dervish; hermit.
sülüğen Red lead.
sülük Leech; tendril *of a vine etc.*
sülümen Corrosive sublimate. **tatlı** ~, calomel.
sülün Pheasant. ~ **gibi**, tall and graceful: ~ **Bey**, a brisk, lively little man, Mr. Mouse.
sülüs, –lsü A third; a style of Arabic script with large letters. ~**an** (··⁴) two-thirds.
sümbük, –kü Hoof.
sümbül Hyacinth. ~**e**, a single ear of grain; a spike of flowers; the constellation Virgo. ~**î** (··–¹), cloudy, overcast.
sümkürmek *vn.* Expel mucus from the nose.
sümmek *va.* (Of a young animal) to bunt the udder when sucking; push about roughly.
sümmettedarik (¹··–·) *Lit.* 'then the preparation', *said of stg. entered on without preparation*; on the spur of the moment.
sümsük Imbecile; uncouth.
sümük Mucus, *esp. that of the nose.* ~**lü**, covered with mucus; slimy; snivelling. ~**lüböcek**, slug.
sümün An eighth.
sümürmek *v.* sömürmek.
sündüs Silk brocade.
süne Drake; an insect pest of cereals (*Eurygastrum*).
sünepe Slovenly; sluggish.
sünger Sponge. ~**le silmek**, to wipe off the slate: **ev** ~**i**, dry rot: ···**in üzerinden** ~ **geçirmek**, to pass the sponge over, to cancel: ⌐**yüzü kasab** ~**iyle silinmiş**⌐, hardbitten; brazen-faced. ~**kâğıdı, –nı**, blotting-paper. ~**taşı, –nı**, pumice-stone.
süngü Bayonet; spine. ~**sü ağır**, slow-moving: ~**sü düşük**, subdued, depressed, crestfallen: **ocak** ~**sü**, poker. ~**lemek**, to bayonet.
sünnet, –ti Moslem practices and rules *not laid down in the Koran but due to the Prophet's own habits and words;* ritual

circumcision. ~düğünü, circumcision feast:
~ etm., to circumcise; to amend: ~ olm.,
to be circumcised: ehli ~, orthodox, Sunni
Moslems. ~ci, circumciser. ~leme,
like Mohammed's beard, i.e. round and
short (beard). ~lemek (*sl.*), to eat up
entirely, to finish off. ~li, circumcised.
~siz, uncircumcised.

sünnî (·⸍) Orthodox; Sunnite.

sünuh (·ᵛ) A *matter's* occurring to the
mind. ~at (·—ᵛ), –tı, thoughts that occur
to the mind; inspiration.

süphan *etc. v.* sübhan.

süprü·lmek *vn. pass. of* süpürmek. Be
swept. ~ntü, sweepings; rubbish.
~ntücü, dustman. ~ntülük, dust-heap,
rubbish-heap.

süpürge Broom; brush. saçını ~ etm., (of
a woman) to work hard in the house: ~
darısı, sorghum: ~otu, heather: ~ sapı
yemek, to 'get the stick'. ~ci, maker *or*
seller of brooms; street-sweeper.

süpür·mek *va.* Sweep; brush; sweep away;
clear the dish. ~ücü, sweeper.

süpya (ᵛ·) Squid.

sürahi (·—⸍) Decanter, waterbottle.

sürat, sür'at, –tı Speed, velocity; haste.
~le, quickly: ~i intikal, quickwittedness,
perspicacity. ~li, quick; hurried.

sürc Stumble; slip; mistake. ~mek, to
stumble; to make a mistake. ~ülisan,
slip of the tongue, 'lapsus linguae'.

|| süre Period: extension.

sürek A drove *of cattle*; duration; fast
driver. ~ avı, drive (shooting). ~li,
lasting, prolonged. ~siz, transitory.

Süreyya The Pleiades.

sürfe Caterpillar; maggot; teredo.

sürgü Harrow; roller; bolt *of a door*;
plasterer's trowel; cursor; sliding bar; till.
~lemek, to harrow (a field); bolt (door);
roll (a road); smooth (plaster); ~lü,
bolted; sliding: ~ pergel, beam-compasses.

sürgün Banishment; place of exile; an
exile; shoot, sucker; diarrhoea. Exiled.
~ avı, drive, battue: ~ etm., to banish.
~lük, exile; place of exile; diarrhoea;
purgative.

sürme Anything drawn; bolt; drawer;
aperient; kohl; move (chess *etc.*); smut *of
wheat etc.* Sliding, drawing in and out.
~ pencere, sash window: ⸢adamın gözünden
~yi çalar⸣, 'he would steal the salve off a
man's eye' (*of a very crafty person*). ~dan,
pot for eye-salve.

sürmek *va.* Drive in front; drive away;
drive (a vehicle); banish; push along; push
forth (buds *etc.*); rub on, smear; plough;
sell; spend (time, life). *vn.* Push on, go on;
continue, extend; (of time) to pass; ger-

minate. sürüp atmak, to drive away,
expel: sür gitsin!, let it be!, don't worry!:
at ~, to push a horse on: ayak ~, to do stg.
slowly and unwillingly: boy ~, to shoot up,
grow tall: boya ~, to lay on paint: çift ~,
to plough: çok sürmedi, it did not last long;
it was not long before ...: ···e el ~, to
touch, to meddle with; işe el sürmemek, not
to lift a finger *to do stg.*: hüküm ~, to prevail: hükûmet ~, to govern: içi ~, to have
diarrhoea: ileri ~, to put forward (suggestion, proposal): kalp akçe ~, to pass false
money: öne ~, to bring up *a matter etc.*
(*with an innuendo of cunning*); to put *s.o.*
forward to meet a difficult situation:
saltanat ~, to reign: safa ~, to lead a
pleasant life: yağ ~, to spread butter, to
rub on oil: yüz ~, to prostrate oneself
humbly.

sürme·lemek *va.* Bolt (a door); put on
eye-salve. ~li, having a bolt; bolted;
sliding; tinged with eye-salve: ~ kumpas,
slide gauge, sliding calipers. ~taşı (·ᵛ··),
–nı, antimony (*used for blackening the
eyebrows*).

sürre Purse; gifts *formerly sent annually
by the Sultan to Mecca.* ~ alayı, the procession which accompanied the sürre: ~
devesi, an oddly-dressed person; ~ devesi
gibi dolaşmak, to loaf about with an air of
being busy: ~ emini, the official entrusted
with the delivery of the sürre.

sürtmek *va.* Rub *one thing* against another;
rub with the hand; wear down by friction.
vn. Wander about aimlessly. ⸢sürt Allah
kerim⸣ (*said of vagabonds*): sokak sokak ~,
to lounge about through the streets: taban
~, to walk incessantly.

sürtük (Woman) always walking the streets.

sürt·ülmek *vn. pass. of* sürtmek. Be
rubbed *etc.* ~ünmek, to rub oneself
against stg.; drag oneself along; creep;
toady; seek a quarrel, behave in a provocative manner.

sürur (·ᵛ) Joy; pleasure.

sürü Herd; flock; crowd, gang; a lot of.
~ ~, in droves, in flocks: ~den ayrılmamak
or ~ye katılmak, to join the throng, to
do as others do; (of a child) to cease to be
a baby and go in company with others:
~sine bereket (*sl.*), heaps of: ~ sepet, all
together; all the lot; in great numbers.
~cü, drover; driver *of a vehicle*; man in
charge of post-horses, *esp.* those carrying
the mail.

sürük·lemek *va.* Drag; drag along the
ground; drag *s.o.* somewhere against his
will; carry *one's audience, one's readers*
with one; involve, lead to, entail. atalete ~,
to bring to a standstill, to render useless.

~**lenmek,** to drag oneself; to be dragged; to drag on, be protracted. ~**leyici,** fascinating, attractive.

sürülmek *vn. pass. of* sürmek. Be rubbed *etc.* **ayağına yüz sürülecek bir adam,** a man worthy of the highest respect.

sürüm Act of driving *etc., v.* sürmek; rapid sale, great demand *for some article.* ~ ~, *used to strengthen the meaning of* sürünmek, *q.v.* ~**lü,** finding a ready sale; in great demand. ~**süz,** hard to sell; not in demand.

sürümek *va.* Drag along the ground; procrastinate. **ayak** ~, to shuffle along; to be very reluctant about stg. one has agreed to do : **ipini** ~, to lead a life of crime and deserve the gallows.

sürünceme Delay; a matter's dragging on. ~**de kalmak,** to drag on, to be long drawn out. ~**li,** dilatory.

süründürmek *va.* Bring into utter misery. || **sürüngen.** Reptile.

sürünmek *va.* Rub in *or* on. *vn.* Drag oneself along the ground; grovel; live in misery.

sürür (·ᵛ) Sulphide of mercury; vermilion varnish.

sürüş·mek *vn.* Rub together. ~**türmek** *va.,* to rub together; rub in slowly and gently; massage.

sürütme Drag-net, trawl; a kind of fishhook.

sürütmek *va. caus. of* sürmek. Cause to drag *etc.* ⌐**iti öldürene sürütürler**⌐, 'they make the killer of the dog drag it away', one must clear up the mess one has made.

Süryani (·—ᵎ) Syrian Christian (of Northern Irak); Syriac language. ~**ce,** Syriac.

süs Ornament, decoration; elegance of dress; toilet; luxury. ~ **saltanat,** great luxury : **kendisine** ... ~**ünü vermek,** to play the part of ... : **kaza** ~**ü vermek,** to pass off as an accident.

süsen (ᵎ·) Iris. ~ **kökü,** orris-root.

süs·lemek, ~**lendirmek** *va.* Adorn; embellish. ~**lenmek,** to adorn oneself, deck oneself out. ~**lü,** ornamented; decorated; carefully dressed; luxurious.

süsmek *va.* Butt, toss; gore.

süt, –tü, –dü Milk; milk-like juice. ~ **ağzı,** beestings (colostrum) : ~ **beyaz,** milk-

white : ~**ü bozuk,** base; without character; unprincipled : ···**in** ~**üne havale etm.,** to leave *stg. to another's* sense of honour : ~ **kardeş,** foster-brother *or* sister : ~ **kesildi,** the milk has turned sour : ~ **kesimi,** weaning; ~**ten kesmek,** to wean : ~ **kırı,** milk-white horse : ~ **kuzusu,** sucking lamb; baby : ⌐**ağzı*** ~ **kokuyor**⌐, he behaves like a child : **aslan** ~**ü,** raki : **kuş** ~**ü,** 'bird's milk', stg. impossible to find; **kuş** ~**ünden gayrı her şey var,** nothing is lacking.

süt·ana, ~**anne** (ᵎ··), wet-nurse; foster-mother. ~**baba,** foster-father. ~**başı, –nı,** cream. ~**çü,** milkman, dairyman. ~**çülük,** dairying, trade of a milkman. ~**dişi, –ni,** milk-tooth. ~**hane** (·—ᵎ), dairy. ~**laç,** rice-pudding. ~**leğen,** spurge, euphorbia. ~**liman** (ᵎ··), dead calm : **ortalık** ~, everything is perfectly quiet; 'the coast is clear!' ~**lü,** milky; in milk. ~**lüce,** petty spurge. ~**lük,** dairy. ~**nine,** ~**ne,** wet-nurse; foster-mother. ~**oğul, –ğlu,** foster-child. ~**otu, –nu,** milkwort, polygala. ~**süz,** without milk; base, ignoble. ~**vurğunu, –nu,** (child) suffering from bad milk; rickety.

sütun (·ᵛ) Column; pillar; column (in a newspaper); beam *of light.*

süvari (·—ᵎ) Cavalryman; captain *in the navy;* mounted police; cavalry. ~ **askeri,** cavalryman. ~**lik,** career and duties of a cavalryman *or* a captain.

süve *v.* söve.

süveter Sweater.

Süveyş Suez.

süz·geç Filter; strainer; rose *of a watering-can.* ~**gü,** fine filter. ~**gün,** languid; half-closed (eye); grown thin. ~**me,** filtered; strained; run (honey).

süzmek *va.* Strain, filter; examine closely; half-close the eyes, look attentively at *stg.* through half-closed eyes. **birine göz** ~, to cast amorous glances at s.o.

süzük Drawn, strained (face *etc.*).

süzülmek *vn. pass. of* süzmek. Be strained *or* filtered; become thin; become languorous; be very closely examined; slip *or* creep away; glide along swiftly and silently. **süzüle serile,** lolling languidly : **gözleri*** ~, for the eyes to be half-closed; to be sleepy.

Ş

şa (*abbrev. for* **yaşa**) Long live ...!; hurrah!

şab (–) Youth; young. ~ı **emred,** beardless youth.

şaban (–¹) *The eighth month of the Moslem year.*

şablon Pattern (*mech.*).

şabrak Horse-cloth; saddle-cover.

şad, şadan, şaduman Joyful, happy. ~i (–¹), ~**umani,** joy, happiness.

şadırvan Tank of water *with a jet in the middle*; tank *attached to mosques for ablutions.*

şaduman (–·¹) *v.* **şad.**

şafak, –kı (*Originally*) twilight, dusk; (*now*) dawn. ~ **atmak,** for dawn to break; birisinde ~ **atmak,** for s.o. to turn pale with fright: ~**la beraber,** at dawn : ~ **sökmek,** for dawn to break.

şafi (–¹) Health-giving; satisfactory; categorical (answer).

şâfi (–¹) Interceding.

şâfiî (–·⊥) The Shafi sect of Islam. ~ **köpeği,** a dirty-faced fellow.

şaft, –tı Shaft.

şaful Wooden tub *for carrying honey.*

şah¹ (*) Shah. ┌ben ~ımı bukadar severim┐, I can't risk any more; don't count on me any further.

şah² Fork; horn. ~**a kalkmak,** (of a horse) to rear.

şahab Flame; meteor.

şahadet (·–¹) *v.* **şehadet.**

şahane (––¹) Royal, imperial; regal, magnificent.

şahbaz Royal falcon; champion, hero. Fine. ┌şahtı (şah idi) ~ oldu┐, 'finer and finer!' (*only used ironically*).

şahdamar (¹··), **şahdamarı, –nı** Aorta.

şaheser (–·¹) Masterpiece.

şahım, –hmı *n.* Fat.

şahıs¹, –hsı Person; individual; personal features. ~**a mahsus,** personal. ~**landırmak,** to personify.

şahıs² (–¹), **–hsı** Surveyor's rod.

şahi (·⊥) Royal, imperial. Kingship; shahi (Persian coin); ancient form of muzzle-loading cannon; a kind of sweetmeat *made of starch and egg.*

şahid (–¹) Witness; example (*gram.*); control (in an experiment); example *from a well-known work.* ~ **tutmak,** to call on one to witness, to accept as witness: kırk ~ lâzım, one can hardly believe it: ···e ~ olm., to witness. ~**lik,** a giving evidence, testimony; a being witness *to stg.*

şâhika (–·¹) Summit.

şahin (–¹) Peregrine falcon. ~ **bakışlı,** with fierce and piercing eyes : ┌alacağına ~ **vereceğıne karga┐,** he is fierce to his debtor but humble to his creditor. ~**ci,** falconer in charge of the peregrines.

şahlanmak *vn.* (Of a horse) to rear; become angry and threatening; get out of hand.

şahmerdan Battering-ram; pile-driver; beetle (heavy hammer).

şahm·ı *v.* **sahım.** ~**î** (·⊥), adipose, fatty.

şahname (·–¹) Poetical history; epic. ~**ci,** court poet.

şahnişin Bay-window on an enclosed balcony.

şahrah Main road, highway (*also fig.*).

şahrem *Only in* ~ ~ **çatlamak** (yırtılmak), (of the skin) to be covered with cracks; (of cloth) to be much torn.

şahs·an (¹·) Personally; in person. ~**ı,** *v.* **sahıs.** ~**î** (·⊥), personal, private. ~**iyat** (··ℓ), –**tı,** personalities; personal matters : ~**a dökülmek,** (of a discussion) to descend to personalities. ~**iyet, –ti,** personality; important person.

şahsüvar Fine horseman.

şahtane Large pearl; a grain of hempseed.

şahtere Fumitory.

şahtur Large raft-like boat *used as a ferry on large rivers.*

şaibe (–·¹) Stain; defect. ~**dar,** stained; tarnished.

şair (–¹) Poet; minstrel; public singer. ~**ane** (–·–¹), poetical; in a poetical manner. ~**lik,** the quality of a poet *or* minstrel.

şak¹ Difficult, arduous.

şak², –kı A clacking noise (*as of wood against wood, the crack of a whip, a box on the ear*).

şak³, –kkı A splitting; crack; fissure. ~**kı şefe etm.,** to open the lips, to speak.

şaka Fun; joke; jest. ~**ya boğmak,** to try to pass off *a matter* with a joke : ┌~ **derken (iken) kaka olur┐,** 'a joke may easily become a serious matter': ~**ya gelmez,** (a matter) not to be joked about; (a man) who can't take a joke; who is not to be joked with, severe : ~ **götürmez,** serious, not a joking matter : ~ **kaldırmak,** to be able to stand a joke : ~ **maka (derken),** by making light of *a difficulty one overcomes it*: ~**ya vurmak,** to pretend to take stg. as a joke : ~**sı yok,** in earnest; not to be trifled with : bu bana ~ gibi geliyor, this is incredible : el ~**sı,** practical joke : hoyrat ~**sı,** horse-play.

şakacıktan (i) As a joke; (ii) (to do stg. serious) under the pretence of a joke.

şakak Temple (of the head).

şakalaşmak *vn.* Joke with one another.

şakavet *v.* şekavet.

şakayık, –kı, –ğı Peony.

şakımak *vn.* (Of a nightingale or canary) to sing loudly.

şakır *In* ~ ~, *imitating the noise of rain, of splashing, of a continuous rattle or jingle.* ~ **şakur** (şukur), *imitates a hollow rattling and banging noise.* ~**damak,** to make the noises expressed by şakır; rattle, jingle; sing vociferously (nightingale). ~**tı,** continuous clatter or rattle, *v.* şakır.

şakıt, –tı Lamprey.

şâki (–¹) Complaining.

şakî (·⸍) Brigand; rebel; outlaw.

şakir (–¹) Thankful, grateful. ⌜ne verseler ana ~ ne kılsalar ana şad⌝, 'he is grateful for whatever they give him and happy whatever they do to him', *used to describe a contented man, who finds all right with the world.*

şakird (–¹) Pupil; apprentice. ~**lik,** quality of a pupil *or* apprentice; apprenticeship; wages paid to an apprentice.

şakketmek (¹··), –**eder** *va.* Cleave; split.

şaklaban Mimic; jester; buffoon; amusing fellow; charlatan. ~**lık,** mimicry; buffoonery.

şak·lamak *vn.* Make a loud cracking noise, *v.* şak². ~**latmak,** to crack (whip); cause a loud cracking noise to be made.

şakrak Noisy; mirthful; vivacious; chatty. ~ **kuşu,** bullfinch.

şakşak Slap-stick; large castanet; applause; toadying. ~**çı,** toady; 'yes-man'. ~**çılık,** base adulation.

şakul (–¹) Plumb-line; plummet. ~**î** (––⸍ *or* –·⸍), perpendicular. ~**lamak,** to set up with a plumb-line; plan; measure.

şal Shawl, *esp.* a Cashmere shawl; pall.

şalgam Turnip.

şali (–¹) Alpaca; camlet; bunting.

şallak Naked; shameless. ~ **mallak,** stark naked; a mob of roughs.

şalter Switch (*elec.*).

şalupa (·¹·) Sloop.

şalvar Turkish baggy trousers. ~**lı,** wearing baggy trousers.

Şam¹ Damascus. ~ **fıstığı,** pistachio nut.

şam² Evening.

şama Wax taper. ~**lı kibrit,** vesta match.

şamama (·¹·) Musk melon; undergrown, weak (child or man).

şamandıra (·¹··) Buoy; float *for a wick*; burner *of a paraffin lamp*; ball *of a ballcock.*

şamar Slap; box on the ear.

şamata Great noise, uproar, hubbub. ~**cı,** a noisy, uproarious person. ~**lı,** noisy.

şambabası (¹···), –**nı** A kind of sweet pastry.

şambrnuvar (*Fr. chambre noire*) Darkroom.

şamdan Candlestick.

şamfıstığı (¹···), –**nı** Pistachio nut.

şamil (–¹) Comprising; including; comprehensive.

şamme (–¹) The faculty of smell.

şampanya (·¹·) Champagne.

şampanze Chimpanzee.

şampiyon Champion.

şampuvan Shampoo.

şan Fame, renown; glory; reputation; state, quality, aspect; display; importance. ~**ına* düşmek (yakışmak)** *or* ~**ından* olm.,** to befit one's station or dignity; ~**ından* olm.,** *also* to be peculiar to, to be characteristic of: **her kese ~ vermek,** to become known to all; to acquire fame.

şangır *etc. v.* şıngır *etc.*

şanlı Glorious; famous; fine-looking. ~ **şöhretli,** fine and imposing.

şano (¹·) Stage (theatre).

şans Chance; luck. ~**lı,** lucky. ~**sız,** unlucky.

şansız Without renown, unknown; undistinguished. ~ **şöhretsiz,** insignificant in appearance.

şantaj (*Fr. chantage*) Blackmail.

şantöz (*Fr. chanteuse*) Female singer.

şap¹, –pı Alum; coral reef. ~ **gibi donmak (kalmak),** to be embarrassed or disconcerted: ~ **gibi dönmek** *or* ~ **kesilmek,** to become bitter: ~ **illeti,** foot-and-mouth disease: ~**a oturmak,** to be grounded on a coral reef; to be in a hopeless dilemma; to be greatly disconcerted: **kızıl ~,** light purple colour: ⌜**ne ~ ne şeker⌝,** neither one thing nor the other.

şap² şap *Imitates the sound of kissing.*

Sapdenizi (¹···), –**ni** The Red Sea.

şaphane (·–¹) Alum factory.

şapır *In* ~ ~ *or* ~ **şupur,** *imitates the smacking of lips.* ~**damak,** to make a smacking noise (in kissing or eating). ~**tı,** smacking noise of the lips.

şapka (¹·) Hat; truck *of a mast*; cowl *of a chimney.* **supap** ~**sı,** valve head. ~**cı,** hatter. ~**lı,** wearing a hat; having a circumflex.

şaplak Smack on the face.

şap·lamak *vn.* Make a smacking noise *with the lips or hand.* ~**latmak,** to cause to make a smacking noise: **bir tokat ~,** to give a resounding slap.

şaprak Saddle covering.

şapşal Untidy; slovenly.

şar şar *Imitates the sound of slashing.*

şarab Wine. ~**cı**, wine-merchant. ~**hane** (··—ᴵ), wine factory; storehouse for wine; large wine-cask, vat.

şarampol Palisade; stockade.

şarapnel Shrapnel.

şarbon (*Fr. charbon*) Anthrax; smut *of wheat etc.*

şarıl Sound of running water. ~ ~ **akmak**, ~**damak**, to flow with a splashing noise. ~**tı**, a gurgling, splashing noise.

şâri (—ᴵ), **–ii** Legislator.

şa'rî (—ᴸ) Capillary. ~**yet**, **–ti**, capillarity.

şarib (—ᴵ) *In* ~**ül leyl vennehar**, a hopeless drunkard.

şarih (—ᴵ) Commentator; annotator.

şark, **–kı** The East. ~**ı karib**, the Near East (*now* **Yakın Doğu**).

şarkadak (ᴵ··) *Imitates the noise of a thing falling.* ~ **bayılmak**, to fall down in a faint.

şark·an (ᴵ·) In *or* from an easterly direction. ~**î** (·ᴸ), eastern, oriental. ~**ıyat**, **–tı**, orientalism; the study of Oriental languages and literature.

şarkı Song. ~ **söylemek**, to sing. ~**cı**, song-writer; singer.

şarlamak *v.* **şarıldamak**.

şarpa (ᴵ·) Scarf.

şart, **–tı** Condition, stipulation; article of an agreement; conditional clause; oath *with the words* '~ **olsun!**' (*may I be divorced from my wife if this be not true*). ~**ı âzam**, indispensable condition: ~ **koşmak**, to lay down a condition. ~**etmek** (ᴵ··), **–eder**, to invoke a divorce *under certain conditions, v.* **şart**; to lay down a condition. ~**î** (·ᴸ), conditional. ~**lamak**, to wash clothes *or* vessels in accordance with the requirements of canon law. ~**laşmak**, mutually to agree to conditions. ~**lı**, having a condition attached; who takes the oath called **şart** *q.v.* ~**name** (·—ᴵ), list of conditions; specification; contract.

şasi Chassis.

şâşaa (—·ᴵ) Glitter, sparkle; splendour. ~**lanmak**, to sparkle; to be magnificent *or* pompous. ~**lı**, sparkling; resplendent; gorgeous.

şaşalamak *vn.* Be bewildered *or* confused.

şaşı Squinting, squint-eyed. ⌈**körle yatan** ~ **kalkar**⌉, 'who sleeps with a blind man will get up with a squint', 'evil communications corrupt good manners'.

şaşılacak Surprising; wonderful.

şaşır·lamak *vn.* Squint. ~**lık**, squint, squinting.

şaşır·mak *va.* Be confused about *stg.*;

lose *the way etc. vn.* Become bewildered *or* embarrassed; lose one's head. ~**tma**, a misleading *or* confusing; zigzag; tonguetwister; transplanting. ~**tmaca**, tonguetwister; puzzle. ~**tmak**, to confuse, bewilder; mislead; transplant (seedlings *etc.*).

şaşkaloz Cross-eyed.

şaşkın Bewildered, confused; stupid. ⌈**ne** ~ **ol basıl, ne taşkın ol asıl!**⌉, 'don't be stupid and get caught and don't be too clever and get hanged!', 'be moderate in everything'. ~**lık**, bewilderment; stupidity.

şaşmak *vn.* Miss one's way, go astray; deviate; be surprised *or* bewildered. **şaşa kalmak**, to be bewildered: **şaşacak şey**, a surprising thing: **şaşmamak**, not to go astray; not to deviate; not to go wrong; to be punctual, to keep exact time (of a clock); **ben söylediklerimden şaşmam**, I will not budge an inch from what I have said.

şat[1] Flat-bottomed boat; lighter.

şat[2], **–ttı** Large river, *esp.* the united Tigris and Euphrates, *also called* **Şattülarab**.

şatafat, **–tı** Luxury; ostentatious living. ~**lı**, pretentious, showy.

şathiyat (··ᴸ), **–tı** Flippant and satirical writings.

şatir Gay, vivacious; agile. Running attendant *formerly employed by high officials when on horseback.*

şatranc Chess.

şavul *v.* **şakul**.

şayak Serge.

şayan (—ᴸ) Fitting; suitable; worthy; deserving. ~**ı dikkat**, worth attention, notable: ~**ı takdir**, praiseworthy.

şayed (ᴸ·) If perchance; lest; perhaps.

şayegân (—·ᴸ) Fit, proper; extensive, plentiful.

şayeste (—·ᴵ) Worthy; deserving.

şayi (—ᴵ), **–ii** Divulged; commonly known; shared in common. ~**a** (—·ᴵ), news spread about, rumour. ~**at**, **–tı**, *pl. of* **şayia**.

şayka (ᴵ·) *A kind of boat used in the Black Sea.*

şaz Contrary to the general rule; irregular; exceptional. Exception.

şeamet (·—ᴵ), **–ti** A being inauspicious; evil omen. ~**li**, inauspicious, ill-omened.

şeb Night.

şebab Youth.

şebboy Wallflower; stock. **sarı** ~, wallflower; **kırmızı** ~, stock.

şebek Baboon; *a kind of boat with a long narrow stern, used in the Mediterranean.*

şebek·e Net; lattice-work; grating; network *of railways etc.*; band *of robbers etc.*;

şebih ring *of dealers etc.* ~**î** (··-²), reticulated: **tabakai** ~**ye**, retina.

şebih (·-²) Like, similar.

şebiyelda (···-²) The longest night of the year.

şebnem Dew.

şebpere Bat.

şecaat (·-²), **-ti** Bravery, courage. ᴦ ~ **arz ederken (merdi kıptı sırkatını söyler)**ᴚ, 'the gipsy, boasting of his courage, tells of his theft'; when boasting of one's qualities to reveal one's defects. ~**li**, brave.

şecer Tree. ~**e**, genealogical tree, pedigree. ~**eli**, of good family, with a pedigree.

şeci (·-²) Brave, bold.

şedaid Severities; adversities.

şedde *Arabic sign for a doubled consonant.* ~**li**, bearing the sign **şedde**, doubled (consonant); complete, utter (ass, fool *etc.*).

şedid (·-²) Hard; strong; violent; severe. ~**en** (·-²·), violently, strongly. ~**üş-şekime** (·-··-²), hard-mouthed; determined, unyielding.

şef (*Fr. chef*) Chief, leader. ~**garson**, head waiter. ~**lik**, duties of a chief; chief office: **istasyon şefliği**, stationmaster's office.

şefaat (·-²), **-ti** Intercession. ~**ci**, intercessor.

şefe Lip. ~**vî** (··-²), labial.

şeffaf Transparent; diaphanous:·

şefkat, **-ti** Compassion; affection; solicitude, concern. ~**li**, compassionate; affectionate. ~**siz**, without pity; without affection.

şeftali (·-²) Peach; kiss.

şeftren (*Fr. chef de train*) Guard *of a train.*

şehadet; (·-²), **-ti** A witnessing; testimony; evidence; a thing witnessed; a testifying to Islam; death in battle (*of a Moslem only*); martyrdom. ~ **etm.**, to bear witness (to = *dat.*): ~ **getirmek**, to pronounce the formula 'there is no God but God, Mohammed is the apostle of God': ~**e nail olm.**, to gain martyrdom, to die on the field of battle: ~ **parmağı**, the index finger. ~**name** (·-·-²), testimonial; diploma; certificate.

şehamet (·-²), **-ti** Boldness coupled with efficiency. ~**li**, bold and efficient. ~**lû**, valorous and successful (*title formerly given by the Turks to the Shak of Persia*).

şehbaz *v.* şahbaz.

şehbender Turkish *or* Persian consul. ~**hane** (····-²), consulate. ~**lik**, rank and duties of a consul.

şehid Martyr; (*of Moslems only*) one who dies in battle *or* in the service of his country, *now often used of the victims of an accident.* ~**lik**, martyrdom, death in battle *etc.*, *v.* **şehid**: cemetery *or* monument for those who died in battle.

şehik, **-ki** Inspiration of breath; sob; hiccough.

şehir¹, **-hri** Month.

şehir², **-hri** Large town, city. ~**dışı**, **-nı**, suburb. ~**li**, townsman, citizen.

şehîr (·-²) Celebrated.

şehislâm *v.* şeyhülislâm.

şehlâ Having a slight cast in the eye.

şehrah *v.* şahrah.

şehrayin (·-²) Illumination of a town *for a festival etc.*

şehr·emaneti (²·-·²), **-ni** Prefecture of a large town. ~**emini**, **-ni**, prefect of a large town.

şehr·i *v.* şehir. ~**î**¹ (·-²), urban; urbane. ~**î**², monthly; every month. ~**ilik**, urbanity.

şehriyar The sovereign; the Sultan.

şehriye¹ *fem. of* şehrî. Monthly salary.

şehriye² Vermicelli. **arpa** ~**si**, pearl-barley.

şehtane *v.* şahtane.

şehvanî (·-²) Lustful; sensual.

şehvet, **-ti** Lust; sensuality. ~**engiz**, appetizing; exciting; aphrodisiac. ~**li**, sensual; voluptuous. ~**perest**, sensual; enslaved by lust.

şehzade (·-²) (*pl.* ~**gân**) Prince, *esp.* a Sultan's son.

şek, **-kki** Doubt; uncertainty. ~ **ve şübhe**, doubt and misgiving.

şekavet (·-²), **-ti** Brigandage.

şeker Sugar; a sweet; darling. Sweet. ~**im**, my darling: ~ **bayramı**, *name of the feast during the first three days after the Ramazan fast*: ~ **illeti**, diabetes: ~ **kamışı**, sugar-cane.

şeker·ci, sweet-seller; sugar-merchant; confectioner: ~ **boyası**, poke-weed (*Phytolacca*). ~**leme**, candied fruit; sugar-plum; doze, nap. ~**lemek**, to sugar, to preserve in sugar. ~**li**, sugared; sweetened with sugar. ~**renk**, whitish brown; uncordial, cool (relations): **araları** ~, their relations are somewhat cool, they are not on very good terms.

şekil, **-kli** Form; shape; figure; plan; diagram; kind; manner; features. **bir şekle girmek**, to take a form *or* shape: **bir şekle koymak**, to manage somehow *or* other: **şekle riayeten**, for form's sake.

şekil·lendirmek to give a form or shape to; to form. ~**siz**, shapeless; uncouth; without diagrams.

şekl·en (²-) In form; in appearance. ~**i**, *v.* şekil. ~**î** (·-²), relating to form; having diagrams.

şekva (·-²) Complaint.

şelâle Waterfall.

şem, –mmi A smelling; sense of smell.

şema (¹·) Outline; sketch; plan, diagram.

şem'a Taper; candle. ⌈perde kurup ∼ yakmak⌉, 'to set up the curtain and light the candle' (for a Karagöz show); to have all ready for the performance.

şemail (·–¹) Features.

şemi, –m'i Wax; candle.

şemis v. şems.

şemm·e A single sniff; a whiff; a very small quantity; hint (of reproach etc.). ∼î (·–¹), pertaining to smell; olfactory.

şems Sun. ∼e, ornamental figure of the sun. ∼î (·–¹), solar. ∼isiper, peak of a cap; handkerchief for protecting the head from the sun. ∼iye, parasol, umbrella. ∼iyeci, umbrella maker or seller. ∼iyeli, carrying an umbrella.

şen Joyous, cheerful; inhabited, cultivated, civilized.

şenaat (·–¹), –ti Foulness; wickedness.

şenayi (·–¹) pl. of şenia. Disgraceful acts.

şendere Stave of a cask; thin board; a kind of Red Mullet.

şenelmek v. şenlenmek.

şeni (·–¹) Disgraceful, vile, immoral. ∼a (·–¹), vile or immoral act.

şe'nî (·–¹) Real. ∼yet, –ti, reality.

şen·lenmek vn. Become cheerful, gay, joyful; become inhabited and prosperous. ∼lik, gaiety, cheerfulness; public rejoicings, illuminations etc.; prosperity, increase in amenities.

şeppere Bat.

şer, –rri Evil; wickedness; harm; quarrel. Bad, wicked. serrine* lânet, a curse upon his wickedness! may God curse him!

–şer, –şar Suffix to numerals making them distributive. ikişer, two each, two at a time.

şerafet (·–¹), –ti A being illustrious; nobility; a being descended from the Prophet.

şerait (·–¹), –ti pl. of şart. Conditions.

şer'an (¹·) In accordance with canon law.

şerare (·–¹) Spark.

şerayin (·–¹) pl. of şiryan. Arteries.

şerbet, –ti Sweet drink; sherbet; infusion; medicinal or aperient draught. ∼ or gübre ∼i, liquid manure: ∼ almak, to take an aperient. ∼çi, seller of sherbet. ∼çiotu, –nu, hop (plant). ∼lenmek, to be rendered immune to a disease. ∼li, with sherbet; infused; immune, bewitched against .ıake-bites etc.; notorious, hardened. ∼lik, anything used for making sherbet.

şeref Honour; glory; excellence; legitimate pride, exaltation; superiority, distinction.

∼ bulmak, to be honoured; to increase in value: kesbi ∼ etm., or naili ∼ olm., to have the honour of .... ∼bahş, ∼bahşa (···–¹), ∼efza (···–¹), that honours, who honours (by his presence etc.). ∼e, gallery of a, minaret whence the call to prayer is made. ∼iye, tax on the increase in land value due to building. ∼lenmek, to acquire honour, be honoured; increase in value. ∼li, honoured, esteemed; favoured or distinguished (district). ∼reşan, bringing honour. ∼yab (··–¹), honoured.

şeremet, –ti A loquacious scoundrel; virago.

şerh Explanation; commentary. ∼etmek (¹··), –eder, to explain, comment on.

şerha Cut; split (of the lips); wound; slice. ∼ ∼ doğramak, to cut to pieces.

şer·i, –r'i The Moslem religious law, sheri. ∼'î (·–¹), pertaining to the religious law: hileyi ∼ye, a legal way of getting round the law. ∼at (·–¹), –ti, canonical obligations; the religious law: ⌈∼in kestiği parmak acımaz⌉, 'just punishment is not resented'. ∼ci, (formerly) an official in the office of the Sheikhulislam; (now) an upholder of the Religious Law.

şerid Ribbon; tape; band, belt; film (cinema); tapeworm. ∼ arşın, tape-measure. ∼lemek, to bind or ornament with ribbon or tape. ∼li, beribboned.

şerif Noble; descended from Mohammed; formerly a title of the Governor of Mecca.

şerik, –ki Partner; shareholder; companion. ∼i cürüm, accomplice in crime. ∼lik, partnership; companionship.

şerir Bad, wicked; rebellious. Scoundrel.

şerm Bashfulness; modesty.

şerr·i v. şer. ∼ülhalef, a successor in evil.

şeş Pers. num. Six, only used in backgammon and in: ∼i beş görmek, to squint; to be thoroughly confused: sana ∼i beş gösteririm!, I'll knock stars out of you!

şetaret (·–¹), –ti Merriment, gaiety, cheerfulness.

şetim, –tmi Abuse, invective. şetmetmek (¹··), –eder, to revile, abuse.

şev Slope; glacis; bevel. Sloping. ∼ ∼ine, sloping; not at right angles.

şevahik (·–¹), –ki pl. of şahika. Summits.

şevaib (·–¹) pl. of şaibe. Stains; defects.

şevk¹, –ki Desire; ardent yearning; eagerness; mirth. ∼e gelmek, to become eager; to grow merry. ∼î¹ (·–¹), ∼li, eager, desirous; gay. ∼siz, without eagerness; cold; dull.

şevk², –ki Thorn. ∼î² (·–¹), thorny; spinal.

şevket, –ti Majesty, pomp. ∼li, ∼lû, ∼meab, majestic (title of a sovereign).

şev·lenmek *vn.* Slope; incline. ~li, sloping; bevelled.

şevval, -li *The tenth month of the Moslem lunar year.*

şey Thing; *often used when one cannot find the right word or name,* what d'you call it, what's his name. bir ~, a thing, something: bir şeyler, something or other: bir ~ değil, it is nothing; it doesn't matter; not at all! (*in reply to thanks etc.*): ⌐bir ~dir oldu⌐, 'I'm sorry it happened, but it can't be helped now': çok ~ !, really!; how strange! : hiç bir ~, nothing.

şeyatin (·–¹) *pl. of* şeytan. Devils.

şeyb Greyness of the hair; hoariness.

şeyda (·–¹) Madly in love.

şeyh Old man; elder; sheikh; head of a family *or* tribe; head of a religious order. uhat (·–¹), -ti, ~uhiyet, -ti, old age. ülharem, the Governor of the town and province of Medina. ~ülislâm, Sheikh-ulislam (*formerly the Minister responsbile for all matters connected with the Sheri or Canon Law, religious schools, etc., and coming next to the Grand Vizier in precedence*).

şey'î (·–¹) Objective.

şeyn Disgrace; vice; defect.

şeytan Satan; devil; crafty man; sharp little devil (child). ~ arabası, floating thistledown *or* dandelion seeds; hand-driven trolley *used by railwaymen;* bicycle: ~ın ard ayağı *or* kıç bacağı, a limb of Satan, a crafty fellow: ~ları ayaklandı, his evil propensities were aroused: ⌐~ azabda gerek⌐, it serves you (him *etc.*) right!: ~ın bacağını kırmak, to overcome temptation, *v. App.* : ~ boku (tersi), asafoetida: ⌐~a çarık giydirir⌐ *or* ⌐~a külâhını giydirir⌐, 'he could cheat the Devil himself, he is very cunning': ~ diyor ki, I am very tempted *to do stg.* foolish: ⌐~ı eşeğe ters bindirir⌐ *or* ⌐~ı şişeye sokar⌐, 'as cunning as the Devil': ⌐~ın işi yok⌐, 'by pure bad luck': ~ları tepesine çıktı, he lost his temper: ~ tırnağı, a hangnail: ~ tüyü, a talisman *supposed to give personal attraction*: ~a uymak, to let oneself be led astray; to yield to temptation: aksı ~, as bad luck would have it; 'how provoking!': ⌐insan insana ~ıdır⌐, one man leads another to evil.

şeytan·bezi, -ni, velveteen. ~et, -ti, act of devilry; malice; craftiness. ~î (·–¹), diabolical. ~lık, devilry; slyness; malicious cunning.

şık¹, -kkı Half of anything cut in two; one of two alternatives.

şık² (*Fr. chic*) Chic; smart. ~lık, smartness.

şıkır *In* ~ ~, *imitates a jingling or clinking noise; also used of dazzling light.* ~damak,

to rattle, jingle: cebleri* ~, to have plenty of money. ~tı, a jingling noise.

şıkşıka Small rings on a door *imitating the large knocker.*

şıldır *In* ~ ~ bakmak, (of a baby) to stare with wide-open eyes.

şıllık Gaudily dressed (woman). Loose woman.

şımar·ık Spoilt (child); saucy, impertinent; stuck-up. ~mak, to be spoilt by indulgence; to get above oneself; to lose one's self-control. ~tmak, to spoil *a child.*

şınanay Refrain, fol-de-rol, tra-la-la.

şıngıl *v.* çıngıl.

şıngır *In* ~ ~, *imitates the noise of breaking glass.* ~damak, to crash, to make the noise of breaking glass. ~tı, the noise of breaking glass.

şıp, -pı Noise of a drop falling; a sudden slight noise. Easily, quickly, at once. ~ diye geldi, all of a sudden he came: ~ın işi, very quickly and easily: beş dakikada ~ın işi bitirim, I'll polish it off in five minutes.

şıpıdık (¹··) Low-heeled shoe *or* slipper.

şıpıldamak *vn.* (Of water) to make a lapping noise, to lap.

şıpır *In* ~ ~, falling in drops. ~tılı, splashing: ~ hava, rainy weather.

şıpka (¹·) Rope *or* wire net *used on a ship;* torpedo-net.

şıppadak (¹··), **şıpsak** Quickly, at once.

şıpsevdi (¹··) (*sl.*) Quick to fall in love; susceptible.

şıpşıp Slipper without any back.

şıra (¹·) Must, unfermented grape-juice. ~ lı, juicy.

şırak *Imitates a sudden sharp noise.*

şırfıntı *A term of contempt for women;* bitch (*of a woman*).

şırıl *In* ~ ~, *imitates the noise of gently running water.* ~damak, to make such a noise. ~tı, noise of running water, splashing, gurgling.

şırınga (·¹·) Syringe; enema; hypodermic syringe; injection.

şırlağan Oil of sesame.

şırlamak *v.* şırıldamak.

şırlop Eggs fried in yoghourt.

şırp, şırpadak *v.* şıp, şıpadak.

şırvan, şırvanı Loft over a shop.

şıvgar *v.* şivgar.

Şîa The Shiite sect of Moslems.

şiar Badge; sign; countersign, watch-word; war-cry; habit, characteristic, trait.

-şiar *Suffix.* Marked by .... rahmetşiar, merciful.

şibih, -bhi A similar thing; *in compounds means* resembling ..., *e.g.* ~maden, metalloid; ~cezire, peninsula: ~münharif, trapezoid.

şiddet, -ti Hardness; strength; violence; severity. ~i sefalet, extreme poverty. ~li, violent; vehement; severe.

şifa (·⌣) Restoration to health; healing. ~ bulmak, to recover health: ~yı bulmak (kapmak), (iron.) to fall ill; to turn out badly: ~ olsun!, 'may it bring you health!', said to one having a drink or taking medicine: ~ vermek, to restore health. ~bahş, ~lı, healing; wholesome. ~hane (·—⌣), hospital; lunatic asylum ~yab, restored to health.

şifah·en (·⌣·) Orally, verbally. ~î (·—⌣), oral, verbal.

şifre (⌣·) Cipher; code. ~ açmak (çözmek), to decode, decipher. ~li, in cipher; with initials.

şiğil, şiğir Hobble; ring without a stone.

Şiî (—⌣) Shiite. ~lik, a belonging to the Shiite sect, Shiism.

şiir Poetry; poem.

şikak, -kı Strife; discord.

şikâr (·⌣) The chase; hunting; game killed in the chase; prey, victim; anything rare and much sought after; booty. ~ bir şey mi?, is it such a rarity?: ~ pazar, a cheap bargain.

şikâyet (·—⌣), -ti Complaint. ~ etm., to complain; ···i ~ etm., to complain about. ~çi, complainant. ~name (·—·—⌣), written complaint.

şikem Belly; womb. ~perver, glutton; gluttonous.

-şiken Pers. suffix. Breaking ...; haysiyet-şiken, humiliating.

şikest Break, fracture; destruction. ~e, broken; the Persian style of Arabic writing.

şil¹ Javelin.

şil² Bloodshot and purulent (eye).

şile Wild marjoram.

şilep Tramp steamer; cargo boat.

Şili Chili.

şilin Shilling.

şilte Thin mattress or quilt.

şimal, -li The North. ~ yıldızı, the Pole Star. ~en (·⌣·), to or from the north. ~î (·—⌣), northern, north.

şimden v. şimdiden. ~geri (·⌣··), henceforth, from now on.

şimdi (⌣·) The present. Now. ~den, henceforth; already: ~den tezi yok, the sooner the better; with all speed: ~ye kadar (değin), up till now. ~cik (⌣··), this very moment, now at once. ~ki, the present; the actual. ~lik, for the present.

şime (—⌣) Natural quality or habit.

şimi (Fr. chimie) Chemistry.

şimşek Lightning. ~li fener, flashing light (lighthouse).

şimşir¹ (·⌣) Sword.

şimsir² Box (tree). 'kel başa ~ tarak', 'a boxwood comb for a bald head', an absurd luxury.

şin Disgrace.

-şinas Pers. suffix. Knowing ...; hakşinas, who knows the right, just.

şinaver (·—⌣) Floating. Swimmer.

şinik Measure for cereals equalling a quarter bushel (10 litres).

şinşile Chinchilla.

şip A kind of coarse gauze.

şir (—) Lion; milk.

şira¹ (·⌣), -aı Purchase or sale. beyü ~, buying and selling, commerce.

şira² v. şıra.

şiraze (——⌣) Head-band of a bound volume; a thing that holds other things together; order, regularity. ~den çıkmak, to lose one's mental balance: ~sinden çıkmak, or ~si bozulmak, (of a matter) to deteriorate beyond recovery.

şirden The second stomach of ruminants.

şirid v. şerid.

şirin Sweet; affable; charming. ~lik, sweetness; amiability.

şiringa (·⌣·) v. şırınga.

şirk, -ki Polytheism. Tanrıya ~ koşmak, to attribute a partner to God, i.e. to be a polytheist.

şirket, -ti Partnership; joint ownership; joint-stock company. ~ vapuru, Bosphorus ferry steamer: ... anonim ~i, the ... Company, Ltd.

şirlan v. şırlağan.

şirpençe Carbuncle; anthrax.

şirret, -ti Evilly disposed, malicious. Malicious person; tartar, shrew, virago. ~lik, malice; evil disposition.

şiryan Artery. ~î (·—⌣), arterial.

şist, -ti Schist.

şiş¹ Spit; skewer; rapier; knitting-needle; axle. ~e geçirmek, to skewer: 'ne ~ yansın ne kebab', so that neither the skewer nor the mutton be burnt, i.e. so that neither party suffers damage.

şiş² Swelling; tumour. Swollen.

şişane (·—⌣) Rifling of a gun; rifled gun. 'altı kaval üstü ~', 'smoothbore below and rifled above', a paradoxical absurdity; wearing clothes that do not go with one another.

şişe Bottle; lamp-glass; cupping-glass; moulded or planed lath. ~hane (··—⌣), glass-works.

şişek Year-old lamb; teg.

şişirmek va. Cause to swell; inflate; exaggerate; (sl.) do stg. hastily and carelessly; 'cram' for an exam.: stab.

şişkin Swollen; puffed up. ~lik, distension, puffiness, swelling.

şişko ($\cdot\dot{-}$) Very fat (man).

şişlemek *va.* Spit, skewer; stab.

şişman Fat. **~lık,** fatness, obesity.

şişmek *vn.* Swell; become inflated; grow fat; become swollen; be distended; (of a runner) to be unable to continue for want of breath. **kafası ~,** to be distraught or dazed *by noise etc.*

şita ($\cdot\dot{-}$) Winter.

şitab ($\cdot\dot{-}$) Speed; haste. **~an** ($\cdot-\dot{-}$), hurried; in haste: **~ olm.,** to hasten. **~etmek** ($\cdot\dot{-}\cdot\cdot$), **~eder,** to hurry, hasten.

şiv *v.* şev.

şive ($-\dot{-}$) Accent, pronunciation; idiom; gracefulness; style. **~kâr, ~li,** graceful, elegant, stylish. **~siz,** unidiomatic, with a bad accent or pronunciation; without grace or style.

şivgar Whipple-tree of a gun-carriage.

şlep Cargo boat.

şoför Chauffeur; driver of a motor-car.

şol *Old form of* şu.

şom Inauspicious; sinister, gloomy. Evil omen. **~ağızlı** ($\dot{-}\cdot\cdot\cdot$), who always predicts misfortune.

şont Shunt (dynamo *etc.*).

şorolop *Imitates the sound of a thing gulped down.*

şose ($\dot{-}\cdot$) (*Fr. chaussée*) Macadamized road.

şoven (*Fr. chauvin*) Chauvinistic.

şöhret, ~ti Fame; reputation; name by which a man is known, pseudonym. **~ hastası,** one who seeks notoriety. **~li, ~gir, ~şiar,** famous; notorious.

şölen Feast, *esp.* feast given in honour of s.o.

şömine (*Fr. cheminée*) Fireplace; European style of open fire.

şövaliye (*Fr. chevalier*) Knight. **~ yüzük,** ring with a crest on it. **~lik,** chivalry.

şöyle In that manner; so; just. Of that sort, such. **~ bir baktı,** he just glanced at, *or* he looked with contempt: **~ böyle,** so so; not too well; roughly speaking: **~ dursun,** ... let alone ..., *e.g.* **çalışmak ~ dursun görmek bile imkânsızdır,** it is impossible even to see, let alone work: **~ ki,** in such a manner that; as follows; that is to say. **~ce** ($\dot{-}\cdot\cdot$), in this manner; in such wise. **~lik,** this way; this manner: **~le,** in this way.

şu, ~nu (*pl.* **şunlar**) This; that (şu *is between* o = that there *and* bu = this here); this person; this thing. **~nu bunu bilmem,** I won't hear of any excuses or objections: **~dur budur diyecek yok,** there is nothing to be said against it: ⌜**~nun bunun ~su busu ile alâkadar olmıyan**⌝, not interested in other people's private affairs: **~na buna,** to this person and that, to all

sorts of people: **şundan bundan** (**şuradan buradan**) **konuşmak,** to talk about this and that: **~ kadar,** *v.* şukadar.

şua ($\cdot\dot{-}$), **~aı** Ray of light.

şuabat ($\cdot\cdot\dot{v}$), **~tı** *pl. of* şube. Branches *etc.*

şuara, şüera ($\cdot\cdot\dot{-}$) *pl. of* şair. Poets. **~ tezkiresi,** biographies of poets.

şubat, ~tı February.

şube ($-\dot{-}$) Branch; section; branch office. **~lenmek,** to branch out, ramify.

şuh Lively; full of fun; coquettish; pert. **~luk,** liveliness, playfulness; coquettish-ness.

şukadar ($\dot{-}\cdot\cdot$) So much; so many; so; this much. **~** (var) **ki,** moreover, it remains to be said: **bundan ~ sene evvel,** many years ago: **şimdilik ~ını söyliyelim ki ...,** for the present let us say this much about it that ... .

şule ($-\dot{-}$) Flame. **~dar, ~li,** flaming, blazing; brilliant. **~lenmek,** to flame, to blaze.

şum *v.* şom.

şuncağız *dim. of* şu. This little one.

şundan, şunu, şunun *v.* şu.

şûra ($-\dot{-}$) Council. **Şûrayı Devlet,** the Council of State.

şura ($\dot{-}\cdot$) This place; that place. **~m,** this part of me: **~da,** here; **~da burada,** here and there: **~ya,** hither: **~dan,** hence: **~ları,** these places: **~larda,** in these parts: **~sı muhakkaktır,** this much is certain. **~cık** ($\dot{-}\cdot\cdot$), just here; close by. **~lı** ($\dot{-}\cdot$), belonging to this place; inhabitant of this place. **~sı** ($\dot{-}\cdot\cdot$), **~nı,** this place; this fact: **~nı unutmamalı,** one must not forget this point.

şurdan *for* şuradan, *v.* şura.

şure ($-\dot{-}$), **şürezar** ($-\cdot\dot{-}$) Salty brackish soil; barren soil.

şûride ($--\dot{-}$) Upset, confused. **~dil,** sore at heart.

şûriş ($-\dot{-}$) Confusion, tumult.

şurub Syrup; sweet medicine.

şuun Events; news; chronicle.

şuur ($\cdot\dot{v}$) Comprehension; intelligence; conscience; mind. **~u bozuk,** out of his senses: **~u gitti,** he is out of his mind. **~altı,** subconscious. **~î** ($\cdot\cdot\dot{-}$), pertaining to the mind *or* conscience. **~lu,** intelli-gent; conscious (will, *etc.*); being con-scious of; with comprehension, sensible, judicious. **~suz,** unconscious (deed *etc.*); callous, heedless; unreasonable.

şübban ($\cdot\dot{-}$) *pl. of* şab. Youths.

şübhe Doubt; suspicion; uncertainty. **···den ~ etm.,** to suspect, *e.g.* **kızamık olmasından ~ ediyorum,** I suspect measles (I think it is probably measles), *but* **kızamık olması bence ~li,** I doubt it being measles: ~ bırakmak, to leave a doubt behind, to instil a suspicion: ~ye düşmek, to begin to suspect, to have a suspicion: işin ~ götürür yeri yok, the matter leaves no room for doubt: ne ~ ?, what doubt can there be!, most certainly!

şübhe·lenmek, to have a suspicion or doubt (about = den). ~li, doubtful; causing suspicion. ~siz, doubtless; sure; giving no reason for suspicion: ~ !, no doubt !, of course! ~ sizlik, certainty.

şüera ($\cdots$) v. şuara.

şüf'a Right of pre-emption in respect of land adjoining one's own or of which one is part owner.

şüheda ($\cdots$) pl. of şehid. Martyrs etc.

şühud ($\cdot$) pl. of şahid. Witnesses.

şükr·an Thankfulness; gratitude. ~etmek ($\cdots$), –eder, to feel grateful; be thankful (for = dat.): ˹bir yiyip bin ~˺, to be very thankful for one's circumstances. ~ü, v. şükür.

şükûfe Flower.

şükür, –krü Thanks; gratitude. ~ ki or

Allaha ~, thanks to God: ˹˹˹in şükrünü bilmek, to be grateful for .... .

şümul ($\cdot$), –lü An including or comprehending; comprehensiveness. ~ü olm., to include, cover, embrace. ~lendirmek, to amplify, extend, generalize. ~lü, comprehensive.

şüphe v. şübhe.

şürekâ ($\cdots$) pl. of şerik. Partners etc.

şüru ($\cdot$), –uu Commencement. ...e ~ etm., to commence ....

şüt, –tü Shot (football). ~ çekmek, to shoot (football).

şütum pl. of şetim. Imprecations.

şüun pl. of şe'n. Events; news; things, affairs.

şüyu[1] ($\cdot$), –uu Publicity; divulgation. ~ bulmak, to be noised abroad, to become common gossip: ˹bir şeyin ~u vukuundan beterdir˺, the news of an event is often more harmful than its happening.

şüyu[2] ($\cdot$) Undivided shares in a property. izalei ~, the dividing up of a property amongst various owners.

T

ta[1] And, v. da[1].

ta[2] (~) Even; even as far as; even until. ~ ki, so that, in order that: ~ kendisi, his very self: hakikatin ta kendisidir, it is the very truth.

taab Fatigue, exhaustion.

taabüd Worship, adoration; devotion. ···e ~ etm., to adore, worship.

taacüb Wonder, astonishment. ···e ~ etm., to marvel, be astonished at.

taaddi ($\cdots$) Oppression; transgression; aggression.

taaddüd A multiplying; plurality. ~ etm., to multiply, to become frequent. ~üzevecat, –tı, polygamy.

taaffün Putrefaction; stink.

taahhüd Undertaking or engagement to do stg.; registration of letters etc. ~ etm., to undertake, engage to do. ~at, ($\cdots$), –tı, pl. of taahhüd: âza ~ı, membership fees. ~lü, registered (letter). ~name ($\cdots$), written undertaking; contract.

taakul, –lü Comprehension; thought.

taalâllah ($\cdots$) In ˹tevekkel ~˺, pop. pronunciation of tevekkeltu alâllah, I resign myself to God, i.e. I resign myself to my fate; I need not do anything about it.

taallûk, –ku Connexion; relation; attachment. ···e ~ etm., to have connexion

with, to concern. ~at ($\cdots$), –tı Relations; family connexions.

taallül A seeking a pretext or excuse for avoiding stg. ···de ~ etm. (göstermek), to try to evade ...; to make excuses for not doing stg.

taallüm A studying.

taam Food; meal. ~ etm., to have a meal. ~iye, subsistence allowance; revenue formerly devoted by religious institutions to the feeding of the poor.

taammüd An acting intentionally; premeditation. ~en ($\cdots$), intentionally; with premeditation.

taammüm A becoming general. ~ etm., to become general, to spread.

taannüd Obstinacy; persistence.

taarruz Attack; aggression; assault; molestation. ···e ~ etm., to attack, assault; violate (a woman); ···le ~ etm., to be in conflict with. ~î ($\cdots$), aggressive; offensive (attacking).

taassub Bigotry; fanaticism; zeal, earnestness. ~kâr, fanatical.

taaşşuk, –ku A falling in love. ···e ~ etm., to fall in love with.

taat (~) –ti Act of obedience to God; piety.

taayyün A being manifest, evident, determined. ~ **etm.**, to become clear or manifest; to be defined or determined.

taayyüş A getting a living; means of subsistence. ~ **etm.**, to manage to live, to find the means of subsistence.

taazzi or **taazzuv etm.** *vn.* Form organs, become a living organism; develop.

taazzum A pretending to be great; arrogance.

tab (–) Power, strength; radiance. ~**ü tüvanı kalmadı**, he has no strength left.

tabaat (·–ᴵ), **–ti** Printing.

tababet (·–ᴵ), **–ti** The science of medicine.

tabahat (·–ᴵ), **–ti** Cooking.

tabak¹ Plate; dish; sheet; layer. ~ **gibi**, quite flat.

tabak² Tanner. ~**hane** (···–ᴵ), tannery. ~**lık**, trade of a tanner.

tabaka¹ Layer; stratum; sheet (of paper); fold; class. ~**t** (··ᴵ), **–tı**, layers; strata; classes; geology (*also* ~**ülarz**).

tabaka² (·ᴵ·) Tobacco or cigarette box.

tâban (–ᴵ) Bright, shining.

taban Sole (of a foot or a shoe); heel; firmness, pluck; girder, wall-plate; floor; base; plateau; fine steel; agricultural roller; bed of a river; a long narrow piece of velvet *attached to two rods of sandalwood, formerly wound round the feet of babies.* ~ **inciri**, small sweet figs ripening last: ~**ı* kaldırmak**, to take to one's heels: ~ **kılıc**, sword of Damascus steel: ~**a kuvvet**, by dint of hard walking: ~**ı* sızlamak**, for one's soles to ache from fatigue: ~ **tepmek**, to walk a long way, to tire oneself by walking: ~**ları* yağlamak**, to prepare to go to a distant place on foot: ~ **~a zıd**, diametrically opposed.

tab'an (ᴵ·) Naturally.

tabanca (·ᴵ·) Pistol.

taban·lı Soled; brave, firm. ~**sız**, soleless; cowardly, weak. ~**vayla**, on foot (*comic variation of* tramvay).

tabasbus A cringing or fawning. ···e ~ **etm.**, to fawn and flatter.

tabayi (·–ᴸ), **–ii** *pl. of* **tabiat**. Natural qualities.

tabelâ (·ᴵ·) Table (list); soldier's ration-book; list of food *in schools, hospitals etc.*; card of treatment *hung on a patient's bed in hospitals*; sign *of a shop or firm*. ~**cı**, sign-painter.

tab'etmek (ᴵ··), **–eder** *va.* Print.

tabı, **–b'ı** Natural quality, disposition: a printing or stamping; an edition.

tabıh, **–bhı** Cooking. **şaheseri** ~, a culinary masterpiece.

tabıl Drum; tympanum.

tâbi (–ᴵ), **–ii** Following; dependent; imitating; subject; conforming; submissive. Subject *of a state*; tributary *of a river.* ···e ~ **olm.**, to follow; to be dependent on; to be subject to; to imitate: **bu, havanın keyfine** ~**dir**, this depends on the state of the weather: **tıbbî muayeneye** ~ **tutulmak**, to be subjected to a medical examination.

tabi (–ᴵ), **–ii** Printer; editor; publisher.

tabiat (·–ᴵ), **–ti** Nature; character, natural quality, disposition; habit; regularity *of the bowels*; taste, refinement. ~**ile**, naturally, of itself: ···i ~ **etm.**, to make a habit of ...: ~ **sahibi**, a man of taste. ~**li**, having *such and such* a nature; possessing good taste. ~**siz**, devoid of good taste. ‖ ~**üstü**, supernatural.

tabib (·ᵛ) Doctor, physician.

tabiî (·–ᴸ) Natural; normal. Naturally, of course. **def'i** ~, a going to stool; **ulûmu** ~**ye**, or ~**yat**, **–tı**, natural sciences. ~**ye**, natural history. ~**yeci**, teacher of or specialist in natural history. ~**yun** (·–·ᴸ), naturalists; natural philosophers.

tâbiiyet, **–ti**, **tâbilik** Nationality; a conforming; dependence.

tâbir (–ᴵ) Word; phrase; expression; explanation; interpretation of dreams. ~**i diğerle**, in other terms: ~ **etm.**, to express in words; to name; to interpret a dream: ~ **olunmak**, to be called, to have the name of. ~**at**, **–tı**, *pl. of* **tâbir**. ~**ci**, interpreter of dreams. ~**name**, book explaining the interpretation of dreams.

tâbiş (–ᴵ) Glow; splendour.

tâbiye (–·ᴵ) Tactics. ~**vî** (–··ᴸ), tactical.

tab'iye Cost of printing.

tabla (ᴵ·) Circular tray; ash-tray; scale of a balance; flat surface; disk. ~**kâr**, itinerant vendor of foodstuffs (*carrying them on his head on a* tabla); servant charged with carrying trays of food.

tablo (*Fr.* tableau) Picture.

tabnak, tabende (·ᴵ·) Shining; brilliant.

tabu Taboo.

tabulga *v.* tavulga.

tabur Battalion. ~**cu**, discharged from hospital, *esp.* soldier passed fit for service after an illness: ~ **edilmek**, to be sent back to his battalion.

tabure (*Fr.* tabouret) Footstool.

tabut, **–tu** Coffin; bier; large egg-box. ~**luk**, place in a mosque where coffins are laid. ~**üssekine**, ~**ül'ahd**, the Ark of the Covenant.

tabya (ᴵ·) Bastion; redoubt; fort.

tac Crown; diadem; crest *of a bird.* ~ **giymek**, ~**lanmak**, to be crowned: **baş** ~**ı**, loved and honoured above all (*mainly of a person*). ~**dar** (–ᴸ), crowned head. sovereign.

Tacik Persian inhabitant of Turkestan.

tâcil (‒⸜) **etm.** *va.* Hasten; accelerate.

tacir (‒⸝) Merchant.

tâciz (‒⸜) A bothering *or* worrying. ~ **etm.**, to annoy, worry, disturb. ~**at, ‒tı,** ~**lik,** a worrying; importunity.

tadad (‒⸜) a counting, enumeration. ~ **etm.**, to count, enumerate. ·

tad·almak *and* ~**ı** *v.* tat. ~**ıcı,** taster. ~**ım,** the faculty of taste. ~**ımlık,** just a taste.

tadil (‒⸜) Adjustment; rectification; modification. ~ **etm.**, to adjust, modify, moderate. ~**ât** (‒‒⸜), ‒**tı,** modifications. ~**en** (‒⸜·), by way of modification *or* rectification.

tafahhus etm. *va.* Investigate, inquire closely into.

tafdil (·⸜) A deeming superior, preference. ~ **etm.**, to prefer: ismi ~, comparative *or* superlative (*gram.*).

taflan Cherry laurel. Dark green (eyes). frenk ~**ı,** Portugal laurel.

tafra Conceit; pride. ~ **satmak,** to give oneself airs. ~**cı,** conceited. ~**furuş,** conceited; boastful.

tafsil (·⸜) Detailed explanation; detail. ~ **etm.**, to explain in detail. ~**ât, ‒tı,** details, particulars. ~**en** (·⸜·), in detail.

tafta (⸝·) Taffeta.

tagaddi (··⸜) A being fed, nutrition. ~ **etm.**, to be fed, be nourished.

tagallüb Usurpation; domination; tyranny; mastery. ~ **etm.**, to usurp power: ···e ~ **etm.**, to make oneself master of; to subjugate.

taganni (··⸜) A singing. ~ **etm.**, to sing *or* chant.

tagayyüb Disappearance. ~ **etm.**, to disappear.

tagayyür Change, variation; deterioration; lesion; a becoming spoilt *or* putrid. ~ **etm.**, to change *or* alter.

tağdiye A feeding; feed, input. ~ **etm.**, to feed, nourish.

tağşiş (·⸜) Adulteration.

tağyir (·⸜) Change; deterioration. ~ **etm.**, to change; spoil.

tahaccür Petrification. ~ **etm.**, to become petrified.

tahaddüs A coming into existence; occurrence. ~ **etm.**, to occur.

tahaffuz A guarding oneself. ~ **etm.**, to take care of oneself: ···den ~ **etm.**, to guard against. ~**hane** (····⸝), quarantine station.

tahaffüf A becoming light *or* thin.

tahakkuk, ‒ku A proving to be true; a being realized; verification. ~ **etm.**, to prove true; to be realized; to come into existence: ~ **ettirmek,** to certify, verify;

realize (a desire *etc.*): ~ **memuru,** official charged with the final assessment of a tax: ~ **tarihi,** date when a tax becomes due.

tahakküm Arbitrary power; dictation; oppression. ~ **etm.**, to dominate, tyrannize, oppress.

tahallûs A becoming free *or* safe; adoption of a pseudonym. ~ **etm.**, to escape (a danger *etc.*); to adopt a pseudonym.

tahallül A being dissolved *or* decomposed. ~ **etm.**, to dissolve, become decomposed.

tahammuz Oxidization.

tahammül A supporting a burden; endurance, patience, forbearance. ~ **etm.**, to endure, support, put up with: ~ olunmıyacak derecede, to an intolerable degree. ~**fersa** (····⸜), ~**sûz** (···⸜), intolerable. ~**süz,** intolerant, impatient.

tahammür Fermentation. ~ **etm.**, to ferment.

tahan *v.* tahin.

taharet (·‒⸝), ‒**ti** Cleanliness; canonical purification. ~ **bezi,** a very small towel *used for canonical ablutions*: ~ **kâğıdı,** toilet-paper.

taharri (···⸜) Search; research; investigation. ~ **etm.**, to investigate, seek: ~ (memuru), plain-clothes police, detective. ~**yat, ‒tı,** *pl.* of taharri.

taharrük, ‒kü Motion; vibration.

taharrüş Irritation; itching.

tahassul, ‒lü A resulting; an occurring. ~ **etm.**, to be produced, to result.

tahassun etm. *vn.* Shut oneself up in a fortress.

tahassür Regret for stg. lost; longing. ~ **etm.**, to grieve *or* long for *stg. lost or absent.*

tahassüs A being moved *or* impressed; feeling; sensation. ~**at, ‒tı,** impressions, feeling (being touched). ~ **etm.**, to feel.

tahaşşüd A collecting together; concentration.

tahattur An occuring to the mind. ~ **etm.**, to call to mind.

tahayyül Imagination; fancy. ~ **etm.**, to imagine, fancy. ~**ât, ‒tı,** ideas; fancies.

tahayyür Amazement; bewilderment.

tahayyüz An attaining distinction *or* importance.

tahdid (·⸜) Limitation, circumscription; delimitation; definition. ~ **etm.**, to limit, circumscribe; to fix boundaries; to define. ~**at** (·‒⸜), ‒**tı,** limitations.

tahdiş (·⸜) A disturbing the mind. ~**i** ezhan etm., to perturb public opinion: ~**i** hatır etm., to cause trouble of mind *to a person.*

tahfif (·⸜) Alleviation; assuagement. ~ **etm.**, to lighten, relieve, mitigate.

tahın, -hnı A grinding.

tahin (–¹) Flour, *esp.* sesame flour; sesame oil. ~ **helvası,** sweetmeat *made of sesame seed with honey or sugar.* ~**î** (–·¹), of a yellowish-grey colour.

tahir (–¹) Undefiled, pure.

tahkik (·⁴), **-ki** Verification; investigation. ~**etm.,** to verify, ascertain, investigate. ~**at** (·–⁴), **-tı,** investigations; research; inquiry.

tahkim (·⁴) Appointment of an arbitrator; act of strengthening *or* fortifying. ~ **etm.,** to strengthen; to fortify. ~**at, -tı,** fortifications. ~**name** (···–¹), arbitration agreement.

tahkir (·⁴) A treating with contempt *or* insult. ~ **etm.,** to despise, insult.

tahkiye Narration, story-telling.

tahlif (·⁴), **etm.,** *va.* Administer an oath to; adjure.

tahlil (·⁴) Analysis. ~ **etm.,** to analyse. ~**î** (·–⁴), analytical.

tahlis (·⁴) A liberating *or* rescuing. ~ **etm.,** to free, to rescue. ~**iye** (·–·¹), lifeboat service: ~ **sandalı,** lifeboat: ~ **simidi,** lifebuoy.

tahlit (·⁴), **-ti** A blending; adulteration. ~ **etm.,** to mix; adulterate; amalgamate.

tahliye An emptying; discharge (of cargo); evacuation. ~ **etm.,** to discharge (cargo); empty; set free. ~**ci,** stevedore.

tahmil (·⁴) A loading *or* imposing. ~**etm.,** to load (ship); to impose (a burden); to impute.

tahmin (·⁴) Estimate; conjecture, guess. ~ **etm.,** to estimate, conjecture, calculate: **göz** ~**ile,** by eye (*in judging distance, weight etc.*). ~**en** (·–⁴), approximately. ~**î** (·–⁴), approximate; conjectural: ~ **kıymeti,** the estimated value.

tahmis¹ (·⁴) A making to be five; a dividing into fifths; the writing of a poem by adding four lines to each one of another poet.

tahmis² (·⁴) A parching *or* roasting; coffee roasting and grinding establishment. ~ **etm.,** to roast (coffee *etc.*). ~**çi,** a roaster and grinder of coffee.

tahmiz (·⁴) Oxidization.

tahnetmek (¹··), **-eder** *va.* Grind (flour).

tahnit (·⁴), **-ti** Embalming *of the dead;* stuffing *of animals or birds.*

tahra Pruning hook.

tahrib (·⁴) Destruction; devastation. ~ **etm.,** to destroy, devastate, ruin. ~ **maddesi,** explosive: ~ **tanesi (mermisi),** high-explosive shell: ~**at** (·–⁴), **-tı,** destructions. ~**kâr,** destructive, deadly.

tahrif (·⁴) Distortion; falsification *of a document by erasure or addition;* fraudulent alteration. ~ **etm.,** to falsify, distort, misrepresent, alter fraudulently.

tahrik (·⁴), **-ki** A moving; incitement; instigation; provocation. ~ **etm.,** to incite, instigate, provoke, impel. ~**amiz** (·––⁴), subversive, provocative. ~**kât** (·–⁴), **-tı,** movements, instigations; subversive acts.

tahrilli *In* ~ **göz,** an eye that naturally looks as if the eyelids had been artificially darkened.

tahrim (·⁴) Prohibition. ~ **etm.,** to prohibit, to declare unlawful.

tahrir (·⁴) A writing; a setting forth in words; essay; a registering. ~**i emlâk,** land registry: ~ **etm.,** to draw up (a document); to set down in writing: ~ **müdürü,** sub-editor. ~**at** (·–⁴), **-tı,** documents; dispatches; *as sing.* official letter; circular note: ~ **kalemi,** secretariat; ~ **müdürü,** secretary-general. ~**en** (·⁴·), in writing. ~**î** (·–⁴), written.

tahrirli *v.* tahrilli.

tahris (·⁴) **etm.** *va.* Make covetous; incite to get *stg.*; arouse ambition.

tahriş (·⁴) Irritation.

tahsil (·⁴) Production; acquisition; collection of taxes; study, education. ~ **etm.,** to produce; acquire; collect (dues *etc.*); study. ~**i emval kanunu,** law concerning the collection of taxes and legal penalties: ~ **görmek,** to study: hasılı ~ **etm.,** to produce what already exists, to 'carry coals to Newcastle': **ilk** ~**,** elementary (primary) education. ~**at** (·–⁴), **-tı,** moneys collected; dues, taxes. ~**dar,** Tax-collector; agent.

tahsin (·⁴) Approbation; admiration; certificate *formerly given as a prize in schools.* ~ **etm.,** to approve, admire.

tahsis (·⁴) Assignment; appropriation. ~ **etm.,** to assign *to a special purpose or person.* ~**at** (·–¹), **-tı,** moneys devoted to a special purpose; appropriations; allowance; her müdüre otomobil ~**ı** diye para verilir, every director is given money as car allowance. ~**en** (·⁴·), specially.

tahşid (·⁴) An assembling; concentration. ~ **etm.,** to assemble, to concentrate (*esp.* troops). ~**at** (·–⁴), **-tı,** concentrations.

tahşiye Annotation; marginal note.

taht¹, -tı Throne. ~**a geçmek,** to succeed to the throne: ~**tan indirmek,** to dethrone: ~**a oturtmak,** to enthrone.

taht², -tı Under surface; space under; *as prefix,* under-, sub-. ~**ıma,** under me: ~**ından,** from under him (it): ~**ı temine almak,** to ensure, to make certain of.

tahta Board, plank; sheet (of metal); bed *in a garden;* wood. Wooden. ~**ya çamaşıra gitmek,** to go as charwoman to a house:

~ya kaldırmak, to make a pupil go to the blackboard: ⌐bir ~sı eksik⌐, having 'a screw loose'; half-witted: bostan ~sı, garden-bed: iman ~sı, the breast: yaş (çürük) ~ya basmak, to fall into a trap: yazar bozar ~sı, child's slate: yek ~da, at one go.

tahta·biti, –ni, bed-bug. ~boş, raised platform on a roof *with posts for clotheslines*. ~kurusu, –nu, bed-bug. ~lı, planked, boarded; wood-pigeon: ~ köy (*sl.*), cemetery: ~köye gitmek, to die.

tahtanı (·—⌣) Lower; ground-floor (room *etc.*).

tahta·pabuc Slippers. ~perde, fence *or* partition of boards. ~puş, *v.* tahtaboş. ~revalli (···⌣·), see-saw.

taht·elârz (*accent on this and following words is on the first syllable*) Subterranean. ~elbahir, submarine. ~elcild, subcutaneous. ~elhıfız, under escort. ~essıfır, below zero. ~eşşuur, subconscious.

tahtıravan Litter; palanquin.

tahtie etm..*va.* Accuse of error; deem to be in error.

tahtim (·⌣) Act of sealing. ~ etm., to seal.

tahvif (·⌣) Threat; intimidation. ~ etm., to frighten *or* threaten.

tahvil (·⌣) A transforming *or* converting; conversion *of debt*; draft, security. ~ etm., to convert, transmute. ~ât, –tı, securities; debentures.

tahzir (·⌣) etm. *va.* Put *s.o.* on his guard, warn (against = den).

taın, –a'nı Censure.

taife (—·⌣) Body of men, crew, gang; class; tribe.

tâir (—⌣) Flying. Bird.

tak¹ *Imitates a knocking sound.* canına* ~ demek (etmek), to become intolerable.

tak² (—), –kı Arch; vault. ~ı zafer, triumphal arch.

tak³ *imp. of* takmak. süngü ~ vaziyetinde, with bayonets fixed.

taka (⌣·) Small sailing-boat *used in the Black Sea.*

takabbuz A being contracted *or* shrivelled.

takaddüm Precedence; priority. ···e ~ etm., to precede, to anticipate.

takallûb Change; transformation. ~ etm., to be transformed.

takallûs Contraction *of muscles etc.* elleri ~ etm., to clench the hands.

takarrüb Approach; proximity. ~ etm., to approach.

takarrür A being established; a being decided. ~ etm., to be decided *or* confirmed.

takas A setting off claims against each other; clearing (*fin.*); exchange of goods;

compensation. ~ etm. (olm.), to balance off (mutual claims, debts *etc.*): ~ odası, clearing-house. ~lamak, to compensate. ~tukas olm., to be all square (of claims, accounts *etc.*).

takat (—⌣), –ti Strength; power. ~i kalmadı, he has not the strength to ...: buna ~ getirmez, this is beyond his strength: bende buna ~ yok, I can't afford so much; I can't bear it. ~siz, powerless; exhausted. ~sizlik, exhaustion; weakness.

takatuka (·⌣⌣·) Noise; tumult; a kind of roller *used in printing*; (*formerly*) a kind of large ash-tray.

takav Horseshoe. ~cı, farrier.

takayyüd Attention; care. ···e ~ etm., to pay attention to, to take care of. ~at, –tı, precautions, precautionary measures.

takayyüh Suppuration.

takaza (·—⌣ *but coll.* ···⌣) Taunt.

takbih (·⌣) Disapproval; blame. ~ etm., to disapprove; to blame, censure.

takbil (·⌣) Kissing.

takdim (·⌣) A giving precedence; presentation; offer. ~ etm., to give precedence *or* preference; to present, offer; introduce *one person to another*: ~ ve tehir, transposition of terms: ehemmi muhimme ~ etm., to do the most important thing first. ~e (·—⌣), offering to a superior, presentation.

takdir (·⌣) Predestination, fate; appreciation; supposition; case. ~ etm., to foreordain, prearrange; know the value of, appreciate; understand; suppose; take for granted; allot (a task): ~ böyle imiş, it was so fated: ~i ilâhî, Divine dispensation: ⌐~ tedbiri bozar⌐, 'man proposes, God disposes': hakkı ~, valuer's commission: gidemiyeceğim ~da, in case I am unable to go: iki ~da, in either case: o ~da, in that case.

takdir·amiz (·——⌣), appreciative. ~en (·⌣·), virtually; in consideration of; appreciating the fact that; by supposition. ~î (·—⌣), taken for granted; virtual; supposed. ~kâr, appreciative; admirer.

takdis (·⌣) Sanctification; consecration; veneration. ~ etm., to sanctify, revere; to celebrate the memory of.

takıldak *v.* çakıldak.

takılış Banter, raillery.

takılmak *vn. pass. of* takmak. Be affixed; be stuck; attach oneself *to a person.* *va.* (*with dat.*) Deride; banter; ridicule; worry. ···e gönlü ~, to be interested in: ···e gözü* ~, for one's eye to be caught by *stg.*: ···e zihni* ~, to apply one's mind to *a problem etc.*

takım A set, lot, *or* number *of things*; tea (dinner *etc.*) service; suit *of clothes*; suit *of cards*; squad of men, crew, gang, team; class *of people*; cigarette-holder. ~ ~, in sets, in lots; in classes : **av** ~ı, shooting *or* fishing tackle : **ayak** ~ı, the common people : **bir** ~, a lot of : **çalgı** ~ı, orchestra : **ev** ~ı, the people of a household : **yatak** ~ı, bedclothes.

takımadalar (·˙···) Archipelago.

takın·mak *va.* Attach to oneself; put on, wear; assume (attitude), put on, affect. ꜰ**tel(ler) takınsın**꜒, ' well, let him rejoice (but *I* certainly shall not)! ': ꜰ**terbiyeni takın!**꜒, behave yourself; ~**tı**, small debt; temporary failure to pass an exam.; connexion *with a person*; affair *with a woman*.

takır ~ ~, *imitates the noise of horses' hooves etc.* ~ **tukur**, *imitates an alternate tapping and knocking noise*. ~**damak**, to make a tapping *or* knocking noise. ~**tı**, a tapping or knocking noise.

takıştırmak *va.* Fasten on neatly; wear as an ornament; dress up. **takıp** ~, to ornament oneself.

takızafer (−··˙) Triumphal arch.

takib (−˙) Pursuit; persecution. ~ **etm.**, to follow, pursue, follow up. ~**at** (−−˙), −**tı**, (kanunî) ~, legal proceedings, prosecution.

takid (−˙) A tying or knotting; obscurity of language.

tâkim (−˙) Sterilization. ~ **etm.**, to sterilize; to render fruitless.

takke Skull-cap; night-cap. ~**sini havaya (göğe) atmak**, to throw one's hat into the air for joy : ꜰ**al** ~ **ver külâh**꜒, a squabble, a coming to blows; familiar joking and talk; a being on very intimate terms.

takla, taklak Somersault. ~ **atmak**, to turn a somersault : ~ **attırmak**, to twist *s.o.* round one's little finger : ꜰ**kırk paraya dokuz** ~ **atar**꜒, he'd do anything for money. ~**cı**, tumbler, acrobat.

taklavat *In* **takım** ~, bag and baggage; the the whole family; the whole lot of them.

taklib (·˙) Inversion; reversal.

taklid (·˙) Imitation, counterfeiting. Counterfeit, sham. ~ **etm.**, to gird on to another; confer (an office); follow blindly; imitate; feign, sham; ~**i seyf**, the girding on by the Sultan of the sword of Osman (*the former Turkish equivalent of our coronation*) : ···**in** ~**ini yapmak**, to mimic *s.o.* ~**î** (·−˙), imitative; counterfeit.

taklil (·˙) Diminution; reduction. ~ **etm.**, to diminish.

takma *verb. noun of* **takmak**. Act of attaching *etc.* Stuck on; attached; false (beard *etc.*); that can be fitted together; prefabricated (house). ~ **aletleri**, make-up appliances.

takmak *va.* Affix, attach; put on; give (a name *etc.*); give as a present *to a bride*; (*sl.*) incur a debt; (*sl.*) surpass; (*sl.*) *abbrev. for* **kancayı** ~, *v.* **kanca**: **adam** ~, to appoint a man to accompany another: **adamı adama** ~, to set one man against another : ···**e çelme** ~, to trip up, to play a dirty trick on : **kulp** ~, to explain away *stg.*; to find a pretext to use against s.o.: **yumurtaya kulp** ~, to seek for pretexts *or* quibbles.

takmamak *neg. of* **takmak**. (*sl.*) Take no notice of.

takoz Wooden wedge; prop *used to shore up a ship on the ways*.

takrib (·˙) A making *or* letting approach; approximation; pretext; means. **bir** ~**le**, by some means : ~ **etm.**, to bring near; to approximate. ~**en** (·−˙·), approximately, about. ~**î** (·−˙), approximate.

takrir (·˙) A making stationary; a confirming; deposition, statement, memorandum; report; official note; official notification of transference of real property; delivery (manner of speaking of lecturer *etc.*); motion (in an assembly). ~ **etm.**, to make stationary; to establish, confirm; depose, state, set forth : ~ **sahibi**, the mover of a motion : ~**i sükûn**, the establishment of public order: **ders** ~ **etm.**, to give a lesson : **sual** ~**i**, interpellation.

takrirlik Paper of the proper size for official documents; foolscap.

takriz Eulogy of a book; favourable review; appreciatory preface by an important literary man to another's book.

taksa (˙·) Postage due. ~**pulu, −nu**, postage-due stamp.

taksi (˙·) Taxicab.

taksim (·˙) A dividing into parts; division; partition; distribution; reservoir whence water is distributed; preliminary rendering of the first bars of a tune; instrumental solo. ~ **etm.**, to divide into parts; share out; distribute; divide (*arith.*) : ~**i gurema**, proportional division among creditors of a debtor's assets. ~**at** (·−˙), −**tı**, divisions; compartments of a building : **idarî (mulkî)** ~, administrative divisions (vilayets *etc.*).

taksir (·˙) Failure in duty, remissness; fault. ~ **etm.**, to abbreviate; to be remiss : **aç** ~, fasting, hungry. ~**at** (·−˙), −**tı** *pl. of* **taksir** *also used as sing.*; fault; sin : ꜰ**Allah** ~**ını affetsin!**꜒, *said when criticizing a dead person*: **kendi** ~**ı haricinde**, through no fault of his.

taksit (·˙), −**ti** Instalment.

taktak Wooden instrument for beating washing.

takti (·⸴), **-ii** A cutting up; a scanning a verse.

taktir (·⸴) Distillation; a pouring drop by drop; a dribbling.

taktuk¹ *Imitates the sound of knocking.*

taktuk² Case hung from the shoulder; quiver.

taktuka *v.* takatuka.

takunya (·⸴·) Clog; sabot.

takuş *In* ~ tukuş, with a clatter.

takva (·⸴) Fear of God; piety.

takvim (·⸴) Almanac, calendar.

takviye Reinforcement. ~ etm., to reinforce, strengthen.

takyid (·⸴) A binding; a putting a condition; restriction. ~ etm., to bind; to limit with conditions; to restrict. ~at (·⸴), **-tı,** restrictions (*also used as sing.*).

talab·ık Palpitation; agitation. ~ımak, to palpitate, throb; to be desirous, strive.

talâk, -kı Divorce. ~ı selâse, final and irrevocable divorce.

talâkat (·—⸴), **-ti** Eloquence. ~li, eloquent.

talamak *va.* Pillage; carry off as booty.

talan Pillage; raid. **alan** ~, in utter confusion.

talapsımak *vn.* Be on heat (of a female animal).

talaş Wood shavings; sawdust; filings. ~ kebabı, a kind of meat patty.

talaz Wave, billow; (of silk *etc.*) a being ruffled up. ~lanmak, (of the sea) to be rough; (of silk *etc.*) to be ruffled up, to swell out; (of driven sheep) to surge into a mass. ~lık, washboard *of a ship.*

taleb Request; demand; desire. ~ etm., to request, ask for, seek for: arzu ~, supply and demand. ~kâr, desirous; who asks (for = *dat.*): applicant; suitor. ~name (··—⸴), written request.

talebe *pl. of* talib; *as sing.* Student; pupil.

taler Thaler, Austrian dollar.

tali¹ (−⸴), **-i'i** Pollen.

tali² (−⸴) *v.* talih.

tâli (−⸴) Following; secondary (education); subordinate.

talia Vanguard.

talib (−⸴) Who requests; desirous. Applicant; suitor; customer. ···e ~ olm., to seek after, aspire to, strive for.

talih (−⸴) Good fortune; luck; one's star. ~i yok, he has no luck: birinin ~ine bakmak, to cast s.o.'s horoscope, to tell s.o.'s fortune. ~li, lucky. ~siz, unlucky.

talik (−⸴), **-kı** Suspension; a making a thing depend on stg. else; Persian style of Arabic writing. ~ etm., to suspend; put off, defer; to attach to, to make depend on; to refer.

talika (·⸴·) Four-wheel cart suspended on straps.

tâlil (−⸴) Deduction. ~ yapmak, to deduce.

talili (−−⸴) Lucky.

talim (−⸴) A teaching; instruction; practice; drill. ~ ve terbiye, instruction, training: ~ etm., to teach; drill; practise: ~ fişeği, blank cartridge. ~at (−−⸴), **-tı,** exercises; instructions. ~atname (−··—⸴), book of instructions; drill-book. ~hane (−·—⸴), parade ground; drill-hall. ~î (−−⸴), pertaining to instruction. ~li (−·⸴), instructed, practised, drilled. ~name (−·—⸴), manual of instruction; drill-book.

talimar Cutwater *of a ship.*

talisiz Unfortunate.

talk, -kı Talc.

talkin *Coll. form of* telkin, *v.* salkım.

tallahi (⸴—·) *Usually in conjunction with* vallahi, by God!

taltif (·⸴) A gratifying; kindness; favour; appreciation; recompense. ~ etm., to gratify; treat with kindness; show favour to; make kind remarks about: ···le ~ etm., to confer (a rank *etc.*).

talyon Marsh-mallow; plaster of vegetable juices.

tam¹ Complete, entire; perfect. Completely; exactly. ~ kalkacağı sırada, just as he was going to get up: ~ adamına düşmüşsün, you've struck the very man *for the job, or for whom you are looking etc.*: ~ tertib, fully, thoroughly: ~ vaktinde, at just the right moment: ~ yol, full speed.

tam² A polishing (of copper *etc.*). ~ çarkı, a polishing-lathe.

tamaan (·⸴·) Out of greed (for = *dat.*).

tamah, tama Greed, avarice; stinginess. ···e ~ etm., to covet, desire: ⌜az ~ çok ziyan verir⌝, a little greed may cause much harm; 'don't spoil the ship for a ha'p'orth of tar!' ~kâr, greedy; avaricious; stingy.

tamam (·⸴) Completion; end; whole; complement. Complete; finished; ready; 'pat', just right; true, correct. ~!, that's right!, that's it!, *or used to express unpleasant surprise,* 'there you are!'; ~ile, wholly, in its entirety: ~ etm., to complete; to terminate: ···e ~ gelmek, to just suit: ~ olm., to be completed, be finished: ~ yerine gelmek, to reach the point of perfection; to get exactly into place.

tamam·en (·⸴·), completely, entirely. ~î (·—⸴), complementary; integral. ~i (·—⸴), completeness; integrity. ~iyet (·—⸴), **-ti,** completeness; wholeness; integrity. ~iceyb (·⸴·), cosine. ~ikati (·⸴···), cosecant. ~imümas (·⸴···), cotangent. ~lamak, to complete, finish; make good *a defect.*

tambur A kind of guitar. ~**a** (·¹·), a small tambur: ağız ~**sı**, Jews'-harp. ~**acı**, player of the tambura. ~**î** (·−⁻), player of the **tambur**.

tâmik (−⁴), −**ki** Profound investigation; research. ~ etm., to go deeply into *stg*.

tamim (−⁴) A making general; generalization; circular. ~ **etm.**, to make general; generalize; circulate: ~ **olunmak**, to be circulated. ~**en** (−⁻·), by circular.

tamir (−⁴) Repair; restoration. ~ **etm.**, to repair, mend: ···**i** ~**e vermek**, to hand over for repair. ~**at** (−−¹), −**tı**, repairs.

tampon Buffer; wad, plug (*med.*).

tamtakır (¹··) Absolutely empty.

tamters (¹·) The exact opposite; exactly the reverse.

tamu Hell.

tan Dawn.

tân (−) Wounding words; reproach; calumny.

tanassur Conversion to Christianity. ~ etm., to become a Christian.

tandır Oven *made in a hole in the earth*; heating arrangement *consisting of a brazier put under a table with a covering right over the table and the legs of those sitting round it.* ~ **ekmeği**, bread baked in an earth oven. ~**name** (···¹), an old wives' tale.

tane (−¹) Grain; seed; pip; piece; bullet, cannon-ball; a single thing. ~ ~, in separate grains; one by one; ~ ~ **söylemek**, to speak each word distinctly: ~**ye gelmek**, to form seed *or* berries: **kaç** ~ **?**, how many?: **üç** ~ **elma**, three apples: **ver bir** ~, give me one.

tane·cik (−·¹), unique, only: granule. ~**lemek**, to separate into grains; granulate. ~**lenmek**, to produce grains *or* berries; to be separated into grains. ~**li**, having grains *or* berries; in separate grains.

tanen Tannin.

tanetmek (−··), −**eder** *va.* Reproach; abuse.

tangır tungur Loud clanging noise.

tango (¹·) Tango; loudly-dressed woman.

tanık Witness. ~**lık**, evidence.

tanı·mak *va.* Know, be acquainted with; recognize; acknowledge; listen to. **tanımamak**, to pay no attention to; **çocuklar şimdi ana baba tanımıyorlar**, *not* 'children today don't know their parents', *but* 'don't pay any attention to them'.

tanı·nmak, ~**lmak**, *vn. pass. of* **tanımak**. ~**şıklık**, mutual acquaintance. ~**şmak**, to make acquaintance with one another; be acquaintances. ~**tmak**, *caus. of* **tanımak**, to introduce *one person to another*.

tanin (·⁴) A booming, buzzing, *or* humming noise. ~**endaz**, resounding, booming.

tanlamak¹ *vn.* Be amazed.

tan·lamak² *vn.* Dawn. ~**layın**, at dawn.

tannan Resounding; ringing.

Tanrı God. ~ **dağı**, the Tien Shan range: ~**nın günü**, every blessed day. ~**lık**, divinity: divine.

tansif (·⁴) Halving; bisection. ~ etm., to cut in half.

tansiyon (*Fr. tension*) Blood-pressure.

tansuk Rare and exquisite thing.

tantana Pomp, display; magnificence. ~**lı**, grand; magnificent.

tantuna In ~ **gitmek** (*sl.*), to be lost, ruined, dismissed.

tanyeri (¹··), −**ni** East; dawn. ~ **agarıyor**, dawn is breaking.

tanzifat (·−⁴), −**tı** *pl. used as sing.* Town scavenging service.

tanzim (·⁴) A putting in order; an organizing. ~ etm., to put in order; organize; reorganize; arrange; edit. ~ **satışı**, sale of foodstuffs by a municipality in order to regulate prices. ~**at** (·−⁴), −**tı**, reforms; reorganization; the political reforms of Abdulmejid in 1839. ~**atçı**, reformer.

tanzir (·⁴) An imitating a poem. ~ etm., to imitate; to produce a similar. ~**en** (·−·), copying, imitating.

tapa (¹·) Fuse; *v.* tıpa.

tapan Harrow.

tapın·ak Temple. ~**ış**, worship; adoration. ~**mak**, to bow down in worship; worship, adore (*with dat.*).

tapıştırmak *va.* Cause to be sought, found, and brought; order (goods *etc.*).

tapkur In ~ **kolanı**, girth, surcingle.

tapmak *va.* (*with dat.*) Worship.

tapon Discarded; common, second-rate.

tapşırmak *v.* tapıştırmak.

taptaze (¹··) Absolutely fresh.

tapu (¹·) Title-deed.

tapyoka (·¹·) Tapioca.

tar¹ Thread; fibre.

tar² Dark.

tarab Joy; merrymaking.

tarac (−⁻) Pillage; plunder. ~ etm., to pillage.

taraça (·¹·) Terrace.

taraf Side; direction; district; part; end; party *to a cause or dispute*; protector. ~ ~, on this side and that: ... ~**ına**, towards: ... ~**ıma**, towards me: ... ~**ından**, on the part of ..., by ..., from the direction of ...: **o** ~**a**, in that direction: **bu** ~**lar**, these parts, this neighbourhood: ···**in** ~**ını tutmak** (*or* ···**den** ~**a çıkmak**), to take the part of, to side with: **ona** ~ **çıktı**, he became his protector.

taraf·dar, partisan; adherent: ···**e** ~ **olm.**, to be in favour of. ~**darlık**, partiality, partisanship. ∼**eyn,** *dual of* **taraf** : the two parties *or* sides. ∼**gir,** partisan : partial, biased. ∼**girlik,** partisanship. ∼**lı,** having sides; having supporters : supporter : **bunu yapmak** ∼**sı görünüyordu,** he appeared to be in favour of doing this. ∼**sız,** neutral, impartial. ∼**sızlık,** neutrality, impartiality.

tarak Comb; rake; harrow; weaver's reed; crest (of a bird) ; drag ; gills *of a fish* : instep ; scallop ; serrated pattern *on cloth etc.* ∼ **dubası,** dredger : **ayak tarağı,** tarsus : **kar** ∼ **makinesi,** snow-plough : ┌**kırk (bin)** ∼**ta bezi var**┐, 'he has cloth on a thousand looms', he looks after a host of things, he has many irons in the fire : **vida tarağı,** screw chaser.

tarak·çı, maker *or* seller of combs. ∼**lamak,** to comb; rake; harrow; dredge; paint with zigzag lines. ∼**lı,** crested (bird) ; broad-footed. ∼**otu** (·˺··), **−nu,** teazle.

tarama Act of combing *or* dredging; search; soft roe; red caviare. ∼ **muayene,** a searching investigation : ∼ **resim,** shaded drawing, hachure : **arama** ∼, search *by police etc.*

tara·mak *va.* Comb; rake; harrow; dredge; search minutely. **arayıp** ∼, to search carefully for *stg.* ; to make minute inquiries about *s.o.'s* whereabouts : **demir** ∼, to drag anchor. ∼**nmak,** to comb oneself; be combed, raked *etc.*

tarassud A watching; observation. ∼ **altında,** under surveillance : ∼ **etm.,** to watch, observe. ∼**at, −tı,** observations.

tarator Sauce made with vinegar and walnuts.

taravet (·−˺), **−ti** Freshness; juiciness; the bloom of youth. ∼**li,** fresh, juicy; ruddy.

tarayıcı That combs *or* dredges. **mayn** ∼ **gemi,** minesweeper.

taraz Combings; fibres combed out. ∼ ∼ (**turaz**), dishevelled. ∼**lanmak,** to become rough by combing *or* friction; be frayed; be dishevelled.

tarbuş Fez; skull-cap.

tarçın Cinnamon.

tard Expulsion, repulsion. ∼ **etm.,** to drive away; expel; degrade (an officer).

tarh[1] Flower-bed; garden border.

tarh[2] Subtraction; imposition *of taxes.* ∼ **etm.,** to lay down, establish; regulate, plan; impose (tax); subtract (a number); compose (a poem).

tarhana Preparation of dried curds and flour; soup made of this.

tarhun Tarragon.

‖**tarım** Agriculture.

tarınmak *In* **arınıp** ∼, to be thoroughly cleaned.

tari (−˫) **olm.** *vn.* Happen; befall.

tarif (−˫) Description; definition; recipe. ∼ **etm.,** to describe, define : ∼**e uymak,** to answer the description *of a person.*

tarife (−·˺) Tariff; time-table.

tarih (−˺) Annals; history; date; epoch; chronogram. ∼ **atmak,** to put the date : ∼**a karışmak,** to be out of date, to be a thing of the past : ∼ **yazmak,** to write a history.

tarih·çe, short history. ∼**çi,** historian. ∼**en** (˺··), historically. ∼**î** (−·˺), historical. ∼**li,** dated .... ∼**nüvis,** historian. ∼**siz,** undated.

târik (−˺) Who forsakes *or* neglects. ∼**i dünya,** who forsakes the world, hermit, nun : ∼**i edeb,** neglectful of good manners.

târîk (−˺) Dark; gloomy.

tarik (·˫) Way, road; method; means; hierarchy; order of dervishes. ∼ **bedeli, road-tax** : ∼**i hak,** the right course. ∼**at** (·−˫), **−tı,** way, path; religious order. ∼**atçı,** member of a religious order, dervish.

târiz (−˺) Allusion; hint; innuendo. ···**e** ∼ **etm.,** to censure by innuendo.

tarla (˹·) Arable field; garden bed; expanse of water. ∼**kuşu, −nu,** lark.

tarlakoz Fishing-boat with two pairs of oars.

tarpan The wild horse of Tartary.

tarraka (·−˺) Crash; loud knocking; squib.

tarsi (·˺) An ornamenting with jewels; composition of rhymed prose.

tarsin (·˺) A consolidating *or* making firm.

tartaklamak *va.* Pull to pieces; tease out (fibres); tease, worry, badger, harass; manhandle, assault; lift *stg.* up to test its weight.

tartı Act of weighing; weight; balance; scale. ∼**ya gelmez,** imponderable : ∼**ya vurulmak,** to be pondered. ∼**lı,** weighed; balanced; well-pondered. ∼**lmak,** *vn. pass. of* **tartmak;** be weighed; totter; vacillate; speak hesitatingly; intrude; be unwilling to go; throw oneself on another. ∼**sız,** unweighed; unbalanced; not well thought out : **eli** ∼, inconsiderate; rash. ∼**şmak,** to weigh one thing with another; struggle; ‖ argue, dispute.

tartkı Girth buckle; a gradual pulling in of a horse.

tartma Act of weighing. Weighed; by weight.

tartmak *va.* Weigh; ponder well; estimate; weigh up (a person); brandish.

tartura Turner's wheel; wheel of a spinning-wheel.

tarumar (−·˺) Scattered; in disorder. ∼ **etm.,** to rout.

tarz Form, shape, appearance; manner; method; sort; demeanour. ∼**ı hâl,** method of solution (of a difficulty *etc.*) :

~ı hareket, behaviour: ~ı itilâf compromise.

tarziye Apology; 'amende honorable'; a satisfying. ~ **vermek** to give satisfaction *to an offended person*, to make an apology.

tas Bowl *or* cup *with a rounded bottom*. ~ı **tarağı toplamak**, to pack up and go: başı ~, bald-headed: ⌐eski hamam eski ~⌐, the same old story: hamam ~ı, metal bowl *used for throwing water over oneself in a bath*: saat ~ı, the bell of a striking clock.

tasa Worry, anxiety, grief. ~sını çekmek, to suffer grief or regret for *s.o. or stg.*; ⌐~mın on beşi⌐, 'I don't care a hang!': ⌐~sı sana mı düştü?⌐, 'why worry, it doesn't concern you!': ~ **vermek**, to cause anxiety. ⌐o ~ bu ~⌐, we've got enough to worry about as it is.

tasaddi (··⌐) A setting oneself to do stg.; a daring to do stg. ···e ~ **etm.**, to set out to, to dare to.

tasadduk, –ku A giving of alms.

tasalı Anxious; grieved.

tasallût, –tu Usurpation of power; aggression; outrage. ~ **etm.**, to usurp power: ···e ~ **etm.**, to behave aggressively towards; to make a violent attack on.

tasallüb etm. *vn.* Become hard. ~ü şerayin, arteriosclerosis.

tasallüf Wheedling, blandishment; a being vain and presumptuous. ~**kâr**, presumptuous.

tasannu (··⌐), **–uu** An affecting to be skilful; feint, pretence; meretricious decoration; artifice.

tasar Project; draft. ~ı, ‖ bill, draft law. ~**lamak**, to plan, project; draft, sketch out: **tasarlıyarak öldürmek**, to kill with premeditation.

tasarruf A having the ownership and disposal of a thing; possession; economy, saving. ~**umda**, at my disposal: ~ **etm.**, to save, economize: ···e ~ **etm.**, to have the use and disposal of; to possess: ···in ~**unda olm.**, to be in the possession and at the disposal of: ~ **sandığı**, savings-bank. ~**kâr**, economical, thrifty.

tasarsız Extempore; improvised.

tasasız Free from care; light-hearted; thoughtless.

tasavvuf Mysticism; sufism. ~î (····⌐), mystical; sufic.

tasavvur Imagination; idea; conception. ~ **etm.**, to imagine, picture to oneself; project: ~**unda olm.**, to have the idea of, to propose to. ~î (···⌐), imaginary; theoretical.

tasdi (·⌐), **–ii** (*Originally*) a giving a headache; (*now*) *polite form for* paying a visit. ~ **etm.**, to pay a visit to *s.o.*

tasdik (·ᶥ), **–ki** Confirmation; affirmation; ratification. ~ **etm.**, to confirm, affirm, ratify, certify. ~**li**, certified. ~**name** (···⌐), letter of confirmation; certificate.

tasfiye A cleaning *or* clarifying; purification; liquidation; clearance; elimination. ~ **etm.**, to clean, clarify, refine; clear up (a matter); liquidate; eliminate: ~ **bankası**, clearing-house: ~ **memuru**, liquidator: hesabları ~ **etm.**, to wind up accounts. ~**hane** (···–⌐), refinery.

tasgir (·ᶥ) A making smaller. ~ **etm.**, to diminish (*va.*): ismi ~, diminutive (*gram.*).

tashih (·ᶥ) Correction; rectification; reading of proofs. ~ **etm.**, to correct, rectify; read proof sheets: ~**i mizac etm.**, to recover one's health. ~**at** (··⌐), **–tı**, corrections.

tasımlamak *va.* Plan, project; imagine.

tas'ib (·⌐) **etm.** *va.* Render difficult.

tâsir (·⌐) **etm.** *va.* Press *fruits* for the juice.

taskebabı (⌐···), **–ni** Meat cut in small pieces and roasted.

taslak Anything in the rough; draft; sketch; model. Naked; hairless. **adam taslağı**, a boor, clown: **hekim taslağı**, an incompetent, bungling doctor. ~**çı**, pattern-maker.

taslamak *va.* Pretend to *stg.* one does not possess; make a show of.

tasma Collar (of a dog *etc.*); strap *of clogs*.

tasmim (·ᶥ) Resolution; intention. ~ **etm.**, to firmly resolve upon.

tasni (·⌐), **–ii** Fabrication; invention. ~ **etm.**, to fabricate (lies *etc.*). ~**at**, **–tı**, inventions, falsehoods.

tasnif (·ᶥ) Classification; composition. ~**i ara**, scrutiny of votes: ~ **etm.**, to classify, compose, compile.

tasrif (·ᶥ) Declension *or* conjugation *of words*. ~ **etm.**, to decline (noun), conjugate (verb).

tasrih (·ᶥ) Clear interpretation *or* expression. ~ **etm.**, to make clear, specify. ~**at** (·–ᶥ), **–tı**, explanations (*also used as sing.*). ~**en** (·⌐·), by way of clarification.

tastamam (⌐··) Quite complete; perfect.

tasvib (·ᶥ) Approval, approbation. ~ **etm.**, to approve. ~**en** (·⌐·), with approval.

tasvir (·ᶥ) Design; picture; likeness. Handsome; sweet (*cf. the 'picture' of a horse*). ~ **etm.**, to depict, draw, represent.

taş Stone; rock; precious stone; piece *or* man (chess, draughts *etc.*); allusion, innuendo. Stone; hard as stone. ···e ~ **atmak**, to throw a stone at; to direct an unpleasant allusion or innuendo at *s.o.*: ~ **çatlasa**, whatever happens, under any circumstances: ~ **çekmek**, to whet (a

knife *etc.*) : ···e ~ çıkar(t)mak, to give
points to, to be greatly superior to *s.o.* :
~ düşürmek, to pass a gall- (bladder-)
stone : ~ı gediğine (yerine) koymak, to give
as good as one gets; to make a clever
retort : ~ kesilmek, to be petrified : ⌐~ı
sıksa suyunu çıkarır⌐, he is incredibly
strong; he succeeds in whatever he undertakes : ~ tutmak, to pelt with stones, to
stone to death : ⌐~ yağar kıyamet koparken⌐,
'it rains stones and hell breaks loose', *used
to describe a great disaster* : ⌐~ yerinde
ağırdır⌐, the value of anything depends on
its proper use : ···e ~ yuvarlamak, to make
bitter allusions to *or* inveigh against *s.o.* :
bağıra ~ basmak, to resign oneself, to
suffer without complaint : baltayı ~a basmak (vurmak), to 'drop a brick' : başını
~tan ~a vurmak, to repent bitterly :
dağ ~, a whole heap of, *e.g.* çamaşır dağ ~
yığıldı, there's a regular pile of dirty
linen : ⌐hangi ~ı kaldırsan altından çıkar⌐,
he always turns up everywhere; he has a
finger in every pie (*in a good sense*).

taşak Testicle. ~lı, having testicles; virile,
bold.

taş·bademi (¹···), **–ni** Wild almond.
~balığı, **–nı,** non-migratory fish. ~bas-
ması, **–nı,** lithograph. ~çı, stonemason;
quarryman : ~ kalemi, stonemason's chisel.

taşım A coming to the boil. bir iki ~
kaynatmalı, one must bring it to the boil
once or twice.

taşıma *verb. n. of* taşımak. Carried. ⌐~ su
ile değirmen dönmez⌐, 'a mill won't turn
with carried water', an enterprise cannot
succeed with inadequate means.

taşımak *va.* Carry; transport; bear; pass
on *another's words*; spread *gossip.*

taşınmak *vn. pass. of* taşımak. Be carried
etc.; move one's belongings to another
place; change one's abode; go too often *to
a place*; turn things over in one's mind.
düşünüp ~, to ponder deeply.

taşırmak *va. caus. of* taşmak. Cause to
overflow. *vn.* Go beyond the bounds of
decency, go too far; (of a horse) to injure
its hoof by excessive work. ⌐bardağı
taşıran damla⌐, 'the drop that makes the
glass overflow', the straw that breaks the
camel's back', the 'last straw'.

‖ **taşıt** Transport; vehicle.

taşıtmak *va. caus. of* taşımak.

taşkaldıran The Turnstone (*Arenaria
interpres*).

taşkın Overflowing; overlapping; excessive; exuberant; insolent. ~lık, excess;
impetuosity; insolence.

taş·lama Stoning; grinding (*mech.*).
~lamak, to stone; to pave with stones;

to grind. ~lı, stony, rocky; set with
stones. ~lık, stony, rocky place; paved
courtyard; stone threshold; gizzard.

taşmak *vn.* Overflow; boil over; lose one's
patience; be in a ferment; go too far; get
above oneself; be insolent; overlap. artıp
~, to increase and overflow; to exceed
bounds.

taşocağı (¹···), **–nı** Stone quarry.

taşra (¹·) The outside; the provinces. ~lı,
living in the provinces; provincial. ~lık,
conditions of provincial life; the provinces.

taş·tahta (¹··) Slate *for writing.* ~yürekli,
stony-hearted, cruel.

tat[1] Taste; flavour; relish; charm. tadını
almak, to acquire a taste for; to enjoy:
tadında bırakmak, not to overdo *stg.*:
tadını çıkarmak, to get the utmost enjoyment out of *stg.*: tadı damağında* kalmış,
the flavour of it still lingers in one's palate;
one still hankers after it : tadını (tuzunu)
kaçırmak (bozmak), to spoil the enjoyment
(of a party *etc.*); artık tadını kaçırıyorsun!,
you are going a bit too far! : tadı (tuzu)
kalmadı, it no longer gives any pleasure :
tadına varmak, to get the full flavour of,
to enjoy : tadından yenmez, delicious;
(*iron.*) insipid : ağız tadile, with zest;
ağzının tadını bilmek, to be a gourmet :
⌐ağza ~ boğaza feryad⌐, 'the mouth enjoys the taste, the belly cries for more',
said of a very small amount of delicious food :
⌐ağzımın tadını bozma!⌐, don't spoil my
enjoyment! : evin tadı, domestic peace.

tat[2], **–tı** *Name formerly given in derision by
the Turks to subject Persians and Kurds*;
poor wretch.

tatar Tartar; courier (*also* ~ ağası).
~böreği, **–ni,** a kind of dough pasty *made
with minced meat and yaourt.*

tatarcık Sandfly; midge. ~ humması,
sandfly fever.

tatar·ı Undercooked (food). ~sı, rather
like a Tartar; *as* tartarı.

tatbik (·⸗) Adaptation; application; comparison. ~ etm., to apply (a rule, an
expedient *etc.*); to adapt; to compare *one
thing with another*; to fit (a lid *etc.*.) : ~
edilmek, to be brought into application, to
come into force (of a law *etc.*) : ~ sahasına
koymak (çıkarmak), to put into practice.
~an (·⸗·), conformably (to); according
to. ~at (·–⸗), **–tı,** applications (of a
law *etc.*); putting into practice; manœuvres
(*mil.*) : ~ta, in practice. ~î (·–⸗), comparative; practical.

tathir (·⸗) Cleaning; purification; disinfection. ~ etm., to clean, purify, disinfect.
~at (·–⸗), **–tı,** *pl. of* tathir, *also used as
singular.*

tatık, tatım A taste; small bit eaten to try the taste.

tatil (–ᵛ) Suspension of work; stoppage (of any activity); holiday; rest. Closed (of an office *etc.*) for a holiday. ~ **etm.**, to suspend, to cause to cease : ~ **olm.**, to be closed (for a holiday) : ~ **yapmak**, to take a holiday. ~**ieşgal** (–ᴸ···), stoppage of work, strike. ~**name** (··–¹), order of suspension *of a newspaper.*

tâtir (–ᵛ) **etm.** *va.* Perfume.

tatlamak *va.* Sweeten; flavour.

tatlı Sweet; agreeable; (of water) drinkable, not salt. Sweetmeat; sweet. ~ **belâ**, 'a sweet curse', *term of endearment for a child* : ~ **dil**, soft words; a pleasant way of speaking : ···**i** ~**ya bağlamak**, to settle *a matter* amicably : ···**e** ~ **yerinde nihayet vermek**, to bring *stg.* to a conclusion in time *to avoid complications* : **canı** ~, who avoids any personal discomfort or labour. ~**ca**, sweetish; rather agreeable. ~**cı**, maker *or* seller of sweetmeats : fond of sweet things, sweet-toothed. ~**lık**, sweetness; kindness. ~**msı**, sweetish. ~**su** (·¹·), drinking water; fresh water (*as opp. to* salt water). ~ **Frengi**, Levantine.

tatlik (·ᵛ), –**ki** A divorcing. ~ **etm.**, to divorce.

tatmak, –dar *va.* Taste; try; experience.

tatmin (·ᵛ) A tranquillizing reassurance. ~ **etm.**, to satisfy (a curiosity, a desire); to calm, reassure. ~**kâr**, satisfactory.

tatsız Tasteless; disagreeable; insipid. ~ **tuzsuz**, insipid; stupid and dull. ~**lık**, insipidity, dullness; disagreeable behaviour. ~**lanmak**, to become insipid; to behave in a disagreeable manner.

tatula (·¹·) Datura, thorn-apple; evil-tasting thing.

tatvil (·ᵛ) Prolongation.

tatyib (·ᵛ) **etm.** *va.* Calm; console; satisfy.

taun (–ᵛ) Pest; plague; epidemic. ~**î** (––ᴸ), pertaining to a plague; epidemic.

tav *The exact state of heat, dampness, etc., required for the manipulation of a material*; proper heat *for tempering or hammering a metal*; opportune moment; well-nourished condition, fatness; water sprinkled *on paper, tobacco, etc., before pressing*; a doubling of the stakes *at gambling.* ~**ını bulmak**, to acquire the right condition *for working* : ~ **fırını**, tempering furnace : ~**ı geçti (savdı)**, the best moment (for working) has passed : ~**a getirmek** *or* ~**ını vermek**, to bring to the correct heat; ~**ına getirmek**, to bring to the right condition (*fig.*) : ~**ı kaçırmak**, to miss the right moment; to let slip a suitable opportunity : ~ **sürmek**, to double the stakes : ~ **vermek**, to bring

to the requisite degree of dampness : **her şeyin** ~**ında olduğuna hükmetti**, he judged that everything was just right (for action).

tava Frying-pan; fried food; ladle *for melting metal*; trough *for slaking lime*; ditch *for letting sea-water into a salt-pan.*

tavaf The ceremony of going round the Kaaba at the pilgrimage to Mecca. ···**i** ~ **etm.**, to keep going round *a place.*

tavaif (·–¹) *pl. of* **taife**. Tribes. ~**i mülûk**, the petty kingdoms into which a great empire breaks up.

tavan Ceiling; highest point reached *by an aircraft or a projectile.* ~ **arası**, garret : ~ **başa geçmek**, to be crushed *or* ruined; to be overcome by fear *or* shame.

tav'an (¹·) Voluntarily; spontaneously. ~ **ve kerhen**, willingly or under compulsion, willy-nilly.

tavassut, –tu Intervention; mediation. ~ **etm.**, to intervene, to act as mediator.

tavaşi (·–ᴸ) Eunuch.

tavattun etm. *vn.* Settle *in a place*; make a home *in a country.*

tavazzuh etm. *vn.* Become clear *or* manifest.

tavcı Accomplice in a swindle, *who runs up the price at an auction or pretends to put a high value on a worthless thing.* ~**lık**, the quality *or* profession of such a swindler.

tavhane (·–¹) Shelter for the poor; hot-house.

tavır, –vrı Mode, manner; kind; attitude; arrogant manner. ~ **satmak**, to give oneself airs : **hali tavrı yerinde**, worthy, well-conducted. ~**lı**, having *such and such* a manner; arrogant.

tavik (–¹), –**ki** A hindering *or* delaying. ~ **etm.**, to hinder, delay, prevent : **bilâ** ~, without delay : ~**li bomba**, delayed-action bomb.

tavil Long; tall; lengthy.

taviz (–ᵛ) Substitution; compensation; replacement; concession; compromise. ~**at** (––ᵛ), –**tı**, compensations *etc.* : ~**ta bulunmak**, to make concessions. ~**en** (–ᴸ·), by way of replacement; as a substitute; in compensation.

tavla¹ (¹·) Backgammon. ~ **pulu**, a piece at backgammon. ~**cı**, backgammon player.

tavla² (¹·) Stable; place where horses are tethered. ~ **halatı**, tether-rope : ~ **uşağı**, ~**cı**, stable-boy.

tav·lamak *va.* Bring *a thing* to its best condition, *v.* **tav**; sprinkle water on *paper, tobacco etc. before pressing*; deceive, swindle, *v.* **tavcı**. ~**lanmak**, *pass. of* **tavlamak**; *also* (of an animal) to get fat. ~**lı**, at its best condition, *v.* **tav**; damped (paper, tobacco); red-hot (iron); in prime condition (animal).

tavrı *v.* **tavır.**

tav·samak *vn.* Lose its **tav** *q.v.*; fall away from its prime; cool down; decline, decay. **pazar** ~, for the market to become dull. ~**satmak,** to let *stg.* decline; lose the opportunity for; delay; cool down; slow up. ~**sız,** not heated sufficiently; not tempered; not in prime condition.

tavsif (·⸴) Description; eulogy. ~ **etm.,** to enumerate the qualities of *stg.*; describe; eulogize.

tavsit (·⸴) **etm.** *va.* Cause to mediate; use as an intermediary.

tavsiye Recommendation. ~ **etm.,** to recommend. ~**li,** recommended. ~**name** (····—¹), letter of recommendation.

tavşan¹ Joiner, cabinet-maker. ~**lık,** fine joinery, carving.

tavşan² Hare. **ada –ı,** rabbit: ⌐~ı araba ile avlamak⌐, 'to hunt hares in a carriage', to do stg. calmly and easily: ⌐~ bayırı aştı⌐, 'the hare has topped the brow'; it will never be seen again; it's gone for ever: ⌐~ boku gibi (ne kokar ne bulaşır)⌐, 'like a hare's droppings (neither smelly nor messy)', harmless but useless: ~ **dudağı,** hare-lip: ⌐~a kaç tazıya tut (demek)⌐, '(to say) to the hare"run !" and to the hound "catch !"'⌐, ⌐to run with the hare and hunt with the hounds⌐: ~ **kanı,** bright carmine colour: ⌐~ın suyunun suyu⌐, a very distant connexion, *v. App.*: ~ **uykusu,** sleep with the eyes half-closed; inattention; pretended sleep: ~ **yürekli,** timid.

tavşan·cıl, eagle, vulture. ~**kulağı, –nı,** cyclamen. ~**lamak,** to become as thin as a hare. ~**yemez,** *nickname given to the Shiite sect called* **Kızılbaş.**

tavuk Hen. ⌐**benim başıma gelen pişmiş tavuğun başına gelmedi⌐,** 'a boiled fowl never suffered what I have suffered'; you can't think what I've been through !: ~ **balığı,** *a local name for* the whiting.

tavuk·göğsü (·⸴··), **–nü,** sweet dish *made with milk and the pounded breast of a fowl.* ~**götü, –nü,** wart. ~**karası, –nı,** night-blindness, nyctalopia. ~**kanadı, –nı,** fan *for fanning a fire.*

tavulga, tabulga (·¹·) (?) A species of buckthorn; (?) purple willow; (?) arbutus.

tavus Peacock. ~ **kuyruğu,** peacock's tail; (*sl.*) violent vomiting.

tavzif (·⸴) **etm.** *va.* Entrust *s.o.* with a duty; appoint as salaried official.

tavzih (·⸴) A making plain; clear explanation; explanatory correction. ~ **etm.,** to make clear, explain. ~**en** (·⸴·), by way of explanation.

tay¹ Foal.

tay², –yyı The traversing of a space *of time or place*; cancellation *or* erasure *of words.*

tay³ Half a beast's load; bale; counterpoise.

taya Child's nurse. ~ **çocuğu,** a spoilt child.

tayaran A flying; a being volatile.

tayf Spectre, ghost; spectrum. ~**î** (·⸴), spectral.

tayfa Band; troop; crew; gang; sailor.

tayfun Typhoon.

tayın Ration, *esp.* small loaf issued to soldiers (*also* ~ **ekmeği**).

tayib (–⸴) A finding fault; a reproaching.

tâyin (–¹) Appointment; designation. ~ **etm.,** to appoint; decide, fix, settle, determine.

tâyinat (–·⸴), **–tı** *pl. of* **tâyin** and **tayın.** Rations.

taylak Yearling camel.

taylan Well-made (youth *etc.*).

taylasan The hanging down end of a turban.

Taymis (¹·) Thames; Times newspaper.

tayyar Flying; volatile. ~**e** (·—¹), airplane: ~ **böceği,** dragon-fly. ~**eci,** airman, aviator. ~**ecilik,** aviation, flying.

tayyör (*Fr. tailleur*) Tailor-made costume.

tazallüm A complaining of wrong. ~ **etm.,** to complain of an injustice; to excite compassion; to play the martyr: ~**ü hal,** a complaining about one's condition.

tazammun A comprising *or* comprehending; implication. ~ **etm.,** to comprise, contain; imply; denote.

tazarru (··⸴), **–uu** A humbling oneself; supplication. ~ **etm.,** humbly to beg.

taze (–⸴) Fresh; new, recent; young; tender. Young girl. ~ **yaprak,** fresh vine-leaves. ~**lemek,** to freshen up; renew. ~**lenmek,** ~**leşmek,** to become fresh; be renewed; become young. ~**lik,** freshness; tenderness; youth.

tazı Greyhound; sleuth. ~ **gibi,** thin, peaked, pinched, ~**lamak,** to become thin.

tazib (–⸴) A torturing *or* tormenting.

taz'if (·⸴) Reduplication, multiplication. ~ **etm.,** to double, multiply; to weaken.

tâzim (–⸴) An honouring; respect; reverence. ~ **etm.,** to do honour to, respect, revere. ~**at** (——⸴), **–tı,** honours; homage. ~**en** (—⸴·), out of respect; as an honour.

tazir¹ (·⸴) Reproof. ~ **etm.,** to reprove, reprimand.

tazir² (–⸴) A seeking an excuse; a putting forth a vain excuse. ~**etm.,** to seek an excuse; to be remiss.

taziyane (··—¹) Whip; stimulus; means; plectrum.

taziye (–·¹) Condolence. ~ **etm.,** to offer

condolence. ~**name** (–···–¹), letter of condolence.

taziz (·⁴) An honouring the memory *of a person*; a holding in esteem. ~ **etm.**, to honour the memory of.

tazmin (·⁴) Indemnification; indemnity; quotation. ~ **etm.**, to indemnify; to accept as surety; to quote from another's works. ~**i zarar etm.**, to make good damage or loss. ~**at** (·–⁴), **–tı**, indemnities; reparations.

tazyik (·⁴), **–ki** A squeezing; pressure; oppression. ~ **etm.**, to tighten, press, put pressure on; to oppress; to reduce to extremity.

te And; also; *v.* **da¹**.

teadül (·–¹) A being equal *in weight or value*; equilibrium. **zaman** ~**ü**, equation of time.

teahhur A being behind *or* late; delay. ~ **etm.**, to be late, be postponed, be retarded.

teakub (·–¹) A following one after the other. ~ **etm.**, to follow in succession.

teali (·–¹) Elevation; loftiness. ~ **etm.**, to be elevated.

teamül (·–¹) Custom, practice; chemical reaction. **kadim** ~ **kanun gibidir**, custom has the force of law.

tearuz (·–¹) Mutual opposition. ~ **etm.**, to oppose; to be in contradiction; to conflict.

tearüf (·–¹) A recognizing *or* being acquainted with one another. ~ **etm.**, to recognize, know.

teati (·–¹) Exchange. ~ **etm.**, to give to one another, to exchange.

teavün (·–¹) Mutual assistance. ~ **etm.**, to help one another.

tebaa *pl. of* **tâbi.** Subjects; *used as sing.* Subject *of a state.*

tebaan (¹··) In conformity with (*dat.*).

tebadül (·–¹) Substitution; exchange.

tebadür (·–¹) Sudden inspiration. ~ **etm.**, to occur to the mind; (of an idea) to strike one.

tebah Wasted; spoilt.

tebahhur¹ Evaporation. ~ **etm.**, to evaporate.

tebahhur² A going deeply into a subject; erudition.

tebaiyet, –ti Allegiance; submission; a conforming. ~ **etm.**, to submit (to), become subject (to); conform.

tebarüz (·–¹) **etm.** *vn.* Become manifest *or* prominent. ~ **ettirmek**, to show clearly, to emphasize, to demonstrate.

tebaud (·–¹) A being *or* becoming distant; withdrawal; divergence.

tebayün (·–¹) A being mutually different, inconsistent *or* incommensurate; contrast.

tebcil (·⁴) Veneration; honouring. ~ **etm.**, to treat with great honour and respect; to glorify.

tebdil (·⁴) Change, alteration; conversion; exchange. In disguise, incognito. ~ **etm.**, to change, alter: ~ **gezmek**, to go about in disguise: ~**i hava**, change of air: ~**i kıyafet**, disguise: ~ **olunmak**, to be changed. ~**en** (·⁴·), in exchange; as a change; in disguise, incognito.

tebeddül A being changed; alteration; vicissitude. ~ **etm.**, to undergo a change, alter. ~**ât** (···⁴), **–tı**, changes.

tebel Fold; wrinkle; corrugation.

tebelbül Confusion of tongues; babel.

tebelleş olm. Pester, worry.

tebelluğ etm. *vn.* Receive an official communication; be informed.

tebellür Crystallization. ~ **etm.**, to crystallize; to become crystal clear.

tebenni Adoption *of a child.*

teber Axe; halberd. **haber** ~, news.

teberru (···⁴), **–uu** Charitable gift; donation. ~ **etm.**, to offer as a free gift. ~**an** (·¹··), as a gift; as a charitable donation. ~**at**, **–tı**, donations.

teberrüd A becoming cold.

teberrük etm. *va.* Regard as a blessing; consider as a good omen. ~**en** (·¹··) counting *stg.* as a blessing *or* as a good omen; as a compliment; (of a holy man) bringing his blessing.

tebessüm Smile. ~ **etm.**, to smile.

tebeşir Chalk.

tebevvül Urination. ~ **etm.**, to make water.

tebeyyün etm. *vn.* Become clear; be evident; be proved.

tebhir (·⁴) Vaporization; fumigation; disinfection. ~ **etm.**, to fumigate, disinfect, vaporize. ~**hane** (···–¹), fumigating station.

teb'id (·⁴) A sending to a distance; banishment. ~ **etm.**, to drive away, banish. ~**en** (·¹··), by removing to a distance; by banishment.

tebliğ (·⁴) Transmission; communication. ~ **etm.**, to transmit, communicate; deliver *a message etc.*: **resmî** ~, official communiqué. ~**at** (·–⁴), **–tı**, communications; reports.

tebrid (·⁴) Refrigeration. ~ **etm.**, to cool, refrigerate.

tebrik (·⁴), **–ki** Congratulation. ~ **etm.**, to congratulate. ~**ât** (·–⁴), **–tı**, congratulations. ~**name** (···–¹), letter of congratulation.

tebriye Acquittal; exoneration; a clearing oneself; a being set free; absolution. ~ **etm.**, to acquit, absolve, exonerate. ~**i zimmet etm.**, to prove one's innocence.

tebşir (·‑ᴗ) A communicating good news; glad tidings. ~ **etm.,** to bring good news, to cheer with glad tidings.

tebyiz (·ᴗ) A making a fair copy. ~ **etm.,** to make a fair copy.

tecahül (·‑ᴗ) Feigned ignorance. ~ **etm.,** to pretend ignorance (of = **den**) : ~**ü arifane,** making uses of an assumed ignorance for the purpose of satire or irony.

tecanüs (·‑ᴗ) Homogeneity.

tecarüb (·‑ᴗ) *pl. of* **tecrübe.** Experiments *etc.*

tecasür (·‑ᴗ) A daring. ~ **etm.,** to dare, presume.

tecavüz (·‑ᴗ) Transgression; excess; aggression, attack, offensive. ~ **etm.,** to go beyond the bounds; transgress; attack (*with dat.*): **ademi** ~, non-aggression: **haddini** ~ **etm.,** to go too far, to be insolent. ~**î** (·‑·ᴗ), aggressive, offensive. ~**kârane** (·‑·—ᴗ), aggressive *or* offensive (action).

Teccal Antichrist; impostor; fearing neither God nor man.

tecdid (·ᴗ) Renewal. ~ **etm.,** to renew; to renovate.

teceddüd A being renewed, renovated, regenerated; renovation; reform. ~ **etm.,** to be renewed *etc.*

tecehhüz etm. *vn.* Be prepared *or* equipped.

tecelli (··ᴗ) A being manifest; manifestation; destiny; luck; Transfiguration. ~ **etm.,** to be manifested, to be shown; to appear; to happen. ~**siz,** ill-fated, unfortunate. ~**yat** (··‑ᴗ), **-tı,** the manifestations of Nature; strokes of fate.

tecellüd Daring; open bravery; display of unflinching firmness; moral courage.

tecemmül Adornment. ~**ât, -tı,** odds and ends; a lot of junk.

tecen Wild goat.

tecennün A becoming insane. ~ **etm.,** to become insane.

tecerrüd A giving up worldly interests for religion; celibacy; isolation. ~ **etm.,** to divest oneself of (*abl.*); withdraw from; remain single.

tecessüd An assuming a material form; incarnation.

tecessüm A becoming a solid body; an appearing to be a solid body; personification. ~ **etm.,** to assume, *or* appear like, a solid body; to be personified : ~ **ettirmek,** to personify.

tecessüs Inquisitiveness; curiosity.

tecezzi (··ᴗ), **-ii** A being divided into pieces; disaggregation. ~ **etm.,** to disaggregate (*vn.*).

techil (·ᴗ) **etm.** *va.* Show up *s.o.'s* ignorance.

techiz (·ᴗ) A fitting out *or* equipping. ~ **etm.,** to equip, fit out; to lay out *a corpse.*

~**at** (·‑ᴗ), **-tı,** *pl. of* **techiz** *as sing.,* equipment, *esp.* the rigging out of a ship.

tecil (‑ᴗ) A granting a respite *or* delay. ~ **etm.,** to defer, postpone (*esp.* military service, or punishment).

teclid (·ᴗ) Binding *of a book.* ~ **etm.,** to bind *a book.*

tecnis (·ᴗ) A punning, play upon words.

tecrid (·ᴗ) A denuding; a separating *or* isolating; isolation. ~ **etm.,** to strip, denude; to free from (*abl.*); to isolate. ~**hane** (···ᴗ), prison cell for solitary confinement.

tecrim (·ᴗ) **etm.** *va.* Find guilty, inculpate; fine.

tecrübe Trial; test; experiment; experience. ~ **etm.,** to try, test, assay; experiment; experience : ~**sini etm.,** to try *stg.* out, to experiment on: ⌐~**yi göge çekmediler ya !**¬, there's no reason why one shouldn't try it : ~ **tahtası,** stg. that can be experimented on with impunity; 'corpus vile': **kalem** ~**si,** essay.

tecrübe·li, experienced; proved by trial. ~**siz,** inexperienced; not yet tested. ~**î** (··ᴗ), experimental.

tecsim (·ᴗ) A making material *or* corporeal.

tecvid (·ᴗ) Art of reading *or* reciting the Koran with proper rhythm.

tecviz (·ᴗ) A regarding as lawful; permission. ~ **etm.,** to declare lawful, permit.

tecziye[1] **etm.** *va.* Divide into parts.

tecziye[2] Punishment. ~ **etm.,** to punish.

tedabir (·‑ᴗ) *pl, of* **tedbir.** Plans; dispositions; measures.

tedafuî (·‑·ᴗ) Defensive. **tecavüzî ve** ~ **ittifak,** an offensive and defensive alliance.

tedahül (·‑ᴗ) Arrears; interaction. ~**de,** in arrears.

tedai (·‑ᴗ) Association of ideas.

tedarik (·‑ᴗ), **-ki** Preparation; provision; a getting together of needed things. ~ **etm.,** to procure, obtain, prepare, provide. ~**ât, -tı,** preparations. ~**li,** prepared; fitted out : ~ **bulunmak,** to be prepared with all requirements.

tedavi (·‑ᴗ) Medical treatment; cure.

tedavül (·‑ᴗ) Circulation; currency. ~ **etm.,** to circulate, to be current.

tedbir (·ᴗ) Precaution; plan; disposition; measure; course of action; circumspection, foresight. ⌐~**e takdir uymıyor**¬, 'man proposes, God disposes'. ~**li,** provident, thoughtful; cautious. ~**siz,** improvident; thoughtless.

tedehhüş A being terrified.

tedenni (··ᴗ) Retrogression; decline; a falling back; decadence. ~ **etm.,** to decline; (of prices) to fall; be retrograde.

tederrüs A taking lessons; study.

tedeyyün A falling into debt.

tedfin (·⸜) An interring; burial. ~ etm., to bury.

tedhiş (·⸜) A terrifying. ~ etm., to terrify.

tedib (—⸜) A teaching manners; punishment. ~ etm., to correct, punish. ~î (——⸜), correctional, punitive.

tedirgin Who does not like his present place and grumbles at the next; restless, discontented. ~ etm., to disturb, upset.

tediye (—⸜) Payment. ~ etm., to pay. ~li, cash on delivery (C.O.D.).

tedkik (·⸜), –ki Close examination; scrutiny. ~ etm., to investigate carefully, to examine closely, to go into a matter. ~at (·—⸜), –tı, investigations; researches.

tedmir (·⸜) Devastation, destruction.

tedric (·⸜) An advancing by degrees. ~en (·⸜·), by degrees, gradually. ~î (·—⸜), gradual.

tedris (·⸜) Instruction, teaching. ~ etm., to teach by lessons : ~ ve tederrüs, teaching and learning. ~at (·—⸜), –tı, instruction; course of lessons. ~î (·—⸜), pertaining to teaching; instructional.

tedvin (·⸜) etm. va. Collect the works of an author; codify; register.

tedvir (·⸜) A causing to revolve; direction (of a business). ~ etm., to cause to revolve; to administer *a business*; to make round.

teeddüb A showing good manners; a refraining (from good manners) from some action. ···den ~ ederim, I hardly venture *to say or to do* .... ~en (·¹··), out of politeness.

teehhül A marrying. ~ etm., to marry.

teehhür Postponement; delay. ~ etm., to be postponed; to be late.

teellüm A being grieved *or* distressed. ~ etm., to be distressed *or* pained.

teemmül Reflection; deliberation; caution. ~ etm., to reflect, deliberate.

teenni (···⸜) A being deliberate; slowness; composure.

teessüf Regret; a being sorry. ~ etm., to regret; to be sorry for (*dat.*).

teessür A being affected; emotion; grief. ~ etm., to be affected, to grieve.

teessüs A being founded *or* established.

teeyyüd A being strengthened *or* confirmed; support, aid. ~ etm., to be strengthened, confirmed.

tef Tambourine. ···i ~e koymak (~e koyup çalmak), publicly to speak ill of, to hold up to public ridicule.

tefahhum Carbonization. ~ etm., to be carbonized.

tefahhus Investigation; research.

tefahür (·—¹) Boasting; arrogance. ~ ~ etm., to boast (about = ile).

tefavüt (·—¹), –tü Difference, disparity. ~ etm., to differ *one from the other*.

tefazulî (·—·⸜) Differential. ~ hesab, differential calculus.

tefe Machine for winding silk; hank of spun silk; flap of a saddle.

tefeci Usurer. ~lik, usury.

tefecik Very small. ufacık ~, tiny; delicate, dainty.

tefehhüm etm. *va.* Understand gradually; perceive.

tefek *Only in* ufak ~, small; insignificant : ufak ~ şeyler, various trifles.

tefekkür Reflection. ~ etm., to think, meditate.

tefeli Of close texture (cloth *etc.*).

tefelsüf A philosophizing.

tefennün A becoming versed in arts and sciences.

teferru (···⸜), –uu Ramification; a being subdivided. ~ etm., to ramify, branch out; be subdivided; (*with dat.*) to belong to ... *as a branch*. ~at, –tı, ramifications, branches; details; accessories.

teferrüc Pleasure trip; a stroll for pleasure; diversion; excursion. ~gâh, pleasure resort; promenade; excursion spot.

teferrüd etm. *vn.* Stand out from others; to distinguish oneself.

teferrüs Perspicacity. ~ etm., to perceive by intuition, to discern by sagacity.

tefessuh Decomposition; putrefaction. ~ etm., to fall to pieces by decay; to putrefy.

tefeül etm. *vn.* Consult an oracle; ···le ~ etm., to draw an augury from *stg.*; ···den ~ etm., to take *stg.* as a good omen.

tefevvuk, –ku Superiority. ···e ~ etm., to be superior to, to surpass.

tefevvühat (···⸜), –tı Insults. ~ta bulunmak, to use insulting *or* blasphemous words.

tefeyyüz Progress; prosperity. ~ etm., to make progress, to prosper; to profit (morally).

teffiz (·⸜) A handing over *or* committing to the charge of *s.o.* ~ etm., to hand over, to commit to the charge of *s.o.*

tefhim (·⸜) etm. Cause *s.o.* (*dat.*) to understand *stg.* (*acc.*); communicate *stg.* to *s.o.*

tefne (¹·) Bay-tree.

tefrih (·⸜) etm. *va.* Gladden; cause to rejoice.

tefrik (·⸜), –ki Separation; distinction. ~ etm., to separate, to distinguish *one thing from another*.

tefrika Discord; supplement *of a newspaper*. ···i ~ya düşürmek, to sow discord between.

tefriş (·⸜) A spreading *a carpet etc.*; a

carpeting or furnishing *a room*. ~ etm., to spread (carpet *etc.*); to furnish; to cover (a floor). ~at (·-ᵛ), –tı, furnishings.

tefrit (·ᵛ), –ti A doing less than one's duty; remissness; deficiency. **birinci ifrattı, ikincisi ~ oldu**, the first was excessive, the second not enough: **ifrattan ~**, from one extreme to the other.

tefsir (·ᵛ) Commentary; interpretation.

teftiş (·ᵛ) Investigation; inspection. ~ etm., to investigate, inspect.

tefviz *v.* **teffiz**.

tegafül (·-ᵛ) Feigned ignorance or inattention. ~ etm., to pretend to be unaware or unmindful: ~ **göstermek**, to feign ignorance.

teğelti Saddle-pad; numdah.

‖ **teğmen** Lieutenant.

tehacüm (·-ᵛ) A rushing or crowding together; concerted rush or attack. ···**e ~ etm.**, to make a concerted rush on.

tehalüf (·-ᵛ) Difference, dissimilarity. ~ etm., to differ from one another; to vary.

tehalük (·-ᵛ), –kü A throwing oneself eagerly on to stg.; keenness, zeal; ardent desire. ~**le arzu etm.**, to desire ardently.

tehassür Grief for stg. lost; regret. ~**etm.**, to grieve for, to regret, to fret for.

tehaşi (·-ᴵ) Avoidance. ~ etm., to withdraw, to keep aloof.

tehcir (·ᵛ) etm. *va.* Cause to migrate; deport.

tehdid (·ᵛ) Threat. ~ etm., to threaten. ~**âmiz** (·--ᵛ), threatening.

tehekküm Mockery.

tehevvür Sudden outburst of anger, fury; rash impetuosity. ~ etm., to burst into anger.

teheyyüc Excitement; emotion. ~ etm., to become excited; to be overcome by emotion.

tehi (·ᴵ) Empty.

tehie etm. *va.* Prepare.

tehir (–ᵛ) Delay; postponement. ~ etm., to defer, postpone.

tehlike Danger. ~**ye atılmak**, to court danger: ~**ye atmak**, to risk: ~**ye sokmak**, to endanger ~**li**, dangerous. ~**siz**, without danger; inoffensive.

tehlil (·ᵛ) The recitation of the Moslem formula 'there is no God but God'.

tehniye(t) Congratulation. **hacı ~si**, solemn congratulations to returning pilgrims.

tehvin (·ᵛ) A lightening; alleviation; facilitation. ~ etm., to alleviate, facilitate; cheapen.

tehyic (·ᵛ) etm. *va.* Excite.

tehzib (·ᵛ) A correcting or setting right; moral improvement. ~**i ahlâk**, moral education: ~ etm., to correct or set right.

tehzil (·ᵛ) etm. *va.* Ridicule; mock.

tehziz (·ᵛ) etm. *va.* Shake about; cause to vibrate.

tek, –**ki** A single thing; odd number; fellow, mate. Single; unique; alone, solitary; odd (not even). Only, merely; once; as long as, provided that. ~ ~, odd ones, not a pair: ~ **başına**, apart; on one's own: ~ **durmak (oturmak)**, to sit by oneself; to be quiet: ~ **elden**, under one management or command; from one centre: ~**e** ~ **kavga**, single combat: ~ **tük**, here and there, now and then: **bir** ~ **atmak** (*sl.*), to have a drink: **çift mi** ~ **mi ?**, odd or even?

tekabbül etm. *va.* Receive willingly; undertake (a task *etc.*).

tekabül (·-ᵛ) A coming face to face; meeting; compensation. ···**e** ~ etm., to correspond to, to be proportional to; to meet (a need *etc.*).

tekâlif (·-ᵛ) *pl. of* **teklif**. Proposals; terms; duties, taxes.

tekâmül (·-ᵛ) A being perfected; evolution. ~ etm., to be in the process of being perfected; to mature, develop: ~ **kanunu**, the law of evolution.

tekâpu (·-ᴵ) Sycophancy. base flattery. ···**e** ~ etm., to toady to ... .

tekarrüb, tekarrür *v.* **takarrüb, takarrür**.

tekâsüf (·-ᵛ) Condensation; density. ~ etm., to condense (*vn.*), to become dense.

tekâsül (·-ᵛ) Negligence; laziness.

tekâsür A becoming numerous. ~ etm., to multiply, increase in number.

tekattur Distillation.

tekatu (·-ᵛ), –**uu** Intersection. ~ etm., to intersect.

tekaüd (·-ᵛ) Retirement; pension. Retired; pensioned. ~ **maaşı**, half-pay; pension: ~**e sevketmek**, or ~ etm., to pension off. ~**iye**, pension; deduction from salary for pension. ~**lük**, a being pensioned; retirement on a pension.

tekbaşına (ᵛ···) All by himself; all on his own.

tekbir (·ᵛ) A proclaiming the greatness of God in the formula 'Allahu ekber' (God is most great). ~**lamak** (~ **getirmek**), to pronounce that formula.

tekdir (·ᵛ) Scolding; reprimand. ~ etm., to scold, reprimand.

teke He-goat. ~**den süt çıkarmak**, to be very skilful in getting what one wants: **deniz** ~**si**, prawn.

tekebbür A being proud; haughtiness. ~ etm., to be haughty, to give oneself airs.

tekeffül A becoming bail or surety. ···**i** or ···**e** ~ etm., to stand surety for, to guarantee.

‖ **tekel** Monopoly.

tekelemek *vn.* (Of a he-goat) to be sexually excited.

tekellüf A taking great pains; a giving oneself unnecessary trouble; false display; ceremoniousness, formality. **akraba arasında teklif ~ olmaz**, there must be no standing on ceremony amongst relatives. **~lü**, on which great care has been expended; ornate; sumptuous; elaborate; bombastic. **~süz**, plain; not overdone.

tekellüm Talking. **~ etm.**, to speak.

tekellüs Calcification.

tekemmül A being perfected; perfection; evolution. **~ etm.**, to be perfected.

teker[1] One at a time; **~ ~**, one by one.

teker[2], **tekerlek** Wheel. Circular, round. **~ arası**, width of track; **~ tabanı**, tyre of a cart-wheel.

tekerleme Rigmarole; stereotyped formal way of speaking; the use of similarly sounding or rhyming words to produce a meretricious effect in speech or writing; roller (wave).

teker·lemek *va.* Roll; let slip out inadvertently; blurt out. **~lenmek**, to roll round (*vn.*); turn head over heels; fall over; (*sl.*) die; (*sl.*) to be sacked. **~meker** (·¹··), head over heels.

tekerrür Repetition. **~ etm.**, to be repeated, to repeat itself.

tekessür Increase, multiplication. **~ etm.**, to increase, multiply (*vn.*).

teketek (¹··) *In* **~ harb** (**kavga**), single combat.

tekevvün A coming into existence. **~ü maraz**, pathogenesis: **~ etm.**, to come into being, to originate, arise.

tekfin (·⁴) **etm.** *va.* Wrap in a winding-sheet.

tekfir (·⁴) *va.* Accuse *a Moslem* of heresy *or* blasphemy.

tekfur Prince of the Byzantine Empire.

tekgözlük (¹··) Monocle.

tekid (−⁴) Confirmation; corroboration; repetition (of a message or order). **~ etm.**, to confirm; repeat. **~en** (−¹·), in confirmation; as a repeat.

tekin Unique, sole; empty, deserted; quiet; free from spirits (djinns); of sound mind. **~ değil**, of unsound mind; inauspicious, haunted, ill-omened; dangerous; uncanny; taboo; (man) with whom it is best to have nothing to do. ‖ **~siz**, taboo.

tekir Tabby (cat). **~ balığı**, striped red mullet.

tekke Dervish Convent. ⌐**~yi bekliyen çorbayı içer**⌐, he who serves (a party *etc.*) patiently will be rewarded eventually.

teklif (·⁴) Proposal; offer; motion *before an assembly*; etiquette, formal behaviour,

ceremony; custom; tax, obligation. **~ etm.**, to propose; offer formally; submit; move (a motion); bid, tender: **~ sahibi**, mover *of a motion or bill*; bidder; one who submits a tender: **~ ve tekellüf**, the rules of etiquette and decorum: **~ yok**, there is no need for ceremony.

teklif·at (·−⁴), **−tı**, proposals; formalities. **~li**, with whom one must stand on ceremony; with decorum; observing the rules of etiquette. **~siz**, without ceremony; free-and-easy, familiar, unconstrained. **~sizlik**, unceremoniousness; absence of compliments.

teklis (·⁴) Calcination.

tekme Kick. **~ atmak**, to give a kick: **~ yemek**, to get a kick, receive a blow; to fall into disgrace. **~lemek**, to kick (*va.*).

tekmil (·⁴) A completing *or* perfecting. All; the whole of. **~ etm.**, to complete, finish: **~ olm.**, to be completed.

tekne Trough; hull; craft. **~ kazıntısı**, 'the last scraping of dough from the trough', *used about the youngest child of a numerous family*: **kuru ~**, the bare hull.

tekn·ik Technique. **~isyen**, technician.

tekrar Repetition; recurrence. Again. **~ ~**, over and over again: **~ etm.**, to repeat: **~ olm.**, to happen again, to recur. **~lamak**, to repeat.

tekrim (·−¹) A treating with respect; deference; mark of respect. **~ etm.**, to treat with deference.

tekrir (·−¹) Repetition.

teksif (·⁴) A making dense. **~ etm.**, to condense, compress; render opaque.

tektük (¹·) Here and there; now and again. One or two; occasional.

tekvin (·⁴) Creation; production. **~ etm.**, to produce.

tekzib (·⁴) Contradiction; a declaring to be a lie. **~ etm.**, to contradict; to proclaim false; to give the lie to.

tel Wire; fibre; a single thread *or* hair; string *of a musical instrument*; silver or gold thread used to decorate a bride's hair; telegram. Made of wire. **~ çekmek**, to draw wire; to enclose with wire; to send a wire (*also* **~ vurmak**); **~ kafes**, iron cage: ⌐**başına ~ler taksın!**⌐, *said of one who has cause to rejoice over others*, 'that's one up to him!': **her ~den çalmak**, to know a bit of everything, to be a jack-of-all-trades: **birinin hassas ~ine dokunmak**, to touch s.o. on his tender spot.

telâ (¹·) Horsehair stiffening *of coat collars etc.*

telâffuz Pronunciation. **~ etm.**, to pronounce.

telâfi (·−¹) A making up for stg. lost;

compensation. ~ etm., to make up for, compensate: ~si imkânsız, irreparable. ~imafât (·—·—¹) etm., to make good the past; to repair an error *or* a loss.

telâhuk, –ku Conjunction. ~ etm., to join one another; to follow *or* succeed one another.

telâki (·—¹) A meeting one another. ~ etm., to meet.

telâkki (···¹) Reception; mode of receiving *or* regarding; interpretation, view. ~ etm., to receive (a piece of news); to regard (as good or bad *etc.*); to consider.

telâro Casement.

telâsuk etm. *vn.* Stick together, adhere to one another.

telâş Flurry, confusion; alarm; hurry; embarrassment; anxiety. ~a düşmek, to be confused, flurried, alarmed *etc.* ~lı, flurried, confused; agitated, upset. ~sız, calm, composed.

telâtin Russia leather.

telâtum The dashing together of waves.

teldolab (¹··) Meat-safe.

telebbüs A putting on of clothes. ~ etm., to put on clothes, to dress.

telef Destruction; ruin; death. ~ etm., to destroy, ruin, kill: ~ olm., to be destroyed *or* ruined, to be killed. ~at, –tı, casualties (*mil.*); losses of life *in an accident etc.*: ~ vermek, to suffer losses *in battle*: ~ verdirmek, to inflict losses.

telefon Telephone.

telehhüf Sigh; lament; regret.

teleme *In* ~ peyniri, fresh unsalted cheese. ~ peyniri gibi, soft, flabby.

teles Threadbare. ~imek, to become threadbare.

teleskop, –pu Astronomical telescope.

televvün A changing colour; caprice, fickleness. ~ etm., to change colour; to be changeable *or* inconstant.

teleyyün A becoming soft.

telezzüz Pleasure, enjoyment. ~ etm., (*with abl. or* ile) to enjoy the taste of, to take pleasure in.

telfik etm. *va.* Put together; compile.

telgraf Telegraph. ~hane (···—¹), telegraph office. ~lamak, to telegraph. ~name (···—¹), telegram.

telh Bitter.

telhis (·⁴) Abstract, summary. ~ etm., to summarize, make an abstract of. ~çi, (*formerly*) an official charged with making summaries of reports for the Sultan.

telif (–⁴) A reconciling; composition, compilation; compromise. ~ etm., to reconcile, to square (conflicting facts); to write *or* compile: ~i beyn etm., to reconcile two contending parties: hakkı ~, copyright:

···le kabili ~, compatible with ... . ~at (—⁴), –tı, compositions; literary works.

telih etm. *va.* Deify.

tel'in (·⁴) A cursing. ~ etm., to curse.

telkadayıf (¹···) Sweet dish *of thin shreds of batter baked with butter and syrup.*

telkâri, –ni Woven of gold or silver thread. Stuff thus woven; filigree.

telkib (·⁴) etm. *va.* Give a nickname *or* surname to.

telkih (·⁴) Grafting; inoculation; vaccination. ~ etm., to graft, inoculate, vaccinate.

telkin (·⁴) Suggestion; inspiration; inculcation; final rites at a funeral; inculcation to a novice of the Moslem articles of faith. ~ etm., to suggest, inspire, inculcate: binefsihi ~, auto-suggestion. ~at (·—⁴), –tı, harmful suggestions: ~a kapılmak, to be influenced by suggestions. ~li, ~ tedavi, faith-healing.

tellâk, –kı Bath attendant; masseur; shampooer.

tellâl Town-crier; broker; middleman. parasız ~, (unpaid crier), one who spreads news about matters that are no concern of his. ~iye, fee paid to a tellâl. ~lık, profession of a tellâl.

tellemek *va.* Adorn with gold wire *or* thread; deck out; embellish (a story); praise extravagantly; wire (telegraph). telleyip pullamak, to deck out with gold thread *etc.*, to cover with decorations; embroider *a narrative with exaggerations.*

tellendirmek *vn.* (*sl.*) Enjoy a smoke.

telli Wired; decorated with gold *or* silver wire *or* thread. ~ bebek, extravagantly dressed; dandy: ~ pullu, decked out: ~ turna, the Crowned Crane.

telmih (·⁴) Allusion; hint.

telörgü (¹··) Barbed wire fence *or* entanglement; wire-netting.

telsiz Without wire. Wireless. ~lemek, to radio.

teltik Deficiency; defect; small balance of an account. teltiği temizlemek, to pay off a small balance of an account. ~li, *account* with a small balance owing; *sum of money with a fractional amount, not a round sum.* ~siz, round *sum*; without fractions; complete, whole; fully paid.

telüre, telöre Casement.

telve Coffee-grounds. ~ falı, fortune-telling by the appearance of coffee-grounds.

telvin (·¹) A colouring. ~ etm., to colour. ~at (·—⁴), –tı, the painting *of buildings.*

telvis (·⁴) A soiling. ~ etm., to defile, soil.

telyin (·⁴) A softening *or* mitigating; a loosening the bowels.

temadi (·–⸗) A continuing uninterruptedly. ~ etm., to contine (vn.).

temaruz (·–⸗) A feigning sickness. ~ etm., to pretend to be ill, malinger.

temas Contact. ···e ~ etm., to touch; to touch on (a subject etc.) : ···le ~ etm., to make contact with, to get in touch with : ~ noktası, point of contact.

temasül (· ⸗) etm. vn. Become like or equal to one another.

temaşa (·–⸗) A walking about to see things; public promenade; spectacle, show, scene; the theatre. ~ya çıkmak, to go out for a walk, to stroll about and watch things : ~ etm., to look on at, to enjoy the scene. ~ger, spectator.

temayül (·–⸗) Inclination; bias; tendency; liking. ···e ~ etm., to have an inclination towards or a tendency to.

temayüz (·⸗⸗) etm. vn. Be distinguished or privileged.

tembel Lazy. Lazy man. ⌐~e iş buyur sana akıl öğretsin⌐, if you ask a lazy man to do something, he will give you better advice, i.e. he will try to get out of it. ~hane (···⸗), leper-house; office where work is neglected. ~lik, laziness.

tembul Betel leaf.

temcid A glorifying God; canticle intoned from minarets before dawn. ~ pilâvı, a thing that grows wearisome from repetition.

temdid (·⸗) Prolongation; extension. ~ etm., to prolong, extend, stretch.

temdin (·⸗) etm. va. Civilize.

temeddüh Boasting. ~ etm., to boast.

temeddün A leaving the nomadic life; a becoming civilized. ~ etm., to become civilized.

temekkün etm. vn. Settle down in a place.

temel Foundation; base. ~inden, fundamentally; at bottom : ~ atmak, to lay a foundation : ~ taşı, foundation-stone : ~ çivisi çakmak (kakmak), to have every intention of staying in a place or in the world : ~ tutmak, to become firm in its place; to settle down permanently.

temel·lenmek, to acquire a permanent foundation; to be firmly settled or based. ~leşmek, to become firmly established; to settle down permanently. ~li, wellfounded; permanent; fundamental : ~ oturmak, to settle permanently in a place : ~ gitti, he went for good. ~siz, without foundation; baseless.

temellûk, –ku A fawning servility; sycophancy. ~ etm., to fawn and flatter.

temellük, –kü A taking possession. ~ etm., to take possession of.

temenna (···⸗), **temennah** Oriental salute

bringing the fingers of the right hand to the lips and then to the forehead. ~ etm. (çakmak), to salute as above.

temenni (··⸗) Desire, wish. ~ etm., to desire, request : ~ sıygası, optative mood : iyi yolculuk ~ etm., to wish s.o. a good journey.

temerküz Concentration. ~ etm., to be concentrated : ~ kabinesi, coalition Cabinet : ~ kampı, concentration camp.

temerrüd Obstinacy; perverseness; default in payment. ~ etm., to be obstinate.

temessük, –kü A taking firm hold; bill acknowledging a debt or claim; titledeed.

temessül An assuming a form; a being assimilated; a being absorbed into a foreign community. ~ etm., to take on a form; to be assimilated, to be absorbed into a foreign community.

temeşşük, –kü A taking as model or pattern; practice in writing etc.

temettü, –üü Profit, gain; dividend. ~ etm., to profit, to use with advantage : ~ vergisi, tax on profits.

temevvüc The rising and falling of waves; fluctuation, undulation. ~ etm., to fluctuate, undulate; (of flags) to wave.

temevvül A becoming wealthy.

temeyyü, –üü A becoming liquid; liquefaction.

temeyyüz A being distinguished; distinction. ~ etm., to become distinct or distinguished.

temhil (·⸗) A granting a delay or respite.

temhir (·⸗) A sealing. ~ etm., to put a seal to, to sign with a seal.

temin (–⸗) A making safe or sure; assurance; confidence. ~ etm., to assure, ensure; render secure; inspire confidence. ~at (––⸗), –tı pl. of temin, used as sing. security; deposit; guarantee; assurance.

temiz Clean; pure; honourable. ~e çekmek, to make a fair copy of a writing : kendini ~e çıkarmak, to clear oneself (of a charge etc.) : ~e çıkmak, to be cleared, to prove innocent : ~ bir dayak, a sound thrashing : ~ giyinmek, to dress respectably : ~e havale etm., to clean up; to kill : ~ kan, oxygenated blood as it issues from the lungs : ~ konuşmak, to talk in a correct and polished manner : ~ para, net sum of money (after deductions) : ~ raporu, certificate of good health : ~ yemek, to eat good food in good places.

temiz·ce, fairly clean : cleanly, nicely. ~leme, act of cleaning : ~ işleri, public cleaning services. ~lemek, to clean; clean up; clear away; despoil, rob; (sl.) to kill. ~leyici, cleansing : cleaner. ~lik, cleanliness; purity; honesty; act of cleaning; purge; ~ **işleri**, scavenging service.

temkin (·ˈ) Self-possession; dignity; composure. ~**li**, grave, dignified; self-possessed.

temlik (·ˈ) A putting in possession. ~ **etm.**, to give formal possession *of a property*.

temmuz July.

tempo Time (*mus.*).

temren Head of an arrow *or* spear.

temrin Exercise *given to a pupil*; practice.

temriye A skin disease, lichen.

temsil (·ˈ) Representation (agency); performance *of a play*; assimilation; comparison; parable; symbol; saying, maxim; copy *of a book*; edition. ~ **bürosu**, Press Bureau of a Ministry: ~ **etm.**, to represent; present (play); assimilate; compare: **birinci** ~, first edition: **söz** ~**i**, for instance. **temsil·en** (·ˈ·), representing. ~**î** (·–ˈ), pertaining to a representation *etc.*; representative.

temyiz (·ˈ) A separating *or* distinguishing; discernment; soundness of judgement; appeal (law). ~ **etm.**, to distinguish; to appeal (*jur.*): ~ **mahkemesi**, Supreme Court of Appeal: **erbabı** ~, those who have reached years of discretion: **sinni** ~, years of discretion. ~**en** (·ˈ·), on appeal (legal).

ten The body; flesh. ~ **fanilâsı**, vest: ~ **rengi**, flesh-colour.

tenafür (·–ˈ) Mutual repugnance; incongruity; incompatibility.

tenakus (·–ˈ) Decrease, diminution. ~ **etm.**, to decrease, diminish.

tenakuz (·–ˈ) Contradiction.

tenasüb (·–ˈ) Proportion; symmetry. ~**î** (·–·ˈ), proportional.

tenasüh (·–ˈ) Metempsychosis.

tenasül (·–ˈ) Reproduction, generation. ~ **aleti**, the organ of generation. ~**î** (·–·ˈ), genital; sexual.

tenavüb (·–ˈ) A taking turns; alternation.

tenavül (·–ˈ) **etm.** *va.* Take *food or drink*.

tenazur (·–ˈ) A being symmetrical.

tenbih (·ˈ) Warning; order, injunction; stimulation. ~ **etm.**, to warn; enjoin; excite (nerves). ~**at** (·–ˈ), **-tı**, warnings; orders.

tencere (ˈ··) Saucepan. ⌜~ ~**ye dibin kara demiş**⌝, 'the pot called the kettle black': ~ **kebabı**, dish cooked in a stewpan with embers on the lid: ⌜~**de pişirip kapağında yemek**⌝, to cook in a saucepan and eat from its lid, to live very economically: ⌜~ **tava hepsi bir hava**⌝, everyone goes their own way; nobody cares a straw: ⌜~ **yuvarlandı kapağını buldu**⌝, 'the saucepan rolled and found its lid', ⌜birds of a feather flock together⌝.

tendürüst Healthy; robust. ~**lük**, soundness of health and body.

tenebbüh Vigilance; stimulation. ~ **etm.**, to become wiser from some experience.

tenebbüt, -tü Vegetable growth. ~ **etm.**, to grow (of plants).

tenef Guy rope of a tent.

teneffü etm. *vn.* Benefit; profit.

teneffür Aversion; disgust. ···**den** ~ **etm.**, to feel an aversion for, to be disgusted with.

teneffüs Respiration; pause for breath (*cf.* 'a breather'). ~ **etm.**, breathe; to pause for breath. ~**hane** (···–ˈ), recreation room; place for resting.

teneke Tin; tinplate; a tin (*esp.* a paraffin tin); amount held by a paraffin tin. (**arkasından**) ~ **çalmak**, to boo *s.o.* publicly: ~**sini eline vermek**, to give *s.o.* the sack: ~ **mahallesi**, the squalid outskirts of an eastern town *composed of huts built mainly of old paraffin tins*: (**yüzü**) ~ **kaplı**, brazen-faced: ~ **peynir**, a kind of cheese made of sheep's milk: **sarı** ~, brass. ~**ci**, tinsmith. ~**li**, tinned: **geçmişi** ~, cursèd.

teneşir Rite of washing a corpse for burial; the bench on which the corpse is washed (*also* ~ **tahtası**). ~**e gelesi !**, (*a curse*) 'may he die!': ~**e sürmek**, (of a bad habit *etc.*) to last till death: ⌜**onu ancak** ~ **paklar**⌝, 'only death can cleanse him', *said of a great scoundrel*. ~**lik**, place for washing corpses *in the courtyard of a mosque*.

tenevvü, -üü Variation. ~ **etm.**, to vary.

tenevvür A being illuminated *or* made clear; enlightenment. ~ **etm.**, to be made clear; to be enlightened.

tenezzüh Pleasure walk, excursion, jaunt. ~**etm.**, to go out for a pleasure trip; to take the air.

tenezzül A coming down; decline; condescension. ~ **etm.**, to decline, diminish, abate; to deign, condescend: ···**e** ~ **etm.**, to deign to ...; to deign to accept ... . ~**en** (·ˈ··), condescendingly; graciously; without being too proud.

tenfir (·ˈ) **etm.** *va.* Cause aversion (for *or* from = ···**den**).

tenha Solitary; alone; lonely; deserted (place). ~**laşmak**, to be alone; to become deserted *or* empty (of places). ~**lık**, solitude; deserted *or* lonely place: deserted, lonely.

te'nis[1] (–ˈ) A making feminine; a putting *an adjective etc.* into the feminine.

te'nis[2] (–ˈ) **etm.** *va.* Familiarize, accustom; tame.

tenkâr, tenkâl Crude borax; tincal.

tenkid (·ˈ) Criticism. ~ **etm.** *or* ~**atta bulunmak**, to criticize. ~**ci**, critic.

tenkih etm. *va.* Perform the service of betrothal or marriage *on s.o.*; cause to be engaged or married (*v.* **nikâh**).

tenkîh (·ᵛ) A pruning *of a composition*; a cutting down *of expenses or salaries.* ~ **etm.**, to cut down *the number of employees etc.*; to reduce *expenses or wages.* ~**at** (·–ᵛ), **-tı**, reductions in expenses; economies.

tenkil (·ᵛ) Repression *of a revolt.* ~ **etm.**, to repress *a rebellion.*

tenkis (·ᵛ) A diminishing; diminution. ~ **etm.**, to curtail, diminish.

tenkit¹ *v.* **tenkid.**

tenkit² (·ᵛ), **-ti** The vocalization of Arabic words by putting in the vowel points; punctuation.

tenkiye A cleaning; clyster.

tenmiye A causing to grow; an adding fuel to a fire; feeding, sustaining; investment *of money.* ~ **etm.**, to make grow; to nourish; develop; invest (capital); cultivate (friendly relations).

tennure (·–¹) Dervish's skirt.

tenperver Who takes great care of himself; fond of comfort; soft. ~**lik**, fondness of comfort and ease; softness *of living.*

tensib (·ᵛ) Approval. **bunu sizin ~inize bırakıyorum**, I leave this to your discretion: ~ **etm.**, to approve.

tensik (·ᵛ), **-kı** Arrangement; organization; a putting in order. ~ **etm.**, to reorganize, reform. ~**at** (·–ᵛ), **-tı**, reforms; reorganization; a combing out of inefficient officials.

tenşit (·ᵛ) **etm.** *va.* Make lively, enliven.

tente (¹·) Awning. ~**li**, with an awning.

tentene (¹··) Lace. ~**li**, ornamented with lace.

tentürdiyot Tincture of iodine.

tenvim (·ᵛ) A causing to sleep.

tenvir (·ᵛ) Illumination. ~ **etm.**, to illuminate; to make clear: ~ **fişeği**, flare (*mil.*): ~ **mermisi**, star shell: ~ **tabancası**, Very pistol. ~**at** (·–ᵛ), **-tı**, lighting *of a street etc.*

tenzih (·ᵛ) A considering free from defect; a declaring God to be free from defect. ~ **etm.**, to absolve.

tenzil (·ᵛ) A lowering *or* diminishing; reduction (of prices); subtraction (*arith.*); divine revelation; the Koran. ~ **etm.**, to lower, diminish, reduce; cause to alight. ~**ât** (·–ᵛ), **-tı**, reductions (of prices *etc.*). ~**âtlı**, reduced in price: ~ **satış**, bargain sale.

tepe¹ *v.* **tepmek.**

tepe² Hill; summit; crown of the head; crest *of a bird.* ~**den**, in a superior manner, condescendingly: ~ **aşağı gitmek**, to fall

headlong; (of a business) to go downhill: ~**si* atmak**, to be infuriated: ···**e ~den bakmak**, to look down on, to despise: ~ **camı**, skylight: ~**sine* çıkmak**, to presume on *s.o.'s kindness etc.*: ~**sine* dikilmek**, to worry, to insist: ~**den inme**, sudden, unexpected; from above, from a higher authority: ~**den tırnağa**, from head to foot: ~ **taklak**, on one's head, upside-down, head foremost: ~ **üstü**, upside-down, head first, headlong: **acısı ~mden çıktı**, I felt very sore about it: **aklı ~sinden yukarı**, thoughtlessly, absent-mindedly.

tepe·cik, little hill. ~**göz**, with an upward squint; whose forehead is so narrow that his eyes seem near his hair; star-gazer (fish, *Uranoscopus*); a legendary monster in Turkish epics (*cf.* Cyclops). ~**leme**, brimful: mound, heap: a killing; sound thrashing. ~**lemek**, to knock on the head; kill; thrash unmercifully. ~**li**, crested (bird). ~**lik**, ornamental knob *formerly worn on headgear.*

tepengi Thick pad of a pack-saddle; broad girth.

tepinmek *vn.* Throw one's legs and arms about; kick and stamp; dance *with joy or in anger.*

tepir Hair sieve. ~**lemek**, to pass through a fine sieve.

tepişmek *vn.* Kick one another; quarrel violently. ⌐**atlar tepişir eşekler ezilir**⌐, 'the weak go to the wall'.

tepme Kick; relapse (in illness). ~ **atmak**, to kick: **geri ~**, recoil.

tepmek *vn.* Kick; recoil; (of an illness) to recur. *va.* Kick; spurn; underestimate. ⌐**teptim keçe oldu, sivrilttim külâh oldu**⌐, 'I kicked and it became a felt mat, I rolled it to a point and it became a conical hat', *used of people who interpret stg. in a way to suit themselves*: **tepe tepe kullanmak**, to wear *a garment* continuously and give it rough usage: **at ~**, to spur on a horse: **bir fırsatı ~**, to spurn an opportunity: **nimeti ~**, to spurn a piece of luck.

tepremek, teprenmek *vn.* Struggle; bestir oneself.

tepreşmek *vn. As* **tepremek**; (of an illness) to recur.

tepsi Small tray.

ter¹ Sweat, perspiration. ~ **alıştırmak**, to wait till one's sweat has dried: ~**e batmak**, to sweat heavily: ~ **dökmek** (**basmak**), to sweat; to labour hard; to sweat with terror *or* anxiety: ~**e yatmak**, to make oneself sweat by hot drinks and many blankets: **soğuk ~ler döktürmek**, to cause to break out in a cold sweat *from terror*: **kan ~**, profuse sweat; **kan ~ içinde**

kalmak, to be in a profuse sweat; to undergo great exertion.

ter² Moist; fresh; green; juicy. ~ bıyık, youth whose moustache has just sprouted.

teradüf (·—¹) Succession; a being consecutive; a being synonymous.

terahhum etm. *va.* (*with dat.*) Take pity on.

terahi (·—⸸) Supineness; sluggishness.

terakki (···⸸) Advance, progress; increase. ~ etm., to make progress, to advance; increase. ~**perver**, progressive. ~**yat**, **–tı**, advances; improvements.

teraküm (·—¹) Accumulation. ~ etm., to collect, accumulate (*vn.*).

terane (·—¹) Tune; refrain; yarn, concocted story; subterfuge.

teravi (·—¹), **teravih** Prayer special to the nights of Ramazan. **Arnavudu kızdıran ~**, *v.* inad *in App.*

terazi (·—¹) Balance; pair of scales.

terazî (·—⸸) Mutual consent.

terbıyık *v.* ter².

terbi (·⸸), **–ii** Quadruplication; a squaring; quarter *of the moon.* ~ etm., to make four; to square: **ilk (son) ~**, first (last) quarter of the moon. ~**an** (·⸸·), by squaring.

terbiye A bringing up; education; training; good manners; a teaching manners; correction, punishment; sauce; rein. ~ etm., to bring up, educate, train; correct; teach manners; punish; flavour *with a sauce etc.*: ~**sini vermek**, to teach *s.o.* his manners; to reprimand: **beden ~si**, physical training, gymnastics.

terbiye·ci, one who educates; pedagogue; trainer. ~**li**, well brought up; good-mannered; educated; flavoured *with a sauce etc.* ~**siz**, badly brought up; ill-mannered; uneducated; without a sauce or seasoning. ~**sizlik**, bad manners; rudeness; lack of education. ~**vî** (···⸸), educational.

tercih (·⸸) Preference; priority. ~ etm., to prefer. ~**an** (·⸸·), preferably, in preference.

terciibend (·—·¹) Poem in which each stanza ends with the same couplet.

tercüm·an Interpreter; translator; dragoman. ~**anlık**, office or profession of an interpreter: ~ etm., to act as interpreter. ~**e**, translation: ···**e** ~ etm., to translate into .... ~**eihal**, **–li**, biography; memoirs.

terdid (·⸸) The art of giving a surprising end to a story.

terdif (·⸸) etm. *va.* Send as escort or guide; cause to accompany. ~**en** (·⸸·), as escort; as company.

terdöşeği (¹···), **–ni** Childbed.

tere Cress. ~**ci**, seller of cress: ⸢~**ye tere**

satmak¹, 'to teach your grandmother to suck eggs': ~**ye tere satma !**, don't try to take me in !

tereddi (···⸸) Degeneration; deterioration. ~ etm., to deteriorate.

tereddüd Hesitation; indecision. ~ etm., to hesitate: **bilâ ~**, without hesitation.

tereffü, **–üü** Elevation. ~ etm., to be elevated; to rise (of prices *etc.*).

tereke Estate of a deceased person; heritage; sale of a dead man's effects.

terekküb A being composed *or* compounded. ~ etm., to be composed *or* compounded.

terelelli (···¹·) Feather-brained; frivolous.

terementi (···¹·) Terebinth; turpentine.

terennüm A singing *or* warbling. ~ etm., to sing, hum, warble.

tereotu (·¹··), **–nu** Dill.

teres Cuckold; pimp; scoundrel.

teressüb Sediment, precipitation. ~ etm., to be precipitated; to be deposited as sediment.

teressüm etm. *vn.* Be pictured; become evident.

tereşşüh An oozing *or* trickling. ~ etm., to ooze *or* trickle: (of secrets, news *etc.*) to ooze out. ~**at**, **–tı**, things that ooze out (secrets *etc.*).

terettüb etm. *vn.* Be incumbent (upon = *dat.*).

tereyağ (·¹·), **tereyağı**, **–nı** Fresh butter. ⸢~**ından kıl çeker gibi**¹, skilfully and easily.

terfi (·⸸), **–ii** Promotion; advancement. ~ etm., to be promoted: ~**i rütbe**, promotion in rank. ~**an** (·⸸·), by way of promotion; on promotion.

terfih (·⸸) A causing to live in prosperity. ~ etm., to bring prosperity to; to better the condition of.

terfik (·⸸) etm. *va.* Send as escort *or* companion. ~**an** (·⸸·), as companion; by way of escort.

tergib (·⸸) A causing to desire.

terhib (·⸸) A threatening *or* terrifying; severe deterrent punishment. ~**î** (·—⸸), terrorizing; deterrent (punishment).

terhin (·⸸) etm. *va.* Pawn; pledge.

terhis (·⸸) Authorization, permission; discharge *of a soldier after serving his time.* ~ etm., to authorize; to discharge (soldier); to demobilize: ~ **tezkeresi**, discharge papers *of a soldier.*

‖ **terim** Term; technical term.

terk, **–ki** Abandonment; renouncement; omission; neglect. ~**i hayat**, dying: ~**i dünya**, a renouncing the world. ~**etmek** (¹···), **–eder**, to abandon; renounce; relinquish; neglect; leave (an inheritance, a post *etc.*).

terkeş Quiver.

terki Anything strapped to the back of a saddle. ∼ bağı, strap for fastening things to the back of a saddle: ∼ye almak or ∼mek, to take as pillion rider. ∼şmek, to take turns riding pillion.

terkib (·ᵏ) A joining or compounding; composition; compound; structure; compound word; phrase; synthesis. ∼ etm., to compose, compound; constitute. ∼at (·—ᵏ), –tı, compositions; compounds. ∼î (·—᷍), relating to composition; compound; composite; synthetic. ∼ibend, a poem, the stanzas of which are connected by a refrain.

terkim (·ᵏ) A marking; a putting a figure on. ∼ etm., to mark with a figure; to write.

terkin (·ᵏ) Cancellation. ∼ etm., to cancel, cross out.

terkos (¹·) Mains water-supply; water laid on (in Istanbul).

terkuva Collar-bone.

ter·lemek vn. Sweat, perspire; be covered with dew (of a glass); start growing (of a moustache); be very tired; be embarrassed. ∼letici, sudorific; hard, fatiguing (work). ∼letmek, to cause to sweat; greatly fatigue. ∼li, sweating, perspiring: ∼ su içmek, to drink water when perspiring.

terlik Slipper.

termim (·ᵏ) A mending or repairing. ∼ etm., to mend; to set (a bone). ˑ

termometre Thermometer.

termos Thermos flask.

ternöv (Fr. Terre-neuve) Newfoundland dog.

ters Back or reverse of a thing; wrong or reverse direction; excrement. Reverse; wrong; opposite; inside out; peevish, contrary, surly, wrong-headed; unfortunate, ill-timed. ∼ ∼ bakmak, to look sourly: ∼i* dönmek, to lose one's bearings: ∼ gelmek, to be the wrong way about; to be in the opposite direction: ∼ gitmek, to go wrong, to turn out badly: ∼ine* olm., to happen contrary to one's wishes: ∼inden okumak, (i) to misunderstand; (ii) to be very quick-witted: ∼ pers, very inverted; all wrong; falling backwards; quite the reverse of what was desired; disconcerted; disappointed: ∼ine yazmak, to write the reverse way: ∼ yüz, empty-handed, disappointed: ∼ yüz etm., to turn (a suit of clothes): elin ∼i, the back of the hand.

tersane (·—¹) Dockyard; maritime arsenal (esp. that at Istanbul). ∼li, attached to the maritime arsenal; (formerly) naval officer or rating.

tersib (·ᵏ) Precipitation. ∼ etm., to deposit, precipitate.

tersim (·ᵏ) etm. va. Picture; design, draw. ∼î (·—᷍), pertaining to designing or drawing: ∼ hendese, descriptive geometry.

ters·lemek vn. va. Scold; answer harshly; snub; dung; befoul with dung. ∼lenmek, to be in a bad temper; to behave in a peevish contrary way: to be snubbed. ∼lik, a turning out in the reverse of what was hoped; a being reversed or wrong; contrariness, vexatiousness. ∼pers, ∼yüz, v. ters.

terşih (·ᵏ) Filtration. ∼ havuzu, filter-bed.

tertemiz (¹··) Absolutely clean.

tertib (·ᵏ) Arrangement; order; disposition; plan, project; recipe; medical prescription; composition; setting-up of type; format of a book. ∼ etm., to arrange, put in order; to plan; prepared beforehand; to compose; organize; to prescribe (med.): hafif ∼, slightly, just a little: tam ∼, fully, thoroughly.

tertib·at (·—ᵏ), –tı, arrangements; dispositions; apparatus; installations. ∼ci, good at organizing; who is always planning. ∼î ((·—᷍), organizing; arranging. ∼iye (·—·᷍), cost of setting-up for printing. ∼lemek, to organize, arrange. ∼lenme, arrangement; disposition (mil.). ∼li, well-organized; well-prepared. ∼siz, without system; ill-prepared; badly planned. ∼sizlik, bad organization; lack of system.

tertil (·ᵏ) A chanting of the Koran in slow time.

terütaze Quite fresh.

tervic (·ᵏ) A making current; encouragement; advocacy of a plan etc. ∼ etm., to make current; to cause to be accepted; to advocate, encourage.

terzi Tailor. ∼ sabunu, French chalk (soapstone). ∼hane (··—¹), tailor's shop; clothing factory. ∼lik, tailoring.

terzil (·ᵏ) etm. va. Treat with ignominy; humiliate before others; ill-treat; insult.

tesadüf (·—¹) A meeting by chance; chance event; coincidence. ···e ∼ etm., to meet by chance, come across; to coincide with; to happen by chance: ∼e bak ki !, what a strange coincidence ! ∼at, –tı, coincidences; chance events. ∼en (·᷍··), by chance; by coincidence. ∼î (·—·᷍), chance (event etc.), fortuitous.

tesadüm (·—¹) etm. vn. Collide with one another.

tesahüb (·—¹) A making oneself owner; a becoming a patron or protector. ∼ etm., to take possession of; to support, protect: ···e ∼ etm., to claim to be the owner or the author of.

tesalüb (·—¹) Cross-breeding. ∼ ettirmek, to cross breeds.

tesamüh (·—ˡ) Condonation.

tesanüd (·—ˡ) Mutual support; co-operation; solidarity.

tesavi (·—ˡ) Equality between two things; parity.

tesbih (·ⁱ) Rosary. ~ ağacı, Indian lilac, bead-tree (*Melia Azedarach*) : ~ çekmek, to tell one's beads. ~böceği, –ni, woodlouse.

tesbit (·ⁱ), –ti A fixing *or* establishing; stabilization; fixation. ~ etm., to establish, stabilize; prove, confirm; (*mil.*) to tie down *an enemy* : hesabı ~ etm., to make up an account.

tescil (·ⁱ) An inscribing in the rolls of a Court; registration. ~ etm., to register, record. ~ât (·—ⁱ), –tı, State Registries.

tesdis (·ⁱ) A dividing into sixths; a making six *or* hexagonal. ~ vaziyeti, sextile aspect (*astron*.).

teselli (···ˡ) Consolation. ~ bulmak, to console oneself : ···e ~ vermek, to console *s.o.* ~bahş, consoling, consolatory. ~yab (···—ˡ), who finds consolation.

tesellüm A taking delivery; receipt. ~ etm., to take delivery : ~ tecrübesi, full-power trials *of a ship before delivery*.

teselsül A following in a continuous series like the links of a chain; concatenation; continuous succession; train of ideas; sequence of events. ~ etm., to follow in an uninterrupted series.

tesemmüm A being poisoned. ~ etm., to be poisoned (inadvertently).

tesettür A being veiled *or* hidden. ~ etm., to veil oneself; to conceal oneself.

teseül Begging, mendicity. ~ etm., to beg (as a beggar).

teseyyüb Negligence, slackness. ~ etm., to act negligently *or* thoughtlessly.

teshil (·ⁱ) A making easy. ~ etm., to facilitate. ~ât (·—ⁱ), –tı, facilities.

teshin (·ⁱ) A heating. ~ etm., to heat. ~at (·—ⁱ), –tı, heating installation.

teshir¹ (·ⁱ) Fascination; enchantment. ~ etm., to enchant, bewitch, fascinate.

teshir² (·ⁱ) Conquest; subjugation.

tes'id (·ⁱ) Celebration, festival. ~ etm., to celebrate *a feast*.

tesir (−ⁱ) Effect; impression; influence. ···e ~ etm., to affect, to cause an impression on; to influence : ~ olunmak, to be affected *or* impressed. ~at (−−ⁱ), –tı, impressions; effects; influences. ~li, touching, moving; impressive; efficacious. ~siz, ineffective; without influence; free, without being influenced. ~sizlik, inefficacy.

tesis (−ⁱ) A laying a foundation, a basing *a matter on stg*. ~ etm., to found, establish,

institute, base. ~at (−−ⁱ), –tı, institutions; establishments; plants (industrial).

teskere (¹··) Litter; stretcher; bier; hand barrow. ~ci, stretcher-bearer.

teskin (·ⁱ) etm. *va*. Pacify, calm; assuage.

teskiye *v*. tezkiye.

teslih (·ⁱ) An arming. ~ etm., to arm. ~at (·—ⁱ), –tı, armament(s).

teslim (·ⁱ) A handing over; delivery; payment; surrender, submission; acknowledgement *or* admission *of an argument or fact*. ~ almak, to take delivery of : ~ etm., to hand over, deliver; to give up, surrender; to pay over *money*; to admit *an argument* : ~ olm., to surrender, give oneself up : ~i ruh etm., to give up the ghost : ~ ve tesellüm, the handing over of an office to a successor. ~at (·—ⁱ), –tı, instalments (of money *etc*.). ~iyet (·—·ˡ), –ti, submission; resignation : arzı ~ etm., to surrender.

teslis (·ⁱ) A making into three; triplication; dividing into three; a boiling till two-thirds have evaporated; belief in the Trinity.

tesliye Consolation.

tesmim (·ⁱ) A poisoning. ~ etm., to poison.

tesmiye A naming. ~ etm., to name, designate : ~ olunmak, to be named, called.

tesniye Dual (*gram*.).

tespih, tespit *v*. tesbih, tesbit.

tesri (·—ˡ), –ii A hastening; acceleration. ~ etm., to accelerate.

tesrir (·ⁱ) etm. *va*. Gladden.

testere (¹··) Saw. kayış ~si, band-saw : kıl ~, fretsaw : kollu ~, hacksaw. ~balığı, –nı, sawfish. ~burun, goosander.

testi Pitcher; jug. ⌐~yi kıran da bir, suyu getiren de⌐, *said reproachfully when a deserving person is no better treated than an undeserving one* : ⌐su ~si su yolunda kırılır⌐, ⌐the pitcher goes often to the well but is broken at last⌐; one must take the risks of one's occupation.

tesvid (·ⁱ) Rough draft. ~ etm., to blacken; to make a rough draft.

tesvil (·ⁱ) A falsely representing a thing to be good; delusion. ~ât (·—ⁱ), –tı, *pl. as sing*., delusion, misrepresentation : ~a kapılmak, to be taken in by a false appearance or representation.

tesviye A making equal *or* level; arrangement; payment, settlement (of an account); adjustment; smoothing, planing; fitting; free pass (railway *etc*.) *given to travelling soldiers*. ~ etm., to equalize, level; settle; arrange; smooth, plane : ~ atölyesi, fitting-shop; ~ hududu, contour line: ~ ruhu, spirit-level: ~i türabiye (*now* toprak ~si), levelling of the ground: bir ihtilâfın hallü ~si, the smoothing-out of a difference: kum ~si, ballast *of a railway or road*. ~ci, fitter; one who levels the ground. ~cilik, fitting (*mech.*).

teşahhus A taking concrete form; personification. ~ etm., to take concrete form; to take the form of a person: ~ ettirmek, to personify.

teşaub (·—¹) Ramification; bifurcation.

teşaur (·—¹) A pretending to be a poet.

teşbih (·⅄) Comparison; simile. ⌐~te hata olmaz¹, only for the sake of comparison; let it not be misunderstood.

teşci, –ii Encouragement; ~ etm., to encourage.

teşdid (·⅄) Intensification; aggravation; redoubling (of efforts *etc.*): doubling a consonant. ~ etm., to intensify, aggravate; redouble (efforts *etc.*).

teşebbüs Enterprise; effort; initiative. ···e ~ etm., to set to work at ..., to undertake, start *an enterprise etc.* ~at, –tı, enterprises; efforts: ~ta bulunmak, to take steps towards *doing stg.*

teşeddüd A being aggravated; a becoming more violent *or* severe. ~ etm., to become aggravated *etc.*

teşekki (···⅃) A complaining. ~ etm., to complain.

teşekkül A being formed; formation; organization; association. ~ etm., to be formed *or* constituted. ~ât, –tı, formations, associations.

teşekkür A giving thanks. ~ etm., to thank: ~ ederim, thank you!

teşemmüs A being exposed to the sun; sunstroke.

teşennüc Convulsion, spasm. ~î (···⅃), spasmodic.

teşerrüf A being honoured. ~ etm., to feel honoured: ~ ettim, I am honoured (to meet you).

teşettüt, –tü Disposal; scattering.

teşeüm etm. *vn.* Draw an evil omen. ···den ~ etm., to consider ... as inauspicious.

teşevvüş Confusion.

teşfiye A curing. ~ etm., to cure: ~i sadır etm., to feel happy; to make *s.o.* feel happy.

teşhir (·⅄) A drawing (of the sword *etc.*); a making public *or* notorious; an exposing to the public view; exhibition. ~ cezası, the punishment of the pillory: ~ etm., to make public, divulge; to expose to the public view, to exhibit; to pillory: ~i silâh etm., to draw the sword.

teşhis (·⅄) Recognition; identification;

diagnosis. ~ etm., to identify, recognize, diagnose.

teşkil (·⅄) Formation; organization. ~ etm., to form; organize; constitute. ~ât (·—⅄), –tı, organizations, formations; *as sing.*, organization; reorganization: ~ı esasiye kanunu, the constitution. ~âtçı, organizer. ~âtlamak, to organize. ~âtlı, organized.

teşmil (·⅄) Extension; generalization. ~ etm., to extend to, to include.

teşne Thirsty; parched; longing for (*dat.*).

teşri (·⅃), –ii Legislation. ~î (·—⅃), legislative: ~ kuvvet (kuvvei ~ye), the legislative power: ~ masuniyet, the immunity of legislators.

teşrif (·⅄) A conferring honour; *polite form for* visit, arrival *or* departure. ~ etm., to honour *by one's presence*: ···e ~ etm., to come to: ···den ~ etm., to go from: ~ nereye?, where are you going?: ~ mi?, must you be going so soon?

teşrif·at (·—⅄), –tı, ceremonies; ceremonial; official etiquette, protocol: *the department of the Foreign Office concerned with such matters*. ~atçı, Master of the Ceremonies. ~atî (···—⅃), pertaining to ceremonial.

teşrih (·⅄) Dissection; anatomy. ~i marazî, pathological anatomy: ~ etm., to dissect; to examine minutely. ~hane (···—¹), dissecting-room.

teşrik (·⅄), –ki A making partner. ~ etm., to make partner, to associate: ~i mesai, joint effort, co-operation.

teşrini·evvel (·—···¹) October (*now* Ekim). ~sani (·—···⅃), November (*now* Kasım).

teşvik (·⅄), –ki Encouragement; incitement. ~ etm., to encourage; incite. ~kâr, encouraging.

teşviş (·⅄) A confusing *or* complicating. ~ etm., to confuse, disorder.

teşyi (·⅃), –ii A seeing s.o. off. ~ etm., to accompany *a departing guest*, to see *s.o.* off; to follow a funeral.

teşyid (·⅄) etm. *va.* Strengthen; consolidate.

tetabu (·—⅃), –uu Uninterrupted succession; long series of words connected by izafats.

tetabuk (·—¹), –ku Conformity; accord; concord (*gram.*). ···e ~ etm., to correspond to, to conform with.

tetanos Tetanus.

tetebbü, –üü Study; investigation; research. ~ etm., to study, investigate. ~at, –tı, studies, researches.

tetevvüc Coronation. ~ etm., to be crowned.

tetik Trigger. Vigilant; agile, quick. tetiğini bozmamak, to keep a cool head: ~

bulunmak *or* ~ üzerinde olm., to be vigilant, to be on the qui-vive : **adımı** ~ **almak,** to proceed with caution : **alt** ~**te,** at halfcock : **üst** ~**te,** at full cock. ~**lik,** a being very alert, promptness, agility.

tetimmat (··⸍), **–tı** Supplements; accessories; accompaniments; complementary parts.

tetkik *v.* **tedkik.**

tetre Sumach.

tetvic A crowning, coronation. ~ **etm.,** to crown.

tevabi (·—⸍), **–ii** *pl. of* **tâbi.** Followers; dependants; dependencies.

tevafuk (·—⸍), **–ku** Agreement; compatibility; conformity. ···**e** ~ **etm.,** to agree with, conform to, correspond to.

tevaggul, –lü A being preoccupied with *stg.* ···**le** ~ **etm.,** to be engrossed in.

tevahhuş A being frightened; a being wild and timid (like a wild animal). ~ **etm.,** to be frightened *or* wild.

tevakki (···⸍) A taking care of oneself; a being on one's guard *against stg.* ···**den** ~ **etm.,** to beware of.

tevakkuf A stopping, tarrying, *or* sojourning; a depending *on stg.* ~ **etm.,** to stop, to stay : ···**e** ~ **etm.,** to depend on, to require (thought, time *etc.*) : ~ **mahalli,** stopping-place (of a tram *etc.*).

tevali (·—⸍) Uninterrupted succession. ~ **etm.,** to follow in uninterrupted succession.

tevarih (·—⸍) *pl. of* **tarih.** Annals, histories.

tevarüd (·—⸍) Coincidence; unintentional composition of the same verse by different poets.

tevarüs (·—⸍) An inheriting. ···**e** ~ **etm.,** to inherit.

tevatür (·—⸍) Hearsay; generally current report; *stg.* confirmed by unanimous report. ~**ile malûm olm.,** to be known by a general consensus of reporters : ~ **olunduğuna göre,** according to general report. ~**en** (·⸍··), by common report : ~ **sabıt,** known to all.

tevazu (·—⸍), **–uu** Humility; modesty; lack of conceit. ~**kârane** (·——·⸍), modest; modestly.

tevazün (·—⸍) A being of equal weight; equilibrium. **bütçenin** ~**ü,** the budget's being balanced : ~ **etm.,** to balance one another.

tevbih (–⸍) Rebuke, reprimand. ~ **etm.,** to rebuke, reprimand. ~**kâr,** reproachful.

tevcih (·⸍) A turning towards; a conferring an office; appointment; an explaining *or* accounting for. ~ **etm.,** to turn towards (*va.*); to direct *one's words or looks* towards; to confer (an office *or* rank); to nominate :

~ **olunmak,** to be awarded (a decoration *or* post of honour).

tevdi (·⸍), **–ii** A committing to the safe keeping of another. ~ **etm.,** to entrust (an affair *or* secret); to deposit (money); to commit *to the charge of* another; to present, tender. ~**at** (·—⸍), **–tı,** deposits (in a bank *etc.*).

teveccüh A turning towards; favour, kindness, goodwill. ~**ünüz efendim !,** it's kind of you to say so (*in reply to a compliment*) : ···**e** ~ **etm.,** to turn towards (*vn.*); to turn one's attention to; to face; (of a duty) to fall to one's lot. ~**at, –tı,** favours, kindnesses.

tevehhüm An imagining, fancying; groundless apprehension *or* foreboding. ~ **etm.,** to imagine *stg. that is not there,* to fancy.

tevekkeli By chance; without reason. ~ (*followed by a neg.*), it was not without reason that ...; it was not for nothing that ... .

tevekkül A putting one's trust in God; resignation. ~ **etm.,** to put one's trust in God; to be resigned.

tevellüd Birth. ~ **etm.,** to be born; to arise *or* spring *from.* ~**lü,** born *in such and such a year.*

tev'em Twin; pair; similar.

teverrüm A swelling; tumefaction; tuberculosis. ~ **etm.,** to become consumptive.

tevessü, –üü A being spacious *or* extensive; extension, expansion. ~ **etm.,** to expand.

tevessül etm. *vn.* (*with dat.*) Approach; have recourse to; take steps to; have in hand : proceed.

tevettür Tension. **yüksek** ~ **pili,** high-tension battery. ~**lü,** having *high or low* tension.

tevezzü, –üü Distribution.

tevfik (·⸍), **–ki** Guidance (*esp.* divine); adaptation; success. ~ **etm.,** to adapt; to make agree : ···**e** ~**i hareket etm.,** to conform to ... : ~ **vermek,** (of God) to grant guidance and success. ~**an** (·⸍·), in accordance *or* conformity (with = *dat.*). ~**at** (·—⸍), **–tı,** *pl. as sing.,* Divine guidance and assistance.

tevhid (·⸍) Unification; consolidation; monotheism. ~ **etm.,** to unite.

tevil (·⸍) An explaining away; forced interpretation. ~ **etm.,** to explain away *stg.*; to put a forced construction on. ~**siz,** that cannot be explained away.

teviye *In* **bir** ~, continuously.

tevki (·⸍), **–ii** The Sultan's signature (tughra); imperial rescript. ~**ci,** *former official who drew the Sultan's signature.*

tevkif (·⸍) Detention; arrest; custody. ~ **ateşi, àrtillery barrage** : ~ **etm.,** to detain, arrest, stop; to deduct (a sum of money). **~at** (·–[·]), **–tı,** deductions (from wages *etc.*); stoppages of pay; arrests. **~hane** (···–¹), place of custody of arrested persons.

tevkiî (·–[–]) *As* **tevkici** *v.* **tevki.**

tevkil (·[·]) **etm.,** *va.* Appoint as representative *or* deputy.

tevkir Respect, deference. **~ etm.,** to treat with respect, to show honour to.

tevlid (·[·]) A giving birth; an acting as midwife; a causing *or* producing. **~ etm.,** to give birth to; to create; cause; act as midwife to.

tevliyet, –ti Appointment of a **mütevelli** *q.v.*; office of **mütevelli.**

Tevrat, –tı The Pentateuch. **~î** (··–[–]), biblical.

tevris (·[·]) **etm.** *va.* Appoint as heir.

tevriye A hiding one thing behind another ; use of an ambiguous word. **~ üzere söylemek,** to speak in hints.

tevsi (·–[–]), **–ii** Enlargement; extension. **~ etm.,** to enlarge, extend.

tevsik (·[·]), **–kı** A making firm *or* trustworthy. **~ etm.,** to confirm, prove; prove by documentary evidence.

tevsim (·[·]) **etm.** *va.* Name.

tevzi (·–[–]), **–ii** Distribution; delivery (of letters *etc.*). **~at, –tı,** distributions; postal deliveries.

tevzin (·[·]) **etm.** *va.* Balance.

teyakkun Certainty; conviction. **~ etm.,** to be convinced of *stg.*

teyakkuz A being awake; vigilance; circumspection. **~ etm.,** to be awake; to be on one's guard.

teybis (·–[·]) Desiccation. **~ etm.,** to dry, desiccate.

teyel Coarse sewing, tacking. **~lemek,** to sew coarsely, tack. **~li,** tacked.

teyelti *v.* **teğelti.**

teyemmüm Ritual ablution with sand or earth in default of water; a looking longingly at stg. one cannot have.

teyemmün A regarding as lucky. **~ etm.,** to regard as lucky; to rejoice in *stg.* as a piece of good luck. **~en** (··¹··), as a token of good luck; as an act of piety.

teyid (–[·]) Corroboration; confirmation; assistance. **~ etm.,** to strengthen; to corroborate *or* confirm.

teyze (¹··) Maternal aunt; *used also by a stepson addressing his stepmother.* **hanım ~,** *polite term of address for any elderly lady*: **~ kadın,** procuress. **~zade** (··–¹), cousin (child of a maternal aunt).

tez¹ Quick. Quickly, promptly. **~ elden,** without delay, in haste : **bugünden ~i yok,** this very day, immediately : **yarından ~i yok, işe başlamalı,** tomorrow at the latest

the work must be begun : **canı (içi) ~,** hustler, energetic; impatient.

tez² (*Fr. thèse*) Thesis; question.

tezad, –ddı Contrast; contradiction; incompatibility.

tezahür (·–¹) Manifestation. **~ etm.,** to become manifest, to appear. **~at, –tı,** public demonstration; ovation.

tezauf (·–¹) **etm.** *vn.* Be doubled.

tezayüd (·–¹) An increasing; growth. **~ etm.,** to increase, multiply (*vn.*).

tezcanlı (¹··) Hustling; energetic; impatient of delay.

tezebzüb Confusion; disorder.

tezehhür A flowering; efflorescence.

tezek Dried dung *used as fuel.* **yer tezeği,** peat.

tezekkür Discussion; consultation. **~ etm.,** to discuss, consider.

tezelden (¹··) Without delay; in haste.

tezellül Abasement. **~ etm.,** to demean onself.

tezelzül Agitation; convulsion; shock. **~ etm.,** to be agitated; to quake; to be shaken.

tezene Plectrum.

tezevvüc A taking a wife; matrimony. **~ etm.,** to marry (*vn.*).

tezeyyün An adorning oneself.

tezgâh Loom; work-bench; counter; ship-building yard; workshop; machine-tool. **~ başı yapmak** (*sl.*), to have a drink at a bar : **dikiş ~ı,** bookbinder's stitching-frame. **~dar,** one who serves at a counter; shop-assistant.

tezhib (·[·]) A gilding *or* inlaying with gold.

tezkâr Remembrance; reminiscence; mention. **~ etm.,** to call to mind; to mention.

tezkere (¹··) Note; memorandum; official certificate *or* receipt; soldier's discharge papers; biographical memoir. **~sini eline vermek,** to give s.o. 'the sack': **av ~si,** shooting licence : **nüfus ~si,** identity papers : **unvan ~si,** trade-licence : **yol ~si,** permit to travel. **~ci** (¹···), (*formerly*) official charged with duty of writing official memoranda; discharged soldier; reservist. **~lik,** paper used for official notes; soldier due for discharge.

tezkir (·[·]) A reminding; a making masculine (*gram.*). **···in ~i namı için,** to perpetuate the memory of ... .

tezkiye Purification; praise; *part of the Moslem funeral ceremony, where the Hodja asks the congregation to confirm the deceased's good qualities, hence* : **~sini* düzeltmek,** to reform oneself; **~si bozuk,** who has a bad reputation : **~ etm.** to clear *s.o.'s* character.

tez·lenmek vn. Make haste; be impatient. ~**lik**, speed; haste; impatience.

tezlil (·ᵻ) A humiliating. ~ **etm.**, to humiliate, vilify, insult.

tezvic (·ᵻ) **etm.** va. Unite in matrimony; cause to marry.

tezvir (·ᵻ) Wilful misrepresentation; falsehood, deceit; malicious instigation. ~**atta bulunmak**, to engage in malicious misrepresentations.

tezyid (·ᵻ) Augmentation, increase. ~ **etm.**, to increase, multiply (va.).

tezyif (·ᵻ) A deeming contemptible; derision; mockery. ~ **etm.**, to deride, caricature; to hold in contempt.

tezyil (·ᵻ) **etm.** va. Add as a supplement or appendix.

tezyin (·ᵻ) An adorning; decoration. ~ **etm.**, to adorn, embellish. ~**at** (·—ᵻ), –**tı**, adornments. ~**î** (·—ᷢ), decorative.

tıb, –**bbı** The science of medicine; therapeutics. ~**ben** (ᵎ·), medically. ~**bî** (·ᷢ), medical. ~**biye**, medical faculty or school. ~**biyeli**, medical student.

tıf·ıl, –**flı** Infant; infantile person. ~**lâne** (·—ᵎ), infantile; in a childish manner.

tığ Crochet-needle; bodkin; awl; knitting-needle; plane-iron. ~ **gibi**, slender but strong and active, wiry : ~ **örgüsü**, crochet.

tığala (·ᵎ·) Gum euphorbium.

tığlamak va. Lance; pierce with a needle; (sl.) slaughter (an animal). vn. (Of a wound) to give a piercing pain.

tıhal Spleen.

tık tık Imitates a ticking noise.

tıka In ~ **basa**, crammed full. ~**ç**, plug; stopper; gag. ~**lı**, stopped up; plugged.

tıkamak va. Stop up; plug; gag. **burnunu*** ~, to hold the nose : ···**in çanına ot** ~, to stop the mouth of ..., to reduce to silence; to render impotent : **hakikate kulaklarını*** ~, to refuse to listen to the truth : **iştahı** ~, to spoil the appetite : **sözü ağza** ~, to interrupt s.o. speaking, to shut s.o. up.

tıkan·ık Stopped up; choked. ~**ıklık**, choking; suffocation; a being stopped up; interruption of communications (mil.); lack of appetite. ~**mak**, v.n. pass. of **tıkamak**, to be stopped up; to choke; be suffocated; to lose one's appetite.

tıkınmak vn. Stuff oneself; eat in haste; gulp down one's food.

tıkır Imitates a clinking or rattling or tapping noise; (sl.) money, 'chink'. ~ ~, with a clinking or rattling noise : ~ ~ **işlemek**, (of a clock etc.) to go perfectly; to go 'like clockwork' : ~**ını** or ~**ına uydurmak**, to put into good order : **işler** ~**ına girdi**, the matter is going well; things have taken a favourable turn : **işler** ~**ında gidiyor**, business is

going well : **keyfim** ~**ında**, I am in the best of spirits.

tıkırdak Wild duck.

tıkır·damak vn. Make the sounds indicated by **tıkır** q.v. ~**dı**, ~**tı**, a rattling or clinking sound : ~**lı telgraf âleti**, sounder (telegraphy).

tıkış·mak vn. Be crammed or squeezed together. ~**tırmak**, to cram into a small space; to bolt (food).

tıkız Fleshy; hard; tightly packed together.

tıklım tıklım Brimful; filled to overflowing.

tıkmak va. Thrust, squeeze or cram into. **çanına ot** ~, v. **tıkamak** : **deliğe (hapse)** ~, to clap into jail : **lâkırdıyı ağza** ~, to cram down s.o.'s throat an assertion he has made.

tıknaz Plumpish; stout.

tıknefes (ᵎ··) Short of breath; asthmatic.

tıksır·ık A suppressed sneeze. ~**mak**, to sneeze with the mouth shut.

tılâ (·ᷢ) Gold ink or paint; ointment. ~ **etm.**, to smear; to rub in (an ointment etc.).

tılsım Talisman; charm; spell. ~ **bozmak**, to break a spell : ~**ı bozuldu**, the spell is broken; he (it) no longer has any influence. ~**lı**, having a charm or spell; spell-binding.

tım In ⌐**kim kime** ~ ~**a** (or **dum duma**)⌐, nobody will take any notice; nobody knows (knew) anything about it!

tımar Attention to a sick man or beast; dressing of wounds; grooming a horse; pruning of trees; formerly a kind of fief granted by the Sultan to soldiers. ~ **etm.**, to groom. ~**cı**, holder of a fief.

tımarhane (···ᵎ) Lunatic asylum. ~ **kaçkını**, escaped lunatic : ⌐~**cinin gözü kör olsun !**⌐, 'damn the asylum warder (for letting you escape)!', you ought to be shut up!

tın tın Imitates metallic sounds.

tınaz Stack of hay or corn. ~ **gibi**, a whole heap of ... .

tıngadak (ᵎ··) Imitates the sound of a thing falling.

tıngıldamak etc. v. **tıngırdamak** etc.

tıngır or ~**sız** (sl.) Stony-broke. ~ ~ or ~ **mıngır**, imitates the sound of metallic things knocking together; cash down. ~**damak**, to tinkle, clink, clang. ~**tı**, clinking, clanking noise; noisy conviviality.

tınlamak vn. Tinkle, ring (of metal etc.).

tınmak vn. Make a sound; usually only in a negative form. **tınmamak**, not to utter a sound; to take no notice; to pretend not to see or hear : **tınmayıvermek**, simply to take no notice : **tınmaz**, who pays no attention, who takes no notice; who says nothing; **tınmaz melâike** (*iron.*), quiet, aloof; non-committal.

tınnet, –ti Tone; timbre.

tıp *v.* **tıb.**

tıpa, tapa Stop; plug; cork; mop *for oiling guns*; fuse.

tıpatıp ($\cdot \cdot$) Exactly; absolutely. ~ **yetişmek,** to arrive exactly on time : **hakikate** ~ **uygun olmayan,** not entirely in accordance with the truth.

tıpır·damak *vn.* Make a noise as of drops falling; walk with little noise; (of the heart) to go pit-a-pat. ~**dı,** sound of drops falling *or* of light footsteps.

tıpış tıpış *Imitates the noise of the small steps of a child.* ~ ~ **gitmek,** to walk with small steps; to go willy-nilly.

tıpkı ($\cdot \cdot$) Exactly like; in just the same way. ~**sı,** exactly like it; the very image of ... .

tırabzan Hand-rail; banister. ~ **babası,** newel, post with knob at the end of a banister; a father who has no influence over his children.

tıraş Shaving; the hair which grows between shaves; boring talk; bragging ~ **etm.,** to shave; to cut; to tell lies to, to take *s.o.* in; to bore : ~**ı gelmiş (uzamış),** needing a shave : ~ **olm.,** to shave oneself, to get a shave : ~**a tutmak,** to detain *s.o.* by idle talk; to buttonhole *s.o.*

tıraş·çı, boring talker; braggart; swindler. ~**ide** ($\cdot$——^{1}), pared; smoothed; polished (style). ~**lamak,** to prune; to thin out trees. ~**lı,** needing a shave; shaved, clean-shaven, unbearded (*the context will usually show which of these contradictory meanings is right*) : ~ **geldi,** he came unshaved.

tırfıl Trefoil; clover.

tırhallı *v.* **turhallı.**

tırhandil Small boat *used in the Mediterranean and either rowed or sailed.*

tırık *Imitates the noise of two hard things striking against each other; usually used with* **tırak.**

tırıklamak *va.* (*sl.*) Steal.

tırıl Naked; thinly clad; 'stony-broke'. ~ ~, shivering. ~**lamak,** to shiver with cold; to be 'broke'. ~**lık,** a being 'stony-broke'.

tırıs Trot. ~ **gitmek,** to trot. ⌐**bana** ~ **gider**⌐, I don't care two hoots!

tırkaz Bar behind a door to keep it shut.

tırmak *v.* **tırmık.**

tırma·lamak *va.* Scratch; worry, annoy; offend (the ears, the taste). ~**nmak,** to cling with the claws *or* the finger-tips : ⸱⸱⸱**e** ~, to climb (a tree, a mountain *etc.*).

~**şmak,** to climb by the claws *or* fingers *or* toes.

tırmık Scratch; rake; harrow; drag-hook. ~**lamak,** to scratch, rake, harrow.

tırnak Finger-nail; toe-nail; claw; hoof; ejector *of a gun*; fluke *of an anchor*; catch (*mech.*). ~ **çekici,** claw-hammer : ~ **işareti,** inverted commas : ⌐**tırnağının kiri bile olamaz**⌐, 'he couldn't be even the dirt in his finger-nails', he's not fit to lick his boots : **tırnağını* sökmek,** to torture : **birine** ~ **takmak,** to have one's knife into a person : **dişinden tırnağından artırmak,** to pinch and scrape : **dişi tırnağı döküldü,** he worked himself to death : **tepeden tırnağa,** from head to foot.

tırnak·çı, pickpocket. ~**lamak,** to scratch with the nails. ~**lı,** having nails *or* claws; spiked (wheel).

tırpan Scythe; trepan. ⸱⸱⸱**e** ~ **atmak,** to exterminate.

tırpana ($\cdot \cdot$) Skate (fish).

tırtık Unevenness; raw spot. ~ ~, uneven, jagged; fleecy (cloud). ~**çı** (*sl.*), pickpocket; rogue. ~**lamak,** to pull to pieces; pluck; rob. ~**lı,** rough; uneven; jagged.

tırtıl Caterpillar; milling *of a coin*; knurl; perforation *of a stamp*. ~**lı,** having a milled edge : ~ **tekerlek,** caterpillar wheels.

tırtır Tartar.

tıs Goose's hiss. ~ !, hush! : ~ **dememek,** not to make the slightest noise; not to raise the slightest objection. ~**lamak,** to hiss like a goose; to spit like a cat.

tıynet, –ti Temperament, disposition; natural character. ~**siz,** of low character.

ti *In* ~ **işareti,** a bugle call.

ticaret ($\cdot$—^{1}), **–ti** Trade, commerce; profit. ~**i bırakmak,** to show a profit : ~ **etm.,** to engage in commerce; to earn, make a profit : **T~ Odası,** Chamber of Commerce. ~**gâh,** centre of commerce; business quarter : having an active commerce. ~**hane** ($\cdot$—$\cdot$—^{1}), business house; firm; place where a man has his business. ~**li,** profitable.

ticarî ($\cdot$—^{1}) Commercial.

tifo ($\cdot \cdot$) Typhoid fever.

tiftik Mohair; fine soft wool *clipped from sheep in spring.* ~ ~ **etm.,** to unravel, to pull into threads : ~ **gibi,** very soft : ~ **kecisi,** Angora goat : **keten tiftiği,** lint. ~**lenmek,** to become unravelled *or* frayed.

tifüs ($\cdot \cdot$) Typhus.

tiğ (–) Sword.

tik[1], **–ki** Teak.

tik[2], **–ki** (*Fr. tic*) Twitching; mannerism, trick.

tike ($\cdot \cdot$) Piece, patch. ~ ~, patched.

tiksin·mek *vn.* (*with abl.*) Be disgusted with; loathe. ~**ti**, disgust; loathing.

tilâvet (·—¹), **–ti** Religious reading *or* chanting.

tilki Fox; cunning fellow. ⌜~**nin dönüp dolaşıp geleceği yer kürkçü dükkânıdır**⌝, 'the fox after all his wanderings will end up in the furrier's shop'; (i) you (he) will end up there anyhow; (ii) you (he) can't help coming back here (or to the same job) however hard you try to avoid it: ~ **tırnağı**, the Spotted Orchis *from which the drink* salep *is made*. ~**leşmek**, to become crafty. ~**lik**, craftiness.

tilmiz Disciple; pupil.

tim Team.

timi A gipsy game; swelling *caused by the bite of an insect*.

timsah (·¹) Crocodile.

timsal (·⁴), **–li** Image, picture, representation; symbol; model, example.

tin *In* ~ ~ **yürümek**, (of a baby) to toddle; (of a very old man) to toddle along briskly; to move with unexpected agility.

tip, –pi (*Fr. type*) Type; queer specimen.

tipi Blizzard, snow-storm. ~**lemek**, to blow a blizzard, snow heavily.

tipik Typical.

tipula *In* ~ **kurdu**, leather-jacket : ~ **sineği**, crane-fly, daddy-longlegs.

tir¹ (–) Arrow.

tir² *As* tiril *q.v.*

tiraj (*Fr. tirage*) Circulation *of a newspaper*.

tirak *v.* tiryak.

tiramola (··¹·) *Naut. interj.* Haul (on a rope)! A kind of capstan. ~ **etm.**, to tack ship; to go about.

tirandaz Popular form of tirendaz, *but meaning* trim, well-dressed; dexterous, skilful.

tirbuşon (*Fr. tire-bouchon*) Corkscrew.

tirdan Quiver.

tire¹ Sewing cotton. Cotton (*a.*).

tire² (*Fr. tiret*) Dash, hyphen.

tirendaz Archer; *v. also* tirandaz.

tirenti (·¹·) Fall (of a pulley); boat-falls.

tirfillenmek *vn.* Become threadbare.

tirid Bread soaked in gravy; feeble old man. **suyuna** ~, without substance; perfunctory : **suyuna** ~ **geçinmek**, to live on next to nothing. ~**leşmek**, to become old and feeble.

tiril *In* ~ ~ **titremek**, to tremble like an aspen leaf. ~**demek**, to shiver.

tirit *v.* tirid.

tiriz Lath, batten; moulding (*architecture*); piping (*dressmaking*).

tirkeş Quiver.

tirlin (*Fr. tire-ligne*) Drawing-pen.

tirpidin, tirpit. Small mattock.

tirsi balığı, –nı Shad.

tirşe Vellum. Pale green.

tiryak Theriac; antidote to poison. ~**i** (·—¹), addicted to alcohol, tobacco, opium *etc.*; tiresome, 'difficile'; great smoker; addict *to anything*; **tavla** ~**si**, keen backgammon player. ~**ilik**, a being addicted to *stg.*; the thing to which one is addicted; obsession; smoking.

titiz Peevish, captious, hard to please, 'difficile'; fastidious, sensitive; meticulous, particular, extremely careful. ~**lenmek**, to be tiresome and hard to please; to become annoyed. ~**lik**, peevishness, captiousness, irritability; a being too punctilious *or* fastidious; pedantry; extreme accuracy, great attention to detail; delicacy, sensitivity; fastidiousness.

titre·k Trembling. ~ **kavak**, aspen. ~**me**, trembling; vibration. ~**mek**, to shiver; to tremble : ···**in üzerine** ~, to love *s.o.* so tenderly that one is always on tenterhooks about him. ~**şmek**, (of two or more) to tremble *or* shiver together.

tiyatro (·¹·) Theatre. ~**cu**, theatre owner; actor.

tiz High-pitched. **yarım ton** ~, sharp (*mus.*).

tizreftar (⌐·̱··) Quick-paced. ⌜~ **olanın payına damen dolaşır**⌝, 'the skirts of one in haste get entangled with his legs', ⌜more haste less speed⌝.

toğdarı The Greater Bustard.

toğrul Gerfalcon (?).

tohaf *v.* tuhaf.

tohum Seed; grain; semen; eggs (of insects). ~**a kaçmak** *or* **bağlamak**, to go to seed; ~**a kaçmış**, *also* aged, past its prime : **fesad** ~**u saçmak**, to sow sedition *or* discontent. ~**luk**, suitable for seed; kept for breeding; garden bed : ~ **buğday**, seed wheat.

tok Satiated; full; deep (voice); closely-woven, thick (cloth). ⌜~ **ağırlamak güç olur**⌝, 'it is hard to feast one whose belly is full', *i.e.* it is hard to do a favour to one who has no need of one : ⌜~ **evin aç kedisi**⌝, well off but still not content : ~ **gözlü**, contented; not covetous : ~ **satıcı**, a reluctant seller, one who has no need to sell at once : ~ **sözlü**, who does not mince his words, outspoken : ~ **tutmak**, (of a food) to be filling : **gözü** ~, contented, free from greed, not self-seeking : **karnım** ~, I am not hungry : I can't be taken in *by that sort of talk*.

toka¹ Buckle. ~**lı**, having a buckle; buckled.

toka² A shaking hands; a clinking glasses. ~ **etm.**, to shake hands; to clink glasses;

tokaç (*sl.*) to give, pay. **~laşmak**, to shake hands.

tokaç Mallet; bat *for beating out washing.*

tokat Cuff, box on the ears. **···e ~ aşketmek** (atmak) *or* **···i ~lamak**, to give *s.o.* a box on the ears.

tokaz *v.* tokuz.

toklu Having pendent glands (goat); yearling lamb.

tokluk Satiety; thickness *or* density *of cloth.* **boğaz tokluğuna çalışmak**, to work in return for one's board.

tokmak Mallet; beetle (*implement*); doorknocker; clapper *of a bell*; wooden pestle; block of wood *used as a seat*; balls of flour. **~ gibi**, chubby (baby).

tokur *In ~* alınlı, with a protruding forehead.

tokurcun Stook *of wheat etc.*; *a game played with pebbles or marbles.*

tokur·datmak *va.* Make *a hookah* bubble. **~tu,** the bubbling noise of a hookah.

tokuş *v.* dokuş.

tokuş·mak *vn.* Butt one another; collide. **~turmak**, to cause to collide; to clink *glasses*; to cannon (billiards).

tokuz Thick, closely-woven (cloth).

tolga¹ Helmet.

tolga² *v.* tavulga.

toloz Arched vault.

tomar Roll *or* scroll (of paper *etc.*). Cylindrical. **top ~ı,** rammer *or* swab *for a gun.*

tombak Gold-plated copper; copper zinc alloy.

tombalak Round as a ball; plump.

tombaz Barge; punt; pontoon. **~lardan yapılmış sal,** ferry (*mil.*); **zincirli ~,** chainferry.

tombola (¹··) Tombola; lotto.

tombul Plump.

tomruk Bud; heavy log; stocks (punishment); square boulder; prison. **~ vurmak,** to put in the stocks. **~lanmak,** to put forth buds.

tomşuk Curved beak *like that of a parrot.*

tomurcuk Bud.

ton¹ (*Fr. thon*) Preserved tunny.

ton² Ton. **~aj,** tonnage.

tondura Tundra.

tonel *Vulg. for* tünel, *only in* **~ geçmek** (*sl.*), to be absent-minded, to be wool-gathering.

tonga Trap, trick. **~ya basmak** (düşmek), to fall into a trap, to be deceived.

tonilâto (··¹·) Tonnage; ton. **~luk,** having a tonnage of ...; a ton's weight of ... .

tonluk Of *so many* tons.

tonoz¹ Vault.

tonoz² **~ etm.**, to warp *a ship*: **~ balığı,** tunny: **~ demiri,** kedge-anchor.

tonton Darling.

top¹, –pu Round; collected together; in a mass. Ball; any round thing; cannonball; the whole mass of anything; a whole; roll (of cloth or paper). **~ ~,** in groups, in lumps; **~u ~u,** in all: **~tan,** wholesale; as a whole: **~unuz,** all of you: **~unu birden,** one and all: **~ gibi,** willy-nilly, without question.

top², –pu Gun, cannon. **~ atmak,** to fire a gun: **~ or ~u atmak,** to 'go bust'; to be 'ploughed' *in an exam.*: **~un ağzında,** the one most in danger: **~a tutmak,** to bombard *a place*: **~ yoluna gitmek,** to be uselessly sacrificed.

topaç Top (plaything), teetotum; the thick rounded part of a Turkish oar. **~ gibi,** sturdy (child).

topak Roundish lump; inner side of a horse's fetlock. Short and fat.

topal Lame. Cripple. ⌐**~ eşekle kervana karışmak**⌐, 'to join a caravan with a lame donkey', to undertake stg. with inadequate means. **~lamak**, to limp. **~lık,** lameness.

topalan, topalak (?) Buckthorn.

topaltı, –nı Field of fire *of a gun*; terreplein *of a fort.*

toparlak Round. Limber (*mil.*).

topar·lamak *va.* Collect together; pack up; roll up (*mil.*). **kendini ~,** to pull oneself together. **~lanmak,** *vn. pass. of* toparlamak, to be collected together *etc.*; to pull oneself together.

topatan An early oblong kind of melon.

topçeker Large gunboat; tractor for pulling guns.

topçu Artilleryman; gunner; the artillery; (*sl.*) one who looks like being 'ploughed' in an exam. **~luk,** gunnery; duties and profession of a gunner.

topla Three-pronged winnowing fork.

toplamak *va.* Collect together; convene; gather; sum up; fold up (clothes); tidy up; clear away; put on weight. **ağzını topla!,** shut up! *said to a person who is insulting one*: **aklını başına ~,** to collect one's wits, to pull oneself together: **kendini ~,** to recover *from an illness.*

toplan·ılmak *vn. impers. form of pass. of* toplamak; *as* toplanmak. **~mak** *vn.*, to collect, assemble, come together; regain one's health; put on flesh; (of a boil) to come to a head: **derlenip ~,** to pull oneself together. **~tı,** assembly, gathering, meeting.

toplaşmak *vn.* Gather together; (of a dish cooking) to get hard lumps in it.

toplu Having a knob *or* round head; compact; collected together, in a mass; well-arranged, tidy; plump; collective; (*for*

~ **iğne)** pin. ~ **ateş,** concentrated fire
(*mil.*): ~ **iğne,** pin: **derli** ~, orderly, tidy.
~**luk,** a being collected together; compact-
ness; community; gathering: ‖ ~ **ismi,**
collective noun.

toprak Earth; soil; land; the grave.
Earthen; earthenware; made of clay;
earth-coloured. ~ **altı,** the subsoil:
ʳ**toprağı bol olsun!**ʰ, 'may he rest in
peace!' (*referring to s.o. dead*): ~ **boya,**
paint in powder form: ʳ**gözlerini ~ doyur-**
sunʰ, they won't be satisfied till they are
dead, *said of very rapacious people*: ~
sokak, unpaved street: **eski** ~, old but well-
preserved (person): **kara** ~, the grave.

toprak·bastı, tax on goods or beings entering a town. ~**lamak,** to cover with earth.

toptan Wholesale; in the mass. ~**cı,**
wholesaler. ~**cılık,** wholesale trading.

toptaşı (¹··), **–nı** *Name of a district in*
Istanbul where there was a well-known
lunatic asylum, hence: a lunatic asylum;
Bedlam. ~**ndan farksız,** a regular Bedlam:
~**na göndermeli,** he ought to be shut up.

topu topu In all; all told.

topuk Heel; ankle; fetlock; bar *of a river*;
heel *of a shoe*; heel *of a mast.* ~ **çalmak,**
(of a horse) to 'brush' the fetlock of one
foot with the shoe of the opposite foot.

topuz Mace; knob (on a stick *etc.*); knot of
hair. Short, thick (man).

topyekûn (¹··) Total.

tor Net; tissue. ~**ağ,** fine-meshed fishing-
net.

torak Charcoal pit; kiln; dried skim milk.

toraman Young, wild and untamed.
Robust young man; pet animal.

torba Bag; scrotum; cyst. ~**dakiler,**
something, hitherto unsuspected, in a
man's nature: ~ **yoğurdu,** yaourt strained
in a bag: ʳ**ağzında ~ mı var?**ʰ, have you
lost your tongue?: ʳ**olan oldu ~ doldu**ʰ,
what has happened has happened: **yem(lik)**
~**sı,** nose-bag.

torik Large **palamut.**

torina (·¹·) Grampus.

torlak Unbroken colt; wild youth. ʳ**hiç**
yoktan ~ yektirʰ, better an unbroken colt
than no horse at all.

torluk Mud hut; charcoal kiln.

torna (¹·) Lathe. ~ **etm.,** to turn *on a*
lathe: ~ **aynası,** potter's wheel; lathe
chuck. ~**cı,** turner.

tornavida (··¹·) Screwdriver.

tornistan¹ (¹··) **etm.** *vn.* Go astern; give
up a project *etc.*

tornistan² (¹··) Turned (suit of clothes).

Toros Taurus.

torpil Mine (explosive); torpedo; (*sl.*) a
'friend at court'. ~**lemek,** to torpedo.

torpito, torpido Torpedo; torpedo-boat.
~ **kovanı,** torpedo-tube.

tortop (¹·) Quite round.

tortu Deposit; dregs; sediment. **şarab** ~**su,**
crude tartar. ~**lu,** having sediment; turbid.

torun Grandchild; two-year-old camel.

tos A blow with the head. ~ **vurmak,** to
butt. ~**lamak,** to butt; (of a ship) to have
a slight collision *or* (*sl.*) to pitch; (*sl.*) to
pay.

tostoparlak (¹···) Quite round.

tosun Young bull; fine robust young man.

toy¹ The Greater Bustard. Raw, inexperienced, 'green', amateur. **göl** ~,
curlew.

toy² Banquet.

toygar A kind of lark.

toyluk Inexperience; rawness.

toz Dust; powder. Like dust; in powder
form. ~ **almak,** to dust: ~**u dumana**
katmak (karışmak), to raise clouds of
dust; to make a great ado; to create confusion: ~ **etm.,** to raise the dust: ~ **kopar-**
mak, to kick up a dust: ~ **silkmek,** to beat
out the dust, to dust; ~**unu silkmek,** to
give s.o. 'a dusting': **ayağının** ~**u ile,** at
the moment of arrival, without delay:
hatırınıza ~ konmasın (amma), don't take
offence, but ..., *said when about to say stg.*
that might hurt a person's feelings: **ortalığı**
~ **pembe görmek,** to see the world through
rose-coloured spectacles: ···**in üzerine ~**
kondurmamak, not to allow anything to be
said against ..., not to hear any criticism
of ... .

toz·amak, to raise the dust: ʳ**vurdukça**
tozuyorʰ, the more one beats, the more
dust there is, *i.e.* the more one insists the
worse one makes it. ~**armak,** to become
dust; to go to powder. ~**koparan,** place
exposed to strong winds. ~**lanmak,** to
become dusty. ~**lu,** dusty. ~**luk,**
gaiter; dusty place.

tozmak In **gezip** ~, to saunter about and
enjoy oneself.

toz·pembe (¹··) *v.* **toz.** ~**untu,** any fine
thing like dust: **gezinti** ~, stroll, excursion. ~**utmak,** to raise a dust; to go too
far, become unreasonable; to go mad.

töhmet, –ti Suspicion that s.o. is guilty of
a crime; imputation; guilt; offence. ~**li,**
under suspicion; guilty. ~**siz,** not
suspected; innocent.

tökesimek, tökezlemek *vn.* Stumble.

tömbeki The Persian tobacco *smoked in*
hookahs.

töre Custom; rule; law.

‖ **tören** Ceremony; celebration.

törpü Rasp; file. **ömür** ~**sü,** an exhausting task; a trying person. ~**lemek**, to rasp, file.

törü v. töre.

tövbe Repentance; vow not to repeat an offence. ~!, pax!; enough!: ···**e** ~ **etm.**, to repent having done *stg.* and vow not to do it again: ~ **istiğfar**, to repent and ask God's pardon: ~**ler olsun!**, I'll never do it again!: ~**ler** ~**si**, *as* ~**ler olsun**, *but more emphatic; also in such phrases as*: '~**ler** ~**si bu adam gene geldi**', Good Heavens! that man's come again!: **yedi ceddine** ~ **etm.**, to swear one will give up *stg.* for good and all.

tövbe·kâr, penitent: ~ (**kadın**), reformed prositute. ~**li**, penitent; under a vow not to sin again *or* not to do stg. again.

töz *Word used to back an animal.* ~**kürmek**, to back (a horse). ~**kürü**, (of a horse) backwards.

Trablus (¹·) Tripoli. ~**ugarb**, Tripoli in Africa: ~**uşŞam**, Tripoli in Syria.

Trabzon (¹·) Trebizond. ~ **hurması**, dateplum: *v. also* **tırabzan.**

trahom Trachoma.

trahoma (·¹·) Dowry (of a non-Moslem).

trahunya, trakonya (·¹·) Greater Weever fish.

trak v. **trank.**

Trakya (¹·) Thrace.

trampa (¹·) Barter; exchange. ~ **etm.**, to exchange one thing for another.

trampete (.¹.) Side drum.

tramplen (*Fr. tremplin*) Spring-board.

tramvay Tram. ~**cı**, tram-driver.

trank *Imitates the clanking of metal (usually in connexion with the payment of cash).*

transit, –**ti** Passage of goods without paying custom dues; through (traffic).

traş, traşide v. **tıraş.**

trata (¹·) Small fishing smack.

travers (*Fr. traverse*) Railway sleeper. ~**e** **çıkmak**, to sail to windward by tacking.

tren, tiren Train.

trimestr School term.

tringa (¹.) (*sl.*) Smart, chic.

trinketa (·¹·) Foresail.

trişin Trichina.

trup, –**pu** Troupe; theatrical company.

tu *Interj.* expressing disgust.

tuba (–¹) *Name of a tree in Paradise, supposed to have its roots in the sky and its leaves in the earth;* happiness, good fortune.

tufalamak va. (*sl.*) Pinch, pilfer.

tufan (–¹) Violent rainstorm; flood; the Flood.

tufeyli (··¹) Parasite; sponger; toady.

tufuliyet (·–·¹), –**ti** Infancy.

tuğ Horse-tail *attached to a helmet or flag-*

staff as a sign of rank. **üç** ~ **vermek**, to confer three horse-tails (*i.e.* the highest rank of Pasha): **yedi** ~ **çıkmak**, to go forth with seven horse-tails (*i.e.* for the Sultan to take the field).

|| **tuğ·amiral** Rear-Admiral. ~**ay**, brigade. ~**bay**, brigadier. ~**general**, brigadier-general.

tuğla (¹·) Brick. ~ **harmanı**, brick-yard. ~**cı**, brickmaker.

tuğlu Wearing a crest of horsehair *v.* **tuğ.** **üç** ~ **paşa**, a Pasha of three horse-tails, *i.e. of the highest rank.*

tuğra v. **tura.** The Sultan's monogram. ~**keş**, *employee in the office where the imperial monogram was inscribed on documents.*

tuğyan A breaking bounds; overflowing, flooding; insubordination, rebellion. ~ **etm.**, to overflow; to rebel.

tuhaf Uncommon; curious, odd; comic, amusing. ~! *or* ~ **şey!**, that's odd!, how curious!: ~**ıma gitti**, it seemed odd to me: **işin** ~**ı**, the odd thing about it is ... . ~**çı**, *v.* **tuhafiyeci.** ~**iye** (·–·¹), millinery, drapery. ~**iyeci**, milliner, draper, fancydealer. ~**lık**, a being odd *or* funny: ~ **yapmak**, to make funny remarks.

tul (–), –**lü** Length; longitude. ~ **dairesi**, meridian: ~**ümerc, mevc** ~**ü**, wave-length: ~**ü emel sahibi**, worldly minded. ~**ânî** (––¹), longitudinal; in length. ~**en** (–¹·), in length; lengthwise. ~**î** (–¹), longitudinal.

tulga Helmet.

tulû (·¹), –**ûu** Rising *of the sun or a star;* appearance *of a tooth etc.;* birth *of an idea.* ~**at**, –**tı**, sudden ideas; improvisations; *as sing.* popular theatre *where the actors improvise.* ~**atçı**, actor who improvises.

tuluç (?) Snipe.

tulum, tuluk Skin made into a bag *to hold water etc., or used as a float for a raft* (**kelek**); tube *for toothpaste etc.;* overalls; pair of fur squares *for making into a cloak.* ~ **gibi** *or* **yağ** ~**u**, as fat as a pig: ~ **peyniri**, a kind of cheese made in a skin.

tulumba (·¹·) Pump; fire-engine; waterspout. ~ **tatlısı**, a sweetmeat *made of dough soaked in syrup.* ~**cı**, a member of the old independent fire brigades; a rough, rowdy; an unmannerly youth: ~ **koğuşu**, a dormitory for firemen; an assembly of roughs.

tulun Full moon.

tuman Long wide drawers *or* trousers.

tumba (¹·) Tilting-truck; a turning upside down; (of children) a tumbling into bed.

tumturak Bombast; pompous speech. ~**lı**, bombastic; high:flown.

Tuna The Danube.

tunc Bronze.

Tunus (ˌ·) Tunis. ~ **gediği,** a thing got without trouble; a rich woman married for her money. ~**lu,** Tunisian.

tur[1] (*Fr. tour*) Tour; promenade.

tur[2] *In* ~ **yağı,** a vegetable oil *made at a factory called Tur.*

tura (ˌ·), **tuğra** The Sultan's monogram; the imperial cipher; skein (of silk *etc.*); a game *played with a knotted handkerchief.* **yazı mı** ~ **mı?,** heads or tails?; **yazı** ~ **atalım,** let's toss for it.

turac Francolin.

Turanî (——ˈ) Turanian.

turb(a) (*Fr. tourbe*) Peat (for fuel).

turfa Anything held unclean to eat by the Jews. Unclean; not fresh (food). ~ **olm.,** to fall into disesteem, to be despised. ~**lamak,** to despise, treat with contempt.

turfanda Early fruit *or* vegetables; (*jokingly*) novice, new. **son** ~, the last fruit *etc.* of the season. ~**lık,** garden for growing early fruit *etc.*

turgay A kind of lark.

turhalli (ˌ··) *Only in* ⌐**her halli** ~⌐ *or* ⌐~ **bir halli**⌐, everyone is in as bad a state as his neighbour; all in confusion.

turhan Nobleman; chief; prince.

Turisina Mount Sinai.

turlak *v.* torlak.

turlamak *va.* Make up into a bundle.

turna Crane (bird). ~ **balığı,** pike; garfish: ~ **geçidi,** spring storm: ~ **gözü,** colour of a crane's eye, light yellow: ⌐~**yı gözünden vurmak**⌐, to hit the mark (*fig.*); to do a good stroke of business: ~ **katarı,** a flock of cranes; a procession of people: ~ **kırı,** ashen grey colour.

turna·cı, *originally* a keeper of the cranes *at the Imperial Palace, later* the 73rd regiment of Janissaries. ~**gağası, –nı,** crane's bill, geranium.

turne (*Fr. tournée*) Tour.

turnike (*Fr. tourniquet*) Turnstile.

turnsol (*Fr. tournesol*), **turnusol, –lü** Dyer's croton; turnsole (purple dye); litmus paper.

turnuva (ˌ··) (*Fr. tournoi*) Tourney; tournament.

turp, –pu Radish. ~ **gibi,** robust, 'as sound as a bell': ⌐**aklına** ~ **sıkayım**⌐, (*sl.*), 'what rot!'

turre A lock of hair; a roll of any tissue; ball of silk wound from cocoons.

Tursina Mount Sinai.

turşu Pickle. ~ **gibi,** very weary: ~ **kesilmek** (olm.), to turn sour; (of food) to go bad; to become slack, to have no energy: ~ **kurmak,** to pickle; ⌐~**sunu mu kuracak-**

sın?⌐, 'do you want to pickle it?', *or* ⌐~**sunu kur!**⌐, 'pickle it!', *angry retorts to one who has refused to give stg.*; 'all right, keep it then!': ~ **suratlı (yüzlü),** sour-faced.

turşu·cu, maker and seller of pickles. ~**luk,** material suitable for pickling.

turuk, –ku *pl. of* tarik. Roads, ways.

turunc Seville orange. ~**u,** orange colour.

tuş (*Fr. touche*) Key (of piano, typewriter *etc.*).

tuta On account (part payment).

tutam *Amount that can be grasped by the fingers*; small handful; way of going on, behaviour.

tutamak Anything to be taken hold of; handle; habitual custom; proof, evidence; means of livelihood. ~ **bulmak,** to find a pretext: ~ **noktası,** stg. to catch hold of: ~ **vermek,** to afford a pretext. ~**lı,** provided with a handle *or* a grip; high-principled, to be depended on. ~**sız,** without a grip *or* handle *or* support; without principles, not to be depended on.

tutar Epilepsy, seizure, fit; total, sum. Holding, seizing, *v.* tutmak.

tutarak Seizure, fit; kindling wood, tinder. **tutarağı tuttu,** he had a seizure; he has a fit of obstinacy.

tutı (–ˈ) Parrot.

tutkal Glue; size. ~ **gibi,** *used of a person one can't get rid of*: **balık** ~**ı,** isinglass. ~**lamak,** to glue.

tutkun (*with dat.*) Affected by; given to; in love with.

tutma Act of holding; grip, hold.

tutmak 1. *va.* Hold; hold on to; keep, retain; preserve; take, catch, seize; stop, detain; esteem, account, reckon, suppose; contain, hold; agree with, tally with; take the part of, favour; listen to *advice etc.*; engage (servant); hire (house *etc.*); spread to, reach (a district); (of a ship) to touch at *a port*; (*sl.*) have as wife. 2. *vn.* Take root; (of seeds, grafts, vaccination *etc.*) to take; succeed; (of a curse) to take effect; hold on, endure, last; (of a sum of money, an account *etc.*) to amount to, to reach; stick, adhere; come into one's head, occur to one; (of rain *etc.*) to begin; (of an illness or pain) to come on, to attack one; (of wine *etc.*) to go to the head. **tutalım ki,** let us suppose that: **tutuyor musun?** (*sl.*), 'have you any cash?': **tuttu, İstanbula gitti,** it occurred to him to go to Istanbul: **atıp** ~, to blame, to criticize; to rant; to talk boastfully *or* airily: **ayağına çabuk tut!,** 'get a move on!': **başı*** ~, for one's head to ache *from noise or worry*: **birbirini tutmaz şeyler,** incompatible things;

things that don't make sense: **bu listeler birbirini tutmuyor**, these lists do not tally: **bu on lirayı borcunuza tutacağım**, I will consider these ten pounds as part payment of your debt: **deniz (tren** *etc.***)** ∼, for the sea (a train *etc.*) to cause one to feel sick: ···**den tutun da** ... **kadar**, starting from ... to ..., e.g. 'kazma kürekten tutunuz da traktörlere kadar her turlu âletler', 'every kind of implement from picks and shovels to tractors': **dişim tuttu**, my tooth has begun to ache again: **dümen (***etc.***) tutmuyor**, the rudder (*etc.*) is not working, is having no effect: **elinden** ∼, to give s.o. a helping hand: **elini çabuk tut!**, get on with the job!: **ev** ∼, to rent a house: **iş** ∼, to work, to have a job: **kar tutmadı**, the snow did not lie: **kendimi tutmadım**, I could not restrain myself, I could not help ...: ···**i lâfa** ∼, to detain *s.o.* by talking to him: **bu dükkân bir turlu müşteri tutmuyor**, this shop attracts no customers: **bir işi sağlam** ∼, to start stg. on a sound basis: **sözünü*** ∼, to keep one's word: ···**in sözünü** ∼, to listen to ..., to take *s.o.'s* advice: **şahid** ∼, to bring forward as a witness: **hiç bir yerim tutmuyor**, I feel rotten all over: **yolu** ∼ (*sl.*), to make off, to clear out: ···**e yüzü* tutmamak**, not to have the face to ..., not to dare to ...: **o akşam sinemaya gideceğimiz tuttu**, we took it into our heads to go to the cinema that evening: **bunu görenin güleceği tutar**, anyone seeing this would feel like laughing: **ben altmışı tuttum**, I was in my sixties: **herifin edebsizliği tutunca da tutar ha!**, when the fellow is rude, he *is* rude.

tutsak Prisoner, captive. ∼**lık**, captivity.

tutturmak *va. caus. of* tutmak. Cause to hold *etc.*; begin; cause to catch on *or* succeed. *vn.* Begin and continue; hit the mark; keep bothering *s.o.* to do *stg.* (like a spoilt child). **tuttura bildiğini fiatı istemek** *or* **tuttura bildiğine satmak**, (of a shopkeeper *etc.*) to ask a price *or* to sell at a price without regard to real value but only thinking of the maximum he can get out of any particular customer.

tutuk Paralysed; having had a stroke; stopped up; impeded; embarrassed; tonguetied; stuttering; slow, hesitant; (*sl.*) 'gone on', in love with. ∼**luk**, *any of the states described by* tutuk; breakdown, stoppage. **göğüs tutukluğu**, shortness of breath.

tutulma *verb. n. of* tutulmak. Act of being held *etc.*; a falling in love. **güneş** ∼**sı**, an eclipse of the sun: **dil** ∼**sı**, an impediment of speech; a being tongue-tied.

tutulmak *vn. pass. of* tutmak. Be held *etc.*; be struck with, fall in love with;

be angered; succeed, catch on; be stopped up; be closed; be rented *or* hired; be seized with illness; stutter, be tongue-tied. ···**e** ∼, to fall in love with, to be mad about ...; to be furious with ...: **ay tutuldu**, the moon is in eclipse: **boynu*** ∼, to have a stiff neck: **dili*** ∼, to be tongue-tied; to be struck dumb *by fear etc.*: ⌐**hay dilin tutulasıca!**⌐, 'curse your tongue!', *said to one who has said what he ought not to:* **elle tutulur**, tangible: **kendi ağzile tutuldu**, he is given away by his own words *or* he contradicts himself: **sesi** ∼, to become hoarse: **tifoya** ∼, to catch typhoid.

tutum Manner, conduct, procedure; economy, thrift. ∼**lu**, thrifty.

tutun *v.* tutmak *and* tutunmak.

tutunmak *va.* Apply to oneself; wear. *vn.* Hold on, cling, take a hold. **bu moda çabuk tutundu**, this fashion caught on quickly: **örtü** ∼, to put on a wrap: **sıkı tutun!**, hold tight!: **sülük** ∼, to apply leeches to oneself.

tutuş·mak *vn.* Catch hold of one another; quarrel; catch fire, be on fire; flare up *in anger*. **bahse** ∼, to bet: **etekleri*** *or* **eli* ayağı** ∼, to be in a great fright; to be in desperation: **kavgaya** ∼, to quarrel; to come to blows. ∼**turmak**, *va. caus. of* tutuşmak, to set on fire; set *persons* by the ears, cause to quarrel; press into a person's hand (*esp.* a bribe): ··· **için yanıp** ∼, to be violently in love with ... .

tutya (¹·) Zinc.

tuvalet (*Fr. toilette*), –**ti** Toilet; articles of toilet; toilet table; lavatory.

tuvana (·—¹) Strong.

tuyur *pl. of* tayır. Birds.

tuz Salt. ···**e** ∼ **ekmek**, to add salt to ...: ∼ **biber ekmek**, to make things worse; to be the last straw: **bu o işin** ∼**u biberidir**, this is a necessary addition; ∼**u biberi yerinde**, properly seasoned; nothing lacking, all right: ∼**la buz olm.**, to be smashed to bits; to be utterly routed: ∼ **ekmek hakkı**, gratitude towards a benefactor; ∼ **ekmek haini**, ungrateful to a benefactor: ∼**u kuru**, well-off, in easy circumstances; without worries: **ingiliz** ∼**u**, Epsom salts: **tadı** ∼**u yok**, tasteless, insipid.

tuzak Trap. ···**e** ∼ **kurmak**, to lay a trap for *s.o.*

tuz·la (¹·), ∼**lak** Saltpan; salt-mine. ∼**lama**, act of salting: salted; pickled in brine. ∼**lamak**, to salt, pickle in brine: ⌐**tuzlayım da kokma**⌐, *stg. like* 'utter nonsense!'; 'you must be off your head!' ∼**lu**, salt, salted; pickled; expensive: ∼ **oturmak** *or* ∼**ya mal olm.**, to cost dear. ∼**luca**, oversalted; rather expensive. ∼**luk**, salt-

cellar. ~**luluk,** saltiness, salinity. ~**ruhu**
(ˡ··), **–nu,** hydrochloric acid; spirit of
salt. ~**suz,** unsalted; insipid.
tüb Tube.
tüccar *pl. of* **tacir** *used as sing.* Merchant.
tüfek Gun, rifle. ~ **çatmak,** to pile arms.
dolu ~, 'a loaded gun', *said of a choleric
person*: **makinalı** ~, machine-gun. ~**çi**
gun-maker; armourer; (*formerly*) guard at
the Imperial Palace. ~**hane** (···ˡ),
armoury.
tüh *Interj. expressing regret or annoyance.*
~ **sana!,** shame on you!
tük·enmek *vn.* Be exhausted; come to an
end; give out. ~**enmez,** inexhaustible;
a kind of syrup *made of fruit juice, to which
water is constantly added.* ~**etmek,** to exhaust; use up; spend: **nefes** ~, to wear oneself out in trying to explain stg.: **sıfırı** ~,
to have come to the end of one's resources.
tükür·mek *va. & vn.* Spit; spit out.
tükürdüğünü yalamak, to eat one's words:
ᒧ**aşağı tükürsem sakalım, yukarı tükürsem
bıyığım¹,** 'if I spit down it will be my beard,
if I spit up, my moustache', I'm between
the devil and the deep blue sea: ᒧ**yüzüne
tükürsen yağmur yağıyor sana (der)¹,**
'if you spit in his face he tells you it's
raining', *said of one devoid of shame*:
ᒧ**birbirinin ağzına tükürmüş gibi¹,** 'as
though they had spit into each other's
mouths', *said of two people who give exactly
the same version of an event.*
tükürük, tükrük, spittle, saliva: ~
bezleri, salivary glands: ~ **otu,** Star of
Bethlehem, ornithogalum: **ağzında tükü-
rüğü kurudu,** he talked himself hoarse.
tül Tulle.
tülbend Muslin; gauze. ~ **kuruyuncaya
kadar,** in a very short time.
‖ **tüm·amiral** Vice-Admiral. ~**general,**
Major-General.
tümen Great number; great heap; ten
thousand; a Persian gold coin; division
(*mil.*). ~ ~, in vast numbers.
tümör Tumour.
tümsek Small mound; protuberance.
tümselmek *vn.* Rise *out of the ground*;
become round; be protuberant.
tün Night. ~**aydın,** good evening!
tünek Perch *in a hen-house etc.* ~**eklemek, tünemek,** to perch (of birds).
tünel Tunnel. ~ **geçmek,** *v.* tonel.
tüp Tube.
türab (·⁴) Earth; dust. ···**in ayağının** ~**ı
olm.,** to humiliate oneself before .... ~**î**
(·—⁴), pertaining to dust *or* earth; earthy:
tesviye ~**ye,** a levelling of the ground.
türâbâ (·—⁴) *Only in* **haraben** ~, tumble-
down, utterly ruined.

türbe Tomb, grave, mausoleum. ~**dar,**
keeper of a tomb.
türe·di One who has sprung up from anywhere; upstart; parvenu. ~**mek,** to spring
up suddenly; come into existence; appear.
Türk, –kü Turk. Turkish. ~**çe,** the Turkish language; in Turkish: ~**si,** in plain
Turkish, *i.e.* the long and the short of it
(*cf.* '*in plain English*'). ~**çü,** admirer and
supporter of Turkish language and culture.
~**iyat, –tı,** the study of things Turkish.
~**iye** (ˡ··), Turkey. ~**iyeli,** belonging to
or originating from Turkey. ~**leşmek,** to
adopt Turkish habits; become like a Turk.
~**lük,** the quality of being a Turk. ~**men,**
Turcoman.
türkü Folk-song. ~ **söylemek,** to sing:
ᒧ**kimin arabasına binerse onun** ~**sünü
çağırır¹,** he changes the tune to suit the
occasion.
türlü Sort, kind, variety; a dish of meat
with various kinds of vegetables. ~ ~, of
all sorts, various: ~**sünü görmek,** to have
varied experiences of *stg.*: **bir** ~, in some
way, somehow; (*with neg.*) in no way whatever, not at all; on no account; **bir** ~
yapamadı, he couldn't do it at all; **bir** ~
gelmedi, he just *wouldn't* come: **her** ~,
every sort of.
türrühat (··⁴), **–tı** Nonsense.
tüs *Only with* **tüy.** Down. **tüyü** ~**ü yok,**
the hair has not sprouted on his cheeks.
tütmek *vn.* (Of a chimney *etc.*) to smoke.
gözünde* (**burnunda***) ~, to be longed for;
bir böylesi gözümde tütüyor, I long for one
like that; **İstanbul burnunda tüttü,** he
longed for Istanbul; **pilâf burnumda
tütüyor,** oh! for a pilaf!: **toprakta bahar
tütüyordu,** the earth was seething with
spring.
tütsü Fumigation; fumigant; incense; the
use of incense in sorcery. ~**lemek,** to
fumigate; to cure *meat etc.* by smoking:
kafayı ~, to become tipsy. ~**lü,** fumigated;
smoked: **kafası** ~, befuddled, tipsy.
tütün Smoke; tobacco. ~ **balığı,** smoked
fish: ~ **içmek,** to smoke (tobacco). ~**cü,**
tobacconist; grower of tobacco. ~**lemek,**
to cure by smoking.
tüvan (·⁴) Power, strength. ~**a** (·—⁴),
strong, robust.
tüveyc Corolla.
tüy Feather; down; hair. ~ **gibi,** as light as
a feather, agile: ~**lerim ürperdi,** my hair
stood on end: (**dilde**) ~ **bitmek,** to be weary
of repeating *stg.*: **bu her şeye** ~ **dikti,** this
was the last straw. ~**kalem,** quill-pen.
~**lenmek,** to grow feathers; to start to
grow a beard; to be well-feathered, to be
rich. ~**lü,** feathered; well-to-do. ~**süz,**

unfeathered; unfledged; young. ~tüs, *v.* tüs.

tüymek *vn.* (*sl.*) Slip away.

|| tüzük Rules and regulations *of a society etc.*

U

ubudiyet (·–·ᵛ), –ti Loyal devotion to God; slavery, servitude.

ubur (·ᵛ) A passing; passage; crossing. ~ etm., to pass, cross: müruru ~, street traffic.

uc Tip, point; extremity; end; frontier; top; direction, course; cause, motive; steel pen; ploughshare. ~ ~a, end to end; point to point: ~dan ~a, from one extreme to the other: ~ bölüğü, leading company (*mil.*): ~u bucağı bulunmaz (yok), vast, endless: ~unu bulmak, to find a clue to *stg.*; to find a way of bringing *stg.* to a successful conclusion: ~u dokunmak, to involve *or* affect *one*; to entail: ~ ~a gelmek, to be just enough: ~u ~una getirmek *or* ~ ~a· karşılamak, to make both ends meet: ···in ~unu göstermek, to drop a hint of *stg. advantageous as an inducement*: ~unu kaçırmak, to lose the thread of a matter: ~unu altına kaçırmak, to be on the downward path (through mismanagement *etc.*): ~unu ortasını bulmak, to get to the bottom of a matter: bu işin ~u ortası belli değil, one doesn't know how to tackle this matter: işin ~unda para var, there is money to be made out of it: ···in ~unda bir şey olm., for there to be some secret purpose behind *stg.*: ~ vermek, to appear; to sprout, grow; (of a boil) to come to a head: bir meselenin alt'~u, the purpose *or* consequence of a matter: ayakların ~una basarak, on tiptoe: başı ~unda, by his side: burnunun ~unu görmemek, to be blind with pride: dilinin* ~una gelmek, for *stg.* to be on the tip of one's tongue (and which one refrains with difficulty from saying); dilinin* ~unda olm., to be on the tip of one's tongue (of *stg.* one is trying to recollect): dünyanın bir ~unda, at the other end of the world: ⌜dünyanın ~u uzundur⌝, the world is a very big place, *i.e.* all sorts of strange things happen: iki ~unu bir araya getirmek, to make both ends meet; to make a success of a business *etc.*

uca Stump; coccyx.

uclu Pointed; having a nib in it (penholder).

ucra (·–) Remote; out-of-the-way; solitary.

ucsuz Without a point; with no nib (penholder). ~ bucaksız, endless, vast.

ucube (––ᵛ) Strange thing; a wonder; curiosity; abortion; monstrosity.

ucun ucun Partially; bit by bit.

ucuz Cheap. ~ kurtulmak, to get off lightly; to escape cheaply: ~ satmak, to sell cheaply; to think *stg.* easy to get *or* do: sudan ~, dirt cheap. ~cu, who sells cheaply; bargain hunter. ~lamak, to become cheap, to go down in price. ~luk, cheapness; place where living is cheap.

uçak Climbing plant; || aeroplane. ~savar (·ᵛ··), anti-aircraft.

uçar Flying; volatile. ~ı, who flies in the face of all decency; dissolute: ~ çapkın, debauchee, rake: ~ takımından, an arrant scoundrel.

uçkun Spark. Flying.

uçkur Belt; band for holding up trousers. harama ~ çösmek, to have illegitimate sexual relations. ~luk, seam for passing band through top of trousers.

uçmak[1] *vn.* Fly; evaporate; fall *from a great height*; fade away, disappear; act outrageously, go beyond all bounds; be wild *with joy etc.* uçan kuşa borclu, in debt to everybody: benzi uçtu, he turned pale.

uçmak[2] Heaven, Paradise.

uçucu Flying; volatile.

uçuk[1] *In* rengi (benzi) ~, whose colour has fled, pale.

uçuk[2] Blain on the lips; vesicle; herpes. ~lamak, to have vesicles break out on the lips.

uçur·mak *va. caus. of* uçmak. Cause to fly *etc.*; fly (an aeroplane); exaggerate; boast about; praise excessively. kellesini ~, to cut off a person's head: kuş uçurmamak, to not let a living thing pass, to be very vigilant. ~tma, kite (paper). ~tmak, *va. caus. of* uçurmak, *but used as caus. of* uçmak, to cause *or* allow to fly *etc.* ~um, precipice; abyss.

uçuş Flight *of a plane.* ~ meydanı, landing-ground, aerodrome.

uçuşmak *vn.* Fly together, fly in a flock; fly about; flap the wings and fly noisily.

ud Lute. ~î (–ᵛ), lute player.

uf *Interj. expressing boredom, annoyance, fatigue.* ~ puf demek, to sigh, to express annoyance.

ufacık (ᵛ··) Very small, tiny.

ufak Small. ~ **tefek,** small; of no account; small and short (man); trifles, small things: ~ **tefek görmek,** to regard as of no account: **ekmek** ~**ları,** crumbs: **un** ~, as fine as flour. ~**lı,** *in* **irili** ~, large and small together. ~**lık,** ~**para,** small change; lice.

ufal·amak *va.* Reduce in size; break into small pieces; crumble; break up. ~**mak,** to become smaller, diminish. ~**tmak, ufatmak,** to reduce in size. ~**anmak, ufanmak** to be broken up small; crumble, disintegrate.

ufarak Smaller; very small.

ufk·an (⸱·) Horizontally. ~**î** (··⸱), horizontal. ~**u,** *v.* **ufuk.**

uflamak *vn.* Say 'oof' *expressing boredom or annoyance.*

ufucuk olm. (*Infantile*) be ill.

ufuk, –fku Horizon.

ufûl A sinking; setting (of the sun *etc.*); passing away *of a person.* ~ **etm.,** to pass away, die.

ufunet (·–⸱), **–ti** Putrefaction; putrid smell; inflammation. ~**lenmek,** to putrefy; become inflamed and putrid. ~**li,** putrefying; putrid; stinking (of an inflamed wound *etc.*).

uğalamak, uğmak *etc.,* *v.* **oğalamak** *etc.*

uğrak Place through which one passes. **seyyah uğrağı,** place frequented by travellers: **sert rüzgârlar uğrağı bir iklim,** a region swept by violent winds: **yol uğrağı,** place lying on one's road.

uğramak *va.* (*with dat.*) Stop *or* touch at *a place;* meet with (an accident); suffer (an illness); look in on *s.o.;* undergo (a change *etc.*). *vn.* Be possessed by an evil spirit: **ahalı sokağa uğramış,** everybody has come out into the street: **gözleri dışarıya uğramış,** his eyes started out of his head: ···**in semtine uğramamak,** not to go near ...: **sütçü her gün uğrıyor,** the milkman calls every day.

uğraş Struggle, fight. ~**mak,** to struggle or fight with one another; to strive hard, to take great pains: ···**le** ~, to be busy with *stg.;* to have a down on *s.o.* ~**tırmak,** *caus.* of **uğraşmak;** *also,* to cause annoyance to, to disturb.

uğratmak *va. caus.* of **uğramak.** Cause to stop at, *etc.;* cause to encounter: expose *s.o. to a danger etc.;* send away.

uğru¹ *v.* **uğur.**

uğru² Place touched at; line, direction; thief. ~**lamak,** to steal.

uğul·damak *vn.* Hum; buzz; (of the wind) to howl. ~**tu,** humming *or* buzzing noise; a singing in the ears.

uğur, –ğru Good luck; good omen; bird's dropping (*as an omen of good luck*). ~**lar olsun!,** good luck!; good journey! (*said to one departing*): ···**in uğruna (uğrunda),** for the sake of ...; on account of .... ~**lamak,** to wish *s.o.* good luck; bid godspeed to *s.o.,* see *s.o.* off *on a journey.* ~**lu,** lucky; auspicious: ~ **kademli,** bringing good luck, a happy omen: **ayağı** ~ **gelmek,** to bring luck. ~**samak,** to consider *stg.* to be a good omen, to regard as lucky. ~**suz,** inauspicious; bringing bad luck; ill-omened: rascal: **ayağı** ~ **gelmek,** to bring bad luck. ~**suzluk,** ill omen; a being unlucky.

uğuşturmak, uğuz *v.* **oğuşturmak, oğuz.**

uhde Obligation; charge; duty, responsibility. ···**in** ~**sinde olm.,** to be entrusted to ..., to be in the charge of ...: ···**in** ~**sinden gelmek,** to carry out the task of ..., to discharge the duty of ...: ~**sine geçirmek,** to charge *s.o.* with the duty *etc.* of ... .

uhrevî (··⸱) Pertaining to the next world.

uhud (·⸱) *pl.* of **ahid.** Contracts; obligations.

uhuvvet, –ti Brotherly feeling; brotherhood; affection; sincerity.

ukab Eagle; the constellation Aquila.

ukalâ (··⸱) *pl.* of **âkil.** Sages, wise people; *as sing.* wiseacre, know-all, prig. ~**dümbeleği, –ni,** pretentious quack; wiseacre. ~**lık,** quality of a wiseacre; pretence of being clever; conceitedness; wisecrack.

ukba (·⸱) The next world.

ukde, ukte Knot; ganglion; sore subject; stg. that sticks in the throat. **adamın içine** ~ **olur,** it's a thing one can't get over; it rankles: **hayat** ~**si,** nerve centre (*also fig.*).

uknum (·⸱) Root, basis; person of the Trinity.

ukubet (·–⸱), **–ti** Retribution; punishment (*esp.* in the next world); torture.

ukul (·⸱), **–lü** *pl.* of **akıl. erbabı** ~, wise men.

ulâ (·⸱) First; earliest. **kurunu** ~, ancient times: **rütbei** ~, first grade of civil functionaries.

Ulah Wallachian.

ulak Courier. **el ulağı,** messenger-boy, page: **bana el ulağı oluyor,** he helps me in small jobs.

ulama Consecutive, uninterrupted. Appendix. ~**k,** to join *one thing to another;* to bring into contact.

ulan My good fellow!; man alive!

ulaş·ık Reaching; touching; arrived. ~**mak,** (*with dat.*) reach, arrive at; come into contact with; meet; have an interview with. ~**tırma,** a causing to reach; communication: ~ **Bakanı,** Minister of Communications (Transport).

ulema ($\cdots\frac{\cdot}{\cdot}$) *pl. of* **âlim**. Learned men; ulema, doctors of Moslem theology. ~**yı rüsum**, *formerly* a hierarchy of theological scholars, *nowadays often used derogatively of the scholar class*.

uleyk Convolvulus, bindweed.

ulu¹ *pl. of* **zu**. Possessors of. ~**lemir**, rulers.

ulu² Great. Great man. ~**larımız**, our great men. ~**geyik**, red deer. ~**lamak**, to extol, honour. ~**lanmak**, to be honoured; to be puffed up. ~**luk**, greatness.

ulûfe (*Formerly*) the pay of a soldier for the fodder of his horse. ~**ci**, member of the old cavalry corps.

ulûm *pl. of* **ilim**. Sciences.

uluma The howling *of dogs*. ~**k**, to howl.

uluorta ($\cdot\cdot\cdot$) Openly; clearly; without reserve; rashly, recklessly. Unfounded, gratuitous (assertion).

ulus Tribe, *esp.* one of the four great Turanian tribes; people, nation.

uluşmak *vn.* Howl together in packs (wolves *etc.*).

ulüv, -vvü (*In compounds*) greatness, highness. ~**vücenab**, magnanimity: ~**vühimmet**, high aspirations.

ulvan ($\cdot\downarrow$) Haughtiness. ~ **satmak**, to be arrogant, to put on airs.

ulv·î ($\cdot\frac{\cdot}{\cdot}$) High; sublime; celestial. ~ **bir noktai nazar**, a lofty point of view. ~**iyat** ($\cdot\cdot\downarrow$), -**tı**, sublime *or* celestial matters. ~**iyet**, -**ti**, superiority; loftiness; sublimity.

umacı Ogre *or* bogy man (to frighten children).

umde Prop, support; principle; *a man who is the main prop and stay of an institution or cause*.

umk, -ku Depth; thickness (*as opp. to length and width*). ~**an** ($\cdot\cdot$), in depth.

umma Hope; expectation. $\cdots$**i** ~**ya uğratmak**, to disappoint *s.o.* ~**dık** ($\cdot\cdots$), unexpected.

ummak *va.* Hope; expect. ⌈**ummadığın taş baş yarar**⌉, 'it's the unexpected stone that wounds the head'; ⌈**misafir umduğunu değil, bulduğunu yer**⌉, 'the guest eats, not what he hoped for, but what he gets', one has to put up with what one finds.

umman ($\cdot\downarrow$) Ocean; the Indian Ocean.

umran ($\cdot\downarrow$) A being in good condition *or* well-built (of a house); a being well cultivated and prosperous (of a country). ~**î** ($\cdot-\frac{\cdot}{\cdot}$), pertaining to the good condition and prosperity of a land.

umud Hope.

umulmak *vn. pass. of* **ummak**. Be hoped *or* expected.

umum ($\cdot\downarrow$) General; universal; all. The public; people in general. ~**a açıktır**, open to all, free entry: ~ **millet**, the whole nation: ~ **muvacehesinde**, publicly, before everyone: ~ **müdür**, director-general.

umum·en ($\cdot\frac{\cdot}{\cdot}$), generally; universally. ~**hane** ($\cdots\cdot$), brothel. ~**î** ($\cdot-\frac{\cdot}{\cdot}$), general; universal; public: **efkâri** ~**ye**, public opinion: **emniyeti** ~**ye**, public security. ~**iyet** ($\cdot-\cdot$), -**ti**, generality; universality: ~**le**, in general: ~ **itibarile**, on the whole, as a whole; generally speaking.

umunmak *va.* Set one's hopes on.

umur ($\cdot\frac{\cdot}{\cdot}$) *pl. of* **emir**. Affairs; matters; *as sing.* a matter of importance; concern. ~**u devlet**, affairs of State: ~ **etmemek**, not to trouble about *stg.*: ~**unde* bile olmamak**, not to care; to be indifferent: **ne** ~**un?**, what's that to you?: **ne** ~**unda!**, what did he care! ~**samak**, to be concerned about: to consider important. ~**sanmak**, to become a matter of concern.

un Flour; meal. **has** ~, fine white flour: ⌈~**umu eledim, eleğimi duvara astım**⌉, 'I've sieved my flour and hung up my sieve', *i.e.* I've finished with this sort of thing; I'm too old; I've done it all before: ~ **ufak**, as fine as flour. ~**cu**, flour merchant.

unalmak *vn.* Heal up; be cured.

unarmak *va.* Mend; set to rights.

unf Roughness; harshness; violence. ~**en** ($\cdot\cdot$), roughly; violently. ~**î** ($\cdot\frac{\cdot}{\cdot}$), rough; harsh; violent.

unfuvan The first bloom of beauty *or* youth.

unk, -ku Neck.

un·lamak *va.* Sprinkle with flour. ~**lu**, prepared with flour; farinaceous.

un·madık ($\cdot\cdots$) Incurable; that will not heal. An unlucky person. ~**mak**, to heal; to get well. ~**maz**, that will not heal; incorrigible; unlucky.

unsur Element; root; component part. ~**î** ($\cdot\cdot\frac{\cdot}{\cdot}$), elemental.

unulmaz *v.* unmaz.

unut·kan Forgetful. ~**kanlık**, forgetfulness. ~**mabeni** ($\cdot\cdot\cdots$), forget-me-not.

unut·mak *va.* Forget. ⌈**(havada bulut) sen onu unut!**⌉, you'll never see it again. ~**ucu**, forgetful.

unvan ($\cdot\downarrow$) Title; superscription; address *on a letter*; show, parade; pride. ~ **satmak**, to give oneself out as; to give oneself airs: ~ **tezkeresi**, trading licence. ~**lı**, bearing the title of ...; entitled; who gives himself airs.

upuzun ($\cdot\cdots$) Extremely long.

ur Wen; tumour; goitre; excrescence.

urağan (*Fr.* ouragan) Hurricane.

urba *Pop. form of* ruba, dress, robe.

urban Bedouin Arabs.

urgan Rope.

uruc (·ᵛ) Ascent; ascension. ~ **etm.**, to ascend.

uruk, –ku *pl. of* ırk. Races.

urup *An old measure,* ⅛ *of an* **arşın,** *i.e. approx.* 3 *in.*

uryan *v.* üryan.

us Right state of mind; discretion; good behaviour.

usan Boredom; disgust. ~**ç,** boring, tedious: boredom, tedium: ···**den** ~ **gelmek,** to be bored by .... ~**dırıcı,** boring, tedious. ~**dırmak,** to bore, sicken, disgust. ~**mak,** (*with abl.*) to become sick of, bored *or* disgusted with.

usare (·–¹) Sap; expressed juice *of a fruit etc.*

usat (·ᵛ), **–tı** *pl. of* asi. Rebels.

uskumru (·¹·) Mackerel.

uskunca (·¹·) Sponge *for a gun.*

uskur (*Eng. screw*) Screw, propeller; screwdriven ship.

uskut Silence!; shut up!

usla·ndırmak *va.* Bring *s.o.* to his senses; make *s.o.* behave. ~**nmak,** to become sensible, discreet, well-behaved; come to one's senses. ~**tmak,** *v.* uslandırmak.

uslu Well-behaved; good (child); quiet (horse); sensible. ~ **oturmak,** to sit still, keep quiet. ~**luk,** a being well-behaved *or* sensible.

usta Master *of a trade or craft*; master workman; craftsman; foreman; overseer; *formerly* a woman superintendent of servants and slaves. Skilled; clever; experienced. ~ **olm.** (**çıkmak**), to finish one's apprenticeship and become a master workman. ~**lık,** mastery *of a trade or craft*; proficiency; master-stroke. ~**lıklı,** masterly; cleverly made; cunningly devised.

ustunc Portable case of instruments.

ustura (¹·· *or* ·¹·) Razor. ~ **tutmak,** to use a razor, to shave.

usturlab Astrolabe.

usturmaça (··¹·) Fender, collision-mat.

usturpa (·¹·) Mop of rope ends; scourge.

usturuplu (*sl.*) Striking, impressive; right, decent, 'comme il faut'.

usul (·ᵛ), **–lü** *pl. of* asıl. Fundamental principles; systems; *as sing.* method; system; manner; procedure; time (*mus.*). Gently, carefully, quietly. ~**la,** carefully, gently: ~**ü dairesinde,** in the recognized way: ~**ü defteri,** book-keeping: ~**ü muhakeme,** judicial procedure: ~ **vurmak,** to beat time (in Turkish music).

usul·acık (·¹··), very slowly, gently *or* quietly. ~**süz,** unmethodical; without system; irregular; contrary to rules.

uşak Boy, youth; male servant; shop assistant. ~**kapan,** Lammergeier. ~**lık,** childhood; profession of a man-servant.

uşkun A kind of wild rhubarb.

uşşak (·ᵛ), **–kı** *pl. of* âşık. Lovers; dervishes; wandering minstrels: *name of a mode in Turkish music.*

ut *v.* ud.

utan·acak Shameful. ~**c,** shame; modesty; bashfulness. ~**dırmak,** to make ashamed; put to shame; cause to blush; cause to look foolish. ~**gac,** ~**gan,** ~**ık,** bashful; shy; shamefaced. ~**ış,** a being ashamed. ~**ma,** act of being ashamed.

utan·mak *vn.* Be ashamed; be shy *or* bashful; blush with shame *or* embarrassment. ~**maz,** shameless; impudent. ~**mazlık,** impudence, shamelessness.

Utarid The planet Mercury.

utmak *v.* yutmak.

utufet (··–¹), **–ti** Kindness, benevolence. ~**lû,** benevolent; *formerly a title given to certain people of high rank.*

uvalamak, uvmak, uvuşturmak *v.* oğalamak *etc.*

uyan·dırıcı Awakening; arousing. ~ **saat,** alarm-clock. ~**dırmak,** to awaken; arouse; revive (a fire *etc.*); stir *a country into activity and prosperity.* ~**ık,** awake; vigilant, wide awake, smart. ~**ıklık,** a being awake; vigilance, smartness.

uyanmak *vn.* Awake; wake up; (of a fire) to burn up: (of plants) to start growth; revive, come to life.

uyar Conformable; like. ~**ı yok,** incomparable.

uyarmak *v.* uyandırmak.

uydurma Invented; false; made-up (story, excuse, *etc.*).

uydurmak *va.* Cause to conform *or* agree; make to fit; adapt; invent, make up; find a way of doing *or* getting *stg.* **anahtar** ~, to use a false key: ···**e ayak** ~, to keep in step with ...: **işi kitaba** ~, to manage an affair cleverly: **pazarlığı** ~, to make a good bargain: 'yine işini uydurdu!', he's brought it off again! (*of a person who is always successful*).

uydurmasyon (*sl. and jokingly*). An invented word for invention, fable; made-up, concocted.

uygun Conformable; in accord; fitting; agreeable; favourable; in tune; cheap, reasonable (price); just right. **hali** ~, in easy circumstances: **işimiz** ~, our affairs are all right. ~**luk,** a being appropriate *or* fitting. ~**suz,** not conforming; unsuitable; unseemly: ~ **bir kadın,** an immoral woman. ~**suzluk,** unsuitability; unseemliness; impropriety; bad behaviour.

uyku Sleep. ~**m açıldı** (**dağıldı**), my sleepiness has passed off: ~sunu* açmak, to shake off one's drowsiness: ~sunu* almak, to have a good night's rest: ~ basmak, for sleep to overcome one: ~ çekmek, to sleep: ~ya dalmak, to fall asleep: ~m geldi (var), I am sleepy: bütün gece gözüme ~ girmedi, I haven't slept a wink all night: ~ ilâcı, sleeping-draught: ~m kaçtı, I can't get to sleep: ~ kestirmek, to have a nap: ~ sersemliği, drowsiness: ~ya varmak, to go to sleep: ~ya yatmak, to lie down to sleep.

uyku·cu, fond of sleep. ~suz, sleepless. ~suzluk, sleeplessness, insomnia.

uykuluk Neck sweetbreads of a lamb.

uyluk Thigh. ~ kemiği, femur.

uymak vn. Conform; agree; fit; suit; answer; harmonize; adapt oneself; follow; listen to; be fitting or seemly; be arranged or settled. uyup ulaşmak, to follow up with abuse: aklına* ~, to yield to some temptation: ˹dakikası dakikasına uymaz˺, he changes his mood every five minutes; hard to get on with: o kimseye uymaz, he goes his own way, listening to no one: iyi ki size uymadım, it's a good thing I didn't listen to you: sözleriniz biribirine uymuyor, your words do not agree with one another; you contradict yourself: şeytana ~, to be tempted and led astray: ˹zaman sana uymazsa sen zamana uy˺, if the times don't suit you, you must suit yourself to the times.

uysal Conciliatory; easy-going; weakminded; who always agrees with everyone.

uyuklamak vn. Dose.

uyumak vn. Sleep; go to sleep; be negligent or slothful; come to a standstill, make no progress; clot, coagulate.

uyun (·ᵏ) pl. of ayn. Eyes.

uyun·mak impers. of uyumak. burada uyunur mu?, can one get any sleep here? ~tu, half-asleep, lazy.

uyur Sleepy; lethargic; dormant; still.

uyuşmak¹ reciprocal of uymak. Come to a mutual understanding. üç aşağı beş yukarı ~, to arrive at an agreement of sorts.

uyuş·mak² reciprocal of uyumak. Become numb or insensible; (of pain etc.) to relax, slacken. ~turan, benumbing; the Electric Ray (fish). ~turmak, to benumb; assuage; deaden (pain etc.). ~turucu, that benumbs or deadens: ~ ilâc, anodyne, narcotic. ~uk, numbed; insensible; indolent. ~ukluk, numbness; laziness.

uyut·mak va. caus. of uyumak. Send to sleep; bore; keep quiet or put off s.o. by vague promises etc.; let a matter become dormant, put off indefinitely. ~ucu, soporific.

uyuz Itch; mange; scab. Having the itch; mangy; scabby. ~ otu, scabious.

uz¹ In az gittik ~ gittik, we went on and on and on.

uz² Good, capital; fitting, seemly; quiet, well-behaved. Excellence; suitability. az olsun ~ olsun, let it be little but let it be good: eli ~, deft, skilful.

uzak Distant, remote, far off (in time or space); improbable; contrary, not in accordance. Distant place; the distance. uzağa, in the distance: ~tan, from far off; ~tan akraba, a distant relative; bir şeye ~tan bakmak, to look on at stg. from a distance, i.e. to take no part in it: uzağa düşmek, to be far from one another: ~tan merhaba, a distant greeting, expression used to indicate that a certain person's acquaintance is not desired: ~tan tanımak, to know s.o. by sight: gözden ~ tutmamak, to keep a close eye upon.

uzak·ça, rather far off. ~laşmak, to retire to a distance; to be far away. ~lık, distance; remoteness; difference.

uza·mak vn. Go to a distance; stretch; grow longer; extend; be prolonged. ···e dili* ~, to criticize or attack presumptuously. ~nmak, to be prolonged or extended; to stretch oneself out; expand; exceed one's rights: ···e ~, to extend to, to go as far as. ~tmak, to extend, stretch out; postpone; prolong; make tedious or tiresome; allow to grow long (hair, beard): to be prolix; be importunate: uzatmıyalım, 'to come to the point!', in short: dil ~, to be forward; to criticize presumptuously: el ~, to seize, to lay hands on; to meddle.

uzlaşma Agreement, understanding. ~k, to come to an agreement or understanding.

uzlet v. üzlet.

uzma (·⸜) comp. of azim. Very great; greatest.

‖ uzman Expert.

uzun Long; long-winded; in detail. ~ boylu, tall, long, lengthy: ~ etm., to hold forth at great length; ~ etme!, that's enough!, don't keep on about it!; or oh! come on!, don't maintain that attitude!: ~ oturmak, to sit with outstretched legs: ···i ~ tutmak, to drag out a job etc.: ~ uzadıya, at great length: ···den bir baş ~, a head taller than ...: eli ~, pilferer, pickpocket.

uzun·ca, somewhat long or tall. ~kulaklı, long-eared. ~luk, length, lengthiness, height.

uzuv, –zvu Member (of the body); organ; limb.

uzv·î (·⸜) Organic; pertaining to a member of the body. ~iyet, –ti, organism.

Ü

übüvvet, –ti Fatherhood; paternity.

ücra (··¹) Remote, out-of-the-way.

ücret, –ti Pay; wage; fee; cost (of postage, telegram *etc.*); price (of a railway ticket). **mekteb** ~**i,** school fees. ~**li,** receiving pay : ~ **memur,** *an official who, although receiving a salary, can be dismissed at any time and does not receive a pension (as opp. to* **aylıklı** *or* **maaşlı memur,** *a permanent and pensionable official).* ~**siz,** unpaid; without payment; gratis.

ücurat (··⅄), –**tı** *pl. of* **ücret.** Salaries, fees *etc.*

üç Three. ~ **aşağı beş yukarı,** after some haggling; ~ **aşağı beş yukarı dolaşmak,** to walk up and down aimlessly *or* anxiously : ~**te bir,** a third : ~ **büçük atmak** (*sl.*), to be very frightened; ~ **büçük cahil (serseri** *etc.*), a handful of ignoramuses (vagabonds *etc.*). **üç·ambarlı** (¹···), three-decker (man-of-war). ~**aylar,** the three sacred months of Islam, *viz.* Rejeb, Shaban, and Ramazan. ~**büçük,** three and a half : ···**den** ~ **atmak,** to be in a funk about … . ~**er,** three each; three at a time. ‖ ~**gen,** triangle. ~**köşeli,** triangular, three-cornered. ~**leme,** triple; three-stranded *rope etc.* ~**lemek,** to make three; divide by three; make *rope* of three strands; hire a farm for a third of the produce : **evlerini üçledi,** he has bought a third house. ~**leşmek,** to amount to three. ~**lü,** consisting of three; marked with the number three. ~**lük,** of the value of three *piastres etc.*; for three persons (coffee *etc.*). Trinity. ~**üncü,** third. ~**üncülük,** a being third; third place. ~**üz,** triplets; one of a triplet. ~**üzlü,** triple : ~ **bir taret,** turret with three guns.

üdeba (··¹) *pl. of* **edib.** Literary men, men of letters.

üflemek *va.* Blow out *a candle etc.*; blow upon; blow up (toy balloon *etc.*); blow *a musical instrument. vn.* Blow, puff, pant. ꜥ**sütten (çorbadan) ağzı yanan ayran üfliyerek içer**꜒, ꜥa scalded cat fears cold water꜒.

üftade (··¹) Fallen; prostrate; in misery; in love.

üful (·⅄), –**lü** A sinking or setting; extinction; death.

üfür·mek *vn.* Blow, puff. *va.* Blow upon; blow up *with the breath*; cast a spell upon *or* cure by breathing on. **canına** ~ (*sl.*), to ruin. ~**ük,** a breathing on a sick person to cure him. ~**ükçü,** sorcerer who claims

to cure by such breathing. ~**üm,** puff; blast.

üğendire, ~**ğendirek** Ox-goad.

üğü Large owl.

ülema *v.* **ulema.**

üleş Portion, share. ~**mek,** to divide with one another; go shares. ~**tirmek,** to distribute; share out.

ülfet, –ti Familiar intercourse; familiarity; friendship; familiar habit. ~ **etm.,** to be on sociable and familiar terms.

ülke Country; province.

Ülker The Pleiades.

ülûhiyet (·—¹), –**ti** Divinity.

ümem *pl. of* **ümmet.** Religious communities; peoples, nations.

ümera (··¹) *pl. of* **emir.** Chiefs; staff officers.

ümid (·⅄) Hope; expectation. ꜥ~ **dünyası bu**꜒, hope never dies : ~ **etm.,** to hope; to expect; ~ **etmediği felâket başına geldi,** an unexpected catastrophe befel him : ···**den** ~**ini kesmek,** to give up hope of … : ~**im var,** I hope : **kat'ı** ~ **etm.,** to abandon hope.

ümid·bahş, hopeful; that gives hope. ~**gâh,** person *or* thing on which one's hopes are fixed. ~**lendirmek,** to make hopeful, to fill with hope. ~**lenmek,** to be hopeful; to conceive hopes. ~**siz,** without hope; hopeless; desperate : **âtiden** ~, despairing of the future. ~**sizlik,** hopelessness, desperation. ~**var,** hopeful.

ümmet, –ti Community *of the same religion*; people, nation. ~**i Muhammed,** Moslems; *often used to mean* people, folk *in general.*

ümmî (·⅄) Illiterate.

ümniye Hope; desire; purpose.

ün Voice, cry; fame, reputation. ~ **salmak,** to become famous : **kuru** ~, a mere name, an empty sound. ~**lemek,** to cry out; sing. ~**lü,** famous; honoured.

üniforma (··¹·) Uniform.

ünsiyet, –ti Familiarity; a being on friendly terms with *s.o.* ···**le** ~ **etm. (peyda etm.),** to be intimately acquainted with.

ürcufe (·—¹) False rumour.

Ürdün Transjordan.

üre Urea.

‖ **üre·ğen** Productive; prolific. ~**m,** increase. ~**me,** reproduction, procreation. ~**mek,** to multiply, increase (*vn.*). ~**tmek,** to cause to multiply; breed.

ürgün Pond *or* backwater *caused by the overflow of a river or the sea.*

ürkek Timid, fearful. ~**lik,** timidity.

ürk·mek *vn.* Start with fear; be frightened (of = den); (of a horse) to shy. ~üntü, sudden fright; panic. ~ütmek, to startle, scare.

ürper·mek *vn.* (Of the hair) to stand on end; shiver. ~tmek, to make the hair stand on end: tüyleri ürperten, hair-raising.

ürümek Howl (of dogs *etc.*).

‖ **ürün** Product.

üryan Naked; bare. ~i (·–ᴵ), a kind of thin-skinned plum; plum or prune skinned and dried.

üs, -ssü Base; basis; exponent, index (*math.*). ~sübahrî (deniz ~sü), naval base: ~sülhareke (hareket ~sü), base of operations (*mil.*): ~sü mizanı doldurmak, to reach the required standard (in an exam.).

üsera (·-ᴵ) *pl. of* esir. Prisoners-of-war. ~ karargâhı (kampı), prisoners-of-war camp.

Üsküdar Scutari. ⌐atı alan ~ı geçti⌐, 'the horsethief has passed Scutari', too late, nothing to be done!

üsküf Knitted cap with a tassel, *formerly worn by officers of the Janissaries*; falcon's hood; wire covering *put over the bowl of hookah to keep out the wind.*

üslûb (·ᴥ) Manner; form; style of writing.

üssü *v.* üs.

üst, -tü *v. also* üzeri. Upper *or* outside surface; the top *of a thing*; the space over *a thing*; clothing; superior (*n.*); remainder; change (from a shilling *etc.*); address *of a letter.* Upper, uppermost. (*with poss. suffix*) On; over; on the top of. ~ ~e, *v.* üstüste: ~te, above; on top: ~ten, superficially: ~ü açık, obscene, 'smutty': ~üne* almak, to take upon oneself; to put on *clothes etc.*; to take (a remark *etc.*) as being directed against oneself; to row ahead; ~ten almak, to talk *or* behave in a superior manner: ~ünden* atmak, to try to avoid *or* get rid of: ~üne basmak, to hit the nail on the head: ~ü başı, *v.* üstbaş: ~üne bırakmak, to quit, to give up: ⌐in ~üne çevirmek (geçirmek), to turn over to ..., to transfer to ...; ~ çıkmak, to win; ~e çıkmak, to pretend to be innocent; ~üne çıkmak, to come to the top; to get the better of: ~ fırçası, clothes-brush: ~ünden geçmek, to violate (a woman); bunun ~ünden beş sene geçti, five years elapsed after this: ~ gelmek, to surpass, to prevail; ~üne gelmek, to turn up, *to appear when one is doing stg.* (*with a suggestion that the appearance will bring either good or bad luck*): ~ümde para yok, I have no money on me: ⌐in ~ tarafı, the rest of ..., the remainder: ~ü temiz, he is cleanly dressed: ~üne* varmak, to keep on at

s.o.; to put on an extra price; to bid higher *at an auction*; ~üme varma!, don't come near me!; don't keep on at me!; don't insist!: ~e vermek, to give in addition; to suffer loss in a business transaction; ~ yan, next door (in a street); a little farther on: ⌐in ~üne yapmak, to make over *stg.* to *s.o.*: ⌐in ~üne yaşamak, to outlive *s.o.*: adı ~ünde, as the name implies; as befits the name: baş ~ünde tutmak, to honour, revere: kış ~ü, at the coming of winter: senin ne ~üne lâzım?, what business is that of yours?

üstad (·ᴥ), **üstaz** Master; teacher; expert. ~ ve amatör, professional and amateur. ~ane (·-–ᴵ), masterly; in a masterly fashion.

üstbaş (*both words declined*) Dress, attire. üstüne başına etm., (i) (of a child) to foul its clothing; (ii) to abuse *s.o.* violently: ~ kalmamak, to have no clothes left.

‖ **üstderi** (ᴵ··) Epidermis.

üste Further; in addition. işin ~sinden gelmek, to succeed, to cope with a matter. ~leme, relapse. ~lemek, *va.* to put on top of *stg. else*; *vn.* to increase; to become dominant; (of an illness) to recrudesce; to dwell on stg. *with regret or desire*; to persist: gelmek istemiyor, fazla üsteleme!, he doesn't want to come, don't press the matter! ~lik, furthermore; in addition.

‖ **üsteğmen** (ᴵ··) First lieutenant.

‖ **üstinsan** (ᴵ··) Superman.

üsture (·-ᴵ) Legend; myth. ~vî (·-·ᴵ), legendary; mythical.

üstübec White lead.

üstün Superior; victorious. ~ gelmek, to come out superior; to be victorious: ~ tutmak, to consider superior, to prefer: ⌐el elden ~dür (arsa çıkıncaya kadar)⌐, there is always one superior (right up to the throne of God). ~körü (·ᴵ··), superficial; only on the surface; superficially. ~lük, superiority.

üstüne *v.* üst *and also* üzerine.

üstüpü Oakum, tow; mop *for cleaning guns.*

üstüste (ᴵ··) One on top of the other. iki sene ~, two years in succession.

üstüvan·e (·-ᴵ) Cylinder; cylindrically shaped thing. ~î (·-–ᴵ), cylindrical.

üşek A small kind of lynx or caracal.

üşen·geç, üsengen Lazy, slothful. ~iklik, laziness, sloth.

üşenmek *vn.* (*with dat.*) Be too lazy to do *stg.*; not to take the trouble to do a thing; do with reluctance.

üşmek *vn.* Flock to a place.

üşne A kind of moss *used as a perfume.*

üşniye Algae.

üşümek *vn.* Feel cold; catch cold.

üşüntü A flocking together; crowd, mob.

üşür, -şrü Tenth; tithe. ~lenmek, to be decimated.

üşürmek va. caus. of üşmek. Collect together; gather into a crowd; cause to make a concerted attack.

üşüşmek vn. Crowd together; make a concerted attack.

üşütmek va. caus. of üşümek. Cause to feel or catch cold.

ütmek vn. dial. for yutmak. Win in a game (children).

ütü Flat-iron; crease made by ironing. bu kumaş ~ tutmuyor, this cloth won't take the iron: bu pantolonun ~sü bozuldu, these trousers have lost their crease (want ironing), ~cü, ironer; laundress. ~lemek, to iron; to singe the hair off sheep's trotters etc.; kafa ~ (sl.), to bore s.o. stiff. ~lü, ironed, singed.

ütüme Roasted fresh wheat.

üvendire Ox-goad.

üvey-. Step-. ~ana, stepmother; ~baba, stepfather, etc. etc. birine ~ evlâd muamelesi yapmak, to treat s.o. unkindly.

üvey·k Turtle dove. ~mek, to coo.

üvez Rowan tree and berry.

|| üye Member (of a council etc.).

üzek Pole of an ox-cart.

üzengi Stirrup. ayağı ~de, ready to start: çanak ~, cylindrical stirrup. ~lemek, to spur a horse with the stirrup (eastern stirrups having pointed corners for this purpose).

üzenmek v. özenmek.

üzere, üzre On, upon; according to; about; on the subject of; on condition of; for the purpose of; at the point of, just about to. güneş batmak ~ iken geldi, he came just as the sun was setting: istasyona gitmek ~ evden çıktım, I left the house to go to the station: tren hareket etmek ~dir, the train is on the point of starting:

üç ay içinde ödenmek ~, to be paid within three months.

üzeri Upper or outer surface of a thing; space above a thing; remainder, change (money). On; over; about. üzeri is practically interchangeable with üst and many phrases under üst can equally well be used with üzeri. ~ne* almak, to take it upon oneself to do stg.: ~mde para yok, I have no money on me: ~nde* kalmak, to remain on one as a debt or a charge: ~ temiz, he is cleanly dressed: kabahati kendi ~nden atmak, to exculpate oneself: kabahati birisinin ~ne atmak, to throw the blame on s.o.

üzerlik Rue seeds used as a fumigant.

üzgeç Rope ladder.

üzgü Oppression; cruelty.

üzgün Weak, invalid, ill; anxious, worried. ~ balığı, Dragonet.

üzlet, -ti A retiring into seclusion; a becoming a devotional recluse; solitude; isolation. ~gâh, place of retirement; hermitage. ~nişin, who lives the life of a recluse.

üzmek va. Treat harshly; cause to break down from grief or anxiety; strain to breaking point.

üzre v. üzere.

üzülmek vn. pass. of üzmek. Be worn out; be weakened by illness; be sorry or worried; regret having been unable to do stg.

üzüm Grape. ⌐~ ~e baka baka kararır⌐, 'evil communications corrupt good manners': ⌐~ünü ye de bağını sorma⌐, 'eat your grapes and don't ask what vineyard they came from', i.e. if you get a pleasure or a benefit, there is no need to worry about its source. ~suyu, -nu, grape-juice; wine.

üzüntü Anxiety; dejection; fatigue. ~lü, tedious; requiring great care and painstaking; anxious.

V

vabeste (−·¹) Dependent; depending (on = dat.).

vacib (−¹) Incumbent; bounden; necessary. ~e (−·¹), incumbent duty; obligation. ~üleda (−···¹), that must be done or performed. ~ülinfaz, that must be carried out (order etc.). ~ültediye that must be paid, payable.

vade (−¹) Fixed term or date; maturity of a bill etc. ~ ile borcetmek, to borrow with a fixed date for repayment: ~si gelmek, to

fall due: ~si geçmiş, of which the date of payment has expired. ~li, maturing at a certain date: ~ mevduat, deposit account which can only be withdrawn after a definite period, as opp. to vadesiz mevduat, deposit which can be drawn 'at sight', i.e. current account.

vadetmek (⌐··), -eder va. Promise.

vadi (−⌐) Valley; sense, tenor. bu ~de, in this sense; in this sphere, in this line: her ~den, on every subject.

va'di (–ı) v. vaid.

vafi (–ı̱) Abundant. ꜔kâfi ve ～꜒, enough and more than enough.

vaftiz Baptism. ～ anası, godmother : ～ ～ babası, godfather : ～ etm., to baptize.

vagon Railway wagon. yataklı ～, sleeping-car. ～li (Fr. wagon-lit), sleeping-car. ～lu, having so many wagons or trucks. ～luk, truck load.

vah Interj. expressing pity or regret.

vaha (–ı) Oasis.

vahamet (·–ı), –ti A being fraught with serious consequences; gravity, seriousness (of a situation). ～li, fraught with serious consequences; grave; dangerous.

vahdaniyet (·–·ı), –ti The Unity of God. ～e inanmak, to believe in the Unity of God, to be a monotheist.

vahdet, –ti Unity; uniqueness; solitariness. ～i vücud, pantheism.

vahi (–ı̱) Futile, silly.

vâhid (–ı) One. ～e irca etm., to reduce to one. ～en (ı̱··), one at a time; by oneself, individually. ～ikıyasi (–····–ı̱), unit of measurement.

vahîd (·ı̱) One; sole; unique.

vahiy, –hyi Divine inspiration; God's revelation to a prophet.

vahlanmak vn. Say 'alas!', 'what a pity!'

vahş·et, –ti Wildness, savageness; gloom; terror; melancholy; solitude. ～etgâh, lonely terrifying spot. ～i (·ı̱), wild; savage; brutish, bestial; shy, afraid of man; (med.) lateral, outer (side). ～ice (·ı̱·), ～iyane (·–·ı), wild; brutal; savage : in a wild, brutal or savage way. –ilik (·–ı), wildness; savageness; bestiality, brutality.

vahy·etmek (ı··), –eder va. Inspire; (of God) to reveal. ～i, v. vahiy.

vaız, –a'zı Admonition; sermon.

vaid, –a'di Promise. va'dinde durmak or va'de vefa etm., to abide by one's promise. ～leşmek, to make promises to one another.

vaiz (–ı) One who admonishes; preacher.

vak The Lesser Bittern.

vak'a Event, occurrence; event of historical importance, such as a great battle; case of plague etc.

vakaâ v. vakıâ.

vakar v. vekar.

vakayi (·–ı̱), –ii pl. of vakıa. Events; calamities; battles. ～name (··–ı), chronicle.

vaketa (·ı·) Calf-skin leather.

vakfe Stop; pause; interval.

vakf·etmek (ı··), –eder va. Devote property to a pious foundation; devote or dedicate oneself (or time) to some purpose. ～iye, deed of trust of a pious foundation. ～ı, v. vakıf.

vakfon Nickle-plated copper or iron.

vakıa (–·ı) Fact; dream, vision. bu bir ～dır, inkâra mahal yok, this is a fact which cannot be denied.

vakıâ (ı̱·–) In fact, actually; it is true that; indeed.

vakıf, –kfı Pious foundation; Wakf. ～name (··–ı), deed of trust of a pious foundation.

vâkıf (–ı) Aware, cognizant; wide awake; who devotes property to a pious foundation. ～ gözlerle, with appraising eyes, with eyes of an expert: ···e ～ olm., to be aware of ... , to be cognizant of ... . ～lık, cognizance; information.

vaki¹ (–ı̱) Protecting; protective. ... karşı ～ tedbir, preventive measure against ... .

vaki² (–ı̱), –ii Happening, taking place; true, actual; existing; situated. What actually happens; reality. ～ olm., to happen, befall.

vakit, –kti Time; (with a participle) when. ～ile, in its proper time; in times past: ～inde, at the right time : ～ ～, at times, from time to time : ～ler hayır olsun!, good day! : bir ～, once, once upon a time : her ～, always, every time : hiçbir ～, never : ne ～?, when? : o ～, then, in that case : o ～ bu ～, from then till now; as it was then, so it is now : hali vakti yerinde, in easy circumstances, well-off.

vakit·li, done at the right time; in due season. ～ vakitsiz, in season and out of season; at all sorts of times. ～siz, unseasonable; inopportune; at the wrong time; premature, untimely.

vakom v. vakum.

vakt·aki (·–ı) When, at the time that ... . ～i, v. vakit. ～ihal, financial circumstances : ～ yerinde, in easy circumstances. ～ile (·ı̱·), in the past; at one time : ～ görmüş geçirmiş, who has seen better days.

vakum (ı·) Vacuum; (·ı), Vacuum oil.

vakur Grave, dignified. ～ane (·––ı), grave or dignified (behaviour etc.); in a grave or dignified manner.

valâ (–ı̱) High; eminent. alayi ～ ile, with great pomp and ceremony (iron.).

valf Valve.

vali (–ı) Vali; Governor of a province (vilayet).

valid (–ı) Begetter; father. ～e (–·ı), mother. ～eyn, the two parents.

valih (–ı) Bewildered. ～ane (–·–ı), in a bewildered manner.

vallah (ı·), vallahi (·ı·) By God!; I swear it is so!

vanilya (·ı·) Vanilla. kâzib ～ çiçeği, heliotrope.

vantilâtör Ventilator; fan.

vantuz (*Fr. ventouse*) Cupping-glass; sucker of an octopus etc.

vapur Steamer. kara ~u (*vulg.*), train.

var[1] Existent; present; at hand; available. Belongings, possessions; wealth. There is, there are. *Used with possessive suffixes for the verb* to have, *e.g.* kitabım ~ *or* bende kitab ~, I have a book; paranız ~mı?, have you any money? ~ etm., to cause to be present, to create; yoktan ~ etm., to make stg. out of nothing: ~ kuvvetile, with all possible force; with all his strength: ~ mışın?, I dare you to do it; I bet you can't do it: ~ olm., *v.* varolmak: ~ı yoğu, all that he has; ~ım yoğum, all that I possess; ~ını yoğunu kaybetti, he lost his all: ~sa ... yoksa ..., he thinks of nothing else than ..., *e.g.* ~sa oğlu yoksa oğlu, he just lives for his son: altmışında ~ yok, he must be about sixty: bir ~ bir yok, at one moment there, at another not there; transitory, uncertain: ne ~ ?, what's the matter?: ne ~ ne yok?, what's the news?: ne ~ ne yok, whatever there is; whatever one possesses.

var[2] *v.* varmak.

varak, -kı Leaf; petal; sheet of paper. altın ~, gold-leaf: bakır ~, copper-foil: ⸢~ı mihri vefa! kim okur, kim dinler?⸣, 'a letter of love and fidelity; who reads?, who listens?, *i.e.* 'who cares two hoots?' *or* 'no one listens to what I say (he says)'.

varak·a, a single leaf; note, letter, document. **–çı**, a worker in gold-leaf, gilder. **~î** (··⸜), leaf-like; pertaining to a leaf. **~lamak**, to ornament with gold-leaf. **~lı**, ornamented with gold-leaf, gilded. **~pare** (··–⸜), scrap of paper; worthless document; humble request; 'rag' (newspaper).

varan *In such phrases as*: ~ dört!, that makes four!, that's number four!

varda (⸝··) Look out!; keep clear!; make way! **~cı** (⸝··), *formerly a man who ran in front of a great person to clear the way; then a guard who shouted out* varda! *to clear the way for a tram*; promoter *or* propagandist (*in a bad sense*).

vardakosta (··⸝·) Coastguard vessel; fat but imposing person.

vardatopu (·⸝··), **–nu** Signal gun.

vardavelâ (··⸝·) Rail of a ship. kıç ~sı, taffrail.

vardırmak *va. caus. of* varmak. Allow to reach; cause to arrive.

vardiya (⸝··) Watch (on board ship).

vardula (·⸝·), **vardolos** Welt of a shoe.

varek Seaweed, kelp.

vâreste (–·⸜) Free; exempt. kendini ···den ~ etm., to free oneself from ... .

varetmek (⸝··) *v.* var.

vargel ~ tezgâhı, shaper.

varılmak *impers. of* varmak. oraya iki saatte varılır, one reaches there in two hours.

varış *verb. n. of* varmak. Arrival *etc.*; *also* quickness of perception. ⸢~ına gelişim (tarhanına bulgur aşım⸣, 'you visit me, I come to you'; (in return for your soup I give you porridge), *i.e.* as you treat others, so will they treat you. ~gidiş, a coming and going; familiarity.

–vari *Pers. suffix.* Similar to ..., like ..., *e.g.* haçvari, crosswise; ingilizvari, in the English manner.

varid (–⸜) That which arrives *or* happens; probable; admissible. bu ~ değildir, it is unlikely to happen: hatıra ~ olm., to come into the mind: bu iddia ~ olamaz, this claim cannot be admitted. ~at (–·⸜), **–tı**, revenues, income. ~e (–·⸜), sudden thought; incoming papers: ~ defteri, register of incoming documents.

varil Small cask.

varis (–⸜) Varicose veins.

vâris (–⸜) Inheriting. Heir.

variyet (–·⸜), **–ti** Wealth, riches; income. ~li, well-to-do, wealthy.

varlık Existence; presence; self, personality; possessions, wealth; easy circumstances. varlığa çıkarmak, to bring into existence: ~ göstermek, to make one's presence felt; to achieve *stg.*: böyle işler ~la olur, one must be well-off to do such things: bütün varlığımızla dileriz, we wish with all our hearts: genc nesli bir varlık diye tanımıyanlar, those who ignore the existence of the young generation. ~lı, well-to-do.

varmak, –ır *vn.* (*with dat.*) Go towards; arrive; reach, attain; approach; succeed in understanding; result, end in; (of a woman) to marry. varsın, *v.* varsın: var istediğini yap!, do whatever you like! (a challenge): varıncaya kadar, up to, to; orada teleskoptan kömür kovasına varıncaya kadar her şeyi bulmak kabildir, there one can find everything from a telescope to a coal-scuttle: çoğa ~, to cost a lot: dili* ~, to dare to say; dilim varmıyor, I can hardly bring myself to say it: eli* ~, to dare to do: ···in farkına ~, to perceive, to notice: fenaya ~, to turn out badly: kocaya ~, to marry a husband: bu iş neye varacak?, what will be the end of this?: zevka ~, to give oneself up to pleasure.

varmış *past of* var *and of* varmak. ⸢bir ~ bir yokmuş⸣, 'once upon a time'.

varolmak (⸝··) *vn.* Exist. varol!, 'may you live long!' well done!, bravo!: varolsun!, 'long may he live!'

varoş Suburb.

varsağı A kind of scimitar *peculiar to the Varsak nomad tribe*; a special form of song.

varsam Lesser Weaver *or* Sting-fish.

varsın *In such phrases as*: ~ gelsin, let him come if he likes: ~ gelmesin, it doesn't matter whether he comes or not: ~ o da keman öğrensin, well, if he wants to learn the violin, let him (it's not a bad idea).

varta Abyss; great peril. ~yı atlatmak, to escape great danger.

varyemez Miserly.

varyos, balyos Sledge-hammer. ~çu, a smith's striker *or* hammerman.

vasat, -tı Middle; average. Middling; mediocre. ~î (··-̲), central, middle; mean. Mean, average. ···in ~sini almak, to take the mean *or* average of ... .

vasf·etmek (¹··), -eder *va.* Describe; qualify. ~î (·-̲), qualifying. ~ı, *v.* vasıf.

vasıf, -sfı Quality; description; eulogy; epithet, adjective. **vasfa gelmez**, indescribable: **vasfı mümeyyiz**, distinguishing quality, characteristic: **vasfı terkibî**, a compound adjective. ~landırmak, to qualify; describe.

vâsıf (-¹) Who describes *or* qualifies; who eulogizes.

vasıl, -slı Union; meeting; attainment. **vâsıl** (-¹), arriving, joining. ~ olm., to arrive; to join one's beloved.

vasıta Means; channel; intermediary, go-between; vehicle. ···in ~sile, by means of : sizin ~nızla, by means of you, through you. ~sız, without intermediary; direct.

vasi (-¹) Executor; trustee; guardian. ~lik, executorship; trusteeship; guardianship.

vâsi (-̲) Extensive, wide; abundant.

vasiyet, -ti Will, testament; last request of a dying person. ~ etm., to bequeath; to give as one's last injunction. ~name (···-¹), written will.

vasl·etmek (¹··), -eder *va.* Unite; join. ~ı, *v.* vasıl.

vaşak Lynx; fur of the lynx.

vat, -tı Watt.

vatan One's native country, motherland. ~daş, compatriot; fellow countryman. ~daşlık, a being a compatriot. ~î (··-¹), pertaining to one's native land. ~perver, ~sever, patriotic; patriot. ~perverlık, patriotism, love of one's country.

vatoz Thornback Ray. iğneli ~, Sting-ray.

vaveylâ (-·-̲) Alas! Cry of horror *or* lament. ~yı koparmak, to raise a cry of horror *or* lament.

vay *Interj. expressing surprise or regret.* ~ sen misin!, hullo, is that you!: ~ başım, oh, my poor head!: ~ başıma!, woe is me!: ~ canına!, how amazing!

vaye (-¹) Share, portion. ~dar, who participates.

vazaif (·-¹) *pl. of* vazife. Duties; obligations.

vaz'an (¹·) In position, according to position.

va'zetmek, vâzetmek (-̲··), -eder *va. & vn.* Admonish; preach.

vaz'etmek (¹··), -eder *va.* Put; place; lay (foundation); impose (tax).

vazgeçirmek (¹···) *va. caus. of* vazgeçmek.

vazgeçmek (¹··) *va. (with abl.)* Give up; cease from; abandon (a project).

va'zı (-¹) *v.* vaız.

vazı, -z'ı Act of putting down *or* laying; a depositing; an imposing (a tax); arrangement; attitude, manner, behaviour. ~esas, the laying of a foundation. ~hamil, -mli, parturition: ~ etm., to give birth. ~yed, a laying hands on; seizure: ···e ~ etm., to seize, confiscate; to take up *a matter*.

vâzı (-¹), -ıı Who lays down *or* institutes. ~ıkanun, legislator. ~ulimza, signatory: ben aşağıda ~, I, the undersigned.

vazıh (-¹) Open; clear, manifest. ~an (-̲··), clearly.

vazife (·-¹) Duty; obligation; task; salary; school fees. ~ etm., *or* ~sinden olm., to care, to mind, to be interested; bunu hiç ~ etmiyor, he doesn't trouble about that; ~si mi?, what does he care!: bir saat sonra ~ almalıyım, in an hour's time I must be on duty *or* I must take my turn: ne ~n *or* ne üstüne ~?, what's that to you? **vazife·dar**, charged with an official duty; competent authority: bu işin ~ı kimdir?, who is responsible for looking after this affair? ~siz, without an official duty; who neglects his work, careless, slack. ~şinas, dutiful; conscientious.

vaziye Co-ordinate.

vaziyet, -ti Position; situation; attitude. ~ almak, to stand to attention.

vazo (¹·) Vase.

vazolunmak (¹···) *vn. pass. of* va'zetmek.

vâzünasihat, -ti Admonition; sermon (advice).

ve And. ~ saire, etcetera (*abbrev.* v.s.).

veba (·-̲) Plague, pestilence. ~î (·-̲), pertaining to the plague *or* a pestilence.

vebal, -li Sin *that will be punished in the next world*; evil consequence. ~i boyuna, on his (your) head be it!

vebalı Stricken with the plague.

veballi That will be punished in the next world.

veca (·-̲), -aı Pain; colic. ~ı cenb, pleurodynia. ~lı, painful; in pain.

vecahet (·-¹), -ti Beauty; nobility of aspect.

vecaib (·–ı) *pl. of* **vecibe.** Obligations.

vecd, vecid, –cdi Ecstasy; rapture. **~aver** (·–ı), ecstatic; causing rapture.

vech·e Direction; side. ···e ~ **vermek,** to direct *s.o.* **~en** (ı··), in face; by face; in some way *or* manner: ~ **minelvucuh,** somehow or other; *(with neg.)* by no manner of means. **~i,** *v.* **vecih. ~î** (·⸱–), facial.

vecih, –chi Face; surface; direction; manner; cause, reason; means. **vechi meşruh üzere,** in the manner described: **ber vechi muharrer,** as set out above: **ber vechi peşin,** in advance, in anticipation: **bir vechile,** in some way: **hiçbir vechile,** in no wise, by no means: **ne vechile olursa olsun,** in whatever way: **lâyıkı vechile,** in a worthy manner, as it should be done: **vechi tesmiye,** the reason for naming ...: **çok ~li,** polyhedral.

vecîh (·⸱–) Of pleasing aspect; prepossessing.

veciz Laconic, terse. ~e (·–ı), terse saying; epigram; aphorism.

veda (·⸱–), **–aı** Farewell; leave-taking. ···e ~ **etm.,** to bid farewell to ...: ···e ~a **gitmek,** to pay *s.o.* a farewell visit. **~laşmak,** to bid each other farewell. **~name** (·––ı), letter of farewell.

vedaatile (···⸱–·) By means of; through the medium of.

vedad Love; friendship.

vedia (·–ı) A thing deposited *or* given into safe-keeping.

vefa (·⸱–) Fidelity; loyalty; faithfulness. ···e ~ **etm.,** to be true to *one's word etc.*: ···e ömrü ~ **etmedi,** he did not live long enough to ... **~dar, ~kâr. ~lı,** faithful, loyal, constant. **~sız,** faithless; disloyal; untrustworthy. **~sızlık,** faithlessness; disloyalty; untrustworthiness.

vefat (·⸱), **–tı** Death; decease. ~ **etm.,** to die.

vefik, –ki Agreeing, conforming. Companion.

vefiyat (··⸱), **–tı** *pl. of* **vefat.** Deaths; mortality.

vefk, –ki Conformity; agreement; amulet.

vefret, –ti Abundance.

vega (·⸱–) Clamour, hubbub; strife.

Vehabî (·–ı) Wahhabi; Wahhabite.

vehbî (·⸱–) Due to God's generosity; natural, inborn.

vehham Given to forebodings; apprehensive; suspicious. **~lık,** a being given to empty forebodings.

vehim, –hmi Foreboding; groundless fear; surmise; illusion; delusion. **Ali fransızca bildiği vehmindedir,** Ali is under the delusion that he knows French. **~nak,** given to groundless fears; suspicious.

vehle Moment, instant. **~i ulâda,** at the first onset, for the first moment. **~ten** (ı··), for the first moment, just at first.

vehm·etmek (ı··), **–eder** *va.* Forebode; fear; surmise; have the illusion that ... . **~i,** *v.* **vehim. ~î** (·⸱–), imaginary; conjectural. **~iyat, –tı,** imaginary things; groundless forebodings; conjectures.

vekâlet (·–·), **–ti** A being agent *or* representative of another; attorneyship; Ministry *(Turkish only)*. ···e ~ **etm.,** to represent *s.o.*; act as agent *or* attorney for *s.o.* **~en** (·⸱–··), as representative *or* deputy of another; by proxy. **~name** (·–·–ı), power of attorney.

vekar Staidness, gravity; dignity; dignified calmness. **sahte ~,** false dignity; one who affects to be dignified. **~lı,** grave, dignified; calm. **~sız,** lacking in dignity *or* seriousness. **~sızlık,** lack of dignity.

vekil (·⸱) Agent; representative; deputy; attorney; proxy; Minister of State *(Turkey only)*. ~ **etm.,** to appoint as one's representative: ···e ~ **olm.,** to represent *or* act as deputy for *s.o.* **~harc,** steward *or* majordomo *in a great house.* **~lik,** quality *or* duties of a **vekil**; agency; attorneyship.

velâdet, –ti Birth.

velâkin (·–·) But still.

velâyet (·–ı), **–ti** Guardianship; trusteeship; saintship.

veled Child; progeny; *(for ~izina)* bastard; rascal. **~i maderbehata,** illegitimate child: **~i manevî,** adopted child.

veleh Stupefaction; violent emotion.

velena (·ı·) Staysail.

velense (·ı·) Kind of thick blanket; horserug.

velev, velevki (·ı·) Even if; even though.

velfecri *Lit.* 'and the dawn'; *name of the 89th chapter of the Koran, which begins with this word.* ⌐gözleri ~ okumak¬, to give the impression of being very astute and wide awake *(slightly derogatory)*.

velhasıl (ı–·) In fine, in short.

veli (·⸱–) Guardian *of a child etc.*; friend of God, saint. **~ahd,** heir to the throne. **~lik,** qualities and duties of a guardian; quality of a saint. **~nimet, –ti,** benefactor, patron.

velime (·–ı) Wedding-feast.

velûd (·⸱–) Prolific; productive. **~iyet, –ti,** prolificacy; productivity.

velvele Outcry; clamour, hubbub; flourish of trumpets *(iron.)* **~li,** tumultuous, noisy.

velyetmek (ı··), **–eder** *vn.* Follow in succession.

Venedik (·ı·) Venice. **~li,** Venetian.

ventil Valve; cock.

vento (¹·) Topping-lift; guy.

veraset (·—¹), **–ti** Inheritance; heritage.

verd·î (·—¹) Pertaining to the rose; rose-coloured. **~iye,** the Rosaceae.

vere (¹·) Capitulation, surrender. Continuously. **~ bayrağı,** flag of surrender: **~ vermek,** to capitulate.

verecek Debt.

verem Tuberculosis. Tuberculous, consumptive. **~li,** tuberculous.

verese *pl. of* **varis.** Heirs.

veresi, veresiye On credit. **~ tekâlif,** requisition without payment (*mil.*).

veretmek (¹··), **–eder** (*sl.*) *va.* (*with dat.*) Keep on hitting; give several blows to.

verev Oblique; diagonal; slanting.

vergi Gift; tax. **Allah ~si,** gift of God, talent: **Allaha ~,** only God can do that: **Ali Paşa ~si,** a gift the return of which is expected: **···e ~ olm.,** to be special to, to be the speciality of ...; **bu ona ~dir,** only he can do that. **~li,** generous.

verici Who *or* which gives. **iştah ~,** that which gives an appetite, appetizing.

verid (·⁴) Vein. **~ iltihabı,** phlebitis. **~î** (·—¹), pertaining to veins, venous.

verile *Lit.* 'let it be given'. **~ emri,** order for payment of government money, *v.* **ita.**

verim Produce; return; profit; output. **~li,** profitable; productive.

veriş Mode *or* act of giving. **alış ~,** trade, commerce. **~mek,** to give to one another, exchange.

veriştirmek *vn.* Utter abuse; swear (at = *dat.*).

vermek, –ir *va.* Give; deliver; pay; offer; sell; attribute; undergo (losses); teach. *As aux. verb implies easiness and quickness, e.g.* **anlayıverdi,** he readily understood; *it sometimes implies a courteous request, e.g.* **kapıyı açıver !,** would you mind opening the door? **ver elini Boğaziçi (dedik gittik),** we decided to go up the Bosphorus and off we went: **açık ~,** to have a deficit: **alıp verem2memek,** to disagree: **ara ~,** to suspend, to interrupt: **başbaşa verdiler,** they laid their heads together: **bel ~,** to sag: **ben bu hareketi size veremedim,** I wouldn't have thought you would have done this: **borcunu verdi,** he paid the debt: **ona borc verdim,** I gave him a loan: **···i çocukluğuna* ~,** to overlook *stg.* as due only to youthfulness: **ele ~,** to hand over, to betray: **bu kitaba on lira verdim, vermedi,** I offered 10 lira for this book; he wouldn't sell it (he wouldn't take that price): **bu mektebde inglizceyi kim veriyor?,** who gives the English lessons at this school?: **patlak ~,** (of a secret) to get out, to be divulged: **ʳser ~ sır vermemekʾ,** better die than give

away a secret: **···i talihsizliğe ~,** to put *stg.* down to bad luck: **ver yansın,** *v.* **veryansın.**

vernik Varnish. **~lemek,** to varnish.

veryansın (¹··) **etm.** *vn.* Squander; get excited *or* enthusiastic; let oneself go; exaggerate.

vesaif (·—¹) *pl. of* **vesile.** Pretexts.

vesaik (·—¹), **–kı** *pl. of* **vesika.** Documents.

vesait (·—¹), **–ti** *pl. of* **vasıta.** Means. **~i nakliye,** means of transport: **zengin ~li,** richly equipped.

vesatet (·—¹), **–ti** Mediation; intermediary. **~ etm.,** to act as an intermediary; to be a channel *or* means.

vesaya (·—¹) *pl. of* **vasiyet.** Injunctions; warnings; advice.

vesayet (·—¹), **–ti, vesaye** Executorship; trusteeship; injunction, warning.

vesi (·¹) Vast; ample, abundant.

vesika (·—¹) Title-deed; document; document proving identity; ration card. **~ ile** by coupon (rationed). **~lı,** licensed (prostitute).

vesile (·—¹) Means; cause; pretext; opportunity. **~ buldukça,** on any pretext: **bir ~ ile,** by some means, under some pretext: **bu ~ ile,** by this means, taking this opportunity: **bu ~i hasene ile,** taking advantage of this excellent opportunity. **~cu** (···¹), who seeks a pretext; who is on the look out for an opportunity.

vesim Pretty.ʿ

vesselâm (¹··) So that's that!; so that's an end of the matter! **anlaşılmaz insansın ~ !,** you're an odd creature and that's all about it !

vestiyer (*Fr. vestiaire*) Cloak-room; coat-peg.

vesvese Anxiety; secret fear; preoccupation; scruple. **~ etm.,** to be inwardly unhappy *or* anxious, to have misgivings.

veşim, –şmi Tattooing.

veted Stake; tent-peg; sphenoid bone.

veter Bowstring; string *of a musical instrument*; tendon, sinew; chord of an arc. **~ikaime** *or* **kaim ~,** hypotenuse.

vetire (·—¹) Path; track; mode, manner; septum.

veya (·—¹), **veyahud** Or.

veyl Alas!; **···e ~ !,** woe to ...!

veyselkarani *In* ʳyemen ellerinde ~ʾ, completely lost; utterly at a loss.

vezaif (·—¹) *pl of* **vazife.** Duties.

vezaret (·—¹), **–ti** Vizierate.

vezin, –zni A weighing; weight; metre (poetry).

vezir (·⁴) Vizier, Minister; queen (chess). **~iazam** (·—·—¹), the Grand Vizier. **~lik,** office and duties of a Vizier.

vezne Balance, gauge; treasury; pay-office; powder-flask. **~dar,** treasurer; cashier.

vezniyet, –ti Momentum.

vıcık Half liquid half solid; sticky; dirty. **~ ~,** *expresses the squelching noise of walking through thick mud*: ortalık ~ ~, the whole place was a quagmire. **~lamak,** to make sticky *etc.*

vık *Expresses the noise made by s.o. in great straits.* içi* ~ ~ etm., to be very impatient.

vınlamak *vn.* Buzz; hum.

vır *In* ~ ~, *imitating continuous and exasperating talk.* ~ ~ başının* etini yemek, to keep on nagging at *s.o.* **~ıldamak,** to talk incessantly; to keep complaining querulously. **~ıltı,** tiresome talk; nagging; querulousness. **~lamak,** to nag.

vız Buzz. ~ gelmek ,to be a matter of indifference: ⌐~ gelir tırıs gider⌐, I don't care two hoots. **~ıldamak,** to buzz, hum; keep on complaining. **~ıltı,** a buzzing *or* whirring noise; querulous complaining. **~ır ~ır,** *imitates the whirring of a machine and used to describe stg. that can easily and quickly be done.* **~lamak,** *v.* **vızıldamak.**

via Blood-vessel.

vicah (·ᵛ) A being face to face; personal presence. **~en** (·ᴸ·), face to face; in the presence of; not by default. **~î** (·ᴸ–), done in the presence of s.o.

vicdan (·ᵛ) Conscience. **~azabı,** the pangs of conscience. **~en** (·ᴸ·), in accordance with one's conscience. **~î** (·–ᴸ), pertaining to conscience. **~lı,** conscientious; honest. **~sız,** without a conscience; unscrupulous. **~sızlık,** lack of a conscience; unscrupulousness.

vida (¹·) Screw. **~lamak,** to screw; to screw down. **~lı** (¹··), screwed: ~ cıvata, screw-bolt.

vidala, videle (·¹·) Box-calf; calfskin.

vifak (·ᵛ), **–kı** Agreement, concord.

viğle (¹·) Observation post at a dalyan, *q.v.*

vikaye (·–¹) Protection; prophylaxis. ···den ~ etm., to protect from ..., to ward off.

vilâdî (·–ᴸ) Inborn, congenital.

vilâyet (·–¹), **–ti** Province governed by a Vali, vilayet; country. **~li,** of *such and such a* vilayet; fellow countryman.

vinç Crane; winch.

vira (¹·) *Interj. giving the* order to set a crane going. (ᴸ·) Continuously.

viraj (*Fr. virage*) Curve of a road. bir ~ı dönmek, to go round a bend.

viran (–ᵛ) Devastated, ruined. ⌐~ olası hanede evlâdü ayal vardı⌐, 'I have a wife and family in that cursed house', *i.e.* 'I am not free to act', *used as an excuse for one's*

inaction. **~e** (––¹), ruin. **~elik** (–––·¹), a place of ruins. **~lık,** a being a ruin; ruin.

vird Portion of scripture recited daily; constantly repeated saying. **~etmek** (¹··), **–eder,** to repeat constantly. **~izeban,** stg. repeated constantly.

virgül (*Fr. virgule*) Comma. noktalı ~, semicolon.

visal (·ᵛ), **–li** Meeting; lover's union.

viski (¹·) Whisky.

vişne (¹·) Morello cherry. **~çürüğü, –nü,** purplish-brown colour.

vites (*Fr. vitesse*) Gear; gears. ~ kolu, gear-lever: ~ kutusu, gear-box.

vitir, –tri Odd, single *or* unique thing.

vitrin (*Fr. vitrine*) Shop window.

viya (¹·) *Order to steer straight after altering course.*

viyak *In* ~ ~, squawking.

viyol·a Viola. **~on,** violin. **~onsel,** violoncello.

viza, vize (¹·) Visa. **~lı** (¹··), with a visa.

vizita (·¹·) Medical visit; doctor's fee.

vizon (*Fr. vison*) Mink.

volan (*Fr. volant*) Fly-wheel.

voli (¹·) Space covered by a cast of a circular fishing-net; (*sl.*) successful stroke of business. ~ çevirmek, to cast a net.

volkan Volcano.

volta (¹·) A round turn (knot); tack; a turn *in walking up and down.* ~ vurmak (etmek), to go to windward by tacking; to cruise about; to walk up and down; to beat about the bush: meze ~, half-hitch.

vonoz Young mackerel *or* bonito.

votka (¹·) Vodka.

v.s. *Abbrev. for* ve saire. Etcetera.

vuku (·ᴸ), **–uu** Occurrence, event. ~ bulmak, to happen, to take place: ~u hal, the fact of the matter: bunun ~u vardır, this has happened, such an event has occurred. **~at** (·–ᵛ), **–tı,** events, incidents.

vukuf (·ᵛ) Knowledge; information. ···e ~ kesbetmek, to get information about, to inquire into ...: ···e ~u tammı var, he has a thorough knowledge of ...: ehli ~, one who knows, expert, connoisseur. **~lu,** well-informed; well up *in a matter.* **~suz,** without knowledge; ignorant; badly informed. **~suzluk,** lack of information, ignorance.

vurdumduymaz (*Lit.* 'I hit him but he felt it not') Insensitive; thick-skinned; blockhead.

vurgu Accent, stress.

vurgun Struck; (*with dat.*) in love with; 'gone on'. Booty; good stroke of business; profiteering. ~ vurmak, to make a successful speculation, to do a good deal. **~cu,** speculator; profiteer.

vurmak, –ur *va. (with acc.)* Hit *stg. (acc.)* against *stg. (dat.)*; put *one thing (acc.)* on *another (dat.)*; hit and kill, shoot dead; apply (paint *etc.*); chafe, gall, blister; (of pickpocket) to steal; swindle. *va. (with dat.)* Strike, hit, knock; take (a road *or* direction); (of the sun) to beat down on; (of wind, light *etc.*) to penetrate into; to pretend to be. ⌐vur deyince öldürmek⌐, to exceed one's orders *or* advice; vur dedikse öldür demedik ya!, I told you to hit him, not to kill him! (*used fig.*): ⌐vur patlasın çal oynasın⌐, squandering money on pleasure; going 'on the bust': ···i açığa ~, to divulge (secret *etc.*): adam ~, to kill a man; adamı ~, to kill the man; adama ~, to strike a man: baş ~, (of a ship) to pitch; ···e baş ~, to have recourse to ...; başına* ~, (of wine) to go to the head; (of fumes *etc.*) to give one a headache: bilmezliğe ~, to feign ignorance: boynunu* ~, to decapitate: deliliğine ~, to feign madness: ···i demire ~, to put *s.o.* in irons: dışarı (içeri) ~, (of a disease) to affect one externally (internally): ···e el vurmamak, not to lift a finger *to do stg.*: harbde haylı vurmuştu, he is said to have made a pile of money during the war (*with a hint of profiteering*): kalbının temizliği cehresine vurmuş, the honesty of his heart was reflected in his features: ormana ~, to take the forest road: para ~, (i) to steal by pickpocketing; (ii) to make money by dubious means, to profiteer: yağmur içeriye vuruyor, the rain is coming in (to a room *etc.*): yakı ~, to apply a blister: kendini yerden yere ~, to roll on the ground in agony: (hayvana) yük ~, to load an animal: ···i birinin yüzüne ~, to cast *stg.* in *s.o.'s* teeth: zavallı adam kim vurduya gitti, the poor fellow was killed, but nobody knows by whom.

vurulmak *vn. pass. of* vurmak. Be struck *etc.* ···e ~, to be in love with *s.o.*: beyninden vurulmuşa döndü, he was thunderstruck.

vuruş Blow. ~mak, to strike one another, fight.

vuslat, –tı Union *with one's beloved.*

vusta (·⊥) Middle, central. kurunu ~, the Middle Ages.

vusul (·◡) **, –lü** Arrival. ~ünde, on his arrival.

vuzuh (·◡) Clearness; clarity *of speech etc.* ~suzluk, lack of clearness, obscurity.

vücub (·◡) A being obligatory; a being incumbent *as a religious duty*; obligation, duty; necessity. ~î (·—⊥), necessitative (*gram.*).

vücuh (·◡) *pl. of* vecih. Faces *etc.*

vücud, –dü Existence, being; the human body. ~ bulmak *or* ~e gelmek, to come into existence, to arise: ~e getirmek, to bring into being, to produce. ~ca (·◡·), bodily; physically. ~lü, large in body, heavily built. ~süz, bodiless; nonexistent; small, weak.

vükelâ (···⊥) *pl. of* vekil. Ministers. ~ heyeti, Council of Ministers, Cabinet. ~lık, post of Minister.

vüreyka A little leaf.

vürud (·⊥), **–dü** Arrival. ~ünde, on his arrival; on the arrival (of papers, post *etc.*): ~ etm., to arrive.

vüsat, vüs'at, –ti Spaciousness; abundance; extent; capacity; means. ~ine göre, as far as one's means *or* capacity allow: ~i hal, easy circumstances. ~li, spacious; extensive.

vüsuk (·◡) **, –ku** Trust, confidence; trustworthiness, authenticity, confirmation. ~ bulmak, to be confirmed.

vüsü, –s'ü Ability, competence.

vüzera (···⊥) *pl. of* vezir, Ministers.

Y

ya¹ Ah indeed!; oh!; then!; so!; especially; don't forget! ...; after all; yes, of course! ~ ben ne yapayım?, well then, what shall I do?: ~ duyarsa?, yes, but what if he hears?: ~ gelmezse?, and if he doesn't come, what then?: ~ öyle mi?, ah! is that so?: gördün mü ~!, there! you see what happens!: istediğin oldu ~!, after all you got what you wanted!: 'Niçin söylemedi?' 'Söyledi ~!', 'Why didn't he say?' 'He *did* say!': öyle ~!, yes, indeed!

ya² O ...!; oh!; hi! ~ rabbi!, oh!, my God!

ya³ Or. ya ..., ya ..., either ..., or ....

yaba Wooden fork *with three to five prongs for winnowing, carrying hay, etc.* ~lamak, to winnow *or* carry hay with a yaba.

yaban Desert; wilderness. *In compounds (the other word having the 3rd pers. possessive suffix)* wild-, *e.g.* ~asması, wild vine; ~keçisi, wild goat. ~ın köpeği, an outcast: sözüm ~a, excuse the expression!; *also* the 'so-called ...'.

yaban·cı, stranger; foreigner; foreign: ···in ~sı, a stranger to .... ~cılık, a being yabis [390] yahudi

a stranger *or* foreigner. ~i (·–¹), belonging to the desert *or* wilds; untamed, wild; boorish, unmannerly. ~ilik, wildness; boorishness. ~lık, visiting *clothes*; one's best clothes: wild place; wildness.
yabis (–¹) Dry.
yad¹ Strange; alien; enemy. Stranger. ~ elde, in a foreign land; away from home: ~ ellere satmak, to sell to foreigners: ⌐Allah kimseye gördüğünden ~ etmesin⌐, Heaven save one from coming down in the world!
yad² (–) Remembrance; mention. ···i ~a getirmek, to call to mind. ~etmek (–·). ~eder, to recollect; mention. ~igâr (–·–), keepsake; souvenir; scoundrel: notorious.
yadırgamak *va.* Regard as a stranger; find *stg.* strange *or* odd; (of a child) to cry at a stranger. bizimkileri yadırgıyorum, our own people are strangers to me: bulunduğum vaziyeti yadırgadım, I found my situation strange.
Yafa (¹·) Jaffa.
yafta (¹·) Label; placard (*esp. one hung round the neck of a condemned person and describing his crime*).
yağ Oil; fat; grease; ointment. ~ bağlamak, to put on fat: ~ bal olsun!, I hope you'll enjoy it (food), 'bon appetit!'; araları ~ bal, all is well between them, they get on excellently with one another; eğer on lira kazanırsan ~ bala ver, you can count yourself lucky if you earn ten pounds: ⌐~dan kıl çeker gibi⌐, with the greatest of ease: ekmeğine ~ sürüldü, that was an unexpected bit of luck; *v. also* ekmek: içi* ~ bağlamak, to feel pleased and relieved: ⌐kendi ~ile kavrulmak⌐, to manage by oneself, to get along with one's own resources; to live very modestly: paltosunun yakası ~ olmuş, his coat collar was greasy: ⌐o sineğin ~ını hesab eder⌐, he is so mean that he charges for the fat of a fly (in the butter): yürek ~ı, happiness, content: yüreğim ~ bağladı, I was overjoyed: yüreğimin ~ı eridi, I was prostrated with grief.
yağ·cı, maker *or* seller of butter *or* oil; an unctuous person. ~cılık, trade of a dealer in fats *or* oils. ~dan, ~danlık, grease-pot; oil-can. ~hane (·–¹), oil-mill; butter factory; creamery. ~ımsı, oily; greasy.
yağdırmak *va. caus. of* yağmak. Rain down *bombs etc.*; pour out *money etc.*
yağı Enemy.
yağır Withers *of a horse*; saddle-gall.
yağış Manner of raining; rain. ~lı, rainy.
yağız Black (horse); very dark (man).
yağ·lamak *va.* Grease; oil; butter; flatter;

grease the palm of; cause to make money. yağlayıp ballamak, to paint in glowing colours: tabanı ~, to run at full speed. ~lanmak, *vn. pass. of* yağlamak, to be greased *etc.*; to become dirty with grease; to be benefited, to gain a profit. ~lavı, large frying-pan. ~lı, fat; greasy; oily; dirty with grease; rich, free with money; profitable: ~ ballı olm., to be on the sweetest of terms: ~ kapı, a rich employer: ~ kuyruk, the fat tail of a sheep; a 'milch-cow'; a profitable business: ~ lokma, a rich windfall: ~ müsteri, a profitable customer; a 'milch-cow'; (*iron.*) a hard bargainer. ~lık, napkin, handkerchief. ~lıkçı, (i) dealer in handkerchiefs *etc.*; (ii) man who hires out wedding garments.
yağma Booty; loot. ⌐~ Hasan'ın böreği⌐, *phrase used to describe an irresponsible waste of other people's (or public) money*: ~ etm., to plunder: ⌐~yok!⌐, 'nothing doing!', 'you can't get away with that!' ~cı, ~ger, plunderer, pillager. ~cılık, pillage.
yağmak *vn.* Rain; be poured out in abundance. dolu ~, to hail: kar ~, to snow: yağmur ~, to rain.
yağmur Rain. ⌐~dan kaçarken doluya tutulmak⌐, 'out of the frying-pan into the fire'; ⌐~ olsa kimsenin tarlasına yağmaz⌐, 'if he were rain itself he would not rain on anyone's field', *used to describe an uncharitable and disobliging person.*
yağmur·ca, fallow deer. ~cın, ~kuşu, plover. ~lamak, to become rainy. ~lu, rainy. ~luk, raincoat; transom *of a door, etc.*
yağsız Without fat *or* oil; skim milk *or* cheese.
yahey (–¹) *Interj. expressing a feeling of comfort.*
yahni A meat stew with onions. ⌐ucuz etin ~si tatsız olur⌐, you get what you pay for; if a thing is cheap you can't expect much of it.
yahşi Pretty; agreeable; good. ⌐anan ~ baban ~⌐, using the most honeyed words.
yahu (–·) *Interj. calling s.o. or emphasizing a remark (often rather reproachfully).* bu da geçer, ~!, don't worry, this will pass!: ~ dün niçin bize gelmedin?, why didn't you come to us yesterday? (*reproachfully*).
yahud (–·) Or.
yahudi (·–¹) Jew. Jewish. ~ baklası, lupin: ~ pazarlığı, hard bargaining: ⌐~ züğürtleyince eski hesabları (defterleri) karıştırmış⌐, 'when a Jew is hard up he searches his old accounts', *often used of one who refers to his past achievements or wealth*

etc., *to excuse his present lack of the same*: yıllanmış ~ aklı, great cunning.

yahudi·ce (·–᳹·), Hebrew language. **~lik**, quality of a Jew; Jewish method of business; stinginess.

yaka Collar; bank, shore, edge; edge *or* corner of a sail. **~sı açılmadık küfür**, an unusual and obscene oath, *hence* **~sı açılmadık**, unusual, unheard-of : **~dan atmak**, to get rid of : ···**in ~sını bırakmamak**, not to let *s.o.* go; **~mı bırak!**, leave me in peace!: **~yı ele vermek**, to be caught *or* arrested : ~ **~ya gelmek**, to come to blows : ~ **ısırmak**, to express horror; to say 'God forbid!': ~ **kavramak**, to make earnest entreaty: **~yı kurtarmak (sıyırmak)**, to escape : ~ **paça etm.**, to seize by the collar and trousers and chuck out : **~sından** (*or* **–(sını) tutmak**, to hold responsible; to keep hold of, not to let escape : ~ **silkmek**, to be disgusted, 'fed up': ···**in ~sına yapışmak**, to hold responsible; to force *s.o.* to do stg. : ⌐iki **~sı bir araya gelmemek**⌐, to fail to get on; to make a mess of things (financially) : ⌐iki **elim ~nda!**⌐, I won't let you get out of this!: **lâkırdı ~sı açmak**, to bring up again an old and unpleasant subject : **öte ~**, the other side *or* shore : **ruzgârı ~ya almak**, to luff (a boat).

yaka·lamak, to collar, seize; find; hold responsible. **~lık**, stuff suitable for collars; collar of a shirt. **~paça**, *v.* **yaka**.

yakamoz Phosphorescence in the sea.

yakarış Entreaty, prayer.

yakarmak *Only in conjunction with* **yalvarmak**, to implore.

yakaza Wakefulness. **beynennevm vel~**, half-awake.

yakı Cautery; blister; plaster. ~ **açmak**, to apply a cautery : **pehlivan ~sı**, actual cautery (burning) *or* cautery by applying a caustic substance; **pehlivan ~sını açmak**, to cause great pain.

yakıcı Burning, smarting; biting *to the taste*.

yakılmak *vn. pass. of* **yakmak**. Be burnt *etc.*; pour out one's woes.

yakın Near (in place or time). Nearby place, neighbourhood; recent time; near future. From near at hand; closely, thoroughly; *frequently confused with* **yakin** (yakîn), *q.v.* **~mızda**, close to us, in our neighbourhood : **~da**, **~larda**, near by; in the near future; recently : ~ **akraba**, near relation : **~dan alâkadar**, closely interested : ~ **amir**, immediate superior (*mil.*) : **~dan bilmek**, to be closely acquainted with : **~a getirmek**, to bring near; (of a telescope) to magnify : ~ **muharebe**, close action (*mil.*) : ~ **zamanda**, not long ago : ⌐akıl var ~ var⌐, it's only common sense.

yakın·laşmak, to draw near, approach. **~lık**, nearness, proximity.

yakıotu (·᳹·), **–nu** Willow-herb.

yakışık Suitability; most suitable way; apparent truth, plausibility; beauty. ~ **almak**, to be suitable : ~ **almaz**, it is 'not done'. **~lı**, suitable, becoming; comely, handsome; well set up. **~sız**, unsuitable, unbecoming; ugly. **~sızlık**, unsuitability; unbecoming appearance.

yakış·mak *vn.* Be suitable *or* becoming; be proper *or* fit: look well, be pretty *or* handsome (of a thing or dress). **size yakışmaz**, it does not become you; it is not worthy of you. **~tırmak**, *va. caus. of* yakışmak, to think *stg.* becoming *to a person*; to expect *stg. of a person*: **bunu sana yakıştıramadım**, I would not have expected that of you: **yakıştırıp takıştırmak**, to embellish, decorate : **yakıştırıp uydurmak**, to invent *stg.* suitable to the occasion : **giydiğini yakıştırır**, he dresses well.

|| **yakıt**, **–tı** Fuel.

yakin, **yakîn** (·᳙) Certainty (*v. also* **yakın**). **~en** (·᳙·), for certain, positively. **~î** (·–᳙), known with certainty. **~iyat** (·–·᳝), **–tı**, certainties.

yaklaşılmak *vn.* Be approached; be approachable.

yaklaşmak *vn.* (*with dat.*) Draw near; approach; approximate; resemble.

yakmak *va.* Burn; set on fire; scorch; light; inflame with love; apply (poultice, henna); dupe. ···**e abayı ~**, to fall in love with ... : ···**in başını ateşe ~**, to bring misfortune on *s.o.* : **can ~**, to oppress; to hurt : **dil ~**, (of pepper *etc.*) to burn the tongue : ⌐dışarısı seni yakar içerisi beni yakar⌐, he (she, it) looks attractive to those who don't know about him (*etc.*) : **elektriği ~**, to turn on the electric light : **türkü ~**, to compose a song : 'yaklaşma, yakarım!', 'don't come near or I'll fire!': ⌐yere bakar yürek yakar⌐, he's not as innocent as he looks.

Yakubi (––᳙) Jacobite (Christian sect in Irak).

yakut (–᳝), **–tu** Ruby. **gök ~**, sapphire : **lâl ~**, garnet : **mor ~**, amethyst : **sarı ~**, topaz.

yal[1] Bright, shining; smooth, level.

yal[2] *Only in* **~ü bal sahibi**, handsome and well set up; well-to-do.

yalab·ık Shining; gorgeous. Glitter, sparkle. **~ımak**, to shine, sparkle.

yalak Trough; drinking-basin *at a fountain*.

yalama Licking; sore; erosion, abrasion; wear, play (*mech.*). ~ **resim**, wash-drawing.

yalamak *va.* Lick; graze; (of artillery fire *etc.*) to sweep over *a place*. **avucunu* yalamak**, to go away empty-handed : ⌐bal tutan

parmağını yalar[1], one connected with a
profitable business is bound to get pickings:
çanak ~, to toady: imzayı ~, to dishonour
one's signature: mürekkeb yalamış, having
some education: tükürdüğünü ~, to swallow
one's words.

yalan Lie, falsehood. False. ~dan, not
seriously, only for appearance; ~dan
söylemek, not to mean what one says;
~dan yıkamak, to wash superficially:
birinin ~ını çıkarmak, to show up s.o.'s
lies; to give the lie to s.o.: ~ çıkmak, to
turn out untrue: birinin ~ını tutmak, to
catch s.o. out in his lying: ~ yanlış, false
and erroneous; carelessly, superficially:
~ yere yemin etm., to perjure oneself: iş
bitirici ~, a lie for a good purpose, a white
lie.

yalan·cı, liar; false; deceitful; imitation:
~ çıkarmak, v. çıkarmak: ~ dolma, vine-
leaves or vegetable stuffed with rice:
⌐~nın mumu yatsıya kadar yanar⌐, 'a liar's
candle only burns till bed-time', a lie has
only a short life: başkasının ~sıyım, '(...
so I was told), if it be not correct it is not
I that lie'. ~cıktan, superficially; not
meaning it; in pretence. ~cılık, lying
mendacity. || ~lamak, to deny, contra-
dict.

yalanmak vn. Lick oneself; get a little
profit out of stg.

yalap yalap In a sparkling manner.

yalatmak va. caus. of yalamak. Graze; let
s.o. get a small profit.

yalavac Messenger; prophet.

yalayıcı Licking. ~ ateş (mil.), grazing
fire, fire with a flat trajectory.

yalaz Flame. ~lanmak, to flame up, blaze
up.

yalçın Rugged; steep; bare; slippery.

yaldırak Shining, brilliant.

yaldız Gilding; superficial finish; false
decoration; superficial accomplishment.
~dan ibaret, superficial. ~cı, gilder.
~lamak, to gild; to put a false finish to.
~lı, gilt; lacquered; falsely adorned.

yalelli (·¹·) Arab song; orgy; amusement.
~ gibi, unending, monotonous.

yalgın Glitter; glow; mirage.

yalı Shore; beach; waterside residence.
~ çapkını, kingfisher: ~ kazığı, tall thin
person: ~ mevsimi, the summer season:
~ uşağı, one born and bred by the seaside.

yalım[1] Blade of a sword etc.; stock; kind;
nature. dağ ~ı, steep slope, cliff, head-
land.

yalın[1], yalım[2] Flame; glitter; lightning.
~lamak, to blaze; glitter.

yalın[2] Single; bare, stripped; naked (sword).
~ayak (·¹··) barefooted: ⌐~ başı kabak⌐,

bareheaded and barefooted, in rags. ~ca,
~cak (·¹·), all alone; quite naked; poor.
~gac, any tree that sheds its bark
naturally. ~kat (·¹·), single-fold, not
double; superficial, shallow; having a
veneer. ~kılıc (·¹··), naked sword, drawn
sword.

yallah (¹·) interj. (abbrev. of ya Allah!)
Come!, go! ~ ~, at most.

yalman The pointed cutting part of a
weapon; steep and jagged mountain peak.

yalnız (¹·) Alone; solitary. Only. ~
başına*, by oneself, single-handed. ~ca
(·¹·), alone; by oneself. ~lık, solitude;
loneliness.

yalpa The rolling of a ship. ~ vurmak, (of
a ship) to roll; (of a drunken man) to sway
about, to lurch. ~lık, gimbals: ~ omurga,
bilge-keel.

yalpak Friendly.

yaltak Fawning; sycophantic; cringing.
~lanmak, to fawn, flatter obsequiously.
~lık, fawning, cringing flattery.

yalvac v. yalavac.

yalvar·ıcı Entreating, imploring. ~ışmak,
(of several persons) to entreat, implore.
~mak, to entreat, beg, implore.

yama Patch. ~ gibi durmak, to look out
of place, as though it did not belong:
⌐~ küçük delik büyük⌐, the means are insufficient for the end: ~ vurmak, to put on
a patch. ~cı, patcher; repairer of clothes,
boots etc.; skinflint.

yamac Slope of a hill; side.

yamak Assistant, mate. aşcı yamağı,
under-cook; kitchen-maid.

yamalak Only in yarım ~, defective, half
done etc. yarım ~ bir türkçe ile, in broken
Turkish.

yama·lamak va. Patch. ~lı, patched;
with scars on the face. ~mak, to patch;
stick on; impose s.o. or stg. on to s.o.

yaman Bad, disagreeable; strong, violent,
cruel; capable, smart, efficient.

yamanmak vn. pass. of yamamak. Be
patched on; instal oneself, get a footing;
settle down in a job etc.; foist oneself on
s.o.

yamçı Thick rough cape; felt saddle-cover.

yampüri v. yanpiri.

yamrı Only in ~ yumru, uneven and
lumpy; gnarled.

yamyam Cannibal. ~lık, cannibalism.

yamyassı (¹··) Quite flat; as flat as a pancake.

yan Side; flank; vicinity of a thing; presence of a person; direction, bearing. ~a,
v. yana: ~dan, from the side; sideways;
in profile: ~ıma, to my side, towards me;
~ımda, at my side; by me; in my opinion;

~ımdan, from my side; from me: ~ında,
at his (your) side; by him (you); in his
(your) opinion: ~ ~, sideways, sidelong: ~
~a, side by side: ···in ~ında, in comparison
with ...: bir ~dan bir ~a, from one side
to the other: ~ına* almak, to take into
one's service: ~ ateşi, flanking fire, en-
filade: ~ atmak, to enjoy oneself lazily: ~
bakmak, to look askance, to cast unfriendly looks; ⌈varmı bana ~ bakan?⌉, 'is
there anyone who dares to quarrel with
me?'; ⌈~ baksın kabahat⌉, every little
error is brought up against me: ~ basmak,
(sl.), to have one's hopes dashed; to 'come
a cropper'; to be deceived: ~ı başında, at
his side, close by him: ~ına* bırakmamak (koymamak), not to leave unpunished: ~ çizmek, to sneak off; pretend
not to see; pay no heed to; shirk: ~ gelmek, to take one's ease, to make oneself
comfortable: ~ gözle bakmak, to look at
s.o. out of the corner of the eye; to look at
s.o. or stg. with evil intentions: ~ına kalmak, to remain unpunished; araba ücreti
~ına kalmak için, to save the carriage
fare: bunu ~ına koymam!, I shan't forget that, you'll pay for it!: ~ında oturmak, to sit down by him; to lodge with
him: ···in alt ~ını sormak, to inquire
further into a matter: dört ~a bakmak, to
look in every direction: ellerim ~ıma
gelecek, I shall die one day (so I must tell
the truth); hilâfım varsa iki elim ~ıma
gelsin!, may I die if I am telling a lie!:
orası ne ~a düser?, whereabouts is that?:
'ben yeni bir işe başlıyorum, sen bir ~dan
eskisine devam et!', 'I'll start a new job,
you get on with the old one!': o zamandan
bu ~a, since that time.

yana¹ dat. of yan, also used as a prep. (with
dat.) Towards; (with abl.) as regards, concerning; in favour of, on the side of. ···den
~ olm., to be on the side of ..., to take the
part of ... .

yana² gerund of yanmak. ~ ~ or ~ yakıla,
in a moving way; pouring out one's sorrows.

yanak Cheek. yanağından kan damlıyor,
his cheeks are ruddy with health.

yanar v. yanmak. Inflammable. ~dağ
(·¹·), volcano. ~döner, shot (silk etc.).

yanaş·ık Adjacent; contiguous. ~ nizam
(mil.), close order. ~ılmak, to be approached; be approachable: yanaşılmaz,
unapproachable; inaccessible. ~ma, act
of approaching; casual labourer, hireling.

yanaşmak vn. (with dat.) Draw near,
approach (of a ship) to come alongside:
accede to a request; incline, seem willing.

yanayakıla v. yana².

yanazlanmak vn. Disagree; object (to =
dat.).

yancık Horse's armour; flank armour.

yançizmek v. yan.

yandık Camel-thorn.

yangabuç Lop-sided; distorted.

yangelmek (¹··), -ir vn. Take one's ease;
enjoy oneself lazily.

yangın Burnt; burning; suffering. Conflagration, fire; victim of a fire etc. (also fig.).
~ bombası, incendiary bomb: ~dan çık-
mış gibi, destitute: ~a gitmek, to go in
great haste: ~ var!, fire! fire!

yanıbaşı (·¹··), -nı Place by the side of a
person. ~nda*, by the side of ..., close
by ... .

yanık Burn, scald; blight; stinking smut;
bunt. Burnt, scorched; tanned; blighted;
lighted, turned on (electric light etc.); dole-
ful, piteous, touching, pathetic. ~ ~, in a
moving way: ~ kokmak, to smell of burning; to have a smoky flavour. ~kara,
bubo of plague. ~yağı (·¹··), -nı, ointment for burns.

yanılmak¹ vn. Complain or fret at a lost
opportunity.

yanıl·mak² vn. Make a mistake; go wrong.
~maz, who does not err; unfailing; fault-
less worker etc. ~tmac, tongue-twister
(like 'she sells sea-shells'). ~tmak, to
cause to make a mistake; lead into error.

yanısıra (·¹··) By the side of.

yani (⌐·) That is to say; i.e.; namely.

Yani Greek prop. name. ⌈kırk yıllık ~ olur
mu Kâni?⌉, ⌈can the leopard change his
spots?⌉

yankesici (¹···) Pickpocket.

yankı, yanku Echo; ‖ reaction. ~lamak,
to echo.

yanlış Error, blunder. Wrong, incorrect;
formidable (man). ~ herif, a man not to be
trifled with: ~ kapıyı çalmak, 'to knock
at the wrong door by mistake'; to be out
in one's reckoning; to make a bad shot:
~ yere, wrongly, falsely. ~lık, mistake,
blunder.

yanma Burning, combustion.

yanmak vn. Burn; be alight; catch fire; be
burnt or over-roasted; (of a plant) to be
blighted by heat or cold; be painful, hurt;
be very thirsty; be ruined, be 'done for';
feel grieved or sorry; recount one's woes;
become invalid or forfeited; lose one's turn
in a game. yana yana, complaining bitterly: yanıp yakılmak, to pour out one's
woes piteously: ···e ~, to be consumed
with passion for ...: ···den ağzı ~, to 'burn
one's fingers' with stg.: o adamın başında
ateş yanıyor, that man is haunted by
disaster: başkasının derdine ~, to suffer

on account of, or for the sake of, another:
canım yandı, I have suffered; I was hurt:
derd ~, to pour out one's sorrows: ···in
elinden ~, to suffer wrong at the hands of
...: haline ~, to complain of one's circumstances: haydi yandı!, time's up! (a turn on
a roundabout etc.): içi ~, to suffer: ···in
narına ~, to suffer or be ruined through
another's fault: yüreği yanmış, distressed,
afflicted.

yanpırı, yanpiri Leaning to one side;
distorted; awkward; crabwise.

yansı Lop-sided.

yanşak Dull, tedious; stupid.

yanyana (¹··) Side by side; contiguous.

yap yap Gently; slowly; by degrees.

yapak, yapağı Wool, esp. the wool of a
sheep shorn in the spring (as opp. to yün,
the shorter wool of an autumn-shorn sheep).
~çı, wool-merchant. ~lı, well-fleeced
(sheep); woollen.

yapalak Great owl.

yapayalnız (¹···) Absolutely alone.

yapı Building, edifice; build of the body.
yerden ~, low-built. ~cı, maker; builder;
constructor: creative; constructive.

yapık Horse-blanket; a kind of shaggy
cape.

yapı·lı Made; of such and such a construction or build: genc ~, of youthful build;
hafif ~, lightly constructed. ~lış, method
of construction; process of building.
~lmak pass. of yapmak, to be made etc.;
to become rich; to be drunk.

yapıncak¹ Rug to protect a horse from rain;
a kind of shaggy coat.

yapıncak² A variety of white grape from
the village of that name.

yapınış Affected or hypocritical air.

yapınmak va. Have made for oneself
(clothes etc.).

yapış In ~ ~, sticky. ~ık, stuck on, attached: ~ kulaklı, with closely adhering
ears. ~kan, sticky; adhesive; pertinacious, importunate. ~kanlık, stickiness;
pertinacity. ~kanotu, -nu, pellitory.

yapış·mak vn. Stick, adhere; stick to one
(as a bore); set about stg. (dat.). ···in
eteğine ~, to hang on to s.o.'s coat in entreaty: bir işe dört elle ~, to show the
greatest energy in a job. ~tırma, act of
sticking on; a thing stuck on; transfer
(picture); ornaments stuck on a bride's
face. ~tırmak, to stick on, attach; to
say stg. in quick reply: tokat ~, to give a
box on the ear.

yapıtaşı, -nı Building stone.

yapkın Wealthy; drunk.

yapma Act of doing or making. False,
imitation, sham. yerden ~, very short,

squat. ~cık, artificial; feigned; false:
affectation.

yapmak va. Do; make; construct; arrange;
set to rights; make ready. yapma!, incredible!: yapacağımı ben bilirim, you just
see what I'll do! (a threat): yapacağını
yap!, do your worst!: bana yapacağını
yaptı, he did me all the harm he could:
ᒣamma yaptın (ha)!ᒣ, is it possible!; you
don't say so!: geçen kış çok soğuk yaptı,
last winter was very cold: gülmeden
yapamadım, I couldn't help laughing:
gönül (hatır) ~, to satisfy, to content: ne
yapıp yapıp, in some way or other; by every
possible means: ᒣsanki iş yaptın değil mi?ᒣ,
a fine lot of use you are!

yaprak Leaf; vine-leaf; sheet of paper;
flake; layer. ~ aşısı, budding: ~ biti,
aphis: ~ dolması, stuffed vine-leaves: ~
kurmak, to pickle vine-leaves: ~ sıgara,
cigar: ~ tutun, tobacco in the leaf.

yaprak·dökümü, -nü, the fall of the leaf;
autumn. ~lanmak, to come into leaf;
become flaky; (of a sail or flag) to flap in
the wind. ~lı, leafed; leafy; flaky; having
so many leaves. ~sız, leafless; bare
(tree).

yapyalnız (¹··) Absolutely alone.

yar¹ Precipice; abyss. ~dan uçmak, to fall
down a precipice: ᒣdeveyi ~dan uçuran bir
tutam ottur¹, a handful of grass may cause
the camel to fall over a precipice, i.e. a
small incident may cause a great disaster.

yar², yâr, -ri Friend; lover. ~ü ağyar,
friend and foe, all the world: ~i gar, intimate friend: ~ olm., to be a helping friend,
to assist.

yara¹ Strength, power.

yara² Wound; sore, cut; boil. ~ açmak,
to wound: ~yı deşmek, to open a wound;
to touch a sore spot: ···in ~sına dokunmak,
to touch s.o. on his tender spot: ~ toplamak, for a boil to come to a head (also fig.):
~ya tuz ekmek, to put salt on a wound, to
increase another's pain by one's words:
dil ~sı, a wounding of the feelings by a
bitter word.

Yarabbi (¹··) My God!

yaradan Creating. The Creator. ~a
kurban olayım!, expression of admiration on
seeing a beautiful child: ~a sığınırım!, God
help me!; ~a sığınıp vurmak, to strike a
violent blow.

yaradılış Creation; nature, temperament;
constitution.

yarak, yarağ Arms; implements; provisions; penis.

yara·lamak va. Wound; hit a ship with a
shell. ~lı, wounded: kalbden ~, afflicted,
grieved.

yara·mak *vn.* Be serviceable *or* useful; be of use, be suitable. **işe yarar,** serviceable, useful for the purpose in hand : **işe yaramaz,** useless : **sana iyilik yaramaz ki,** it's no good treating you kindly. **~maz,** unserviceable; good-for-nothing; naughty. **~maz-lık,** unserviceableness; naughtiness; rudeness, bad behaviour.

yâran *pl. of* **yar.** Friends; lovers. **~ gay-reti,** favouritism.

yaranış A currying favour; polite attention.

yaranmak *vn. (with dat.)* Make oneself serviceable; offer one's services; curry favour; pay polite but insincere attentions. **ne yaptımsa kendisine yaranamadım,** I did everything I could to please, but all in vain.

yarar Serviceable, useful; capable; brave. Use; advantage. **~lık,** usefulness; capability; courage.

yarasa Bat.

yaraşık Pleasing appearance; suitability. **~ almaz,** it is unsuitable. **~lı,** suitable; pleasing in appearance; elegant. **~sız,** unsuitable; unpleasing.

yaraş·mak *vn.* Be suitable; be pleasing in appearance; harmonize, go well with *(dat.).* **güzele ne yaraşmaz?,** a beauty looks well in anything. **~tırmak,** to make suit; to deem suitable *or* becoming; invent (a lie *etc.*).

yaratan *v.* **yaradan.**

yaratıcı Creative; creating.

yaratılış *v.* **yaradılış.**

yaratmak *va.* Create. ⌐Allah yaratmış dememek⌐, to be merciless : ⌐Allah seni dünya boş kalmasın yaratmamış⌐, God didn't create you just to fill up space (but to do stg. useful) : ⌐küçük dağları ben yarattım diyor⌐, 'he says "I created little hills"', he is incredibly conceited.

‖ **yarbay** Lieutenant-colonel.

yarda (¹·) Yard. **~lık,** *so many* yards long.

yardak Assistant; mate; accomplice. **~çı,** helper; accomplice; lickspittle. **~çılık,** aid; complicity.

yardım Help, assistance. ···e **~ etm.,** to help, succour : ···ın **~ına yetişmek,** to come to the aid of .... **~cı,** helper, assistant; auxiliary : **~ fiil,** auxiliary verb. **~cılık,** quality of a helper; assistance. **~cısız,** without a helper; without assistance. **~laşmak,** to help one another.

yaren Friend. **~lik,** friendly conversation *or* joking.

yargı A splitting; split, fragment; decision in a court of law; ‖ lawsuit. ‖ **~ç,** judge. **~lamak,** to hear a case; try; judge. ‖ **yargıtay,** Supreme Court of Appeal.

yarı Half. **~ ~ya,** on a fifty-fifty basis, taking equal shares : **~ çekili bayrak,** half-masted flag : **~da kalmak,** to be left half-finished, to be broken off in the middle : **~ yolda,** half-way; **~ yolda bırakmak,** to leave half-finished, to give up before completion.

yarıbuçuk Small; insufficient; 'only half a ...': **~ askerle,** with only a handful of soldiers.

yarıcı¹ Who splits; wood-chopper; who breaks through the enemy's line.

yarıcı² One who works another's land for half the profit. **~lık,** the working of land on that basis.

yarıgece (·¹··) Midnight. At midnight.

yarık Split, cleft, cracked. Crack, fissure.

yarılamak *va.* Be half-way to *a place*; be half-way through *a job or a period.* **Ağustosu yarılamadık,** we are not half-way through August.

yarılmak *vn. pass. of* **yarmak.** Be split *etc.*; crack. ⌐yer yarılıp içine girmiş⌐, 'the earth must have cracked and it dropped into the crack', *said of stg. that can't be found.*

yarım Half. **~ ağızla,** not seriously meant *(as of an invitation etc.)*: ⌐~ elma gönül alma⌐, a very small kindness may win a heart : **~ kan,** half-bred : **~ saat,** half an hour.

yarım·ada (·¹··), peninsula. **~ca** (·¹·), megrims, severe headache. **~lamak,** to be half-way through *stg.*; to half finish. **~pabuc** (·¹··), pauper; vagabond; prostitute. **~sağ,** half right *(mil.).* **~sol,** half left *(mil.).* **~yamalak,** perfunctory; only half *done, learnt etc.*: incompletely.

yarın (¹·) Tomorrow. **~ değil öbür gün,** the day after tomorrow. **~ki** (¹··), of *or* belonging to tomorrow.

yarış Manner of splitting; race; competition. **~ etm.,** to race : **at ~ı,** horse-race : **çene ~ı,** empty chatter.

yarış·mak *vn.* Race; compete. **~tırmak,** cause to race *etc.*: **çene ~,** to wag the jaw incessantly, to chatter nonsense.

yarıyarıya, yarıyolda *v.* **yarı.**

yarlığ Command, edict.

yarlığamak *va.* (Of God) to pardon sins.

yarlık¹ A place of precipices.

yarlık² *v.* **yarlığ.**

yarlık³ Friendship; kindness.

yarma Act of splitting; cleft, fissure; break-through *(mil.);* railway cutting; large coarse man. Cleft, split; coarsely ground (wheat *etc.*). **~ muharebesi,** battle aiming at a break-through : **~ şeftali,** free-stone peach.

yarmak *va.* Split; cleave; cut through; break through *(mil.).* **başını gözünü ~,**

to smash s.o.'s face; to make a mess of, to mangle (a lesson, a language etc.): **kafa göz ~**, to be very tactless: **kılı kırk ~**, to split hairs.

yarmalamak va. Cut or tear in half lengthways.

yarpuz Pennyroyal. **su ~u**, water-mint.

yas Mourning. **~ tutmak**, to be in mourning.

yasa Law; code of laws.

yasak Prohibition; interdict. Forbidden, prohibited. **~ etm.**, to forbid: **~ savmak**, to serve in case of need, to 'do' when nothing better is available; to do stg. merely to comply with a rule: **~ savar**, (stg.) that will do for the time being.

yasakçı (Formerly) a man who went in front to clear the way for a great person; guard for an ambassador or consul.

yasamak va. Make laws; govern, control.

yasavul (Formerly) An official charged with the arrangement of state processions.

yasemin (–·¹) Jasmine.

yasla·mak va. Support; bolster up. **~nmak**, leans against stg.; support oneself.

yaslı In mourning.

yassı¹ v. **yatsı**.

yassı² Flat and wide. **~kadayıf** (·¹···), small cakes of batter soaked in syrup. **~lanmak**, **~laşmak**, **~lmak**, to become flat and wide. **~lık**, flatness; broadness of surface.

yastağac Bream.

yastamak, yastanmak etc. v. **yaslamak** etc.

yastığac Pastry-board.

yastık Bolster, pillow; cushion; pad; nursery-bed (garden). **~ yüzü**, pillow-case: **bir yastığa baş koymak**, to get married: **bir ~ta kocamak**, to have a long married life: **başı* ~ görmemek**, not to sleep a wink: **bıyık yastığı**, part of the beard left unshaven to support the end of long moustaches: **sıcak ~**, hot-bed: **yüz yastığı**, pillow.

yastım Squat; flat-nosed.

yaş¹ Wet; damp; fresh. Wetness, moisture; tears. **~a bastırmak**, to deceive, cheat: **~ dökmek**, to shed tears: **~ içine akıtmak**, to hide one's grief: **~ odun**, green wood: **~ tahtaya basmak**, to be cheated, to be taken in: ⌈**ağac ~ken eğilir**⌉, 'as the twig is bent the tree is inclined'.

yaş² Age. **~ını başını almış**, of mature years; **~ına başına bakmadan**, regardless of his (your) age: **~ında değil** or **daha ~ı yok**, he is not yet one year old: **~ı ne başı ne!**, he's too young! ⌈**akıl ~ta değil baştadır**⌉, age is no guarantee of wisdom:

ben ~ta, of my age: **biz ~takiler**, people of our age: ⌈**bir ~ıma daha girdim**⌉, I am astonished; also, I am older and wiser, I have learnt stg. over this: **bu ~tan sonra böyle giyinmek size yakışmaz**, it does not become you to dress like this at your age: **kaç ~ındasın?**, how old are you?: **on ~ına girdi**, he is in his tenth year.

yaşa Long live ...!

yaşama Living; the art of living.

yaşamak vn. Live; know how to live. **yaşadınız çocuklar!**, you are in luck!, said to congratulate s.o. on a piece of good fortune.

yaşanmak impers. of **yaşamak**. **burada iyi yaşanıyor**, one lives well here.

yaşanmış True to life.

yaşarmak vn. Become wet; become fresh. **gözleri yaşardı**, tears came to his eyes.

yaşasın Long may he live!; long live ...!

yaşatmak va. caus. of **yaşamak**. Cause or allow to live; keep alive; represent as alive (on the stage).

yaşayış Method of living; life; livelihood.

yaşdaş, yaşıt Of the same age.

yaşlanmak¹ vn. Become wet.

yaşlanmak² vn. Grow old.

yaşlı¹ Wet; suffused with tears.

yaşlı² Aged. **~başlı**, of mature years. **~ca**, getting on in years. **~lık**, old age; advanced years.

yaşlık Wetness; damp weather; juiciness.

yaşmak Veil worn by oriental women. **~lamak**, to veil; to put on a **yaşmak**. **~lanmak**, to be veiled; to put on the veil; to become nubile. **~lı**, veiled.

yat¹, -tı Armour; arms.

yat², -tı Yacht.

yat³ v. **yad**.

yatağan Heavy curved knife; yataghan.

yatak Bed, couch; lair; anchorage, berth; bearing of a shaft; chamber of a gun; receiver of stolen goods; screen for illicit enterprises; place of congregation, mart; river-bed; ore-bed. **yatağa düşmek**, to take to one's bed: **av yatağı**, place frequented by game: **bilye yatağı**, ball-bearing: **zengin yatağı**, the residential quarter of a town.

yatak·hane (··—¹), dormitory. **~lı**, furnished with a bed; having so many beds; deep-channelled (river): **~ bıyık**, trained moustache: **~ vagon**, wagon-lit, sleeping-car: **yüz ~ bir hastahane**, a hospital of 100 beds. **~lık**, bedstead; place for storing beds; a being a receiver of stolen goods: for so many beds: **~ hasta**, ill enough to have to go to bed: **~ kadın**, (contemptuously of a woman) only fit to go to bed with. **~odası, -nı**, bedroom.

yatalak Bedridden.

yatı A lying down; a going to bed; place

where one rests; halting-place. ~ **mektebi,** boarding-school: **gece** ~**sı,** staying the night as a guest. ~**lı,** where one sleeps: ~ **mekteb,** boarding-school.

yatık Leaning to one side; gently rising (ground). ~ **yollu top,** gun with a flat trajectory: **30 derece** ~, (ship) with a list of 30 degrees: *v. also* **yatkın.**

yatır Place where a saint is buried. ~ **çeşme,** saint's tomb with a fountain.

yatırım Deposit; investment.

yatırmak *va. caus. of* **yatmak.** Lay down; cause to lie down; make lean *or* slope; throw to the ground; overthrow; deposit *money in a bank etc.*

yatısız Home-boarder (at a school).

yatış·mak *vn.* Calm down; become quiet. ~**tırmak,** to calm, tranquillize.

yatkı Crease; fold.

yatkın Laid down; leaning to one side; inclined; that has laid too long, deteriorated, stale. **eli** ~ *(with dat.),* accustomed to, fairly skilled at *some job.*

yatmak *vn.* Lie down; go to bed; be in bed; pass the night; be bedridden; become flat; (of a ship) to lie at anchor; be broken in, be used to *work etc.;* yield, consent; stay in prison. ···**e** ~, to lie on; lean towards; agree to: **eli* yatmak,** to be used (to work *etc.*), to be fairly skilful: **bir yerde yatıp kalkmak,** to live *or* lodge at a place: **sulha (subhana)** ~ *or* **yola** ~, to be (with some difficulty) brought to reason *or* to agreement: **bir şeyin üstüne** ~ *(sl.),* to 'hang on to' stg. *that does not belong to one*: **yan** ~, to lean over to one side.

yatsı¹ Time of going to bed; ~ (namazı) prayer said by Moslems two hours after sunset. ⌈~**dan sonra ezan okumak⌉,** to do stg. too late or at an unsuitable moment.

yatsı² Levelled; smooth; flat.

yatuk, yatuğan Any musical instrument held in the lap while being played.

yavan Plain, dry *food*; without oil; tasteless, insipid. ~**lamak** *(sl.),* to be 'stonybroke'. ~**laşmak,** to be tasteless *or* insipid. ~**lık,** a being dry *or* without fat or oil; insipidity.

yavaş Slow; gentle, mild; soft (sound); docile. ~ ~!, gently!; steady!; don't be in a hurry!: ~ **konuşmak,** to talk in a low voice: ~ **yürümek,** to walk slowly; to walk quietly.

yavaşa Farrier's barnacles.

yavaş·ça, ~**çacık** Gently; slowly. ~**lamak,** to become slow *or* mild; to slow down; (of rain) to slacken. ~**lık,** slowness; gentleness; mildness.

yave (–¹) Foolish talk. Silly; commonplace. ~**gû,** who babbles nonsense.

yaver (–¹) Helping. Assistant; aide-decamp. ~**lik,** status and duties of an aide-de-camp.

yavru The young *of an animal or bird*; cub; chick; *affectionate term for a child.* ~**çıkarmak,** (of a bird) to hatch out chicks: **kapı** ~**su,** a wicket gate: **konak** ~**su,** a little mansion. ~**cuk,** *dim. of* **yavru.** ~**lamak,** (of an animal) to bring forth young.

yavsı A kind of stinging cricket.

yavşak Young louse, nit.

yavşan Thorny, spiny. ~ **otu,** *Artemisia fragrans* (?).

yavuk Token of betrothal; betrothal. ~**lamak,** to give a token of betrothal; to become engaged (to). ~**lu,** betrothed, engaged.

yavuz *(Originally* stern, ferocious, cruel); resolute; efficient; good, excellent. ⌈~ **hırsız ev sahibini bastırır⌉,** a bold thief will bluff the owner of the house, *said of one who is in the wrong but who carries the day by bluff*: ~ **Selim,** Selim the First *(known as Selim the Grim, but the real meaning to the Turks was rather 'the inflexible', 'the inexorable').*

yay Bow (of an archer); bow (violin). ~ **burcu,** the constellation of Sagittarius: **araba** ~**ları,** the springs of a carriage: ⌈**ok** ~**dan fırladı⌉,** the thing has happened, there can be no recall.

yaya, yayan On foot; pedestrian; of little account; without skill. ~ **kalmak,** to be compelled to go on foot *for want of a horse or vehicle*; to be in a difficult situation, to get oneself into a pretty pass: ⌈~ **kaldın tatar ağası⌉,** now you're stranded!; you are in a sorry plight; you're on the wrong track!

yayakaldırımı, –nı Foot pavement.

yayanlık A going on foot.

yaygara Shout; outcry, clamour. ~**yı basmak (koparmak),** to raise an outcry; to make a great to-do about nothing. ~**cı,** noisy; brawling; noisy fellow, brawler; cry-baby: loud (in taste).

yaygı Something spread out as a covering.

yayık¹ Spread out; broad, wide. ~ ~, in a dawdling manner; drawling one's words.

yayık² Churn.

yayılma Act of being spread out *etc.*; deployment *(mil.);* ‖ publication. ~**k,** *vn. pass. of* **yaymak,** to be spread out; spread, be disseminated; be stretched out on the ground *by a blow or fainting*; ‖ be published. ‖ **yayın¹** Distribution; publication.

yayın², ~**balığı** Sheat-fish, silurus.

yaylâ High plateau; summer campingground. ~**k,** summer pasture on high ground. ~kiye, rent paid for a yaylâk. ~mak, to pass the summer in a yaylâ; to graze on a yaylâk.

yaylı Armed with a bow; having springs. Carriage with springs *used for long journeys.* ~ gözlük, pince-nez.

yaylım *In* ~ ateş, volley; drum-fire.

yayma Act of spreading *etc.*; small dealer's stall. ~cı, small dealer *whose goods are spread out on a stall.*

yaymak *va.* Spread; scatter; disseminate; || publish.

yayvan Broad; spreading out; slack. ~ ~ gülmek, to laugh uproariously: ~ ~ konuşmak, to drawl: ağzı ~, garrulous.

yaz Summer. ⌐bir çiçekle ~ olmaz⌐, 'one swallow does not make a summer'.

yazboz tahtası School slate.

yazdırmak *va. caus. of* yazmak. Cause to write *or* be written; have inscribed *or* registered.

yazı¹ Plain; flat place.

yazı² Writing; calligraphy; manuscript; inscription; destiny; a written article. ~ makinesi, typewriter: ~ tahtası, blackboard: ~ taşı, slate: alın ~sı, the decrees of Fate; bu benim alnımın ~sıdır, this is my destiny.

yazı·cı, writer; clerk; secretary. ~hane (···–¹), writing-table, desk; office.

yazık A pity; a shame; deplorable; what a pity!; what a shame! ~lar olsun!, shame!: adama ~ oldu, it was a pity that this happened to the man.

yazı·lı Written; inscribed, registered; decreed by Fate, destined. ~lış, method of writing; spelling. ~lmak, *vn. pass. of* yazmak, to be written *etc.*; be registered *or* enrolled; be entered *at a school or university, etc.*

yazın (¹·) In summer.

yazış Manner of writing. ~mak, to write to one another, correspond.

yaz·lamak *vn.* Pass the summer *in a place.* ~lı, *only in* ~ kışlı, summer and winter alike. ~lık, suitable for the summer: summer clothing; rent for the summer.

yazma Act of writing; hand-painted *or* hand-printed kerchief *or* bedspread. Written, manuscript; hand-painted. ~cı, one who paints or prints fine stuffs (muslin *etc.*).

yazmak *va.* Write; inscribe; register; enrol; *(auxiliary verb, used in the past only)* to have been on the point of ...; düşe-yazdı, he all but fell. yazıp bozmak, to give an order and then a counter-order; to be capricious: ~ çizmek, to compose in writing: yüz ~, to decorate the face of a bride.

ye *v.* ya³.

Yecuc (–¹) *In* ~ Mecuc, *vaguely connected with* Gog and Magog *of the Bible; also the name of a* dwarf people *supposed to appear at the Day of Judgement.*

yed Hand; possession; assistance. ~i adil, ~i emin, depositary, trustee: ~i kudret, the hand of power, *i.e.* Providence: ~i tasarruf, possession, power of disposal: ~i tulâ, power; capability. ~beyed (¹··), from hand to hand; direct.

yede Jade; *(esp. a piece of jade given to Noah by Gabriel, which enabled him to control rain).*

yedek Halter; tow-rope; led animal; reserve horse; reserve; spare part. Spare; in reserve. yedeğe almak, ~ (~te *or* yedeğe) çekmek, to take in tow, to tow: ~ parçaları, spare parts: ~ subay, supplementary officer, reserve conscript officer: yedeğe vermek, to have *a horse* led *or a boat* towed: gıda ~leri, reserves of food.

yedek·çi, man who leads a spare horse; man who tows a boat: ~ yolu, towpath. ~li, in lead; in tow; having a spare horse; provided with a spare part. ~lik, serving as a reserve *or* spare part.

yedi¹, ~emin *v.* yed.

yedi² Seven. ~ adalar, the Ionian Islands: ~ başlı (yılan), a seven-headed hydra; venomous woman; dangerous man: ~ canlı, having seven lives, invincible.

yedi·gir, the constellation of Ursa Major, the Great Bear. Y~kule, the citadel of the Seven Towers *at Istanbul:* ~ marulu, *name of a much-esteemed lettuce.* ~li, having seven *parts etc.*; of seven *piastres etc.*: the seven *of a suit of cards.* ~lik, costing, weighing, measuring seven: piece of seven *piastres etc.*; clothes given to the bride by the bridegroom *to be worn on the seventh day of the marriage.* ~nci, seventh.

yedirme *verb. noun* of yedirmek. A preparation of hemp, lime, and oil *used to make a watertight joint in pipes.*

yedirmek *va. caus. of* yemek. Cause to eat *or* be eaten; feed; cause to swallow; let *oil etc.* be absorbed; expend, lose *money:* nefsine ~, to swallow *an insult etc.*: ···e para (rüşvet) ~, to bribe *s.o.*

yedişer Seven each; seven at a time.

yeditasarruf, yeditulâ *v.* yed.

yediveren Any prolific plant; plant producing several crops a year.

yedmek *va.* Lead *or* tow with a rope.

yeğ *v.* yey.

yegân Singly; one by one; individually. ~e (·–¹), sole, unique.

yeğen Nephew; niece.

yeğin Victorious; active; violent.

yeğni, yeğnik Light; easy.

yeğrek v. yeyrek.

yek¹ v. yey.

yek² One. ~ten, all at once; without any reason: ~ kalem, straightway. ~çeşim, one-eyed. ~diğer, one another; each other. ~dil, of one heart and mind. ~emel, having the same purpose.

yeke Tiller.

yekinmek vn. Make a great effort.

yek·nasak In a single row; uniform; monotonous. ~nasaklık, uniformity; monotony. ~nazarda (ˡ···), at a single glance; for the first moment. ~pare (·−ˡ), in a single piece: ~ buzlar, ice-floes.

yekrek Better; preferable.

yek·renk All of one colour; of the same mind; constant. ~san, one with; level; together; yerle ~, levelled to the ground. ~ser, from end to end; all together; all at once. ~ta (·ˡ·), single, sole, unique; matchless. ~ten, all at once; without any reason.

yekûn (·ˡ·) Total; sum. lâfa ~ çek!, enough of that!, oh! shut up!

yek·vücud United; one with ... . ~zeban, unanimous.

yel Wind; flatulence; rheumatism. ~ gibi gelmek, to slip in unobserved: ⌐~ üfürdü su götürdü¬, the wind blew and the water carried (the boat), easily and without effort: ~e vermek, to scatter to the winds, to destroy: ⌐o lâfı ~ler alsın!¬, said too ne who says stg. indecent or unlucky: ⌐yerinde ~ler esiyor¬, the place knows him no more; it no longer exists.

yelda (·ˡ·) Only in şebi ~, the longest night of the year.

yeldeğirmeni, –ni Windmill.

yeldirme A kind of light cloak formerly worn by women.

yele Mane. ~li, maned: uzun ~, having a long mane.

yelek Waistcoat, vest; wing-feather, pinion; feather of an arrow.

yelengec v. yalıngac.

yelim¹ Swift movement.

yelim² Mucilage; gum.

yelken Sail. ~ açmak, to hoist sails: ~ gemisi, sailing-ship: ~leri indirmek or mayna etm., to lower sails: ~i suya indirmek, to humble oneself, to knuckle under; for s.o.'s anger to blow over: ⌐(yel yeperek) ~ kürek¬, in a great hurry.

yelken·bezi, –ni, sailcloth, canvas. ~ci, sailor on board a sailing vessel; sail-maker. ~li, fitted with sails: sailing-boat.

yelkovan Minute-hand of a watch; weather-cock; eaves-board; smoke-cowl; the Bosphorus shearwater (Puffinus yelkovanus).

yel·lemek va. Blow upon; fan. ~lenmek,

break wind, fart. ~li, windy; flatulent; rheumatic.

yellim In ~ yeperek (yepelek), running swiftly; in great haste.

yelloz Whore.

yelmek vn. Run; move hurriedly and in confusion.

yelpaze (·−ˡ) Fan. ~lemek, to fan. ~lenmek, to fan oneself.

yelpik Severe asthma.

yeltenmek va. (with dat.) Strive or dare to do stg. beyond one's powers or rights.

yelve Woodcock; (in some districts) snipe.

yelyeperek v. yel.

yelyutan A disease of horses (? crib-biting); Alpine swift.

yem Food; a ration of food; fodder; bait; priming of a muzzle-loading gun. ~ borusu, bugle-call for horse fodder; ~ borusunu çalmak, to put s.o. off by empty promises: ~ kestirmek, to stop and feed the horses.

yemek¹ (yer, yiyor, yiyecek, yiyen) va. & vn. Eat; feed; consume; spend; dissipate; suffer (an infliction, a beating etc.); take a bribe. ⌐yeme de yanında yat!¬, said of a delicious food almost too good to touch: yiyip bitirmek, to consume utterly, to exhaust: ···in başını ~, to ruin, to kill; başının* etini ~, to worry the life out of ..., to nag at: ceza ~, to receive punishment: ···in hakkını (parasını) ~, to do s.o. out of his rights (money): içi* içini* ~, to be consumed with impatience or anxiety: kendi kendini ~, to worry oneself to death: kumarda ~, to gamble away: miras ~, to come into an inheritance: yağmur ~, to be wetted through by rain.

yemek² n. Food; a meal; a dish or course of food. ~ borusu, bugle-call for food. ~hane (···−ˡ), dining-hall. ~li, with food; with a meal; of so many courses or dishes. ~lik, serving as food; edible: a thing destined as food; money for food. ~siz, without food; without a meal.

Yemen (ˡ·) The Yemen. ~ zafranı, dyer's rocket, yellow-seed. ~li, native or inhabitant of the Yemen.

yemeni A kind of light shoe, worn by peasants; coloured cotton handkerchief. ~li, wearing a yemeni.

yemin The right hand; the right side or direction. ~ bozmak, to violate an oath: ~ etm., to swear, to take an oath: ~ ettirmek, to administer an oath: ⌐~ etsem başım ağrımaz¬, 'if I swear it, it won't give me a headache', I can say with a clear conscience (meaning that the speaker is telling a half-truth): bir şeyin üzerine ~ etm., to swear by a thing. ~li, bound by oath:

~yim oraya ayak basmam, I have sworn never to set foot in the place again.

yemiş Fruit. ~ **vermek,** to bear fruit. ~**çi,** fruiterer. ~**li,** fruit-bearing. ~**lik,** fruit-garden; fruit-store; fruit-dish.

yemleme Bait; alluring words; priming *of a muzzle-loader.* ~**k,** to bait *a hook or trap;* prime *a gun;* entice.

yemlik Suitable for food *for animals.* Trough, manger; nose-bag; bribe; an easy prey (in gambling).

yemyeşil (¹··) Very green.

yen Sleeve; cuff.

yencilmek *vn. pass. of* **yençmek.** Be crushed *etc.;* smash, fly to pieces.

yençmek *va.* Crush; smash; hurt the feelings of.

yenge (¹·) A woman's sister-in-law *or* aunt-in-law; elderly woman who helps and attends a bride.

yengec Crab.

yeni New; recent; raw, inexperienced. Recently. ~**den,** over again from the beginning; afresh, anew; ~**den** ~**ye,** always over again, ever anew: ~ **çıkma,** newly brought out; new-fangled: ~ **yapmak,** to do over again.

yeni·bahar, pimento. ~**baştan** (·¹··), over again, anew, afresh. **Y~cami,** *name of a famous mosque in Istanbul:* ~ **traşı,** a rough-and-ready haircut. ~**ce,** fairly new *or* recent. ~**den** (¹··), *v.* **yeni.**

yeniçeri (·¹··) Janissary; the Corps of Janissaries; swashbuckler, bully. ~ **traşı,** a rough-and-ready, not very skilful haircut. ~**ağası,** –**nı,** the Commander-in-chief of the Janissaries.

yenidünya (·¹··) The New World, America; the Japanese medlar, loquat; glass ball *used as an ornament in a room.*

yenik Place nibbled or gnawed by insects *etc.;* moth-eaten place.

yeni·lemek *va.* Renew; renovate. ~**lik,** newness; novelty; rawness, inexperience.

yenilmek¹ *vn. pass. of* **yemek.** Be eaten; be edible. **bu yenilir yutular şey değil !,** this is intolerable!

yenilmek² *vn. pass. of* **yenmek².** Be overcome; lose *at a game.*

yenir Edible.

yenirce Canker of trees.

yenişmek *vn.* Try to beat one another; wrestle; fight. **yenişememek,** to tie, to dead-heat.

yenli Having sleeves.

yenmek¹, –**ir** *vn. pass. of* **yemek.** Be eaten *etc.;* be edible; be worn *or* frayed. '**yenenle yanana ne dayanır',** food and fuel don't last long.

yenmek², –**er** *va. vn.* Overcome, conquer;

be victorious; win *at a game.* **suyu yenemiyoruz,** we cannot get the better of the water coming in (in a damaged ship).

yepermek *vn.* Run quickly *or* in starts; rush about in confusion.

yepyeni (¹··) Brand new.

yer¹ *v.* **yemek.**

yer² The earth; ground; place; space; room; landed property; situation, employment; mark *left behind by a thing.* ~**de,** on the ground; on the Earth: ~**inde,** in its place; suitable; to the point, well put; correct, right: ~**e bakmak,** to cast one's eyes to the ground *from modesty or shame;* ⌐~**e bakar yürek yakar**⌐, not so innocent as he looks; artful dodger: ~**e batmak,** to perish: ~**den bitme,** short, squat: ~ **bulmak,** to find a place, to get a situation; ~**ini bulmak,** (of an order *or* a request) to be carried out; (of a man) to find his right job: ~**e düşmek,** (of a command) to be disregarded: ~ **etm.,** to leave a mark; to impress, make an impression: ~**e geçmek,** to feel ready to sink into the earth for shame; ~**e geçsin !,** may he perish!: ~**ine** * **geçmek,** to replace *s.o.:* ~**ine gelmek,** to come into place, to come all right: ~**ine getirmek,** to carry out (an order *etc.*): ~**de kalmak,** not to be appreciated: ~**ine koymak,** to replace *stg.:* ⌐~**in kulağı var**⌐, 'walls have ears': ~**e vurmak,** to defeat; to discredit; ~**den** ~**e vurmak,** to throw violently to the ground; **kendini** ~**den** ~**e vurmak,** to be violently excited, to throw oneself about in a rage: ~**i yok,** it is uncalled for, it is out of place: **başı** * ~**ine gelmek,** to recover oneself; **çok yoruldum, bir sigara içmezsem, başım** ~**ine gelmiyor,** I am very tired, I shan't be myself again until I've had a cigarette: **baş üzerinde** ~**i var,** he is esteemed and respected: **boş** ~**e,** in vain, uselessly: **bunlara verilen paralar** ~**ine masruftur,** money given to these will be well spent: **bunu yapsa** ~**idir,** if he does this he will be quite right: **sen beni abdal** ~**ine koyuyorsun,** you take me for a fool.

yer·altı (¹··), –**nı,** ground below the surface; tunnel; underground chamber: ~ **kablosu,** subterranean cable. ~**çamı** (¹··), –**nı,** a kind of heath. ~**elması** (¹···), –**nı,** Jerusalem artichoke. ~**eşeği** (¹···), –**ni,** woodlouse. ~**fesleğeni** (¹····), –**ni,** dog's mercury. ~**fıstığı** (¹···), –**nı,** peanut. ~**göçkeni** (¹···), –**nı,** mole.

yerinmek *va.* (*with dat.*) Feel regret for; be sorry about.

yer·kabuğu (¹···), –**nu** The Earth's crust. ~**katı** (¹··), –**nı,** ground-floor.

yerleş·ik Settled; established. ~**mek,** to settle down; become established; get into an employment *or* office. **~tırmek,** *caus. of* **yerleşmek,** to put into place; arrange in proper order; put into an employment; settle *s.o. into a place of residence.*

yerli Local; indigenous; native. **~ ~si,** a local inhabitant: **~ dolab,** a fixed cupboard: **~ mal** *or* **malı,** local produce: **~ yerinde,** in its (his) proper place; **~ yerine,** each to his post.

yermek *va.* Loathe; blame; criticize. **aş ~,** to turn from one's proper food and long for stg. else (*used esp. of a pregnant woman*).

yer·siz Without a home; out of place. **~sıçanı** (¹····), **–nı,** mole. **~yüzü** (¹··), **–nü,** the face of the earth: **~nde öyle bir şey yok,** there is no such thing in the world.

yesar The left; left hand.

ye'si *v.* **yeis.**

yestehlemek *vn.* Go to stool, relieve nature.

yeşermek *vn.* Become green; bloom.

yeşil Green, verdant; fresh. **Y~ay,** the Green Crescent (Turkish Temperance Society). **~bağa,** Tree-frog. **~baş,** the mallard drake (*the duck is* **~in geri** *or* **tekir ördeği**). **~imtrak,** greenish. **~lenmek,** to become green; be freshened: ···e **~,** to be amorously excited by .... **~li,** mixed with green. **~lik,** greenness, verdure; meadow; salad; green vegetables, greens.

yeşim Jade.

yet *v.* **yed.**

yeter Sufficient. Enough! ‖ **~lik,** competence, capacity, qualification. ‖ **~sizlik,** insufficiency, inadequacy.

yetim (·ẋ) Orphan; fatherless child. Rare, unique. **dürrü ~,** 'a pearl of great price'. **~e** (·–¹), a priceless pearl. **~hane** (··–¹), orphange. **~lik,** quality of an orphan; orphanage.

yetinmek *vn.* Be contented (with = **ile**).

yetiş·kin *v.* **yetişmis. ~me,** *verb. noun of* **yetişmek:** arrived at full growth; ripe; perfected. **alaydan ~,** risen from the ranks; not professional.

yetişmek *vn. & va.* (*with dat.*) Reach; attain; suffice; attain maturity, grow up; be brought up; be ready *or* on hand in time; catch (a train *etc.*); arrive to the help of; live to see *a certain event etc.*; have lived long enough to have seen *a person or event*; (of plants) to grow. **yetişin!**, help!: **yetişme** (yetişmiyesi), 'may you (he) never grow up!' (*a curse*): **ben size yetişirim,** I'll catch up with you: **ben yalnız başıma bu kadar işe yetişemem,** I can't cope with all this work by myself: **trene yetişemedim,** I missed the train.

yetiş·miş, arrived; reached maturity; grown up. **~tirici,** breeder *of animals.*

~me, ···**in ~si,** brought up by .... **~tirmek,** *caus. of* **yetişmek,** cause to reach *etc.*; bring up, educate; breed (animals); convey (news), send (information); be unduly precipitate in passing on unnecessary information.

‖ **yetki** Competence; qualification. **~li,** competent; qualified.

yetmek¹ *v.* **yedmek.**

yetmek² *vn.* Suffice; reach, attain. **canına* ~,** to become intolerable; **artık canıma yetti,** I've had enough of it: ···**e gücü ~,** to be capable of, to have the strength to .... .

yetmiş Seventy. **~er,** seventy each. **~inci,** seventieth. **~li,** containing seventy. **~lik,** of the value of seventy *piastres etc.*; weighing seventy *kilos etc.*; seventy years old: seventy seventy years old.

yevm Day. ⌜**~ün cedid rıskün cedid**⌝, living from hand to mouth. **~î** (·⸱), daily. **~iye,** daily pay; day-book.

yey, yeğ Better; preferable. ⌜**akıllı düşman cahil dosttan ~**⌝, an intelligent enemy is better than a stupid friend.

yeyni, yeğni Light; easy.

yeyrek, yeğrek Better; best; preferable.

Yezdan God.

yezid, yezit Impious; cruel; vile fellow.

yığılı Heaped, piled up.

yığılmak *vn. pass. of* **yığmak.** Be heaped up; crowd together; fall in a faint; collapse.

yığın Heap; pile; crowd. **~ ~,** in heaps: **~la ...,** heaps of .... **~ak** (*mil.*), concentration. **~mak,** to be concentrated. **~lık,** crowd; mass. **~tı,** accumulation; heap; crowd.

yığışmak *vn.* Crowd together.

yığmak *va.* Collect in a heap; pile up; accumulate; mass (troops).

yıkama Act of washing. **~ makinesi,** washing-machine.

yıka·mak *va.* Wash. ···**den elini* yüzünü* ~,** to wash one's hands of .... **~nmak,** to wash oneself; have a bath; be washed.

yık·ıcı Destructive. Breaker-up (of old ships or buildings); junk dealer. **~ık,** demolished; fallen down; ruined. **~ılmak,** *pass. of* **yıkmak,** be demolished *etc.*; fall down; become decrepit; take oneself off, clear out. **yıkıl git!**, clear out! **~ım,** ruin; crash (bankruptcy). **~ıntı,** heap of ruins; debris. **~kın,** ruinous; about to collapse.

yıkmak *va.* Pull down; demolish; ruin, overthrow; unload (an animal). **ev ~,** to bring ruin to a home; to sow domestic discord: **yakıp ~,** to destroy utterly.

yıl Year. **~ başı,** New Year's Day: ⌜**~ uğursuzdur**⌝, 'the times belong to the rascals', said of undeserving people who get money or position : ⌐ar ∼ı değil kâr ∼ı¬, one can't be squeamish about money matters these days : **ayda ∼da bir**, very rarely : **kırk ∼da bir**, very seldom; just for once : **kırk ∼ın başında**, just for once.

yılan Snake. ∼ **gibi**, treacherous; repulsive : ∼ **gömleği**, snake-skin : ∼ **hikâyesi**, a long-winded story; stg. that never ends : ∼**ın kuyruğuna basmak**, to arouse the spite of a venomous and powerful person : ⌐**uyuyan ∼ın kuyruğuna basma !**¬, 'let sleeping dogs lie !'

yılan·balığı, –nı, eel. ∼**cı,** snake-charmer. ∼**cık,** erysipelas. ∼**cıkçı,** quack doctor who pretends to cure erysipelas by incantations etc. ∼**cıl,** the Sacred Ibis. ∼**kavı** (··–¬), spiral, winding. ∼**yastığı, –nı,** arum.

yılbaşı (¹··), **–nı** The New Year; New Year's Day.

yıldırak Bright, shining.

yıldırıcı Terrifying; one who causes fear and anxiety.

yıldırım Lightning, thunderbolt. ∼ **cezası,** fine levied on the spot, automatic fine : ∼ **telgrafı,** urgent telegram : ∼**la vurulmuşa döndü,** he was thunderstruck with terror.

yıldırmak va. Frighten, daunt, cow.

yıldız Star; Pole star; north; destiny. ∼**ı** ···**ile barışmak,** to be on good terms with ..., to get on with ...; ∼**ı dişi,** sympathetic, popular : ∼**ı düşkün,** ill-fated : ∼**ı parlak,** whose star is in the ascendant, lucky. ∼**böceği, –ni,** firefly; glow-worm. ∼**çiçeği –ni,** dahlia.

yıldönümü (¹···), **–nü** Anniversary.

yılgın Cowed, daunted. ∼**lık,** a being cowed : **göz yılgınlığı,** terror.

yılışık Sticky; importunate; grinning unpleasantly.

yılışmak vn. Grin unpleasantly; smile impudently.

yıl·lamak vn. Be a year in one place; become a year old. ∼**lanmak,** to become a year or several years old; remain several years; grow old; (of a matter) to drag on for a long time. ∼**latmak,** to keep for a year or several years; to delay for a very long time.

yıllık One year old; so many years old. One year's rent; a year's salary; year-book, annual. **bunca ∼ dost,** a very old friend. ∼**çı, ∼lı,** who receives a yearly salary; who pays a yearly rent : servant paid by the year.

yıl·mak vn. Be afraid; ···**den ∼,** to dread : ···**den gözü ∼,** to be terrified of .... ∼**maz,** undaunted; not to be cowed : dreadnought.

yıpranma Wear and tear.

yıpranmak vn. Wear out; be worn by friction or use; grow old prematurely.

yıprat·ıcı That wears out; exhausting; toilsome. ∼**ma,** act of wearing out : ∼ **harbi,** war of attrition. ∼**mak,** to wear out (va.); wear by friction etc.

yırak Thin and weak (horse).

yırlamak vn. Sing.

yırt·ıcı Tearing, rending. ∼ **hayvan (kuş),** beast (bird) of prey. ∼**ık,** torn, rent; ragged, tattered; broken in (horse); shameless, brazen-faced : ∼ **pırtık,** all in pieces; in rags.

yırtılmak vn. pass. of yırtmak. Be torn or rent; (of a horse) to be broken in. (yüzünün perdesi) ∼, to become insolent or shameless.

yırtınmak vn. Shriek in desperation or fear; be fearfully perturbed; struggle hopelessly.

yırtışmak Tear each other's clothes; scratch one another's face.

yırtlak Gaping as though torn.

yırtmac Slit in a sleeve etc.

yırtmak va. Tear, rend; burst; tear to pieces; break in a horse; assault, violate the person. ···**in yüzünü ∼,** to render insolent; to encourage s.o. to be too forward.

yısa v. yisa.

yiğit, –ti Young man; fine manly youngster; hero. Brave, stout-hearted. ⌐**her ∼in kârı değil¬,** it's not a thing anybody can do; it's not as easy as all that.

yiğit·başı, –nı, (formerly) man responsible for carrying out the regulations of a guild. ∼**lenmek,** to grow up; become brave; pluck up courage. ∼**lik,** courage, pluck, heroism: **yiğitliğe leke sürmemek,** to save one's face.

yilim Mucilage; gum. **ağız ∼i,** phlegm, mucus.

yine (¹·) v. gene.

yirmi Twenty. ∼ **yaş dişi,** wisdom-tooth. ∼**li,** costing, weighing, measuring twenty ... . ∼**lik,** of the value, weight, length of twenty ... : twenty para or twenty piastre piece : ∼ **bir genc,** a twenty-year-old youth. ∼**nci,** twentieth. ∼**şer,** twenty each; twenty at a time.

yisa (¹·) Hoist away !; pull !

yitik Lost. ∼**çi,** one who searches for a lost thing.

yit·irmek va. Lose; cause to go astray, ruin. ∼**mek,** to be lost; go astray; go to ruin.

yiv Groove; rifling of a gun; chamfer; hem; stripe. ∼**li,** grooved; chamfered; rifled.

yiy·ecek Edible; to be eaten. Food. v. **yemek.** ∼**en,** v. yemek. ∼**ici,** who eats; glutton; greedy; corroding (sore). ∼**inti,**

anything edible; edibles; foodstuff. **~ip,** *v.* **yemek.** **~iş,** manner of eating: ⌜**her yiğitin bir yoğurt ~i var**⌝, everyone has his own way of doing things.

yobaz Big; coarse; boor; *epithet jokingly applied to a country bumpkin when he first arrived at one of the old religious schools*; (*now*) a dangerous religious fanatic.

yoğrulmak *vn. pass. of* **yoğurmak.**

yoğun Thick; stout; coarse; big; gross, unmannerly.

yoğuna *v.* **yok.**

yoğurmak *va.* Knead.

yoğurt Yaourt (a kind of sour milk). **~ çalmak,** to make yaourt: ⌜**yoğurdu üfliyerek yemek**⌝, to blow upon one's yaourt before eating it, *i.e.* to be unnecessarily cautious: ⌜**hiç kimse yoğurdum kara demez**⌝, nobody runs down his own handiwork, 'nobody cries "stinking fish!"': ⌜**sütten ağzı yanan yoğurdu üfler de yer**⌝, 'a scalded cat fears cold water'. **~çu,** maker *or* seller of yaourt.

yok Non-existent; absent. Non-existence; nothing. No. There is not; **yok** *is used with possessive suffixes to make the negative of the verb 'to have', e.g.* **babam ~,** I have no father; **evi ~,** he has no house; **paraları ~,** they haven't any money. **yoğuna,** vainly; for nothing: **~ değildir,** there are (it is) not wanting, there are (is): **~ etm.,** to annihilate, to render non-existent: **evde ~tum,** I was not at home: **~ olm.,** to be annihilated, to cease to exist: **~ pahasına,** for a mere song: **yoğuna vermek,** to give for nothing, to sell for a mere trifle: **~ yere,** without reason; uselessly: **Londrada ~ ~,** there is nothing that is not to be found in London: ⌜**hiç ~tan azı hoş görmeli**⌝, 'half a loaf is better than no bread': **hiç ~tansa ona da razı olduk,** we agreed to that as better than nothing: **ne var ne ~ ?,** what's the news?: **var ~,** there is very little if any: **varı yoğu,** all he possesses, his all: **varımı yoğumu oğluma vereceğim,** I shall give everything I have to my son.

yoketmek (ˈ..), **-eder** *va.* Render non-existent; annihilate.

yoklama Examination; inspection; roll-call; call-up *of recruits.* **~cı,** military inspector; official in charge of the personal records of a military unit.

yoklamak *va.* Feel with the fingers *or* hand; examine, inspect; search; try, test; visit *a sick person.* **yoklaya yoklaya gitmek,** to feel one's way along: **···in ağzını ~,** to sound *a person,* to try to learn his opinion.

yoklaştırmak *va.* Feel; search minutely.

yokluk Absence; non-existence; lack; poverty. ⌜**adam yokluğunda**⌝, 'for want of a man', *used as an expression of modesty,* because they could not get anyone else.

yoksa (ˈ.) If not; otherwise; or; if there be not; but not; I wonder if. **~ gelmiyecek mi ?,** perhaps he isn't coming after all: **insan hayatta örnek vermeli ~ yalnız nasihat değil,** a man should set an example and not merely give advice.

yoksul, yoksuz Possessing nothing; destitute; in need of; lacking. **dayak ~u,** who deserves a beating: **fırsat ~u,** one who always looks out for an opportunity *to do stg. wrong*; **namus ~u,** devoid of honour. **~luk,** destitution.

yokuş Rise; ascent; slope. Rising (ground). **~lu,** rising (ground); sloping upwards.

yokyere (ˈ..) Without due cause; in vain, uselessly.

yol Road; way; street; channel, canal; means, medium; manner, method; behaviour; rule, law; journey; career; rate of speed; stripe. **~ ~,** striped; in lines: **~una,** for, for the sake of, *e.g.* **vatan ~una,** for one's country's sake; **Hak ~una,** for God: **~unda,** for the sake of; in order, going as it should, *e.g.* **bütün işler ~undadır,** everything is going as it should, all goes well: **~unda, ~undaki,** in the sense that, to the effect that: **~iyle** (**~u ile**), via; by way of; properly, duly: **~ almak,** to acquire momentum, to get up speed; to advance: **···in ~una bakmak,** to await *s.o.'s* arrival: **···in ~unu beklemek,** to lie in wait for ...: **~ bilmek,** to know the way; to know how to do *stg.*; to know how to behave: **~unu bulmak,** to find a way of doing *stg.*: **~undan çıkarmak,** to mislead, pervert: **~dan çıkmak,** to go off the rails; to go astray, to go to the bad: **···e ~u* düşmek,** for one's road to lead one to ..., *e.g.* **oraya ~unuz düşerse,** if you are going that way: **~a düşmek,** to set out, to set forth on a journey; **~lara düşmek,** to set out in search of s.o. (*implies an emergency*): **~ erkân,** social conventions: **~a gelmek,** to come round, to think better of *stg.*; to come to reason, to listen to advice: **~a getirmek,** to bring *s.o.* round to the right view *or* course, to bring to reason, to persuade: **~una girmek,** (of a matter) to come right: **~ iz bilmek,** to know the rules of social behaviour: **~dan kalmak,** to be kept back, to be detained; **~larda kalmak,** to be delayed on the road: **~ kesmek,** to waylay a road, to stage a hold-up; **~unu kesmek,** to stop *s.o.*: **~una koymak,** to set right; **~undan koymak,** to prevent, detain, delay: **~ üslûb,** mode, manner: **~üstü,** on the road: **~ vermek,** to give passage, to make way; to give *a horse* his head; to let go his own way; to discharge, dismiss from service; ···e ~ **vermek**, to open the way to, to cause: ~ **vurmak**, to waylay a road, to stage a hold-up; ~a **vurmak**, to see *s.o.* off *on a journey*: bir **yol** (*provincial*), once: ⌐**bize ~ göründü**¬, we must be going: **top ~una gitmek**, to die obscurely: to perish miserably; to punish along with others although innocent: **bu vapurun ~u yok**, this steamer has no speed: ⌐(**sıçanın geçtiğini aramam ama**) ~ **olur**¬, I don't mind it once, but it might become a precedent.

yol·bilir, who knows how to comport himself *or* how things should be done; well-mannered; adroit. ~**bilmez**, unmannerly, awkward; maladroit. ~**cu**, traveller; passenger; child about to be born; one at the point of death; woman of the streets: ~ **geçirmek**, to accompany *s.o.* on the start of a journey: ⌐~ **yolunda gerek**¬, a traveller's place is on the road; one should stick to what one is doing: **yine ~ olduk**, I must start on my travels again. ~**culuk**, travelling, travel: ~ **ne zaman?**, when do you set out? ~**daş**, fellow traveller; comrade: **can ~ı**, a very intimate friend, a faithful friend; s.o. to keep one company: **kapı ~ı**, fellow servant; in the same employment. ~**daşlık**, a being a fellow traveller; comradeship, fellowship.

yoldurmak *va. caus. of* **yolmak**. Cause to pluck *etc.* ···e ot ~, to make *s.o.* work hard.

yolgeçen *In ~ hane, used of a place which is much frequented (though not on account of its natural function, such as a post office).*

yol·harcı (¹··), -**nı** Travelling expenses; journey-money. ~**kesici**, highwayman, brigand.

yollama Act of sending; Goods Department of a railway; military transport service; large beams of building timber. ~ **müdürü**, railway official in charge of the Goods Department.

yol·lamak *va.* Send; dispatch. ~**lanmak**, be sent off; set off *on a journey etc.*; advance.

yollu Having *such and such* roads; striped; having *such and such* a way *or* manner; proper, correct, regular; fast (ship *etc.*). Of the nature of, by way of. ~ **yolsuz işler**, irregular actions: **nasihat ~**, of the nature of advice.

yolluk Provisions for a journey; journey-money.

yolmak *va.* Pluck; tear out; strip; despoil. **saçını başını ~**, to tear one's hair; to tear out *s.o.'s* hair.

yolsuz Roadless; irregular, contrary to law

or custom; (of a tradesman) banned by his guild *for some fault*; without speed (ship, motor-car *etc.*). ~**luk**, irregularity; impropriety; punishment of a tradesman (*v.* yolsuz).

yoluk Plucked; hairless.

yolunda *v.* yol.

yolunmak *vn. pass. of* **yolmak**. Be plucked; be robbed; lose one's money *at* gambling; tear one's hair *with grief*.

yolüstü (¹··) (Place) lying on one's road; (window *etc.*) looking on the road.

yom *v.* yum.

yoma Cable-laid (rope). ~ **bağı**, carrick bend.

yonca Clover; trefoil; lucerne.

yonda Under-feathers *of a bird*.

yonga Chip, chipping; kindling. ⌐**ağır ~yı yel kaldırmaz**¬, the wind does not blow away a heavy chip, *said of one who has influential friends and cannot easily be removed from a post*: ⌐**mal canın ~sıdır**¬, possession is a bit of one's being, *i.e.* it is hard to part with anything one owns.

yonma, yonmak *v.* yontma, yontmak.

yont, -**tu** Wild unbroken mare; water-wagtail.

yontma Act of chipping. Chipped, cut. ~ **taş**, dressed stone.

yont·mak *va.* Cut, chip into shape; dress (stone); pare (nails); sharpen (pencil). **kendinden yana ~**, to turn to one's own advantage, to look after number one. ~**ulmamış** (·¹··), not chipped *or* hewn; rough, uneducated.

yoramak *v.* yormak².

yordam Agility; dexterity. **el ~ı**, feeling with the hand; **el ~ile**, by touch: **yol ~ bilmek**, to know the proper way to do *stg.*; **yolunu ~ını şaşırmak**, to lose one's bearings; not to know where one is. ~**lı**, *in* yollu ~, in the proper way, 'comme il faut'.

yorga Jog-trot. Going at a jog-trot.

yorgan Quilt. ⌐~ **gitti kavga bitti**¬, 'the dispute is ended', *said ironically when the subject of a dispute no longer exists, v. App.*: ⌐**ayağını ~a göre uzatmak**¬, 'to cut one's coat according to one's cloth'. ~**cı**, quilt-maker; upholsterer. ~**iğnesi**, -**ni**, quilting-needle. ~**lık**, suitable for making quilts. ~**yüzü**, -**nü**, outer covering of a quilt.

yorgun Tired, weary. ~ **argın**, dead tired. ~**luk**, weariness, fatigue: ~ **almak**, to rest from one's fatigue: ~ **kahvesi**, coffee to revive one when tired.

yorma¹ Act of tiring.

yorma² Interpretation of a dream *or* an an omen.

yormak¹ va. Tire, fatigue. **ağız ~**, to talk or plead in vain: **çene ~**, to chatter, talk nonsense.

yormak² va. Interpret a dream or omen; presage; attribute. **hayra ~**, to interpret favourably, to regard as auspicious: **üstüne ~**, to take a remark etc. as directed against oneself.

yortu Christian feast.

yorucu Fatiguing, wearisome.

yorulmak¹ vn. pass. of **yormak¹**. Be tired; tire oneself out in vain.

yorulmak² vn. pass. of **yormak²**. Be interpreted etc.

yorum Interpretation of a dream or omen; a counting as auspicious. ‖ **~cu**, commentator. ‖ **~lamak**, to comment on, explain.

yosma Pretty; graceful; attractive. Pretty and attractive person; coquette. **~m**, my pet! **~lık**, gracefulness; charm.

yosun Moss. **~ bağlamak**, to become covered with moss: **deniz ~u**, seaweed: **taş ~u**, lichen. **~lu**, mossy, covered with moss.

yoz Untrained, wild. **~laşmak**, to become wild; to lose qualities that have been acquired.

yön Direction; quarter; regard, relation. **gıda ~ünden**, as regards food: **ne ~den?**, in what respect? **~elme**, direction, course. **~eltmek**, to direct; turn towards. ‖ **~etim**, direction, administration, management: **sıkı ~**, martial law. **~lü**, directed or turned towards.

yöre Side; neighbourhood; ‖ suburb.

yörük v. **yürük**.

yörünge Course taken by a thing; orbit; trajectory.

yudum Mouthful; draught of water etc.

yuf Interj. expressing scorn and disgust. **~ borusu çalmak**, to boo: **~ sana!**, shame on you!

yufka Thin; weak; poor. Thin layer of dough; wafer; unleavened bread in thin sheets. ⌈**arkası ~**⌉, (jokingly) there's nothing more (to eat)!: **cebi ~**, penniless: **sırtı ~**, scantily clad: **yüreği ~**, compassionate, soft-hearted. **~lık**, flour suitable for flake pastry; thinness; poverty; soft-heartedness.

yuğurmak v. **yoğurmak**.

yuha (⸳⸳) A shout of contempt or derision. **~ya tutmak** or **···e ~ çekmek**, to hold up to derision; to hoot.

yukar·da On high; above; overhead. **~dan**, from above: **~ almak**, to behave in a condescending manner.

yukarı High; upper; top. Above; upwards; on high; up. Upper or topmost

part. **~ya yığmak**, to pile up high; to exaggerate.

yulaf Oats.

yular Halter. ⌈**başında ~ı eksik**⌉, 'he wants a halter', i.e. he's an ass.

yum Good luck; good omen. **~lu**, auspicious. **~suz**, inauspicious.

yumak¹ va. Wash.

yumak² Ball (of wool, string etc.). **~lamak**, to wind into a ball.

yummak va. Shut; close (eye, fist). ⌈**ağzını açıp gözünü ~**⌉, to lose one's temper and say bitter things without reflection; to let oneself go: **el ~**, to be close-fisted: **gözünü* ~**, to shut the eyes (physically); **···e göz ~**, to shut the eyes to, to wink at ..., to pretend not to see; **göz yummamak**, not to wink at or condone; not to sleep a wink.

yumru Round, globular. Round thing; boil; tubercle (bot.). **~ burun**, bottlenose: **boyun ~su**, goitre.

yumrucak v. **yumurcak**.

yumruk Fist; blow with the fist. **~larını sıkmak**, to clench the fists; to threaten with the fists. **~lamak**, to hit with the fist; pound with the fist, knead. **~luk**, in ⌈**bir ~ canı var**⌉, one blow and he's a dead man.

yumru·lmak, **~lanmak** vn. Become swollen; get a boil. **~luk**, roundness; swelling (of a boil etc.).

yumşak v. **yumuşak**.

yumuk Closed by swelling (eye); half-shut (eye); plump; soft.

yumulmak vn. (Of the eye) to become closed by swelling.

yumurcak Bubo; plague; pestilential child. **~ olm.**, to be stricken by the plague.

yumurmak v. **yumrulmak**.

yumurta Egg; darning mushroom. **~ akı**, the white of an egg: ⌈**~ kabuğunu beğenmemiş**⌉, 'the egg did not like its shell', said of one who runs down those who brought him up or educated him: ⌈**~ kapıya gelince**⌉, at the very last minute; or when the situation has become serious: **~ ökçeli ayakkabı**, shoes with oval high heels, worn by town roughs: **~ patlıcanı**, aubergine bearing white fruits: **~ sarısı**, the yolk of an egg.

yumurta·lık, ovary; egg-cup. **~lamak**, to lay eggs; spawn; invent a story; blurt out, say stg. indiscreet.

yumuşacık Rather soft or mild.

yumuşak Soft; mild; yielding. Soft part of anything. **~ başlı**, docile: **yüzü ~**, too kind to refuse. **~lık**, softness; mildness.

yumuşamak vn. Become soft; become pliant or yielding; calm down.

yuna Small felt numnah.

yunak, yunaklık Wash-house; place for washing clothes on a river bank.

Yunan, ~istan Greece. **~ca** (·¹·), ancient Greek or modern Greek as spoken in Greece (modern Greek as spoken in Turkey is rumca). **~î**, pertaining to ancient Greece. **~lı**, Greek.

yunmak vn. Wash oneself.

Yunus Jonah. **~balığı, –nı**, porpoise; dolphin.

yura Steep slope.

yurak Spoke of a wheel.

yurd Native country; home; habitation; estate. **yeri ~u yok (bellisiz)**, homeless, vagabond. **~daş**, fellow countryman, compatriot. **~lanmak**, to settle in a place; to cease being a nomad and live a settled existence: to acquire an estate. **~luk**, estate, domain. **~sever**, patriotic.

yurdu Eye of a needle.

yurtmak vn. Wander about aimlessly; (of a horse) to amble along.

yusufçuk A small kind of turtle-dove; dragonfly.

yusufî (··¹) A peaked turban formerly worn by great personages.

yusyumru (¹··) Quite round; very swollen.

yusyuvarlak (¹···) Quite round.

yutkunmak vn. Swallow one's spittle; gulp in suppressing one's emotions. **bir şey karşısında ~**, to resign oneself to doing without stg.

yutmak va. Swallow; gulp down; swallow an insult; endure an injury in silence; believe a lie, swallow a tall story; win at cards; appropriate wrongfully; fail to see a joke. **yuttum oturdum**, I raised no protest, I didn't open my mouth: **kazık (baston) yutmuş gibi**, as stiff as a poker: **riyaziyeyi yutmuş**, he knows mathematics from A to Z: **zehir ~**, to swallow poison; to brood over a thing.

yut·turmak va. caus. of yutmak. Cause to swallow etc., esp. cause to swallow a lie, swindle. **~turulmak**, pass. of yutturmak, to be taken in by a lie etc. **~ucu**, who swallows or devours; who wins at cards. **~ulmak**, pass. of yutmak, be swallowed etc.; lose at cards: ⌐ekmek bile çiğnenmeden yutulmaz⌐, even bread must be chewed before it can be swallowed, i.e. no reward without effort. **~um**, v. yudum.

yuva Nest; home; socket; seating of a valve. **~ kurmak**, to build a nest; to set up a home: ···in **~sını* yapmak**, to give s.o. 'what for', to teach him a lesson: ⌐garib kuşun ~sını Allah yapar⌐, God builds the nest of the stranger bird, i.e. cares for all. **~lamak**, to nest.

yuvarlak Round, spherical. Ball; marble; limber of a gun; cylinder of a printing-press. **~lık**, roundness.

yuvar·lamak va. Rotate; roll; roll up; swallow greedily; utter a lie; toss off (a glass of wine). **~lanmak** vn., to revolve, turn round; roll; topple over; be tormented by grief or worry; lose one's job, be sacked; (sl.) die suddenly: **yuvarlanıp gitmek**, to worry along somehow. **~latmak**, to cause to rotate etc.; make round.

yüce, yücel High; exalted person or position. High place. **~lenmek, ~lmek**, to become high; rise. **~lik**, height; loftiness; exalted rank.

yük, –kü Load; burden; heavy task or responsibility; cargo; unborn young; 100,000 piastres; large cupboard for bedding. **~ünü almak**, to become crowded; to take all it can hold: **~ün altından kalkamamak**, to find one's duties too much for one: **~ arabası**, wagon: ⌐~te hafif pahada ağır⌐, small in bulk but valuable: **~ hayvanı**, pack-animal: **~ünü tutmak**, to become rich: **~ü üzerinden atmak**, to decline or shift a responsibility: ···e **~ vurmak**, to load an animal: **~ünü yüklenmiş**, wealthy.

yük·lemek, to load; place a load on; throw the blame on; impute; attribute. **~lenmek** pass. of yüklemek, to be loaded etc.; take a load upon oneself; ···e **~**, to throw oneself upon, attack; keep on at s.o. **~letmek**, to place a load on; load (a ship etc.); impose a duty, an expense etc.; impute, attribute. **~lü**, loaded (with= nom.); pregnant; drunk; overburdened with work; in debt; rich: **kömür ~**, loaded with coal. **~lük**, large cupboard or closet for bedding.

yüksek High; loud (voice). High altitude. **~ten atmak**, to boast: ···e **~ten bakmak**, to look down upon: **~lerde dolaşmak**, to aim high, to be ambitious: **~ten kopmak**, to set out with great pretensions: **~ sesle okumak**, to read aloud: **~ten uçmak**, to be ambitious or presumptuous. **~lik**, height, elevation.

yüksel·mek vn. Mount; rise; be promoted; (of a ship) to gain the open sea. **~tmak**, to cause to rise; raise; promote; praise excessively.

yüksük Thimble. **~le ölçmek**, to dole out stingily: **~ otu**, foxglove.

yüksünmek va. & vn. (Of an animal) to flinch under a heavy load; show temper in the performance of duty; regard as burdensome; grudge giving or fulfilling a promise.

yül·gü Razor. **~cü**, barber. **~ük**, shaven; smooth. **~ümek**, to pluck, to shave.

yümün, –mnü A being lucky; prosperity.

yün Wool. Woollen. ~**lenmek,** to become woolly; to be frayed. ~**lü,** woollen.

yürek Heart; stomach; centre of the affections; courage, boldness. [*In many idioms* **yürek** *is used instead of* **iç** *or* **gönül**; *if the phrase cannot be found under* **yürek** *consult* **iç** *and* **gönül**]. ~**ler acısı,** a heartbreaking event *or* condition: **yüreği* atmak,** for one's heart to palpitate from emotion: **yüreği* (içi) bayılmak,** to be very hungry: ~ **çarpıntısı,** palpitation of the heart; misgivings: **yüreği dar,** impatient: ~ **dayanmaz,** unbearable; heartbreaking: **yüreği delik,** full of woes: **yüreğine* inmek,** to be struck with great fear, agitation *or* shame: **yüreği* kabarmak,** to be nauseated; to suffer trouble *or* pain: **yüreğini* kaldırmak,** thoroughly to upset *or* excite *s.o.*: **yüreği* kalkmak,** to be alarmed; to be very upset: **yüreği katı,** obstinate, obdurate: **yüreği* katılmak,** to suffer greatly: **yüreği* oynamak,** to have a fluttering of the heart; to have misgivings: **yüreği pek,** stouthearted: **yüreği* tükenmek** *or* ~ **tüketmek,** to wear oneself out *in trying to explain stg.*: ~ **vermek,** to hearten, to give courage: **yüreği* yağ bağlamak,** to have a load taken off the heart, to feel relieved: **yüreğinin* yağı erimek,** to be terribly anxious *or* grieved: **yüreği* yanmak,** to be grieved; to feel pity; to meet with disaster: ... ···**se ·yüreğim yanmaz,** it wouldn't have been so bad if ...: **yüreği yufka,** easily moved; compassionate.

yürek·lenmek, to take heart, be emboldened. ~**li,** stout-hearted, plucky; -hearted. ~**siz,** faint-hearted, timid; apathetic, lukewarm. ~**sizlik,** faint-heartedness, timidity; lukewarmness.

yürük Fast, fleet. Nomad; (*formerly*) a class of Janissary soldiers.

yürüme *verb. n. of* **yürümek. kan** ~, congestion of blood.

yürümek *vn.* Walk; advance, make progress; hurry along; (*sl.*) die; ‖ come into force, have effect. ⌐**Allah yürü ya kulum demiş**¹, 'Allah said "advance, my slave!"', *said, rather enviously, of one who has made rapid progress*: ... **modası aldı yürüdü,** the fashion of ... has grown: ···**in üstüne** ~, to 'go for' *s.o.* (physically): **üzerine** ~, to march against, to attack.

yürünmek *vn. impers. of* **yürümek.** Be walked. **on saat yüründü,** a march of ten hours was made.

‖ **yürürlük** A being in force; validity.

yürütmek *va. caus. of* **yürümek.** Cause to walk *etc.*; put forward (an idea, a proposal *etc.*); (*sl.*) 'walk off with', pilfer; (*sl.*)

'sack', dismiss; ‖ put into force. **faiz** ~, to reckon up and pay interest.

yürüyüş Gait; march; assault. ~ **kapısı,** wicket-gate: **mevzun** ~, marching in step.

yüz¹ Face; surface; the face *or* right side (of cloth *etc.*); the outer covering of a thing; motive, cause; boldness; effrontery. ~**ünde,** on, on the surface of: ~**ünden,** for the sake of, on account of: ~ **akı,** *v.* **yüzakı:** ⌐~**ü ak olsun!**¹, *phrase expressing gratitude,* 'bless him!', 'may his shadow never grow less!': ~ ~**e bakmak,** *in such phrases as:* **ona bu kadar hakaret etme, yine** ~ ~**e bakacaksınız,** don't insult him like this; after all you'll have to meet him again; ~ ~**e bakamam,** I can't look him in the face (*because of some past injury I have done him*): ~**üne bakılır** *or* ~**üne bakılacak gibi,** good-looking; ~**üne bakmağa kıyılmaz,** one can't help looking at her (him), very beautiful; ~**üne bakılmaz,** ugly, horrible: ~ **bulmak,** to be emboldened; to become presumptuous; to be spoilt *by kind treatment:* ~**ünden* çekmek,** to suffer at the hands of ...: ···**den** ~ **çevirmek,** to be estranged from *s.o.*; to turn away from: ~**e çıkmak,** to come to the surface; to be insolent; arrogantly to maintain an untenable position: ~ **etm.,** to hand *stg.* over; to face up *two boards that are to be joined together:* ~**e gelen,** select, superior: ~ ~**e gelmek,** to come face to face with, to meet; ⌐**bir gün olur** ~ ~**e gelirsin**¹, don't make an enemy of anyone, you may meet him again some day: ~ **geri,** *v.* **yüzgeri:** ~ **göre,** just to please *or* flatter: ~**ü görmek,** *in such phrases as:* **bir az rahat** ~**ü görmek,** to find a little peace; **para** ~**ü görmek,** to get a bit of money: ~ **göz olm.,** to be too intimate *or* familiar; ~**ünü gözünü açmak,** to talk to a child about unseemly things, *esp.* sex: ~**ü* gülmek,** to be happy *or* delighted; ~**ü güler,** with smiling face, happy: ~**üne* gülmek,** to smile at, to be friendly towards (*with a hint of insincerity*); **her taraf insanın** ~**üne gülüyor,** everything is tidy and clean: ~**üne* kan gelmek,** to recover one's health: ~**ü kara,** one who in the past has done stg. to be ashamed of: ~ **karası,** dishonour, disgrace: ~ **kızartıcı,** shameful, disgusting: ~**ünden okumak,** to read (**okumak** *alone often means* ' *to recite*'): ~**u* olmamak,** not to dare, not to have the face to; to be unable to refuse; to be unable to face: ~**ü pek,** brazen-faced: ~**ü soğuk,** dour: ~ **suyu,** honour, self-respect; **babasının** ~**ü suyu hürmetine,** out of respect to his father; thanks to his father: ~ **tutmak,** to begin; to take a turn towards; **ona bunu söylemeğe** ~**üm tutmaz,** I can't bring myself to tell him this: ⌐ ∼ ∼**den utanır**¬, it is difficult to say such things to a person's face; it is hard to refuse personally: ∼ **üstü,** *v.* **yüzüstü:** ∼ **vermek,** to be indulgent *to,* to spoil; to give encouragement: ···**e** ∼ **vurmak,** to have recourse to; ∼**üne*** **vurmak,** to cast *stg.* in a person's teeth; to reproach *s.o.* with *stg.*: ∼ **yazısı,** decorations stuck on to the face of a village bride: ∼**ü*** **yok,** he has not the face, he dare not; one can't hold out against; **sıcağa** ∼**üm yok,** I can't face the heat; **kumara** ∼**ü yok,** he can't resist a gamble: **ne** ∼**le geldin?,** how have you the face to come?: **ne** ∼**le söyleceğim?,** how shall I bring myself to tell him?: **ne** ∼ **ünden?,** for what reason?, under what pretext?

yüz² Hundred; one hundred. ∼**lerce,** by hundreds; hundreds of ...: ∼**de beş,** five per cent.

yüzakı (¹··), **-nı** Personal honour; *both words declined in such phrases as:* **işten yüzümün akile çıktım,** I came out of the affair with unblemished honour; **yüzünün akile buradan çekil git!,** clear out of here before I show you up!

yüzbaşı Captain (army). ∼**lık,** rank of captain.

yüzde Per cent. Percentage; rate per cent. ∼**lik,** percentage: **tesbit edilen kâr** ∼**leri,** fixed percentages of profit.

yüzdürme *verb. n. of* **yüzdürmek.** ∼ **kuvveti (kabiliyeti),** buoyancy. ∼**k,** *caus. of* **yüzmek,** to float (a sunken ship *etc.*).

yüzer A hundred each; a hundred at a time.

yüzgeç Swimming; floating; knowing how to swim. Fin; float *of a seaplane.*

yüzgeri *In* ∼ **dönmek,** to face about, to turn around; to retreat.

yüzgörümü (¹···), **-nü** Present given by the bridegroom *on first seeing the face of the bride.* **yüzgörümlüğü,** the thing given as such a present.

yüzlemek *va.* Accuse *or* reproach *a person* to his face, *producing some positive proof in support of the accusation.*

yüzlerce (·¹·) In hundreds; in great numbers.

yüzleş·mek *vn.* Meet face to face; be confronted with one another. ∼**tirmek,** to bring face to face; confront.

yüzlü¹ With *such and such* a face *or* surface. **güler** ∼, smiling: **pek** ∼, brazen-faced: **iki** ∼, double-faced.

yüzlü² Having a hundred ...

yüzlük¹ Cover *or* protection for the face.

yüzlük² Costing, worth *or* weighing one hundred .... A hundred para *or* piastre piece.

yüzlülük State of having *such and such* a face. **iki** ∼, a being double-faced, duplicity.

yüzmek¹ *vn.* Swim; float.

yüzmek² *va.* Flay; skin; despoil. ⌐**yüzdük yüzdük kuyruğuna geldik**¬, the main job is done, the lesser one will easily be done; *or* 'a little patience, we're nearly there': **birinin derisini** ∼, to 'skin' s.o. of his money.

yüzsüz Brazen-faced, shameless. ∼**lük,** effrontery.

yüzük Ring. ∼ **çevirmek,** to play the **yüzük oyunu** *or* **fıncan oyunu,** a parlour game *resembling our 'Up Jenkins'*: **yüzüğü geri çevirmek,** to break off an engagement.

yüzükoyun (·¹··) Face downwards, lying on one's face, upside-down.

yüzüncü Hundredth.

yüzüstü (¹··) Face downwards; as things are. ∼ **bırakmak,** to leave things as they are *or* incomplete: **beni buralarda** ∼ **bırakma!,** don't leave me to my fate in these regions!: ∼ **kapanmak,** to be prostrate with one's face on the ground.

‖ **yüzyıl** Century.

yüzyüze (¹··) Face to face; *v.* **yüz.**

Z

zabıt, -btı A holding firmly; a taking possession; conquest; forcible seizure; comprehension; a taking down in writing, a recording; minutes; legal proceedings. ∼ **kâtibi,** clerk of the court; clerk charged with the duty of recording the proceedings of any assembly: ∼ **tutmak,** to take legal proceedings: **zabtı sabık,** minutes of the last meeting.

zabıta (-·¹) Police. ∼**ca görülen lüzum üzerine,** it is considered necessary by the police that .... ∼**lık,** a matter for the police; a person whom only the police can deal with.

zabıtname (···¹) Minutes *of a meeting etc.*; proceedings; protocol.

zabit (—¹), **-ti** Officer. Capable of command, who can keep discipline. ∼ **namzedi,**

gentleman cadet. ~**an**, officers. ~**lik**, rank, status and duties of an officer; commission.

zabt·etmek (¹··), –**eder** *va.* Hold firmly; seize; take possession of; restrain, master; grasp, understand; take down in writing. ~**iye**, gendarmerie, gendarme. ~**ı** *v*, zabıt. ~**urabt, –tı**, orderliness; discipline.

zac Vitriol; sulphate of iron. ~**ı kıbrıs**, sulphate of iron: **ak** ~, sulphate of zinc. ~**yağı** (¹··), –**nı**, sulphuric acid.

zade (–¹) Born; noble. Son; (*in compounds*) son of ... . ~**gân** (–·¹), nobles: noble: ~ **sınıfı**, the nobility. ~**gânlık**, nobility of birth; the belonging to a noble family. ~**lik**, noble birth.

zâf *v.* **zaıf.**

zafer Success; victory. ~ **bulmak**, to be successful *or* victorious. ~**yab** (··¹), successful; victorious.

za'fı *v.* **zaıf.**

zafiyet (–·¹), –**ti** Weakness; thinness.

zağ¹ Crow; rook.

zağ² Keenness of edge *of a sword etc.*

zağanos Large owl *trained to hunt*; *v. also* **çağanoz.**

zağar Hound. ~**cı**, houndsman; keeper of the hounds *in the household of the old sultans*; *name of one of the Janissary regiments.*

zağara Fur collar *to a coat.*

zağlamak *va.* Give a keen edge to; polish (sword, knife).

zahair (·–¹) *pl. of* **zahire.** Provisions; foodstuffs; corn.

zahır, –hrı The back; the other side. **zahrına!**, p.t.o., 'see back!'

zâhib (–¹) Who forms *or* follows *a doctrine.* ···**e** ~ **olm.**, to follow *a doctrine*; to incline *to an idea*; to surmise.

zâhid (–¹) Piously abstemious, ascetic. ~**lik**, asceticism for religious reasons; piety.

zâhif (–¹) Creeping, crawling. ~ **hayvanlar**, reptiles. ~**e** (–·¹), reptile.

zâhir (–¹) Outward, external; apparent. Outside, exterior; outsider. Clearly, evidently. ~ **olm.**, to be *or* become evident. ~**en** (¹··), outwardly; to outward appearance. ~**î** (–·¹), external, outward.

zahîr (·¹) Helper, supporter, backer.

zahire (·–¹) Store of grain *or* provisions; provisions. ~ **ambarı**, granary.

zahm Blow; wound.

zahmet, –ti Trouble; difficulty; distress; fatigue. ~ **buyurdunuz**, you have put yourself to great trouble: ~ **çekmek**, to suffer trouble *or* fatigue: ~**ine değdi**, it was worth the trouble: ~ **etm.**, to give oneself trouble, to put oneself to inconvenience; ~ **etmeyiniz**, don't trouble yourself! : ~**e**

sokmak *or* ~ **vermek**, to cause pain *or* trouble: **size son bir** ~**im daha olacak**, I'll trouble you for one last thing.

zahmet·li, troublesome; painful; difficult; fatiguing. Plus. ~**siz**, free from trouble; easy. ~**sizce** (··¹·), easily, without trouble.

zahrî (·¹) Pertaining to the back, dorsal. ~**ye**, docket *or* title *put on the outside of a document.*

zaıf, –a'fı Weakness.

zaid (–¹) Additional; redundant, superfluous. Plus; above zero. ~ **işareti**, the plus sign: **uzvu** ~, supernumerary member.

zaika (–·¹) The faculty of taste.

zâil (–¹) Declining; transitory, passing; disappearing; past. ~ **olm.**, to go away, to disappear.

zaîm (·¹) Feudal chieftain *holding the fief known as* **zeamet.**

zair (–¹) Visitor; pilgrim.

zakkum Oleander; a tree that grows in Hell *according to the Koran.* Very bitter.

zalâm (·¹) Darkness; the dark; oppression.

zalim (–¹) Unjust; tyrannical; cruel. Tyrant. ~**lik**, cruelty, oppression, tyranny.

Zaloğlu *In* ~ **Rüstem**, *a hero in Persian legend*; *type of a very strong man.*

zam, –mmı Addition. ~**mı maaş**, increase in salary: **kıdem** ~**mı**, increase in salary for seniority.

zamaim (·–¹) *pl. of* **zamime.** Supplements; additions.

zamân (·–) Guarantee; surety.

zaman (·⁴) Time; period. (*with participle*) When. ~**ında**, in his day; in its season; at the right time: ~**la**, in the course of time: ~ **adamı**, opportunist: ~**ın hükümdarı**, the ruler of the day, the then ruler: ~**a uymak**, to conform to the requirements of the time: **aman** ~ **yok**, without respite: **bir** ~ *or* **bir** ~**lar**, at one time; formerly, once: **gel** ~ **git** ~, after a certain time; in due course: **hiçbir** ~, never: **ne** ~**dır**, how long ago it is that ... : **o** ~, then.

zaman·e (··¹), the age; the present time; fortune. ~ **adamı**, opportunist: ~ **çocukları**, the children of today. ~**en** (·¹·), according to the time; as regards time.

zambak Lily.

zamime (··¹) Addition; supplement. ~**ten** (·¹··), in addition; by way of supplement.

zamin (–¹) Who stands surety. ~ **olm.**, to be guarantee, to make oneself responsible for.

zamir (·¹) Heart; inner consciousness; secret thought; (·¹) personal pronoun. ···**in** ~**ine*** girmek, (of a thought) to enter *s.o.'s* mind.

zamk, –mkı Gum. ~lamak, to gum. ~lı, gummed.

zamm·etmek (^{1}··), –eder *va*. Add; increase. ~ı, *v*. zam.

zampara Womanizer, rake. ~lık etm., to run after women.

zan, –nnı Opinion; surmise; suspicion. ~nımca *or* ~nıma göre, in my opinion : ... ~nındayım, I am of the opinion that ... : ~nı galib, the prevailing opinion; the fairly certain presumption.

zanaat, –tı Craft; handicraft.

zanetmek *v*. zannetmek.

zangır *In* ~ ~, trembling; with the teeth chattering; making a clanking *or* rattling noise. ~damak, to have the teeth chatter through fear; tremble; clank; rattle. ~tı, a clanking *or* rattling noise.

zangoç Verger of a church.

zani (–^{1}) Adulterer. Adulterous. ~iye, adulteress.

zanka (^{1}·) Horse-drawn sleigh.

zann·etmek (^{1}··), –eder *va*. Think; suppose. ~ı, *v*. zan.

zânû (–$^{\_}$) Knee. ~bezemin, kneeling.

zaparta (·^{1}·) Broadside; severe scolding.

zaptetmek *etc. v*. zabtetmek *etc*.

zar^{1} Membrane; film; thin skin *of an onion etc*. kulak ~ı, ear-drum : beyin ~ı veremi, cerebral meningitis.

zar^{2} Dice. ~ atmak, to throw dice : ~ tutmak, to cheat in throwing dice.

zâr (–) Weeping bitterly; miserable; thin, wan. Bitter weeping. ahu ~, bitter lamentation.

zarafet (·–^{1}), –ti Elegance; grace; delicacy. malûmu ~leri, *courteous way of saying* 'as you well know, Sir'.

zarar Damage, injury; loss; harm. ~ etm., *or* görmek, to suffer harm : ~ına satmak, to sell at a loss : ~ vermek, to cause harm *or* loss : ~ı yok, it doesn't matter! ; never mind! : ne ~, what does it matter !

zarar·dide (···–^{1}), who has suffered injury *or* loss. ~lı, harmful; who suffers harm : ~ çıkmak, to come out the loser. ~sız, harmless; innocent; safe, unhurt; not so bad; pretty good.

zarb, darb Act of striking; blow; multiplication (*arith*.). ~ işareti, the multiplication sign : para ~ı, the minting of money. ~etmek (^{1}··), –eder *va*, to strike; to mint *money*; to multiply (*arith*.).

zarf Receptacle; envelope; cover; case; cupholder *in which a cup of hot* coffee is placed; adverb. ~ ile mazruf, outward appearance and inner substance; style and content *of a book, i.e*. the way it is written and the substance of the writing : bir ay

~ında, during a month; for a month; within a month.

zarfçı Crook; confidence trickster.

zargana (·^{1}·) Garfish.

zarı *In* ~ ~ ağlamak, to weep bitterly.

zarif Elegant, graceful; delicate; witty, clever (idea, speech *etc*.). ~lik, elegance; delicacy.

zarta (^{1}·) Fart.

zartzurt *Imitates loud and domineering words*. ~ etm., to give orders *or* to talk in a loud and blustering manner.

zaruret, -ti Need; want; necessity; poverty. ~ halinde, in case of necessity : ~inde kalmak, to be obliged to ..., to be under the necessity of ... : hayatî ~ler, the necessaries of life.

zarurî (·–$^{\_}$) Necessary; indispensable; unavoidable; involuntary.

zarzor (^{1}·) Willy-nilly; barely.

zat (∗), –tı, –ti Essence, substance; person, individual; (*in compounds*) possessor of ..., endowed with ... . ~ı aliniz (alileri) your exalted person, *polite for* you : ~ işleri, personal affairs : ~ı mesele, the essence of the matter, the real point : ~a mahsus, personal, not transferable : ~ı Şahane, Your Majesty : haddi ~ında, in itself, in its essence.

zaten (–$^{\_}$) Essentially; in any case; as a matter of fact. 'bu adam ingilizce iyi konuşuyor'; '~ ingiliz!', 'this man speaks English well'; 'Of course he does, he's English!' : 'bu doktor romatizmayı heman anlıyor' : '~ mesleği bu!', 'this doctor recognizes rheumatism at once!'; 'Well, that's his profession!' : 'ona ben söylemedim, ~ biliyormuş', 'I didn't tell him, he knew already' : *where the Turks use* zaten *we frequently merely use intonation, e.g.* ⌐~ her zaman geç geliyor⌐, he *always* comes late.

zati (–^{1}) *Vulg. for* zaten.

zatî (–$^{\_}$) Essential; original; personal. menfaati ~ye, personal interests. ~yat (–·$^{\_}$), –tı, personal matters.

zat·ilcenb, ~ilkebed *etc. v*. zatülcenb, zatülkebed *etc*. ~irrie, *v*. zatürrie. ~issedaye (–···–^{1}), mammal. ~işerif, Your Honour; (*sarcastically*) you. ~ülcenb, pleurisy. ~ülkebed, inflammation of the liver. ~ülkürsü, the constellation Cassiopeia. ~ürrie, pneumonia.

zavahir (·–^{1}) *pl*. of zâhire. Outside; visible parts; appearance. ~e kapılmak, to be taken in by the outward appearance of a thing *or* man : ~i kurtarmak, to save appearances.

zavallı (^{1}··) Unlucky; miserable. ah ~!, poor chap!

zaviye (–·') Corner; cell *of a recluse*; angle. ~i hadde, acute angle: ~i kaime, right angle: ~i münferice, obtuse angle: görüş ~si, angle of vision.

zayetmek ('..), –eder *va.* Lose.

zayıf Weak; thin; weakly; of little weight *or* authority. ~lamak, to become enfeebled; become thin. ~lık, weakness, debility; emaciation.

zayi (–·'), –ii Lost; destroyed. ~ etm., to lose: ~ olm., to be lost, to perish: ~inden vermek, to issue a duplicate of a lost document (*identity papers etc.*). ~at (–··ᵥ), losses: ~ vermek, to suffer casualties: ~ verdirmek, to inflict losses.

zayiçe (––') Astronomical table; horoscope.

zayolmak ('··) *vn.* Be lost; perish.

zeamet (·–'), –ti A large fief, *formerly held by feudal chieftains with the title of* zaîm.

zeban (·ᵥ) Tongue; language. ~dıraz, insolent; intemperate in speech.

zebani (·–·') Demon of hell; cruel monster.

zebanzed Commonly used in speech.

zebellâ, zebellâyi Huge; thick-set. Huge man.

zeberced Chrysolite; beryl; topaz. Pale bluish-green.

zebih, –bhi A cutting of the throat; ritual slaughter. **zebhetmek** ('··), –eder, to slaughter *an animal* ritually. **zebhiye**, tax on slaughtered animals.

zebil *v.* sebil.

zebun (·ᵥ) Weak, helpless; exhausted. ihtiraslara ~ olanlar, those who are powerless against their desires: yanlış bir düşüncenin ~u, the dupe of an erroneous idea.

zebun·küş, who oppresses the weak or defenceless; cruel and cowardly. ~küşlük, oppression of the weak; cowardly cruelty. ~lamak, to become weak and emaciated. ~luk, weakness; helplessness.

zebur The Psalms of David.

zecir, –cri Restraint; violence; a compelling to labour unwillingly.

zecr·en ('·) With violence; forcibly. ~î (·'), violent; compulsory; forcible. ~iye, *fem.* of zecrî: tax on alcoholic liquors.

–zede *Pers. suffix.* Stricken by ..., *e.g.* kazazede, overtaken by disaster, shipwrecked; taunzede, stricken with the plague.

zedelemek *va.* Damage by striking; maltreat; bruise.

zefir¹ Deep sigh; expiration.

zefir² Zephir (tissue and garment).

zehab (·ᵥ) Belief; imagination. ~ı batıl, a vain belief *or* supposition: ···in ~ı

hilâfına olarak, contrary to the belief held by ... .

zeheb Gold. ~î (··'), golden.

zehî (·') What a ...! ~ hayal!, what an illusion!

zehir, –hri Poison; anything very bitter. zehri hand, a bitter smile: beyaz ~, cocaine, heroin *etc.*: ⌐içime ~ (zemberek) oldu¬, it spoilt my enjoyment. ~lemek, to poison. ~li, poisonous, venomous; poisoned (food). ~nâk, containing poison; poisoned (food, dagger).

zehri *v.* zehir.

zekâ (·') Quickness of mind; intelligence; perspicacity.

zekât (·'), –tı Alms *prescribed by Islam* (*one fortieth of income*); tax for the relief of the poor. ⌐malın kadar ~ın olsun!¬, *said as a reproach to s.o. who gives very little.*

zekâvet (·–'), –ti *v.* zekâ.

zeker The male organ.

Zekeriya (··'·) Zachariah. ~ sofrası kurmak, to prepare a dinner of various sorts of dried fruit *to which guests are invited and at which the host makes some solemn wish.*

zeki Sharp, quick-witted, intelligent.

zelil Low, base, contemptible.

zelle Error; sin.

zelzele Earthquake.

zem, –mmi Blame; censure; disparagement. ~mu kadih dâvası, action for libel.

zemaim (·–') *pl. of* zemime. Faults; vices.

zeman *v.* zaman.

zemberek Spring (of a watch *etc.*); any very bitter thing. zehir ~, bitter as poison; a very cantankerous person. ~li, fitted with a spring.

zembil Basket *woven of rushes or palmleaves.* ⌐gökten ~le insen bile¬, 'no matter what you do' (you can't please these people *etc.*): ⌐gökten ~le inmemiş ya!¬, he's nothing out of the way; he's just the same as anybody else: ~ otu, quaking-grass. ~ci, make *or* seller of these baskets. ~li, carrying a zembil.

zemherir, zemheri Extreme cold; the depth of winter. ~ zürafası, one who wears very inadequate clothes in winter.

zemim (·ᵥ) Reprehensible. ahlâkı ~e, bad moral qualities, bad character. ~e (·–'), reprehensible trait, vice.

zemin (·ᵥ) The earth, the world; ground; ground *of a design*; subject-matter *of a discourse*; meaning, sense. ···e ~ açmak, to give grounds for ...: ~ katı, groundfloor: ~ü zaman, conditions of time and space: bu ~de bir şey yaz! write stg. in this sense! ~lik, underground room;

dungeon; hidden road; road made of gratings *etc.* on the earth (*mil.*); underground shelter; cave.

zemmetmek (¹··), **–eder** *va.* Censure; denigrate, slander.

zemzem Name of the sacred well at Mecca. ⌜**~ kuyusuna işemek**⌝, 'to urinate into the well of Zemzem', *i.e.* to do stg. monstrous merely to acquire notoriety, *v.* **bevval**: çoklarına nisbetle ~le yıkanmış gibidir, he is a perfect paragon compared with most of them.

zemzeme A humming *or* murmuring.

zenaat *v.* zanaat.

zencefil Ginger.

zenci (·⁻) Negro. ~ ticareti, the slave-trade.

zencifre Vermilion; cinnabar.

zencir *v.* zincir.

zend Forearm; wrist. ~ kemiği, ulna.

zendost Fond of women; rake.

zeneb, –nbi Tail; retinue.

Zengibar Zanzibar.

zengin Rich. Wealthy man. **~lemek**, to become rich. **~lik**, riches, wealth.

zenne The female sex; female; male taking a female part *in old Turkish theatre.* Female (clothes *etc.*). **~ci**, seller of women's clothes.

zephetmek *v.* zebhetmek.

zer¹ Gold.

zer² *v.* zeri.

zeravend (·–¹) Aristolochia, birthwort.

zerd Yellow.

zerdali (·–¹) Wild apricot.

zerdava Beech marten.

zerde Dish of sweetened rice coloured with saffron *served at weddings.*

zerdeçal, zerdeçav Turmeric.

zerduz Embroidered with gold thread. ⌜**~ palan vursan eşek yine eşek**⌝, 'an ass is still an ass even if you put a gold-embroidered saddle on him'.

Zerdüşt, –tü Zoroaster. **~i**, Zoroastrian; fire-worshipper.

zeren *v.* zerrin.

zer·'etmek (¹··), **–eder** *va.* Sow. ~i (·⁻), **–r'i**, a sowing; sown seed; seed for sowing. **~iyat** (··⁻), **–tı**, sowings; crops; cultivation.

zeria (·–¹) Cause; motive; reason.

zerk, –ki Injection. **~etmek** (¹··), **–eder,** to inject, give an injection of.

zerişan Inlaid with gold.

zerrat (·⁻), **–tı** *pl. of* zerre. Atoms.

zerre Atom; mote. ~ kadar, in the slightest degree; **~nin ~si**, absolutely nil.

zerrin Golden; like gold. Jonquil.

zerzevat, –tı Vegetables. **~çı**, greengrocer.

zevahif *pl. of* zahife. Reptiles.

zevahir *v.* zavahir.

zevaid (·–¹) *pl. of* zaide. Superfluities.

zeval (·⁴), **–li** The sinking of the sun after noon; noon; decline; decadence; adversity. ~ bulmak, (of a nation *etc.*) to decline: ⌜elçiye ~ olmaz⌝, an ambassador is sacrosanct; an ambassador cannot be blamed for his mission.

zeval·î (·–⁻), reckoned from noon: ~ saat ikide, two p.m.; two by European time. **~napezir**, permanent, imperishable. **~pezir**, transitory; subject to decline. **~siz**, unfading; everlasting, permanent.

zevat (·⁴), **–tı** *pl. of* zat. Persons.

zevaya (·–¹) *pl. of* zaviye. Angles.

zevc One of a pair; mate; pair; consort; husband. **~e**, wife. **~eyn**, a married couple, man and wife. **~î** (·⁻), marital, matrimonial. **~iyet, –ti**, the married state, matrimony.

zeveban Melting; fusion. noktai ~, melting-point.

zevecat (··⁴), **–tı** *pl. of* zevce. Wives. taadüdü ~, polygamy.

zevil·hayat (···⁴), **–tı** Living things. **~ukul** (···⁴), **–lü**, rational creatures.

zevk, –kı, –ki The sense of taste; taste, flavour; appreciation *of a thing*; good taste; enjoyment, pleasure. ···i ~a almak, to make fun of ...: ~ına bak!, enjoy yourself!: ~ı bediî, aesthetic pleasure: ···in ~ını bozmak, to spoil *s.o.'s* pleasure: ···in ~ını çıkarmak, to enjoy stg. to the full: ~ına* gitmek, to appear amusing *or* pleasant to one: ~ına meclûb (mecbur), voluptuary: ~ını* okşamak, to please: ~inda* olm., to be enjoying *or* amusing oneself: ~ ve safa, amusement, pleasures: ~ı selim, good taste; ~ı selim sahibi, a man of taste: ~ına varmak, to appreciate stg.

zevk·ıyab, who enjoys *or* finds pleasure: ···den ~ olm., to take pleasure in .... **~lendirmek**, to delight, amuse: birini kendile ~, to be the butt of *s.o.*, to be the object of *s.o.'s* derision *or* amusement. **~lenmek**, to amuse oneself: ···le ~, to mock at, to make fun of .... **~li**, pleasant; amusing. **~siz**, tasteless; ugly; in bad taste. **~sizlik**, bad taste.

zevrak, –kı Small boat.

zevzek Silly; giddy; talkative. **~lenmek**, to behave in a silly manner; to say stupid things. **~lik**, silly flighty behaviour; senseless chatter.

zeybak, –kı Quicksilver.

zeybek *A class of the population in the Smyrna and Aidin districts; formerly a kind of light infantryman.* ~ oyunu, the Zeybek folk-dance.

zeyç, –çi Astronomical tables.

zeyl, zeyil, –yli Appendix; addendum, postscript. **~en** (¹··), by way of appendix *or* postscript.

zeyrek Intelligent, wide awake.

zeyt, –ti Oil.

zeytin Olive. **~ci**, dealer in olives. **~lik**, olive grove. **~yağı, –nı**, olive-oil: **~ gibi üste çıkmak**, to come off best; to get the better of an argument.

zeytuni (·–¹) Olive-green.

zıbarmak *vn.* Become torpid from drink; (*contemptuously*) to go to bed, to sleep; to die.

zıbın Wadded jacket for a baby.

zıcret, –ti Distress, oppression (*med.*).

zıd, –ddı The contrary; the opposite; opposition; detestation. ···**in ~dına* basmak**, to do stg. to spite *s.o.*: ···**in ~ına* gitmek**, to act contrary to the wishes of ...; to oppose. **~diyet, –ti**, opposition; repugnance, antipathy; contrast.

zıh Edging; border; fillet; moulding. **~lamak**, to put a border *or* edging to.

zııf, –ı'fı The double *of a number*.

zıkkım The food of the damned; any bitter *or* unpleasant food. **~lanmak**, to stuff oneself with food (*only used in anger or contempt*).

zıl, –llı Shadow, shade; protection. **Zılullah**, the shadow of God (title of the Caliph).

zılgıt (*sl.*) Threat; scolding. **~ vermek**, to scold: **~ı yemek**, to get a scolding.

zılıf, –lfı Cloven hoof.

zıman Surety, bail.

zımba Drill; punch. **~lamak**, to drill, punch; (*sl.*) stab. **~lı**, perforated; with a hole punched in it.

zımbır·datmak *va.* Twang; strum *on a stringed instrument*. **~tı**, a twanging *or* strumming noise.

zımn·en (¹·) By implication; between the lines; tacitly. **~ anlatmak**, to imply: **~ itiraf ediyorlar**, they are as good as confess. **~î** (·–¹), implied, indirectly or tacitly understood. **~ında**, with a view to; for the purpose of.

zımpara Emery. **~ kâğıdı**, emery paper; sandpaper.

zıncan *v.* sıncan.

zındık Misbeliever; atheist.

zıngıl *v.* zıngır.

zıngır *In ~ ~, imitates the noise of violent trembling.* **~damak**, to tremble violently; rattle. **~tı** A rattling *or* trembling noise.

zınk *Imitates the noise of a moving thing brought to an abrupt standstill.* **otomobil ~ diye durdu**, the motor-car came to an abrupt stop.

zıp Suddenly; pop! **~ diye çıkmak**, to pop up all of a sudden: **~ ~ sıçramak**, to jump about wildly. **~çıktı**, a foppish bounder; upstart: **~ bir halde**, dressed in a ridiculous manner.

zıpır Hare-brained; madcap.

zıpka (¹·) A kind of tight-fitting breeches.

zıpkın Fish-spear; harpoon.

zıplamak *vn.* Jump, skip *or* bounce about.

zıppadak (¹··) Suddenly, unexpectedly; with one bound.

zıpzıp, –pı Marble (plaything).

zır zır *Imitates a continuous and tiresome noise.*

zırdeli (¹··) Raving mad.

zırh Armour; crease; braid down the side of trousers. **~lı**, armoured; armour-plated; braided (trousers): battleship. **~sız**, unarmoured; without braid (trousers).

zırıl *In ~ ~, in streams.* **~damak**, to keep up an incessant chatter *or* clatter. **~tı**, continuous chatter *or* clatter; squabble; (*sl.*) dirty, silly, useless. **kaynana ~sı**, rattle: **kocakarı ~sı**, the cackle of old women.

zırlak Senselessly yelling; bawling. Cricket (insect).

zırlamak *vn.* Keep up a continuous noise; bray; (*contemptuously*) weep.

zırnık Orpiment; yellow arsenic. **~ bile almazsın**, you won't get a farthing *out of him*: **adama ~ vermez**, not a red cent will he give.

zırt zırt Frequently; at unexpected *or* unsuitable times.

zırtapoz Crazy.

zırva Sheep's trotters stewed with garlic; a kind of rice pudding; silly chatter. '**~ tevil götürmez**', it's no use trying to make sense out of foolish talk. **~lamak**, to talk twaddle.

zırzop, –pu Silly ass.

zıt *v.* zıd.

zıvana (·¹·) Inner tube; tenon (mortise); mouthpiece of a cigarette. **~dan çıkmak**, to be befuddled; to be in a rage: **~ testeresi**, tenon-saw. **~lı**, having a tube at the end (cigarette). **~sız**, crazy.

zıya (·¹·), **–aı** Loss. **~ı ebedi**, eternal loss (of a death).

zıyk, –kı Tightness; oppression. **~ı nefes** *or* **~ısadır**, asthma.

zibidi Oddly dressed; eccentric, crazy; upstart.

zifaf (·¹) Entry of the bridegroom to the nuptial chamber. **~ gecesi**, the first night of wedded life.

zifir Deposit in a pipe stem. Bitter; dark. **dili ~**, of caustic tongue. **~i**, pitch-black.

zifos Splash of mud. Useless, in vain. **~ yemek**, to be bespattered with mud.

zift, -ti Pitch. Pitch-black; very bitter.
~ **yesin** or ~**in pekini yesin,** he may starve
for all I care. ~**lemek,** to daub with
pitch. ~**lenmek,** to be daubed with
pitch; overeat; *used contemptuously for*
yemek, eat, consume, squander; to put to
one's own use (not too honestly). ~**li,**
daubed with pitch.

zihayat (−·¹) Alive, living.

zihin, -hni Mind; intelligence; memory.
zihnini* bozmak (bulandırmak), to make
one suspicious: **zihnim durdu,** my mind
ceased to work, I couldn't take anything
in: ~ **hesabı,** mental arithmetic: **zihni***
karışmak, to be confused; ···**in zihnini***
karıştırmak, to confuse *s.o.*: ···**e zihni***
takılmak, for one's attention to be caught
by some striking fact or knotty point: ~**de**
tutmak, to bear in mind: ~ **(zihnini*)**
yormak, to think hard, to rack one's brains:
sarfı ~ **etm.,** to apply the mind to *stg.*

zihn·en (¹·) Mentally; in one's mind. ~
hesab etm., to reckon in one's head. ~**î**
(·-¹), mental; intellectual. ~**iyet, -ti,**
mentality.

zikir, -kri Remembrance, recollection;
mention; recitation of the attributes of
God; dervish religious service.

zikıymet (−·¹) Precious, valuable.

zikr·etmek (¹··), **-eder** *va.* Mention;
intone religious formulae or prayers. ~**i,**
v. **zikir.** ~**icemil,** honourable mention,
praise: '~**iniz geçti',** *(politely)* you were
mentioned. ~**olunmak,** to be mentioned.

zikzak Zigzag. ~**vari** (··−¹), zigzagging.

zil Cymbals; bells on a tambourine; gong;
bell. ~ **takınmak,** to make merry:
etekleri ~ **çalıyor,** he is in transports:
karnım ~ **çalıyor,** I feel peckish.

zil·hicce *The twelfth month of the Moslem
year.* ~**kade** (·−¹), *the eleventh month of
the Moslem year.*

zillet, -ti Abasement, degradation.

zilli With cymbals or bells; having a bell;
badly behaved. ~ **bebek,** doll which, when
squeezed, strikes cymbals: ~ **maşa,**
jingle, jingling Johnny.

zilyed Owner, possessor; holder. **bir şeye**
~ **bulunmak,** to be in possession of a thing.
~**lik,** ownership.

zilzurna (¹··) Blind drunk.

zimam (·⁴) Reins. ~**ı idare,** the reins of
government. ~**dar** *(pl.* ~**an),** one who
holds the reins *of government etc.;* statesman; leader.

zimem *pl. of* **zimmet.**

zimmet, -ti Duty; obligation; charge;
debt; debit side *of an account.* ~**inde,** to
his charge; ~**inde bin lira alacağım var,** I
am his creditor for 1,000 lira: ~**ine iki**

bin lira geçirmiş, he has misappropriated
(embezzled) 2,000 lira: ~**te kalmak,** to be
owing: **tebriyei** ~ **etm.,** to relieve oneself
of a responsibility; to get one's discharge
of a debt: ~**i tebriye edildi,** he has got the
discharge of his debt.

zina¹ Bumble-bee.

zina² (·¹) Adultery; fornication. ~**kâr,**
adulterous.

zincifre Vermilion; cinnabar.

zincir, zencir Chain; fetters; succession,
series. ~**ini koparmak,** (of a madman) to
run amok: ~**i koparmak** or **aklın** ~**ini**
koparmak, to lose all control of oneself:
···**i** ~**e vurmak,** to put s.o. in chains: **gemi**
~**i,** anchor chain.

zincir·leme, in a continuous series: act of
chaining; a proceeding continuously:
temsil ~ **usulüne göre devam ediyor,** the
show goes on continuously (as in a cinema):
perakendeciler birbirlerine ~ **usulile mal**
satıyorlar, the retailers sell goods to one
another in succession, *each time taking the
legally allowed profit and selling to the public
at a high price, thus evading the anti-
profiteering laws.* ~**lemek,** to chain; to
connect in a series. ~**li,** provided with a
chain; chained; in a continuous manner: ~
han, old-fashioned inn. ~**lik,** chain
locker *(naut.).*

zindan (·⁴) Dungeon; dark place. Very
dark. ⌜**dünya başına*** ~ **olm.,**⌝ for the world
to become a place of darkness, *i.e.* suddenly
to feel very depressed. ~**cı,** warden of a
dungeon; jailer. ~**delen,** medium-sized
bonito **(palamut).**

zinde Alive; active, energetic. ~**gi** (··¹).
~**lik,** life; animation, activity.

zinhar Beware!; take care!; by no
means.

zir (−) Lowest or under part; top string of
a lute; *(with izafat)* under. ···**in** ~**i idare-**
sinde, under the direction of ... .

zira (¹·) Because.

zirâ (·¹), **-âı** Cubit.

zira·at (·−¹), **-ti** Agriculture. ~**î** (·−¹),
agricultural.

zirde Underneath, below.

ziruh (−¹) Alive. Animate object.

zirüzeber (¹···) Upside-down.

zirve Summit; peak.

zivoma (¹·) Carpenter's square.

ziya (·¹) Light. ~**dar,** luminous; well
lighted (room *etc.).*

ziyade (·−¹) Increase; more; surplus;
excess. More; much; too much; excessive,
superfluous. Too; very. ···**dan** ~, more
than ... : ~**sile,** to a great degree; largely:
⌜**Allah** ~ **etsin!**⌝, *a form of thanks for a
meal:* **hadden** ~, beyond measure: **pek** ~,

extremely, excessively. ~ce, rather more, somewhat. ~leşmek, to increase (vn.).

ziyafet (·−¹), **-ti** Feast, banquet; dinner-party. ~ çekmek, to give a feast.

ziyan (·ⁱ) Loss; damage. ~ına, at a loss: ~ çekmek (görmek), to suffer loss or damage, to suffer prejudice: ~ sebil olm., to be wasted: ~ı yok!, no matter! **ziyan·cı**, ~kâr, prejudicial, injurious. ~lı, injured; who suffers loss: bu işten ben ~ çıktım, it is I who came out the loser in this business. ~sız, harmless; not so bad, pretty good.

ziyaret (·−¹), **-ti** Visit; pilgrimage. ~ etm., to pay a visit; to perform a pilgrimage: ⌐hem ~ hem ticaret⌐, to combine a visit with business: yarın ~inize geleceğim, I will pay you a visit tomorrow. ~çi, visitor; pilgrim. ~gâh, a much visited place; place to which a pilgrimage is made.

ziynet, **-ti** Ornament; decoration. ~lemek, to adorn, embellish. ~li, ornamented; embellished.

zoka (¹·) Artificial bait; spinner. ~yı yutmak, to be duped.

zom (sl.) Drunk.

zonklamak vn. Throb with pain.

zor Strength; violence; difficulty; compulsion. Difficult, hard; fatiguing; forced (marriage). With difficulty; only just. ~la, by force; with difficulty: ~ belâ, by great efforts, after great trouble: ~a gelmek, or ~u altında kalmak, to be forced or constrained: ⌐~la güzellik olmaz⌐, no good can be achieved by force: ~u* ne? or ne ~u*?, what's th ematter with him; what does he want?; why should he do it (he is not obliged to)?: ~un ne?, what's the trouble?, what's the matter with you?; ~ları ne imiş?, what did they want?, etc.: ... ~unda olm. (kalmak), to be obliged to ... : aklında ~u var, he's off his head.

zoraki Forced; involuntary; under compulsion; by force. ~lik, a forced thing: iltifatlarında bir ~ sezdim, I felt his courtesy was rather forced.

zorba Who uses force; rebel; bully. Violent; brutal. ~lık, the use of force; violence; bullying.

zor·lamak va. Force; use force; exert one's strength; handle roughly; misuse; oblige; urge strongly. kendini ~, to force oneself; to exert oneself. ~lan, v. zorla (under zor). ~lanmak, to force oneself; make vain efforts; be forced; be roughly handled. ~laşmak, to grow difficult, become harder. ~lu, strong; violent; powerful, influential. ~luk, difficulty; arduousness. ~zoruna (¹···), with great difficulty.

zuaf Zouave.

zuafa (··−) pl. of zayıf. Weak ones.

zucret, **-ti** Distress; annoyance.

zuhur (·ⁱ) A becoming manifest; appearance; happening. ~ etm., to appear; come to pass; come into existence; become a man of mark: ~a gelmek, to happen: ~a getirmek, to cause to happen, to bring to pass: sahib ~, a man who rises from obscurity to power.

zuhur·at (·−ⁱ), **-tı**, sudden occurrences; chance events; unexpected events; the turn of events; unexpected expenses: ~a tâbi olm., to depend on events. ~i (·−¹), a clown in the old Turkish theatre: ~ye çıkar gibi, dressed in a ludicrous manner: ~ kolu, a band of clowns.

zulmanî (·−−) Pertaining to darkness; dark.

zulmen (¹·) Wrongfully; cruelly.

zulmet, **-ti** Darkness.

zulmetmek (¹··), **-eder** va. (with dat.) Do a wrong to; treat unjustly or cruelly.

zulumba (·¹·), **zulumpad** Zedoary (aromatic root).

zulüm, **-lmü** Wrong; oppression; cruelty. ~kâr, oppressive; tyrannical; cruel.

zurna A kind of shrill pipe usually accompanied by a drum; the Saury Pike (Scombresox saurus). çatlak ~, a garrulous man: davul ~ ile, publicly; ostentatiously. ~cı, ~zen, player of the zurna.

zuum, **-u'mu** Unfounded opinion; false assumption.

zübde Lit. cream; the cream of anything; quintessence.

zücac (·ⁱ) Glass. ~i (·−¹), glassy, vitreous. ~iye (·−·¹), glassware.

züğürt Destitute; bankrupt; 'stony-broke'. ~ tesellisi, cold comfort: akıl züğürdü, of poor intelligence: çehre züğürdü, lacking in good looks: terbiye züğürdü, uneducated. ~lük, indigence; bankruptcy; a being 'stony-broke'. ~lemek, to become destitute; go bankrupt.

Zühal, **-li** Saturn.

zühd Pious asceticism.

Zühre The planet Venus. ~vi (··−), venereal: emrazı ~ye, venereal diseases.

zühul (·ⁱ), **-lü** Negligence; omission; forgetfulness. ~en (·−·), by error; through forgetfulness.

zükûr pl. of zeker. Males.

zül, **-llü** Degradation; humiliation.

zülâl (·ⁱ), **-li** Cool, pure water; albumen. ~î (·−¹), albuminous.

zülfikar The two-bladed or cleft sword of Ali.

zülfüarus Flower-branches of the caracalla bean.

zülfüyar (The beloved one's curl), *only in* ~a **dokunmak,** to touch a tender spot; to 'put one's foot in it'.

zülkarneyn 'The two-horned one', Alexander the Great; *also* cuckold.

zülmaaşeyn (··—¹) Amphibious; amphibian.

zülûbiye, zülbiye A cake made with honey and almonds.

zülüf, –lfü Side-lock of hair; love-lock; tassel. ~**lü,** having love-locks; wearing a tasselled cap : ~ **baltacı,** *formerly a class of Palace guards.*

zülvecheyn Two-faced; two-sided.

zümre Party; body; set of people; group; class. ~ **dersi,** a group of studies embracing different subjects : ~**i düveliye,** a group of states or Powers : **halk** ~**si,** the common people. ~**vi** (··⸱—¹), belonging to *such and such* a class *or* group.

zümrüd Emerald; emerald green. ~**i** (··⸱—¹), ~**in,** emerald green. ~**üanka,** a fabulous bird *said to inhabit the Caucasus*;

phoenix; a will-o'-the-wisp : ⌜~ **gibi ismi var cismi yok**⌝, 'like the phoenix it has a name but no body', *said of stg. that does not really exist.*

zünnar Rope girdle *formerly worn by Christians in Turkey*; (*med.*) shingles.

zünüb, –nbü *pl. of* **zanb.** Sins.

züppe Fop; coxcomb; affected person. Affected; snobbish. ~ **münevver,** one who affectedly pretends to be an intellectual. ~**lik,** foppishness; affectation; snobbery.

zürafa (·—⸱—¹) Giraffe.

zürdeva *v.* **zerdava.**

zürefa (··⸱—¹) *pl. of* **zarif.** Witty people; *as sing.* Lesbian.

zürra (·⸱—¹), –**aı** *pl. of* **zarı'.** Cultivators, farmers.

zürriyet, –ti Issue, progeny; descendants. ~**i kesildi,** his family has died out for want of heirs.

züvvar *pl. of* **zair.** Visitors; pilgrims.

züyuf (·⸱—¹) Base money; spurious coins.

züyut ((·⸱—¹), –**tu** *pl. of* **zeyt.** Oils.

APPENDIX

Note. N.H. stands for Nasreddin Hodja, the semi-historical character, to whom are attributed so many Turkish witticisms and good stories.

barut. A great personage visiting a town asked why no salute had been fired. The local commander said, 'Because we had no powder', and then proceeded to give a lot of other reasons. He was told that the first was sufficient and no further explanation was necessary.

bayram. ⌈Bayram değil, seyran değil, eniştem beni niçin öptü?⌉ 'It's not a feast-day, it's not an outing, why did my brother-in-law kiss me?' The remark (in a well-known story) of a naïve girl on being kissed by her brother-in-law, who 'had an eye' on her. Often quoted when someone is puzzled by something, the reason of which is obvious to everyone else. Sometimes it merely means 'for no apparent reason'.

boncuk. N. H. gave each of his two wives a blue bead, telling each not to tell the other. One day the two wives were pestering him to say which of them he loved the most. He replied, 'My heart is with the one who has the blue bead', and they both departed satisfied.

çömlek. Just before one Ramazan (the month of fasting) N. H. said to himself, 'Why should I just copy other people and go on fasting as long as they do? I'll get a pot and put a stone in it every day and when there are 30 stones in it I shall know the fast is over and shall celebrate the feast (Bayram)'. So he got a pot and put in a daily stone. But his little daughter saw him do this and now and then put in a handful of stones on her own account. One day they asked the Hodja what day of the month it was. The Hodja told them to wait a minute while he found out. He turned out his pot and counted 120 stones. He said to himself, 'If I tell them the truth they will never believe me', so he went back and told them it was the 45th of the month. 'But Hodja', they said, 'there are only 30 days altogether in the month'. The Hodja replied, 'What I am telling you is reasonable; if you go by the pot reckoning it is the 120th of the month.'

dam. N. H. was sleeping on his roof, as is usual in the summer. Being unable to sleep he got up to go for a stroll, and, forgetting he was on the roof, fell off it on to the ground. The neighbours heard him

groaning and moaning and ran to see what was the matter. All he would say was, 'Have any of you fallen off a roof?' 'Why do you keep asking that?' they said. The Hodja replied, 'Only he who has fallen off a roof can understand how I feel.'

deve. 'Deveye yokuşu mu seversin inişi mi diye sormuşlar, deve düz yol ne güne duruyor demiş.' They asked the camel whether he preferred going up hill or down. He replied, 'Why not have a level road?' Used when someone is offered two alternatives, both unpleasant, and suggests a third and simpler way.

dost. At one time N. H. used to buy eggs at nine a penny and then go to another market and sell them at ten a penny. They said to him, 'Hodja, what sort of trading is this, always at a loss?' The Hodja replied, 'I'm not out for profit, I only want my friends to see me engaged in commerce.'

eleğimsağma. ~ altından geçmek, to pass under the rainbow. There is a belief that a child passing under a rainbow changes its sex.

fincancı. N. H. while walking one day in a cemetery slipped and fell into an open grâve. His clothes were covered in dust and mud and he took some of them off to clean them. Just then some potters approached the cemetery, driving their mules laden with pottery. The Hodja heard a great noise of bells, of running animals and shouting men; he couldn't understand what was happening, but suddenly a thought occurred to him and he cried out, 'Alas! what an unlucky day for this to have occurred; it must be the Day of Judgement!', and frightened to death, he jumped out of the tomb half naked and tried to run away. At that moment the mules had just reached the spot and seeing this strange figure suddenly leap out of the earth, they panicked and rushed about and ran into each other. The whole cemetery was strewn with broken bowls and plates and pots and dishes. The potters rushed at N. H. saying, 'Who are you and what are you doing here?' The Hodja said, 'I belong to the other world and have come to have a look at this one.' 'We'll give you something to look at!' they cried and gave him an unmerciful beating. The Hodja with difficulty crawled home, which he reached at midnight. To the anxious inquiries of his wife he replied, 'I fell into a grave and got mixed up with people from the other world.' 'And what is going on in the other world?' asked his wife. The Hodja replied, 'Nothing happens there unless you frighten potters' mules.'

inad. An Albanian and his boy brought vegetables to town one night to sell in the morning. They came to a mosque, where the prayers known as **teravih** were being recited. The Albanian told the boy to stay with the horse while he went in to pray. He did not know that the **teravih** was a very lengthy affair and thought that the Imam was prolonging it on purpose, in order to test his patience; so, after a while, he went out and said to the boy, 'You had better go on to the market, because it has become a question of obstinacy to see who can hold out the longest and I may be here all night.'

ip. A neighbour came to N. H. and asked for the loan of his rope. The Hodja went indoors and then came out and said that the rope was not available because the womenfolk were spreading flour on it. The neighbour said, 'What's the meaning of this? Can one spread flour on a rope?' and continued to protest; whereupon the Hodja replied, 'If I don't want to lend my rope, flour can be spread on it.'

islim. A Shah of Persia embarked on a steamer that was to take him to Europe. He expected the ship to move off as soon as he had come on board and when it did not do so he inquired angrily why they did not start. He was told that they were waiting for steam. 'Let the steam come on behind!' he commanded.

kedi. A man about to be married asked a friend if he could give him any tips. The friend said, 'Unless you are very careful your wife and your in-laws will dominate you; in order to make sure that this should not happen to me, on the wedding night I got a cat and put it in the bed. When we came up I said to my wife, "What is that in the bed?" She said, "It's a cat." "A cat!" said I angrily and seized the animal and tore it in two. That showed her the sort of man I was.' After the marriage the friend asked the newly-wed bridegroom how matters had gone. 'Alas!' he said, 'I forgot about the cat the first night; I put it in the bed the second night, but it was too late; she had already sized me up.'

kulak. When the Muezzin recites the Call to Prayer from the minaret he holds both hands open behind his ears. When, therefore, he is seen to put his hands up to his ears, you know that the Call to Prayer is about to begin.

kuş. N. H. caught a stork one day. He cut off half its beak and half its legs and then said to it, 'Now you have been turned into a bird!'

kürk. N. H. went to a feast in his ordinary clothes. Nobody paid any attention to him. He slipped away home, put on his best clothes and his fur coat and returned to the feast. He was at once met at the door, conducted to the top table and offered the choicest food. He stretched out his coat to the food and said, 'Eat, my fur coat, eat!' They said, 'Hodja, what are you doing?' The Hodja replied, 'Since it is to my coat that honour is paid, it is only right to offer food to it.'

post. This meaning of **post** has nothing to do with the English word. It was a sheepskin rug, used to sit on by anyone holding an important position and so it comes to mean the office or post itself.

prasa. 'I couldn't even eat a leek', meaning 'Thank you, I am not hungry', (used also sometimes figuratively). The Albanians are supposed to be so fond of leeks that they eat them at every meal. One of them, when invited to a meal, when he had already eaten, made this reply.

sarmısak. N. H. said to a friend, 'I have invented a new dish, honey eaten with garlic; but, to tell the truth, I don't care very much for it.'

sormak. One day a man brought a closed box to N. H. and asked him to keep it until he came back. After some days the man had still not returned and the Hodja's curiosity got the better of him. He opened the box and found it contained the finest run honey. He put a finger in and tasted it and liked it so much that there was soon no honey left. Then the owner returned, opened the box and, on finding it empty said, 'Sir, what about the honey?' The Hodja replied, 'Don't you ask and then I needn't say.'

şeytan. A phrase, very difficult to translate, originating from the idea that the Devil sometimes prevents one from doing what one would like, or ought, to do, and, therefore, by breaking his leg one gets rid of the spell he has cast on one; the following examples may help: 'nihayet bugün şeytanın bacağını kırıp şu satırları yazıyorum', 'at last today I have made an effort and brought myself to write these lines'; 'şeytanın bacağını (ayağını) kır!', (*to a child*)

'Give up being so obstinate (bad-tempered, lazy etc.)!'

tavşan. A peasant brought N. H. a hare. The Hodja entertained him in the best possible manner. Next week the man came again. The Hodja did not recognize him and asked who he was. He said, 'I am the man who brought you the hare.' So the Hodja asked him to a meal and set some soup before him, saying jokingly, 'Pray have some soup made from the gravy of the hare.' Next week three or four peasants came and explained that they were the neighbours of the man who had brought the hare. So the Hodja gave them a meal. Next week yet more peasants arrived and when N. H. asked them who they were they said, 'We are the neighbours of the neighbours of the man who brought you the hare.' N. H. set before them a bowl of water. They looked at it with astonishment and said, 'Sir, what is this?' The Hodja said, ⌈Tavşanın suyunun suyunun suyu!⌉ ('it is the gravy of the gravy of the gravy of the hare').

yorgan. One night at midnight there was a row outside N. H.'s door. Wishing to ascertain what the squabble was about, he wrapped a blanket round him and went out. While he was endeavouring to find out what was happening, someone snatched the blanket off him and ran away. The Hodja returned to his house much perplexed. When his wife asked what was the matter, he replied, 'The quarrel was about our blanket. The blanket's gone, the quarrel is over.'

PRINTED IN GREAT BRITAIN
AT THE UNIVERSITY PRESS, OXFORD
BY VIVIAN RIDLER
PRINTER TO THE UNIVERSITY